To Andrea,
you are the brightest, hardest working, most joyful, and kind person I know. Thank you for the opportunity to teach you. I've learned a lot! Much Love,
Melody

Research-Based Practices
in Special Education

Bryan G. Cook

University of Hawaii

Melody Tankersley

Kent State University

Boston Columbus Indianapolis New York San Francisco Upper Saddle River
Amsterdam Cape Town Dubai London Madrid Milan Munich Paris Montreal Toronto
Delhi Mexico City São Paulo Sydney Hong Kong Seoul Singapore Taipei Tokyo

Vice President and Editorial Director: Jeffery W. Johnston
Executive Editor: Ann Castel Davis
Editorial Assistant: Andrea Hall
Vice President, Director of Marketing: Margaret Waples
Marketing Manager: Joanna Sabella
Senior Managing Editor: Pamela D. Bennett
Project Manager: Sheryl Glicker Langner
Senior Operations Supervisor: Matthew Ottenweller
Senior Art Director: Diane C. Lorenzo

Cover Designer: Candace Rowley
Cover Image: Background: © Lora liu/Shutterstock;
Photo: © Orange Line Media/Shutterstock
Full-Service Project Management: S4Carlisle Publishing
Services
Composition: S4Carlisle Publishing Services
Printer/Binder: Edwards Brothers Malloy
Cover Printer: Lehigh-Phoenix Color/Hagerstown
Text Font: Times LT Std

Every effort has been made to provide accurate and current Internet information in this book. However, the Internet and information
posted on it are constantly changing, so it is inevitable that some of the Internet addresses listed in this textbook will change.

Library of Congress Cataloging-in-Publication Data
Research-based practices in special education / [edited by] Bryan G. Cook, Melody Tankersley.
    pages cm
    Includes bibliographical references and index.
    ISBN-13: 978-0-13-702876-4—ISBN-10: 0-13-702876-8
    1. Special education—Research—United States.   2. People with disabilities—Education—Research.   I. Cook, Bryan G.
II. Tankersley, Melody.
    LC3981.R385 2013
    371.9—dc23

                                                                                                2012005638

10 9 8 7 6 5 4 3 2 1

ISBN 10:   0-13-702876-8
ISBN 13: 978-0-13-702876-4

Dedication

We dedicate this to our families, who help us remember what life is really about.

To Lysandra, Zoe, and Ben. – BC

To Bebe and Jackson. – MT

Preface

Research-Based Practices in Special Education was born of discussions over many years between special education practitioners and researchers regarding the need for a reliable and practical guide to highly effective, research-based practices in special education. Providing this type of information is a primary focus of the Council for Exceptional Children's Division for Research (CEC-DR), which the Division has pursued in many ways—sometimes with considerable success, sometimes with disappointment. At a meeting of the Executive Board of CEC-DR, then President Dr. Robin McWilliam suggested that the division consider producing a textbook to meet this need that would be unique in its emphasis on research-based practices. And so began concrete discussions that led to the book you are now reading.

You have probably read or heard something about the research-to-practice gap in special education—when practice is not based on research and, although less often emphasized in the professional literature, when research is not relevant to practice. This gap is not unique to special education; it occurs in general education and many other professional fields, including medicine. It is unlikely that the gap between research and practice will ever disappear entirely; indeed, it may not be desirable to thoroughly commingle the worlds of special education research and practice. However, when the gap between research and practice becomes a chasm, with practice being dictated more by tradition and personal trial-and-error than reliable research, the outcomes and opportunities of students suffer unnecessarily. Simply stated, special educators need to use the most effective instructional practices so that students with disabilities can reach their potentials; all too often, that does not occur.

We believe that this text is made all the more timely and important given the recent explosion of information on the Internet. The wealth of information available on the Internet (as well as from other, more traditional sources of recommendations on instructional practice such as professional development trainings, textbooks, and journals) can sometimes represent powerful opportunities. However, it often has a stultifying effect, leaving many of us drowning in a sea of information overload, without the time or expertise to determine what is truly credible and what is not. By implementing practices with solid research support, such as those featured in this text, special educators can feel confident that they are using the practices most likely to result in improved performance for their students.

That being said, it is important to recognize that research is not a panacea. Perfect research studies do not exist; even the most effective, research-based practices do not work for everyone (there are nonresponders to every practice); and contextual factors (e.g., school and classroom environments, student characteristics) found in practice seldom align perfectly with the research studies supporting most practices. Therefore, teachers will have to rely on their professional wisdom to select and adapt research-based practices to make them work in their classrooms, for their students. Nonetheless, having practices identified as effective on the basis of sound research, knowing what the research says about those practices, and understanding how those practices work represent critical, initial steps in effective special education practice.

In *Research-Based Practices in Special Education*, researchers, teacher trainers, policy makers, practitioners, family members, and other stakeholders can find information about research-based practices shown to generally produce desirable outcomes in the core areas of academics, behavior, and assessment, and for targeted populations of learners. This core content is also available in four separate volumes: *Research-Based Strategies for Improving Outcomes in Academics, Research-Based Strategies for Improving Outcomes in Behavior, Research-Based Approaches for Assessment,* and *Research-Based Strategies for Improving Outcomes for Targeted Groups of Learners.* We believe that *Research-Based Practices in Special Education* will be one of CEC-DR's considerable successes in producing reliable and practical guidance to help bridge the research-to-practice gap in special education.

Acknowledgments

Very little is accomplished in isolation, and that was certainly true for this text. It is important for us to acknowledge the many professionals whose hard work is responsible for *Research-Based Practices in Special Education*. We first acknowledge the chapter authors. We were fortunate to have some of the foremost authorities in the field of special education author chapters in this work. We thank them for sharing their expertise and working so diligently and agreeably with us throughout the entire process. We thank Ann Davis, our editor at Pearson, for her unflagging support and insightful assistance. We also express our appreciation to Dr. Christine Balan, Dr. Lysandra Cook, Luanne Dreyer Elliott, and Norine Strang for their excellent and professional editing. We owe a huge debt of gratitude (and probably a few glasses of wine) to our incredible team of section editors—Dr. David J. Chard, Dr. Timothy J. Landrum, Dr. Kathleen Lane, Dr. John Wills Lloyd, and Dr. Robin A. McWilliam. You consistently amaze us with your expertise, collegiality, and patience. We are privileged to have collaborated with these leaders in the field. Thank you to our reviewers: Mary E. Cronin, University of New Orleans, and E. Paula Crowley, Illinois State University. And most importantly, we acknowledge our families, without whose support and forbearance this work could not have been accomplished.

Bryan G. Cook
University of Hawaii

Melody Tankersley
Kent State University

Contents

Introduction to Research-Based Practices in Special Education

Bryan G. Cook | *University of Hawaii*

Melody Tankersley | *Kent State University*

*T*his is not a typical introductory textbook in special education that provides brief overviews of a large number of student characteristics and instructional practices. Textbooks with this focus serve important purposes. For example, individuals who are just beginning to explore the field of special education need to understand the breadth of student needs and corresponding instructional techniques that have been and are being used to teach students with disabilities. This text addresses a different need—the need for extensive information on selected, highly effective practices in special education. Stakeholders such as advanced pre-service special educators, practicing special education and inclusive teachers, administrators, parents, and many teacher-educators are more directly involved with the instruction and learning of children and youth with disabilities and as a result need in-depth treatments of the most effective practices that they can use to meaningfully impact and improve the educational experiences of children and youth with and at risk for disabilities.

In this textbook we provide extensive (rather than cursory) information on selected, highly effective practices (rather than on many practices, some of which may be less than effective) in special education. This endeavor begs an important question: What are the most highly effective practices identified in special education? That is, how do we tell "what works" for children and youth with and at risk for disabilities?

Traditionally, special educators have relied on sources such as personal experience, colleagues, tradition, and experts to guide their instructional decision making (e.g., Cook & Smith, in press). These resources have served teachers well in many ways. Special education teachers are skilled professionals who learn from their personal experiences and refine their teaching accordingly. Traditions and custom represent the accumulated personal experiences of whole groups and cultures and therefore can be imbued with great wisdom. And experts most often know of which they speak (and write) and make many valid recommendations. Yet, just as in other aspects of life, the personal experiences that lie at the root of these sources of knowing are prone to error and can lead special educators to false conclusions about which practices work and should be implemented with students with disabilities.

Limitations of Traditional Methods for Determining What Works

Chabris and Simons (2010) described five everyday illusions documented in the psychological literature (i.e., illusions of attention, memory, confidence, knowledge, and cause) that cast doubt on whether teachers can use personal experiences (their own, or those of their colleagues) to determine reliably whether practices work for their students. Chabris and Simons noted that although people assume that they attend to everything within their perceptual field, in reality many stimuli—especially those that contrast with one's expectations—"often go completely unnoticed" (p. 7). That is, people tend to focus their attention on what they expect to happen. Moreover, even when people actively attend to phenomena, their memories are unlikely to be wholly accurate and also are biased by their preconceptions. "We cannot play back our memories like a DVD—each time we recall a memory, we integrate whatever details we do remember with our expectations for what we should remember" (p. 49). Moreover, people tend to hold false illusions of confidence (e.g., most people think of themselves as above-average drivers) and knowledge (e.g., people tend to falsely believe that they know how familiar tools and systems work). Finally, "Our minds are built to detect meaning in patterns, to infer causal relationships from coincidences, and to believe that earlier events cause later ones" (p. 153), even though many patterns are meaningless, many associations are coincidental, and earlier events often simply precede rather than cause later occurrences.

Special education teachers—just like other people in their professional and day-to-day lives—may, then, not attend to events in a classroom that they do not expect (e.g., when using preferred practices, teachers may be more likely to focus on students who are doing well but not recognize struggling students); may construct memories of teaching experiences that are influenced by their preconceptions of whether a practice is likely to work; may be more confident than warranted that a favored instructional approach works when they use it; may believe that they fully understand why and how a practice works when they do not; and may believe that a practice causes positive changes in student outcomes when it does not. We are not suggesting that special educators are more gullible or error prone than anyone else. Nonetheless, these documented illusions show that using one's perceptions of personal experiences is an error-prone method for establishing whether instructional practices cause improved student outcomes.

Traditional wisdom shares many important traits with scientific research (e.g., refining understanding based on empirical input over time; Arunachalam, 2001). Indeed, many traditional practices are shown to be valid when examined scientifically (Dickson, 2003). Yet, tradition and custom often are based on incomplete science or consist of inaccurate superstition and folklore. History is replete with examples of traditional thinking that science subsequently has shown to be incorrect—from the flat-earth and geocentric models of the solar system to the direct inheritability of intelligence and ineducability of individuals with various disabilities. Accordingly, although many traditional instructional practices for students with disabilities may be effective, others have been passed down through generations of teachers even though they do not have a consistently positive effect on student

outcomes. Basing instruction on the individual learning styles of students with disabilities, for example, is an accepted, traditional teaching practice despite the lack of supporting evidence (see Landrum & McDuffie, 2010).

As with personal experience and tradition, expert opinion is often faulty. Indeed, a common logical fallacy is the appeal to authority, in which one argues that a statement is true based on the authority of who said it. Not surprisingly, so-called authorities such as new-age gurus and celebrities often support less than effective products. But experts more commonly considered credible, such as textbook authors, also frequently provide inaccurate guidance. "The fact is, expert wisdom usually turns out to be at best highly contested and ephemeral, and at worst flat-out wrong" (Freedman, 2010, p. 7). In special education, "experts" have a long history of advocating for ineffective practices such as avoiding immunizations, facilitated communication, colored glasses or prism lenses, and patterning (e.g., Mostert, 2010; Mostert & Crockett, 2000). Thus, special educators need to be wary of basing instructional decisions on unverified expert recommendation.

Unlike their nondisabled peers, who often experience success in school while receiving mediocre or even poor instruction, students with disabilities require the most effective instruction to succeed (Dammann & Vaughn, 2001). As Malouf and Schiller (1995) noted, special education serves "students and families who are especially dependent on receiving effective services and who are especially vulnerable to fraudulent treatment claims" (p. 223). It appears, then, that those who teach and work with students with disabilities need a more reliable and trustworthy method for determining what works than personal experience, tradition, or expert opinion. Scientific research can provide a meaningful guide to special educators and other stakeholders when making decisions about what and how to teach learners with disabilities.

Benefits of Using Research to Determine What Works

It is the professional and ethical duty of special educators to implement the instructional techniques most likely to benefit the students they serve. Indeed, the Council for Exceptional Children's (CEC) standards for well-prepared special education teachers specify that special educators should keep abreast of research findings and implement research-based practices with their students (CEC, 2009). Moreover, the No Child Left Behind Act and the Individuals with Disabilities Education Act of 2004 both place considerable emphasis on practices that are supported by scientifically based research (e.g., Hess & Petrilli, 2006; A. Smith, 2003; H. R. Turnbull, 2005). Using research as the preferred method to determine what and how to

Figure 1 Relation between educator's judgments and reality regarding the effectiveness of instructional practices.

	REALITY	
	Works	**Does Not Work**
EDUCATOR'S JUDGMENTS — Does Not Work	False Negative	Hit
EDUCATOR'S JUDGMENTS — Works	Hit	False Positive

teach makes sense because research can address many of the shortcomings of other traditional approaches for identifying what works.

False Positives and False Negatives

When examining a practice's effectiveness, four possibilities exist to represent the relation between reality (Does the practice actually work for the children in question?) and educators' judgments (Do I believe that the practice works?) (see Figure 1). Educators can be right, or hit, in two ways: they can conclude that the practice (a) works, and it actually does, or (b) does not work, and it actually does not. They can also be wrong, or miss, in two ways. First, educators can commit a false positive by concluding that the practice works when it actually *is not* effective. Second, educators can commit a false negative by concluding that the practice does not work, when it actually *is* effective. The goal of any approach to determining what works is to maximize the number of hits while minimizing the likelihood of false positives and false negatives.

As discussed in the previous section, using personal experience, colleagues, tradition, and expert opinion leaves the door open to false positives and false negatives, which results in ineffective teaching and suboptimal outcomes for students with disabilities. Sound scientific research reduces the likelihood of false positives and false negatives in a number of ways, such as (a) using credible measures of student performance,

(b) involving large and representative samples, (c) using research designs that rule out alternative explanations for change in student performance, and (d) engaging in the open and iterative nature of science (Lloyd, Pullen, Tankersley, & Lloyd, 2006).

Safeguards in Scientific Research

Credible Measures

Teachers' perceptions of students' behavior and academic performance are often based on subjective perceptions and unreliable measures and therefore do not correspond strictly with actual student behavior and performance (e.g., Madelaine & Wheldall, 2005). In contrast, sound scientific research uses trustworthy methods for measuring phenomena. Whether using direct observations of behavior, formal assessments, curriculum-based measures, or standardized rating scales, high-quality research utilizes procedures and instruments that are both reliable (i.e., consistent) and valid (i.e., meaningful) to accurately gauge student behavior and performance.

Large and Representative Samples

Educators typically interact with a limited number of students, whose performance and behavior may differ meaningfully from other students. Consequently, personal experience (as well as the experiences of colleagues or experts) may not generalize to other students. That is, just because a practice worked for a few students does not mean that it will work for most others. In contrast, research studies typically involve relatively large and often representative samples of student participants across multiple environments and educators. When research has shown that a practice has been effective for the vast majority of a very large number of students, the results are likely to generalize to others in the same population. It is true, however, that most single-subject research studies and some group experimental studies involve a relatively small number of participants. In these cases, confidence in research findings is obtained across a body of research, when multiple studies with convergent findings show that an intervention works for a substantial number of students within a population.

Ruling Out Alternative Explanations

When educators informally examine whether a practice works, they might implement the technique and observe whether students' outcomes subsequently improve. If outcomes do improve, it might seem reasonable to conclude that the intervention worked. However, this conclusion might be a false positive. The students may have improved because of their own development, or something else (e.g., a new educational assistant, a change in class schedule) may be responsible for improved outcomes. Group experimental and single-subject research studies are designed to rule out explanations for improved student outcomes other than the intervention being examined. In other words, causality (i.e., an intervention generally *causes* improved outcomes) can be inferred reasonably from these designs (B. G. Cook, Tankersley, Cook, & Landrum, 2008).

Group experimental research incorporates a control group (to which participants are randomly assigned in true experiments) that is as similar as possible to the experimental group. Ideally, the control and experimental groups comprise functionally equivalent participants and the only differences in their experiences are that the experimental group receives the intervention whereas the control group does not. Under these conditions, if the experimental group improves more than the control group, those improved outcomes must logically be ascribed to the intervention (e.g., L. Cook, Cook, Landrum, & Tankersley, 2008).

In single-subject research studies, individuals provide their own control condition. A baseline measure (e.g., typical instruction) of a student's outcomes over time serves as a comparison for the student's outcomes in the presence of the intervention. Single-subject researchers strive to make conditions in the baseline and intervention phases equivalent, except for the intervention. Of course, it is possible that the student's outcomes improved in the presence of the intervention relative to the outcome

trend during baseline because of a number of phenomena outside the control of the researcher (i.e., not the intervention; e.g., new medication, a change in home life). Accordingly, single-subject researchers must provide at least three demonstrations of a functional relationship between the intervention and student outcomes. When the intervention is introduced or withdrawn and student outcomes change in the predicted direction at least three times, educators can then be confident that the intervention was responsible for changes in the student outcomes (e.g., Tankersley, Harjusola-Webb, & Landrum, 2008).

Open and Iterative Nature of Science

Although many safeguards exist at the level of individual studies to protect against false positives and false negatives, scientific research is inevitably an imperfect enterprise. No study is ideal, and it is impossible for researchers to control for all possible factors that may influence student outcomes in the real world of schools. Furthermore, researchers can and sometimes do make mistakes, which may result in reporting misleading findings. The more general process and nature of scientific research protects against spurious findings in at least two additional ways: public examination of research and recognizing that knowledge is an iterative process.

When reporting a study, researchers must describe their research (e.g., sample, procedures, instruments) in detail. Additionally, before being published in a peer-reviewed journal (the most common outlet for research studies), research studies are evaluated by the journal editors and blind-reviewed (the reviewers' and authors' identities are confidential) by a number of experts in the relevant field. Authors also must provide contact information, which readers can use to make queries about the study or request the data for reevaluation. These processes necessitate that published research undergoes multiple layers of scrutiny, which are likely to (a) weed out most studies with serious errors before being published and (b) identify errors that do exist in published studies.

Finally, it is critical to recognize that research is an iterative process in which greater confidence in a practice is accrued as findings from multiple studies converge in its support. Even with the safeguard of peer review and public scrutiny of research, published studies do sometimes report inaccurate findings. However, the iterative nature of science suggests that conclusions are best examined across entire bodies of research literature made up of multiple studies. For truly effective practices, the possible erroneous conclusions of one or two studies will be shown to be incorrect by a far larger number of studies with accurate findings. Thus, in contrast to relying on personal experience or on expert opinions, science has built-in self-correction mechanisms for identifying spurious results (Sagan, 1996; Shermer, 2002).

Caveats

Research-based practices represent powerful tools for improving the educational outcomes of students with disabilities, yet special educators need to understand a number of associated caveats and limitations. Specifically, research-based practices (a) will not work for everyone, (b) need to be implemented in concert with effective teaching practices, (c) must be selected carefully to match the needs of targeted students, and (d) should be adapted to maximize their impact.

Special educators cannot assume that a practice shown by research to be *generally* effective will be automatically effective for *all* of their students. No number of research participants or studies translates into a guarantee that a practice will work for each and every student, especially for students with disabilities who have unique learning characteristics and needs. Nonresponders, or treatment resistors, will exist for even the most effective instructional approaches. Therefore, although research-based practices are highly likely to be effective and special educators should therefore prioritize these practices, special educators should also always systematically evaluate the effects of these practices through progress monitoring (e.g., Deno, 2006).

Furthermore, research-based practices do not constitute good teaching but represent one important component of effective instruction. Research on effective teaching indicates that effective instruction is characterized by a collection of teacher behaviors, such as pacing instruction appropriately, emphasizing academic instruction, previewing instruction and reviewing previous instruction, monitoring student performance, circulating around and scanning the instructional environment to identify learner needs, recognizing appropriate student behavior, exhibiting enthusiasm, displaying "withitness" (an awareness of what is happening throughout the classroom), and using wait time after asking questions (Brophy & Good, 1986; W. Doyle, 1986). When educators implement research-based practices in the context of generally *ineffective* instruction—instruction that occurs in the absence of these hallmarks of effective teaching—the practices are unlikely to produce desired outcomes. As such, research-based practices cannot take the place of and should always be applied in the context of good teaching (B. G. Cook, Tankersley, & Harjusola-Webb, 2008).

Another important caveat is that a practice demonstrated by research studies to be effective for one group may not work for others. It is therefore important that special educators are aware of the student group for which a practice has been demonstrated to be effective when selecting instructional and assessment practices to use with their students. For example, although a practice may have been shown by research studies to be effective for elementary students with learning disabilities, it may not work or even be appropriate for high school students with autism. However, highly effective practices tend to be powerful and their effects robust, and as such, they typically work for more than one specific group of children. For example, the use of mnemonic strategies has been shown to be effective for nondisabled students, students with learning disabilities, students with emotional and behavioral disorders, and students with intellectual impairments at a variety of grade levels (Scruggs & Mastropieri, 2000). Therefore, when reading about a practice that has been validated by research as effective with, for example, students with learning disabilities, special educators working with children and youth with other disabilities should not simply assume that the practice will be similarly effective for their students. But neither should they automatically assume that the practice will be ineffective. Rather, we recommend that special educators use their unique insights and knowledge of their students to evaluate the supporting research, underlying theory, and critical elements of a practice to determine the likelihood that a research-based practice will work for them.

Furthermore, special educators will need to consider whether and how to adapt research-based practices to meet the unique needs of their students. Although implementing a practice as designed is important (e.g., if a practice is not implemented correctly, one cannot expect it to be as effective as it was in the supporting research), recent research has indicated that overly rigid adherence to research-based practices may actually reduce their effectiveness (e.g., Hogue et al., 2008). It appears that teachers should adapt research-based practices to match the unique learning needs of their students and make the practice their own (McMaster et al., 2010). Yet they must do so in a way that preserves the integrity of the essential elements of the research-based practice to avoid rendering it ineffective.

These caveats notwithstanding, because of its many safeguards protecting against false-positive and false-negative conclusions regarding what works, scientific research is the best method available for special educators to identify effective instructional practices. By making decisions about how to teach on the basis of collective bodies of peer-reviewed research studies, special educators can identify with confidence practices that are likely to work for their students.

The Research-to-Practice Gap in Special Education

"Educational research could and should be a vital resource to teachers, particularly when they work with diverse learners—students with disabilities, children of poverty, limited-English speaking students. It is not." (Carnine, 1997, p. 513). The research-to-practice gap describes the commonplace occurrence of children and youth being taught with unproven practices while practices supported through research are not implemented. It is a complex phenomenon with many underlying causes that defies simple solutions. Kauffman (1996) suggested that the research-to-practice gap may be particularly extreme in special education, illustrating that an inverse relationship may actually exist between research support and degree of implementation for instructional practices in special education.

Despite reforms and legislation supporting the role of research in education, research findings indicate that the gap between research and practice continues to persist. For example, special educators reported using research-based practices no more often than ineffective practices (M. K. Burns & Ysseldyke, 2009; M. L. Jones, 2009). Jones also observed that some special education teachers over-reported their use of research-based practices, suggesting that the actual implementation rate of research-based practices may be even lower than reported. To make matters worse, when special educators do implement research-based practices, they often do so with low levels of fidelity (or not as designed; e.g., B. G. Cook & Schirmer, 2006)—potentially rendering the practices ineffective. Furthermore, many special educators report that they do not trust research or researchers (Boardman, Arguelles, Vaughn, Hughes, & Klingner, 2005) and find information from other teachers more trustworthy and usable (Landrum, Cook, Tankersley, & Fitzgerald, 2002, 2007).

The research-to-practice gap has clear and direct implications for the educational outcomes of students with disabilities. Using practices shown to have reliable and positive effects on student outcomes is the most likely way to improve student performance. Using research-based practices should, therefore, be a professional and ethical imperative for educators. This is true for all teachers. But as Dammann and Vaughn (2001) noted, whereas nondisabled students may perform adequately even in the presence of less than optimal instruction, students with disabilities require that their teachers use the most effective instructional practices to reach their potentials and attain successful school outcomes.

This Textbook and Addressing the Research-to-Practice Gap

Bridging the research-to-practice gap in special education represents a significant challenge. Many issues will have to be addressed, such as improving teachers' attitudes toward research, providing ongoing supports for teachers to adopt and maintain research-based practices,

and conducting high-quality research that is relevant to special education teachers (see B. G. Cook, Landrum, Tankersley, & Kauffman, 2003). But perhaps the most fundamental issues for bridging the research-to-practice gap are (a) *identifying* those practices that are research-based in critical areas of special education and (b) *providing the relevant information* (e.g., supporting theory, critical elements of the research-based practices, specific information on the supporting research studies) necessary to guide special educators in deciding whether the practice is right for them and their students and how to implement it. Without these critical first steps of identifying and providing special educators relevant information about research-based practices, the field of special education is unlikely to make significant progress in bridging the gap between research and practice.

Turning to original reports of research is an unsatisfactory alternative for the vast majority of special educators. Most teachers do not have the training to critically analyze technical research reports that often are geared for audiences with advanced training in statistics and research (Greenwood & Abbott, 2001). And even for those educators with advanced training in these areas, their full-time teaching jobs should and typically do occupy their time. It is simply not realistic for teachers to read through, synthesize, and critically analyze entire bodies of research literature for every instructional decision with which they are faced.

Textbooks focused on methods of instruction and assessment seem an ideal place to provide educators with useful information on research-based practices that can be used to bridge the research-to-practice gap. Unfortunately, much of teacher education—both preservice and inservice—is based on expert opinion and the personal experiences of those conducting the training or writing the training materials (e.g., textbooks). For example, textbook authors frequently recommend practices with little justification. Discussion of supporting research, if provided at all, is often too brief and incomplete for educators to make informed decisions about the appropriateness of the recommended practice for their classrooms. For example, Dacy, Nihalani, Cestone, and Robinson (2011) analyzed the content of three teaching methods textbooks and found that when prescriptive recommendations for using practices were supported by citations, authors predominantly cited secondary sources (e.g., books, positions papers) rather than provide discussions of original research from which their readers might arrive at meaningful conclusions regarding the effectiveness of the practices.

To address special educators' need for trustworthy, detailed, and teacher-friendly summaries of the research literature regarding what works in special education, the chapters in this text provide thorough synopses of the research literature supporting research-based practices in core areas of special education: academics, behavior, assessment, and targeted groups of learners. Specifically, in this volume on improving the academic outcomes of students with disabilities, chapter authors, who are documented experts on the topics of focus, address how to improve the outcomes of students with disabilities in critical academic content areas: early literacy, reading fluency, reading comprehension, vocabulary, mathematics computation, mathematics reasoning, written expression, the content areas (e.g., social studies, science), and co-taught classrooms. Chapter authors discuss and recommend practices and approaches based on supporting research available for the practices. Chapter authors also provide readers with descriptions of the underlying theory supporting the practices; supporting research studies, including information such as the research designs, the number and type of participants, and the degree to which the recommended practices positively affected student outcomes; and the critical elements of each research-based practice. Using this information, special educators can (a) make informed decisions about which research-based practices best fit their needs and (b) begin to implement the practices and improve the educational outcomes of their students with disabilities.

Conclusion

Special educators clearly want to use the most effective practices to enhance the educational outcomes and opportunities of the students they teach. However, given traditional methods for determining what works and the rapid proliferation of information on teaching techniques on the Internet (Landrum & Tankersley, 2004), much of which is misleading, it is increasingly difficult and complicated to know what works, what doesn't, and how to know the difference. Research is the most trustworthy method for determining what works in special education. This text provides readers with a wealth of information on specific research-based practices in critical areas of special education.

PART 1

Research-Based Strategies for Improving Outcomes in Academics

CHAPTER 1

Strategies for Improving Student Outcomes in Emergent Reading:
Advances in the Field of Early Literacy Instruction

Jill H. Allor | *Southern Methodist University*

Stephanie Al Otaiba | *Florida State University*

F ar too many children do not learn to read within the primary grades and consequently have limited opportunities for future education and employment. Recent statistics from the National Assessment of Educational Progress (NAEP; National Center for Educational Statistics, 2007) show that nearly a third of all fourth graders and about half of students from minority backgrounds do not read on grade level. Over two decades ago, Juel (1988) showed that roughly 90% of children would remain poor readers if they were poor readers at the end of first grade. Ten years later, the seminal work *Preventing Reading Difficulties in Young Children* (Snow, Burns, & Griffin, 1998) presented a synthesis of research and identified three areas of difficulty that negatively impact early reading development: (a) the inability to acquire and apply the alphabetic principle, resulting in dysfluent and inaccurate word reading

skills; (b) poor verbal knowledge and comprehension strategies; and (c) poor initial motivation or the failure to develop an appreciation for the benefits of reading.

More recently, three seminal reviews of the research on reading have emphasized the importance of preventing reading difficulties through effective early literacy instruction (e.g., National Early Literacy Panel [NELP], 2008; National Reading Panel [NRP], 2000a; Sweet & Snow, 2002). Converging evidence from these reviews has identified five critical early literacy intervention components: phonemic awareness, phonics, fluency, vocabulary, and comprehension. Evidence indicates that these components should be taught explicitly and systematically in order to prevent most reading difficulties. However, researchers have shown that a small number of students who do not learn to read despite having received comprehensive instruction need (and benefit from) more

This work was supported by (a) Mental Retardation and Reading Center Grant H324K040011-05 from the Institute of Education Sciences in the U.S. Department of Education, and by (b) Multidisciplinary Learning Disabilities Center Grant P50HD052120 from the National Institute of Child Health and Human Development.

intensive help that is individualized according to their needs (for review see Al Otaiba & Torgesen, 2007).

This knowledge about what works and the need for early intervention provided in layers of increasing intensity to match students' assessed needs is incorporated into new educational policy. Response to Intervention (RtI) is an important aspect of the Individuals with Disabilities Act (IDEA; 2004). RtI is a focus of Chapter 17 by Burns and Scholin in this volume, but for the purposes of this chapter, we briefly describe RtI to help readers think about how each of the interventions we discuss might be used.

In RtI, Tier 1 is primary reading instruction (and assessment to inform instruction including screening and progress monitoring) and is the foundation for all children. If Tier 1 is not successful, extra tiers of supplemental intervention are provided by classroom teachers, by well-trained and supervised nonteacher tutors, or by interventionists. Students with the most persistent challenges will require instruction provided by more highly trained interventionists. Methods for increasing intensity include reducing the group size, increasing the length and/or frequency of instructional sessions, and individualizing instruction based on student needs. Frequent progress monitoring is used to ensure that students are responding to additional tiers and to guide decisions regarding whether students should need to receive more or less intense and individualized instruction. Typically, specialists such as special educators, reading coaches, and highly-trained teachers provide Tier-3 instruction.

In the present chapter, we highlight three research-based early literacy interventions: Peer-Assisted Learning Strategies, Sound Partners, and Early Interventions in Reading. We describe the research base for each program and teachers can deliver the program to improve reading outcomes. These programs vary in their intensity and individualization and so are useful resources or tools for schools and teachers to implement at different tiers within RtI. Although these programs are research-based, we emphasize they have been successful when implemented *as intended*. This is a very important consideration because, if programs are not implemented with fidelity, they will not be as effective as they could be (Al Otaiba & Fuchs, 2006). For example, a school may decide to implement an intervention program that was shown by research to be successful when implemented 4 days a week, but if the intervention is only provided twice a week, it will likely not be as successful (Al Otaiba, Schatschneider, & Silverman, 2005). Thus, we provide guidelines for ensuring implementation fidelity. Finally, we discuss suggestions for implementation of these three programs within RtI contexts in the primary grades.

Before discussing each of these three programs, we describe our theoretical framework for emergent literacy development.

Theoretical Framework

Our theoretical framework for this chapter is the Simple View of Reading, in which Gough (1996) described reading comprehension as dependent on two broad sets of skills: (a) accurate and fluent word recognition and (b) language comprehension. Research is clear that good readers fully process print, meaning that they attend to internal structures (i.e., complete spellings) of words as they read (Adams, 1990; Ehri, 2002; Torgesen, 1998). They do this quickly and effortlessly. Once readers learn to recognize words with automaticity, they can shift the majority of their attention to the meaning of text (Torgesen, 1998). The underlying processes of comprehension are more complex, depending on a variety of factors including listening comprehension, linguistic abilities, relevant knowledge, understanding of story structure, and the ability to monitor comprehension (Perfetti, Landi, & Oakhill, 2005). In sum, good readers effortlessly recognize words and build mental representations of the message of the text, which in turn adds to their overall knowledge.

Owing to years of research and current technological advances, particularly those enabling researchers to examine brain activity, we are rapidly increasing our knowledge about underlying reading processes. Learning to read is a remarkable, complex process that requires students to connect experiences cracking the alphabetic code with oral language and background knowledge. In spite of this complexity, researchers agree that most individuals progress through predictable stages as they learn to read (Chall, 1983; Ehri, 2002). Early on, phonological awareness, print awareness, and expressive and receptive oral language skills develop. Later, decoding skills—including morphographic knowledge, or understanding the meaning of different word parts such as prefixes, suffixes, and roots—increase. Finally, students quickly and effortlessly retrieve both the pronunciation and meaning of individual words from long-term memory, enabling them to read fluently with deep understanding. Stage theories recognize that reading is an integrated process and that instruction at all stages focuses on development in multiple areas. For example, vocabulary and general knowledge are addressed in all stages of reading development, with early instruction focused on oral activities and later instruction focused on print-based activities. The Simple View of Reading and theory about how reading develops undergird the rationale for the early interventions presented in the remainder of this chapter.

Peer-Assisted Learning Strategies (PALS)

What Is PALS, and How Does It Work?

Converging findings from more than two decades of research demonstrate the efficacy of class-wide peer-tutoring interventions as a strategy for improving reading outcomes in the primary grades (Greenwood, Carta, & Hall, 1988). For the purposes of this chapter, we focus on one of the most widely researched peer-tutoring programs, Peer-Assisted Learning Strategies (PALS; see McMaster, Fuchs, & Fuchs, 2007). PALS is recommended as a supplement to classroom core reading programs and typically takes between 20% to 25% of a 90-minute reading block (i.e., approximately 30 minutes, three times per week).

During PALS lessons, dyads of higher- and lower-performing readers work together to practice critical skills including word recognition, fluency, and comprehension. Kindergarten and first-grade PALS include practice with phonological awareness and word recognition, as well as basic comprehension strategies. The classroom teacher introduces these components in a systematic and explicit fashion, and includes PALS activities that are designed to incorporate cumulative review and practice. The components and design reflect stage theories of reading development (Ehri, 2002) and the recommendations of the NELP (2008) and NRP (2000a) as students are first taught the internal structure of words and then systematically apply those skills in increasingly difficult lesson passages and trade books. Comprehension strategies are incorporated into all PALS programs, but PALS for grades 2 and higher emphasizes building fluency and engaging in structured dialogue about text (i.e., discussing main ideas and predictions). The comprehensive nature of PALS assists students in integrating skills so that they can comprehend text more fully, which is also consistent with our theoretical framework recognizing the complexity of reading with deep comprehension. Both higher- and lower-performing readers take turns being the reader and being the coach, so that each student in the pair has an opportunity to practice key skills. A typical PALS lesson is described in Table 1.1, and sample lessons are available online (http://store.cambiumlearning.com and http://kc.vanderbilt.edu/pals).

The structure of PALS enables teachers to efficiently increase the amount of reading practice and provide differentiated instruction during a manageable whole-class activity. During PALS, students receive increased opportunities to respond as compared to typical instruction, thereby increasing the amount of practice with important early literacy skills. Simply put, students spend more time practicing key skills during PALS, because at all times half

Table 1.1 Overview of Typical First-Grade PALS Lesson

Activity	Brief Description
1. What sound?	Teacher presents new letter–sound correspondences, and pairs of students practice identifying them.
2. Sound it out and say it fast.	Teacher models decoding words, and students practice.
3. What word?	Teacher models sight–word reading, and students practice.
4. Story reading	Students practice reading simple stories composed of previously taught decodable and sight words.
5. Story sharing	Students "pretend read" a picture book, looking at the pictures and telling what is happening. Students "read aloud" the storybook two or more times. Students "retell" the events in the story, using the pictures as needed.

of the students are reading or practicing key reading skills while the other half of the students are coaches whose job is to follow along, assisting the reader and discussing the text. Thus, students are more actively engaged during PALS than typical instruction. Active engagement that increases opportunities to use literacy skills, time spent reading, and opportunities to engage in structured dialogue about stories have all been associated with long-term positive effects for students who are English Language Learners (ELLs) (A. W. Graves, Gersten, & Haager, 2004).

Although all students within the classroom follow the same structure, PALS allows teachers to tailor instruction to meet individual needs by assigning texts and lessons at levels appropriate for each pair. For example, a teacher may choose a specific text for a student who is an ELL, ensuring that it is of the appropriate difficulty level and includes content the student is likely to comprehend based on the student's current level of English proficiency. PALS provides students with opportunities to engage in meaningful conversation with their peers, and it also enables teachers to move around the classroom, monitoring student performance and providing brief feedback as needed. For example, as students discuss whether a new prediction is reasonable, the teacher is free to listen to these discussions and guide pairs to discuss why a prediction is reasonable or not. In these ways, teachers provide instructional support, or scaffolds, for different learner types. Scaffolded instruction and increased opportunities to engage in dialogue about text are particularly important for struggling readers and for students who are ELLs. Thus, PALS can assist teachers as they address linguistic diversity within their classrooms by ensuring the meaning of stories is understood by students who are ELLs and the needs of students who are native English speakers are also met.

PALS Research Base

An impressive line of rigorous empirical research has demonstrated that participating in PALS three to four times per week for 16 to 20 weeks improves reading achievement for students in kindergarten through 12th grade (D. Fuchs & Fuchs, 2005; D. Fuchs et al., 2001; D. Fuchs, Fuchs, Mathes, & Simmons, 1997; Mathes & Babyak, 2001; Mathes, Howard, Allen, & Fuchs, 1998; D. C. Simmons, Fuchs, Fuchs, Mathes, & Hodge, 1995). Furthermore, across these studies, researchers have carefully documented that teachers and students can implement PALS with a high degree of fidelity, meaning that they successfully follow PALS procedures as designed. Teachers have been surveyed to show that they enjoy PALS, agree that it is easily implemented, and that they attribute student gains to the PALS activities.

A series of experimental studies show that participating in PALS led to improved reading outcomes for first graders who were high, average, and low achieving (Mathes & Babyak, 2001; Mathes et al., 1998). In these studies, researchers compared students engaged in PALS to a control group who received typical reading instruction. Students in PALS consistently showed statistically greater gains on measures of phonological awareness and word reading. Across these studies, effect sizes, which explain the degree of difference between PALS and control students, indicate that students engaged in PALS outperformed the control group by a 0.5 standard deviation or greater. For example, Mathes and colleagues (1998) reported an overall average effect size (ES) of 0.55, and Mathes and Babyak (2001) reported an ES of 0.60 for high-achieving, 0.94 for average-achieving, and 0.67 for low-achieving students. In other words, the differences between the PALS and control groups were large and meaningful.

The effect of PALS was also tested in kindergarten, when formal reading instruction begins (D. Fuchs et al., 2001) and a subsequent study followed student progress through third grade (Al Otaiba & Fuchs, 2006). Researchers randomly assigned 33 kindergarten teachers in eight culturally diverse urban schools to a control group or to one of two treatments in order to compare the efficacy of (a) a teacher-directed phonological awareness intervention, Ladders to Literacy (or Ladders; O'Connor, Notari-Syverson, & Vadasy, 1998) (totaling 15 hours), or (b) a combination of Ladders activities and Kindergarten Peer-Assisted Learning Strategies (K-PALS; D. Fuchs et al., 2001) (totaling 35 hours). On average, students receiving this combined approach outperformed controls on a variety of measures. The differences among low-achieving

students were moderate to large on phonological awareness measures (blending and segmenting), with effect sizes ranging from 0.45 to 1.27, and were small to large on reading and alphabetic measures, with effect sizes ranging from 0.28 to 1.28. Differences were even larger for average-achieving students, with effect sizes ranging from 1.97 to 2.10 on phonological measures and 0.73 to 1.42 on reading and alphabetic measures. The following year, researchers randomly assigned all first-grade teachers in the same eight schools to first-grade PALS or control conditions. First graders in the PALS condition outperformed controls across most measures of reading achievement, and notably large effects favored students with the weakest initial skills at the start of the study.

At the end of the 2-year study, D. Fuchs and colleagues (2001) examined the degree to which students had benefited from PALS. Encouragingly, only about 2% of students had word-attack skills below the 30th percentile on a standardized reading measure, and only 4% had similarly low word-identification scores. In addition, Al Otaiba and Fuchs (2006) examined the characteristics of "less-responsive" students and reported that those students made less growth in phonological and early reading skills than the sample average. These less-responsive students began kindergarten with significantly weaker vocabulary, rapid letter naming, and verbal memory, and had relatively more teacher-rated problem behaviors than their peers. Thus, an important cautionary implication is that even well-implemented PALS was not intensive or individualized enough to prevent reading problems for some children with very low vocabulary, with phonological processing deficits, or who experienced serious attention and behavior issues. An examination of less-responsive students' school records at the end of third grade revealed that all but one student was receiving special education services in reading. Therefore, these studies suggest that well-implemented peer tutoring can be incorporated into Tier-1 instruction to reduce the number of students who might need more intensive intervention.

Another smaller-scale experimental study (B. Calhoon et al., 2006) shows the promise of PALS as a strategy for improving reading outcomes for Hispanic students who have varying degrees of English proficiency. The study was conducted in six predominately Hispanic Title I first-grade bilingual classrooms in a U.S./Mexico border town. Nearly 80% of the 76 participating students were Hispanic; of these, 24 were identified as ELLs. Thus, in addition to examining the overall impact of PALS on students' reading scores, researchers also explored the degree of student responsiveness on various measures depending on English proficiency. Consistent with other first-grade PALS studies, statistically significant differences favored students in the PALS condition over the control condition on measures of phoneme segmentation and nonsense word fluency. Students who were English proficient and participating in PALS showed greater growth on phoneme segmentation and oral reading fluency, with large effect sizes of 0.85 and 0.56, respectively. However, the performance of students who were ELLs in PALS was more similar to controls', with negative to very small effect sizes on these same measures (i.e., ES = -0.60 on phoneme segmentation and 0.03 on oral reading fluency). By contrast, effect sizes for students who were ELLs in PALS were 1.29 on nonsense word fluency and 1.15 on letter naming fluency; whereas, students who were English proficient in PALS performed similarly to controls on these two measures. These different patterns of findings appear related to students' oral language proficiency in English, but could also be explained by the initial weak skills in phonological and alphabetic awareness among the students who were ELLs. This finding is consistent with two reviews of responsiveness to early literacy interventions that were conducted predominantly with native English speakers (Al Otaiba & Fuchs, 2002; J. R. Nelson, Benner, & Gonzalez, 2003).

How Is PALS Implemented?

Preparation and Planning

Preparing and planning to implement PALS is straightforward, and all materials (except trade books) are provided with PALS programs, including detailed manuals describing how to implement programs. The first step is to select the appropriate program for the participating classrooms. Some PALS programs are available commercially (Mathes, Torgesen, Allen, & Allor, 2001; Mathes, Torgesen, & Clancy-Menchetti, 2001), and others are available through Vanderbilt University (D. Fuchs, Fuchs, Svenson, et al., 2000; D. Fuchs, Fuchs, Thompson, et al., 2000; kc.vanderbilt.edu/pals/). All PALS programs are fairly inexpensive and have research support, so selecting the appropriate program should generally be based on how well the scope and sequence matches the current needs of students. Obviously, the range of ability level varies from classroom to classroom, so it is more important to consider students' skills rather than their actual grade level. For example, one kindergarten classroom may need a version of PALS designed for kindergarten, and another classroom, especially at the beginning of the spring semester, may need a version of PALS designed for first grade.

After obtaining materials, teachers should receive training similar to that provided to teachers who participated in the research studies. Researchers usually incorporate a one-day workshop for teacher participants, with informal assistance provided to them occasionally throughout the year. In workshops conducted during research studies, teachers observed while professional development staff modeled each activity and then participated in role-plays and practice of each PALS activity. Experts familiar with PALS, many of whom participated in the research studies, are available to conduct workshops. Alternatively, because the PALS materials are detailed and complete, an experienced and knowledgeable reading specialist can be effective in providing this training. The manual provides clear directions about how to implement the program, including pairing students, placing students in appropriate lessons, and preparing materials. Scripts to teach students how to conduct PALS are also provided. Costs for materials are nominal. Black-line masters are provided, and no special texts or other materials are needed.

Key Implementation Issues

As we have emphasized, positive outcomes for students may be jeopardized if programs are not implemented in the same manner as they were conducted in research studies. Monitoring the quality and intensity of implementation is therefore important. For example, to ensure high fidelity of implementation across the PALS studies, research assistants (typically experienced teachers) visited classrooms to provide ongoing support, answer questions, and offer corrective feedback (e.g., D. Fuchs et al., 1997). Thus, teachers followed scripted lessons that included teacher presentation, student practice, and teacher feedback to students. Typically, within these published studies, researchers assessed treatment fidelity by direct observations using an observational checklist to record whether teachers and students implemented PALS components correctly. The fidelity scores for K-1 PALS implementation are typically high (on average, above 90%).

One distinct advantage of PALS is that ongoing planning is straightforward and requires relatively little teacher time. However, it is very important that the skills being practiced during PALS match the needs of the students. Although this recommendation seems self-evident, student needs are moving targets and always challenging to determine, particularly in general education classes with many students with varying needs. We strongly recommend the involvement of a reading specialist or coach in monitoring the implementation of PALS. Specialists should ensure that students are following procedures accurately and that teachers are regularly moving among the pairs of students, listening carefully (though briefly) to each pair of students, providing needed scaffolding and feedback as well as praise and reinforcement for appropriate behaviors. PALS provides a great opportunity for teachers to provide brief (1 to 2 minutes) assistance to individual pairs of students. PALS is also an excellent vehicle for differentiated instruction, because all pairs do not need to be reading from the same text or lesson sheet; however, some teachers may require the encouragement and assistance of a reading coach or specialist to differentiate effectively.

In summary, PALS has been shown to be an effective technique in helping teachers adapt instruction for students with different levels of achievement (i.e., high, average, low, with learning disabilities; D. Fuchs et al., 1997; D. Fuchs, Fuchs, Thompson, et al., 2001; Mathes et al., 1998) and for students with different levels of English proficiency. However, students who show a poor response to PALS are likely to require more intensive individualized reading instruction.

We next describe two programs that can be used to intensify instruction for struggling students: Sound Partners and Early Interventions in Reading.

Sound Partners

What Is Sound Partners and How Does It Work?

Sound Partners (Vadasy et al., 2004) is a code-oriented (phonics-based), structured, supplemental tutoring program designed for struggling readers in kindergarten through second grade. Intended to be implemented by volunteers or para-educators for 30 minutes, four times each week, the program consists of 100 scripted, code-oriented lessons that follow a structured routine and include learning letter–sound correspondences, decoding words with familiar sounds or from common word families, practicing sight words, demonstrating fluency on decodable text, and monitoring comprehension. Although vocabulary is not specifically addressed, tutors are encouraged to address vocabulary during lessons as the need arises. Sound Partners provides instruction and practice that proceeds from early decoding skills to fluent passage reading and is consistent with stage theory of reading development (Ehri, 2002). Tutors are trained and supervised by a reading coach, reading teacher, or special education teacher. The goal of the program is to improve student outcomes so they can read grade-level text and participate successfully in the core reading program. A typical Sound Partners lesson is described in Table 1.2, and sample lessons are available on the Internet (http://store.cambiumlearning.com).

Several program characteristics are key to successful implementation of Sound Partners. First, although Sound Partners is specifically designed to be implemented by nonteachers with relatively limited training, tutors do need some training and regular support. This training is minimal when compared to typical professional development for reading teachers. The program is well organized, and lessons are scripted and easy to implement. Second,

Table 1.2 Overview of Typical Sound Partners Lesson

Activity	Brief Description
1. Say the Sounds (and Write Sounds)	Student says the sounds for all letters printed in the lesson. Student writes letters that represent the sounds the tutor says.
2. Segmenting	Student orally breaks words into parts.
3. Word Reading (and Spelling)	Student sounds out and says fast words that are printed in the lesson book. Student spells selected words from the list.
4. Sight Words	Student reads and orally spells high-frequency words that are printed in the lesson book.
5. Sentence Reading	Student reads sentences that are printed in the lesson book.
6. Book Reading	Student reads books orally.
7. Letter–Sound Dictation	Student writes the letters for the sounds the teacher says.
8. Sounding Out	Student sounds out words that are printed in the lesson book.
9. Connected Text	Student reads text orally that is printed in the lesson book.

the instructional design of the program is consistent with research-based reading instruction and incorporates multiple elements of effective instruction including explicit modeling, scaffolding and feedback, cumulative review, and application of skills to text, making it consistent with the Simple View of Reading (Gough, 1996) and recommendations of the NRP (2000a). Third, it is individually administered, providing supported intensive practice of key skills at an appropriate level of difficulty for each student. The program has a proven track record when it is implemented fully by tutors who are provided with appropriate (though not extensive) training and ongoing support to ensure accurate implementation of lessons that are at the appropriate difficulty level.

Sound Partners Research Base

Since 1993, Sound Partners has been actively field tested and validated through a program of research studies (e.g., Jenkins, Vadasy, Firebaugh, & Profliet, 2000; Vadasy, Jenkins, Antil, Wayne, & O'Connor, 1997; Vadasy, Jenkins, & Pool, 2000; Vadasy, Sanders, & Abbott, 2008; Vadasy, Sanders, & Peyton, 2006). Multiple studies have demonstrated that Sound Partners can be an effective tool for improving the reading performance of at-risk students in the early grades. In each of these studies, Sound Partners was implemented by nonprofessional tutors who had participated in training and were paid to tutor. In some of these studies, community members were recruited, including parents, grandparents, college students, and high school students. In other studies, schools identified para-educators to serve as tutors. Participants in the studies were students at risk for developing reading problems and included students with special education, Title I, or ELL status. In the following paragraphs, we describe three studies in detail. We selected these to demonstrate the effectiveness of the program with kindergarten through second grade, as well as to discuss factors that predicted students for whom the intervention would be most effective and students who would likely need additional support.

Vadasy et al. (2006) found that Sound Partners was effective when provided by para-educators to at-risk kindergarten students identified in the middle of their kindergarten year. In this study, Vadasy et al. selected students from schools with high minority enrollment, as well as large numbers of students who were from high-poverty backgrounds. More than half of the students received Title I, ELL, or special education services. Researchers identified students as at risk based on scores on several measures and randomly assigned them to groups, with the final sample including 36 students in the treatment group and 31 students in the control group. Para-educators participated in an initial 4-hour training session and received ongoing assistance provided by the researchers. The para-educators tutored participants four times each week for 30 minutes per session, for an average of approximately 27 hours of individual instruction per student.

Students who received the tutoring outperformed those who did not receive tutoring, demonstrating gains in reading and spelling at the end of kindergarten. The largest differences between the groups were for reading accuracy (ES = 1.02) and oral reading fluency (ES = 0.81). Differences were moderate for reading efficiency (ES = 0.61) and developmental spelling (ES = 0.57). Average reading accuracy and efficiency scores were at the 45th and 32nd percentiles at the end of kindergarten, as compared to the 25th percentile for the control group. Approximately one fourth of the tutored students were considered to be no longer at risk by the end of kindergarten based on performance on phoneme fluency and nonsense word fluency. All of the students in the control group were considered to be at risk according to these measures. The authors concluded that para-educators can effectively implement supplemental Sound Partners instruction, thereby reducing the number of students at risk for reading failure. However, Vadasy et al. (2006) caution that the level of intensity provided in their study is not sufficient to bring all students to adequate levels of performance. Further, this type of instruction could

assist schools in identifying students who require more intensive and typically more expensive intervention.

The second study we chose to highlight was conducted by the same research group and found Sound Partners to be effective for at-risk first graders who were followed through spring of second grade (Vadasy et al., 2000). Researchers selected at-risk first-grade students based on teacher recommendation and pretest scores. The authors then randomly assigned the resulting sample of 46 students to either the treatment or control group. Approximately two thirds of the students were members of minority groups, and almost half were eligible for free or reduced-price lunch. Tutors in this study were nonprofessionals recruited from the community (primarily parents) and paid a nominal hourly rate. Tutors received 8 hours of training before tutoring and 6 hours across the school year. Tutors were also observed and assisted by an experienced, certified special education teacher who provided expert feedback.

The results strongly supported the effectiveness of Sound Partners when implemented by nonteacher tutors to at-risk first graders. Students who were tutored performed better on all measures, with very large and statistically significant differences on all but one measure. Effect sizes ranged from 0.42 to 1.24, with the smallest effect size for reading in context and the largest effect size for nonword reading. By the spring of second grade, the tutored group continued to outperform the control group on measures of phonics and spelling, but not word recognition or fluency.

The third study we describe followed students through third grade with 79 students participating in Sound Partners in first grade and a subgroup of these students also receiving tutoring in second grade (Vadasy et al., 2008). Although this study did not compare treatment students to a control group, its findings provide key information about (a) the long-term reading outcomes that are likely for at-risk students who receive the Sound Partners intervention from nonteacher tutors for 1 or 2 years and (b) which students are likely to require more intensive interventions. In first grade, students were assessed on measures that in other studies have been found to be predictive of later reading ability, including receptive language, phoneme segmentation, and rapid letter naming. Researchers collected outcome measures in the fall and spring of first grade and then in the spring of both second and third grade. These measures included decoding (word attack/nonword reading), word reading (real-word identification), spelling, fluency, and comprehension.

Primary conclusions were that (a) benefits of Sound Partners were evident through the third grade and (b) receptive language and rapid letter naming in the first grade were important predictors of third-grade outcomes.

For each outcome measure, researchers calculated average predicted scores indicating that the typical student participating in first-grade tutoring would earn scores at the 48th percentile on decoding, the 42nd percentile on word reading, the 30th percentile in spelling, and the 37th percentile in comprehension. Additionally, a score of 129 words correct per minute on passage reading was predicted, which corresponds to a percentile rank estimated to be between the 50th and 75th percentiles. Considering students in this study were performing near the 20th percentile at the beginning of first grade when the study began, these long-term gains are impressive. The second primary finding of the study was that rapid letter naming and receptive language were the best predictors of long-term reading performance. This finding informs practice by providing schools with some guidance in determining who may require more intensive intervention, that is, students who demonstrate significant weaknesses on measures of rapid letter naming and receptive language.

How Is Sound Partners Implemented?

Preparation and Planning

The Sound Partners program includes all materials needed for implementation, including an implementation manual, lesson book, and tutor handbook, as well as sets of decodable books for use during lessons. The implementation manual provides detailed information about the organization of the program, as well as how to train tutors. The program thoroughly describes all routines, which are easily implemented by individuals with little or no knowledge or experience tutoring struggling readers.

The first step in preparing for the implementation of Sound Partners is determining who will be the supervisor. This person may be a reading coach, reading teacher, reading specialist, or special education teacher who will oversee the tutoring. Although this individual certainly may delegate many tasks related to implementation, it is key that someone knowledgeable about teaching reading is responsible for the tutoring program. In addition to being knowledgeable about reading instruction, this individual should have strong interpersonal and organizational skills and be able to share knowledge (e.g., modeling procedures, providing feedback to tutors) effectively and positively. The amount of time a supervisor will need to devote to a tutoring program depends on the number of students being tutored, the number of different tutors, and the experience and skills of the tutors.

Even enthusiastic teachers are likely to be unable to allocate sufficient time to this task, unless they are released from some of their teaching responsibilities. Primary duties include recruiting and training tutors, determining which students should be tutored, collaborating with teachers and tutors to schedule tutoring sessions, providing technical assistance on instructional and management problems, and monitoring students' success and progress. In research studies, Sound Partners was typically implemented four times each week in 30-minute sessions. It is important that a supervisor has time to recruit, train, and monitor tutors. In research studies tutors were provided with approximately 2 to 6 hours of initial training and approximately the same amount of follow-up training, in addition to assistance during tutoring sessions.

Selecting students who are in need of tutoring should be linked to screening and assessment procedures already used by the school. Generally, measures of phonemic awareness, rapid letter naming, and language should be used to identify students who are likely to struggle learning to read. Students with the lowest scores on these measures should be monitored carefully. If they respond slowly to Sound Partners tutoring provided by a paraprofessional, other more intensive interventions, particularly those provided by a specialist, should be considered. Of course, these decisions must be made based on the resources available to the school.

In research studies, Sound Partners has been implemented by a variety of people, including community-based tutors (e.g., parents, college students) and para-educators. The educational backgrounds of the para-educators in the Sound Partners studies averaged 14 years (e.g., high school plus 2 years), which is similar to current No Child Left Behind (NCLB, 2001) requirements for para-educators. Fortunately, the cost of nonteacher tutors is relatively small, and the evidence is clear that employing them as tutors can result in long-term gains for many students.

Key Implementation Issues

The supervisor should monitor tutoring sessions regularly. First and foremost, the supervisor should monitor whether sessions are being implemented according to the schedule. We recommend the use of monitoring forms so the supervisor can quickly determine who is being tutored, by whom, and for how long. If the sessions are not occurring on a regular basis, the supervisor should determine the cause of the problem and identify possible solutions (e.g., changing the schedule, contacting a parent regarding excessive absences, assisting a tutor with time management). Second, through direct observation, the supervisor should determine whether the lessons are being implemented effectively. Supervisors can also learn about the appropriateness of tutoring by tutoring students themselves occasionally, either substituting for an absent tutor or providing additional sessions. By tutoring, supervisors quickly learn whether the lesson is at the right difficulty level and whether students can participate in lessons successfully and apply strategies. Finally, supervisors should monitor student progress. If lessons are being implemented appropriately, yet students are making slow progress toward grade-level reading ability, other more intensive interventions should be considered. Options would be simply increasing the length or number of sessions provided each week or placing the student in an additional or separate intervention taught by a reading specialist (e.g., reading specialist provides tutoring two times each week, and para-educator provides tutoring three times). One program to consider for those needing more intensive intervention is Early Interventions in Reading, described in the following section.

Early Interventions in Reading

What Is Early Interventions in Reading and How Does It Work?

Early Interventions in Reading—Level 1 (EIR; Mathes & Torgesen, 2005) is a comprehensive, structured small-group reading intervention designed for struggling readers in grades 1 and 2; it is consistent with the recommendations of NELP (2008) and NRP (2000a), providing for explicit and systematic instruction in multiple strands, including phonemic awareness, letter knowledge, word-recognition fluency, connected text fluency, vocabulary, and comprehension. The program consists of 120 highly detailed lesson plans that are constructed so that each of the critical strands are practiced daily in 7 to 10 short, interrelated activities, including application of skills in context. Lessons progress in a manner consistent with stage theory of reading development (Ehri, 2002), as students proceed from foundational skills to automaticity and fluency with connected text. For most struggling readers, a complete lesson can be implemented in one session, but when necessary, lessons can continue from one session to the next. Lesson plans provide teachers with concise language to model, practice, scaffold, and reinforce critical skills facilitating the delivery of explicit, highly interactive instruction. Many activities require students to respond in unison followed by brief individual practice. Other activities require students to write in a workbook or read to a partner. Although a second level of the intervention is also available to address more advanced skills, our focus in this chapter is on Level 1. A typical lesson early in Level 1 is described in Table 1.3, and sample lessons are available on the Internet (www.sraonline.com).

Table 1.3 Overview of Typical Early Interventions in Reading Lesson

Activity	Brief Description
1. Tricky Words/ Story-Time Reader	Students read high-frequency irregular words from flashcards and then read a decodable book in unison. Students make predictions before reading and check predictions after reading.
2. Letter–Sound Introduction	Teacher presents new letter sound and students practice new sound.
3. Thumbs Up–Thumbs Down	Teacher says words beginning or ending with the new sound and students put their thumbs up if the word begins with the new sound or thumbs down if it ends with the new sound.
4. Letter–Sound Review	Students say the sounds for all letters printed in the presentation book.
5. Stretch and Blend	Students orally repeat words and then stretch words by saying them one sound at a time.
6. Writing the Letter	Students write the new letter, saying its sound each time they write it.
7. Letter–Sound Dictation	Students write the letters for the sounds the teacher says.
8. Sounding Out	Students sound out words that are printed in the presentation book.
9. Connected Text	Students read text orally that is printed in the presentation book.

As is the case with PALS and Sound Partners, EIR is consistent with current theory of reading development and scientifically based reading instruction. When implemented with sufficient intensity, the program is effective in improving the performance of even extremely challenged learners, including students who are at risk, are ELLs, or have intellectual disabilities (Allor, Mathes, Roberts, Jones, & Champlin, 2010; Mathes et al., 2005; S. Vaughn, Cirino, et al., 2006). Its effectiveness is a result of very careful instructional design, as well as careful, intense implementation in small groups. The program closely follows principles of the theory of instruction or Direct Instruction model (Engelmann & Carnine, 1982; Coyne, Kame'enui, & Simmons, 2001). Lesson plans provide teachers with tools to minimize student confusion and maximize practice opportunities. The lesson activities provide for extensive cumulative review, systematic introduction of increasingly more complex skills, and specific instruction in applying skills to more complex skills and to connected text (e.g., letter-sound knowledge is quickly applied to sounding out words, which is in turn applied to connected text). Students are taught to become flexible decoders (using decoding skills to produce a pronunciation that is close enough to the actual word to figure it out) and to approach comprehension strategically. Effective implementation requires initial teacher training (i.e., approximately 2 days of workshops) and ongoing professional development, particularly when teaching extremely challenging students.

Early Interventions in Reading Research Base

The research base for EIR provides evidence of its effectiveness for greatly reducing the number of students who experience significant difficulty learning to read. It has been found to be effective for first graders who are at risk for reading difficulty and typically not identified as learning disabled at this early age (Mathes et al., 2005; Mathes, Kethley, Nimon, Denton, & Ware, 2009). It has also been found to be effective for first graders who are ELLs and also at risk for reading difficulty (S. Vaughn, Cirino, et al., 2006; S. Vaughn, Mathes, et al., 2006), as well as students with mild or moderate intellectual disabilities (i.e., mental retardation: Allor, Mathes, Roberts, Cheatham, & Champlin, 2010; Allor, Mathes, Roberts, Jones, et al., 2010). Following, we highlight studies with first-grade students.

In the first study, Mathes and colleagues (2005) compared the reading performance of students participating in one of two intensive interventions, EIR and Responsive Reading, to students receiving typical instruction alone. In this large-scale study (252 participants), students in both interventions significantly outperformed the students in the control condition on measures of phonological awareness, word reading, and passage fluency. Effect sizes were moderate to large.

Importantly, by the end of first grade, only 7% of the Responsive Reading intervention students and 1% of the EIR students were still below the 30th percentile on basic reading skills, compared to 16% of the students in the typical classroom condition. This sample was drawn from students performing in the lowest 20th percentile at the beginning of first grade, and it therefore demonstrates that the total number of poor readers would likely be less than 1% of the broader student population if interventions such as EIR were routinely and appropriately implemented.

When effect sizes for each intervention (relative to the typical classroom condition) were compared, the effect sizes for EIR were somewhat higher on measures related to decoding, including phonological awareness, timed and untimed nonword reading, and untimed word reading. In contrast, effect sizes for Responsive Reading (relative to classroom condition) were somewhat higher on oral reading fluency. Another difference was

that fewer students in the EIR condition remained at or below the 30th percentile on basic skills.

Research studies have also supported the effectiveness of an enhanced version of EIR with first-grade students who were ELLs and at risk for developing reading difficulties (S. Vaughn, Cirino, et al., 2006; S. Vaughn, Mathes, et al., 2006). In these studies, 10 minutes of focused oral language and vocabulary practice were added to each EIR lesson. Language support was also incorporated throughout the EIR lessons. Language supports varied and included the use of instructional scripts with pictures, use of gestures, additional explanations of vocabulary, explicit instruction in English language usage, and opportunities to give elaborated responses. In both studies, students were randomly assigned to either the treatment group who received enhanced EIR in small groups of three to five students or to a control group that participated in instruction typically provided by the schools. Although the S. Vaughn, Cirino, et al. (2006) study included a sample of students who were learning to read in Spanish, discussion in this chapter is limited to the sample of students who were learning to read in English.

The findings in these studies were similar; students participating in the intervention significantly outperformed students in control groups on multiple measures. Effect sizes were found to be substantively important, according to What Works Clearinghouse (2006). In the S. Vaughn, Mathes, et al. (2006) study, the treatment and control groups performed similarly on measures of picture vocabulary and oral reading fluency; however, the effect sizes on all other measures showed positive and meaningful gains for the treatment group, ranging from a modest 0.26 (listening comprehension) to a strong 1.24 (phonemic awareness). Differences on seven of these measures were statistically significant. In the S. Vaughn, Cirino, et al. (2006) study, the treatment and control groups performed similarly on rapid letter naming, letter-word identification, and oral language measures, but the treatment group outperformed the control group on other measures, with effect sizes ranging from 0.36 (letter-sound identification) to 0.42 (word attack). These differences were statistically significant on four measures.

How Is Early Interventions in Reading Implemented?

Preparation and Planning

The EIR program includes all materials needed for implementation, as well as professional development materials to ensure that teachers are fully prepared to implement EIR. In addition to a staff development guide, teacher's editions with detailed lessons, and an assessment guide, a Teaching Tutor CD-ROM is also provided that details the teaching techniques with explicit instructions and video examples. The first step in implementing EIR is determining which students would most likely benefit from the program and identifying teachers to provide instruction. Generally, students who exhibit weaknesses on measures that predict future reading performance will benefit from EIR. Moreover, EIR is particularly appropriate for students who do not respond to less-intensive interventions. In a recent study analyzing the effectiveness of EIR when implemented on a large scale by school districts, the importance of both the quality and quantity of intervention implementation was documented (Mathes et al., 2009). This finding points to the importance of administrators' ensuring that teachers (a) provide instruction that is high quality, implementing EIR as it was designed, and (b) provide a "full dose" of the intervention (daily lessons across the entire first-grade year). In addition to providing teachers with training on effective implementation of EIR, administrators must allocate adequate teacher time for the intervention and plan ways to ensure that this time is uninterrupted.

Key Implementation Issues

Teacher implementation and student performance should be monitored throughout the school year to ensure that instructional and behavioral techniques critical to the success of EIR lessons are effective. Teachers benefit from the assistance and support of reading coaches or specialists, particularly when teaching students who experience significant difficulty learning how to read. The scripted and straightforward lessons allow teachers to model skills clearly and focus on responding to students appropriately; however, teachers must make many decisions as they implement EIR lessons, including pacing and how to respond to student errors. The program calls for unison responses to increase opportunities for students to practice, but it is critical that teachers also require frequent individual responses in order to assess students adequately. Quick pacing and positive reinforcement are also important to keep students actively engaged. For students who have low IQs, including those with intellectual disabilities, teachers should take particular care to pace EIR lessons according to student needs. Mastery of content may require repeating lessons or sets of lessons multiple times and specifically teaching students to transfer skills learned during EIR lessons to connected text. For further information about implementing EIR with this type of student, see Allor, Mathes, Champlin, and Cheatham (2009) and Allor, Mathes, Jones, Champlin, and Cheatham (2010).

Discussion

A strong, well-developed research base supports understanding why students have difficulty learning to read and which methods can help prevent most reading difficulties. In this chapter, we focused on beginning reading stages and described three specific emergent literacy interventions: PALS, Sound Partners, and EIR. Our discussion illustrated how educators can use these research-based programs to teach all students to read, specifically within an RtI model, and we drew from our own research to provide some helpful procedural guidelines and to describe some potential challenges with implementation. Next, we suggest some adaptations for using these programs with students who are ELLs and students with intellectual disabilities. Finally, we conclude with directions for future research.

Using PALS, Sound Partners, and EIR within a Multitier RtI Model

The three programs we reviewed, PALS, Sound Partners, and EIR, have been rigorously tested; beginning readers made educationally important reading gains when the programs were implemented faithfully at the intended intensity. Consistent with the recommendations of NELP (2008) and the NRP (2000a), each program incorporates explicit instruction and practice applying the alphabetic principle to support decoding, as well as reading connected text to build reading vocabulary and develop comprehension strategies. In addition to increasing instructional time, the programs also incorporate, albeit to varying degrees, motivation and behavioral supports. These programs also complement one another in that they use a similar direct instruction approach. Thus, although the programs' scopes, sequences, and specific activities differ, they are similar enough that students could transfer skills learned in one program to another.

Within Tier 1 of an RtI model, PALS is particularly effective as a supplement to core instruction, because it is a manageable method for greatly increasing practice time on critical beginning reading skills that would be taught in any core reading program consisting of NRP-recommended components (NRP, 2000a). Further, the entire class participates, and teachers may use the text from the core reading program during PALS, allowing time for all students to read assigned text within a structure that is proven to be effective. Although teachers report that time is a frequent barrier to sustaining research-based practices (Gersten, Chard, & Baker, 2000), PALS could replace some of the independent seat work or independent center time activities typically conducted during a language arts block. Because PALS is conducted with the entire class, the teacher moves throughout the room to ensure all students are on task and that their lessons are at the appropriate instructional level. Effective PALS teachers ensure that the entire class actively participates by frequently providing positive reinforcement, including praise and awarding points to pairs of students that are engaged, helpful to one another, and showing good effort. To further keep all students motivated, teachers have an option to divide students into teams that compete to earn the most points. Keep in mind that in the research studies, the PALS intervention was supported by weekly or biweekly visits by research staff; thus, a reading coach or even a trained para-educator could be similarly helpful, at least during the initial training of students in following PALS procedures. Another important consideration is that research has shown that students who responded less well to PALS had lower levels of language, relatively weaker initial skills, and relatively more attention and behavior issues (Al Otaiba & Fuchs, 2006).

Another delivery option would be for a para-educator to monitor the whole-class implementation of PALS. This option would free the teacher up during PALS time to provide additional teacher-directed small-group intensive and individualized instruction to the lowest-performing students receiving Tier-2 and Tier-3 services. Another similar option is for pairs of teachers to combine students and co-teach. For example, one teacher conducts PALS with a large group, and the second manages a small group of students in Tier 2. It is vital that teachers regularly monitor how students respond to PALS to identify individual students who are not making adequate gains relative to their peers (see Chapter 18 in this volume) and may, therefore, require more intensive supports associated with Tiers 2 and 3 of a typical RtI model.

Sound Partners could be appropriate as a Tier-2 intervention for students who did not fully benefit from Tier 1 (whether Tier 1 involved PALS, or just well-implemented classroom instruction). Typically, Tier-2 intervention is provided in small groups by someone other than the classroom teacher. Sound Partners is specifically designed to be implemented by individuals with little knowledge or experience with tutoring struggling readers, meaning that it is carefully scripted to support fidelity of implementation and may be implemented by a variety of individuals. In our own research, we have enlisted high school students participating in service learning, college students, retired teachers, Ameri-Corps members, parents, or other community members. However, Vadasy and co-workers' (2006) use of para-educators may be an easier solution for many schools. Similarly, teachers or reading specialists could also implement Sound Partners to students with the greatest need. This flexibility makes Sound Partners highly feasible as a Tier-2 intervention.

As we have learned from experience, it can be challenging to ensure that programs implemented by someone other than the classroom teacher (as is common in Tier-2 interventions) are well-supervised and that tutors understand the balance between following a program and individualizing that program. For instance, some students need a slower pace and more frequent repetition and scaffolding; others benefit from a faster pace. Training and ongoing supervision to ensure that tutors provide positive reinforcement for on-task behavior is vital. Inattention and behavioral problems may co-occur with reading problems, but we have observed these problems are exacerbated when tutors move too quickly or too slowly within a program. Going too fast can prevent children from mastering and applying skills. For example, if a tutor moves too quickly, students may not master reading a sound, which will then compromise their ability to read that sound in a word, which in turn makes it unlikely that they will read that word correctly in connected text. In contrast, going too slowly can be boring and lead to off-task behavior.

Because EIR is the program demonstrated to succeed with students who experience the most significant learning challenges, it is appropriate for students with the greatest need. Thus, it can be used as a Tier-2 or -3 intervention for students who have not succeeded with other, less-intensive and less-individualized interventions. The hallmark of Tier-3 instruction is that it is delivered by an expert teacher who provides highly tailored instruction designed to meet the specific needs of individual students who are experiencing severe learning challenges. When implemented appropriately, instructors pace EIR lessons according to student needs and repeat lessons or lesson components until students have fully mastered content. Because EIR is implemented in small groups (or individually), experienced and knowledgeable teachers can provide both individual instructional and behavioral support in the form of explicit modeling, expert feedback, and reinforcement. For EIR to succeed with the most challenging students, interventionists would ideally be the most carefully trained in terms of initially placing students on an appropriate lesson, pacing, individualizing, supporting behavior, matching books to students' instructional levels, and managing grouping assignments. Teachers or tutors ideally should instruct small groups of three to four children, and groups need to be carefully monitored and adjusted. Paraprofessionals or less-experienced teachers can be successful with EIR as well, if adequate professional development is provided. However, students with more severe learning difficulties (e.g., children in Tier 3) are likely to require instruction or support from a reading specialist with extensive expertise in individualizing reading instruction.

Adaptations for Learners with Limited Language and other Special Needs

Classrooms in America are rapidly changing. First, demographics are changing, and an increasing number of students are learning English while learning to read (Kindler, 2002). Second, more students with disabilities participate in general education than ever before, and RtI is recognized as a tool for improving collaboration between general education and special education (Gersten, Compton, et al., 2008). Therefore, we emphasize that interventions used within RtI will likely also be provided to a diverse student population. Generally speaking, considerable evidence shows that well-implemented reading instruction for all students should include both code- and meaning-focused components, as well as fluency components. For learners who are learning English as a second language, instruction may initially include a relatively strong focus on building vocabulary so that words that are sounded out are meaningful and immediately linked to meaning. Similarly, reading passages should include extensive discussion of meaning to support comprehension. For many students with higher IQs and stronger first-language skills, these needs are likely to be met through a combination of Tier-1 and English as a second language (ESL) strategies. However, as we described earlier in this chapter, an emerging research base supports the efficacy of both PALS and EIR with students who are ELLs.

Students identified with intellectual disabilities are also likely to benefit from the three programs we have reviewed, although they likely will need individualized pacing to ensure mastery of skills. EIR has been demonstrated to be effective with students with intellectual disabilities, although extensive practice over a much longer period of time is needed for students to acquire skills (Allor, Mathes, Roberts, Cheatham, et al., 2010; Allor, Mathes, Roberts, Jones, et al., 2010). For these students, it is vital to begin reading familiar words and to ensure mastery learning through a slow pace and cycle of cumulative review and practice.

Conclusion and Directions for Future Research

Research on early reading instruction provides educators with strategies that produce strong outcomes when implemented as designed. More research and refinement of techniques are needed for students with low language levels, such as students who are ELLs and students with low IQs, including those with intellectual disabilities. Further research is also needed with regard to how to use these interventions and similar interventions in a coordinated fashion to prevent and greatly minimize reading failure. The current national focus on prevention and early intervention brings fresh optimism to efforts to teach all children to read.

CHAPTER 2

Strategies for Improving Students' Reading Fluency

Beth Harn | *University of Oregon*

David J. Chard | *Southern Methodist University*

Reading fluency, a neglected aspect of reading instruction for many decades, has received increased attention over the past few years (Rasinski, Rueztel, Chard, & Linan-Thompson, 2010). More and more, discussion and promotion of reading programs, assessments, and standards includes expectations that students will achieve measureable growth in reading fluency as part of their overall reading development. Many researchers have argued that fluent reading is critical to understanding text and to motivating readers to read more and, subsequently, is key to success in school and beyond (e.g., Logan, 1988; Therrien, 2004). Clearly, the most important point about this renewed emphasis on reading fluency is that it is directly related to *understanding* what is read.

Theoretical Framework

A significant and positive relationship exists between oral reading fluency and reading comprehension (Pinnell et al., 1995). For example, T. Harris and Hodges (1985) described fluency as the "freedom from word identification problems that might hinder comprehension" (p. 85). Several studies and reviews of research have emphasized the connection between fluency and meaning by describing *fluency* as simultaneously being able to process text while reflecting on the syntax and semantic features of the text and attending to its meaning (Chard, Pikulski, & McDonagh, 2006; Hudson, Mercer, & Lane, 2000; LaBerge & Samuels, 1974; Perfetti, 1985). The relationship between fluency and comprehension is complex, however, with research seeming to suggest that they contribute to one another in a reciprocal manner (S. K. Stecker, Roser, & Martinez, 1998). This reciprocity led Pikulski and Chard (2005) to develop a comprehensive definition of reading fluency that acknowledges the relationship of fluency to comprehension and all of its dimensions.

> Reading fluency refers to efficient, effective word recognition skills that permit a reader to construct the meaning of text. Fluency is manifested in accurate, rapid, expressive oral reading and is applied during, and makes possible, silent reading comprehension. (p. 3)

Pikulski and Chard's (2005) definition emphasized that fluency is part of a developmental process of building oral language and decoding skills that ultimately support reading comprehension. Described as a "deep construct view" (p. 40), this definition explicates four specific dimensions of fluency: rate, accuracy, and quality of oral reading, as well as reading comprehension. This deep construct view promotes the explicit connection between the development of early reading skills, including oral language, phonemic awareness, alphabetic principle, and decoding to the development of comprehension. Despite the increased instructional attention placed on reading fluency and the recognition that it is intimately related to comprehension development, evidence suggests that many children still struggle to develop fluent reading, particularly students with learning disabilities (LDs) (Therrien, 2004; Vellutino et al., 1996).

Perhaps what is most important about ensuring that students develop reading fluency in the early elementary grades is the benefits it affords readers as they progress through school. For example, fluent readers can synchronize their skills of decoding, knowledge of vocabulary, and comprehension strategies to focus their attention on understanding the text (Stanovich, 1986). In addition, they can read with sufficient speed and accuracy so that what results sounds like language. Finally, because they are more facile with reading, they are better able to interpret text and make connections between the ideas in the text, ideas in other texts, and the world around them. In contrast, students who have not achieved fluency focus their attention almost entirely on decoding and accessing meanings of individual words. In addition, their reading is slowed by frequent errors, resulting in few cognitive resources being available to dedicate to comprehension (R. G. Nathan & Stanovich, 1991).

Torgesen, Rashotte, and Alexander (2001) identified five factors that impact a child's ability to read fluently:

1. *The proportion of recognized words in text.* Reading words as orthographic chunks (i.e., word parts such as *ing*, *igh*, etc.) increases word-recognition speed, thereby allowing the reader to focus on text meaning. Rapid word recognition is strongly related to reading rate in connected texts (Torgesen et al., 2001).

2. *Variations in speed of sight-word processing.* Depending on the number and quality of exposures to words, students vary in the speed with which they process sight words (Ehri, 1997; Logan, 1988). Difficulty processing smaller orthographic units (e.g., letters, word parts) results in slower processing of larger orthographic units (e.g., words) (M. Wolf, Bowers, & Biddle, 2000).

3. *Speed of identifying novel words.* Reading new words requires careful analysis including decoding, recognizing familiar word parts, and guessing from the context or meaning of the passage (Torgesen et al., 2001). All aspects of this process slow reading.

4. *Use of context to increase word identification.* Fluent readers do not rely on context for word identification, but struggling readers and beginning

readers do (Pressley & Afferbach, 1995). Relying on passage context during reading likely contributes to slow, effortful reading and may be less helpful than accurate word identification in supporting comprehension (I. L. Beck, McKeown, & Kucan, 2002).

5. *Speed with which word meanings are identified.* When students can accurately decode and identify the meaning of a word while reading connected text, they can maintain speed, and comprehension can occur. If students cannot recognize the meaning of a word rapidly and must actively reflect on word meanings while reading, both fluency and comprehension will decline (Torgesen et al., 2001).

In light of these factors, it seems straightforward that the development of fluency for struggling readers should encompass instruction and practice in multiple skill areas, including phonemic awareness, decoding, vocabulary, oral language, and connected text reading. Instruction across these multiple skills has the potential to positively impact both independent text reading fluency and comprehension and should be considered when planning, scheduling, and providing instructional and practice opportunities to struggling readers including students with disabilities.

In this chapter, we review two practices that are commonly used in classrooms to improve reading fluency for struggling readers including students with disabilities: repeated reading and a multidimensional approach to fluency. We provide an overview of each practice, discuss critical instructional elements required for each practice, detail the theoretical underpinnings of each practice, and describe the available research with regard to its impact on student fluency development.

Repeated Reading

Repeated reading has been defined in a number of ways based on theoretical orientation or program emphasis, but a definition across approaches is that repeated reading requires students to "read passages in connected text or word lists more than once" (Chard, Ketterlin-Geller, Baker, Doabler, & Apichatabutra, 2009, p. 266). This definition emphasizes both word-level and sentence- or passage-level fluency as recommended within factors that impact fluency development (Torgesen et al., 2001). Although numerous approaches and programs emphasize repeated reading, they can be grouped by the manner in which they are delivered: (a) by the teacher directly or (b) within a peer-tutoring approach. A common research-based program that is teacher-delivered is Read Naturally (Hasbrouck, Ihnot, & Rogers, 1999). The most common research-based peer-tutoring approaches are Classwide Peer Tutoring (CWPT; Arreaga-Mayer, Terry, & Greenwood, 1998) and the more recent and widely implemented Peer-Assisted Learning Strategies (PALS) by Fuchs and colleagues (D. Simmons, Fuchs, Fuchs, Pate, & Mathes, 1994). We review both Read Naturally and PALS in this chapter; first we present the critical features these repeated reading interventions share.

Critical Elements of Repeated Reading Interventions

Therrien (2004) completed a meta-analysis of published repeated reading interventions studies conducted between the 1990s and early 2000s. From this review, Therrien identified essential intervention features in effective repeated reading interventions: (a) having students read to an adult, (b) ensuring students were explicitly told that becoming a more fluent reader will help them understand what they are reading, (c) establishing an explicit student-specific goal, (d) providing corrective feedback, and (e) having students repeatedly read a passage three to four times. Each of these components can be found in the repeated reading interventions discussed in this chapter (i.e., Read Naturally and PALS). We provide specific examples of each in the following descriptions and emphasize these examples in the respective research reviews.

Read Naturally

An experienced Title 1 teacher developed Read Naturally (RN; Hasbrouck et al., 1999) for use in her elementary school setting. The initial version of the program was designed to be implemented in small groups (i.e., 3 to 10 students) three times a week for about 30 minutes each time. Read Naturally was designed to supplement a more comprehensive reading intervention by providing students systematic opportunities to practice rereading carefully selected and developed reading passages. The general approach of RN has the teacher determine a student's instructional level when reading connected text (i.e., reading passages students can read with about 90% accuracy) within the RN passages. The RN program does note that teachers should use their judgment and past experience with the student in determining the level at which they should be placed to build fluency. The program has developed at least three sets (20 passages per set) of nonfiction passages per grade level that have been grouped to be of comparable difficulty based on common readability formulae (i.e., Spache readability formula and Fry Graph readability formula; see A. Harris & Jacobson, 1980). After determining a student's instructional level, the teacher

assigns that student to the appropriate set of instructional materials.

Read Naturally provides standard steps for reading each passage. The student begins by completing a "cold" reading of the passage to the teacher. This reading is referred to as "cold" because it is not previously practiced. During this phase the student reads the unfamiliar passage independently and the teacher determines the number of words read correctly in 1 minute and notes quantity of errors and trends in the types of errors made. The teacher then provides the student corrective feedback on the errors and provides practice on new sight words that are in the passage. Next, the teacher determines a fluency goal for the student based on the "cold" reading. The goal is typically to improve on the cold reading by reading 30% more words correctly in 1 minute after completing the remaining steps of the intervention. Students graph their "cold" reading time, visually see their goal, and then move to the repeated reading aspect of the intervention.

A unique aspect to RN is the process of listening and reading along with a recorded model of expressive and fluent reading. The student reads along (audibly subvocalizing) with a recording that models reading with good prosody (i.e., reading with accuracy and natural conversational expression). The read-along model is done three times, with each consecutive reading paced more quickly than the previous. The final reading sounds like a proficient reader. After these multiple models, the student conducts a self-timing for 1 minute, reading the passage independently to determine if the goal is reached.

In general, students will reach the goal within two to four repeated readings. After achieving the predetermined goal, the student answers the associated comprehension questions and writes a brief retell about the passage (i.e., one to two sentences summarizing what the student remembered). The comprehension questions are designed to measure both inferential and literal aspects of the passage as well as the main idea and vocabulary specific to the topic of that passage. After completing the independent comprehension step, the student rereads the passage again while being timed by the teacher to determine the number of words read correctly in 1 minute. The student then graphs her score on the chart to determine if she met her goal. The teacher and the student review and discuss the student's answers to the comprehension section, and the student practices words that she missed. The program provides guidelines about how many passages in a row a student should "pass" before either increasing the student's goal or moving on to more difficult passages.

As mentioned, the original version of RN was developed for use with audiotapes. More recently, the modeled readings have been provided on compact discs. The passages are designed to be of high interest to students, present factual information across a range of topics, and vary in length from about 100 words (first-grade level) to 300 words (grades 5 and up). More recent passages have been developed with a range of multicultural themes as well as some passages developed in Spanish. In addition, a computerized version of RN has been developed. Research findings published on each of these versions will be reviewed.

Research on Read Naturally

The initial study of RN completed by Hasbrouck et al. (1999) included 25 third-grade students, both at risk for and identified as having LD, within an urban school setting in Minnesota. Students received their general education instruction in a traditional core reading program that was supplemented with small-group phonics and fluency building with RN three times a week. Results indicated that all students demonstrated significant improvements in reading fluency across the duration of intervention (i.e., an average improvement of more than two words read correctly per week). Although this was not an experimental study (i.e., no random assignment of students to RN or a control group), it does provide initial support for the intervention and was published in a peer-reviewed research journal. However, because the students all received instruction that included more than RN, it is difficult to determine how much of the improvement in reading fluency was directly tied to RN or the other intervention components.

Although the publisher's Web site provides numerous "case studies" documenting the efficacy of RN in a range of different settings (e.g., rural, large urban schools), grade levels, and student populations (i.e., English Language Learners [ELLs]), none of these case studies are designed to support the notion that the RN program alone caused improved reading fluency. The program has been widely used in schools for decades with strong support from educators as to its utility; however, the body of peer-reviewed research on the program is extremely limited. More information is available from the publisher's Web site, http://www.readnaturally.com/.

Read Naturally—Software Edition (RN-SE) was developed around 2005 to provide a computer-delivered version of the program. The computer automates many of the steps of the original RN program. The teacher still determines the instructional level of the student, but the program provides a suggested goal for the student. The teacher can modify as needed. When the student logs on to the system, the computer matches the instructional level to the student, and the student chooses the story he prefers from the set. During the "cold," timed reading step, the software prompts the student to begin reading and click on words that are difficult or unfamiliar. The program pronounces highlighted words at the end of the timing. Next, the computer presents the key words to the student visually and orally, reviews words the student indicated were difficult, and prompts the student to write a prediction. Similar to the original version, the student then reads along with the model of good fluency and prosody, with each successive model increasing its pace. The student then proceeds to answer the comprehension questions, writes a retell, and signals to the teacher that he is ready for the final check out or "hot timing." The program presents the student an automated graph of both the cold and hot timings on that story as well as a history of prior repeated reading practices.

At this writing, no peer-reviewed study of the RN-SE program has been published. However, the RN Web site provides a study completed by Christ and Davie (2009) from the University of Minnesota (http://www.readnaturally.com/company/news_seStudyUMn.htm). The authors report that the monies used to complete the study were provided by the publishers of RN. In the reported study, researchers randomly assigned 109 low-performing third-grade students from six elementary schools to either the RN-SE or the control (business as usual) condition and monitored reading performance for 10 weeks. Students in the RN-SE condition received the computerized intervention for 20 minutes daily across the intervention. Results indicated that students who received the RN-SE program performed significantly better on multiple measures of fluency (i.e., word and connected text) and on one measure of word accuracy, although effect sizes were small. No significant differences were found between conditions on multiple measures of comprehension. Although this is an experimental study, it has not been published in a peer-reviewed journal and must be viewed within that context.

Peer-Assisted Learning Strategies

Peer-Assisted Learning Strategies (PALS; D. Simmons et al., 1994) was initially designed as a strategy for use in general education classrooms to supplement comprehensive reading programs by increasing student opportunities to read aloud, receive feedback, and practice answering comprehension questions (D. Simmons et al., 1994). Since its inception, it has been modified across grade levels (preschool, elementary, middle and high school), content areas (reading and math), and student populations such as students with LD (D. Fuchs & Fuchs, 1998; D. Simmons, Fuchs, & Fuchs, 1995) and students who are ELLs (Sáenz, Fuchs, & Fuchs, 2005). Across each of these areas, the general steps and method of implementation are the same and will be discussed next, with more specific research findings following.

The theoretical basis for PALS is found in the research on the effectiveness of reciprocal teaching developed by A. L. Brown and Palincsar (1987) and the practical basis is the CWPT approach (Arreaga-Mayer et al., 1998) previously mentioned.

The general process of implementing PALS requires the teacher to create student pairs that vary in reading skill level. The higher performer is called the "coach" and the lower performer is the "player." Within these dyads both students receive structured and efficient opportunities to practice reading letter sounds, words, or both (depending on grade/skill level); reading connected texts; and identifying and discussing the main ideas and essential information to develop comprehension. The teacher trains the coach and player how to interact (training materials provide explicit scripts for students to follow) while moving through the teacher-selected materials (i.e., each dyad has individually chosen instructional materials), and the teacher supervises and supports implementation through each of the phases of practice.

The developers designed PALS to be implemented two to three times a week in 20- to 30-minute sessions (D. Fuchs, Fuchs, & Burish, 2000). Implementation can occur in small-group or whole-group situations. After the teacher trains the students on the specific approach of moving through the phases of PALS, the teacher signals the coach to begin the first phase (Partner Reading), and the coach reads the words/passage while the player watches. It is assumed that the coach will have sufficient skills to complete the task accurately and will be a successful model for the player. They then switch roles, and the player reads the words/passage with the coach providing feedback as needed. This reciprocal approach (coach and player taking turns and discussing) is used across the three phases of PALS: Partner Reading, Paragraph Shrinking, and Prediction Relay. For each phase, the teacher provides initial training on the essential steps and expectations in each phase. After training the teacher typically will be the timer and facilitator to ensure students are successful and on track.

The first phase of PALS is Partner Reading, which the coach begins by reading a passage for 5 minutes while the player follows along. The player then rereads the same section. The coach uses specific error-correction procedures when the player makes an error or does not know a word (e.g., "Can you figure it out?" If not, the coach provides the word and has the player reread the sentence). After the reread is complete, the player provides a 2-minute retell. Within the retell, the coach prompts the player to answer the following questions: "What did you learn first?" "What did you learn next?" "What did you learn next?" To keep motivation high for students, the dyad earns points for successful reading and accurate retell.

Next, the pair moves to the second phase, called Paragraph Shrinking. In this phase, students continue to read the material a paragraph at a time to practice identifying the main idea and important information. The coach goes first and does this for 5 minutes; they switch roles, and then they repeat. After finishing a paragraph the listener (either the coach or player) prompts the reader to achieve the following: identify the main point/person (who or what), identify the most important thing about the "who or what," and then summarize the main idea in less than 11 words. If the coach and player succeed, they earn additional points for their team.

The final phase is the Prediction Relay, in which students predict what will happen in the next section and earn points for being correct. Instead of going a paragraph at a time as in the prior phase, the Prediction Relay covers larger chunks of material (e.g., half a page). After reading half the page, the nonreader asks the student to predict what may happen next. When they finish the page, the nonreader then asks, "Did your prediction come true?" and then they switch roles for the next page. Students take turns making and confirming predictions about the text. If dyad members don't agree about the accuracy of the prediction or are wrong, they are expected to go back to that paragraph and use the Partner Reading activities to clarify.

Students are also trained to administer a traditional timed oral reading fluency (ORF) assessment, which is an assessment of the number of words read correctly in 1 minute. They administer an ORF to each other and graph scores to monitor progress at the end of each session. In addition, the teacher completes ORF assessments at least twice a month to formally evaluate progress. D. Simmons et al. (1994) suggested that teachers modify dyad pairings every 4 to 6 weeks to keep things fresh and interesting for the students.

Research on PALS

Numerous published research articles demonstrate PALS's efficacy across grade levels for students who are at risk, have LD, have behavior disorders (BDs), and who are ELLs (D. Fuchs, Fuchs, & Burish, 2000). For this review, we focus only on research involving students included in general education classrooms who have LDs, emotional and behavioral disorders (EBDs), and students who are ELLs. In one of the initial studies using PALS, 118 students in grades 2 to 5 in five elementary schools participated. The authors reported that 58 of the students were identified as having LD, 27 were below average readers, and the remaining 33 were average readers. All students received explicit reading instruction, but half were randomly assigned to explicit teaching plus PALS for the 14-week intervention. Because this was the initial study measuring the efficacy of PALS, there were four conditions that students were randomly assigned to, including the current prescribed PALS steps previously described. Results indicated that students who received the full PALS condition performed significantly better on a measure of fluency (medium effect size) and comprehension (large effect size) when compared to the control condition. Within this study the researchers also demonstrated the efficacy of the comprehension discussion steps that students completed (i.e., shrinking and prediction), because these students showed the most growth on comprehension during the study.

An early version of the PALS intervention was also used with students who not only had significant reading delays but also corresponding attention and behavioral difficulties. Locke and Fuchs (1995) used a single-subject withdrawal design to measure the impact of on-task behavior of three fifth- and sixth-grade boys by implementing PALS. After baseline was established, students had 5 days of PALS intervention, then 4 days of withdrawal, and then 4 more days of PALS, followed by a corresponding withdrawal phase. Results indicated that on-task behavior improved markedly across all students during the PALS reading in comparison to typical reading instruction. This study did not measure reading performance but demonstrates how the PALS approach may also provide the structured experience that some students need to maximize instructional time.

The utility of using PALS with students who are ELLs was investigated in a study completed by Sáenz et al. (2005). All students ($n = 132$) were native Spanish speakers in grades 3 through 6 including students who were LD, as well as low-, typical-, and high-achieving readers. The teachers were randomly assigned to use PALS three times a week for 15 weeks, and student performance was contrasted with the reading performance of comparable classrooms during this same time. Results indicated that although the overall growth between PALS and the control condition were similar at the average class-level on the fluency measure, the students with LD demonstrated significantly more growth across the PALS condition (large effect size) than students with LD in the control condition. All students in the PALS condition performed significantly better on a measure of comprehension than the control group, with all learner types displaying large effect sizes.

Whereas PALS was initially developed for use with elementary-aged students, it has also been extended for use in high schools. L. S. Fuchs, Fuchs, and Kazdan (1999) completed a study in which they randomly assigned special education and remedial reading teachers to use PALS two to three times a week within their traditional reading instruction and compared fluency, comprehension development, and student attitudes to

comparable classrooms that did not use PALS. The students who were monitored across the study included some students with reading disabilities but also any students who were reading below the sixth-grade level. PALS was implemented for 16 weeks with only a minor adjustment to the typical PALS steps. The intervention included the typical steps of partner reading, paragraph shrinking, prediction relay, and use of points for motivation. The modifications included changing partners at least weekly as well as daily tangible reinforcement for successful completion of activities. Researchers believed this would make the intervention more palatable and motivating for high school students. Results indicated that although growth on fluency measures was comparable across conditions, the PALS condition demonstrated significantly larger improvements in reading comprehension than students in the control classrooms, with a medium effect size reported. When compared to students who did not receive PALS, students in the PALS condition indicated that they were more likely to enjoy working collaboratively with their peers and reported a greater sense of self-efficacy in their approach to reading (e.g., "In this class, I have worked hard to improve my reading skills").

As previously mentioned, numerous studies document the efficacy of PALS across grade levels and disability types (i.e., LD, BD), as well as ELLs. We have provided just a summary of key articles documenting the range of empirical studies. PALS has been reviewed by the What Works Clearinghouse and found to have positive effects at improving not only fluency but also word analysis/phonics and comprehension skills (see review at http://ies.ed.gov/ncee/wwc/reports/beginning_reading/pals/).

Multidimensional Approach to Improving Reading Fluency: RAVE-O

A more recent approach to fluency development for students with LD in reading has been developed by Maryanne Wolf and colleagues (Wolf, Barzillai, et al., 2009). This approach takes a multidimensional approach to developing fluency. In contrast to the repeated reading approach that emphasizes successful, accurate rereading of connected text, Wolf et al. asserted that students need more practice and opportunities across all reading dimensions (i.e., semantic, or word meaning; orthographic, or print; morphologic, or meaningful word parts; phonologic, or sounds; and syntactic, or word order). Wolf and her colleagues have developed a reading intervention called Retrieval, Automaticity, Vocabulary, Engagement with Language, and Orthography (RAVE-O) that has primarily been used with struggling readers in second and third grade. The 60-minute intervention has two components and is delivered in small groups of one to four students through computer-assisted instruction. The first 30 minutes focus on developing phonological awareness, letter-sound understanding, and phonological recoding to support word-reading development using an explicit, systemic intervention called Phonological Analysis and Blending (PHAB; Lovett, Steinbach, & Frijters, 2000). Using this as the base, the second 30 minutes includes a systematically integrated approach to developing students' semantic, orthographic, morphologic, and comprehension skills through the use of unique teacher- or computer-delivered activities. The intervention is implemented over 70 total hours, and the research on its efficacy is just emerging (Morris et al., 2010; Wolf, Barzillai, et al., 2009).

Critical Elements of RAVE-O

Wolf and colleagues developed the RAVE-O program using theoretical perspectives from cognitive psychology, neuroscience, and linguistics that view reading disabilities as a breakdown across a range of dimensions (M. Wolf & Katzir-Cohen, 2001). One of the hallmark characteristics for students with reading disabilities is dysfluent reading, which these researchers believe to be influenced not only by deficits in phonological processing (as many reading interventionists do), but also by deficits in cognitive and linguistic processing. They believe that successful reading "depends on the integrity, speed, and automatic connections" across each of these subprocesses (M. Wolf, Barzillai, et al., 2009, p. 86). This approach is influenced by work on the "Double-Deficit" hypothesis initially developed by M. Wolf and Bowers (1999), which indicated that the most significantly impaired readers have deficient skills not only in phonological processing but also in rapid automatized naming (i.e., the ability to quickly name colors, letters, or objects under timed conditions). According to this approach, all aspects of reading (e.g., semantic, orthographic, phonologic) are important and intertwined to support the efficient cognitive processing of reading for understanding. Therefore, RAVE-O strives to provide students with daily, repeated, and varied practice with linguistic stimuli that will improve the efficiency of the connections across all subprocesses to support reading development. It is theorized that this multidimensional approach will improve fluency development more effectively and efficiently than interventions that focus primarily on phonologic processing or repeated reading separately.

As previously mentioned, the first 30 minutes of RAVE-O instruction consists of the PHAB intervention, which uses explicit and systematic approaches to teach phonological awareness, word analysis, some orthography, and connected text reading. Skills are sequentially organized and systematically delivered using careful wording, corrective feedback, and active pacing. After completing the PHAB, students move into the RAVE-O activities that link to the skills taught in the PHAB. Recent publications have also used other explicit and systematic phonics-based interventions for this first 30-minute intervention time (Morris et al., 2010). Each RAVE-O lesson has several major dimensions that are linked to one another to provide students repeated and varying approaches to developing the subprocesses by addressing the critical elements discussed previously.

In the RAVE-O lesson, several core words are introduced. For example, core words for the -*it* rime may be *fit, sit, split*. The meanings of the words are discussed, and then the words are taught on rime cards with separable, color-coded onsets. Students are taught to segment and combine onsets (e.g., /f/, /s/, /sp/) and rimes (e.g., /it/) for about five words each week while learning to recognize other words containing the same rime. They also play a computerized game and engage in other activities to increase automaticity. These activities are combined with writing to enhance automaticity with decoding and word recognition. Finally, multiple meanings of core words are taught. To help students to retrieve the word meanings, they engage in multimodal activities and cognitive monitoring activities. The core words were carefully selected and sequenced to teach critical phonologic, semantic, and orthographic principles of reading. The words were also specifically chosen to link to the skills taught in the PHAB, teach the most essential letter sounds, and have multiple meanings (i.e., ram=animal, physical act, or computer processor). Teachers introduce a group of core words each week of the intervention and use and review these words across the duration of the intervention. These core words are the base to which all additional activities are strategically linked to support students' understanding of the multiple dimensions involved in reading (Wolf, Barzillai, et al., 2009; Wolf, Miller, & Donnelly, 2000).

The core words are used in activities to develop *semantic* skills through the use of (a) pictures to teach and demonstrate the words' multiple meanings, (b) word webs showing varying linkages to words of similar meaning, (c) a computer activity prompting students to use specific strategies to discover the missing word in a game called "Sam Spade Detectives," and (d) "minute stories" that integrate the words within connected text during a repeated reading activity. *Orthographic* skills are addressed through the daily use of a computer game called "Speed Wizard" to systematically provide practice and increase the speed of retrieval of common orthographic patterns. For example, if students were learning the word part *-ight,* the student would have multiple exposures to words of this type but the computer would expect them to recognize/identify it more quickly through each round to spur retrieval efficiency. *Morphologic* skills are developed through activities demonstrating how changing specific aspects of words change their meaning in a game-like activity called "Ender Benders." *Phonologic* skills are taught through activities such as dice and cards with high-frequency spelling patterns on them that students use to build words; high-frequency word drill practice; and "sound sliders" that have onsets, rhymes, and blends on word strips for word building. *Syntactic* skills are taught within the context of sentence and paragraph reading where students are shown how varying morphemes can change the grammatical role of a word within the passage.

So, for example, one of the core words is *jam.* The teacher explicitly teaches students how to phonologically segment the word (/j/ /a/ /m/) and then link it to meaning (semantics) and discusses its syntactic variations as a noun (jam you eat) or a verb (to be in a jam). Additionally, students are shown how adding different morphemes (i.e., *ing, ed, s*) changes the root word meaning. The goal of this multicomponent approach is to provide students multiple and differential exposure to all processes involved in reading to provide a greater depth of reading for meaning (Wolf, Gottwald, & Orking, 2009). The core words are systematically introduced and used across the entire intervention and in each domain to develop an integrated approach to maximize reading development. Each lesson has at least one activity related to each of the five dimensions to improve reading fluency and comprehension (Wolf, Gottwald, et al., 2009; Wolf, Miller, et al., 2000).

Review of RAVE-O Research

RAVE-O is a recently developed intervention, and only one study has been published. The initial study worked with 279 second- and third-grade students identified as having a reading disability; 135 were African American and the remaining Caucasian. Students received 70 hours of intervention from October to March in one of the following conditions: (a) PHAB + RAVE-O, (b) PHAB + PHAST (Phonology Plus Strategy Training), (c) PHAB + study skills, or (d) classroom control. Results indicated that the RAVE-O condition significantly outperformed

the other conditions on multiple measures of vocabulary and comprehension. The RAVE-O group also significantly outperformed students in the PHAB + study skills and control conditions on measures of fluency, decoding, and word reading. Similar performance was found for students in the RAVE-O condition when compared to the PHAB + PHAST condition on word attack, word identification, fluency, and one comprehension measure. Additional studies and modifications to the intervention are currently underway, and as data are analyzed, additional insights for various learner types may be available (M. Wolf, Barzillai, et al., 2009). Additional studies and replication of results on other student populations are needed to more fully understand how this multidimensional intervention may impact fluency development differently than other approaches.

Conclusion and Directions for Future Research

The hallmark characteristic of students with reading disabilities is a slow, deliberate, and often inaccurate approach to reading connected text (G. R. Lyon, 1998). As such, it is not surprising that reading for these students is not the enjoyable experience that typical readers encounter. Moreover, whereas regulating reading speed can be used by good readers to assist in focusing on sophisticated aspects of a passage of text, struggling readers and those with reading disabilities often read so slowly that it impairs their comprehension (Breznitz, 2006). The most common approach to addressing dysfluency has been through a combination of continued practice in word analysis but also sufficient time for students to read and reread passages that are at an instructional level that they can read with greater pace to facilitate comprehension. The repeated reading interventions reviewed here have been around in various iterations for over 20 years and have strong research backing their efficacy at improving not only fluency but also comprehension. The more recently developed multidimensional approach to addressing fluency (e.g., RAVE-O) provides a multidimensional alternative for conceptualizing and addressing reading needs. Although initial research is promising, further investigation is needed to determine whether the effects of this new approach are similar to or perhaps exceed those associated with traditional approaches for improving reading fluency, such as repeated reading and PALS. Tables 2.1 to 2.3 provide a comparison of the reviewed interventions with regard to effective repeated reading interventions and skills taught, as well as general descriptions of intervention delivery components.

Table 2.1   Features of Effective Fluency-Building Interventions Across Reviewed Interventions

	Interventions		
Intervention Feature	*RN*	*PALS*	*RAVE-O*
Student reads to an adult	X	Periodically	X
Students are told the goal of intervention effort is to improve comprehension	X	Implied	Implied
Student has a specific reading goal	X	Not discussed	Not discussed
Students are provided feedback within session	By teacher	By student	By teacher
Repeated reading of materials	X	X	X

Note: RN = Read Naturally; PALS = Peer-Assisted Learning Strategies; RAVE-O = Retrieval, Automaticity, Vocabulary, Engagement with Language, and Orthography; X = explicit component of intervention.

Table 2.2   Content and Skill Coverage Across Reviewed Fluency-Building Interventions

	Interventions		
Skill	*RN*	*PALS*	*RAVE-O*
Word analysis/phonics	X	Varies by level	X
High-frequency words	X	Varies by level	X
Connected text	X	X	X
Comprehension	X	X	X
Orthographic patterns			X
Morphological analysis			X
Semantics and syntax			X

Note: RN = Read Naturally; PALS = Peer-Assisted Learning Strategies; RAVE-O = Retrieval, Automaticity, Vocabulary, Engagement with Language, and Orthography; X = explicit component of intervention.

Table 2.3   Recommended Delivery Features of the Reviewed Fluency-Building Interventions

	Interventions		
Delivery Feature	*RN*	*PALS*	*RAVE-O*
Group size	Flexible up to 15	Whole class	1:4
Time (minutes)	15–30	20–30	30 for Phonics Component + 30 for RAVE-O
Frequency	3 times per week	2–3 times per week	Daily
Daily role of teacher	Direct and facilitating	Facilitating	Direct teaching
Grade level	1–8	K–12	1–4

Note: RN = Read Naturally; PALS = Peer-Assisted Learning Strategies; RAVE-O = Retrieval, Automaticity, Vocabulary, Engagement with Language, and Orthography.

CHAPTER 3

Using Collaborative Strategic Reading to Improve Reading Comprehension

Alison Gould Boardman | *University of Colorado at Boulder*

Elizabeth Swanson | *University of Texas at Austin*

Janette K. Klingner | *University of Colorado at Boulder*

Sharon Vaughn | *University of Texas at Austin*

"I think [Collaborative Strategic Reading] has been an incredible innovation in my teaching. . . . I hadn't done cooperative groups in middle school Language Arts, and it's incredible."

From *Now We Get It!: Boosting comprehension with collaborative strategic reading* (Jossey-Bass/John Wiley & Sons, Inc.).

Overview of Reading Comprehension

The goal of reading instruction is to develop skills students will need to understand and learn from text. While this goal is easily attainable for typical readers, for many students with disabilities, especially the 1.7 million adolescents with a learning disability (LD; U.S. Department of Education, 2009), this task is difficult, at best. Reading comprehension combines the basic components of reading, discussed in Chapters 2 and 4 and in upcoming chapters (e.g., decoding, fluency, vocabulary knowledge), with cognition (e.g., processing, memory), motivation (e.g., interest, perseverance), and the demands of different text types within which reading takes place (e.g., reading a textbook, a sports magazine). It involves extracting meaning from the words on the page as well as interacting with a written language to bring those words

to life (RAND, 2002). This composite set of skills that is reading comprehension is a prerequisite for the *prose literacy* needed in the workplace of the 21st century (Kaestle, Campbell, Finn, Johnson, & Mikulecky, 2001) and, of equal importance, is needed to manage the multiple daily encounters with text that can range from text messages to technical manuals and canonical literature. Although many students with disabilities struggle with reading comprehension (Snow, Burns, & Griffin, 1998), we focus much of our discussion on students with LDs because problems with reading and reading comprehension are primary characteristics of this population (Kavale & Reese, 1992). The majority of students with LD initially struggle to read at the word level and then continue with word and comprehension difficulties as they progress through school. Thus, instruction in components of word reading such as phonological processing (understanding that words are made up of sounds), the alphabetic principle (knowing that sounds are represented by letters that make up words), decoding (applying letter sounds and chunks of letters to read words), fluency (reading words accurately, automatically, and with expression), and vocabulary is essential for students who lack skills in those areas. Reading comprehension is negatively influenced when students have difficulties with any of the components of reading. Consider the amount of attention it takes to sound out a long and unfamiliar word. For students with LD, laboring over word reading requires tremendous cognitive energy and limits the attention they can focus on understanding the text. Yet, a deficit in word-reading skills is not the sole contributor to breakdowns in comprehension. In fact, students with LD who read fluently often struggle to understand what they read (M. S. Edmonds et al., 2009; Englert & Thomas, 1987; J. P. Williams, 1998, 2000). This may be a result of many other factors contributing to comprehension including vocabulary knowledge, background knowledge, and the ability to read strategically.

Given comprehension's important role in helping individuals develop as successful readers and the difficulty struggling readers experience in text comprehension, one would expect teachers to focus a substantial amount of instructional time on practices that improve reading comprehension skills. Historically, this has not been the case. More than 30 years ago, Dolores Durkin (1978–1979) conducted a seminal classroom observation study that revealed a broad weakness in the quality of comprehension instruction. Durkin characterized classrooms that lacked in both quantity and quality of comprehension instruction. More often than not, a teacher would *mention* a skill (e.g., "after you read, write down the main idea"), offer opportunities to *practice* with skill sheets or workbooks, and then *assess* students' success or failure at applying the target skill. These traditional methods do not provide struggling readers with necessary instruction or models that teach them how to perform important reading skills and strategies. Furthermore, there was an overall lack of instructional time devoted to reading comprehension. Although much has been learned about comprehension instruction in the last 30 years, observations of classrooms indicate a continued lack of instruction in essential comprehension strategies (e.g., Pressley, 2006).

Recently, Klingner, Urbach, Golos, Brownell, and Menon (2008) observed 124 reading lessons taught by 41 special education teachers to determine the extent to which and in what ways they promoted their students' reading comprehension. In approximately one third of their observations, Klingner and colleagues did not observe any comprehension instruction. When teachers did provide comprehension instruction, it consisted of prompting students to use a strategy more often than

providing explicit instruction. The researchers concluded that special education teachers missed many opportunities to promote their students' reading comprehension and still seemed unsure how to teach reading comprehension strategies.

Perhaps more promising is a recent review of the five most common elementary core reading programs (Dewitz, Jones, & Leahy, 2009). Although the review of curriculum does not include observations of classroom practice, the authors conclude that more time is devoted to reading comprehension instruction than has been previously reported, including higher emphasis on modeling and guided practice. Still, these programs tend to teach skills in isolation, lack the research-supported focus on the metacognitive processes associated with each strategy (e.g., knowing why the strategy is used and when to use it), and none of the programs contain the opportunities for dialogue and higher-order thinking skills that support active engagement with text (National Institute of Child Health and Human Development [NICHD], 2000). Although quality comprehension strategy instruction has rarely been documented in classes that serve students with LD and other disabilities, the growing research base can inform teacher practice. In this chapter, we will present a summary of the literature on components of effective strategy interventions, followed by a literature review and description of Collaborative Strategic Reading (CSR)—a set of comprehension strategies that are effective for students with LD and other children at risk for problems with reading comprehension.

Summary of Literature on Strategy Instruction

Support and rationale for reading comprehension strategy instruction for students with disabilities has originated primarily from two lines of research: how successful readers understand text and effects from reading comprehension intervention studies.

Researchers have identified strategies successful readers use with the goal of teaching students with disabilities how to mimic these strategies during their own reading. These studies were often conducted by asking successful and poor readers to "think aloud" while reading. Researchers also question readers' actions before, during, and after reading text (e.g., Dole, Duffy, Roehler, & Pearson, 1991; Jimenez, Garcia, & Pearson, 1995; Klingner, 2004; Rudell & Unrau, 2004). Additional studies have investigated neuropsychological processes such as the study of eye movement to determine how individuals process text as they read (e.g., Starr, Kambe, Miller, & Keith, 2002). Overall, successful readers appear to be more strategic as they read than poor readers. These readers integrate a complex set of skills that they employ before, during, and after reading as necessary, to support text comprehension (A. H. Paris, Wasik, & Turner, 1991):

Successful readers:

- Read words fluently and accurately.

- Set goals for reading.

- Understand text structure and the organization of text.

- Make predictions, and modify predictions as needed while reading.

- Monitor understanding while reading.

- Generate main ideas as they read, connect what was read previously, and infer about what will come next.

- Connect ideas from what they are reading with prior knowledge.

- Make inferences.

- Use visualizations or other mental images to help them understand and remember.

When compared with successful readers, poor readers are less strategic in their selection and application of reading strategies (A. H. Paris, Lipson, & Wixson, 1983). Furthermore, struggling readers do not deduce comprehension strategies without specific instruction in what strategy to use, how to use it, when to use it, and why (Pressley, 2002). Students with LD most often approach reading tasks as inactive learners (Torgesen & Licht, 1983). They may lack motivation, content knowledge, vocabulary knowledge, necessary basic reading skills, and they often do not monitor their understanding as they read.

Several reviews of intervention research have reported positive outcomes for students with LD and struggling readers who are taught to use comprehension strategies (e.g., M. S. Edmonds et al., 2009; Gajria, Jitendra, Sood, & Sacks, 2007; Gersten, Fuchs, Williams, & Baker, 2001; Mastropieri, Scruggs, Bakken, & Whedon, 1996; Mastropieri, Scruggs, & Graetz, 2003; NICHD, 2000; H. L. Swanson & Hoskyn, 2001a; Talbott, Lloyd, & Tankersley, 1995; S. Vaughn, Gersten, & Chard, 2000). Other reviews analyze the effectiveness of unique components of comprehension instruction (see Maccini, Gagnon, & Hughes, 2002 for review of technology approaches; Kim, Vaughn, Wanzek, & Wei, 2004 for review of graphic organizers; and De La Paz & MacArthur, 2003 and Gajria et al., 2007 for reviews of strategy instruction for expository text type). Taken together, the following practices are associated with improved reading comprehension outcomes for students:

1. Facilitating students' familiarity and understanding of narrative and expository text structures, using strategies to figure out the meaning of unknown words, accessing prior knowledge, monitoring understanding during reading, using or creating graphic organizers, generating questions about what is read, and using cooperative learning to increase engagement are associated with improvements in reading comprehension.

2. Using explicit strategy instruction benefits both elementary- and secondary-age students with LD, struggling readers, and typically achieving students.

3. Providing explicit instruction in several strategies that can be used together (e.g., preview text, monitor comprehension, and formulate main ideas) is particularly effective at improving reading comprehension outcomes.

4. Whereas interventions in decoding and fluency may contribute to increased outcomes in reading comprehension for those with deficits in basic reading skills, explicit instruction in reading comprehension strategies is essential to growth in reading comprehension.

Teaching Reading Comprehension Strategies

The growing body of research on reading comprehension has given us information about what works with students with disabilities. Good readers combine a complex set of reading processes in order to understand and remember what they read. Thus, teaching students to be more strategic readers involves not only teaching strategies that good readers use, but also how to integrate the strategies together into a reading routine. Traditionally, reading comprehension instruction includes a session after reading in which the teacher asks questions about passage content to which students respond. When students struggle to come up with a correct response, teachers might provide additional support in the form of hints from the story, by paraphrasing key ideas, offering suggestions for where to find the answer, and so on. Students with LD are the least likely to raise their hand to respond or to be called on during such whole-class question-and-answer sessions, putting them at a great disadvantage (Alves & Gottlieb, 1986; R. McIntosh, Vaughn, Schumm, Haager, & Lee, 1993). Although this type of questioning may be effective at helping some students understand the content of what they have just read, it does not provide students with information that will increase their comprehension when they read the next time.

Strategy instruction presents a different focus, creating students who are more actively engaged throughout the reading process. Students are taught specific comprehension strategies that activate cognitive processes before, during, and after reading. For example, when students are taught to find the main idea, they learn methods for identifying the most important information in a section of text and how to synthesize that information into a succinct main idea sentence. Instruction includes teacher modeling with think alouds, scaffolding, and opportunities to practice with feedback. In strategy instruction, the teacher focuses both on comprehension strategies and the content to be learned.

Several multicomponent reading approaches, including reciprocal teaching (Palincsar, 1986), transactional strategies instruction (Pressley, El-Dinary, et al., 1992) and Collaborative Strategic Reading (CSR; Klingner & Vaughn, 1999; Klingner, Vaughn, Dimino, Schumm, & Bryant, 2001), incorporate similar strategies such as predicting, monitoring understanding, summarizing, and generating questions. In addition, all these strategies include peer discussion as a critical component to developing understanding about how to use reading strategies and about the content that was read.

Collaborative Strategic Reading

Collaborative Strategic Reading (CSR) was designed to promote content learning, language acquisition, and reading comprehension in diverse classrooms (Klingner, Vaughn, et al., 2001) and has been effective at increasing reading comprehension outcomes for students with LD, students at risk for reading difficulties, average- and high-achieving students (e.g., Bryant et al., 2000; Klingner, Vaughn, & Schumm, 1998; S. Vaughn, Chard, et al., 2000), and students who are English Language Learners (ELLs)

(Klingner & Vaughn, 1996). CSR consists of a series of before, during, and after reading strategies that allows students at varying levels to engage with grade-level text more independently than in traditional teacher-led discussions (Klingner, Vaughn, & Boardman, 2007). Before reading, students preview the text, brainstorm what they know about the topic, and predict what they will learn. During reading, students identify breakdowns in understanding and follow a series of steps to "fix up" the breakdowns. Students also write several "gist," or main idea, statements. After reading, students generate questions and write a short summary statement containing the most important information from the passage.

What distinguishes CSR from other comprehension approaches is the deliberate and well-specified manner in which cooperative learning (e.g., D. W. Johnson & Johnson, 1989) and reading comprehension strategy instruction (e.g., Palincsar & Brown, 1984) are integrated. In CSR, students use assigned cooperative learning expert roles in which each person has a unique job that contributes to the group. Students engage in a recursive process of working individually and then sharing with their group. For each strategy, students first record their own ideas and then discuss them with their group members before moving on. Figure 3.1 presents CSRs *before, during,* and *after* reading strategies. Although CSR has been used primarily in content area classrooms with expository text, teachers have succeeded in using CSR with narrative texts as well (Klingner et al., 2012).

Theoretical Foundation

Based on cognitive psychology (Flavell, 1979) and Lev Vygotsky's (1978) sociocultural theory, CSR includes three important instructional features: explicit instruction, scaffolding, and peer-mediated learning.

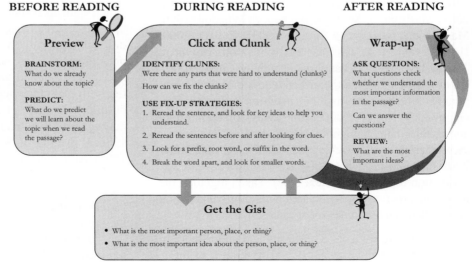

Figure 3.1 Collaborative Strategic Reading plan for strategic reading.
Source: Adapted with permission from Klingner, J. K., Vaughn, S., Dimino, J., Schumm, J. S., & Bryant, D. (2001). *Collaborative Strategic Reading: Strategies for improving comprehension* (p. 106). Longmont, CO: Sopris West. Cambium Learning Group-Sopris.

BEFORE READING

Preview

BRAINSTORM:
What do we already know about the topic?

PREDICT:
What do we predict we will learn about the topic when we read the passage?

DURING READING

Click and Clunk

IDENTIFY CLUNKS:
Were there any parts that were hard to understand (clunks)?
How can we fix the clunks?

USE FIX-UP STRATEGIES:
1. Reread the sentence, and look for key ideas to help you understand.
2. Reread the sentences before and after looking for clues.
3. Look for a prefix, root word, or suffix in the word.
4. Break the word apart, and look for smaller words.

AFTER READING

Wrap-up

ASK QUESTIONS:
What questions check whether we understand the most important information in the passage?

Can we answer the questions?

REVIEW:
What are the most important ideas?

Get the Gist

• What is the most important person, place, or thing?
• What is the most important idea about the person, place, or thing?

Explicit Instruction

A focus on explicit instruction in reading is grounded in a line of research in which teachers were taught to provide instruction in reading skills using defined teaching procedures. Results from these studies identified common practices that were associated with positive student outcomes (Carnine, 2000; Rosenshine & Stevens, 1986). These include teacher practices such as explicit teaching of skills in small steps and providing guided practice with feedback until students have a high rate of successful responses. Throughout the learning process, explicit instruction provides students with the metacognitive knowledge and self-regulation skills they need to read independently and successfully. Thus, when students learn a strategy, explicit instruction enables them to understand both its intent and its application, which, over time, translates into students' applying strategies effectively (e.g., a student learns to use fix-up strategies to find the meaning of unknown words or ideas while reading) and efficiently (e.g., the student knows how to identify the types of words or ideas that lend themselves to using fix-up strategies and knows to apply these strategies after reading a short section of text). Especially pertinent to students with disabilities, CSR does not require students to deduce or to discover the strategy or how it is used on their own. Teachers provide instruction that is clear and focused. Students learn to answer and internalize the following questions about each strategy they learn (Klingner, Vaughn, et al., 2001): What is the strategy? When is the strategy used? Why is the strategy important? and How do I carry out the strategy?

Scaffolding

In sociocultural theory, learning occurs in a student's zone of proximal development, the target area of instruction. The zone of proximal development is thought of as the difference between what students can do with help from the teacher and what they can do on their own (Vygotsky, 1978). The task for teachers is to provide just the right support to their students and then to gradually release responsibility as students become more proficient at a reading comprehension strategy. This enables students to reach their maximum learning potential.

During CSR lessons, teachers scaffold student learning. First, the teacher thinks aloud as she performs a new strategy. During this phase, you might hear a teacher say, "Watch me while I write a gist statement. Listen to the way I think about writing a gist. First, I identify the most important who or what. . . ." Slowly, the teacher turns more of the task over to students, resulting finally in students' independent application of the strategy. In sum, teachers have a plan for strategic reading, they include students in the plan, and they carefully scaffold learning through extensive modeling, guided practice, and independent practice with teacher feedback and support.

Peer-mediated Learning

Peer-mediated learning is another important component of CSR. In sociocultural theory, interaction between peers is a critical aspect of learning and cognitive development (Gallimore & Tharp, 1990). Students can assist each others' performance by providing immediate feedback at a level and in a manner that is appropriate for the group. Consider this interaction regarding a main idea, or gist statement, during CSR. Two students have just written their own gists and are sharing what they wrote:

Student A: I put that, "Scientists are making fabrics out of chicken feathers."

Student B: Okay, but I think that's a detail. And you are missing the part about the bad stuff. That fabrics use too much petroleum and that's why scientists need to make new fabrics.

Student A: Oh . . . [pause while student reworks gist]. How about "Scientists are making new fabrics that don't hurt the environment."?

Student B: Okay, I think that gets both the environmental part and that they don't use the bad stuff. And it's 10 words, right?

Student A: Good, are we ready to go on to the next section?

The influence of student–student feedback is notable. The teachers we work with are often impressed by students' ability to explain and encourage each other in cooperative learning groups. One of the strengths of CSR is the focus on strong teacher instruction and feedback in conjunction with teaching students to support each other during engaging conversations about what they are reading. Teachers encourage active learning through a cooperative learning structure (D. W. Johnson & Johnson, 1989) that includes the use of group roles, clear expectations for group work, teaching group-work skills to students, and lots of modeling and practice about how to make cooperative learning successful.

Research Support for CSR

Collaborative Strategic Reading was designed to improve the reading comprehension of struggling readers, including students with LD (Klingner, Vaughn, et al., 2001) and is supported by a corpus of promising research findings resulting from several experimental and quasi-experimental studies focused on effectiveness of

CSR among students with LD and descriptive studies of teacher implementation.

Effectiveness Studies

Early studies of CSR focused on evaluating its effectiveness within science and social studies content area instruction. In one such study (Klingner, Vaughn, & Schumm, 1998), one researcher taught CSR to intact, heterogeneous fourth-grade classes for 45 minutes per day during an 11-day Florida state history unit. The comparison group of intact classes received instruction reflective of the school's typical practice. Students in the CSR group made greater gains in reading comprehension and equal gains in content knowledge. In a separate study (Klingner & Vaughn, 2000), fifth graders who were ELLs were provided with CSR instruction for 30–40 minutes per day, 2 to 3 days per week, over a 4-week period during science instruction. Students frequently engaged in verbal discourse that supported vocabulary and content knowledge development. Students who were ELLs as well as low-, average-, and high-achieving students who were non-ELLs made gains in target vocabulary over time using CSR.

In another series of studies, researchers provided teachers with extensive professional development and coaching in CSR. Bryant and colleagues (2000) provided 10 sixth-grade teachers with three full-day workshops where they learned the Word Identification Strategy (Lenz, Schumaker, Deshler, & Beals, 1984), Partner Reading (Delquadri, Greenwood, Whorton, Carta, & Hall, 1986), and CSR. Following training, all teachers received coaching from workshop leaders and participated in teacher–researcher meetings twice per month to discuss ideas and solve implementation problems. Teachers implemented all three strategies over a 4-month period. On a measure of word identification, students with LD made statistically significant gains from pre- to post-test on measures of word identification (effect size [ES] = 0.64) and fluency (ES = 0.67). However, they did not exhibit statistically significant gains on a curriculum-based measure of reading comprehension (ES = 0.22).

In a similar study, S. Vaughn, Chard, and colleagues (2000) studied the differential effects of partner reading and CSR instruction on reading outcomes for students with LD and low- to average-achieving third graders. In this study, eight third-grade teachers received either CSR or partner reading training that consisted of 5 hours in professional development sessions, co-teaching and modeling by researchers, and support group meetings twice during the semester. Each strategy was implemented two to three times per week over a 12-week period. Each CSR session lasted approximately 45 minutes, and partner-reading sessions lasted approximately 25 minutes. Authors reported that CSR and partner reading groups performed equally well on tests of oral reading rate and accuracy as well as reading comprehension. Although small sample sizes precluded comparing outcomes of students with reading disabilities to students in other achievement groups, pre- to post-test gains for students with reading disabilities who participated in either CSR or partner reading varied, with effect sizes ranging from 0.14 on comprehension to 0.83 on oral reading rate.

In a third study, Klingner, Vaughn, Arguelles, Hughes, and Leftwich (2004) provided a group of five fourth-grade teachers with CSR training and in-class demonstrations. Teachers implemented CSR twice per week over an unspecified period of time. A comparison group of teachers provided instruction as usual. On a norm-referenced, distal measure of reading comprehension (a measure of the skill that was not directly taught in the program), students in the CSR group outperformed students in the typical practice comparison group (ES = 0.19). Whereas only gains made by high/average-achieving students were statistically significant (ES = 0.25), pre- to post-test effect sizes for students with LD and low-achieving students were medium in size (ES = 0.38 for students with LD; ES = 0.51 for low-achieving students).

Finally, a computer-adapted version of CSR was investigated in Kim and colleagues' (2006) experimental study of sixth- through eighth-grade students with LD who were randomly assigned to either a computer-based CSR intervention or typical school practice comparison groups. Students in the treatment group were provided with 20 to 24 sessions, 50 minutes in duration, of computer-based CSR. On a norm-referenced measure of passage comprehension, students in the CSR group outperformed students in the comparison group (ES = 0.50). Effects were larger in magnitude for students in the CSR group on more proximal measures of main idea (ES = 0.95) and question generation (ES = 1.18).

Implementation Studies

The final set of studies (Klingner, Arguelles, Hughes, & Vaughn, 2001; Klingner, Vaughn, Hughes, & Arguelles, 1999; S. Vaughn, Hughes, Schumm, & Klingner, 1998) used descriptive research designs to report teachers' perceptions of CSR before, during, and after implementation. S. Vaughn, Hughes, and colleagues (1998) worked with seven general education teachers who taught in a school recently restructured to include students with LD in the general education classroom full-time. CSR was one of four reading and writing practices implemented over the course of a 1-year period of professional development and coaching. Researchers documented the level of implementation and teachers' perceptions of effectiveness of the four practices. Findings indicated that only one teacher was familiar with CSR before professional development, and initial reactions to CSR were not positive, though teachers' enthusiasm increased after implementation. Of the four instructional practices, CSR had the lowest implementation, with only two teachers implementing it on a "consistent" basis. Facilitators to implementation of the strategies included the ability to adapt and modify the strategy and students' acceptance of the strategy. Barriers included the time it took to cover material using the approach and the perceived need to prepare students adequately for standardized tests.

Three years later, researchers (Klingner et al., 1999) returned to these teachers' classrooms to ascertain the level to which the four strategies continued to be implemented. Through focus group interviews, classroom observations, a facilitators and barriers checklist, and individual interviews, researchers found that five teachers reduced their level of CSR implementation over the 3-year period, while one increased implementation, and one maintained a high level of implementation. Two reasons were cited for the decrease in CSR implementation: the need for ongoing professional development, and CSR being viewed as appropriate only for content-area learning. Conversely, two teachers cited several facilitators to sustained use, including a support network that incorporated coaching from an experienced teacher, administrative backing, and student benefits.

In the third in this series of studies, Klingner, Arguelles, et al. (2001) conducted a follow-up study to the series of implementation studies previously described (Klingner, Arguelles, et al., 2001; Klingner, Vaughn, et al., 1999; S. Vaughn, Hughes, et al., 1998) to determine the extent to which the instructional practices they had taught had spread to other teachers' classrooms. They found that 57 of the 98 teachers in two schools had tried CSR, and 31 continued to use it regularly. Understandably, intermediate-level teachers were much more likely to use it than primary-grade teachers. Special education and ELL teachers also learned it. Teachers gave many reasons for choosing to learn CSR, but the primary reason was that they expected that CSR would benefit their students. Although only two of the seven teachers who had participated in the original professional development program had sustained their usage of CSR, they were influential teachers who were able to convince their colleagues to try CSR and were willing to help them learn it.

These findings support the claim that CSR is a complex set of strategies that are difficult to implement without high-quality support and modeling from expert teachers. Based on these findings, we note several trends for effectively implementing CSR. First, teachers should commit to implementing CSR over an extended period of time. It seems that far more than 30 sessions are needed to produce gains among students with LD. Second, it takes time for teachers to become facile at teaching the CSR strategies. One should seek out experts (i.e., master teachers) to provide support and guidance in mastering the strategy and cooperative grouping components of CSR.

How to Teach CSR

CSR includes four reading strategies for use before, during, and after reading (Klingner, Vaughn, et al., 2001). Before each CSR lesson, the teacher identifies an appropriate selection of text (e.g., a section of a textbook chapter, a short article, a chapter from a novel), divides the text into sections (usually three to four), identifies key vocabulary or concepts for preteaching, and formulates model gist statements. In this way, the teacher can support content learning and prepare to provide meaningful feedback to students. For instance, with preparation, a teacher can easily identify if a student's gist statement is a detail from the section or if it encompasses the most important information.

Before Reading Strategies

Preview

The purpose of previewing is to help students identify what the text will be about, to make connections to their prior knowledge about the topic, and to generate interest in reading the text. Teachers and students engage in a four-step procedure to complete the before-reading, preview strategy. First, the teacher introduces the topic in a whole-class setting. If students lack background knowledge about the topic presented in the passage, this is an ideal time for teachers to provide some base knowledge. For example, if prerequisite knowledge about the coral life cycle is necessary to understand an article about the development of coral reefs, then before reading, the teacher can provide a description or graphic that describes the structure of coral and its life cycle. Teachers may also introduce key terms such as important proper nouns or vocabulary words that can't be figured out using the "clunk" fix-up strategies (described following). Second, students activate their background knowledge by brainstorming what they already know about the topic. Third, students briefly preview the passage, looking at headings, subheadings, pictures or tables and their captions, as well as bold words and other features that stand out. The goal during this step is for students to learn as much as possible in a very short period of time. Finally, based on the knowledge gained during the text preview, students predict what they might learn. Students first record both brainstorming and predictions individually in the learning log and then share them within small groups for feedback and discussion. Figure 3.2 presents a short passage and a student's completed learning log on bison.

Figure 3.2 Sample reading passage and corresponding Collaborative Strategic Reading student learning log.

Bison

The largest mammal

The bison is the largest land mammal in North America. Males, called bulls, weigh up to 2,000 pounds. That is about as heavy as a car. Despite their large size, bison are herbivores, feeding mostly on grass varieties. Bison live on large grassy ranges in the Western Plains.

On the go

Bison are migratory animals. The time and route for migration varies depending on the weather and where food is most plentiful. It is common for bison to move towards winter migration ranges when snowfall increases. Many of these routes, carved into the earth from thousands of hoofs year after year, passing by water sources and fertile ground, were followed by Native Americans, explorers, and pioneers.

CSR Learning Log for Informational Text

Name _____ Date_____

Today's Topic *Bison* _____

BEFORE READING: Preview

Brainstorm: Connections to prior knowledge

I saw a bison when I was on a vacation in Yellowstone National Park.

Predict: What I might learn about the topic

I will learn how big a bison is. Also I'll read about where it lives.

DURING READING: Section 1

Clunks		**Fix-up Strategies**
herbivore = *animal that eats grass*		① 2 3 4

Gist:

Bison are very large but they only eat grasses.

DURING READING: Section 2

Clunks		**Fix-up Strategies**
Plentiful = *lots; there is plenty*		① 2 3 ④
Migratory Range = *area to live in winter*		1 ② ③ 4

Gist:

Bison's migration routes were also used by people.

AFTER READING: Wrap-Up

Questions: Write questions and answers.

What is a male bison called?
A male bison is called a bull.
Why did explorers and Native Americans follow the bison's migratory routes?
They probably followed the routes because they were already made into paths and went near food and water.
How are bison similar to and different from horses?
Horses also are herbivores. Horses used to live on open ranges but now they mostly live on ranches. You can ride a horse but I bet you can't ride a buffalo.

Review: Write one or two of the most important ideas in this passage.
        Be prepared to justify your ideas.

Bison live on ranges. They are herbivores and they have to migrate to avoid snow and find food when it is cold.

Source: Information from Klingner, J. K., Vaughn, S., Dimino, J., Schumm, J. S., & Bryant, D. (2001). *Collaborative Strategic Reading: Strategies for improving* comprehension (p. 105). Longmont, CO: Sopris West. Cambium Learning Group-Sopris.

During Reading Strategies

Click and Clunk

Students use the click and clunk strategy to monitor understanding during reading. When students understand what they read, everything "clicks." When something doesn't make sense, or "clunks," students must stop to figure out what went wrong. The click and clunk component of CSR involves the following steps. After reading a short section of text (e.g., one or two paragraphs), students record their clunks individually on the learning logs. Next, the clunk expert guides students to use fix-up strategies to figure out the meaning of the difficult words or concepts. In this way, students learn to monitor their comprehension and to actively work to repair misunderstandings. CSR uses four fix-up strategies:

1. Reread the sentence without the word. Think about what would make sense.
2. Reread the sentence with the clunk and the sentences before or after the clunk, looking for clues.
3. Look for a prefix, suffix, or root in the word.
4. Break the word apart, and look for smaller words you know.

Fix-up strategies are also provided to students on cue cards that can be referred to easily during reading. In their learning logs, each student writes a brief definition next to their clunk. Teachers can review clunks to see which words or ideas the students are struggling with as they read. After reviewing the clunks, teachers may decide to provide additional instruction to support vocabulary learning.

Get the Gist

Teaching students to identify and restate the main idea of passages they read is associated with improved understanding of text (Klingner et al., 2007). During "get the gist," students write the central ideas of a paragraph or short section of text. Students are taught a three-step procedure for writing a gist statement. First, students name the most important "who or what" in the paragraph. Second, they identify the most important information about the "who or what," leaving out details. Third, they write a sentence using approximately 10 words. "Get the gist" helps students distinguish between important information and details, use key concepts and vocabulary, use their own words, and write only what is needed to present the main idea. Students record their gist statements on their learning logs after reading each section of text (see Figure 3.2).

After Reading Strategies

Wrap-Up

Students learn to "wrap-up" their reading by generating questions and answers about what they have read and by reviewing key ideas. The purpose of "wrap-up" is to increase knowledge and memory for what was read, to further engage with text, and to monitor understanding. Students are taught to use question starters (i.e., who, what, when, where, why, and how) to write questions that capture key information from the text. Questions should be related to the text and should be answered either by reading the passage or by combining background knowledge with information from the reading. In most classrooms, students write individual questions and answers on their learning logs first and then share their questions with their group. Finally, students review what they have learned by writing one or two of the most important ideas from the passage and justifying why their ideas are important when they share with their group (see Figure 3.2). As with the other strategies, students first write their ideas on their own and then discuss and revise when they share with their group members. Many teachers also conduct a quick whole-class wrap-up where students can ask and answer each others' questions and present their most important ideas. At this time the teacher can also call students' attention to key ideas from the text and connect to what has been learned previously or what will be learned in future lessons.

Introducing CSR

Multicomponent reading comprehension strategies require teachers to invest planning and instructional time in order for students to achieve proficiency and to benefit from strategy use. Introducing CSR generally requires about 12 to 14 lessons (about 4 to 5 weeks) before students can work through all the strategies together in their cooperative groups. Many teachers implement CSR two to three times each week. When teachers initially introduce CSR, they model the entire process of CSR with a short passage, demonstrating how to use learning logs and discussing the benefits of CSR. Teachers may choose to show a video of students engaged in a CSR lesson or to bring in a small group of experienced student CSR users to demonstrate in front of the class. CSR includes the following explicit instructional cycle to introduce and to practice each strategy individually until all strategies are integrated into the reading routine.

During the *modeling phase,* teachers begin by providing explicit instruction in the strategy, telling students what the strategy is, why it is used, when to use it, and finally, how to use the strategy. Teachers show students how the strategy works by thinking out loud as they record their ideas on their learning log. For example, you might hear the following from a fourth-grade teacher conducting a think aloud of writing a gist after reading a passage about the Caddo Indians:

> Listen as I get the gist of this paragraph [teacher reads paragraph aloud]. There is a lot of information in this paragraph, but let's see whether we can figure out what it is mostly about. First, I'm going to identify the most important "who" or "what." This paragraph is mostly about The Caddo Indians [teacher writes "the Caddo" on blackboard]. Now, I need to decide on the most important information provided about the Caddo. The Caddo were farmers. There is also information about helping their neighbors with planting and making pottery. This seems to mostly be about the Caddo culture and some of the things the Caddo people did. So, I think the most important thing about the Caddo is that they were farmers and made pottery to trade [teacher models how to write a gist, a short sentence containing the most important information].

In the *teacher-assisted phase,* students join the teacher in using the strategy and may begin to practice in pairs or small groups. The teacher-assisted phase is a key scaffolding component as teachers monitor how well students grasp the strategy and adjust practice opportunities to meet their needs. For instance, while teaching the "get the gist" strategy, teachers may first determine the most important "who or what" with the class, and then have students create a class list of the most important ideas. Students then work in pairs to combine those important ideas into a gist statement. The teacher can then evaluate student gists as a group, pointing out examples and nonexamples of gists and highlighting key features. For example, for our sample passage on bison (see Figure 3.2), the following gists were shared with the class for the reading section titled, "On the Go": (a) *Bison migrate in winter* (too general, not all important information is included); (b) *Migration and depending on weather and to find food* (too detail focused; not a complete sentence; missing connection to people who used routes); and (c) *Bison's migration routes were also used by people* (contains the most important "who or what" and the most important ideas about the "who or what"). The teacher can lead the class in evaluating the gists and discussing features of a high-quality gist.

Another key feedback component occurs when students provide support and feedback to each other in their cooperative learning groups. Teachers gauge how long students work in the teacher-assisted phase according to student proficiency at using a strategy. The goal is that students can perform the strategy successfully on their own.

During the *independent phase* of CSR, students combine the strategies they have learned so far in their cooperative groups. Teachers are very engaged in student learning during group work, spending time with each group (about 2 to 5 minutes each) to provide substantive feedback and guidance. A benefit of strategy instruction is that it can support the feedback process for teachers. Consider the student who has written a detail for her main idea. The entry point for feedback is to draw attention to the strategy. The teacher might ask questions such as, "What is the most important 'who or what?'" "Is that 'who or what' included in your gist?" "This is a detail that is included but does not capture the most important information in the section." Teachers also address issues or problems that they observe across multiple groups by discussing them with the entire class. The teacher's role during group work also includes spending extended time with each group at least once every 2 weeks, monitoring the performance of each group, monitoring the performance of each group member, highlighting the performance of students and groups who are implementing CSR well, and supporting low-achieving students.

Cooperative Learning Group Roles

CSR uses cooperative group roles to facilitate peer-mediated discussion and learning. Groups of three to five students use the following group roles:

- *Leader:* Leads the group in the implementation of CSR by saying what to read or which strategy to do next.
- *Clunk expert:* Leads the group in trying to figure out difficult words or concepts.
- *Gist expert:* Guides the group toward the development of a gist and determines that the gist contains the most important ideas but no unnecessary details.
- *Question expert:* Guides the group to generate and answer questions.
- *Encourager:* Watches the group and gives feedback. Looks for behaviors to praise. Encourages all group members to participate and assist one another.
- *Time-keeper:* Sets the timer for each portion of CSR and lets the group know when it is time to move on. Helps keep the group on task.

Grouping is an important component of cooperative learning and CSR. Teachers assign students to heterogeneous groups, taking into consideration student characteristics such as leadership qualities, reading level, and ability to work well in groups. Because teachers vary group size according to the needs of their classrooms, roles may also vary. Essential roles are the "leader," the "clunk expert," the "gist expert," and the "question expert." When groups are smaller than four students, teachers can assign two roles to one student. For instance, one student could be the gist expert during reading and the question expert after reading. In some cases, the teacher may take on a role such as the timekeeper or the encourager. High-quality cooperative learning has several features (D. W. Johnson & Johnson, 1989) that are incorporated into the structure of CSR. These are presented in Figure 3.3. For an extensive discussion of how to implement cooperative learning, please see D. W. Johnson, Johnson, and Holubec (2008). Introducing cooperative learning can be challenging, especially in classrooms where students are not used to working together (D. W. Johnson & Johnson, 2009). CSR roles (leader, clunk expert, gist expert, question expert, timekeeper, and encourager) are taught to students so that each student becomes a valued and contributing member of the group. There are two ways that teachers introduce cooperative learning with CSR, and both have strengths. The first is to teach the CSR strategies to students in a whole-class format and to provide opportunities for pairs or triads of students to practice together and to begin providing feedback and support to each other regarding their strategy use and content learning. Once students gain proficiency at using the strategies, teachers then introduce the CSR roles and cooperative learning procedures. The strength in this method is that students become strong CSR users before learning to work together in groups. A drawback is that once students are comfortable working on their own, they may not readily see the benefit of discussing with and supporting peers during group learning. If this occurs, teachers should show students how learning is advanced with cooperative learning and demonstrate how discussion and engagement are increased when students work together in groups.

An alternative method for introducing cooperative groups within CSR is to integrate the learning of roles and group-work skills with instruction of comprehension strategies. For example, a teacher might model how to use preview in one lesson and then provide guided practice in the next lesson. On the third lesson, the teacher introduces group roles and teaches students to conduct preview in cooperative groups, using group roles. The strength in this method is that students learn group work skills as part of CSR and thus see reading comprehension strategies and cooperative group learning as interconnected parts of CSR from the beginning (Klingner et al., 2012).

Whether students first become proficient at CSR strategies or learn cooperative group roles along with the CSR strategies, it is imperative that teachers provide students with skills to function effectively in groups. Structuring cooperative group activities is not enough to help students learn to work together effectively in groups. Teachers should take time to explicitly teach the responsibilities of each group role. Just as teachers scaffold learning when teaching clunks or gist, so do teachers scaffold learning cooperative group roles. For example, teachers may provide a model of students who are experienced at CSR either with a small-group demonstration or a video. Students can then come together in role-alike groups (i.e., all "leaders" meet in one group, all "clunk experts" meet in another, etc.) and discuss how to perform their roles and why they are important. In addition, students need to be taught the rules and procedures of group work and may need explicit instruction in group-work skills such as how to support ideas with evidence and how to provide feedback to group members. Finally, students need support to process how well their group work is going. The role of the encourager guides students to debrief the quality of their group work. Teachers can also build on the encourager's role to help students recognize what worked and what they can do better the next time they do CSR. In sum, do not expect students to perform their roles, provide effective feedback to one

Figure 3.3 Features of cooperative learning (D. W. Johnson & Johnson, 1989) incorporated into Collaborative Strategic Reading.

Positive interdependence: Unique and important roles support positive interdependence because students feel that their work benefits others in group.

Face-to-face interaction among students: Group members encourage, support, and assist each other in small groups through structured sharing of responses and discussion led by expert roles.

Individual accountability: Students complete individual learning logs and understand that their individual performance is assessed regularly.

Positive social skills: Teachers provide instruction in group work skills so that students can be successful working together.

Evaluation and reflection: The encourager role leads students in reflecting how well the group worked together and in identifying strengths and shortcomings of their group work.

Figure 3.4 Sample Collaborative Strategic Reading cue cards.

Leader	Clunk Expert	Gist Expert	Question Expert
Before Reading Preview *What topic?* Prompt group to brainstorm about topic Review titles, headers, pictures Predict			
During Reading Prompt group to Read Click and Clunk Get the Gist	**During Reading** Help group identify clunks and figure out word meanings *Does someone in the group understand?* Yes! Explain No? Use fix up strategies	**During Reading** Help group identify most important who or what and the most important information about the who or what in 10 words or less	
After Reading Wrap up Prompt questions, review, share			**After Reading** Help group think of questions that check for understanding Ask and answer questions

Source: Based on Klingner, J. K., Vaughn, S., Dimino, J., Schumm, J. S., & Bryant, D. (2001). *Collaborative Strategic Reading: Strategies for improving comprehension.* Longmont, CO: Sopris West.

another, and support their ideas with evidence from the text without explicit instruction in these skills. Allow planning time to prepare for these lessons and decide before CSR implementation how the introduction of cooperative learning will be worked into the initial lessons used to get CSR up and running in the classroom.

CSR Materials

Several materials aid students and teachers in implementing CSR. Learning logs are used by students to record before, during, and after reading activities (see Figure 3.2). Learning logs are important because they provide a vehicle for individual processing and accountability and become a tool for follow-up activities, as well as a way for teachers to monitor student progress and provide feedback. Learning logs are easily adapted for younger students by providing additional space for students to write and picture cues for each strategy or for older students by decreasing the font size and including additional sections as needed. Teachers can also create a scoring rubric that includes the components of each CSR strategy and aids evaluation of student learning logs.

Another set of materials that supports CSR implementation is the CSR cue cards (see Figures 3.4 and 3.5) (Klingner, Vaughn, et al., 2001). Cue cards provide prompts about how to perform a given cooperative group role. For example, the question expert role card cues the student in this role to guide her group through the question-generation strategy and to lead students in asking and answering questions in the group (see Figure 3.5).

Figure 3.5   Sample CSR cue card: Question expert card.

Question Expert

Job Description

The question expert guides the group in coming up with questions that address important information from the reading. The question expert makes sure that students ask different levels of questions. The question expert checks to see that all students write questions and answers.

AFTER READING

Wrap-Up

- Let's think of some questions to check whether we really understood what we read. Write your questions and the answers in your learning log.

  Remember to write different types of questions:

  a. "Right there"

  b. "Think and search"

  c. "Author and you"

  [After everyone is finished writing questions, ask:]

- Who would like to share his or her best question?

  [Check that the question begins with "who," "what," "when," "where," "why," or "how."]

- Who would like to answer that question?

- Where did you find the information to answer that question?

Question Types

LEVEL ONE: "RIGHT THERE"

- Question can be answered in one sentence.

- Answers can be found word-for-word in the story.

Example: *The answer to "What is the capital of Texas?" is found in one of the sentences of the text: "The capital of Texas is Austin."*

LEVEL TWO: "THINK AND SEARCH"

- Questions can be answered by looking in the text.

- Answers require one sentence or more.

- Information is found in more than one place and put together.

Example: *To answer "How did ranchers get their cattle to the markets?" several sentences are needed to describe the steps that are presented on different pages of the text.*

LEVEL THREE: "AUTHOR AND YOU"

- Questions cannot be answered by using the text alone.

- Answers require thinking about what the reader just read, what the reader already knows, and how it fits together.

Examples: *How is the vampire bat different from other bats we have read about?*
Why did Jackie Robinson need to prove he could win at baseball?

Students appreciate the support of the cue cards as they build confidence and become experts at their given roles. Our observations and reports from teachers indicate that many students who were previously quiet and inactive during reading activities increase on-task behavior and engagement in reading when they participate in CSR cooperative groups.

Text Selection

Selecting Text to Use with CSR

CSR can be used with a variety of reading passages. We recommend using text that contains important information for students to learn and that is relevant to their curriculum. For teachers who find themselves avoiding having students read in content classrooms or replacing student reading with teacher read alouds, CSR is an excellent way to help students gain access to text. In social studies or science, teachers may select sections of the textbook or identify additional readings that focus on the content to be learned. Students at a variety of levels can work together to tackle the dense, content-heavy text that is often found in textbooks (Mastropieri et al., 2003). In language arts, reading, and special education classrooms, teachers often choose expository text that supports a novel or unit of study. For example, when reading the *Diary of Anne Frank,* teachers may choose selections on the holocaust, diary writing, and Germany. During a unit on poetry, teachers may select text that provides background readings on poetry genres and the poets that are being studied.

Teachers introduce CSR with passages that are relatively short (one to two pages or less) and convey clear information that lends itself to the target reading strategies. Many teachers choose to begin with short sections from content-area textbooks or weekly news magazine-type articles. When focusing on a specific strategy, such as clunks or gist, short paragraphs may provide enough text to practice the strategy.

Using Narrative Text

Teachers have also used CSR with novels and narrative selections. Small adaptations to the learning log facilitate using CSR with narrative text. For example, on the learning log, brainstorm might be changed from, "what I already know about the topic" to, "what we read about yesterday." In addition, because narrative text is not usually as information laden as expository text, students may be able to read longer sections before stopping to generate a gist statement. With longer sections, the number of words used to write the gist might also be increased. Comprehension strategies support reading in a variety of contexts. As with any reading materials, when using narrative text, teachers should be sure that the strategies in CSR support their goals for reading and provide students with strategies that will help them actively engage in reading, monitor their understanding, and improve comprehension.

Conclusion

Collaborative Strategic Reading provides both teachers and students with a systematic approach to reading comprehension. With explicit teaching that includes scaffolding instruction, students with LD and struggling readers gain the deep understanding they need to apply their newly learned strategies when they read. Still, the teaching of reading comprehension strategies does not simplify the complex decisions teachers make as they approach the profundity of content that is to be learned in their classrooms (M. W. Conley, 2008). Furthermore, the implementation of CSR and other multicomponent reading comprehension strategies is not easily accomplished. Each strategy on its own is complex and requires a unique knowledge base. Teachers who are successful at teaching CSR tend to implement CSR regularly (two to three times each week) and are responsive to student needs and adjust instruction to ensure student mastery. These teachers focus on helping students internalize and apply the cognitive strategies they are learning in CSR and provide the tools students need to do so. For example, when teaching fix-up strategies, students who have limited knowledge of prefixes and suffixes will need instruction in how to use the third fix-up strategy ("Look for a prefix, suffix, or root in the word"), but will also need to learn the affixes required to apply the strategies.

Teachers can use CSR in general education classrooms where students with special needs are included for instruction (Klingner et al., 2004) as well as in special education settings (Klingner & Vaughn, 1996). CSR takes time to learn, both for teachers and for students. Teachers who integrate the instruction of reading comprehension strategies into their curriculum, taking time for students to gain mastery in the strategies and in the skills needed to work effectively in groups, are rewarded by increased reading comprehension outcomes for students.

CHAPTER 4

Vocabulary Instruction for Students at Risk for Reading Disabilities: *Promising Approaches for Learning Words from Texts*

Joanne F. Carlisle, Christine K. Kenney, and **Anita Vereb** | *University of Michigan*

From birth, children learn words that are used by others in their homes and at school. Differences in the depth and breadth of their vocabulary begin early. Once they start school, better language learners and readers might learn as many as 5,000 to 7,000 words a year, while the students at risk for reading problems might learn as few as 1,000 words a year (e.g., I. L. Beck & McKeown, 1991). For some, challenges acquiring word knowledge stem from language impairment, hearing impairment, or reading disability. Others are learning English as a second language. Vocabulary knowledge is important in its own right but particularly for school-aged students because of the strong relationship of vocabulary and achievement in reading comprehension (Cunningham & Stanovich, 1997; R. K. Wagner, Muse, & Tannenbaum, 2007). In this chapter, we examine approaches for teaching students ways to learn words and habits to engage in word learning that have the potential to improve their word knowledge and to prevent the onset of pervasive difficulties with reading comprehension.

About 90% of the approximately 3,000 words students learn each year are learned through exposure to words in their classrooms and home environments—through a process referred to as *incidental word learning* (Carlisle, Fleming, & Gudbrandsen, 2000). Students typically learn only a small number of words through teachers' instruction or activities related to the educational programs in school. Incidental word learning may sound like an aspect of language development outside the influence of the teacher, but this is a misconception. Using strategies that we describe in this chapter, teachers can assist students to become more adept at learning words from context, and these techniques have the potential advantage of providing students with life-long habits of thinking about and reflecting on the meanings of words they hear and read. Because of the demonstrated benefits to students' word learning, this chapter focuses on methods to help students learn words from texts, whether with adult or technical support or on their own.

To date, no major reviews of vocabulary instruction report on methods of instruction in word learning through reading for students with or at risk for learning and other disabilities. In fact, the National Reading Panel (NRP) (2000a) reported on the limited number of high-quality studies of instruction in vocabulary of any kind and recommended that research on vocabulary instruction be regarded as a high priority. The need to determine methods of vocabulary instruction that foster improvements in students' word learning is underscored by research that shows powerful and lasting effects of vocabulary knowledge on students' reading comprehension through the school-aged years (Cunningham & Stanovich, 1997). As Roberts, Torgesen, Boardman, and Scammacca (2008) pointed out, for older students in particular, accurate and fluent word identification receives considerable attention from researchers, but fluent reading gets you nowhere if you don't know the meanings of the words you are reading. Comprehension is contingent on students' vocabulary knowledge and their ability to infer the meanings of unfamiliar words that they encounter as they read.

Even students who do not have particular challenges in acquiring vocabulary benefit from support in learning how to learn words, as vocabulary affects comprehension in content areas, whether through oral or written language. Unfortunately, recent analysis of classroom observations and surveys has indicated that little time is devoted to vocabulary instruction (E. A. Swanson, Wexler, & Vaughn, 2009). Because students with reading difficulties also spend less time reading than their peers, E. A. Swanson et al. (2009) emphasized the critical role of teachers in providing guidance for students' learning of strategies to support their word and text comprehension.

If we accept that the goal of vocabulary development is to improve students' language and reading comprehension, what methods might be most promising? Two reviews of instruction in vocabulary for students with or at risk for learning disabilities have reported research on effective vocabulary interventions (Bryant, Goodwin, Bryant, & Higgins, 2003; Jitendra, Edwards, Sacks, & Jacobson, 2004). In these reviews, most interventions focused on techniques to assist memory of taught words. Jitendra et al. (2004) found 27 studies that provided instruction in the key-word method, cognitive strategy instruction, direct instruction, constant time delay, activity-based instruction, and computer-aided instruction. Bryant et al. (2003) reported that the major emphasis of the interventions in their review was also memorization and practice of specific words out of context. The various techniques for memorizing individual words used in these studies have one important limitation: students learn a limited number of words. If they learn 10 words each week, they would work on about 400 words during a school year, perhaps 300 of which they will remember. Direct instruction can account for only a small portion of the 3,000 words that, on average, students learn in a year. Students therefore need more fluid approaches that aid in problem solving when they encounter unfamiliar words as they read.

Our focus is on methods of instruction that help students learn words while reading. Even in the preschool years, children can become accustomed to thinking about how words are used in specific contexts, to developing ways of anticipating what these words might mean, and to sharing ideas and experiences related to these words. In addition, these reflective techniques engage students in the critical process of monitoring their understanding of words and texts. As Nagy (2007) pointed out, word-learning strategies can also serve as comprehension-repair strategies.

Of course, teaching students strategies to infer word meanings as they read (or listen to) a text is not the only approach to vocabulary instruction teachers might consider using. Indeed, researchers have recommended a broad-based approach to building students' vocabulary, including direct instruction, teaching students to use resources such as dictionaries, and creating a classroom environment that stimulates word consciousness (I. L. Beck & McKeown, 1991; M. F. Graves, 2006; Jenkins, Matlock, & Slocum, 1989; Nagy, 2007). However, because our goal was to synthesize research on vocabulary instruction that might benefit not only word learning but also reading comprehension, we searched the research literature for methods teachers might use to foster students' understanding of unfamiliar words while reading. In the next three sections, we discuss studies we found in three very different areas, drawing as often as possible on methods that have been used to improve the vocabulary of students at risk for reading disabilities. The areas we focus on are (a) word learning during storybook reading, (b) word- and context-analysis strategies during reading, and (c) technological supports for word learning during reading.

We provide information about research-based instruction that might benefit students' vocabulary development in each of these three areas. Each section provides a rationale, a description of the theoretical framework, an overview of research in that area, a description of practices that have been explored, and discussion. We then discuss the extent to which the studies we reviewed have identified research-based practices, and we provide recommendations for further research.

Approaches for Learning Words During Storybook Reading

Rationale

Shared storybook reading has an established reputation as an approach to improving both the language and reading skills of young children that has lasting effects (R. C. Anderson, Hiebert, Scott, & Wilkinson, 1985).

In a review of literature on this approach, Scarborough and Dobrich (1994) identified storybook reading as an activity that particularly influences children's language development. Yet others view shared storybook reading as an opportunity to support children's vocabulary development, in particular (e.g., Senechal, 1997). The following section highlights the teaching procedures and learning activities that, when coupled with storybook reading, have been found to positively influence the vocabulary learning of young children at risk for reading disabilities.

Theoretical Framework

Within the shared storybook reading context, natural social learning takes place when adults and children work together to construct meaning (e.g., Crain-Thoreson & Dale, 1999; Sulzby, 1985). The book-reading context allows more capable readers (often parents or teachers) to facilitate the language and vocabulary growth of children who either are unable to read independently or are just beginning the reading process. While reading a story aloud, more capable readers model the mechanics of reading written texts. Regular engagement in story reading creates a predictable and safe learning environment where children can feel comfortable asking questions and making comments, including taking on the role of storyteller (Crain-Thoreson & Dale, 1999; Crowe, Norris, & Hoffman, 2000). In effective storybook read alouds, adults adjust their reading strategies to enable children to expand their thoughts and to explore use of the language of the text. With experience, children gradually show awareness of story structure and book vocabulary and improved story comprehension; regular involvement in storybook reading is likely to support development of their reading and language (Bus, van Ijzendoorn, & Pellegrini, 1995; Scarborough & Dobrich, 1994).

Storybook reading has been found to be particularly useful for the development of vocabulary. I. L. Beck and McKeown (2007) explained that when children participate in storybook readings, they are often exposed to words and language structures they would not otherwise come across in their independent reading or conversations with others. These researchers recommended that the books chosen for storybook readings contain challenging concepts and some unfamiliar words—characteristics that make them a valuable vocabulary-teaching tool. Through the adult–child partnership necessary for successful storybook reading, children can hear, discuss, and practice vocabulary they may not encounter on their own.

Unfortunately, children with limited word knowledge often do not benefit from storybook readings in the same manner as peers with higher vocabulary proficiency (Marvin & Mirenda, 1993; L. Wood & Hood, 2004). Children with smaller vocabularies are less likely to learn new words incidentally, simply through hearing a story read aloud (Coyne, Simmons, Kame'enui, & Stoolmiller, 2004; Robbins & Ehri, 1994). In addition, it is possible that adults have different levels of expectation for children with lower vocabulary skills than for children who are developing typically. Marvin and Mirenda (1993) surveyed parents and found that the expectations of parents when reading to their children with disabilities focused mainly on very basic tasks, such as pointing to pictures, turning pages, or listening. This is in contrast to the seemingly more lofty academic goals for their children without disabilities, including understanding more advanced concepts of print and story comprehension.

All in all, storybook reading has been shown to influence vocabulary development in young children; however, because children with disabilities might not reap the same benefits from storybook reading as their peers, we need to look closely at those studies focusing specifically on storybook reading and vocabulary development in children with or at risk for reading failure in order to ascertain if and how book reading impacts their overall vocabulary knowledge.

Overview of Studies on Word Learning Through Story Reading

A large number of studies have focused on the benefits of shared book reading for children who are typically developing (e.g., DeBaryshe, 1993; Elley, 1989; Senechal, 1997). A review of the research literature, however, yielded few studies that focused on vocabulary learning through storybook reading for children with or at risk for reading disabilities. One reason for this gap in the research literature might be the age at which children are typically identified as having a reading disability. The research associated with storybook reading characteristically focuses on the early childhood (often preschool) years, before children have learned to read and also before they are likely to have been identified as having a reading disability. We therefore focus on the potential benefits of storybook reading for students at risk for reading disabilities. The "at-risk" label covers a variety of conditions, including speech and language or attention difficulties. For purposes of examining approaches to vocabulary instruction through storybook reading, we are less interested in the reasons children were referred to as at risk than the features of studies that contribute to the effectiveness of the instructional approaches.

In our review of the literature, two oral word-learning approaches surfaced, both of which have been found to result in improvements in vocabulary of children at risk for reading disabilities. One of these approaches focused on training adults to use questioning and commenting styles to expand the language of children during storybook reading (e.g., Crain-Thoreson & Dale, 1999; Hargrave & Senechal, 2000; Whitehurst et al., 1994). Appropriately training the adults who participate in storybook reading in particular techniques such as the dialogic reading approach (described in the next section) greatly increases the effectiveness of the overall storybook-reading experience. The second vocabulary approach involved studies that found explicit, direct, and extended instruction of targeted vocabulary words during storybook reading to be an effective word learning approach for at-risk children (e.g., I. L. Beck & McKeown, 2007; I. L. Beck, McKeown, & Kucan, 2002; Coyne, McCoach, & Kapp, 2007; Coyne, McCoach, Loftus, Zipoli, & Kapp, 2009; Wasik, Bond, & Hindman, 2006). As discussed earlier, directly teaching specific words often involves memorization of the meanings of individual words. Through such instruction during storybook reading, children are also exposed to the use of decoding strategies, context clue strategies, and the use of prior knowledge to interpret illustrations that help convey the meaning of the passage and perhaps some words included in the story. These strategies, when internalized, may assist children in future word learning while reading independently.

In the following section we provide a brief summary of the dialogic reading approach as well as a more in-depth discussion of explicit and extended word instruction. We also outline studies that exhibit clear examples of each approach.

Description of Practices

The first approach found to improve the language skills of children at risk for reading disabilities involves questioning and commenting while reading a story. Whitehurst and colleagues (1994) studied a storybook reading method called *dialogic reading;* a goal was to equip adults with the skills necessary to read aloud to children in order to advance their vocabulary knowledge. In this study, 3-year-old children attending subsidized preschools participated in storybook reading with adults. The adults were taught to follow the lead of the child and to allow the child to take on the role of storyteller. For example, while reading a story using dialogic strategies, an adult might incorporate questions such as, "What is happening on this page?" or, "Tell me what you think might happen next," to encourage children to use longer and more elaborate language and vocabulary. Whitehurst and colleagues (1994) found that both parents and teachers used dialogic reading effectively. In addition, increased student vocabulary was demonstrated for children exposed to the dialogic reading principles.

The second vocabulary approach looked at explicit and extended word instruction. Teachers can learn a great deal about vocabulary instruction through storybook reading by studying *Bringing Words to Life: Robust Vocabulary Instruction* by Beck et al. (2002). In this book and in subsequent articles, these researchers explained how to explicitly teach children at risk for reading difficulties "rich words" through storybook readings. They also have provided guidelines about how to prepare teachers to deliver vocabulary instruction during reading with their students in the classroom environment. Their work examined the effects of a program called Text Talk, in which teachers used trade books to promote word knowledge and meaning construction among kindergarten and first-grade students. A main focus of the approach was the importance of selecting words from trade books that were "sophisticated words of high utility for mature language users and that [were] characteristic of written language" (I. L. Beck & McKeown, 2007, p. 253). These "tier-2" words were thought to be especially important for at risk learners who would be less likely to learn them independently (Curtis, 1987). Examples of tier-2 words selected by I. L. Beck and McKeown (2007) from the trade book *Mrs. Potter's Pig* (Root, 1996) were *clinged, clutched,* and *shrieked.*

Within the Text Talk program, instruction in word meanings typically took place following the storybook reading, thus allowing teachers to capitalize on the story by teaching words in a recognizable context. In addition, teachers in the treatment conditions of studies received scripted lessons for each book and were trained to deliver word instruction following the same steps for each target word. I. L. Beck and McKeown (2007) delineated the steps used in delivering the word instruction. The following section explains the steps in this instructional routine, using the word *shrieked* as an example:

Each word is discussed using the story context as a reference. For example, the teacher might say,

"In the story we read, the woman shrieked when she saw the pig in the stroller."

1. The teacher gives the definition of the word and discusses it with the children. The teacher might say, "When people shriek, they make a loud, high-pitched sound; like a scream."

2. The teacher asks children to say the word aloud with an emphasis on the phonological pronunciation of the word, "Now, everyone try saying the word aloud, *shrieked.*"

3. The children and the teacher discuss the target word using examples other than the story itself. The teacher might say, "Sometimes people shriek when they are surprised by another person, or when they see a bug crawling on the floor."

4. The teacher asks students to decide what does and does not constitute an example of the target word. For example, the teacher might ask, "If someone bumped into you and you said 'ouch' in a quiet voice, is that a shriek?"

5. Children receive opportunities to share their own examples and ideas pertaining to the target word, "Does anyone remember a time when they shrieked?"

Teachers enrolled in the study were also asked to extend students' experience with the target words by using them in other parts of the school day. For example, a teacher might insert a discussion of the word *shrieked* into the morning circle time when talking about the previous night's occurrences, "Last night I shrieked. Do you want to know why?"

Teachers who used Text Talk were fully trained in word selection and in the process of discussing these words, whereas teachers in the comparison group read aloud daily to their students using age-appropriate trade books but without specific discussion of vocabulary. I. L. Beck and McKeown's (2007) results revealed that both kindergarten and first-grade children who were enrolled in an experimental study and received direct, explicit, and extended word instruction during storybook reading showed greater gains in target word knowledge than those children in the control group who did not receive this instruction.

Other studies have used methods similar to those used by I. L. Beck and McKeown (2007); these focused on learning new words either through extended instruction or through incidental exposure during storybook reading (Coyne, McCoach, et al., 2007; Coyne et al., 2009). Coyne and his colleagues used a smaller number of words, and the researchers themselves taught the children. The following is a summary of the steps the authors used to teach targeted words (Coyne, McCoach, et al., 2007):

1. Introduce the targeted words before reading the story. Ask the children to say each of the target words aloud.

2. While reading the story, prompt children to listen carefully for the "magic words." Whenever a targeted word is identified, reread the sentence containing the word.

3. Provide a definition for the target word, for example, "Oh here is the word *scrumptious*; that means the food tastes very good."

4. Encourage children to again say the target word aloud in order to practice the phonological pronunciation.

The reader repeats the same process whenever encountering a target word within the story. Following the reading, children receive opportunities to interact with the target words outside the story context. For example, the children may be asked to describe food they find scrumptious. In contrast to this explicit word instruction, other selected words were taught incidentally; that is, students heard these words within the story but were given no additional instruction or discussion. The authors found greater gains in word knowledge when words were taught explicitly while reading a story aloud, rather than when words were encountered incidentally in the story (Coyne, McCoach, et al., 2007).

Discussion

Clearly, both dialogic reading (Whitehurst et al., 1994) and Text Talk (I. L. Beck & McKeown, 2007) assist young children in their vocabulary development. However, for either approach to influence a child's word learning substantially, adults must be able to scaffold a child's knowledge and language. Scaffolding during storybook reading is not easy; adults must know which words to focus on, what questions to ask, when to ask them, when to relinquish control, and much more. As the research discussed in the preceding section shows, some work focuses on training teachers or parents to deliver word-learning interventions during storybook reading. I. L. Beck and McKeown's (2007) work stressed the importance of training teachers to implement Text Talk. Whitehurst and colleagues (1994) trained both teachers and parents in their dialogic reading approach. The process of training teachers and parents to deliver a successful word-learning intervention may be complicated and time-consuming, but the impact on word learning is greatly increased as children participate in greater numbers of effective storybook readings where vocabulary development is a goal. The more research focuses on training teachers and parents to incorporate word-learning instruction into storybook reading (especially when working with at-risk children), the better off children will be in their vocabulary development.

Strategies for Understanding and Learning Unfamiliar Words While Reading

Rationale

The RAND report (2002) stressed the importance of providing students with strategies for working out the meanings of unfamiliar words in texts, given the impact these strategies are likely to have on reading comprehension. Earlier, the NRP (2000a) report noted that relatively few studies focused on methods to teach strategic word analysis during reading; this is a neglected area of research on vocabulary instruction. In this section, we review practices that hold promise for assisting students at risk for reading disabilities in their analysis and understanding of words while reading. These methods have been studied in contexts that apply to all students (i.e., general education classrooms) as well as in clinical settings with a focus on methods appropriate for students with or at risk for reading or learning disabilities.

Theoretical Framework

Students at risk for reading disabilities commonly have limitations in their knowledge (e.g., background knowledge, vocabulary) and tend not to initiate actions to address problems they encounter during reading, as compared to same-age, skilled readers (Gersten, Fuchs, Williams, & Baker, 2001; G. Roberts et al., 2008). They give up easily when asked to read texts with unfamiliar words and concepts and sometimes develop an aversion to reading altogether. In theory, this problem can be addressed by equipping students with strategies for figuring out the likely meanings of the unfamiliar words that impede their comprehension during reading (e.g., Nunes & Bryant, 2006). The two word-analysis strategies that are most useful for this purpose are context analysis and morphological analysis. As Nagy and Scott (2000) stated, "context and morphology (word parts) are the two major sources of information immediately available to a reader who comes across a new word" (p. 275). As with other methods of strategy instruction, students need to understand how to apply these strategies and how the strategies can help them understand the texts they read for school and pleasure. However, they also need ample practice and guided opportunities to use the strategies on their own. What are at first deliberately applied strategies need to become habitual reading behaviors.

Word-analysis strategies provide assistance with word recognition (linked to decoding strategies, perhaps) and initial understanding of the meanings of unfamiliar words. *Morphological analysis* refers to analysis of the morphemes or units of meaning within words. This strategy is particularly useful because, from the late elementary years on, about 60% of unfamiliar words in texts are morphologically complex (e.g., base words with prefixes and/or suffixes), and most of these words are sufficiently transparent so that meaning can be inferred from the word parts (Nagy & Anderson, 1984). Through morphological analysis, students can identify the separate morphemes. These help students pronounce the word, recognize known parts, and infer the meaning of the whole. For example, students with reading problems can work out the meaning of *misplacement,* once they recognize the three parts (*mis-place-ment*).

When a student uses morphological analysis to infer the meaning of a word, analysis of the context in which the word is read also provides clues to its meaning. Context clues come from information found in text (e.g., synonyms and definitions, antonyms, examples) that help readers infer the meaning of a word. Analysis of context is useful, even when a word is not morphologically complex. In the following example (from Baumann et al., 2002, p. 161), the clue for the unfamiliar word (*befuddled*) is a synonym (*confused*): "Erica was confused about how to subtract fractions. She was usually excellent in math, but this topic had her *befuddled*."

Overview of Studies of Word and Context Analysis Strategies

Studies of instruction in context analysis have had mixed results (see Fukkink & deGlopper, 1998, and Kuhn & Stahl, 1998, for reviews of this research). Some have shown that students taught context analysis made greater gains in vocabulary than students in a no-treatment control group (e.g., Buikema & Graves, 1993). Others did not find significant improvements in word knowledge for students trained to use context analysis (Patberg, Graves, & Stibbe, 1984). A limitation of this strategy, when used alone, is that most passage contexts provide few cues to the meaning of specific words. Nonetheless, researchers have reported that, with sufficient support, context analysis can be an effective strategy for students with poor vocabulary or language/learning disabilities (Cain, Oakhill, & Elbro, 2003; Goerss, Beck, & McKeown, 1999; Nash & Snowling, 2006; Tomesen & Aarnoutse, 1998). For example, Nash and Snowling (2006) found that students with poor vocabularies who were taught context analysis performed better than those taught definitions on tests of taught words, transfer words, and reading comprehension.

Researchers have developed methods to teach morphological analysis to students with reading disabilities as well as students who achieve at normal levels (e.g., Elbro & Arnbak, 1996). Morphological analysis has been taught both as a decoding strategy and as a strategy for inferring the meanings of morphologically complex words in texts. Results of a number of studies suggest that teaching students to use morphological and context analysis helps them decode, spell, and understand unfamiliar words in texts (e.g., Berninger et al., 2008; M. Henry, 1993; Lovett, Lacerenza, & Borden, 2000).

Morphological and context analysis, taught together, are likely to be more effective than either one taught alone. Students taught these strategies might perform better not just because of their knowledge of specific clues or prefixes but rather because of heightened sensitivity to analytic methods to make sense of words in texts. In two recent studies, the two strategies were taught together (Baumann et al., 2002; Baumann, Edwards, Boland, Olejnik, & Kame'enui, 2003). The results of the first of these studies showed that fifth graders taught either the context or morphological strategy performed better on inferring meanings of new words than the no-treatment control group. Furthermore, students taught both strategies performed better on new words than students taught either one of these strategies (Baumann et al., 2002). However, no significant improvements occurred on transfer passages. Baumann et al. observed that fifth graders taught the combined strategies were significantly more likely to infer the meanings of unfamiliar complex words in new passages after training than students who were taught words from their social studies texts (Baumann et al., 2003). Here, too, results were significant for new words (including delayed posttests) but not for transfer passages.

Combined context and morphological analysis has also been effectively taught to small groups made up of both normally achieving and underachieving fourth-grade readers (Tomesen & Aarnoutse, 1998). These researchers used explicit instruction combined with a dialogic method to engage small, mixed-ability groups of students in discussion of unfamiliar words in passages. The less-skilled readers benefited at least as much as the skilled readers on a measure of application of strategies to analyze unfamiliar words when reading new texts.

The positive results from studies carried out in classroom settings (Baumann et al., 2002; Baumann et al., 2003) and by teaching small groups of students with diverse learning abilities (Tomesen & Aarnoutse, 1998) suggest that the word-analysis strategies methods might be useful to practitioners in inclusive general education classrooms in various content areas. Still, further research is needed to determine methods to ensure that students transfer strategies to texts they read in content area courses.

Description of Practices

What are the characteristics of effective practices in context and morphological analysis strategies? First, an effective intervention program should have the goal of helping students become analytic and engaged readers. An important goal is to help them overcome habits of skipping hard words when reading and overrelying on prior knowledge in interpreting the text (L. Baker & Brown, 1984). To achieve this goal, students need to be invested in learning and using the strategies. Only then are they likely to become better at comprehension monitoring and learning new words. Based on this framework, we should not be surprised to find that researchers make motivating learning activities a key feature of their

programs. They want students to perceive the strategies they are learning as do-able and engaging. Sometimes researchers achieve this by presenting problems that engage students' reasoning and imagination. For example, in Nunes and Bryant's program (2006), they might pose problems such as the following: "What is the important difference between a bicycle and a tricycle? What is it about the word that gives you a clue to this difference?" (p. 91). Other researchers have given students the role of "word detectives," a clever technique to motivate older, struggling readers (e.g., Tomesen & Aarnoutse, 1998).

Second, effective programs have provided explicit instruction in the purpose and use of the strategies, accompanied by guided practice. Most use a "release of responsibility model," wherein the teacher begins by modeling and explaining the strategies but gradually encourages students to take over the role of identifying and analyzing unfamiliar words themselves. Quite often, this involves explicit instruction. This might involve studying the meanings of prefixes and suffixes, such as the ending *-ian* in *musician* and *electrician* (Nunes & Bryant, 2006). Baumann et al. (2002) covered one prefix "family" in each session (e.g., the "not" family including *un-*, *in-*, and *im-*, as in *unfriendly* and *impossible*); each context strategy session covered a different context cue (e.g., synonyms or appositives).

Third, combined strategy instruction has been studied with varied amounts and kinds of support for students' practice and application. For example, Ebbers and Denton (2008) adapted the "vocabulary rule" of Baumann et al. (2003) to guide students when they encounter an unfamiliar word in text:

1. First, look outside the word, at context clues in the neighboring words and sentences.

2. Then, look inside the word, at the word parts (prefix, root, suffix).

3. Next, reread the section, keeping the meaningful word parts in mind. Make an inference: What do you think the word might mean? (Ebbers & Denton, 2008, p. 98)

Ebbers and Denton suggested that students benefit from numerous opportunities to apply the vocabulary rule during guided reading (2008). For example, engaging students in think-aloud procedures helps by making cognitive processes more transparent, which in turn should support students' efforts to understand how to use the two strategies and the vocabulary rule.

Somewhat similarly, emphasis on guided application characterizes a program called "close reading," designed by L. A. Katz and Carlisle (2009), which placed high priority on instructional time devoted to practice using strategies while reading. In an initial study using the program with three fourth-grade struggling readers, half of each training session was devoted to shared reading of a book of African tales. During shared reading, the teacher initially took the lead, modeling his identification and analysis of unfamiliar words that stood in the way of understanding the text. Over time, the teacher guided the students to take increasing responsibility for identifying and analyzing unfamiliar words. The teacher and students then discussed the meaning of the word and passage. Other researchers have also used a dialogic process to ensure that students learn to apply the strategies they have been taught. For example, Goerss et al. (1999) taught fifth- and sixth-grade less-skilled readers to use a five-step process to infer meanings of words from context: read/reread, discuss, make initial hypothesis, place constraints or develop hypothesis, and summarize. Each student met individually with the researcher/ teacher so that instruction could be designed to meet the student's needs.

Discussion

Nash and Snowling (2006) refer to teaching children to derive meanings of words from context as a self-teaching device. This characterization is true of morphological analysis as well. This term highlights a critical goal of strategy instruction—that is, to ensure that students are better able to infer independently the meanings of words in passages that were not used for training purposes. Ideally, we should also find that application of the strategies leads to improved comprehension. However, few studies have reported significant transfer effects.

An important consideration in designing instruction in strategies for learning words during reading is the amount and kind of practice provided (Kuhn & Stahl, 1998). In particular, Nash and Snowling (2006) pointed out that students with low vocabulary (and other language and reading difficulties) need substantial support for their learning and, with sufficient guidance and practice, can learn to derive meanings of unfamiliar words in passage contexts. This is promising, given previous findings that students with low vocabulary lack the semantic knowledge and linguistic flexibility so critical to success in inferring the meanings of words from context (e.g., McKeown, 1986).

An additional finding that might be important for classroom teachers is that word-analysis strategies have been successfully taught in both small-group and classroom settings (e.g., Nunes & Bryant, 2006). Furthermore, Baumann and co-workers' (2003) study suggested that word-analysis strategies can be successfully taught in content-area courses (i.e., social studies). Carlo, August, Snow, Lively, and White (2004) taught a set of vocabulary strategies, including morphological

analysis, to fifth-grade classes made up of both students who were English Language Learners (ELLs) and students who spoke only English. The authors reported significant effects of the instruction on a measure of text comprehension. The finding that instruction in word analysis for struggling readers can be delivered effectively in general education classrooms enhances its value for many teachers.

Technological Aids for Learning Vocabulary During Reading
Rationale

Interest is growing in the use of technology to support literacy learning not only for students who are typical learners but also for students who are ELLs and students with disabilities. As the capabilities of technology continue to develop rapidly, and the number of classrooms with access to technology and the World Wide Web increases, the ways in which technology can extend and support students' literacy learning are constantly expanding. This potential for enhancing students' literacy learning was acknowledged in the NRP Report (2000a), which identified the use of technology as a promising avenue for providing effective reading instruction. In this section, we review technology-incorporating practices that hold promise in improving word learning through reading for students with reading disabilities.

Theoretical Framework

As noted earlier, students with reading disabilities often have limited vocabulary knowledge compared to their peers, which affects their reading comprehension and their motivation to work at understanding difficult texts. Technology offers ways to address these challenges; in effect, it serves as a viable instructional tool because of its flexibility, its ability to scaffold students' learning, and its ability to enhance students' motivation and engagement.

The adaptability and multimodality of technology open the door for improved word-learning opportunities, especially for children with reading disabilities. I. L. Beck and McKeown (1991) argued that the most effective way to improve students' vocabulary knowledge is to provide them with an assortment of techniques, including multiple exposures to unfamiliar word meanings in context. An immediate problem is that struggling readers don't engage in much reading because their basic skills aren't sufficiently developed and/or they find written texts very difficult to understand. Such features of technology as speech production, hypertext, graphics, word processing, and streaming videos are particularly valuable because they provide accommodations for basic difficulties and in doing so make it more likely that students will engage in more reading. As a result, students with reading disabilities have greater opportunities to learn word meanings through reading—including texts presented through a variety of modalities.

Another important factor is that technological features can be customized to meet individual students' needs and preferences (e.g., different fonts and font sizes, volume and rate of speech production, number of repetitions). The fact that technology can be customized to provide appropriate instruction for individual learners is a key component to what A. Meyer and Rose (1998) have termed a Universal Design for Learning (UDL). UDL is not a "universal" system in the sense that one program fits all, but rather a system that is flexible enough to support differentiated instruction to meet the needs of individual students. Integrating the features of technology (e.g., large print, speech production) into practice enables students with disabilities greater access to otherwise inaccessible or challenging text. This is of critical importance considering the current movement to educate students with mild disabilities in general education classrooms (G. Fitzgerald, Koury, & Mitchem, 2008).

As the capabilities and features of technology have advanced, the way in which practitioners and researchers use technology to support students' word learning has shifted to focus on the integration of technology into classroom instruction. In a review of the literature, Fitzgerald and co-workers (2008) addressed how the use of technology for students with high-incidence disabilities has evolved from what researchers referred to as computer-assisted instruction (CAI) to computer-mediated instruction (CMI). CAI mainly focused on software-guided, drill-and-practice activities, with the aim of learning words in isolation; it was primarily used and studied in resource room settings. Because CAI provided students with opportunities to learn and practice on their own, special education teachers had more time to focus on higher-level literacy tasks with students. In this sense, the use of technology was viewed more as a practice tool. In recent years, the focus has shifted to CMI, where the emphasis is on how to effectively integrate computers into practice maximizing students' learning and enabling students with disabilities greater opportunities for learning in a mainstreamed setting. With CMI, technology is not viewed as a separate component of instruction but an integrated one, designed to help students build on prior knowledge, to encourage the use of problem solving skills, and to scaffold students' learning of higher level strategies (e.g., predicting, monitoring),

in turn, supporting word learning and comprehension (Fitzgerald et al., 2008). CMI moves beyond drill and practice and focuses on the use of technology to scaffold students' literacy learning.

In addition to technology's capabilities to scaffold students' learning, the use of technology provides students with an opportunity to participate actively in their learning in ways that can positively influence their reading achievement (Guthrie & Wigfield, 2000). Student motivation and engagement have been shown to increase with the use of technology, as students are often provided greater autonomy over their learning (Dalton & Proctor, 2008; Strangman & Dalton, 2005). Students can choose the words they want to highlight, Web sites to explore, or graphics to display, thereby creating an interactive learning experience that can lead to greater exposure to content and new vocabulary, as well as improved motivation to read. Relevant to vocabulary learning, the use of the Internet gives students with limited background knowledge opportunities to engage in real-world experiences. Viewing a video from www.youtube.com about tornados, the subway, or farming provides life-like vibrancy and contextual depth in a way that picture books alone cannot.

The use of technology holds promise in improving word learning through reading for students with reading disabilities because of its flexibility, its ability to scaffold students' learning, and its ability to enhance students' motivation and engagement. The following section provides a review of the literature on research-based practices related to supporting word learning through reading for students with or at risk of reading disabilities.

Overview of Studies on Word Learning with the Aid of Technology

Research demonstrating the effectiveness of technology to support students' word learning includes students who are typical learners (Kolich, 1991), students who are ELLs (Proctor, Dalton, & Grisham, 2007; Proctor, Uccelli, Dalton, & Snow, 2009), children with hearing loss (Barker, 2003), children with autism (Bosseler & Massaro, 2003; M. Moore & Calvert, 2000), and children with learning disabilities (Hebert & Murdock, 1994; J. Xin & Rieth, 2001). Despite the increased attention on the use of technology to improve students' literacy, systematic research identifying research-based instructional practices in this area remains sparse (Fitzgerald et al., 2008; Strangman & Dalton, 2005). The majority of studies on the use of technology to support reading instruction focus on decoding skills, fluency, and reading comprehension as primary outcomes measures and address vocabulary development only indirectly. Although research in this area is limited, results imply the potential of multimedia technology as an effective tool to support students' word learning. As the integration of multimedia technology becomes more commonplace in the classroom, we expect that teachers will gradually become familiar with methods that hold promise for improving students' word learning through reading, including the use of speech feedback (otherwise referred to as text-to-speech [TTS]), hypertext, and instructional practices that combine these various features of technology. In turn, additional research will likely be conducted to better establish these technological supports and their effectiveness in improving students' literacy outcomes. For a detailed overview of the present research in this area, refer to Strangman and Dalton (2005).

One area of research on technology examines the use of video to anchor students' learning in a real-world context to support word learning and reading comprehension. J. Xin and Rieth (2001) studied the effects of video technology as a means for enhancing word learning for elementary students with learning disabilities. Instruction occurred over a 6-week period, and teachers used a videodisc about the 1989 San Francisco earthquake to anchor students' word learning in a real-world context. Results showed that students who received video-anchored instruction had significantly higher gains on a word-definition test, compared to students who received traditional instruction with a dictionary and printed texts. Although performance on a delayed post-test was not significant, J. Xin and Rieth (2001) concluded that the use of videodiscs holds promise as an effective tool in motivating and engaging students in understanding word meanings in an interactive context.

Another area that has received some attention in the literature examines the use of speech feedback, or what is often referred to as the text-to-speech (TTS) capabilities of technology. Several studies have been conducted to investigate the use of technology and speech feedback in remediating struggling readers' deficits in word recognition and phonological decoding while engaging in computer-assisted storybook reading (Olson & Wise, 1992; Wise et al., 1989; Wise, Ring, & Olson, 2000). In these studies children were instructed to click the computer's mouse on unfamiliar words they encountered when reading. Depending on their assigned study condition (i.e., whole word, syllable, or onset/rime), when students clicked on the word, they saw and heard different segments of the word to provide word-decoding support. Wise and co-workers (2000) found that children made significant gains in phonological decoding and word-reading measures, compared to classroom controls, regardless of the size of segmentation support they received.

Besides using TTS as a remediation tool to support children's word-reading skills, other researchers have examined the use of TTS as a compensatory tool to provide students with reading disabilities greater exposure to the kinds of cognitive challenge in higher-level texts that might lead to improved reading comprehension (Dalton & Proctor, 2008; Elkind, Cohen, & Murray, 1993; Montali & Lewandowski, 1996). As a compensatory tool, TTS allows struggling readers to bypass the challenges of word recognition and fluency in order to focus greater attention on constructing meaning from the text—thus, also enhancing their opportunities for learning words through reading. Hebert and Murdock (1994) examined students' gains in word learning following computer instruction with and without TTS support. They provided sixth-grade students with learning disabilities access to TTS, either synthesized or digitized speech, when reading vocabulary words, definitions, and sentences from digital text. The vocabulary words, definitions, and sentences were taken directly from the glossaries and context of the students' sixth-grade reading, science, math, and social studies textbooks. Study findings revealed that students made significant gains in vocabulary when reading digital text paired with TTS, as compared to reading digital text without TTS support. The results demonstrated the benefits of this feature of technology as a viable tool to support students' language and literacy learning.

Other researchers (e.g., Boone & Higgins, 1993; Higgins & Raskind, 2005; Proctor et al., 2007, 2009) further examined the benefits of TTS but in the context of combining TTS with additional enhancements of technology, such as hypertext, hypermedia, and access to an online glossary. These scholars examined how various features or capabilities of technology can be integrated into practice to improve the word learning and reading comprehension of students with reading difficulties. Combining these various capabilities of technology increases students' opportunities to learn word meanings through multiple modalities and sources of information.

Higgins and Raskind (2005) conducted a study to explicitly examine reading comprehension of students with learning disabilities using the Quicktionary Reading Pen II. The Reading Pen is a hand-held device that allows students to scan printed text either one word or one line at a time; the text is then displayed on the LCD screen and read aloud using the pen's TTS feature. Single words can be segmented by syllables and displayed on the screen. In addition the speech rate, volume, font size, background colors, and various enhancements of the Reading Pen can be customized to meet an individual student's needs. One enhancement of the Reading Pen is a definition function, which students can activate to provide them with primary and secondary definitions of words during reading. Even though students' vocabulary gains were not formally assessed, the study demonstrated the potential of improved word learning with use of the Reading Pen.

After using the Reading Pen for 2 weeks, students were assessed using a formal reading inventory, with and without the Reading Pen. Results revealed significant differences between the two conditions with higher passage comprehension with use of the Reading Pen. In addition, study field notes revealed that several students were motivated to examine novel vocabulary encountered by accessing the glossary while using the Reading Pen. Researchers noted that students engaged in word play, breaking words into various parts by using their knowledge of phonology and morphology to analyze unfamiliar words. This study demonstrates the promise of the Reading Pen and its multiple capabilities as a tool to support students' reading disabilities with word learning during reading.

In the next section, we discuss in greater depth promising research on an instructional practice that incorporates multiple features of technology including TTS via a scaffolded digital reading environment to support word learning and comprehension in students with or at risk for reading disabilities.

Description of Practices

Current practices in the use of technology to support word learning from texts primarily take the form of indirect, compensatory systems that increase the likelihood that students will engage in reading challenging texts. These systems may increase students' opportunities to learn strategies to address unfamiliar vocabulary and monitor comprehension. Because technological practices are becoming increasingly prevalent, teachers interested in research-based practices would benefit from becoming familiar with the affordances of technology—qualities that allow technology to offer opportunities to teach and learn or to provide supports for teaching and learning. We have selected a study examining the use of a scaffolded digital reading (SDR) environment to illustrate practices shown to be effective.

Proctor and his colleagues (2007) investigated the affordances of working in an SDR environment to support learning vocabulary and reading comprehension strategies for students with reading difficulties, including students who are ELLs, and students with learning disabilities. The SDR environment provides a variety of embedded supports (e.g., TTS functionality, hyperlinks for vocabulary, Spanish–English translations, a digital word wall, coaching of comprehension strategies) for students to access during their reading of digital text. Proctor et al. (2007) conducted a 4-week intervention study with 30 fourth-grade struggling readers, including students who were Spanish-speaking ELLs. Students engaged in an SDR environment for 45 minutes, three times per week, for 4 weeks, in a computer lab where they read and interacted with narrative and informational digital texts. The researchers purposefully chose challenging texts in order to examine how struggling readers accessed and used the various digital supports (e.g., TTS, hyperlinks, the glossary, strategy instruction prompts) to decode unfamiliar words, understand the vocabulary, and comprehend the text. In the initial step, the prereading phase of the SDR environment, students in the study were introduced to five "power words" important to the text. Students were given access to a number of embedded learning supports in the digital reading environment, including an audio pronunciation of the word, a brief definition, a contextual sentence, and graphics illustrating the word. After reviewing these, students were asked to begin reading the digital texts. While engaged in reading, students had access to a virtual coach who could model various comprehension strategies, additional hyperlinks to obtain a definition, or audio pronunciation of an unfamiliar word. Students were also required to add three unfamiliar words to their personal glossary. At the end of each page of the digital text, the system automatically prompted students to think about the story and apply a particular comprehension strategy (i.e., summarization, prediction, or questioning) to provide a written response. On completion of reading the digital texts, students engaged in a postreading retelling computer-based activity to assess their progress of reading comprehension and vocabulary knowledge.

To monitor students' progress, researchers tracked which supports readers were accessing via a remote server that maintained a usage log for each text for each individual student. Results showed that lower-performing students accessed these supports more often than their higher-functioning counterparts. In addition, increased use of the various supports (e.g., hyperlinked glossary terms or coaching avatars) was positively associated with gains at posttest in vocabulary and reading comprehension (Proctor et al., 2007). One reason for the success of the SDR environment might be that it provided students with multiple representations of new words in context, thus promoting language and literacy learning in students with reading difficulties. Furthermore, the intentional use of a meaningful purpose for accessing the supports (e.g., requirement that students add three words to their personal glossary) could have contributed to its success. In this study, the SDR environment provided a balance between student choice of using embedded supports and explicit instruction on when to use them. More information on this research and other literacy projects incorporating the UDL framework can be found at the Center for Applied Special Technology (CAST) Web site (www.cast.org).

Discussion

Research in the area of technology to aid literacy learning has largely focused on software or computer features to support the reading of text. The traditional concept of literacy—the assumption that print is the primary source of information in our culture—is changing rapidly. Digital technology, including the Internet, is quickly becoming a primary carrier of information, and this has significant implications for education (Leu, Kinzer, Coiro, & Cammack, 2004). Increasingly, students are surfing the Web for information, instead of going to the library to gather information from an encyclopedia. They are participating in social networks, such as Facebook, MySpace, and Twitter, which have their own rules of sharing information through reading and writing. We have provided an overview of current research in the area of technology that supports students' vocabulary and comprehension development. While research-based practices are limited at this time, evidence indicates that technology can help struggling readers compensate for word reading and fluency problems as well as facilitate their use of content-rich learning environments likely to foster vocabulary growth (e.g., Hiebert & Murdock, 1994; Higgins & Raskind, 2005; Proctor et al., 2007). With an increased reliance on technology both in and out of school, future research will undoubtedly identify various ways in which technology can foster word learning during reading and exploring multimedia resources.

Analysis of Research Quality

The studies on research-based approaches for learning words from texts vary widely in the quality of research design and method. Some meet standards for high-quality research, including random assignment to condition, evaluation of fidelity of treatment, and efforts to determine whether effects of the treatment are lasting. However, many of the studies we reviewed fall short of current standards for high-quality research (e.g., Gersten et al., 2005).

It is important to appreciate the preliminary efforts made by a number of researchers in developing and studying a program of instruction; one goal was to determine whether the instructional techniques were sufficiently promising to warrant further study (e.g., Nunes & Bryant, 2006). We have referred to various exploratory studies in our overview of studies. These include short-term studies in clinical settings with no comparison group (e.g., Goerss et al., 1999), as well as truly novel treatments, such as the Quicktionary

Reading Pen (e.g., Higgins & Raskind, 2005). Exploratory research serves an important purpose. When results show learning gains, such studies provide evidence of the promise of innovative methods for improving vocabulary through reading and exploring words in texts—and in the long run, reading comprehension as well. The next step is to carry out larger and more rigorously designed studies, and these represent the research-based practices in the preceding review (e.g., Baumann et al., 2003; I. L. Beck & McKeown, 2007; Coyne et al., 2009).

In the area of storybook reading, results suggest that enhancing the word learning of young students might engender a habit of thinking about words as they read, possibly preventing later reading difficulties. Studies in this area were based on pretest/post-test control group designs, where the researchers thoughtfully identified the sample and teacher characteristics and measured for equivalency of groups in the area of vocabulary knowledge at pretest (e.g., I. L. Beck & McKeown, 2007; Whitehurst et al., 1994). Researchers carefully outlined the intervention materials and procedures (including examples of scripted lessons), monitored for fidelity of implementation, and used assessments that showed the extent to which children had learned the target words.

In studies of instruction in word-analysis strategies, Baumann and his colleagues (2002, 2003) and Carlo et al. (2004) designed studies that meet current criteria for high-quality research reports. Most of the remaining studies were exploratory, often employing a convenience sample and sometimes without a control group (e.g., Goerss et al., 1999; L. A. Katz & Carlisle, 2009). Overall, instruction in word-analysis strategies has been shown to foster students' understanding and use of word-analysis strategies; however, to date, the effects on vocabulary development and reading comprehension have been modest.

Similarly, many studies of the use of technology to improve literacy learning in students with reading difficulties have been exploratory. The majority used experimenter-designed dependent variables, had short intervention time frames, provided little information on transfer or long-term benefits of the intervention, and rarely addressed issues of fidelity. The studies that were more rigorous in design show the benefits of text-to-speech support for struggling readers (e.g., Wise et al., 1989) and positive influences of various supports for reading digital texts (Proctor et al., 2007, 2009). Technological supports for word learning while reading are changing at a rapid rate, and this situation makes it hard for researchers and teachers to stay abreast of current practice. Still, both theory and the evidence suggest the value of various technological supports for struggling readers.

Discussion and Directions for Future Research

We selected three areas of research for which research-based evidence shows that instructional practices can help students learn words from texts. Our choice of approaches was based on current views that students with or at risk for reading disabilities, even preschoolers, can benefit from engaging in analysis of meanings of unfamiliar words in texts and that doing so will lead to positive engagement and a can-do attitude toward reading challenging texts. These are important goals, as all too often students lack persistence and interest in reading (Gersten et al., 2001). Teachers need established practices to guide them in teaching students how to read texts, and they need to provide more guided practice for their students than is currently the case (E. H. Hiebert, 2009). However, our review of the literature has shown us that research in the three areas we investigated is still limited with regard to the impact of interventions on the vocabulary development of students with reading disabilities. Nonetheless, much can be learned from these studies, both for practitioners and researchers. We start by summarizing what we see as promising practices in the three areas we investigated. Then we provide suggestions for further research.

Research results show that the preschool years are not too early to begin to teach children to analyze and reflect on word meanings when adults are reading with them. In storybook reading, methods used with children before they are themselves readers lay a foundation of word knowledge that is critical for development of their vocabularies. Enhancing the word learning of young students might engender a habit of thinking about words as they read, possibly preventing later reading difficulties. We found two approaches that were effective in teaching young children to engage in analysis of word meanings. One involved teachers' selection of several high-utility words from a storybook and their guidance of the discussion of these words after reading (e.g., I. L. Beck & McKeown, 2007). The other involved dialogic reading, in which parents or teachers provided children opportunities to talk about and even tell stories about the text that they were reading together (Whitehurst et al., 1994). Both have been shown to lead to gains in students' word learning.

Researchers have also studied explicit instruction in two word-analysis strategies that can help students learn words and improve their understanding of texts. Results have shown that together context analysis and morphological analysis strategies support students' learning of unfamiliar words through deriving meaning from word parts and context. The two strategies work better together than either one alone (Baumann et al., 2002).

It is possible that students are not just learning specific analytic techniques, such as looking for synonyms of unfamiliar words, but rather are acquiring habits of monitoring their comprehension as they read, making an effort when necessary to figure out the meaning of words, sentences, and longer passages.

Research on these two strategies has shown that all students can benefit, whether they have reading difficulties or not, and some research indicates that students benefit whether they are in general education classrooms or working with a tutor in a "pull-out" or clinical setting. One critical factor is that students with low vocabulary knowledge need more structured learning and more extended support (Nash & Snowling, 2006). With sufficient guidance, students with reading problems have been found to make as much progress as their peers (Tomesen & Aarnoutse, 1998).

Our review showed benefits for reading and understanding words in texts that are made possible by various kinds of technology. The affordances that can come with electronic technologies are such that it might seem that students don't need teachers to guide their learning, but this turns out not to be the case (Wise et al., 2000). Hypermedia and Internet links certainly can provide very rich learning opportunities for students—opportunities that offer experiential and visual support, not just linguistic cues to meaning. However, students need help learning when and how to use such features as speech or pictorial representations of words. Still, in the area of technological advances, we found more theory than empirical support for practices that teachers might want to employ—a sign that this is still an emerging area of research. Preliminary results show the promise of technological supports for acquisition of vocabulary, word knowledge, and reading comprehension.

Our review of current research has suggested several specific areas where further research is needed. One area is the benefits of continuing to use read-aloud techniques beyond the first years of formal schooling, coupled with discussion of words in the texts, to foster students' vocabulary development. This practice is used in preschool and kindergarten, but it is likely that older students and students with (or at risk for) reading disabilities would benefit from guided discussion of text vocabulary as well.

A second area concerns technological, compensatory supports that are increasingly available and potentially helpful in improving students' understanding of words and texts. Studies have shown the value of speech-to-text options, but additional technological supports, such as those studied by Proctor et al. (2007) (e.g., text-to-speech, hyperlinks for vocabulary, Spanish–English translations), offer additional ways to make it possible for students with reading difficulties to read challenging texts. Most important, more research is needed to determine the extent to which such supports, when properly used, lead to improvements in word knowledge and comprehension.

A third area in which we see the need for further research is the effectiveness of instruction in word-analysis skills in content-area courses, particularly to arrive at a better understanding of the extent to which students with reading difficulties benefit from such instruction. In this area, as in the other two areas included in this review, studies that have included students with disabilities have generally focused on students with reading disabilities (or at risk for such disabilities); however, students with various disabilities (e.g., those with hearing impairment or autism) often experience problems understanding vocabulary while reading texts. Research should be expanded to more fully investigate the impact of interventions on these students' vocabulary development. For all students, we see particular promise in vocabulary instruction focused on learning words through reading in content area courses. Learning how to make sense of the many new words and concepts introduced in, for example, science and history textbooks offers the possibility of building students' word and topical knowledge—both of which matter for their performance in school. Support in content area vocabulary development should help students become more invested in their reading and learning in school.

CHAPTER 5

Instructional Practices for Improving Student Outcomes in Solving Arithmetic Combinations

Diane Pedrotty Bryant, Brian R. Bryant, and **Jacob L. Williams** | *The University of Texas at Austin*

Sun A. Kim | *Queens College, The City University of New York*

Mikyung Shin | *The University of Texas at Austin*

Success in mathematics achievement is a critical component for competitive advancement to post-secondary education and to enhance opportunities for careers and employment (National Mathematics Advisory Panel [NMAP], 2008). However, national indicators of mathematical achievement have shown that although overall average scores have improved for fourth and eighth graders since 1990, scores in the most recent few years do not indicate significant changes. In fact, between 2007 and 2009, scores remained unchanged for fourth graders and only slightly improved for eighth graders (National Assessment of Educational Progress [NAEP], 2009). Additionally, NAEP findings indicate a problem of underachievement that is particularly severe for students with disabilities. This lack of significant improvement in mathematics achievement for students with disabilities is of grave concern for their future educational and career opportunities. Given that math performance remains low, one can only conclude that a need exists for educators to provide high-quality instruction to teach important mathematical ideas that lead to improved performance for all students, including students with all disabilities.

The issue of poor mathematics performance of students with disabilities underscores the need for focused attention on critical foundation skills that are prerequisites for success with higher levels of math at the secondary level, such as algebra (NMAP, 2008). For example, the NMAP recommended proficient performance with addition and subtraction of whole numbers by the end of third grade and proficiency with multiplication and division by the end of fifth grade. Specifically, students should possess "the automatic recall of addition and related subtraction facts, and of multiplication and related division facts" (p. 17). Unfortunately, all too often students with disabilities reach the secondary level

The work on this article was supported in part by a grant # R324B070164 from the U.S. Department of Education, Institute of Education Sciences. No official endorsement should be inferred.

ill-equipped on basic critical foundation skills. Yet, these students are often required to tackle curriculum that proves overwhelming to them because of the lack of mastery of concepts and skills on which more advanced mathematics (e.g., algebra) is based. Thus, high-quality instruction in solving arithmetic combinations must begin in earnest at the elementary level.

Arithmetic Combinations

In 2006, the National Council of Teachers of Mathematics published the *Curriculum Focal Points (CFPs) for Prekindergarten through Grade 8 Mathematics: A Quest for Coherence*, herein called the Focal Points, to provide guidance to school districts as they organize their curriculum standards. According to recommendations in the Focal Points, in the early grades, students should develop an understanding of the *meaning* of addition, subtraction, multiplication, and division. For example, students should be able to visually depict multiplication combinations by using area models, arrays, and number lines to construct multiplication situations before engaging in procedural activities that focus only on building fluency.

The Focal Points also include standards that focus on students learning effective strategies for solving arithmetic combinations to help develop fluent or automatic retrieval (i.e., quick recall) of the answers. Automaticity with arithmetic combinations is important because of the role it plays with more advanced mathematics, such as finding common multiples or solving algebraic equations that require factoring (Woodward, 2006). Also, quick retrieval of facts facilitates everyday living skills that involve making change, measuring for cooking purposes, computing distance and time, and so forth.

Difficulties with Arithmetic Combinations Related to Instruction

According to Siegler (2007), students with mathematics disabilities are "not only worse at retrieval of arithmetic facts, but also at understanding mathematical concepts, executing relevant procedures, choosing among alternative strategies, . . . and so forth" (pp. xix–xx). Difficulties with arithmetic combinations may stem from a variety of sources, including causes that are inherent to the individual (e.g., working memory, processing speed deficits). Empirical evidence supports the view that child-level variables can explain at least part of student performance in arithmetic combinations (Passolunghi & Siegel, 2001; H. L. Swanson & Beebe-Frankenberger, 2004). Instruction in math also plays an important role in determining students' mathematical achievement. For the purposes

of this chapter, because instruction is a more malleable factor, we chose to examine difficulties from an instructional perspective.

For many students with learning disabilities (LD) in mathematics, difficulties with fluent or automatic retrieval of arithmetic combinations may be linked to a variety of instructional issues. One issue is the insufficient development of fundamental understandings of whole numbers, the relationships among the four operations, and whole-number properties. For example, students may not understand the relationship between addition and subtraction (e.g., addition and subtraction as inverse operations, addition facts and related subtraction facts), and multiplication and division (e.g., multiplication and division as inverse operations, multiplication and related division facts). Lack of understanding of these inverse relationships limits the ability to recognize fact families (e.g., $3 + 7 = 10, 7 + 3 = 10, 10 - 7 = 3, 10 - 3 = 7$) as a strategy for solving arithmetic combinations.

Another issue that may hamper fluency or automatic retrieval is lack of understanding of the meaning of arithmetic properties. Students may have a limited understanding of the commutative (i.e., $A + B = B + A$; $A \times B = B \times A$) and associative (i.e., $[A + B] + C = A + [B + C]$; $[A \times B] \times C = A \times [B \times C]$) properties of addition and multiplication, and the distributive property (i.e., $A \times [B + C] = [A \times B] + [A \times C]$). Knowledge about these properties can help students solve more facts accurately (e.g., $5 \times 3 = 3 \times 5$) and derive answers more effectively for difficult problems (e.g., $4 \times 12 = 4 \times 10 + 4 \times 2 = 40 + 8 = 48$) (NRC, 2009). Lack of an understanding of whole-number properties hinders the ability to tackle harder arithmetic combinations strategically by using the properties to reason about how to efficiently and effectively solve problems (NRC, 2009).

Opportunities to learn, practice, and master effective and efficient fact strategies may be yet another instructional issue for students with mathematics disabilities. Students with mathematics disabilities do not master and become fluent in using efficient fact strategies such as more advanced counting strategies (e.g., Count-On strategy, described later in this chapter) and derived strategies (e.g., $9 + 6 = 9 + [1 + 5] = [9 + 1] + 5 = 10 + 5 = 15$) to solve addition, subtraction, multiplication, and division problems without focused practice and review to learn how to use the strategy correctly (Woodward & Rieth, 1997). For example, Geary (1990) found that students with mathematics difficulties did not differ significantly from typically achieving students in the *types* of strategies (e.g., counting on, use of fingers, verbal counting, retrieval) used to solve problems. Rather, students with mathematics difficulties made more errors in the *use* of these strategies than the typically achieving peer group. In sum, students with mathematics disabilities exhibit problems solving arithmetic combinations that may stem primarily from inadequate instruction. Thus, educators need to identify practices that are research based to improve student outcomes in solving arithmetic combinations.

The purpose of this chapter is to describe research-based instructional practices that are intended to promote accurate and fluent or automatic retrieval of arithmetic combinations when teaching students with LD. The studies we identified focus on intervention research that was conducted with students with LD. We think it is important to examine this body of literature to identify evidence-based intervention practices because students with LD typically exhibit difficulties learning arithmetic combinations. Thus, their teachers should employ practices that are grounded in the research. Also, although we just examined literature specific to students with LD, many other children with disabilities at the elementary and secondary level experience similar problems with mathematics; it is quite possible that the practices described in this chapter will benefit them as well.

Instructional Practices for Arithmetic Combinations

Overview, Rationale, and Supporting Theory

In this section, we briefly describe three empirically supported instructional practices—explicit practices, strategic practices, and the use of visual representations—to teach arithmetic combinations to students with LD, as well as discuss the underlying rationale and supporting theory for each approach.

Explicit Instructional Practices

Explicit instructional practices focus on a series of behavioral practices that are systematically implemented to teach mathematical ideas and procedures. A substantial body of research shows the effectiveness of systematic, explicit instruction for teaching computation to students with mathematical difficulties (S. Baker, Gersten, & Lee, 2002; NMAP, 2008; M. Stein, Kinder, Silbert, & Carnine, 2006). Explicit instructional practices are based on the behavioral theory of learning, which is linked to the early work of notable researchers such as Ivan Pavlov, B. F. Skinner, Edward Lee Thorndike, and John B. Watson. Early behavioral psychology studies focused on how behavioral changes were influenced by the arrangement of antecedents (i.e., classical conditioning) or how behavioral changes were effected by the arrangement of consequent events (i.e., operant conditioning) (Tawney & Gast, 1984). Applying the behavioral theory

of learning to education focuses on improving instructional behavior (e.g., increasing the number of facts computed correctly in a minute) by manipulating consequent events (e.g., providing reinforcement for improved academic or social performance). The influences of the behavioral theory of learning are found in educational research (e.g., H. L. Swanson, Hoskyn, & Lee, 1999) that has identified practices associated with explicit (direct) instruction that foster improved instructional performance. Additionally, the NMAP (2008) stressed that struggling students need explicit mathematics instruction on a consistent basis, particularly on foundation skills and conceptual knowledge. Thus, a teacher might use explicit instruction to teach an addition algorithm with regrouping by:

- Preteaching addition facts
- Preteaching place value concepts such as regrouping
- Modeling how to perform the algorithm by verbalizing the steps and providing an explanation of when and why it is necessary to regroup
- Providing examples illustrating when it is necessary to regroup and when it is not
- Carefully sequencing examples to show easier to more difficult problems with regrouping
- Providing multiple opportunities for students to practice
- Correcting errors immediately so students do not practice errors
- Monitoring student progress

An explicit approach to instruction includes important practices (e.g., modeling, high rates of responding and practice, repetition, error correction, review and distributed practice, frequent monitoring of performance) that help students with mathematics disabilities learn mathematical ideas. Consistent application of these practices is well supported in the research as necessary for struggling students (H. L. Swanson et al., 1999).

Strategic Instructional Practices

Strategic instructional practices focus on the rules and process of learning, including cognitive and meta-cognitive (e.g., self-regulatory) cues and the use of mnemonics for memory retention and retrieval (H. L. Swanson & Beebe-Frankenberger, 2004). Strategic instructional practices include a rationale for learning the strategy and specific steps to activate cognitive and meta-cognitive processes. Some evidence suggests that students with mathematics disabilities can benefit from learning strategies for solving arithmetic combinations with fluency (Woodward, 2006).

Strategic instructional practices are based on information processing theory, which focuses on how individuals perceive, encode, represent, store, and retrieve information (e.g., Sternberg, 1985). Regarding arithmetic combinations, individuals must possess efficient and effective strategies in order to retrieve the solutions to arithmetic combinations directly or automatically. By doing so, theoretically, this automaticity reduces the cognitive load (Sweller, 2005, p. 1) for learning higher-order mathematics skills. Moreover, the use of strategies promotes flexibility with numbers (Cumming & Elkins, 1999) and a knowledge base (Isaacs & Carroll, 1999) that can facilitate retention and retrieval (Woodward, 2006).

Use of Visual Representations

Visual representations are concrete or physical models and pictorial depictions that are intended to promote understanding of mathematical ideas. Examples include manipulatives, tallies, pictures, and number lines. Cramer, Post, and del Mas (2002) noted the importance of using multiple representations to help students develop mathematical understanding. Gersten, Beckmann, et al. (2009b) explained that students' understanding of the relationships between visual representations and abstract symbols can strengthen their understanding of mathematical concepts. In their meta-analysis, Gersten, Chard, et al. (2009) found positive, moderate effects for the use of visual representations in mathematics instruction and positive effects on mathematics performance when the use of visual representations was paired with other instructional elements (e.g., systematic instruction) in computation. Thus, students should be taught how to visually represent mathematical ideas and to translate their representations into symbolic representations.

In the next section, we report on research studies investigating the application of explicit practices, strategic practices, and the use of visual representations to teach arithmetic combinations to students with LD. The discussion of research is organized into two sections: (a) studies on practices that promote the acquisition or learning of arithmetic combinations, and (b) studies on practices that promote the fluent or automatic responding of answers. In reviewing the literature, we found that researchers often combined practices in a study. So, for example, a study might include explicit instructional practices and visual representations to teach arithmetic combinations. We grouped the studies accordingly (e.g., explicit instructional practices and visual representations) and present findings from the studies in each section of this chapter. We also provide discussions of the specific instructional steps used in selected studies.

Research-Based Practices for the Acquisition of Arithmetic Combinations

Despite the importance of teaching arithmetic combinations (NCTM, 2006; NMAP, 2008) at the elementary level, we identified only nine studies that examined research-based instructional practices to help students with LD acquire or learn arithmetic combinations. We used a variety of strategies and criteria to identify studies. For example, we conducted a systematic search of psychological and educational databases (PsycINFO, Educational Resources Information Center [ERIC], and Academic Search Complete) published from 1990 to June, 2009. We examined peer-reviewed special education journals (e.g., *Exceptional Children, Journal of Learning Disabilities*) that frequently include articles of the type we were seeking. We were interested in studies that involved students with identified LDs and that focused on an intervention to teach arithmetic combinations to elementary-level students. Finally, the intervention had to include explicit instruction, strategic instruction, and/or visual representations as a major component of the intervention.

Across the nine studies, a total of 82 students with identified LD participated. The amount of time devoted to instructional practices to teach arithmetic combinations varied, with a low of eight sessions (Tournaki, 2003) to a high of 111 sessions (J. C. Mattingly & Bott, 1990). Not surprisingly, researchers designed studies that typically included a combination of instructional practices. Of the nine studies, most of the research included pairing the instructional practices. Explicit and strategic practices were paired (Beirne-Smith, 1991; Tournaki, 2003), as were explicit practices with visual representations (D. M. Williams & Collins, 1994). Studies with a combination of explicit and strategic practices with visual representations (C. A. Harris, Miller, & Mercer, 1995; D. Wood, Frank, & Wacker, 1998; Woodward, 2006) were also identified. Finally, the use of explicit practices only was found in two of the studies (J. C. Mattingly & Bott, 1990; Stading, Williams, & McLaughlin, 1996).

When examining the types of arithmetic combinations that were the focus of the studies, only Beirne-Smith (1991) and Tournaki (2003) taught addition combinations with sums 0 to 18; the remaining studies taught multiplication combinations, and one study included multiplication and division (S. P. Miller & Mercer, 1993). Missing from this group of studies was research on subtraction and more research on division combinations, which tend to be more difficult for students to master. Moreover, although teaching students the connections between the operations (addition and subtraction; multiplication and division) is a recommended practice (NCTM, 2009), none of the studies that we reviewed examined the practice of teaching combinations as fact families to help students with LD learn about the relationship between addition and related subtraction combinations, and multiplication and related division combinations. Although research is limited in the area of instructional practices that focus on explicit practices, strategic practices, and using visualizations, research findings overall hold promise for teaching students with LD arithmetic combinations (specifically, addition and multiplication).

Explicit Practices

We located two studies that focused solely on the use of explicit practices (not in combination with strategic practices or visual representation) to teach arithmetic combinations. Both studies focused on the teaching of multiplication. In the first study, J. C. Mattingly and Bott (1990) taught four students (two fifth graders, two sixth graders) in a resource room program. They examined the effects of a Constant Time Delay procedure as a means for teaching multiplication combinations 0 to 9 written on 3×5 index cards. Constant Time Delay involves the teacher presenting a task (reading a fact and saying the answer in this case) to the student and systematically increasing the time interval between the teacher's directions ("Read the problem. Say the answer.") and the prompt (reading the fact and saying the answer). The teacher provided the prompt systematically within a certain time frame. For example, given 3×4 and the teacher's directions, the student's answer should be "three times four equals twelve." The time interval for students to respond started with 0 seconds and was increased to 5 seconds between the teacher's directions and the prompt. In the 0-seconds condition, the teacher read the problem and said the answer. The goal was for the student to read the problem and state the answer within 5 seconds without a teacher prompt. Explicit practices that were used as part of the Constant Time Delay intervention included near-errorless learning, multiple opportunities to respond, and systematic prompting.

At the beginning of this multiple-probe, single-subject research study, 25 trials at 0-seconds delay were used with a continuous reinforcement system that involved giving a token for each correct answer. The criterion for mastery was 100% correct for three consecutive days. As part of the review process, mastered combinations were interspersed within the set of combinations to be learned to promote discrimination among learned arithmetic combinations. Under this condition, the criterion for mastery was 100% for two consecutive days. Results showed a high percentage of accuracy that continued in both the follow-up maintenance and generalization phases.

In another study that focused on multiplication, Stading and co-workers (1996) studied the effects of a Copy-Cover-Compare (CCC) technique for teaching $\times 2$, $\times 3$, $\times 4$, and $\times 5$ multiplication combinations with one third-grade girl with LD as part of home instruction using a single-subject multiple baseline across problem sets research design. During 15- to 20-minute sessions for 20 days, the student completed four new problems from one set (e.g., $\times 3$) and reviewed previously taught combinations (e.g., $\times 2$). A mixed probe (new and previously taught combinations presented together) was administered daily following the CCC technique. Explicit practices included a limited amount of instructional content taught at any one time, high rates of correct responding, immediate corrective feedback, and mixed review on the probe.

After the intervention, the student took a test (sheet of problems) with 16 multiplication combinations including the four most recently practiced and previously mastered combinations. Results from this test were part of the procedures for monitoring the student's progress with mastering sets of targeted combinations. Overall, results showed significant improvement at the conclusion of the acquisition phase of instruction from a mean of 35% correct during baseline to a mean of 100% correct after 20 days of instruction. No maintenance or generalization phases were identified.

Instructional steps for CCC. The CCC technique followed a systematic, explicitly taught step-by-step procedure, which included having the student provide a written response to match to the model and a written response from memory. An error-correction system was also built into the technique (Stading et al., 1996). The student received four new multiplication combinations on flash cards to study before the implementation of the CCC technique. The following steps were used for the student to learn the combinations:

Step 1: Copy. The student was taught to look at the written multiplication combination, read the problem aloud, and provide the answer while copying the problem and answer.

Step 2: Cover. The student covered the problem and answer and then wrote the problem and answer again from memory.

Step 3: Compare. The student compared her written problem and answer to the original problem and answer.

Step 4: If the student was correct, she proceeded to the next problem and repeated the same steps. If the student was incorrect, she repeated the steps with the same problem (error correction).

Explicit and Strategic Practices

We identified two studies that examined the potential benefits of combining explicit and strategic practices for instructional purposes. In an experimental study, Beirne-Smith (1991) examined two methods in separate instructional groups along with a control, or no-treatment, group. The study took place in four schools (two urban and two rural) in self-contained classes. Twenty students with LD who were identified through a pretest (i.e., scored 60% or less on addition facts) were randomly assigned to the treatment condition; 10 students to Method A and 10 students to Method B. Also, an additional 10 students who scored below 60% on the pretest were randomly assigned to the no-treatment control group. The treatment group included students with a mean age of 8.7 and the control group had a mean chronological age of 8.5.

Method A, which included explicit practices and a Count-On strategy, was compared to Method B, which emphasized explicit practices combined with a rote memorization strategy. Sets of related combinations (e.g., first digit held constant and second digit increased by 1; e.g., 2 + 1, 2 + 2, 2 + 3) were the instructional skill set for both methods. In Method A, combinations were systematically taught and the interrelationship of combinations was stated. That is, students were told that each combination started with a number (2, in our example) and the next quantity was added on. These procedures have been found successful when teaching students the Count-On strategy (Carnine & Stein, 1981). In Method B, the arithmetic combinations in the sets were presented randomly and no interrelationship was noted (i.e., the Count-On strategy was not demonstrated).

A cross-age peer-tutoring arrangement was used for instructional purposes. The pairs were matched based on scores on an arithmetic combinations test, so a stronger student without LD was paired with a student with LD who did not score as well on the test. Cross-age tutors were chosen to serve as "teachers" based on their scores of 80% or above on a pretest. Tutors were taught in two 45-minute sessions how to provide explicit instruction and either Method A (Count-On strategy) or Method B (rote memorization). Instruction occurred in 30-minute sessions. Students needed to earn five consecutive correct responses on all steps and tasks (different sets of related arithmetic combinations) for acceptable performance and advancement to the next task set. Then, the arithmetic combinations were mixed with previously learned arithmetic combinations for a review session.

Beirne-Smith (1991) found that students in the tutoring conditions (Method A and Method B) significantly outperformed students in the control group; yet no differences resulted between the two tutoring conditions.

Beirne-Smith suggested that the explicit practices, controlled materials, multiple opportunities to respond, high rates of repetition, error-correction procedures, reinforcement, and cumulative review (which were included in both methods) explained the lack of significant differences between the methods and the overall gains that exceeded the control condition.

Using a true experimental design with random assignment of participants to conditions, Tournaki (2003) also examined procedures that included explicit practices in a drill-and-practice group and strategic plus explicit practices in a Count-On group. These practices were very similar to those used by Beirne-Smith (1991) with the exception of the instructor. Eighty-four second-grade students participated in the study, 42 students with LD who had a mean age of 8.9 and 42 general education students with a mean age of 7.53. The ethnic groups represented in the school district included 75% European American, 13% African American, 10% Hispanic, and 2% Asian. One quarter of the students qualified for free/reduced lunch. The study was conducted in a classroom separate from the general education class.

Graduate research assistants (GRAs) demonstrated and verbalized (think aloud) the Count-On strategy; and the students also verbalized the strategy. The GRAs provided error correction immediately when mistakes were made. In the drill-and-practice group, neither demonstration nor verbalization was provided as part of instruction. Students were told to work as quickly as they could to complete the problems. The GRAs noted errors and asked the students to recompute the problems. The GRAs told students the answer if the correct solution was not provided. There were eight 15-minute sessions. Students moved from lesson to lesson after achieving 90% accuracy in 80 seconds. Tournaki's findings showed that students with LD in the Count-On strategy group outperformed their counterparts in the drill-and-practice (effect size of 1.5) and control (effect size of 1.35) groups when computing addition combinations. These differences were statistically significant, and the effect sizes represent meaningful differences between the treatment and control groups. These findings offer initial evidence in support of teaching students a counting strategy, such as Count-On, in combination with explicit practices to solve addition combinations.

Instructional steps for the Count-On strategy and explicit practices. Beirne-Smith (1991), who used cross-age tutors as instructors, followed several steps in implementing the Count-On strategy with explicit instruction. In Method A, Counting On, the tutor first showed the tutee a file folder with the designated addition combinations with the answers and then turned over the file folder to show the combinations without the answers. The procedures included the following:

1. The tutor stated the Count-On rule: start with the bigger number, count on by the smaller number.

2. The tutor demonstrated how to apply the strategy to solve a combination using the Count-On strategy (e.g., for the problem $6 + 3$, the teacher says "6 . . ., 7, 8, 9" while counting to 3 on her fingers).

3. The students in unison stated the rule and how to apply it.

4. The students took individual turns in using the steps.

5. Testing.

During testing, the tutor presented the flash-card sets, asking the tutee to read the problem and give the answer. Cards were shuffled and the process was repeated.

In Method B, which involved rote memorization, the tutor displayed the file folder with the combinations but without the answers. The tutor modeled how to say and answer the problems. The Count-On strategy was not taught. The file folder was removed from view, and the tutee was asked for answers to random problems within the task set. The tutee read the problems presented in random order and provided answers. Beirne-Smith's (1991) findings for the two tutoring groups, Method A and Method B, showed that they performed better than the control group but no significant differences existed in performance between the two methods. As noted, the use of the Count-On strategy was the difference between the two methods; explicit practices were used in both studies. One might conclude that using explicit practices for teaching combinations in and of itself is sufficient; however, findings from other studies (e.g., Tournaki, 2003; Woodward, 2006) show that the use of cognitive strategies (e.g., Count-On strategy) help students with LD learn arithmetic combinations.

Explicit Practices with Visual Representations

In examining the literature, one study was identified that investigated the use of explicit practices paired with visual representations for improving the acquisition of arithmetic combinations for students with LD. Using a single-subject, multiple-probe across groups of facts design, D. M. Williams and Collins (1994) compared two procedures, Constant Time Delay + Teacher-Selected Prompts and Constant Time Delay + Student-Selected Prompts, to teach $\times 6$, $\times 7$, and $\times 8$ multiplication combinations to four male students with LD. The four students were White and ranged in age from 9.6 years to 13.10 years; they received instruction in a self-contained day school.

The Constant Time Delay procedures were similar to those used by Mattingly and Bott (1990). The prompts (i.e., visual representations), which included poker chips, number lines, and fingers, were introduced to help students solve problems if they were not able to answer the problems correctly during the time-delay procedure. The two instructional conditions were teacher-selected prompt and student-selected prompt. During the teacher-prompt condition, if the student gave the wrong answer or did not provide an answer within 5 seconds, the teacher instructed the student to use a visual prompt. Instruction continued on the facts and involved the teacher's using a hierarchy of prompts from most to least intrusive across 9 days of instruction. The prompts included 3 days of chips, 3 days with the number line, and 3 days counting on fingers. In the student prompt condition, for incorrect or no responses within the designated 5-second time period, students could choose one of the three material prompts they wished to use.

The teacher taught a set of multiplication facts ($\times 6$, $\times 7$, $\times 8$) for 15-minute sessions five times per week for a total of 35 sessions. Students were not permitted to move to a new problem until giving a correct answer. Each student completed 30 trials per session.

Results showed that the time needed to reach criterion to move to another problem and the number of errors were less during the student-selected prompt condition, although no pattern was noted across the four students in choice of prompt and accuracy on probes. Three of four students performed above 90% correct on probes during the maintenance condition. Moreover, all of the students generalized knowledge of the target facts to two- and three-digit problems and to story problems. The findings demonstrated that although both conditions were effective, perhaps self-selection had some motivating appeal for students in this study.

Explicit and Strategic Practices with Visual Representations

We located two studies that focused on combining explicit practices, strategic practices, and using visual representations for acquisition of arithmetic combinations. In one study that used the combined practices, D. Wood, Frank, and Wacker (1998) used a multiple-baseline design across three 10-year-old students with LD to examine the effects of an instructional package on student performance in solving multiplication combinations $\times 0$ to $\times 9$. The school was located in a multiethnic district; two students in the study were White and one student was Black. All three students were identified as low socioeconomic status. The students were taught individually, separate from one another and the other students in the class.

Multiplication combinations were categorized as zeros, ones, doubles, fives, nines, and pegword (the remaining 18 combinations) facts. For instance, 4×4 was a double and belonged in the doubles group. Students were taught explicitly to say the steps for solving the arithmetic combinations in each group for facts. For example, for zeros facts, students were taught to look for a zero in the problem and then to write a 0 for the answer. For the ones facts, students were taught to look for a 1 in the problem, ignore it, and write the other number in the fact as the answer.

For doubles facts, real objects were introduced (e.g., skateboard has 2 sets of 2 wheels = 4 wheels, two toy octopi with 8 legs each = 16 legs) to illustrate the facts followed by pictures that depicted doubles. Students then practiced the double facts using flash cards with the mnemonic pictures. Participants were taught to solve five facts (e.g., 3×5) by counting by fives (e.g., 5, 10, 15). Students were taught to solve nine facts in three lessons. In the first lesson, they were taught to associate or link the numbers that add up to 9 (i.e., 1 and 8, 2 and 7, 3 and 6, 4 and 5). In the second lesson, they were taught to solve for the first digit of the answer by subtracting one from the number by which 9 is being multiplied. For example $9 \times 6 = 5\_$, because $6 - 1 = 5$. In the final lesson on nine facts, teachers provided instruction on solving for the second digit in the answer by adding the linked number. For example, $9 \times 6 = 54$ because 4 is linked with 5, which was identified in the previous step.

A pegword mnemonic strategy was used to teach the remaining 18 combinations. Pegwords are pictorial (visual) representations that are associated with key rhyming words for a particular item (see Chapter 26, this volume). D. Wood et al. (1998) provided the example of depicting an elf (pegword for 12) standing in a door (pegword for four) of a tree (pegword for three) to help students remember that $4 \times 3 = 12$. Students were first taught pegwords for numbers. For each combination, they were then presented with flash cards, then taught verbal elaborations to accompany the mnemonic (e.g., "an elf is in the door of the tree"), and finally solved the combinations by saying the verbal elaboration without the flash card.

A special education teacher administered the intervention for about two months with 20 to 40 minutes of instructional time per day in small groups. Results showed that during baseline one student scored 15% accuracy and two students scored 4% accuracy. At the end of the study, two students scored above 90% accuracy while one student scored 87% accuracy. Overall, results showed that all three students with LD made substantial gains from testing to intervention training and maintained a high percentage of accuracy. Moreover, as a result of the instructional package, "participants appeared to be more enthused about math instruction," resulting in multiplication assignments being "completed quickly and often chosen first, with few or no negative comments" (D. Wood et al., 1998, p. 336).

In another study that used combined practices, C. A. Harris and colleagues (1995) reported two simultaneously administered studies that evaluated the effectiveness of several instructional components on the math performance of students with LD when taught by their general education teachers. In one study, 12 students with LD and one student with emotional disturbance participated. All of the students were White. Nine of the 13 students were eligible for free/reduced lunch; their ages ranged from 7.11 to 9.6 years. In the other study, the 99 participants did not have disabilities; 83 were White, 15 were Black, and 1 was Hispanic. The ages ranged from 7.1 to 9.4, and of the 99 students, 42 qualified for free/reduced lunch.

Using a multiple-baseline design across three classes, multiplication combinations ($\times 0$ to $\times 9$) were taught using a concrete-representational-abstract (CRA) instructional sequence, rule instruction (e.g., any number $\times 0 = 0$; any number $\times 1 =$ the number), and the DRAW strategy (defined in the following section). The CRA sequence and the DRAW strategy have been previously validated (e.g., S. P. Miller & Mercer, 1993). C. A. Harris et al. (1995) were interested in knowing the effects of the intervention when taught in a larger group setting.

The CRA sequence began with concrete objects or manipulatives to develop conceptual understanding, including paper plates used to represent groups and plastic counting discs to show the objects in each group. At the visual representational level, the manipulatives were exchanged for pictures of boxes with dots or tallies to show the multiplication problems. After six lessons at the concrete and representational levels, the students moved to the abstract and symbolic level. Two mnemonic strategies were taught to help students remember how to solve the problems.

The DRAW strategy is a mnemonic intended to help students recall the steps of problem solution (DRAW). The strategy includes a mnemonic in which each letter of the word signals a procedure for students to follow (e.g., D = Discover the sign). The mnemonic features of the DRAW strategy are described in detail in the following section.

The CRA sequence used explicit practices along with concrete objects and pictures; rule instruction involved repetition; and the DRAW strategy was taught explicitly. A total of 21 lessons over 8 weeks were conducted with all participants (C. A. Harris et al., 1995). As part of each lesson, students independently completed a Learning Sheet with 10 problems; the lesson was retaught to students who did not achieve a score of at least 80% accuracy. Additional student progress-monitoring data included completion of a Multiplication Minute sheet under timed conditions throughout the study.

Instructional steps for the DRAW strategy. The lessons were teacher directed and included describing and modeling the process for solving the problems, providing guided practice and error correction, and having students complete 10 problems independently as part of monitoring their progress (C. A. Harris et al., 1995). When teaching students this strategy, the teacher (a) explained the purpose of the lesson; (b) modeled, using "think alouds," how to use the mnemonic to solve problems; and (c) taught students the mnemonic (i.e., "say the mnemonic, name the letters, and tell what action to do for each letter"). The DRAW strategy includes a semi-concrete component (i.e., draw). Teachers used the following steps to teach students the mnemonic strategy:

D = Discover the sign (The student looks at the sign to figure out the operation.)

R = Read the problem (The student says the problem aloud.)

A = Answer or draw and check (The student thinks of the answer or draws tallies to solve the problem.)

W = Write the answer. (The student writes the answer in the answer space.)

Once students set up the problem, they use DRAW to solve the computation. The goal is that students learn the mnemonic steps and apply them independently to successfully solve both multiplication and word problems. Findings showed that all students with LD improved their performance, ranging in improvement from 50 to 85 percentage points. When using the DRAW strategy, the students with LD performed similarly to their typically achieving peers on instructional probes.

Research-Based Practices for Building Fluent Responding with Arithmetic Combinations

In this section, we identify and describe the instructional practices—explicit practice, strategic practices, and visual representations—that researchers used to promote fluent or automatic retrieval of arithmetic combinations. Again, we found that researchers frequently combined instructional practices in their studies. Quick retrieval (i.e., fluent responding) of arithmetic combinations (i.e., addition and related subtraction combinations; multiplication and related division combinations) is a critical element of mathematics instruction and a foundation

skill for algebra success in later school years (Gersten, Beckmann, et al., 2009b; NCTM, 2009; NMAP, 2008).

We located only three studies in this category. One study (McIntyre, Test, Cooke, & Beattie, 1991) focused on explicit practices and strategic practices; one study included explicit practices and visual representations (Miller & Mercer, 1993); and one study consisted of explicit practices, strategic practices, and visual representations (Woodward, 2006). A total of 21 elementary-level students participated in these three studies in three different settings (i.e., resource room, general education classroom, media center). Each of the studies included approximately 20 instructional sessions.

Explicit and Strategic Practices

Using a multiple-probe design, McIntyre et al. (1991) examined the effects of the Count-By strategy on fluency with multiplication combinations for which other strategies are not typically employed (i.e., $\times 4$, $\times 7$, $\times 8$) for one African American fourth-grade boy with LD. The Count-By technique is rooted in studies that examined effects of "attack" strategy training whereby students are taught procedures that can then be applied to the solving of multiplication problems (Lloyd, Saltzman, & Kauffman, 1981). The Count-By strategy was taught explicitly using the Model-Lead-Test procedure in which the teacher modeled the procedures, then guided or led the student through the steps, followed by the student performing the steps independently while being assessed. The student first practiced counting by one set of numbers until fluency (e.g., saying "4, 8, 12, 16, 20, 24, 28, 32, 36, 40" in 10 seconds or less). The student was then taught to turn a multiplication combination into a Count-By problem. For example, 7×4 would be solved by counting by 7 four times—7, 14, 21, 28. Practice consisted of oral and written responses. Then, a test was conducted (i.e., 1-minute timing of the combinations) to determine how many more combinations the student answered correctly during each timing. Overall, findings showed that it took the student nine sessions to learn the $\times 4$ facts, 11 sessions to learn the $\times 7$ facts, and 21 sessions to master the $\times 8$ facts. On the generalization test across time, the student improved from 6 digits per minute to 49 digits per minute on a test of all multiplication facts.

Explicit Practices and Visual Representations

S. P. Miller and Mercer (1993) examined the effect of a Concrete-Semiconcrete-Abstract (CSA) instructional sequence on the mathematics performance of addition arithmetic combinations with sums from 10 to 18 and division arithmetic combinations with quotients from 0 to 9 using a multiple-baseline across subjects design.

Six boys and three girls ranging in ages between 7.7 and 11.3 years were involved in this study; five students were identified as having LD, one student had developmental disabilities, and three students were at risk for LD. The students with disabilities received their instruction in resource rooms; the students were in first to fifth grade.

The CSA routine is the same as the CRA routine discussed earlier in this chapter (see C. A. Harris et al., 1995). The teacher taught ten 20-minute lessons. During the concrete phase, the teacher used various concrete materials (e.g., buttons, coins, popsicle sticks) as part of instruction to promote generalization of responding across objects. In the semi-concrete phase, students were taught to represent problems using drawings; the drawings were then replaced by the use of tally marks. In the abstract phase, students were instructed not to use drawings or tallies when solving problems.

One-minute timings were done each day to collect fluency data that included the number of correct and incorrect responses. Results indicated that all students demonstrated significant improvement at the abstract level (i.e., on daily 1-minute timings) as noted in increased correct rate and decreased error rate scores. Findings showed that students in this study required three to seven lessons in concrete and semi-concrete activities using manipulative devices and pictures before they could transfer their learning to a test sheet (e.g., correct responses per minute were higher than error responses per minute) that was at the abstract level.

Explicit and Strategic Practices with Visual Representations

In a true experiment, Woodward (2006) studied the effects of Integrated Strategy Instruction (i.e., strategies and timed practice drills) compared to Timed Practice Drills on student fluency with a range of multiplication combinations including common, hard, and extended (more than one digit) problems. The teacher provided instruction in the general education classroom for 25 minutes per day, 5 days per week, for 4 consecutive weeks. Fifty-eight students participated in the study; 15 students had identified LD. Participants were matched by pretest score, and one member of each pair was randomly assigned to either the integrated condition or the timed practice drills-only condition. Six boys with LD and two girls with LD, of which five were Black and three were White, were assigned to the integrated condition. In the timed practice drills-only condition, seven participants were classified as LD—four boys and three girls, three White and four Black. The average age was 9 years and 5.6 months.

The Integrated Strategy Instruction method included strategic and explicit practice with visual (pictorial) representations. Daily instruction consisted of teaching combinations using different strategies depending on the nature of the combinations. Rule-based strategies were taught for relatively simple combinations (i.e., perfect squares, 0s, 1s, 2s, 5s, 9s). More difficult problems were taught using derived and doubling approaches coupled with number lines or arrays (e.g., blocks). For example, using the derived approach, the answer for 6×7 was derived from the previously mastered problem 6×6 by breaking down 6×7 into $6 \times 6 + 6$. As represented on a number line, 6×6 was shown as a series of "hops" (i.e., hopping in increments of 6 from 6 to 12 to 18 and so on) to reach 36. Then 6×7 simply involves one additional hop of 6, showing the answer to be 42. Thus, students were taught explicitly to use their knowledge of one combination to find the answer to a more difficult combination (e.g., neighbors on the number line). The doubling and doubling again strategies also used students' knowledge of relatively basic multiplication and applied them to combinations that involve 4, 6, or 8 as a multiplier. For example, $4 \times 7 = 2 \times 7$ doubled (i.e., $14 + 14$). This can be represented on either a number line or with manipulatives during instruction. Strategies and corresponding combinations were introduced in order of difficulty.

Strategies were also included to extend students' understanding of solving single-digit multiplication combinations to combinations involving two- and three-digit numerals. Extended combination instruction consisted of linking number line knowledge of single-digit combinations to combinations with two- or three-digit multipliers. For example, knowledge of $4 \times 7 = 28$, represented by making 7 hops of 4 on the number line, was extended to the multidigit problem of $40 \times 7 = 280$ by making 7 hops of 40 on a number line in 10-digit increments. Similarly, using blocks, students' knowledge that $4 \times 2 = 8$, as represented by 2 sets of 4 blocks, was extended to $40 \times 2 = 80$ by showing two sets of four 10-block rows. More difficult multiplication combinations involving a one-digit multiplier and a two- or three-digit multiplier were taught using the partial product algorithm. This algorithm breaks down multiple-digit combinations into a series of combinations that the students can solve based on their previously learned strategies. For example, 6×387 can be broken down into $6 \times 7 + 6 \times 80 + 6 \times 300$, all of which students had been taught to solve.

In the timed practice drills-only condition, instruction focused on teaching facts using explicit practices. Daily instruction consisted of teachers eliciting choral responses to teach new combinations (e.g., "7 times 3 is 21. What is 7 times 3?") or review previously taught combinations (e.g., "3 times 4 is what?"). Combinations were taught using a hierarchical approach from easiest to hardest facts (e.g., $\times 2$ facts to $\times 8$ facts). Instruction also involved students completing computation sheets using traditional computation algorithms to solve previously taught math combinations.

Findings showed that both interventions were effective in helping students to achieve fluency with multiplication combinations. Although the study found no differences between the two groups' performance on the difficult multiplication combinations, students in the integrated strategy instruction group did better than students in the timed practice drills-only group on the extended combinations. Furthermore, students' scores in the integrated timed strategy instruction group remained at mastery level from post-test to maintenance, whereas students in the timed practice drills-only group did not.

Instructional steps for the integrated strategy instruction method and timed practice drills-only method. The two methods involved the following steps:

Method 1: Daily Instruction in the Integrated Strategy Condition

1. *Phase 1:* Students were introduced to a new strategy or reviewed previously taught strategies. Overheads or number lines were used as visuals. Students were encouraged to discuss the strategy and contrast it to previously taught strategies.

2. *Phase 2:* Students completed a 2-minute timed practice drill. Teacher dictated answers following the drill. Students circled any incorrect answers and wrote correct response. When 70% of students in the class achieved 90% or greater on the drill, the teacher moved to the next skill.

3. *Phase 3:* Students extended and applied their knowledge of the strategies taught in Phase 1 in different ways. On some days, students were taught the relationships between one-digit problems and extended multiplication combinations through number lines and manipulatives (e.g., blocks). On other days, the partial product algorithm was taught (e.g., $243 \times 6 = 6 \times 3 = 18, 6 \times 40 = 240, 6 \times 200 = 1,200; 18 + 240 + 1,200 = 1,458$). Approximation and rounding were taught using number lines on some days. And on other days students completed word problems as a class.

Method 2: Timed Practice Drills Only

1. Students were introduced to or reviewed previously introduced combinations (no strategy instruction took place) in teacher-directed instruction. The teacher introduced combinations and answers, followed by students repeating combinations and answers chorally.

2. Students completed 2-minute timed practice drill in the same manner as the integrated instruction.

3. Students completed worksheet practice on computational problems.

Summary and Directions for Future Research

Summary of the Instructional Practices

We located nine studies for teaching arithmetic combinations to students with LD. We identified only three studies for teaching fluency. In terms of the instructional practices, the findings reinforce extensive previous research (e.g., the importance of *explicit practices* as part of an intervention to teach arithmetic combinations to students with LD). All 10 studies included the following hallmark characteristics of explicit practices: modeling, high rates of responding and practice, repetition, error correction, review and distributed practice, and frequent monitoring of performance. These practices are well documented as effective in promoting mathematics performance in students with LD and low achievement (S. Baker et al., 2002; Bryant, Bryant, Gersten, Scammacca, & Chavez, 2008; Bryant, Bryant, Gersten, Scammacca, Funk, & Winter, 2008; Gersten, Beckmann, et al., 2009b). Moreover, 6 of the 10 studies also included *strategic practices* (e.g., Count-On strategy for addition arithmetic combinations, DRAW to cue memory for multiplication procedures, Count-By strategy for multiplication arithmetic combinations) for prescribed sets of related arithmetic combinations, which were effective in promoting student performance related to acquisition and fluency.

This combined instructional focus, explicit practices and strategic practices, has been documented as most effective when teaching students with LD (H. L. Swanson et al., 1999). Yet, interestingly, findings were mixed when examining strategic practices compared to timed drills/ rote memorization. Beirne-Smith (1991) found that although students in the strategy and rote memorization conditions did better than the control group, no differences were noted between the two methods. However, in Tournaki's (2003) study, students in the strategy condition did better than students in the timed drill condition. And Woodward (2006) found that although students in the integrated strategies condition did better than students in the timed drill condition in both mastery and maintenance, no differences were found between groups for the harder combinations.

Finally, results across studies showed that *visual representations* were important for students to acquire, master, and develop fluency in arithmetic combinations. However, because the studies combined visual representations with other practices (e.g., explicit, strategic), it is not possible to determine which specific practices might be more or less beneficial. More research that involves unpacking multicomponent interventions to test the effectiveness of visual representations appears warranted.

Limitations and Directions for Future Research

First, the overall sample size across the studies was relatively small, and most of the studies occurred in special education settings. Moreover, with the exception of two studies (Tournaki, 2003; Woodward, 2006), all of the studies were conducted in the 1990s. Clearly, given that most students with LD who are struggling with mathematics now receive their instruction in general education settings, more studies are needed in the general education setting with interventions delivered by a general education teacher alone or by a pair of co-teachers.

Second, missing from this review was research on the effect of these practices when teaching subtraction and division arithmetic combinations. Research that examines the effects of teaching both subtraction and addition, as well as both division and multiplication, is needed. Students must conceptually understand inverse operations to help them see and make connections across mathematical concepts.

Third, it is widely accepted practice and expected in intervention research that sufficient information about participants is provided to demonstrate that they have the learning problems presented; thus, the procedures for how districts identified students as having LD (or other disabilities) is necessary. The participants must be described with sufficient detail to allow replication of the study. Information such as age, gender, ethnicity, primary language, and achievement is necessary to better understand the characteristics of the participants (Gersten et al., 2005; R. H. Horner et al., 2005; Rosenberg et al., 1992). Inclusion of these participant characteristics varied across the articles, and information about primary language was absent in all of the studies. Thus, the degree to which findings apply to English Language Learners is unclear and should be investigated in future research.

Conclusion

Robinson, Menchetti, and Torgesen (2002) proposed that instruction for students with poor mastery of arithmetic combinations should include providing interventions that develop conceptual knowledge of the four operations and fluent retrieval of answers to arithmetic combinations. Additionally, students must have ample time and opportunity to practice the strategies to develop meaning as well as fluency (NCTM, 2009). In sum, the overall findings from the studies in this chapter support and reconfirm the effectiveness of *explicit practices, strategic practices,* and *visual representations* when teaching arithmetic combinations (specifically addition and multiplication) to students with LD in mathematics. Not only must students master combinations, they must also be able to automatically retrieve answers to basic combinations. In closing, this chapter was not an exhaustive review of effective practices for promoting acquisition, mastery, and automatic retrieval of arithmetic combinations for students with mathematics disabilities at the elementary level. Certainly, findings from other studies (e.g., computer-based technology, early elementary "prevention" studies) can provide a more comprehensive view of effective instructional practices for students who struggle with mathematics. The findings from studies in this chapter, however, do shed important light on ways to help students with LD become more proficient in foundation skills.

CHAPTER 6

Strategies for Improving Student Outcomes in Mathematics Reasoning

Asha K. Jitendra | *University of Minnesota*

Marjorie Montague | *University of Miami*

"All young Americans must learn to think mathematically, and they must think mathematically to learn."

(National Research Council, 2001a, p.1)

*T*he centrality of mathematical reasoning is clear, as indicated in the National Council of Teachers of Mathematics' (NCTM) *Principles and Standards for School Mathematics* (NCTM, 2000):

> Being able to reason is essential to understanding mathematics. By developing ideas, exploring phenomena, justifying results, and using mathematical conjectures in all content areas and—with different expectations of sophistication—at all grade levels, students should see and expect that mathematics makes sense. . . . Systematic reasoning is a defining feature of mathematics. (pp. 56–57)

Learning mathematics goes beyond recalling facts and fluency with algorithms to mathematical reasoning and critical reflection. Yet despite 20 years of research and reform in mathematics education emphasizing students' thinking and reasoning, many students continue to engage in rote thinking (J. Hiebert, 2003; Lithner, 2008; National Research Council, 2001a) and are often "unprepared for complex and novel problem solving" (Nathan & Kim, 2009, p. 91). Students with disabilities, in particular, experience difficulties employing effective problem-solving

strategies in making sense of mathematical situations (Jitendra, 2008).

Traditional forms of instruction that focus on getting the correct answer to word problems using the key-word strategy, for example, exacerbate the problems these children experience in applying mathematical skills in flexible ways to solve novel problems. Consider the following problem:

> One morning, Maya was cleaning out her bookshelves in her room and decided to give away 12 books from her collection of Babysitter's Club to her cousin, Tanya. That afternoon, she gave away 20 of her books. How many books did she **give away** that day?

Keisha, a third-grade student, solved the problem by using the key-word method. Her answer was eight books, because she reasoned that the key word *give away* implies subtraction as the operation. In this example, rather than engaging in sophisticated mathematical reasoning, Keisha applied a simple, rote procedure that ignores the meaning and structure of the problem. In the situation above, the rule associating the key word with the operation is misleading; thus, use of the key-word approach would not result in successful problem solving.

In fact, "mathematical reasoning is no less than a basic skill" (Ball & Bass, 2003, p. 28). Students must be able to verbalize their reasoning processes and explanations as well as critically reflect on their understanding of the underlying concepts. Toward this end, teaching all students, including students with disabilities, complex mathematical reasoning and critical reflection is of great importance. At the same time, it is important to address learner characteristics and scaffold instruction for students with disabilities, who may have memory and conceptual difficulties, background knowledge deficits, linguistic and vocabulary difficulties, strategy knowledge and use difficulties, and self-regulation problems (S. K. Baker, Simmons, & Kame'enui, 1995).

In the sections that follow, we review two practices—schema-based instruction (SBI) and cognitive strategy instruction (CSI)—that research has shown to be highly effective in facilitating mathematical reasoning of higher-order problem-solving skills for students with disabilities. For the purpose of this chapter, we define reasoning as "the line of thought adopted to . . . reach conclusions in task [problem] solving" (Lithner, 2008, p. 257).

Schema-Based Instruction

Schemata are hierarchically organized, cognitive structures that are acquired and stored in long-term memory. According to schema theory, the acquisition of the problem schema, or semantic structure of the problem, is critical to successful problem solving (Sweller, Chandler, Tierney, & Cooper, 1990). Working memory load during cognitive processing is reduced when recognizing a problem's schema, because multiple elements of information are grouped into and conceptualized as a single schema (Kalyuga, 2006). Although the initial acquisition of problem schemata requires working memory resources, with practice the use of schemata becomes automated and requires minimal working memory resources (Kalyuga, 2006).

In the domain of arithmetic word problems, the most comprehensive set of schemata described in the relevant literature include Change, Group, Compare, Restate, and Vary (Marshall, 1995). These schemata are separated into two problem categories, additive and multiplicative structures. Change, Group, and Compare problems belong to the additive field in that the solution operation is either addition or subtraction; the multiplicative field involves Restate (i.e., Multiplicative Compare) and Vary (i.e., Equal Groups and Proportion) problems, because the solution operation is either multiplication or division (Christou & Philippou, 1999). Solving word problems requires mentally representing the different elements described in the problem text. Therefore, the difficulty of the problem may be a function of the difficulty in understanding the problem situation.

Our instructional model uses schema training to focus students' attention on the problem schema (e.g., Change, Compare) and helps them represent the relations between the different elements described in the text using schematic diagrams (e.g., Hegarty & Kozhevnikov, 1999; Janvier, 1987). Unlike pictorial representations of problems that include concrete but irrelevant details, which "are superfluous to solution of the math problem" (Edens & Potter, 2006, p. 186), a schematic diagram depicts the spatial relations between objects in the problem text (Hegarty & Kozhevnikov, 1999). The nature of representations in our SBI model not only facilitates recognition of the problem schema (e.g., Compare) and organization of problem schema knowledge, but also emphasizes information (nonmathematical) contained in the situation model (Van Dijk & Kintsch, 1983). The situation model "is a temporary structure stored in working memory [that] . . . corresponds to a level of representation that specifies the agents, the actions, and the relationships between the events in everyday contexts" (Thevenot, Devidal, Barrouillet, & Fayol, 2007, p. 44).

Given that many students with disabilities, especially learning disabilities (LD), lack skills to translate word problems, SBI focuses on comprehending the sentences (nonmathematical information) in word problems, especially sentences that express a relation between two quantities. For example, consider the following problem:

> Music Mania sold 56 CDs last week. It sold 29 fewer CDs last week than this week. How many CDs did it sell this week?

(Jitendra, 2007, p. 118). Instruction in SBI emphasizes that compare words such as "fewer than" in this problem can cue the learner to the schemata (e.g., Compare) and identify the key comparison or relational sentence as, *"It (Music Mania) sold 29 fewer CDs last week than this week."* Further, SBI teaches that the comparison sentence can help the student figure out the two things compared (i.e., number of CDs sold last week and number of CDs sold this week) as well as identify the bigger quantity in the problem. Students trained in SBI would then deduce that the bigger quantity is the number of CDs sold this week, because the number of CDs sold last week is *fewer than* the number of CDs sold this week. In addition, SBI instruction would focus on the need to determine the difference between the two things being compared in the comparison sentence. Finally, information in the remaining verbal text specifies the known and unknown quantities for the two things compared necessary to solve the problem.

Successful problem solvers can translate and integrate information in the problem into a coherent mental representation that mediates problem solution (R. E. Mayer, 1999; Mayer & Hegarty, 1996). For students with LD, teaching them to represent the situation described in the problem using schematic diagrams is critical to reduce working memory resources. The use of schematic representations as a means to identify the underlying structure of problems is a key recommendation in the practitioner literature on Response to Intervention (RtI) in mathematics (Gersten, Beckman, et al., 2009a). At the same time, helping students with LD collectively use language and representations to reason and solve problems is of great importance (Hegarty, Mayer, & Monk, 1995). As Ball and Bass (2003) argued, "these things [mathematical reasoning and solving problems] need to be taught and learned if they are to be known" (p. 40). In sum, SBI focuses on teaching students to comprehend the problem, represent the problem, plan to solve the problem using appropriate strategies, and reflect on the solution. Teachers therefore play an important role in scaffolding the use of problem-solving processes (e.g., representing, reasoning) via "think alouds." Following is a description of how SBI in conjunction with self-questioning to monitor the learning process can be used to help students develop mathematical reasoning in solving word problems (e.g., Compare).

Teaching Problem Solving and Mathematical Reasoning with SBI

The SBI intervention described here is based on our work with elementary school students with learning difficulties (see Jitendra, 2007). In our word problem-solving program, we have used a four-step strategy to anchor student learning, called FOPS:

F—Find the problem type

O—Organize the information in the problem using the diagram

P—Plan to solve the problem

S—Solve the problem

The teacher uses a checklist based on the strategy steps to scaffold the cognitive processes as she thinks aloud to solve word problems (see Jitendra, 2007). See Figure 6.1 for a checklist for applying FOPS to a Compare problem.

Figure 6.1   A checklist for applying FOPS to a compare problem checklist.

COMPARE PROBLEM CHECKLIST

Step 1.   Find the problem type

☐ Did I read and retell the problem?

☐ Did I ask if it is a compare problem? (Did I look for compare words – taller than, shorter than, more than, less than?)

Step 2.   Organize information using the compare diagram

☐ Did I underline the comparison sentence or question and circle the two things compared?

☐ Did I reread the comparison sentence or question and ask, "Which is the LARGER amount and the SMALLER amount?" and write names of things compared in the diagram?

☐ Did I underline important information, circle numbers and labels, and write numbers and labels in the diagram?

☐ Did I write a "?" for what must be solved? (Did I find the question sentence?)

Step 3.   Plan to solve the problem

☐ Do I add or subtract? (If the "Total" or "Whole" is given, subtract. If the "Total" or "Whole" is not given, add.)

☐ Did I write the math sentence?

Step 4.   Solve the problem

☐ Did I solve the math sentence?

☐ Did I write the complete answer?

☐ Did I check if the answer makes sense?

Given the question of how many CDs Music Mania sold this week (described earlier), the teacher identifies the problem type using Step 1 of the strategy by reading, retelling, and examining information in the problem to recognize it as a Compare problem via self-instructions (e.g., Are there compare words in the problem that tell me about a comparison? Does the *comparison* statement tell what the problem is comparing?). In addition, the teacher makes the connection between previously solved problems (e.g., Change, Group) by noting that this problem differs from a Group problem solved earlier, because the problem compares two distinct, disjoint sets (i.e., last week's sale of CDs and this week's sale of CDs) that are not combined into a new, pooled set. In contrast, Group problems involve two disjoint sets (e.g., red crayons, blue crayons) that combine to make a new set (i.e., red and blue crayons). It is also unlike a Change problem, in which a permanent change occurs over time in the starting quantity when a direct or implied action causes an increase or decrease of that quantity to result in a changed quantity (e.g., Toshi had 56 CDs in her music collection. Then her brother borrowed 29 of her CDs. How many CDs does Toshi have now?).

For Step 2, the teacher demonstrates how to organize information using the schematic diagram. This step includes self-instructions to read the problem to identify critical information and represent it using the appropriate schematic diagram. For example, questions such as, "What does this problem compare?" (i.e., number of CDs sold last week and number of CDs sold this week) and "What does the comparison sentence tells us about?" (i.e., the difference between the number of CDs sold last week to number of CDs sold this week), are used to make sense of the problem schema. Specifically, the questioning makes clear the difference amount (i.e., 29), which is first represented in the diagram followed by reading the comparison sentence to find the bigger and smaller sets and writing the terms associated with those sets (i.e., this week's sales of CDs is the bigger set, and last week's sales is the smaller set). Next, the quantities for each of the two sets are identified by reading the problem text and writing the given amount(s) or a "?" for what must be solved in the diagram. The teacher then analyzes the problem situation using the completed diagram in Figure 6.2 as follows: "This week's sales of CDs is more than last week's sales of 56 CDs. The difference between this week's sales and last week's sales is 29 CDs. We need to solve for the number of CDs sold this week."

Step 3 involves translating the information in the diagram into a number sentence. During this step, students also learn to discriminate between instances when addition or subtraction is appropriate based on whether or not the whole (i.e., total) is known. In this instance, students learn that the bigger quantity is the whole, which is unknown. The teacher models using self-instructions by asking, "Do I add or subtract to solve for the '?' or the whole?" The teacher reasons that addition would be the operation, because the whole (bigger amount) is the sum of the parts (smaller amount and difference amount). Then, the teacher writes the number sentence: $56 + 29 = ?$

Finally, Step 4 has the students solve the problem using the operation identified in Step 3, justify the derived solutions using the schema features as anchors for explanations and elaborations, and check the accuracy of not only the computation but also the representation. The following provides an illustration of a teacher modeling the mathematical reasoning to make sense of the answer:

> Let's see . . . the number of CDs sold this week is 85 and the number of CDs sold last week is 56. This seems right, because the number of CDs sold this week (85) should be more than the number of CDs (56) sold last week. So, the answer 85 CDs sold this week, which is more than 56 CDs sold last week, seems right. I will also check the answer by subtracting: $85 - 56 = 29$, which is the difference amount.

In sum, SBI encourages student think alouds to monitor and direct problem-solving behavior along the following dimensions: (a) problem comprehension

Figure 6.2   Sample compare schematic diagram.

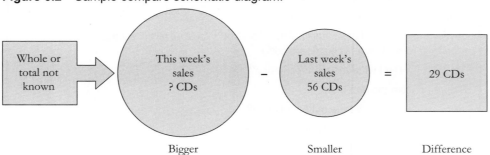

(e.g., "Did I read and retell the problem to understand what is given and what must be solved?" "Why is this a Compare problem?" "How is this problem similar to or different from ones I already solved?"), (b) problem representation (e.g., "What diagram can help me adequately represent information in the problem to show the relation between quantities?"), (c) planning (e.g., "How can I set up the number sentence? What operation can I use to solve this problem?"), and (d) problem solution (e.g., "Does the answer make sense?" "How can I verify the solution?") (see Jitendra et al., 2007, 2009).

Research Evidence in Support of SBI

Since the 1990s, researchers have investigated the effectiveness of SBI to help students struggling in mathematics solve arithmetic and algebra word problems. These investigations have typically involved schema-based instruction or external modeling emphasizing the semantic structure of problem types (L. S. Fuchs, Seethaler, et al., 2008; Hutchinson, 1993; Jaspers & Van Lieshout, 1994; Jitendra et al., 1998, 2007, 2009; Jitendra, DiPipi, & Perron-Jones, 2002; Jitendra & Hoff, 1996; Jitendra, Hoff, & Beck, 1999; Y. P. Xin, 2008; Y. P. Xin, Jitendra, & Deatline-Buchman, 2005; Y. P. Xin, Wiles, & Lin, 2008; Zawaiza & Gerber, 1993) and schema-broadening instruction focusing on transfer (SBI-T) (L. S. Fuchs, Fuchs, et al., 2008; L. S. Fuchs, Fuchs, Finelli, Courey, & Hamlett, 2004; L. S. Fuchs, Fuchs, Hamlett, & Appleton, 2002; Owen & Fuchs, 2002). Although SBI-T, not unlike SBI, teaches students to recognize problems as belonging to specific problem types (e.g., Shopping List, Half, Buying Bags, Pictograph), the problem types are not based on the common set of schemata for arithmetic word problems (e.g., Change, Group, Compare, Multiplicative Compare, Equal Groups) described in the literature (Marshall, 1995). In addition, SBI-T focuses on transfer by teaching students to search novel problems for familiar problem types that may seem different based on different format, different key vocabulary, additional or different question, and irrelevant information. A total of 758 students participated in these studies, including students with LD and students with mild intellectual disabilities, as well as students who were English Language Learners (ELLs) and students without disabilities struggling in mathematics. Students ranged in age from 8-10 to 26-7 years. SBI research focused on elementary, middle, and high school students; SBI-T research focused primarily on elementary school students.

Schema-Based Instruction

The early work on schema training focused on modeling the semantic structure of arithmetic word problems using a number line (Zawaiza & Gerber, 1993) or concrete materials (Jaspers & Van Lieshout, 1994) and emphasized schema development by embedding metacognitive strategy instruction to represent and solve algebra word problems (Hutchinson, 1993). SBI that emphasized modeling the semantic structure of word problems using schematic diagrams was studied extensively by Jitendra and colleagues in a series of single-subject and randomized controlled group design studies examining mathematical problem solving for elementary and middle school students. For example, in two single-subject studies (Jitendra & Hoff, 1996; Jitendra et al., 1999), students with LD who were provided SBI intervention in solving addition and subtraction problems involving Change, Group, and Compare not only demonstrated improved word problem-solving performance (mean increase ranged from 47% to 69%), but also maintained their problem-solving performance 2 to 4 weeks following the intervention. Further, transfer effects from one-step to two-step problems were seen for three of the four middle school students in the Jitendra et al. (1999) study. Interestingly, the mean gains on one-step problems for all four students were comparable to those for a normative sample of third graders. However, the mean performance on two-step word problems was substantially higher for students with LD trained in SBI (71% correct) compared to the normative sample (28% correct).

While these two studies suggested that SBI is a potentially promising approach for improving the word problem solving of students with LD, other studies by Jitendra et al. (1998, 2007) used randomized controlled trials to validate its effectiveness for elementary school students with disabilities (e.g., LD, intellectual disabilities, emotional and behaviorial disorders [EBDs]) and students at risk for poor problem-solving outcomes. Results of the Jitendra et al. (1998) study showed that students in the SBI group not only scored significantly higher than the control group, but also performed at the same level as average-achieving students on math problem-solving post-tests. Further, results revealed transfer effects to novel problems for students in the SBI group. Effects sizes comparing SBI with the control condition were $d = 0.65$ at post-test, $d = 0.81$ at delayed post-test, and $d = 0.74$ for generalization, all medium-to-large effect sizes.

Jitendra et al. (2007) improved on the SBI approach by embedding metacognitive strategy instruction, described earlier, in a study conducted in five third-grade classrooms ($N = 88$ students) in a high-poverty elementary school with a sample of mostly low-achieving students, including students with LD, students who were ELLs, and Title I math students. General education teachers provided all instruction during their regularly scheduled mathematics class. Results suggested that SBI was more effective than typical classroom instruction in improving students' mathematical problem-solving skills (post-test: $d = 0.52$; 6-week delayed post-test: $d = 0.69$). Moreover, students in the SBI group outperformed the comparison group on the state assessment of mathematics performance ($d = 0.65$).

The next set of studies by Jitendra and colleagues extended this work on SBI to the domain of multiplication and division word problem solving involving Multiplicative Compare and Proportion problems. In a single-subject research study, Jitendra et al. (2002) found that four middle school students with LD who received SBI not only improved their word problem-solving performance on both problem types (mean improvement ranged from 50% to 71%), but also maintained their performance 2 to 10 weeks following the end of the intervention and generalized to more complex problems, including multistep problems. Y. P. Xin et al. (2005) and Jitendra et al. (2009) further validated the effects of SBI using randomized controlled trials. Y. P. Xin et al. (2005) worked with 22 students with LD, behavior disorders, and students at risk for poor problem-solving outcomes. Results showed that students receiving SBI significantly outperformed a comparison group on an immediate post-test ($d = 1.69$), delayed post-tests ($d > 2.50$), and a transfer test ($d = 0.89$) that included items from standardized mathematics achievement tests.

Jitendra et al. (2009) provided professional development on SBI to seventh-grade general education teachers in preparation for using SBI as part of the curriculum on ratios and proportions. Students were taught the concepts of ratio and rate and also how to solve proportion word problems using multiple solution methods (e.g., unit rate, equivalent fractions, cross multiplication). Seventh graders from eight classrooms in one middle school ($n = 148$) in a large, urban school district participated in a 10-day intervention. The students who received SBI instruction outperformed students in the comparison classrooms on the problem-solving post-test ($d = 0.45$) and on a 4-month delayed post-test ($d = 0.56$). Thus, the research conducted by Jitendra and colleagues suggests that SBI is effective for solving various types of math problems (2009).

Other research teams have also investigated the impact of SBI on students' problem-solving performance. For example, Xin and colleagues (Y. P. Xin, 2008; Xin et al., 2008; Xin & Zhang, 2009) modified SBI by using schematic diagrams and word-problem story grammar instruction to test what they term "conceptual model-based problem solving" to improve student learning. This series of single-subject design studies showed promising results for studies of Equal Groups, Multiplicative Compare, and Part-Part-Whole (e.g., Group) problems. L. S. Fuchs, Seethaler, et al. (2008) and L. S. Fuchs et al.

(2009) tested the efficacy of schema training on the math problem-solving performance of third-grade students with math and reading difficulties. In these studies, the intervention not only focused on recognizing addition/subtraction word problem types, but also emphasized "transfer solution methods to problems that include irrelevant information, 2-digit operands, missing information in the first or second position in the algebraic equation, or relevant information in charts, graphs, and pictures" (p. 155). Results of the study by L. S. Fuchs, Seethaler, et al. (2008) conducted with 35 participants indicated that the schema-training group made significantly greater gains when compared to the control group at post-test ($d = 1.80$), although transfer to a standardized math word problem was not evident.

L. S. Fuchs et al. (2009) extended their research on SBI to evaluate whether difficulties in mathematics only or a combination of reading and math difficulties differentially impact word problem-solving learning. Across two sites, the authors stratified the 133 participants by mathematics disability status and randomly assigned them to three conditions: number combinations tutoring, word problem-solving tutoring (i.e., SBI), and control (no tutoring). Both tutoring groups outperformed the control group on number combinations ($d = 0.55$) and word problem-solving skills ($d = 0.62$); differences between tutoring groups were not significant.

Schema-Broadening Instruction Focusing on Transfer

L. S. Fuchs and colleagues validated the effectiveness of SBI-T for elementary students with LD, intellectual disabilities, or at risk for poor problem-solving outcomes in four randomized controlled studies. In all four studies, the control-condition group received instruction from a district-adopted mathematics textbook. Results of the study by L. S. Fuchs et al. (2002) conducted with 40 students with mathematics disabilities indicated that both the problem-solving tutoring group and problem-solving tutoring plus computer-assisted practice group showed significantly greater math problem-solving scores on the post-test as well as on transfer tests than students in the computer-assisted practice only and control groups (d ranged from 0.83 to 2.10).

Owen and Fuchs (2002) worked with 24 students with LD, intellectual disabilities, speech and language disorders (SLDs), or attention deficit hyperactivity disorder (ADHD) to examine the differential effects of problem-solving treatments compared to a control condition on solving one-step word problems involving "half" problems (e.g., "Every day Tony spends 8 hours at school. Yesterday he got sick and had to go home after 1/2 of the school day. How many hours was he at school?"). Students in the acquisition treatment condition received a six-step method that included drawing circles to represent the given number and distributing circles evenly into each half of a rectangle over 4 days. Students in the low-dose acquisition + transfer condition received both acquisition instruction (an abbreviated dose of instruction over 2 days) and instruction on how to transfer skills to solve novel problems. The full-dose acquisition + transfer condition was the same as the low-dose acquisition condition, except for the duration of the acquisition instruction (which occurred over 4 days, as in the acquisition condition). Effect sizes comparing the treatment groups with the control condition showed that the full-dose acquisition + transfer condition outperformed the other groups (*d* ranged from 0.93 to 1.63). This study showed that a combination of problem-solving instruction and transfer instruction was more effective than either component alone.

Similarly, L. S. Fuchs et al. (2004) compared the differential effects of SBI-T, expanded SBI-T, and a control condition with 30 students with disabilities. SBI-T involved teaching solution rules for solving similar problem types and emphasized transfer skills (identifying similar problem structure by searching for superficial changes such as cover story, quantities); expanded SBI-T focused additionally on challenging problem features (e.g., irrelevant information, combining problem types, combining superficial problem features). Results indicated significant improvement in math problem solving for students in the treatment groups compared to the control group on all four transfer problem-solving measures (*d* ranged from 1.28 to 1.76 for expanded SBI-T and from 1.03 to 2.02 for SBI-T).

A recent study by L. S. Fuchs, Fuchs, and colleagues (2008) with 243 at-risk students for poor problem-solving outcomes supported the added value of supplemental SBI-T instruction (*d* ranged from 1.34 to 1.52) to either classroom SBI-T or conventional classroom instruction on a range of proximal (*d* ranged from 0.23 to 1.52) and distal (*d* ranged from 0.23 to 0.49) measures of word problem solving. In addition, on proximal measures of word problem solving, students at risk who received only supplemental tutoring in SBI outperformed or performed as well as students not at risk.

Findings from these 20 studies indicate that schema training is effective for many different groups of students, including students with LD, ADHD, EBD, and SLD as well as students who are ELLs and students who are not disabled and are struggling in mathematics. Schema training appears to be effective whether the focus is on SBI, external modeling to emphasize the semantic structure of problem types, or teaching for transfer as in schema-broadening instruction. The positive outcomes of SBI were found for students instructed in general education

classrooms, special education classrooms, and outside the students' classrooms by either researchers or classroom teachers. Further, instruction was effective whether implemented individually, in small groups, or class-wide. Our review of the 20 studies indicated that the supports provided in studies with positive effects included explicit instruction via modeling and/or elaborative explanations of the strategy using visuals (e.g., a number line, schematic diagrams), prompt cards containing critical information, and posters or checklists of strategy steps. In some studies, manipulatives (e.g., L. S. Fuchs, Fuchs et al., 2008) and calculators (e.g., Y. P. Xin et al., 2005) were used to further scaffold student learning. Partner learning in some studies presented additional opportunities for students to immerse themselves in problem solving and reasoning as well as to communicate orally with their peers when they shared their solutions and explanations (e.g., Jitendra et al., 2007).

In sum, SBI is a research-based, conceptual teaching approach that meets the diverse needs of students in classrooms in several ways. SBI promotes understanding and reasoning by moving away from direct translation methods to problem representation using relevant semantic cues. Also, it reduces cognitive memory load for students struggling in mathematics. Finally, it provides the kind of scaffolding (e.g., explicit explanations) that is necessary to support these students as they make sense of word problems and independently solve word problems. In the next section we describe CSI research and its application to math problem solving.

Cognitive Strategy Instruction

SBI and CSI are complementary interventions in that they are cognitively based and specifically develop students' ability to represent mathematical problems. However, SBI is more specific than CSI in its emphasis on recognizing different problem types and constructing an appropriate schema or symbolic representation to reflect the unique problem type (e.g., Compare, Change), whereas CSI provides a cognitive routine that can be applied across problem types. CSI is more generic in its emphasis on the cognitive processes that help students translate and transform the linguistic and numerical information into symbolic representations of the problem that serve to organize the information and set up the solution plan.

CSI focuses on teaching students a range of cognitive and metacognitive processes and strategies that facilitate learning. These strategies may be relatively simple or complex, depending on the difficulty of the task and the context. Strategic learners and successful problem solvers have a repertoire of strategies and use them effectively and efficiently when they understand, analyze, represent, execute, evaluate, and solve problems. They are self-regulating and motivated problem solvers who know what strategies to use and when and how to use them (Pressley, Borkowski, & Schneider, 1987). In contrast, students with learning difficulties and disabilities such as LD and ADHD usually have not acquired strategies needed for successful problem solving, have difficulty selecting and using strategies appropriate to the task, do not abandon ineffective strategies, do not adapt previously learned strategies, and do not generalize strategy use to other tasks or settings (H. L. Swanson, 1990, 1993)—and therefore typically need explicit strategy instruction. Thus, CSI—which teaches students how to think and behave like successful problem solvers—appears to meet the needs of many students with learning difficulties and disabilities.

CSI is grounded in cognitive theory and considers students' development and how they process information. The approach provides instruction in cognitive processes (e.g., visualization) and metacognitive or self-regulation strategies (e.g., self-questioning). To illustrate, Montague's (2003) model designed for students in middle school includes seven cognitive processes critical to solving mathematical word problems: (a) reading the problem for understanding, (b) paraphrasing by putting the problem into one's own words, (c) visualizing by drawing a schematic representation, (d) hypothesizing or setting up a plan, (e) estimating or predicting the answer, (f) computing, and (g) checking that the plan and answer are correct. The model also incorporates self-regulation in the form of a "SAY, ASK, CHECK" procedure whereby students give themselves instructions, ask themselves questions, and monitor their performance as they solve problems.

The instructional format for CSI is explicit instruction, which is characterized by highly structured and organized lessons that include techniques and procedures such as appropriate cues and prompts, guided and distributed practice, cognitive modeling, interaction between teachers and students, immediate and corrective feedback on performance, positive reinforcement, overlearning, and mastery (Montague, 2003). The basic CSI routine has several stages (Graham & Harris, 2003). First, teachers develop and activate students' background knowledge. Then they discuss the strategy and model its application with the targeted task. Students are required to memorize the strategy. Then teachers provide the necessary guidance and support as students learn and practice the strategy until they can apply it independently. Modeling the strategy is critical to the success of CSI. Cognitive modeling, sometimes referred to as process modeling, is simply thinking aloud while demonstrating a cognitive

activity. The teacher and then students model how successful problem solvers/strategic learners think and behave as they engage in the academic tasks (e.g., math problem solving). This technique stresses learning by imitation and provides students the opportunity to observe and hear how successful problem solvers understand and analyze a problem or task, develop a plan to complete the task, and evaluate the outcome. CSI thus teaches students both cognitive and metacognitive processes and strategies using a specific and explicit instructional routine.

Teaching Problem Solving Using CSI: Solve It! Instruction

The CSI intervention described here is Solve It!—an instructional program designed to teach students with LD how to solve math word problems. Solve It! teaches the cognitive processes that are necessary for developing and applying declarative, procedural, and strategic knowledge of arithmetic when solving math word problems. *Declarative knowledge* refers to the ability to recall math facts from memory, *procedural knowledge* is knowledge of basic algorithms, and *strategic knowledge* can be described as a storehouse of multiple strategies that enable individuals to approach math tasks and problem solving effectively and efficiently.

Math problem solving has two major phases: problem representation and problem execution (R. E. Mayer, 1985). Problems can be represented with physical objects or manipulatives, a symbolic representation written on paper, a carefully constructed arrangement of the problem information in one's mind, or a combination of these levels of representation (Janvier, 1987). Problem representation strategies are needed to comprehend and integrate problem information, maintain mental images of the problem in working memory, and develop a logical plan to solve the problem (Silver, 1985). Problem solvers must be able to translate and transform the linguistic and numerical information in math problems into verbal, graphic, symbolic, and quantitative representations that show the schemata or relationships among the information in the problem (R. E. Mayer, 1985; Montague & Applegate, 1993; van Garderen & Montague, 2003) in order to develop a plan to solve it. Then the problem solver executes the solution. Problem execution requires the problem solver to develop the plan and move between the problem information, problem representation, and the solution path. If students cannot or do not represent the problem correctly, they cannot solve it. The Solve It! intervention places particular emphasis on teaching students how to represent mathematical problems by paraphrasing problems, using visualization strategies such as diagram drawing or mental imaging, and hypothesizing or setting up a plan.

Specifically, the Solve It! intervention introduces cognitive processes and self-regulation strategies that students memorize by using verbal rehearsal. Verbal rehearsal is a memory strategy that enables students to recall automatically the math problem-solving processes and strategies. Solve It! uses the acronym RPV-HECC to help students remember and internalize the labels and definitions for the processes and strategies (R = Read for understanding, P = Paraphrase in your own words, V = Visualize—draw a picture or diagram, H = Hypothesize–make a plan, E = Estimate—predict the answer, C = Compute—do the arithmetic, C = Check—make sure everything is right). Cues and prompts are used to help students as they memorize the processes and their definitions. The ultimate goal of the program is to have students internalize the cognitive processes and metacognitive strategies and use them automatically. Figure 6.3 presents the cognitive processes and metacognitive strategies that are the foundation for the Solve It! intervention.

Solve It! is flexible because it allows teachers to adapt the teaching routine and tailor instruction to

Figure 6.3   Solve It! math problem-solving cognitive routine.

READ (for understanding)

Say: Read the problem. If I don't understand, read it again.

Ask: Have I read and understood the problem?

Check: For understanding as I solve the problem.

PARAPHRASE (your own words)

Say: Underline the important information. Put the problem in my own words.

Ask: Have I underlined the important information? What is the question? What am I looking for?

Check: That the information goes with the question.

VISUALIZE (a picture or a diagram)

Say: Make a drawing or a diagram. Show the relationships among the problem parts.

Ask: Does the picture fit the problem? Did I show the relationships?

Check: The picture against the problem information.

HYPOTHESIZE (a plan to solve the problem)

Say: Decide how many steps and operations are needed. Write the operation symbols (+, −, ×, and /).

Ask: If I …, what will I get? If I …, then what do I need to do next? How many steps are needed?

Check: That the plan makes sense.

ESTIMATE (predict the answer)

Say: Round the numbers, do the problem in my head, and write the estimate.

Ask: Did I round up and down? Did I write the estimate?

Check: That I used the important information.

COMPUTE (do the arithmetic)

Say: Do the operations in the right order.

Ask: How does my answer compare with my estimate? Does my answer make sense? Are the decimals or money signs in the right places?

Check: That all the operations were done in the right order.

CHECK (make sure everything is right)

Say: Check the plan to make sure it is right. Check the computation.

Ask: Have I checked every step? Have I checked the computation? Is my answer right?

Check: That everything is right. If not, go back. Ask for help if I need it.

Source: From Montague, M. (2003). *Solve It: A mathematical problem-solving instructional program.* Reston, VA: Exceptional Innovations. Copyright by Exceptional Innovations. Permission to photocopy this figure is granted for personal use only.

accommodate the strengths and weaknesses of students. It includes a detailed instructional guide, informal assessments, curriculum-based measures, scripted lessons that facilitate explicit instruction, instructional materials, and procedures for helping students apply, maintain, and generalize skills and strategies. The time frame for initial instruction can range from 3 to 15 days, which makes this program feasible and practical as a complement and supplement to the standard curriculum. Weekly practice sessions across the school year with word problems drawn directly from the school and/or district curriculum provide the application and distributed practice vital to developing not only effective but efficient problem solving. The mathematical problems used for initial instruction and practice include typical textbook problems; state assessment-type problems; and authentic, situated, real-life problems, such as the following:

- *Typical textbook problem:* A store sells shirts for $13.50 each. On Saturday, it sold 93 shirts. This was 26 more than it had sold on Friday. How much did the store charge for all the shirts sold on both days?

- *State assessment-type problem:* It costs an initial fixed cost of $2 plus an additional $1.50 per mile to rent a taxi. What is the total cost for a 5-mile trip?

- *Real-life problem:* Your group is planning to go to a matinee movie on Saturday and then to Burger King for dinner. How much money will each person need? What will be the total cost for the group?

In this way, students are engaged in a variety of problem-solving applications and have many opportunities to solve problems independently, in teams, and in cooperative groups. After students have mastered the Solve It! routine and have had sufficient independent practice, they can pair up for solving problems where one student models the routine while the other student acts as the coach. Group problem solving is most effective when students work together to solve a real-life problem, such as the movie and Burger King problem mentioned in the preceding list. Solve It! ensures that students are actively engaged during instruction, develop the ability to communicate about mathematics with their peers, become competent in demonstrating what they have learned, and learn to correct errors and reinforce themselves for accuracy and progress over time. To illustrate, Figure 6.4 presents an example of a Solve It! introductory lesson that focuses on conceptual understanding of paraphrasing as a translation and comprehension process (Montague, 2003).

Research Evidence in Support of Using Solve It! to Improve Math Problem Solving

All of the research studies that have focused on CSI for improving math problem solving used Montague's (2003) Solve It! or used a cognitive routine similar to Solve It! (L. P. Case, Harris, & Graham, 1992; Cassel & Reid, 1996; K. H. Chung & Tam, 2005; Hutchinson, 1993; Montague, 1992; Montague, Applegate, & Marquard, 1993; Montague & Bos, 1986). A total of 142 students with LD or mild intellectual disabilities ranging in age from 8-4 to 16-7 years participated in these studies. For a detailed review of these studies, see Montague and Dietz (2009). Solve It! was designed to teach students how to understand, analyze, solve, and evaluate mathematical problems by developing the processes and strategies that effective problem solvers use. Montague's research focused primarily on middle and high school students with LD and, most recently, also on middle school students in general education classes who were identified as at risk for mathematics failure (Montague, Enders, & Dietz, 2009).

The first study was a single-subject, multiple-baseline design with six secondary students with LD (Montague & Bos, 1986) who met participation criteria (e.g., minimum reading level, computation competence). Following intervention, all students improved to criterion (at least 70% correct on at least three of four consecutive tests of math problem solving) and also generalized strategy use to more difficult problems. Additional validation studies using both single-subject and group designs were then conducted as part of a federally funded grant to improve mathematical problem solving for middle school students with LD (Montague, 1992; Montague et al., 1993).

In the group study (Montague et al., 1993), 72 middle school students with LD were given the Solve It! intervention and, following intervention, they performed at the same level as average-achieving students on math problem-solving tests and maintained performance over a 4-month period. Within-group pretest/post-test analyses produced large effect sizes based on pretest performance ($d = 1.09$ post-test, $d = 1.08$ maintenance at 1 month, $d = 0.74$ maintenance at 2 months, and $d = 1.25$ following a booster session). Furthermore, participants generalized the problem-solving routine to more complex problems. This study also indicated that the combination of cognitive and metacognitive components of instruction was more effective than either component alone. Daniel (2003) used Solve It! and also found significant improvement in math problem solving for middle school students with LD compared with a control group. She reported that their knowledge and awareness of strategies improved

Figure 6.4 Example of a Solve It! introductory lesson.

Teacher: Yesterday you began to learn a routine for solving math problems. What is the name of the routine? (Call on a student.) Yes, that's right. The problem-solving routine is called *Solve It!* What was the acronym for *Solve It!*? (Call on a student and write RPV-HECC on the board.)

That's right. RPV-HECC. Together, let's review what the acronym stands for. (Point to the Master Chart and read the routine.) R ... Read ... P ... Paraphrase ... V .... Visualize .... etc.

Now, let's review the entire *Solve It!* routine. (Review the entire RPV-HECC routine. The teacher leads a group recitation of the routine.)

Teacher: Now I want to talk more about the paraphrasing process. Remember, good problem solvers put the problem into their own words and they remember the information. What does paraphrase mean?

Students in unison (S): Put the problem in your own words.

Teacher: Again. What does paraphrase mean?

Students: Put the problem in your own words.

Teacher: What does that mean ... put the problem in your own words? (Elicit student responses and write them on the board.)

Teacher: Excellent ideas. Okay, you said that paraphrasing has to do with using different words to say the same thing. It also has to do with eliminating unimportant or unnecessary information to get the meaning only. Paraphrasing gets at the basic meaning of the message or, in this case, the math problem. Paraphrasing helps us to understand what we read. Sometimes we call paraphrasing "retelling," which means telling it again. Any other ideas, questions, or comments?

Let's look at this problem (on overhead projector). (Read the problem to the students. Then read in unison.)

Jose and Nancy are selling greeting cards to raise money for the school camping trip. Together they sold cards totaling $88.50. Nancy sold $67.00 worth of cards. How much money did Jose make selling cards?

(Distribute the problem.) Now I want you to underline the important information. Go ahead.

What did you underline? (Call on students and ask why that information is important and then, on the transparency, underline the important information.) Now, put the problem in your own words. Say it aloud. Okay, let's have some examples of paraphrasing. (Call on students individually and discuss each person's "paraphrase.")

Very good! So, when you paraphrase a math problem, what do you do to locate the important information? (Elicit responses, for example, use important information only, names of people are not important, the question is important, etc.)

Let's try another problem. (Use the same procedures.)

Look at the Paraphrase process in RPV-HECC. (Use Master Class Charts.) First you say to yourself (Recite as a group):

Say: Underline the important information. Put the problem in my own words.

Then you ask yourself (Recite as a group):

Ask: Have I underlined the important information? What is the question?

Finally, you check yourself (Recite as a group):

Check: That the information goes with the question.

Let's try another problem. (Use the **Say – Ask – Check** procedure for additional problems.)

to the level of average-achieving students following Solve It! instruction. Thus, the program was validated in four studies of students with LD, a group of students who frequently struggle with mathematics (Geary, 1994; Jitendra & Xin, 1997). These students characteristically have limited cognitive strategies, particularly problem representation strategies, poor self-regulation, and low motivation and self-efficacy.

Researchers have also established that Solve It! has the potential for addressing students with other types of disabilities. Coughlin and Montague (2011) successfully adapted Solve It! for three adolescents with spina bifida.

As a result of a pilot study, the researchers eliminated the estimation process, provided manual support for visual representation, and built in a graduated program whereby students demonstrated mastery with one-step problems before they advanced to two-step problems. All students improved to criterion on both types of problems. Whitby (2009) successfully adapted Solve It! and improved the problem-solving performance of three middle school students with high-functioning autism/ Asperger's syndrome by adding a video modeling component and gradually increasing the difficulty level of the problems.

Solve It! is the focus of a federally funded U.S. Department of Education study (Montague et al., 2009) that provided general education math teachers with professional development to incorporate Solve It! instruction into the prescribed curriculum. Results from the first year of the study indicated that students in grades 7 and 8, including average-achieving students as well as at-risk students and students with LD ($n = 185$), made significantly greater growth in math problem solving over the school year than students in the comparison group ($n = 127$) on curriculum-based measures of textbook-type problems ($d = 0.44$). They also made significantly greater growth in math problem-solving self-efficacy and math confidence over the school year than students in the comparison group ($d = 0.37$). Year 2 results, with grade-8 students ($n = 719$), indicated that students who received the Solve It! intervention demonstrated significantly greater increases across the school year on the curriculum-based measures compared with students in the control condition who received typical classroom instruction only ($d = 0.91$). By the end of the school year, students with LD in the Solve It! condition performed significantly better than the average-achieving students in the control condition.

In sum, the research conducted thus far has suggested that CSI is a promising approach not only for teaching students math problem solving but also for teaching other higher-order skills such as reading comprehension and composition. For a review, see Wong, Harris, Graham, and Butler (2003). Like SBI, it meets the diverse learning needs of students with and without disabilities who are at risk for mathematics failure.

Recommendations for Practice

Promoting effective problem-solving and reasoning skills using SBI and CSI requires adhering to several guidelines. One important consideration for students struggling with mathematics is to ensure that students understand problem representation and develop the ability to represent problems accurately using schematic representations that show the relationships among the problem parts. Students with and without disabilities who struggle with mathematics have difficulties in generating coherent problem representations that mediate problem solving (van Garderen & Montague, 2003). SBI provides them with schematic representations that illustrate the mathematical relationships between objects and facilitates translating information from the diagram into an appropriate number sentence (Hegarty & Kozhevnikov, 1999). Similarly, CSI explicitly teaches students problem-representation processes (i.e., paraphrasing and visualization) that provide the foundation for deciding on an appropriate solution path.

Another consideration in the case of SBI is that a four-step problem-solving process is used to guide problem solving. However, it is critical that students become actively engaged in the process of reasoning rather than simply applying the steps in a rote fashion to obtain the correct answer. That is, coherently representing information in the problem using a diagram requires more than following the steps. It involves identifying the problem schemata (i.e., Change, Group, Compare), understanding the various features and semantic relations that characterize the problem, and integrating the information to accurately represent it. Students struggling in mathematics may prematurely focus on the problem solution without understanding the problem situation that is essential to successful problem solving. Therefore, initial tasks could include story situations with no unknown information to inhibit direct translation methods (e.g., the word *altogether* suggesting the use of addition) that ignore mathematical reasoning.

Specifically, the focus of instruction should be on critical thinking and reasoning as students learn to represent information in the problem using the schematic diagram. For example, students should read to understand the problem situation to first find the two things compared in the Compare problem before identifying the larger and smaller quantities, which may pose difficulties for some students when there is irrelevant information and the comparison statement describes the compared quantity to be less than the referent quantity. In the following story situation, "Mahesh, a shoe salesman, works at Harry's Shoes. He sold 68 shoes last month. He sold 12 fewer shoes this month than last month. Mahesh sold 56 shoes this month." "Mahesh, a shoe salesman, works at Harry's Shoes" is irrelevant information. Although "shoes sold this month" and "shoes sold last month" are the two things compared from the comparison statement, it is important for students to understand that the order of information presented in the comparison statement does not translate to "shoes sold this month" is the bigger quantity to represent in the diagram. The same caveat is true for CSI. Students must be provided with ongoing, distributed practice with a variety of problem types to ensure that the acquired processes and strategies are "overlearned": that is, they are internalized and used automatically.

Clearly articulated explanations are critical to help students identify and eliminate irrelevant information and ensure that they understand problems conceptually, represent problems accurately, and develop a logical plan to solve them. To do this, students must understand the problem situation. Finally, checking to see whether the answer makes sense or is reasonable is another crucial component of both SBI and CSI. Checking the answer should emphasize reasoning and critical thinking, which involves going beyond checking the computation to having students check the problem-solving process. This often involves working backward and may include having students check whether their diagram accurately represents the problem.

Conclusion

Meaningful differences related to children's mathematical problem-solving skills are evident when children enter first grade (National Research Council, 2001a). These differences grow wider over time and are difficult to ameliorate without "direct school-based instruction" (National Research Council, 2001a, p. 19). For several reasons, the research on SBI and CSI is promising for improving mathematical reasoning by focusing on math word problems. First, the benefits of SBI and CSI for students struggling with mathematics are evident from the research base showing that students' math problem-solving skills improve significantly and substantially following systematic and explicit instruction in these approaches.

Second, many of the studies addressed maintenance and transfer aspects of word problem-solving skills that are particularly difficult for students with mathematics disabilities. These students struggle to transfer their learning to novel problems, particularly if their original exposure to word problems is superficial and is not reinforced over time. Therefore, it may be necessary to specifically teach transfer to novel situations (e.g., L. S. Fuchs, Seethaler, et al., 2008). Third, the content addressed in SBI and CSI studies ranged from arithmetic word problems involving all four operations to algebra problems, including two-variable two-step equations. While the approaches have been successful with varying types of problems, future research should also address word problems representing other mathematical content strands (e.g., fractions, measurement, geometry). For example, in recent SBI research (Jitendra et al., 2009), positive outcomes for improving student learning of ratios, proportions, and percents have been noted.

In sum, both SBI and CSI provide direction to facilitate students becoming more effective and efficient problem solvers, which in turn helps students to become more independent problem solvers. As a consequence, improved math problem solving should have a positive impact on students' overall math performance, as has been documented in the research. Theoretically, these approaches may also positively impact other student outcomes such as high-stakes test performance and graduation rate.

CHAPTER 7

Strategies for Improving Student Outcomes in Written Expression

Linda H. Mason | *The Pennsylvania State University*

Karen R. Harris and **Steve Graham** | *Vanderbilt University*

"The pages are still blank, but there is a miraculous feeling of the words being there, written in invisible ink and clamoring to become visible."

Vladimir Nabokov

Many students with disabilities likely share Nabokov's sentiment that the words remain invisible and the pages are blank, or close to blank, as they produce few ideas and little detail when they write (Graham & Harris, 2003). An important educational goal for these students is to make sure that they have the tools to improve this situation so that their thoughts and ideas take form in writing, becoming both visible and powerful. This chapter presents research-based instructional practices that provide teachers with tools for meeting this goal.

Why is it important for students with disabilities to develop as writers? Writing is critical to students' school, occupational, and social success. Poor writing directly impacts students' learning in classroom contexts (Mason & Graham, 2008). Writing is an important educational tool, as it provides students with a means for personalizing information as well as reformulating and extending it (Langer & Applebee, 1987). Over 90% of white-collar workers and 80% of blue-collar workers indicate writing is important to job success (National Commission on Writing, 2007). Writing has also become a primary means for communicating and keeping in touch with friends, colleagues, and others, as electronic forms of communication, such as e-mailing, texting, and blogging have become so prominent. Thus, students who do not learn to write well are increasingly at risk in almost all facets of life.

This presents major problems for students with disabilities, as the overwhelming majority of them have not developed the writing skills needed for success. When compared to students without disabilities, they are not as effective in using writing as a tool for communication, expression, or learning (K. R. Harris & Graham, 1999; Mason, 2010). Results from the National Assessment of Educational Progress 2007 writing test, however, make it clear that writing is a challenge for most students in our schools: approximately 74% and 95% of students without disabilities in eighth and twelfth grades did not meet the proficiency skill level in writing (Salahu-Din, Persky, & Miller, 2008).

Students with disabilities experience even greater difficulties than their normally achieving peers mastering the process of writing (K. R. Harris & Graham, 1999), as a result of multiple factors. Their knowledge about different writing genres and tasks is typically incomplete, resulting in selection of inefficient and ineffective strategies for planning, drafting, monitoring, evaluating, and revising what they write (K. R. Harris, Graham, & Mason, 2003). They experience difficulties managing or regulating these same processes (H. L. Swanson, Hoskyn, & Lee, 1999) and, just as importantly, they exhibit little goal-directed behavior, persistence, or effort when writing (Graham & Harris, 2003). Further, their writing performance is often affected negatively by conditions such as attention problems, hyperactivity, acting out, withdrawal, or other behaviors (Bos & Vaughn, 2006). Other difficulties, such as memory and poor language abilities, provide additional barriers to their writing development.

Fortunately, considerable evidence indicates that teachers can overcome each of these barriers and that children with disabilities can learn to be skillful writers (Graham & Perin, 2007; Rogers & Graham, 2008). Perhaps the most significant roadblock to achieving this goal, however, resides in the classroom. While many teachers do an excellent job of teaching writing, too often teachers simply provide too little writing instruction (Kiuhara, Graham, & Hawken, 2009), or the instruction provided in both general education and special education settings is ill-defined, providing inadequate development for students (Cutler & Graham, 2008; Graham & Harris, 2003). Such instruction is contrary to what has been shown to be effective in research: students who struggle with writing need explicit and systematic instruction that helps them master and regulate critical aspects of the writing process (Graham, 1999; Schumaker & Deshler, 2003). Effective instruction for these students should include careful progress monitoring; planning that considers flexible groupings, adaptation, and scaffolding; appropriate pacing for individual students; plenty of opportunity to be actively engaged; and positive and facilitative feedback. Fortunately, researchers have developed and validated well-designed instructional methods for teaching students writing skills, strategies, processes, and knowledge. This includes teaching the essential building blocks of composing: the processes of planning, organizing, and revising text; taking ideas and shaping them into interesting and syntactically correct sentences; and transcribing these sentences onto paper through handwriting/word processing and spelling.

In this chapter, we present research-based instructional programs for developing these basic building blocks in writing for students with disabilities. The first program, the Center on Accelerating Student Learning (CASL) Handwriting/Spelling Program, addresses basic transcription skills for young students with disabilities (Graham & Harris, 2006). The next program,

the Strategic Instruction Model (SIM), focuses on strategies instruction for adolescents with disabilities (Schumaker & Deshler, 2003). In this chapter, we highlight SIM strategies for sentence construction and paragraph writing. Finally, we present the Self-Regulated Strategy Development (SRSD) model for teaching strategies for planning, drafting, and revising text as well as self-regulation procedures for carrying out these processes. SRSD has been validated for students with disabilities from elementary through secondary grades (Graham & Harris, 2003).

Effective Practices for Teaching Writing-Transcription Skills

Students with disabilities often have difficulty with both handwriting and spelling (Graham, 1990). These difficulties can interrupt the composition processes, interfere with intended messages, constrain writing development, and impact vocabulary use in writing (Graham, Harris, et al., 2008). In addition, difficulties with handwriting and spelling may lead students to avoid writing and to believe they cannot write (Berninger, Mizokawa, & Bragg, 1991). Given the potential negative impact of poor transcription skills, students with disabilities would benefit from effective handwriting instruction that teaches efficient ways for writing letters and words legibly and fluently (Graham, Harris, et al., 2008). Furthermore, students with disabilities should be taught how to spell words they use frequently in writing, generate reasonable spellings for unknown words, check and correct spelling errors using multiple resources, and develop a desire to spell correctly (Graham, 1999).

Effective handwriting instruction for students with disabilities should include (a) individualization to meet a student's needs; (b) teaching skills through frequent and short lessons; (c) modeling how to form letters; (d) comparing and contrasting letter features; (e) providing facilitative supports such as marks for paper placement on student desks and tripod grip molds for pencils; (f) teaching students how to independently evaluate and improve their handwriting; (g) promoting handwriting fluency; and (h) teaching letter formation in isolation, quickly followed by application in context (Graham, 1999).

Based on the available empirical evidence (Graham, 1999), effective instruction for spelling difficulties includes explicitly teaching spelling words, skills, useful rules, and phonological awareness. This includes mastery of words students are likely to use when writing and individualized instruction as needed. In addition, word-study approaches, such as word sorting by spelling patterns, have proven effective for students with disabilities.

Maintenance and generalization should be supported by continual review of previously learned words and integration of spelling words with students' reading and writing. The CASL Handwriting/Spelling Program includes these recommended instructional practices in a program that addresses both handwriting and spelling.

CASL Handwriting/Spelling Program

> My spelling is Wobbly. It's good spelling but it Wobbles, and the letters get in the wrong places.
>
> A. A. Milne

The CASL Handwriting/Spelling Program was designed to improve developing spellers' skills in writing the letters of the alphabet, handwriting fluency, knowledge of sound–letter combinations, spelling patterns involving long and short vowels, and words commonly used when writing (K. R. Harris & Graham, 2009). Before starting the lesson units, a pretest of 94 of the most commonly used words in young children's writing is given (Graham, Loynachan, & Harris, 1993). Misspelled words from this list, as well as words misspelled during instruction, combined with a spelling phonics sequence, are used for the handwriting/spelling lessons. The phonics unit sequence includes: (a) Unit 1: short /a/ and /o/; (b) Unit 2: short /o/ and /e/; (c) Unit 3: short /i/ and /u/; (d) Unit 4: short and long /a/; (e) Unit 5: short and long /i/; (f) Unit 6: short and long /o/; (g) Unit 7: short and long /e/; and (h) Unit 8: long /a/. In Unit 8, three spelling patterns are contrasted: long /a/ with silent e, /ai/, and /ay/.

Lesson Activities Overview

Forty-eight 20-minute lessons, divided into the eight units previously noted (six lessons per unit), are included in the program. Each unit includes six short activity-based lessons (see Table 7.1). Five different activities are included in Lessons 1 through 5. Lesson 6 has one activity.

Activity 1. Across the 48 lessons, students work on 46 different sound–letter combinations during a 2-minute Phonics Warm-up activity. Each sound–letter combination is represented on a card with a picture on one side (e.g., in Unit 2, a picture of a bed) and corresponding letters on the other side (e.g., "b," "e," "d"). The teacher holds up a card and says, "What letter(s) make the sound you hear at the (beginning, middle, or end) of this word?" If an incorrect response is given, the teacher says the correct letter and repeats the process. The purpose of this activity is to improve students' skills in correctly identifying the letter(s) that correspond to sounds for consonants, blends, digraphs, and short vowels.

Table 7.1   CASL Program for Handwriting/Spelling

	Description	Purpose
Lessons 1–5		
Activity 1	2-minute Phonics Warm-up	Letter identification
Activity 2	5-minute Alphabet Practice	Letter formation
Activity 3	4-minute Word Building	Spelling
Activity 4	4-minute Word Study	Spelling
Activity 5	5-minute Writing	Letter formation practice
		Word selection
		Skill application
Lesson 6	Word Sorting	Rules for spelling patterns

Activity 2. In a 5-minute Alphabet Practice activity, students are taught how to form letters of the alphabet previously determined on a letter-writing pretest to be written incorrectly, inefficiently, or both. Two letters are taught in each lesson, starting with lower-case letters and moving to capital letters after the lower-case letters are mastered. During the first two lessons, the teacher models how to form each letter. Using cards with numbered arrows indicating the order and direction of strokes for each letter, the teacher models by tracing and discussing aloud letter formation. Next, the student imitates the teacher, tracing each letter while describing how to write it. This letter-writing activity is followed by a discussion about how the two target letters are similar and different. The student then practices by tracing, copying, and writing each letter. Finally, the student circles her best-formed letters.

Procedures for Alphabet Practice in the next two lessons replicate the ones used in Lessons 1 and 2, with two differences. First, teacher and students do not discuss similarities and differences in how target letters are formed. Second, practice in tracing, copying, and writing individual letters is reduced and substituted with additional practice in copying words containing the target letters (e.g., "bad" for the letters "b" and "d"). One additional modification is made for Lesson 5. In this lesson, students copy "hinky-pinkys" that contain the target letter (e.g., "muddy-buddy" for the letter "d"). Students are asked to circle their best-formed word or "hinky-pinky," respectively, in Lessons 3 to 5.

Activity 3. The third activity is a 4-minute Word Building. Word Building is based on the rime introduced in the lesson's previous Phonics Warm-up activity. For example, in the Unit 2 lesson for short /e/ and short /o/, the teacher begins by showing a card containing the rime (i.e., the part of a syllable that consists of its vowel and the consonant sounds that come after the vowel) "ed" and says the sound that the rime makes. The teacher then models building a word by placing a card containing either a consonant (e.g., "b") or blend (e.g., "sl") in front of the rime. The student then builds as many real words as he or she can by adding consonants, blends, and diagraphs to the rime. During Lesson 2 students build words on a worksheet instead of with cards. Procedures in Lessons 3 and 4 are identical to Lessons 1 and 2 except that a new rime is introduced (e.g., "en"). Students review rimes taught in the previous unit by using these rimes to build words via a worksheet activity in Lesson 5.

Activity 4. A 4-minute Word Study is the fourth activity in Lessons 1 to 5. Students practice learning to spell correctly words previously missed on the pretest or during Activity Five: Writing (see the following section). The words are studied using the "add-a-word" method described by Graham (1999). The teacher selects five words that the student misspelled on the pretest/ writing for the student to study. Each word is written on a card, which in turn is attached to a ring. Students study the misspelled word by saying it, studying its letters, writing it from memory, and then checking for spelling accuracy. The word is corrected if it is not spelled correctly. Once a word is spelled correctly six times in a row over a period of two lessons, it is removed from the ring, and a new word is added. Periodically, mastered words are reviewed and restudied as needed.

Activity 5. The final activity is 5-minute Writing. The Writing activity serves three purposes: (a) writing provides a context in which students can apply skills taught in Alphabet Practice; (b) writing provides a source for selecting words for students to learn during Word Study; and (c) writing provides a context in which to apply skills learned in Word Building, Word Study, and Word Sorting (a Lesson 6 activity described in the following section). The prompt for the writing task asks students to write a story or personal narrative that incorporates words practiced during Word Building (e.g., students are asked to write a story during Unit 2 about "Fred wanting to buy a red sled bed" when working on the "ed" rime). The teacher and the student place a star next to any word that the child uses in the story with the target rime pattern practiced during Word Study and emphasized during Word Sorting (e.g., the short /e/ during Unit 2).

Activity for lesson 6. During the sixth lesson of each unit, students participate in a Word Sorting activity (Graham, Harris, & Loynachan, 1996). Word Sorting is designed to help students learn the rule for each of the spelling patterns emphasized in the phonics unit. For example, in Unit 2, words are sorted into two categories: CVC-type words containing the short-vowel sounds of /e/ (e.g., bed) and /o/ (e.g., top). The teacher begins the Word Sorting by placing a master word card for each category next to each other (e.g., "bed" and "top"). The teacher pronounces each master word and then says the word again, emphasizing the target feature (e.g., short-vowel sound for /e/ in bed and /o/ in top). Students are asked to consider how the master words are similar and different. The teacher focuses students' attention on critical features, such as how the letter "e" is pronounced in the master word, and the combination of consonants and vowels in the master word.

The teacher then tells students that they are going to look at other words and decide within which category they should be placed, with the idea of figuring out the rule for why the letter "e" makes the short /e/ sound in "bed" and the "o" makes the short /o/ sound in "top." Using a pack of 12 cards (containing an equal number of words that fit each pattern), the teacher draws a card, reads and says the word (emphasizing the target sound), thinks out loud about where to place the word, and places it under the appropriate master word card. The teacher continues to do this until the students understand the process. Students are then encouraged to think out loud while categorizing and placing the remaining word cards under the appropriate master card. If an error is made in placing a word card, the teacher corrects it and models out loud thinking about where to place the word card. Once all of the words are appropriately placed, the teacher helps students state a rule for the patterns emphasized in the word sort. Students then generate words of their own, writing them on blank word cards, and placing them under the appropriate master target card. If time permits, students are encouraged to hunt for words in their writing that fit these patterns. Finally, it should be noted that the word-sorting, word-study, and word-building activities all focus on strengthening the same set of spelling patterns.

Tips for Implementation

The manual for the CASL Handwriting/Spelling program can be obtained by contacting Steve Graham (steve.graham@vanderbilt.edu). It is necessary to create or obtain some materials to implement the program (these are detailed in the manual), and it is better to obtain or develop all of these materials before putting the program into place. It is also useful to practice presenting one or two units before using the program with students.

Research Base for CASL Handwriting/ Spelling Program

The full program has been validated in one study with first-grade students (Graham & Harris, 2006); the handwriting portion of the program and the spelling portion were validated in studies with grade-1 (Graham, Harris, & Fink, 2000) and grade-2 students (Graham, Harris, & Fink-Chorzempa, 2002), respectively. All three studies took place in inner-city schools, where the majority of the students were culturally and linguistically diverse. Each student scored at or below the 25th percentile on a norm-referenced story-writing measure before instruction, and a variety of children with disabilities were included in the three studies, including children with learning disabilities (LDs), attention deficit hyperactivity disorder (ADHD), and behavioral problems. Instruction was provided in sessions outside the regular classroom, and each instructor was taught to apply the instructional procedures until he or she could do so correctly and fluently. All three studies were randomized field trials, with high levels of implementation fidelity, and comparison groups that received either phonological awareness instruction (Graham & Harris, 2006; Graham et al., 2000) or math instruction (Graham et al., 2002). Across the three studies, students' spelling improved dramatically, as did their handwriting legibility and fluency. All three of these studies were randomized control trials, and effect sizes for handwriting and spelling measures ranged from 0.54 to 1.46. The studies also demonstrated positive carryover effects to the students' writing (sentence construction skills and output when writing improved) and reading skills (word-recognition and word-attack skills improved). These effect sizes were in the moderate to large range (0.76 to 1.21).

Effective Instruction for Composition Skills

Good writers spend time recursively planning, revising, monitoring, evaluating, and regulating the writing process (K. R. Harris & Graham, 1999). Students with disabilities, on the other hand, tend to spend little time involved in such processes, focusing much of their attention on lower-level transcription skills (i.e., handwriting, spelling, capitalization, and punctuation). A process approach to writing (prewriting by planning and organizing, drafting, revising, editing, and publishing) combined with strategy instruction and self-regulation procedures has been validated as a highly effective instructional approach for improving performance in higher-level skills for composition (Graham & Perin, 2007). In this chapter we describe two evidence-based approaches that use effective instruction in strategy development for teaching composition. As noted previously, the first approach, SIM, has been validated as effective in improving sentence and paragraph writing abilities among adolescents with high-incidence disabilities (Schumaker & Deshler, 2003). The second approach, SRSD, has been validated as effective in improving planning, composing, and revising for students who are normally achieving and students with high-incidence disabilities from elementary through secondary grade levels (Graham & Harris, 2003).

SIM for Sentence and Paragraph Development

> A perfectly healthy sentence, it is true, is extremely rare.
> Henry David Thoreau

Writing research focused on adolescents with LD began in the late 1970s and early 1980s, as Deshler, Schumaker, and their colleagues began to conceptualize and validate learning strategy interventions for adolescents with disabilities (e.g., Deshler & Schumaker, 2006). They developed a Learning Strategies Curriculum with three major strands: the acquisition strand, storage strand, and expression strand. The expression strand includes strategies for sentence writing, paragraph writing, error monitoring, spell checking, and organizing and writing short themes. Research has been reported and evidence established on teaching the strategies for writing sentences and paragraphs using the SIM approach (Mason & Graham, 2008; Schumaker & Deshler, 2003).

The goal of instruction using SIM is to support students in acquiring the knowledge, motivation, and practice necessary to successfully use a strategy as needed for tasks in the general education setting. All strategies included in the Learning Strategies Curriculum share common features. Each strategy consists of a set of sequenced steps leading to a specific, successful outcome. The strategy steps cue students to use specific cognitive and metacognitive activities; students learn to select and use required procedures, skills, and rules that are observable. The strategy steps are kept short and are expressed in an easily remembered mnemonic (e.g., COPS for Capitalization, Organization, Punctuation, Spelling). The learning strategies are typically seen as strategy systems, because any one step can often cue the use of multiple cognitive or metacognitive strategies for a given task (Deshler & Schumaker, 2006; Schumaker & Deshler, 2009). SIM instruction includes eight instructional stages as described later. Lessons are mastery based; that is, students are required to demonstrate the skill taught before moving to another intervention component.

SIM for Sentence Construction

The Sentence Writing Strategy program includes two parts, Fundamentals in the Sentence Writing Strategy and Proficiency in Sentence Writing Strategy (Schumaker & Sheldon, 1985). With these two SIM programs, students are taught to apply a series of formulas and steps for writing four types of sentences: simple, compound, complex, and compound-complex. The mnemonic PENS (Picks, Explores, Noted, and Subject) prompts students to remember the steps for writing a sentence. Students learn to apply 14 different sentence formulas, with each formula corresponding to a specific sentence structure. To write a sentence, a student first picks a formula and then explores words to fit the formula. Once the student decides on which words to use, these are noted or written down, and the student checks to make sure the sentence is complete (i.e., contains a subject and verb).

SIM for Paragraph Development

The Paragraph Writing Strategy program is used to teach students to write four types of paragraphs (Schumaker & Lyerla, 1991): paragraphs that list or describe, show sequence, compare/contrast, and demonstrate cause and effect. The mnemonic SLOW CaPS prompts students to remember the strategy for writing paragraphs. Each letter (with the exception of the small "a") reminds students to carry out a step or process: (S)—show the type of paragraph in the first sentence; (L)—list the type of details you plan to write about; (O)—order the details; (W)—write the details in complete sentences; and cap off the paragraph with a (C) concluding, (P) passing, or (S) summary sentence.

Instructional Overview

The teacher emphasizes mastery at each of the eight stages of SIM instruction and provides specific and individual feedback after each lesson (Schumaker & Deshler, 2009). Lessons are scaffolded so that students initially apply the strategy to a simple task, with the goal of teaching students to apply the strategy to grade-level tasks. The SIM instructional sequence includes eight stages of strategy acquisition.

Pretest and make commitments. Students' preskills are tested in the first SIM instructional stage. A purpose for using the strategy for writing sentences/paragraphs is established, and the benefits of using the strategy for the specific task are presented. The students and teacher collaboratively set goals for learning the strategy, for memorizing the mnemonics for the strategy steps, and for applying the strategy to the task (e.g., sentence and paragraph writing).

Describe. In the next stage, the teacher describes the purpose of the strategy and how each strategy step helps with the skill to be learned. The teacher explains how to use the strategy for the target skill; describes when the strategy should be used (and when it should not be used); and tells the students why the strategy is important for helping with sentence and paragraph writing skills.

Model. Modeling, the third instructional stage, is the heart of effective strategy instruction. To be an effective model, the teacher thinks out loud each step of strategy application for the targeted skill. The teacher also clearly demonstrates effective use of instructional support materials such as graphic organizers or strategy mnemonics while using the strategies to write sentences/paragraphs.

Verbal practice. In the fourth instructional stage, the teacher conducts practice activities that enable the students to memorize the strategy steps. The goal is for students to become fluent so that they can self-instruct while applying the strategy to the target skill.

Controlled practice. During the initial stages of acquisition, students practice using the strategy with easy tasks. In the fifth instructional stage, practice is scaffolded by increasing task difficulty only after easier tasks are mastered. The teacher provides specific and individual feedback after each practice attempt.

Advanced practice. By the sixth instructional stage, students practice the strategy in grade-level contexts. Writing assignments may come from the students' teachers or may be developed by the SIM instructor.

Post-test and obtain commitment for generalization. In the seventh instructional stage, students' skills are post-tested. The teacher also obtains the students' commitment to continue to use the strategy and to use the strategy in other settings.

Generalization. In the eighth and final instructional stage, students are supported in generalizing application of the strategies learned to the general education classroom and maintaining strategy use across the school years. Teachers create situations that give students chances to use the strategies learned across tasks, situations, and settings. Four phases of generalization instruction are required.

1. Orientation: awareness of the variety of opportunities for generalization is stressed.

2. Activation: students are given numerous opportunities to generalize with feedback provided.

3. Adaptation: focuses on helping students learn to modify the strategy to meet demands in different settings.

4. Maintenance: consists of periodic probes to see if the student continues to use the strategy effectively in multiple settings.

Tips for Implementation

SIM developers note that positive results are typically found when the eight-stage instructional methodology is implemented. Daily lessons with multiple opportunities for practice and teacher feedback are recommended (Schumaker & Deshler, 2003). SIM instruction highlights the importance of explicit instruction and guided practice for strategy acquisition in writing for adolescents with LD. Professional development is a critical component of SIM instruction, as is the support of administrators and general education teachers in order to achieve generalization across classrooms and writing tasks (Deshler & Schumaker, 2006). Coaching may be very helpful for teacher development, and fidelity needs to be addressed through frequent classroom observations, monitoring of student performance, and meetings with teachers. Most SIM instructional materials, including the sentence writing and paragraph writing programs, are available only in conjunction with professional development provided by certified SIM Professional Developers. Contact the University of Kansas, Center for Research on Learning (KU-CRL's) director of professional development at crl@ku.edu for information. Further information including newsletters, videotapes/DVDs, and CDs that can be ordered is found at www.kucrl.org/.

Research Base for SIM

Effects of SIM instruction for sentence writing for 64 urban, suburban, and rural school students in grades 6 to 12 have been examined in five single-subject studies (Beals, 1983; Eads, 1991; First, 1994; C. S. Johnson, 2005; Schmidt, Deshler, Schumaker, & Alley, 1988). As summarized by Rogers and Graham (2008), students with disabilities, primarily LDs, were included in the five studies. Sixty-six percent of the students in these studies were male. Race/ethnicity was reported in four studies, with a total representation of 47% Hispanic, 44% Caucasian, 7% African American, and 2% Hispanic and African American across the studies. Results of the five studies indicated that students' writing of complete sentences improved with a range of 78% to 100% for the percentage of nonoverlapping data (PND), with a mean PND of 83% (PND > 0.90 are considered very effective, PND between 0.70 and 0.90 are effective; Scruggs, Mastropieri, & Casto, 1987). These

results indicate that SIM instruction for sentence writing was effective to very effective.

Four single-subject studies examined the effects of SIM instruction for paragraph writing for students who were average and low achieving in grades 8 and 9 (Dowell, Storey, & Gleason, 1994; Moran, Schumaker, & Vetter, 1981; Sonntag & McLaughlin, 1984; G. W. Wallace & Bott, 1989). Two thirds of the suburban and urban participants were male students with LD; race/ethnicity was not reported. SIM instruction for paragraph writing was effective to very effective, with results of 89% to 100% PND (for structural elements of a paragraph; Rogers & Graham, 2008).

Some caution must be applied in interpreting the effectiveness of SIM writing instruction, because experimental control was not adequately established in any of the sentence or paragraph writing studies. For the 11 quality measures (R. H. Horner et al., 2005) assessed in the studies reviewed by Rogers and Graham (2008), for example, these single-subject studies averaged addressing 61% of the quality indicators for sentence writing and 58% of quality indicators for paragraph writing. This finding places these studies slightly below the mean of quality indicators addressed across all single-subject design studies in writing. Furthermore, although researchers have noted that SIM instruction for sentence and paragraph writing have been used effectively with elementary school-aged students (Schumaker & Deshler, 2003), no study, to date, has empirically documented effects of SIM for younger students.

SRSD for Planning, Composing, and Revising

> A writer is somebody for whom writing is more difficult than it is for other people.
>
> Thomas Mann

One approach for teaching written expression to students who struggle with writing, SRSD, blends explicit instruction in self-regulation procedures with cognitive strategy instruction. SRSD was, and continues to be, developed by integrating research on learning and teaching from multiple theoretical perspectives (K. R. Harris & Graham, 2009). Six strategy-acquisition stages are typically included in SRSD regardless of the genre (e.g., persuasive writing, informative writing) and for any planning, composing, and revision strategies being taught: (a) develop background knowledge, (b) discuss the strategy, (c) model the strategy, (d) memorize the strategy, (e) guided practice, and (f) independent performance. Students' self-regulation of strategy use is supported by teaching students to use four procedures (i.e., goal setting, self-monitoring, self-instruction, and self-reinforcement) throughout the writing process. SRSD instruction is recursive and criterion-based; lessons, instructional stages, and principles are repeated and revisited based on individual student needs. Instruction continues until each student has mastered the strategy. SRSD has been used effectively for teaching planning, drafting, and revising strategies across narrative, persuasive, and expository genres to students with disabilities (Graham & Harris, 2009).

Planning and Composing Strategies

A well-constructed planning and composing strategy will guide students to organize their writing for narrative, persuasive, and expository writing. While different genres require different strategies, a general writing strategy can be paired with a genre-specific strategy (K. R. Harris, Graham, Mason, & Friedlander, 2008). The POW (*P*ick an idea, *O*rganize notes, and *W*rite and Say More) strategy, for example, guides students to: (a) think about, brainstorm, and pick ideas before writing; (b) select a genre-specific planning strategy to help with organizing notes; and (c) write from a plan and remember to add new information while writing. Researchers have validated a number of planning and drafting strategies for stories (e.g., K. R. Harris, Graham, & Mason, 2006), persuasion (e.g., Mason & Shriner, 2008), and expository text (e.g., De La Paz, 2001). Table 7.2 highlights examples of evidence-based planning and composing strategies.

Revising Strategies

Two different revising strategies (see Graham & MacArthur, 1988; MacArthur, Schwartz, & Graham, 1991) have been taught and tested within the SRSD framework. We highlight the more general revising strategy here (MacArthur et al., 1991) because it can be applied more broadly and has been tested in more than one experiment. With this peer-editing strategy, each student receives and gives feedback for revising and editing to another student. Once each student has finished a first draft, she reads it to her partner. The partner first identifies strengths and the goals met and then provides constructive feedback on specific aspects of the composition, such as places where more detail would be helpful or text that is unclear. The students then use this feedback to revise their papers. After revision, the partner provides specific editing feedback, concentrating on issues of form such as spelling, punctuation, and so forth.

SRSD Stages of Instruction

As noted, six recursive, flexible stages of instruction are typically used to introduce and develop planning and

Table 7.2 Examples of Self-Regulated Strategy Development Planning and Composing Strategies

Narrative Writing	*POW + W-W-W, What = 2, How = 2*
	Pick my idea.
	Organize my notes—Use W-W-W, What = 2, How = 2!
	Write and say more.
	+
	Who is the main character?
	Where does the story take place?
	When does the story take place?
	What does the main character do or want to do?
	What happens next?
	How does the story end?
	How do the characters feel?
Persuasive Writing	*POW + TREE*
	Pick my idea.
	Organize my notes—Use TREE!
	Write and say more.
	+
	Topic Sentence—Tell what you believe!
	Reasons—3 or more
	Why do I believe this?
	Will my readers believe this?
	Explain reasons—Say more about each reason.
	Ending—Wrap it up right!
Expository Writing	*PLAN and WRITE*
	P = Pay attention to the prompt, set goals
	L = List main ideas to develop your essay
	A = Add supporting ideas (details, examples, etc.)
	N = Number major points in the order you will use them
	and
	W = Work from your plan to develop a thesis statement
	R = Remember your goals
	I = Include transition words for each paragraph
	T = Try to use different kinds of sentences
	E = Exciting, interesting, $1,000,000 words

Note: For complete strategy lesson plans and materials see: Harris, K. R., Graham, S., Mason, L. H., & Friedlander, B. (2008). *Powerful writing strategies for all students.* Baltimore: Brookes.

composing strategies, revising strategies, and self-regulation knowledge: Develop Background Knowledge, Discuss It, Model It, Memorize It, Support It, and Independent Performance (see Figure 7.1 for an overview of the Stages of Instruction). These stages provide a general format and guidelines for teachers and students as they acquire, implement, evaluate, and modify the strategies. One or more days of instruction occurs in each stage,

Figure 7.1 Stages of self-regulated strategy development instruction.

Develop and Activate Knowledge Needed for Writing and Self-Regulation

- Read model papers in the genre being addressed (stories, persuasive essays, informative), to develop students' knowledge of genre characteristics and components.
- Develop students' appreciation of effective writing (e.g., how did the writer make the story fun to read?).
- Explore and discuss both writing and self-regulation strategies to be learned; may begin development of self-regulation by introducing goal setting and self-monitoring.
- Continue developing students' knowledge through the next two stages as needed until all key knowledge and understandings are clear.

Discuss the Strategy

- Explore students' current writing and self-regulation abilities, their attitudes and beliefs about writing, and what they are saying to themselves as they write.
- Introduce graphing (self-monitoring). Prior compositions may be used to assist with goal setting. Skip graphing prior writing if the student is likely to react negatively.
- Further discuss strategy to be learned by focusing on the purpose and benefits.
- Discuss how and when the strategy can be used appropriately (begin generalization).
- Establish the students' commitment to learn the strategy and to act as collaborative partners.
- Establish role of student effort and strategy use.

Model How to Use the Strategy

- Model and/or collaboratively model how to use the strategy and self-regulation procedures for the writing tasks, resulting in an appropriately written composition.
- Analyze and discuss strategies and the model's performance, making changes as needed.
- Model self-assessment and self-recording by graphing the components of the composition.
- Continue the students' development of strategy and self-regulation procedures across composition and other tasks and situations (continue generalization support).

Memorize Strategy Mnemonics and Steps

- Typically begun in earlier stages by providing student practice in memorization of strategy steps, mnemonic(s), and self-instructions.
- Continue to support memorization in the following stages.
- Students should have strategy steps and mnemonics memorized, as well as what each means, before Independent Performance.

Support Students' Strategy Use

- Initially, teachers and students use writing and self-regulation strategies collaboratively to achieve success in composing. Prompts such as strategy charts, self-instruction sheets, and graphic organizers are used to support students' writing.
- Collaboratively establish challenging initial goals for genre elements and characteristics of writing with individual students; criterion levels increased gradually until final goals are met.
- Prompts, guidance, and collaboration are faded individually (e.g., graphic organizer replaced with student creating mnemonic on scratch paper) until the students can compose successfully alone.
- Goal setting, self-instructions, self-monitoring, and self-reinforcement are all being used by this stage; monitor students' use of these procedures.
- Self-regulation components not yet introduced may begin (e.g., environmental control, use of imagery, and so on, may be used as desirable).
- Discuss plans for maintenance, continue support of generalization.

Independent Performance

- Students are able to use writing and self-regulation strategies independently; teachers monitor and support as necessary.
- Fading of overt self-regulation may begin (e.g., graphing may be discontinued).
- Plans for maintenance and generalization continue to be discussed and implemented.

Source: Data from Harris, K. R., & Graham, S. (2007). Marconi invented the television so people who couldn't afford radio could hear the news: The research on powerful composition strategies we have, and the research we need. In M. Pressley (Ed.), *Shaping literacy achievement: Research we have, literacy research we need.* New York: Guilford.

with some stages expected to take longer than others, depending on student needs and rate of progress. Changes to this typical framework and individualization to differing student needs should be made as needed (cf. Lane et al., 2008; Sandmel et al., 2009).

Develop and activate background knowledge.

During this initial stage of instruction, students acquire the vocabulary, knowledge, and concepts needed to use the writing and self-regulation strategies they will be learning. This stage begins with a teacher-led discussion about what good writers do when writing. The strategy parts are introduced and each step is described. For example, for the POW strategy, the teacher would explain that the first step or thing to do when planning is "Pick a good idea." Additional "tricks" used by good writers, such as writing a catchy opening, are discussed. The teacher and students then read one or more model compositions for the genre (written at the students' level) and identify how the author used each strategy part for planning and composing or revising. Self-regulation is introduced as students set a goal to learn and use the strategy, with the instructor committing to do her best in teaching the strategy. In this and each subsequent lesson, the teacher provides students time to practice memorizing the strategy steps and the corresponding mnemonic; then the teacher tells students that they will be asked to share the steps from memory in the next session. In addition, students may begin sharing opportunities and ideas for transfer of this strategy to other settings or tasks as appropriate; this continues throughout the rest of instruction. The teacher, if possible, should arrange opportunities for such transfer and scaffold student success in other settings once strategies are learned.

Discuss it.

Although a great deal of discussion obviously takes place during stage 1 and in later stages, stage 2 is called "Discuss It" because not only does the initial discussion of the strategy continue, but also discussion expands when the teacher asks students to evaluate and discuss their previous writing using what they have learned. The teacher asks students to evaluate a composition they wrote before they began learning the new strategies by: (a) counting how many of the genre elements (i.e., the required parts of a composition, such as a topic sentence for an informative essay or setting for a story) their composition contained, (b) editing for ways to revise, and (c) identifying strengths in the composition. The teacher stresses that it is not a problem if the paper is imperfect: "Of course, the story/essay does not have all the parts; you hadn't learned POW yet!" The teacher and students then discuss what could have been done to improve their papers. Students record their prior performance on a graph and learn that they will

continue to use this graph to self-monitor their writing as they plan and compose or revise new compositions. Students set a goal to include all of the genre elements next time they write, and set individualized goals to improve other elements of their writing. Students proceed to stage 3 (Model It) when the teacher determines they have developed the necessary background knowledge, vocabulary, and understanding of what they are learning and why they are learning it.

Model it.

In the third stage, the teacher models the complete writing process, using the strategies to plan, compose, and/or revise a paper. Strategy acquisition is supported by developing self-instructions and teaching students self-monitoring and self-reinforcement strategies. Following memorization practice, the teacher models, while thinking aloud, how to use the strategies. The teacher also models how and when to use instructional support materials such as mnemonic chart reminders, graphic organizers for planning and organizing, and charts for self-monitoring performance. The teacher thinks out loud while planning, composing, and revising, using six types of self-instruction (i.e., problem definition, strategy use, focusing of attention, coping, self-evaluation, and self-reinforcing self-statements). The teacher models how to monitor strategy use during and after writing and how to self-reinforce success in using the strategies. Students can participate by helping the teacher plan and make notes on a strategy step graphic organizer and write the first draft. Following the teacher's modeling, students develop and record personal self-instructions in their own words to be used while thinking of good ideas ("Relax," "Take my time, good ideas will come"), while working ("What is my first strategy step?" "I can do this"), and to check work ("Do I have all of my parts?" "Perfect!").

Memorize it.

While listed here as a separate stage, memorizing the mnemonic and the strategy step procedures has been occurring since stage 1. The goal is for students to have the strategy memorized and to be able to write the mnemonic on blank paper so they can make notes in the future using the mnemonic without a graphic organizer. Students who need it are provided more practice of the mnemonic and its meaning (including why each step is important) until it is memorized. As one student we worked with said, "You can't use what you can't remember!"

Support it.

This stage is typically the longest. Research indicates, however, that students may make the biggest jump in performance in this stage, and that support in using the strategy is necessary even after the explicit, collaborative modeling in stage 3 (K. R. Harris & Graham, 1999). At first, students work with the teacher to plan and write a first draft. For example, students may provide ideas for the paper while the teacher writes the notes. The teacher re-models and provides any assistance necessary. At first, students keep out their mnemonic chart and list of self-statements while they work, and use the graphic organizer. The student continues to set goals, self-monitor, self-instruct, and self-reinforce while applying the strategy. Over time, the teacher provides less help, and students begin writing independently; pace is individualized to students' needs.

Independent performance. At this point, students can write successfully without teacher or peer support. Students are encouraged to write the genre mnemonic and element steps on blank paper before writing; the graphic organizer is no longer used. Graphing of performance can be continued for one or two more compositions. Once students can independently apply the strategies to the writing task, the student can be asked to plan, compose, and/or revise in a different academic class with a different teacher, or to generalize strategy use in other ways (i.e., to determine when these strategies, or some subset of them, can be used for other writing tasks).

Tips for Implementation

It is critical to remember that the six stages are not intended to be implemented in a rigid or linear format. Stages should be repeated and revisited based on the needs of individual students. Instruction should continue until students demonstrate mastery in applying these strategies to their writing. SRSD instruction takes time, practice, and careful planning (K. R. Harris et al., 2008). Further, students need to be able to write a complete sentence before beginning SRSD. SRSD is meant to supplement, not supplant, the writing curriculum. Research indicates that for most struggling writers, all six instructional stages and all four self-regulation procedures (i.e., goal setting, self-monitoring, self-instruction, and self-reinforcement) are important (Graham, Harris, & Mason, 2005).

SRSD has been used successfully with whole classes, small groups, individual students, and in tutoring situations. K. R. Harris et al. (2008) do not recommend a prescribed set of strategies taught in a specific order; teachers and administrators should decide what strategies to use with whom, and at what time, based on student needs and the larger writing curriculum. Students who are already writing effectively in a given genre do not need to be taught basic genre strategies; this may actually encourage them to do less than they are capable of. These students should work with their teachers to set individualized goals and learn additional strategies for refining their writing (K. R. Harris et al., 2008). Finally, learning validated strategies using the SRSD approach is only a beginning for all students, because learning to write is a complex, developmental process.

Detailed lesson plans and support materials for instruction are provided in K. R. Harris et al. (2008), and a detailed example of classroom implementation is provided by K. R. Harris, Graham, and Mason (2003). All of the stages of instruction can be seen in both elementary and middle school classrooms in the video *Teaching Students with Learning Disabilities: Using Learning Strategies* (Association for Supervision and Curriculum Development, 2002). Online interactive tutorials on SRSD are available at http://iris.peabody.vanderbilt .edu/pow/chalcycle.htm. Finally, lesson plans and student support materials for elementary students (grades 1 through 3) can be found online at http://hobbs.vanderbilt .edu/projectwrite/.

Research Base

Since 1985 more than 40 studies conducted by K. R. Harris, Graham, and their colleagues or independent researchers using the SRSD model of instruction have been reported in the area of writing involving students from the elementary grades through high school. These studies have included students with LDs, emotional and behavioral disorders (EBDs), at-risk for EBDs, other disabilities (e.g., ADHD), and normally achieving students (cf. Graham & Harris, 2009; Lane et al., 2008). Four recent reviews have reported the effectiveness of SRSD for students with disabilities (S. K. Baker, Chard, Ketterlin-Geller, Apichatabutra, & Doabler, 2009; Graham & Perin, 2007; K. R. Harris, Graham, Brindle, & Sandmel, 2009; Rogers & Graham, 2008; Taft & Mason, 2011). Summary of the primary findings from these reviews follows.

Results of a meta-analysis of 15 group planning studies indicated that SRSD has large positive effects, improving the quality, number of essay elements, and length of students' writing (K. R. Harris et al., 2009). The average weighted effect size (ES) for writing quality at post-test, for example, was 1.20 (J. Cohen, 1988, considered ES >0.80 large). These group studies involved a broad range of students in second- to eighth-grade settings.

Equally positive effects have been obtained for SRSD planning studies investigated using single-subject design methodology. A total of 108 suburban and urban second- through eighth-grade students have participated in 21 SRSD single-subject planning studies reviewed by Rogers and Graham (2008). Of these students, 55% were Caucasian, 37% African American, 5% Turkish, 2% Hispanic, and 1% Asian. Effect sizes from comparing post-instruction to baseline performance for 18 single-subject studies ranged from 67% to 100% PND at post-instruction and 25% to 100% for maintenance. The majority of students, in 18 of the 21 studies, were struggling writers or students with LD.

Fourteen single-case studies have investigated the effects of SRSD planning strategies for students with EBD, at-risk for EBD, ADHD, speech and language impairments, Asperger's syndrome, autism spectrum disorder, and mild intellectual disability (Taft & Mason, 2011). Students ranged from second to eleventh grade. Of these participants, 61% were male, 39% female; 60% were Caucasian, 32% African American, 7% Turkish, and 1% Hispanic. PND at post-test ranged from 83% to 100% for number of text parts written for these students.

Only a few studies have examined the effectiveness of SRSD with revising strategies. MacArthur et al. (1991) obtained an effect size of 1.09 for improvements in writing quality (see Graham & Perin, 2007) for the peer revising strategy described earlier. Stoddard and MacArthur (1993) obtained 100% PND for number of revisions at post-test, maintenance, and generalization in a single-subject design study (see Rogers & Graham, 2008). Both of these studies involved students with LDs in self-contained classrooms.

The overall quality of SRSD research studies was assessed in Graham and Perin (2007) and Rogers and Graham (2008). In both of these meta-analyses, study quality was high and treatments were delivered with fidelity. This was confirmed in part by an independent review by S. K. Baker et al. (2009) assessing the quality of five group experimental and quasi-experimental studies and 16 single-subject studies. All group studies met standards established for high-quality research. Of the 16 single-subject studies reviewed, 9 met all of the standards required for high-quality single-subject research.

Conclusion and Directions for Future Research

Once a pond time. There was a boy named Sam. It happen at 11 2000. In the math and science center. Sam wanted to be a writer. Ms. Smith came to the school. Ms. Smith tried to teach Sam how to writing. Then she taught him POW. Then he became a great writer. He feel so happy that he will be a story writer went he grow up.

Sam, second-grade student with a disability
(K. R. Harris, Graham, & Mason, 2006)

Learning to write well is a challenging task for all students; it is a particularly difficult one for students with disabilities. During the last 30 years, researchers and teachers have learned much about how to effectively teach writing to students with disabilities. Although much still remains to be done, and we do not yet have research-based practices that represent a complete writing curriculum, we now have a number of well-validated practices that research shows to be effective for teaching core writing skills and processes to these students. This includes effective practices for teaching handwriting, spelling, sentence construction, paragraph development, planning, drafting, and revising. A strength of the types of instructional practices presented here is that evidence shows that they work, and the positive effects obtained were replicated in multiple studies (such replication is a central hallmark of scientific investigation). Moreover, confidence can be placed in these findings, as the research was generally of high quality.

It is important to note, however, that these practices have not been tested in all possible contexts, and in most instances (with the exception of SRSD), they have involved a small range of disabilities. Although a larger number of studies have been conducted involving the SRSD approach, numerous research issues and challenges remain, such as maintenance and generalization of strategy use (K. R. Harris et al., 2009; K. R. Harris & Graham, 2007, 2009). Further, implementing research-based treatments is a difficult and complex task. A procedure's effectiveness in the studies included in this chapter does not guarantee that it will be effective in all other situations. Consequently, the safest course of action for teachers is to carefully monitor the effects of evidence-based practices as they are implemented in their classes to gauge directly whether they are effective under these new conditions.

Because learning to write is a complex, developmental process, students' growth as writers will be enhanced only if their writing programs engage them in frequent and extended writing; broaden their knowledge about writing and writing genres; automatize basic text transcriptions skills (i.e., handwriting and spelling); facilitate the development of flexible and facile sentence and paragraph construction skills; enhance the ability to plan, draft, monitor, evaluate, and revise text; and promote a positive, "I can do this" attitude toward writing. Although research-based practices exist for some of these elements, they do not exist for all. As a result, to meet the writing needs of students with disabilities and other struggling writers, teachers must apply a judicious mixture of research-based practices and practices not yet validated, which increases the importance of teachers monitoring the effectiveness of their writing practices. Clearly, further research is needed to identify additional effective writing practices and to determine how these practices can be combined to successfully meet the needs of students with disabilities.

CHAPTER 8

Improving Academic Outcomes in the Content Areas

B. Keith Ben-Hanania Lenz | *SRI International*

Janis Bulgren | *University of Kansas*

Twenty years ago, components of the standard K–12 curriculum could be easily characterized based on grade levels. During grades K–3, the curriculum focused on teaching basic skills (e.g., phonics, word reading, basic computation). During grades 4 to 6, the curriculum focused on teaching students how to use the basic skills and strategies learned in the earlier grades to learn the foundational vocabulary, concepts, and ideas to be learned in content areas such as social studies, science, language arts, and mathematics. This focus constituted the introduction of formal content areas or "subjects." Also at this level, students were introduced to textbooks, lectures, and content area tests. In grades 7 to 12, the curriculum focused on exposure to an increasingly complex set of content elements in courses requiring a high level of independent learning by the student.

Today, the K–12 curriculum is not so easily characterized. Instead, it now reflects national efforts to improve student achievement on high-stakes tests, address the increasing role of technology in our economy, improve our nation's international performance in math and science, support higher-order reasoning and collaborative problem-solving efforts, and close the achievement gap between higher-achieving and underperforming groups of students (e.g., students from minority groups, students

with disabilities, others at risk for failure). Specifically, today's K–12 curriculum, as reflected in the Common Core Standards (www.commoncorestandards.org), introduces more complex content elements earlier in school. At the same time, direct instruction and practice of both learning strategies and thinking skills are being extended into secondary school. As a result, the lines have blurred that had once distinguished when skill instruction and content area instruction occur.

Challenges for All Students

To succeed in our increasingly complex and specialized society, it is imperative that individuals think divergently and creatively and see the relationships between and among seemingly diverse concepts (F. J. King, Goodson, & Rohani, 1998). Many adolescents have developed sufficient literacy skills in reading and writing to pass basic literacy tests. Nonetheless, these students may not be able to apply successfully the sophisticated thinking skills required to succeed in core content courses and pass content area subtests of state assessments (M. W. Conley, 2008; R. Heller & Greenleaf, 2007). As a result, too many high school graduates have difficulty with the tasks required in contemporary content area curricula, such as formulating and solving problems, evaluating and incorporating reference material appropriately, developing a logical and coherent argument or explanation, interpreting data or conflicting points of view, and completing their assignments and projects with precision and accuracy (D. T. Conley, 2008). In fact, many high school students arrive at college largely unprepared for the intellectual demands and expectations of postsecondary education.

Challenges for Students with Disabilities

The curricular shifts have had a significant impact on what students with disabilities are now expected to learn, how they are expected to learn it, and which instructional settings and personnel will be involved. Students with disabilities are now more likely to (a) be enrolled in more rigorous content area courses reflecting a move to increase success in the regular education curriculum; (b) be required to pass courses in algebra in order to graduate from high school; (c) experience use of technology to support content area learning, which can occur in the form of a major course component to support learning or as a specific accommodation provided to support learning for a student with a specific disability; and (d) be provided with direct instruction of strategies to increase content area learning as part of a class in special education.

Students with disabilities may also receive additional instruction in the same strategies in the content area classroom in order to provide additional tiers of supportive and aligned instruction with a goal of improving student performance in literacy on high-stakes measures (Deshler et al., 2001; Fore, Hagan-Burke, Burke, Boon, & Smith, 2008; M. Kennedy & Deshler, 2010). Instruction in and reinforcement of the same strategies related to acquiring, storing, retrieving, and expressing information and demonstration of competence increase the likelihood that students will learn the strategies and see how they can be applied in different content area courses. For example, the language arts teacher might instruct and model for students the use of a mnemonic device in literature using the first-letter mnemonic device to help students remember that there are four types of poetry: lyric, epic, narrative, and descriptive. The first letters of each of the types of poetry can be used to create the word "LEND." Then, the students and teacher create a reminding sentence to link the mnemonic device to the content: "Will you LEND me your poetry book?" To consolidate the learning, the special education teacher instructs and models how to use the same mnemonic,

reinforces instruction provided by the language arts teachers, provides more practice, and helps the student apply the strategy to other content area work.

Although the shifts in expectations and curriculum reflect a desire to improve student outcomes, progress in improving the outcomes of students with disabilities has been slow. According to the U.S. Department of Education (2006b), students with disabilities drop out of school at a significantly higher rate than their peers without disabilities. In addition, in the 2001 to 2002 school year, only 51% of students with disabilities graduated from high school with a standard high school diploma, indicating that they are not succeeding in the general education curriculum. Many factors must be considered as teachers and educators respond to the challenges faced by students with disabilities.

A Framework of Approaches for Responding to the Challenge

Helping students learn the types of thinking required in today's world must begin with recognizing that students with diverse learning abilities, including students with disabilities, will be present in many content classes. Furthermore, given the difficulties involved in promoting content area learning for students with disabilities, it is important to begin by identifying a general framework for organizing how we might think about and respond to the challenge. Figure 8.1 presents a basic framework for considering intervention approaches for students with disabilities who are expected to successfully participate and succeed in content area classes.

IEP-Related Learning Goals

At the top of Figure 8.1, we list three primary goals associated with improving content area learning based on specific learning barriers. These goals are typically addressed on a student's individualized education program (IEP). The first goal focuses on improving how a student initially acquires content area information. Interventions designed to address this goal are developed when a disability interferes with the student's ability to understand and comprehend information presented in the typical learning activities provided in the content area classroom. The second goal focuses on improving a student's storage of information in short- and long-term memory and the appropriate retrieval of this information when required. Interventions designed to address this goal are developed from the assumption that the student may understand new content but may have difficulty storing information in notes, making important content

Figure 8.1 Approaches to ensuring content mastery.

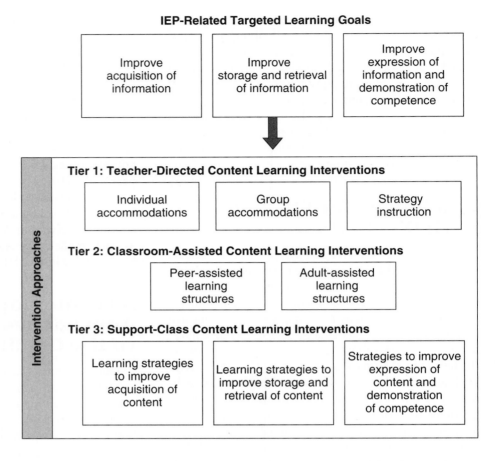

associations that put the information into perspective, or remembering information when it is needed. The third goal focuses on improving how a student expresses what has been understood and remembered—verbally, in writing, on assignments, and on various formative and summative assessments. These three goals point to the inherent learning barriers that must be addressed to promote learning for students with different types of learning problems.

The IEP should play an important role in defining how teachers or teams of teachers should help students gain access to the general education content area curriculum by focusing on two critical efforts. One effort is to ensure mastery of critical content when specific disabilities prevent students from being able to access the content independently. For example, the teacher might plan to be more explicit in his instruction to the whole class by using more visual representations of the content in order to make the most important content more concrete. The second effort involves providing direct instruction to teach the skills and strategies necessary to learn independently without content area supports. For example, the teacher might teach the specific skills or strategies for interpreting visuals used to display content or for paraphrasing passages and summarizing sections so that students learn to monitor comprehension of text.

These efforts must be achieved within and among the different types of educational services provided. Some services are provided by the content area teacher, some by the special education teacher, and some via collaboration between the content area teacher and the special education teacher.

Tiered Intervention Approaches

Approaches to using interventions that help teachers promote content area learning for students with disabilities generally fall into three categories. The interventions in the first category are designed to improve learning outcomes through teacher-directed learning activities as part of ongoing content area instruction. In a Response-to-Intervention (RtI) or a multi-tiered system of supports (MTSS) context, these interventions are typically considered first-tier interventions. The interventions in the second category are designed to improve learning outcomes through assisted learning arrangements in which peers or adults other than the primary teacher work to enhance content area learning in an academically diverse group of learners. These interventions are typically considered second-tier interventions. The interventions in the third category are designed to improve learning outcomes by providing instruction in learning strategies provided outside the content area classroom that will enable students to learn independently once they are in content area classes. These interventions are typically considered third-tier interventions.

This chapter will build on the basic framework presented in Figure 8.1. A brief description of the intervention areas will be provided in the next section. Because of the critical role that the content area teacher plays in providing effective whole-group instruction, we will highlight intervention areas that have been found to improve the performance of students with disabilities in that context. In addition, two teacher-directed interventions (i.e., the Question Exploration Routine and the Recall Enhancement Routine) will be described more extensively in the second part of the chapter.

Content Area Intervention Approaches

As shown in Figure 8.1, we conceptualize contemporary models of content area teaching as falling into one of three tiers: Tier 1 (teacher-directed interventions), Tier 2 (classroom-assisted interventions), and Tier 3 (support-class interventions). In this section, we briefly describe the primary instructional approaches associated with each tier.

Teacher-Directed Content Area Interventions

Teacher-directed interventions consist of three approaches: individual accommodations, group accommodations, and strategy instruction.

Using Individual Accommodations to Support Content Area Learning

A central part of planning and supporting content area learning for students with disabilities is the use of specific accommodations that reduce or eliminate the impact of a disability. Nolet and McLaughlin (2000) described an instructional accommodation as "a service or support that is provided to help a student fully access the subject matter and instruction as well as to demonstrate what he or she knows" (p. 71). An accommodation does not change the content or expectations for what must be learned or the required level of competence that must be demonstrated. Because a disability may impact a student's ability to acquire, store, retrieve, or express what the student has learned in content area classes, accommodations may be needed. Accommodations are used during content area learning and evaluation activities to ensure that a student who has the intellectual ability to

master content demands has an opportunity to learn content that she would be able learn without the disability. Some examples of individual accommodations include audio books, special seating arrangements, note takers, alternate or modified assignments or assessments, text-to-speech devices and software, and talking calculators. These accommodations are compensatory supports intended to reduce the impact of a disability and to ensure access to the general education curriculum in content area classes.

Using Group Accommodations to Support Content Area Learning

Some scholars have called for equal access to content area knowledge and skills through universal design for learning (UDL) (e.g., Rose & Meyer, 2002). One approach to implementing UDL is to provide a group accommodation, defined as an instructional activity used as part of whole-group instruction to promote learning for students with specific learning needs. However, the use of the accommodation can lead to benefits in learning that may be realized for all students in the class. The study of teaching adjuncts or mediators (e.g., graphic organizers, teaching routines, guided notes, study guides) to enhance or promote content area learning of students with disabilities has been steadily growing since the 1980s (for a review of early studies, see Bulgren & Schumaker, 2006).

Based on some of the same principles as those embodied in UDL, an approach to promoting content area learning for struggling students is represented in a set of well-researched interventions called Content Enhancement Routines (CERs; Lenz & Bulgren, 1995; Schumaker, Deshler, & McKnight, 2002). CERs were designed to move explicit, direct, strategic, organized instruction found to be successful with struggling learners (H. L. Swanson & Deshler, 2003) into large-group, content area classroom instruction. When a CER is used correctly, a teacher introduces an instructional device, such as a graphic organizer, to the whole class and teaches the class how to use the device. The teacher then identifies the content and expected learning outcome that must be achieved and leads the class through a co-constructed process to complete the strategic thinking process required to learn and review the information. Once initiated, the teaching process involved in the use of the device to achieve an intended learning outcome (e.g., compare concepts) is repeated throughout the course. The goal is that it becomes routine for both the teacher and students to use the strategy to manipulate the information. We will highlight a more detailed example of the components and procedures related to the implementation of CERs later in this chapter.

Strategy Instruction in the Content Area Classroom

Use of the CERs provides a type of compensatory instruction required when students do not have good learning strategies to ensure content learning. Some students, however, may not acquire a learning strategy unless the teacher explicitly teaches the strategy. While teaching subject matter material, teachers can look for opportunities to point out to students particular strategies that would help them manipulate the information being taught. For example, a teacher may teach, model, and prompt the use of paraphrasing, prediction, or self-questioning to learn content. In this scenario, teachers not only tell students about a strategy that would be helpful for them to use, they also explain how to use the strategy, model its use, and then require students to use the strategy in relation to their content assignments.

The purpose of doing this is to teach students "how to learn" the subject matter material. By teaching students strategies that are directly relevant to the demands of their course, teachers shift from a single instructional emphasis on learning course content to simultaneously helping their students acquire the underlying cognitive processes that will enable them to independently understand and remember the content. Some students need support to recognize and use the underlying cognitive processes, and these students can be guided by instruction in strategies associated with different cognitive demands. Embedding explicit instruction in learning strategies—especially strategies tied to literacy (e.g., reading comprehension strategies) as part of instruction provided in content area courses in middle and high school—reflects a departure from traditional approaches to teaching content. However, the national trend toward adoption of the Common Core Standards by states indicates that secondary general educators teaching the core courses required for graduation will be required to provide a variety of instructional supports that help students engage in a continuum of content area learning and strategic thinking and reasoning (Porter, McMaken, Hwang, & Yang, 2011).

Several approaches are effective for embedding strategy instruction in content area learning. One approach is to link strategy instruction to a group accommodation. For example, almost all content supports are provided because one or more students lack a good strategy for doing a task independently. To illustrate, as part of group instruction, a teacher may provide a set of guided notes to the entire class because the teacher realizes that one or more students do not know how to detect main from supporting details—a key strategy for successful note taking. As content supports are provided to ensure that content is mastered, the strategies associated with a specific content support (e.g., note taking) can be taught. Similarly, when a CER is used, the specific strategy associated with each CER (e.g., those described in the following section) can be explicitly taught and practiced as part of the content learning experience.

As supports are provided to ensure content area learning and higher-level thinking, strategy instruction is also provided to students so they can eventually apply the strategies independently. These are often higher-level thinking strategies such as those that help students understand a concept, answer important questions, make comparisons, or explain causation. In addition, more general strategies may be taught in the content area classroom. General strategies include those that support paraphrasing, self-questioning, or summarizing. Finally, those general strategies can be cued by the content area teacher if students have been taught those strategies in another setting. All of these strategies may be embedded in content area instruction.

Classroom-Assisted Content Area Interventions

Many content area teachers use interventions that promote the use of assisted learning structures within the content area classroom. Classroom-assisted interventions are designed to provide adult or peer assistance to students in the content area classroom other than those provided by the primary content area teacher. These arrangements can include the use of special-education teachers, paraprofessionals, within-class tutors, and peers. Although assisted learning structures for students with disabilities have not been shown to be as effective in promoting student learning as teacher-directed instruction (H. L. Swanson & Hoskyn, 2001b), content area teachers often use these types of learning structures to individualize instruction. In fact, secondary teachers reported that having students work in groups to learn content was one of the top three instructional strategies that they used in order to individualize instruction to meet the needs of students in an academically diverse group of learners (Lenz, Schumaker, & Deshler, 1991). Teachers therefore need information on effective assisted learning structures that can be used within content area classrooms.

Peer-assisted learning structures have been described in the literature as peer tutoring, student learning teams, and cooperative learning. In peer-assisted learning structures, students are expected to help each other learn content or complete tasks; however, the teacher is expected to plan for and monitor peer-assisted learning activities. Peer-assisted learning structures allow the teacher to shift teaching responsibilities to a student's peers. Although peer-assisted learning structures can be used in many ways to improve content learning outcomes, they are used most often to promote understanding of course content, to provide practice opportunities, or to help students complete assignments or perform tasks (see Bulgren & Schumaker, 2006).

Adult-assisted learning structures are learning activities provided to individuals or small groups of students in which an adult supports content area learning. These activities typically are implemented in supportive co-teaching arrangements in which a special education teacher or paraprofessional helps students learn the content. Content area tutoring is an example of these types of activities frequently found in schools. One model for providing content area tutoring that has demonstrated some empirical support is strategic tutoring (Hock, Pulvers, Deshler, & Schumaker, 2001). In strategic tutoring, the tutor teaches students strategies in how to learn the content for a specific content area class.

Support-Class Content Area Interventions

Another approach to improving content learning outcomes involves interventions that teach learning strategies to students in a support class (e.g., a reading class) or special education class. This approach has generated a considerable amount of research evidence (Schumaker & Deshler, 2010). Proponents of these interventions argue that learning strategies (e.g., paraphrasing, self-questioning, textbook usage, note taking, test preparation, mnemonic strategies) that are taught in a support class (e.g., learning strategies or study skills class) or in special education settings (e.g., resource room) should be directly linked to improving outcomes in the general education content classroom. That is, the teacher should spend instructional time teaching students how to generalize the strategies that they are learning in support classes to their general education content courses (e.g., language arts, history, biology, algebra).

Descriptions of Effective Practices: Content Enhancement Routines

Content Enhancement Routines: Principles, Learning Supports, Procedures, and Research

The term *content enhancements* refers to a type of group accommodation that includes a variety of instructional adjuncts or mediators that teachers can use to facilitate or enhance students' organization, understanding, and remembering of content as part of whole-group instruction. Researchers at the University of Kansas Center for

Research on Learning who were designing and studying instructional interventions for use with students with learning disabilities (LD) and other students who were low achieving developed CERs. These researchers found that instructional interventions required systematic, intensive, and explicit instruction sustained over a long period of time in order to be effective (Deshler, Schumaker, & Lenz, 1984). In the following section, we describe the guiding principles, learning supports, procedures, and research associated with CERs.

Content Enhancement Routine Principles

CERs are based on four key principles: (a) content area teachers must select the critical features of the content and then transform that content in a way that promotes learning for academically diverse groups of students, (b) the instruction must meet the needs of both the group and the individuals in the group, (c) the process must not compromise the integrity of content by watering down important ideas, and (d) teachers and students must engage in a co-constructive partnership (i.e., the teacher and student must work together to generate and transform the content) that honors the role of each in the learning process (Bulgren, Deshler, & Lenz, 2007).

Content Enhancement Routine Learning Supports

Several learning supports are common to many of the CERs. Among these are graphic organizers that provide a visual representation of how information may be organized and suggest relationships between chunks of information through the use of geometric shapes and drawing elements. The organization of the shapes shows the relationships among the ideas or chunks of information. Because graphic organizers can only hold a limited amount of information, only the most critical information can be displayed. Thus, the teacher's selections for inclusion in a graphic organizer significantly influence student learning.

The relationships shown in the graphic organizer may or may not be supported by verbal cues provided directly on the graphic organizer. However, Pashler et al. (2007) found that graphic presentations (e.g., graphs, figures, charts, maps) that illustrate key processes and procedures that have the most research support are those used with verbal descriptions and presentations provided by the teacher. Therefore, the provision of explicit instruction is another common learning support provided in CERs. Finally, embedded cognitive learning strategy prompts are common across CERs; most of the embedded strategies are scaffolded by acronyms to facilitate recall and by cueing them on the graphic organizer.

Content Enhancement Routine Procedures

The teaching methods in the CERs are sequenced within three instructional phases: "CUE," "DO," and "REVIEW." The purposes of the phases are summarized in the following list:

- *CUE:* The purpose of CUE is to ensure that students (a) are aware of the graphic organizer unique to each CER; (b) understand the importance of the learning goal; (c) understand how the graphic organizer provides a framework for organizing, understanding, and remembering the information needed to reach the learning goal; and (d) understand expectations for their participation in the co-construction of the organizer and learning. This is a verbal preview led by the teacher using the appropriate blank graphic organizer that has been copied and distributed to each student.

- *DO:* The purpose of DO is to ensure that students (a) understand how to process and organize the information, (b) work with the teacher to co-construct the information that is placed on the graphic organizer, and (c) succeed in achieving the learning goal as a result of participation in a carefully scaffolded learning process. In the DO phase, teachers engage students in a carefully scaffolded learning process that consists of a series of instructional steps to guide learners through the use of a cognitive processing strategy. For example, the strategy steps related to independently analyzing, exploring, and answering a question are presented to students as part of the Question Exploration Routine. The teacher uses these steps to lead the class through this question exploration process, as presented later in this chapter. Each strategy is unique to the learning goals of the CER. The teacher engages students in dialogue and construction to promote understanding at each step in whole-group or small-group instruction, or with support from a special education teacher in the classroom.

- *REVIEW:* The purpose of REVIEW is to ensure that students (a) are aware they have achieved the learning goal and can independently summarize learning, and (b) can describe how the graphic organizer and the strategic process of its development helped them learn and reach the learning goal. The teacher leads the review by asking students to summarize the information in the graphic organizer, how decisions were made that led to the information being recorded on the graphic organizer, and how the graphic organizer might be used to study and learn the information.

The CUE-DO-REVIEW instructional procedures are common to all CERs. However, the major portion of each CER, the DO component, is designed to respond to a unique learning goal (e.g., recall information; understand a concept; manipulate information to make comparisons, determine causation, or answer critical questions).

Content Enhancement Routine Research

The effectiveness of CERs has been tested in inclusive secondary settings such as science, social studies, and English/language arts classes. These were classes that contained groups of students of diverse abilities, including those who were high achieving (HA), average achieving (AA), and low achieving (LA), as well as students with disabilities, including LD. Research conducted at the University of Kansas Center for Research on Learning has occurred across a variety of content topics with a range of experimental designs. Results have shown that teachers can use CERs to enhance students' scores on tests that measure retention of factual information (Bulgren, Deshler, & Schumaker, 1997; Bulgren, Schumaker, & Deshler, 1994), comprehension of conceptual information (Bulgren, Schumaker, & Deshler, 1988), knowledge of a concept by analogy (Bulgren, Deshler, Schumaker, & Lenz, 2000), comparison of critical concepts (Bulgren, Lenz, Schumaker, Deshler, & Marquis, 2002), determining causation and making decisions about competing choices and options (Bulgren et al., 1998), and argumentation and evaluation of a statement of claim (J. D. Ellis & Bulgren, 2009).

To illustrate the types of interventions that might be used to promote content learning, in the following sections we describe two specific CER interventions that can be implemented for large-group instruction in content area classrooms: the Question Exploration Routine and the Recall Enhancement Routine.

The Question Exploration Routine

The Question Exploration Routine (QER) is based on a wealth of previous research. For example, the use of questions and questioning is supported by reviews of empirical literature (Pressley et al., 1992; Rosenshine, Meister, & Chapman, 1996). Researchers support the use of questions to set the stage for reasoning and the eventual application of content knowledge to practical situations (Graesser, Person, & Hu, 2002), provide fundamental guides for basic reasoning (Graesser, Baggett, & Williams, 1996), lead students to integrate ideas (A. King, 1994), help organize knowledge (Graesser et al., 2002), promote deep reasoning (Graesser, McNamara, & VanLehn, 2005), facilitate deeper comprehension (Rouet, Vidal-Abarca, Erboul, & Millogo, 2001), and help students transfer learning from one context to another (Perkins & Salomon, 1992).

Research focusing on the QER specifically showed it is effective in helping students who had disabilities, such as those with LD, as well as LA, AA, and HA students without disabilities, succeed on both quantitative and qualitative assessments (Bulgren, Marquis, Lenz, Deshler, & Schumaker, 2011; Bulgren, Marquis, Lenz, Deshler, & Schumaker, 2009). It is an example of a group accommodation that focuses on student mastery of content that requires higher-level thinking in the form of analysis, synthesis, and generalization.

This routine shows how teachers use a graphic organizer combined with some explicit verbal supports to scaffold learning. The goals associated with the use of the graphic organizer and verbal supports are to promote interactive student–teacher co-construction of learning and to provide a cognitive strategic scaffold that can be used as part of whole-group instruction to more effectively teach content to groups of students of diverse abilities. The QER supports acquisition and retention of content information, understanding about a topic by analysis of a critical question, development of a clear answer, and generalization of what the student has learned.

The Question Exploration Guide

The Question Exploration Guide (QEG) is a graphic organizer teaching device (see Figure 8.2) designed to help teachers lead students through the scaffolded learning experience provided in the QER. Students are prompted to explore and answer questions that teachers have

Figure 8.2 A sample Question Exploration Guide.

Text Reference __________________ Name __________________
Course ________ Title ________________________
Critical Question # ________ Unit ________ Date ________
Lesson ________________________________

(1) What is the Critical Question?

(2) What are the Key Terms and explanations?

(3) What are the Supporting Questions and answers?

(4) What is the Main Idea answer?

(5) How can we Use the main idea again?

(6) Is there an Overall Idea? Is there a real-world use?

Source: Bulgren, J. A., Lenz, B. K., Schumaker, J. B., & Deshler, D. D. (2002). *The Concept Comparison Routine* (p. 53). Lawrence, KS: Edge Publications, Inc. Reprinted with permission.

determined to be critical to improving content learning outcomes. Figure 8.3 defines the different sections of a completed QEG for a language arts course focusing on a component of narratives in literature. The guide can be used to launch learning on a topic with a critical question, to record learning tied to the question as a topic is covered, and to confirm that learning tied to the question has occurred. The embedded cognitive strategy is represented by the acronym ANSWER, as described next.

Implementation of the Question Exploration Routine

Effective implementation of the QER is described in detail in the QER guidebook (Bulgren, Lenz, Deshler, & Schumaker, 2001). The QER uses the CUE-DO-REVIEW sequence common to all CERs, but the DO component is uniquely tailored to supporting a strategic approach to answering critical content area questions.

Figure 8.3 Sections defined on a completed Question Exploration Guide from a language arts course.

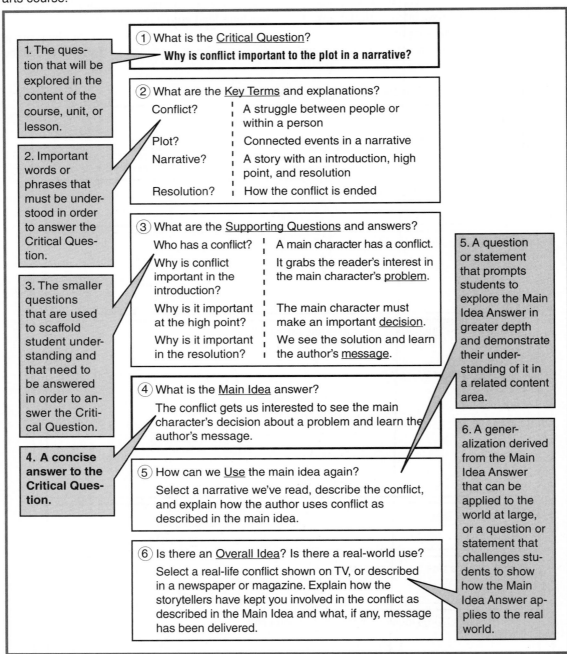

Source: Bulgren, J. A., Lenz, B. K., Deshler, D. D., & Schumaker, J. B. (2001). *The Question Exploration Routine* (p. 7). Lawrence, KS: Edge Publications, Inc. Reprinted with permission.

During the CUE phase, the teacher notes the important question and the importance of understanding and answering it, cues the use of and explains the graphic organizer, and prompts expectations about the students' participation in the co-construction of learning. For example, a teacher might indicate that, as a class, the group will explore why conflict is so important to the plot in a literature narrative, explaining that analysis of conflicts in the plots of short stories, novels, and plays is an important, recurring challenge throughout the course. The teacher will pass out blank QEGs to students and remind them to take notes and participate in a discussion of the important question.

During the DO phase, the part of the routine in which the most time and instructional energy is spent, the teacher and students co-construct the QEG by following a set of six strategic steps, enumerated in Figure 8.3. The six steps are prompted by the acronym ANSWER, which was constructed from the first letter of the first word of each of the six steps: (a) Ask a Critical Question; (b) Note and explore key terms and basic knowledge needed to answer the Critical Question; (c) Search for Supporting Questions and answer those Supporting Questions; (d) Work out or formulate a clear, concise main-idea answer to the Critical Question; (e) Explore the Main Idea Answer in a related area; and (f) Relate the Main Idea to today's real world. The teacher presents a critical question to the class that is tied to the attainment of specific content standards; the teacher then uses the strategy steps to lead the whole class in the exploration and answering of the question. To further enhance student learning, the teacher might also embed general strategies such as paraphrasing, self-questioning, and summarizing as they proceed through the ANSWER steps. In summary, the acronym ANSWER guides students in learning a higher-order strategy associated with answering a critical question.

The routine was designed so the steps can be flexible in the sense that instruction is often delivered to the whole group. However, depending on teacher preferences, part of the procedures can be developed as small groups or even as individual assignments. The only portion of the development that is largely under teacher control is the selection of the critical question based on standards, assessments, and learning demands. However, when teachers and students become familiar with the routine, teachers can often involve students in developing the critical questions based on their interests or previous questions. Thus, this sequence involves exploring a critical question, developing supporting questions, and answering those questions. It also includes ways for students to apply and transfer or generalize new knowledge both to their course content and the world around them.

Finally, in the REVIEW phase, the teacher and students review both the information covered in the DO Phase and the process used to answer the Critical Question. For example, the critical understanding is found in the main idea answer: "The conflict gets us interested to see the main character's decision about a problem and learn the author's message." The critical cognitive process is that the steps of the ANSWER strategy allowed the group to carefully develop their understanding; in the early stages of implementation, the teachers may review the steps with the students.

Research on the Question Exploration Routine

Three research studies have been conducted on the QER. One study was conducted in an experimentally controlled setting with instruction delivered by a researcher (Bulgren et al., 2011). Over 100 students, including those with disabilities, in seventh- and eighth-grade science and social studies classes were randomly assigned to experimental or control conditions. Results indicated that students who received instruction with the QER correctly answered a significantly higher percentage of all questions on the tests than did students who received traditional lecture-discussion instruction. Effect sizes were large to very large on each of two tests designed to assess student understanding of a critical question and its answer.

A second study was conducted to determine the feasibility of use of the QER by general education teachers as they taught regularly scheduled content, and the effectiveness of the QER to enhance learning under those conditions (Schumaker, Deshler, Lenz, Bulgren, & Davis, 2006). The study took place in ninth-grade language arts classrooms during instruction on Shakespeare's *Romeo and Juliet*. Over 130 students, including those representing groups of students with diverse abilities, participated. Tests assessed students' ability to explain their understanding of two critical main ideas. Answering the assessment questions required students to indicate overall understanding by providing examples of the main ideas from the play, and to generalize those ideas to other settings. On average, students who received instruction with the QER correctly answered a significantly higher percentage of all questions on both tests than did students who received traditional lecture-discussion instruction. Effect sizes were large on two tests associated with critical questions from the play.

A third study investigated the effects of using the QER to help students of diverse abilities, including those with LD, answer critical essay questions related to content area learning (Bulgren et al., 2009). In this study, researchers randomly assigned 36 students in grades 9 through 12 to experimental or control conditions, and all participated in the instruction about the ozone layer on the first day. On the second day, some students participated in a review using the QER while the other students saw a film that repeated and reinforced all the information from the previous day. Students' responses on an essay were scored in two ways. One assessed students' essays in response to the critical question using the 6-Trait Model of Analysis Scoring, part of the 6-Trait Model of Writing Instruction (Kozlow & Bellamy, 2004). Independent scorers certified in 6-Trait scoring analysis and blind as to which essays were written by students in the experimental or control conditions scored the essays. Results showed statistically significant differences and moderately large effect sizes for students in the experimental condition compared to students in the control condition. The essays were then scored by two independent scorers for accuracy of knowledge and understanding of the

content about the ozone. Results showed significant differences and very large effect sizes for students in the experimental condition compared to students in the control condition with regard to knowledge and comprehension of content about the topic taught.

Examples of how the QEG has been used across additional subject areas (i.e., science, history, and math) are provided in Figures 8.4 through 8.6. As is illustrated in section 3 in Figures 8.4 to 8.6, the supports used in the questioning process to scaffold instruction can be quite varied. In addition, the questions posed on the guide can be whole-course questions that can be revisited across the year, unit questions that can be used to guide learning across the study of topics in a unit, or lesson questions that are posed to guide the discussion of a specific topic or issue that is important for unit- and course-level

Figure 8.4 Completed Question Exploration Guide in science.

① What is the Critical Question?

Why is a four-chambered heart two pumps in one?

② What are the Key Terms and explanations?

Chamber	An enclosed space.
Heart	A muscle that pumps blood to the lungs through the body.
Pump	A device for moving liquid from one place to another.

③ What are the Supporting Questions and answers?

A. What are the four chambers?

What is the function of . . .

B. The right atrium?
C. The right ventricle?
D. The left atrium?
E. The left ventricle?

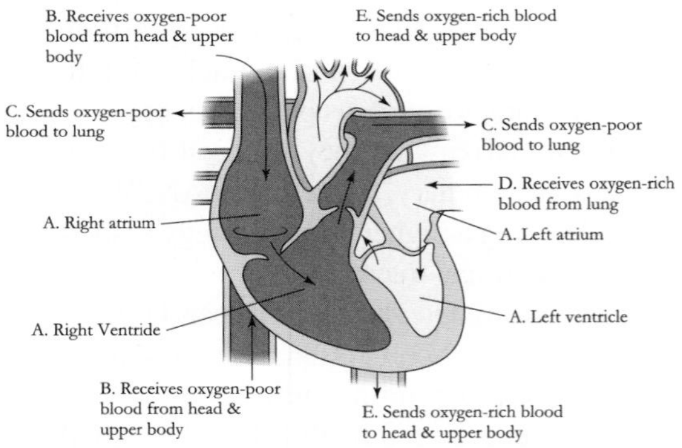

④ What is the Main Idea answer?

The right side of the heart pumps oxygen-poor blood to the lungs, and the left side pumps oxygen-rich blood through the body. (The right side is one pump; the left is the second pump = 2 pumps.)

⑤ How can we Use the main idea again?

Why do the walls of the left ventricle have to be thicker than the walls of the right ventricle?

⑥ Is there an Overall Idea? Is there a real-world use?

If a person smokes, which pump is most affected and why?

Source: Bulgren, J. A., Lenz, B. K., Deshler, D. D., & Schumaker, J. B. (2001). *The Question Exploration Routine* (p. 59). Lawrence, KS: Edge Publications, Inc. Reprinted with permission.

Figure 8.5   Completed Question Exploration Guide in history.

① What is the <u>Critical Question</u>?

How has the search for human and civil rights been a major theme of U.S. history?

② What are the <u>Key Terms</u> and explanations?

Human rights	What is due every person as a citizen of the Earth.
Civil rights	What is due every person under law.
Theme	Runs through from beginning to end.

③ What are the <u>Supporting Questions</u> and answers?

What human rights were involved?	Freedom; people are not property.
How is this part of our history?	People violated human rights because of economic and social values (both in North and South).
What civil rights were involved?	Because slaves were property, they were not equal under law. When they were recognized as not being property, it opened the door to being covered by laws and civil rights.
How is this part of our history?	Disagreement over both issues led to war, which allowed progress in gaining more human and civil rights.

④ What is the <u>Main Idea</u> answer?

During the Civil War, our nation struggled over what were the human rights of people being treated as slaves. Protecting human rights opened the door for civil rights.

⑤ How can we <u>Use</u> the main idea again?

The Declaration of Independence states that all people are equal—a major idea of human and civil rights. How does the Declaration of Independence address human and civil rights?

⑥ Is there an <u>Overall Idea</u>? Is there a real-world use?

O.I.: Human rights must be guaranteed before you have civil rights. How do examples from different periods of our history illustrate the relationship between human rights and civil rights?

Source: Bulgren, J. A. (2002). *The Question Exploration Guide: Trainers' Guide* (p. 85). Lawrence, KS: Edge Publications, Inc. Reprinted with permission.

learning. However, regardless of the level, the question answering should be aligned with assessments and ensure that targeted content learning outcomes are achieved. The QER represents a response to instructional needs of all students to engage in higher-level thinking.

The Recall Enhancement Routine

Although higher-order thinking and reasoning are the focus of many of the CERs, the developers also recognized the need to help students acquire, recall, and demonstrate understanding of important information; this was the basis for the development of the Recall Enhancement

Routine (RER) (Schumaker, Bulgren, Deshler, & Lenz, 1998). This routine helps students acquire and use a variety of mnemonic devices. Mnemonic devices help students to acquire and store information for use in more complex levels of thinking. The RER is another example of a group accommodation that also focuses on embedding strategy instruction into content area instruction to help students recall important foundational information and prior knowledge. A significant amount of research has been completed supporting the positive effects of mnemonic devices with students with disabilities (e.g., Mastropieri & Scruggs, 1992; Mastropieri, Scruggs, & Fulk, 1990).

Figure 8.6   Completed Question Exploration Guide in math.

① What is the <u>Critical Question</u>?

What is the algorithm and an associated acronym for multiplying binomials?

② What are the <u>Key Terms</u> and explanations?

Algorithm	A set of steps for performing a math operation.
Binomial	A mathematical expression comprised of two terms joined by a plus sign $(+)$ or a minus sign $(-)$.
Acronym	A word formed by the first letters of different words.

③ What are the <u>Supporting Questions</u> and answers?

What is step 1?   F = Multiply the First terms in each binomial
$(2x-y)(3x+2y)$ $2x * 3x = 6x^2$

What is step 2?   O = Multiply the Outside terms in each binomial
$(2x-y)(3x+2y)$ $2x * 2y = 4xy$

What is step 3?   I = Multiply the Inside terms in each binomial
$(2x-y)(3x+2y)$ $-y * 3x = -3xy$

What is step 4?   L = Multiply the Last terms in each binomial
$(2x-y)(3x+2y)$ $-y * 2y = -2y^2$

What is step 5?   S = Set up and Summarize the answer

$6x^2 + (4xy-3xy)-2y^2 = 6x^2 + xy - 2y^2$

④ What is the <u>Main Idea</u> answer?

The algorithm contains 5 steps involving multiplying the terms in a sequence and summarizing the answer. The word "FOILS" is an acronym that can be used to remember the steps.

⑤ How can we <u>Use</u> the main idea again?

Solve this new problem using the FOILS algorithm. $(3x + 4y)(2x + 2y)$

⑥ Is there an Overall Idea? Is there a real-world use?

Explain how the FOILS acronym helps you as a learner. Create your own memory device for another math algorithm.

Source: Bulgren, J. A., Lenz, B. K., Deshler, D. D., & Schumaker, J. B. (2001). *The Question Exploration Routine* (p. 66). Lawrence, KS: Edge Publications, Inc. Reprinted with permission.

Systems to help students remember information can include very simple strategies such as rehearsal. In the early school years, rehearsal is one of the first methods used by teachers to help students remember. For example, teachers often create rhymes, poems, or songs from important information to help young children's recall. As students mature, and as they are expected to remember larger and more complex sets of information, more sophisticated strategies and mnemonic devices can be used to help students develop strategic ways to remember information when it is needed.

The RER illustrates how teachers can help students acquire strategic approaches to recalling small but critical sets of facts needed in content areas. Research on the RER points to a number of elements that teachers should include when embedding mnemonic strategies in large-group content area instruction. These elements include (a) providing information to students regarding the types of mnemonics that can be used and the types of information that are best suited for each type of mnemonic; (b) teaching how content area information should be selected, organized, and effectively applied to the construction of a mnemonic; (c) teaching how information captured by mnemonics is practiced and used to remember the information; and (d) using the principles of direct instruction to ensure that the mnemonic is learned (Schumaker et al., 1998).

The strategic steps associated with the RER include formatting the information, analyzing the information and selecting a device, creating the recall device, and tying the mnemonic together. These steps not only guide instructional procedures and development of the device, but also contain an embedded strategy cued by the acronym FACT. A number of mnemonic devices are taught to the students in the RER. These include variations on mental images or picture devices, keyword devices, stories, symbols or associations, acronyms and acrostics, series or location cues, and other devices such as rhyming and coding in which letters serve as substitutes for numbers.

The Recall Device Sheet

The Recall Device Sheet is used as a central part of the direct instruction process to organize information and practice. Figure 8.7 shows a graphic organizer, the Recall Device Sheet, that teachers and students can use

to approach the use of mnemonics. It extends the FACT acronym to FACTOR to guide students to format the information, analyze the information and select a device, create the recall device, tie it together, organize some questions, and review the plan. Figure 8.8 shows a completed Recall Device Sheet, with a list entitled "Classes of Fishes."

Implementation of the Recall Enhancement Routine

The instructional procedures use the CUE-DO-REVIEW sequence common to all CERs and already illustrated with the QER. After cueing the use of the graphic organizer, the importance of answering the question, and expectations regarding participation and note taking, the DO component is implemented. In the first step, the students and teacher write the important information that needs to be remembered and select the format of the

Figure 8.7   Blank Recall Device Sheet.

Format the Information   Type of Information: ❏ List ❏ Pair ❏ Trio ❏ Definition ❏ Other

Analyze the Information & Select a Device

Type of Memory Device: _____

Create the Recall Device

Tie it Together

Organize Some Questions

Review Plan

Source: Schumaker, J., Bulgren, J., Deshler, D., & Lenz, B. K. (1998). *The Recall Enhancement Routine* (p. 20). Lawrence, KS: The University of Kansas Center for Research on Learning. Reprinted with permission.

Figure 8.8 Completed Recall Enhancement Routine Device Sheet from a science course.

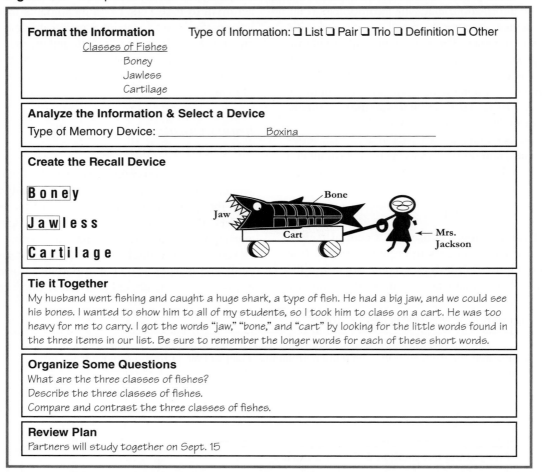

Source: Schumaker, J., Bulgren, J., Deshler, D., & Lenz, B. K. (1998). *The Recall Enhancement Routine* (p. 20). Lawrence, KS: The University of Kansas Center for Research on Learning. Reprinted with permission.

information. In the next step of the graphic organizer, the student examines the information and selects the best type of mnemonic that might be used to remember the information. Figure 8.8 shows that the students have chosen to use a variation on the keyword method called "boxing" as the appropriate memory device. In this method a key syllable is identified, boxed off from the rest of the word, and used as part of the complex mnemonic that can also involve mental pictures and stories.

To illustrate, the next segment of the graphic organizer shows how the students "boxed" part of each word in the list to identify the key part of the word that would be used in the memory device. Then the students and teachers collaboratively think of a story that links the key words together. Figure 8.8 shows how students draw a picture to help remember the associations. The class then discusses and collaboratively ties this mnemonic together by writing a few sentences that make explicit the connections between the content and the mnemonic used. The students then develop some questions they will use to test the use of the mnemonic and to commit the information to memory. This step also includes the

creation of study cards for use during the study process. And in the final steps of the Recall Device Sheet, the teacher guides students to develop a plan related to how and when studying will occur. At the conclusion, the REVIEW step is completed to check on understanding of the information and the process of developing the device.

Research on the RER

Bulgren and co-workers conducted two studies on the RER in inclusive general education classrooms. In the first study conducted on this routine, Bulgren et al. (1994) randomly assigned 41 students with LD and students without disabilities in seventh- and eighth-grade social studies classes to experimental and control groups. All of the students received the same lecture on the history of American journalism in which 40 facts on a social studies unit were embedded. Students in the experimental group collaboratively reviewed 20 important facts in the lecture using mnemonic devices and the RER. The review for the control group included collaborative review of the same important information, but without the mnemonics.

All of the students took a 40-item multiple-choice test (half of the items were related to reviewed facts, and half were related to nonreviewed facts). Results showed that students with LD and without disabilities in experimental classes answered significantly more test items related to reviewed facts when the routine was used than did students in the comparison classes.

Another experimental study on the same routine (Bulgren et al., 1997) showed that nine teachers in secondary (junior high and high school) content area classes could be taught to use the RER at mastery levels in their classrooms after a 3-hour workshop. It also showed that students were more likely to identify the most appropriate type of mnemonic device to be used for particular factual items (e.g., correctly selected devices for recalling listed information when lists were present, selected

visual imagery devices when the information required imagery) when their teacher had used that device in comparison to students in the comparison group.

Evaluation of Content Enhancement Routines

Teachers, administrators, and professional developers can evaluate the effectiveness of a teaching routine and its intended use in a group of students with disabilities along three dimensions, which we will illustrate with evaluation materials for the QER. The first evaluation dimension focuses on the accuracy of the content that is placed in the QEG and whether the information that is provided is appropriately ordered in the question unpacking process. Figure 8.9 provides a checklist that has

Figure 8.9 Question Exploration Routine content checklist for the Question Exploration Guide.

Teacher _____   Observer _____

School _____   Subject _____

Date _____

Directions: Put a checkmark (√) by each component that is present/observed.

Critical Question   **Refer to pp. 7 and 21 in the Question Exploration Routine (QER) guidebook**

_____ is a Big Idea question that students need to answer to succeed in the course (usually a "how" or "why" or broader "what" question).

NOTE: A question may consist of an interrogatory statement signaled by "explain," "describe," etc., but must elicit in-depth consideration as a question would.

Key Term and Explanations   **Refer to pp. 7 and 23–24 in the QER guidebook**

_____ are the important words or phrases (implicit or explicit) that must be understood to discuss and answer the question;

_____ are each explained briefly but clearly.

NOTE: Key terms and explanations may be added at any point in the lesson as needed.

Supporting Questions and Answers   **Refer to pp. 8 and 24–25 in the QER guidebook**

_____ are supporting questions leading to the Main Idea answer to the Critical Question;

_____ are answers for each supporting question that are clearly developed.

NOTE: The answers to the supporting questions, viewed as a sequence of written statements, often represent a coherent short-answer response.

Main Idea Answer   **Refer to pp. 8 and 22 in the QER guidebook**

_____ is a concise answer to the Critical Question that can be used later in a variety of ways.

Use in a Related Area   **Refer to pp. 8 and 25 in the QER guidebook**

_____ is a question prompting students to explore the Main Idea answer in greater depth within the same subject;

_____ results in an application of the Main Idea.

Real-World Use   **Refer to pp. 8 and 25 in the QER guidebook**

_____ is a question prompting students to explore the Main Idea answer as it applies to the real world;

_____ results in a generalization of the Main Idea answer (Overall Idea) OR is a Challenge Question or activity.

Source: Information from Bulgren, J. A., Lenz, B. K., Deshler, D. D., & Schumaker, J. B. (2001). *The Question Exploration Routine.* Lawrence, KS: Edge Publications, Inc.

been used for evaluating the information placed in the device during classroom instruction.

The second evaluation dimension focuses on the degree to which a teacher provides direct, explicit, guided instruction in the CUE-DO-REVIEW process. Because the verbal supports related to using the guide are so important to its effectiveness, the CUE-DO-REVIEW process described earlier is critical to its success. Figure 8.10 provides an example of a checklist for evaluating the teacher's adherence to the process.

The third evaluation dimension focuses on the degree to which the device is used routinely in the course with frequency and intensity. If a teacher is not using the routine over the course of the year, the teacher can be

Figure 8.10   Question Exploration Routine Implementation Checklist.

Teacher _____   Observer _____

Date _____   Subject _____

Question Exploration Routine Implementation Checklist

Cue

The teacher…
_____ named the Question Exploration Guide.
_____ explained how it will help students learn important ideas.
_____ handed out blank guides.
_____ explained expectations for note taking and participation.

Note: Score points only if the teacher writes each item on a Question Exploration Guide that is visible to the students.

Do

Step 1:
The teacher…
_____ announced the Critical Question.

Step 2:
The teacher…
_____ noted Key Terms.
_____ explained or developed explanations for Key Terms with students.

Step 3:
The teacher…
_____ guided discussion of the supporting questions to elicit *all* needed information.
_____ elicited/co-constructed answers to the supporting questions in a logical, sequenced flow.

Step 4:
The teacher…
_____ co-constructed a brief, but concise Main Idea answer with students.

Step 5:
The teacher…
_____ announced or co-constructed a question prompting students to apply the Main Idea answer in a related area.

Step 6:
The teacher…
_____ announced or co-constructed a question prompting students to generalize the Main Idea answer in a real-world or extended area.

Review

The teacher…
_____ asked questions prompting the students to ensure their *understanding* of the Main Idea.
_____ asked questions prompting the students to reflect about and review the *process* of exploring critical questions.

Source: Information from Bulgren, J. A., Lenz, B. K., Deshler, D. D., & Schumaker, J. B. (2001). *The Question Exploration Routine.* Lawrence, KS: Edge Publications, Inc.

judged as not implementing the routine correctly. That is, in order for students to become comfortable with the routine, the teacher must use it sufficiently throughout the course in order for students to become familiar with its use. Some indications that a teacher is using a teaching routine sufficiently include that students immediately recognize the device and how it will be used during the CUE phase, contribute and participate in the completion of information during the DO phase, and can use the device to independently summarize the information included on the device in the REVIEW phase.

Conclusion

The purpose of this chapter has been to discuss approaches that have emerged in the research literature related to promoting content area learning for groups of students of diverse abilities and achievement, including students with disabilities. The content enhancement intervention approaches described here and the methods we have highlighted provide windows on practices that can significantly help students with disabilities learn in content area classrooms. However, the effectiveness of both of these interventions depends on the careful selection of content and the explicit and intentional use of the procedures to address the learning problems of students with disabilities. Ensuring access to content relies on teachers' striking a careful balance between those strategies that students can ultimately use to learn content independently and the critical need to provide teacher-directed supports and instruction for content attainment regardless of students' proficiency in using good learning strategies.

The two highlighted CERs address the content area learning needs of students with disabilities in a number of ways. The use of CERs can be specified in the IEP process as ways to respond to the learning needs of students who may, for example, learn better when information is presented in visual as well as a verbal format. In addition, CERs conform to UDL principles in that they have been designed and tested to be responsive to the learning needs of all students. In terms of instructional procedures, the routines have been developed to be flexible enough that teachers can use them to support learning in small, peer groups as well as large-group instruction.

In addition, CERs incorporate instructional components shown to be effective practices. For example, in terms of learning supports, the graphic organizers used in CERs provide a method of collaboration and efficient communication about important content and thinking when general education teachers work with adult tutors or special education teachers in support classes. In addition, the routines include explicit instruction about learning goals and procedures as well as co-constructive procedures that help all students build understandings based on different sets of prior knowledge. The routines also contain embedded cognitive strategies, both general and higher level, which may be used in different content areas. The goal is that use of integrated sets of routines combined with teacher prompts about using effective strategies will result in increased metacognitive abilities on the part of students. Ultimately, the attention that these routines gives to the selection of proven instructional procedures has been shown to help all students as they acquire, store, and retrieve information; demonstrate their understanding of content information; and engage in the strategic thinking required to improve academic outcomes in content areas.

CHAPTER 9

Strategies for Improving Student Outcomes in Co-Taught General Education Classrooms

Naomi Zigmond | *University of Pittsburgh*

Kathleen Magiera | *State University of NY Fredonia*

Rhea Simmons | *State University of NY Fredonia*

Victoria Volonino | *University of Pittsburgh*

With the 2004 reauthorization of the Individuals with Disabilities Education Act, students with disabilities were mandated not only to have access to the general education curriculum, but also to take the state accountability assessments. This most recent reauthorization of the federal special education law reinforced the provisions of the No Child Left Behind Act of 2001 that emphasized accountability for the performance of all students, with and without disabilities. As general education classrooms have become increasingly populated with diverse learners, all of whom are expected to meet annual achievement benchmarks, co-teaching has been advocated as a way to enhance instruction and facilitate learning for all students, but especially for students with disabilities in general education classrooms. In fact, co-teaching has become the strategic centerpiece of both special and general education reform movements during the past several years (Hyatt, Iddings, & Ober, 2005; Mariage & Patriarca, 2007; Saxon, 2005).

Co-teaching has enormous intuitive appeal and has been widely implemented in schools across the nation. Several state education agencies support the use of co-teaching through statewide policies and teacher trainings (Muller, Friend, & Hurley-Chamberlain, 2009). Nevertheless, research on the instructional validity of co-teaching (i.e., whether it actually provides the assumed instructional benefits) and on student outcomes (i.e., increased student achievement) as a result of its implementation is extremely limited. A review of the literature reveals gaps and omissions in the research evidence for the actual contribution of co-teaching to the teaching–learning process. In this chapter, we provide a brief overview of that literature and research on co-teaching and identify approaches for implementing co-teaching that are based in the research literature and may facilitate attaining improved student outcomes in co-taught classes. We begin with a discussion of definitional issues that have affected both implementation and research on co-teaching.

Co-Teaching Models and Practices

The traditional definition of co-teaching has been described by several researchers (Bauwens, Hourcade, & Friend, 1989; L. Cook & Friend, 1996; S. Vaughn, Bos, & Schumm, 2006). These authors have noted that co-teaching occurs when a special educator and a general educator teach together in a general education classroom during some portion of the instructional day to accommodate the needs of students with and without disabilities. They also emphasize various formats of the co-teaching model in which students learn within smaller groups (i.e., not whole-class instruction). Recently, in a more "functional" definition of co-teaching, Kloo and Zigmond (2008) reiterated the importance of focusing on the strategic grouping of the students rather than on the interactions between the two teachers. Their "functional" definition suggests that small-group instruction should be the norm in a co-taught classroom.

In this chapter, we focus on co-teaching as a service that is recommended for students with high-incidence disabilities (e.g., learning disabilities [LD], emotional disturbance, mild intellectual disability). Although their individualized education programs (IEPs) typically call for instruction to be adapted, students with high-incidence disabilities are placed in co-taught classes with the expectation that they will participate and make progress in the general education curriculum in content areas such as reading, mathematics, social studies, or science. Co-teaching is also recommended for students with low-incidence disabilities (see Hunt & Goetz, 1997; J. Katz & Mirenda, 2002; Santamaria & Thousand, 2004), but the curricular focus of co-teaching for these students may be more individualized—a topic we do not consider in this chapter. Further, we limit our review of co-teaching to situations in which one general educator and one special educator share responsibility for planning, delivering, and evaluating instruction for a diverse class of students, some of whom are students with disabilities. Typically, the general education teacher instructs students with disabilities in the general education curriculum while the special education teacher provides greater access to that curriculum through accommodations and supports (Thousand & Villa, 1989).

One of the earliest models of co-teaching was described by Friend and Cook (1992). They described the following "traditional" approaches in which either teacher can assume any role:

1. The *one teaching and one assisting* variation requires one teacher to retain the instructional lead in the classroom, while the other teacher circulates through the room providing assistance and support to the students as needed.

2. The *one teaching and one observing* approach requires one educator to assume responsibility for instruction while the other educator actively observes and assesses the learning of target students.

3. *Station teaching* involves students rotating through three instructional groups with each teacher assuming particular instructional responsibility for one group while a third group works independently.

4. *Parallel teaching* requires teachers to jointly plan instruction, but then each teacher delivers the content to half of the students.

5. *Alternative teaching* allows for a large- and small-group configuration with each group led by one of the teachers.

6. *Team teaching* occurs when teachers continually alternate the role of primary instructor within individual lessons.

A model offered by S. Vaughn, Schumm, and Arguelles (1997) builds on the options of parallel teaching, station teaching, and team teaching, but provides adaptations to enhance the instructional aspects of the one teaching/one assisting approach. In their model, while one teacher leads the class, the other teacher provides brief intensive instruction to individual students, student pairs, or small groups. Walther-Thomas, Korinek, McLaughlin, and Williams (2000) further extended the co-teaching model. They retained the co-teaching options of parallel teaching, station teaching, and alternative teaching, but replaced the option of one teaching/one assisting with a variation referred to as *interactive teaching*. In this interactive teaching format, instruction is presented to the whole group, with the educators alternating the role of instructional leader for periods of 5 to 10 minutes. As the lead teacher role changes frequently, both teachers are afforded several opportunities to serve as the primary educator (Walther-Thomas et al., 2000).

Co-Teaching Research

Given the popularity of co-teaching as a service-delivery model for students with high incidence disabilities, one might expect to find a sizable research base supporting the practice. Unfortunately that is not the case. Most of the published literature on co-teaching is not empirical or evaluative; instead it describes logistics and recommends procedures such as ongoing co-planning, compatibility in teaching philosophy, and strong administrative support (Bauwens et al., 1989; Friend & Cook, 2003;

Gately & Gately, 2001; Reeve & Hallahan, 1994; S. Vaughn et al., 1997; Walther-Thomas et al., 2000). Some researchers provide rich descriptions of co-teaching implemented in elementary, middle school, or high school classrooms (J. Baker & Zigmond, 1995; Walther-Thomas, 1997; Weiss & Lloyd, 2002), though these studies often focus solely on the one particular arrangement that participating teachers have adopted.

Several authors have reported high levels of satisfaction among all constituents once co-teaching has been implemented (Pugach & Johnson, 1995; Purkey & Smith, 1985; D. L. Voltz, Elliot, & Cobb, 1994). General education teachers, often initially skeptical about sharing their classroom space, generally come to enjoy having a second adult in the classroom who can assist students. On the other hand, special education teachers respond positively to reaching more students in the general education classroom.

Questions remain, however. Does co-teaching work? Does it provide students with high-incidence disabilities more and better instructional opportunities and lead to improved student outcomes? Research on the effectiveness of co-teaching is still emerging (Weiss & Brigham, 2000; Zigmond, 2003), and data on achievement outcomes for students with disabilities in co-taught classes have been particularly elusive. Klingner, Vaughn, Hughes, Schumm, and Elbaum (1998) studied co-teaching at an elementary school that implemented "responsible" inclusion. They followed 25 students with LD assigned into six general education classrooms in one elementary school and calculated gains in academic achievement over one school year using pretests and post-tests. Their study did not include a control group of students with LD taught in general education classrooms without co-teaching or students with LD taught in pullout settings. Although Klingner et al. found that students with disabilities, as well as students at risk for educational failure, made small but significant increases in fall-to-spring reading achievement in co-taught classrooms, the gains were not significant for math achievement.

Welch (2000) completed a descriptive analysis of team teaching using qualitative and quantitative methods in an approach referred to as a "formative experiment" (Reinking & Pickle, 1993). He tracked the progress of eight students with LD, five in one classroom and three in another, and their classmates in two schools implementing co-teaching for 16 to 19 weeks. Again, this study included no control group of students with LD who did not receive co-teaching. Welch found that team teaching improved the reading fluency and word-recognition skills of *all* students in the two elementary-level classrooms, but the overall increase in mean performance of students with LD was not statistically significant.

Rea, McLaughlin, and Walther-Thomas (2002) investigated the relationship between placement in the special education program and academic and behavior outcomes for eighth-grade school students with LD in two middle schools, one providing inclusive, co-taught services ($n = 36$) and the other providing pullout services ($n = 22$). They used a retrospective approach, gathering extant data for a cohort of students who had been served in two distinct service-delivery models in the middle schools of a single suburban district. Although students were not randomly assigned to the treatments/schools, several student-level variables established the equivalence of the two groups of students at the start of the study. The authors reported that students with LD taught in the general education classrooms with co-teaching services received higher course grades in language arts, math, science, and social studies than their peers in pullout programs. Rea et al. reported significant findings also favoring co-taught students with LD for scores on the Iowa Test of Basic Skills (ITBS) in language and math, and for attendance. However, the groups earned comparable scores on state achievement tests; comparable scores on the ITBS in reading, science, and social studies; and comparable numbers of school suspensions.

K. C. Fontana (2005) also examined the effect of co-teaching on eighth graders with LD. Students with LD who were randomly assigned to a control group ($n = 16$) were taught in a traditional one-teacher classroom for English and math. Students with LD who were randomly assigned to the target group ($n = 17$) were randomly placed in English and math classes co-taught by three general education teachers who volunteered to co-teach. Students with LD in both the control and target groups received one period of resource room support. The only comparisons between the outcomes of the two groups involved English and math grades. Grades (calculated from objective measures such as unit tests and quizzes) of target, co-taught students were significantly higher at the end of eighth grade than they had been at the end of seventh grade. Grades of students with LD in solo-taught eighth-grade classes showed no significant improvement over their previous year's grades.

Murawski (2006) conducted a randomized block design experiment to study outcomes of co-taught, solo-taught, and resource room English classes for 38 ninth graders with LD and 72 students without disabilities in one urban high school. The four experimental conditions included a general education class with no included students with disabilities, two solo-taught inclusive classes, two co-taught inclusive classes, and one special education class. A block design was called for because students with LD were assigned to an inclusive or special education class based on student ability and family preference, not at random. However, students with LD selected for an inclusive class were randomly assigned to a co-taught ($n = 12$) or a solo-taught class ($n = 8$). After co-varying for pretest and ability scores, Murawski found no significant main effects for treatment condition for standardized tests of spelling, math, vocabulary, reading comprehension, or writing after the 10-week intervention for students with LD in resource room, solo-taught, or co-taught classes, and no main effects for students without disabilities in classes with one teacher (with or without included students with LD) or with two teachers (and included students).

In addition to outcomes on academic skills, studies have also evaluated outcomes related to socialization. Co-teaching all day long was not as effective as a consultation/collaborative teaching model of service delivery (with co-teaching for only part of the day) in increasing peer acceptance ratings and overall friendship quality for elementary-aged students with LD. Vaughn and colleagues (Vaughn, Elbaum, Schumm, & Hughes, 1998) found that the number and quality of students' friendships improved when students transitioned from exclusionary educational settings back into the general education classroom, but students in the co-teaching school did not fare as well as those in the comparison school. The authors acknowledge that the results could be attributed to differences in the ratio of students with LD to students without disabilities in the two settings: in the co-teaching school, half the classes of 27 to 35 students were students with LD, while in the consultation/collaborative teaching, only 3 to 8 of the 31 to 37 students in each classroom were students with LD. It was also difficult to separate setting effects from teacher and other home and school effects despite the authors' attempts to match schools in terms of overall achievement scores and ethnicity of the student population.

In a review of the overall research base of co-teaching, Murawski and Swanson (2001) conducted a meta-analysis. Unfortunately, only six quantitative studies that met their inclusion criteria were identified. Only one study (Self, Benning, Marston, & Magnusson, 1991) involved students in kindergarten through third grade, and this study yielded an effect size of 0.95. Two studies (Klingner, Vaughn, Hughes, et al., 1998; S. Vaughn, Elbaum, et al., 1998) reported on 11 outcome measures for students in grades 3 through 6; the total effect size of 0.19 indicated a low effect for elementary students. Finally, three studies analyzed for their effects on high school students (Lundeen & Lundeen, 1993; Rosman, 1994; J. M. Walsh & Snyder, 1993) yielded a total effect size on nine measures of 0.30. Measures of student outcomes spanned a range of dependent variables that included grades (mean effect size of 0.32), special education referrals (mean effect size of 0.43), attitudes (no effect), and academic achievement in reading (mean effect size of 1.59) and mathematics (mean effect size of 0.45).

Murawski and Swanson (2001) concluded that co-teaching was moderately effective in influencing student outcomes (overall mean effect size of 0.40), although they cautioned that because so little quantitative research evaluated the effectiveness of co-teaching, it is difficult to draw meaningful conclusions about the practice. Further, their meta-analysis did not include the Boudah, Schumaker, and Deshler (1997) landmark study of co-taught classes at the high school level in which academic achievement for students with mild disabilities actually decreased.

The lack of empirical support for co-teaching is not surprising; co-teaching may be a service, but it is not a "treatment" that can be imposed with fidelity on an experimental group and withheld with equal fidelity from a control group. Researchers who have attempted to contrast student outcomes in co-taught vs. solo-taught classrooms or co-taught vs. pullout instruction, whether through quasi-experimental designs or true random assignment of students, assume they have specified the treatment when they claim that co-teaching is occurring, yet the intervention is often defined merely as "a variety of co-teaching methods" (K. C. Fontana, 2005, p. 20).

Collaboration is the process whereby special and general education teachers implement co-teaching (Magiera, Simmons, Marotta, & Battaglia, 2005). Most often, the collaboration is described in terms of the roles assumed by the two teachers. Several descriptive studies have sought to determine whether the potential for co-teaching to provide enhanced learning opportunities actually materializes in co-taught classes. Magiera and Zigmond (2005) studied co-taught and solo-taught classrooms at the middle school level and reported that the instructional experience for students in co-taught classrooms was similar to the instructional experience in solo-taught classrooms. McDuffie, Mastropieri, and Scruggs (2009) found that students with disabilities in four solo-taught classes interacted significantly *more* often with their teachers than did students in four co-taught classes.

In secondary co-taught classes observed by Weiss and Lloyd (2002), and in a later study reported by Zigmond and Matta (2004), researchers failed to observe significantly enhanced instructional experiences. In fact, a recent meta-synthesis of qualitative research on co-teaching by Scruggs, Mastropieri, and McDuffie (2007) showed that true collaboration between co-teachers seldom has been achieved. They found that special educators frequently assume the role of instructional aide and that a variety of factors inhibit their ability to provide specialized instruction within the general education classroom. Further, Scruggs et al. concluded that the benefits of co-teaching services related to "curriculum needs, innovative practice, and appropriate individualization—ha[ve] largely not been met" (p. 412).

Despite the research base providing limited support for co-teaching, proponents continue to emphasize that co-taught classrooms provide a venue for the integration of the complementary skills of general and special educators (Friend & Cook, 2003). That is, the general educator brings to co-teaching content knowledge and group instructional skills, while the special educator brings expertise in the diagnosis and remediation of individual learning problems or challenges. By interfacing these instructional skills, instruction in the general education classroom should be sufficiently enhanced such that the needs of both students with disabilities and those at-risk for educational failure can effectively be met (Kauffman & Hallahan, 2005). However, future researchers will need to specify the actual instructional practices under consideration (e.g., collaboration) in their attempts to document desired student outcomes.

A Key to More Successful Co-Teaching: The Collaboration Process

Teachers require professional socialization to learn to become more collaborative (Friend & Cook, 2003; R. J. Simmons, Magiera, Cummings, & Arena, 2008). Without consistent training and follow-up, teachers make up their own ways of implementing a co-teaching model. For example, R. J. Simmons and Magiera (2007) observed 10 secondary co-taught classes and interviewed 22 co-teachers in three different high schools within the same school district and found strikingly different degrees of implementation of the co-teaching model in this single school district. These findings are consistent with the conclusions of other researchers (e.g., Adelman & Taylor, 2003; Magiera, Smith, Zigmond, & Gebauer, 2005; Salend, Gordon, & Lopez-Vona, 2002; R. J. Simmons & Magiera, 2007) that only a systematic approach to implementing the process of collaboration within a school district will lead to greater access to the general education curriculum for students with disabilities.

Based on previous foundational research and their own studies of co-teaching, Magiera, Simmons, and Hance (2008) have delineated a six-step "quality process" to ensure that co-teachers are truly collaborating. The implementation process begins by establishing a common understanding of co-teaching to be implemented among all co-teachers and administrators. To become more collaborative, several researchers (Caron & McLaughlin, 2002; Magiera et al., 2005; R. J. Simmons & Magiera, 2007) have recommended a tiered approach to professional development (see Figure 9.1). Magiera and her colleagues (2008) suggest that the first step is joint planning meetings involving district leaders, staff development specialists, and higher education partners to establish a vision of co-teaching for the district. A common and consistent framework for co-teaching may be essential for successful collaboration.

Professional development opportunities for administrators and co-teaching pairs are the second step in laying the co-teaching foundation. Essential to this foundational staff development is the establishment of a common vocabulary and a consistent understanding of the co-teaching service for administrators and co-teachers (M. J. McLaughlin, 2002). In a large-scale co-teaching initiative involving 132 teachers, Magiera, Simmons, et al.

Figure 9.1 Essential elements for developing a quality collaborative process for co-teaching.

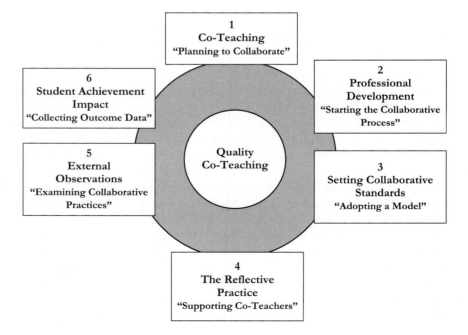

(2005) found administrative and teacher knowledge was critical to establishing a consistent foundation for co-teaching.

Setting collaborative standards is the third step. This involves making transparent and observable the "best practices" of collaborative behaviors that are being fostered (Caron & McLaughlin, 2002; Dieker, 2001; Salend et al., 2002). Caron and McLaughlin (2002) have called for measurable indicators of these practices so that implementation of co-teaching can be monitored and improved. In their work in four elementary and two middle schools involving 12 special education teachers and 17 general education teachers, Caron and McLaughlin identified "critical indicators" related to successful collaboration among special and general education teachers. Following classroom observations of co-teaching, teachers discussed various patterns of collaboration. The researchers found that setting clear expectations for all students including students with disabilities within the context of teaching the general education curriculum was critical to the collaborative process.

A. I. Nevin (2006) has identified three available tools that may help with successful collaboration: the Co-Teacher Relationship Scale (Noonan, McCormick, & Heck, 2003), which focuses on matching up potential co-teaching pairs; the Are We Really Co-Teachers Scale (Villa, Thousand, & Nevin, 2008), which focuses on teaching interactions and behaviors in a co-taught classroom; and finally the Magiera-Simmons Quality Indicator Model of Co-Teaching (Magiera & Simmons, 2005), designed to help teachers become more collaborative in co-taught classrooms. These tools yield formative teacher data critical to ensure that co-teaching implementation goes beyond the "one teach/one assist" as noted by Scruggs et al. (2007).

Setting standards and collecting data are not sufficient. Therefore, the fourth step in establishing collaborative practices is reflection. Co-teachers need time and opportunities to review the observation data, to ask questions, to clarify their roles, and to reinforce their initial learning of the collaborative process. They do this as they plan together. The iterative process of data collection followed by reflection helps co-teaching pairs refine their collaborative instructional practice (Caron & McLaughlin, 2002; Dieker, 2001; Magiera et al., 2008; R. J. Simmons & Magiera, 2007). Dieker (2001) found in a study of nine pairs of teachers (seven pairs at the middle school level and two pairs at the high school level) that student outcome data were used during planning time to guide teachers' selection of the co-teaching support model to be implemented. Teachers valued this planning time and reported that "sanctity" of team planning time was essential to the co-teaching model.

The fifth step involves an examination of collaborative practices with or by an objective, independent evaluation team. This step is highly recommended by Salend and his colleagues (2002) as a useful balance to self-study and self-reflection. Salend et al. (2002) described various sources of evaluation data such as interviews, surveys, best practices checklists, observations, journals, and teaching portfolios to identify strengths and concerns of co-teachers. After reviewing the overall progress of the collaborative processes, the independent evaluation team (often including a higher-education partner) can help guide the school administrators' and teachers' next steps in the implementation process.

Consistent with M. J. McLaughlin's work (2002) on the usefulness of collaborative communities, Magiera, Smith, et al. (2005) found in their research that a strong learning community of administrators and special and general educators is the precursor to student success. Supporting co-teachers through ongoing administrative follow-up was key to implementing the co-teaching model with fidelity. Because of the community, co-teaching pairs were actually willing to take risks and more fully implement varied groupings in their classrooms for the benefit of all students, with and without disabilities (Magiera et al., 2008).

The final step for developing a quality collaborative process involves appropriately measuring student outcomes. Murawski and Swanson (2001) in their meta-analysis of co-teaching research found that in the limited number of studies in which teachers provided joint instruction and had common planning time, co-teaching had a positive impact on student achievement, particularly in reading and language arts. Future research in the area of co-teaching should examine the impact of the collaborative process on student achievement. However, while the ultimate goal of collaboration is overall improved student performance, Friend, Hurley-Chamberlain, and Cook (2006) caution against judging the value of a co-teaching service solely on the basis of student outcomes.

Another Perspective on Co-Teaching: Reconfigure the Dance

Collaboration among general and special educators is often described as a delicate dance enacted in a single classroom. Kloo and Zigmond (2008) provide yet another way of framing the co-teaching partnership. They delineate three broad "lesson configurations" made possible when two fully certified teachers are in the classroom co-teaching: (a) both teachers actively instructing a single group of students; (b) each teacher actively instructing their own group of students; and (c) neither teacher involved in group instruction (students working independently, working on group projects, watching a film, etc.). They argue that the purpose and content of the lesson should determine which of these configurations is used, not the preferences or teaching styles of the two teachers involved. Both teachers actively instructing a single group of students works well for teaching content subjects like literature, science, or the social studies. Each teacher actively instructing his or her own group of students fits well with the skills orientation of reading and math instruction. And if students are engaged in independent work, both teachers are mere observers.

Content Subjects: Two Teachers, One Instructional Group

In content subject classes, the norm is a single, whole-class lesson or assignment; classes in science, social studies, or English are generally characterized by large-group lecture or discussion followed by individual or small-group assignments or projects. Small-group *instruction* is not a common practice in content subject classes, particularly at the high school level (Zigmond, 2006; Zigmond & Matta, 2004). Kloo and Zigmond (2008), drawing on the extensive research base on effective instructional techniques for struggling learners, suggest that the job of the special education teacher in content subject instruction is to provide *S-U-P-P-O-R-T*, not only to the students with disabilities in the classroom but also to the general education partner (see Figure 9.2).

Study the Content

To support students' understanding of content, special education teachers should have a working knowledge of the curriculum. They must become familiar with the content or relearn concepts and principles of the subject

Figure 9.2 Activities of the special education teacher in a co-taught content subject class.

S-tudy the content.

U-nderstand the Big Ideas.

P-rioritize course objectives.

P-lan with the general education teacher.

O-bserve the students in the class as they listen to instruction.

R-ephrase, repeat, redirect.

T-each your co-teacher to do it all on her own.

being taught. This is, perhaps, one of the greatest challenges for special education teachers, particularly at the secondary level (Weiss & Lloyd, 2002). However, special education teachers need not become content experts in that classroom.

Understand the Big Ideas; Prioritize Course Objectives

General education teachers plan courses of study for content subjects using logic and experience to determine how much can be accomplished in one grading period, one semester, or one school year. Students with disabilities generally start each school year knowing less than their classmates, have more to learn, and take longer to learn it (Zigmond, 1996). The special education teacher should work collaboratively with the general education teacher to set priorities within the general education curriculum. The curriculum for students with disabilities, as well as for students without disabilities, is often focused on what will be assessed on the statewide test. For students with disabilities who already struggle to learn, the curriculum probably needs to be narrowed even more to allow time for teachers to teach high-priority content deeply and to ensure student mastery (Schumm, Vaughn, & Harris, 1997).

Plan with the General Education Teacher

Lack of co-planning time for special and general educators is one of the major obstacles to successful collaboration (Bauwens & Hourcade, 1995; Walther-Thomas, 1997). To be effective, co-teachers need to learn to work together so that each performs relevant and meaningful tasks that promote student learning (S. C. Trent, 1998). When co-teachers plan together, this agenda moves forward by identifying instructional responsibilities and possible accommodations for the students who will need them (Schumm et al., 1997).

Observe Students in Class as They Listen to Instruction; Rephrase, Repeat, and Redirect, as Needed

In content subject classes, special and general education teachers may take turns leading and supporting instruction. The supporting teacher (often the special education co-teacher) assumes the critical role of observing and evaluating students' learning. The special education teacher actively observes and "diagnoses" student engagement, interest, and understanding. At the first sign of student confusion, the special education teacher redirects the flow of instruction by elaborating and clarifying difficult concepts.

Teach Your Co-teacher to Do it All on Her Own

None of the advocates for co-teaching (e.g., Bauwens & Hourcade, 1995; L. Cook & Friend, 1996; Vaughn et al., 1997; Walther-Thomas et al., 2000) have proposed that co-teaching is a vehicle for training general education teachers to become strategy specialists, but we do. Part of the job of the special education co-teacher must be to make explicit to the general education partner the rationale for the accommodations provided in the IEPs so that, over time, the general education teacher can make appropriate accommodations decisions on her own.

Skill Subjects: Two Teachers, Two Instructional Groups

Educational researchers have long known that to increase students' learning of skill subjects like reading and mathematics, teachers need to increase students' opportunities to respond to and engage in the instruction (Shulman, 1985). In a co-taught classroom, two teachers are available to monitor student engagement and provide corrective feedback. As a result, Kloo and Zigmond (2008) suggest that when two teachers are in the classroom and a basic skills lesson is being taught (i.e., reading, writing, spelling, mathematics), the job of the special education teacher would be to *T-E-A-C-H* (see Figure 9.3). Small-group instruction, rather than whole-class instruction, should be the norm with increased use of parallel teaching, station teaching, or alternative teaching.

Target the Skills and Strategies a Particular Student Needs to Learn

Ample evidence indicates that most students with disabilities in general education classrooms are far behind their peers in the mastery of basic skills and are unlikely

Figure 9.3 Activities of the special education teacher in a co-taught skills-based class.

T-arget the skills and strategies a particular student needs to learn.

E-xpress enthusiasm and optimism.

A-dapt the instructional environment.

C-reate opportunities for small-group or individual, direct, intensive instruction.

H-elp student apply skills learned to content classes.

to benefit from large-group skill instruction moving at a normal pace (Thurlow, Altman, & Vang, 2009). These students are also unlikely to cover the entire curriculum for that grade level in the time available (U.S. Department of Education, 2007). Kloo and Zigmond (2008) recommend that the special education teacher in a co-taught class help target the skills and strategies a particular student with a disability needs to learn and, in collaboration with the general education teacher, help set curricular priorities.

Express Enthusiasm and Optimism

Students with disabilities need to work longer and harder than students without disabilities. However, the learning environment and their own learning histories often prevent them from investing vigorously in their learning (Guthrie & Davis, 2003; Margolis & McCabe, 2004). F. J. Brigham, Scruggs, and Mastropieri (1992) demonstrated that a teacher's positive attitude, high expectations, and high levels of enthusiasm can turn around students' negative reactions to learning. Brigham et al. taught each of two classes using both enthusiastic and unenthusiastic presentations in a cross-over design in which each classroom received both presentation styles in counterbalanced order. After 2 weeks of enthusiastic and unenthusiastic teaching, they reported that students learned more and had been on task more when enthusiastic teaching variables were employed. Additionally, independent observers viewing randomly selected videotape segments rated students much higher on learning and motivations variables when those students were taught in the enthusiastic condition.

Adapt the Instructional Environment

General education classrooms are often noisy and confusing settings, not conducive to focused, intensive, teacher-directed instruction. One major drawback to the inclusive classroom may well be the high level of distraction (J. Baker & Zigmond, 1995). Special education teachers in co-taught classrooms must take the lead in adapting the instructional environment, the seating arrangements, and the instructional dynamics to maximize instructional outcomes for students with disabilities.

Create Opportunities for Small-Group or Individual, Direct, Intensive Instruction

Students with disabilities need to learn more in less time in order to make up lost ground (Tomlinson, 1999). The special and general education teachers should collaborate to create opportunities for small-group or intensive teacher-directed instruction. In a review of the research literature, Vaughn and colleagues conclude that small groups produce better learning outcomes than whole-class instruction by increasing students' opportunities for responding and for receiving corrective feedback (S. Vaughn, Hughes, Moody, & Elbaum, 2001).

Help Students Apply Skills Learned to Content Classes

Multiple research studies have shown that students with disabilities often fail to apply effective learning strategies across relevant learning contexts but can be taught to do so. For example, Chan and Cole (1986) taught 11-year-old students with LD to remember what they read by learning to ask a question about the text and/or underline interesting words in the text. Schumaker and Deshler (1992) build explicit instruction for generalization into their learning strategies teaching model so that teachers will facilitate student application of a newly learned strategy in other academic and nonacademic settings. This is an important role for the special education teacher in a co-taught skills class.

Kloo and Zigmond (2008) contend that efforts to evaluate the effectiveness of co-teaching on student learning outcomes will be fruitless until teachers understand more precisely what they are supposed to be doing and researchers can be assured of some fidelity of treatment implementation in their research designs. Although Kloo and Zigmond provide a research base to support each component in their TEACH/SUPPORT suggestions, it is important to remember that to date no empirical data support the effectiveness of their service-delivery model.

Conclusion and Directions for Future Research

Co-teaching should be planned deliberately and implemented dynamically. It should also marry the science of specially designed instruction and effective pedagogy with the art of reorganizing resources.

Developing collaborative skills among co-teachers requires a strategic process involving administrators and co-teaching partners. Based on empirical data collected in case studies of six exemplary schools, Caron and McLaughlin (2002) suggest that co-teaching helps to foster a strong "professional community" (p. 307) by building capacity among school personnel that will ensure that collaborative partnerships are sustained over time. In McLaughlin's introduction to the special issue of the *Journal of Educational and Psychological Consultation* that reports on the Beacons of Excellence research projects, she observes that, when co-teaching is implemented well, the impact can be far greater than that of two individual teachers simply sharing a common task (M. J. McLaughlin, 2002).

Large-scale, long-term research is needed that explicitly defines co-teaching practices and carefully monitors fidelity of implementation. Ideally, also needed are controlled experimental research designs using random assignment to co-taught and solo-taught comparison classrooms to examine academic and behavioral outcomes for students with disabilities.

Co-teaching is an example of a service that has been embraced by some researchers and practitioners as a solution to the problem of access and mastery of the general education curriculum by students with disabilities. However, the research base is limited in its support of effective co-teaching instruction. Future research must uncover the collaborative practices that lead to "added value" in the educational experiences of students with disabilities.

PART 2

Research-Based Strategies for Improving Outcomes in Behavior

Research-Based Strategies for Improving Outcomes in Behavior

CHAPTER 10

Positive Behavior Support: *A Framework for Preventing and Responding to Learning and Behavior Problems*

Kathleen Lynne Lane | *University of North Carolina, Chapel Hill*

Holly Mariah Menzies | *California State University, Los Angeles*

Wendy P. Oakes and **Jemma Robertson Kalberg** | *Vanderbilt University*

eachers, administrators, and support staff working in K–12 school systems are confronted with a number of responsibilities. For example, they are expected to teach highly rigorous content; ensure that all students make adequate yearly progress academically; serve an increasingly diverse student population; support students with exceptionalities in inclusive environments; and teach social and behavioral competencies necessary to maintain a safe, positive climate (Kauffman, 2010; Lane, Kalberg, & Menzies, 2009; MacMillan, Gresham, & Forness, 1996; No Child Left Behind Act, 2001). The last objective is particularly formidable, given the rise of antisocial behavior among our nation's youth, which is reflective of the growing incivility of society as a whole (H. M. Walker, 2003). For example, a national survey on school crime and safety found that violent incidents were reported by 75.5% ($n = 62,600$) of schools surveyed, with a total of 1,332,400 violent acts in one school year (Neiman & DeVoe, 2009). Further, 20,260 acts were student threats of physical attack with a weapon. In 2007, students ages 12 to 18 were more likely to become a victim of a nonfatal crime at school (1.5 million) than

away from school (1.1 million; Dinkes, Kemp, & Baum, 2009). It is not surprising that many school-site personnel feel overwhelmed and challenged, particularly when it comes to managing student behavior (Lane, Menzies, Bruhn, & Crnobori, 2011).

National estimates suggest that between 3% and 6% of school-age students have emotional and behavioral disorders (EBDs), with less than 1% of students meeting the inclusionary criteria necessary to qualify for services under the Individuals with Disabilities Education Act (IDEA, 2004). Consequently, it is the job of the general education community to identify and support students with and at risk for EBD. Students with EBD include individuals with externalizing (e.g., aggression, coercion, noncompliance, delinquency), internalizing (e.g., anxiety, social withdrawal, depression), and comorbid conditions. Clearly, teachers are more apt to notice students with externalizing behaviors, because their behavior patterns often impose safety concerns and impede the teacher's ability to deliver instruction—posing significant challenges to the educational environment (Kauffman & Brigham, 2009; H. M. Walker, Ramsey, & Gresham, 2004). For example, in a recent national survey, 34% of teachers reported that student behavior interfered with their teaching (Dinkes et al., 2009). In fact, such challenging behavior is a major determinant in teachers' decisions to leave the field of education (Brouwers & Tomic, 2000; L. Harris, 1991; Martin, Linfoot, & Stephenson, 1999).

Not only does student behavior affect instruction, but teachers themselves are victims of student violence. Teachers of secondary (8%) and elementary (7%) schools report being victims of violent threats, whereas elementary teachers are more often (6%) attacked by students than are secondary teachers (2%; Dinkes et al., 2009). Many schools have increased safety procedures to address such trends. For example, 99% of schools require visitors to sign in, 90% maintain locked and monitored facilities, 43% have electronic procedures for alerting the building and community of a threat, 55% monitor safety with security cameras, and 55% require adults to wear security badges with photos. These procedures also serve as daily reminders of the potential safety threats to students and teachers. Thus, concerns surrounding school safety are warranted, and attempts to address these concerns are evident. Although teachers and support staff may not have expected that they would be responsible for addressing social and behavioral considerations in addition to academics, this is clearly the case (Lane, Kalberg, & Menzies, 2009).

During the last 10 years, a number of legal and legislative mandates have been established that require schools to establish safe, nonviolent environments. For example, Title IV of Improving America's Schools Act of 1994, The Safe and Drug-Free Schools and Communities Act (1994), called for states and local educational agencies (LEAs) to design school-wide violence and drug abuse prevention programs (A. Turnbull et al., 2002). Title IV may have also prompted the zero-tolerance policy for drugs and weapons that was also included in the IDEA (1997). In addition, the White House issued a charge calling for systemic changes to guarantee a safe, nonviolent environment for all students (Dwyer, Osher, & Warger, 1998; Kern & Manz, 2004). To this end, the Surgeon General's *Report on Youth Violence* offered the following recommendations to address antisocial behavior that occurs in schools: (a) eliminate antisocial networks, (b) boost students' academic performance, (c) establish prosocial school climates, and (d) adopt a primary prevention agenda that focuses on designing, implementing, and evaluating prevention efforts (Satcher, 2001). IDEA (2004) includes parallel language specifying "incentives for whole-school approaches, scientifically based early reading programs, positive behavior interventions and supports, and early intervening services to reduce the need to label children as disabled in order to address the learning and behavioral needs of such children" (p. 4). Thus, the expectation is clear: schools need to establish safe, nonviolent environments to facilitate both instruction and the personal safety of all individuals (students, faculty, and staff; American Psychological Association [APA] Board of Educational Affairs Task Force on Classroom Violence Directed Against Teachers, 2011).

To meet this charge, many school sites and districts across the country have adopted three-tiered models of prevention that are grounded in systemic change and data-based decision making to better meet students' academic, behavioral, and social needs. A variety of models have been developed such as (a) positive behavior support (PBS) models (Lewis & Sugai, 1999; Sugai & Horner, 2002), which, initially, focused predominantly (if not solely) on behavior; (b) Response to Intervention (RtI; Gresham, 2002b; Sugai, Horner, & Gresham, 2002) models, which focus mainly on meeting students' academic needs and providing alternative methods of identifying students for special education services under the specific learning disabilities category; and (c) integrated, comprehensive, three-tiered (CI3T) models that include features of PBS and RtI models, with a goal of supporting students' combined academic, behavioral, and social needs. We contend that integrated models pose particular benefit, given that academic and behavioral concerns do not appear in isolation, but rather interact to influence one another—a transactional relation mediated by many other variables (e.g., teacher–student interactions [see Chapters 12 and 13, this volume], social competence [see Chapter 16, this volume], and instructional techniques [see Part 1, "Research-Based Strategies for Improving Outcomes in Academics," Chapters 1 through 9 of this volume], Lane & Wehby, 2002).

The concept of three-tiered models is not new; they originated in the mental health industry and were adapted to provide a new delivery of instructional and behavioral support in the educational system (Lane, 2007). One of the main theoretical benefits of such models, particularly for students with and at risk for EBD, is that they ideally provide a seamless delivery of increasingly intensive supports (a) to prevent the development of learning and behavioral problems through the use of primary prevention (Tier 1) supports and (b) to respond to existing learning and behavioral problems through the use of secondary (Tier 2) and tertiary (Tier 3) supports. No longer are learning and behavioral challenges viewed solely as within-child problems. Instead of traditional models that require students to fail before supports can be offered, three-tiered models subscribe to a proactive, instructional approach to provide the necessary level of supports based on individual student needs within this larger prevention framework (R. H. Horner & Sugai, 2000; Lane, Robertson, & Graham-Bailey, 2006). Ideally, school-wide data collected as part of regular school practices are used to determine which students may benefit from secondary and tertiary efforts. These decisions are made by leadership teams who meet regularly to engage in this data-based decision-making process.

In this chapter we write to both practitioner and researcher audiences. We begin by describing an integrated, comprehensive three-tier model of prevention that includes key features of PBS and RtI models, *not* with an emphasis on identifying students for special education services, but with a focus on meeting the academic, behavioral, and social needs of students. Specifically, we describe each level of prevention—primary, secondary, and tertiary—with an emphasis on primary prevention efforts. We conclude the chapter by offering a summary of the strengths of the model as well as areas for improvement in future inquiry.

Primary Prevention: Building a Comprehensive Base Program

At the base of a three-tiered model is the primary prevention component, which can be referred to as school-wide, universal, or Tier-1 prevention. Tier 1 has no screening or eligibility determinations: *all* students participate just by virtue of attending school (Lane, Kalberg, & Edwards, 2008). The intent of Tier-1 support is to *prevent harm* from occurring by providing a support that is accessed by all students (H. M. Walker & Severson, 2002). This same logic is evident in a medical model. For example, in a medical model, parents may elect to have their children receive a vaccination for the flu. The intent of receiving the vaccine is to *prevent* their children from getting the virus.

Ideally, in a school-based model, prevention would include three core components: academic, behavioral, and social. Specifically, the school-site leadership team would construct a primary prevention plan that addresses each of these three components. For example, an elementary-level team may select the Scott Foresman reading program (see www.sfreading.com) as the base curriculum to teach reading and the Second Steps Violence Prevention Program (SSVP; Committee for Children, 2007) as their social skills component. Strong evidence bases support the feasibility and efficacy of each program to increase academic performance and decrease problem behaviors, respectively (e.g., Frey, Hirschstein, & Guzzo, 2000; S. D. McMahon & Washburn, 2003; Wehby, Lane, & Falk, 2005).

The team may decide to design its own school-wide positive behavior support (SW-PBS) program for the behavioral component. This would involve establishing school-wide expectations for behavior (e.g., respect, responsibility, and best effort) that are operationally defined in all relevant settings (e.g., hallways, bathrooms, classrooms, cafeterias, buses, drop-off and pick-up areas; see Table 10.1 for an example of an expectation matrix). We recommend using a data-based method of identifying those expectations that faculty and staff view as essential for students' success (Lane, Kalberg, & Menzies, 2009). One method is to have school-site personnel rate the importance of the 30 social skills items specified on the Social Skills Rating System (SRSS; Gresham & Elliott, 1990). Rather than rating each item for each individual student, teachers and staff rate the extent to which each item is essential for student success in their class (e.g., *listens to instructions*, *makes assistance needs known in an appropriate manner*). Each item is rated on the same 3-point Likert-type scale as specified in the manual: 0 (*not important*), 1 (*important*), or 2 (*critical*). Then, these data can be analyzed using frequency counts to determine which items are rated by the majority (>50%) of faculty and staff as critical for success (rated as a 2). This information is used to construct the teacher-expectation matrix (see Lane, Kalberg, & Menzies, 2009, for additional details on the planning process).

After the expectations are established and all adults (e.g., administrators, teachers, custodians, secretaries) in the building have reached consensus, the next step is to teach these expectations explicitly to students. This can be done through school-wide lessons and other instructional activities (e.g., posting of expectations, videos, assemblies). Then, students should be afforded opportunities to practice and receive reinforcement for meeting these expectations. The reinforcement typically occurs by allocating PBS tickets that are delivered intermittently in response to students exhibiting target behaviors and are paired with behavior specific praise (J. O. Cooper, Heron, & Heward, 2007). Students then exchange these tickets for secondary reinforcers that allow students to access (positive reinforcement) or avoid (negative reinforcement) attention (e.g., lunch with a teacher); activities, tasks, or tangibles (e.g., homework pass); and sensory experiences (e.g., listen to music during independent seat work; Lane, Kalberg, & Menzies, 2009; Umbreit, Ferro, Liaupsin, & Lane, 2007).

Assessment Considerations

When implementing such a model, it is important to monitor all aspects of the program including treatment integrity, social validity, and student performance. In the

Table 10.1   Sample Expectation Matrix for Use at the Elementary Level

	Settings					
	Classroom	*Hallway*	*Cafeteria*	*Playground*	*Bathroom*	*Bus*
Respect	Follow directions. Use kind words and actions. Control your temper. Cooperate with others. Use an inside voice.	Use a quiet voice. Walk on the right side of the hallway. Keep hands to yourself.	Use an inside voice. Use manners. Listen to and follow adult requests.	Respect other peoples' personal space. Follow the rules of the game.	Use the restroom, and then return to class. Stay in your own bathroom stall. Little talking.	Use kind words toward the bus driver and other students. Listen to and follow the bus driver's rules.
Responsibility	Arrive to class on time. Remain in school for the whole day. Bring your required materials. Turn in finished work. Exercise self-control.	Keep hands to yourself. Walk in the hallway. Stay in line with your class.	Make your choices quickly. Eat your own food. Choose a seat, and stick with it. Clean up after yourself.	Play approved games. Use equipment appropriately. Return equipment when you are done. Line up when the bell rings.	Flush toilet. Wash hands with soap. Throw away any trash properly. Report any problems to your teacher.	Talk quietly with others. Listen to and follow the bus drivers' rules. Remain in seat after you enter the bus. Use self-control.
Best Effort	Participate in class activities. Complete work with best effort. Ask for help politely.	Walk quietly. Walk directly to next location.	Use your table manners. Use an inside voice.	Include others in your games. Be active. Follow the rules of the game.	Take care of your business quickly. Keep bathroom tidy.	Listen to and follow the bus drivers' rules. Keep hands and feet to self.

Source: Information from Walker, H. M., Ramsey, E., & Gresham, F. M. (2004). *Antisocial behavior in school: Evidence-based practices* (2nd ed., p. 138). Belmont, CA: Wadsworth.

sections that follow, we define each of these constructs and discuss issues of measurement and relevance.

Treatment Integrity

Treatment integrity refers to the extent to which the plan is implemented as intended (Gresham, 1989; Yeaton & Sechrest, 1981). Treatment integrity is an essential, but often omitted, measure (see Lane, Kalberg, Bruhn, Mahoney, & Driscoll, 2008). If treatment integrity data are not collected, we cannot establish that the plan actually occurred as intended. Consequently, we cannot be certain that the change in students' performance (or absence of changes) was the result of the intervention effort or some other extraneous variables (e.g., the introduction of hall monitors, which was not in the original plan).

Monitoring the integrity of school-wide plans is challenging, particularly in middle and high schools,

because the buildings are larger and the number of persons involved (e.g., teachers and students) is greater than elementary settings. Nonetheless, if a school-site leadership team or research team wants to draw accurate conclusions regarding the effect of primary prevention efforts on student outcomes, treatment integrity must be measured. Some methods of measurement include teacher self-reports using behavioral checklists with intervention components specified; outside observers (e.g., research assistants, behavior specialist, principal) completing behavioral checklists; and teacher self-reports of the same period for which the outside observer is present, with a comparison of the two perspectives used as coaching information (see Lane, Kalberg, Bruhn, et al., 2008, for a detailed explanation of how to collect and use treatment integrity data collected using these perspectives).

Standardized measures such as the School-wide Evaluation Tool (SET; Sugai, Lewis-Palmer, Todd, & Horner,

2001) can also provide treatment integrity data. The SET includes 28 items that make up seven key features of SW-PBS (R. H. Horner, Todd, Lewis-Palmer, Irvin, Sugai, & Boland, 2004). Specifically, subscales measure the degree to which the following occur: (a) school-wide behavior expectations are defined; (b) school-wide expectations are taught to all students and rewards are provided for meeting school-wide behavior expectations; (c) a consistently implemented continuum of consequences for problem behavior is utilized; (d) problem behavior patterns are monitored, and the data are used as part of ongoing decision-making; (e) an administrator actively supports and is involved in the SW-PBS program; and (f) the district provides support to the school (e.g., functional policies, staff training opportunities, and data collection; Horner et al., 2004). Each item is scored on a 3-point Likert-type scale ranging from 0 (*not implemented*), to 1 (*partially implemented*), to 2 (*fully implemented*). Subscale summary scores are formed by computing the percentage of possible points for each of the seven key features. An overall summary score is computed by averaging the seven subscale scores. The SET has strong psychometric properties (alpha coefficient of 0.96; Horner et al., 2004).

In addition to assisting with the interpretation of intervention outcomes, data collected using each of these techniques can be used to inform the coaching process. Specifically, treatment integrity data can assist school-site leadership team members in identifying those features of the plan that are and are not being implemented as designed. For example, a core construct of a reinforcement plan is to pair the delivery of the reinforcement (e.g., a ticket) to students with behavior-specific praise that is tied to school-wide expectations. If a leadership team finds, through the use of the SET, that faculty and staff are giving the reinforcer (tickets) but are unable to state the school-wide expectations, the leadership team may want to provide a refresher for faculty on the expectations and provide examples with practice in using behavior-specific praise (e.g., "Sarah, you have earned a ticket for being responsible in remembering your homework today").

One factor that may influence teachers' level of implementation integrity is their perceptions of the plan, or social validity. Namely, if teachers believe that a plan targets meaningful goals, has reasonable procedures, and is likely to "work," they may be more likely to implement the plan as designed—with treatment integrity.

Social Validity

Social validity refers to the social significance of the goals, the acceptability of intervention procedures constituting the plan, and the social importance of the effects (either expected or actualized; Kazdin, 1977; Lane & Beebe-Frankenberger, 2004; M. M. Wolf, 1978). When monitoring the social validity of a primary prevention plan, we recommend administering measures of social validity (either formally or informally) before implementing a school-wide model, and again following each year of implementation. In 2002, the Intervention Rating Profile-15 (Witt & Elliott, 1985) was modified for use with primary-level interventions. In an initial validation study of the modified version, the Primary Intervention Rating Scale (PIRS; Lane, Robertson, & Wehby, 2002) was found to be a one-factor measure with high internal consistency in elementary, middle, and high school settings with alpha coefficients of 0.97, 0.98, and 0.97, respectively (Lane, Kalberg, & Menzies, 2009). Furthermore, site-level mean scores on the PIRS predicted mean levels of treatment integrity (measured using a teacher-completed behavioral checklist) during the first year of implementation ($r = 0.71$, $p = 0.005$), suggesting that high social validity may promote treatment integrity. Additional studies are necessary before using the PIRS on a wide-scale basis.

Social validity data collected before implementation can provide important information that educators can use to identify areas of concern and subsequently modify a plan before implementing it. And (as indicated previously) the data may predict the extent to which the intervention is implemented as intended. Social validity data collected after the first year of implementation can be used to inform revisions. Educators should remain mindful of the fact that primary prevention plans should not be modified during an academic year if the school would like to evaluate the extent to which the plan is associated with changes in student outcome measures. In other words, if the plan continually shifts throughout a school year, it is not possible to evaluate it accurately. Essentially, the plan becomes a moving target. It is more effective to wait until the end of each academic year to collect social validity data from teachers, students, and parents to inform revisions that can occur before the onset of the next academic year (see Lane, Kalberg, & Menzies, 2009, for a more detailed explanation). The intent of each revision is to ensure that the plan is customized to the ever-changing community of students that the school serves, with an overall goal of creating an environment that facilitates learning. This is accomplished by creating a context that is safe for all students (physically, intellectually, and otherwise), so that students are motivated and encouraged to take risks to extend their learning. To determine if these lofty goals are achieved, it is necessary to measure students' performance in order to inform ongoing refinement of the primary prevention plan as well as to monitor each individual student's performance.

Student Performance

To monitor student performance, school-wide data collected as part of regular school practices are used to monitor (a) overall level of performance for the school or grade levels as a whole and (b) how individual students respond over time to identify those students who may need more assistance. Table 10.2 shows a sample assessment schedule that features school-wide data such as curriculum-based measures to monitor academic performance (AIMSweb; Pearson Education, 2008), attendance (unexcused tardies and absences), office discipline referrals (ODR), behavioral screeners (Systematic Screening for Behavior Disorders [SSBD], H. M. Walker & Severson, 1992), and referrals to counseling. When determining which measures to include in an assessment schedule, it is important to attend to issues of reliability, validity, and feasibility. For example, data should be accurate in terms of measurement and practical, given the constraints of the school day.

ODRs, for instance, are a frequently used outcome measure in SW-PBS, in large part due to the feasibility of collecting this data (e.g., takes limited teacher time, already is required by the district; e.g., Clonan, McDougal, Clark, & Davison, 2007; K. McIntosh, Campbell, Carter, & Zumbo, 2009). However, without using specific procedures to ensure the consistency with which ODR and other school-based outcomes are measured, reliability of the data can be problematic; the school's overall level of risk and the identification of students for secondary or tertiary supports therefore may not be accurate (Lane, Kalberg, Bruhn, et al., 2008; J. R. Nelson, Benner, Reid, Epstein, & Currin, 2002). For example, use of a system such as the School-Wide Information System (SWIS; S. May et al., 2000) is important to ensure that the procedures are clear for determining which behaviors do and do not warrant an ODR (minor or major offenses). Furthermore, ensuring that such a system is implemented as planned

Table 10.2   Sample Elementary School Assessment Schedule

Measure	Aug	Sept	Oct	Nov	Dec	Jan	Feb	Mar	April	May
Report cards and progress reports		X		X		X			X	
Writing assessment		X			X				X	
Curriculum-based measures (CBMs)	X	X	X	X	X	X	X	X	X	X
State-wide assessment										X
Office discipline referrals (ODRs)	X	X	X	X	X	X	X	X	X	X
Student Risk Screening Scale (SRSS; Drummond, 1994)		X			X				X	
Systematic Screening for Behavior Disorders (SSBD; H. M. Walker & Severson, 1992a)		X			X				X	
Attendance	X	X	X	X	X	X	X	X	X	X
Counseling referrals	X	X	X	X	X	X	X	X	X	X
Bullying referrals	X	X	X	X	X	X	X	X	X	X
Social Validity Survey: Primary Intervention Rating Scale (PIRS; Lane, Robertson, & Wehby, 2002)		X							X	
School-wide evaluation tool (SET; Sugai, Lewis-Palmer, Todd, & Horner, 2001)		X							X	
Treatment integrity: self-report and direct observations by an outside observer	X	X	X	X	X	X	X	X	X	X
Rate of access to reinforcement (PBS Tickets)		X							X	
Effective behavior supports (EBS; Sugai, Horner, & Todd, 2000)		X							X	

Source: Information from Lane, K. L., Kalberg, J. R., & Menzies, H. M. (2009). *Developing schoolwide programs to prevent and manage problem behaviors: A step-by-step approach* (p. 105). New York, NY: Guilford Press.
Note: PBS = positive behavior support.

(with procedural fidelity) is also necessary, so that the school-site leadership team can be certain that the data are reliable and that the decisions made based on these data are valid.

Concerns about the reliability and validity of ODR data have prompted some researchers and practitioners to choose validated systematic screening tools such as the SSBD, the Strengths and Difficulties Questionnaire (SDQ; R. Goodman, 1997), the Student Risk Screening Scale (SRSS; Drummond, 1994), the Behavior and Emotional Screening System (BESS; Kamphaus & Reynolds, 2007), and the Social Skills Improvement System: Classwide Intervention Program (SSiS; S. N. Elliott & Gresham, 2007). These measures have strong psychometric properties suggesting that they accurately identify students who do and do not exhibit the characteristics of the behavior pattern of interest (e.g., externalizing or internalizing; SSBD). It is beyond the scope of this chapter to provide a complete discussion of the features, psychometric properties, strengths, and limitations of each screening tool. However, this information is presented elsewhere (see Lane, Menzies, Oakes, & Kalberg, 2012).

These screening tools can be administered at multiple times during an academic school year such as 4 to 6 weeks after the onset of the school year, before winter break, and before year end. Data from these time points within and across school years can be compared to examine how the level of risk shifts over time within a building. Also, these data can be used either in isolation or in conjunction with other data (e.g., curriculum-based measure [CBM] data or course failures) to identify specific students who might benefit from secondary and tertiary supports as provided by the school's three-tiered

model of prevention. For example, consider the SDQ, a factor analytically derived tool with different versions for different age groups and different raters. It is designed to assess students' (ages 3 to 17) strengths and deficits in sociobehavioral domains (R. Goodman, 2001; R. Goodman, Meltzer, & Bailey, 1998). The SDQ contains teacher-completed, parent-completed, and self-report forms (ages 11 to 17, only) available at no cost. When teachers complete the SDQ, they complete one page for *each* student in their class, rating each student on the 25 items constituting the SDQ on a 3-point, Likert-type scale (*not true* = 0, *somewhat true* = 1, *certainly true* = 2). These items are equally distributed across five factors: emotional symptoms, conduct problems, hyperactivity, peer problems, and prosocial behavior. Subscale scores range from 0 to 10, with high scores indicating higher degrees of risk for the first four factors, and higher prosocial skills for the final factor (prosocial behavior). The total score ranges from 0 to 40, which includes the first four factors. Each subscale as well as the total score place students into one of three discrete categories: normal, borderline, or abnormal.

Figure 10.1 shows SDQ data from the hyperactivity scale. In Panel A, Fall 2006 and Winter 2007 data are presented for an elementary school serving students in grades K–4 (Lane & Eisner, 2007). When the primary prevention program was initially implemented, 76.80% of the students in the school scored in the normal range on the hyperactivity subscale score, with 3.61% placing in the borderline range, and 19.59% placing in the abnormal range. By the winter SDQ administration (approximately 3 months later), the overall student body showed improvement, as evidenced by an increase in the percentage of students placing in the normal category (82.32%) and a decrease

Figure 10.1   Strength and Difficulties Questionnaire (SDQ) data.

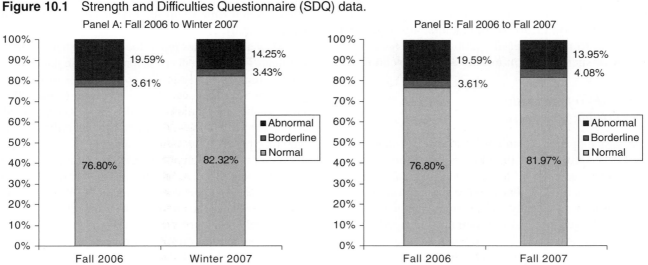

Source: Data from Lane K. L., & Eisner, S. (2007). *Behavior screening at the elementary level.* Paper presented at Metropolitan Nashville Public Schools. Nashville, TN.

in the students placing in the abnormal category (14.25%). The school-site team can use these data in conjunction with other data (e.g., CBMs) to (a) identify students for secondary interventions, and (b) inform the selection of secondary supports. For example, the students still scoring in the abnormal category on the hyperactivity who also fall below the CBM benchmark for their grade level may benefit from secondary interventions to, for example, improve oral reading fluency (e.g., repeated readings; Chard, Ketterlin-Geller, Baker, Doabler, & Apichataburta, 2009) and academic engagement (e.g., self-monitoring; Mooney, Ryan, Uhing, Reid, & Epstein, 2005).

Behavior screening can also be used to examine the overall level of risk evident in a building over time (Lane, Kalberg, Bruhn, et al., 2008). For example, Figure 10.1, Panel B, illustrates SDQ hyperactivity scores from Fall 2006 to Fall 2007. These data also suggest improvements; however, it is imperative not to draw causal conclusions from such descriptive analyses. This is an important point and is one we will return to when we consider the research that examines the impact of primary prevention efforts.

Supporting Literature

Since the late 1990s, an extensive body of research has been developed that examines the utility of primary prevention efforts that include behavioral supports in elementary, middle, and high school settings. To date, more cases of primary prevention efforts have been documented in elementary settings than in middle and high school settings. However, the standard for SW-PBS was developed in middle schools (Gottfredson, Gottfredson, & Hyble, 1993; G. R. Mayer, Butterworth, Nafpaktitis, & Sulzer-Azaroff, 1983). While findings of systematic literature reviews can be found elsewhere, we highlight a few features of the studies conducted to date. See Lane, Kalberg, and Edwards (2008) for a systematic review of primary prevention efforts at the elementary level, and see Lane, Robertson, et al., (2006) for a systematic review of such efforts in middle and high schools.

Methodological Design and Student Outcomes

The vast majority of studies conducted to date have used descriptive rather than experimental procedures. Numerous studies provide illustrations or case studies of implementation over one or more years. Given that the school is the unit of analysis, random assignment should occur at the school level in group design experimental studies. However, very few studies have used random assignment when assigning schools to either treatment or comparison conditions (e.g., T. D. Cook et al., 1999;

Stevens, De Bourdeaudhuij, & Van Oost, 2000). In some instances, school administrators selected treatment and comparison schools (Gottfredson et al., 1993; Sprague et al., 2001), with the lack of a formal experimental comparison acknowledged as a weakness of the study. Similarly, efficacy and scaling up studies of SW-PBS are highly limited. To date Horner and colleagues (R. H. Horner et al., 2009) are the only research team to have conducted a randomized, wait-list controlled trial to examine the impact of primary prevention efforts (SW-PBS) at the elementary level. In this study, training and technical assistance in SW-PBS were provided by state personnel over a 3-year period in Hawaii and Illinois. Results suggested that improved use of SW-PBS was functionally related to improvements in the perceptions of school safety and the proportion of third-grade students who met or exceeded state standards for reading performance.

According to studies conducted to date, primary prevention programs have been associated with improved student behavior. For example, at the elementary level, results suggested decreases in ODRs, suspensions, and expulsions (e.g., McCurdy, Manella, & Eldridge, 2003; J. R. Nelson, 1996; J. R. Nelson, Martella, & Galand, 1998; T. M. Scott & Barrett, 2004; Todd, Haugen, Anderson, & Spriggs, 2002). In addition, evidence indicates improvement in school climate (Netzel & Eber, 2003) and academic skills (Ervin, Schaughency, Goodman, McGlinchey, & Matthews, 2006). Similar findings are noted in middle and high school settings. Specifically, school-wide interventions with primary prevention components that included a behavioral emphasis exhibited decreases in ODRs (Lohrmann-O'Rourke et al., 2000; Metzler, Biglan, Rusby, & Sprague, 2001; Taylor-Greene et al., 1997; Taylor-Greene & Kartub, 2000), detentions (Luiselli, Putnam, & Sunderland, 2002), physical and verbal aggression (Metzler et al., 2001), and noise in hallways during lunch time (Kartub, Taylor-Green, March, & Horner, 2000).

Only a few studies report the use of systemic screening data. This is a concern given that these data can be used to reliably (a) assess the overall index of the level of risk present at a school site over time (Lane, 2007; Lane, Kalberg, Bruhn, et al., 2008; Lane, Kalberg, et al., 2011; Lane & Menzies, 2005) and (b) identify students who may benefit from targeted supports (e.g., secondary or tertiary intervention efforts; Cheney, Blum, & Walker, 2004; Kalberg, Lane, & Menzies, 2010; Kalberg, Lane, & Lambert, 2012; Lane et al., 2003; Lane, Wehby, et al., 2002; B. Walker, Cheney, Stage, & Blum, 2005).

Overall, results of these investigations suggest that primary prevention efforts improve behavior and, to a lesser extent, school climate and academic performance. Although it is very important to avoid drawing causal conclusions from correlational or descriptive research, evidence suggests that primary prevention programs are associated with positive impacts on school climate and students' outcomes.

Treatment Integrity

Another factor to consider when interpreting the research on primary prevention efforts is the presence or absence of treatment integrity. For the reasons we discussed previously, this is a critical feature of all intervention research. In a systematic review of primary prevention at the elementary level (Lane, Kalberg, & Edwards, 2008), only five of the 19 studies reviewed monitored and reported treatment integrity results (Ervin et al., 2006; Leff, Costigan, & Power, 2003; Marr, Aduette, White, Ellis, & Algozzine, 2002; McCurdy et al., 2003; Sprague et al., 2001). Similar findings were noted in a parallel systematic review of primary prevention efforts in middle and high schools. Specifically, only 5 of the 14 studies reviewed measured treatment fidelity; 3 used team or teacher surveys or reports (T. D. Cook et al., 1999; Gottfredson et al., 1993; Sprague et al., 2001), 1 used parent phone interviews (Cook et al. 1999), and 1 used process measures (Metzler et al., 2001). Direct observation techniques rarely have been used to monitor treatment integrity of primary prevention efforts (Lane, Kalberg, Bruhn, et al., 2008; Lane & Menzies, 2002, 2003). It is encouraging to note, however, that several investigators reported the absence of treatment integrity data as a limitation (Colvin, Sugai, Good, & Lee, 1997; Leedy, Bates, & Safran, 2004; Lewis, Powers, Kelk, & Newcomer, 2002; Lewis, Sugai, & Colvin, 1998; J. R. Nelson, 1996; J. R. Nelson et al., 1998; J. R. Nelson, Martella, & Marchand-Martella, 2002; T. M. Scott, 2001; T. M. Scott & Barrett, 2004). Clearly, the field recognizes the importance of treatment integrity and is aware that the absence of this information limits the internal and external validity of findings (Gresham, Gansle, & Noell, 1993; Lane, Kalberg, & Menzies, 2009).

Social Validity

Another noteworthy construct in this literature is social validity. Yet, like treatment integrity, studies infrequently have attended to this construct. A few studies at the elementary level have mentioned and reported social validity from the teacher perspective (Ervin et al., 2006; Leff et al., 2003; McCurdy et al., 2003; J. R. Nelson, 1996; Nelson, Martella, et al., 2002; Todd et al., 2002). However, parent and student views were not considered. A few studies implemented in middle and high school settings have attended to social validity from teacher, students, and/or parent view points (e.g., Gottfredson et al., 1993; Kartub

et al., 2000; Metzler, Biglan, Rusby, & Sprague, 2001; Taylor-Green et al., 1997; Taylor-Green & Kartub, 2000). In addition, some studies (e.g., T. D. Cook et al., 1999) have actually measured and reported social validity from all three perspectives.

In sum, this growing body of research points to several important considerations for both practice and research. It appears evident that time and resources spent on designing and implementing primary prevention plans can result in positive outcomes for schools and students. Additionally, primary prevention is appropriate for all levels of schooling, although less evidence supports its utility at the high school level. As new studies are conducted, increased emphasis should be put on random assignment, measuring treatment integrity, and assessing social validity. Improving the methodological rigor of studies will provide more reliable and valid information that enhances the decision-making abilities of school personnel.

Secondary Prevention: Targeted Supports for Students Who Need More

Approximately 80% of the student body is likely to respond to primary prevention efforts (Gresham, Sugai, Horner, Quinn, & McInerney, 1998; Sugai & Horner, 2006). However, such global prevention efforts are not expected to meet all students' needs. Consequently, secondary supports that have the potential to *reverse harm* (H. M. Walker & Severson, 2002) should be in place. In other words, a school site needs to have supports available for students who are identified with low-level concerns but who have not responded adequately to the primary prevention program. Such concerns may pertain to academic performance (e.g., poor oral reading fluency), limited social interactions (e.g., difficulty interacting with peers during unstructured activities), and interfering behavioral problems (e.g., verbal aggression toward peers and adults). Secondary supports typically include small-group, whole-class, or other low-intensity strategies, some of which you will read about in subsequent chapters.

Some secondary supports include services that are currently available at many school sites such as social skills groups led by school counselors, divorce recovery groups led by school psychologists, homework clubs led by paraprofessionals during after-school care, or Tier-2 reading interventions led by the classroom teacher during a regularly scheduled literacy block. Other secondary supports may be more formalized interventions such as the Behavior Education Program (Crone, Horner, & Hawken, 2004; Hawken, MacLeod, & Rawlings, 2007) or high-intensity academic interventions such as self-regulated strategy development for writing (K. R. Harris, Graham, Mason, & Friedlander, 2008). Other secondary supports can address both academic and behavioral domains, such as behavior contracts (Downing, 2002) and self-monitoring strategies (Mooney et al., 2005). Still others may focus on shaping teacher behaviors with an emphasis on low-intensity strategies such as active supervision; effective instructional techniques (e.g., proximity, withitness, appropriate use of praise, providing opportunities to respond, instructive feedback); and use of high-engagement strategies such as offering choice and preferred activities (Lane, Menzies, et al., 2011).

The remaining chapters in Part 2, "Research-Based Strategies for Improving Outcomes in Behavior," present a wide range of strategies for secondary prevention. For example, in Chapter 11, Jolivette, Alter, Scott, Josephs, and Swoszowski present three strategies to prevent and respond to problem behaviors that include choice making, precorrection, and self-management. In Chapter 12, Sutherland and Wright introduce three strategies to improve academic engagement: increasing students' opportunities to respond, improving teachers' use of praise, and the Good Behavior Game. Davis and McLaughlin, in Chapter 13, introduce compliance training and high-probability requests to improve students' compliance. And in Chapter 16, Gresham, Libster, and Menesses introduce three strategies to improve students' social competence: social skills training, replacement behavior training, and positive peer reporting. These strategies are designed to reverse harm by providing additional supports (either by shaping teacher behavior or introducing more student-directed practices) to meet students' individualized needs via low-to-moderately intensive procedures.

Secondary support practices should be grounded in research, with the ultimate goal of implementing practices that are evidence based (e.g., Self-Regulated Strategy Instruction Development for Writing; K. R. Harris et al., 2008). Evidence-based practices are those that have been rigorously studied to suggest that they are effective for use with a particular group of students when delivered by a designated professional (or paraprofessional) within a given context; or as Mark Wolery would say, who is doing what to whom and under what conditions (Lane, Wolery, Reichow, & Rogers, 2006).

Recently, much discussion has surfaced in the literature about how to determine whether a practice is evidence based (see Gersten, Fuchs, Compton, Coyne, Greenwood, & Innocenti, 2005, and R. H. Horner, Carr, Halle, McGee, Odom, & Wolery, 2005, for a discussion of determining evidence-based practices using group design and single-case methodologies, respectively). To determine whether a practice is evidence based, reviewers evaluate research studies on a practice, examining whether each study meets indicators of methodological quality associated with trustworthy research. Reviewers then determine whether a sufficient number of high-quality research studies support the practice as causing meaningfully improved student outcomes. For example, Horner et al. require that five high-quality single-case studies support a practice as effective for it to be considered evidence based.

In our work with school-site teams interested in designing, implementing, and evaluating three-tiered models of prevention, we encourage schools to develop secondary intervention grids that contain a master list of all secondary supports available at their school site (see Table 10.3). Then, the school-site leadership team (a) describes the service, including who will implement the support, under what conditions, and information regarding "dosage" (i.e., how long and how often the service is implemented); (b) identifies how students will be identified for possible participation; (c) specifies how treatment integrity data will be monitored to ensure implementation; (d) delineates how data will be collected and monitored to determine how secondary support shapes student performance; and (e) states the criteria for terminating the service.

Central to this model is accurate identification of which students may benefit from extra support. For this reason, we highly recommend the use of reliable behavior and academic screening tools to determine which students need support. Table 10.2 includes an example of the various screening measures that were collected at a school site as part of regular school practices. Curriculum-based measures were used to monitor academic performance, and attendance data were collected to look for problems with truancy or tardiness. Other measures were implemented so that the school could collect systematic data on student behavior. For example, although the school kept records of ODRs, they decided to also administer the SSBD (H. M. Walker & Severson, 1992a) so that they would have additional, and perhaps more reliable, data about students' individual behavior.

Another benefit of this model is that it provides a forum for conducting scientific inquiry using group (e.g., Lane, Harris, et al., 2011; Kalberg et al., 2012) and single-case research designs (Lane, Wehby, Menzies, et al., 2002, 2003) to examine how well these intervention efforts support students (Lane, 2007). Within the context of this applied research model, the teaching community benefits from on-site supports and the research community benefits from gaining knowledge regarding the effects of interventions in applied contexts. The same benefits apply to the next level of prevention—tertiary supports.

Table 10.3 Secondary Intervention Grid: Elementary Level

Support	Description	School-wide Data: Entry Criteria	Data to Monitor Progress	Exit Criteria
Study Skills Group	Identified students meet 3 days a week during the enrichment block, in which 30-min lessons are taught focusing on study skill strategies. This group can be run by teachers, trained parent volunteers, or paraprofessionals in a designated classroom, an office, or in the school library or cafeteria.	• Report cards: earned a "needs improvement" score on study skills or a C− or lower in any academic content area, or • Below proficient on curriculum-based measures, or • Scored in the bottom quartile on standardized state assessments.	• Weekly grades collected by the teacher (accuracy percentage) • Weekly completion collected by the teacher (percentage of assignments completed)	Complete the program when they: (a) demonstrate mastery of study skills taught on a criterion-referenced assessment, and (b) weekly teacher records reflect a minimum of 80% accuracy and 90% work completion over a 3-week period.
Behavior Education Program (BEP; Crone, Horner, & Hawken, 2004)	The BEP is designed for students with persistent behavior concerns that are not dangerous. The BEP provides a daily check-in/check-out system that helps teachers provide students with (a) immediate feedback on their behavior by completing a Daily Progress Report (DPR) and (b) additional opportunities for positive adult interactions. Parents participate by signing off on daily sheets.	Academic and Behavioral Concerns: *Academic* • Report cards: earned a "needs improvement" score on study skills or a C− or lower in any academic content area, or • Below proficient on curriculum-based measures, or *Behavioral* • Behavioral Student Risk Screening Scale (SRSS) score in the moderate risk range, or • Systematic Screening for Behavior Disorders (SSBD) score exceeding normative criteria on externalizing, or internalizing behavior on Stage-2 rating scales	Daily progress-monitoring forms collected by teacher and viewed by parent might note what is monitored (e.g., an operationally defined target behavior)	Move into the maintenance self-monitoring phase when they meet their goals for 3 consecutive weeks. Self-monitoring phase ends when the next academic reporting period and behavior rating results indicated the absence of risk following the same criteria stated in the inclusion criteria.
Incredible Years Training for Children	This curriculum builds skills in anger management, school success, and interpersonal problem solving. It is delivered as a "pull out" for small groups in a designated classroom or office. (See *Blueprints for Violence Prevention* www.colorado.edu/cspv/index.html for further details.)	• Scored in the moderate risk range on the SRSS with a 2 or higher on item 4 (peer rejection) or 5 (low achievement), or • 2 or more bullying referrals turned in, or • 3 or more major office discipline referrals (ODR)	• Information pertinent to elements of intervention are established, then collected and analyzed (e.g., results of social skills training, academic tutoring) by teacher.	• Students complete the curriculum components and then are assessed and compared to initial inclusionary criteria. • Students exit if they score in the low-risk range on the SRSS during the next systematic screening period and do not receive bullying referrals or ODRs for 3 consecutive weeks during the same rating period.

(continued)

Table 10.3 Secondary Intervention Grid: Elementary Level (*continued*)

Support	Description	School-wide Data: Entry Criteria	Data to Monitor Progress	Exit Criteria
Social Skills Group	Identified students meet 3 days/week during the enrichment block for 30-min lessons focused on improving specific social skills deficits. Students meet with school psychologist or interns 2 days/week for 30-min lessons for 10 weeks in the student's specific areas of concerns (see Lane et al., 2003; M. J. Miller, Lane, & Wehby, 2005). This group would be held in a designated classroom or office.	Behavioral Concern: *Internalizing Group* • SSBD score exceeding normative criteria on internalizing behavior on Stage-2 rating scales, or • 1 or more unexcused absences or 3 or more unexcused tardies during the first 6 weeks of school. *Externalizing Group* • SSBD score exceeding normative criteria on externalizing behavior on Stage-2 rating scales, or • 1 or more office discipline referrals for major offenses during the first 6 weeks of school.	School Psychologist monitor: *Internalizing Group* • Daily attendance patterns • Daily social interactions on the playground *Externalizing Group* • Daily discipline records • Daily social interactions on the playground	Concludes the social skills group when (a) teacher-completed SSRS (Gresham & Elliott, 1990) scores indicate average performance on the social skills and problem behavior subscale scores and (b) the SSBD scores collected during the next behavior rating period indicate the absence of risk.

Source: Information from Lane, K. L., Kalberg, J. R., & Menzies, H. M. (2009). *Developing schoolwide programs to prevent and manage problem behaviors: A step-by-step approach* (pp. 130–131). New York, NY: Guilford Press.

Tertiary Prevention: Increased Intensity

Tertiary supports are the most intensive level of prevention offered within the three-tiered model and are designed to *reduce harm* (H. M. Walker & Severson, 2002). Approximately 3% to 5% of the student body is likely to require tertiary supports because they will have (a) not responded to primary prevention or secondary prevention efforts as measured by school-wide data, (b) been repeatedly exposed to multiple risk factors that place them at heightened risk for school failure, or (c) experienced both these conditions (Kern & Manz, 2004). Such interventions are highly ideographic in nature and must be customized to meet an individual student's comprehensive needs.

Examples of tertiary prevention efforts include both process and programmatic supports such as function-based interventions (Umbreit et al., 2007); the First Step to Success program (see Chapter 15, this volume); the Multisystemic Therapy program (MST; Henggeler, 1998); and highly intensive, individualized reading interventions (e.g., Clarke-Edmands, 2004; Wilson, 2000). Because not all students experience externalizing issues, it is also important to have tertiary supports in place for students who have internalizing issues. To this end, Kern, Hilt-Panahon, and Mukherjee (Chapter 14, this volume) discuss three research-based supports to address internalizing behaviors (i.e., cognitive behavior therapy, anxiety management/relaxation training, and pharmacological intervention) that teachers can use as tertiary interventions.

As with secondary supports, we recommend that school-site teams establish tertiary intervention grids to delineate the supports available for students who require this level of prevention. The same procedures we described for establishing secondary intervention grids should be followed. Again, we contend that it is important to design, implement, and evaluate tertiary supports that are grounded in research. Given the investments that these supports require in terms of personnel and student time, money, effort, and otherwise, it is essential to make wise decisions when establishing the scope of these services at each school site. We encourage the use of *only* evidenced-based practices (as previously described) for tertiary supports to ensure the (a) best possible outcomes for students in the greatest need of intervention and (b) most efficient use of teacher and other school-site personnel's time. Likewise, it is paramount that these supports include the necessary features in terms of intervention design (e.g., control features that ensure that the intervention, and not other variables [e.g., introduction of a student teacher], was responsible for changes in students' behavior); outcome measures (reliable, valid, clearly defined); treatment integrity; and social validity to ensure that accurate conclusions can be drawn in terms of intervention outcomes (R. H. Horner et al., 2005). If the student does respond to the tertiary intervention and attains the desired behavior, then she may return to the primary plan in isolation or perhaps receive a secondary support (e.g., behavioral contract) to promote maintenance of the new behavior. If the student does not respond to the plan, then a different tertiary support may be necessary, or perhaps a referral to determine special education eligibility may be warranted.

Summary: Strengths and Considerations

As we conclude this chapter, we highlight some strengths as well as areas to consider as educators seek to improve comprehensive, three-tiered models of prevention. First, this systemic approach focuses on the school as the unit of change (and the unit of analysis) allowing school-site personnel to establish an integrated approach that addresses school-wide, class-wide, and noninstructional areas of concern, as well as individual student needs (Sugai & Horner, 2006). One benefit of this model is that this approach moves away from viewing problems as "within the child" and instead views concerns from an integrated, systemic approach.

Second, this integrated model includes a continuum of supports based on individual student needs. Central to this model is a data-driven approach to preventing and responding to learning and behavioral challenges. Specifically, it is imperative that educators make accurate decisions about which students may benefit from targeted intervention, whether secondary or tertiary levels of prevention. Movement between these levels of prevention should not be arbitrary and instead should be guided using data-based decision procedures involving reliable, valid measures. For example, rather than making decisions on which students need behavioral supports using ODR data, we recommend using measures with documented reliability such as behavior screening tools. Furthermore, we recommend analyzing data from academic screening tools (e.g., CBM) and behavioral screening tools (e.g., SSBD) in conjunction with one another to obtain a complete view of students' individual needs. A concern we hold is that too often the decision-making process can be incomplete when decisions are made using (a) measures that lack sufficient psychometric properties to yield accurate decisions and (b) data that reflect only one dimension of student functioning (e.g., ODRs in isolation from academic performance data) to obtain a view of students' needs.

Third, we view this model as being particularly beneficial for students with and at risk for EBD (Lane, 2007). While many teachers enter the field of education fully expecting to work with students who struggle to meet academic expectations, teachers often feel less prepared to identify and support students with behavioral challenges (Schumm & Vaughn, 1995). Specifically, some teachers need additional training in a range of strategies that include low-intensity strategies (e.g., choice making and increasing opportunities to respond), moderate-intensity (e.g., behavioral contracts and self-monitoring techniques), and functional assessment-based interventions (Umbreit et al., 2007) to prevent and respond to problem behavior, with an ultimate goal of facilitating instruction (Lane, Menzies, et al., 2011). Teachers need this full continuum of supports in order to adequately, and quickly, meet the needs of students who require more intensive assistance. This integrated three-tiered model provides a structure and context that supports teachers to work with all students—including those with behavioral challenges, who may or may not have academic deficits as well (Lane, 2007).

Fourth, this model also provides an incredibly useful forum for conducting additional scientific inquiry. We are encouraged that the research and teaching communities are beginning to capitalize on this opportunity by conducting scientifically rigorous studies using group and single-case methodologies to examine the additive benefit of academic and behavioral supports when implemented as secondary prevention efforts within the context of three-tiered models of prevention. For example, Karen Harris, Steve Graham, and colleagues have begun to explore the relative benefits of self-regulated strategy development in writing for students with behavior concerns as a secondary support in the elementary school settings (e.g., Sandmel et al., 2009). Jemma Kalberg and colleagues have explored the utility of social skills and conflict resolution strategies for middle school students with low academic performance and combined behavior concerns (Kalberg et al., 2012; Robertson & Lane, 2007).

And Doug Cheney and colleagues have examined the effects of addressing social domains within a three-tiered RtI model for elementary students at risk for developing EBD (Cheney, Flower, & Templeton, 2008). These efforts are particularly encouraging given that until relatively recently the secondary prevention efforts had received somewhat limited attention within the three-tiered model of prevention. Moving forward, it will be important to explore the feasibility and effectiveness of these supports in the absence of university assistance. However, at this time, a strong partnership between school sites and university-supported projects are providing (a) service to the local school systems and (b) a venue for scientific inquiry for university personnel.

Finally, the research community has offered several guidelines for conducting high-quality studies in order to identify evidence-based practices that can support school-personnel in their day-to-day activities (Gersten et al., 2005; R. H. Horner et al., 2005). However, too often these standards are not met when conducting applied investigations at the school-site level. Consequently, we encourage research teams to ensure that procedures are clearly articulated, with clear specification of the responsibilities involved for all key parties, for each level of prevention. Furthermore, student performance data should be collected for primary, secondary, and tertiary levels of prevention using reliable, valid measures to monitor the behaviors (academic, social, and behavioral) targeted for change. In addition, treatment integrity and social validity data should be collected and examined to assist in interpreting intervention outcomes so that they may subsequently be used to revise intervention efforts.

In sum, comprehensive, integrated, three-tiered (CI3T) models of prevention have many valuable features. These models provide an important framework for meeting students' multiple needs in a respectful, efficient, data-driven fashion. We encourage the continued exploration of these models, with particular attention to (a) improving the methods by which students are identified for additional supports and (b) the rigor with which we test the utility of secondary supports implemented within the context of this model.

CHAPTER 11

Strategies to Prevent Problem Behavior

Kristine Jolivette | *Georgia State University*

Peter Alter | *Saint Mary's College of California*

Terrance M. Scott | *University of Louisville*

Nikki L. Josephs | *Xavier University of Louisiana*

Nicole C. Swoszowski | *The University of Alabama*

R esearchers and classroom practitioners alike are focusing on changing environmental variables so that student inappropriate behaviors become irrelevant, ineffective, and inefficient (R. H. Horner, 2000), while student appropriate behaviors become more relevant, effective, and efficient within their environment. The effects of problem behavior within the classroom, community, and home negatively affect students, peers, and adults. Such effects include (a) increased adult time dealing with inappropriate behavior, (b) lost valuable instructional time for both student and peers, (c) disruption to family routines within the home, and (d) problems assimilating into the community.

The purpose of this chapter is to describe richly, from less to more intrusive, three specific behavioral strategies used to prevent and reduce problem student behavior in school, community, and home settings. These three strategies are pre-correction, choice making, and self-management. Each strategy has literature bases that vary in their extensiveness to address student problem behavior. We discuss the definitions and theoretical framework, steps for implementation, brief literature review, and future directions for each strategy.

Pre-Correction

The intervention strategy of pre-correction is perhaps the simplest application of the statement, "If we can predict problem behavior, we can prevent problem behavior." Setting students up to succeed by providing brief reminders of desired behavior can be an effective method to stop challenging behaviors before they start or develop into a pattern. For many adults who work with students who engage in problem behavior, this strategy is one they have used often, even when they did not know what to call it. By being aware of emerging behavior patterns, adults can be in the position to "stop it before it starts." For example, a teacher who notices that a group of students excludes a specific peer during free time may mention right before free time begins, "Don't forget, it is important to play with everyone and to treat each other respectfully." This prompt, in essence, pre-corrects the problem behavior of exclusion by providing a reminder of expectations.

Definition and Theoretical Framework

Pre-correction is defined as "an antecedent instructional event designed to prevent the occurrence of predictable problem behavior and to facilitate the occurrence of more appropriate replacement behavior" (Colvin, Sugai, & Patching, 1993, p. 145). In other words, pre-corrections are brief prompts, often verbal questions, statements, or gestures, directed to a student or group of students just before the students enter a context in which predictable problem behaviors often occur (e.g., "We are about to line up for lunch. What are you going to do with your hands and feet?"). Pre-corrections specify the desired behavior (which is typically incompatible with the problem behavior) in close temporal proximity to environments that are predictive of these problem behaviors. By using pre-correction right before the problem context, teachers can increase the probability of students' success (e.g., student engages in the desired behavior rather than the problem behavior) for two reasons. First, the reminder of appropriate behavior is fresh in the student's mind as he initiates the task. Second, the pre-correction alerts the student that the teacher will be monitoring his behavior.

Grounded in the theoretical underpinnings of a wide range of disciplines including school-wide positive behavior support (SW-PBS; Lewis, Colvin, & Sugai, 2000), prevention science, and applied behavior analysis, pre-correction is one of the least-intrusive prevention strategies available. Moreover, it is efficient. The efficiency of the use of pre-correction is that by preventing the error before it occurs, the step of "unlearning" the wrong way to do something and relearning the right way to do it is simplified through pre-correction. Students are prompted to do it correctly the first time.

Pre-correction has four key features. First, pre-correction is *predicated on accurate prediction.* Clearly, no one can identify all of the contexts that precede problem behavior, but in both theory and process the need for accurate prediction is clear: by anticipating the inappropriate behavior in advance of its occurrence, we can provide prompts that will direct students to use a more appropriate behavior instead. To anticipate the problem behavior, it is helpful to make note of when problem behaviors occur, the environments in which they occur, and the antecedents of the behaviors. Synthesizing such information over time allows us to notice patterns in responding. Once you have established a pattern (e.g., talking loudly in the hallways, touching others when lining up for recess, complaining after being given directions to get out one's math book, entering class late), you can

use pre-correction questions, statements, and/or gestures to proactively prompt the appropriate behavior.

Second, pre-correction is *simple.* It is brief; effective pre-correction does not require long drawn out exchanges between teacher and student. Rather, it is a quick verbal question, brief statement, or succinct gesture that identifies the desired replacement behavior. Fading pre-corrective statements to more subtle forms, such as signals or environmental cues, is an important element to using this process effectively. If a teacher can use a brief gesture (e.g., a finger pressed to the lips to remind the student of the behavioral expectation in the hallways) rather than having to use verbal statements (e.g., "Silence in the hallways"), then pre-correction becomes even more efficient and effective.

Third, pre-correction is used *consistently to enforce rules, routines, and procedures.* The use of pre-correction to model and enforce expectations should be as predictable as the occurrences of the problem behavior. Predictability allows students consistent instruction and, over time, helps in fading the overt prompts to more subtle forms. The brief question of "What are you going to do with your hands and feet when we line up?" asked consistently can soon become the teacher's simply modeling having their hands to their sides until students often reach a point where they say, "I know, I know, keep my hands and feet to myself when we line up." Consistent implementation leads to fading and ultimately self-enforcement of the rule by students.

Fourth, if pre-correction is ineffective in curbing problem behavior, it can certainly be *combined with other more intensive interventions or abandoned.* Action is implicit in the name "pre-correction." If prompting questions, statements, or gestures do not stop or "correct" problem behaviors before they become apparent, then pre-correction has not occurred, and the intervention should be modified or discarded. Steps for implementation capture these four key features and lead to the use of an efficient and effective process.

Steps to Implementing Pre-Correction

Figure 11.1 presents the effective use of pre-correction as a step-by-step process summarized by Colvin et al. (1993). The steps that follow are an expanded version of that checklist and include an example of effective implementation.

First, *identify the predictors within various contexts and environments* that lead the student or students to engage in problem behavior. A number of effective tools for predicting patterns of challenging behavior have been developed largely as a result of work in the area of functional behavior assessment. Although some

Figure 11.1 Essential steps in implementing pre-correction.

1. Identify the predictors within various contexts and environments that lead the student or students to engage in problem behavior.

2. Identify the predictable problem behavior and the desired replacement behavior.

3. Ensure that the desired replacement behavior is in the student's repertoire by teaching and conducting rehearsals.

4. Provide a prompt regarding the appropriate replacement behavior at the appropriate time just before the behavior is warranted.

5. Listen to the student's response and assess accuracy.

6. When the student engages in the appropriate replacement behavior, provide reinforcement to ensure future occurrences of the same behavior.

7. Collect data on the occurrences of desired behaviors and occurrences of problem behavior.

8. When behavior is occurring at an acceptable rate, fade pre-corrects to be less frequent and more subtle.

Source: Information from Colvin, G., Sugai, G., & Patching, B. (1993). Pre-correction: An instructional approach for managing predictable problem behaviors. *Intervention in School and Clinic, 28*, 143–150.

instruments focus only on the function or what environmental events occur *after* the problem behavior, many others also include measures to determine what occurs *before* the problem behavior. These tools include direct observation-recording devices such as scatter plots and Antecedent-Behavior-Consequence (ABC) worksheets, as well as indirect measures such as the Functional Analysis Interview (FAI; O'Neill et al., 1997) and the Functional Assessment Checklist for Teachers and Staff (FACTS; R. March et al., 2000). Predictors of problem behavior may be related to time of day, type of activity (or a specific activity), proximity of specific people (other students and adults,) or just proximity of people in general. For example, based on an analysis a teacher might identify that, "Student pushes, trips, and hits others on the way to lunch line-up each day."

Second, *identify the predictable problem behavior and the desired replacement behavior.* The desired replacement behavior is often a behavior that is incompatible with the problem behavior. That is, the student cannot engage in the problem behavior while performing the desired replacement behavior. Questions to guide what the replacement behavior should look like may include, "What do other students do in this situation?" and "What does the teacher want the process to look like?"

An identified replacement behavior for the pushing, tripping, and hitting problems may be, "Walk to the line and stand with hands and feet to self in single file."

Third, *ensure that the desired replacement behavior is in the student's repertoire by teaching and conducting rehearsals.* Teachers can use modeling, role-plays, and guided practice to ensure that the student understands what behavior the teacher is looking for from the student. This instruction needs to be explicit. Teaching the desired behavior within the context that it occurs (e.g., teach appropriate behavior for clearing lunch trays in the cafeteria rather than the classroom) will increase its salience and therefore its effectiveness. For example, the teacher may talk to students about how to line up and allow practice with feedback. The teacher can instruct students to role-play examples of the appropriate replacement behavior such as keeping hands to yourself and respecting other people's personal space, while the teacher role-plays the problem behavior.

Fourth, *provide a prompt regarding the appropriate replacement behavior* at the appropriate time just before the behavior is warranted, such as asking the student a question about what behavior is expected. Rhode, Jenson, and Reavis (1992) identify a number of variables that will increase compliance when providing these types of prompts including having close proximity to the student, using a quiet voice, and giving the student an opportunity to respond appropriately before repeating the prompt. For example, the prompt may be, "It's almost lunch time. When we line up today, what will you do?"

Fifth, the teacher should *listen to the student's response and assess accuracy.* If the student responds correctly, the teacher has an opportunity to provide positive, specific praise for the appropriate response, such as, "You're right! Keep your hands to yourself when we line up. Good for you!" Also, this statement cues the student that praise will be available again if she engages in the correct behavior (Conroy, Sutherland, Snyder, Al-Hendaawi, & Vo, 2009). Increasing rates of praise is one effective practice teachers may use to increase future occurrences of desired behaviors. If the student does not respond correctly, the teacher should use this as an opportunity to briefly re-teach and emphasize the important characteristics of the desired replacement behavior. Feedback for an incorrect response may be, "Think again. Your hands will be at your sides and kept to yourself. Where are your hands going to be when I give the direction to line up?"

Sixth, when the student engages in the appropriate replacement behavior, it is vital that the teacher *provide reinforcement to ensure future occurrences of the same behavior.* A consideration of function can help in providing the student with equivalent outcomes for the desired appropriate behavior, making the problem behavior inefficient, ineffective, and irrelevant. For example, if the student's goal is to get to lunch quickly, a similar outcome would be that good line-up behavior moves the student to the front of the cafeteria line and poor line-up behavior does not allow the student to be at the front of the line.

Seventh, it is important for teachers to *collect data on the occurrences of desired behaviors and occurrences of problem behavior*. The teacher should bear in mind the number of times the student was in the context that was predictive of problem behavior and view these as opportunities. This number of opportunities becomes the denominator, and the number of either successful or unsuccessful behaviors will become the numerator for calculating the percentage of positive or negative behaviors occurring in relation to the opportunities for response. This way a teacher can systematically determine the effectiveness of the use of pre-correction on the student's behavior. For example, the data may indicate that the *student lines up correctly 95% of the opportunities available*, which may be determined as satisfactory.

Eighth, now that the behavior is occurring at an acceptable rate, the teacher can *fade these pre-corrects* to be less frequent and more subtle. For example, the teacher may give a pre-correction reminder only every other time the behavior should occur or move from verbal questions to a hand gesture or a quick nod. Decreasing the student's need for overt pre-corrects increases student independence and allows an opportunity to be increasingly more self-directed about his behavior. For example, right before lunch time, the teacher makes eye contact with the student and quickly models keeping hands by your side. The teacher then gives the direction to line up for lunch.

Pre-Correction as an Intervention for Students with Problem Behavior

To accurately describe the research base of pre-correction, we need to clarify terminology. *Pre-correction* is the application of an instructional strategy to remediate problem behaviors through prompts. A large body of research supports the use of prompts as a strategy to help strengthen students' ability to discriminate when a response is required to help prevent academic or behavioral errors. In fact, the use of prompts could be described as one of the foundational strategies of applied behavior analysis (see Wolery & Gast, 1984, for a review). Yet, using the term *pre-correction* to describe the use of prompts may make the literature base supporting this practice seem artificially thin. Ultimately, although pre-correction may be broadly considered as the use of prompts to prevent problem behavior, the prescriptive nature with which pre-correction is described in initial

articles including the seven-point checklist (Colvin et al., 1993) may indicate its more specific use and application. Thus, this literature review is restricted only to empirical research articles that use the term *pre-correction* (or *precorrection*) and describe primary research using pre-correction strategies to address problem behaviors. A total of six articles met these criteria. The pre-correction articles are described in terms of participants and settings, level of support, and the effect of the intervention on outcome measures.

Although pre-correction can be implemented for increasing positive behavior or for reducing problem behavior, all six studies reviewed for this chapter described the reduction of problem behaviors as a result of the prescribed intervention package (i.e., pre-correction was one aspect of the package). For example, one study used office discipline referrals (ODRs) as the outcome measure (Haydon & Scott, 2008), while the other five used problem behaviors that are best summarized in the description by Stormont, Smith, and Lewis (2007) as "off-task, oppositional, disruptive, aggressive and other types of externalizing behavior" (p. 283). Most of these studies reported decreases in problem behaviors from baseline to intervention. For example, Haydon and Scott reported decreases from 77 ODRs during baseline to 12 with the use of pre-correction, and Lewis, Sugai, and Colvin (1998) produced a decreasing trend in problem behaviors during transitions using pre-correction (but not an overall meaningful level change for the other settings).

Pre-correction can be effective in a variety of settings. Five of the six studies reviewed occurred in elementary schools, and the sixth (Stormont et al., 2007) was implemented at a Head Start center. Four of the six studies targeted whole schools as the populations for change, with a range of 110 to 475 students, and the pre-correction intervention occurred in a variety of settings including recess (Lewis et al., 2000; Lewis et al., 1998), cafeteria (Lewis et al., 1998), and morning gym (Haydon & Scott, 2008), and in the doorways and hallways during transitions (Colvin, Sugai, Good, & Lee, 1997; Lewis et al., 1998). One study targeted a single sixth-grade classroom ($N = 26$) (Depry & Sugai, 2002), and one study targeted three small-group learning activities with seven or nine students in the group ($N = 25$) (Stormont et al., 2007).

Research has also shown that pre-correction is a relatively easy and efficient intervention to implement. For all reviewed studies, the teachers and other school staff (e.g., paraprofessionals) served as the implementers of the intervention and were trained in relatively short amounts of time, with an average of 2 hours of training. In some examples, pre-correction was included as part of a larger training such as a 2-day workshop on

School-wide Positive Behavior Support (Lewis et al., 1998) and always as one part of a multi-pronged intervention package. For one study, feedback on the use of pre-correction was provided throughout the intervention (Stormont et al., 2007), but for all other studies, researchers simply collected baseline data, provided training for school practitioners, and collected data during the intervention phase. Three of the six studies identified the ease and efficiency of training teachers how to use pre-correction as a strength of the intervention and a rationale for its continued use.

Future Research Directions

Pre-correction is a strategy grounded in research regarding the use of prompts to effectively elicit desired behaviors when initial discriminative stimuli are ineffective at transferring stimulus control. However, as an identified strategy used and applied in classrooms, a dearth of evidence supports the application of this practice alone. Due to this shortage, future research is warranted. Specifically, future research should investigate the effectiveness of pre-correction with students of various ages with specified variables regarding setting, cultural and linguistic diversity, exceptionality, and other demographics. Such information would provide evidence of the robust nature of intervention. Because most studies evaluated its effectiveness on generic problem behavior and ODRs, research focusing on more specific dependent variables is needed. Moreover, future research should investigate the effects of pre-correction as the sole intervention on a variety of problem behaviors, rather than as a part of an intervention package. Such investigations should also evaluate the fidelity of pre-correction implementation (Lewis et al., 2000) as well as the social validity of pre-correction as a school, home, or community strategy to address problem behavior.

Regardless of these future directions, pre-correction has shown to be a promising strategy used to prevent the occurrence of problem behavior. This strategy is cost-effective, easy to implement, and requires minimal training to implement. In addition, in its broad form as a behavioral prompt, it is a common practice that has been used in schools and homes. A second strategy used to address problem behavior, choice making, shares these same characteristics with pre-correction.

Choice Making

The extension of opportunities for students to make choices is a critical aspect of a high-quality education (F. Sigafoos & Dempsey, 1992), especially when students have histories of displaying problematic behaviors. In fact, some researchers have pointed to choice making as an important aspect of teaching and learning, and Bambara, Koger, Katzer, and Davenport (1995) even stated that "the absence of choice making can have a devastating effect on students' quality of life and emotional development" (p. 185). As intervention, choice-making strategies have demonstrated positive, clinical significance for students across ages, disabilities, and behaviors. As K. M. McCormick, Jolivette, and Ridgely (2003) suggested, "if you provide choices instead of demands, children are more likely to respond in a positive manner" (p. 8).

Shogren, Faggella-Luby, Bae, and Wehmeyer (2004) conducted a meta-analysis of 13 choice-making studies that used either task-order choice (choice of order of task to complete) or either/or choice (choice of two activities) to intervene with student problem behavior. They found that the intervention was effective overall, and the greatest effect was found for younger students (4- to 7-year-olds), for students with emotional and behavioral disorders, and for aggressive behavior.

Although the use of choice making has been shown to be an effective intervention, few studies have attempted to establish the naturally occurring rates of choice-making opportunities for students with and without disabilities typically available in most classroom situations (before manipulations of the number and types of choices provided). For example, during structured activities, Jolivette, Stichter, Sibilsky, Scott, and Ridgely (2002) observed the natural provision of choice-making opportunities provided to 14 students (seven with speech and language disabilities or developmental delay and the other seven at risk for school failure) ages 4 to 5 years old in a university-based preschool program. They found that choice-making opportunities were provided to the students with disabilities at a rate of 0.17 per minute and at a rate of 0.12 for those at risk. In addition, Jolivette, McCormick, McLaren, and Steed (2009) observed naturally occurring choice-making opportunities provided by an interdisciplinary team in two inclusive preschool classrooms with a total of 42 students, ages 2 to 3 years, who were typically developing, had disabilities, or were at risk for disabilities. They found that choices were provided at an overall rate of 0.51 per minute for 26 hours of observations. Differences in the types of choices, areas in the room in which choice was provided, and choice-delivery methods were observed across the interdisciplinary team members. Such differences may be due to the goal/objectives of the learning centers, team member purposefulness of the use and type of choice, and specific classroom conditions.

Establishing the rate of choice-making opportunities within a variety of educational settings and across ages is an important first step in understanding the natural occurrences of choice before intervention. Knowing the rates provides a context in which a researcher, teacher, or parent may manipulate the number, types, and complexity of choice-making opportunities as a means to improve behavior.

Definition and Theoretical Framework

The provision of a choice-making opportunity as a teaching or intervention method is simply the manipulation of existing variables such as items, task demands, situations, and reinforcers. Shevin and Klein (1984) defined choice as "the act of a student's selection of a preferred alternative from among several familiar options" (p. 160). For example, a teacher may say, "After you accurately complete the worksheet, would you like to listen to your CD, draw a picture, or read a book at your desk?" Such options are choices. Choice-making interventions may be conceptualized as a prevention method, as choices are typically provided before the occurrence of problem behavior based on known behavioral patterns. With choice making rooted in behaviorism and applied behavior analysis, choice making is an operant response as students indicate and access a preferred option, thus increasing rates of reinforcement (Morgan, 2006).

Steps to Implementing Choice Making

Most research studies implementing choice making as an intervention follow a similar set of steps, whether implicitly or explicitly stated, as suggested by J. Sigafoos, Roberts, Couzens, and Kerr (1993). The six steps, as summarized in Figure 11.2, include (a) offering, (b) asking, (c) waiting, (d) responding, (e) prompting, and (f) reinforcing.

Figure 11.2   Essential steps in implementing choice making.

1. Offer the student or group of students a choice of at least two options.
2. Ask the student or group of students to make a choice based on the options provided.
3. Wait for the student or group of students to make their choice.
4. The student responds.
5. Prompt the student to make a choice if, after waiting the predetermined amount of time, the student has yet to make a choice.
6. Reinforce the choice option, giving the selected item to the student.

After identifying a student or group of students for the choice-making intervention and selecting an environmental context for implementation, the teacher is ready to begin the first step. First, *offer* the student or group of students a choice of at least two options. An offer of a choice typically is provided through orally verbalizing a statement, signing the statement, or showing the actual options. For example, a teacher may say, sign, or indicate by holding up items in succession, "Do you want a, b, or c?" A combination of the offer method (e.g., verbalizing while holding up the two options) also can be used. The offer method depends on the developmental, cognitive, and communication skills of the students being provided with the choice. Additionally, the number of choice options extended will be influenced by the student's developmental and cognitive abilities as well as the learning objectives/goals within the context.

Second, *ask* the student or group of students to make a choice based on the options provided. The asking must be clear and concise so that the students can unmistakably understand their options. When extending more than two choice options, the specificity of the choice options becomes even more critical. For example, a teacher may provide a choice to a student with attention deficit hyperactivity disorder (ADHD) and say, "Would you like to use a mechanical pencil, a black pen, or blue gel pen (holding just these three in her hand) to write your spelling words?" This example highlights the exact options being offered free of other distractions. A nonexample would be to say, "Mechanical, black, or blue?" That question is not explicit or specific, and the student may not know the context of the statement or that a choice is being offered. In fact, the nonexample may inadvertently become an antecedent to further problem behavior from the student, because it could promote disengagement, discussion, negotiation, or noncompliance, leading to overall increased levels of off-task behaviors.

Third, *wait* for the student or group of students to make their choice. Typically, 5 to 10 seconds of wait time is provided per student to make a choice, although the specific wait time will depend on the student's or group's abilities. If administering choice-making opportunities to a small or large group of students, 5 to 10 seconds may be too intrusive to the learning environment. In this case, the teacher may provide a time construct within step two by adding a specific length of time for the students to respond. Also, teachers may conduct steps one and two with a small group of students to minimize the effects of student wait time on instructional time. For example, when working with a small group of students, the students should be purposefully grouped depending on ability (e.g., all students in the group typically take the same amount of time to respond), the choice offering and asking can be together, and the options the same for each member.

Fourth, the student *responds*. How students respond will vary based on their unique communication characteristics. For example, a student may orally verbalize or sign his selection; or gesture (e.g., nodding, blinking) toward, point to, or touch his selection. To illustrate, for a student with severe disabilities and limited communication skills who has a history of inappropriate behavior during meal times (e.g., food refusal, screaming), the teacher may provide a snack choice using the actual two options as prompts. With the two boxes directly in front of the student, the teacher orally states, "Do you want to have pretzels [while pointing to the pretzels and placing the student's hand on the box] or crackers [while pointing to the crackers and placing the student's hand on the box] for snack [orienting the student's hand in the middle of the two options]?" The teacher may repeat this option several times before removing physical guidance (depending on the student's communication abilities and styles) and waiting for the student to place his hand on one of the items.

Fifth, *prompt* the student to make a choice if, after waiting the predetermined amount of time, the student has yet to make a choice. It is possible that when choice is first introduced to a student, the student may not fully understand that he is permitted to exert control over the situation and make a selection. If a student does not make a choice within 10 seconds, then the teacher should provide steps one and two again. In some cases, it may be necessary to add to step two additional verbal, gestural, model, or physical assistance prompts to the student. For example, if a teacher has offered a choice (e.g., "Would you like to jump like a rabbit, walk like a person, or walk like a robot to lunch?"), asked for a response, waited a specified amount of time, and received no response, the teacher may offer additional assistance. In relation to the previous example, the teacher may also model what each option looks like—hopping, walking naturally, and walking in a stiff manner—before continuing with the steps.

Sixth, *reinforce* the choice option, giving the selected item to the student. This reinforcement should be immediate and match the item selected. As a caveat, some researchers have permitted students to change their minds about their initial choice option selection during the intervention session. If this is an option a teacher would like to extend to the student, then a statement indicating this needs to be part of step two. For example, the teacher might say, "Once you begin the task, if you change your mind and want to select one of these other choices, you may." This may be helpful to students who engage in problem behavior as a means to exert control over their environments. If the option to change one's mind is being offered, then the teacher needs to consider (a) how the student is to indicate this change of mind, (b) the repercussions of accepting partially completed

tasks (e.g., half-completed worksheets), and (c) how many times students may change their minds. Kern and State (2009) contend that even before the six steps to choice-making opportunities are implemented several tasks are necessary for the teacher to prepare the environment for choice:

> (1) create a menu of choices you would be willing to provide your students, (2) look through your choice menu before planning your lesson, (3) decide what types of choices are appropriate for your lesson, (4) decide where choice-making opportunities fit best in your lesson, (5) incorporate the choices you decided as appropriate into your lesson, and (6) provide the planned choices while delivering the lesson. (Kern & State, 2009, p. 5)

Once the steps have been successfully completed, the teacher can evaluate the student's performance across academic and social domains to determine whether choice making has resulted in improved academic or social behavior of the student. For example, a teacher may academically measure student performance on the number of problems attempted/completed, the accuracy of the work product, the time it took to complete the work product, and the overall quality of the product to judge the intervention effectiveness. Socially, the teacher may measure student performance on the percentage of on-task, off-task, disruptive, noncompliant, compliant, or aggressive behaviors and peer interactions. Whether measuring academic and/ or social student behavior during and after choice-making opportunities, it is critical to monitor the effectiveness of the choice-making interventions, because some students may not benefit from choice.

Choice-Making Interventions for Students with Problem Behaviors

Choice-making interventions and their effects on student problem behavior as well as academic and social deficits have been more widely investigated than pre-correction. In this section, we review the literature on choice making in relation to the variety of conditions (e.g., types of behavior, disability populations, age groups, and environments) in which it has been studied.

The provision of choice-making opportunities has been investigated across varying types of problem behavior. Investigations include measuring the effects of choice-making opportunities on (a) student task performance, attempted task problems, and problems correct (e.g., C. L. Cole & Levinson, 2002; Jolivette, Wehby, Canale, & Massey, 2001; Kern, Mantegna, Vorndran, Bailin, & Hilt, 2001); (b) off-task behavior, disruption, and noncompliance (e.g., Dunlap et al., 1994; Dyer, Dunlap, & Winterling, 1990; Jolivette et al., 2001; Romaniuk et al., 2002); (c) aggression (e.g., Haynes, Derby, McLaughlin, & Weber, 2002; Kern, Mantegna, et al., 2001;

B. Vaughn & Horner, 1997; see Chapter 15 in this volume for additional strategies to address aggression); (d) self-stimulation (e.g., Dattilo & Rusch, 1985); and (e) spontaneous speech (Dyer, 1987).

For example, Carlson, Luiselli, Slyman, and Markwoski (2008) investigated the effects of two clothing choices provided several times a day to address the disrobing and incontinence behaviors of a 13-year-old female with autism and a 5-year-old male with pervasive developmental disorder. The decision to provide clothing choices was based on the results of a functional behavioral assessment indicating that both students used their inappropriate behavior to gain access to preferred clothing items. Both students demonstrated decreases in their disrobing and incontinence behaviors to near-zero levels when they were provided the opportunity to make choices about what they would wear. In addition, maintenance 6 months afterward for the female remained at near-zero levels.

The provision of choice-making opportunities as an intervention began with students with severe disabilities (e.g., Bambara et al., 1995; Dattilo & Rusch, 1985; B. Vaughn & Horner, 1997; for a review, see Lancioni, O'Reilly, & Emerson, 1996) to address problem behavior as well as a means to build autonomy and self-determination. Since then, choice-making opportunities have been extended to those with other disabilities such as emotional and behavioral disorders (EBDs; e.g., Dunlap et al., 1994; Jolivette et al., 2001; Kern, Mantegna, et al., 2001) and developmental disabilities (e.g., Carlson et al., 2008; C. L. Cole & Levinson, 2002; Kern, Mantegna, et al., 2001; Romaniuk et al., 2002), as well as those with typical development (e.g., Tiger, Hanley, & Hernandez, 2006). For example, for students with EBD, Ramsey et al. (2010) investigated the effects of choice of task sequence on five students, ages 14 to 16 years, with EBD in a residential facility who displayed problematic behavior related to low levels of on-task behavior, task completion, and accuracy during academic tasks. Results suggested that four of the students demonstrated overall increases in on-task behavior and task completion when provided choice in the order of their task completion, but had mixed results on the accuracy of the products.

Additionally, choice-making opportunities have been implemented across various age groups including preschool (e.g., S. M. Peck et al., 1996; Tiger et al., 2006), elementary (e.g., Jolivette et al., 2001; Umbreit & Blair, 1996; B. Vaughn & Horner, 1997), middle school (e.g., Kern, Bambara, & Fogt, 2002), high school (e.g., Seybert, Dunlap, & Ferro, 1996), and adult (e.g., Bambara et al., 1995) learners as a means to address problem behavior. For example, Seybert et al. investigated task choice on the problem behavior (i.e., self-stimulation, inappropriate use of objects, inappropriate vocalizations, noncompliance, and off-task) of

three high school students, ages 14 to 21 years, with intellectual disabilities during school domestic and vocational tasks. Results suggest that the choice condition resulted in a greater than 50% reduction in problem behavior for all three students when compared to behavior during nonchoice conditions.

Choice-making opportunities also have been implemented in varying environments such as in the school, community (e.g., E. G. Carr & Carlson, 1993), and home (B. Vaughn & Horner, 1995). The ease of implementation and naturally occurring choice options within each environment makes the provision of choices a flexible and useful intervention amenable to most contexts. For example, Jolivette et al. (2001) studied the effects of choice versus no choice of task sequence in an elementary self-contained math class for three students with EBD. Two of the students decreased their off-task and disruptive behaviors and increased their attempted math problems and correct problems.

Strengths and Future Directions

Multiple strengths to providing choice-making opportunities to students who exhibit problematic academic and social behavior within the school day, out in the community, or in the home setting have been noted in the literature. The provision of choice making is simple and easy without causing additional burden in time and preparation to those providing the choice (Carlson et al., 2008; Kern & State, 2009) and can be embedded within regular routines across environments (C. L. Cole & Levinson, 2002). K. M. McCormick et al. (2003) state embedding choice is important because it "supports decision making, social competence, and autonomy" (p. 5) while promoting engagement in tasks/activities selected by the student. Moreover, the provision of choice making requires no special training beyond following the choice-making steps outlined and thinking ahead of time how choice will be implemented within the lesson and classroom (Kern & State, 2009).

Given the mixed yet promising results of choice making as an intervention on reducing student problem behavior and increasing student positive behaviors, many future directions might be fruitfully explored. Future research should continue to investigate the effects of choice-making opportunities on task engagement in terms of the amount of work completed, the time required to complete the work, and the accuracy of the work completed for students who display chronic and persistent problem behavior (von Mizener & Williams, 2009). Research should also investigate the generalizability of the effects of choice making to other problematic behaviors or settings in which problematic behaviors occur (Carlson et al., 2008) as well as the long-term effect of choice-making interventions on student academic and social behaviors after the withdrawal of the intervention. It would also be helpful to know if, once students are exposed to choice-making opportunities, student-initiated choices are recognized and reinforced by teachers. It is also unclear if differential effects result from choice-making opportunities based on a student's disability and the severity of the disability (Morgan, 2006) or why choice-making is effective for some participants but not others. These future directions provide a focus for empirical inquiries of choice making as educators seek interventions to reduce and prevent student problem academic and social behaviors.

Even with questions remaining, evidence points to choice making as an effective and efficient prevention-focused intervention strategy. In brief, choice-making opportunities should be consistent, be frequent, range from basic to complex, and be reinforced (Jolivette, Ridgely, & White, 2002). In addition, implications for practice include being realistic when first providing choice-making opportunities, focusing on curricula areas where the student will benefit most, viewing choice-making opportunities on a continuum, and being consistent in presentation and reinforcement of the selection of the choice as a means to prevent problem behavior (Jolivette, Stichter, & McCormick, 2002). Kern and State (2009) contend that the provision of choice-making opportunities "is well worth the time, especially because teachers of students with EBD spend a considerable amount of time dealing with problem behaviors. This time could be used more effectively to prevent problems by planning how to make choices available" (p. 11). Another proactive strategy to address problem behavior that is also well worth the time and effort is self-management.

Self-Management

Teaching students self-management skills shifts the locus of control from teacher-mediated external reinforcement (e.g., teacher praise, tangible rewards) to student-directed intrinsic reinforcement (Fitzpatrick & Knowlton, 2009). Researchers have reported many benefits associated with self-management including (a) increased probability of maintenance of learned behavior because of student implementation, (b) less teacher time and resources required for addressing classroom problems, (c) increased autonomy of students, and (d) a greater sense of ownership of and responsibility for one's actions.

Definition and Theoretical Framework

Self-management is a process through which a student is taught to control her own behavior (McDougall, 1998). Generally, self-management is a procedure with multiple components including self-monitoring, self-instruction, self-assessment/self-evaluation, and self-reinforcement

(Mooney, Ryan, Uhing, Reid, & Epstein, 2005); however, no prescribed order of implementation is necessary for success of a self-management intervention (Niesyn, 2009). Self-management is founded on the principles of behaviorism, cognitive theory, and social cognitive theory. The theory of behaviorism (and most specifically operant conditioning), which is founded on the three-tier contingency model of antecedent, behavior, and consequence, perhaps offers the most direct explanation of self-management (Schunk, 2004). Self-management involves a consistent and predictable routine for providing immediate feedback for behavior. Students are not expected to delay gratification but are taught to reinforce their own behavior through self-praise or tangible reinforcement according to a schedule and agreed-upon criteria for reinforcement, which works to increase the likelihood of future desirable behavior. Furthermore, the principles of behaviorism are evident in the antecedent manipulations associated with some self-management interventions. Having students write the steps for completion of a specific academic task such as the steps to complete a multi-step division problem, or a mnemonic for the mathematical order of operations (e.g., *Please Excuse My Dear Aunt Sally* for remembering **p**arentheses, **e**xponentiation, **m**ultiplication, **d**ivision, **a**ddition, **s**ubtraction) are examples of antecedent modifications.

Cognitive theory and social cognitive theory are also apparent in the theoretical foundation of self-management. The concepts of self-talk and self-efficacy are evident when students are taught to manage independently their own behavior. Students cognitively process demonstrations of behavior, communicate and process desired behavior, and evaluate whether they demonstrate the targeted behavior. Furthermore, in line with social cognitive theory, students must feel they are capable of increasing or decreasing the target behavior; that is, they must have a sense of self-efficacy (Bandura, 1979, 1993).

Components to Implementing Self-Management for Students with Problem Behavior

Implementing self-management with students exhibiting problem behavior has four components: self-monitoring, self-instruction, self-evaluation/assessment, and self-reinforcement. Each is described in the following sections, and specific steps for each component are summarized in Figure 11.3.

Self-Monitoring

A major component of self-management is self-monitoring. Self-monitoring includes teaching students two tasks: (a) to realize the absence or presence of a

Figure 11.3   Essential steps in implementing self-management.

Self-monitoring

1. Identify the target behavior(s) of concern, and operationally define the behavior(s).
2. Develop a plan for how students will be cued to record their behavior (e.g., tone played on an audio recorder, visual prompt on a form) and a schedule for monitoring.
3. Meet with the student to explain the management plan.
4. Develop a self-monitoring sheet for data collection.
5. Teach the students how to use the self-management plan by first modeling for the student the act of self-recording while verbalizing the steps out loud.
6. Assess for accuracy of recording.
7. Fade the plan.

Self-instruction

1. Identify the problem.
2. Attend to the situation.
3. Plan during the phase.

Self-assessment/evaluation

1. Conduct a performance assessment.
2. Set observable and attainable goal(s).
3. Develop a schedule for evaluation.
4. Compare student performance to a goal for performance.

Self-reinforcement (external)

1. Determine desirable reinforcers for the student.
2. Establish a schedule for reinforcement.
3. Establish rules for reinforcement.

---

target behavior, and (b) to record the occurrence or non-occurrence of that behavior (Hallahan & Sapona, 1983; McDougall, 1998). Self-monitoring is a key component in the self-management process. In order for students to effectively self-manage their actions, they must first be taught the skills to monitor their own behaviors, which involves seven key steps. First, *identify* the target behavior(s) of concern, and *operationally define the behavior(s).* The target behavior needs to be observable and measurable. For example, the target behavior may be "keeping hands to self" with an operational definition of "the absence of any part of the elbow to fingertip touching another person anywhere on his body or any of his possessions."

Second, develop a plan for how students will be *cued to record their behavior* (e.g., tone played on an audio recorder, visual prompt on a form) as well as a *schedule for monitoring.* The schedule and cue may vary based on the student's level of functioning. For example, an elementary-age student may require an auditory prompt such as a tone or bell, while a middle or high school student may be prompted by the time on a clock.

Third, meet with the student to *explain the management plan.* The student and teacher discuss examples and nonexamples of the expected behaviors. For example, the teacher may ask the student "Where should your hands be during line-up time?" If the student says "At my side," the teacher reinforces the response and says, "Yes, at your side. Let me show you what that looks like and then you show me." The teacher and student should practice this several times and expand the example to include other settings (e.g., where hands should be when walking in the hallway, when sitting at a desk). For the nonexamples, the teacher should model examples of what the behavior would not look like (e.g., touching items, touching others).

Fourth, develop a *self-monitoring sheet* that can be used as a data collection method for teacher and student alike. The data collection form should be easy to use and portable so the student can bring it to other classrooms or settings if necessary. It may be beneficial for the form to have prominent visual or written prompts (e.g., "Am I keeping my hands to myself?") with a column for yes or no responses where the student can easily place a circle or tally mark to indicate self-evaluation of behavior.

Fifth, *teach the students how to use the self-management plan* by first modeling for the student the act of self-recording while verbalizing the steps out loud. For example, at the cue the teacher may say, "OK. That was the cue. Was I keeping my hands to myself? Yes! I was keeping my hands to myself so I'll check the 'yes' column and get back to work." Then the student models the steps by verbalizing the steps for the teacher to complete. Next the student performs the entire plan while also verbalizing all steps. It is important for the teacher to provide time to teach the student and for the student to practice the accurate implementation of the strategy before data collection. The student should exhibit mastery of the plan under the teacher's supervision before implementing it independently.

Sixth, *assess for accuracy of recording.* After the student can complete the plan without teacher assistance, the intervention period begins, and the teacher assesses for accuracy of recording. For example, a teacher may systematically assess the student's use of the plan and data collection by conducting independent checks every couple of sessions. If the teacher and student data match for the session, then the student receives an additional reinforcer. Initially, teachers provide reinforcement for correct recording but fade this level of assistance throughout the intervention period. The student should know that the teacher will be monitoring him; however, the actual occurrence of these checks should be completed without the student's knowledge. If the two data sets do not match, then the teacher needs to repeat step six and reteach to mastery.

Seventh, *fade the plan.* A teacher will know when the student is ready to have her plan faded when the student meets her performance goal for an extended period of time. To fade, the teacher may first remove the cue for recording and then gradually remove other elements of the program (Maag, 2004; Patton, Jolivette, & Ramsey, 2006; L. A. Wilkinson, 2008).

Self-Instruction

As part of the overall procedure of self-management, students can be taught the process of self-instruction. Teachers can teach students the steps for self-instruction in a variety of ways. The following is a three-step sequence example adapted from K. R. Harris (1982).

First, *identify the problem.* For example, a student working on task completion and accuracy may ask himself, "What am I supposed to be working on?" The student may need to be taught to use a mnemonic such as the steps to solve mathematical problems (e.g., **Please Excuse My Dear Aunt Sally**).

Second, *attend to the situation.* In this example, the student may say, "I have to concentrate on my work" to cue himself to focus on the task at hand. He may then verify that the steps were completed in the correct order (e.g., exponents before multiplication).

Third, *plan during the phase.* The student may remind himself to "work on one thing at a time." In this case, the student looked at the entire math problem, then looked for the operations involved, then decided the order in which to complete the problem.

Self-Assessment/Evaluation

Self-assessment/evaluation is a process through which each student is taught the method of evaluating her own progress. Self-assessment/evaluation works in collaboration with other elements of self-management as it involves comparing data from the self-monitoring portion to a goal for performance (Rhode et al., 1983; Rosenbaum & Drabman, 1979). For self-assessment/evaluation to be most effective, it is essential to include a few basic steps. The following discussion highlights the essential steps for self-assessment/evaluation.

First, *conduct a performance assessment.* The teacher observes the student to determine her current level of performance. Using standardized or individualized data, the teacher then identifies the performance level the student should grow toward. This process provides information that helps lead to the second task, *to set observable and attainable goal(s).* The goal for

performance is typically agreed upon by the student and teacher and is related to the baseline performance data collected. If, for example, a student is talking out an average of 10 times per class period, the student and teacher may agree to an initial performance goal of 5 or fewer talk outs during a class period. While talking out 5 times during a class period may still be disruptive to the learning of the student and her classmates, it is recommended that initial goals be set at a point that is both realistic and attainable. Setting the goal too high may cause frustration for students, as they may feel the goal is unreachable and therefore may discontinue use of the intervention. It will be necessary to shape the goal over time to a more acceptable and less disruptive level (e.g., moving to 0 to 1 displays of talking out during a class period).

Third, *develop a schedule for evaluation.* After the student reaches the agreed-upon performance goal, the teacher should determine a schedule for evaluation. The teacher determines how often the data will be compared to the goal. It may be necessary to evaluate more frequently at the start of an intervention (i.e., after each class) and to fade the schedule for evaluation over time (i.e., one to two times per day).

Fourth, *compare student performance to a goal for performance.* The final step involves the comparison of actual student performance to the goal. Additionally, the teacher will want to offer reinforcement for correctly evaluating performance. According to L. A. Wilkinson (2008), it may be common for the teacher and student to disagree initially, but the teacher ratings are always the standard assessment of performance, and an agreement is only achieved if the teacher data indicate the criterion were met.

Self-Reinforcement

Although students can be taught to self-reinforce in two ways, externally and internally (Maag, 2004), we focus on the process of external reinforcement because it is more overt and within the teacher's control to shape the steps associated with it. Determining and implementing conditions associated with internal self-reinforcement, by contrast, is given wholly to the student herself, making the role of the teacher less central (Bandura, 1976). Following are the steps for external reinforcement.

First, *determine desirable reinforcers for the student.* The teacher should engage the student in a discussion to determine which items the student finds motivating. Over time, what motivates a student may change, so conversations on reinforcers may need to occur frequently.

Second, *establish a schedule for reinforcement.* The teacher then establishes a schedule for reinforcement to inform the student of when the desired reward will be received. For example, the student may initially reinforce himself for reaching his performance goal each time. This schedule should then be thinned over time.

Third, *establish rules for reinforcement.* Additionally, the teacher establishes rules for reinforcement (i.e., must choose from reward menu, only one choice per time). For example, if the student has a choice of computer time or free reading time for meeting a performance goal, then the teacher needs to (a) make sure the student has access to the reinforcement, and (b) ensure that the student can have/use the reinforcement at the time of achievement.

Self-Management for Students with Problem Behavior

Researchers have investigated self-management in numerous ways and have demonstrated positive outcomes for those who display problem behavior. For example, self-management has been used successfully across multiple grade levels (e.g., Blick & Test, 1987; Callahan & Radenmacher, 1999; Rock, 2005) within general education settings (e.g., DiGangi, Maag, & Rutherford, 1991; Maag, Reid, & DiGangi, 1993). For example, Blick and Test used self-management to increase the on-task classroom behaviors of 12 students with high-incidence disabilities in grades 9 to 12 in general education classrooms. The students responded to an audible cue played from an audio tape at 5-minute intervals by recording a "+" or "−" on a recording sheet if they were on task at the signal and recorded the total number of "+"s, receiving reinforcement if their criterion was met. Results suggest on-task behavior significantly increased with the use of self-management.

Self-management has been successful with students with disabilities (e.g., Coyle & Cole, 2004; DiGangi et al., 1991; Todd, Horner, & Sugai, 1999), including students with EBD (e.g., Mooney et al., 2005), learning disabilities (e.g., Todd et al., 1999), attention deficit disorder (e.g., Hoff & DuPaul, 1998), and autism (e.g., L. A. Wilkinson, 2008). For example, Prater, Hogan, and Miller (1992) used self-monitoring to improve the classroom behavior of a 14-year-old male diagnosed with a specific learning disability who displayed inappropriate classroom behaviors including interrupting others, getting out of seat during instruction, and refusing to complete assignments. Using a time-sampling procedure to record his behavior, the student decreased his inappropriate behaviors across mainstream classroom settings (resource room, mathematics, and English classrooms) over the period of the study.

Self-management also has demonstrated positive results for a variety of behavioral outcomes (e.g., on-task behavior, work completion, hand raising). For example, Todd et al. (1999) documented the use of a self-management package including self-monitoring, self-evaluation, and self-recruited reinforcement on the on-task behavior and work completion of a 9-year-old fourth grader diagnosed with ADHD and conduct disorder. Data were collected on the use of appropriate language, verbal responses to adult requests, and refraining from harassment and intimidation of peers during a reading period and project time. Results show that the self-monitoring package was successful in significantly increasing the on-task classroom behavior while simultaneously decreasing problem behaviors in both settings.

A new application of self-management is the incorporation of technology as a means for students to self-manage. For example, Gulchak (2008) evaluated the impact of self-monitoring using a mobile handheld computer on the on-task behavior of an 8-year-old male with EBD. Results indicated that on-task behavior improved and that the student was able to use the handheld computer with 100% fidelity.

Future Directions

Although self-management is supported as an effective, evidence-based practice, it is not without limitations. Future research should investigate (a) to what extent teachers and adults can implement self-management within natural contexts without external supports (e.g., researchers), (b) the role of technology in self-management procedures, (c) which student populations are most responsive to self-management strategies and what adaptations may need to be made to meet students' unique needs, and (d) what process should be followed to determine student reinforcement for performance goal attainment. These future directions will expand the self-management literature to address more fully the social and academic needs of students with problem behavior.

Conclusion

Overall, when students display problem behavior, whether at school, in the home, or in the community, teachers and adults need to implement strategies to prevent the occurrence of such behavior in the future. Teachers and adults may use pre-correction, choice making, or self-management to do that. Each of these strategies has shown promising outcomes in reducing and preventing future problem behaviors across disabilities, ages, behaviors, and settings. The literature base could be strengthened for these three strategies related to their application across learners of culturally and linguistically diverse populations as well as the systematic measurement of fidelity of the strategies used. However, teachers and adults should consider use of these three strategies for their students and children, because all three are easy to use, cost-effective, and can be used to address a plethora of behaviors.

CHAPTER 12

Students with Disabilities and Academic Engagement: *Classroom-Based Interventions*

Kevin S. Sutherland and **Stephen A. Wright** | *Virginia Commonwealth University*

Research has demonstrated a consistent and strong positive association between academic engagement and achievement (e.g., Greenwood, Horton, & Utley, 2002; Klem & Connell, 2004). Although the exact linkage between these two constructs can be elusive, several factors within the classroom environment appear to influence this relationship. For example, individual student characteristics such as inattention, hyperactivity, noncompliance, and aggression are likely to have a detrimental effect on engagement (Greenwood et al., 2002). At the same time, even for students who exhibit problem behavior, differential effects on engagement can be associated with classroom contextual factors (J. A. Baker, Clark, Maier, & Viger, 2008). Because many classroom contextual factors are malleable (e.g., instructional grouping, instructional pacing, teacher behavior), researchers have targeted these areas. Identifying an evidence base for increasing student academic engagement may be particularly salient for students with and at risk for disabilities, given both their documented risk for academic problems (M. Wagner, Newman, Cameto, Levine, & Garza, 2006) and data that suggest that both elementary (e.g., Kemp & Carter, 2006) and secondary (E. W. Carter, Sisco, Brown, Brickham, & Al-Khabbaz, 2008) students with disabilities have low rates of engagement. The importance of

increasing the academic engagement of all students is further highlighted by research suggesting a reciprocal relationship between academic achievement and engagement; that is, increased academic achievement is also associated with increased academic engagement (Urdan & Schoenfelder, 2006).

Academic Engagement Defined

Yell, Meadows, Drasgow, and Shriner (2009) differentiate between allocated instructional time (e.g., amount of time the teacher sets aside for instruction) and academic engaged time (e.g., the amount of time a student is actively involved in instruction). Furthermore, academic engagement can be defined on a continuum from passive to active engagement. J. A. Baker et al. (2008) offered a broad definition of engagement that indicates "active involvement in classroom tasks and activities that facilitate learning, while inhibiting behaviors that detract from learning" (p. 1876). Within academic engagement, active student responding has been defined as observable and measurable student responses to specific academic stimuli (Gunter & Sutherland, 2005) and is the most

153

direct measure of student responding during academic instruction (Heward, 1994).

Classroom Contexts and Academic Engagement

Classroom contexts are dynamic, complex systems where moment-to-moment interactions between teachers and students (not to mention students and their peers) exert influence on academic engagement. Individual student characteristics certainly play a role in student learning, but modifiable teacher behaviors and instructional factors also play a role. For example, proactive classroom management, whereby teachers actively promote prosocial behaviors associated with academic engagement, is associated with increased academic engagement (Kern & Clemens, 2007). J. A. Baker et al. (2008) found that instructional arrangements (e.g., direct instruction, small groups, individual seat work, interactive teaching) had a differential effect on students' engagement, with small-group and interactive teaching resulting in more engagement than direct instruction and individual seat work for students with behavior problems. Finally, research has shown the positive effects of a variety of instructional strategies on academic engagement, including but not limited to shortening task duration (Kern, Childs, Dunlap, Clarke, & Falk, 1994), frequent reinforcement (R. G. Smith & Iwata, 1997), and matching task demands to meet students' skill levels (L. M. Roberts, Marshall, Nelson, & Albers, 2001).

Given the dynamic nature of classroom environments, it is helpful to conceptualize the classroom environment as a system comprising multiple interrelated subsystems. From a theoretical perspective, this conceptualization involves behavioral principles (B. F. Skinner, 1953) embedded in social transactions (Sameroff, 1983), all the while recognizing the role of the ecology (Bronfenbrenner, 1979) on students' academic engagement. To illustrate, behavioral principles serve as the foundation for key instructional practices that serve as antecedents and consequences for academic engagement. For example, data indicate the role that antecedent instructional behavioral stimuli (e.g., providing frequent opportunities to respond during instruction) as well as behavioral reinforcement (e.g., feedback and contingent praise) serve as strategies for increasing academic engagement (e.g., Sutherland, Alder, & Gunter, 2003; Todd, Horner, & Sugai, 1999). The application of transactional theory to the classroom environment suggests that teacher–student interactions are reciprocal in nature (Sutherland & Oswald, 2005); thus, improvements in students' academic engagement likely will result in an improved classroom learning environment through both improvements in classroom behavior and learning opportunities as well as increased effective classroom-based instructional practices. Finally, from an ecological perspective, multiple influences affect students' academic engagement in the classroom, including peer and teacher influences.

In light of these multiple, interactive influences on students' academic engagement, the purpose of this chapter is to critically review the literature across a selective, yet interrelated, layer of classroom influences. Specifically, we will review the effects of (a) opportunities to respond to academic requests (OTR; antecedent procedure); (b) the Good Behavior Game (GBG; contextual procedure); and (c) praise (consequent procedure) on the academic engagement of students with or at risk for disabilities. Search criteria for experimental or quasi-experimental studies across the three procedures included the following: (a) the independent variable was either OTR, GBG, or teacher praise; (b) the dependent variable was student engagement, either self-reported or observational (including active and/or correct academic responding); and (c) research participants were students with or at risk for disabilities, including students identified as having problem behavior. Following a brief description of each procedure, including the underlying theoretical framework, we provide an implementation fidelity checklist. We then review the literature for each procedure with a focus on strengths and limitations of the research base. Finally, we discuss the implications for both practice and future research.

Opportunities to Respond

Research has shown OTR to improve the academic and social behavior of students with high-incidence disabilities, including students with emotional and behavioral disorders (EBD). Specifically, research has shown that increasing opportunities for students to academically respond is associated with increased task engagement and correct responding. In addition, as teachers increase OTR, students' disruptive behaviors decrease (Conroy, Sutherland, Snyder, & Marsh, 2008; Sutherland et al., 2003; Sutherland & Wehby, 2001). Given its ease of implementation, OTR can be an effective and inexpensive means to helping students receive better and more desirable outcomes in the academic setting. Adequate rates of OTR are necessary, as Gunter, Hummel, and Venn (1998) note. It is also important for students to have a high rate of correct responding (80% to 90%). Although OTR is important for student learning, especially for students with or at risk for disabilities, descriptive research suggests that classroom teachers rarely provide adequate OTR and require additional supports to do so (Sutherland & Wehby, 2001).

Description and Fidelity Checklist

OTR is an instructional strategy initiated and used by teachers that serves as a prompt for student academic responding. It can be defined as a questioning strategy that is used as a stimulus that begins or ends a learning trial (Carnine, 1976; Sutherland et al., 2003). A learning trial consists of a three-term, stimulus–response–consequent contingency sequence (C. H. Skinner, Fletcher, & Hennington, 1996). An OTR is used as an antecedent stimulus in the beginning of a learning trial, followed by a verbal, written, or physical student response. An example of a learning trial is when a teacher presents a question to a student (i.e., stimulus), the student answers the question (i.e., response), and the teacher delivers feedback or praise (i.e., consequence). Increasing the quantity and improving the quality of learning trials have been associated with higher learning rates (Carnine, 1976), and researchers have shown that increasing the number of learning trials can also increase learning levels during the acquisition, fluency building, and maintenance stages of learning (C. H. Skinner, Smith, & McLean, 1994).

The fidelity checklist for OTR is simple and concise. Completing the steps on this checklist before instruction allows the teacher to review the academic content to be taught and to design the OTR to use during instruction. In addition, teachers must determine the format of OTR to provide. For example, for younger students, a teacher may want to use choral responding to increase the rate of OTR and student responding, while a teacher of older students might want to use response cards (any sign, such as yes/no cards or dry erase boards, which individual students can use and can be held up simultaneously by all students in response to a teacher prompt). Three other common types of OTR are guided notes (handouts that guide a student through the lecture with standard cues), electronic response systems (remote systems that allow all students to respond simultaneously with outcomes projected publicly), and individual prompting (one student is prompted to respond). All students, including those with disabilities who may have a difficult time responding to complex questions, should have the opportunity to respond correctly to academic questions; by varying the wait-time and difficulty level, teachers may increase the likelihood of students' achieving this goal. As for increasing OTR during instruction, a teacher may decrease the intertrial interval between OTR (i.e., the amount of time between OTR); it remains desirable, however, to have a list of possible OTR available for reference. See Figure 12.1 for a fidelity checklist of procedures for OTR.

Research on OTR

Sutherland and Wehby (2001) reviewed the literature on the relationship between OTR and classroom (academic and behavioral) outcomes of students with EBD. The studies reviewed suggested that lower rates of disruptive behavior and increased rates of task engagement and academic achievement were associated with the occurrence of increased rates of OTR. Since the time this review was published, few studies have been conducted that examined the effects of OTR in the classroom settings. Following is a review of 11 studies that met the criteria for inclusion in our review; six of these studies (Carnine, 1976; C. H. Skinner, Belfiore, Mace, Williams-Wilson, & Johns, 1997; C. H. Skinner, Ford, & Yunker, 1991; C. H. Skinner & Shapiro, 1989; C. H. Skinner et al., 1994; West & Sloane, 1986) were reviewed in Sutherland and Wehby (2001), while four were conducted since that review (Sutherland, Wehby, & Yoder, 2002; Sutherland et al., 2003;

Figure 12.1   Opportunities to Respond (OTR) fidelity checklist.

Behavior	Yes	No	NA
Before Instruction			
Identify students' academic levels.			
Review academic content.			
Identify OTR format.			
Create OTR.			
OTR represent range of difficulty levels.			
During Instruction			
Present OTR at brisk pace (3–5 per min).			
Students respond correctly at rate of 80% or higher.			
Distribute OTR across students.			
Present corrective feedback and/or praise.			

Tincani & Crozier, 2008; Haydon, Mancil, & Van Loan, 2009). A final study, Darch and Gersten (1985), was not included in the Sutherland and Wehby (2001) review but did meet inclusion criteria for this review.

Study Designs

Sutherland et al. (2002) used a correlational design to measure the magnitude of the relationship between OTR and correct responding, while the remaining studies used single-subject designs. Darch and Gersten (1985), Haydon et al. (2009), Sutherland et al. (2003), and Carnine (1976) used withdrawal designs to analyze the increased rate of OTR on students' classroom outcomes. Tincani and Crozier (2008) and West and Sloane (1986) used single-subject multi-element designs, while C. H. Skinner and colleagues (1989, 1991, 1994, 1997) used alternating treatment designs.

Effect of OTR on Outcome Measures

All studies reviewed indicated positive effects of OTR on outcome measures. Carnine (1976) increased OTR by increasing the teacher's presentation rate with two first-grade students identified by the teacher as having high rates of off-task behavior. Results suggest that increased OTR were associated with increased percentages of correct responses and participation and decreased percentages of off-task behavior for the target students. In a similar study, West and Sloane (1986) examined the effects of increased OTR with five students (two boys and three girls) between the ages of 7 and 9 years. Presentation rate (fast = 20 seconds between presentations; slow = 60 seconds between presentations) was used as the independent variable in addition to a reinforcement procedure (token economy system that varied the delivery rate of point delivery for correct responding). The percentage of intervals with disruptive behaviors, academic accuracy, and correct response rate were dependent variables. Results indicated no difference among dependent variables between high and low delivery rate for reinforcement. However, a higher OTR presentation rate resulted in fewer occurrences of disruptive behaviors and increased correct response rate, although academic accuracy was slightly better during the slow OTR presentation rate.

Three additional studies also investigated the effects of increased presentation rate, resulting in increased OTR. C. H. Skinner et al. (1994) examined the effect of both a 5- and 1-second intertrial interval (ITI) procedure on the number of words mastered under each condition of three students (two boys and one girl) with EBD between the ages of 9 and 11. Results indicated that both 5-second and 1-second ITI increased presentation rate

for OTR resulted in more mastered words than the no-treatment condition. During both 5- and 1-second ITI, students were given three OTR per target reading word, compared to one OTR per target reading word during the no-treatment condition. Although the results show no difference between the 5- and 1-second ITI interventions, results do suggest that the number of responses (three) required during the intervention conditions, compared to the one response required during the no-treatment condition, may have impacted the students' mastery of the reading words. Further, the 5-second presentation rate took an average of 103 seconds longer per session than the 1-second presentation rate, so the 1-second rate may represent a more efficient use of instructional time.

Tincani and Crozier (2008) examined the effect of a wait-time procedure (brief v. extended) on response opportunities, academic responding, percentage of correct responding, and disruptive behavior of two students (ages 6 and 7 years) with challenging behaviors. The setting for this study was an empty classroom in a private clinic for students with behavior problems. Results suggest that brief wait-time had a positive effect on all of the dependent variables. When wait-time was brief, researchers noted an increase in OTR and increased responding for both students. Both students also tended to increase correct responding during the condition with increased response opportunities; while less definitive, decreases in disruptive behavior were noted during the brief wait-time condition as well. Finally, Darch and Gersten (1985) examined the effects of increased presentation rate (increased OTR) and praise on both the percentage of correct responding and percentage of on-task behavior of four students (3 boys; 7.8 to 8.6 years) with learning disabilities (LD) during reading instruction in a special education classroom. Results indicate that students' mean levels of correct responding and on-task behavior increased during the increased presentation rate phases. In sum, the research on increased presentation rate suggests that increased OTR results in desirable learning and behavioral outcomes.

C. H. Skinner and Shapiro (1989) examined the effect of increased OTR using taped words (two OTR), drill interventions (two OTR), and continuous and intermittent assessment (one OTR) on words read correctly and incorrectly per minute using an alternating-treatments design. During the taped words intervention, participants read along with a tape recording of vocabulary words, whereas in the drill condition, they read the list of vocabulary words out loud before completing an assessment (two OTRs). During the continuous and intermittent assessment, participants simply read from the list of vocabulary words (one OTR). Results indicated that the two OTR interventions resulted in 78.4 words read correctly and 3.9 words read incorrectly per minute, while having one OTR resulted in 54.4 words read correctly and 5.6 words read incorrectly per minute for five students between the ages of 14 and 18 years, suggesting that a relationship may exist between the increase in OTR and performance on the reading task.

The two remaining C. H. Skinner et al. studies (1991, 1997) examined the effect of verbal cover, copy, and compare (VCCC) and writing cover, copy, and compare (WCCC) on math responding of two students with EBD, ages 9 and 11 years old. To illustrate, during the WCCC condition, the participants looked at a math problem and wrote the answer, covered the problem and answer, wrote the problem and answer, and uncovered the problem and answer to evaluate what was written. During the VCCC condition, the procedures were the same, except that the participant stated the problem and answer verbally rather than in writing, resulting in increased OTR for participants in this condition. Across students, both the mean percentage of problems correct (74% for the VCCC intervention and 68% for the WCCC intervention and no treatment combined) and digits correct per minute (28 for the VCCC intervention and 20 for the WCCC intervention and no treatment combined) favored the condition with increased OTR. C. H. Skinner et al. (1997) further examined the effect of increased OTR using the VCCC and WCCC interventions on the number of multiplication problems completed and digits correct per minute of two students with EBD. The VCCC intervention again resulted in an increase in learning trials for both students (86 and 83 for VCCC, compared to 26 and 33 for WCCC for both students, respectively), and the data suggest that the accuracy (number of problems correct) and fluency (digits correct per minute) of one of the students increased during the VCCC intervention. Results from these two studies suggest that the increased efficiency of the VCCC condition (verbalizing responses rather than writing responses) resulted in more learning trials and, over time, more OTR, which may be associated with improved academic outcomes.

Sutherland et al. (2002) examined the relationship between teacher praise and opportunities for students with disabilities to respond to academic requests. The sample consisted of 20 teachers and 216 students (183 boys and 33 girls) identified with disabilities (112 EBD, 48 with LD, 20 with developmental disabilities, and 36 identified with other disabilities). Results indicated a significant positive correlation between OTR and students' correct responses ($r = 0.94$, $p < 0.01$). Sutherland et al. (2003) also increased OTR as the independent variable to analyze the effects on students' correct responses, disruptive behaviors, and on-task behaviors. Participants were nine students (eight boys and one girl) with EBD who ranged in age from 8 to 12 years old. Results showed mean increases in correct responding and on-task behavior, as well as decreases in students' disruptive behavior.

Finally, Haydon et al. (2009) examined the effect of increased rates of choral responding OTR on the on-task behavior, correct responding, and disruptive behavior of a fifth-grade girl identified as at-risk for EBD. The setting was a fifth-grade general education science classroom with 19 students and a male teacher. Increased rates of OTR were associated with decreased disruptive behavior and increased task engagement. Increases in correct responding were also noted during the treatment phase.

Procedures

In general OTR was increased in the reviewed studies by an increase in presentation rate during academic instruction. Two studies (Carnine, 1976; West & Sloane, 1986) simply instructed the teacher to increase presentation rate, while Darch and Gersten (1985) instructed the teacher to provide an OTR immediately following a student response. Similarly, C. H. Skinner et al. (1994) decreased the intertrial interval between OTR, and Tincani and Crozier (2008) decreased wait time between response opportunities and student responses. Two studies (C. H. Skinner et al., 1991, 1997) used a VCCC strategy to increase OTR, simply requiring students' verbal responses rather than written responses. An observation feedback intervention was used in both Sutherland et al. (2003) and Haydon et al. (2009), whereby the teacher received feedback on his use of OTR following each observation session. In each case the teacher also set a goal for his use of OTR.

Implementation Fidelity

Nine of the eleven studies reviewed provided some form of treatment fidelity data. The lack of an intervention in Sutherland et al. (2002) precludes the need for fidelity data, while Darch and Gersten (1985) provided no data to indicate that rates of OTR actually increased during their intervention. Haydon et al. (2009) and C. H. Skinner et al. (1989, 1994) used various forms of checklists to measure treatment fidelity. For example, Haydon et al. (2009) used a checklist on 25% of the sessions to record the steps of the choral responding sequence, noting 100% fidelity. Similarly, C. H. Skinner et al. (1989) noted 100% fidelity on 17% of the sessions, and C. H. Skinner et al. (1994) noted 100% fidelity for 11 intervention-phase sessions. Treatment fidelity was measured by direct observation in five studies (Haydon et al., 2009; C. H. Skinner et al., 1989; Sutherland et al., 2003; Tincani & Crozier, 2008; West & Sloan, 1986), which strengthens the findings from these studies by providing evidence of increased rates of OTR.

Strengths and Limitations of Research on OTR

Findings across the 11 studies reviewed here are consistent: Increases in OTR are associated with increased academic achievement and task engagement and decreased disruptive behavior. The measurement of treatment fidelity (9 of 10 intervention studies reported treatment fidelity data) is a strength of this literature, increasing our ability to link increases in dependent variables to actual increases in OTR. At the same time two significant limitations in the research must be noted. First, only three of the eleven reviewed studies (Haydon et al., 2009; Sutherland et al., 2003; Tincani & Crozier, 2008) provided information on the race/ethnicity of student participants; additionally, these three and Sutherland et al. (2002) also provided race/ethnicity information for teacher participants. Second, the lack of a reintroduction of the intervention in Haydon et al. (2009) limits the interpretation of experimental effects in this study. Nonetheless, research on the antecedent procedure of OTR suggests that it can be a useful tool for teachers attempting to provide instruction for students with and at risk for disabilities. We will next review the literature on a contextual intervention on academic engagement, the Good Behavior Game.

Good Behavior Game

The Good Behavior Game (GBG), which has its theoretical roots in behavioral psychology, has been described as a behavioral vaccine (Embry, 2002). Embry defines a behavioral vaccine as "a simple procedure that can dramatically change an adverse outcome" (p. 274). Hallmark characteristics of effective behavioral vaccines related to our discussion include their ability to be combined with other treatments in a synergistic manner as well as their low costs and generalizability (Embry, 2002). In 1969 Barrish, Saunders, and Wolf published the first study on the GBG, and in the ensuing years both empirical studies (e.g., Lannie & McCurdy, 2007, Salend, Reynolds, & Coyle, 1989) and reviews of the literature (e.g., Embry, 2002; Tingstrom, Sterling-Turner, & Wilczynski, 2002) have documented the positive effects of the GBG on a variety of developmental outcomes, including proximal decreases in disruptive behavior and increases in prosocial behavior as well as more distal outcomes such as problem behavior and drug or alcohol use in young adulthood (Poduska et al., 2008; Tingstrom et al., 2002).

Description and Fidelity Checklist

The GBG is a group-contingency classroom management procedure that may occur during any group activity and is designed to reduce problem behavior. Before implementing the GBG, the teacher first (a) identifies and operationally defines up to three negative behaviors to be targeted for change (e.g., talking out, out-of-seat behavior, aggression); (b) assigns students to one of three to four teams (three to four students per team), taking care to create heterogeneous groups based on behavior (externalizing and internalizing); (c) collects baseline data on team behavior to ensure that teams are similar on base rates of behavior; and (d) reorganizes groups if necessary based on baseline data showing marked differences in behavior between groups. During the pre-implementation phase, the students do not know that the teacher is collecting data on these behaviors.

Before implementation of the game, the teacher describes the game and provides examples and nonexamples of the behaviors. Each team may appoint a team leader and assign their team a group name. The teacher then informs the students that groups that receive fewer than a certain number of check marks (e.g., five during a 15-minute session) may receive a predetermined reward at the end of the activity. Throughout the activity period, the teacher monitors the students for occurrences of the targeted behaviors. If a student displays any one of the behaviors, she earns a check mark for her team, thus holding the group responsible for the behavior of each of its members. If all groups exceed the determined number of check marks, then the group with the fewest number wins the reward. If all teams tie or have fewer than the criterion number of checks, all students on those teams receive the reward. The team leaders are then responsible for dispensing the rewards (if tangible) to their team members and marking their team's reward on a progress chart. Once the students are familiar with the game, the teacher may begin the game unannounced at any time, thus teaching students to consistently self-monitor their behavior. See Figure 12.2 for a fidelity checklist of procedures for the GBG.

Research on the GBG

After the initial study on the GBG (Barrish et al., 1969), a series of studies documented the positive effects of the GBG on a variety of youth outcomes. Perhaps the most well-known evaluation of the GBG is a series of studies conducted by Kellam and colleagues (e.g., Kellam, Ling, Merisca, Brown, & Ialongo, 1998; Poduska et al., 2008) in a randomized control trial with a longitudinal design in 19 elementary schools in Baltimore, Maryland. A review of this literature is well beyond the scope of this chapter, and only a small subset of these studies ($N = 4$) met the criteria for inclusion in our review of measuring a dependent variable of student engagement. However, it is important to mention that the effects of the GBG on both proximal and distal measures of disruptive behavior

Figure 12.2   Good Behavior Game (GBG) fidelity checklist.

Behavior	Yes	No	NA
Before Implementation (1–2 Weeks)			
Identify and define undesirable behaviors.			
Create teams.			
Collect baseline data.			
Reorganize teams based on baseline data (if necessary).			
Implementation			
Announce game before beginning.			
Announce group members before beginning.			
Read the classroom rules.			
Explain the classroom rules.			
Explain the requirements to win.			
Explain the rule violation process.			
Set the game timer.			
Announce the start of the game.			
Handle disruptive behaviors appropriately.			
Review scores.			
Review rules.			
Record proper information.			
Provide reinforcement.			

and aggression, particularly for high-risk students, have been overwhelmingly positive. Following is a review of the four studies (Darch & Thorpe, 1977; Darveaux, 1984; Fishbein & Wasik, 1981; Lannie & McCurdy, 2007) that met the criteria for inclusion in our review.

Study Designs

Two of the studies (Darveaux, 1984; Lannie & McCurdy, 2007) used an ABAB single-subject design, while one (Darch & Thorpe, 1977) used an ABACA single-subject design. The reversal design used in these studies allows for an evaluation of the effects of the independent variable on dependent variables as the participants serve as their own controls. Fishbein and Wasik (1981) used an ABCB single-subject design, which limits the interpretation of results due to a lack of experimental control.

Effect of the GBG on Outcome Measures

All studies reviewed indicated positive effects of the GBG on outcome measures. Similar to the majority of studies on the GBG, three of the four studies reviewed included a measure of disruptive behavior (Darveaux, 1984; Fishbein & Wasik, 1981; Lannie & McCurdy, 2007), and data indicated that students' disruptive

behavior covaried with the introduction and implementation of the GBG across studies. Two studies (Darch & Thorpe, 1977; Lannie & McCurdy, 2007) included a measure of student on-task behavior, and results also indicated that on-task behavior covaried with the introduction and implementation of the GBG. For example, Lannie and McCurdy reported that on-task behavior increased from 53.3% and 47% in the two baseline phases to 68% and 75.6% in the two treatment phases when the 22 first-grade students in their study played the GBG. Similarly, Darch and Thorpe reported that on-task behavior increased from 26%, 51%, and 34% during baseline conditions to 86% (for GBG with group consequences) and 75% (for GBG with individual consequences) for the 10 highest-risk students in a disruptive fourth-grade classroom. Interestingly, the students' level of on-task behavior during the reintroduction of the GBG without group contingency (i.e., students worked for individual rather than group consequences) was not as high as the group contingency condition, suggesting the importance of the peer-group reinforcement in this study.

Results for outcomes other than on-task behavior have also been positive. For example, Darveaux (1984) found that assignment completion rates increased from 40% to 75% for two second-grade boys identified as high risk when their classroom participated in the GBG.

In addition, Fishbein and Wasik (1981) found increases in task-relevant behaviors, such as answering or asking lesson-related questions, writing, and raising a hand, and decreases in off-task behaviors of 25 fourth-grade students who had been identified as disruptive when the GBG was introduced. Interestingly, in the third phase of this study, winning teams received verbal reinforcement rather than a tangible (e.g., fun classroom activity) reinforcer, and rates of both task-relevant and off-task behavior decreased to approximate levels demonstrated during the baseline phase, indicating the importance of tangible reinforcement in this study.

Procedures

Embry (2002) noted that a strength of the GBG is its relatively easy implementation procedures. Of the four studies reviewed here, only two reported the level of support provided to implement the procedures of the GBG. Darveaux (1984) noted that a school psychologist provided a total of 1 hour of training to the teacher, and Lannie and McCurdy (2007) noted that the researcher provided training to the teacher in GBG procedures, although the amount of time and training was not provided.

Several adaptations were made to the GBG in reviewed studies that warrant mention. Three of the studies (Darveaux, 1984; Fishbein & Wasik, 1981; Lannie & McCurdy, 2007) used reinforcement rather than punishment procedures as the students in these studies earned points for desirable behaviors. This adaptation is notable, particularly as it relates to students with and at risk for disabilities, given the long history of beneficial effects of positive reinforcement on students' academic and behavioral outcomes. Darveaux also used an innovative procedure whereby students could use earned points to "take away" negative check marks that teams had earned; this strategy might be particularly useful when teams have exceeded a set criteria for negative behaviors, allowing them to continue working toward a reward rather than "giving up" for the session. Finally, an adaptation in Darch and Thorpe (1977) involved the principal's acknowledging winning teams by coming into the classroom once a day and providing verbal reinforcement.

Implementation Fidelity

Unfortunately, only one study (Lannie & McCurdy, 2007) provided data on implementation fidelity. These researchers used a checklist that was rated for 29% of the observed GBG sessions. Results indicated that across sessions, 88% of the procedures were implemented.

Strengths and Limitations of the Research on the GBG

Interpreting the research on the effects of the GBG on student engagement is made difficult by the small number of studies reviewed. Again, however, it is important to note that the research base for the GBG is much larger than that reviewed here; the vast majority of research studies on the GBG did not meet criteria for inclusion in this review. That said, several limitations in the reviewed studies should be taken into account when considering outcomes. First, none of the four studies in this review included information on the race or ethnicity of their participants, limiting the generalizability of results. Second, the lack of a return to baseline in the Fishbein and Wasik (1981) study did not allow for a demonstration of experimental control. Finally, of the four studies reviewed, only one (Lannie & McCurdy, 2007) provided treatment fidelity data. This omission limits the interpretation of findings from the research reviewed on the GBG, particularly given the number of procedural steps necessary to implement the intervention with fidelity. Results of the reviewed research, even in light of these limitations, do suggest that a contextual intervention such as the GBG can have positive effects on the engagement of students with and at risk for disabilities. We next review the literature on teacher praise—a consequent procedure—and its effect on students' academic engagement.

Praise

Teacher praise is widely recognized as an effective consequent strategy for promoting desirable student classroom behavior (Gable, Hester, Rock, & Hughes, 2009). Teachers use praise to communicate positive evaluations of a student's performance or effort to the student (Henderlong & Lepper, 2002), and praise can be used to promote both academic responding and behavioral skills. Effective praise can increase intrinsic motivation, promote appropriate behavior, and decrease disruptive behavior (Henderlong & Lepper, 2002; Stormont, Smith, & Lewis, 2007). Although providing effective praise can be a simple consequent strategy for a teacher to use, it may be difficult to find opportunities for praise within the ongoing dynamic classroom environment. This assertion is supported by descriptive research that suggests that praise statements, particularly for students with or at risk for disabilities, are delivered infrequently (Van Acker, Grant, & Henry, 1996; Wehby, Symons, Canale, & Go, 1998). Ironically, students with academic or behavioral deficits are precisely the ones who need the most positive attention (Haager & Klinger, 2005).

Description and Fidelity Checklist

Praise is a social reinforcer and is one of the most effective and convenient positive reinforcers teachers can use to manage student behavior. It is inexpensive, because it costs nothing but the teachers' observation and time. Paine, Radicchi, Rosellini, Deutchman, and Darch (1983) report that effective praise has several important components:

- Good praise adheres to the "if–then" rule, which states that if the student is behaving in the desired manner, then (and only then) the teacher praises the student.
- Good praise frequently includes students' names.
- Good praise is descriptive.
- Good praise conveys that the teacher really means what is said (i.e., it is convincing and sincere).
- Good praise is varied.
- Good praise does not disrupt the flow of individual or class activities.

In addition, researchers (Dweck, 2007; Sutherland & Singh, 2004) recommend that praise be effort related. That is, praise should be focused on the process of responding, whether academic or behavioral. Process praise focuses on students' effort and strategies that are modifiable when faced with difficult tasks, resulting in maintained high expectations and more positive affect (Kamins & Dweck, 1999). This focus differs from person praise (e.g., "You're so smart!"), which is related to characteristics of the student that are not modifiable. See Figure 12.3 for a fidelity checklist for teacher praise.

Research on Teacher Praise

A large literature base has examined the effect of praise on a variety of student outcomes. However, only five studies met criteria for inclusion in this review (Connell & Carta, 1993; Darch & Gersten, 1985; Sutherland, Wehby, & Copeland, 2000; Sutherland et al., 2002; Todd et al., 1999).

Study Designs

Sutherland et al. (2002) used a correlational design to measure the magnitude of the relationship between praise and correct responding, while the remaining studies used single-subject designs. One study used a multiple baseline design across participants to determine whether the implementation of the self-assessment intervention influenced rates of student active engagement, competing behavior, and teacher prompting to the target students during in-class transition (Connell & Carta, 1993). Another study (Todd et al., 1999) began with a functional assessment and then employed withdrawal and multiple baseline design elements. Two studies (Darch & Gersten, 1985; Sutherland et al., 2000) used withdrawal of treatment designs.

Effect of Praise on Outcome Measures

We described the setting and measurement of two studies (Darch & Gersten, 1985; Sutherland et al., 2002) earlier. Sutherland et al. found a positive association between teacher praise and correct academic responding ($r = 0.49$, $p < 0.05$) in 20 classrooms for students with EBD, while Darch and Gersten noted increases in both

Figure 12.3   Praise fidelity checklist.

Behavior	Yes	No	NA
Before Instruction			
Identify desirable social behavior.			
Identify desirable academic behavior.			
Generate list of possible praise statements.			
During Instruction			
Provide praise for desirable social behavior.			
Provide praise for desirable academic behavior.			
Praise is contingent on desirable behavior ("if–then rule").			
Praise statement includes student name.			
Praise is descriptive (e.g., behavior specific).			
Praise is sincere.			
Use a variety of praise statements.			
Praise is related to effort.			

correct responding and on-task behavior when praise was increased for four students with LD, particularly when these increases were paired with increases in OTR.

Connell and Carta (1993) investigated an intervention package that combined a self-assessment procedure with teacher praise for appropriate behavior during transition time in three early childhood special education classrooms. Participants included one student from each of the three classrooms and the corresponding teachers who were all certified in early childhood special education. Results suggest that the intervention resulted in mean increases in students' engagement across classrooms; however, praise was included as part of an intervention package including students' self-assessment of behavior, and as such the effects of praise on engagement are difficult to ascertain. Results of this study do suggest, however, that teaching students to self-assess performance of in-class transition skills, accompanied by moderate levels of teacher praise, can have a positive effect on student active engagement and independent responding.

Todd et al. (1999) examined the effects of a self-management procedure in the context of positive behavior support, including increased teacher praise. Participants were nine third- and fourth-grade students (one target student with LD and eight randomly selected students) in a mixed third- and fourth-grade classroom with 29 students and one teacher. Results suggest that implementation of self-monitoring, self-recruitment of teacher attention, and increases in teacher praise were associated with decreases in problem behaviors, increases in on-task behavior, and increases in task completion. In a similar study, Sutherland et al. (2000) examined the effect of increases in a teacher's behavior-specific praise on the on-task behavior of nine fifth-grade students with EBD in a self-contained classroom. Using an observation/feedback procedure, the teacher set a goal of six behavior-specific praise statements per 15-minute observation period and received feedback on his use of praise statements. Increases in the teacher's behavior-specific praise were associated with increased on-task behavior.

Procedures

Procedures for increasing rates of praise varied across the five studies reviewed, although it should be noted that the Sutherland et al. (2002) study was descriptive in nature and thus measured naturally occurring rates of teacher praise. Darch and Gersten (1985) simply instructed the teacher to increase rates of praise during treatment phases; no other procedures were noted. Similarly, Connell and Carta (1993) instructed the teachers in their study to praise desirable student behavior at least when students were transitioning between activities during the treatment phases. Additionally, the teachers

completed a self-assessment scale following transitions that allowed them to note occurrences of students' target behavior. Finally, the researcher in Sutherland et al. (2000) provided the teacher with feedback immediately following observations on the teacher's rate of behavior-specific praise related to the teacher's goal of six praise statements per observation period.

Implementation Fidelity

Given the descriptive nature of Sutherland et al. (2002), fidelity data were not noted, although rates of teacher praise and correct responding were provided. Darch and Gersten (1985) did not provide rates of teacher praise; thus, interpreting the effect of their increased praise condition on student engagement is limited. Connell and Carta (1993) used a checklist to measure treatment fidelity across phases of their study. These authors noted that fidelity of implementation of the praise component were 93%, 56%, and 84% across three classrooms. Todd et al. (1999) used direct observations of teacher behavior to document increases in teacher praise; results indicated increased means during treatment phases with some data overlap. Sutherland et al. (2000) reported direct observation data on the teacher's use of behavior-specific praise statements; results indicated that the teacher's rate of praise statements was 1.3 and 1.7 per minute during baseline phases and 6.7 and 7.8 per minute during intervention phases.

Strengths and Limitations of the Research on Praise

The small number of studies makes it difficult to generalize the findings of the research reviewed here; however, results suggest a positive association between teacher praise and various measures of students' academic engagement. The treatment fidelity data in two of the studies strengthen these findings. However, one study (Darch & Gersten, 1985) did not provide data on rates of teacher praise, making it difficult to link any increases in praise to improvements on the measured variables. Finally, only one of the five reviewed studies (Sutherland et al., 2000) provided race/ethnicity for student participants, while an additional study (Sutherland et al., 2002) provided race/ethnicity information for teacher participants, limiting the generalizability of findings from this research.

Summary

The purpose of this chapter was to review the effects of three classroom-based interventions on academic engagement among students with disabilities. OTR to academic requests (antecedent strategy), the GBG (contextual strategy), and teacher praise (consequent strategy) were evaluated, and this review resulted in a total of 18 studies that met criteria for inclusion. Following is a discussion of the collective strengths and limitations of the research reviewed, as well as recommendations for research and practice.

Strengths of the Research Base

Overall the studies reviewed in this chapter suggest positive effects of the independent variables on a variety of student engagement measures. Because 17 of the 18 studies reviewed used single-subject methodology, the criteria for determining whether a study meets acceptable methodological rigor recommended by R. H. Horner et al. (2005) are helpful in identifying both strengths and limitations of the reviewed studies. In general, both dependent and independent variables were provided with operational and replicable precision. The variety of student engagement measures, including correct academic responding (including reading, math, and science responding), off-task behavior, and task engagement, showed desirable change across studies, a finding that suggests that the interventions can have a positive effect on both passive and active student engagement. Demonstrations of experimental effects were evident across studies and at a minimum were replicated across participants. In addition, given the association between student engagement and academic achievement, the dependent variables in the research reviewed are socially valid, and the independent variables, particularly OTR and teacher praise, are practical and cost-effective to implement.

A relative strength of the OTR and praise literature reviewed was the reporting of treatment fidelity data. Of 13 intervention studies that examined the effect of OTR or praise, 12 provided some form of treatment fidelity data. Only Darch and Gersten (1985) failed to provide fidelity data, and this limits the interpretation of findings from this study, because it is not clear that rates of OTR and praise actually increased. Finally, although all of the research studies examining the effects of the three interventions reviewed do not necessarily meet the criteria for methodological rigor suggested by R. H. Horner et al. (2005), confidence in the effects of the three interventions reviewed is enhanced by the number of different research teams and geographical locations represented by the studies. To illustrate, of the 11 OTR studies reviewed, 7 were conducted by different research teams, while all 4 of the GBG studies and 4 of the 5 praise studies were conducted by different research teams.

Limitations of the Research Base

Although the results of the research reviewed in this chapter are promising, several significant limitations in this literature were evident. First, R. H. Horner et al. (2005) note the importance of describing research participants with sufficient detail. Of the reviewed 18 studies, only 4 provided information on the race/ethnicity of student participants, with one more providing information on the race/ethnicity of teacher participants. This limitation significantly limits the generalizability of the reviewed research and raises questions about the potential effects of the interventions on students from culturally and linguistically diverse backgrounds. Second, methodological limitations were noted in several studies. Specifically, the lack of a return to baseline in the Fishbein and Wasik (1981) study did not allow for a demonstration of experimental control, and the lack of a reintroduction of the intervention in Haydon et al. (2009) limits the interpretation of experimental effect in this study. Finally, of the four GBG studies reviewed, only one (Lannie & McCurdy, 2007) provided treatment fidelity data. This omission limits the interpretation of findings from the research reviewed on the GBG, particularly given the number of procedural steps necessary to implement the intervention with fidelity.

Recommendations for Future Research

Limitations of the reviewed research should inform future studies examining the effects of classroom-based interventions on the active student engagement of students with and at risk for disabilities. For example, studies should provide data on the race/ethnicity of student and teacher participants in order to help determine the potential effects of interventions for all students, including those from culturally and linguistically diverse groups. Additionally, collecting data on treatment fidelity is crucial as the field attempts to determine if particular interventions are associated with desirable student outcomes. Specifically, it is important that educators do not discount interventions with potential positive effects on student outcomes due to weak treatment effects when fidelity of implementation was poor or unexamined.

While encouraging practitioners to implement interventions with fidelity has been of interest to school-based researchers for some time, the science of measuring implementation of interventions remains behind that of the development and identification of these practices (McLeod, Southam-Gerow, & Weisz, 2009). Thus, it is critical that researchers not only measure treatment fidelity but also be thoughtful in the development of fidelity measures so as to capture those characteristics of fidelity that are most related to treatment effectiveness. From an educational perspective, *adherence* to a treatment protocol (e.g., base rates of target behavior) and *quality* (e.g., purposeful use of target behavior) might have differential effects on students' task engagement. Although many of the studies reviewed in this chapter used observed rates (i.e., *adherence*) of OTR and praise as measures of treatment fidelity, the *quality* with which these strategies were used was not measured. Mediational models of analysis can provide important information to researchers about the relationship between treatment fidelity and treatment outcomes, allowing for more targeted intervention packages that have the potential for greater treatment gains.

The selection of interventions to review in this chapter was purposeful. Each represents a different layer in a complex, interactive classroom system, and examining these interventions in concert therefore might be useful. To illustrate, Sutherland et al. (2002) found a sequential association between teacher praise and OTR, such that OTR were likely to occur with 5 seconds of a teacher praise statement at a rate higher than suggested by chance occurrence. Given that these two strategies are part of a learning trial (and given the promising results of each in isolation per this review), examining the effects of increased rates of praise and OTR might yield particularly powerful effects on student outcomes. In addition, examining the effects of increased rates of praise and OTR within the context of the GBG might also be a worthwhile research focus. For example, three of the GBG studies reviewed in this chapter (Darveaux, 1984; Fishbein & Wasik, 1981; Lannie & McCurdy, 2007) utilized reinforcement rather than punishment procedures as a procedural modification, and this adaptation might hold promise for students with and at risk for disabilities.

Recommendations for Practice

Although the limitations of the studies reviewed here provide some hesitation in the strength of recommendations, a few general suggestions for practitioners can be made. The research does suggest that increasing OTR is associated with improved student engagement, and increasing learning trials therefore should be a goal for teachers. A variety of means to increase rates of OTR are available to teachers, including decreasing intertrial interval, response cards, and choral responding. Selecting the method for increasing OTR should be based on a variety of factors, including but not limited to the age and developmental level of the students, the material to be learned, and the teacher's professional judgment. Additionally, teachers should attempt to identify and praise students' desirable behavior, both academic and social, as research strongly suggests the positive effects of praise. Delivering high-quality praise (e.g., behavior specificity, sincerity, contingent on target behavior) and appropriate, frequent OTR should be consistent goals of all practitioners. Finally, the GBG does appear to hold promise for students with and at risk for disabilities. Although adhering to the treatment protocol of the GBG is critically important, it may also be important for students with and at risk for disabilities to receive instruction on desirable behaviors and to have opportunities to be reinforced for performing desirable behaviors. Findings from three of the four studies on the GBG reviewed in this chapter, in which teachers provided points for desirable behavior rather than punishment procedures for undesirable behavior, support this assertion (Darveaux, 1984; Fishbein & Wasik, 1981; Lannie & McCurdy, 2007).

CHAPTER 13

Strategies to Improve Compliance

Carol Ann Davis and **Annie McLaughlin** | *University of Washington*

Following instructions is one of the basic readiness skills children need as they move into public school settings (Ladd, Kochenderfer, & Coleman, 1997). Without this skill, a child is less likely to perform well in school and more likely to have poor social relationships (Shores & Wehby, 1999). Long before children reach age 5, parents and day-care workers struggle with preschool children who do not follow instructions or are considered noncompliant (Webster-Stratton, 2006). In fact, Gilliam and Shahar (2006) reported preschool expulsion rates as 27 per 1,000 students. This alarming rate reflects not only those children with known disabilities but is indicative of the behavioral difficulties of the general population of young children (Patterson & Reid, 1973; G. R. Walker, 1993). Recent reports have listed noncompliance, or not following directions, as one of the primary causes for children being asked to leave their day-care settings. Children and youth who are noncompliant are at greater risk for exclusion from the day-care or general education classrooms and have fewer opportunities to engage in a variety of activities in the community (e.g., Gilliam & Shahar, 2006).

Noncompliance has been defined as a failure to initiate an adult request or direction in a timely manner, or as a failure to complete the task requested of the individual (Schoen, 1983). The study of compliance has a long history in the field of education and parenting (Engelmann & Colvin, 1983; Forehand & McMahon, 1981). In fact, compliance to typical routine instructions within the educational environment is a critical skill for students to succeed in school. Issues related to compliance therefore affect the amount of instructional time a teacher can provide and, thus, directly influence students' success (Belfiore, Basile, & Lee, 2008).

While the primary purpose of this chapter is to discuss research-based strategies for improving compliance, it is important to acknowledge this literature's influence on other areas of instruction and behavior and provide a rationale for why we, as educators, should still be interested in a literature that focuses on compliance and compliance training. Much of what we know about improving compliance comes from the early work of Forehand, MacMahon, Patterson, and other colleagues examining family interactions (Forehand & McMahon, 1981; Forehand, Wells, & Sturgis, 1978; Patterson, 1982). These researchers, along with several others, studied interactions in the home and school and differentiated the types of requests delivered to children and students and their corresponding compliance to those requests (S. M. Johnson, Wahl, Martin, & Johansson, 1973). Findings showed that higher rates of compliance were associated with higher rates of "initiating commands," which required the student to begin an activity (e.g., "Please sit down") as opposed to "stop commands," which required the student to stop doing something (e.g., "Stop touching the glass"). H. M. Walker, Ramsey, and Gresham (2004) suggest it is important to deliver instructions that are specific (i.e., explicitly telling the student what to do), direct (e.g., "Please put the paper down" rather than questioning, e.g., "Could you put the paper down?"), and simple (e.g., not wordy, one request at time). This body of research on the delivery of requests, taken together, provides guidelines regarding ways to improve students' overall compliance by simply changing how adults deliver requests. The literature also provides several demonstrations of the successful use of compliance training with requests "to do" as well as "to stop doing" something (see Houlihan & Jones, 1990; Neef, Shafer, Egel, Cataldo, & Parrish, 1983).

Much of the early work on compliance assisted the field of special education in determining ways to increase appropriate responding and improve compliance. That is, we know how to change the environment, context, and type of request to increase the likelihood that students will engage or stay engaged in an activity (i.e., comply). We also recognize the importance of how teachers and other adults respond (or do not respond) to student noncompliance. That is, researchers have indicated that inconsistent responding to a child's noncompliance is likely to contribute to continued problems with noncompliance (e.g., Patterson, 1982; Dishion & Patterson, 2006). In addition, we know that increasing reinforcement (i.e., attention) when a learner follows a direction is likely to result in continued or improved compliance (Madsen, Becker, & Thomas, 1968; Sutherland, Wehby, & Copeland, 2000).

What we know about working with students with challenging behavior has evolved over time. The field has shifted its emphasis to focus on preventing and teaching skills rather than relying on only changing the consequence to influence the behavior. This shift in focus is evident in the expansive work on effective instruction and functional behavioral assessment. The literature, as well as chapters in this book, offers many strategies that if implemented can increase engagement and therefore increase compliance (see Chapter 12 in this volume).

More recently, appropriate strategies for increasing compliance have focused on determining the function of noncompliance and identifying a replacement behavior for noncompliance. Some perceive compliance training negatively (I. M. Evans & Meyer, 1990; A. McDonnell, 1993; L. Meyer & Evans, 1989), as it seems to focus only on conformity and does not address the underlying issue or mislearning that has occurred. Said differently, some professionals believe that the use of effective instruction and functional behavioral assessments to inform prevention efforts or identify a replacement behavior for noncompliance has alleviated the need for strategies that focus on the somewhat mechanistic procedures of compliance (i.e., simply "do as I say" approach). For example, we can change the environment or the conditions under which we deliver the requests to alleviate

noncompliance rather than direct intervention only at student compliance.

Nonetheless, we believe some situations and some learners may benefit from direct strategies to improve compliance. Take, for example, the adolescent who refuses to sit down and buckle the seat belt when asked by the airplane attendant or the fourth grader who still refuses to engage in the academic task, even when the teacher has increased the power of the consequence or opportunities to respond in the activity. In these instances, using effective instruction such as opportunities to respond or teaching a replacement behavior will not result in an acceptable alternative. Yet, the lack of compliance to a request or rule is likely to have dire consequences for those individuals. These instances provide us with examples to consider the need for strategies that increase a student's engagement (i.e., improving compliance) that other research-based strategies (e.g., increasing opportunities to respond, addressing the function of behavior) do not provide.

As acknowledged in the previous paragraph, our field's shift to applications of preventive and function-based approaches provides us with many strategies that increase the likelihood a learner will engage in the learning activities or respond appropriately to a request. However, some learners are particularly resistant to the typical interventions that increase engagement. In some cases, it may be necessary to first implement strategies that teach the skill of "compliance" or "following directions" so the learner may be ready or more willing to access those instructional strategies that increase or maintain engagement. The two strategies discussed within this chapter—compliance training and high probability requests—focus on improving compliance. In the sections that follow, we will present definitions, provide some theoretical background for the strategies, and list in a "how-to" format the steps of the strategies.

Compliance Training
Definition and Theoretical Background

Compliance training is simply the use of reinforcement to establish a particular behavior under stimulus control of an instruction or a request. For example, a teacher identifies those requests to which the learner does not respond appropriately, delivers one request, and then provides reinforcement when the appropriate response occurs. If the student does not respond within 10 seconds (typically) or engages in an incorrect behavior, a correction procedure is used by redelivering the request and providing prompts or assistance to complete the request.

The teacher provides reinforcement for the student's responding appropriately and does not provide reinforcement when the student does not respond appropriately. Differential reinforcement (i.e., reinforcing appropriate responses and not reinforcing inappropriate responses) is used to teach the student that appropriate response to a task demands occasional reinforcement. Several studies have indicated that providing reinforcement for following a subset of similar requests (also known as a response class) increases "instruction-following" behavior for other requests (Neef et al., 1983; Russo, Cataldo, & Cushing, 1981).

More recently, the more traditional procedures for compliance training have been modified to incorporate what Ducharme, Sanjuan, and Drain (2007) refer to as "errorless compliance training." This procedure structures the instructional trials (i.e., the delivery of a request, student compliance behavior, and the delivery of reinforcement) in phases that are categorized by the type of request. The types of requests are defined by the likelihood the student will respond. That is, level-1 requests are those that the student will respond to 75% to 100% of the time, level-2 requests are those that the student will respond to 51% to 75% of the time, level-3 requests are those that the student will respond to 26% to 50% of the time, and level-4 requests are those that the student will respond to 0% to 25% of the time. During the first phase, the interventionist or teacher delivers level-1 requests that the student will respond to 76% to 100% of the time. The interventionist starts at this level to ensure that the student will experience success by responding appropriately and thus begin to pair the reinforcement with the instruction and subsequent appropriate responding. Once the student demonstrates stable responding to level-1 requests, the interventionist begins to deliver only level-2 requests. Once the student responds to level-2 requests consistently, the teacher moves to level-3 and then level-4 requests, typically delivering only one level of request at a time (Ducharme, Harris, Milligan, & Pontes, 2003). In the section that follows, we offer a "how-to" guide for conducting compliance training in the classroom.

A "How-To" Guide

Identify the Instructions or Task Demands

For most teachers, identifying instructions that an individual does not consistently complete or does not complete in a timely manner is easy. These are typically the instructions (e.g., "Get out your book," "Come to circle time," "Clean up your activity") that we are most aware of because they cause us great concern or take many opportunities for the individual to accomplish them. For some learners, it is often a group of instructions (i.e., stimulus class) that are not followed consistently. A group of instructions (i.e., stimuli) can be defined by the elements they share. These common instructions may make up a stimulus class. In this case, the group of instructions or the stimulus class is defined by their effects on the behavior (i.e., noncompliance). The group of instructions that produce noncompliant responses is individual to each learner. For some learners, the group of instructions that result in noncompliance might include "Come here," "Put the _____ away," "Hand me the _____." For other students the instructions may be related to academic tasks and include "Begin working now," "What is the capital of Texas?" or "It is your time to read out loud."

Identify Reinforcers

Much has been studied and written about the use and role of reinforcement in the stimulus–response paradigm, particularly the role it plays in stimulus (or instructional) control. A stimulus is defined as a condition or event that occurs before a response or behavior that elicits its occurrence. A reinforcer is defined by the effect it has on the increased occurrence of a particular behavior (J. O. Cooper, Heron, & Heward, 2007). That is, a stimulus provided contingent on the production of a behavior that maintains or increases that behavior is termed a *reinforcer*. Consider, for example, a situation when a student responds to an instruction or request (i.e., stimulus) and a teacher provides praise contingent on that response. If the student's responses to the teacher's requests increase, then teacher-provided praise is considered reinforcement, and the student's response is likely to occur again when the teacher gives that request or instruction in the future. Much has been studied and written about the identification of reinforcers (J. E. Carr, Nicolson, & Higbee, 2000). Although reinforcers are individually determined and specific to each learner, we do have reliable and valid ways to ensure we identify stimuli that serve as reinforcers (Morgan, 2006; Piazza, Fisher, Hagopian, Bowman, & Toole, 1996) through direct observation and choice assessment.

When preparing to directly teach "instruction following," it is necessary to identify and validate reinforcers for the learner. This can be done by observing which items or activities the learner engages with during a "free-choice" condition in which items that are likely to function as reinforcers are accessible. Reinforcers can also be identified by presenting likely preferred items to the learner in a forced choice condition. That is, the interventionist provides a choice of potential reinforcers (typically two to three items or activities selected from a larger pool) and then asks the learner to choose among them. The interventionist records the learner's selection and then presents another choice of two to three potential reinforcers (items and activities from the larger pool may be represented). Choice of items or activities is presented repeatedly, and a hierarchy of preferred items are then identified based on the frequency with which the learner chose a particular item.

Decide on a Correction Procedure

As with all interventions or teaching trials, it is important to remember that a behavior is not under the control of the stimulus until it has been paired with reinforcement. On those occasions early in the teaching cycle, it is important to identify what the procedure will be when the desired behavior (e.g., instruction following) does not follow after the stimulus (e.g., instructions). The consequence for noncompliance or correction procedure can include physical guidance, time-out, or ignoring. Physical guidance is the process of physically guiding the learner through the desired behavior. That is, if the instruction is to "Give me the paper" and the learner does not respond, the interventionist would physically prompt the student to give the paper (or provide physical assistance to the learner to hand the paper to the interventionist). If a teacher chooses to use time-out as the consequence for noncompliance, she would move the student to an area of the room in which all reinforcement is removed and unavailable for the learner to access. Finally, a teacher might decide to ignore the noncompliance by not providing any feedback or verbal redirection. The literature on functional assessment indicates that we should choose an intervention that will not provide the learner with reinforcement for the noncompliance. For example, if the noncompliance is a function of escape, the teacher should avoid choosing time-out or ignoring, because these two consequences would lead to reinforcing the function of the noncompliant behavior.

Provide Opportunities to Follow Instructions and Receive Reinforcement

Once the components have been identified, the interventionist provides opportunities for the student to respond, and when the learner provides the target response, the learner receives reinforcement. For example, the teacher says, "Please put down your pencil," and delivers the reinforcer to the student immediately when the student puts down her pencil. The teacher repeats the set of steps (instruction, behavior, reinforcement) over and over to provide numerous opportunities for the learner to experience both the instruction and the reinforcement. It is through multiple trials of the three-part contingency of the (a) teacher delivering the stimulus, (b) student

Table 13.1   Steps to Implementing Compliance Training

Steps	Examples
1. Deliver the instruction.	"Johnny, sit down."
2. Student responds.	Johnny sits in his chair.
3a. Teacher delivers reinforcement for instruction following.	"Nice sitting, Johnny," while the teacher gives Johnny a high-five.
3b. Teacher delivers corrective feedback for incorrect responding.	If Johnny does not sit down, the teacher may physically guide him to his seat.

responding appropriately, and (c) student receiving the reinforcement that compliance is taught. See Table 13.1 for an illustration of steps to implementing compliance training.

Consider, for example, a teacher who wants a student to sit down so she will stop wandering the classroom. The teacher gives the student the direction, "Sit down." If the student responds by sitting down, the teacher delivers the reinforcer by stating, "Great following directions, thank you for finding your seat." Of course, at any time the student does not respond by sitting down, the teacher delivers the correction procedure (e.g., physically guides the student to sit down) as previously described.

Errorless Compliance Training

Errorless compliance training is based on the same principles as errorless learning. That is, errorless learning structures the teaching opportunities in a way that increases the likelihood the learner will succeed and provide the correct response. Errorless compliance training is a specific form of compliance training that involves exposing the learner to increasingly and successively more challenging instructions at a pace that provides many opportunities for the student to experience success and gain reinforcement.

When implementing errorless compliance training, one of the first tasks is to identify a set of requests and categorize them into four categories related to the student's ability to perform them: easy requests (i.e., those the student has a history of completing), easy moderate requests, moderate requests, and hard requests. Clearly, some of these requests will be those for which the learner responds, and other requests will be those for which the student does not respond. In order to ensure success, the instruction begins with delivering easy requests and continues to deliver easy requests until the student is successful 80% of the time. Once the easy requests are mastered, the instruction then moves to the next level of requests, easy moderate, and so on until all requests have been

Table 13.2 Steps to Implementing Errorless Compliance Training

Steps	Examples
1. Identify requests (i.e., instructions), and categorize the requests into four groups (easy, easy moderate, moderate, and hard).	Make a list of requests the student always follows, usually follows, sometimes follows, hardly ever follows.
2. Deliver instruction for easy requests.	Deliver a request in which the student will always follow, "What is your favorite after-school activity?"
3. Deliver reinforcement for instruction following (ignore inappropriate responding).	Deliver some form of reinforcement, "That sounds like a great thing to do."
4. Provide many opportunities for the student to succeed at responding appropriately to the request.	Deliver requests in which the student always follows until you have 80%–100% compliance across 10 opportunities.
After teaching easy requests (to 80% responding for all requests), provide instruction on the next level of requests.	Deliver requests in which the student usually follows and so on until you are delivering instructions that the student typically does not follow.

taught. While appropriate responding is provided reinforcement (typically contingent praise), inappropriate or no responding is ignored. That is, errorless compliance training is based on the use of differential reinforcement; reinforcement is provided when the learner follows the direction, and reinforcement (or any other correction procedure) is not provided when the learner does not follow the instruction. See Table 13.2 for illustrative steps to implementing errorless compliance training.

Research Base

The literature on compliance training has a long history and influenced much of how we now prepare teachers to provide instruction in the classroom. However, this research is primarily focused on young children and involves parent training programs (R. McMahon & Forehand, 2003; Webster-Stratton, 2006). For the purpose of this chapter, we will provide a brief summary of the literature on compliance training and errorless compliance training together (see R. McMahon & Forehand, 2003, for a comprehensive review of the parent training literature).

Populations

Given the importance compliance, or responding to requests, plays in the early interaction of parents and

children, it is not surprising that the majority of this research has been conducted with young children, primarily 3 to 8 years of age (Bernhardt & Forehand, 1975; Ducharme et al., 2010; Forehand & Scarboro, 1975; M. Roberts, McMahon, Forehand, & Humphreys, 1978; Scarboro & Forehand, 1975). These participants have included learners who are typically developing (Ducharme, Popynick, Pontes, & Steele, 1996; Ford, Olmi, Edwards, & Tingstrom, 2001), with parents who use physical punishment (Ducharme, Atkinson, & Poulton, 2001), and learners with developmental disabilities (Ducharme & Di Adamo, 2005; Ducharme & Popynick, 1993; Russo, Cataldo, & Cushing, 1981).

Settings and Interventionists

The early research occurred in clinical settings, which allowed the researchers to isolate particular attributes of the instructional package to be evaluated (see summary of literature in R. McMahon & Forehand, 2003), and subsequently in the home setting (Ducharme, DiPadova, & Ashworth, 2010; Ducharme & Drain, 2004; Ducharme & Popynick, 1993). This research conducted with families laid the ground work for what we know about increasing compliance and effective instruction and has led to applications in preschool and school settings (Ducharme et al., 2010; Ducharme & Harris, 2005; Ford et al., 2001; Neef, Shafer, Egel, Cataldo, & Parrish, 1983). A range of individuals have implemented the intervention in research studies, beginning with parents who were prompted by the researchers (Ducharme & Popynick, 1993; Forehand & Scarboro, 1975; M. Roberts et al., 1978), and have included clinical therapists (Russo et al., 1981), researchers (Ducharme & DiAdamo, 2005), and teachers (Ducharme et al., 2010; Ford et al., 2001).

Delivery of Intervention

Compliance training is a package of several components related to the delivery of instructions, the prompted responses, and consequences provided upon the learner's response. We know that limiting the number of instructions (Forehand & Scarboro, 1975), using instructions that are clear and concise (M. Roberts et al., 1978), and providing instructions that require a learner to "do" something rather than "don't" do something (Neef et al., 1983) lead to increased compliance. In addition, the research literature indicates it is important for those implementing this intervention to use a consequence based on the learner response. If a learner follows the instruction, interventionists can increase compliance in the future by reinforcing the behavior through attention (J. Kotler & McMahon, 2003) or specific praise (Bernhardt & Forehand, 1975). On the other hand, interventionists can increase the likelihood of future compliance by implementing time-out (Hobbs, Forehand, & Murray, 1978; M. Roberts et al., 1978; Yeager & McLaughlin, 1995), ignoring (Davies, McMahon, Flessati, & Tiedemann, 1984), or physical guidance (Neef et al., 1983; Parrish, Cataldo, Kolko, Neef, & Egel, 1986) when the learner does not follow the instruction. Interestingly, McMahon and his colleagues found that including a verbal rationale along with the time-out procedure increased learner compliance and parental satisfaction with the intervention. Finally, the literature indicates that intervening on compliance can lead to changes in other behavior (Parrish et al., 1986).

General Strengths of the Research

As mentioned previously, compliance training has a long history demonstrating how to increase compliance. From the research findings of evaluating the implementation of compliance training, we have learned what types of requests or instructions are likely to lead to compliant responses (i.e., following directions). The research that forms the literature base is rich and varied. Studies have been conducted in a variety of settings such as clinics, homes, and schools, and effectiveness of compliance training has been documented in multiple replications. Much of the literature regarding compliance training has established the basis for what we know about effective instruction and the prevention of problem behavior.

General Limitations of the Research

Compliance training, while clearly effective, sometimes suffers from a lack of social validity, particularly from indirect consumers. That is, it is not often considered by caregivers and other educators as "functional" or meaningful learning when a student is repeatedly asked to perform simple tasks or instructions (e.g., "Come here," "Hand me the pencil"). This perspective may be due to the historical nature of the research (A. McDonnell, 1993). Much of the compliance training literature is older and was conducted at a time when education did not see the value of embedded instruction. That is, students were taught to read during reading class and to do calculations during math class. Thus, instruction often looked like "drill and practice." Many studies have taken place in clinical settings and under conditions in which mass trials of the same (or a limited group of) instructions have been taught instead of in actual classrooms. This is not to say the strategy itself is not effective or does not have social validity; in fact, parents and interventionists report meaningful changes in outcomes for learners and agree the intervention is easy to use (Ducharme et al., 2007). However, the way in which the strategy has been reported to have been implemented in the past possibly contributes to the sometimes negative perceptions of the intervention.

Recommendations for Future Research

Following instructions continues to be a critical skill in the classroom and is clearly linked to the future success of students, both academically and socially. Most of the research in this area to date has been in clinical or segregated settings. With the contemporary emphasis on inclusion, compliance training should also explore ways in which the intervention can be delivered within the context of less restrictive environments. Such research might consist of examining the ways in which the intervention can be embedded within the school day or the dosage of the intervention necessary to be effective.

High-Probability Requests
Definition and Theoretical Background

The high-probability requests (HPRs) teaching strategy is designed to increase a learner's compliance with instructions to which she does not usually comply. By providing a series of requests with which the learner is likely to respond favorably (HPRs) before providing the request with which the learner is not likely to respond (low-probability request), results have shown increases in compliance. Since the mid-1990s, a plethora of research has been conducted examining the use of HPR sequences on compliant responses to a variety of task demands across a variety of learners (C. A. Davis, Brady, Hamilton, McEvoy, & Williams, 1994; Killu, Sainato, Davis, Ospelt, & Paul, 1998; Zarcone, Iwata, Hughes, & Vollmer, 1993). Most often, HPR sequences have been implemented when the target outcome is to increase instances of following instructions or completing tasks and the function of the noncompliant behavior is escape (e.g., to avoid tasks that are difficult or uninteresting, to get away from social situations). HPRs have also been associated with or noted as being similar to "pre-task requesting" (G. H. Singer, Singer, & Horner, 1987) and "interspersed requesting" (R. H. Horner, Day, Sprague, O'Brien, & Heathfield, 1991).

HPR sequences is an intervention package consisting of an interventionist delivering three to five quick requests to which the student has a history of responding (HPR) immediately before delivering a request to which the student does not typically respond (low-probability request). The student is provided with reinforcement after he has responded appropriately to each request.

Table 13.3   High-Probability Request Sequence Examples

Request (high- and low-p)	Student Response	Teacher Response
"Clap your hands." (high-p)	Student claps hands.	Teacher praises student's response.
"Give me five." (high-p)	Student claps teacher's hand.	Teacher praises student's response.
"Touch your nose." (high-p)	Student touches nose.	Teacher praises student's response.
"Clean up toys." (low-p)	Student cleans up toys.	Teacher praises student's response.

Request (high- and low-p)	Student Response	Teacher Response
"Put your name on the paper." (high-p)	Student writes name on paper.	Teacher praises student's response.
"How many problems are on the paper?" (high-p)	Student says, "Ten."	Teacher praises student's response.
"Point to the fifth problem." (high-p)	Student touches problem number 5.	Teacher praises student's response.
"Start work now." (low-p)	Student begins work.	Teacher praises student's response.

A high-probability (high-p) request is a request to which the individual typically complies with 80% to 100% of the opportunities. A low-probability (low-p) request has been defined as a request in which the person typically complies with 50% or less of the presented opportunities. The HPR sequence, then, is made up of the interventionist delivering (a) a series of three to five high-p requests, (b) a low-p request, and (c) reinforcement for the compliance to each high- and low-p request. The requests, both high-p and low-p, are individually determined. An example of the implementation of this intervention is located in Table 13.3.

A considerable amount has been written about the possible theoretical explanations for the success of HPR. Although considerable discussion of and challenges to these explanations exist (see Houlihan & Brandon, 1996; Mace, 1996; J. A. Nevin, 1996), we focus on the two most frequently cited explanations in the research: behavioral momentum and response generalization.

Behavioral Momentum

Behavioral momentum is an analogy frequently used to describe the behavior principles at work in the HPR sequence (Mace et al., 1988). In Newton's law of physics, momentum is the product of an object's mass and velocity. For example, a car traveling at 60 mph (velocity) has more momentum than the same car traveling at 20 mph. Therefore, it would be more difficult to stop the car traveling at 60 mph. J. A. Nevin, Mandell, and Atak (1983) applied Newtonian physics and the associated concept of momentum to describe behavior such that the behavior response strength is analogous to mass and response rate is analogous to velocity. The product of the response strength (behavioral mass) and the response

rate (behavioral velocity) is a behavior's momentum. A behavior's momentum can increase when the response rate or response strength is increased. When a behavior's momentum is increased, the behavior is less likely to change and more likely to persist across time. A behavior with a high momentum, then, is likely to persist over time even when conditions change. For example, the behavior's (i.e., compliant responding) velocity is increased by increasing the response rate (i.e., presenting three to five high-p requests in close proximity). The mass, or response strength, is increased by delivering continuous reinforcement for the compliant responses to the high-p requests. This succession of request/compliance/reinforcement creates a momentum for compliant responding even when the more difficult task, the low-p request, is presented.

Response Generalization

HPR sequences have also been explained using the principles of response generalization (R. H. Horner et al., 1991). In their article using interspersed requests, Horner and colleagues suggest the sequence of high-p requests serves as varied stimuli from the same stimulus class of "instructions." That is, a learner begins to follow one "instruction" and then generalizes this response to other instructions. These instructions are followed by the learner's correct responses, all representing the same response class of "instruction following," and reinforcement. The authors suggest that the reinforced responses to the varied instructions increase the probability of the learner responding to the low-p request (i.e., a request from the same stimulus class of "instructions") because response generalization has occurred.

Regardless of the explanation for the phenomena, sequencing several high-p requests before initiating a low-p request can help students learn to successfully respond to low-p requests. In the section that follows, we offer a "how-to" guide on how to conduct HPRs.

A "How-To" Guide

Identify Low-P Requests

Teachers can typically easily identify low-p requests. Students refuse to follow these requests, delay starting them, or fail to complete them in a timely manner. Before beginning the HPR sequence, it is important to make sure the teacher directs the student to the complete task clearly and explicitly. For example, the language the teacher uses should be task-oriented (e.g., "Begin writing") and not in the form of a question (e.g., "Are you ready to begin writing?") and should use minimal words (e.g., "Begin writing" instead of "If you are ready to begin writing now you can go ahead and get started"). The teacher should also ensure that the student understands the expectation and is capable of responding appropriately. Only tasks that students can perform but are not performing well or are refusing to perform should be included in the HPR sequence. To identify low-p requests, the teacher can consult with those who frequently work with the student and create a list of possible low-p requests. Once these requests have been identified, teachers can validate the low-p requests by observing that they are not complied with at least 50% of the time.

Identify High-P Requests

High-p requests should be tasks or requests to which the student has a history of responding and readily completes. In addition, these requests should be instructions that can be completed in a relatively short amount of time (i.e., seconds versus minutes). Easy directives to which the student can respond to quickly, such as "Give me five," "Touch your nose," "Tell me your name," "Point to the light," are the focus of high-p requests. To identify possible high-p requests, interview those who typically work with the student and/or observe the student within her usual routine. It is important to make sure that you identify a pool of high-p requests from which to draw the three or four to make an HPR sequence and to later develop new sequences. Davis and Reichle (1996) found that HPR sequences that used the same three high-p requests were less successful than those sequences that were chosen from a variety of high-p requests. After identifying these high-p requests, it is necessary to validate that the learner will actually respond to the requests at least 80% of the time. If the sequences are built from requests the learner does not readily complete, the intervention will be ineffective.

Validate High-P and Low-P Requests

To validate low-p requests, simply provide the student with opportunities to complete a task, and record the student's response (see Figure 13.1). Those requests to which the student responds 50% of the time or less are considered low-p requests. To validate the requests as high-p, create a list from the interview and observation. Over the course of a few days and within a typical routine, ask the student to perform the high-p request. Spread the tasks out over the course of the school day. Over approximately five trials, record whether the student complied with the request. Requests that result with 80% success or better can be considered high-p requests.

To determine high-p requests for written assignments, develop one high-p worksheet and one typical worksheet. Both worksheets should contain the same number of letters or numbers. For example, if you are assessing addition, the low-p worksheet has five two-digit-by-two-digit problems (20 digits, total). The high-p worksheet needs to have 20 digits as well: 10 one-digit-by-one-digit problems. This equality ensures that the assessment focuses on the type of task and not the amount of work. Place one type of each worksheet on the desk, and ask the student to pick one of them. Over the course of a few days, repeat this procedure approximately five times. Record the student's choice each time. Again, the type of worksheet the student chooses 80% or more of the time can be considered to contain high-p content. If the student does not select one of the choices 80% of the time, you should re-evaluate the choices of high-p requests. Find different potential high-p requests and repeat the process again.

Select the HPR Sequences

Because we know that delivering the same or a select number of high-p sequences decreases the effectiveness of the intervention (Davis & Reichle, 1996), it is helpful for the interventionist to select and determine a pool of sequences before implementing the intervention. For example, the pool could include 10 different high-p requests so that whenever the interventionist uses an HPR sequence, plenty of options are available instead of repetitions of the same requests.

Implement the HPR Sequence

The considerations for implementing HPR sequences for verbal requests differ from those for written requests. When implementing the HPR sequence with verbal instructions, the sequence is initiated by asking the learner to complete the first high-p request. On completion of the high-p request by the learner, the interventionist delivers

Figure 13.1 Verify high-probability and low-probability requests.

Request	1	2	3	4	5	Percentage	High- or Low-p?

a reinforcer. The reinforcer can be in the form of verbal praise or a tangible (Mace et al., 1988; Mace, Mauro, Boyajian, & Eckert, 1997). The second and third high-p requests should be delivered within 5 to 15 seconds from the delivery of the reinforcement for the previous request. Some evidence indicates that the longer the intertrial interval, the less effective the intervention seems to be (C. A. McLaughlin & Davis, 2010). After the delivery of the reinforcer for the third high-p request, the interventionist should deliver the low-p request quickly (typically within 5 seconds) (Mace. et. al., 1988). The interventionist then provides reinforcement for completion of the low-p request, as well. Figure 13.2 provides an implementation checklist for the HPR sequence intervention.

When implementing the high-p request sequence for written tasks, arrange the written tasks with three to five high-p tasks (e.g., single-digit addition problems) immediately before the low-p task (e.g., double-digit addition problems). Provide reinforcement for completion of the low-p task. For some written tasks, reinforcement is not provided following the high-p requests until the learner has finished the low-p request. This differs from the verbal HPR sequences.

Evaluate the Effectiveness of the Intervention

In evaluating the success of HPR, the interventionist should consider collecting data on both high-p and low-p compliance (Figure 13.2 also serves as a data collection sheet). Monitoring the rate of compliance to high-p requests allows the interventionist to determine the fidelity of the intervention. That is, if the learner is not complying with the high-p requests, then the high-p request is not functioning as a stimulus for reinforcement, and the intervention will not work. The compliance to high-p requests does not need to be monitored for each sequence, but compliance should remain at about 80%. It is also important to monitor compliance with low-p requests. For verbal low-p requests, record compliance to the request, and for written low-p requests,

Figure 13.2   High-probability requests implementation checklist and data collection form.

Type of request	Student Response		Reinforcement w/in 5 s	
High-p: (write request)	C	IC	Y	N
High-p	C	IC	Y	N
High-p	C	IC	Y	N
Low-p	C	IC	Y	N

Type of request	Student Response		Reinforcement w/in 5 s	
High-p: (write request)	C	IC	Y	N
High-p	C	IC	Y	N
High-p	C	IC	Y	N
Low-p	C	IC	Y	N

Type of request	Student Response		Reinforcement w/in 5 s	
High-p: (write request)	C	IC	Y	N
High-p	C	IC	Y	N
High-p	C	IC	Y	N
Low-p	C	IC	Y	N

Type of request	Student Response		Reinforcement w/in 5 s	
High-p: (write request)	C	IC	Y	N
High-p	C	IC	Y	N
High-p	C	IC	Y	N
Low-p	C	IC	Y	N

Type of request	Student Response		Reinforcement w/in 5 s	
High-p: (write request)	C	IC	Y	N
High-p	C	IC	Y	N
High-p	C	IC	Y	N
Low-p	C	IC	Y	N

Request	Total delivered	Total correct	Percentage ([Total Correct/Total #] x 100)
High-p requests			
Low-p requests			

record the number of letters or numbers that the student completes. Evaluate whether the student is completing more of the low-p requests over time.

Fade the Intervention

Eventually, you can begin to fade the intervention by reducing the number of high-p requests delivered before the low-p request (Ducharme & Worling, 1994).

Although some evidence indicates that fading is not necessary (C. A. Davis, Brady, Williams, & Hamilton, 1992), other research leads us to recommend the interventionist systematically reduce the number of high-p requests slowly (Ducharme & Worling, 1994). If compliance to low-p behaviors decreases, then it may not be appropriate to decrease the high-p requests at that time. Implement the HPR sequences again, and plan to fade its use in the future.

Research Base

Research has provided a great deal of understanding regarding the effects of HPR. To date, over 40 peer-reviewed articles from a variety of researchers examine not only the efficacy of HPR, but also what variables or components of the strategy contribute to its effectiveness. The following is a summary of the literature on HPR.

Populations

HPR has been validated among individuals with a range of disabilities, as well as individuals without disabilities (Ardoin, Martens, & Wolfe, 1999; Austin & Agar, 2005; Rortverdt & Miltenberger, 1994; Bullock & Normand, 2006). Specifically, HPR has shown to be successful with people with behavior disorders (Belfiore, Lee, Scheeler, & Klein, 2002; C. A. Davis, Brady, Williams, & Hamilton, 1992), developmental disabilities (Killu et al., 1998; Mace et al., 1988; Zarcone et al., 1993), learning disabilities (Wehby & Hollahan, 2000), autism (Romano & Roll, 2000; Ray, Skinner, & Watson, 1999), and traumatic brain injury (D. L. Lee & Laspe, 2003). In addition, HPR has been used successfully across a variety of ages, including toddlers (Bullock & Normand, 2006), preschoolers (Rortverdt & Miltenberger, 1994), elementary-aged students (Ray et al., 1999; C. A. Davis et al., 1994), high school-aged students (Belfiore, Lee, Vargas, & Skinner, 1997), and adults (Fisher, Adelinis, Thompson, Worsdell, & Zarcone, 1998; Romano & Roll, 2000).

Outcomes

Most of the research on HPR has focused on increasing compliance to general requests. However, researchers have also targeted other behaviors, such as increasing social interactions (Davis et al., 1994; McComas et al., 2000), increasing functional communication skills (Sanchez-Fort, Brady, & Davis, 1995), improving academic skills (Belfiore et al., 1997), increasing compliance to a medication routine (Harchik & Putzier, 1990), decreasing task duration and response latency to instruction following (Mace et al., 1988; Belfiore et al., 1997; Wehby & Hollahan, 2000), decreasing transition latency (Ardoin et al., 1999), and decreasing challenging behaviors (R. H. Horner et al., 1991; Zarcone, Iwata, Mazaleski, & Smith, 1994). The different behaviors shown to be affected by using HPRs are wide in variety and indicate versatility in its application.

Variety of Settings and Interventionists

HPR studies have been conducted in both clinical and applied settings. These settings include schools (C. A. Davis & Reichle, 1996; Houlihan, Jacobson, & Brandon, 1994; Wehby & Hollahan, 2000), preschools and day-care centers (D. L. Lee, Belfiore, & Ferko, 2006; Santos & Lignugaris-Kraft, 1999), family homes (Bullock & Normand, 2006; Ducharme & Worling, 1994), hospitals (McComas, Wacker, & Cooper, 1998), and group homes (Romano & Roll, 2000). In schools, HPRs have been used in various locations on school grounds, such as general education classrooms (Ardoin et al., 1999), self-contained/segregated special education classrooms (Belfiore et al., 2008), hallways (Banda & Kubina, 2006), and inclusive classrooms (C. A. Davis et al., 1994).

The majority of the studies have used one interventionist to implement the HPR sequence with one individual (Banda & Kubina, 2006; Belfiore et al., 2008). However, Ardoin et al. (1999) delivered the HPR sequence to a class with three students targeted for intervention. Use of HPR increased compliance and decreased response latency for two of the three targeted students. In addition, G. H. Singer et al. (1987) implemented the intervention to a class of students when returning from recess with 100% success for two of the target students and 97% success for two other target students.

Interventions have been implemented by researchers or trained research assistants (Belfiore et al., 1997; Bullock & Normand, 2006; Zarcone et al., 1994) and by teachers or teacher assistants (Banda & Kubina, 2006; Belfiore et al., 2008; C. A. Davis et al., 1994). Additionally, peers have been trained to deliver the HPR sequence within the context of classroom activity (C. A. Davis & Reichle, 1996). A social validity survey and direct follow-up observations in C. A. Davis, Reichle, and Southard (2001) indicate that the intervention is practical for teachers to use on a daily basis in their classrooms. Overall, HPR sequences have been used in a variety of settings, spanning a large range of ability levels, and implemented by different people as interventionists.

Delivery of High-P and Low-P Requests

Much of the research regarding HPR has defined high-p requests as those requests to which the participant complies with 80% or more of instances of the requests being delivered (Ardoin et al., 1999; Belfiore et al., 2008; C. A. Davis & Reichle, 1996; Zarcone et al., 1994). However, Romano and Roll (2000) examined the use of high-p sequences (>80% compliance) and medium-p request sequences (50% to 70% compliance) to increase compliance of individuals with developmental disabilities. Romano and Roll showed that no systematic differences existed between the medium- and high-probability sequences on increasing the compliance with low-p requests. The results of this study indicate that both high- and medium-probability requests may be successful antecedents to low-p requests.

When examining research regarding the implementation of HPR sequences, we know that it is important to vary the individual high-p requests. C. A. Davis and Reichle (1996) used high-p requests to increase initiated social interactions of young children with behavioral disorders and found that using variant high-p request sequences was more effective than using invariant sequences. Research has also indicated that it is important to attend to the time between the delivery of the reinforcers and the high-p and low-p requests (intertrial intervals). For example, Mace et al. (1988) examined differences in 5 seconds and 15 seconds between the delivery of the reinforcer for the last high-p request and the delivery of the low-p request (interprompt time). They found that the 15-second inter-prompt time failed to elevate the rates of compliance above baseline; instead, shorter inter-prompt times increased the rate of reinforcement, and compliance with low-p requests persisted over time. These findings were replicated by Houlihan et al. (1994) and Kennedy, Itkonen, and Lindquist (1995). Moreover, C. A. McLaughlin and Davis (2010) found that HPR sequences were more effective when the intertrial intervals between the reinforcer of the high-p requests and the next high-p request are in close temporal proximity (e.g., 5 seconds).

Reinforcer Quality

In addition to varying the high-p requests in sequences and shorter intertrial intervals, Mace et al. (1997) found that increasing the quality of the reinforcer increased the compliance to low-p requests. For example, Mace et al. (1997) used social praise alone and then food as reinforcers for compliance to the low-p requests. They found that using food (a higher-quality reinforcer) produced higher rates of compliance. Additionally, Mace et al. (1997) found that responding to multiple low-p requests persisted better when a higher-quality reinforcer such as food was used.

Consequences for Not Responding to Low-P Requests

When using HPR, we typically expect the learner to comply with the low-p request when followed by a sequence of high-p requests. However, as with most interventions, the use of an HPR sequence does not always produce the effects or compliant responding to the low-p request that is targeted. Zarcone and her colleagues (1993, 1994) examined the use of escape extinction on noncompliant responding to the low-p requests. For example, if a student engages in noncompliance to escape having

to do the task, using escape extinction would look like not allowing the student to escape the task. That is, if a teacher asks a student to put away his materials and the student does not comply, the teacher's physically prompting the student to put away the materials would be an example of escape extinction. Zarcone's research indicated that using escape extinction for noncompliance to the low-p request produced more effective results than when the noncompliant responding was ignored. However, several studies also indicate positive effects when noncompliant responding to the low-p request was ignored (C. A. Davis, Brady, Williams, & Hamilton, 1992; C. A. Davis et al., 1994).

General Strengths of the Research

The research on HPR has shown positive outcomes for individuals with a range of disabilities as well as individuals without disabilities. The research has also shown an influence on a variety of outcomes, with most being conducted in applied settings with practitioners implementing the intervention. The applied nature of the research base allows teachers in schools to envision a variety of opportunities in which the HPR sequence might be utilized.

General Limitations of the Research Reviewed

Although HPR clearly has been documented as a successful invention, as with compliance training, some professionals consider its perceived contrived nature as a limitation (I. M. Evans & Meyer, 1990). For example, most of the research using the HPR sequence with people with intellectual disabilities often uses one-step directions (high-p requests) that peers without disabilities may not comply with due to social disapproval. That is, many interventionists cannot imagine an adolescent complying with being asked to "Give me five." However, the breadth of this literature provides opportunity to identify socially and contextually valid high-p requests (either verbally or nonverbally) that are effective with a variety of individuals and in a variety of situations.

Recommendations for Future Research

As with any intervention, once the strategy has been validated as successful, it is up to researchers and practitioners to work together to provide further information about its utility in applied settings. In addition, when we examine intervention packages such as HPR, it is also helpful to have a better understanding about the influence of fidelity of implementation on the effectiveness on the intervention. Moreover, as HPR continues to be studied across a wide variety of learners and in a variety of settings, it will be important for us to consider the impact of the context on the implementation of the intervention. For example, examining how the age of the participant influences which high-p requests are used, or how the preferences of the interventionists (e.g., teacher, parent) impact whether or not escape extinction is plausible would be important contextual variables that would further our understanding.

Conclusion

Compliance, or the lack thereof, influences the interactions between learners and adults in school and other settings in ways that can adversely affect a student's outcomes and future opportunities for learning. In this chapter, we reviewed the procedures and supporting literature for two effective and straightforward strategies that are supported by research as improving compliance—compliance training and HPRs. Each of these strategies not only has provided teachers and families with specific interventions that can increase compliance, but also has contributed to our understanding of (a) how to increase effective instruction in schools, (b) how to increase positive interactions in families, and (c) how these strategies work in combination with other research-based strategies to provide an optimal learning environment for both students and teachers. Although both practices are supported by strong research bases and are relatively simple to implement, it is important to remember these strategies should be used in the classroom alongside the other advances in our field (i.e., functional assessment and positive behavior support).

CHAPTER 14

Strategies to Address Internalizing Behavior Problems

Lee Kern | *Lehigh University*

Alexandra Hilt-Panahon | *Minnesota State University, Mankato*

Anuja Divatia Mukherjee | *University of Texas Health Science Center at Houston*

Overview of Internalizing Problems

The mention of youth emotional and behavioral problems usually brings to mind externalizing or acting out behaviors, such as aggression and disruption (e.g., see Chapters 10 and 15, this volume). Because these types of behaviors are evident to others in the environment and usually disrupt learning and order in classroom and school settings, they beseech the most attention. Equally problematic, however, are behaviors that are not readily observable, yet cause individual interruptions in learning, social relationships, and everyday functioning. Problems of this nature, classified as *internalizing behaviors,* are directed inwardly and represent overly controlled patterns of behavior (Gresham & Kern, 2004).

Internalizing problems pose unique challenges for identification and assessment, particularly for school-based practitioners, for a number of reasons. First, the covert and nonintrusive types of behaviors that characterize internalizing problems are often overlooked by teachers and other school-based practitioners. This is because they are seldom disturbing or disruptive to

others (Algozzine, 1977). Second, unlike externalizing behaviors, internalizing behaviors do not challenge a teacher's authority or ability to manage the classroom and provide instruction. Third, the definition of emotional disturbance, as specified in the Individuals with Disabilities Education Act (IDEA), does little to facilitate identification of students needing intervention. Specifically, the IDEA denotes three limiting criteria for identification, including the presence of a disorder: (a) of sufficient severity or "to a marked degree," (b) exhibited for a "long period of time," and (c) that "adversely affects educational performance." These criteria are extremely subjective and provide particularly little guidance in identifying internalizing disabilities, especially given their covert nature (e.g., Kauffman, 2001). Finally, the academic performance of many students with internalizing problems is not adversely affected to an extent that most schools or districts require for special education identification. This does not diminish the need for intervention, but rather eliminates the possibility that it will be mandated through the educational system. Exclusion for this reason is particularly unfortunate because, although the large majority of students with emotional health needs do not receive services, for those who are able to access intervention, schools are the primary provider (B. J. Burns et al., 1995). Specifically, schools provide 70% to 80% of the services that school-age students receive for their emotional problems.

A comprehensive definition of internalizing disorders requires familiarity with two systems of classification, education and psychiatry. The IDEA definition of "emotional disturbance" encompasses both externalizing and internalizing problems, but a close inspection reveals that the majority of criteria pertain to internalizing problems. Specifically, "emotional disturbance" is defined as:

(i) . . . a condition exhibiting one or more of the following characteristics over a long period of time and to a marked deter which adversely affects school performance: (a) an inability to learn which cannot be explained by intellectual, sensory, or health factors; (b) an inability to build or maintain satisfactory relationships with peers and teachers; (c) inappropriate types of behaviors or feelings under normal circumstances; (d) a general mood of unhappiness or depression; (e) a tendency to develop physical symptoms or fears associated with personal or school problems.

(ii) The term includes children who are schizophrenic. The term does not include children who are socially maladjusted, unless it is determined that they also are emotionally disturbed.

As the federal definition reflects, students with internalizing problems typically experience difficulties with learning, relationships with others, feelings, moods, and/or physical symptoms/fears. To reiterate, the definition is quite ambiguous and lacks clarity, providing little direction for school-based practitioners when determining eligibility.

The *Diagnostic and Statistical Manual of Mental Disorders IV,* published by the American Psychiatric Association (1994), specifies a number of types of internalizing disorders and describes characteristics of those disorders. Disorders falling under the category of internalizing problems, and their definitions, are provided in Table 14.1. This system of classification, the most commonly used for identifying psychopathology in the United States, provides more specificity than the IDEA definition. Still, this system has limitations, particularly with respect to use in schools (Gresham & Gansle, 1992). One issue is that diagnosis, even by skilled clinicians, has been unreliable (e.g., Sattler & Hoge, 2006). In addition, the descriptions focus on associated feelings or behaviors, rather than related environmental events (e.g., S. T. Watson & Robinson, 1998). The absence of focus on environmental triggers and responses to internalizing

behavioral problems or symptoms is an important omission because it does facilitate the development of strategies to address associated environmental events, a critical component of a comprehensive behavior plan. In spite of the limitations, it is important to understand both the educational and psychiatric classifications, given that students with internalizing disorders may meet diagnostic criteria for a DSM IV diagnosis but not IDEA classification and vice versa.

It is essential for educators to understand effective interventions for reducing internalizing behaviors for numerous reasons. First, without effective intervention, internalizing problems are associated with a range of negative outcomes, including low self-esteem, social withdrawal, sadness, physical health problems, lack of concentration, poor academic performance in school, disrupted day-to-day functioning, and, in severe cases, even suicide. These problems last far past the school years, interfere with productive adult functioning, and cause a tremendous burden to the individual herself as well as society. Effective intervention is imperative for healthy development and long-term quality of life. In addition, the large numbers of students who experience internalizing problems during the school-age years underscore the need for services. For instance, research indicates that as many as 8% of adolescents in the United States experience depression (K. A. Collins, Westra, Dozois, & Burns, 2004; Costello, Erkanli, & Angold, 2006). Estimates of the prevalence of mental health issues suggest that more than 30% of students will experience a significant problem during their school career (Hammen & Rudolph, 1996). Also, as noted, it is unlikely that students will receive intervention if it is not provided in schools. Finally, growing evidence indicates that intervention is most effective if delivered when symptoms first emerge, before problems become severe (Kern et al., 2007). Hence, providing intervention at the early stages of internalizing disorders will prevent the development of associated problems and will require less intensive efforts.

Because internalizing problems have garnered less attention than externalizing problems, a relative paucity of research supports intervention effectiveness. Further, although some interventions, such as medication, have been tested with adults, far fewer evaluations have been conducted with school-age students. In the following sections, we review the interventions that are most commonly used, have the most empirical support, and appear to be either efficacious or promising: cognitive behavior therapy, anxiety management/relaxation training, and pharmacological intervention. Due to the large and diverse number of internalizing problems, we focus primarily on the most common two, depression and anxiety.

Table 14.1   DSM IV Internalizing Disorders and Characteristics

Disorder	Description
Adjustment disorder	Emotional or behavioral symptoms in response to an identifiable stressor or stressors. There are six subtypes of adjustment disorders, depending on whether symptoms include depressed mood, anxiety, mixed anxiety and depressed mood, disturbance of conduct, mixed disturbance of mood and conduct, or are unspecified.
Anorexia nervosa	An eating disorder characterized by an obsessive fear of gaining weight and resulting in extremely low body weight and body image distortion. Body weight is often controlled through voluntary starvation, excessive exercise, or diet pills and diuretic drugs.
Bulimia nervosa	An eating disorder characterized by recurrent binge eating, followed by compensatory behaviors (e.g., self-induced vomiting, purging, fasting, use of laxatives, over exercising) to avoid weight gain.
Dysthymic disorder	A chronic mood disorder with low-grade depression, less severe than major depressive disorder. In children, the disorder may be characterized by irritability, rather than sadness.
Generalized anxiety disorder	Excessive, uncontrollable, and generally irrational worry that is disproportionate to the actual source of worry.
Major depressive disorder	Low mood, low self-esteem, and loss of interest or pleasure in nearly all activities. In children, the disorder may be characterized by irritability, rather than sadness.
Obsessive-compulsive disorder	Recurrent intrusive thoughts, which may include feeling compelled to perform irrational, time-consuming behaviors.
Posttraumatic stress disorder	Severe ongoing emotional reaction to an extreme and traumatic stressor, such as someone's death, a threat to own or another's life, serious physical injury, or unwanted sexual act.
Reactive attachment disorder of infancy or early childhood	Disturbed and developmentally inappropriate ways of relating socially in most contexts, ranging from failure to initiate or respond to displaying excessive familiarity with strangers. The disorder begins before age 5.
Selective mutism	Failure to speak in person given situations, or to specific people, when capable of speech.
Separation anxiety disorder	Excessive anxiety regarding separation from home or from people to whom the person has a strong attachment.
Social anxiety disorder	Excessive distress and impaired functioning in social situations, particularly pertaining to a fear of being embarrassed or humiliated by one's actions or being judged by others.
Somatization disorder	Chronic and persistent complaint of varied physical symptoms with no identifiable physical origin.

Source: Information from American Psychiatric Association. (2000). *Diagnostic and statistical manual of mental disorders* (4th ed.). Washington, DC: Author.

Effective Practices

Cognitive Behavioral Therapy

Definition and Theory for Effectiveness

The term *cognitive behavior therapy* (CBT) describes techniques that incorporate both cognitive and behavioral methods of intervention. Cognitive approaches are rooted in the work of Aaron Beck, who developed a treatment for depression based on cognitive theory. Specifically, he hypothesized that people experienced depression because of deficits in information processing that cause a negative self-view, as well as a negative outlook of the world and the future (Kazdin & Marciano, 1998). This negative world view then leads

to maladaptive thought processes, such as a short-term focus, excessively high performance standards, and lack of self-reinforcement. In fact, research has shown that students with depression can exhibit a wide range of cognitive distortions including low self-esteem and selective attention to negative events (Kendall, Stark, & Adam, 1990; McCauley, Burke, Mitchell, & Moss, 1988). Given these distorted and negative views, the goal of cognitive therapy is to confront, challenge, and modify maladaptive thought processes.

Unlike cognitive interventions that attempt to change the thoughts of an individual with depression, behavioral interventions focus on changing specific behaviors that will then lead to decreased symptoms. According to behavioral theory, depression leads to decreases in engagement in pleasurable activities due to a restricted range of response-contingent reinforcement, fewer social reinforcers, and inadequate social skills. Behavioral interventions for depression therefore are designed to teach skills and provide opportunities to increase positive social experiences and pleasurable activities (i.e., reinforcers). When combined, these two types of interventions target both the thoughts and actions of individuals with depression.

Implementation

Although many variations of cognitive-behavioral therapy exist, all CBT treatments have several common features (Harrington, Whittaker, & Shoebridge, 1998). The overarching commonality is that both cognitive and behavior techniques are combined to affect change in thoughts and behavior. In addition, several other common features exist in all CBT programs. First, the focus of CBT is the child/adolescent. Although intervention also may involve parents or family members peripherally, the focus of change is on the individual. Another common feature is that the therapist is an active participant in therapy, collaborating closely with the child to solve problems and identify solutions. The therapist acts as a teacher, providing instruction to the child on how to monitor his thoughts and behavior. The child also is taught to keep a record of thoughts and behavior for later reflection (Harrington et al., 1998).

One advantage of CBT is that it can be implemented in relatively brief periods of time. Intervention typically lasts 5 to 12 weeks, and requires 8 to 15 sessions, ranging in length from 30 to 90 minutes per session. In addition, CBT is most frequently conducted in group sessions, making it cost-effective.

In a recent review of school-based interventions for students at risk for depression, Hilt-Panahon, Kern, Divatia, and Gresham (2007) identified the most common techniques and combinations of techniques used in CBT interventions. Among 15 studies identified, cognitive restructuring was used in the majority of studies ($n = 8$). Cognitive restructuring involves teaching students to challenge distorted and negative cognitions about themselves and their environment and to replace those cognitions with more realistic ones. This technique is based on the assumption that students are depressed due to a maladaptive style of information processing (i.e., interpreting events as negative). If cognitions are more realistic (and potentially more positive), then the individual should experience less depression.

Problem solving, also considered a CBT approach, was the second most frequently implemented technique,

occurring in six studies. Problem solving involves teaching students to evaluate stress-provoking situations by gathering relevant information, thinking about alternative responses, and choosing the best response. For example, students may be taught how to identify social conflict and then develop appropriate ways to handle those situations (Cardemil, Reivich, & Seligman, 2002). Pleasant activity scheduling is an intervention that entails systematic planning of students' daily activities to incorporate pleasant and desirable events, and it was implemented in five studies. For instance, students generated a list of preferred activities, which were incorporated into their daily routines to increase positive experiences. Weisz, Thurber, Sweeney, Proffitt, and LeGagnoux (1997) incorporated this technique into CBT by focusing therapy sessions on the student's learning to both identify and engage in activities that the student found to be mood enhancing.

Self-management, in many forms, is also a major component of CBT. For students to begin to think and act differently, they must be able to identify and address their own thoughts, feelings, and actions. Several specific techniques fall into this category including self-change (making self-evaluations and changing behavior as a result), self-instruction, self-modeling, and attribution retraining (teaching students to make more realistic and adaptive attributions). In addition, activities to link thoughts, feelings, and behavior (teaching students how all three are linked and influence each other) can assist students in managing their own behavior. For example, Jaycox, Reivich, Gillham, and Seligman (1994) taught children to understand the link between their own thoughts and feelings and how one influenced the other. Participants in the therapy learned how to develop a list of potential explanations for the negative events in their lives and then to identify the most plausible explanation based on what they know about the situation.

As highlighted by Hilt-Panahon et al. (2007), it is important to emphasize that these interventions have been used in schools with great success in the context of research protocols; however, little is known about the feasibility of implementation of CBT in schools with school staff as intervention agents. In fact, of the studies reviewed, only one used school personnel to implement the intervention, and that was with the collaboration and supervision of the researcher. In addition, extensive training and supervision were provided in a number of studies reviewed, regardless of who was implementing the intervention. CBT is designed to be implemented by or in conjunction with someone who has been trained in its use.

As described in the previous sections, CBT is not a specific intervention but rather a combination of therapeutic techniques. These interventions should be implemented in conjunction with a professional trained in the use of CBT. Figure 14.1 provides guidelines for the implementation of CBT by school personnel. Given that many possible components can be implemented in combination, it is difficult to provide a specific protocol for implementation. Instead, in the following sections, we provide an example of an intervention protocol, as described as part of an efficacy study conducted by Reynolds and Coats (1986).

The intervention package was designed to be delivered over a short period of time. Intervention was intense, with students participating in small groups for 10 sessions, each 50 minutes in duration, across a 5-week period. Students received reinforcement contingent on their participation and attendance. Intervention was conducted at the high school the students attended. The program consisted of three phases that emphasized the training of self-control and self-change skills. Specific techniques used in the intervention package included self-monitoring, self-evaluation, and self-reinforcement. In addition to the specific skills taught, the participants

Figure 14.1   Steps for implementation of cognitive-behavior therapy.

1. Operationally define problem behavior.
2. Collect data to determine frequency and severity of problem behavior.
3. Is the problem behavior frequent and severe enough to impact the student's socioemotional well-being?
   a. Yes—go to step 4.
   b. No—intervention not indicated.
4. Consult with experienced professionals to determine the benefits of referral for cognitive–behavioral interventions.
5. Consult the school district's policy for such referrals.
6. If cognitive behavior therapy (CBT) is implemented, determine the roles of different school personnel for the following tasks:
   a. Implementation of intervention (must be conducted by or under the supervision of someone with extensive training in cognitive–behavioral techniques).
   b. Behavior-progress monitoring.
   c. Home–school communication.
7. Establish data collection procedures, such as:
   a. Develop a checklist for monitoring intervention fidelity.
   b. Conduct behavioral observation techniques for behavior-progress monitoring.
   c. Establish home–school communication through home–school note system.
8. Implement CBT:
   a. Identify most appropriate intervention components for individual student or students.
   b. Identify time, place, and content of sessions.
   c. Implement with fidelity.
   d. Review discussion in text of detailed research protocol.
9. Continue to collect data.
10. Review data periodically, answering the following questions:
    a. Are CBT procedures being implemented as indicated?
    b. Has the problem behavior reduced to desired level?
    c. Are parents/guardians informed regularly by the school about the students' behavioral progress?
    d. Is the school informed regularly by the parents about any changes at home?
11. Make data-based decisions such as:
    a. Continue the current intervention if data indicate high fidelity of implementation and progress in student behavior.
    b. Reconsider school-based CBT if behavioral data indicate a lack of desired level of progress.
    c. Refer for private/community services if depression is still clinical after treatment.

also were provided training in basic techniques for developing a self-change plan that they could use when applying the self-control skills.

The general format of each session consisted of a presentation and a discussion of self-control principles followed by the assignment of homework exercises and a review of the preceding session's assignment. Session 1 began with an introduction to the program that included a description of CBT as well as the theory behind the intervention's effectiveness. The remainder of the first session focused on how to self-monitor and the importance of accurate self-observation. All participants were asked to complete daily log forms, monitoring their positive activities and moods that day. Each subsequent session began with a short summary of the rationale and format of the last assignment.

In Session 2, an exercise was used to highlight the relation between the two aspects of mood and activity related to depressive behavior. Students graphed the number of both positive activities and mood ratings daily. This exercise was designed to show the connection between the activities that the students engaged in and the way that they felt (mood). Research has shown that depressed individuals tend to focus on the immediate rather than long term-effects of their behavior (Reynolds & Coats, 1986). This faulty self-monitoring resembles Lewinsohn's (1974) concept that depressed behavior functions to elicit immediate rather than more important delayed forms of reinforcement. Session 3 therefore focused on activities designed to aid students in attending more closely to the delayed positive consequences of behavior, facilitated by an immediate versus delayed effects exercise.

Beginning in Session 4 the focus of therapy changed to individual self-evaluation. Given the distorted self-views that depressed individuals hold, the importance of evaluating oneself accurately was stressed. According to cognitive theory (A. T. Beck, Rush, Shaw, & Emery, 1979), depressed persons often hold faulty beliefs about their responsibility for events. Thus, students were taught to look closely at assumptions people make in assigning credit, blame, or responsibility for events. In Session 5, students were presented with strategies for developing a self-change plan. These methods included (a) defining the problem, (b) collecting baseline data, (c) discovering antecedents and consequences, (d) setting goals, (e) contracting, and (f) obtaining reinforcement (Lewinsohn, Munoz, Youngren, & Zeiss, 1978). Students were asked to identify a specific problem to work on and begin collecting baseline data while paying attention to antecedent and consequent events. Session 6 focused on setting realistic and obtainable goals as part of a self-change plan. Students were encouraged to identify goals that were positive, attainable, overt, and within their own

control. The students were asked to continue to collect baseline data regarding their target problems and then identify appropriate goals. Session 7 began the self-reinforcement phase of the program. The therapist presented general principles of reinforcement and related these to the problems of depression. The therapist highlighted how errors in an individual's thinking can often lead to too much self-punishment and too little self-reward. In addition to the identification of negative interpretations, students also created a "reward menu." As students met goals identified in earlier sessions, they administered rewards to themselves from the menu as points were earned. Session 8 included a brief presentation relating both covert self-reward and self-punishment to depression, followed by an activity on covert self-reward. Students were asked to monitor themselves and to use covert self-reinforcement (e.g., state "I'm doing well" to oneself) in addition to other rewards, according to their plans. The remaining two sessions were arranged to obtain information indicating how subjects complied with treatment instructions, to work on remedial efforts, and to provide a review of the program. Students were encouraged to continue using cognitive-behavioral procedures in the future and were given extra copies of log sheets and related forms.

Research Base

A strong research base exists to support the use of CBT for individuals with depression, including school-age students. Several literature reviews have summarized the evidence to support CBT for use with adult (Gillham, Shatte, & Freres, 2000) and child (Curry, 2001) populations. Specifically, research has shown that individuals who participate in CBT show symptom reduction and are less likely to relapse than individuals treated with other interventions, particularly psychopharmacology (M. D. Evans et al., 1992; Paykel et al., 1999). Researchers hypothesize that the reduced rate of relapse with CBT occurs because CBT teaches individuals the skills necessary to cope with stressful situations. After therapy is complete, individuals continue to use the skills learned. This differs from medications, which, when removed, leave individuals with no means to deal with stress, and depressive symptoms are likely to return (Gillham et al., 2000). In addition, CBT has been shown to lead to more rapid reduction of symptoms than other interventions (Brent et al., 1997).

Although a great deal of evidence supports the efficacy of CBT interventions, the majority of studies have focused on its use in clinical settings. For example, a review by Curry (2001) examined the effectiveness of psychosocial interventions for childhood and adolescent depression. Curry reviewed a total of 15 studies, and the findings indicated that CBT was both efficacious and superior to control (no intervention) and other types of intervention (e.g., family therapy, relaxation training). These findings were encouraging; however, the majority of studies (*n* = 10) were conducted in clinical settings. Considering that the vast majority of students receive mental health intervention at school, it is imperative to examine effectiveness when implemented in school settings (e.g., Kahn, Kehle, Jenson, & Clark, 1990).

The aforementioned review by Hilt-Panahon et al. (2007) examined interventions for school-age students at risk for depression. Those authors identified 15 studies that met inclusion criteria, and they evaluated a variety of variables related to intervention implementation and effectiveness. CBT emerged as the intervention with the strongest evidence base for effectively reducing depressive symptoms. Eleven studies implemented CBT in the school setting, with effect sizes ranging from 0.16 to 2.22. The effect sizes across the majority of studies were moderate to large, with low effect sizes found in only two studies. In one study (Hains & Szyjakowski, 1990), an effect size of 0.18 for depressive symptoms was hypothesized by the authors to be a result of low levels of initial symptoms in both experimental and control groups. The low effect size for the other study (Cardemil et al., 2002) was attributable to a subgroup of participants. That is, the same intervention program was provided to two ethnically diverse groups of students at two different schools. While results were positive for the Latino students (ES = 1.01), little positive effects were noted for the African American participants (ES = 0.16). The authors provided several possible explanations for these results, including regression to the mean, differential expression of symptoms across ethnic groups, and ethnic variation in the response to different intervention components.

CBT has been used in both public and private school settings, as well as at the middle and high school levels (Hilt-Panahon et al., 2007). To date, no studies have evaluated the effectiveness of school-based implementation of CBT with an elementary school population. School-based CBT interventions have primarily been implemented in a group format, although about a third of reviewed studies have implemented a combination of group as well as individual sessions. Group size has been as small as 2 students to as many as 12.

Anxiety Management/Relaxation Training

Definition and Theory for Effectiveness

Anxiety management/relaxation training (AM/RT) interventions are derived from the body of literature

supporting that stressors, both major life events as well as minor hassles, can contribute to depression (Reynolds & Stark, 1987). An individual's response to those stressors has a major impact on mood and levels of anxiety. By teaching a person more appropriate ways to respond to stressful life events, the negative effects can be reduced. Although the intervention does not specifically align with any of the major theories of depression (Reynolds & Coats, 1986), several empirical studies have shown AM/RT to be an effective means of reducing depressive symptoms (e.g., Biglan & Dow, 1981). As a result, AM/RT has been used in the treatment of depressive symptoms and anxiety.

Implementation

Descriptions of AM/RT vary in the literature but have several similar components. First, an explanation of the intervention is provided. Next, the relationship between anxiety, stress, and depressive symptoms is discussed. It is important for students to understand how their stress and anxiety are related to feelings of depression and how managing their reactions to stress can lessen depressive symptoms. Finally, students are taught through therapy that these are techniques that they can use at any time and that are under their control (Reynolds & Stark, 1987).

A second common feature is some form of progressive relaxation training (PRT). PRT consists of training individuals to systematically tense and release each of 16 muscle groups within the body. This technique was developed and modified based on the seminal work by Jacobsen (1938). Individuals are taught to tense and relax the various muscle groups, which then leads to a release of tension and increased relaxation. These procedures have been used in connection with the treatment of numerous disorders including anxiety and depression.

Muscle groups are tensed, the position held for a short period, and then relaxed in progressive order, causing the body to feel relaxed. To begin PRT, the student makes a tight fist with the dominant hand, holds the position, and then releases the muscles. Then, with the dominant bicep, the student pushes his elbow down against a chair. The student repeats these actions for the nondominant hand and bicep. To tense the forehead, the student lifts the eyebrows as high as possible and for the central section of the face, the student squints and wrinkles his nose. For the lower face and jaw, the student bites hard and pulls back the corners of the mouth. To tense the neck, the student pulls the chin toward (but not touching) the chest. Then, to tense the chest, shoulders, and upper back, the student pulls the shoulder blades together and makes his stomach hard to tense the abdomen. To tense the legs, the student then tightens the top and bottom muscles of the dominant upper leg and to tense the calf, the student pulls the toes of the dominant calf toward his head. Finally, the student points and curls the toes of the dominant foot inward to tense them. This tensing sequence is then repeated for the nondominant leg, calf, and foot. Descriptions in the literature of the implementation of PRT have indicated that as an individual becomes more skilled at the technique of PRT, the number of muscle groups used can be decreased without an apparent loss of effects (e.g., Hains, 1992; Kahn et al., 1990). PRT can be conducted alone (e.g., by oneself) or in a group setting, a flexibility that makes it an ideal intervention for classroom implementation. For those interested in implementing relaxation techniques in the classroom, see Figure 14.2 for an implementation checklist.

Research Base

Hilt-Panahon et al. (2007) identified three studies that evaluated relaxation training in isolation implemented in the school setting. Effect sizes were large, ranging from 1.14 to 2.45. In a study by Reynolds and Coats (1986), the effectiveness of both CBT and relaxation training interventions was evaluated for reducing

depression in 30 high school-age adolescents with moderate depression. Participants in both intervention groups met in small groups for ten 50-minute sessions. Sessions were held over a 5-week period at the students' school. CBT consisted of training participants in self-control and self-change skills. Relaxation training sessions were implemented following a general introduction to the program, which included a presentation of a rationale for the treatment that highlighted the relation between stress-related problems and depression. It was explained that the goal of relaxation training was to understand the relation between stress, muscle tension, and depression and to learn specific skills to facilitate self-relaxation. Students were asked to practice the techniques they would learn during the sessions as homework assignments. Then, in subsequent sessions, students were taught to implement PRT as described previously. Sessions 2 to 5 focused on teaching students the specific procedures outlined by Jacobsen (1938), which consisted almost exclusively of practicing standard progressive muscle-relaxation exercises and of reviewing homework assignment log sheets. The next four sessions (6 to 9) were devoted primarily to helping students generalize the techniques learned in previous sessions. In the final session, the procedures were

Figure 14.2   Steps for implementation of relaxation training techniques.

1. Provide an explanation of the intervention to the student including rationale for effectiveness.
2. Explain the relationship between anxiety, stress, and depressive symptoms.
   a. Stress and anxiety are related to feelings of depression.
   b. Managing stress can reduce feelings of depression.
3. Teach students Progress Relaxation Training (PRT).
   a. Make a tight fist with the dominant hand, hold for a short period, and then release.
   b. Push elbow down against a chair for the dominant bicep.
   c. Repeat steps a and b for the nondominant hand and bicep.
   d. Tense the forehead by lifting the eyebrows as high as possible.
   e. Squint and wrinkle the nose to tense the central section of the face.
   f. Bite hard and pull back the corners of the mouth to tense the lower face and jaw.
   g. Pull the chin down toward (but not touching) the chest to tense the neck.
   h. Tense the chest, shoulders, and upper back by pulling the shoulder blades together.
   i. Tense the abdomen by making the stomach hard (pull in the stomach muscles).
   j. To tense the legs, tense the top and bottom muscles of the dominant upper leg.
   k. To tense the calf, pull the toes toward the head.
   l. Finally, point the toes of the feet and curl them inward.
4. Practice PRT until students are fluent.
5. Help students to generalize skills outside of the therapy situation.
   a. Practice in other settings and situations.
   b. Students may reduce the number of muscle groups tensed at one time based on their own needs.
6. Encourage students to use skills whenever they feel stress or anxiety.

reviewed and the students were encouraged to continue using the skills in tension-producing situations.

Results of the Reynolds and Coats (1986) study indicated that both CBT and relaxation training were superior to a wait-list control condition for reducing depression in adolescents. Participants, who had moderate depression pre-intervention, showed no depression at post-test as well as at 5 weeks' follow-up. In addition, the researchers found no difference in effects across the two interventions. In other words, relaxation training was as effective as CBT in reducing depression in the students who participated in the intervention. This result is important to note, given the simplicity of relaxation training and the relatively little training that is needed for implementation, especially as compared to CBT.

In a second study, Kahn et al. (1990) compared the effects of CBT, relaxation training, and self-modeling on the depressive symptoms of 68 middle school students. Relaxation training was similar to interventions described in other studies. Sessions began with an introduction to and rationale for the intervention. The link between anxiety, stress, and depression was highlighted, along with how the techniques could reduce feelings of anxiety and stress, leading to a reduction of depressive symptoms. This session was followed by several sessions in which progressive relaxation techniques were modeled and practiced. After this, generalization procedures were taught as well as alternative methods of relaxation, including the use of fewer muscle groups, imagery, and counting. Results indicated that all three interventions were superior to wait-list control in the reduction of depressive symptoms.

The third study, by Hains (1992), evaluated the effects of anxiety management training with a traditional cognitive restructuring technique. Participants in the anxiety management intervention were taught to recognize cues that signaled the onset of anxiety and then to react to those cues using relaxation techniques including visualization and progressive relaxation training. As treatment progressed, control was gradually shifted to the students rather than the therapist. Results indicated that treatment succeeded in reducing levels of anxiety, anger, and depression, and the results were maintained at 11 weeks' follow-up.

AM/RT has been implemented as an intervention in both public and private school settings and at both the middle and high school levels. Moreover, intervention has been delivered in a group format, with group sizes ranging from 2 to 12 students, with the duration of intervention of 9 to 12 sessions over 5 to 8 weeks, and with sessions ranging from 30 to 50 minutes in length. A promising feature of this intervention is that it appears to be quite simple to implement and could be conducted with relatively little training.

Pharmacologic Intervention

Definition and Theory for Effectiveness

In addition to CBT and AM/RT, psychotropic medication or psychopharmacological intervention is an important and widely used intervention for internalizing disorders, such as depression and anxiety. Psychotropic medications are prescribed by a primary care physician, pediatrician, or a psychiatrist and are typically taken orally. Although originally developed for and used with adults, psychotropic medications are now commonly used to address internalizing disorders in students. With new research regularly emerging to document the efficacy of medications for internalizing disorders in students, their use has increased substantially in the last decade (Abrams, Flood, & Phelps, 2006). It should be stressed that medications are recommended to supplement, *not substitute for*, behavioral or cognitive–behavioral interventions (Abrams et al., 2006; Merrell, 2001).

The use of medications for internalizing behavior disorders, such as anxiety or depression, is based on the theories that postulate anomalous functioning of the different neural channels and chemicals in the brain of individuals with symptoms of psychological disorders (Reiter, Kutcher, & Gardner, 1992). Specifically, pharmacological agents in psychotropic medicines affect the malfunctioning neurotransmitter systems in the brain, and consequently reduce the symptoms of the psychological disorder that an individual experiences.

Implementation

The first step with respect to the use of pharmacologic interventions for internalizing behavior difficulties is determining need. Before a recommendation of medication (or concurrent with, in very extreme cases), behavioral or cognitive behavioral interventions should be implemented. Medications are generally restricted to students whose symptoms of internalizing disorders reach very high levels of severity and cannot be reduced through nonpharmacological interventions. Although school personnel cannot prescribe specific medications, as members of the multidisciplinary team, school personnel can play an important role in helping parents decide whether pharmacological interventions should be considered for a child or adolescent. Merrell (2001) provided a comprehensive guideline to help the multidisciplinary team with this decision. Some of the important considerations for a medication referral include severity or symptoms, chronicity of symptoms, interference of symptoms with students' socioemotional and academic functioning, threat of harm to self or others, symptoms of psychotic behavior (i.e., hallucinations, abnormal thought process, delusions), persistent failure of other sound and evidence-based psychological or behavioral interventions, and strong family history of mental disorders (Merrell, 2001). If one or a combination of these symptoms is present for a child or adolescent, a referral for pharmacological intervention may be appropriate. If a teacher or school psychologist has little experience in this area, it is advisable to consult more experienced colleagues as well as to consult the school's policy before making such a recommendation.

Medications should *not* be viewed as an exclusive or superior treatment for internalizing disorders. Medications should not replace, but rather supplement, other evidence-based behavioral interventions. Studies comparing behavioral and pharmacological treatments for students with anxiety and depression have consistently found that treatments combining cognitive behavioral therapy and medications yielded greater efficacy as compared to exclusively pharmacological interventions (Bernstein et al., 2000; Forness, Freeman, & Paparella, 2006; Pediatric OCD Treatment Study Team, 2004; Treatment for Adolescents with Depression Study Team, 2004). These results signify the importance of continuing behavioral, cognitive–behavioral, or other school-based intervention with students, regardless of the medical treatment they obtain.

After a student is placed on medication, monitoring is needed by school personnel. Because medications are often taken multiple times during the day and many students receive their medications at school, one form of monitoring involves ensuring that students take the medications as prescribed. Typically, the school nurse provides the medications and monitors ingestion.

In addition to ensuring that medications are taken, it is important for the teachers, school psychologists, and other relevant school personnel who interact with a student to understand the type of medications the student is prescribed, the symptoms for which they are taken, the expected effects on students' behavior, and the potential side effects. In case of deviations in the student's typical behavior, the medication-monitoring data can be particularly important. For example, a student who begins taking a new medication or experiences a dosage change may engage in atypical types of behavior (e.g., initial fatigue). When school personnel know that the student has begun a new medication, they can evaluate whether the medication change is influencing her behavior. Conversely, a student may revert back to maladaptive behavior if medications are not taken as prescribed. A teacher who notices such changes in the student's behavior can refer to the medication-monitoring data to determine whether the student took the medications as prescribed.

It also is important for school-based practitioners to evaluate specific behaviors to determine medication effectiveness. Although medical doctors (general practitioners, pediatricians, and psychiatrists) prescribe medications, given their infrequent contact with the student, they cannot regularly monitor behavior changes in response to the medication. More typically, they rely on parent reports and student self-report to determine medication effectiveness, which can be very subjective. School personnel, on the other hand, have the advantage of being in close contact with the student for several hours every day. Given this frequent and close contact, they can play a vital role in monitoring a student's behavior during the pharmacological intervention.

When monitoring medication effects, it is important to again note that even when medication is considered necessary, best practice suggests continuation of behavioral, cognitive–behavioral, or other effective psychological interventions in addition to the pharmacological interventions (Forness et al., 2006). Thus, it is critical that school personnel ensure students are receiving a comprehensive package of interventions, including evidence-based psychosocial approaches. In addition, it is important for school-based practitioners to assist in monitoring the effectiveness of medications.

Ideally, psychosocial interventions (i.e., cognitive behavioral therapy) should begin before the implementation of medications. If effective, medications may not be warranted. If, however, nonpharmacologic interventions are not sufficient, data can provide an interesting and important analysis of the combined effects of the two interventions versus the effects of a behavioral intervention in isolation. If the progress-monitoring data show that medications provide very little or no effectiveness beyond the behavioral interventions, the implementation of medications may be reconsidered.

To determine whether medications are having the intended effects, it is best to collect periodic data on a target behavior or set of behaviors. In the case of internalizing problems, the behaviors will be those associated with the disorder, such as withdrawal, somatic complaints, or anxiety-related behaviors. Data collection to assess and monitor the level of internalizing behavior challenges can be conducted in numerous ways. For example, a teacher may collect frequency data on the number of somatic complaints made by a student. For internalizing problems that are more difficult to observe, behavioral indicators can be identified. For instance, social anxiety might be operationally defined as lack of interpersonal interaction and/or refusal to respond to social initiations by peers or adults. These behaviors can be measured using duration data to indicate the amount of time the behaviors occurred throughout a school day. This type of ongoing data collection not only provides information on whether or not medications are effective in reducing problem behaviors, but also on their level of efficacy. If such progress-monitoring data reveal a lack of change in behaviors, the medications (i.e., the type of medication and the dosage) as well as other interventions can be reevaluated.

In addition to monitoring medication effectiveness, school personnel can facilitate communication between individuals involved in the intervention and coordination of intervention. Students frequently receive multiple services at doctor's offices, the school, the home, and outpatient settings. This is particularly true for students who are prescribed medications. Thus, it is important that all intervention agents and stakeholders communicate with each other and coordinate their interventions in order to best serve the student. School personnel can play an important role in coordination of services. Home–school communication is important for medication monitoring as well as for behavior intervention monitoring. Home–school communication can be conducted by the regular exchange of notes between the parents and teachers. It also is important to communicate with the student's doctor to maintain updated information about the prescribed medications. In addition, physicians and/or psychiatrists should be provided all data, particularly objective data that are collected to evaluate medication effects (both beneficial effects and side effects). Family members also should be involved in data collection regarding medication effects. Checklists, on which each respondent can mark whether or not medications were administered as prescribed and whether or not various expected positive effects and potential negative effects of the medications were observed, may be best suited for this purpose. This is a feasible system that is likely to be more objective than other formats (e.g., notes) and will allow the individual prescribing the medications to fully evaluate if the desired outcome is achieved and whether the dosage is optimal. A regular schedule of communication should be arranged. Generally, home–school communication should be daily, especially when new medications are evaluated, while communication with physicians or psychiatrists may be less frequent (e.g., bi-weekly, monthly, just before scheduled visits). To establish communication with the doctor prescribing the medication, it is important for the school personnel to obtain consent from the parents. Subsequently, communication arrangements can be made that are mutually agreeable and optimally beneficial for all parties. See Figure 14.3 for an implementation checklist.

Research Base

Most psychotropic medications are categorized into classes based on the biochemical brain system they impact, the disorder or symptoms they target, or both (Abrams et al., 2006). The three main classes of medication for pediatric internalizing disorders are tricyclic

antidepressants (TCAs), selective serotonin reuptake inhibitors (SSRIs), and benzodiazepines. Other medications, such as monoamine oxidase inhibitors (MAOIs) and Buspirone, commonly used with adults, are understudied with students. The few studies assessing the efficacy of MAOIs and Buspirone had weak research designs and resulted in contradictory findings. Therefore, we will discuss only the three main classes of medications, tricyclic antidepressants (TCAs), selective serotonin reuptake inhibitors (SSRIs), and benzodiazepines, which have been systematically evaluated in a number of double-blind research studies specifically with school-age students.

Tricyclic antidepressants (TCA) were one of the first medications used to treat symptoms of depression and anxiety disorders in children (Wolraich, 2003). TCAs are termed tricyclic because of their three-ring antihistaminic structure. TCAs increase the supply of norepinephrine and serotonin in the brain, which allows the flow of nerve impulses to return to normal levels, thereby reducing the symptoms of depression and anxiety. Some of the commonly used TCAs include amitriptyline (Elavil), clomipramine (Anafranil), desipramine (Norpramine), imipramine (Tofranil), and nortriptyline (Pamelor).

Literature to support for the efficacy of the TCAs for internalizing disorders is somewhat inconclusive. Although some double-blind studies have found the TCAs to be more effective than placebos for pediatric depression (Braconnier, Le Coent, & Cohen, 2003; Sallee, Hilal, Dougherty, Beach, & Nesbitt, 1998; Sallee, Vrindavanam, Deas-Nesmith, Carson, & Sethuraman, 1997) and anxiety (Gittelman-Klein & Klein, 1971), others have found that they are no more effective than placebos (Barney, Klovin, & Bhate, 1981; Geller, Reising, Leonard, Riddle, & Walsh, 1999; Klein, Koplewicz, & Kanner, 1992). Common side effects of the TCAs include dry mouth, drowsiness, tremors, visual difficulties, sleep disorders, and impacted cognition (Abrams et al., 2006; Velosa & Riddle, 2000). In addition, overdoses of TCAs can increase the risk of seizures. The overdose of desipramine, in particular, has been reported to have lethal effects in some cases (Riddle, Geller, & Ryan, 1993; Varley & McClellan, 1997; Velosa, & Riddle, 2000).

In the 1990s, TCAs were very popular medications for depression and anxiety. Their popularity as the primary pharmacological treatment for pediatric internalizing disorders has decreased significantly. The reduced use is a result of contradictory research evidence on their efficacy in treating pediatric internalizing disorders, their potentially serious side effects, and the availability of alternative medications (e.g., SSRIs) with stronger efficacy and milder side effects (Merrell, 2001).

Selective serotonin reuptake inhibitors (SSRI) work by blocking the reabsorption, or reuptake, of a

Figure 14.3   Steps for school professionals working with students receiving pharmacological interventions.

1. Operationally define problem behavior.
2. Collect data to determine frequency and severity of problem behavior.
3. Determine whether the problem behavior is frequent and severe enough to impact the student's socioemotional well-being.
   a. If Yes—go to step 4.
   b. If No—attempt relatively nonintrusive classroom-based interventions.
4. Determine whether behavioral interventions alone might address the problem behavior.
   a. If Yes—implement intervention (e.g., CBT, relaxation techniques).
   b. If No—consider concurrent pharmacological intervention referral.
5. Consult experienced professionals to determine the benefits of referral for pharmacological interventions.
6. Consult the school district's policy for such referrals.
7. If pharmacological intervention is implemented, determine the roles of different school personnel for the following tasks:
   a. Medication monitoring.
   b. Behavior progress monitoring.
   c. Home–school communication.
8. Establish data collection procedures, such as the following:
   a. Develop a checklist for medication monitoring.
   b. Conduct behavioral observation techniques for behavior progress monitoring.
   c. Establish home–school communication through a home–school note system.
9. Continue to collect data.
10. Review data periodically, answering the following questions:
    a. Are medications being administered as prescribed?
    b. Has the problem behavior reduced to the desired level?
    c. Are parents/guardians informed regularly by the school about the student's behavioral progress?
    d. Is the school informed regularly by the parents about any changes in the prescribed dosage or types of medications?
11. Make data-based decisions such as the following:
    a. Continue the current intervention if data indicate high fidelity of implementation and progress in student behavior.
    b. Enhance medication monitoring methods if data indicate that medications are not taken as prescribed.
    c. Reconsider the type and dosage of medication if behavioral data indicate a lack of desired level of progress.

neurotransmitter in the brain called *serotonin,* consequently increasing its overall level in the brain. Low levels of serotonin have been found to be associated with symptoms of mood and behavioral disorders. Hence, increased levels of serotonin, as a result of SSRIs, help reduce symptoms related to mood disorders. Some of the common SSRIs are fluoxetine (Prozac), sertraline (Zoloft), paroxetine (Praxil), fluvoxamine (Luvox), and citalopram (Celexa).

SSRIs, as a group, have the strongest research support as medications for internalizing disorders in children (Abrams et al., 2006; C. J. Whittington et al., 2004; Velosa & Riddle, 2000; Wolraich, 2003). Fluoxetine is the most widely researched SSRI for the treatment of depression and anxiety in children. A number of recent double-blind randomized control studies have demonstrated significantly higher efficacy of fluoxetine for reducing symptoms of depression and anxiety when compared with a placebo (Birmaher et al., 2003; Emslie et al., 2002; Treatment for Adolescents with Depression Study Team, 2004). Additionally, other SSRIs, such as sertraline (J. S. March et al., 1998; Rynn, Siqueland, & Rickels, 2001), paroxetine (Braconnier et al., 2003; Keller et al., 2001), and fluvoxamine (The Research Unit on Pediatric Psychopharmacology Anxiety Study Group, 2001, 2002) also have demonstrated efficacy in treatment of anxiety and depression in children in double-blind studies.

The previously cited research base evaluating the efficacy of the SSRIs included nine double-blind randomized control trial studies conducted since 2000. The studies collectively included 1,593 children and adolescents aged 5 to 20 years. Females were slightly overrepresented (61%) as compared to males in the collective sample. Only six studies reported the details of ethnic and linguistic diversity of the sample. The samples of these studies included the highest proportion of Caucasians (above 80%), followed by African Americans, Hispanics, Asian Americans, biracial, and other racial groups consisting of about 15% or less in each respective sample. All studies were implemented in the clinic or home, wherein the medications were delivered to the participants' parents on their weekly or biweekly clinic visits. While five studies mentioned medication-monitoring services provided by a case manager or a nurse on the clinic visits, none of the studies provided sufficient detail to determine integrity procedures. This emphasizes the point that, given the lack of close and constant contact, clinic-based practitioners may not be in the best position to thoroughly monitor medication intake.

In the cited research, the symptom reduction was measured by a number of standardized informant and self-rating scales. All studies found the SSRIs to be effective in reducing the symptoms of depression and anxiety, with one study demonstrating positive medication effects lasting up to 6 months in a follow-up assessment (The Research Unit on Pediatric Psychopharmacology Anxiety Study Group, 2002). Overall, the research indicated strong support for SSRIs to address internalizing difficulties in children and adolescents. More research in the area of involvement of school personnel; better communication between clinics, homes, and the schools; and home- and school-based implementation fidelity assessment may overcome the current limitations in the existing literature base.

SSRIs have relatively mild side effects, which include nausea, dry mouth, diarrhea, headaches, and insomnia. The overdose of SSRI does not have fatal effects. Given the strong empirical evidence and relatively milder side effects, SSRIs have replaced TCAs as the most commonly prescribed medication for anxiety and depression in children. In fact, in one survey, 91% of family care physicians and 58% of pediatricians reported having prescribed an SSRI for depression at least once (Rushton, Clark, & Freed, 2000).

Benzodiazepines are typically used to address symptoms of anxiety in children. They are effective because of their sedative, anticonvulsant, and muscle relaxant effects, which help reduce the symptoms of anxiety. Commonly prescribed benzodiazepines include alprazolam (Xanax) and clonazepam (Klonopin). Although benzodiazepines have been extensively researched with adults, research on their efficacy with children is sparse and contradictory. A few early double-blind studies have demonstrated that alprazolam (Simeon & Ferguson, 1987) and clonazepam (Biederman, 1987; Kutcher & Mackenzie, 1988) were significantly more efficacious than placebos. A number of later studies, however, failed to demonstrate statistically significant differences between benzodiazepines and placebos (Bernstein, Garfinkel, & Borchardt, 1990; Graae, Milner, Rizzotto, & Klein, 1994). The literature to date, and particularly more recent research, is equivocal regarding the use of benzodiazepines with school-age children.

Summary of the Research Base of CBT, AM/RT, and Pharmacologic Interventions and Recommendations for Future Research

The research base suggests that CBT and SSRIs benefit from the strongest research support for decreasing depression and anxiety in school-age children and adolescents. To support this conclusion, we applied criteria developed by Chambless and Hollon (1998) to identify empirically supported efficacious interventions. Their criteria include (a) a randomized control trial with results superior to no treatment or equivalent or superior to another treatment of known efficacy; (b) the use of a treatment manual, a specified population, valid and reliable outcome measures; and (c) the use of appropriate statistical analyses. Further, the criteria must have been met in studies conducted in at least two different research settings. Applying these criteria, both CBT and SSRIs are considered efficacious, evidence-based interventions.

In addition, the research regarding AM/RT interventions, to date, shows that this approach is promising for addressing internalizing behaviors. Although this type of intervention does not yet meet the definition of an evidence-based practice, as defined by Chambless and Hollon (1998), the only criterion that was not met was the use of a treatment manual, an implementation variable that was absent in two of the three studies. Thus, we consider it a promising practice.

The research regarding tricyclic antidepressants yielded mixed findings, and that class of medications is less frequently used at the present time, in favor of SSRIs with more consistent and overall positive research support. The research on benzodiazepines also is inconclusive with respect to efficacy for treating internalizing problems.

For those effective and promising interventions (CBT, SSRIs, AM/RT), in spite of research support, a number of limitations remain in the literature base. First, few research studies have considered contextual variables related to implementation and outcomes. Specifically, in all but one research study, CBT and AM/RT procedures were implemented by trained clinicians. Consequently, it is unclear whether these interventions could be implemented as effectively by typical school personnel. Further, involvement by school personnel is essentially absent in the SSRI research.

A related concern pertains to feasibility of implementation in school settings. The CBT and AM/RT interventions required an average of approximately 10 hours of implementation, which seems a minimal amount of time given the high risk of negative sequelae absent intervention. Still, it is important to determine whether school personnel will find time for such interventions—time related to implementation as well as time devoted to training professionals.

In light of these limitations, future research should determine the type and amount of training and supervision required for school personnel to implement CBT and AM/RT with integrity. In addition, research is needed to document how schools can make critical behavioral and mental health interventions a part of ongoing school practices. Finally, future research might identify barriers to implementation and delineate strategies to overcome such barriers.

Another limitation is the paucity of evidence-based research with elementary-age students experiencing depression and anxiety. Although medication trials have included this age group, CBT and AM/RT research has been conducted only with middle and high school-age adolescents. Given that disorders may be most easily and effectively treated when symptoms initially emerge, it is critical for future research to examine whether these and other interventions are efficacious with younger children as well.

The absence of research to support intervention efficacy across racial and ethnic groups is another limitation. This is particularly concerning in light of the differential effectiveness of CBT across racial groups found by Cardemil et al. (2002). Given that the intervention had little effect on the depression of African American participants, while large effects were found for Latino children, additional research is needed to determine whether CBT and other interventions are effective with racial, ethnic, and other subgroups. Similar research across

diverse groups is needed for medications. Although some of the research on SSRIs included somewhat diverse racial/ethnic samples, outcomes were not parceled out by subgroup. Thus, in addition to including diverse students as study participants, outcome data also must be differentially analyzed.

In general, a great deal of additional research is needed in the area of internalizing problems, and research in this area, unfortunately, appears to have slowed over time. To illustrate, only 2 of the 15 studies evaluating CBT or AM/RT were conducted after 2001. This is particularly discouraging given the need to further evaluate issues related to the applicability and feasibility of these interventions with existing school-based resources.

In light of the current research base, we recommend that practitioners begin arranging for implementation of CBT and AM/RT in schools. Evidence for effectiveness is sufficient at the present time. Further, given that youth are unlikely to receive intervention unless provided by their schools, these evidence-based strategies become particularly urgent. Although training is required for CBM implementation, no specialized certification or skill base for practitioners was evident in the research literature. AM/RT appears to be a somewhat easier intervention to implement, requiring less training, and therefore could be rapidly implemented. Finally, the combined use of medication and psychosocial interventions can be improved greatly via data collection and communication. Simple checklists, as described in this chapter, provide a means to thoroughly and more objectively evaluate the additive effectiveness of medications across settings, which can be regularly communicated to those who are prescribing.

Given only preliminary evidence for effectiveness of CBT and AM/RT, particularly in school settings and when implemented by natural intervention agents, along with limited evaluation/communication regarding medications, we recommend collection of procedural and outcome data to guide decisions. Further, responsiveness should be examined individually to determine effectiveness on students of different age, racial, and gender groups. In the case of medication, desirable effects must be carefully considered and balanced in terms of unwanted side effects. Practical applications should be carefully documented and publicly disseminated. Such documentation will greatly inform science and practice, particularly around issues of feasibility.

CHAPTER 15

Strategies for Decreasing Aggressive, Coercive Behavior: *A Call for Preventive Efforts*

Kathleen Lynne Lane | *Vanderbilt University*

Hill Walker | *University of Oregon*

Mary Crnobori, Regina Oliver, Allison Bruhn, and **Wendy P. Oakes** | *Vanderbilt University*

Students with emotional and behavioral disorders (EBD) represent between 2% and 20% of school-age youth, with conservative estimates approximating 6% (Kauffman & Landrum, 2009). This category includes students with externalizing (e.g., aggression, coercion) and internalizing (e.g., anxiety, depression) behaviors. Clearly, these students experience a host of short- and long-term negative outcomes within and beyond the school setting, as evidenced by grade-level retentions, school dropout rates, impaired social relationships, high rates of mental health services, unemployment, and even criminality (Stouthamer-Loeber & Loeber, 2002; M. Wagner, Kutash, Duchnowski, Epstein, & Sumi, 2005). Yet, only 1% of students are likely to qualify for special education services under the category of emotional disturbance (ED; Individuals with Disabilities Education Improvement Act [IDEA], 2004). Thus, many of these students will spend their educational careers in K–12 general education settings with teachers who report feeling ill-prepared to meet the multiple needs of these students (Lane, Menzies, Bruhn, & Crnobori, 2011).

Students with externalizing behavior patterns are most recognized for their antisocial behavior tendencies, which include a propensity to misinterpret social cues, engage in high rates of negative social interactions despite average levels of positive social interactions, and invoke aggressive tactics as a means of resolving conflicts and getting their own needs met (Cullinan & Sabornie, 2004). Given these social skills acquisition and performance deficits, it is not surprising that these students' behaviors escalate quickly, resorting to an aggressive mode of interacting with peers and adults (Colvin, 2004). Without intervention these aggressive behaviors tend to become intractable over time (Kellam, Ling, Merisca, Brown, & Ialongo, 1998).

In addition, students with externalizing behaviors do not fare well academically. They exhibit low levels of academic engagement (DeBaryshe, Patterson, & Capaldi, 1993), which are associated with low levels of compliance with teacher directives, low rates of homework completion, and poor academic performance (Greenwood, Hart, Walker, & Risley, 1994). These students have broad-based academic deficits in core academic areas (e.g., reading, writing, mathematics) that tend to remain stable or even decline over time (Landrum, Tankersley, & Kauffman, 2003; J. R. Nelson, Benner, Lane, & Smith, 2004). G. R. Mayer (1995) suggested that academic failure may serve as a setting event for antisocial behavior tendencies. Namely, these students may act out to escape demands that are beyond their skill set (Penno, Frank, & Wacker, 2000).

Regardless of the nature of the link between multiple deficits, what is clear is that the collective behavioral, social, and academic characteristics pose significant challenges to educators, parents, and the students themselves, as well as to society as a whole (Kauffman & Brigham, 2009; Lane, 2007; H. M. Walker, Ramsey, & Gresham, 2004). Consequently, early detection and socially valid, evidence-based supports are critical to improve outcomes on multiple levels. For example, not only is it important to prevent student-to-student violence, it is also important to prevent student-to-teacher violence (American Psychological Association [APA] Classroom Violence Directed Against Teachers Task Force, 2011). It may surprise some to learn that approximately 6% of elementary teachers and 8% of secondary teachers have been threatened with injury by students, and 4% of elementary teachers and 2% of secondary teachers have been physically attacked by students (Dinkes, Kemp, & Baum, 2009). In fact, school-based violence and lack of safety in some schools and communities are keystone factors in some teachers' decisions to exit—or even not enter—the field of education (Dinkes, Kemp, Baum, & Snyder, 2008).

A teacher's ability to prevent and respond to aggressive behaviors as manifested in the form of verbal or physical aggression, or even property destruction, is paramount to providing a safe, productive learning environment. Yet, this is a challenging task given that aggression is a powerful means to achieve a desired outcome. From a behavioral perspective, aggression is a reliable, efficient tool in the sense that it typically allows the student who exhibits aggression to access (positive reinforcement) or avoid (negative reinforcement) attention, tasks, or sensory experiences (J. O. Cooper, Heron, & Heward, 2007). In short, aggressive behavior works for students to "get their way." Rather than engage in other, more constructive, prosocial strategies that may or may not lead to their desired source of reinforcement, many students resort to aggression, thereby challenging the behavior management skills of even highly trained teachers.

The Importance of Early Intervention

Given that aggressive behavior is so efficient for some students, it is wise to intervene early at two critical junctures: (a) on initial school entry when students are most amenable to intervention efforts (Kazdin, 1987) and (b) early in the acting-out cycle by responding effectively to lower levels of undesirable behaviors (e.g., disruption, noncompliance) before *behavior earthquakes* occur (Colvin, 2004). The first intervention goal is to intervene before students become highly efficient in their use of aggression by providing a comprehensive approach to teaching and reinforcing prosocial, productive behavior. First Step to Success (FSS; H. M. Walker, et al., 1997) is one such program designed to meet this charge. In brief, FSS provides school-based and home-based instruction on key social skills necessary for academic success by involving key social change agents in the child's life: parents, teachers, and peers. Ideally, all students who need this level of support could be detected on initial school entry using methodical screening tools such as the Systematic Screening for Behavior Disorders (SSBD; H. M. Walker & Severson, 1992b) or the Student Risk Screening Scale (SRSS; Drummond, 1994) and subsequently supported with FSS.

Educators also need other effective practices for students who are not identified early. For example, it is important to have evidence-based practices to support older students whose aggressive tendencies may develop later in life (e.g., late-onset conduct disorders; Moffitt, 1993) or for those who have continued to be nonresponsive to primary and secondary prevention efforts (Lane, Kalberg, Parks, & Carter, 2008). As a result, the second intervention goal is to intervene early in the acting-out cycle to prevent low levels of disruptive behavior from escalating. In this instance, the ultimate goal is to prevent the damaging consequences of violence and facilitate a productive, safe instructional environment (Colvin, 2004). A clear understanding of the progression of aggressive behavior is necessary so that (a) interventions can be targeted early in the escalating behavior chain to prevent aggression; (b) the student can be taught problem-solving strategies and academic skills if necessary; and (c) aggressive behavior is not inadvertently reinforced. A functional assessment-based intervention (FABI) is one approach that can be used to meet this charge. In brief, FABIs focus on identifying the reasons why the target behavior is occurring and then teaching students functionally equivalent behaviors that are more reliable and efficient in meeting their objectives. Such interventions involve modifying antecedent conditions, adjusting rates of reinforcement, and extinguishing reinforcers that previously maintained the undesirable behavior (Umbreit, Ferro, Liaupsin, & Lane, 2007).

In sum, it is important for teachers to have evidence-based practices to prevent and respond to aggression during the early school years to prevent antisocial behaviors from becoming stable (e.g., FSS). At-risk students need to learn new ways to get their needs met so that they will not resort to less desirable (yet efficient) coercive behaviors (e.g., FABI).

Purpose

In this chapter we review two highly effective practices to prevent and respond to aggressive behavior patterns: First Step to Success (FSS) and functional assessment-based interventions (FABIs). To rigorously evaluate each of these practices, we conducted a systematic review of the literature to identify the full scope of treatment outcome studies. Specifically, we identified articles by using a systematic search process that included electronic searches using specific key words, hand searches in relevant journals, and personal queries with authors who had contributed to these bodies of literature. A total of 9 articles pertaining to FSS and 31 related to FABI met inclusion criteria and were evaluated.

In the sections that follow, we provide (a) a definition of the practice, including the theoretical underpinnings; (b) a description of the practice; and (c) a review of the treatment-outcome literature base. We conclude by discussing (a) the strengths and limitations of each literature base, (b) recommendations for future research, and (c) recommendations for practice.

First Step to Success

First Step to Success Definition and Description

FSS is a manualized program designed to interrupt the progression of antisocial behavior for at-risk students on school entry (H. M. Walker, Stiller, Severson, Feil, & Golly, 1998). FSS has three components: (a) proactive universal screening, (b) school intervention, and (c) parent training (see Table 15.1 for procedures). This early intervention program involves parents, teachers, and peers as key social agents in the student's developmental process. A school professional coordinates and delivers

the program by acting in the role of behavioral coach to the teacher and parents (i.e., FSS consultant).

The first component requires screening of all kindergarten students to identify those who may require intervention on initial school entry. Early identification is crucial to determine which students demonstrate the initial indicators of antisocial behavior and later delinquency. Then, treatment may be implemented when it has the greatest likelihood of success, before adolescent involvement in deviant peer groups and delinquency (Patterson, Reid, & Dishion, 1992). Screening procedures range from teacher nominations to more complex three-stage gating procedures (H. M. Walker & Severson, 1992b). These stages include (a) teacher nominations and rank ordering of nominated students on external and internal behavior dimensions, (b) assessment of student behavior using teacher behavior ratings, and (c) direct observations in the school setting.

In the initial stage of screening, students are nominated by their teachers, based on externalizing and internalizing behavioral characteristics. Five students per class are nominated as at risk for externalizing and five for internalizing behavior problems and then rank ordered from most-like to least-like the characteristics provided. The three highest-ranked students enter the next screening stage, where teachers rate each student on specific critical behaviors and frequency of adaptive and maladaptive behavior. Students exceeding predetermined normative cut scores are then observed directly in the classroom and on the playground to determine the quality and duration of their academic engagement and social interactions with peers. Students exceeding normative criteria at this final stage are typically identified as having severe behavioral adjustment problems and referred for early intervention. This screening process is conducted after students have been in school for at least

Table 15.1 First Step to Success Procedures

FSS Component	Implementer	Time Line	Duration	Goal
Systematic Screening	Consultant with input from teachers.	After 6 weeks of attending school year.	1–2 days to collect data.	Identify students who are at risk for aggression.
Contingencies for Learning Academic and Social Skills (CLASS)	Consultant with fading to classroom teacher.	Begins after student is identified. • Initially 2- to 20-min sessions with extension to ½ or full day once teacher takes over.	Typically 30 days.	Teach important social skills with short lessons, and provide feedback on behavior through the use of a behavior card and rewards.
Home Base	Consultant works with parents. Parents work with child.	Begins on day 10 of implementation. • 45-min daily consultant sessions with parents. • 15- to 20-min daily parent sessions with child.	Typically 6 weeks.	Reinforce social skills taught in CLASS component at home with parents. Improve parent–child interactions.

30 days, allowing the teacher sufficient exposure to the student to make screening decisions.

After students are identified and parents are brought into the process (e.g., parental consent), the FSS school component is implemented. The school component consists of an adapted version of the Contingencies for Learning Academic and Social Skills (CLASS) Program for Acting-Out Child developed by Hops and Walker (1988) with the key components of (a) frequent adult praise and monitoring of student performance; (b) awarding points to the student based on program guidelines and student performance; and (c) individual, group, and home rewards. Features of the classroom-based component teach important prosocial behaviors by using powerful behavioral strategies such as frequent monitoring and feedback, positive reinforcement, and group contingencies that provide positive peer social involvement (Lane, Menzies, et al., 2011).

Initially, two 20-minute sessions occur daily (one in the morning and then another in the afternoon) and are conducted by the consultant in the classroom (M. H. Epstein & Walker, 2002). The consultant sits by the student to accomplish behavioral monitoring and to provide feedback. A red and green card is used to signal the student about his behavior, to record points, and to note praise and bonus points. Sample behaviors are provided on the cards (e.g., follows directions, works quietly, gets along with others), but the teacher may add or change an additional two behaviors based on the goals for the student. The green card is placed face up when the student is performing appropriate behaviors and is immediately turned over to the red side if the student exhibits any inappropriate behavior. The changing of the card acts as a cue to the student and provides immediate visual feedback. Verbal feedback is also provided when the student responds to the red card (e.g., "You made a good choice." "You know how to work."). Points are awarded, and verbal praise provided, during predetermined intervals established for each day of the program. If the student reaches 80% of the criteria for that program day, the whole class is given a reward. The card goes home at the end of the day for a parent signature, and the student receives home privileges contingent on meeting the performance criteria for that day.

The consultant sits farther away from the student once the student demonstrates success. Students can progress to the next program day only after they have mastered the criteria; otherwise, the program day is repeated. Student performance goals progressively increase, and reinforcement is faded (e.g., every other day), making meeting the criteria more challenging while shaping behavior. Eventually, the program is extended to half day or full day, and the teacher assumes control of implementation after the sixth day of the program. The teacher uses the green/red card in the same way as during the consultant phase, with the criteria for student success becoming increasingly

difficult. The program requires at least 30 days to complete, although it typically takes longer as students repeat program days that are not mastered initially (H. M. Walker, Stiller, et al., 1998). A maintenance phase is built into the program to fade out the use of the card and classroom reinforcement, typically around day 30.

Parents of targeted students are enlisted to support the school component with the home-based FSS program component shortly after the school component is initiated. Home base begins on day 10 and typically lasts 6 weeks. Parents are trained by the consultant to teach their children important school success skills such as accepting limits, cooperation, and problem solving. The home-based component contains lessons, guidelines, and games and activities that parents can use with their child for 10 to 15 minutes daily. Parents teach and reinforce skills being taught in the school-based component. The goal of involving parents in the process is to build a partnership with the school to support their child's development and improve home–school communication (M. H. Epstein & Walker, 2002). The home-based component also indirectly teaches parents valuable parenting skills and interrupts the coercive interaction patterns responsible for aggressive behavior (Patterson et al., 1992).

First Step to Success: Theoretical Underpinnings

FSS is a comprehensive early intervention program for aggressive children in grades Pre-K–3 who are at risk for developing antisocial behaviors and later delinquency (H. M. Walker, et al., 1997). It is based on a social learning model of antisocial behavior developed by Patterson and colleagues (1992). Early aggressive behavior patterns begin at home with coercive cycles of parent–child interactions. These patterns are developed over time and are a result of the bidirectional influence of caregiver–child interactions. Contextual variables such as family stress, divorce, poverty, or parental antisocial behavior establish a family system marked by inconsistent and harsh discipline, poor monitoring, and overall poor family management skills. In fact, families with antisocial children tend to rely heavily on coercion in their daily interactions, exchange high rates of aversive initiations, maintain longer durations of negative interactions, and use more negative reinforcement strategies (Patterson et al., 1992).

Coercive interaction patterns develop through a system of escape conditioning (Patterson et al., 1992) that begins with overly harsh parental discipline, to which the child responds with aversive behaviors such as crying, aggression, or tantrums. The caregiver responds by removing any demands previously issued or by engaging in conversation and negotiation with the child, which stops the aversive child behavior. The child and caregiver are both negatively reinforced by removal of these undesirable events (e.g., demands, crying). This cycle escalates with inconsistent parenting and increased use of coercion during parent–child interactions, thus creating a breakdown in parental effectiveness that inadvertently teaches the child to use aggression to achieve desired outcomes. As such, it is critical to involve parents and the home context in any comprehensive intervention program to stop this cycle in the home.

The next stage of the coercion model begins when the child enters school unprepared to handle the social and academic demands of schooling. Children who enter school with antisocial, coercive behavior patterns already established at home often use the same coercive techniques with teachers and peers (Patterson et al., 1992). As a result, the student experiences rejection by teachers and peers and associated poor academic outcomes. Having experienced teacher and peer rejection, students with antisocial tendencies tend to seek out students with similar behavior patterns that perpetuate and reinforce coercive interactions. Without early intervention, these students often do not learn important social skills such as cooperation, problem solving, negotiating, and friendship making. Over time, they tend to demonstrate increasing levels of aggressive behavior, substance use, and delinquency. Thus, the school becomes a critical context for arresting the progression of antisocial behavior and the development of prosocial behavior patterns and appropriate peer interactions.

Given the nature of the progression of antisocial behavior, intervention should be targeted as early as possible in the developmental sequence to divert students with aggressive tendencies from this trajectory (Kazdin, 1987). Comprehensive intervention for aggressive, antisocial behavior should involve the family context as well as the school context to address this cycle of behavior. The FSS program areas address issues in both these critically important contexts.

Research Base

Of the nine FSS articles reviewed, data are reported for all 342 included participants (see Appendix 15.1 at the end of this chapter for details). The majority of participants were young boys (77%), ranging in age from 5 to 10 years in first through third grades (72%), who did not have a disability (77%), but who were identified through systematic screening tools. Most students were Hispanic (54%) or Caucasian (30%). All interventions occurred in elementary schools, with one school located on an Indian reservation (Diken & Rutherford, 2005).

Purpose

The purpose of the initial studies using FSS was to evaluate the multicomponent intervention as an approach to

preventing antisocial behavior in schools. Over a 4-year period, the initial evaluation (H. M. Walker, Kavanagh, et al., 1998) examined two cohorts of kindergarteners with follow up into first grade. All three components (i.e., universal screening, CLASS, home base) were implemented by an FSS consultant with fading of implementation gradually to the classroom teacher. To confirm previous findings and explore issues of feasibility, subsequent studies replicated these initial results and expanded the research goal to evaluating social validity (e.g., Golly, Stiller, & Walker, 1998).

Intervention

Nearly all studies implemented all three components of the FSS intervention. All studies used universal screening procedures and the classroom-based intervention (i.e., CLASS). In addition, home-based intervention occurred for 99% ($n = 339$) of participants, with only three participants receiving school-based intervention only (D. R. Carter & Horner, 2007; Golly, Sprague, Walker, Beard, & Gorham, 2000). One study also used a FABI consisting of check-in procedures, various antecedent adjustments, and skill-building strategies for a participant who did not respond to the FSS intervention (D. R. Carter & Horner, 2007). Screening measures used to determine risk status and treatment eligibility were limited to the Early Screening Project (ESP; H. M. Walker, Severson, & Feil, 1994; $n = 3$), Systematic Screening for Behavior Disorders (SSBD; H. M. Walker & Severson, 1992; $n = 3$), and Student Risk Screening Scale (SRSS; Drummond, 1994; $n = 2$), with one study omitting information regarding the type of screening measure used.

Design and Dependent Variables

Of the nine studies, five (56%) used a group design to evaluate the effects of FSS, while the other four (44%) used single-case methodology. A randomized cohort group design was used for three of the five group studies (Seeley et al., 2009; H. M. Walker, Kavanagh, et al., 1998; H. M. Walker et al., 2009) and the remaining two studies used a nonrandomized pretest/post-test group design (Golly et al., 1998; S. Overton, McKenzie, King, & Osborne, 2002). Of the studies using single-case methodology, multiple baseline was the predominant design, two across participants (Golly et al., 2000; Lien-Thorne & Kamps, 2005) and one across groups (Diken & Rutherford, 2005), with one study using a within-subjects reversal design (D. R. Carter & Horner, 2007).

The number of dependent variables measured within studies ranged from 2 to 10 ($M = 5.7$), with greater numbers of dependent measures in group studies ($M = 7.4$) compared to studies using single-case methodology

($M = 3.75$), resulting in a total of 34 separate measures across studies. The dependent measures themselves evaluated a range of behaviors from specific (e.g., talk outs, out of seat) to broad behavioral constructs (e.g., maladaptive, adaptive) with a variety of those measured through direct observation (e.g., academic engaged time) or reports from teachers or parents (e.g., Child Behavior Checklist—Teacher Report; Achenbach, 1991b). The most common measure was direct observations of academic engagement, used in eight studies (88.8%).

Components Related to Valid Inference Making

Reports of the reliability of the dependent variable, treatment integrity, and social validity are all important variables necessary to make valid inferences about study outcomes (R. H. Horner, et al., 2005). Fortunately, all studies reported reliability for the dependent measures. However, treatment integrity and social validity were reported less frequently. Only two studies (Seeley et al., 2009; H. M. Walker et al., 2009) discussed data collection procedures and reported outcomes for treatment integrity for both CLASS and home-base components. Three studies (D. R. Carter & Horner, 2007; Diken & Rutherford, 2005; S. Overton et al., 2002) discussed treatment integrity data collection and reported outcomes for the CLASS component only, while two studies (H. M. Walker, Kavanagh, et al., 1998; Lien-Thorne & Kamps, 2005) mentioned that treatment integrity was considered but did not report outcomes. Similar patterns were found for social validity. Social validity data were reported in five studies (Diken & Rutherford, 2005; Golly et al., 1998; S. Overton et al., 2002; Seeley et al., 2009; H. M. Walker et al., 2009), with one study (Lien-Thorne & Kamps, 2005) mentioning it without reporting, and one study (Golly et al., 2000) offering anecdotal reports.

Outcomes

In general, significant decreases in antisocial behaviors and increases in prosocial behaviors were found across studies, although variability was found based on type of behavior and who was reporting. In terms of antisocial behavior, teachers reported significant decreases in maladaptive and aggressive behavior in two group studies (Golly et al., 1998; H. M. Walker, Kavanagh, et al., 1998), and significant decreases in externalizing behavior were reported by both parents and teachers in another group study (S. Overton et al., 2002). In another group study, parents, but not teachers, reported significant decreases in aggressive behavior. Moderate-to-large effects were also found for maladaptive and problem behavior and for behavior symptomatic of ADHD in group studies

reporting those outcomes (Seeley et al., 2009; H. M. Walker et al., 2009). However, researchers found no significant improvement reported by parents or teachers for withdrawn (Golly et al., 1998; H. M. Walker, Kavanagh, et al., 1998) or internalizing behavior (S. Overton et al., 2002).

Functional relations between FSS and decreases in specific behaviors were found in some single-case studies. Observations of talk outs, out of seat, touching others, and touching property demonstrated initial decreases in behavior across participants ($n = 4$) with slight variability (Golly et al., 2000). Inappropriate behavior decreased and maintained across participants ($n = 3$) for one study (Lien-Thorne & Kamps, 2005). Decreases in problem behavior were also found in one study (D. R. Carter & Horner, 2007) during FSS, and decreased further when a FABI was implemented for the participant ($n = 1$). Also, nonsocial play decreased for three participants with slight variability for the fourth (Diken & Rutherford, 2005). Parent and teacher reports of problematic behavior in studies that used single-case methodology were less clear. Inconsistency in parent and teacher reports was found across participants for two studies (Diken & Rutherford, 2005; Lien-Thorne & Kamps, 2005); parent reports of problem behavior indicated decreases for most participants, while teacher reports indicated variability across participants with little change.

The outcomes for prosocial behavior appeared stronger and more consistent across studies. Adaptive behavior improved significantly (Golly et al., 1998; Seeley et al., 2009; H. M. Walker, Kavanagh, et al., 1998; H. M. Walker et al., 2009), as did social skills based on both parent and teacher reports (Seeley et al., 2009; H. M. Walker, Kavanagh, et al., 1998). The most consistent finding across studies was significant improvement in academic engagement (Golly et al., 1998, 2000; Lien-Thorne & Kamps, 2005; S. Overton et al., 2002; Seeley et al., 2009; H. M. Walker, Kavanagh, et al., 1998; H. M. Walker et al., 2009), with some variability (Golly et al., 2000) for at least one participant. Some indication that these improvements in academic engagement may maintain over time was evident (S. Overton et al., 2002). Academic competence also improved significantly (Seeley et al., 2009; H. M. Walker et al., 2009). The outcomes for studies using nonexperimental designs (Golly et al., 1998; S. Overton et al., 2002), although generally consistent with that of experimental designs in the current review, should be interpreted with caution.

High variability in treatment integrity was found for studies that did report it, with strong correlations between treatment integrity and outcomes. The percentage of items implemented by teachers for the CLASS component ranged from 75% to 100% (S. Overton et al., 2002), 83.3% to 100% (Diken & Rutherford, 2005), and 20% to 100% of intervals (D. R. Carter & Horner, 2007). Two studies examined the relationship between the quality of implementation and study outcomes (Seeley et al., 2009; H. M. Walker et al., 2009). These correlations were found to be strong across parents, teachers, and coaches ($r = 0.52$; $r = 0.67$; $r = 0.93$, respectively), indicating outcomes improved when the quality of implementation was high.

In general, social validity data indicated favorable ratings of FSS, although some variability was found. One study (Golly et al., 1998) specifically examined social validity. Teachers in this study gave favorable ratings to the training content of FSS. Follow-up surveys from teachers indicated the primary reason for lack of implementation was that no students were found to require intervention, with the expense and impracticality of implementation cited next.

Functional Assessment-Based Interventions

Definition and Description

Functional assessment-based interventions (FABIs) refer to interventions that are constructed based on the reason(s) *why* a target (problem) behavior occurs (Umbreit et al., 2007). For example, if the target behavior is physical aggression, the intent of a function-based approach is to determine *why* aggressive behavior is occurring. In other words, what is happening before physical aggression occurs (antecedents) to set the stage for the occurrence? And, what occurs after physical aggression occurs to increase (or decrease) the probability of future occurrences (consequences)? The motive for the specific behavior is identified by conducting a functional behavioral assessment. In brief, a functional behavioral assessment includes the full range of descriptive (e.g., interviews, direct observations of behavior, rating scales) and experimental (e.g., functional analysis) procedures conducted to identify antecedent conditions that prompt a target behavior as well as the maintaining consequences. This information is analyzed to determine a hypothesis statement (e.g., aggression is maintained by peer attention and escape from too-difficult tasks) that can be tested within the context of an experimental (functional) analysis. All behaviors occur to either access (positive reinforcement) or avoid (negative reinforcement) social attention, activities or tasks, or sensory conditions (Umbreit et al., 2007). The intent of these tools is to determine the function of the target behavior (see Table 15.2 for procedures).

Once the function of the behavior is identified and confirmed, an intervention is designed, based on the function of the target behavior. Rather than simply designing topographical interventions that focus on suppressing a specific behavior, such as physical aggression, the intent of a FABI is to teach students a more reliable, efficient, functionally equivalent method of meeting their objective (e.g., accessing peer attention and requesting help or a break from too-difficult tasks; J. O. Cooper et al., 2007). This new behavior is referred to as a *replacement behavior.* In general, function-based interventions contain three core components: (a) antecedent adjustments to set the stage (prompt) for the replacement behavior to occur, (b) modification of reinforcement rates to increase the likelihood that the replacement behavior (and not the target behavior) will occur in the future, and (c) extinction of the target behavior.

After the intervention is designed, then it is implemented using a scientifically rigorous single-subject

Table 15.2   Functional Assessment-Based Interventions Procedures

Step	Sample Tools	Purpose
1. Collect data to determine function of behavior.	Teacher, parent, or student interviews Behavior rating scales Antecedent-behavior-consequence (ABC) observation data Scatter plot Record reviews	To collect data from multiple settings, multiple times of day, over at least 3 days, 3 hours (or 8 instances of the behavior), and multiple respondents. Data provide information about antecedents and consequences that reliably predict target behavior.
2. Analyze data to determine function of target behavior.	Function matrix (Umbreit et al., 2007)	To organize data systematically to identify the function and develop a hypothesis statement.
3. Design the intervention linked to function of the behavior.	Function-Based Intervention Decision Model (Umbreit et al., 2007)	To identify which method, or combination of methods, are needed in the intervention to address the target behavior and identified function.
4. Evaluate the extent to which the intervention produces changes in the desired behaviors.	Progress monitoring Time series graphs	To determine if the intervention is working or if adjustments need to be made.

research design such as a withdrawal (ABAB) or multiple baseline across settings to ensure that a functional relation is established between the introduction of the intervention and changes in the target and/or replacement behavior (Gast, 2010). To draw accurate conclusions regarding intervention outcomes, it is important for (a) reliability of the dependent variable (interobserver agreement), (b) treatment integrity (the accuracy with which the intervention is implemented as planned), (c) social validity (social significance of the goals, social acceptability of the treatment procedures, and social importance of the outcomes; M. M. Wolf, 1978), and (d) generalization and maintenance of student outcomes to be addressed.

One of the challenges associated with describing the step-by-step process of designing and evaluating FABIs is that tremendous variability occurs in the procedures used to (a) collect data to determine the function of the behavior, (b) analyze data collected to determine the function of the target behavior, (c) design an intervention linked to the results of the functional assessment, and (d) evaluate the extent to which a functional relation is established between the introduction of the intervention and changes in the target and/or replacement behavior.

Umbreit and colleagues (2007) attempted to address some of these concerns by developing a systematic approach to designing, implementing, and evaluating FABIs. In their model, they introduce a systematic approach to (a) determining the function of a given target behavior and (b) constructing interventions linked to results of the functional assessment. In brief, this systematic approach involves a new tool, the Function Matrix, which is used to analyze data from all functional assessment tools (e.g., interviews, direct observations, school record searches, behavior rating scales, functional analysis; Umbreit et al., 2007; see Figure 15.1). The Function Matrix is a six-celled grid used to determine if the behavior is maintained by positive and/or negative reinforcement to attention, tangibles/activities/tasks, or sensory stimuli. Data collected from each tool are placed into the

appropriate cell. For example, consider the antecedent-behavior-consequence (ABC) chain in this sequence: teacher again prompts Frank to "get back to work" (A), Frank throws the assignment at the teacher coupled with some colorful words (B), and the teacher sends Frank to on-campus suspension (C). In this instance of the target behavior (#5—the fifth time that the target behavior was observed during ABC data collection), the analysis indicates that the behavior was being maintained by escape from task. Thus, #5 could be placed in the cell that intersects with negative reinforcement and task (meaning that the result of this behavior is that the student avoided the task). After reviewing all data in the Function Matrix, a hypothesis statement describing the function(s) of the target behavior is generated. For example, if the majority of comments from the interviews (teacher, student, and parent) and the direct observation data were coded under negative reinforcement and activity, the teacher might hypothesize that when presented with work that he perceives as too difficult, Frank uses inappropriate language to escape the teacher-assigned task.

Another feature of this systematic approach is the Function-Based Intervention Decision Model (Umbreit et al., 2007; see Figure 15.2). This tool was developed to guide intervention planning using two key questions: (a) Is the replacement skill in the child's repertoire? and (b) Does the classroom environment represent effective practices? Answers to these questions direct the intervention to one of three methods:

- *Method 1: Teaching the Replacement Behavior* is reserved for students who do not have the replacement behavior in their repertoire (acquisition deficit) and when the classroom represents effective practices. This method focuses on explicitly teaching the replacement behavior. For example, a validated intervention designed to teach social skills may be implemented to teach the student specific skills that she lacks.

Figure 15.1 Function matrix for developing functional assessment-based intervention.

	Positive Reinforcement (Access Something)	Negative Reinforcement (Avoid Something)
Attention		
Tangibles/Activities		
Sensory		

Figure 15.2 Function-Based Intervention Decision Model.

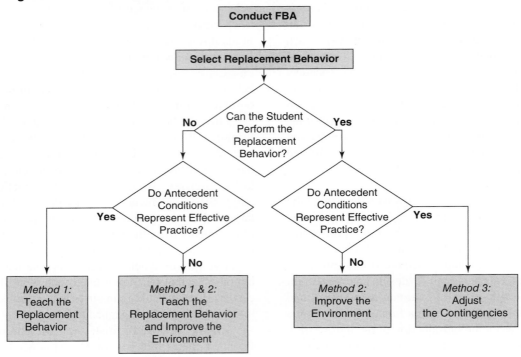

Note: FBA = functional behavior assessment.

Source: Reprinted with permission from Umbreit, J., Ferro, J., Liaupsin, C., & Lane, K. (2007). *Functional behavioral assessment and function-based intervention: An effective, practical approach* (p. 98). Upper Saddle River, NJ: Prentice-Hall.

- *Method 2: Improve the Environment* is reserved for students who have the replacement behavior in their repertoire but are in classrooms where the antecedent conditions may be less than optimal in terms of facilitating instruction (Lane, Weisenbach, Phillips, & Wehby, 2007). This intervention involves (a) adjusting (or removing) existing aversive events and (b) providing a context that supports the replacement behavior. For example, a teacher might withhold reinforcement for the disruptive behavior (i.e., talking out) by using planned ignoring and by asking the student to use communication cups to appropriately signal a need for assistance (communication cups involve students being given a red, yellow, and green cup to arrange on their desk to serve as a signal to the teacher: red = I am stuck and need help before I can move on; yellow = I am a little confused, but I can do some of this task; green = I am clear on the directions and able to do the assignment).

- *Method 3: Adjust the Contingencies* is reserved for students who have the necessary replacement behavior in their repertoire and are in classrooms where antecedent conditions represent effective practices. This intervention method focuses predominantly on adjusting reinforcement rates to decrease the rate for the target behavior and

increasing the rate for the replacement behavior. For example, an escape-motivated student who was previously sent to the office for misbehavior for failing to complete assignments will now gain access to the office contingent on work completion.

Each method includes three core components: teaching or modifying antecedents; reinforcing the occurrence of the replacement behavior; and extinction of the target behavior. Yet, each method has a predominant emphasis tailored to the student needs and environmental context. Once the intervention method is selected, the interventionist designs socially valid (feasible) plan tactics.

The Function-Based Intervention Decision Model is only one approach to conducting functional assessments; a number of other methods also can be used to design, implement, and evaluate FABIs. Ideally, any approach to functional assessment should gather multiple sources of information through the tools mentioned previously to identify converging evidence of the hypothesized function of the target behavior. And regardless of the method for identifying the function, we encourage the reader to intervene early in the acting-out cycle, before aggressive behavior ensues (Colvin, 2004). It is important to measure treatment fidelity of the *intervention* to be implemented as well as the procedural fidelity to measure the *process* of conducting the functional assessment, analyzing data, and designing the plan.

In the following section, we discuss the logic behind FABIs. We also illustrate some of the controversy surrounding applications of this practice within naturalistic contexts (e.g., classrooms).

Theoretical Underpinnings and Legal Foundations

The logic behind FABI is that this approach to intervention recognizes the communicative intent of behavior. Namely, behavior occurs for a reason: to either access (positive reinforcement) or avoid (negative reinforcement) social attention; activities, tasks, or tangibles; or sensory conditions (Umbreit et al., 2007). Once the function of the behavior is determined, the intervention can be developed based on this information. FABIs provide a respectful method of analyzing undesirable behaviors with a goal of providing an intervention designed to expand the student's repertoire by teaching her a new, more adaptive skill or how to use the replacement behavior more consistently and appropriately. Initial studies of functional assessment procedures were conducted in clinical settings with individuals having severe developmental disabilities (e.g., Iwata, Dorsey, Slifer, Bauman, & Richman, 1982).

Functional behavioral assessments have been endorsed by several organizations including the National Association of State Directors of Education (NASDE), National Association of School Psychologists (NASP), and National Institutes of Health (NIH). According to the IDEA (2004), functional behavioral assessments must be conducted by school personnel if a student receiving special education services is (a) assigned to an alternative placement for behavior that poses a threat to the individual or others; (b) assigned to an alternative setting for 45 days resulting from drug or weapons violations; or (c) suspended (or placed in an alternative setting) for more than 10 days or if the suspension constitutes a change in placement (Drasgow & Yell, 2001; Kern, Hilt, & Gresham, 2004). Despite the research support of functional behavioral assessment, questions remain as to whether evidence is sufficient to require FABIs for students with or at risk for EBD or aggressive behavior in naturalistic settings (e.g., Quinn et al., 2001; Sasso, Conroy, Stichter, & Fox, 2001).

In the next section, we present the findings of our systematic review of the literature examining the efficacy of FABIs with students who have a history of aggressive behavior. While it is beyond the scope of this chapter to provide a systematic application of the core quality indicators for single-case methodology as recommended by R. H. Horner and colleagues (2005) to

the articles identified, we will discuss (a) participant characteristics and instructional setting; (b) purpose of the studies conducted; (c) intervention components; (d) research design and dependent variables; (e) functional assessment tools and identified function; (f) components related to valid inference making and level of support; and (g) student outcomes.

Research Base

For the 31 articles reviewed, data are reported for 61 participants who met inclusion criteria (e.g., school-aged students, students presenting with aggressive behavior, studies conducted since 1988, studies that used at least two methods associated with functional behavioral assessment, intervention was function-based; see Appendix 15.2 at the end of this chapter for more details). Consistent with other reviews (e.g., Lane, Bruhn, Crnobori, & Sewell, 2009; Lane, Kalberg, & Shepcaro, 2009; Lane, Umbreit, & Beebe-Frankenberger, 1999; Quinn et al., 2001), the majority of participants were elementary-age (72%) students, and most were male (80%). Ethnicity was reported for only 28 students (46%), five of whom were Hispanic English Language Learners (see Appendix 15.2).

In terms of students' disability status, the majority of students were receiving special education services for emotional disturbances, other health impairments, and comorbid disorders. However, 20 were typically developing students, 2 of whom had been identified as at risk according to systematic screening data (see Kamps, Wendland, & Culpepper, 2006; Lane, Weisenbach, et al., 2007) and one of whom had a mild hearing loss (Liaupsin, Umbreit, Ferro, Urso, & Upreti, 2006). The majority of interventions were conducted with special education students in special education classrooms on general education campuses, self-contained schools, and alternative learning centers. However, it is important to note that 47% of the FABIs conducted since 2007 assessed students in the general education classrooms in public education schools.

Purpose

The purpose of the studies published has shifted somewhat over time. As expected, earlier studies were focused more on issues of efficacy, in the sense that they addressed questions pertaining to whether or not these procedures could work beyond clinical settings with individuals who did not have developmental disabilities (e.g., Knapczyk, 1988, 1992; Umbreit, 1995). Studies continued in this vein, exploring the utility of FABIs conducted in segregated schools for adolescents with EBD (e.g., Penno et al., 2000; Stahr, Cushing, Lane, & Fox,

2006), self-contained classrooms (e.g., Dunlap, White, Vera, Wilson, & Panacek, 1996; Kern, Delaney, Clarke, Dunlap, & Childs, 2001), traditional general education classrooms (e.g., Grandy & Peck, 1997; Todd, Horner, & Sugai, 1999), and inclusive settings (e.g., Umbreit, 1995). In time, the purpose of the studies began to shift beyond exploring efficacy in different settings to exploring the level of support necessary to implement FABIs in naturalistic contexts (e.g., Kamps et al., 2006; Lane, Barton-Arwood, et al., 2007; Lane, Weisenbach, et al., 2007).

Intervention

Although all interventions were function based, interventions contained a range of components. In general, most interventions contained antecedent adjustments. For example, several studies included components related to instructional accommodations or modifications (e.g., Burke, Hagan-Burke, & Sugai, 2003; Kern, Delaney, et al., 2001), and some included an instructional component (e.g., video modeling) to teach alternative responses to aggression (e.g., Knapczyk, 1992). In addition, some interventions incorporated self-management components (e.g., Todd et al., 1999; B. W. Smith & Sugai, 2000). Several studies explicitly mentioned three components: (a) antecedent adjustments, (b) increased reinforcement for the replacement behavior (e.g., differential rates of reinforcement of alternative behavior), and (c) extinction of the target behavior (e.g., C. H. Kennedy et al., 2001). The range of intervention components included in these studies reflects the individualized nature of FABIs.

Design and Dependent Variables

All of the 31 studies reviewed were single-case designs, of which 14 studies employed multiple baseline designs, 12 studies used some variation of an ABAB design, and two studies used alternating treatment designs. One study used a withdrawal design for one participant and a multiple baseline for another participant (Lane, Barton-Arwood, Spencer, & Kalberg, 2007). Two other studies involved combinations of these designs such as a multiple baseline across two settings with a withdrawal component (Stahr et al., 2006; Todd et al., 1999).

Very few studies explicitly monitored aggressive behavior as a student outcome measure (e.g., Knapczyk, 1988, 1992). The vast majority of behaviors monitored focused on target behaviors that occurred earlier in the acting-out cycle, such as disruption (e.g., Grandy & Peck, 1997; Umbreit, 1995), noncompliance (e.g., Fairbanks, Sugai, Guardino, & Lathrop, 2007), inappropriate touching (e.g., Lane, Barton-Arwood, et al., 2007), and off-task behaviors (Y. Lee, Sugai, & Horner, 1999), as well as

more global measures of problem behavior. Global measures focused on multiple behaviors in the response class such as making noises, talking to peers, and playing with other materials (e.g., C. H. Kennedy et al., 2001; Todd et al., 1999). Replacement behaviors often focused on academic-related behaviors such as task engagement, productivity, and accuracy of work completed (e.g., Burke et al., 2003; Filter & Horner, 2009; Kern, Delaney, et al., 2001; Penno et al., 2000; Preciado, Horner, & Baker, 2009; B. W. Smith & Sugai, 2000; Trussell, Lewis, & Stichter, 2008). Other studies focused on other academic-enabling skills such as hand raising, appropriate responding, and appropriate requests for breaks (e.g., Turton, Umbreit, Liaupsin, & Bartley, 2007; Wright-Gallo, Higbee, Reagon, & Davey, 2006). A few studies monitored students' social interactions (e.g., Christensen, Young, & Marchant, 2004; Knapczyk, 1988, 1992; Lane, Weisenbach, et al., 2007).

Functional Assessment Tools

Researchers used a wide range of tools to identify the function of the target behaviors of interest. In the 31 studies reviewed, the most common tools used were teacher interviews (29 studies), direct observation (predominately ABC data collection, 27 studies), and then student interviews (20 studies). Twelve studies conducted school record searches to gain information.

In terms of maintaining functions for the students in this review, 27 students' behaviors were maintained by some form of attention (e.g., peer, teacher, or combined), and 19 were maintained by escape from task demands. For other students, behavior served a dual function of escape from task and teacher attention. In the study by Kamps et al. (2006), for example, the behavior served three functions: accessing peer attention, accessing sensory stimulation, and escaping task demands.

Components Related to Valid Inference Making

In terms of reliability of the dependent variables examined, all 31 studies mentioned and reported interobserver agreement or other relevant reliability information for at least one variable. However, treatment integrity received less attention, with only 18 studies mentioning and reporting the extent to which the intervention was implemented as intended. In looking across the time frame during which these studies were published, treatment integrity data became more the rule than the exception, with 14 of 18 studies published between 2004 and 2009 including treatment integrity. Similarly, social validity was measured (at least anecdotally) and reported for 18 of the 31 studies, again becoming a relatively standard practice beginning in 2002 (R. E. March & Horner, 2002). A total of 12 studies mentioned and reported treatment integrity and social validity (see Table 15.2).

Outcomes

Although it is beyond the scope of this chapter to provide a detailed discussion of student outcomes for each of these ideographic interventions, the majority of the studies established a clear functional relation between the introduction of the intervention (when implemented with fidelity) and changes in student outcome measures. This relationship was true in the earlier studies, when the research teams were responsible for all facets of this multiple-step procedure (e.g., Umbreit, 1995; Umbreit et al., 2004), as well as in more recent research, when teachers assumed more active roles in this process with less-intensive support from local universities (e.g., Kamps et al., 2006; Lane, Barton-Arwood, et al., 2007; Lane, Weisenbach, et al., 2007). The evidence also supports the additional benefit of FABIs relative to nonfunctional assessment-based interventions in increasing task engagement and decreasing problem behavior (Filter & Horner, 2009; Trussell et al., 2008). Moreover, evidence also suggests that FABIs can play a role not only in improving decorum and social interactions (e.g., Lane, Weisenbach, et al., 2007), but also in improved academic outcomes, as evidenced by increases in completed and correct tasks (e.g., Preciado et al., 2009). Finally, social validity data were generally favorable, with the majority of parties indicating that these interventions, although labor intensive, did meet (and in some cases exceed) expectations.

Discussion

As we discussed at the onset of this chapter, aggressive behavior is a hallmark characteristic of students with antisocial behavior patterns and one of the most challenging behaviors to address within and beyond the school setting. Because it is difficult to teach students replacement behaviors that are more reliable and efficient than aggression, it is prudent to intervene at two junctures. First, we recommend intervening at initial school entry, when students are most amenable to intervention efforts before aggressive behavior patterns become highly stable and nonresponsive to intervention efforts (much like interventions for chronic diseases such as diabetes; Kazdin, 1987). Second, we recommend intervening early in the acting-out cycle before aggression is exhibited; the goal here is to respond effectively to lower levels of undesirable behaviors (e.g., disruption, noncompliance, coercion) before behavior escalates into aggression. To address these two objectives, we recommend FSS, a manualized intervention,

to address the first charge and FABIs to meet the second charge. The evidence reviewed in the chapter supports the efficacy of using both practices. Each approach, however, has identifiable strengths and limitations that are important to consider.

First Step to Success: Strengths and Considerations

One strength of FSS is that it is a manualized program involving the school and home contexts as pivotal factors for change. FSS provides explicit instructions to guide intervention training, implementation, and evaluation. It includes clear directions as well as all necessary materials for consultants, teachers, and parents (implementation guide, consultant guide, parent handbook, treatment fidelity-monitoring sheets for the classroom-based component, and even the stopwatch). For many interventions, a barrier to successful implementation is a lack of clarity about procedures related to intervention components. Explicit procedures may provide needed structure to key interventionists and enhance treatment fidelity, which is important to meaningful, lasting change—a long-standing goal of all intervention work (Baer, Wolfe, & Risley, 1968). The use of a consultant also provides much-needed support during start up, when barriers may prevent teachers and parents from initiating and sustaining implementation. Fading of this support to the teacher also programs for maintenance of the intervention within the context of the classroom.

Although social validity data suggest that some teachers view FSS to be too labor intensive, we encourage potential users to consider the costs—financially, emotionally, and otherwise—of dealing with the consequences of antisocial behavior for administrators, teachers, parents, students, and society as a whole (see Kauffman & Brigham, 2009). Fortunately, direction has been offered to guide feasible, effective implementation of FSS. For example, S. Overton et al. (2002) have provided the following points to consider before implementing FSS: (a) results appear to be somewhat less favorable in terms of success with students repeating kindergarten; (b) beginning teachers may struggle to implement the intervention with high fidelity; and (c) characteristics of the consultant influence intervention success, with consultants who lack training in teaching or counseling experiencing less success than consultants who have such training. Also, Diken and Rutherford (2005) suggested that FSS may be less efficacious for students residing in highly chaotic home environments that require more extensive intervention supports than those in more stable homes. Yet, regardless of these challenges, FSS has yielded meaningful changes for many students, as determined by high-quality single-case and group design studies. Thus, we recommend FSS as an evidence-based practice to reverse and reduce risk on initial school entry.

Functional Assessment-Based Interventions: Strengths and Considerations

One strength of FABI is that it is a highly ideographic process that allows for a customized, tertiary prevention effort to design, implement, and evaluate interventions based on the reasons why problem behaviors occur. This is a respectful approach that involves an individualized instructional approach to behavior, ultimately providing students with a more reliable, efficient method of accessing or avoiding relevant conditions (i.e., attention; activities, tasks, or tangibles; and sensory experiences). Such an intervention establishes the student as an effective learner who can acquire more desirable behaviors by modifying antecedent conditions, adjusting reinforcement rates, and using procedures to extinguish undesirable behaviors (Umbreit et al., 2007).

One of the challenges of FABIs is that, in contrast to FSS, it is not a manualized program, making fidelity of the intervention process at times challenging. Systematic approaches are now available for conducting functional assessments. Such approaches include specific guidelines for analyzing data collected from functional assessment tools and procedures, selecting an intervention method that is linked to the function of the target behavior with explicit instructions to guide intervention design, and constructing legally defensible designs to test the intervention effects that include the core components needed to draw accurate conclusions regarding intervention outcomes (Umbreit et al., 2007). Practices used by researchers and practitioners exhibit considerable variability (Sasso et al., 2001), however, which makes synthesis and evaluation activities (e.g., those attempted in this chapter) challenging.

Another challenge associated with FABIs, which is also true for FSS, pertains to social validity. Namely, the costs of conducting FABIs with respect to personnel time to learn the procedures and to develop fluency in the required skills to implement the practice are substantial. However, given the alternative of not intervening, we view the costs as warranted.

Despite these challenges, sufficient evidence suggests that FABIs are an effective, socially valid practice for intervening early in the acting-out cycle. Results from this review indicate FABIs are effective in decreasing problem behaviors that occur earlier in the cycle before aggression (whether physical, verbal, or directed toward property) occurs. Given the deleterious consequences associated with aggression, particularly as students become older, this is encouraging.

Recommendations

We conclude by offering recommendations to researchers and practitioners. First, to our esteemed colleagues, we thank you for the work that has been conducted to prevent the development of antisocial behavior. We are encouraged by the presence of FSS and FABI. And we encourage future inquiry with current practices and in development of new practices.

We recommend scaling up studies such as those funded by the Institute for Educational Sciences to determine how to best build district's and school's capacities to implement these practices. In particular, we encourage studies to determine how best to enable school-site personnel to implement and sustain these practices in isolation from university support (Lane, Kalberg, & Shepcaro, 2009). Additional inquiry to examine the efficacy and effectiveness of these practices when implemented with students whose culture is not the majority to established generalizability is also warranted (J. O. Cooper et al., 2007). Furthermore, because so many students (especially those with early-onset antisocial behaviors; Moffitt, 1993) have already developed their aggression skills as a highly effective, efficient component in their behavioral repertoire, we encourage additional inquiry to identify other secondary and tertiary levels of prevention to manage students who regularly display aggressive behaviors.

To those practitioners working with students who have acquired highly successful repertoires of aggressive and coercive behaviors, we understand and respect the significant challenges you face on a daily basis. Because it is extremely difficult to teach students a replacement behavior that is more reliable and efficient than aggression, we strongly encourage practitioners to intervene early in the student's educational experiences before these behavior patterns become firmly engrained and to intervene early in the acting-out cycle by identifying and preventing behaviors that precede aggressive outbursts. While intervention efforts such as FSS and FABI may be time-consuming, we contend that these procedures are more effective than less-comprehensive interventions (e.g., those that do not involve the families in the early years) and those interventions that do not take into account the communicative function of behavior.

Summary

In this chapter, we reviewed two highly effective practices to prevent and respond to aggressive behavior patterns: FSS and FABI. We provided a review of research studies investigating the efficacy of each practice. Appendixes 15.1 and 15.2 summarize the findings of our literature review of the research base for FSS and FABI, respectively.

Appendix 15.1

Summary of Studies Reviewed for Preventing Aggression: First Step to Success

Author	Participant Characteristics and Instructional Setting	Intervention Components	Outcomes
H. M. Walker, Kavanagh, Stiller, Golly, Severson, & Feil (1998)	$N = 46$; M ($n = 74\%$); Age NS; Ethnicity NS; Grades K and follow-up to 1; SLD ($n = 5$), SLI ($n = 4$), SED ($n = 2$); School and home.	1. ESP 2. CLASS 3. Home base	Significant differences between treatment and control for 4 of 5 measures for both clinical and nonclinical samples. Increases in AET and adaptive behavior and decreases in maladaptive behavior and aggression for the experimental group.
Golly, Stiller, & Walker (1998)	$N = 20$; M ($n = 19$), F ($n = 1$), Age NS; Ethnicity, C ($n = 19$), NA ($n = 1$); Grade K; Typical; School and home.	1. ESP 2. CLASS 3. Home base	Significant effects in the experimental group for adaptive, maladaptive, academic engaged time, and aggression from pre-test to post-test. No effects found for withdrawn behavior.
Golly, Sprague, Walker, Beard, & Gorham (2000)	$N = 4$ (2 sets of twins); M; Age 5; Ethnicity, C; Grade K; Typical; School and home.	1. All for S1 and S2 2. Only school component for S3 and S4	Initial decreases in problem behavior initially with slight variability after. Immediate increases in academic engaged time with variability for S4. S1 and S2 did not complete the program.
S. Overton, McKenzie, King, & Osborne (2002)	$N = 22$; 16 completed; M ($n = 16$), F ($n = 6$); Age 5–6; Ethnicity, C ($n = 5$), AA ($n = 7$), AA and C ($n = 5$), H ($n = 1$), NA ($n = 3$), NA and C ($n = 1$); Grade K; Typical; School and home.	1. SRSS 2. CLASS 3. Home base	Behavioral improvement was significant, but variable. Academic engaged time increased and maintained. Internalizing behavior did not significantly decrease per parent or teacher reports. Externalizing behavior decreased per parent and teacher reports. Aggression decreased per parent, but not teacher.
Diken & Rutherford (2005)	$N = 4$; M ($n = 3$); Age 5–7; Ethnicity, NA; Grade K ($n = 2$) and Grade 1 ($n = 2$); Typical Elementary school of a Southwestern Indian tribe in Arizona and home.	1. SRSS 2. CLASS 3. Home base	Social play behaviors increased for all participants with reductions in variability for S4. Nonsocial play behaviors decreased for S1–S3 with decreased variability for S4. Parent ratings of problem behavior decreased for most. Teacher ratings of class-wide problem behavior indicated little change.
Lien-Thorne & Kamps (2005)	$N = 3$; M ($n = 2$); Age 7–8; Grades 1–2; Ethnicity, C ($n = 2$), AA ($n = 1$); Label, ADHD (S1: SPED); School and home.	1. SSBD 2. CLASS 3. Home base	Academic engagement increased, and inappropriate behaviors decreased and maintained. Variability across participants in post-test measures of risk with little change.
D. R. Carter & Horner (2007)	$N = 1$; M; Age 6; Ethnicity, C; Grade 1; Typical; School and home.	1. CLASS with FABI	Initial decreases in problem behavior from 37% to 3% during the coaching phases of FSS with continued low levels during the teacher phase of FSS plus FABI. Problem behavior increased when FABI was removed.

Author	Participant Characteristics and Instructional Setting	Intervention Components	Outcomes
Seeley, Small, Walker, Feil, Severson, Golly, & Forness (2009)	$N = 42$ (Treatment $= 23$; Control $= 19$); M ($n = 39$); Age 6–8; Ethnicity, H ($n = 30$), NS ($n = 12$); Grades 1–3; ADHD ($n = 42$); School and home.	1. SSBD: Stages 1 and 2 2. CLASS 3. Home base	Significant effects on school-based measures of ADHD and disruptive behavior symptoms, social functioning, and academic performance. Effects of home-based assessments of problem behavior and social skills were nonsignificant.
H. M. Walker, Seeley, Small, Severson, Graham, Feil, Serna, Golly, & Forness (2009)	$N = 200$ (Treatment: 101; Usual care 99); M ($n = 73\%$); Ethnicity, C ($n = 24.5\%$), H ($n = 57\%$), NA ($n = 4.5\%$), A/PI ($n = 0.5\%$), AA ($n = 3\%$), NS ($n = 6\%$); Grade 1 ($n = 83$), Grade 2 ($n = 69$), Grade 3 ($n = 48$). School and home.	1. SSBD: Stages 1 and 2 2. CLASS 3. Home base	Significant gains in problem behavior for treatment (effect sizes: $d = 0.62$ to 0.73). Statistically significant gains for treatment across functional domains with an effect size of $d = 0.54$. Significant gains for treatment on academic competence and academic engaged time, but comparison group had significant gains on Letter–Word ID with no difference between groups on ORF.

Note: A/PI = Asian/Pacific Islander; AA = African American; ADHD = Attention Deficit Hyperactivity Disorder; C= Caucasian; CLASS = Contingencies for Learning Academic and Social Skills (Hops & Walker, 1988); ESP = Early Screening Project (H. M. Walker, Severson, & Feil, 1994); F = Female; FABI = Functional Assessment-Based Intervention; WJ-III = Woodcock-Johnson-III (Woodcock, McGrew, & Mather, 2001); FSS = First Step to Success (H. M. Walker, Stiller, Golly, Kavanagh, Severson, & Feil, 1997); H = Hispanic; M = Male; N = Number; NA = Native American; NS = Not Specified; ORF = Oral Reading Fluency; S = Student; SED = Seriously Emotionally Disturbed; SLD = Specific Learning Disability; SLI = Speech/Language Impairment; SRSS = Student Risk Screening Scale (Drummond, 1994); SSBD = Systematic Screener for Behavior Disorders (H. M. Walker & Severson, 1992b).

Appendix 15.2

Summary of Studies Reviewed for Preventing Aggression: Functional Assessment-Based Interventions

Author	Participant Characteristics and Instructional Setting	Intervention Components	Outcomes
Knapczyk (1988)	S1 Mark; M; Age 13; Ethnicity NS; Grade 7; SPED S2 William; M; Age 14; Ethnicity NS; Grade 8; SPED Public school, special education, part time	Modeling and rehearsal procedures to teach alternative replacement behaviors (social skills).	Functional relation between introduction of intervention and (a) reduction in aggressive behavior, (b) increased initiation–participation events, and (c) decreased initiation–nonparticipation events.
Knapczyk (1992)	*Experiment 1:* S1 Warren; M; Age 16; Ethnicity NS; Grade 10; SPED BD *Experiment 2:* S2 Lonnie; M; Age 15; Ethnicity NS; Grade 9; SPED BD S3 Kenton; M; Age 15; Ethnicity NS; Grade 9; SPED BD S4 Philip; M; Age 16; Ethnicity NS; Grade 10; SPED BD Two rural high schools for students with EBD	Video modeling and behavioral rehearsal to develop alternative responses to aggression. Experiment 1—individually administered; Experiment 2—small-group training sessions.	When participants substituted alternative responses for aggressive responses following the treatment, decreases occurred in the frequency of aggressive behavior and antecedent events associated with the behavior.
Umbreit (1995)	Corey; M; Age 8; Ethnicity NS; Grade, 3; ADHD Public school, general education classroom	1. Independent assignments 2. Cooperative groups without friends 3. Brief breaks 4. Ignore disruption	Functional relation established between the introduction of the intervention and decreases in disruptive behavior in all three inclusive general education classes.
Dunlap, White, Vera, Wilson, & Panacek (1996)	S1 Michael; M; Age 7; Ethnicity NS; Grade 2; SED S2 Gizelle; F; Age 9; Ethnicity NS; Grade 4; SED S3 Ann; F; Age 7; Ethnicity NS; Grade 1: SED Typical public school; EBD classrooms	Individualized, multicomponent plan of curricular modifications.	Functional relation established for all participants demonstrating that task engagement increased and disruptive behavior decreased following the implementation of each intervention.

Author	Participant Characteristics and Instructional Setting	Intervention Components	Outcomes
Grandy & Peck (1997)	S1 M; Age 6; Grade 1; Ethnicity NS; Typical suburban elementary school (K–3), general education	Self-management with fading: participant self-recording; contingent; experimenter attention.	A functional relation was evident between the introduction of the intervention and decreases in disruptive behavior across three settings.
Y. Lee, Sugai, & Horner (1999)	S1 Bill; M; Age 9; Ethnicity NS; Grade 3; EBD S2 Matt; M; Age 9; Ethnicity NS; Grade 3; Label EBD, ADHD Elementary school; Special education self-contained classroom	Component skill instruction on difficult math tasks.	Reductions in problem behavior with inconsistent results based on type of math problem. Reductions in off-task behavior are inconsistent based on the type of math problem. Increases in accuracy but inconsistent across math problem.
Todd, Horner, & Sugai (1999)	S1 Kyle; M; Age 9; Ethnicity NS; Grade 4; LD, physical disability Elementary school; general education classroom (blended 3–4)	Self-monitoring, self-evaluation, and self-recruitment of reinforcement.	Functional relation between the intervention and decrease in problem behaviors, increase in on-task, increase in work completion, increased teacher praise, and increased teacher views of performance.
Penno, Frank, & Wacker (2000)	S1 Andy; M; Age 13; Ethnicity NS; Grade NS; Typical S2 Nick; M; Age 14; Ethnicity NS; Grade NS; ADHD S3 Josh; M; Age 14; Ethnicity NS; Grade NS; LD, BD, ADHD State-funded segregated school for adolescents with EBD	S1: Completing assignments with computer and peer tutor. S2: Shortened assignments and peer tutor. S3: Self-monitoring and working 1:1 with staff.	For 2 students; 2+ modifications resulted in (a) improved productivity and accuracy; (b) decreased behavior problems. Increases in (a) percentage of items completed for S1 and S2 and (b) percent correct for S1 across, (c) number of problems completed for S3.
B. W. Smith & Sugai (2000)	Stu; M; Age NS; Ethnicity NS; Grade 7; Special Education, EBD Self-contained behavioral classroom	Self-management.	Increases in on-task behavior for first intervention phase with slower increases in second. Decreases in off-task during initial intervention, variable performance during second intervention.
C. H. Kennedy, Long, Jolivette, Cox, Tang, & Thompson (2001)	S1 Charles; M; Age 8; Ethnicity, C; Grade 4; Labels: Tourette's syndrome, ADHD, SED S2 Mickey; M; Age 6; Ethnicity, C; Grade 1; ADHD S3 Jolanda; F; Age 6; Ethnicity, AA; Grade 1; Typical S1: SPED resource S2 and S3: General education	Individualized PBS plans including antecedent adjustments, reinforcement, and extinction.	When interventions were implemented with integrity, problem behaviors were reduced and general education participation was either maintained or increased as problem behaviors decreased (one demonstration one replication for each DV).

Author	Participant Characteristics and Instructional Setting	Intervention Components	Outcomes
Kern, Delaney, Clarke, Dunlap, & Childs (2001)	S1 Benjamin; M; Age 11; Ethnicity NS; Grade 5; ADHD, EBD S2 Art; M; Age 11; Ethnicity NS; Grade 5; ED Self-contained classroom for student with EBD	S1 Choice of 3 media to complete the assignment. S1 and S2 Complete assignments using a preferred medium.	S1 preferred medium and choice of medium were both associated with increased engagement and decreased disruption behavior. Interesting assignments were associated with higher levels of engagement and decreased disruptive behavior. S2 preferred medium was associated with higher rates of engagement and lower rates of disruptive behavior and increased number of words written.
R. E. March & Horner (2002)	S1 Andy; M; Age 13; Ethnicity NS; Grade 7; SPED, NS S2 Bill; M; Age 13; Ethnicity NS; Grade 7; Typical S3 Cathy; F; 12; Ethnicity NS; Grade 6; SPED, general education middle school	1. Setting event procedures 2. Antecedent procedures 3. Teaching new skills 4. Consequence procedures	Decreases in level and variability of problem behavior across participants. Increases in academic engagement found across participants.
Burke, Hagan-Burke, & Sugai (2003)	Mario; M; Age NS; Grade 3; Ethnicity NS, ELL; LD Suburban elementary school (K–5), general education classroom	Intervention: preteaching vocabulary concepts.	Functional relation between preteaching vocabulary and on-task behaviors.
Christensen, Young, & Marchant (2004)	S1 Justin; M; Age 8; Ethnicity, C; Grade 3; referred Instructional setting: urban elementary school; third-grade general education classroom	Alternative behaviors/ skill development; self-monitoring; peer and teacher reinforcement; peer mediators.	Functional relationship was established between the introduction of the intervention package and improved socially appropriate classroom behavior.
Maag & Larson (2004)	S1 Allen; M; Age NS; Ethnicity NS; Grade 5; ED; Instructional Setting: general education class S2 Bruce; M; Age NS; Ethnicity NS; Grade 5; SLD Instructional Setting: general education class	S1 Preferred seating. S2 Contingent verbal praise.	Partial evidence (one demonstration; one replication) to suggest a functional relation between introduction of the intervention and decreases in problem behavior for both students.
Newcomer & Lewis (2004)	S1 Matthew; M; Age 9; Ethnicity NS; Grade 3; OHI S2 Emma; F; Age 11; Ethnicity NS; Grade 5; Typical Suburban, elementary school, general education class	Function based: S1: Antecedent, consequence, and instructional manipulations. S2: Instruction in appropriate replacement behaviors, teacher pleaser behaviors; Non-function based: Topography.	Partial evidence of a functional relation in support of function-based interventions; however, comparative data across (a) B and C phases revealed a slight level change during C phase for S2 and (b) A and B phases also revealed improvement.
Umbreit, Lane, & Dejud (2004)	S1 Jason; M; Age 10; Ethnicity, C; Grade 4; Typical Instructional setting: General education classroom at a public elementary school	Providing more challenging academic tasks to meet the ability level of the participant.	A functional relation was established between intervention implementation (challenging tasks) and academic engagement.

Author	Participant Characteristics and Instructional Setting	Intervention Components	Outcomes
Kamps, Wendland, & Culpepper (2006)	Patricia; F; Age 7; Ethnicity, AA; Grade 2; at risk (SSBD, DIBELS) Urban, culturally diverse charter elementary school classroom	*Group Instruction:* 1. Teacher attention, points 2. Self-management 3. Reminders *Independent Seat Work:* 1. Modeling 2. Help tickets 3. Social attention	S1: Functional relation established, with disruptive behavior decreasing and on-task behavior increasing during intervention for independent and group instruction as compared to initial assessments.
Liaupsin, Umbreit, Ferro, Urso, & Upreti (2006)	Fiona; F; Age 14; Ethnicity, C; Grade 7; Typical, mild, unilateral hearing loss Charter school that focused on athletics and academics	1. Antecedent adjustments 2. Reinforcement 3. Extinction	Introduction of the intervention was associated with increases in on-task behavior in both settings; one demonstration and one replication for each setting.
Lo & Cartledge (2006)	S1 Ted; M; Age 7; Ethnicity, AA; Grade 2; Typical S2 Adam; M; Age 8; Ethnicity, AA; Grade 2; Typical S3 Chad; M; Age 9; Ethnicity, AA; Grade 4; ADHD, SPED S4 Sam; M; Age 9; Ethnicity, AA; Grade 4; ADHD SEDPublic elementary school (P–5) S1 2nd grade Gen Ed S2 2/3 Gen Ed S3 Resource room for language arts (21%–50%) S4 51%–60% in SED resource room	*Intervention Components:* 1. Skill training 2. DRA 3. DRI 4. Self-monitor desired and replacement behaviors	Functional relation between introduction of the intervention and reductions in all participants' levels of off-task behavior. AAR behavior data revealed slight improvements in appropriate behavior and decreases in inappropriate behavior for S1 and S2. S3 demonstrated no changes in AAR but IAR declined to a low, stable level during implementation and maintenance. S4 showed inconsistent changes in IAR but AAR increased.
Wright-Gallo, Higbee, Reagon, & Davey (2006)	S1 Mike; M; Age 14.5; Ethnicity NS; Grade NS; SPED; EBD S2 Tim; M; Age 12.75; Ethnicity NS; Grade NS; SPED; EBD Public middle school self-contained special education classroom for students with EBD	Differential reinforcement of alternative behavior.	For both participants, there was one demonstration and one replication of experimental effect demonstrating lower rates of disruptive behavior during treatment (following the functional analysis).
Stahr, Cushing, Lane, & Fox (2006)	Shawn; M; Age 9; Ethnicity, AA; Grade 4; ADHD, internalizing (anxiety), and a SLI; OHI Self-contained school for students with EBD in a large metropolitan city	1. Teaching help seeking 2. Self-monitoring 3. Planned ignoring	A functional relation was established between intervention implementation and increased on-task time during language arts and math.

Author	Participant Characteristics and Instructional Setting	Intervention Components	Outcomes
Fairbanks, Sugai, Guardino, & Lathrop (2007)	S1 Blair; F; Age 7–8; Ethnicity, C; Grade 2; Typical S2 Ben; M; Age 7–8; Ethnicity, C; Grade 2; Typical S3 Marcellus; M; Age 7–8; Ethnicity, C; Grade 2; Typical S4 Olivia; F; Age 7–8; Ethnicity, C; Grade 2; LD General education classroom	Originally CICO, then FABI that included antecedent and reinforcement adjustments with clear consequences for infractions, review of expectations.	Mean intervals with problem behavior were reduced during function-based phases for all participants as compared to baseline and CICO phases.
Lane, Barton-Arwood, Spencer, & Kalberg (2007)	S1 John; M; Age 7; Ethnicity NS; Grade 2; ADHD S2 Thomas; M; Age 6; Ethnicity NS; Grade K; ADHD, OCD, special education—OHI S1 Private school for high-incidence disabilities S2 General education kindergarten, public elementary	*S1:* Curricular modifications Self-monitoring *S2:* Antecedent adjustments Consequence adjustments	S1: Functional relation between introduction of the intervention and interruptions. S2: Functional relation not established between introduction of the intervention and inappropriate touches (number of mediation changes). Replacement behaviors were used inconsistently for both students.
Lane, Smither, Huseman, Guffey, & Fox (2007)	S1 Harry; M; Age 6; Ethnicity, C; Grade K; Typical General education classroom in an inclusive school district in Middle TN	*Intervention Components:* 1. Self-monitoring 2. Differential reinforcement 3. Positive scanning	Possible functional relation; (one demonstration, one replication); improvements in disruption and academic engaged time were associated with the intervention despite some variability in treatment fidelity.
Lane, Weisenbach, Phillips, & Wehby (2007)	S1 Margaret; Age 7; Ethnicity NS; Grade 2; Typical, at risk per screening Inclusive, general education public schools in middle TN	*Method 1 and 2:* 1. Antecedent adjustments (teach and prompt desired behavior) 2. Reinforcement 3. Extinction	A functional relation existed between the introduction of the intervention and increases in Margaret's PSI and decreases in her NSI.
Turton, Umbreit, Liaupsin, & Bartley (2007)	S1 Saida; F; Age 16; Ethnicity, Black African (Bermudian); Grade 10; ED and LD Alternative high school for students with SED; received noncategorical special education services	Antecedent adjustments Reinforcement for replacement behavior; extinction of target behavior	Functional relation established between the introduction and increases in appropriate responses. The intervention was rated as socially valid by the teacher, Saida, and her peers.
B. K. Wood, Umbreit, Liaupsin, & Gresham (2007)	Josh; Age 8; Ethnicity NS; Grade 3; Typical General education	*Method 3:* 1. Adjust the antecedents 2. Adjust the contingencies 3. Extinction	Equivocal results produced by the intervention; the level of on-task behavior parallels the teacher's level of implementation.

Author	Participant Characteristics and Instructional Setting	Intervention Components	Outcomes
Trussell, Lewis, & Stichter (2008)	S1 Larry; Age 11; Ethnicity, AA; Grade 5; ED and SLD S2 Dave; Age 8; Ethnicity, AA; Grade 3; ED S3 ED; Jack; Age 7; Ethnicity, AA; Grade 1; ED Midwest school district, at an alternative public school	Targeted Classroom vs. Interventions FABI	S1, S2, and S3: Targeted classroom interventions decreased problem behaviors, which decreased further when individualized interventions based on the function were implemented.
Preciado, Horner, & Baker (2009)	S1 Juan; M; Age NS; Ethnicity, Latino ELL; Grade 2; Typical S2 Julia; F; Age NS; Ethnicity, Latina ELL; Grade 3; Typical S3 Jose; M; Age NS; Ethnicity, Latino ELL; Grade 2; LD S4 Javier; M; Age NS; Ethnicity, Latino ELL; Grade 4; Typical General education classes	Intervention: Language-matched instructional priming (LMIP)	Functional relation for S1, S2, and S3 between the introduction of the language-matched instructional priming and decreases in problem behavior, increases in engagement, increases in completed and correct tasks. Results for S4 were variable. Increased DIBELS and IDEL scores.
Filter & Horner (2009)	S1 Brett; M; Age NS; Ethnicity, C; Grade 4; LD S2 Dylan; M; Age NS; Ethnicity, C; Grade 4; ADHD (not in special education) General education classrooms	Functional-based academic Intervention compared to non-function-based interventions (S1 reading; S2 math)	Functional relation between the academic variables and the problem behaviors; S1 and S2 engaged in lower levels of problem behavior and higher levels of task engagement during function-based intervention than non-function-based interventions.

Note: A/PI = Asian/Pacific Islander; AA = African American; AAR = Appropriate Attention Recruitment; ADHD = Attention Deficit Hyperactivity Disorder; ADHDH = Attention Deficit Hyperactivity Disorder, Hyperactive type; BD = Behavior Disorder; C= Caucasian; CBM = Curriculum-Based Measurement; CICO = Check In/Check Out; DIBELS = Dynamic Indicators of Basic Early Literacy Skills; DRA = Differential Reinforcement of Alternative Behavior; DRI = Differential Reinforcement of Incompatible Behavior; EBD = Emotional/ Behavioral Disorder; ED = Emotional Disturbance; ELL = English Language Learner; F = Female; FABI = Functional Assessment-Based Intervention; FBA = Functional Behavioral Assessment; H = Hispanic; IAR = Inappropriate Attention Recruitment; IDEL = Indicadores Dinamicos del Exito en la Lectura (Good, Bank, & Watson, 2003); LD = Learning Disability; M = Male; NA = Native American; NS = Not Specified; NSI = Negative Social Interactions; OCD = Obsessive/Compulsive Disorder; OHI = Other Health Impairment; PSI = Positive Social Interactions; S = Student; SED = Seriously Emotionally Disturbed; SLD = Specific Learning Disability; SLI = Speech/Language Impaired; SPED = Special Education; TN = Tennessee.

CHAPTER 16

Research-Based Practices for Social Behavior: *Social Skills Training, Replacement Behavior Training, and Positive Peer Reporting*

Frank M. Gresham, Lisa Libster, and **Keri Menesses** | *Louisiana State University*

hildren and youth with emotional, behavioral, and social difficulties present substantial challenges to schools, teachers, parents, and peers. These challenges cut across disciplinary, instructional, and interpersonal domains and frequently create chaotic home, school, and classroom environments. The social, emotional, and behavioral characteristics of children with or at risk for behavior difficulties often overwhelm the capacity of schools to effectively accommodate these students' instructional and disciplinary needs. Schools are charged with teaching an increasingly diverse student population in terms of prevailing attitudes and beliefs, behavior styles, race and ethnicity, language, socioeconomic levels, and risk status (H. M. Walker, Ramsey, & Gresham, 2004). Additionally, pressures for higher academic standards and outcomes for all students currently are approaching nearly unattainable levels, particularly for students with behavioral challenges. Students bringing these behavioral challenges to school often create turbulent classroom and school environments, thereby disrupting the learning and achievement of other students.

Children with or at risk for behavior difficulties experience significant difficulties in the development and maintenance of satisfactory interpersonal relationships,

exhibition of prosocial behavior patterns, and social acceptance by peers and teachers (Gresham, 1997, 1998; Maag, 2005, 2006; H. M. Walker et al., 2004). These social competence deficits can lead to short-term, intermediate, and long-term difficulties in the domains of educational, psychological, and vocational spheres of functioning (Kupersmidt, Coie, & Dodge, 1990; Newcomb, Bukowski, & Pattee, 1993; J. Parker & Asher, 1987). The fact that most children with or at risk for behavior difficulties exhibit severe social competence deficits dictates that we design and implement effective intervention strategies to remediate these children's interpersonal difficulties.

In this chapter we describe and critique three evidence-based practices designed to alter the social behavior of children and adolescents. Specifically, we review the following interventions: (a) social skills training, (b) replacement behavior training, and (c) positive peer reporting. We describe these practices within the context of a multitiered model of intervention delivery (universal, selected, and intensive) and point to directions for future research for each practice. Before reviewing each practice, we briefly review the risk and protective factors in relation to students' developing behavioral difficulties, provide a conceptualization of social competence, and provide a discussion of classi-fication of specific types of social skills deficits. This discussion should provide a context for understanding how each of the three intervention practices addresses different aspects of social behavioral functioning.

Risk and Protective Factors in Serious Behavior Disorders

H. M. Walker and Severson (2002) suggested that children and youth having characteristics of behavioral difficulties or disorders are at risk for a host of negative developmental outcomes, many of which place these individuals on destructive pathways often leading to unfortunate consequences such as school failure and dropout, alcohol and substance abuse, delinquency, social rejection, and violent and destructive behavior patterns. These risk factors interact in complex ways, and it is unlikely that a single risk factor is responsible for the development of behavior difficulties in a particu-lar individual. Given that single risk factors may predict multiple outcomes and that a great deal of overlap occurs among behavioral markers, interventions focusing on risk reduction of interacting risk factors may have direct effects on multiple outcomes (Coie & Dodge, 1983; Dryfoos, 1990). Researchers typically find a nonlinear relationship among risk factors and outcomes, suggest-ing that a single risk factor may have a small effect, but researchers also find that rates of students identified with serious behavior disorders (SBDs) increase rapidly and exponentially with the accumulation of additional risk factors (Rutter, 1979; Sameroff, Seifer, Barocas, Zax, & Greenspan, 1987).

More germane to the present chapter, H. M. Walker and Severson (2002) identified a number of risk and protective factors specifically within the realm of social competence that could be targeted for interven-tion efforts. In particular, poor problem solving, poor social skills, lack of empathy, bullying, and peer rejec-tion represent important risk factors for students who may develop behavior disorders. A recent synthesis of the meta-analytic literature of the risk and protective factor literature also found that controversial, rejected, and neglected sociometric statuses as well as poor social skills were significant risk factors for children and youth with externalizing (e.g., noncompliance, aggression, or coercive behaviors) and internalizing (e.g., social withdrawal, anxiety, or depression) behavior concerns (Crews et al., 2007).

Although children and youth with behavioral diffi-culties have a number of social competence risk factors, a number of protective factors buffer the negative outcomes created by risk factors. Protective factors are variables that reduce the likelihood of maladaptive outcomes, given conditions of risk. Protective factors in the realm of social competence include social-cognitive skills, prosocial be-havior patterns, and peer acceptance. In a meta-analytic synthesis, Crews et al. (2007) found that positive play activities, popular sociometric status, and prosocial be-havior patterns served as significant protective factors for individuals with both externalizing and internalizing behavior patterns.

This brief review of the risk and protective factor literature indicates that individuals with characteristics of SBD experience a number of risk factors that inter-act in complex ways to produce negative developmental trajectories. Unfortunately, many of these risk factors are immutable and are not amenable to change by schools. On the positive side, a number of risk factors, particularly within the realm of social competence, can be targeted for intervention by schools. Moreover, the literature has dem-onstrated that many behaviors that make up the construct of social competence serve as important protective factors that buffer the pernicious effects of risk factors associated with behavioral difficulties. This chapter reviews three strategies designed to teach social skills to children and youth who are at risk for or who have behavioral concerns.

Conceptualization of Social Competence

Since the 1990s, we have seen an explosion of pro-fessional interest and investment in the development of children's social competence in general and those of at-risk students in particular (Elksnin & Elksnin, 2006; Gresham & Elliott, 1990; Maag, 2006; Merrell & Gimpel, 1998). An important distinction in the theoreti-cal conceptualization of social behavior is the distinction between the concepts of *social skill* and *social compe-tence*. Social skills are a specific class of behaviors that an individual exhibits in order to complete a social task. Social tasks might include things such as peer-group en-try, having a conversation, making friends, and playing a game with peers. Social competence, in contrast, is an evaluative term based on judgments (given certain criteria) that an individual has performed a social task adequately. These judgments are made by social agents with whom the individual interacts within natural envi-ronments (e.g., school, home, community). Given this conceptualization, social skills are specific behaviors exhibited in specific situations that lead to judgments by others that these behaviors were competent or incompe-tent in accomplishing social tasks.

Gresham (1986) suggested that evaluations of social competence might be based on three criteria: (a) relevant judgments of an individual's social behavior (e.g., by peers, teachers, parents); (b) evaluations of social behavior relative to explicit, pre-established criteria (e.g., number of steps successfully completed in the performance of a social task); and (c) behavioral performances relative to a normative standard (e.g., scores on social skills rating scales). It is important to note that social behaviors, in and of themselves, cannot be considered "socially skilled" apart from their impact on the judgments of social agents in a given social environment.

Definitions of Social Skills

Numerous definitions of social skills have been developed since the 1980s. Merrell and Gimpel (1998) identified at least 15 definitions of social skills that have appeared in the professional literature. Despite these myriad definitions, social skills are perhaps best conceptualized as a behavioral *response class,* because specific social behaviors are grouped under the generic category of "social skill." Conceptually, social skills make up a set of competencies that (a) facilitate the initiation and maintenance of positive social relationships, (b) contribute to peer acceptance and friendship development, (c) result in satisfactory school adjustment, and (d) allow for individuals to cope with and adapt to the demands of the social environment (Gresham, 1998, 2002a). For purposes of the current chapter, social skills can be defined as socially acceptable learned behaviors that enable an individual to interact effectively with others and to avoid or escape unacceptable behaviors that result in negative social interactions with others (Gresham & Elliott, 1984, 1990, 2008).

A useful way of conceptualizing social skills is based on the concept of *social validity* (Kazdin, 1977; M. M. Wolf, 1978). In this approach, social skills can be defined as social behaviors occurring in specific situations that result in important social outcomes for children and youth (Gresham, 1983, 1986). Socially important outcomes are those that key social agents (peers, teachers, parents) consider significant, adaptive, and functional within specific settings. Put differently, socially important outcomes are those that make a difference in individuals' adaptation both to societal expectations and to the behavioral demands of specific environments in which they function (H. M. Walker, Forness, et al., 1998).

What are socially important outcomes? Research has shown that some of the most socially important outcomes for children and youth include peer acceptance (Newcomb et al., 1993; J. Parker & Asher, 1987), academic achievement, and school adjustment (DiPerma, Volpe, & Elliott, 2002; Hersh & Walker, 1983; H. M. Walker, Irvin, Noell, & Singer, 1992), as well as teacher and parent acceptance (Gresham, 2002c; Gresham & Elliott, 1990). It is well established that children who

are poorly accepted or rejected by peers, who have few friendships, and who adjust poorly to schooling are at much greater risk for lifelong maladaptive outcomes. J. Parker and Asher (1987) showed that children having difficulties in peer relationships often demonstrate a behavior pattern that can be described as antisocial or aggressive and characterized by repeated school norm violations. This behavior pattern is characteristic of many children with or at risk for SBD. In the absence of effective interventions, this behavior pattern is likely to continue and morph into more virulent and resistant forms of maladaptive behavior (Patterson, DeBaryshe, & Ramsey, 1989; J. B. Reid, 1993; H. M. Walker et al., 2004).

Social Skills as Academic Enablers

Researchers have documented meaningful and predictive relationships between children's social behaviors and their long-term academic achievement (DiPerma & Elliott, 2002; DiPerma et al., 2002; Malecki & Elliott, 2002; Wentzel, 1993). The notion of *academic enablers* evolved from the work of researchers who explored the relationship between students' nonacademic behaviors (e.g., social skills and motivation) and their academic achievement (Gresham & Elliott, 1990; Malecki, 1998; Wentzel, 1993; Wigfield & Karpathian, 1991). DiPerma and Elliott (2000) distinguished between academic skills and academic enablers. Academic skills are viewed as the basic and complex skills that are the primary focus of academic instruction. In contrast, academic enablers are attitudes and behaviors that allow a student to participate in and ultimately benefit from academic instruction in the classroom. Research using the Academic Competence Evaluation Scales (ACES; DiPerma & Elliott, 2000) showed that academic enablers were moderately related to students' academic achievement as measured by standardized tests (*Mdn r* = 0.50). In a major longitudinal study, Caprara and colleagues found that social skills of third graders as assessed by teachers were better predictors of eighth-grade academic achievement than achievement test results in third grade (Caprara, Barbaranelli, Pastorelli, Bandura, & Zimbardo, 2000). Even stronger findings were reported by Malecki and Elliott (2002), who showed that social skills correlated approximately 0.70 with end-of-year academic achievement as measured by high-stakes tests. It thus appears that social skills are vitally important academic enablers for children in schools.

Classification of Social Skills Deficits

Another important conceptual feature of social skills that has direct implications for the design and delivery of social skills intervention programs is the distinction between social skills acquisition deficits and social skills performance deficits (Gresham, 1981a, 1981b). This distinction is important because different intervention approaches in remediating social skills deficits are required, and different settings (e.g., general education classroom vs. pullout groups) are indicated, for different tiers of intervention (universal, selected, or targeted/intensive).

Acquisition deficits result from either the absence of knowledge about how to perform a given social skill, an inability to fluently enact a sequence of social behaviors, or difficulty in knowing which social skill is appropriate in specific situations (Gresham, 1981a, 2002a). Based on the preceding conceptualization, acquisition deficits can result from deficits in social-cognitive abilities, difficulties in integrating fluent response patterns, or deficits in appropriate discrimination of social situations. Acquisition deficits can be characterized as "can't do" problems because the child cannot perform a given social skill under the most optimal conditions of motivation.

Performance deficits can be conceptualized as the failure to perform a given social skill at acceptable levels even though the child knows how to perform the social skill. These types of social skills deficits can be thought of as "won't do" problems; the child knows what to do, but does not want to perform a particular social skill. These types of social skills deficits can best be thought of as motivational or performance issues rather than learning or acquisition issues.

Competing Problem Behaviors

Another important component in the conceptualization of social skills deficits is the notion of *competing problem behaviors* (Gresham & Elliott, 1990). Competing problem behaviors effectively compete with, interfere with, or "block" either the acquisition or performance of a given social skill. Competing problem behaviors can be broadly classified as either externalizing behavior patterns or internalizing behavior patterns. For example, a child with a history of noncompliant, oppositional, and coercive behavior may never learn prosocial behavioral alternatives such as sharing, cooperation, and self-control because of the absence of opportunities to learn these behaviors caused by the competing function of these aversive behaviors (Eddy, Reid, & Curry, 2002). Similarly, a child with a history of social anxiety, social withdrawal, and shyness may never learn appropriate social behaviors because of withdrawal from the peer group, thereby creating an absence of the opportunities to learn peer-related social skills (Gresham, Van, & Cook, 2006).

In the sections that follow, we introduce three strategies designed to teach social skills to children and youth who are at risk for or who have SBD: (a) social skills training, (b) replacement behavior training, and (c) positive peer reporting.

Social Skills Training

The importance of social competence for children and youth with SBD has been translated into various service-delivery and instructional approaches to remediate deficits in social competence functioning. One of the most popular of these approaches is *social skills training* (SST), which is designed to remediate children's acquisition and performance deficits and to reduce or eliminate competing problem behaviors (Gresham, Sugai, & Horner, 2001). See Figure 16.1 for a list of steps used in most SST programs. An important question to be answered is whether or not SST is efficacious in

Figure 16.1   Social skills training: treatment integrity checklist.

1. Tell/Coach
   a. Define the skill.
   b. Give examples of the skill.
   c. Discuss steps to perform the skill.
   d. Tell students why the skill is important.
2. Show/Model
   a. Use videos or live modeling to show exemplars and nonexemplars of the skill.
   b. Discuss reasons why models are positive or negative examples of performing the skill.
3. Do/Behavioral Rehearsal
   a. Review skill steps.
   b. Allow students to role-play positive and negative examples of the skill.
   c. Give feedback on student performance.
   d. Discuss reasons why role-plays are positive or negative examples of performing the skill.
4. Practice
   a. Rehearse skill in role-plays.
   b. Encourage students to practice skill in multiple settings.
   c. Assign homework to further encourage practice.
5. Monitor Progress
   a. Ask students to consider how well they perform the skill.
   b. Periodically monitor progress in applying the skill.
6. Generalize
   a. Discuss situations in which the skill should be performed.
   b. Brainstorm ways to improve the skill.
   c. Discuss advanced applications of the skill (e.g., situations that may require modifying the skill).
   d. Discuss when it is easy/difficult to perform the skill.
   e. Review the skill.

remediating social skills deficits. Several narrative and meta-analytic reviews have addressed this question, with some reviews yielding conflicting conclusions.

Narrative Reviews

At least 12 narrative reviews of the SST literature using both group and single-case experimental designs have been conducted since the 1980s (Ager & Cole, 1991; Coleman, Wheeler, & Webber, 1993; Gresham, 1981b, 1985; Hollinger, 1987; Landrum & Lloyd, 1992; Mathur & Rutherford, 1991; R. McIntosh, Vaughn, & Zaragoza, 1991; Olmeda & Kauffman, 2003; Schloss, Schloss, Wood, & Kiel, 1986; Templeton, 1990; Zaragoza, Vaughn, & McIntosh, 1991). These narrative reviews reached the following general conclusions about the efficacy of SST: (a) The most effective SST strategies appear to be some combination of modeling, coaching behavioral rehearsal, and procedures derived from applied behavior analysis; (b) evidence for cognitive-behavioral procedures (e.g., social problem solving, self-instruction) is generally weaker, particularly on direct measures of social behavior in naturalistic settings; and (c) by far the greatest weakness in the SST literature is the absence of consistent, durable gains in prosocial behaviors across situations, settings, and over time (maintenance).

Meta-Analytic Reviews

Eight meta-analyses of the SST literature have been conducted since 1985 (Ang & Hughes, 2001; Beelmann, Pfingsten, & Losel, 1994; C. R. Cook et al., 2008; Gresham, Cook, Crews, & Kern, 2004; Losel & Beelmann, 2003; Quinn, Kavale, Mathur, Rutherford, & Forness, 1999; Schneider, 1992; Schneider & Byrne, 1985). It should be noted that the Gresham et al. (2004) and C. R. Cook et al. (2008) meta-analyses were syntheses of the above six meta-analyses (i.e., they were "mega"-analyses). These meta-analyses focused on children and youth with behavioral difficulties, involved 338 studies, and included over 25,000 children and youth between the ages of 3 and 18 years. We reserve our discussion of the Quinn et al. (1999) meta-analysis for a later section of this chapter because of its methodological problems.

Based on the above-cited meta-analyses, the definition of the construct of social skills appears to be consistent for research synthesis purposes. The meta-analyses suggested that the social skills construct can be divided into three major categories: social interaction, prosocial behavior, and social-cognitive skills. Correlates of social skills fall into two categories: problem behavior (externalizing and internalizing) and academic achievement/performance. These social skills categories and correlates are consistent with other work in the area of social skills conducted

by a number of researchers (Caldarella & Merrell, 1997; Coie, Dodge, & Coppotelli, 1982; Dodge, 1986; Gresham, 2002a; Gresham & Elliott, 2008; H. M. Walker & McConnell, 1995; H. M. Walker et al., 1992).

Gresham et al. (2004) summarized five of the meta-analyses and found a grand mean effect size $r = 0.29$ (range, 0.19–0.40) and Cohen's $d = 0.60$ (range, 0.47–0.89). Using the binomial effect size display (BESD), these data suggest that approximately 65% of the participants in the SST groups improved their social skills compared to only 35% of individuals in the control groups. The BESD shows the effect of group membership (i.e., treatment vs. control students) on the success rate of a given outcome. The BESD is a 2×2 contingency table with the columns representing group status and rows representing success and non-success rates (Rosenthal, Rosnow, & Rubin, 2000). Using J. Cohen's (1977) conventional standards, an effect size of this magnitude would be considered "medium." Considering these five meta-analyses, it is clear that SST produces practically significant changes in social behavior based on percentages of participants in SST groups that show improvement.

In a subsequent meta-analytic synthesis, C. R. Cook et al. (2008) extended the findings of Gresham et al. (2004) by examining the efficacy of SST with secondary-age students (ages 11 to 19 years). These authors analyzed data from five meta-analyses that involved secondary-age students with or at risk for SBD (Ang & Hughes, 2001; Beelmann et al., 1994; Durlak, Fuhrman, & Lampman, 1991; Losel & Beelmann, 2003; Schneider & Byrne, 1985). Because secondary grades entail both middle and high school students, as well as the fact that youth as young as 11 years of age attend middle school, age 11 was used to demarcate secondary from elementary students. The overall weighted mean effect size across the five meta-analyses was $r = 0.32$, $d = 0.63$ (range = 0.41–0.92). An effect size of this magnitude indicates a medium effect size for SST according to J. Cohen's (1977) guidelines. Using the BESD, almost two thirds (66%) of secondary-age students improve with SST compared to only 34% of control students.

The majority of studies analyzed across the meta-analyses included random assignment to intervention conditions, which is the most rigorous procedure that can be employed to ensure the internal validity of a particular intervention. Moreover, the five meta-analyses clearly showed that SST produces *practically* important changes in social behavior according to percentage of youth in the SST groups who showed improvement relative to controls.

These findings also support the external validity of SST for students with behavioral difficulties. That is, all five meta-analyses reviewed showed that SST was an effective intervention for students representative of the SBD population. These findings suggest that SST would likely be an effective intervention for students with emotional and/or behavioral problems beyond those included in different meta-analyses—that evidence in the meta-analyses supports generalization across sample characteristics. That is, across the meta-analyses, SST programs were implemented with students with different types of behavioral issues, and comparison of effect size indices suggested similar benefits of SST for individuals with different social, emotional, and behavioral problems.

Quinn et al. (1999) Meta-Analysis

The Quinn et al. meta-analysis of 35 studies is particularly relevant to the SBD population because it was reported to be based entirely on students labeled as emotionally disturbed (ED) under IDEA (1999). Unfortunately, it appears that the 35 studies in this meta-analysis did not meet the more stringent inclusion criteria of the previously described meta-analyses (Christoff, Scott, Kelley, Schlundt, Baer, & Kelly, 1985; Goldstein & Ferrell, 1987) by requiring a control group and either an experimental or quasi-experimental design. Therefore, the results of the Quinn et al. report, an overall mean effect size of $r = 0.10$ ($d = 0.199$) across the 35 studies, are questioned. Using a BESD, an effect size of $r = 0.10$ suggests that 55% of the participants in the SST groups improved and 45% of the controls improved. However, the Quinn et al. effect size of $r = 0.10$ is far below the average effect size of $r = 0.29$ reported in the meta-analyses reviewed earlier. What explains this divergence in the magnitude of effect sizes between the Quinn et al. and other meta-analyses? One influence on effect size estimation is the nature of the dependent measures on which the effect size is based. Approximately 22% of the effect sizes were based on measures of academic achievement ($r = 0.03$). Although academic competence is an important correlate of social competence, aggregation of academic achievement effect sizes in the overall effect for SST is questionable. Moreover, an additional eight effect sizes were based on personality test measures ($r = 0.06$). Thus, almost 40% of the effect size estimates were based on outcome variables that SST was never intended to impact. It appears that many of the effect sizes calculated in the Quinn et al. meta-analysis are tainted theoretically by construct irrelevant variance (see Messick, 1995). Therefore, the meta-analysis performed by Quinn et al. does not appear to be representative of the true population effect size for SST.

Replacement Behavior Training

Replacement Behavior Training (RBT) is an intensive intervention and is designed primarily for students who are weak responders to other intervention strategies. RBT is designed to remediate resistant social skills performance deficits that are accompanied by well-entrenched competing problem behaviors by identifying positive replacement behaviors that serve the same behavioral function as the problem behavior, and to actively teach the student to use the positive replacement behavior instead. RBT requires a functional behavioral assessment (FBA) and a competing behavioral pathways conceptualization of the relationship between prosocial behavior and competing problem behavior (Sugai, Horner, & Gresham, 2002). See Figure 16.2 for a list of steps used in most RBT programs.

Competing Problem Behaviors

Social skills performance deficits are due primarily to motivational variables rather than a lack of knowledge or learning concerning how to enact a particular social skill. One of the most conceptually powerful and empirically established learning principles used to explain the relationship between social skills performance deficits and competing problem behaviors is the *Matching Law* (Herrnstein, 1961, 1970). The Matching Law states that the relative rate of any given behavior matches the relative rate of reinforcement for that behavior. In other words, response rate *matches* reinforcement rate.

Figure 16.2   Replacement Behavior Training: treatment integrity checklist.

1. Identify the problem behavior that will be replaced.
2. Conduct a functional behavioral assessment to determine the function of the problem behavior.
3. Identify a positive behavior that will serve to replace the problem behavior.
   a. This behavior must already be in the student's repertoire (i.e., the student already exhibits the behavior to some degree).
   b. This behavior cannot be more effortful to exhibit than the problem behavior.
   c. The behavior must occur at a rate sufficient to come into contact with contingencies.
   d. The behavior is likely to contact natural contingencies such that the behavior will continue to be reinforced when the intervention is withdrawn.
4. Identify rewards that will effectively reinforce the occurrence of the positive behavior.
   a. Consider applying the same type of reinforcement that was identified as maintaining the problem behavior to the positive replacement behavior.
5. Consistently and immediately deliver reinforcement each time the positive behavior occurs.
6. Consistently withhold reinforcement during occurrences of the problem behavior.

Matching is studied in a concurrent schedules of reinforcement paradigm, which refers to an experimental arrangement in which two or more responses are reinforced according to two or more simultaneous, but quantitatively different, schedules of reinforcement (i.e., concurrently).

Matching involves *"choice behavior"* in that behaviors having a higher rate of reinforcement will be "chosen" more frequently than behaviors reinforced at lower rates. For example, if aggressive behavior is reinforced, on average, every 3 times it occurs (variable ratio 3 or VR-3 schedule of reinforcement) and prosocial behavior is reinforced, on average, every 15 times it occurs (VR-15 schedule of reinforcement), the Matching Law would predict that, on average, aggressive behavior will be chosen (i.e., performed) five times more frequently than prosocial behavior based on the ratio between the two concurrent schedules of reinforcement (15/3 = 5). Research in naturalistic settings has consistently shown that behavior observed under concurrent schedules of reinforcement closely follow the Matching Law (Martens, 1992; Martens & Houk, 1989; Martens, Lochner, & Kelly, 1992; J. Snyder & Stoolmiller, 2002).

Maag (2005) suggested that one way to decrease competing problem behaviors is to teach *positive replacement behaviors,* or Replacement Behavior Training (RBT). RBT may help solve many of the problems described in the social skills training literature such as poor generalization and maintenance, modest effect sizes, and social invalidity of target behavior selection (C. R. Cook et al., 2008; Gresham, 1998; Gresham et al., 2004). RBT seeks to identify *functionally equivalent* prosocial behaviors to replace the competing problem behaviors. Two or more behaviors are functionally equivalent if they produce similar amounts of reinforcement from the environment (R. H. Horner & Billingsley, 1988).

Conceptualization of RBT

Why does RBT work, and what explains its utility in teaching positive replacement behaviors? RBT is based on the principle of *differential reinforcement,* which requires the reinforcement of one response class and withholding or reducing the amount of reinforcement for another response class (J. O. Cooper, Heron, & Heward, 2007). For example, using differential reinforcement, a student may be reinforced when he asks for an item in a pleasant voice but ignored when he makes a request in an aggressive tone. Although several forms of differential reinforcement exist, two forms are the most frequently used in RBT: *differential reinforcement of alternative behavior* (DRA) and *differential reinforcement of incompatible behavior* (DRI). Both DRA and DRI have the effects of strengthening the behavior that is the desired alternative to or is incompatible with the problem behavior (e.g., appropriate social skills) and simultaneously weakening problem behavior (e.g., aggression).

There are three basic steps in implementing DRA or DRI to increase prosocial behavior and to decrease competing problem behaviors. First, a prosocial alternative or incompatible behavior must be identified to effectively compete with the problem behavior. This prosocial behavior must meet the following criteria: it already exists in the student's repertoire, requires equal or less effort than the competing problem behavior, occurs at a rate that would allow for it to be reinforced, and is likely to be reinforced after the intervention is withdrawn (J. O. Cooper et al., 2007). The second step in using DRA/DRI is to identify and deliver reinforcers for prosocial behaviors that can be delivered immediately and consistently. J. O. Cooper et al. suggest that the magnitude or quality of the reinforcer for behavior is probably less important than its *consistent* delivery and control. The third step in this process is to systematically and consistently withhold reinforcement for the competing problem behavior. In other words, you would "thin" the schedule of reinforcement for problem behavior, which would make the ratio of reinforcement for prosocial behavior and problem behavior greater, thereby inducing the principle of the Matching Law.

A study by Gresham and colleagues demonstrates using DRA to teach social skills in a school setting (Gresham et al., 2006). Four students were taught social skills over a period of 20 weeks, which involved a combination of SST and DRA interventions in the classroom. The SST procedures were delivered in a small-group pullout setting using four basic instruction variables of coaching, modeling, behavioral rehearsal, and performance feedback (see Elliott & Gresham, 1991). All students were classified as having social skills acquisition deficits before the study. The DRA intervention (RBT) consisted of four steps: (a) identify the reinforcer for the competing problem behavior (social attention); (b) identify the reinforcer for the replacement behavior (social attention); (c) specify the DRA time interval (DRA-5 minutes); and (d) eliminate the reinforcer for the competing behavior, and deliver the reinforcer for the replacement behavior instead.

The Gresham et al. (2006) study indicated that students receiving SST and DRA interventions exhibited relatively large decreases in competing problem behaviors and improvement on a measure of teacher-rated social skills (Gresham & Elliott, 1990). These results suggest that a higher intensity or "dosage" of SST than has been reported in the literature produces larger effects on measures of target behaviors and social validation than lower-intensity SST interventions produce. This "dose effect" would seem to argue for simply providing more SST to achieve positive outcomes. Treatment integrity levels, however, may also moderate these findings. The effect of treatment integrity has not been studied extensively in the SST literature.

Positive Peer Reporting

Positive Peer Reporting (PPR) is a peer-mediated social skills intervention used to improve the quality of social interactions and the social status of socially rejected or neglected children. It has been effectively applied with children ages 4 to 16 in a variety of settings including general and special education classrooms and a residential treatment center (Bowers, Cook, Jensen, Snyder, & McEachern, 2008; Bowers, Woods, Carolyn, & Friman, 2000; Ervin, Johnston, & Friman, 1998; Ervin, Miller, & Friman, 1996; Hoff & Ronk, 2006; Johnson-Gros & Shriver, 2006; K. M. Jones, Young, & Friman, 2000; Moroz & Jones, 2002). In PPR, classmates are informed they will be able to earn rewards for reporting a specific classmate's prosocial behavior during a daily reporting session. Next, they are taught to recognize and report prosocial behavior. Examples and nonexamples are provided as models of appropriate praise statements, which must be positive, specific, and genuine. The classmates are then prompted to generate their own examples, and positive or corrective feedback is provided. Finally, the type of reinforcement (e.g., token/points for a class-wide reward or preferred activities/items for individual reporters) is chosen and delivered for each appropriate praise statement reported during the daily reporting session. Treatment effects are monitored through direct observation of social interactions and by sociometric data, such as peer ratings and nominations, which are used to assess changes in peer acceptance. See Figure 16.3 for a list of steps used in most PPR programs.

The goal of PPR is to enhance reinforcement for the selected child's prosocial behaviors by having peers verbally acknowledge these appropriate behaviors and, thereby, increase the performance of similar behaviors in the future. Rather than targeting specific skills, prosocial behaviors are conceptualized as a functional response class in that any positive social behavior can be reported and reinforced (C. H. Skinner, Neddenriep, Robinson, Ervin, & Jones, 2002). This intervention is designed to remediate performance deficits by increasing reinforcement contingent on behaviors already in the child's repertoire but performed infrequently, rather than teaching specific behaviors (i.e., social skills acquisition deficits).

PPR is thought to produce socially valid outcomes by restructuring classroom social ecologies (K. M. Jones et al., 2000; Moroz & Jones, 2002; C. H. Skinner et al., 2002). Research indicates teachers devote more time and

Figure 16.3 Positive Peer Reporting: treatment integrity checklist.

Pre-intervention

1. Inform students that they will be playing a game in which they can earn rewards for noticing and reporting prosocial or "friendly" behavior.
2. Discuss the meaning of prosocial behavior:
   a. Provide examples and nonexamples.
3. Have students provide examples of prosocial behavior, giving positive or corrective feedback.
4. Explain the rules of the game:
   a. A target student will be selected.
   b. Pay attention to the target student during the course of the day.
   c. During a specific period each day, students can earn points toward a reward for reporting instances in which the target student exhibited prosocial behaviors.
5. Determine rewards:
   a. Consider class-wide rewards.
   b. Set a goal for the total number of positive statements.

Intervention

At the beginning of the school day:

1. Remind the class who the target student is for the day.
2. Remind the class to look for positive behaviors displayed by the target student throughout the day or during a certain class period.

During the reporting session:

1. Ask students to raise their hands if they observed the target student displaying positive behavior.
2. Call on students to make praise statements.
3. Give the class a point/token for each appropriate comment reported.
4. Tell the class how many points/tokens they earned today, and remind them of the final goal.
5. Administer rewards when the goal is obtained.

resources responding to disruptive rather than appropriate behavior and have 60% to 90% more interactions with students who have behavior problems (R. H. Thompson, White, & Morgan, 1982). The pattern of interactions establishes an ecology wherein classmates are more likely to attend to and report inappropriate behaviors, a practice that may encourage excessively negative peer evaluations of the students with behavior problems, leading to their social rejection. It should be recalled from our earlier discussion that peer rejection and social isolation are well-established risk factors for the development of SBD (Crews et al., 2007; H. M. Walker & Severson, 2002).

Therefore, in typical classroom ecologies, the children in greatest need of practice with social skills are provided with the fewest opportunities to do so. PPR addresses these issues by explicitly modifying existing contingencies; the selected student's prosocial behaviors are reinforced, whereas classmates receive reinforcement for reporting the student's positive behavior (C. H. Skinner et al., 2002). In addition, PPR influences the social ecology by encouraging classmates to form more positive perceptions of the selected child, thereby establishing protective factors against SBD and related adverse outcomes.

Next, PPR capitalizes on incidental teaching; peers are more likely to notice prosocial behaviors as they naturally occur. A teacher or parent may not observe the occurrence of the behavior due to numerous environmental demands. Prosocial behaviors exhibited by the socially isolated child are more likely noticed by peers, and PPR provides a way for peers to provide reinforcement during the reporting session. Also, the intervention is operating across all times and settings. As peers notice and report incidental prosocial behaviors that occur in novel settings, these behaviors are "trapped" and are more likely to occur in the future (Stokes & Baer, 1977). Moreover, because peer-mediated reinforcement can serve as a type of natural reinforcement contingency (Kohler & Greenwood, 1986), treatment effects are more likely to generalize across settings (Stokes & Osnes, 1989).

Although generalization has been documented (Bowers et al., 2008: Libster, 2008; J. Q. Morrison & Jones, 2007), researchers have mixed findings for the maintenance, or durability, of treatment gains over time (Bowers et al., 2008, Moroz & Jones, 2002). Bowers and colleagues (2008) assessed maintenance 15, 30, and 45 days after PPR was withdrawn and found that some participants showed maintenance throughout this entire duration, whereas others' gains appeared to deteriorate. Maintenance may need to be actively programmed. In fact, Bowers and colleagues (2008) suggest implementing PPR for a longer duration and/or providing periodic booster sessions, which may enhance the durability of treatment effects.

Literature Review

Grieger, Kauffman, and Grieger (1976) were the first to use peer reporting procedures as a class-wide intervention to improve the social behavior of kindergarteners. Ervin and colleagues (1996) further refined PPR as a dependent contingency to improve the social interactions and peer acceptance of a socially rejected girl in a middle school classroom. Studies conducted at the Nebraska Girls and Boys Town program further established the efficacy of PPR procedures across educational and residential treatment center settings (Bowers, McGinnis, Friman, & Ervin, 1999; Bowers et al., 2008; Ervin et al., 1998; K. M. Jones et al., 2000).

Other investigators have successfully applied PPR in a variety of settings and with other populations. Hoff and Ronk (2006) used PPR to improve the quality of social interactions in a special education classroom for children with cognitive delays. Johnson-Gros and Shriver (2006) used a combination of PPR and compliance-training procedures to achieve similar effects in a preschool classroom. Finally, Moroz and Jones (2002) demonstrated the efficacy of PPR in elementary school general education classrooms.

Although a complete narrative review of studies is beyond the scope of this chapter (see Johnson-Gros & Shriver, 2006, and Hoff & Ronk, 2006, for reviews), we will highlight Ervin and colleagues (1996), who targeted the social behavior and peer acceptance of Allison, a socially rejected girl in a middle school classroom. At the end of math class, classmates could earn points (exchanged for privileges) for reporting specific instances in which Allison engaged in prosocial behaviors. Allison's peer interactions during an interactive part of class were directly observed and coded as positive, negative, or neutral. At baseline, Allison engaged in high levels of negative interactions and low levels of positive interactions. When the intervention was introduced, negative interactions immediately ceased to near zero, and a corresponding increase in positive interactions was noted. Behavior returned to near baseline levels on treatment removal, and attained previous levels when treatment was reinstated.

Moreover, Ervin et al. (1996) found the intervention produced changes in Allison's social acceptance. Classmates were asked to rate how much they enjoyed working and playing with Allison, and, following the use of PPR, a slight gain in Allison's peer ratings occurred. This finding has been replicated across many, but not all, participants in subsequent PPR studies (Bowers et al., 2000; K. M. Jones et al., 2000). Although improvements in social acceptance are uniformly small, few interventions produce immediate improvements in social acceptance (Bowers et al., 1999; Coie & Dodge, 1983; DuPaul & Eckert, 1994). However, it is important to note that even small changes may indicate practically important treatment effects (Gresham & Lopez, 1996; Hawkins, 1991).

Class-Wide Applications

PPR can be conceptualized as a selected intervention in which a few students are specifically targeted; however, PPR has also been successfully applied as a primary or universal class-wide intervention (Hoff & Ronk, 2006; J. Q. Morrison & Jones, 2007). In the class-wide variation, there is no selected student; rather, students may report the positive behaviors of any classmate. J. Q. Morrison and Jones (2007) found class-wide PPR was effective in reducing disruptive events in the classroom, as well as in untrained settings (e.g., lunchroom, during transitions). In addition, fewer students were identified as socially isolated after the intervention, evidencing the beneficial effects of PPR on peer acceptance.

Current research suggests that PPR may be effective for children with a range of social difficulties. However, as with any intervention, PPR will not be universally effective or maintainable for some children (Bowers et al., 2008; Libster, 2008; Moroz & Jones, 2002). Differential treatment effects may be due to externalizing or internalizing competing problem behaviors and may require more individualized interventions, such as RBT. Another reason that some students may not benefit or maintain benefits may be the differences in the social ecologies in which children function. Some children may be surrounded by peers who initiate interactions even if the child does not; other children may initiate positive interactions independently. Although hypotheses have been proposed, determining moderators of the effectiveness of PPR will require future systematic research (Bowers et al., 2008; Libster, 2008; Moroz & Jones, 2002).

Conclusions

This chapter discussed the role of social competence in designing and implementing interventions for students with or at risk for severe behavioral difficulties. A conceptualization of social competence was provided in which the concepts of social skills, social tasks, and social competence were delineated. In this view, social skills were seen as specific behaviors, which, when successfully performed, allow for individuals to successfully accomplish specific social tasks. Social tasks were conceptualized as a *response class,* which includes a group of social behaviors (responses) having different topographies that produce the same effect on the environment (J. O. Cooper et al., 2007). Social competence was seen as *judgments* by significant social agents (e.g., peers, teachers, parents) that these social tasks were successfully accomplished.

An important distinction was made between social skills acquisition deficits versus social skills performance deficits. Acquisition deficits indicate that the individual

does not have a particular social skill. These acquisition deficits might arise from deficits in social-cognitive abilities, difficulties in integrating social behavior patterns in a fluent manner, or deficits in appropriate discrimination of social situations. Acquisition deficits therefore require direct instruction of social behavior using evidence-based strategies of modeling, coaching, behavioral rehearsal, and performance feedback (Gresham & Elliott, 2008).

This chapter reviewed six meta-analyses of the SST literature that involved 338 studies and over 25,000 children and youth ages 3 to 18 years. These meta-analyses assumed that students receiving SST have primarily acquisition rather than performance deficits (Gresham et al., 2004). Five of the six meta-analyses showed an average effect size of $d = 0.60$, which indicates that 65% of students who receive SST improve compared to 35% of students who do not receive such training. An effect size of this magnitude is considered to be medium and indicates that most children receiving SST will benefit from this intervention.

The other type of social skills deficit can be classified as performance deficits in which the student fails to perform a particular social skill at acceptable levels even though the student knows how to perform the social skill. Such deficits can be viewed as "won't do" problems and can be best conceptualized as motivational or performance deficits rather than learning or acquisition deficits. PPR is an intervention that is well-suited for the remediation of social skills performance deficits because it assumes that the student knows how to and does perform a specific social skill. PPR is based on the notion that a student's peers notice and report on the student's successful performance of social skills. PPR is based on the principle of social attention as a reinforcer for successful social skills performances. It also takes advantage of the principle of incidental teaching, which allows for the immediate reinforcement of prosocial behavior patterns.

RBT is based on differential reinforcement (DRA or DRI) and incorporates another response class (competing problem behavior) into the social skills intervention process. We used Herrnstein's notion of the Matching Law to explain how and why RBT reduces competing problem behaviors and increases socially skilled behaviors. RBT requires an FBA to determine the function of the competing problem behavior and to identify a socially skilled alternative or incompatible behavior that will serve the same function.

PART 3

Research-Based Approaches for Assessment

CHAPTER 17

Response to Intervention: *School-Wide Prevention of Academic Difficulties*

Matthew K. Burns and **Sarah Scholin** | *University of Minnesota*

*A*ssessment in special education has fundamentally changed since the inception of the Individuals with Disabilities Education Act (IDEA, originally titled the Education for All Handicapped Children Act) in 1975. Diagnostic assessments dominated the early days of special education under IDEA; educators used the data to identify the extremely high- and low-performing students in order to rank them and to identify disabilities (Reschly, 1996). Assessment in Pre-K–12 schools has evolved, however, from establishing a rank order to raising the foundational skills of all students (Stiggins, 2005), and special education has followed suit. Beginning with the seminal work of Deno (1985), assessment within special education became more instructionally relevant and focused on what to teach in addition to identifying students who need to be taught through special education.

The change in Pre-K–12 assessments from assessment *of* learning to assessment *for* learning (Stiggins, 2005) has resulted in a focus on preventing learning difficulties. Prevention science is the process of identifying potential risk and protective factors in order to eliminate or mitigate major human dysfunction (Coie et al., 1993). Prevention efforts have consistently demonstrated effectiveness in many fields (Botvin, 2004; Hage et al., 2007; Stith et al., 2006), but researchers are only beginning

to apply the principles to special education. Academic disabilities are major human dysfunctions that are relevant to special education and could be potential targets of prevention efforts.

School-wide prevention can reduce the number of students identified with disabilities (M. K. Burns, Appleton, & Stehouwer, 2005; VanDerHeyden, Witt, & Gilbertson, 2007) through (a) early identification of difficulties with universal screening and (b) providing interventions through tiers of increasing intensity, both of which are consistent with the principles of prevention science (VanDerHeyden & Burns, 2010). However, prevention science also requires coordinated action (Coie et al., 1993), which suggests that efforts must be school-wide in order to be successful and incorporate general, special, and remedial education.

School-wide prevention of academic difficulties is best accomplished with a Response to Intervention (RtI) model in which assessment data are systemically used to make resource allocation decisions to improve student learning (M. K. Burns & VanDerHeyden, 2006). In addition to the focus on student learning, RtI can also be applied to the identification of students who have educational disabilities and need special education. The 2004 amendments to IDEA stated that local educational agencies "shall not be required to take into consideration whether a child has a severe discrepancy between achievement and intellectual ability" (Pub. L. No. 108-446 § 614 [b][6][A]) when diagnosing a specific learning disability. Instead, schools "may use a process that determines if the child responds to scientific, research-based intervention as a part of the evaluation procedures" (Pub. L. No. 108-446 § 614 [b][6][A]; § 614 [b][2 & 3]), which is commonly referred to as *RtI*. The provision for allowing RtI data to be used to make special education identification decisions bridges the two fundamental purposes for assessment in special education by allowing data that are used to improve instruction to also be used to identify students who need special education.

Most school-wide prevention models (e.g., RtI, school-wide positive behavior supports) are essentially extensions of the same construct (Sandomierski, Kincaid, & Algozzine, 2007), which is data-based problem solving as initially described by Deno and Mirkin (1977). As students progress through the three tiers of intervention commonly associated with RtI, practitioners collect data more frequently (e.g., three times per year for Tier 1, but at least weekly for Tier 3) and more precisely (e.g., general indicators of reading skills for Tier 1, measures of specific skills in Tiers 2 and 3) in order to conduct more in-depth problem analyses (M. K. Burns & Gibbons, 2008). Following are descriptions of the three tiers of interventions frequently used within RtI, the assessment techniques frequently used at each level, and how the resulting data address specific problem-analysis questions.

Tier 1

The first tier of any school-wide prevention model is quality classroom instruction. It is beyond the scope of this chapter to provide a detailed discussion of quality instructional practices. However, core instruction within an RtI framework should address the recommendations from national research councils for reading (Snow, Burns, & Griffin, 1998) and math (Kilpatrick, Swafford, & Finell, 2001).

In addition to quality core instruction, periodic (e.g., three times per year) screening of all students for academic deficits is also a fundamental aspect of services provided within Tier 1. Measurement in an RtI system relies heavily on curriculum-based measurements of reading (CBM-R) and math (CBM-M) because they result in data that are psychometrically adequate (i.e., reliable and lead to valid decisions) and sensitive to student progress or growth (Gresham, 2002b). (For additional information, see Chapter 18 of this volume, where Lembke, Hampton, and Hendricker provide a detailed description of CBM.) Although CBM data are psychometrically sound, other types of data can inform Tier-1 decisions because the primary function of assessment in Tier 1 is to identify individuals or groups of students who need additional support, as opposed to monitoring student progress over time. Thus, some schools conduct universal academic screenings with highly reliable but less sensitive measures such as the Measures of Academic Progress (Northwest Evaluation Association, 2003) and Star Math (Renaissance Learning, 1998).

Tier 2

Meta-analytic research found that an average of 20% of students were not successful despite quality core curriculum and instruction in Tier 1 (M. K. Burns et al., 2005) and required more intensive intervention. The hallmark of Tier-2 interventions is that they are delivered in small homogeneous groups and are often delivered with a standard protocol (i.e., using the same carefully scripted intervention for groups of students with similar needs). Academically, that might involve grouping approximately five students at the elementary level who all require additional assistance in decoding, for example, and delivering a 30-minute phonics-based intervention to the group four or five times each week.

Measurement in Tier 2 must determine whether a student's problem (i.e., low performance) persists but must also indicate specific skills and deficits and must be appropriate for weekly progress monitoring. For example, in Tier 1, school personnel are focused on determining how well the child or classroom reads generally, in order to determine general risk. But in Tier 2, once general risk has been established, educators must determine the specific skill deficits that underlie reading problems in order to improve reading performance (e.g., phonemic awareness, decoding). Moreover, data are collected with Tier-2 interventions once each week or no less than once every other week. These more-frequently collected data are used to monitor progress and to judge the effectiveness of the intervention(s) being implemented.

School-wide prevention efforts for academic difficulties again rely heavily on CBM for Tier-2 decisions because the data can be collected frequently and can monitor student progress. However, data are also needed to identify specific strengths and skills deficits, and CBM does not have strong utility for that purpose (M. K. Burns, Dean, & Klar, 2004; L. S. Fuchs, Fuchs, Hosp, & Hamlett, 2003). Decisions made regarding interventions within Tiers 2 and 3 often depend on subskill mastery measurement (M. K. Burns & Coolong-Chaffin, 2006) to assess skills in a specific domain. Thus, problem-analysis decisions and instructional planning for Tier-2 interventions may rely on data that explicitly assess skills in different domains such as Star Early Literacy (SEL; Renaissance Learning, 2003) or curriculum-based assessment of instructional design (CBA-ID; Gravois & Gickling, 2008). The former is used to assess individual students' skills in the five areas identified by the National Reading Panel (NRP, 2000b) as important aspects of reading instruction (i.e., phonemic awareness, phonics, fluency, vocabulary, and comprehension). The latter assesses the accuracy with which various skills are completed in order to determine skills and instructional material that represent appropriate intervention targets. Both SEL and CBA-ID have been shown to produce data with adequate psychometric properties for instructional decision making (M. K. Burns, Tucker, Frame, Foley, & Hauser, 2000; Ysseldyke & McLeod, 2007).

Tier-2 math interventions represent a special situation from an assessment perspective because assessments of general math skills do not inform how well a student can perform a specific skill and because measures of specific skill performance do not indicate overall math proficiency (Hintze, Christ, & Keller, 2002). Thus, a comprehensive assessment system for math at Tier 2 should include evaluations of specific skills (e.g., single-digit by single-digit multiplication, subtraction with regrouping).

Tier 3

On average, 5% of the student population will require intervention intensity greater than that provided in Tier-1 and Tier-2 interventions (M. K. Burns et al., 2005). For those students, interventions are highly targeted, derived based on individual student need, and often delivered in one-on-one or two-to-one formats. School problem-solving teams develop the interventions through in-depth problem analyses. Problem-solving teams rely on functional assessments of academic problems such as the five hypotheses for student failure outlined in Table 17.1 (Daly, Witt, Martens, & Dool, 1997); curriculum-based evaluation (Howell & Nolet, 2000); or the Review, Interview, Observe, Test–Instruction, Curriculum, Environment, and Learner (RIOT-ICEL) matrix (J. L. Hosp, 2008).

Following the progression of increased precision and frequency, teachers (or other trained education personnel, e.g., reading specialists, math tutors, paraprofessionals) collect data in Tier 3 at least once each week, and usually twice weekly, to monitor progress. Progress-monitoring data collected in Tiers 2 and 3 are often produced by general outcome measures (e.g., oral reading fluency, digits correct per minute on a multiskill math probe), but teachers should also monitor progress in the specific skill being taught (e.g., nonsense-word fluency for a phonics intervention, single-digit multiplication probes). However, even more precise data are used to determine the appropriate intervention, and these data often take into account factors such as the accuracy with which a skill is completed and malleable environmental factors that could contribute to the problem such as instruction, curriculum, and learning environment. Sources from which this information can be gleaned include file reviews; interviews of teachers, parents, and students; observations of student performance; and formal and informal assessments/testing. The RIOT-ICEL problem-analysis matrix (J. L. Hosp, 2008) can be used to collect, organize, and analyze this information. Functionally relevant data for academic problems can be generated by examining the five hypotheses for student failure and tested in a brief experimental analysis, which has resulted in improved student outcomes in reading (M. K. Burns & Wagner, 2008), math (Carson & Eckert, 2003), and spelling (McComas et al., 1996).

Table 17.1 Five Hypotheses for Student Failure and Relevant Assessment

Hypothesis	Data to Evaluate
The student does not want to do the task.	Collect highly sensitive and specific data (e.g., oral reading fluency of a specific passage or single-skill math measure such as double-digit addition of two numbers) with and without providing an incentive to examine differences in performance.
The student needs more practice.	Collect highly sensitive and specific data before and after implementing an intervention that provide practice without teaching (e.g., repeated reading).
The student needs more instruction.	Collect highly sensitive and specific data before and after providing direct instruction in the skill in a one-on-one tutoring setting.
The student has never had to do the task that way before.	Collect highly sensitive and specific data with a typical task and by completing the task in a different manner (e.g., a different setting, orally versus in writing, and with and without manipulative or visual cues).
The task is too difficult.	Collect highly sensitive and specific data from a typical task and from one that represents an instructional level for that student.

Source: Information from Daly, E. J., III, Witt, J. C., Martens, B. K., & Dool, E. J. (1997). A model for conducting a functional analysis of academic performance problems. *School Psychology Review, 26,* 554–574.

Critical Elements of Response-to-Intervention Efforts

RtI may differ in various states, districts, and schools because each system is unique and because the school-wide prevention effort should address the unique needs of the school in which it is implemented. However, RtI is premised on basic core tenets including data-based decision making through universal screening and progress monitoring, problem analysis, efficient resource allocation, tiered interventions, collaboration across disciplines, and treatments based on student need rather than labels or other arbitrarily determined characteristics to enhance outcomes for all students. Next we describe some of the features and elements of successful school-wide prevention models.

Grade-Level Teams

Many practitioners mistakenly assume that a problem-solving team should drive school-wide prevention efforts, but this approach is highly ineffective. Research has consistently found that on average 20% of students need more support than what is provided in typical core instruction (M. K. Burns et al., 2005). Very few schools have the resources necessary to implement effective problem analyses and individualized interventions for 20% of their students. Thus, problem-solving teams are reserved for Tier-3 interventions, which address approximately 5% of the student population.

Grade-level teams, rather than problem-solving teams, should drive the school-wide prevention process at the elementary level, and multidisciplinary professional learning communities (PLCs) often do so at the high school level. Grade-level teams comprise the teachers who teach each grade level, or some other combination of teachers. For example, a school with a small number of teachers at a given grade level could combine teachers to create three grade-level teams (K–1, 2–3, and 4–5). High school models that are driven by a PLC comprise teachers who teach a common group of students and should include English and language arts teachers, as well as appropriate content area teachers. For example, a PLC at a high school could include two Grade-9 English teachers, two Grade-9 Social Studies teachers, one Grade-9 Science teacher, and one Grade-9 Math teacher. We also recommend that the special education teacher, or at least one representative who works with students with disabilities in that given grade, also serve on the grade-level team or PLC.

In middle schools, the instructional system can vary dramatically from school to school. Some middle schools operate with "houses" in which students are assigned to a group of teachers who instruct them in all core areas. The PLC in this scenario would be the teachers assigned to each house. Alternatively, some middle schools function very much like a high school, and the PLC model would mirror the one we described for high schools.

Although the format of the grade-level team and PLC could vary based on the individual school, the process in which they engage remains constant. The primary task of these groups, from a school-wide prevention perspective, is to examine student data and make intervention decisions. There are two kinds of team meetings, one to examine universal screening data that meets three times each year (or how ever often universal screenings are conducted) and one to examine student progress that occurs at least once each month. During the progress-monitoring meeting, the team members examine the growth for each student getting a Tier-2 or Tier-3 intervention to determine whether the intervention is working. Research has not yet developed well-established criteria for comparing student growth data. However, research does support the validity of decisions made with a dual discrepancy (L. S. Fuchs, 2003) in which interventions are deemed as ineffective when a student's (a) postintervention level remains below the grade-level benchmark standard and (b) rate of growth falls at least 1 standard deviation below the average grade-level growth (M. K. Burns & Senesac, 2005).

During the triannual meeting to discuss universal screening data, the grade-level team or PLC examines universal screening data for every student in the building. In doing so, the team attempts to answer the following questions: (a) Is there a class-wide problem? (b) Who needs a Tier-2 intervention? (c) Did we miss anyone? Class-wide problems, discussed further in a later section, are the first agenda item in a benchmark assessment team meeting. After determining that no class-wide problems exist, or that they were successfully remediated, the next step is to determine which students need a Tier-2 intervention. Generally speaking, this is accomplished with straight resource allocation. In other words, approximately 20% of students at a given grade level who are most in need of additional support are designated to receive a Tier-2 intervention. For academics, that simply means students at or below the lowest 20th percentile rank for each grade level on the given measure (e.g., the lowest 20 CBM-R scores of 100 third graders).

Although CBM measures represent psychometrically adequate measures of student academic performance, and the lowest 20% is a reasonable cutoff point to indicate problematic performance, this approach is not a foolproof method, and it may fail to identify all students who need support beyond that provided in Tier 1. Accordingly, after determining who needs a Tier-2 intervention, teams should examine students whose data closely approximate the cutoff criterion (i.e., the CBM-R score that represents the 20th percentile rank) and evaluate other sources of data such as classroom performance to be sure that all students who need Tier-2 intervention supports receive them.

Data Management Team

Ideally, teachers who make up the grade-level teams and PLCs would be well versed in how to analyze and interpret assessment data, but this may not be the case in many K–12 schools. We therefore recommend forming a data management team to assist grade-level teams and professional learning communities in consuming the data. The data management team usually comprises two to three members, often including the school psychologist and one or two of the following: general education classroom teacher, Title 1 teacher, reading specialist, behavioral specialist, or special education teacher. The essential attributes of data management team members are that they know how to analyze and interpret data and have a strong understanding of assessment and data-based decision making. Each elementary school usually has one data management team, but more could be created for large schools. High and middle schools often have one data management team for each grade, depending on the size of the school.

As the name implies, the data management teams help facilitate teachers' and teams' use of data. They ensure that data are given to the teachers by a given time of year soon after the benchmark data are collected (e.g., September 30th, January 30th, and May 30th). The data management team presents assessment results arranged so that each teacher has data for each individual student in his classroom and the representative data for the class and grade level. For example, median CBM-R or CBM-M scores would be reported for each classroom within a grade, as would the grade-level average. Median scores are used with smaller data sets of less than 30 pieces of data to prevent undue influence by outlying data.

Identifying Class-Wide Problems

Our experience with schools has shown that teachers are generally excited to provide interventions for struggling learners, and administrators are eager to start systemic interventions to address the needs of groups of students. However, both groups tend to be less enthusiastic about examining their own practice, though without such evaluation the likelihood of interventions being effective diminishes. Many schools have such a large number of struggling students that they cannot possibly implement more intensive Tier-2 interventions for all of them, for two reasons. First, most schools do not have the resources to implement a Tier-2 or -3 intervention with more than 20% to 25% of the students. Second, and perhaps more important, if more than 25% of the students require a Tier-2 intervention, it is a sign that students' needs are not being met adequately by the core instruction at Tier 1, which makes it unlikely that interventions at higher tiers will be effective. For example, in order for students to learn how to read, they need a solid core curriculum that balances instruction in letter sounds, free-choice reading, writing, and word study (NRP, 2000b; Snow et al., 1998). Typically, effective Tier-2 and -3 interventions represent highly targeted instruction in one of these core areas (M. K. Burns, VanDerHeyden, & Boice, 2008). Thus, a student might receive intensive instruction in letter sounds as a Tier-2 intervention, which might increase ability to sound out words, but without the other aspects of effective reading instruction occurring within the core curriculum, the student will not learn how to read.

The first step in a school-wide prevention model in schools with more than 20% to 25% of students who fall below established benchmarks on universal screeners is to identify class-wide problems, which can then be directly remediated before individual interventions begin (VanDerHeyden & Burns, 2005; VanDerHeyden, Witt, & Naquin, 2003). Class-wide problems are identified for academic domains by comparing the class median on a given measure such as CBM-R to the 25th percentile rank on a national norm (e.g., Hasbrouck & Tindal, 2005). We use the 25th percentile rank because, statistically speaking, the 25th percentile represents the lowest end of the average range for any distribution. Currently no national norms are widely available for math, so we recommend comparing CBM-M data to the instructional level range of 14 to 31 digits correct per minute through third grade, and 24 to 49 digits correct per minute for grades 4 and 5 (M. K. Burns, VanDerHeyden, & Jiban, 2006). Class medians that fall below the instructional level range (i.e., below 14 through third grade and below 24 for fourth and fifth grades) suggest that a class-wide problem exists in math. However, little guidance exists for classrooms above the fifth grade.

The core instruction within each classroom is carefully evaluated when a class-wide problem is identified. First, standards for reading (NRP, 2000b; Snow et al., 1998) and math (Kilpatrick et al., 2001) instruction are used to evaluate the instruction within the classroom. Grade-level teams and professional learning communities discuss the instructional practices to ensure quality instruction is occurring. Next, a class-wide intervention may be implemented to improve student performance. For example, Peer-Assisted Learning Strategies (PALS; D. Fuchs, Fuchs, Mathes, & Simmons, 1997) is a commonly used class-wide intervention for academic difficulties that has a strong research base (D. Fuchs & Fuchs, 2005; McMaster, Fuchs, Fuchs, & Compton, 2005) and has been shown to be an effective intervention for class-wide problems (McMaster & Wagner, 2007; VanDerHeyden & Burns, 2005).

Implementation Integrity

A strong school-wide prevention model is dependent on quality instruction and research-based interventions. However, the strongest interventions available will not result in improved student performance if they are not correctly implemented. Thus, implementation integrity (i.e., implementing plans and interventions as designed) is another aspect of an effective school-wide model that is not considered frequently enough. Indeed, some have identified implementation integrity as the largest obstacle to overcome in school-wide prevention efforts (Noell & Gansle, 2006; Ysseldyke, 2005). Thus, effective school-wide prevention efforts assess the implementation integrity of the grade-level team's and PLC's data-based decision-making process, the problem-solving team process, and the actual interventions used.

Implementation integrity can be assessed in one of two ways. First, checklists for interventions, and grade-level team or PLC or problem-solving team processes, can be created and the implementation observed to provide feedback (M. K. Burns, Wiley, & Viglietta, 2008). Unfortunately, this option may be perceived as threatening by classroom teachers and team members and may be too resource-intensive to be practical. Thus, school personnel could develop a shorter checklist that focuses only on the most critical aspect of an intervention in order to allow for a shorter observation while still providing useful information (Noell & Gansle, 2006); but the observations may not sufficiently represent the entire intervention or team process. Gansle and Noell (2007) recommend using permanent products as well. Most interventions involve creating some product (e.g., flash cards, answer sheets) that can be used to assess whether the intervention occurred. Permanent products with which team processes could be examined include completed summaries of meetings, meeting agendas, or the created list of students within the lowest 20th percentile. A combination of directly observing the critical components of a treatment plan and examining permanent products is likely the most efficient yet valid approach to assess implementation integrity (Gansle & Noell, 2007).

Supplemental (Tier-2) Interventions

Interventions provided at Tier 3 are important to a successful RtI model, but schools often tend to focus on

Tier 3 without first establishing a well-developed Tier 2. Without a well-implemented and effective Tier 2, interventions implemented at Tier 3 have little chance of success because of a lack of resources. Fortunately, research has consistently demonstrated the effectiveness of implementing supplemental interventions. For example, Blachman, Tangel, Bail, Black, and McGraw (1999) implemented supplemental instruction in the alphabetic code with 66 first-grade students and found that these students outperformed the control group in measures of phonological awareness, letter-name and letter-sound knowledge, and multiple measures of word recognition, and further that those differences remained at the end of second grade. Moreover, O'Shaughnessy and Swanson (2000) delivered small-group decoding and word analogy training to high school students during 30-minute sessions three times each week for 6 weeks, which resulted in significantly higher phonological awareness, phonological memory, and word-attack skill in comparison to a control group.

M. K. Burns and colleagues (2006) reviewed research regarding Tier-2 interventions and made recommendations based on that review. Research data from several studies found that Tier-2 interventions should be implemented in small groups of approximately five students but should be as large as possible while maintaining effectiveness. This might mean that the Tier-2 groups among young students (i.e., kindergarten) need to be considerably smaller (e.g., 2 or perhaps 3 students), whereas groups could be larger (e.g., 10 students) among middle school and high school students. More important than the size of the group is how they are grouped. Students in each Tier-2 group should have similar deficits so that interventions can be highly targeted. Moreover, the groups should be led by someone qualified to deliver the intervention, which might be a specialist, a classroom teacher, or a paraprofessional with close supervision by a certified teacher or behavior specialist.

It is important to note that Tier-2 interventions are designed to support core instruction, not to supplant it. Thus, all students participating in a Tier-2 intervention should also participate fully in core instruction. For example, if a student receives a Tier-2 intervention for reading 30 minutes each day, then she would also participate in the 90 to 120 minutes of core reading instruction. Keeping in mind that Tier-2 interventions are always in addition to, and never instead of, core instruction, such interventions usually consist of approximately 30 minutes of intervention 3 to 5 times each week, which may again be modified based on individual school requirements or student needs.

No robust, research-based recommendations exist for the length of an academic intervention at Tier 2, but a measurement perspective sheds some light on the subject. Christ (2006) demonstrated that when using slope of growth to determine intervention effectiveness, slopes were not sufficiently reliable until approximately 8 weeks of data were collected, and that was assuming that two data points were collected each week in an acceptably standardized manner. Thus, it seems that 8 weeks' duration is an acceptable target for Tier-2 interventions. Certainly, a grade-level team or PLC could determine that an intervention is effective in somewhat less time than 8 weeks, or they may decide to change the intervention within Tier 2 in less time, but a move to a more intensive intervention (i.e., Tier 3) should not happen until at least 8 weeks of data are collected.

As we have discussed, implementation integrity is critically important for a school-wide prevention model. VanDerHeyden and Burns (2010) provided a checklist, based on the review of research by M. K. Burns et al. (2006), with which the implementation of Tier-2 interventions in an RtI model can be evaluated. We provide a similar list in Table 17.2. Practitioners can observe Tier-2 interventions with this checklist and present the resulting data to grade-level teams, PLCs, and school-wide leadership teams as evidence of the degree to which interventions are implemented with fidelity.

Continuum of Intervention Intensity

Although many people use time as an indicator of intensity, other factors must be considered. Interventions implemented in Tier 2 should be more intense than those in Tier 1, and Tier 3 interventions should be more intense than Tier 2. Intervention intensity is best conceptualized as the interaction of dose and intervention duration, with *dose* defined as the number of "properly administered teaching episodes during a single intervention session" (Warren, Fey, & Yoder, 2007, p. 71). Thus, *intensity* can be equated with the dosage (number of times a skill is directly taught) delivered over time, and Tier-2 interventions would consist of more teaching episodes of a highly specific skill than during Tier 1. Moreover, as intervention intensity increases, so should assessment frequency and precision.

Validity

Because RtI can be used as part of the special education identification process for a specific learning disability, the resulting data should demonstrate adequate psychometric properties. Research has consistently demonstrated that data obtained from CBM are reliable and result in valid decisions (Wayman, Wallace, Wiley, Ticha, & Espin, 2007), and other commonly used tools to measure academic progress within RtI also demonstrate sufficient psychometric properties (see the Web site for the National Center on Response to Intervention http://www.rti4success.org/ for a review of specific tools). However, decisions made at various critical points in the RtI process should also be considered when evaluating the technical adequacy of the data from school-wide prevention (Barnett et al., 2006).

Barnett et al. (2006) point out that validity for decisions made within a school-wide prevention model should be evaluated with concepts outlined by Messick (1988, 1995). For example, Barnett et al. state that validity data should be collected at each decision point to

Table 17.2   Characteristics of an Effective Tier-2 Response to Intervention System

Item	Observed	Not Observed
Intervention is implemented by a qualified professional with appropriate supervision as needed.		
The group size is appropriate (e.g., approximately 5 in elementary school, and 8–10 in middle and high school).		
The intervention is implemented 3–5 times each week.		
The intervention is implemented for approximately 15–30 minutes each time.		
The intervention is implemented in addition to core instruction (i.e., does not occur during core instructional time).		
The intervention is targeted but is consistent with core curriculum and instruction.		
The intervention is designed to last at least 8 weeks.		
The intervention is research based.		
Individual student progress is monitored with a reliable source of data.		

Source: Information from Burns, M. K., VanDerHeyden, A. M., & Jiban, C. (2006). Assessing the instructional level for mathematics: A comparison of methods. *School Psychology Review, 35,* 401–418.

evaluate the inferences made from the data. Specifically, particular points within each tier should be examined, which are outlined in Table 17.3. School-wide leadership teams should examine these questions and not just rely on using well-constructed measurement tools. No guidelines have been developed regarding criteria to which data obtained to answer the questions in Table 17.3 should be compared. Needless to say, however, the more times the questions can be answered positively, the more confidence leadership teams can have in their process.

Some previous research can inform the validity conversation regarding school-wide prevention. For example, using a dual discrepancy to determine if a Tier-2 intervention is effective leads to consistent judgments of intervention effectiveness (M. K. Burns, Scholin, Kosciolek, & Livingston, 2010), converges with data from standardized measures of reading (M. K. Burns & Senesac, 2005; McMaster et al., 2005; Speece & Case, 2001), and reduces ethnic and gender bias in

the decision-making process (M. K. Burns & Senesac, 2005). These data support the validity of school-wide prevention services, but the validity of RtI processes can be established fully only by examining their effect on student outcomes (Messick, 1988, 1995).

Effectiveness of School-Wide Prevention of Academic Difficulties

A 2009 survey found that 71% of the respondents indicated that their districts were either starting an RtI initiative or had one in place (Spectrum K12 School Solutions, 2009). Despite this impressive level of implementation, effectiveness research is somewhat limited. Ellis (2005) proposed that in order to evaluate the effectiveness of an innovation, research is needed regarding the effectiveness of implementation not only in a well-controlled

Table 17.3   Questions to Address to Examine the Validity of Decisions Made in a School-Wide Response to Intervention Model

Tier	Questions
Tier 1	• Do core curricula match current scientific standards?
	• Are core curricula being implemented with fidelity?
	• Are instructional methods consistent with current best practices?
	• Are universal screening data reliable?
	• Do universal screening data accurately predict meaningful outcomes?
	• Are grade-level teams and PLCs examining universal screening data to identify class-wide problems and to determine who needs a Tier-2 intervention?
	• Do data support the decision-making rule for identifying who needs a Tier-2 intervention?
Tier 2	• Are Tier-2 interventions being implemented with fidelity?
	• Is student progress being monitored with reliable data?
	• Are Tier-2 interventions directly linked to core curriculum and objectives?
	• Do data support the decision rules for increasing/decreasing intensity?
	• Are the goals and outcomes socially valid (seen as important by teachers and parents)?
Tier 3	• Are interventions in Tier 3 more intense and individualized than in Tier 2?
	• Are problem-solving processes being implemented with fidelity?
	• Are intervention targets selected in a reliable manner?
	• Do data support the decision rules for increasing/decreasing intensity?
	• Are the goals, methods, and outcomes socially valid?
	• Do grade-level teams and PLCs examine both level and trend of progress for students?
	• Do teams document that special services are necessary for further progress due to the degree to which interventions differ from typical routines in terms of resources, time, involvement of professionals beyond the child's teacher, and other factors?

Source: Information from Barnett, D., Elliot, N., Graden, J., Ihlo, T., Macmann, G., Natntais, M., & Prasse, D. (2006). Technical adequacy for response to intervention practices. *Assessment for Effective Intervention, 32,* 20–31.
Note: PLCs = professional learning communities.

setting but also on a wide-scale basis. Innovations that are implemented on a large scale, but that lack well-researched effectiveness, may quickly become educational fads that fail to effect meaningful change.

Considerable research has addressed the effectiveness of school-wide prevention models implemented in applied settings, but essentially none has examined such models in well-controlled settings (VanDerHeyden & Burns, 2010). M. K. Burns and colleagues (2005) conducted a meta-analysis of 20 studies that examined the effectiveness of RtI. Some of the studies included in the meta-analysis were evaluations of large-scale implementation (e.g., Ikeda & Gustafson, 2002; McNamara & Hollinger, 2003), and some studied supplemental intervention in a more-controlled trial (e.g., McMaster et al., 2005; Speece & Case, 2001; Torgesen et al., 2001). Large median effect sizes were noted for both large-scale and controlled studies ($d = 1.02$ and 0.86, respectively). A total of 11 studies examined student outcomes (e.g., increased reading scores) and resulted in a median effect size of $d = 0.72$, and 13 studied systemic outcomes (e.g., reductions in students referred to and/or placed into special education) and resulted in a median effect size of $d = 1.28$.

Although most comprehensive evaluations of RtI models use a program evaluation design rather than research designs with strong internal validity, one study examined the effectiveness of an RtI model with a multiple-baseline design. VanDerHeyden and colleagues (2007) implemented an RtI model in five elementary schools across 4 years and saw an immediate reduction in numbers of students referred for evaluation for special education eligibility, as well as those initially placed in special education, after starting RtI. Moreover, approximately 55% of the students referred for a special education eligibility evaluation during the baseline phase were identified with a specific learning disability. However, the proportion of students referred for special education evaluation who were actually identified with a disability increased from 88% to 89% after RtI was modified, indicating a more effective identification model. These data suggested strong systemic effects, but academic outcomes were only anecdotally included.

In addition to research addressing large-scale implementation and supplemental services, research regarding other specific RtI components has found large effects. For example, a core reading curriculum that explicitly taught phonics skills led to better-developed reading skills and fewer students being identified with a specific learning disability in reading (Foorman, Francis, Fletcher, Schatschneider, & Mehta, 1998), and meta-analyses found large effects for formative evaluation ($d = 0.70$, L. S. Fuchs & Fuchs, 1986) and for problem-solving teams ($d = 1.10$, M. K. Burns & Symington, 2002).

Limitations of Empirical Research Base

Research regarding school-wide prevention is still ongoing, which makes it difficult to conclusively summarize the state of the current research. Numerous individual studies and meta-analyses support the effectiveness of school-wide RtI approaches, and considerable research addresses various interventions and model components (e.g., M. K. Burns et al., 2005; McMaster et al., 2005; McNamara & Hollinger, 2003). Moreover, considerable research has addressed assessment tools within RtI (e.g., VanDerHeyden et al., 2007). In a number of areas, the research has been less clear and future research is needed.

In the early 1980s, K. A. Heller, Holtzman, and Messick (1982) recommended RtI as national policy, and by the early 1990s some school districts across the country were using RtI procedures to improve student learning and to make identification decisions regarding specific learning disabilities (Graden, Stollar, & Poth, 2007; Lau et al., 2006). However, relatively little research that meets scientific standards for methodological rigor has addressed RtI models in their entirety. Perhaps the biggest concern that research has yet to adequately address is implementation integrity. Noell and colleagues (Noell, Duhon, Gatti, & Connell, 2002; Noell, Gresham, & Gansle, 2002; Noell et al., 2005) have certainly informed the literature about treatment integrity for individual interventions, and recent research has demonstrated that providing feedback on implementation integrity improved the fidelity of the problem-solving team process (M. K. Burns, Peters, & Noell, 2008). However, implementation integrity was identified as a potentially fatal flaw in RtI (Noell & Gansle, 2006).

Researchers have yet to identify ways to ensure implementation integrity within RtI, and many important questions about what should be implemented remain unanswered. For example, the role of parents in RtI seems to be almost completely absent in research. This is especially concerning, given that prevention science is the theoretical basis for RtI, and prevention depends on coordinated services between home, school, and community (VanDerHeyden & Burns, 2010). Moreover, problem analysis is critical to RtI, but the research evaluating the effectiveness of various approaches to analyses such as curriculum-based evaluation is sparse, and the data about math and writing are very limited.

School-wide prevention models have their bases in grassroots movements, and those initiatives outpaced pre-service training. Fortunately, many colleges of education and school psychology programs graduate personnel with the necessary skills (e.g., curriculum-based measurement, data-based decision making, interventions, consultation, problem-solving), but those skills are rarely directly contextualized within school-wide prevention. The field needs a stronger pre-service focus and needs research regarding how to best provide in-service training to current practitioners. Moreover, school effectiveness research has consistently found that the single variable that contributes most directly to effective schools is effective *instructional* leadership by school principals (Levine & Lezotte, 1990), but research regarding administrators' roles within school-wide prevention is yet to occur. Researchers have made several recommendations for school administration regarding RtI (e.g., Elliott & Morrison, 2008; Kurns & Tilly, 2008), but even those helpful documents do not fully discuss several important issues such as personnel development and human resource issues.

Due to the increased complexity of high schools, more research is needed on successful implementation of RtI at the secondary level. Specifically, educators need research regarding effective measurement tools for high school students, how to best implement Tier-2 interventions, and how to implement problem-solving teams at the high school level.

Effect on Special Education

Because RtI is directly linked to special education through diagnosis of a specific learning disability, it is important to consider the effect of school-wide prevention on special education. Fortunately, previous research has informed this conversation. Most of the research on RtI focuses on student outcomes, which is appropriate given the focus on enhancing student learning (M. K. Burns & VanDerHeyden, 2006). Some have cautioned that RtI would lead to a dramatic increase in the number of children identified with a specific learning disability (J. B. Hale, Naglieri, Kaufman, & Kavale, 2004), but a review of four studies of districts implementing RtI found that an average of 1.26% ($SD = 0.65$) of the student population was referred for a special education eligibility assessment, and an average of 1.68% ($SD = 1.45$) of the population was identified with a special education disability (M. K. Burns et al., 2005); it should be noted that these were based on different studies, which is why the percentage of students identified with a disability was slightly higher than the percentage referred for an evaluation. Moreover, the same review found an average percentage of the student population that was referred to the problem-solving team within the RtI model of 5.98% ($SD = 2.97$), which usually occurs within Tier 3 of an RtI model. If approximately 5% of the student population generally is identified with an SLD

(Lerner, 2002), and students with a specific learning disability and those referred to a problem-solving team within Tier 3 both have severe learning difficulties, then schools that used an RtI model in the previous research had approximately the same number of students experiencing significant difficulties as most schools across the country. However, most of the students experiencing significant difficulties in the RtI schools had their needs met without being identified as a student with a disability.

M. M. Gerber (2005) stated that RtI research does little to inform us about the nature of specific learning disabilities, which appears to be true. Perhaps future research regarding the characteristics of students identified with a specific learning disability through an RtI approach will shed light on the nature of these disabilities. However, the current research focuses on outcomes for students and systems, which is appropriate at this point. What we do know is that RtI results in special education decisions that are not biased by gender (M. K. Burns & Senesac, 2005). Moreover, research with 13 elementary schools in an urban area found that after 2 years of implementation, schools that implemented an RtI model (Instructional Consultation Teams) experienced significant decreases in the risk of minority students being referred to and placed in special education when compared to 9 control schools (Gravois & Rosenfield, 2006). In fact, the likelihood of a minority student's being identified with a disability was cut in half in the participating schools.

Conclusion

Implementing school-wide prevention can be a long and difficult process, but several excellent examples of successful models exist in the literature (Ervin, Schaughency, Goodman, McGlinchey, & Matthews, 2006; Grimes, Kurns, & Tilly, 2006). Sandler and Sugai (2009) describe the conceptual framework, features, and outcomes of a 10-year initiative to establish a model of Effective Behavior and Instructional Support (EBIS) in a district in Oregon. The district observed increasing fidelity of implementation, increasing numbers of students demonstrating sufficient reading skills, and accurate early identification of children with specific learning disabilities. The EBIS model incorporated prevention of both academic and behavioral difficulties, but it provides an example from which practitioners interested in implementing RtI can learn. The legal justification, theoretical framework, and research base suggest that school districts are wise to move to a school-wide model for preventing academic difficulties.

CHAPTER 18

Data-Based Decision Making in Academics Using Curriculum-Based Measurement

Erica S. Lembke, David Hampton, and **Elise Hendricker** | *University of Missouri*

With the passage of the No Child Left Behind Act (NCLB, U.S. Department of Education, 2001), schools are focusing more on accountability and ensuring that all children are learning and progressing in their education. Schools around the country are collecting data, analyzing student performance, and using research-based practices and instruction that are proven advantageous for student success. To achieve these outcomes, many schools have elected to employ a Response to Intervention (RtI) model (D. Fuchs & Fuchs, 2006; Burns, Appleton, & Stehouwer, 2005) to guide their instruction, intervention, and data-based decision making. Making data-based decisions in an RtI model requires educators to use technically adequate tools for universal screening to determine which students are at risk of later difficulties as well as for monitoring student progress over time to gain reliable information regarding the effectiveness of instructional practices.

This chapter specifically focuses on the use of empirically validated practices to make effective decisions regarding student progress and outcomes. After introducing basic concepts about using simple data to determine who needs help and whether the help they receive is resulting in improved performance, we present research examining technical aspects of progress-monitoring methods and the benefits of their use. In the third section, we illustrate the application of data-based decision making by showing how a school would employ the procedures we have presented in the first two sections. Finally, we summarize the case for systematically monitoring progress and present needs for future research about curriculum-based measurement (CBM).

What Does Progress Monitoring Contribute to Making Data-Based Decisions?

This section establishes the background on making data-based decisions using progress-monitoring data. It provides a definition and description of progress monitoring; describes measures typically used for monitoring student performance; recounts historical and legal rationale for their use; and concludes by discussing logical and practical reasons that progress monitoring should be used by classroom teachers to inform instructional decisions and increase student achievement.

Progress monitoring is defined as the assessment of student academic performance on a regular basis using standardized, scientifically validated measurement tools (L. S. Fuchs & Fuchs, 2002). Although current teaching practices may include various assessments to monitor student understanding of curriculum and concepts, these assessment tools are often not scientifically validated, a crucial element of progress monitoring. To ensure the technical adequacy of progress monitoring, educators can administer CBM tools that have been scientifically validated and standardized for use across student populations.

CBM is "a simple set of procedures for repeated measurement of student growth toward long-range instructional goals" (Deno, 1985, p. 221). The cornerstones of CBM are threefold. First, it is simple and efficient for teachers to administer, because the measures that are administered (sometimes called *probes*) have standardized directions and most are 1 minute in duration. Second, CBM uses repeated measurement over time with standardized forms; although all probes differ, they are created at the same difficulty level and assess similar skills across time, which allows teachers to derive information that helps them to evaluate the progress of students, classes, schools, and districts over time. Third, and perhaps most important, because CBM tools for progress monitoring are repeated measures, individual student growth and progress can be monitored; teachers therefore can graph CBM results and use the data and graphs to make decisions about instructional programs and teaching methods for students (Deno, Fuchs, Marston, & Shin, 2001).

Uses of Progress Monitoring

CBM tools have been scientifically validated for use and have over 30 years of research support (L. S. Fuchs, 2004). CBM tools have been found to increase student achievement (L. S. Fuchs, Deno, & Mirkin, 1984; P. M. Stecker, Fuchs, & Fuchs, 2005), because teachers can identify when instructional changes are needed for individuals or groups of students in the classroom (L. S. Fuchs, Fuchs, & Hamlett, 1993). Graphed data provide an objective view of student performance and facilitate communication among teachers, students, and parents about student progress (M. R. Shinn, Habedank, & Good, 1993). CBM tools also have adequate predictive validity and can predict over time which students are likely to succeed on high-stakes assessments (Good, Simmons, & Kame'enui, 2001). CBM can reliably and validly designate which students are at risk or struggling in academic areas, leading teachers to have confidence in the assessment and easily intervene with these students to alter their academic trajectories.

CBM is used traditionally for two purposes: screening and progress monitoring. *Screening,* or *benchmarking,* refers to an assessment window in the fall, winter, and spring of each school year when all students are given CBM measures within a subject area to assess their current level of performance. These screening

measures give teachers, school psychologists, and other educational specialists in the school environment data regarding where each student is performing in comparison to established national norms to determine which students are making effective progress and which students need further intervention strategies. For those students who fall below expected levels of performance, educators can implement progress monitoring using the same CBM measures to monitor academic growth (Brown-Chidsey & Steege, 2005).

Within the school setting, CBM data have many advantages for both students and teachers. Because some commercially available CBM tools have been standardized on thousands of students, progress monitoring can been used to estimate normative rates of student improvement (i.e., Aimsweb.com, dibels.uoregon.edu). This gives teachers an objective, standardized growth rate to determine if students are benefiting from typical classroom instruction (L. S. Fuchs & Fuchs, 2002). When teachers monitor students' performance on a regular basis, the students' performance can be compared either to the performance of a student in the same grade who is average performing or to the students' own past performance. These are the key ways that CBM data help teachers make data-based decisions: The data can be used to identify those students who are not progressing by comparing them with others and can be used to assess growth by comparing scores of the same individual over time. These decisions can be made relatively quickly, rather than waiting for students to fail, which increases the likelihood that interventions can be implemented early in elementary school, which leads to earlier remediation of deficits.

For students who are not benefiting from typical classroom instruction, progress monitoring can help determine their instructional needs or can help monitor the individualized education program (IEP) goals for students who are already in special education. A common source of confusion is the type of information that can be gathered from CBM tools. Because they are quick, general indicators of educational performance, CBM tools do not tell teachers specifically what skills should be taught to certain students. However, CBM tools do indicate reliably when specific children are struggling in a particular academic subject and when the current teaching strategies are not effective for those students and their needs. Teachers can then use various methods, such as follow-up assessments, diagnostic interviews, or error analysis, to make data-based decisions to alter their instructional practices for those students (M. R. Shinn, 1989, 1998).

After monitoring students' progress and objectively determining which students are not making adequate progress, teachers should implement research-based intervention strategies that are both quantitatively and qualitatively different from previous instruction to teach the academic skills. Many struggling students or students with IEPs need more instruction in certain areas, as well as teaching methods that differ from the standard curriculum. During intervention implementation, progress monitoring helps teachers assess the effectiveness of the instruction. This allows teachers to compare the efficacy of different forms of instruction, as well as to design more effective, individualized instructional programs for learners not making adequate progress (L. S. Fuchs & Fuchs, 2002). If it's working, keep doing it. If it's not working, try something else!

Historical, Legal, and Logical Basis for Progress Monitoring

To understand the need and momentum for the use of progress monitoring in the current educational system, it is imperative to examine the historical and legal basis for its use, as well as why it should be used from a logical standpoint. Within the empirical literature, numerous researchers have communicated the need for prevention and early intervention of academic problems (Juel, 1988; Francis, Shaywitz, Stuebing, Shaywitz, & Fletcher, 1996; L. M. Phillips, Norris, Osmond, & Maynard, 2002). Because many programs target children too late in the process, when academic problems have occurred for long periods, the chance of significant change is decreased. In contrast, early intervention programs not only target children when they are young, thus changing their developmental trajectories, but are also cost-effective for society as a whole (Weissberg, Kumpfer, & Seligman, 2003). This window of opportunity between the onset of concerns and later diagnoses of learning disabilities (LD) has forced schools, educators, and researchers to rethink their practices to identify and intervene with at-risk students effectively.

Historically, models of achievement and student progress assumed that students were progressing normally until otherwise noted, often using subjective feelings or instincts of the teacher to make decisions about student progress (Fletcher, Coulter, Reschly, & Vaughn, 2004). This model, often termed "wait to fail," did not provide students with intensive intervention until their academic achievement was significantly below that of their peers. Once this discrepancy occurred, students were diagnosed with LDs and given special education services to remediate their academic skills; however, this model of identification did not result in increased academic skills for these students generally, as many showed few gains and rarely exited special education services (Donovan & Cross, 2002; G. R. Lyon et al., 2001). For example, Chard and Kame'enui (2000) found that students who exhibit delayed reading achievement at the end of third grade show little significant reading

growth into eighth grade and beyond. This knowledge, which highlights the importance of early intervention and prevention, has compelled schools to use valid and reliable screening and progress-monitoring practices to identify problem learners as early as possible.

From a legal perspective, educational legislation such as No Child Left Behind (NCLB) (U.S. Department of Education, 2001) and the Individuals with Disabilities Education Improvement Act (IDEA; U.S. Department of Education, 2004) provides statutes and mandates regarding student achievement and data-based decision making, highlighting the need for and use of progress monitoring in the school setting. Two important mandates of the NCLB legislation are relevant to the use of progress monitoring: First, schools receiving federal funds must employ research-based practices to improve academic outcomes for all students. Second, schools and states must use progress-monitoring tools to ensure that academic programs and curricula are advantageous and effective in meeting the learning needs of students (Brown-Chidsey & Steege, 2005; U.S. Department of Education, 2001). Because monitoring progress with CBM measures is supported by years of research and can be used to monitor student progress toward academic goals, the practice is compatible with the requirements set forth by NCLB, making it a valuable approach employed by many schools around the country.

Within special education law, the 2004 revision of IDEA (IDEIA) defined an alternative approach regarding the procedures schools can use to identify students with LDs. Due to problems with the wait-to-fail model (Fletcher et al., 2004), RtI practices may be used to determine a student's eligibility for special education services (U.S. Department of Education, 2004). In a three-tiered RtI model, in Tier 1, schools must first use a research-based curriculum for all students, ensuring that teaching tools and practices are based on sound empirical research and all students have an opportunity to learn. Using data gathered from CBM screening measures administered to all students, those who are not performing at expected levels would be considered for Tier-2 services, indicating that alternative research-based interventions must supplement the classroom curriculum. Schools must evaluate how students respond to these interventions, with an emphasis placed on data-based decision making for instructional planning and education decision making. Using CBM tools, schools can monitor student progress effectively and determine if Tier-2 interventions are successful. For those students whose CBM data indicate that they have not benefited from the interventions, these data, along with other appropriate evidence, can be used to determine the presence of an LD and the need for intensive special education programming (Brown-Chidsey & Steege, 2005) or, in some cases, more intensive and specific intervention (Tier 3).

Beyond the legal impetus, progress monitoring has many logical, practical uses within the classroom setting. First, progress monitoring using CBM is both efficient and effective for teachers to compare rates of growth over time and has many advantages over other types of assessments. Typical classroom assessment relies on mastery measurement, which focuses on the mastery of single skills throughout the year. These tests are often lengthy to administer and are not administered regularly, as students often take end-of-unit tests or quizzes to determine if they have mastered skills taught within the curriculum. This type of assessment does not offer immediate feedback to the teacher. For example, if students take an end-of-unit test after a month of instruction, and approximately 50% of the class did not master the material, the teacher has not obtained these data until the unit is over. In addition, it is difficult to compare scores and progress over time using these assessments, because different skills are assessed by each assessment. Most importantly, these commonly used assessments are rarely scientifically validated or technically adequate, making it difficult for teachers to understand how trustworthy the test is in assessing student achievement (L. S. Fuchs & Deno, 1991; L. S. Fuchs & Fuchs, 2002). Progress monitoring overcomes many of these deficits: It is efficient and easy for teachers to administer to assess student progress; its reliability and validity have been established; the data can be analyzed to adjust student goals and instructional programs; and the data can be used to assess growth over time, as well as to compare student performance to typically performing peers.

Summary

CBM tools have important uses in general and special education, helping to improve the academic achievement of students at risk of developing academic problems as well as those with identified academic disabilities. Progress monitoring has been developed as a way to improve on historical assessment methods, satisfy educational and legal requirements, and inform teachers regarding student performance to help make instructional decisions based on objective data. CBM tools used for monitoring student progress are reliable and valid. In particular, they have predictive validity. For example, progress-monitoring tools measuring early literacy skills have been found to be predictive of later reading performance, leading teachers to make informed decisions about students at risk of later academic failure (Deno, 2003; Good et al., 2001). Most importantly, research indicates that progress monitoring improves student performance, teaching practices, and instructional decisions (P. M. Stecker et al., 2005). When teachers use progress monitoring, they can make better decisions regarding students in need of different instructional programs and design programs that meet the unique learning needs of students (L. S. Fuchs & Fuchs, 2002).

What Does Research Say About Using CBM in Reading and Mathematics?

As mentioned previously, using CBM for progress monitoring has been well researched for over 30 years. Monitoring progress using CBM demonstrates student growth throughout a school year of instruction in general education classrooms or can be used to evaluate intervention support provided in addition to general education or as part of special education. CBM measures have been developed in academic areas including reading, mathematics, spelling, and written expression, at both the elementary and secondary levels. To date, the preponderance of the research has been done in the areas of reading and mathematics. Although CBM research in reading is extensive, research about CBM of mathematics is gaining significant attention in recent years as federal mandates and statewide assessment requirements have heightened the need for appropriate methods to measure progress over an academic year. Reading and mathematics are the academic areas where students struggle the most, so it makes sense to make them the focal point of this chapter. However, it is important to recognize that, while not the focus of this chapter, much research has been done in other academic areas such as spelling (Deno, Mirkin, Lowry, & Kuehnle, 1980; M. R. Shinn & Marston, 1985; M. R. Shinn, Ysseldyke, Deno, & Tindal, 1986; Tindal, Germann, & Deno, 1983), written expression (Deno, Marston, & Mirkin, 1982; Espin, Wallace, Campbell, Lembke, Long, & Ticha, 2008; Gansle, Noell, VanDerHeyden, Naquin, & Slider, 2002; Marston, 1989; Tindal & Parker, 1991; Espin, De La Paz, Scierka, & Roelofs, 2005), and the content areas such as science and social studies (Espin, Busch, Shin, & Kruschwitz, 2001; Espin, Shin, & Busch, 2005; Tindal & Nolet, 1995).

The technical adequacy of CBM measures for monitoring progress provides teachers and administrators with confidence in measuring students' growth over time by accurately indicating how students, and particularly those students who are academically at risk, are progressing over time. Tindal and Parker (1991) identified four markers that educators can use to assess the technical adequacy of effective assessment procedures. The markers, or criteria, and a brief description of each include (a) consistent administration and reliable scoring methods (teachers use the same directions, time students for the same length of time, and score in the same manner); (b) the ability to discriminate the performance or skill levels of a diverse range of students (the measures provide information about students who are achieving above, on, and below grade level); (c) criterion validity in relation to other validated forms of assessment (the measures compare favorably to other common academic assessments in reading or mathematics); and (d) sensitivity to change (especially growth) in student performance (the measures can be used to monitor growth for even those students who are growing very slowly). Once these technically adequate measures are identified, the most important and useful part of CBM is teacher use of the graphed data to inform changes that might be necessary in instruction. This continued attention to data and use of data-based decision making is what leads to improved student outcomes. In the following sections, we detail examples of research that support progress monitoring in reading and mathematics.

Technical Adequacy in Reading

In this section, we briefly describe some of the CBM progress-monitoring measures that are available in the most prominently researched areas in reading, including oral reading, early literacy measures, and maze. Early research examining CBM validity in reading focused on determining criterion validity of potential CBM measures such as oral reading fluency (ORF; Marston, 1989). Deno, Mirkin, and Chiang (1982) discovered that listening to students read aloud from basal readers for 1 minute was a valid indicator of reading proficiency. Correlation coefficients between ORF and scores on standardized reading measures ranged from 0.73 to 0.91 with the majority of coefficients over 0.80. Since then, other studies have assessed the criterion validity of ORF for both screening and progress monitoring, with coefficients ranging from 0.63 to 0.90 and most above 0.80 (Burke & Hagen-Burke, 2007; L. S. Fuchs, Fuchs, & Maxwell, 1988; L. S. Fuchs, Tindal, & Deno, 1984; Marston, 1982; Tindal, Fuchs, Fuchs, Shinn, Deno, & Germann, 1983). The technical adequacy of CBM measures for first through sixth grade have been well documented in the literature (L. S. Fuchs et al., 1984: L. S. Fuchs & Deno, 1994; M. R. Shinn, Good, Knutson, Tilly, & Collins, 1992; Tindal, 1992).

Given that reading proficiency is critical for academic success, it is important that CBM provide useful information to teachers when they assess progress of their students as they move from pre-literacy skills toward reading competence. M. K. Hosp and Fuchs (2005) examined the relationship between CBM and specific reading progression as a function of grade. They administered CBM reading passages and the Word Attack, Word Identification, and Passage Comprehension subtests of the Woodcock Reading Mastery Test—Revised

(Woodcock, 1987) to 310 participants distributed equally across grades 1 to 4. M. K. Hosp and Fuchs (2005) reported that comparisons across grades for CBM and word reading were highest for grades 1, 2, and 3 compared to fourth grade. The overall results support the notion that CBM assesses different skills across grade levels, and that these skills are aligned with the tenets of instruction that are germane to each grade.

The Dynamic Indicators of Basic Early Literacy (DIBELS; Good & Kaminski, 2007) is also a validated CBM instrument for assessing early literacy. DIBELS is designed for use in early identification of reading difficulties and monitoring progress among elementary students. DIBELS assesses proficiency of a set of early literacy skills identified in the literature as directly related to and foundational for subsequent reading proficiency. Young students' knowledge of letters, phonemic awareness, and sound–symbol relationships in kindergarten have all been identified as important predictors of later literacy proficiency (J. Elliott, Lee, & Tollefson, 2001).

J. Elliott et al. (2001) examined the technical adequacy of four selected DIBELS measures (Letter Naming Fluency, Sound Naming Fluency, Initial Phoneme Ability, and Phoneme Segmentation) for identifying kindergarteners who were at risk for reading difficulties. Seventy-five kindergarteners from four classrooms in three elementary schools in a moderate-sized Midwestern city participated in the study. Elliott and colleagues obtained three types of reliability: inter-rater, test–retest, and alternate form. All reliability coefficients with the exception of Initial Phoneme Ability were 0.80 or higher. Criterion validity received strict scrutiny, which was obtained by correlating "level" estimates (average scores over repeated administration) of the DIBELS measures with (a) the Broad Reading and Skills clusters of the Woodcock Johnson Psycho-Educational Achievement Battery—Revised (WJ-R; Woodcock & Johnson, 1990); (b) the Test of Phonological Awareness (Torgesen & Bryant, 1994); (c) Teacher Rating Questionnaire (Share, Jorm, MacLean, & Matthews, 1984); (d) the Developing Skills Checklist (Clark, 1995); and (e) the Kaufman Brief Intelligence Test (Prewitt, 1992). The DIBELS measures demonstrated the strongest correlations with scores on the Skills Cluster of the WJ-R and the Developing Skills Checklist, with coefficients that ranged from 0.44 to 0.81.

To provide further insight into the relationships between the DIBELS measures and the WJ-R, J. Elliott et al. (2001) conducted hierarchical regression analysis with all analyses statistically significant ($p < 0.01$). Across all analyses, Letter Naming Fluency was the single best predictor of kindergarten achievement scores on the Broad Reading and Skills clusters of the WJ-R and the teacher ratings of student's reading proficiency. This study was particularly important because it examined the technical adequacy of DIBELS measures by increasing the sample size and diversity of participants.

A measure that has been developed and used as a progress-monitoring tool for secondary students is the maze task (L. S. Fuchs & Fuchs, 1992; Espin, Wallace, Lembke, Campbell, & Long, 2010). The maze task is a silent reading task that can be group administered. Students read through a passage in which every seventh word is deleted and replaced with the correct word and three distracters. Students circle the word that they feel makes sense in the sentence. The number that is recorded is the number of correct choices circled in the time limit. At the elementary level, correlations between the maze task and reading comprehension and broad reading scores from standardized tests range from 0.80 to 0.89 (Jenkins & Jewell, 1993; L. S. Fuchs & Fuchs, 1992). At the secondary level, Espin et al. examined the relation between performance on the CBM measures and a state reading test with validity coefficients above 0.70 and reported substantial and significant growth over time for a subset of students ($n = 31$).

Evidence supports the technical adequacy of CBM in reading for monitoring progress of all readers, but especially those who may be at risk of reading failure or struggling with attaining reading proficiency. CBM provides teachers, school psychologists, and administrators with a valuable tool necessary to implement tiered interventions for improving the reading levels of their students. In addition, CBM has been suggested for use in screening and monitoring the progress of students who may have difficulties in mathematics.

Technical Adequacy in Mathematics

With the growing attention that student achievement in mathematics has been receiving, the development of methods for monitoring student progress in mathematics has garnered increased attention among researchers. In a review of the use of CBM in reading and mathematics and subsequent gains in student achievement, P. M. Stecker et al. (2005) suggest that, overall, CBM leads to significant gains in student achievement. Achievement is particularly enhanced when CBM data are paired with decision-making rules, skills-focused feedback, and suggestions for instructional changes. Foegen, Jiban, and Deno (2007) reviewed literature regarding progress monitoring in mathematics. Of the studies included in the review, 17 were for elementary mathematics, while four were conducted in early mathematics and four in secondary mathematics. Research on early mathematics was centered exclusively on measures of numeracy and used participants from the general education classroom, a potential benefit when considering validity and reliability of progress monitoring in math for use in an RtI model. Although researchers have found that ORF and scores on standardized reading tests are highly correlated (0.80–0.90; Deno, Mirkin, et al., 1982), Foegen and colleagues (2007) reported that correlations between CBM mathematics measures across grade levels and criterion validity measures are generally moderate (in the 0.50–0.70 range). It is important to note that these coefficients are similar to the coefficients of many commercial achievement tests of mathematics. Commonly used CBM measures in the studies review by Foegen et al. (2007) included number identification, quantity discrimination, computation, concepts and applications, and word-problem–solving measures.

In the area of early numeracy, Lembke and Foegen (2009) conducted a preliminary investigation into the potential of four early numeracy CBM measures [Number Identification (identifying a number between 1 and 100), Quantity Array (naming the numerical amount after looking at a pattern of dots), Missing Number (identifying a missing number from a pattern of 3 numbers and a blank), and Quantity Discrimination (orally saying the larger of two numbers)] for use in screening students who may have difficulties in early math skills. This foundational study assessed over 300 kindergarten and first-grade students in two states to evaluate the technical adequacy of the measures by administering the four measures three times during the school year. Alternate-form reliability coefficients were strong (0.80–0.90), except for Missing Number in kindergarten at all three administrations. Concurrent criterion validity and predictive validity coefficients with standardized early mathematics tests and teacher ratings were obtained and were varied according to the measure and the grade level. The strongest coefficients for both grades for criterion validity were found in Quantity Discrimination (8 of 13 correlations in the moderate, 0.50–0.66, range) and Missing Number (9 of 13 correlations in the moderate to strong, 0.54–0.75, range), with coefficients generally stronger in first grade. Predictive validity coefficients were strongest for Number Identification (3 of 4 coefficients in the 0.58–0.64 range) and Missing Number (3 of 4 coefficients in the 0.67–0.70 range). The findings indicated that Number Identification, Missing Number, and Quantity Discrimination possessed sufficient technical adequacy to be useful tools for teachers to identify young students who struggle with early math content. Quantity Array did not meet the threshold for technical strength and was subsequently dropped from future examinations (Lembke & Foegen, 2009). These results provide an encouraging springboard for continued examination to determine the utility of these measures for use in screening and monitoring the progress of young students in early mathematics skills.

In an extension of the previous study, Lembke, Foegen, Whittaker, and Hampton (2008) examined the technical adequacy of the Number Identification, Missing Number, and Quantity Discrimination measures to monitor the progress of kindergarten and first-grade students over time. Hierarchical Linear Modeling was used at each grade level to determine the ability of the three measures to model growth over time, an important component of determining technical adequacy for use as progress-monitoring tools. All measures produced growth rates that were significant across time for both grade levels, but linear growth was observed only for Number Identification. Growth rates varied from a low of 0.11 items per week increase for Missing Number in grade 1 to 0.34 items per week for Number Identification in kindergarten. Students grew the most on the Number Identification measure. The findings from this study have implications for teachers as they consider which measures might be used for progress monitoring, in that measures such as Missing Number and Quantity Discrimination that have nonlinear growth might produce student graphs that show variable performance or that do not always capture student growth that is being made. More research is needed on the use of these early numeracy measures across weeks, and up-to-date technical reports can be found on progressmonitoring.org.

Although research examining progress monitoring in mathematics using the general education population yields significant information beneficial for future use within the tiered intervention system of RtI, it is still important to consider the utility of monitoring the progress of students with LDs in mathematics. Many students with LDs experience pervasive difficulties mastering even the most basic mathematical concepts (Owens & Fuchs, 2002). E. S. Shapiro, Edwards, and Zigmond (2005) reported findings from a state-wide project that provided weekly progress monitoring for 120 students (104 elementary students and 16 middle school students) in special education classes. All of the participants were monitored in mathematics computation, and 109 were additionally monitored in concepts and applications. Results showed that weekly growth rates of 0.38 digits per week for computation, and 0.38 points for concepts and applications, were obtained by participants, rates of growth that are similar to the growth rates found in general education settings. These results provide additional evidence (see P. M. Stecker et al., 2005, for a brief summary of earlier work in mathematics) for considering CBM mathematics measures as an appropriate tool for examining the progress of students who receive services in special education environments.

L. S. Fuchs et al. (2007) examined both screening and progress monitoring using CBM by following 225 students from first grade to the end of second grade.

They assessed Number Identification/Counting (writing the final two numbers in a five-number sequence), Fact Retrieval (addition and subtraction single-digit fact fluency on paper), Computation (solving mixed computation facts with 2 to 3 digits), and Concepts/Applications (solving applied types of problems, e.g., graphs, more/less than, and fractions on paper). Number Identification/Counting and CBM Computation were also administered weekly for 27 weeks in order to test technical adequacy for use in progress monitoring. Results indicated CBM Concepts/Applications was the best predictor of two outcome measures administered in the spring of second grade: the WRAT 3-Arithmetic (Wilkinson, 1993) and Jordan's Story Problems (Jordan & Hanich, 2000). Results also showed that CBM computation demonstrated validity for use in monitoring progress, and Number Identification/Counting did not meet the technical adequacy standards created by the authors.

Monitoring progress in mathematics using (a) computation and (b) concepts and applications measures is an important step to improving student achievement in mathematics (Foegen, Jiban, & Deno, 2007; P. M. Stecker et al., 2005), yet students are quickly expected to apply mathematics knowledge on word problems. Word problems require students to integrate their mathematical competence with adequate levels of reading comprehension. Jitendra, Sczesniak, and Deatline-Buchman (2005) examined CBM mathematical word-problem–solving tasks for use as indicators of mathematics proficiency for 77 third graders in the winter and spring of the school year. Specifically, the study assessed the reliability and concurrent and predictive validity of word-problem–solving CBM measures. Results indicated that these CBM measures were technically adequate as indicators of mathematics proficiency of third graders with internal consistency reliability coefficients ranging from 0.76 to 0.83 using the means of two forms and mostly moderate criterion validity coefficients (7 of 8 in the 0.58–0.71 range).

Students in school encounter increasingly complex computation and conceptual tasks as they enter middle and secondary school. Therefore, it is important to identify technically adequate measures to assess student proficiency in the middle school grades. Foegen and Deno (2001) studied the technical adequacy of potential math indicators of growth in the middle school. They gave 100 students four mathematics measures (one involved basic facts, and three involved the concept of estimation) twice in a 1-week period. Results indicated that the measures were reliable: Test–retest reliability coefficients calculated using the mean of two forms ranged from 0.80 to 0.88. Results also indicated that the levels of criterion validity were adequate, with 7 of 8 coefficients in the moderate (0.44–0.63) range with standardized mathematics tests. These measures therefore may be useful as indicators of mathematics competence for children in middle school.

The Effects of CBMs on Students' Outcomes

The evaluation of technical adequacy is an important foundational step in assessing a measurement system's utility for implementation in schools and classrooms. But it is only a part of the equation; one must also consider the benefits for students when using any instructional, assessment, or intervention program for students. All educators and administrators should apply the test of whether a program can demonstrate the ability to improve student outcomes. Monitoring progress using CBM has a large body of evidence to support its ability to improve the outcomes of students in reading and mathematics, but only when teachers use the data to make instructional decisions (P. M. Stecker et al., 2005).

The original intent of CBM was to provide educators with technically adequate, easy-to-use data that document student proficiency and growth over a period of time (P. M. Stecker et al., 2005). The overriding premise of CBM is that by employing these trustworthy data about student proficiency, a teacher can ultimately improve academic outcomes for students. In their review of literature on the utility of CBM in improving student achievement, Stecker et al. found that CBM produced significant gains in student achievement that were associated with using systematic data-based decision rules, skills analysis checklists, and instructional recommendations for making program modifications.

L. S. Fuchs, Fuchs, and Hamlett (1989) explored the value of CBM in planning effective reading programs and reported that students who were exposed to both assessment using CBM and evaluation of instructional programming performed better than a control group exposed to the assessment program only. In a variation on this research, Fuchs and colleagues (L. S. Fuchs, Fuchs, Hamlett, Phillips, & Bentz, 1994) explored the effectiveness of class-wide decision-making structures within the general education mathematics classroom. They found the students of teachers who used CBM and received instructional recommendations designed to better instructional programming realized greater achievement than peers in the classrooms of teachers who just collected the CBM data. In one of many studies addressing the utility of the use of DIBELS measures to improve student outcomes in early reading skills, S. Baker and Smith (1999, 2001) found that introducing teachers to using DIBELS data and helping them focus on early decoding competence resulted in improved student

performance on a wide array of measures of basic reading achievement.

Spicuzza et al. (2001) studied whether implementing an instructional management system that included CBM in mathematics would result in positive changes in the classroom environment and, subsequently, improvement in student achievement. They found that implementing progress monitoring can be beneficial to student math achievement, as evidenced by a positive effect on the math achievement growth demonstrated by students on two math achievement assessments. Some of the mathematics studies detailed earlier also provide evidence of the utility of CBM in mathematics as useful tools for improving student outcomes (L. S. Fuchs et al., 2007; E. S. Shapiro et al., 2005). These studies were preceded by work by L. S. Fuchs, Fuchs, Hamlett, and Stecker (1990) that experimentally contrasted teachers' use of CBM with and without skills analysis with teachers in a control group who did not use CBM. The students in the CBM with skills-analysis group performed better on a computation assessment. In another experimental study (P. M. Stecker & Fuchs, 2000), students with mild-to-moderate disabilities were matched on mathematics ability and were progress monitored twice weekly. Teachers made instructional decisions for one group of CBM students based on their CBM graphs. Teachers incorporated these changes for the matched partner at the same time. After 20 weeks, all students had grown significantly in mathematics, but those students whose teachers made changes based specifically on the students' CBM graphs grew the most.

Summary

Over the past 30 years, an extensive body of evidence has been amassed that lends support for the validity and reliability of CBM measures as screening and progress-monitoring tools in reading and math. The Research Institute on Progress Monitoring (Espin & Wallace, 2004) identified 141 studies in which technical adequacy and instructional utility were examined. This extensive literature base has served to extend CBM beyond its initial focus on special education progress monitoring to now include universal screening, general education progress monitoring, and LD classification within an RtI framework (L. S. Fuchs, 2004). Further empirical support has been established to link the use of CBM for screening and monitoring progress with improved student outcomes, the primary goal of education at the classroom, school, district, state, and national level. Strengths of the CBM literature are its breadth across time, student type, subject area, and grade level. One specific research need is the use of more sophisticated statistical analysis, although this has been increasing since the early 2000s (e.g., see Hintze, Christ, & Keller, 2002).

Recommended Practices for Using CBM Progress-Monitoring Tools

As detailed in the previous sections, progress monitoring using CBM is an excellent tool to monitor the progress of general education students who are at risk for academic problems or students who already have been found eligible for and are receiving special education services in reading, math, or both. Several elements are critical for teachers to address or put into place as they prepare to implement a system of CBM

progress monitoring (Deno, 1985, 2003). These elements include selecting technically adequate measures, organizing materials, scheduling, monitoring reliability of implementation and scoring, graphing data, establishing data-decision rules, making decisions based on a student's graphed data, implementing instructional changes, and continued monitoring. These critical elements for CBM progress monitoring are also summarized in a checklist in Figure 18.1. To illustrate, in the next section, we present the case of a reading specialist, Mrs. Adams, as she and her colleagues work through these elements.

Figure 18.1   Critical elements for implementation of progress monitoring using curriculum-based measurement.

Date Completed	Element	Notes
	1. Select technically adequate measures.	
	2. Complete school-wide screening.	
	3. Select students for progress monitoring using decision-making rules.	
	4. Organize materials.	
	5. Develop a schedule.	
	6. Graph data, including goal setting.	
	7. Monitor reliability of implementation and scoring.	
	8. Make decisions based on a student's graphed data.	
	9. Implement instructional changes.	
	10. Continue monitoring.	

Case Study

Selecting Technically Adequate Measures

It is important to choose measures that are technically adequate. Publishers should provide reports on the reliability and validity of the measures that they are promoting, and teachers who are selecting measures should ask about these important technical features. It is important to know that not just any measures can serve as CBM progress measures. The measures need to have been studied and found to function as reliable indicators of both short- and long-term progress.

Mrs. Adams is working with members of her school team to choose measures for monitoring the progress of the students at risk for reading failure in their school. The team wants to identify measures that have been deemed reliable and valid, but they are also on a tight budget in their district, so they do not have a lot of money to spend. They consult a tools checklist available from the National Center for RtI (rti4success.org) and find measures that fit both of their needs—technically adequate and cost-effective. Because this is the school's first experience with establishing a system of progress monitoring, and because they will monitor reading only, they decide to use the DIBELS measures (Good & Kaminski, 2007). The DIBELS are free for use (if consumers do not purchase the online data management) and also have convincing evidence for use as progress measures on the National Center for RtI's progress-monitoring tools chart. This evidence is provided for reliability and validity of the measures and also for other areas such as reliability of students' slopes over time (the measures demonstrate students' growth consistently over time) and for whether benchmark scores are provided (in this case, for DIBELS, they are). This is a much better method of selecting measures than choosing something that has unknown technical adequacy or developing one's own measures.

School-Wide Screening and Selecting Students for Progress Monitoring

Once the school team has chosen the measures that they will use, the next step is to identify the students who are at risk for or have reading problems and therefore need ongoing progress monitoring. Members of the school problem-solving team (PS team) complete a school-wide benchmarking—meaning that they assess all students in the school using the recommended DIBELS measures for that time of year for that grade. This takes about 10 to 15 minutes per student. These data are entered into an electronic spreadsheet, and students' scores are categorized based on whether they are meeting or not meeting the published and established DIBELS scores for that particular time of year (benchmark scores based on data from all students who have completed the measures at that time of year across the country). Then the PS team meets to examine the data and determine which students are most in need of additional reading help. The students are grouped into tiered levels based on the national norms of the system that the team selected. After looking at the data, PS team members meet with grade-level teams to discuss the data and any students who the teachers feel should or should not be included in progress monitoring and intervention. Because the screening data are reliable and valid, teachers have confidence in the results. However, if teachers have alternative, quantitative classroom data that support placement or nonplacement in intervention, the team also considers those data. If the PS team questions whether a student who is under consideration for intervention needs intervention at this time, the team can schedule a period of progress monitoring before intervention to confirm or disconfirm placement (see Compton, Fuchs, Fuchs, & Bryant, 2006, for one example of a discussion on identifying students for various tiers in an RtI model).

Essentially, the grade-level teams, with assistance from members of the PS team, meet to review screening data and to make determinations about who should receive intervention. These decisions are based primarily on the normative data that group students according to risk status. Mrs. Adams works primarily with students who are at risk for problems but are not in special education. The grade-level and PS teams identify 10 students following screening with whom Mrs. Adams will work during intervention time.

Scheduling, Organizing Materials, Graphing, and Goal Setting

The next steps for teachers implementing the intervention program are logistical in nature—organizing materials and scheduling a time to monitor students' progress. Mrs. Adams works with classroom teachers to schedule times when she will provide reading intervention to the 10 students with whom she works. She wants to meet with the students every day for at least 30 minutes. Because of careful negotiation and planning, the principal at the school has built intervention time into each grade-level schedule, so scheduling is easy. Mrs. Adams's students have very low scores, so the PS team and Mrs. Adams have decided to monitor their progress once per week. Mrs. Adams determines the grade level of the materials that she will use for each child's assessment. For two of the students, this is their grade level, but for the others, Mrs. Adams monitors progress in out-of-grade-level material. She prepares a folder for each student with all of the progress-monitoring probes, as well as a chart to keep track of scores for each student. For the two students being monitored at grade level, their long-range goals are grade-level goals; that is, the target level of ORF is the reading rate typical of students at that grade level. For the students monitored on out-of-grade-level material, Mrs. Adams sets long-range goals according to end-of-year criteria for their instructional levels; this means the target ORF is the reading rate typical for students completing the grade of the materials they are reading.

Regardless of whether students are assessed on materials at or below their grade level, Mrs. Adams adds lines to the graph for each of her students based on her long-range goals for them. To do this she either uses long-range benchmarks that are published as part of the DIBELS system (and are reported for other Web-based systems as well) or she uses a weekly growth rate (i.e., one word growth per week, multiplied by the number of weeks that she will be progress monitoring). The students' median score from the school-wide screening serves as the starting point for the goal line. If the student is being monitored on out-of-grade-level material, three progress-monitoring measures at the student's instructional level are administered, and the starting point is set using the median score from these three measures. The goal line connects this starting level and the long-range benchmark that has been determined for each student.

A sample progress-monitoring graph for one of Mrs. Adams's students, Sonia, is shown in Figure 18.2. Sonia is in fourth grade but is being progress monitored at the third-grade level. Mrs. Adams gives three third-grade passages to Sonia on one day, and her scores are 44, 55, and 66 words read correctly. Mrs. Adams graphs the data and labels it as baseline data. Sonia's median score is 55, so this is the starting point for the goal line for Sonia. The benchmark level for the spring in DIBELS for third grade is a minimum of 110 words read correctly in 1 minute, so Mrs. Adams used 110 as the end point for the goal line.

Figure 18.2   Sample curriculum-based measurement progress-monitoring graph with goal line showing weekly data for Mrs. Adams's student Sonia.

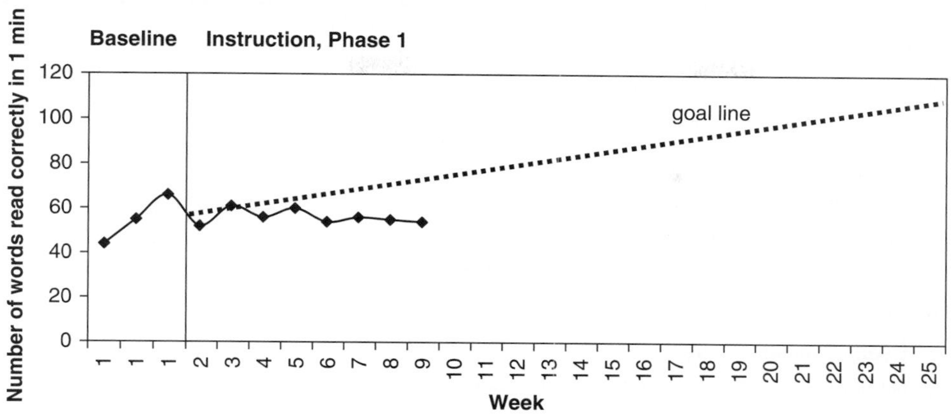

Mrs. Adams decides to assess two students each day. Using this schedule will allow her to have weekly assessments of each of her 10 students. She will score the assessments and enter the data into a computer after the students have left the 30-minute intervention session. The system that the school is using for screening and progress monitoring has a graphing feature, so as Mrs. Adams enters the data, the software creates graphs for each student. Periodically, Mrs. Adams prints these graphs so that she can view them and use the data to make instructional decisions.

Monitoring Reliability of Implementation and Scoring

Before beginning school-wide screening and individual progress monitoring, all school staff members received training on administration of the measures, and they also scored measures as a group to assess the reliability of the scoring. As the year progresses, the PS team recognizes that inconsistencies in administering or scoring the data may have occurred because of lack of review. Members of the team work with each grade level to set up a system of reliability checks; either a grade-level colleague or a PS-team member observes administration and checks scoring as progress monitoring is implemented. A sample administration checklist for CBM ORF is provided in Figure 18.3. As needed, teachers review procedures for administration and scoring at all staff meetings. More detail about scoring procedures for both reading and mathematics measures are provided in administration manuals that are provided with each CBM system (in this case, DIBELS).

Making Decisions Based on a Student's Data

As mentioned previously, the most important aspect of progress monitoring is teacher use of the data, and Mrs. Adams knows that if she wants to see significant growth in her students, she needs to put research-based interventions into place and then assess the effects of those interventions on an ongoing basis. To make the decisions, the teams need to examine data for individual students. Mrs. Adams looks at her students' graphs on a weekly basis and, at least every 6 weeks, she takes student graphs to the appropriate grade-level team meetings for discussion. Using previously established decision-making rules, the teams assess each student's progress. The grade-level team and Mrs. Adams examine the trend of each child's data as compared to the goal line that was set. If the trend line is steeper than the goal line, the teachers consider raising the goal. If the trend line is not as steep as the goal line, they consider changing the intervention they are providing. Decisions are also based on how long the intervention has been in place, with what intensity it has been delivered (student engagement, for instance), whether the intervention is research-based, and with what fidelity the intervention has been implemented. A sample decision-making rubric like the one Mrs. Adams's school uses is included in Figure 18.4. This rubric uses suggested decision-making rules as described in presentations conducted and materials developed by the National Center on Student Progress Monitoring (studentprogress.org), with Lynn and Doug Fuchs as the primary authors. Teams might use the rubric by making determinations about where a student's data fall on each row of the rubric (decision-making rule, class work, behavior, and other). Decisions are listed across the top of the rubric, and the column where the majority of indicators are circled gives teams a suggestion regarding what decision should be made for a student at that time.

When the team examines Sonia's graph and applies the four-point rule (examination of the last four consecutive points in comparison to the goal line), the last four consecutive points are all below the goal line. So in the first row

Figure 18.3   Administration checklist for administration of curriculum-based measurement oral reading fluency aloud.

Administrator _____

Rater _____

Date _____

	Yes	No
1. Presentation of materials		
a. Places student copy in front of the student.	_____	_____
b. Places examiner copy out of view of the student.	_____	_____
2. Reads directions		
a. Reads directions correctly.	_____	_____
b. Demonstrates by pointing when appropriate.	_____	_____
c. Gives appropriate prompts for correct/incorrect examples.	_____	_____
d. Pauses for questions.	_____	_____
3. Timing		
a. Says "begin."	_____	_____
b. Starts/stops timer at the correct times.	_____	_____
c. Times student for 1 minute.	_____	_____
d. Marks student answers on administrator copy.	_____	_____
e. Puts a bracket after the last word said.	_____	_____

Source: Information from Deno, S. L., & Mirkin, P. K. (1977). *Data-based program modification: A manual.* Reston, VA: Council for Exceptional Children.

of the rubric where decision-making rules are applied, the team selects "Trend of data or last four consecutive data points are below the goal line for the past 6 weeks." If the team had access to (or wanted to draw in) a trend line for Sonia's data, they could compare the trend line to the goal line to help make their decision. In the second row, class work is addressed. Mrs. Adams has work samples available, and she had graphed Sonia's scores on weekly reading assignments. Sonia's scores on these classroom assignments clearly are decreasing, so the team circles "Classroom work samples and assessment data indicate that the student is making progress, but not at the expected rate" in the second row of the rubric. In the third row of the rubric, student behavior is addressed. Mrs. Adams feels that Sonia's frustration has been increasingly more evident in class, because she has been delaying starting assignments after they are given, and she has a 70% homework completion rate. This information indicates to the team that on the behavior row of the rubric, they should circle "Inappropriate classroom behaviors are escalating due to frustration with academic performance." Given that two of the three indicators are underneath the decision heading "Student should stay in a tier, and an instructional change should be made," the team determines that at this point, an instructional change needs to be implemented. However, before making the final decision, the team discusses important questions regarding intervention intensity, research base, duration, and fidelity, as detailed in the second part of the rubric.

Implementing Instructional Changes and Continued Monitoring

As the year continues, CBM graphs indicate that several of the progress-monitored students are on track to meet their goals in Mrs. Adams's class, whereas other students are not making adequate progress toward their goal and therefore need changes in their instructional regimens. Based on applying the decision-making rubric to each student's data, Mrs. Adams works with each grade-level team and consults diagnostic data to determine what changes need to be implemented. For Sonia this is just a small refinement of her current intervention plan. This small refinement is made because Sonia's data indicate another change is needed, but Sonia's trend of data is not very far below her graphed goal line. For another student, Mrs. Adams significantly changes the intervention, incorporating a much more explicit and systematic instructional program, because this student's data are far below where the team would expect it to be, given that the student is already receiving intervention. Mrs. Adams uses diagnostic data

Figure 18.4   Decision-making rubric for evaluating student progress and planning intervention.

Decision-making rubric—to be implemented at least every 6 weeks

Three questions to guide discussion on data at problem-solving team meetings:

1. What is the student's goal? Current level?

2. What decision-making rule are we using (four-point; trend; rubric)? Can we apply that now?

3. If a change needs to be made, what do we do?

FIRST, to make a decision on movement/nonmovement between tiers, the following rubric should be applied:

Student should move to a more intensive tier.	**Student should stay in a tier, and an instructional change should be made.**	**Student should stay in a tier with no changes.**	**Student should be moved to a less intensive tier.**
Trend of data or last four consecutive data points are below the goal line for the past 6 weeks, and when the student was checked 6 weeks prior.	Trend of data or last four consecutive data points are below the goal line for the past 6 weeks.	Trend of data or last four consecutive data points are even with the goal line.	Trend of data or last four consecutive data points are above the goal line.
Classroom work samples and assessment data indicate that the student is not making progress in the current curriculum, even after a change has been made.	Classroom work samples and assessment data indicate that the student is making progress, but not at the expected rate.	Classroom work samples and assessment data indicate that the student is making adequate or expected progress.	Classroom work samples and assessment data indicate that the student is making excellent progress and it does not appear that the intervention may be needed.
Inappropriate classroom behaviors are escalating due to frustration with academic performance.	Frustration is evident, although this has not yet manifested in inappropriate classroom behaviors.	Classroom behavior and frustration with academic assignments is status quo or has improved.	Classroom behavior has improved, and frustration is less evident.
Other (i.e. attendance)? Needs to be quantifiable data.	Other (i.e. attendance)? Needs to be quantifiable data.	Other (i.e. attendance)? Needs to be quantifiable data.	Other (i.e. attendance)? Needs to be quantifiable data.

SECOND, if a change needs to be made, the team questions:

1. Has the instruction/intervention been as **intense** as it could be?

    a. Teacher/student ratio, curriculum used, time engaged

2. Has the instruction/intervention been delivered with **fidelity**?

    a. Implementation reports are provided by the teacher, or someone has observed implementation.

3. Is the instruction/intervention **research-based**?

    a. References are provided, or someone has checked on this.

4. Has the **duration** of the instruction been lengthy enough?

    a. Does the team feel that lack of results is due to not having the intervention in place long enough?

Note: This rubric uses suggested decision-making rules as described in presentations conducted and materials developed by the National Center on Student Progress Monitoring (studentprogress.org), with Lynn and Doug Fuchs as the primary authors.

from assessments like running records and teacher-made checklists in her classroom to help determine intervention refinement or selection. Mrs. Adams documents changes on the students' graphs and continues to collect, graph, and examine progress-monitoring data to assess the effects of these changes. When students reach their goals, she sets aside time for a celebration.

Summary

Progress monitoring using CBM is a research-based technique that helps teachers to determine how students are performing compared to national norms or compared to past student performance. Graphed data present a picture of student progress over time and provide teachers with information about whether instruction or intervention is effective for students. Progress monitoring can be conducted in academic areas such as reading and mathematics, and the technical adequacy of measures in both areas has been documented. Measures are available for early elementary, upper elementary, and secondary students, with the largest body of research conducted with elementary students. Progress-monitoring systems have been studied with students who are average achieving or at risk, as well as students who have IEPs.

Teachers who use progress-monitoring systems determine which students in the school are at risk for academic problems through a screening process and then schedule a progress-monitoring routine for those students. The teacher sets a goal for each student and then monitors each student's progress on a frequent basis, graphing and visually examining the data. At least every 6 weeks, the teacher should meet with a grade-level or PS team to share the student's graph and make decisions about future instruction using decision-making rules. Finally, the progress-monitoring regimen should continue as long as the student continues to be deemed at risk. The teacher should continue to examine the graph showing the student's progress on a frequent basis to determine whether instruction needs to be altered or whether it is meeting the student's academic needs.

A weakness of progress monitoring is that sometimes data are misused to target specific instructional areas, rather than to serve as an indicator of overall proficiency in a subject. This might occur, for instance, if a teacher uses ORF to assess student performance solely in oral reading fluency rather than as an indicator of general reading performance. A better course of action would be to assess the student's particular areas of need by conducting follow-up diagnostic assessments when data indicate that a student is not performing well. Another concern arises when teachers use progress-monitoring measures that do not have technical adequacy, including creating their own measures that have unknown technical adequacy. This can result in data that may not be indicative of a student's actual performance or progress. An excellent and easily accessible resource for both screening and progress-monitoring tools are the tools charts available at the National Center for RTI Web site, www.rti4success.org. A technical review committee comprising experts in the field has reviewed CBM screening and progress-monitoring tools and posts results based on the level of evidence available (not convincing to convincing). Finally, a weakness in the progress-monitoring system can result if teachers simply collect data but do not use those data to make instructional decisions. Teachers should engage in ongoing collaboration with their colleagues—either the grade-level or PS team, or both—to appraise progress and apply decision-making rules.

Future research should continue to focus on progress-monitoring measures at the secondary level, including development of measures in all academic areas for high school students, as well as consideration of measures for the content areas. Some work has been completed at the secondary level (for mathematics, see Foegen, 2008, and Foegen, Olson, & Impecoven-Lind, 2008; for writing and reading, see Espin et al., 2008, and Espin, Wallace, Lembke, Campbell, & Long, 2010), but more remains to be done to determine how CBM progress monitoring can be implemented with secondary students. Additional research should also examine measures in other areas outside of reading and mathematics, such as written expression measures for early elementary students, group-administered measures in reading such as maze, and content area measures such as vocabulary matching. More information can be found on current and emerging work in CBM on the Research Institute for Progress Monitoring Web site www.progressmonitoring.org. Continued work needs to focus on teacher supports for implementing progress monitoring, including how to encourage teachers to attend to data and to implement decision-making rules based on data.

Progress monitoring is an important, research-based strategy for teachers that allows them to make more objective, data-based decisions about academic instruction. It is a critical element in an RtI framework and can help both general and special education teachers to more effectively meet the needs of their students. To maximize instruction for students at risk, it is critical that data be examined on a frequent basis so that interventions can be initiated, continued, or changed appropriately. More than 30 years of research suggest that use of CBM data will lead to improved student outcomes.

CHAPTER 19

Best Practices in Assessment for Eligibility Identification

Berttram Chiang | *University of Wisconsin Oshkosh*

Suzanne L. Russ | *Dickinson State University*

Stacey N. Skoning | *University of Wisconsin Oshkosh*

ince its inception in 1975, the Individuals with Disabilities Education Act (IDEA) has specified the types of disabilities that qualify for services, identified the procedures that must be followed to determine eligibility, and required a comprehensive assessment of the referred student to determine whether the child has a disability requiring special education. This seemingly simple process is formidable, however, due to the nuances of the educational system and the complexities of the children who participate in it. Differences in state eligibility criteria relating to the federal definitions and disparate court decisions further complicate the issue. Recent large-scale efforts to increase educational accountability and employ research-based interventions for all students make it more essential to improve the reliability and validity of the special education eligibility determination process. Current practices necessitate broadening the scope of eligibility assessment to include not only disability identification but also a larger prevention and assessment-informed instructional framework.

This chapter explores current eligibility determination processes by clarifying the use of assessment for determining eligibility, extending understanding of the issues underlying the process, and identifying examples of best practices supported by empirical evidence. Three sections serve to meet these purposes: (a) an introductory overview of the historical, legal, and ethical contexts of special education assessment for the purpose of eligibility determination; (b) an overview of the eligibility determination procedures, tools, and individual roles; and (c) a review of empirically supported best practices in eligibility determination for high-incidence disabilities. The chapter concludes with a summary of recommendations for future research and practices.

Historical, Legal, and Ethical Context of Eligibility Determination

The roots of special education eligibility determination can be traced to the Social Security Act of 1956, which stipulated that individuals entitled to services were those "who cannot do work that [they] did before and . . . cannot adjust to other work because of [their] medical condition" (Holdnack & Weiss, 2006, p. 872). This two-part test, examining both the presence of a disorder and its consequential impediment to functionality, became a fundamental tenet for special education eligibility determination. In both the Social Security Act and the later legislation guaranteeing special education services, neither the presence of a disability nor the inability to function in and of itself entitles an individual to benefits; rather, a causal linkage between a documented disability and functional impairment must be established (K. May, 2009). The two-step approach remains the basis for eligibility determination in special education, despite notable differences in the function and objectives of each law.

This two-pronged approach embodied in IDEA has been preserved throughout the reauthorizations since 1975. The most substantive eligibility determination changes before 2004 included (a) the 1986 reauthorization that extended services to preschoolers with disabilities (Part B) and established new discretionary programs for infants, toddlers, and their families (Part C); (b) the 1990 reauthorization's recognition of Autism and Traumatic Brain Injury as separate disability categories, along with the authorization of states to use significant developmental delay as an additional disability category for children ages 3 through 5; and (c) the 1997 expansion of this category to ages 3 through 9. Additionally, the 1997 reauthorization required greater efforts to ensure that children from culturally and linguistically diverse backgrounds were assessed and identified accurately and appropriately. Without necessitating a major paradigm shift, each of these reauthorizations served to influence the general patterns of referrals and the manner in which eligibility determination procedures were implemented.

Unlike previous reauthorizations, however, IDEA 2004 generated a major shift in the eligibility determination paradigm by stipulating that schools may use a Response-to-Intervention (RtI) framework as part of the eligibility determination process for identification of a learning disability. This framework, which typically involves a three-tiered process "that determines if the child responds to scientific, research-based intervention" (PL 108-446, Sec. 614[b][6][B]), includes funding for interventions to children who are at risk but have not yet been placed in special education. This is a marked departure from all prior legislation, in which funding was designated exclusively for the identification and provision of services for children with disabilities.

The implementation of IDEA has presented legal challenges about a range of issues related to eligibility determination due to the relative imprecision of disability definitions and differences in state interpretation of the federal guidelines. Determining the presence of a disability is sometimes a relatively straightforward process requiring little more than a medical diagnosis. Such cases are often diagnosed at or before birth, and the children have noticeable behavioral or physical characteristics. In the high-incidence areas of specific learning disabilities (LD), emotional disturbance (ED), and mental retardation[1] (MR), however, this process is fraught with challenges that occasionally lead to legal conflicts between districts and parents. Each of these disability categories can be difficult to diagnose, because they are bounded by nebulous and subjective parameters that vary across states. Legal issues relating to eligibility decisions tend to revolve around the question of whether the condition is within the child or caused by the environment in which the child was raised or educated. Faced with the ambiguous and implicit language of IDEA, the evaluation team must strive to meet ethical standards while exercising its collective professional judgment to apply local norms and reflect "the perception of the school building personnel in terms of the students at the site most in need of, and likely to benefit from, the services available at that site" (MacMillan & Siperstein, 2002, p. 287). The ethical issues considered herein rest in the following areas: (a) early intervention versus delayed classification, (b) meeting educational needs versus necessity to control costs, and (c) the long-term cost of excluding versus the short-term costs of including children who fall on the borderline of a disability category.

Although applicable to all disability areas, early intervention for LD has proven to be particularly controversial. Before the 2004 IDEA reauthorization, common use of the IQ-achievement discrepancy for eligibility decisions delayed treatment by requiring that academic performance be significantly lower than the student's potential ability indicated by intelligence test scores. Thus, young children with LD may not have met the criteria because of a floor effect: the commonly expected academic skills at that level are simply too low to produce a significant discrepancy from IQ. Because more-advanced academic skills are not developed until the upper grades, the children with a disability must lag further and further behind their peers before receiving the necessary special education support. When the discrepancy is finally shown, often not until the upper elementary grades, the optimal period for efficacious support has passed and the child has lost valuable time for special education assistance (Jenkins, Graff, & Miglioretti, 2009).

Many of the eligibility decisions made by states, districts, and individual evaluation teams seek to balance meeting the needs of exceptional students with conserving costs to the district. To do so, they wrestle with a range of potentially competing interests, including federal legislation, state guidelines, district initiatives, and the will and wishes of the parents and teachers. While IDEA defines disability areas in general terms, states

---

[1]Because this chapter focuses on eligibility, we use the term *mental retardation*, as used in legal phrasing, instead of the preferred term of *intellectual disability*.

are given latitude to further expand on and clarify the federal guidelines. Because guidance from the federal government is minimal and clarification by the states is inconsistent, some evaluation teams find themselves at the heart of an ethical dilemma in which they are forced either to "err on the side of missing students who actually should receive services (minimize false negatives) or on the side of making sure students who do not require services do not get them (minimize false positives)" (Lloyd, 2002, p. 431).

IDEA definitions for LD and ED include specific exclusionary clauses. Students cannot be identified as having LD if it is "primarily the result of visual, hearing, or motor disabilities, of mental retardation, of emotional disturbance, or of environmental, cultural, or economic disadvantage" (PL 108-446, Sec. 602[30][C]). In addition, IDEA clearly excludes LD eligibility determination if the determining factor is "lack of appropriate instruction in reading, math, or limited English proficiency (PL 108-446, Sec. 614(b)[5][A], [B], [C]). Students whose conduct problems stem from social maladjustment cannot qualify for ED services "unless it is determined that they have an emotional disturbance" (34 CFR § 300.8(c)(4)(ii)). These exclusions seem sensible: IDEA is designed to serve children whose impairments originate from disabilities, while other programs such as Title I and English as a Second Language (ESL) are generally in place to assist with challenges originating from factors or etiologies not related to disabilities (e.g., lack of appropriate instruction, limited English proficiency). Nevertheless, children who are denied special education services because of the absence of clear etiology may pay a long-term price, because their needs may remain unmet. Therefore, it remains debatable whether such exclusions contribute to the formation of socially unjust educational systems (Artiles, 2003) or to infringement of the five broad ethical standards for psychoeducational assessment: multifaceted, comprehensive, fair, useful, and valid (Jacob & Hartshorne, 2007).

Assessment Procedures for Eligibility Determination

Assessment Tools and Data Sources

The procedure for determining whether a child is eligible for special education includes three key steps: (a) referral—the school district, parents, or the state make a written request for evaluation and obtain parental consent; (b) evaluation—school professionals evaluate the student to determine whether a qualifying disability is present; and (c) eligibility—school professionals and parents meet to determine whether the child is eligible for special education. To make such decisions

judiciously, a comprehensive assessment may include data related to a child's "health, vision, hearing, social and emotional status, general intelligence, academic performance, communicative status, and motor abilities" (34 CFR § 300.304(c)(4)).

With the exception of severe and sensory disability identification, which is usually diagnosed by medical professionals, evaluation teams tend to use a routine battery of individually administered standardized tests as primary assessment tools supplemented by classroom observations and input from parents and teachers. Specific tools and strategies should be selected and weighed in relation to the suspected disability and the child's developmental, linguistic, and cultural background. For example, the Battelle Developmental Inventory (BDI-2; Newborg, 2005) or Developmental Indicators for the Assessment of Learning (DIAL-R; Mardell & Goldenberg, 1998) provides more useful information for assessing a preschool child with potential developmental delays, while rating scales such as the Behavior Assessment System for Children (BASC-2; C. R. Reynolds & Kamphaus, 1992) and Child Behavior Checklist (CBCL; Achenbach, 1991) give more relevant information about the presence or absence of characteristics of conduct problems or hyperactivity for a child suspected of ED. The Wechsler Intelligence Scale for Children (WISC-IV; Wechsler, 2004) and Vineland Adaptive Behavior Scales II (Sparrow, Cicchetti, & Balla, 2005) are more likely to be used for assessing intellectual functioning and adaptive behaviors if a child is referred for possible MR, but a nonverbal intelligence test such as the Naglieri Nonverbal Cognitive Test (Naglieri, 1997) can yield more valid information about the cognitive abilities of a child with cultural or language differences. Likewise, systematic observation and parent interviews can be important strategies to assess a child with autism, while collecting repeated curriculum-based probes or administering standardized tests such as the Woodcock-Johnson III Tests of Achievement (WJ III; Woodcock, McGrew, & Mather, 2001) or the Wechsler Individual Achievement Test (WIAT-II; Psychological Corporation, 2002) makes more sense for assessing a child considered for LD.

Roles of Individuals in Eligibility Determination

IDEA requires evaluation to be conducted "by a team of qualified professionals and the parent of the child" (PL 108-446, Sec. 614(b)4(A)). A number of professionals such as the school psychologist, speech and language therapist, audiologist, school nurse, social worker, guidance counselor, occupational therapist, or physical therapist may participate, based on the expertise that is needed. The varied composition of the evaluation team helps to ensure an accurate and comprehensive evaluation of the child and reduce the impact of bias on both the process and decisions.

The respective roles assumed by members of the evaluation team differ on a case-by-case basis. However, three members of this team often play distinctly vital roles that have changed with the IDEA 2004 reauthorization: school psychologists, general education teachers, and parents. Historically, school psychologists spent two thirds of their time in special education eligibility determination and administered over 100 individual intelligence tests annually (Reschly & Wilson, 1995). Because of their expertise in cognitive assessment and behavioral consultation, school psychologists have long played a critical role in the evaluation and special education eligibility determination process. According to a survey of 177 school psychologists by Huebner and Gould (1991), 39% of them served as case managers in their schools. A separate survey of 124 school psychologists in Wisconsin revealed that on average they spent 30% of their working hours conducting assessment, 16% writing reports, and 17% participating in individualized education program (IEP) team meetings (Chiang, Rylance, Bongers, & Russ, 1998). Similarly, in eligibility meetings for students with emotional and behavioral disorders, teachers see school psychologists as playing a dominant role in making final decisions (K. F. Martin, Lloyd, Kauffman, & Coyne, 1995).

With the emergence of RtI as a problem-solving model leading to potential special education identification, however, the roles of school psychologists have shifted. The RtI framework demands that school teams ensure empirically driven best practices in the general education setting (Tier 1) before implementing gradually more individualized interventions in Tiers 2 and 3. Thus, school psychologists no longer serve primarily as psychometricians who interpret test scores in a referral-evaluation-eligibility framework. Instead, they assume a more collaborative role as instructional consultants in selecting technically sound tools, interpreting widely varying data, deriving criteria to identify those not responding to the instruction, and identifying effective interventions (M. R. Shinn & McConnell, 1994). In addition to their emerging roles related to instructional consulting, school psychologists also "are well positioned in the schools to advocate, and in some contexts provide leadership for, a proactive and preventive approach to social behavior problems in schools" (Malecki & Demaray, 2007, pp. 161–162). This trend materialized rather dramatically in the Minneapolis Public School District, which reported that school psychologists decreased the proportion of their time spent testing from 58% to 35% after schools switched to a problem-solving model to identify LD and mild mental retardation (MMR) (Marston, Muyskens, Lau, & Canter, 2003). The role of general education teachers, always important because they

are often the first to observe a potential problem, has also shifted somewhat in response to the IDEA 2004 reauthorization. Before the IDEA reauthorization, general educators assumed minimal responsibility in the evaluation process after initiating a referral, being required only to attend the IEP meeting with evidence of the child's present level of performance. Within the RtI framework, general education teachers assumed a much more integrated role. In addition to initiating referrals and describing the child's current level of performance in the general education setting, these teachers are expected to implement research-validated curricular interventions accurately, to monitor student progress by gathering a variety of systematic data, and to collaborate with other building staff to ensure the child's needs are met. Although this integrated role remains predominant in referrals for potential LD, such a shift may begin to influence the role of general educators in other disability areas as well.

Finally, the role of parents in the assessment and eligibility determination process is enhanced still further following the IDEA 2004 reauthorization. Expanding from a time when parent roles were often limited and inconsequential, the reauthorized IDEA continues efforts to make parents genuinely equal partners in the evaluation process. By more actively providing the evaluation team with critical information about family background and the developmental and social history of the child, parents now are often viewed as critical contributors in helping evaluation teams understand the child's performance in terms of general family background and culturally or linguistically relevant differences.

Best Practices in Eligibility Determination for High-Incidence Disabilities

As described earlier, a marked disparity exists in the technical adequacy of special education eligibility determination for the categories of ED, LD, and MR and the medically identifiable categories (e.g., orthopedic impairment, traumatic brain injury, visual impairment, hearing impairment, and severe MR). For high-incidence special education disability areas, however, students' chances of being identified with a disability vary according to the state in which they reside, their minority or linguistic status, the makeup of the evaluation team, the persistence of their parents, and the relative tolerance of the general education teacher.

Emotional Disturbance

Eligibility decisions for students with ED have consistently faced two formidable obstacles: (a) underidentification of children who may benefit from special services (H. M. Walker, Nishioka, Zeller, Severson, & Feil, 2000) and (b) disproportionate representation of children with cultural and linguistic diversity (Harris-Murri, King, & Rostenberg, 2006; Landrum, 2000).

Underidentification

For many reasons, the identification of students with ED typically occurs much later than other disabilities. According to the most current available data from the Office of Special Education (2009) 28th Annual Report to Congress, the number of students identified with ED increased incrementally as the student ages—from 7,109 students identified by age 6 years to a peak of more than eight times that number for 15-year-old students (57,267). Further, students with ED waited an average of 2 years for special education services following onset of difficulties, compared with less than 1 year for other disabilities (M. Wagner, Kutash, Duchnowski, Epstein, & Sumi, 2005). Because behaviors that are sufficiently problematic to necessitate ED identification in ninth or tenth grade are not likely to have emerged with no prior evidence, it is likely that inadequate attention in earlier grades allowed the behaviors to intensify and become intolerable during adolescence. By delaying interventions, therefore, the most promising years for effective services were lost.

Several factors contribute to the tendency to delay intervention. Landrum (2000) attributed the underidentification phenomenon to parents' reluctance to have their child assigned this stigmatizing and pejorative label of ED and to schools' concerns about funding for relatively costly ED programs. Many school administrators are also reluctant to classify students as ED because of the "constraints it imposes on their ability to discipline students experiencing school-related behavior problems" (H. M. Walker et al., 2000, p. 32). Additionally, confusion surrounding the social maladjustment exclusion and the absence of assessment tools that can distinguish ED from social maladjustment further contribute to the tendency toward underidentification (Gresham, 2005).

Disproportionate Representation

Although IDEA reauthorizations placed increased emphasis on culturally appropriate identification procedures, their effect has been only minimally observed in the category of ED. National data of children with ED, in which more than 2,000 carefully sampled parents of elementary- and secondary-aged children were surveyed or interviewed, confirmed the continued existence of significant differences in prevalence rates by gender (males overrepresented), socioeconomic status

(SES; more risk factors associated with low SES), and race (African Americans are overrepresented, while Hispanic students are underrepresented) (M. Wagner et al., 2005). Both system-based (Harry, Klingner, Sturges, & Moore, 2002) and intergroup differences (J. L. Hosp & Hosp, 2001) have been cited to explain this disparity. For example, teachers in low SES schools and schools with high proportions of African American students may have different classroom management styles and competencies, resulting in increased identification rates in the ED category. It is also possible that the interaction styles of males, students from low SES backgrounds, and African Americans may result in higher levels of ED identification because they are misaligned with the interaction styles of teachers, who are often middle class females. Further, while both poverty and race influence prevalence rates in ED, the interaction between the two remains minimal; problems of racial overrepresentation tend to exist more strongly in affluent than in poor schools (Skiba, Poloni-Staudinger, Gallini, Simmons, & Feggins-Azziz, 2006).

Best Practices in Identification of ED

One process appears to hold the greatest empirical support in identifying students with ED. This multiple gating procedure, known as Systematic Screening for Behavioral Disorders (SSBD), has substantial evidence supporting its efficacy. Further, SSBD has been endorsed by a panel of Stanford Research Institute researchers and project managers in the Office of Special Education Programs as the optimal practice in terms of its standardization, normative characteristics, cost-effectiveness, and successful implementation (Severson, Walker, Hope-Doolittle, Kratochwill, & Gresham, 2007).

Addressing the problem of delayed identification of students with ED, H. M. Walker, Severson, and Haring (1985) developed SSBD, which relied on general educators to systematically screen all students for potential ED. SSBD involves three stages, or "gates," through which students must pass in order to be evaluated for ED. In Gate 1, general education teachers rank all students in their class from most to least severe with respect to a list of internalizing (e.g., anxiety, depression) and externalizing (e.g., disruptive, violent behaviors) characteristics. The few students whose characteristics are most severe on either dimension pass to Gate 2, in which teachers complete more detailed measures, such as the Critical Life Events checklist and the Combined Frequency Index for adaptive and maladaptive behaviors, for each of the smaller group of students. The scores on these measures are compared with normative standards, and those whose scores are significantly below the norm pass on to Gate 3. In Gate 3, an outside professional observes and rates the students in natural settings. If both the teacher ratings and the observations are suggestive of a disability, then the child may be referred for special education.

Substantial evidence supports the validity of SSBD. H. M. Walker and colleagues (1988) conducted extensive testing of the procedure and tools during the development process. Their initial field tests involved 18 teachers and 454 elementary school children in Oregon, and they conducted subsequent replications using 58 teachers and 1,468 first- through fifth-grade children in Utah (Walker, Severson, Nicholson, et al., 1994). Both the initial testing and replication used two randomly selected students in each classroom to serve as controls during Gates 2 and 3, and students currently identified with ED served as comparison measures when evaluating the efficiency of the process. Their findings revealed that (a) both internalizers (i.e., those who experience symptoms related to anxiety or depression) and externalizers (i.e., those who experience symptoms such as disruptive or violent behaviors) scored significantly higher than controls on the Gate-2 checklists; (b) observational data confirmed the tendency toward internalizing or externalizing responses; (c) the method effectively discriminated among internalizers, externalizers, and non-referred students; and (d) both time and costs were significantly lower for the SSBD procedure than for the traditional process in which students were referred and evaluated based on teacher perceptions.

Use of a systematic screening procedure was also effective for identifying kindergarten students most at risk for later behavioral problems. One well-designed study randomly placed 48 targeted kindergarteners into either a wait-list or a treatment group exposed to the SSBD procedure before receiving comprehensive interventions (H. M. Walker, Severson, Feil, Stiller, & Golly, 1998). The group exposed to the SSBD procedures experienced significantly greater behavioral improvement than the control group. In a second longitudinal study using at-risk kindergarten students from Montreal, Canada, Charlebois and Leblanc (1994) employed slightly different measures within a two-gate screening system to determine whether a process employed in early childhood could predict later behavior problems. During Gate 1, all students ($n = 84$) scoring above the 70th percentile on the aggressiveness-hyperactivity-distractibility subscale of the Teachers' Preschool Behavior Questionnaire (Behar & Stringfield, 1974) were identified for further assessment. The more detailed assessment in Gate 2 involved both observations for task-inappropriate behaviors in the classroom and at home and mother and teacher ratings using the CBCL. Based on these children's scores on a Self-Reported Delinquency Questionnaire 5 years later, the predictive efficacy of SSBD procedures for later problems with delinquency and maladaptive behaviors was confirmed.

The efficacy of SSBD with older students was supported by Caldarella, Young, Richardson, Young, and Young (2008) in their study with more than 2,100 students attending middle/junior high schools in Utah. In comparison to school-wide averages, students identified as at risk for ED based on the first two gating procedures of the SSBD tended to be suspended more often and have lower grade-point averages. However, some of the identified students actually were suspended less than average or had higher than average grade-point averages. The potentially false-positive identifications may be attributed to (a) the decreased likelihood that students with internalizing disorders present behaviors necessitating suspensions or (b) the absence of Gate-3 procedures in this study, which have been shown to more accurately pinpoint those with ED (Loeber, Dishion, & Patterson, 1984).

H. M. Walker, Severson, and Feil (1995) modified the SSBD items and formats for preschool children and called this downward adaptation the Early Screening Project (ESP). The ESP involves a three-stage process to screen for behavior disorders among preschool children. Teacher ranking constituted the Stage-One screening, teacher rating with normative criteria made up the Stage-Two process, and behavioral observation and parent rating were used as Stage-Three procedures. Feil and Severson (1995) effectively employed a three-stage gating procedure with 3- to 5-year-old children and found that assessment time was reduced up to 16% over other procedures. The ESP was also found to yield no significant racial differences in ED referrals among Oregon's 40 classes of 954 Head Start participants of different ethnic groups (Feil, Walker, Severson, & Ball, 2000), producing a preliminary suggestion that systematic screenings may in fact reduce disproportionality. However, because children attending Head Start come from predominantly lower-socioeconomic classes but racial disproportionality tends to be greater in affluent districts, the impact of ESP on disproportionality requires substantial additional verification.

In summary, determination of an emotional disturbance has been fraught with challenges, resulting in underidentification of children with ED in general, and disproportionate overrepresentation of particular groups (i.e., males, those with low SES, and particular racial or ethnic groups). A more systematic method of identifying and evaluating both internalizing and externalizing behaviors across all children is needed to minimize these outcomes. A multiple-gating approach, as described in this section, may be one way to accomplish this goal.

Mental Retardation

Fewer contentious issues exist in identification of students with MR than the identification of students with

ED or LD, though the criteria are not entirely problem free. Challenges pertain to each aspect of the MR criteria, described by Bergeron, Floyd, and Shands (2008) as "deficits in intellectual functioning, impaired functioning in the daily environment, and onset during the developmental period" (p. 123). Most of the criticisms rest not with the identification of more severe disabilities but rather relate to the larger population of children who would be considered to have MMR. The difficulty with MMR identification is attributed to the fact that characteristics of children with MMR are relatively subtle and often overlap with those children with other disabilities (e.g., LD, attention deficit hyperactivity disorder [ADHD], autism) and those with no disabilities.

Deficits in intellectual functioning are typically assessed through an individually administered intelligence test such as the WISC-IV. Criticisms of the use of IQ tend to relate to (a) the relative importance placed on IQ at the expense of other potentially relevant information (Greenspan, 2006), (b) the absence of agreement on whether subscale rather than full-scale IQ may serve as a more valid measure of intellectual functioning (Bergeron et al., 2008), (c) the use of inconsistent IQ cutoff points that do not consider statistical error of measurement (Scullin, 2006), and (d) the tendency for children from some minority groups to score more poorly and thus be overidentified with MR (Skiba et al., 2006).

Several tools are available to assess deficits in adaptive behaviors, including the Vineland Adaptive Behavior Scales, the AAMR Adaptive Behavior Scale (Lambert, Nihira, & Leland, 1993), the Adaptive Behavior Assessment System—Second Edition (ABAS-II; Harrison & Oakland, 2003), Scales of Independent Behavior—Revised (Bruininks, Woodcock, Weatherman, & Hill, 1996), and the Battelle Development Inventory (BDI-2; Newborg, 2005). General criticisms of such measures include the following: (a) inconsistencies exist across states in terms of which dimensions of adaptive behavior (social, practical, or cognitive) should indicate an impairment (Bergeron et al., 2008; Greenspan, 2006), (b) subtle adaptive behaviors such as gullibility are neglected despite the fact that they create great challenges for those with MMR (Greenspan, 2006), and (c) adaptive behavior measures tend to retain secondary importance relative to IQ scores (Heflinger, Cook, & Thackrey, 1987). IDEA also mandates that deficits in both IQ and adaptive behaviors must be "manifested during the developmental period" (34 CFR § 300.8(c)(6)). This ambiguous age-of-onset definition is complicated by the fact that children with MMR are often misidentified initially as children with LD, ADHD, or other impairments and thus fail to meet the early-onset requirement.

Best Practices in Identification of MR

The framework and tools with which children with MR are identified has varied little in past decades. The relative constancy of MR eligibility determination is somewhat surprising, given that recent IDEA legislation has sought to remedy the overrepresentation of African American students in this category (Allen-Meares, 2008). Given the paucity of best practice assessment models in the literature, the following should be incorporated in MR identification practices:

1. *Balance IQ with adaptive measures:* Because of the challenges addressed with IQ tests, evaluation teams should ensure that both IQ and adaptive measures are considered appropriately. A child who achieves a lower score on an intelligence test but higher adaptive behavior scores should not be more likely to be identified with MR than one who achieves lower adaptive behavior scores but a higher IQ score.

2. *Attend to cultural differences in both IQ and adaptive measures:* Adaptations from standardized procedures "may include removing time restraints, incorporating nonverbal formats, and replacing single procedure and single score instruments with those that are more diverse" (Allen-Meares, 2008, p. 314). For example, a tester can employ language that allows for alternate phrasing or slang terminology or can supplement traditional assessment methods with multidimensional tools such as the Brief Impairment Scale (BIS; Bird et al., 2005). Despite promising efforts a few decades ago, however, little promise has been made in the development of a finely tuned multicultural tool (Allen-Meares, 2008).

3. *Clarify the required domains of adaptive behavior deficits for eligibility criteria:* Because adaptive behavior is typically assessed in terms of social, practical, and conceptual skills, evaluation teams must specify the areas in which a child being assessed for eligibility shows deficits before they identify the child with MR.

4. *Use revised standardized intelligence tests with recent norms in order to avoid the Flynn effect, or systematic increases in IQ scores as norms age (Reschly & Grimes, 2002; Tylenda, Beckett, & Barrett, 2007):* The Flynn effect, in which scores tend to raise by about 3 points per decade due to factors such as better nutrition and increased familiarity with test mechanisms, can lead to inaccurate conclusions if outdated norms are employed.

Specific Learning Disabilities

Since the early 1990s, the dominant method for identifying LD involved a significant discrepancy between intellectual ability as measured by IQ tests and achievement as measured through standardized tests. In 2002, two years before the most recent IDEA reauthorization, 48 of the 50 states relied on significant discrepancy as the primary method of determining eligibility for LD (Reschly & Hosp, 2004). A major shift occurred with the IDEA 2004 reauthorization: states were required to allow other methods for eligibility determination, including an RtI framework. Despite the mandate, however, most states simply added language to their original legislation giving school districts the choice of using significant discrepancy or RtI (Ahearn, 2009). The following paragraphs will examine issues related to the discrepancy approach, issues related to the newly emerging RtI framework, and best practices in LD assessment.

Issues with the Discrepancy Approach

The discrepancy model has received abundant criticism (Donovan & Cross, 2002; Speece, 2002) in recent years. Problems exist in three primary areas: (a) inaccurate or overidentification of students with LD, (b) delayed identification of LD, and (c) low predictive validity.

The first of these challenges, inaccurate or overidentification of students with LD, rests in the overreliance on test scores to determine eligibility at the expense of other potentially important factors. By applying formulas "in a mechanistic, narrow fashion" (Mather & Kaufman, 2006, p. 747), information about attempted interventions, duration of the problem, or the strength of the general education program may be overlooked. Consequently, we may identify children with LD who are disabled by their environment or circumstances (e.g., insufficient support or accommodation) rather than by a true deficit. Because the formulaic nature of the discrepancy model provides a spurious sense of objectivity, it diverts attention from the conditions and potential solutions that could alleviate or prevent the problem.

The second challenge, delayed identification or "wait-to-fail," results from the dubious requirement of obtaining a significant discrepancy between IQ and performance until the child has demonstrated substantial and enduring failure. Because academic learning for younger children is relatively undeveloped, the range of potential achievement is limited. This limited range of achievement, in turn, may mask the seriousness of a performance deficit faced by a child with a potential learning disability. Until the rest of the children have advanced substantially in their learning, the child struggling with LD will simply not be far enough behind to produce a significant discrepancy. Thus, young children with LD will miss out on services during their most formative years, therefore facing mounting failure and frustration while awaiting the actualization of a significant discrepancy.

Finally, the traditional formula has low predictive validity, or accuracy in predicting which students have LD. According to a meta-analysis by Stuebing and colleagues (2002), few differences exist in early indicators of learning problems between struggling readers who are IQ discrepant (IQ and achievement are significantly different) and those who are IQ consistent (IQ and achievement do not differ). If the significant discrepancy formula cannot tease out such differences in young readers, it loses validity as a predictive tool and becomes another factor contributing to unnecessary delay of services.

Issues with the RtI Framework

The inadequacies of the significant discrepancy framework led to the IDEA 2004 mandate that states could no longer require its use in identifying students with LD. RtI has been described most aptly as "a model supported by converging sources of evidence . . . [that] will move the field from an exclusive reliance on eligibility determination into intervention-based practices in the schools for struggling learners" (Gresham, 2007, p. 21). Despite its proven and potential benefits in establishing a closer link between LD identification and treatment, reducing the special education referrals (Ikeda & Gustafson, 2002), and overrepresentation of African American students placed in special education (Marston et al., 2003), the use of RtI to determine eligibility for LD has engendered a number of concerns: (a) timing within the IDEA mandates, (b) paucity of relevant research, (c) ineptitude with decisions regarding students who change schools, and (d) inconsistencies across states.

Timing of special education referrals is clearly stipulated in IDEA: Evaluation must be conducted within 60 days of parental consent. RtI, however, can be a lengthy process that does not fit neatly into such a timeline: Interventions must be planned, implemented, monitored, and modified within each tier of RtI—clearly, a process that could easily exceed the 60-day limit. The issue is further complicated by ambiguity around the beginning and end points of the referral process. Previously, the due process requirements began when the special education referral was initiated. Under RtI, due process requirements may be activated when the concern is first voiced or may be deferred until the student is found nonresponsive to Tier-2 or Tier-3 interventions. This uncertainty, along with a lack of clarity of what might occur if parents act on their right to request a comprehensive evaluation for special education eligibility at any time during the RtI process, suggests that legal clarification will be needed.

Questions persist about the adequacy and appropriateness of using RtI as a diagnostic tool to identify LD based on the limited research in support of such practices (Kavale, Kauffman, Bachmeier, & LeFever, 2008). Current assessment tools for the implementation of RtI are largely limited to the curriculum areas of basic reading and mathematics skills for elementary school students. Because research is scanty and long-term research nonexistent, we risk once again plunging into a new initiative with no sound empirical basis on which to proceed.

Lastly, states and districts apply RtI models inconsistently. Just as the federal government allows states latitude in interpreting its definitions of LD and other disability areas, so is ambiguity present in the new potential uses and practices of RtI. In fact, the inconsistencies may be even greater for RtI as most states simply leave the decision to be made at the district level. Thus, inconsistent application occurs not only among states, but also within individual states or even districts.

Exacerbating the problems of inconsistent application, significant implementation challenges exist in determining eligibility for students who transfer to different schools before the completion of the process. Unlike traditional tests, which use well-publicized standard procedures, protocols, and scores, repeated measures of curriculum-based assessment may vary enormously from one school district to another and thus be nongeneralizable in the public domain. If a student transfers to a different school in the midst of one of the RtI tiers of intervention, interpretation of that student's documents regarding RtI at the transferring school can be a much more daunting task than understanding Woodcock-Johnson achievement battery or WIAT-II scores. Any efforts to continue such an interrupted RtI process at the student's new school requires arduous paperwork and documentation and can be fraught with serious problems of treatment fidelity ("the strategies that monitor and enhance the accuracy and consistency of an intervention to (a) ensure it is implemented as planned and (b) make certain each component is delivered in a comparable manner to all participants over time" [S. W. Smith, Daunic, & Taylor, 2007])—and test validity (the degree to which a test accurately measures what it was designed to measure).

In addition to the aforementioned problems, currently a morass of confusion surrounds nearly every aspect of RtI. Uncertainty exists about the nature of the basic models (Gresham, 2002b), the appropriate number of tiers (Reschly, 2005), the optimal duration of intervention for each tier, criteria to identify students who do not respond to interventions (M. K. Burns, Jacob, & Wagner, 2008; D. Fuchs & Deshler, 2007), and the nature of interventions applied in each tier. Thus, it is essential to begin the process of developing an RtI model that offers consistency across states as we move forward

with more coherent and uniform large-scale implementations (M. K. Burns, Deno, & Jimerson, 2007).

Best Practices in Identification of LD

To illustrate how RtI may address some of the LD-eligibility issues raised in this chapter, the following paragraphs review two programs that employ best practices in eligibility determination: (a) the Minneapolis Public Schools' Problem-Solving Model (PSM; Marston et al., 2003), and (b) Iowa's Heartland Educational Agency Model (Heartland; Tilly, 2003). Both of these frameworks were implemented before the 2004 IDEA reauthorization, paving the way for the broader implementation to come.

The framework employed in Minnesota was initiated through a waiver of typical special education eligibility criteria for LD and MMR. Within this framework, applications of the tiers were clearly outlined. Tier 1 involved 4 to 6 weeks of interventions in the general education classroom, Tier 2 included 6 to 8 weeks of team interventions, and Tier 3 required a comprehensive assessment for possible special education eligibility. Several worksheets were developed to assist classroom teachers in implementing the model, including separate documents for the diverse strategies employed at each tier. A notable feature of the Tier-3 worksheet is the particular attention given to the influences of culture, language, and environment—an often overlooked dimension.

To study the impact of PSM, the district conducted a program evaluation in which they analyzed factors such as identification rates and responsiveness to different plans. Results were promising: (a) identification rates for high-incidence disabilities have remained stable, around 7% between 1994 and 2001; (b) similar students were identified with both PSM and the traditional method (Marston et al., 2003); (c) the number of children referred for Tier 2 more than doubled over the 5-year period; and (d) the number of African American students referred and found eligible for special education declined markedly during the period of PSM implementation.

While the results appear quite promising, the absence of random assignment, the passage of time as additional schools were oriented to PSM, and the absence of information about how schools were selected for participation all minimize the potential claims to causality. Nevertheless, the successful implementation of PSM in a culturally and economically diverse school district provides a beacon for future implementation in similar environments.

The second best-practices model, Heartland (Iowa) has implemented RtI since 1993. Special features of the program include an Instructional Decision Making (IDM) framework for higher-frequency problems (e.g., basic reading or math proficiency concerns) in order to better integrate the problem-solving approach to serve all students. The major concept of IDM includes a core instructional program for all students, a supplemental program for students needing different or additional instruction, and an intensive program for the few students requiring additional support to succeed. Depending on the severity of the problems, different resource levels may be needed to solve low-incidence individual problems at each of the four levels, ranging from Level 1 (consultation between parents and teachers), Level 2 (combination of resources such as Building Assistance Teams), Level 3 (extended consultation team for ongoing support), and Level 4 (special education eligibility or IEP considerations). It has been reported that about 25% of teacher-identified concerns have been satisfactorily resolved at Level 2 or 3 (Ikeda & Gustafson, 2002), and in over 10 years of practice, fewer than 20 IQ or published standardized achievement tests have been administered for over 15,000 initial eligibility evaluations or reevaluations (Ikeda et al., 2007). The RtI process for identifying disability therefore clearly would minimize the need for traditional assessments and instead place more emphasis on systematic prevention efforts before formal referrals for special education.

Conclusion

Assessment for special education identification historically served the primary function of gate keeping in order to determine referred children's eligibility for special education and related services. The general definition provided by IDEA regarding which children are eligible for the disability categories of LD, ED, and MR left ample room for subjective judgment and inconsistent placement decisions. Consequently, "few areas are so thoroughly unsettled, with so few guideposts, as eligibility for special education services under the statute" (Weber, 2009, p. 83). IDEA 2004 generated a major paradigm shift in eligibility determination in order to reduce both false negatives and false positives. Additionally, the shifting philosophy and need to assess for both eligibility and instructional decision-making purposes resulted in a need for collecting and analyzing different kinds of data and a change in the roles of some of those involved in the data collection process. Systematic screening and the use of multiple gates or tiers of assessment support these new developments. However, even these methods are not without their criticisms.

Despite its promising prospect as a viable option for LD identification, infusing culture and linguistic considerations in RtI models has surfaced as one of the greatest challenges in RtI. To answer the crucial question of "what works with whom, by whom, and in what context?" (Klingner & Edwards, 2006, p. 110), educators need to give much greater attention to cultural and language considerations as an integral part of ensuring implementation fidelity. This increased attention is particularly important as educators expand RtI to more students at secondary schools, requiring the use of broader performance measures rather than assessment of specific basic skills such as word recognition or arithmetic computation fluency. Additionally, the culturally responsive use of multiple-gating procedures potentially can reduce the disproportionate minority representation in special education programs for students with ED. In particular, during the problem identification and analysis stages of a problem-solving model, the evaluation team needs to (a) "validate that a referred student was truly exhibiting a problem that merited intervention" (Witt & VanDerHeyden, 2007, p. 347) and (b) direct its attention to a student's response to intervention as well as the intervention's responsiveness to the student (Harris-Murri et al., 2006).

Directions for Future Research

The empirical evidence presented in this chapter described emerging best practices in the field of assessment for eligibility. Outlined next are future eligibility assessment research directions that can inform educational policies and practices in order to positively affect the outcomes for all students.

1. *Develop technology infrastructure:* In moving away from the IQ–achievement discrepancy model, more schools will phase in the implementation of RtI for identification of students with LD. To counter the operational challenges, researchers need to develop and test innovative technology to manage the reams of data generated. Some school districts have already tested and piloted such programs: the interactive Web-based Student Intervention Monitoring System (SIMS), created by Wisconsin's Madison Metropolitan School District (see http://dpi.wi.gov/rti/sims2.html), allows K–12 staff to maintain academic and behavior records and share information about strategies to track and support student progress while considering special education eligibility. Investigations of the effects of incorporating technology into RtI implementation, particularly designed as longitudinal studies, can shed light on the relationship between various RtI parameters (e.g., decision rules, intervention duration) and prevalence rates. Specifically, the data analysis made available through technological

consistency allows for a clearer appraisal of effective and ineffective practices. Other areas of future research that hold the promise of improving the validity and efficiency of eligibility assessment practices include (a) the correlation between RtI progress-monitoring benchmarks (e.g., level, slope, goal) and other student outcome indicators in grade-level standards on the statewide assessment and (b) the roles of professional judgments in problem-solving teams' eligibility decision making (Tilly, Reschly, & Grimes, 1999).

2. *Expand RtI applications:* To advance RtI to district-wide LD and ED identification assessment best practices, we need more controlled studies to validate its diagnostic utility in the social-emotional domain, in academic domains other than basic reading, and for students at the middle and high school levels. As suggested by Kratochwill, Clements, and Kalymon (2007), "a major research agenda in the future must focus on establishing reliability, validity, and utility for a variety of screening measures to be used in the RtI models" (p. 31). Additionally, in the area of eligibility assessment for ED, "continued research on the psychometric integrity and utility of [universal screening instruments such as] . . . SSBD across diverse populations is needed" (Glover & Albers, 2007, p. 131).

3. *Improve discriminative validity:* Another eligibility assessment area that warrants the attention of future research relates to the extent to which students on the mild end of the disability spectrum can be distinguished reliably from one another by the current categorical system and distinguished from other students whose achievement levels are below typical levels and who were found ineligible for any of the aforementioned categories. For instance, the shrinkage of students identified for MR and the simultaneous expansion of the LD category has been well documented and thoroughly analyzed in the existing literature of actual placement committee deliberations (MacMillan & Siperstein, 2002) and in the context of a changing construct of MR and overrepresentation of minority children in the MR category (Donovan & Cross, 2002). It remains an open research question whether the replacement of the IQ–achievement model by the RtI approach will in and of itself produce a more consistent classification and placement system in special education.

4. *Develop early intervention practices:* Given the fact that evaluation of students with ED often involves "reactive school practices in identification" (Donovan & Cross, 2002, p. 266), future research in this area should address the issue of early identification and intervention of emotional and behavior problems with the same rigor and sense of urgency as it did with the "wait-to-fail" model for LD identification. For instance, Nishioka (2001) found that students were often identified with ED 5 or more years after teachers initially documented the presence of behavior problems. The growing number of schools that are embedding positive behavior support within the context of a problem-solving model offer a fertile ground for researchers to identify tools and strategies to provide multi-tiers of proactive interventions for potentially disruptive behavior problems.

A great deal of progress has been made in the practices of special education eligibility assessment since the IDEA reauthorizations in 1997 and 2004. This chapter highlighted the tremendous strides made in the first decade of the 2000s, with school professionals moving away from answering the proverbial question of "to be or not to be" by placing a proper emphasis on preventing students from falling through the cracks of the imperfect classification system. By employing more empirically based decision making regarding eligibility and properly framing the prevention and intervention efforts within the context of general education reform, educators provide reason for great optimism in the future of more effective assessment and services for all students.

CHAPTER 20

Parent Participation in Assessment and in Development of Individualized Education Programs

Katharine G. Shepherd and **Michael F. Giangreco** | *University of Vermont*

Bryan G. Cook | *University of Hawaii*

Parent involvement is a key principle of special education with roots in the field's history, laws, practices, and overall goal to meet the needs of all children and youth with disabilities. The U.S. Congress asserted its belief in the importance of parent participation in the passage of the Education for All Handicapped Children Act of 1975 (EHA; Public Law 94-142), and has affirmed the commitment to the importance of parents as educational partners and decision makers in each of its subsequent reauthorizations of the Individuals with Disabilities Education Act (IDEA) (A. Turnbull, Turnbull, Erwin, Soodak, & Shogren, 2011). Although the literature has identified numerous benefits of parent participation in the special education assessment process and generation of individualized education programs (IEP) (S. W. Smith, 1990b; H. R. Turnbull, Turnbull, & Wheat, 1982), theoretical analyses and empirical research suggest that the realities of participation generally fall far short of the IDEA vision of parents as partners in planning (Harry, 1992a, 2008; A. Turnbull et al., 2011).

In this chapter, we first review the legal and theoretical justification for parental involvement in their children's schooling generally and in the IEP assessment and development process specifically. Second, we review the literature on observed levels of parental involvement and identified roadblocks to higher levels of parental involvement. We conclude with descriptions of two family-centered practices that are supported by research as increasing parental participation in the IEP process: (a) person-centered planning (PCP) approaches (Claes, Van Hove, Vandevelde, Van Loon, & Schalock, 2010), and (b) Choosing Outcomes and Accommodations for Children (COACH) (Giangreco, Cloninger, & Iverson, 2011). Although we acknowledge that these practices do not meet all of the criteria established for evidence-based practices (see B. G. Cook, Tankersley, & Landrum, 2009), they address many barriers to parent participation, are supported in the research literature, and may be described as "promising practices" with implications for future research and practice.

Parent Involvement and General Education

Although it is beyond the scope of this chapter to give full attention to the general issue of parent involvement in education, it is important to situate the construct of parent participation in assessment and IEP generation within this broader context. In some ways, the history of parent involvement in education as a whole has paralleled that of parent involvement in special education, with responsibility for education shifting from families in an agrarian society (Kaestle, 2001) to schools and professionals by the middle of the 20th century (W. W. Cutler, 2000). The increasingly bureaucratic and professionalized nature of schools initially acted as a force that discouraged family involvement in schooling (M. Henry, 1996). However, by the 1990s, researchers and practitioners began to promote parent involvement as a strategy for improving public schools and increasing student achievement, attendance, and attitudes (J. S. Epstein, 2009; Henderson & Mapp, 2002). Legally, federal statutes have given less attention to parent involvement in general education than special education, with the first mention of the importance of parent involvement appearing in the 2001 reauthorization of the Elementary and Secondary Education Act, also known as the No Child Left Behind Act (NCLB).

Research on the relationship between increased family involvement in general education and improved student outcomes continues to emerge, but to date remains inconclusive. A relatively large body of literature supports a connection between parent involvement and student performance; findings suggest that students whose parents are more engaged with school show higher academic and behavioral achievement (C. Ferguson, 2008; Henderson & Mapp, 2002), improved attendance rates, and higher aspirations for postsecondary education (Jeynes, 2005). At the same time, some researchers have cautioned that the disparate definitions of parent involvement (Mattingly, Prislin, McKenzie, Rodriguez, & Kayzar, 2002) and concerns about study design and effect sizes (K. R. White, Taylor, & Moss, 1992) must be considered in drawing conclusions about the impact of involvement on student outcomes.

Historical, Legal, and Theoretical Underpinnings of Parent Participation in Special Educational Planning

Before EHA/IDEA

Historically, the roles of parents of children and adults with disabilities have been viewed in a variety of ways, each of which has influenced expectations for parent participation in educational planning. The eugenics movement of the late 1800s and early 1900s, for example, contributed to a socially constructed notion of individuals with disabilities as deviant and potentially dangerous individuals (A. Turnbull et al., 2011). Societal responses to the perceived "problem" of disability, including institutionalization, typically removed parents from decision-making roles and reinforced the notion that professionals were more knowledgeable and better able to determine the futures of children with disabilities than were their parents. Beliefs about the roles of parents of children with disabilities shifted during the 1940s to 1970s, as a growing number of parents expressed their dissatisfaction and advocated for changes in the residential and educational services available at the time (Yell, Rogers, & Rogers, 1998).

Passage of EHA/IDEA

The efforts of parents, disability advocacy organizations, legislators, and the courts to bring attention to exclusionary and discriminatory practices led to passage of the EHA, now known as the IDEA. IDEA affirmed a new role for parents in the education of their children with disabilities (A. Turnbull et al., 2011), particularly through the requirement for parents to participate in decisions about assessment and educational planning for their children. Further, IDEA articulated the school's responsibility for ensuring parent participation through procedural safeguards and rights, including the right of parents to provide consent to initial evaluations for special education eligibility and placement, revoke consent for services, and pursue their right to due process in the event of disagreements with the school. Bateman (2011) underscored the centrality of the parent participation principle in the IDEA, noting that failure to allow full and equal parent participation can lead to a legal determination that schools have denied a student's right to a free and appropriate public education (FAPE).

Subsequent reauthorizations of IDEA continued to underscore the need for parent participation. Part C of IDEA, enacted in 1986, mandated that services for children from birth to 3 years be delivered through an individualized family services plan (IFSP) that relies heavily on family input to identify the type and extent of special education and related services to be provided to the child (A. Turnbull et al., 2011). IDEA 1990 reaffirmed the importance of parent and student participation by mandating transition planning and the development of goals based on a student's needs, preferences, and interests (Hasazi, Furney, & DeStefano, 1999). The assumption was that although some students would be able to direct the development of their transition plans, parental input would remain critical in many instances.

Theoretical Underpinnings

The definition of parent involvement specified in the IDEA is most connected to sociological theories that emerged in the 1970s and that attributed differences in achievement and social success to differences in opportunity (Foster, Berger, & McLean, 1981). This view proposed that parents who were empowered to take an active role in educational decision making would be more likely to obtain services for their children than parents who were not similarly involved. Moreover, the parent participation principle of the EHA attempted to correct previous practices—such as the exclusion of children with disabilities and discriminatory assessment procedures—by giving parents a role that would hold professionals accountable for implementing IEP services (H. R. Turnbull et al., 1982). The purported benefits of parent participation are also connected to the idea that parents who are active participants in IEP planning will contribute to the development of educational plans with a high likelihood of success (S. W. Smith, 1990b). The IEP planning process has been characterized as a constructive way for parents to gain knowledge of the school setting, for teachers to gain knowledge of the students and their home environments, and for the IEP team to create a mutual understanding that will lead to mutually agreed-upon goals.

Observed Levels of Parental Involvement and Observed Roadblocks

Early Studies of Parent Participation

The IDEA legal provisions for parent participation did not translate into immediate changes in educational practices or the actual roles of parents. In the first 15 years following passage of the EHA, researchers focused on examining the roles of parents in the IEP process and identifying factors that appeared to promote or inhibit their participation (Foster et al., 1981). For the most part, these studies reported that during IEP meetings, parents engaged in less verbal participation than educators, asked fewer questions, and demonstrated behaviors that were assumed to indicate their agreement with professional judgments (Cone, Delawyer, & Wolfe, 1985; S. Goldstein, Strickland, Turnbull, & Curry, 1980; Lusthaus, Lusthaus, & Gibbs, 1981; Vacc et al., 1985; S. Vaughn, Bos, Harrell, & Lasky, 1988). A finding that was initially perplexing was that most parents reported overall satisfaction with the planning process, contradicting the assumption that they would be dissatisfied with IEP meetings in which professionals maintained control over planning and decision making.

Studies focused on teachers' perceptions and behaviors indicated that many educators in fact defined "appropriate" parent roles in a passive rather than an active sense. Analyses of teacher self-reports indicated that the majority felt it was more appropriate for parents to gather and present information than to participate in educational decision making (Yoshida, Fenton, Kaufman, & Maxwell, 1978) and believed that parents should be allowed to waive their right to participation and place educational decision making solely in the hands of professionals (P. L. Gerber, Banbury, & Miller, 1986). Studies of IEP meetings identified additional barriers to parent participation, including teachers' use of unexplained and technical educational jargon in the reporting of test results and insufficient allocation of time for IEP meetings (Hughes & Ruhl, 1987), as well as presentation of completed or nearly completed IEPs that lacked parental input (P. L. Gerber et al., 1986; S. Goldstein et al., 1980).

Reconceptualizing Parent Participation

As the 1980s drew to a close, early characterizations of parents as passive participants who were generally satisfied with the IEP process were called into question. For example, because most participants in the studies were Caucasian mothers from middle class backgrounds, findings could not be generalized to other populations (A. Turnbull & Turnbull, 1990). Moreover, the 1980s witnessed a paradigm shift in which proponents of parent participation and early intervention began to focus on family systems theory and family support models that conceptualized families as social systems with unique characteristics and needs (Blue-Banning, Summers, Frankland, Nelson, & Beegle, 2004). These models posited that professionals should focus their work on identifying families' needs and choices, encouraging family control in decision making, and creating effective and collaborative partnerships that extended beyond the IEP planning context. Family-centered approaches also encouraged parents to establish their own expectations for involvement, acknowledging that some families want to play greater roles in their children's educational programs than others (Bruder, 2000; MacMillan & Turnbull, 1983).

The literature also reflects a shift in language during the 1980s. Whereas the IDEA continued to refer to "parent" participation, researchers and practitioners began to refer to the participation of "families" (Blue-Banning et al., 2004). This change was indicative of the fact that although the IEP process continued to focus on the legal authority of one or more parents, expanded definitions of participation reflected a need to collaborate with the individuals in a student's broader family constellation, both within and outside of the IEP and IFSP processes.

Reconceptualizing Barriers to Parent Involvement

As the research on parent participation moved away from a singular focus on behavior during IEP meetings, it evolved to include a deeper exploration of cultural and contextual barriers to meaningful participation and the development of collaborative relationships between parents and professionals.

Culture and Context

In the 1980s and 1990s, researchers began to explore issues of diversity and their relationship to parent participation in the IEP process (Greene, 1996; E. W. Lynch & Stein, 1983; Sileo, Sileo, & Prater, 1996; Sontag & Schacht, 1994). These studies generally described parents from diverse backgrounds as playing passive roles in the IEP process, but the studies provided alternate explanations for previous deficit views of this dynamic and identified issues of power and differences in cultural values and beliefs that were often subtle but defined many of the relationships between professionals and parents (Harry, 1992a, 1992b, 2008; Geenan, Powers, & Lopez-Vasquez, 2001; Rao, 2000; Sileo et al., 1996).

The literature has identified ways in which definitions of and responses to disability are culturally situated, which, if not understood, may serve as a barrier to effective school and family collaboration (Harry, Allen, & McLaughlin, 1995). For example, Western perspectives of disability as an individual phenomenon with medical, biological, and physical origins and a need for remediation (Kalyanpur & Harry, 1999) are quite different from cultural and religious beliefs that may define disability from a more spiritual perspective (Lamory, 2002). Qualitative studies conducted with Latino mothers of children with developmental disabilities (D. G. Skinner, Correa, Skinner, & Bailey, 2001) and families of children with autism (Jegatheesan, Miller, & Fowler, 2010) identified spiritual and religious lenses on disability that are not generally acknowledged by white, middle class educators and may result in misunderstandings and frustration in the IEP process (Harry, 2008). Additionally, Sileo et al. (1996) noted the ways in which ideals such as efficiency, independence, self-determination, and equity are valued by Americans of European descent but may clash with the values held by families whose cultures prize family associations and the extended family structure.

Relationships, Collaboration, and Language

Barriers related to language have been identified among parents from diverse linguistic backgrounds, as well as among parents who are fluent in English but do not understand the vocabulary and terms used in the IEP process

(Dabkowski, 2004). Parents also report feeling excluded based on subtle messages and nonverbal communication conveyed by professionals. Parents find it difficult to participate when they lack information regarding special education processes, terminology, and parental rights (Lytle & Bordin, 2001), and when they encounter IEPs that have been written before meetings (Spann, Kohler, & Soenksen, 2003). They continue to report that the IEP process is characterized by a lack of trust, poor communication, and failure to develop positive, collaborative relationships that could support effective planning and service delivery (Rao, 2000; Whitbread, Bruder, Fleming, & Park, 2007). This appears to be the case for families of children of all ages, including young children receiving early intervention services (McWilliam, Tocci, & Harbin, 1998) as well as older students preparing for the transition from school to adult life (McNair & Rusch, 1991; Salembier & Furney, 1997).

Strategies for Enhancing Involvement

One set of strategies proposed to enhance parent participation in the IEP process focuses on defining indicators of effective family and professional partnerships and developing related skills among professionals and parents. Blue-Banning et al. (2004) suggested that the field conduct research to operationalize the construct of positive partnerships among families and professionals. They and others maintained that a commonly accepted set of definitions would allow the development of measures that could be used in conducting empirical studies of parent participation, promoting accountability among professionals, and identifying a clear set of competencies and skills that could be addressed through pre-service education. Strategies proposed for enhancing skill development include expanding the pre-service curriculum for educators to include a focus on the development of skills in collaboration, problem solving, and cultural perceptions of difference (Hoover-Dempsey, Walker, Jones, & Reed, 2002); providing joint training and opportunities for dialogue among parents and professionals (Whitbread et al., 2007); fostering self-reflection and awareness among educators regarding cultural sensitivity and cultural reciprocity (Harry, 2008; Kalyanpur & Harry, 1999); and providing information and support to parents regarding special education processes and research-based practices (A. Turnbull et al., 2010).

A second set of strategies focuses on implementing specific approaches for conducting IEP and other planning meetings in a manner that emphasizes families' expertise and creates an environment conducive to building trust, respect, communication, and positive and collaborative relationships (Furney & Salembier, 2000; Geenan et al., 2001). These include PCP approaches

(Claes et al., 2010) and the COACH process (Giangreco et al., 2011), which are discussed in more detail in a subsequent section.

Effectiveness of Strategies for Increasing Parent Participation

Although the literature provides many suggestions for increasing parent participation and positive school and family partnerships, relatively little research has been conducted on the effectiveness of specific strategies. In addition to the empirical literature examining PCP and COACH, reviewed in the following section, Boone (1992) explored the use of a parent-training strategy designed to increase parent participation in transition planning for students with disabilities but found no significant differences between the degree and levels of active participation of parents receiving and not receiving the intervention. Whitbread et al. (2007) concluded that a joint training strategy involving parents of children with disabilities and school professionals improved participants' skills in collaboration, but the authors acknowledged a need to follow-up on long-term effectiveness.

Studies of the relationship between strategies to improve parent participation and student outcomes are even rarer. Poponi (2009) conducted an extensive review of the literature on family involvement in both the IEP and broader school contexts, identifying only one study that measured the relationship between increased parent participation and improved student performance. In this study, McConaughy, Kay, and Fitzgerald (1999) compared outcomes between students in kindergarten whose parents were included in regularly scheduled multidisciplinary team meetings and students whose parents were not included, finding significantly greater reductions in the exhibition of children's problematic behaviors for the first group, as rated by teachers and parents. Poponi's retrospective review of 270 records of students with disabilities found significant differences in students' grades based on their parents' attendance or nonattendance at IEP meetings. This study represents a step toward linking increased parent participation with improved outcomes for students with disabilities; however, it examined participation as a function of attendance, rather than through broader constructs such as active participation, collaboration among families and professionals, or other factors.

Examples of Family-Centered Practices

We turn now to a description of two family-centered practices that are supported by research and show promise for increasing parental participation in the IEP

process: (a) PCP approaches (Claes et al., 2010) and (b) COACH (Giangreco et al., 2011). Both processes are typically conducted before the IEP meeting and focus on creating a planning context that enhances the development of partnerships between professionals and families and encourages family and individual choice and decision making around the identification of educational goals and services.

Person-Centered Planning

In reaction to traditional planning meetings that tended to be dominated by professionals, PCP has emerged as a viable alternative (Keyes & Owens-Johnson, 2003) "that is focused entirely on the interests of an individual with disabilities and keeps them first" (Rasheed, Fore, & Miller, 2006, p. 48). Rasheed et al. noted that although no clearly accepted definition of PCP exists, it can be described generally as a reflective, strength-based planning process attended by and focused on an individual with disabilities and a variety of people close to the individual (typically including parents), which results in a vision of the future for the individual with disabilities (based on his or her preferences) and plans for achieving that vision. As summarized in Figure 20.1, Flannery, Newton, Horner, Slovic, Blumberg, and Ard (2000) delineated nine critical attributes of PCP.

PCP has become a popular planning approach used for individuals (a) with a variety of disabilities, most commonly those with developmental and intellectual disabilities; (b) at varying ages, from young children into adulthood; and (c) in a variety of settings (e.g., school,

Figure 20.1 Nine critical attributes of person centered planning.

1. The individual is present at the meeting(s).
2. The individual participates in the process.
3. The individual (and family/advocates, if appropriate) determines who will be present at the meeting.
4. The people participating in the planning know the individual well.
5. The planning is based on the individual's interests, preferences, and strengths.
6. The planning is based on the individual's vision of the future.
7. The process results in an action plan.
8. The action plan includes a clear process for monitoring implementation of the plan.
9. The process is flexible and informal.

Source: Data from Flannery, K. B., Newton, S., Horner, R. H., Slovic, R., Blumberg, R., & Ard, W. R. (2000). The impact of person centered planning on the content and organization of individual supports. *Career Development of Exceptional Individuals, 23,* 123–137.

home community). Although PCP may involve a variety of processes for eliciting input from participants to envision and plan for the future of an individual with disabilities, PCP often uses an established tool for this purpose, including Essential Lifestyle Planning (ELP; Smull & Sanderson, 2005), Lifestyle Planning (J. O'Brien & Lyle, 1987), the McGill Action Planning System (MAPS; Forest & Lusthaus, 1987; Vandercook, York, & Forest, 1989), Personal Futures Planning (Mount & Zwernik, 1988), and Planning Alternative Tomorrows with Hope (PATH; Pearpoint, O'Brien, & Forest, 1993).

Historical and Theoretical Underpinnings of Person-Centered Planning

As summarized by C. L. O'Brien and O'Brien (2000), PCP evolved out of communities of practice devoted to the principles of normalization in the 1970s and 1980s. The normalization movement posited that all people, including those with intellectual disabilities, should be perceived and treated as developing, full-fledged human beings (Wolfensberger, 1972). The principles of normalization were used to deconstruct the services, supports, and planning provided to individuals with intellectual disabilities. Perceptions of individuals with disabilities as inferior or even subhuman historically led to segregation (e.g., institutionalization) and inadequate provision of services and supports, which in turn perpetuated negative attitudes and low expectations. PCP originated in reaction to these conditions and in the context of social and political activism associated with the 1970s for improving and normalizing the opportunities of individuals with disabilities (e.g., advocacy for and passage of the Rehabilitation Act of 1973 and the EHA in 1975).

The principles of self-determination were a logical outgrowth of the normalization movement that also provided the conceptual foundation for PCP. Wehmeyer (1996a) defined *self-determination* as "acting as the primary causal agent in one's life and making choices and decisions regarding one's quality of life free from undue external influence or interference" (p. 22). Traditionally, professionals have made the critical decisions in the lives of many individuals with disabilities. Self-determination holds that individuals should make their own decisions, regardless of their disability status. PCP bases planning and supports on the hopes and desires of individuals with disabilities with the assistance and input from those closest to them (e.g., family), rather than solely on the basis of professionals' recommendations.

Description of PCP Implementation

Describing the implementation of PCP can be challenging because *person-centered planning* is an umbrella term encompassing a variety of practices meant to be applied flexibly. In this section, we describe the procedures used in an experimental study supporting the effectiveness of PCP for improving parental participation in developing IEPs (Miner & Bates, 1997). Miner and Bates used procedures adapted largely from the Personal Futures Planning model (Mount & Zwernick, 1988). Activities included (a) developing a personal profile, (b) describing a desirable future, and (c) planning for attaining goals. To conduct these activities, the student and family met with a trained facilitator at a location of the family's choosing.

To generate a personal profile, the student and family first developed a circle of support by naming people in the student's life at four levels (represented by four circles): (a) closest and most important people (e.g., family members, close friends), (b) people close to (but not closest to) the student, (c) people in the student's life (e.g., via church, sports teams, clubs), and (d) people paid to be involved in the student's life (e.g., teachers, doctors). The student and family next developed a community presence map, listing community settings the student used. These two processes and the resulting documents provided a frame of reference in subsequent discussions about how the student could "be assisted in developing greater choice and autonomy in community participation" (p. 107). The final steps in the personal profile development involved listing things that work and do not work for the student (e.g., identifying student preferences) and listing the students' gifts and capacities (e.g., "What do people who like the student say about her or him?"). Primary members identified in the circle of support were invited to subsequent planning sessions.

In the next step, describing a desirable future, the planning team answered questions from the facilitator regarding future living situations, community participation, employment, and recreation and leisure. The facilitator stressed that the vision for the student's future being developed should not be based on the perceived limits of the student's disability. In the final step, planning for attaining goals, participants identified three to five activities that could immediately move the student closer to goal attainment. The meeting ended by summarizing the student's future goals, activities identified for moving toward those goals, the needed services and supports for those activities, and the individuals responsible. The facilitator also encouraged the team to meet periodically to review progress and to identify new activities needed to attain the student's vision.

A detailed lesson plan starter—including an objective, setting and materials, content taught, teaching procedures, and method of evaluation—on the PCP procedures used by Miner and Bates (1997) that were shown to result in improved parental participation in the IEP process is available on the National Secondary Transition Technical Assistance Center's Web site (NSTTAC, n.d.). A number of online resources provide further information on implementing PCP (e.g., Inclusive Solutions, n.d.; Interactive Collaborative Autism Network, n.d.).

Research on PCP and Parental Participation in the IEP Process

Research on PCP has examined its effect on outcomes such as social networks, community involvement, choice making, knowledge, reduction of problem behaviors, and process issues (e.g., participation of parents) (see Claes et al., 2010, for a review of this literature). In this chapter, we specifically review research related to PCP and the participation of parents in the IEP process.

Experimental research. In Miner and Bates's (1997) experimental study of PCP, 22 adolescents with intellectual disabilities and their families were matched by program placement, IQ, anticipated year of school exit, and communication skills. One student/family from each pair was randomly assigned to either the experimental (7 males, 4 females) or control group (5 males, 6 females); ethnicity of participants was not described. PCP activities took place at sites selected by each family. All but one opted to meet at their homes; one meeting was conducted at a high school. Procedures were adapted primarily from the Personal Futures Planning model (as detailed in the previous section). The PCP meetings took place with experimental group families approximately 2 weeks before IEP meetings. Materials and results from the PCP meetings were reviewed with and provided to the families by the facilitator approximately 2 days before their IEP meetings. The control group did not receive any support before IEP meetings but were provided opportunities to engage in PCP after their meetings were completed.

An observer recorded who was speaking at all of the IEP meetings using a momentary time sampling approach with 15-second intervals. Two trained observers collected data at six of the 22 (27%) IEP meetings to collect inter-rater reliability data. Mean inter-rater agreement for speakers was 90%. Implementation fidelity was not assessed, although the same experienced, trained special educator facilitated all PCP meetings. Participants completed satisfaction surveys directly after each IEP meeting and again 2 months after the IEP meeting.

Parents were observed speaking at 26% of intervals ($SD = 11.2$) in the experimental group, compared to 14% ($SD = 10.9$) in the control group, a statistically significant difference. Parents in both the experimental and control groups expressed high levels of satisfaction with the IEP meeting related to preparation, input, satisfaction with goals, and likelihood of goal achievement (all means > 4 on a 1 [highly dissatisfied] to 5 [highly

satisfied] scale). Differences between groups were not statistically significant.

On the follow-up survey (2 months after the IEP meetings), participants compared the recently completed IEP meeting with the previous year's IEP meeting on a 1 (much less favorable) to 5 (much more favorable) scale. Although statistical analyses were not conducted, when matched pairs were compared, parents in the experimental group ($M = 4.11$, $SD = 0.59$) gave higher ratings than parents in the control group ($M = 3.47$, $SD = 0.33$) for 10 of the 11 pairs (SDs calculated from data provided in article). Because these data were provided in the article, we were able to conduct a *t*-test, which indicated that parents in the experimental group provided significantly higher ratings than those in the control group ($p < 0.01$), with an effect size (Cohen's *d*) of 1.29. When asked to rate the value of the PCP activities, six parents in the experimental group rated them as extremely valuable, three as valuable, and two as neutral.

Within-group comparison research. Flannery et al. (2000) conducted an evaluation of PCP on a single group of students with disabilities and their families that included examination of parental participation in the IEP-planning process. The study involved 10 students (7 female, 3 male) ages 19 to 21 and their parents. The students were categorized as having intellectual disabilities ($n = 3$), specific learning disability (SLD; $n = 3$), speech and language impairment, hearing impairment, other health impairment and SLD, and orthopedic impairment and SLD. The families had all taken part in PCP meetings facilitated by educators who were trained as part of the Oregon Transition Systems Change Project.

Using a 1 to 4 Likert scale (from "strongly agree" to "strongly disagree"), parents and students indicated statistically significantly higher satisfaction with IEP meetings and planning occurring after PCP training in comparison to before PCP training on these items related to their participation:

- "I was allowed to talk about my hopes and dreams" ($p < 0.05$).
- "At the meeting, I was allowed to contribute to the discussion of the goals, actions, or next steps included on my plan" ($p < 0.05$).

Flannery et al. (2000) also reported that educators rated the structure for family and student involvement ($p < 0.001$), family involvement ($p < 0.001$), and their understanding of the family's goals and desires ($p < 0.001$) as significantly higher at the post-PCP meeting in comparison to the pre-PCP meeting. Moreover, parents and students ($p < 0.05$), as well as educators ($p < 0.001$), indicated a significantly higher level of overall satisfaction with the planning at the post-PCP meetings in comparison to the pre-PCP meetings.

Qualitative research.   Childre and Chambers (2005) studied six students and their families. The students were 10 to 15 years old, with moderate intellectual disabilities ($n = 2$) and orthopedic impairments ($n = 4$); three were African American and three Caucasian. Using established person-centered tools, the researchers developed a new approach to PCP that explicitly emphasized the link to IEP meetings, which they referred to as Student-Centered Individualized Education Planning (SCIEP). The SCIEP uses written forms to guide and document person-centered techniques. Before IEP meetings, families completed three forms: the Relationship Circle, Dreams, and Goals. Students completed two forms: Strengths and Preferences, and Goals and Dreams. A trained special educator facilitated the IEP meetings by incorporating the information on these forms and the perspectives of individuals attending the IEP meeting onto seven forms, which were used to help design the students' IEPs: Relationship Circle, Community Survey (to identify places in the community frequented by the family in order to develop community-based curricula), Now (i.e., present level of functioning), What Works (factors that promote student success), Dreams, Goals, and Who and When (describes team members' responsibilities).

In interviews conducted after the SCIEP process, families reported they generally enjoyed the SCIEP process and found it productive and worthwhile. Specifically related to their involvement in the IEP meetings, parents noted,

> The process encouraged communication, brainstorming, and problem solving between families and professionals. These meetings were characterized by their shift from simple exchange of information between team members toward true collaboration. "Everybody, each one, put in their input and discussed it to the fullest." (p. 226)

Case studies.   The positive effect of PCP on parental participation in the IEP process is also supported by reports from case studies. For example, in a case study of PCP in two culturally distinct communities (one primarily Caucasian, one primarily Latino), Trainor (2007) reported that, "PCP increased the amount and quality of participation of both youth and families" (p. 98) in both communities. Furthermore, the bilingual special education teacher who facilitated PCP meetings in the Latino community noted that, "when you do a PCP, they become the experts. The parents are the ones telling you, the kid is the one telling you, and, if you think about it, that's the way a normal IEP should be, but it's not" (p. 97).

In another case study, Salembier and Furney (1994) described a PCP process based on a modified MAPS procedure that was used to write the transition section of the IEP for Peter, a 10th-grade student with a nonspecified disability, over 2 years. Peter's special education teacher observed that PCP

> really helped his parents take a more active role in planning. By the time of the second MAP, they were more vocal and clearer about Peter's future goals and needs. They now have a feeling that they are partners with the school in making things happen for Peter. (Salembier & Furney, 1994, p. 16)

Finally, Chambers and Childre (2005) provided a case study of PCP on a first-grade student. The authors described and applied the "true directions" model of PCP, which uses the SCIEP tools and forms described previously. The authors reported that the child's parents and grandparents were both active and influential participants in their child's IEP.

Summary of research.   The effectiveness of PCP for improving parental participation in the IEP process is supported by a small number of research studies, including one experimental study with a randomly assigned control group (Miner & Bates, 1997). However, this is the only experimental study we identified on the topic. Accordingly, educators should be cautious in drawing the conclusion that PCP causes improved parental participation in the IEP process until subsequent experimental research replicates these findings. More research also seems warranted related to the impact of different models of PCP. Additionally, component analyses will be important to identify which components of PCP are essential for attaining desired outcomes. Although some initial research (e.g., Trainor, 2007) and theoretical analysis (e.g., Callicott, 2003) have indicated that PCP can be successfully adapted for students and families who are culturally and linguistically diverse, further research is also warranted regarding its application for improving parental participation among diverse populations. Furthermore, given the important role of the facilitator in the PCP process, future researchers should examine facilitator skills and attributes that may be associated with levels of parental participation. Although limited in number and scope of studies, research supporting PCP as a tool for improving parental participation in the IEP process has been conducted by multiple investigators in different settings, and findings suggest that students, families, and educators express satisfaction with PCP (e.g., Flannery et al., 2000; Miner & Bates, 1997).

Choosing Outcomes and Accommodations for Children

Overview of COACH

Now in its ninth version since 1985, COACH is an assessment and planning process designed to assist school personnel in working collaboratively with families to develop IEPs for students with intensive special education needs (Giangreco et al., 2011). A secondary aim of COACH is to assist families in becoming better consumers of educational services and partners in the educational process. COACH is designed primarily to plan for students, ages 3 through 21, with low-incidence disabilities whose curricular content needs extend beyond the typical general education curriculum corresponding to their chronological age. In other words, some of the most important things these students need to learn (e.g., foundational communication, socialization, and academic access skills) have already been mastered by most other students their age and therefore are not reflected in typical general education curricula.

COACH is divided into two parts (Part A, Determining a Student's Educational Program, and Part B, Strategies and Processes to Implement a COACH-Generated Educational Program), including six major steps (see Figure 20.2), and also includes strategies for implementing COACH-generated plans in inclusive classrooms (e.g., scheduling matrix, tools for

planning instruction). Information presented here focuses on the first three steps of Part A of COACH because they include family participation. The Family Interview (Step 1) is the heart of COACH—it provides a unique combination of features to assist families in selecting a small set of the highest-priority learning outcomes for their child. To ensure students have sufficiently broad curricular opportunities, Additional Learning Outcomes (Step 2) assists in identifying a set of learning outcomes from both those listed in COACH and the general education curriculum. General Supports (Step 3) assists in identifying supports to be provided to or for students with disabilities across six categories so they can pursue the learning outcomes identified in Steps 1 and 2.

Conceptual Basis for COACH

COACH is rooted in a set of foundational principles that potential consumers of COACH should consider, so their team, including the family, can make an informed

Figure 20.2   Parts and steps of Choosing Outcomes and Accommodations for Children (COACH).

Part A: Determining a Student's Educational Program

Preparation Checklist

Step 1: Family Interview

Introducing the Family Interview

Step 1.1: Valued Life Outcomes

Step 1.2: Selecting Curriculum Areas to Explore During the Family Interview

(a) Communication, (b) Socialization, (c) Personal Management, (d) Access Academics, (e) Applied Academics, (f) Recreation, (g) School, (h) Community, (i) Vocational

Step 1.3: Rating Learning Outcomes in Selected Curriculum Areas

Step 1.4: Prioritizing Learning Outcomes in Selected Curriculum Areas

Step 1.5: Cross-Prioritization

Step 2: Additional Learning Outcomes

Step 2.1: Additional Learning Outcomes from COACH

Step 2.2: Additional Learning Outcomes from General Education

(a) Language Arts, (b) Math, (c) Science, (d) Social Studies, (e) Physical Education/Health, (f) Foreign Language, (g) Art, (h) Music, (i) Other

Step 3: General Supports

(a) Physical Needs, (b) Personal Needs, (c) Sensory Needs, (d) Teaching Others About the Student, (e) Providing Access and Opportunities, (f) Other General Supports

Part B: Translating the Family-Identified Priorities into Goals and Objectives

Step 4: Annual Goals

Step 5: Short-Term Objectives

Step 6: Program-at-a-Glance

Source: Data from Giangreco, M. F., Cloninger, C. J., & Iverson, V. S. (2011). *Choosing outcomes and accommodations for children (COACH): A guide to educational planning for students with disabilities* (3rd ed.). Baltimore: Brookes.

Figure 20.3 Principles forming the basis of Choosing Outcomes and Accommodations for Children (COACH).

1. All students are capable of learning and deserve a meaningful curriculum.
2. Quality instruction requires ongoing access to inclusive environments.
3. Pursuing valued life outcomes informs the selection of curricular content.
   - Safety and health (physical and emotional)
   - A home—now and in the future
   - Meaningful relationships
   - Control over personal choices (suited to the student's age and culture)
   - Meaningful activities in various and valued places
4. Family involvement is a cornerstone of educational planning.
   - Families know certain aspects of their children better than anyone else.
   - Families have the greatest vested interest in seeing their children learn.
   - Families should be approached in culturally sensitive ways.
   - The family is likely to be the only group of adults involved with a child's educational program throughout his entire school career.
   - Families have the ability to positively influence the quality of educational services provided in their community.
5. Collaborative teamwork is essential to quality education.
6. Coordination of services ensures that necessary supports are appropriately provided.

Source: Information from Giangreco, M. F., Cloninger, C. J., & Iverson, V. S. (2011). *Choosing outcomes and accommodations for children (COACH): A guide to educational planning for students with disabilities* (3rd ed.). Baltimore: Brookes.

decision about whether to use it (see Figure 20.3). Although each step of COACH includes a statement of purpose, forms, explicit directions for use, and helpful hints, it is purposely not standardized. Part of its family-centered approach encourages thoughtful individualization to match variations across the wide range of families schools serve. To maintain the internal integrity of the tool if adapting any aspects of COACH, facilitators are advised to do so in ways that are congruent with its underlying principles.

Some Unique Elements of COACH

Although it shares some similarities with other assessment approaches (e.g., checklists of observable behaviors across multiple curricular domains, scoring based on parent reporting), COACH also embodies elements that distinguish it from other tools and deliberately links the collection of certain types of assessment data (e.g., parent perspectives) with curricular and instructional planning. This section describes a few embedded aspects unique to COACH that have been designed to contribute to its effectiveness.

Posture of listening. Many well-intended parent–professional interactions are dominated by professionals sharing data (often deficit based) they have collected, followed by telling parents what they think is important.

COACH reverses this common and potentially problematic practice, first during the Family Interview by having professionals assume the roles of question asker and listener, with the goal of better understanding what the family thinks is important. An explicitly designed set and sequence of questions, field tested and adjusted over many years, provides a facilitated process culminating in the selection of a small set of high-priority learning outcomes by the student's family. As COACH proceeds through Steps 2 (Additional Learning Outcomes) and 3 (General Supports), it continues to provide a facilitated forum for professionals and parents to listen to each other and establish shared expectations about a student's educational program components. Having shared goals and a productive dynamic that acknowledges the respective expertise of professionals and families is foundational to collaborative teamwork and constructive home–school relationships.

Valued life outcomes. An initial substep within the Family Interview, valued life outcomes (Step 1.1), sets the context for selecting curricular content by asking families a series of carefully crafted questions about the current and desired future status of five valued life outcomes for their child (see Figure 20.2). These questions are purposely worded in broad terms so families can attach their own personal meaning. Step 1.1 ends with the family being asked to rate their level of concern/importance about each of the valued life outcomes. This substep provides valuable information to school personnel in planning an appropriate educational program responsive to a vision for the student identified by the family and emphasizes improving quality of life indicators for individuals with disabilities (Dennis, Williams, Giangreco, & Cloninger, 1993).

Creative problem solving. Professionals with good intentions often seek input from families but with inadequate attention to the methods used. Open-ended questions such as, "What would you like to see on Sam's IEP this year?" or "What are your priorities for Cara?" might work for some families, but all too often such broad queries result in parents' deferring to professionals or making selections that do not adequately reflect their perspectives. This can occur because families are faced with trying to make priority selections based on hundreds of potential options without any strategies to help generate, organize, sort, and select from among a vast array of possibilities.

COACH relies on selected elements of the Osborn-Parnes Creative Problem-Solving Process (CPS) (Parnes, 1988), an approach with a history of documented effectiveness (Parnes, 1992), to gather meaningful input from families and facilitate the selection of priorities for their child. Although COACH does not employ a classic application of the CPS process, it embeds some of its key features, a few of which are presented here. The first three steps in COACH (Part A) offer multiple opportunities to alternate between divergent and convergent thinking to facilitate the selection of desired elements of the students' educational program. The divergent aspects encourage problem solvers to explore and generate possibilities by posing various types of fact-finding questions in an atmosphere of deferred judgment. Convergent aspects encourage analysis of the divergently generated possibilities and fact finding to focus on a smaller set of options, moving toward ultimate selections. The opportunities to alternate between the divergent and convergent aspects of COACH are purposely separated and repeated because generating ideas and attempting to evaluate them at the same time can inhibit informed decision making.

Research Base for COACH

Research on COACH summarized here is separated into two categories: (a) studies that directly informed the development of new or revised elements of COACH, and (b) studies about COACH (e.g., its use and impact). Step 1.1 (Valued Life Outcomes) was developed as a direct result of a qualitative study of 28 Vermont families whose children, ages 3 to 20, had sensory and multiple disabilities (Giangreco, Cloninger, Mueller, Yuan, & Ashworth, 1991). Based on semi-structured interviews, this study sought to better understand parents' perspectives about the impact of educational and related services on the lives of their children. The findings (a) highlighted the importance of connecting the selection of individualized curriculum content to quality of life indicators; (b) resulted in the articulation of the underlying principles of COACH; and (c) offered explicit categories of what parents identified as a "good life" (p. 18) for their children, which are reflected in the Step 1.1 questions and are embedded elsewhere in COACH.

A qualitative document analysis of 46 IEPs of students in grades K–12 with multiple disabilities in nine states (Giangreco, Dennis, Edelman, & Cloninger, 1994) identified a series of problematic characteristics of IEP goals and objectives. Some of these included IEP goals that were so vague (e.g., "Peter will improve communication skills," p. 290) that they were virtually meaningless to an educational team. Other IEP goals (a) lacked observable behaviors, (b) were selected based on what was valued independently by various professionals, or (c) were written with excessive related-services jargon. Many of the IEP documents analyzed were 20 to 30 pages long (one was 49 pages), with dozens of annual goals, rendering them quite improbable to deliver. The numerous negative findings from this study informed alternatives reflected throughout the principles of COACH and practices found in virtually all the steps of COACH (e.g., observable learning outcomes, selection of a small set of parent-selected priorities, and clear distinction between learning outcomes and general supports).

A descriptive, quantitative study followed changes in educational team membership for 18 students with sensory and multiple disabilities in four states over 4 years (Giangreco, Edelman, Nelson, Young, & Kiefer-O'Donnell, 1999). The findings revealed substantial team membership changeover from year to year, including 384 different team members, and identified families as the only constant for all 18 students across all 4 years. Data from this study further strengthened the principles of COACH, particularly those related to the importance of family involvement, and are reflected in practical aspects of facilitating COACH (e.g., COACH participants, team membership and roles, language used in Introducing the Family Interview).

Six studies have been conducted specifically about COACH. A national expert validation of COACH included two descriptive, quantitative studies (Giangreco, Cloninger, Dennis, & Edelman, 1993). The first study included 78 participants from 27 states who met specified criteria from two respondent categories: (a) national and state experts (e.g., university faculty, national technical assistance providers), and (b) field-based experts (e.g., parents, special educators, related services providers). Using a survey instrument, each participant reviewed COACH and rated it as highly congruent with a set of 20 exemplary practices it purports to embody across six categories: (a) family-centered practices, (b) collaborative planning, (c) social responsibility, (d) curriculum planning, (e) individualized instruction, and (f) family–school collaboration. The second study within the national validation (Giangreco et al., 1993) sought to extend the initial qualitative research on parents' perspectives (Giangreco et al., 1991) by exploring how a larger set of parents from geographically diverse states would perceive the valued life outcomes in COACH. From four states, a group of 44 parents of children with sensory and multiple disabilities, ages 5 to 20, validated that the valued life outcomes included in COACH were highly consistent with what they perceived as a "good life" for their children with disabilities.

A mixed-methods study about the use and impact of COACH was based on 30 students, ages 5 to 21, in eight states (Giangreco, Edelman, Dennis, & Cloninger, 1995). Researchers relied on interviews, observations, and document analysis, with data collected from 78 educational team members (e.g., special educators, parents, teachers). In part, the findings documented how COACH contributed to parent–professional relationships (e.g., better collaboration, improved perceptions of families by professionals, more parental involvement in decision making). Specifically related to parental participation, the findings reported the elements and structure of COACH (a) increased parent participation in educational planning, opened dialogue on previously undiscussed topics, and shifted educational decision-making control toward families; (b) provided opportunities that resulted in professionals' viewing parents more favorably; (c) encouraged parents to think about potential priorities in ways that they would not have considered before; (d) helped parents organize and communicate their ideas; and (e) ultimately helped parents identify relevant priorities that contributed to positive changes in valued life outcomes for their children. As one parent stated, "Of everything we've tried, and we've tried lots of different approaches over the years with Sandra of coming up with IEP goals, this just gave us so much assistance in really getting what we wanted for her and helping us crystallize what we really did want" (p. 126). Two single-case studies, one based on a preschool student with Down syndrome (Giangreco, Whiteford, Whiteford, & Doyle, 1998) and the other based on a high school student with deaf-blindness and intellectual disabilities (Edelman, Knutson, Osborn, & Giangreco, 1995), reiterated the positive impact of using COACH on parent participation, educational teams, and students with disabilities.

Lastly, a qualitative, cross-cultural review of COACH was conducted. Fourteen individuals from a wide range of minority cultures in the United States, who met specific selection criteria, reviewed COACH and then participated in interviews about it (Dennis & Giangreco, 1996). The findings presented issues pertaining to cultural sensitivity in family interviewing while avoiding stereotyping and generalizations. Findings from the study were incorporated in the principles of COACH and are embedded in a variety of specific directions, forms, and helpful hints in COACH (e.g., considerations for seating arrangements, use of translators, asking parents whether they want to be asked categories of questions in Step 1.1).

The evidence base for COACH has four main limitations: (a) only a small number of studies about COACH ($n = 6$) have been conducted; (b) all of the studies are descriptive in nature (i.e., no experimental or quasi-experimental studies have yet been published; (c) existing research is dated, and no recent research on COACH is available or known to be forthcoming; and (d) the studies highlighted were conducted by the developers of COACH or close associates. One descriptive study by researchers not involved in developing the program identified COACH as a useful practice to facilitate choosing and planning what to teach students with moderate and severe disabilities in inclusive classrooms (Jackson, Ryndak, & Billingsly, 2000). Although the research base is modest and nonexperimental, few other planning tools report evidence. Because it is designed to be a nonstandardized planning tool with assessment elements, rather than a standardized assessment, and because its potential impact might reasonably be thought of as two or three steps removed from direct student outcomes, COACH is not very amenable to evaluations that use research designs that seek to experimentally verify its impact on student outcomes. The nonstandardized nature of the tool and its directions, which include parents' making informed decisions to use it, presents a self-selection bias that could further hamper experimental comparisons. Despite the modest data available on the impact of COACH, it continues to be used by consumers in the field with some regularity. Future research by nondevelopers of the tool would be a welcome contribution to the literature.

Conclusion

The IDEA identifies a central, specific, and active role for parents in their children's education and IEPs, reflecting the ethical, theoretical, and empirical support for parent involvement in the education of students with disabilities (A. Turnbull et al., 2011). However, research has identified numerous barriers to meaningful parent participation, including differences in culture and context, failure to develop positive relationships, a lack of emphasis on families' wishes regarding their child's future, and challenges related to language and communication. This chapter includes a description of two practices, PCP and COACH, which are identified as promising practices for enhancing parent participation in the IEP process on the basis of their research support. The preceding reviews of the literature suggest that although much has been learned, there is a continued need to identify and conduct research on practices to enhance parents' roles as educational decision makers in the IEP process.

Although PCP and COACH appear promising, we recommend developing the research base on these and other practices for improving parent participation in the IEP process in a number of ways. First, although PCP and COACH are implemented with some frequency in schools, they are hardly commonplace. We recommend that researchers investigate what training and supports are associated with educators using PCP, COACH, and other approaches to enhance parent participation effectively and pervasively throughout schools, districts, or communities. Furthermore, the majority of the studies conducted on parental participation to date have relied on qualitative case studies and interviews, surveys, and observations to collect information. Many of these studies have been critical to expanding our understanding of parents' perspectives on the IEP process and the cultural, linguistic, and relational barriers to participation (Harry, 2008). At the same time, the dearth of experimental studies makes it difficult for parents and educators to draw firm conclusions about the effectiveness of specific strategies. As such, we recommend that researchers conduct more intervention research, including single-subject research studies (e.g., multiple baseline across participants), to examine the effectiveness of specific strategies for improving parent participation in the IEP process.

Future research should also examine the impact of new developments in the educational landscape on parental participation. For example, the context of parental participation in their children's education has changed with the advent of the Internet and social media. Future research should investigate whether parents are accessing information about their legal rights and research-based interventions for their children through these sources, whether they are using that information in planning meetings, and whether online communication tools can be incorporated into existing approaches to increase parent participation in the IEP process to make them even more effective.

CHAPTER 21

Individualized Education Programs:
Legal Requirements and Research Findings

Christine A. Christle and **Mitchell L. Yell** | *University of South Carolina*

According to Yell and Crockett (2011), before the mid 1970s, students' with disabilities access to public education was limited in two major ways. First, many students were completely excluded from public schools. Second, many students with disabilities were admitted to school but did not receive an education that was appropriate to their needs. These students were often "left to fend for themselves in classrooms designed for education of their nonhandicapped peers" (*Board of Education v. Rowley*, 1982, p. 191). Because of these challenges faced by students with disabilities, the U.S. Congress passed legislation to ensure the educational rights of all students with disabilities. In 1975, the Education for All Handicapped Children Act (EHA) was enacted to guarantee that eligible students with disabilities received an education suited to their unique needs. When the EHA was reauthorized in 1990, the name of the law was changed to the Individuals with Disabilities Education Act (IDEA). Note that every 5 or 6 years Congress reauthorizes, and usually amends, the IDEA. These amendments often make significant changes to the law. In this chapter when we address specific changes made in the amendments, we will refer to the specific year in which the law was changed (e.g., IDEA 2004). When we are not referring to these specific changes, we will use the actual name of the law: IDEA.

With EHA and IDEA, Congress granted every eligible student with a disability the right to receive a free appropriate public education (FAPE). Congress believed that the goal of providing a FAPE was best ensured by individualizing a student's education. Toward that end, Congress ensured that students with disabilities would receive an individualized and appropriate education through the use of individualized education programs (IEPs). The purpose of the IEP process was to develop an *individualized* and *appropriate* education program for students with disabilities, which Congress viewed as crucial in achieving the primary goals of the EHA (Zettel & Ballard, 1982). In the IEP process, school-based teams (a) conduct assessments of students' unique educational needs, (b) develop measurable annual goals based on the assessment, (c) determine the special education and related services that will be provided to the student, and (d) establish evaluation and measurement criteria by which a student's progress toward his goals will be monitored. The IEP, therefore, is of critical importance to educators, parents, and students. It is the process by which school-based teams determine the content of a student's program of special education and a written document that is the blueprint of the student's FAPE. Because of the legal and educational importance of the IEP, it is imperative that school-based teams develop IEPs that are both educationally meaningful and legally correct.

Our purpose in this chapter is to (a) review the legal requirements for developing, implementing, and evaluating IEPs; (b) describe the process for developing educationally meaningful and legally sound IEPs; (c) examine the research that has been conducted on IEPs; and (d) provide recommendations for district and school administrators, pre-service teacher educators, and school-based teams charged with fulfilling the IEP requirement. We begin with a brief examination of the IDEA.

Legal Requirements

The IDEA set forth a process by which school-based teams must develop IEPs. A challenge faced by IEP teams is that properly crafted IEPs must address two sets of requirements: procedural and substantive. These requirements guide the development and implementation of a student's FAPE (Drasgow, Yell, & Robinson, 2001). It is critical that practitioners and researchers understand the distinction between procedural and substantive compliance with the IEP requirements of the IDEA. We next examine each set of requirements.

Procedural Requirements

Procedural requirements of the IEP refer to those aspects of the IDEA that compel schools to follow the strictures of the law when developing an IEP. These procedures include the process by which the team develops a student's program of special education and the document itself. The IDEA requires that (a) IEP meetings must be scheduled at a mutually agreeable time and place, (b) the IEP team must consist of mandated team members (see Figure 21.1), and (c) certain components must be included in the IEP (see Figure 21.2).

Figure 21.1   Required participants in the IEP meeting.

- The student's parents
- A student's special education teacher
- A general education teacher who teaches the student
- A representative of the local educational agency
- A professional who can interpret the instructional implications of the evaluation results (one of the preceding members can serve here because members can serve more than one role)
- The student, if appropriate
- Other specialists (e.g., school psychologist, school nurse, representatives of community agencies) can be invited at the discretion of the school and parents but may require parental consent. Additional members must have knowledge or special expertise regarding the student.

Figure 21.2   Required components of the IEP.

A statement of

- Present Level of Academic Achievement and Functional Performance (PLAAFP)
- Measurable annual goals
- Method for collecting and reporting student progress
- Special education and related services
- Extent to which student will not participate in general education classroom
- Student's participation in state-wide or district-wide assessments
- Projected date for beginning services, anticipated frequency, location, and duration
- Transition services (IDEA requires this at age 16, but many states require transition services at a younger age.)

Adherence to these requirements is necessary because major procedural errors on the part of a school district may render an IEP inappropriate in the eyes of a hearing officer or court (Bateman & Linden, 2006; Huefner, 2000; Yell & Drasgow, 2000). According to the IDEA of 2004 (hereafter, IDEA 2004), serious procedural errors include those that (a) impede a student's right to a FAPE, (b) interfere with the opportunity for parents of a student with a disability to participate in the special education decision-making process, or (c) cause a deprivation of educational benefits (IDEA 20 U.S.C. § 1415(f)(1)(B)(i)(3)(E)(ii)(I-III)). The most serious procedural error that IEP teams can make is to fail to involve a student's parents in a meaningful collaboration when developing an IEP. In fact, this error may be the most likely to result in a hearing officer or judge invalidating an IEP. According to Bateman (2011), the IDEA makes parent participation central in all decisions regarding their child's program, and when full and equal parent participation is abridged or denied, a denial of FAPE is likely to be found. Indeed, the U.S. Court of Appeals for the Ninth Circuit ruled that interference with parental participation in IEP development undermines the very essence of the IDEA (*Amanda J. v. Clark County School District,* 2001). Figure 21.3 depicts common procedural errors that IEP teams make (Lake, 2010; Yell, 2009).

Substantive Requirements

Crafting educationally meaningful and legally correct IEPs requires more than following procedures; it demands attention to the development of special education programs that lead to meaningful educational benefit for students. As the President's Commission on Excellence in Special Education (2001) noted, educators unfortunately

Figure 21.3 Common procedural errors in IEP development.

- Failing to notify parents of their procedural rights.
- Failing to obtain informed parental consent when it is required (e.g., to conduct an initial evaluation of a student to determine eligibility, to provide special education services for the first time, to conduct a reevaluation of a student, to excuse an IEP team member from an IEP meeting in which the member's areas or service is being discussed).
- Predetermining a student's placement or IEP services.
- Improperly excusing IEP members from attending IEP meetings (i.e., without parental permission).
- Improper IEP team membership.
- Failing to ensure the availability of a continuum of alternative placements.
- Failing to consider the five special factors (i.e., behavior, limited English proficiency, blind/visually impaired, deaf/hard of hearing, and assistive technology) when developing an IEP of a student when these factors are relevant.
- Making decisions based on the availability of services.
- Making decisions based solely on costs.
- Failing to consider the results of an independent educational evaluation.
- Failing to allow a student's parents meaningful participation in the IEP process.

Figure 21.4 Common substantive errors in IEP development.

- Failing to conduct a full and individualized evaluation of a student that provides the IEP team members with important information that leads to programming decisions.
- Failing to address all of a student's academic and functional needs in the Present Levels of Academic Achievement and Functional Performance (PLAAFP) statements.
- Failing to link a student's needs from the PLAAFP statements to the student's annual goals and special education services.
- Writing annual goals that are not measurable.
- Failing to measure a student's progress toward her annual goals.
- Failing to provide services to meet all of a student's needs from the PLAAFP statements.
- Failing to properly address transition services when necessary.
- Failing to include positive behavior supports and interventions in a student's IEP when necessary.
- Failing to provide the services written in a student's IEP.

often place "process above results, and bureaucratic compliance above student achievement, excellence, and outcomes" (p. 3). Procedurally correct IEPs will not meet legal standards if a student's IEP does not result in her achieving meaningful educational benefit.

According to Drasgow et al. (2001), the crucial determinant in hearings or cases involving the substantive standard of the IDEA is whether the student makes educational progress. Regrettably, school personnel often seem to have a difficult time with the substantive requirements for developing and implementing IEPs. In fact, compliance with the mandate that students show educational progress probably occurs less often than compliance with any other IDEA-related obligation (Bateman & Linden, 2006). IDEA 2004 increases the emphasis on meaningful programming by requiring that IEPs include (a) special education services that are based on peer-reviewed research, (b) measurable annual goals, and (c) progress-monitoring systems. In fact, IDEA 2004 now requires that when hearing officers rule on cases involving IEPs, they base their decisions on "substantive grounds based on a determination of whether a child received a free appropriate public education" (IDEA, 20 U.S.C. § 1415(f)(3)(E)(I)). Whereas the procedural

requirements retain importance, this section of IDEA 2004 requires hearing officers to base their rulings on whether a student makes meaningful academic and functional progress in their special education program. In summary, to provide an appropriate education to a student with disabilities, school professionals and the student's parents must develop an IEP that meets the requirements of the law and provides meaningful educational benefit. To do so requires careful attention to both the procedural and the substantive requirements of the IDEA. Figure 21.4 depicts common substantive errors that IEP teams make (Lake, 2010; Yell, 2009).

Developing Educationally Meaningful and Legally Sound IEPs

The IEP, as both a process and a document, is tremendously important in the special education process. In fact, the document is the embodiment of FAPE, which school districts are required to provide to every student in special education. Because of the crucial nature and legal basis of the IEP, one might assume that special education teachers are prepared to meet both the procedural and substantive requirements of the IDEA when they take part in developing IEPs. Unfortunately, this is frequently not the case. Too often the pre-service and in-service education programs for special education teachers stress the procedural requirements of IEPs and do not include professional development in substantive development of IEPs (Yell, 2009). The problem with such a focus is that an IEP team may develop a procedurally impeccable IEP that is substantively worthless. That is, just because an IEP has passed the procedural litmus test does not mean that the IEP will confer meaningful educational benefit. To ensure that students' IEPs meet the substantive requirement of the IDEA, it is crucial that IEP teams understand the importance of assessment, research-based special educational programming, and progress monitoring.

Assessment

The purpose of the special education assessment/evaluation in the IEP development process is to determine the student's unique educational needs on which the IEP will be based. Thus, the assessment is the keystone of the IEP process. The information gathered from the assessment is, in essence, the baseline information from which annual goals are written, special education services are determined, and educational progress is measured. The importance of the assessment process was directly addressed by a U.S. District Court Judge when he ruled that a school district had denied a student a FAPE because the student's IEP was based on an inadequate assessment. In his opinion, the judge wrote:

> This deficiency goes to the heart of the IEP; the child's level of academic achievement and functional performance is the foundation on which the IEP must be built. Without a clear identification of [the child's] present levels, the IEP cannot set measurable goals, evaluate the child's progress and determine which educational and related services are needed. (*Kirby v. Cabell County Board of Education,* 2006, p. 694)

The assessment results are included in the Present Level of Academic Achievement and Functional Performance (PLAAFP) section of an IEP. When IEP teams develop PLAAFP statements, they must (a) describe the effects of a student's disability on his performance in all areas that are affected by his disability (e.g., reading, mathematics, behavior), (b) write the statement in objective and measurable terms that are easily understood by all members of the team, and (c) describe how a student's disability affects his involvement and progress in the general curriculum. Moreover, the IEP team must ensure that a direct relationship exists between the PLAAFP and the other components of the IEP (e.g., annual goals, special education services, progress-monitoring system). For example, if the PLAAFP statement

describes a reading problem, the IEP must provide an annual goal for reading, a special education service that will address the reading problem, and a data-based method for measuring a student's progress toward her reading goal.

Special Education Programming

Following delineation of the PLAAFP and a discussion of a student's educational needs, team members develop and delineate a student's special education program on the IEP. The special education program consists of (a) measurable annual goals and (b) special education services.

Measurable Annual Goals

The purpose of the annual goals is to measure the progress a student makes in his special education program. The Individuals with Disabilities Education Act Amendments of 1997 (hereafter, IDEA 1997) added the requirements that annual goals must be written in measurable terms and that IEPs must also include a statement about how educators will measure a student's progress toward the goals. Unfortunately, goals are too often not aligned with the PLAAFP statement and frequently lack measurable outcomes, which would very likely invalidate an IEP in the eyes of a hearing officer or judge (Bateman & Linden, 2006). Neither the IDEA nor the regulations implementing the IDEA indicate the specific form that goals are to take, beyond requiring that they be measurable. One method that can be used to ensure that IEP goals are measureable is to use the model first proposed by Mager in 1962. Mager suggested that measurable goals, which he referred to as *instructional objectives,* needed to have three components. These components were (a) a target behavior, (b) the conditions under which the goal was to be measured, and (c) a criterion for acceptable performance. Figure 21.5 depicts a goal with these three components.

Figure 21.5   Measurable annual goal.

Goal:

In 32 weeks when presented with a passage from the second-grade reading textbook, Stacy will read aloud 48 words in 1 minute with no more than two errors.

- *Target Behavior:* Reading aloud.
- *Conditions:* In 32 weeks when presented with a passage from the second-grade reading textbook.
- *Criteria for Acceptable Performance:* 48 words in 1 minute with no more than two errors.

Special Education Services

The services to which students with disabilities with IEPs are entitled include special education services, related services, supplementary services, accommodations, and program modifications. These services represent the educational "strategies that will be most effective in realizing (the student's) goals" (IDEA Regulations, Appendix A). Essentially, the services provided are an IEP team's response to effectively addressing a student's unique educational needs. The special education services, therefore, must be aligned with the PLAAFP and the measurable annual goals in an IEP.

Perhaps the most significant change in IDEA 2004 was the requirement that special education services must be based on peer-reviewed research to the extent practicable (IDEA Regulations, 34 C.F.R. § 300.320(a)(4)). The U.S. Department of Education defines *extent practicable* as "to the extent it is possible," given the availability of peer-reviewed research (*Analysis of Comments and Changes,* 2006). Congress included this peer-review requirement because of the belief that special education had not been achieving the goals of the IDEA because of low expectations for students and an "insufficient focus on applying replicable research on proven methods of teaching and learning" (IDEA, 20 U.S.C. § 1401(c)(4)). Additionally, the U.S. Department of Education defined peer-reviewed research as "research that is reviewed by qualified independent reviewers to ensure that the quality of the information meets the standards of the field before the research is published" (71 *Fed. Reg.* 46664 (Aug. 14, 2006)).

The peer-reviewed research requirement applies to the selection and provision of (a) special education services; (b) related services (e.g., counseling services, occupational therapy, physical therapy, psychological services, speech-language services); and (c) aids, services, and supports provided in regular education settings (Etscheidt & Curran, 2010). The legislative history of IDEA 2004 and the peer-reviewed research requirement reveal that the intent of this section of the law was to ensure that IEP teams' selection of educational approaches reflect sound practices that have been validated empirically whenever possible (Etscheidt & Curran, 2010).

Progress Monitoring

All IEPs must include objectively measurable annual goals. An equally critical requirement is that a student's progress toward these goals must actually be measured. In fact, failing to measure a student's progress most likely would result in a hearing officer's or judge's invalidating an IEP and determining that FAPE had been denied if the IEP were challenged in a due process hearing or court case (Bateman & Linden, 2006). If IEP members do not establish the means to measure a student's progress toward the IEP's goals, then those goals become meaningless and useless (Bateman, 2007a).

Every student's IEP must include a description of how and when a student's progress will be measured. Moreover, a student's progress must be reported to her parents as often as the parents of nondisabled children receive progress reports or report cards, usually every 6 to 9 weeks. An important consideration in determining how progress will be monitored is that the measures must be objective and meaningful. That is, subjective or anecdotal data (e.g., a teacher's general impressions) are not sufficient. If the data show that the student is not progressing, something in her program must be changed. Yell and Stecker (2003) asserted that IEP teams must continuously collect meaningful data to document student progress and, thus, to demonstrate the effectiveness of the special education program. Students' IEP teams can meet these requirements of the IDEA by using appropriate data-collection procedures and using the data to guide instructional decision making. For example, to monitor student progress in reading, a team could collect reading-fluency data using curriculum-based measurement (see Deno, 2003); or if data were being collected on student behaviors, a team could systematically observe and graph the frequency of the occurrence of those behaviors (Kazdin, 2010).

The IEP requirement of the IDEA is the method by which local education agencies (LEAs) provide a FAPE to all students in special education. Unfortunately, the procedural and substantive requirements of IEPs have been challenging to school districts. Clearly, many IEP team members have basic misunderstandings of both the IEP process and IEP document (Simon, 2006). In fact, in interviews and surveys, researchers have found that some special education teachers regard IEPs as paperwork exercises for legal purposes (Yell & Stecker, 2003) and find IEP meetings burdensome (E. C. Lynch & Beare, 1990; Nickles, Cronis, Justen, & Smith, 1992; S. W. Smith, 1990b), rather than understanding the crucial nature of the process and document. We have addressed these challenges in this section by briefly outlining the legal requirements in developing, implementing, and evaluating IEPs, as well as the process for developing educationally meaningful and legally sound IEPs.

Researchers have also examined the issues involved in both the IEP document and the IEP meeting with regard to compliance issues. In fact, J. Gallagher and Desimone (1995) identified a number of problems with IEPs in their review of the literature. They described two major problem areas that emerged from 15 years of IEP research: satisfying content requirements of the IEP document (i.e., procedural issues), and developing and implementing effective IEPs (i.e., substantive issues). Next, we provide a representative sample of the literature about potential problems and recommended practices regarding compliance issues with the IEP document. We follow this with an examination of examples from the literature describing problems and recommended practices in developing and implementing IEPs.

Research on IEP Compliance Issues

The literature on IEPs is vast, especially before 1997, and we have chosen to review a sample of studies from 1990 to the present to illustrate the findings of this literature base. For a more comprehensive review of the literature on IEPs before 1990, see S. W. Smith (1990b); Rodger (1995); and McLaughlin and Warren (1995). See Sopko (2003) for a synthesis of literature on IEPs from 1997 to 2002. In this section, we examine two major areas of IEP research: (a) studies that focus on the extent to which practitioners have written and implemented the required components in the IEP document and (b) studies

involving training practitioners in the development and implementation of the IEP requirement. The research on compliance issues can inform practice by highlighting the need for careful consideration of components that must be included in the IEP document. This research also emphasizes the need for effective practitioner training in writing and implementing educationally meaningful and legally sound IEPs.

Research on IEP Components and Implementation

In this section we provide a sample of studies that represents the literature on the adequacy of IEPs, specifically in relation to IEP goals, IEP accommodations, and IEP transition plans. Table 21.1 provides a summary of findings from these studies.

Research Involving IEP Goals

Although Congress intended for the IEP to be the vehicle to ensure that students with disabilities receive an individualized and appropriate education (Yell & Stecker, 2003),

Table 21.1   Studies Examining IEP Components

Variables Examined	Reference
IEP Goals	
Appropriateness of goals and objectives for students with EBD and MID categories and relationship of IEP goals to classroom instruction.	E. C. Lynch & Beare, 1990
Types of goals for students with EBD and LD and congruence of goals with present levels of performance.	S. W. Smith, 1990a
Appropriateness of goals and objectives for the EBD, LD, and MID categories.	Nickles et al., 1992
Types of goals for students with EBD and congruence of goals with present levels of performance.	M. Epstein et al., 1992
Relationship of IEP goals for students with MID to classroom instruction.	Krom & Prater, 1993
Quality of IEP goals for students with deaf-blindness.	Giangreco et al., 1994
Quality of IEP goals and objectives for students in early childhood special education programs.	Michnowicz et al., 1995
Congruence of IEP goals with diagnosed reading disabilities in basic skills.	Catone & Brady, 2005
IEP Accommodations	
Validity of testing accommodation for students with learning disabilities.	L. S. Fuchs & Fuchs, 2001
Relationship between instructional and assessment accommodations.	Ysseldyke et al., 2001
Definitional, legal, and validity issues involved in decisions on testing accommodations.	S. N. Elliott et al., 2002
Relationship between accommodation assignments, teachers' recommendations, and students' performance data.	Ketterlin-Geller, Alonzo, et al., 2007
IEP Transition Plans	
Quality of transition plans related to federally mandated content.	Shearin et al., 1999
Quality of the transition plans and relationship of transition goals to transition programming.	K. M. Powers et al., 2005

Note: EBD = emotional and behavioral disorder; IEP = individualized education program; LD = learning disability; MID = mild intellectual disability.

it did not offer specific details on how to write the IEP document, particularly IEP goals. It has indeed been a challenge for practitioners to develop IEP goals that are appropriately aligned to students' needs, are measurable, can be understood by IEP team members, and can be effectively implemented in classroom settings. Various studies specifically examined the relationship between IEP goals and present levels of performance, the appropriateness and quality of IEP goals for various students, and the relationship between IEP goals and classroom instruction.

The following three studies represent the research addressing the relationship between IEP goals and present levels of performance. These studies all examined archival data and employed correlational research designs. S. W. Smith (1990a) examined 120 IEPs of fourth-, fifth-, and sixth-grade male students with emotional and behavioral disorders (EBDs) and learning disabilities (LDs) to assess (a) procedural compliance, (b) substantive content, and (c) congruence (i.e., the match between present levels of performance and annual goals). M. Epstein, Patton, Polloway, and Foley (1992) assessed the IEPs of 107 junior high students with EBD to determine the relationship between the students' current behavioral problems listed on their IEPs with their annual goals. Catone and Brady (2005) examined the congruence of the annual goals of 54 high school students who had diagnosed reading disabilities in decoding and word recognition to the listed needs and present levels on their IEPs. The overall finding of these studies revealed substantial problems regarding congruence, most notably, a mismatch between listed areas of need, present levels of performance, and annual goals.

We identified four descriptive studies examining archival data that typify the research on the appropriateness and quality of IEP goals for various students. E. C. Lynch and Beare (1990) examined the IEPs of 48 students identified as having either an EBD or an educable mental handicap (i.e., mild intellectual disability). They found that nearly all of the IEP goals were academic—to the exclusion of social skills, vocational skills, or other functional living skills. They also found that goals and objectives were vague and lacked criteria for successful performance and evaluation. Nickles et al. (1992) examined the categories of objectives in the IEPs of 150 students with EBD, LD, and mild intellectual disabilities. The researchers found a number of deficiencies in the IEP goals and objectives, such as few social/behavioral objectives for the students with EBD, and an insufficient number of goals in basic living skills for the students with intellectual disabilities. Giangreco, Dennis, Edelman, and Cloninger (1994) analyzed the IEP goals for 46 students with deaf-blindness in kindergarten through 12th grade who attended general education classes either full- or part-time. The researchers

identified three major problems with the IEP goals: (a) goals were broad, inconsistent, and inadequately matched to the general education context; (b) goals addressed staff behavior (e.g., repositioning students) rather than student learning outcomes; and (c) goals described broad curricular categories rather than student learning outcomes. And finally, Michnowicz, McConnell, Peterson, and Odom (1995) examined the IEPs of 163 children in early childhood special education programs. The researchers found that most of the goals and objectives were not measurable and that the majority of the IEPs were so vague that students' progress could not be monitored. They also found that nearly half of the IEPs did not include goals for social interactions, even when assessment data showed a need for social interaction interventions with preschool children with disabilities.

Three descriptive studies represent the research addressing the relationship between IEP goals and classroom instruction. In their study of 48 students with EBD and mild intellectual disability, E. C. Lynch and Beare (1990) also examined the relationship between IEP goals and instruction by observing the students in their general and special education classrooms. During the observations, the researchers saw little relationship between IEP goals and instruction. Krom and Prater (1993) compared the IEP goals of 21 intermediate-aged students with mild intellectual disability to the teachers' self-reported subjects and content they taught. The researchers found wide discrepancies between the written IEP goals and the content teachers reported teaching. Giangreco et al. (1994), in their study of students with deaf-blindness, also observed 20 students during their classes and concluded that daily instruction in the general education settings did not incorporate students' IEP goals.

These research studies demonstrate that teachers need instruction, practice, and support in cultivating skills for developing and implementing IEPs, particularly in writing goals. The researchers recommended that teacher preparation programs and professional development programs explore strategies to help practitioners develop quality IEPs. They suggested stressing the importance of the relationship between IEP goals and daily instruction, as well as evaluating the IEP as an instructional tool.

Research Involving IEP Accommodations

IEP teams are entrusted with the difficult task of selecting valid accommodations for individual students before their participation in state proficiency testing (i.e., high-stakes testing). Accommodations are intended to level the playing field for students with disabilities, yet the very nature of individualizing accommodations seems to contradict the purpose of testing standardization that allows for score comparisons across groups. Several researchers have examined issues involved in determining appropriate accommodations for students with disabilities who are required to participate in high-stakes testing. Some of the problems identified in documenting accommodations on students' IEPs include: (a) determining which accommodations are appropriate and valid for individual students, (b) recommending accommodations too frequently, (c) inconsistency between instructional and assessment accommodations, and (d) confusion between accommodations and modifications. Modifications exceed accommodations and refer to changes in the content of curricula or assessments that represent meaningful differences from that given to other students (e.g., excluding certain items from an assessment). Modifications are generally not allowed for state proficiency testing (Ysseldyke, Thurlow, Bielinski, House, Moody, & Haigh, 2001).

The following three studies addressed issues of determining appropriate accommodations for students with disabilities who are required to participate in high-stakes testing. L. S. Fuchs and Fuchs (2001) discussed two controlled experimental studies, one focused on reading (L. S. Fuchs, Fuchs, Eaton, Hamlett, Binkley, et al., 2000) and one focused on math (L. S. Fuchs, Fuchs, Eaton, Hamlett, & Karns, 2000), in which the researchers examined testing accommodations for students with LD. Their studies involved approximately 200 students with LD and 200 without LD in fourth and fifth grades from several schools. L. S. Fuchs and Fuchs (2001) concluded from the results of these studies that teachers granted many more reading and math accommodations to students than were warranted. They further suggested that teachers seemed to base their decisions for accommodations on student demographics, recommending accommodations more frequently for students who were African American, qualified for free/reduced-price lunch, had been retained, had lower IQ scores, and read at lower levels.

Ysseldyke et al. (2001) conducted a descriptive study in which they examined the relationship between instructional and assessment accommodations in the IEPs of 280 students with various disabilities in grades 1 through 8. The researchers found that overall students' instructional accommodations matched their testing accommodations (84%). Some of the problems raters identified on these IEPs for instructional or testing accommodations included (a) lack of documentation, (b) providing more or fewer accommodations than appeared justified, and (c) confusion about terminology (i.e., listing an accommodation as a modification).

Ketterlin-Geller, Alonzo, Braun-Monegan, and Tindal (2007) used a correlational research design to examine the IEPs of 38 third-grade students to assess the consistency of accommodations assigned, teachers'

recommendations, and students' performance data. Ketterlin-Geller, Alonzo, et al. concluded that teachers recommended more accommodations than were designated on the students' IEPs, and that teachers recommended more accommodations than needed, when considering student performance data.

These examples of research studies involving IEP accommodations provide an outline of the issues that practitioners need to address. For example, it appears that IEP team members use subjective judgment to make accommodation decisions. These decisions often lead to unjustifiable accommodations that were not distinctly beneficial to students with disabilities (i.e., leveled the playing field). S. N. Elliott, McKevitt, and Kettler (2002) illustrated this in a summary of four experimental studies examining statistical effects of accommodations on test scores of students with and without disabilities. Results from these studies revealed that teachers recommended accommodations that did not significantly and differentially affect test scores for students with or without disabilities. For example, they found that extended time made no significant difference for students with or without disabilities on a math assessment, and that a read-aloud accommodation gave a boost to both groups.

S. N. Elliott et al. (2002) recommended that practitioners who select testing accommodations need knowledge of (a) the student's abilities, disabilities, and instructional accommodations; (b) state and district testing guidelines; (c) the test's item content and format; (d) tests' validity and how test scores can be invalidated; and (e) any previous accommodations successfully used with the student. IEP teams need support and guidance in fulfilling the difficult task of selecting valid accommodations for individual students with disabilities. Specifically, IEP teams need support and guidance to provide accommodations that address the student's disability, are consistent with instructional accommodations and previously successful testing accommodations, do not invalidate the test, do not contradict testing guidelines, and are consistent with the test's items and content.

Research Involving IEP Transition Plans

Poor outcomes for students exiting from special education have served as an impetus for federal initiatives to improve transition planning. IDEA requires that IEPs include transition goals, services, and plans for students who are 16 years of age, and for younger youth if determined appropriate by the IEP team. Specifically, transition plans must consider the following postschool outcomes: (a) postsecondary education, (b) vocational training, (c) integrated employment, (d) continuing and adult education, (e) adult services, and (f) independent living or community participation. A number of researchers have examined the extent to which transition planning in students' IEPs incorporates the IDEA mandates and effective transition practices.

The following two descriptive studies represent the research addressing the quality of transition plans. Shearin, Roessler, and Schriner (1999) evaluated transition plans in the IEPs of 68 high school students identified as having either LD or intellectual disability. Their results revealed the following inadequacies in transition planning within these IEPs: (a) transition goals addressing future living arrangements, postsecondary education, and employment were vague or missing (e.g., of the 68 documents examined, 43% did not address employment and 78% did not address postsecondary education); (b) few plans referred to self-advocacy and family planning; and (c) few plans specified adult service agencies (e.g., 7% referred to vocational rehabilitation). K. M. Powers et al. (2005) examined 399 IEPs for students aged 16 to 22 with learning, physical, intellectual, and emotional disabilities. The researchers found that transition plans were missing for 24% of the sample and that the overall quality of the plans was low. For example, students' current work experiences were inconsistent with employment goals for 27% of the sample. The authors reported that (a) the transition plans did not provide sufficient detail; (b) the participation of transition specialists and vocational rehabilitation personnel in the IEP process was low; and (c) few IEPs referenced self-determination education, even though self-determination skills have been found to support students' current success and postschool outcomes. The researchers also found that the IEPs of students with developmental disabilities included the lowest-quality transition plans.

These research studies involving IEP transition goals highlight the need for training for practitioners who must write and implement transition goals. Some IEP teams appear to lack basic information about the requirements of IDEA relative to transition goals and objectives, especially regarding access to adult service agencies, and the range of curricular and employment opportunities available for students.

This sample of the literature on compliance issues suggests the need for careful consideration of components that are included in the IEP document. Studies revealed that IEPs often lacked required components and that misconnections or no connections occurred among the components (e.g., Catone & Brady, 2005; Nickles et al., 1992). Additional findings indicated that many IEPs contained inappropriate goals and that goals did not match classroom instruction (e.g., Krom & Prater, 1993; E. C. Lynch & Beare, 1990). Accommodations included in IEPs for students taking state-wide assessments seemed to lack individuality, and practitioners often made subjective decisions based on

student demographics (e.g., L. S. Fuchs & Fuchs, 2001). Researchers questioned the validity of such accommodations when scores improved for both students with and without disabilities, or did not improve for either group (S. N. Elliott et al., 2002). Researchers also found that the quality of transition plans included in IEPs was problematic, with goals either missing or too vague to be meaningful (e.g., K. M. Powers et al., 2005). These studies point to a critical need for practitioner training, guidance, and support. Teacher-preparation programs as well as state and district administrators need to explore strategies to ensure that those who are responsible for the important tasks of developing and implementing IEPs have the knowledge and skills necessary.

Research on Training Practitioners to Develop and Implement the IEP

In the previous section, we focused specifically on required components within the IEP document; now we review intervention studies focusing on the development and implementation of the IEP. Unfortunately, few studies have specifically examined training practitioners to develop and implement IEPs. Nevertheless, the following examples from the literature (see Table 21.2) address training practitioners on writing IEP goals and transition plans, determining and documenting accommodations in the IEP, implementing IEP goals in the classroom, and student participation in the IEP process.

Research on Training Practitioners to Write IEP Goals and Transition Plans

As described previously, investigations of IEP goals and transition plans written by educational personnel often do not meet recommended practice guidelines. Strategies are needed to close this gap between recommended practice and actual practice. In theory, well-developed IEP goals lead to effective instruction, and well-written transition plans lead to positive student outcomes and successful postschool experiences. Researchers have demonstrated that teachers need instruction, practice, and support in cultivating skills for developing and implementing IEPs, particularly in writing goals (e.g., M. Epstein et al., 1992; Nickles et al., 1992). Although states and districts have reported providing an array of training efforts for educators on developing and implementing IEPs, the literature is lacking in studies designed to assess the impact of such training (J. Gallagher & Desimone, 1995). Following are two examples of intervention studies on training practitioners to write goals.

Pretti-Frontczak and Bricker (2000) conducted a quasi-experimental study that involved using a training

Table 21.2 Studies Examining Development and Implementation of IEPs

Variables Examined	Reference
Writing IEP Goals	
Writing IEP goals and objectives using a CBA.	Pretti-Frontczak & Bricker, 2000
Writing IEP Assessment and Participation Accommodations	
Increasing the quality and extent of participation and accommodation documentation on the IEP.	Shriner & DeStefano, 2003
Writing IEP Transition Plans	
Improving the quality of transition components in students' IEPs.	Finn & Kohler, 2009
Implementing IEP Goals	
Embedding instruction of IEP goals for students with disabilities in inclusive classrooms.	Horn et al., 2000
Perceptions of the IEP Requirement	
Comparing perceptions of IEP meeting participants.	Menlove, Hudson, & Suter, 2001
Comparing teachers' and parents' perceptions of the IEP requirement.	J. E. Martin, Marshall, & Sale, 2004; Simon, 2006
Involving Students in their IEP Process	
Using an IEP lesson package to increase student participation in their annual IEP meeting.	Allen et al., 2001
Increasing student participation in IEP conferences.	Hammer, 2004
Review of intervention studies to involve students in their IEP process.	Test et al., 2004
Increasing student participation in IEP meetings.	J. E. Martin, Van Dycke, Christensen, Greene, Gardner, & Lovett, 2006

package to help practitioners write IEP goals. The researchers arranged training for 86 participants from five states. They implemented a training package over 2 days that included information on writing IEP goals and objectives, as well as using a curriculum-based assessment and an evaluation measure. Results indicated statistically significant improvement in IEPs from pre- to post-training. Although this study lacked a control group and did not examine student outcomes, writing quality IEPs is an important first step in the process of achieving desired outcomes for students with disabilities.

In another example of training practitioners to improve the quality of transition planning, Finn and Kohler (2009) conducted a quasi-experimental study in which they analyzed the data from one state on their implementation of the Transition Outcomes Project using the Transition Requirements Checklist (O'Leary & Doty, 2001). The researchers analyzed the content of 166 students' IEPs to determine whether the IEPs complied with the transition requirements of the IDEA at two points: before a 3-day training provided by state transition leaders and 2 years following completion of the training. Mixed results revealed that the content of some students' IEPs showed improvement, whereas others did not. In some cases, compliance of transition items in the IEP did not improve at all, and in other cases compliance declined.

Research on Training Practitioners to Document Accommodations in IEPs

In the previous section on research involving the IEP document, we reviewed several studies that addressed documenting accommodations on students' IEPs and determining which accommodations are appropriate and valid for individual students. Those researchers recommended training IEP teams in this area; however, research on training practitioners to select appropriate accommodations is limited. We identified one study that involved this type of training. To improve decisions regarding state-wide assessments, Shriner and DeStefano (2003) conducted a quasi-experimental intervention study in three school districts in which they provided 8 to 10 hours of training in (a) IDEA requirements regarding participation in state proficiency testing and accommodations in that testing, (b) revising current IEP forms and processes to facilitate and document participation and accommodation decisions, (c) state learning standards, and (d) assessing and documenting students' participation in the general curriculum and their instructional and classroom assessment accommodations. The researchers found that following training, the IEPs in all three districts were more complete in documenting assessment accommodations planned for state testing, and the IEPs reflected planned increases in student participation in state-wide testing.

Research on Training Practitioners to Implement IEP Goals

Teachers' implementation of IEP goals and the resulting student outcomes make up perhaps the most important area researchers should be addressing. Unfortunately, this is another area where a major gap exists in the literature. J. Gallagher and Desimone (1995) found that many teachers viewed the IEP as an administrative rather than instructional task, and once written, they often did not use the IEP for instruction. The authors suggested that when IEP teams neglect progress monitoring of IEP goals, they are not meeting the original intent of the IEP. Indeed, in Hill's (2006) review of federal and state IEP-related court decisions from the years 2000 to 2006, more than 50% of the cases involved procedural violations of the IEP process. This affirms the need to examine the extent to which teachers are implementing the IEP and monitoring progress toward meeting those goals.

The following study is an example of an intervention aimed at helping teachers implement IEP goals and monitor progress. Horn, Lieber, Li, Sandall, and Schwartz (2000) conducted three case studies in which they examined a three-step procedure to assist early childhood inclusive teachers in developing strategies for embedding instruction of targeted IEP goals and objectives for students with disabilities into daily activities. The researchers (a) gave teachers examples of embedding IEP goals and objectives into daily activities, (b) clarified and discussed each student's IEP goals and objectives with the teachers, and (c) guided teachers in designing their own strategies for embedding the goals and objectives into daily activities. In each case, the teachers increased instruction of the targeted IEP goals, and each of the children demonstrated improvement on these targeted goals. This type of study offers important implications for the field in demonstrating that, with varying degrees of support, inclusive teachers can provide instruction on students' IEP goals within existing classroom activities; and when they do, student outcomes on their IEP goals are positive.

Research on Training Students to Participate in the IEP Process

The IDEA requires that educators must invite a student to her IEP meeting when postsecondary goals and transition services are being considered (IDEA regulations, 34 CFR 300.321(b)(1)). In addition, promoting students' self-advocacy and self-determination skills are important goals in special education programs (Wehmeyer, 2005). Thus, involving students in their IEP process should be common practice. Nevertheless, this practice does not appear to be widespread. Teachers have expressed a need and desire for training in how to teach students self-advocacy and self-determination skills as well as a need for information on related curricula (Test et al., 2004). Several researchers have examined interventions designed to increase students' involvement in their IEP process. Test and colleagues conducted a review of this literature from 1972 to 2002 (2004). They found that the use of published curricula (e.g., IPLAN by Van Reusen & Bos, 1990; The Self-Directed IEP by J. E. Martin, Marshall, Maxson, & Jerman, 1997; Next S.T.E.P. by Halpern et al., 1997) as well as person-centered planning (see Miner & Bates, 1997; Timmons & Whitney-Thomas, 1998) effectively increased student participation in their IEP meetings. The results also indicated that providing direct instruction to the student before the meeting as well as the meeting facilitator's behavior during the meeting (e.g., directing questions to students, avoiding jargon, using understandable language), enhanced student performance. We selected the following three studies as examples of training students and teachers to promote student participation in the IEP process.

Allen, Smith, Test, Flowers, and Wood (2001) conducted a single-subject, multiple-baseline research study in which they taught four students aged 15 to 21 with moderate intellectual disabilities the skills needed to manage their own IEP meetings. The researchers modified a multimedia package called The Self-Directed IEP (J. E. Martin et al., 1997), which included a Teacher's Manual, Student Workbook, and two videos. After completing the units, students demonstrated increased participation in mock IEP meetings and in their actual IEP meetings. J. E. Martin, Van Dycke, Greene, et al. (2006) conducted a randomized group experiment to assess the effectiveness of the Self-Directed IEP strategy. The researchers collected and analyzed data from 764 IEP team members participating in 130 middle and high school transition IEP meetings. Students were randomly assigned to the intervention and control groups, with 65 students with various disabilities in each group. The findings revealed that students who were taught the Self-Directed IEP strategies significantly outperformed the control group on the following measures: (a) attendance at IEP meetings; (b) active participation in their IEP meetings; (c) engagement in IEP leadership behaviors; (d) expression of their interests, skills, and limits across transition areas; and (e) recall of IEP goals after the meetings ended. In addition, their postschool vision section on the IEP document included more comprehensive postschool transition statements. Finally, Hammer (2004) conducted a single-subject, multiple-baseline research study in which she used the Self-Advocacy Strategy (Lancaster & Lancaster, 2003) to increase participation in IEP meetings of three students aged 12 to 13. The students learned the IPLAN strategy, which includes the following steps: (a) **I**nventory your strengths, areas to improve or learn, goals, and choices for learning or accommodations; (b) **P**rovide your inventory information; (c) **L**isten and respond; (d) **A**sk questions; and (e) **N**ame your goals. Teachers then role-played IEP meetings with the students. Results indicated that after training using the IPLAN strategy, the three students were more involved with writing goals and participating in their IEP meetings. For example, all three students verbalized relevant statements about their strengths and areas for improvement.

This sample of the literature on compliance issues suggests the need for careful consideration in developing and implementing the IEP. Studies revealed that with training, teachers can improve the quality of written IEP goals, the documentation of mandated transition components on IEPs, the documentation of assessment accommodations, and the implementation of IEP goals within existing classroom activities. Additional findings revealed positive effects of specifically training and instructing students in how to write goals and participate in their IEP meetings.

Summary of Empirical Literature

In this section, we presented examples from the literature involving the IEP requirement. We reviewed several research studies that addressed compliance issues involving components of the IEP document. Researchers found various inadequacies when examining the IEP document, specifically with IEP goals, accommodations, and transition plans. We also reviewed several research studies that addressed the IEP process. The problems found with the process mirrored those found with the content in the IEP document, such as writing and implementing the IEP, as well as students' participating in the IEP meeting. Researchers discovered that specific training improved the writing and implementing of IEPs and students' participation in their IEP meetings.

These research findings make it clear that practitioners are having difficulty fulfilling the mandated IEP requirement of the IDEA. J. Gallagher and Desimone (1995) asserted that the difference between policy development and policy implementation is often vast. Policy makers' mandated requirements often are well intended and based on good theory, yet short on practicality at the local level. For example, policy makers may assume that a team of professionals from different disciplines can collaborate well as a transdisciplinary IEP team. In reality, it is difficult to coordinate schedules and share information among the various professionals to accomplish this (J. Gallagher & Desimone, 1995). A theme that has emerged from the empirical literature to date is the need to narrow this gap between policy and practice.

Most of the empirical literature on implementing the IEP requirement has focused on the content of the IEP document, with a few studies addressing interventions on training practitioners in how to write IEPs. These studies were informative and demonstrated the value of specific training on developing components in the IEP document. Researchers also demonstrated the positive effects of training on student participation in their IEP meetings. Unfortunately, research on the implementation of IEPs and the link between IEPs and student outcomes is scarce. Assessing the implementation and impact of IEPs on student outcomes is critical, and thus future research should address the following issues: (a) the extent to which teachers currently implement IEP goals in classroom settings; (b) the extent to which students master IEP goals; (c) the effect of pre-service training on new teachers' development of IEPs, and implementation of IEP goals, accommodations, and transition plans; (d) the effect of professional development training on teachers' development of IEPs, and implementation of IEP goals, accommodations, and transition plans; and (e) the effect of accommodations on student outcomes during instruction and testing.

Finally, to conduct investigations of the IEP process, researchers need a reliable and valid tool to evaluate the procedural and substantive quality of IEPs. Such a tool could be used as a dependent variable in research to improve the IEP. At least one such instrument, the IEP Quality Indicator Scale (IQUIS), was developed by Yell, Drasgow, and Oh (2008) to analyze IEPs in a study of a web-based IEP tutorial (Shriner, Carty, Trach, Weber, & Yell, 2008). The development of a reliable and valid IEP evaluation instrument is important to research in this area.

Recommendations for Practice

Researchers have repeatedly suggested the need for training at the practitioner level and have recommended that teacher-preparation programs and school district professional development programs provide the needed training in implementing the IEP requirement of the IDEA (Bateman & Linden, 2006; Catone & Brady, 2005; Etscheidt & Curran, 2010; M. Epstein et al., 1992; Huefner, 2000; Nickles et al., 1992; S. W. Smith, 1990b; Yell, 2009). Both teacher-preparation programs and school districts can use the information from the empirical literature to develop training programs that address the observed weaknesses in fulfilling the IEP requirement. Based on the legal requirements and research findings, we suggest recommendations for practice that emphasize a general need for training, guidance, and support for practitioners and students in various aspects of the IEP requirement. Readers should note that we distinguish between *pre-service training* in those skill areas that teachers should possess on leaving their preparation programs and *in-service training,* which refers to professional development opportunities conducted by school districts and state educational agencies to ensure that teachers become fluent in newly developed research-based procedures.

Pre-service teacher trainers should ensure that special education teachers leave their programs with the skills to plan, develop, implement, and evaluate IEPs that lead to meaningful and legally sound educational programs for the students they teach. Pre-service training should specifically address the following five areas: (a) conducting meaningful assessments; (b) developing appropriate, measurable goals; (c) using research-based practices; (d) monitoring the progress of students toward achieving their goals; and (e) collaborating with parents and professionals in IEP development.

First, special education teachers must have the skills to plan, conduct, and interpret meaningful assessments. Whereas assessment begins with eligibility determination, it is crucial that special education teachers understand that a meaningful assessment must also contribute useful and functional information that leads directly to educational programming (Bateman & Linden, 2006; Deno, 2003; Yell, 2009).

Second, teachers need to be able to write goals that are measurable, linked to student deficits, reflect skills needed to access the general education curriculum, and include measurement procedures for monitoring and evaluating performance (Bateman, 2007a; Yell, 2009). The annual goals are statements of what the IEP team believes a student can reasonably be expected to accomplish in 1 year with effective research-based educational programming. For students who are of transition age, IEP teams and students themselves must be able to collaborate with various service agencies to develop meaningful and measurable transition goals that lead to a full range of life, curricular, and employment opportunities.

Third, teachers must be able to develop special education services that are based on the peer-reviewed research (Etscheidt & Curran, 2010; Yell, 2009). Thus, special education teachers must be knowledgeable about peer-reviewed research and be able to integrate effective, evidence-based practices into students' program to facilitate advancement toward their goals. Table 21.3 includes examples of Web sites where teachers and administrators can access and identify empirically validated practices and procedures.

Fourth, special education teachers must understand how to collect and analyze progress-monitoring data (Bateman & Linden, 2006; Deno, 2003; Yell, 2009). The IDEA requires that all IEPs include statements of how students' progress toward their annual goals will be measured and how students' parents will be informed of their children's progress. This will require that the IEP team adopt an effective, data-based method of monitoring students' progress. The most appropriate data collection systems are those that rely on quantitative data in which target behaviors can be measured, graphed, and visually inspected (e.g., curriculum-based measurement, direct observation) to monitor students' progress toward achieving their goals (Yell, 2006). Anecdotal data and subjective judgments are not appropriate for monitoring progress and should not be the basis of a teacher's data collection procedures.

Finally, pre-service programs should also prepare their students in collaborating with parents and other professionals on multidisciplinary teams, working together in IEP meetings, and involving students in their IEPs.

Table 21.3   Web Sites on Research-Based Practices

Web Site	*URL*
Council for Exceptional Children	http://www.cec.sped.org/AM/Template.cfm?Section=Evidence_based_Practice&Template=/TaggedPage/TaggedPageDisplay.cfm&TPLID=24&ContentID=4710
National Center on Response to Intervention	http://www.rti4success.org/tools_charts/instruction.php
National Dissemination Center for Children with Disabilities (NICHCY)	http://www.nichcy.org/Research/EvidenceForEducation/Pages/Default.aspx
National Dropout Prevention Center for Students with Disabilities	http://www.ndpc-sd.org/knowledge/practice_guides.php
National Professional Development Center on Autism Spectrum Disorders	http://autismpdc.fpg.unc.edu/content/evidence-based-practices
National Secondary Transition Technical Assistance Center	http://www.nsttac.org/ebp/ebp_main.aspx
Office of Special Education Programs, Technical Assistance Center on Positive Behavioral Interventions and Supports	http://www.pbis.org/
What Works Clearinghouse	http://ies.ed.gov/ncee/wwc/

School district administrators are responsible for implementing appropriate professional development opportunities for their teachers. Because of the constant expansion of the knowledge base in special education, professional development activities should focus on keeping teachers fluent in the latest peer-reviewed research findings. Professional development activities should also target general educators and help to clarify their roles in the IEP process and how to implement IEP goals and monitor progress. In addition, district and school administrators should develop a system of accountability in which they follow up on team members' performance in developing IEPs and evaluating student performance. They should promote collaboration and communication among IEP team members and provide continued training and opportunities for writing measurable goals, linking goals to instruction, and monitoring student progress. For specific information on how to link assessment, IEP goal development, intervention, and evaluation, see Grisham-Brown, Pretti-Frontczak, Hemmeter, and Ridgley (2002) and Pretti-Frontczak and Bricker (2004).

Practitioners, including all IEP team members, face numerous challenges in attempting to fulfill the IEP requirement of the IDEA. Although professional development and teacher-preparation programs should provide the needed training in implementation of the IEP requirement, practitioners must put the training into practice. In addition to the recommendations provided here, IEP team members should focus on (a) providing specially designed instruction based on assessment data; (b) developing IEP goals for academic and functional areas that are relevant, measurable, and individually meaningful; (c) implementing educational programs that are based on peer-reviewed research; and (d) monitoring student progress toward their IEP goals frequently and systematically using appropriate data collection systems. Additionally, teachers must maintain good communication and effective working relationships with parents and elicit feedback from IEP team members to constantly improve the IEP process.

Practitioners and researchers need to understand the distinction between procedural and substantive compliance with the IEP requirements of the IDEA. Too often, school district personnel assume that procedurally compliant IEPs will result in substantive compliance (i.e., improved education and services and better outcomes for students) with the IDEA. This is clearly not the case. In fact, a procedurally compliant IEP can be substantively useless if the IEP does not provide meaningful educational benefit to a student (Yell, 2009). If IEPs are to meet the promise envisioned when the EHA was passed in 1975, school personnel must understand that the IEP is more than a document; it is in actuality the process by which a student's FAPE is developed and delivered.

CHAPTER 22

Using Assessments to Determine Placement in the Least Restrictive Environment for Students with Disabilities

Frederick J. Brigham | *George Mason University*

Jean B. Crockett | *The University of Florida*

Special education decisions should be deliberative. The actions taken should be based on clear thinking and rooted in data that address the specific issues of concern. In many cases, special education decisions, particularly those involving placement, are made without adequate data to support clear thought and reasoned actions. Actions that are independent of thought and data are unlikely to result in actual benefits for the individuals with disabilities they are intended to help.

Some educators point to recent revisions in federal and state regulations, claiming they are no longer required to conduct many assessments that were a part of special education deliberations in the past; others question the utility of assessment tools in making placement decisions; and others suggest that placement is a moot point because *all* students with disabilities should be taught in general education settings. We contend that these beliefs are incorrect, and in this chapter we examine the ways that regulations continue to require timely and meaningful assessments to make individual placement decisions based on individual needs. We also examine issues surrounding various forms of assessment data in pursuit of the union of data, thought, and action in placement.

Special education in the United States is carried out under requirements of the Individuals with Disabilities Education Act (IDEA), the federal law that ensures each student with a disability receives a free appropriate public education (FAPE) in the least restrictive environment (LRE) for that student. The tool for carrying out these requirements is the student's individualized education program (IEP). At first glance, the meanings of FAPE and LRE appear straightforward and easily understandable. The amount of contention surrounding these concepts, however, suggests that *if* their meaning was ever clear to lawmakers, it is no longer clear to decision makers concerned with determinations of special education eligibility, appropriate services, and the settings or placements in which those services might be provided.

The topic we address is broad, and generalizations that apply uniformly across disability types, various purposes of schooling, and age groups are rare. For this reason, the *I* in IEP stands for *individualized* (not *interchangeable*). Therefore, we limit our focus to academic curricular issues for students of school age with high-incidence disabilities (i.e., specific learning disabilities, emotional or behavioral disorders, and mild intellectual disabilities). We also limit our discussion to students with adequate proficiency in English.

Contextual Bases for Making Instructional Placement Decisions

The contextual background with which one approaches deliberations about instructional placement decisions can greatly influence the questions to be raised and the way that answers should be framed. We consider three contextual referents for educational placement decisions: (a) the legal context, (b) the empirical context, and (c) the conceptual context.

Legal Context

Volumes have been written about behavior issues and the procedural requirements for serving students with frequently occurring disabilities. However, comparatively little attention has been directed toward these students' academic achievement when making instructional placement decisions. Given the alignment of the IDEA with the provisions of the Elementary and Secondary Education Act (currently authorized as the No Child Left Behind Act [NCLB]), the dominant legislation governing American public education, it is surprising that so little attention and research is directed to this topic. NCLB makes clear that the purpose of schooling is academic achievement. The alignment of IDEA with NCLB by extension makes clear that special education similarly targets academic achievement.

The IDEA requires school officials "to ensure that all children with disabilities have available to them a free appropriate public education [FAPE] that emphasizes special education and related services designed to meet their unique needs, and prepare them for further education, employment and independent living" (20 U.S.C. § 1400(d)(1)(A)). School officials must also ensure that students with disabilities are educated in settings alongside classmates without disabilities, to the maximum extent appropriate to the individual learning needs of the students with disabilities.

Placement decisions—or decisions about the instructional settings where an individual student might receive an appropriate education—are governed by the LRE provisions of the federal regulations to the IDEA (34 C.F.R §§ 300.114-120). The LRE requirements set out factors to consider in educating students with and without disabilities together to the maximum extent appropriate (20 U.S.C. § 1412(a)(5)). The law presumes that all students will be taught in general classes, but this presumption is rebutted by convincing evidence that an appropriate placement cannot be delivered in the general education classroom, or that an alternative placement would provide the student with a more appropriate education. As a result, school district officials are required to make a full continuum of alternative placements available, ranging from inclusion in general education classes to special classes, separate schools, residential facilities, hospitals, and home settings.

Under the IDEA, the LRE is not a specific location but the outcome of a decision-making process that places greater weight on the standard of FAPE than on the actual place where instruction occurs. Decisions about where an individual student can be taught appropriately must be made by the team that develops the student's IEP—a group of people that includes parents and others who are knowledgeable about the student, the placement options, and the meaning of the assessment data. Placement decisions for special education students must be reviewed annually, must be based on the IEP, and must give consideration to potentially harmful effects on the child and the quality of the required services (Crockett, 2008). Unless an IEP requires otherwise to achieve FAPE, students should attend a school as close to home as possible or the school they would attend if they did not have a disability.

IEPs and Appropriate Services

Not all disputes about an appropriate education involve concerns about placement, but all disputes about placement in the LRE are determined by the appropriateness of a student's IEP (Crockett, 2008). The meaning of an appropriate education under the IDEA was defined by the Supreme Court in the case of *Board of Education v. Rowley* (1982). Amy Rowley was a girl with a hearing impairment who was denied the services of a sign language interpreter. Her family sued, stating that such services would allow her to reach her optimal level of performance. The court held that the law does not require optimal services, but rather, appropriate services. According to the opinion, when students are attaining passing marks and moving easily from grade to grade, the services provided are appropriate. Since then, the meaning of FAPE has hinged on the provision of an IEP that addresses a student's unique educational needs; in recent years, this has meant considering those needs in the context of standards-based reforms.

IEPs and LRE

To date, the Supreme Court has decided no LRE cases, and consequently, no U.S. standard exists for making instructional placement decisions in students' IEPs. Analytical frameworks for determining LRE were used in several important cases in lower courts from 1984 to 1997, including the Roncker Portability Test, the Daniel Two-Part Test, the Rachel H. Four Part Test, and the Hartman Three-Part Test; these frameworks continue to guide legal determinations of LRE in different parts of the country (see Rozalski, Stewart, & Miller, 2010; Yell, 2006).

Questions to Guide Placements in the LRE

The type of services required for an individual student, as well as the intensity of those services, should be guided by systematic assessment of the student's needs, and his response to the instructional program. The following questions address components embodied in the LRE frameworks, and answers to them rely on the assessment of student-centered data collected throughout the LRE determination process (Yell, 2006). Questions one through three are particularly amenable to assessment information, and we shall return to them later in the chapter.

1. *Has the school taken steps to maintain the child in the general education class?* What supplementary aides and services were used? What interventions were attempted? How many interventions were tried?

2. *What are the benefits of placement in a general education setting with supplementary aids and services versus the benefits of placement in a special education setting for this child?* What are the academic benefits? What are the nonacademic benefits such as social communication and interactions?

3. *What are the effects on the education of other students?* If the student is disruptive, is the education of other students adversely affected? Does the student require an inordinate amount of attention from the teacher and, as a result, adversely affect the education of others?

4. *If a student requires an alternative setting, are appropriate opportunities for integration available?* In what academic settings is the student integrated with nondisabled students? In what nonacademic settings is the child integrated with nondisabled students?

5. *Is the full continuum of alternative services made available across the school system from which to choose an appropriate placement?* (Yell, 2006, p. 326)

Each set of questions about a student's educational placement depends on the union of careful thought, data, and concerted action that begins with assessment

of the individual child and considers the interaction of instruction with the environment where teaching and learning is to occur. Instruction that (a) focuses on different content from the general curriculum, (b) incorporates intensive remedial activities to develop skills already mastered by other students of the same age or grade, (c) progresses at a different pace from the general education program, or (d) employs systematic teaching of cognitive strategies not needed by other students may require specialized settings for the delivery of appropriate services.

Empirical Context for Placement Decisions

Placement decisions are governed by law and should be guided by empirical research (Bateman, 2007b). Empirical evidence is lacking, however, to support the notion that the needs of *all* children can be met in the same environment, even when inclusive classroom strategies such as differentiated instruction (see Tomlinson, 2003) and Universal Design for Learning (see Rose & Meyer, 2006) are used (M. M. Brigham, Brigham, & Lloyd, 2002). The positive response of *some,* or possibly *many,* or even *most* students in no way establishes that *all* students will respond positively, or need *only* these approaches to derive FAPE.

The impact of instructional placements on a student's academic performance remains a debatable point (e.g., Carr-George, Vannest, Willson, & Davis, 2009; Zigmond, Kloo, & Volonino, 2009). Elbaum, Vaughn, Hughes, Moody, and Schumm (2000), however, provided meta-analytic evidence that placement in various instructional groupings can substantially alter students' performance. Multiple-grouping strategies, such as small-group instruction and individual tutoring, resulted in tangible gains in reading compared to whole class or heterogeneous instructional grouping for students with high-incidence disabilities. This evidence suggests that placement for reading instruction in whole-class, individual, or smaller groups makes a difference in the rate at which struggling students acquire skills and progress to higher levels of mastery. These data suggest that more supportive, or restrictive, placements must be maintained for *some* children and that a diversity of educational placements based on instructional need should be celebrated and maintained.

Where a student receives instruction is only one component of a defensible educational plan (Crockett, 2008). Special education settings that afford (a) low expectations and reduced assignments, (b) weak accommodations that undermine employability in the postschool world, and (c) assessments that misrepresent performance levels so that educators and students have a false sense of accomplishment threaten the provision of FAPE in the LRE and should be avoided (Chandler, 2009). Conversely, general education settings in which instruction (a) moves at a faster pace than can be mastered by a given student with a disability (Engelmann, 1997), (b) yields few meaningful opportunities for success (Hallenbeck & Kauffman, 1995), and (c) focuses on skills or conceptual learning that differ from the student's needs (H. L. Swanson, Hoskyn, & Lee, 1999) should also be avoided. Inclusive placements can be difficult to justify as "least restrictive" when conditions impede a student's successful performance.

The default placement for students is the general education classroom, and most special education students have previously demonstrated inadequate response to basic instruction. In cases where FAPE requires instructional elements that extend beyond general education with the supports of supplementary aids and services, other placements must be considered. If an alternative placement makes FAPE possible, that placement is the LRE. From a conceptual perspective, typical placements where a student is failing to make academic and/or social progress despite appropriate supports could be considered more restrictive (in terms of achievement) than are highly specialized settings.

Conceptual Context of Placement Considerations

When the Education for All Handicapped Children Act, the forerunner of IDEA, was enacted in 1975, many individuals with disabilities were excluded from public education, and many others were afforded inappropriate educational programs (Yell, Rogers, & Rogers, 1998). School systems were required to provide educational services to each student but were not required to have every service available within the local district. Children whose needs could not be met appropriately were often sent to neighboring districts, multidistrict service centers, or residential centers at the district's expense. The prevailing sentiment was that highly specialized programs would often be impractical or impossible to create locally, and so children were sent to existing programs within a broad geographical region. Under such circumstances, the place (i.e., physical location) of the program was a highly salient feature.

Over time, specialized aspects of such programs were scrutinized and sometimes found wanting (R. W. Goldman, 1994; Merulla & McKinnon, 1982; S. J. Taylor, 1988). Early efforts to develop effective treatments for students with learning problems focused on interventions aimed at training or repairing the student's cognitive makeup presumed to be different or damaged relative to most other individuals (e.g., perceptual motor training). Such treatments, it was thought, would enable more typical interactions with the world than would otherwise have been afforded to the student. Interventions, in other words, attempted to change individuals in fundamental ways. Over time such approaches to intervention have largely been abandoned.

Kavale and Forness (2000) emphasized the conceptual changes in educating students with disabilities by suggesting that interventions designed to change the individual focus on the SPECIAL in special education: *SPECIAL education* engaged in remedial practices unique to the individual and different from the educational programs provided to most students. In contrast, the alternative was referred to as special EDUCATION. From this perspective, *special EDUCATION* means adapting and modifying the instruction provided to most students so that it is more accessible and beneficial for students with disabilities. The outcomes reported for *special EDUCATION* greatly exceeded those reported for *SPECIAL education* (Kavale & Forness, 2000), and the 2004 reauthorization of IDEA codified that special education programs were to reflect the goals and content of general education programs (S. Gordon, 2006).

Changing the focus of instruction to address the same elements as general education seemed to undercut the need for different placements, because the content and ostensibly the pace of instruction in pursuit of adequate yearly progress goals would be similar for most students. However, data regarding homogeneous placement of heterogeneous groups of students (i.e., full inclusion) remains inconsistent at best (Kavale, 2002). Although the goals may be similar, the methods and supports necessary to attain them may be very different for students with disabilities compared with their peers without disabilities (Weiss & Lloyd, 2001).

An optimal environment or level of support for one individual might be detrimental to another, and "an everyday setting that inclines one individual to feel and function well can push another in the opposite direction" (W. Gallagher, 1993, p. 18). In short, even though people may be working toward the same or similar goals, their educational background, personal characteristics, rates of progress, and instructional needs may respond to instructional approaches that are better carried out in different educational placements than a general education setting.

Summary

The IDEA requires special education students to be educated in environments that provide them with the opportunity to participate and progress in the general curriculum alongside classmates who are not disabled to the maximum extent appropriate to their learning needs. When a student cannot be taught appropriately in a typical setting, a continuum of placement options must be made available so that instruction can be delivered in what is determined by the IEP team to be the least restrictive alternative to the typical class. Decisions about alternative placements are contentious in many cases, but they are also crucial to supporting a student's FAPE. In the next section, we describe some of the assessment tools available for determining placement in the LRE for students with disabilities.

Tools in the Workshop

Skilled artisans have workshops equipped with a variety of tools. The key to excellence in a craft is not so much the possession of a single tool that works all the time, but in appropriately applying a combination of different tools to do the job at hand. Good assessment decisions work the same way. Better tools increase the chances that results will be meaningful, and using the appropriate combination of tools vastly increases the chances of making beneficial decisions. Therefore, we discuss various assessments available to educators responsible for making placement decisions. Our list is not exhaustive, but the categories are illustrative of the kinds of tools available to IEP teams making these important decisions.

Formal, Standardized Tests

The term *standardized* simply means that a test is administered to each individual under the same (standardized) conditions; however, "standardized tests have been the objects of scorn primarily because critics do not understand what they are designed to do and why they are important" (Kauffman & Konold, 2007, p. 81). Standardized tests can provide a constant backdrop of behavioral expectations so that differences in scores can be attributed primarily to an individual's performance and not to differences in testing procedures.

Large-Scale State Assessments

Large-scale assessments are most often associated with state-administered competency measures for accountability and, in many states, graduation requirements (Cortiella, 2006). All students, even students with disabilities, *must* participate in state educational accountability systems in some way. Students might participate in general assessments with or without

accommodations, or in an alternative assessment. Regardless of the manner in which students participate in assessments, the yielded data can help to guide placement decisions.

Passing scores on large-scale assessments.   If a student is passing large-scale tests without special education support, then the student has little need for additional special education supports (see *Alvin Independent School Dist. v. A.D. ex rel. Patricia F*, 2007). For a student who is already receiving special education services, passing scores on state assessments could be a suggestion that the placement and intensity of services currently provided are appropriate, at least relative to the test domain and conditions. Passing scores on state tests could also indicate that the services being provided are beyond those *needed* by the student. However, passing scores are not an automatic indicator that levels of service should be reduced, or that students can be served successfully in less-restrictive environments. It does not necessarily follow that a student who performs well with support can do so independently in a general education classroom.

Failing scores on large-scale assessments.   It is unrealistic to expect that *all* students (even students with appropriate IEPs) will attain passing grades in an era of standards intended "to (a) focus the general education curriculum on a core of important and challenging content and (b) ensure that *every* student in a state or district receives instruction on the *same* challenging content" [emphasis in original] (Nolet, 2005, pp. 6–7). Students may not perform well, even when they use familiar accommodations (Thurlow & Thompson, 2004). Having standards means some will fall short of them; having high standards means a greater percentage of people will fall short of the mark.

Failing scores on a state test do not automatically indicate an inappropriate educational program or placement; however, failing state tests is certainly a prompt to examine the appropriateness of the educational program, including the adequacy of the placement. Identifying the reasons for poor performance can provide relevant information for making decisions regarding instructional needs and corresponding placement options.

False negatives.   Two major causes of false negatives (erroneous failing scores) must be considered before using large-scale assessments in guiding FAPE and LRE placement decisions. First, failure on a state test should be unrelated to extraneous factors such as anxiety or being ill on the day of the test. In such cases, the information yielded by the test is invalid and of no use for making placement or any other kind of decision beyond the decision to discount the data. Second, a student with a disability may fail a large-scale test because required testing accommodations were unavailable. Providing appropriate accommodations is a complicated enterprise. Many teachers insert multiple accommodations into the IEP, hoping that at least one of them will help the student (Thurlow, 2000). Further, accommodations are often assigned based on subjective beliefs unrelated to the individual student's disability characteristics (L. S. Fuchs & Fuchs, 2001). Confusion about the nature and purposes of accommodations appears to be more common than unusual.

The Dynamic Assessment of Test Accommodations (L. S. Fuchs, Fuchs, Eaton, & Hamlett, 2003) is one instrument that can provide guidance in selecting accommodations. However, schools may be unlikely to expend the added time and expense to administer such a personalized instrument in the absence of substantial pressure from state and federal agencies for districts to ensure the appropriateness of accommodations (Della Toffalo & Milke, 2008). Nevertheless, the appropriateness of assessment accommodations for the student and the test should be examined before concluding that the failing grade indicates lack of FAPE or inadequate placements.

Failing scores and FAPE.   Failing scores on a state test could be an accurate measure of student accomplishment, and therefore a valid indicator rather than a false negative. In such cases, the failure could indicate lack of FAPE. One way to *undermine* FAPE is to insist on placement options that prevent the specialized instruction specified in the IEP to be delivered with sufficient frequency or intensity for the student to derive adequate benefit. For example, co-teaching is currently a recommended strategy for many students with high-incidence disabilities. In co-teaching, "the student with disabilities and his/her special education teacher are both integrated into the general education classroom, and the two teachers share instructional responsibilities" (Zigmond & Magiera, 2001, p. 1). In many cases, an arrangement such as co-teaching is profitable for the student, but in other cases, the arrangement provides a seat in the classroom but yields little meaningful progress (Weiss & Lloyd, 2001). When co-teaching provides an inadequate level of service, the student may be *immersed* in the general education curriculum but fail to *master* challenging content. Failing to pass the state proficiency test may suggest that the access to the general education curriculum is not meaningful, and educators need to consider something different.

When students with IEPs fail state examinations, their IEP teams should examine the IEP to determine whether (a) the supports specified on the IEP are adequate and (b) whether those supports can reasonably be carried out in an effective manner within the current placement. If the IEP team determines that additional supports are needed and that they cannot be carried out in the present environment, educators have good reason to consider a different placement. Given the default preference for general education placements, such considerations often suggest the need for more specialized (more-restrictive) environments. Although efforts to make students with disabilities successful in general education settings are clearly worthwhile, educators should not be so enamored of the goal of inclusion that they exchange a seat in a general education classroom for meaningful instruction in another setting.

Individually Administered Tests

Individually administered achievement tests have long been the workhorses of special education eligibility decisions and, therefore, may be helpful in placement decisions. Two examples of such measures include the Kaufman Test of Educational Achievement II (Kaufman & Kaufman, 2004) and the Woodcock-Johnson—III, Tests of Achievement (Woodcock, McGrew, & Mather, 2001).

Individual measures have the distinct advantage of offering greater probability of valid administration than is possible in tests administered to groups; however, they also have the disadvantage of being abstractions of a generalized curriculum, representing performance across the entire nation rather than being tied to local or state standards. Additionally, norm-referenced achievement tests sample the curriculum at a sparse level with as few as one or two items representing an entire school year's growth. The high reliability of these measures is obtained at the cost of sensitivity to small increments of progress (Galagan, 1985). Therefore, these kinds of tests can be problematic if one wishes to measure small increments of progress across time.

Problems in interpretation.   Unlike state tests that are evaluated binomially (pass or fail), individual tests do not typically carry a bright-line marker for adequate scores. No universally accepted set of cut points is available for determining when scores rise from the low range to the "good-enough" range, and then to the high range. Traditional statistical analysis suggests that the average range is determined by the first standard deviation on either side of the mean, but some tests and school district policies set narrower constructions of typical performance.

Even though bright-line tests on such instruments are unwise, some ways of interpreting scores may be helpful in making placement decisions. One of the more common uses of achievement tests is to determine adequacy of progress in comparison to performance predictions from IQ tests. In general, students who perform at a similar level (e.g., standard scores that are similar to each other) on the IQ and achievement tests are often said to be performing at a level commensurate with their ability. How close the scores need to be to each other remains an open and debatable issue. Additionally, some scholars question the utility of IQ tests relative to special education placement decisions (e.g., Kortteinen, Närhi, & Ahonen, 2009; MacMillan & Forness, 1998). Nevertheless, IQ tests are commonly used, and achievement measures that reflect the IQ scores are one suggestion that educational placements may be adequate and yielding appropriate achievement benefits.

Another method of using achievement test scores to demonstrate adequacy of placement is in consideration of scores from repeated administrations of the instrument over time. Norm-referenced tests yield measures of relative standing, so individuals who are making progress that is notably faster than the norm group will attain increasingly high scores from administration to repeated administration. Individuals who keep pace with the norm group will maintain scores of approximately the same level with each administration of the test. Individuals who make notably less progress than their peers will, however, attain scores that are lower from initial to repeated administrations of the measure. Using this method requires educators to be sensitive to the variation in scores that can be attributed to random error. All high-quality assessments provide indicators of the measurement error (standard error of measurement [SEM]) for the test across different scales and characteristics such as the age of the individual test taker. Any gain or decrease in performance must be outside of the estimated measurement error to be meaningful. Scores that vary within the range of performance that can be attributed to measurement error are best interpreted as representing roughly the same level of performance.

Adequate and high scores on individual achievement tests.   Adequate and high scores on individually administered achievement tests are indicators of desirable outcomes and vouch for the adequacy of the educational placement. Administration of these tests is intended to yield a "best-effort" level of performance. Sometimes, students who earn failing grades in a classroom domain or skill directly related to a given subtest can actually attain strong scores in such an assessment. This result represents the difference between what an individual is able to do, and

what she is willing or able to do over a long period of time in classroom conditions. Classroom performance involves more than academic skills. Students who are unwilling or unable to complete homework assignments independently or participate in classroom activities such as discussions may have grades that are actually under-representations of their academic ability. Thus, individually administered achievement tests can help to discriminate between students needing additional academic support (low grades and low test scores) and students who are roughly on target in their skill development but in need of behavioral or organizational supports (low classroom grades but adequate test scores).

Low scores on individual achievement tests.   As was the case for state assessments, low scores can be the result of a variety of conditions unrelated to the student's actual competence. Therefore, the results of these tests, like the results of any other test, should not be taken at face value. In this case, it is easier for a student to underperform (attain a lower score than would be accurate) than it is to overperform (guess right often enough to substantially and meaningfully raise the test score).

All of the caveats for interpreting low scores on state tests apply to individual tests. Low scores suggest that educational programming may be inappropriate and that additional supports might be needed, which may necessitate a change in placement. However, a certain proportion of the population will always attain low normative scores for a variety of reasons (Kauffman & Konold, 2007). The emphasis of the educational goals in the IEP can help to determine the extent to which low scores alone call for additional effort. Like state assessments, individual standardized tests represent only one piece of the puzzle for making placement decisions. Other indicators must be used in conjunction with these kinds of scores.

Examples of Other Standardized Measures

Although IDEA and NCLB align to support academic outcomes and, thus, focus on tests of achievement, other measures of performance affect FAPE and LRE decisions. Among these are (a) behavior rating scales and (b) self-report measures of attitudes toward self and school-related constructs. Other classes of assessment measures exist, but we restrict our discussion here to these two examples.

Behavior rating scales.   A number of behavior rating scales are available to identify, categorize, and evaluate problem behaviors. Two examples that have substantial scientific validation are the Systematic Screening for Behavior Disorders (SSBD; H. M. Walker & Severson, 1992a) and the Behavioral and Emotional Rating Scale (BERS; M. H. Epstein & Sharma, 1998). Teachers and parents complete such instruments by rating the frequency of a variety of behaviors during a given period of time (e.g., 6 months). The SSBD is an example of a "multiple-gating system" where each level of the assessment becomes progressively more precise and demanding. It moves from a general screening of behavior to actual comparison of the target student's behavior to norms constructed from more than 4,500 cases. The BERS is an example of a "strength-based assessment" that examines the presence of social abilities as well as deficits.

High levels of behavioral disorders or low levels of strength relative to the general population may signal the need for additional behavioral supports or instruction. As with academic instruction, some behavioral treatments require more specialized (restrictive) environments than the general education setting.

Self-report measures.   Students are sometimes asked to complete self-rating scales. The Student Self-Concept Scale (SSCS; Gresham, Elliott, & Evans-Fernandez, 1992) is one such instrument that possesses adequate psychometric properties. The SSCS collects information across three content domains (i.e., Self-Image, Academic, and Social) and creates ratings of (a) the individual's self-confidence in performing the behaviors, (b) the importance placed on the various behaviors, and (c) self-confidence that positive outcomes will result from carrying out the behaviors (Gresham, 1995). Although such self-report instruments are highly subjective and open to social expectancy effects (people may report in ways they think are beneficial to them rather than honestly), they may provide insights into the individual's emotional state, which would otherwise be unavailable or at least very difficult to obtain (S. N. Elliott & Busse, 2004).

Student perceptions of various placements are often overlooked in the process of assessment but potentially are useful. Students may express self-efficacy beliefs that suggest the need for more or different supports than are in their IEPs or general education programs. Student preference alone may not be the primary determinant in placement decisions. Nevertheless, when self-report measures suggest that students are developing feelings of inadequacy and hopelessness relative to their studies, the implication becomes clearer that additional support is desirable. Increases in intensity of program or frequency of evaluative interaction with teachers may require IEP changes in programming and placement.

Informal Measures

Informal measures differ from formal, standardized measures by a number of characteristics. In general, informal measures are less reliant on normative comparisons derived from large samples of the population, are more adaptable to immediate needs of educators, have less rigid and well-defined scoring criteria, and have less well-defined administration procedures (Bennett, 1982). The boundaries between formal, standardized assessments and informal assessments are not well-defined, and some procedures share characteristics of both classes of assessment (Vansickle, 2004). Curriculum-based measurement (CBM), for example, is a highly flexible approach to measurement that can be adjusted informally to adjust to classroom needs. CBM can also be standardized so that each student receives the same measure the same way, each time it is repeated. We have chosen to include CBM as an informal measure. Other forms of informal measures include but are not limited to (a) direct observation, (b) teacher opinion, (c) classroom grades, and (d) interviews with students and parents.

Direct Observation

Direct observation of behavior is by far the most frequently used tool for evaluating classroom behavior (Sasso, Conroy, Stichter, & Fox, 2001). Observations completed according to a predetermined structure including operational definitions of target behaviors and time parameters are usually more useful than general narrative observations. Frequently, in addition to observing the target student(s), observers will select one or two individuals who are also present in the environment and take data on their behaviors for comparison purposes. In that way, the behavior exhibited by the target student can be compared to others in the same environment. By examining the behavior of students within the context of the classroom, and relative to the teacher's actions, direct observation efforts can prompt suggestions for change in areas of need, which might be related to changes in placement (Slate & Saudargas, 1986).

Direct observation can range from relatively unstructured narrative approaches, in which the observer writes everything that is seen, heard, and perceived, to highly structured protocols, in which the variables to be observed and the schedule for observing them are specified (T. Thompson, Symons, & Felce, 2000). All observation procedures have their limitations and potential benefits, but the more structured methods appear to have the greatest utility for making decisions relative to placement.

When observational data suggest that other students in a given setting are engaged and responding appropriately to teacher directives, but the target student is unengaged or responding inappropriately, a number of possible implications regarding the adequacy of the educational program emerge. It is possible that the individual is unable to perform the behaviors expected of students in the class; it is possible that the individual does not value the reinforcers in the environment; it is also possible that the individual may believe he is incapable of attaining access to the reinforcers maintaining the behavior of other students. All of these possibilities suggest the need for alterations of instructional and behavioral programs available to the student. Increasing the intensity of instruction, for example, may require consideration of a more specialized and structured environment so that the student is working on missing skills. Conversely, a student may appear disengaged because the placement is overly restrictive and providing supports that the individual does not need. In such cases, a more typical or less-restrictive environment is indicated.

Teacher Opinions as Informal Assessments

The U.S. District Court of South Dakota considered teacher judgment that a student was performing at levels sufficient for reintegration as an adequate form of assessment data (*Geffre et al. v. Leola School District 44-2*, 2009). In this case, teacher opinion was a recognized form of assessment data that was considered when making placement decisions.

Teachers are often the first to notice the performance problems of students with frequently occurring disabilities such as mild intellectual disabilities and learning disabilities, and their judgment regarding the difficulties facing students relative to other classmates is often correct (M. M. Gerber, 2005; M. M. Gerber & Semmel, 1984). Elements such as the resources available to support learning (including materials for instruction and instructional expertise), and competing demands facing the teacher (clerical and other noninstructional duties, as well as the heterogeneity of students' learning needs) combine to form the boundaries of "teachability" in a classroom. Gerber and Semmel proposed that when students fall outside of the bounds of teachability, they are unlikely to receive appropriate instruction. In sum, characteristics of the individual student under consideration, as well as the context in which the student is taught, affect teacher judgment.

Factors affecting teacher judgment.   Contextual pressures on general education teachers (e.g., increased class size, or the behavioral challenges in the school population) are reflected in the number and severity of students referred for evaluation of a suspected disability (Hess & Brigham, 2007). Context can also affect the nature of students identified for special education and placed for instruction within different schools (Wiley, Siperstein, Bountress, Forness, & Brigham, 2009; Wiley, Siperstein, Forness, & Brigham, 2010).

Teachers are intimately familiar with how students interact with the learning environment in a way no assessment can adequately measure. Their informal observations comprise a data set much richer and more comprehensive than any other assessment measure, by taking into account many complex interactions between the student, the teacher, the curriculum, and the environment. Working with students on a daily basis puts teachers in a uniquely well-informed position to determine if a student can or cannot succeed in a given environment. Thus, teacher suggestions that the current educational environment is unsatisfactory should be considered relative to other decision-making data. The triangulation of teacher opinion with achievement and behavioral data can make a powerful case for determining the appropriateness of a placement option.

Classroom Grades as Informal Assessments

Classroom grades can influence educational placement decisions. The classroom teacher has a crucial role in determining the adequacy of educational programs and placements through awarding grades and evaluating student progress in other ways such as behavior reports and statements of a student's ability to manage learning and social behaviors independently.

Teacher grades are important indicators of placement and programmatic adequacy, but they are often constrained by various factors. For example, some schools use modified grading standards for students with IEPs, basing their grades not simply on performance but on a combination of performance and effort (Gersten, Vaughn, & Brengelman, 1996). Thus, it is not always clear what the grades awarded by a specific teacher to a given student mean. Nevertheless, grades should be considered relative to placement decisions. IEP teams should consider whether passing grades suggest that (a) a student has more support than is currently needed and might succeed in a less-restrictive placement, or (b) the current supports and placement are necessary to maintain passing grades. Failing grades may indicate that greater supports and a change of placement are appropriate, but need to be evaluated in terms of the possible reasons for the unsuccessful performance they indicate to make these decisions.

Interviews

Students and parents can provide useful information in support of FAPE and LRE placement decisions. Interviews of students and teachers as well as parents can yield insights that would not otherwise be available (De Groot, 2002). Students with learning disabilities frequently report a preference for more specialized (more-restrictive) settings for their special education programs over receiving supports in general education classes (Klingner, Vaughn, Schumm, Cohen, & Forgan, 1998; S. Vaughn & Klingner, 1998). Students with learning disabilities in inclusive settings also reported higher levels of alienation than did students with emotional/behavioral disorders in self-contained special education programs (Fulk, Brigham, & Lohman, 1998). More recently, groups of high school students with learning disabilities reported that they generally preferred to receive their services in "pull-out" settings (often considered more restrictive than general education settings) for two reasons: (a) special education teachers deliver distinctly different services than do general educators, and (b) it is often difficult to gain access to special education teachers in large co-taught classrooms (Leafstedt, Richards, LaMonte, & Cassidy, 2007).

Interview data provide another window on the adequacy of placements for individual students. In some cases, students and parents may be seeking more supportive or restrictive placements; in other cases, they may be seeking less-restrictive placements. When students are making adequate progress and they or their parents request a less-restrictive placement, educators are well-advised to consider the request. If school officials are uncertain that a less-restrictive placement will yield satisfactory results, they might initiate a trial placement and monitor the results for a set period of time. Continued success would indicate appropriate placement; declining performance would suggest an inappropriate program of instruction and accompanying placement.

Curriculum-Based Assessment and Measurement

Curriculum-based assessment (CBA) and CBM are kinds of formative evaluation that have been demonstrated to substantially raise the achievement of nearly all students with whom it is employed (L. S. Fuchs & D. Fuchs, 1986). These procedures also form a substantial component of Response to Intervention (RtI) programs, described in the following section (F. J. Brigham & Brigham, 2010; T. Wallace, Espin, McMaster, Deno, & Foegen, 2007).

CBA involves the observation and recording of student performance in a local curriculum in order to gather information to make instructional decisions. The test materials used in CBA are developed by the teacher on the basis of a task analysis of the curriculum and presented to students after pretesting identifies target skills for instruction. During instruction, students are repeatedly measured on the selected skills using alternative test forms. Mastery of a skill prompts a move to the next skill in the task analysis. With CBM, student performance is measured repeatedly (e.g., once or twice per week) with test materials that represent an entire curricular domain rather than specific subcomponents of the domain (Espin, Shin, & Busch, 2000).

CBA and CBM are particularly useful for demonstrating adequacy of intervention programs and the placements they require. Other chapters in this volume address CBA and CBM in greater detail (Chapters 23 and 18, respectively), but when student performance is consistently below the rate necessary to meet established goals by the end of a specified time period, some aspect of the instructional program (e.g., focus, method, duration, frequency of instruction) should be addressed. In some cases, increased instruction can necessitate a move to a different placement to facilitate the program.

Response to Intervention

Recent efforts to implement RtI approaches using multiple tiers of instructional support provide another opportunity for assessing students' needs and monitoring progress. RtI was developed through research efforts to (a) increase the accuracy of eligibility decisions for special education, (b) prevent students without disabilities from falling so far behind that they seem to require special education, (c) focus instructional attention on standards-based curricula, and (d) improve the professionalism of educational decision making (F. J. Brigham & Brigham, 2010; see also Chapter 17, this volume). The fundamental premise of RtI is that screening every child regularly on simple performance indicators related to important curricular outcomes allows teachers to recognize students who are showing signs of difficulty and respond to them with increasingly intense levels of support before their instructional problems become insurmountable (F. J. Brigham & Brigham, 2010).

Most RtI models operate in a three-tier model, with each tier involving more substantial supports and frequent progress monitoring (Mellard & Johnson, 2008). A student's responsiveness to intervention is judged according to both the actual performance level and the trajectory, or rate of improvement, compared to peers

(D. Fuchs, Mock, Morgan, & Young, 2003). That is, students who are nonresponsive to intervention not only perform at a lower level than their peers, but also improve at a slower rate. Tier 1 involves universal screening of performance in the general education program. Tiers 2 and 3 are devoted to increasingly intensive interventions for those who make inadequate progress at lower levels.

When students are found to be nonresponsive to Tier 3 interventions, implications arise for changing programming and placement. Nonresponsiveness to targeted treatments that resemble special education at this level suggests substantial amounts of time, and focused instruction needs to be allocated for progress to occur. Timely referral of struggling students for special education evaluations cannot be denied in the RtI process, and decision making that fosters appropriate programming in the LRE must not be delayed (U.S. Department of Education, 2010b).

Using Assessments in Making Placement Decisions

The demonstration that school personnel have systematically considered the student's unique educational needs and the capacity of the program to confer educational benefit is fundamental to defensible decisions for placing students with disabilities in any instructional setting. The determination of a student's educational needs can be based on a variety of information sources, but should be based on careful consideration of meaningful assessment data.

Addressing Fundamental Questions with Assessment Data

Fundamental questions drive decisions about instructional placement for students with disabilities (Yell, 2006). In this section, we revisit these questions and examine assessment procedures that can be used to address them.

What Has Been Done to Maintain the Child in a General Education Class?

Given the legal preference for placements in general education settings, and the sentiments of many educators and parents, it is logical to ask what has been done to ensure that the student is responding to instruction with adequate levels of performance. What supplementary aides and services were used, what interventions were attempted, and how many interventions were tried?

Responding to this set of questions requires development of a historical record, and the assessment/intervention model used in multi-tiered levels of support such as RtI can provide useful tools for documenting (a) areas in need of interventions, (b) the instructional methods used, (c) the intensity (time) of the strategies, and (d) duration (weeks or months) of the interventions. Most RtI models compare student progress with intervention support against the progress expected of students' age- or grade-mates. When research-based interventions have been attempted with documented integrity (i.e., implemented as designed) over a sufficient amount of time, then continued low performance with a trajectory of improvement that is flatter than expected suggests the need to review the appropriateness of the student's programming and instructional placement.

RtI is carried out in the context of general education and can indicate the need to move to more intensive programming and possibly a more-restrictive placement option when students demonstrate poor response to even the best basic instruction. Reliable data on (a) what interventions and supports have been implemented and (b) the effects of those interventions and supports on student outcomes will be useful for IEP teams making justifiable and appropriate placement decisions. It is tempting to claim that data will trump opinion in every case, but that is unlikely. It is certain, however, that educators attempting to defend contentious decisions in the absence of data will find themselves on shaky legal and professional ground.

What Are the Relative Benefits of General Versus Special Education?

Addressing this question involves comparing the advantages of different program options; placement decisions must consider the potential costs and benefits of each environment. Recent policies (e.g., NCLB and IDEA) suggest that it is worth the social costs to address the academic benefits and nonacademic benefits of instruction delivered in either special or general education settings as long as the student's needs are met. In responding to these questions, educators must document the efforts made on the student's behalf, as well as her level of performance on academic measures in response to those efforts. Descriptions of expectations for behavior in a particular setting, as well as engagement in nonacademic activities during the day, could add to the evidence in favor of one setting (e.g., special education) over another (e.g., general education).

Using test data.   Scores from state tests and individual achievement tests can be used to compare the academic benefits of one setting over another. For example, students with low scores in basic skills may have more difficulty keeping pace with their peers in content area classes, even with supplementary aides and services. The student might have a significant need for reading instruction at a level of intensity and duration unlikely to be provided in a general education class, particularly in the upper grades. Difficult decisions might need to be made about the relative value of acquiring fundamental reading skills versus participating in social opportunities. In other cases, adequate scores for students in restrictive settings could suggest they might be able to prosper in a more typical placement with supports. Carr-George et al. (2009) reported that students with high-incidence disabilities taught in general education classrooms with in-class support were twice as likely to fail state tests as their general education classmates. Consequently, it should not be assumed that supplementary supports necessarily enable included students with disabilities to pass state proficiency tests.

Using classroom grades. Before the rise of state testing programs, classroom grades determined a special education student's successful passage from grade to grade (*Board of Education v. Rowley, 1982*). Mead and Paige (2008) noted that the *Rowley* decision was inconclusive regarding the provision of FAPE and a student's progress in the curriculum. Foremost, it is unclear how much progress is sufficient. In a subsequent decision *(Alvin Independent School Dist. v. A.D. ex rel. Patricia F, 2007)*, the court held that earning passing grades in the classroom and demonstrating proficiency on state assessments suggest that a general education student's program was *adequate* enough to not require special education. In cases where a special education student is unable to pass the state's achievement test, but is attaining passing grades, legislative language suggests that the IEP, which includes the student's instructional placement, is questionable (P. T. K. Daniel, 2008).

When grades and test scores align in a positive direction, it is difficult to contest the adequacy of the support. Situations in which grades are positive and test scores are low, or vice versa, could indicate the need for more intensive programming and placement. When both the test scores and classroom grades are low, there is little doubt that the educational program is in need of revision, and a more intensive and specialized placement should be considered.

Using student and teacher interviews. Students may have clear preferences for one setting over another. In cases where students strongly advocate for a general education setting, classroom descriptions and test information can be useful in prompting students to develop their own IEP supports (McGahee-Kovac, 1995; E. P. Snyder & Shapiro, 1997). In some cases, students may become more invested in their education, reducing the need for intensive services; in other cases, they may become more aware of the services they actually need.

There is also precedent for using teacher opinion and interview data in support of placement decisions. In *Geffre ex rel. S.G. v. Leola Sch. Dist.* (2009), the court found the school's unwillingness to consider the judgments of the direct service staff that the student could function well in a more typical environment to be a violation of the LRE provision of IDEA. This case supports the use of teacher judgment as one form of acceptable assessment data.

Combining data from state assessments, individual achievement tests, ongoing classroom performance (including progress-monitoring measures), and teacher judgment with the preferences of the student and the family can make a strong case for one placement over another. When indications point in the same direction, the decision is clear. When data from different sources suggest different options, the team must weigh the relative importance of each source against FAPE as developed in the student's IEP. Regardless of the placement decision, continued monitoring of conditions in the learning environment are essential to ensure adequate responses to instruction, and to make adjustments in the program. CBA and CBM are appropriate tools to use for this purpose because they are more sensitive to small changes over time. Teacher grades can also be an indicator, as can state and individual achievement tests, although grades may be influenced by other (subjective) factors, and achievement tests are not designed to measure small changes in student performance.

How Does This Student Affect the Environment?

Addressing this question acknowledges that the curricular and behavioral needs of a student might demand unusual attention from the classroom teacher. Consequently, the law permits IEP teams to consider the adverse impact on classmates (a) if the student is disruptive, or (b) if the student requires an inordinate amount of attention from the teacher. Responding to this set of questions is likely to be a sensitive issue. In essence, school officials are in the position of convincing a parent, hearing officer, or judge that the needs of the many outweigh the needs of the few. Using data can potentially reduce the adversarial nature of such discussions.

Using behavioral rating scales.   Having some indication that the student's behavior differs from that of age- or grade-mates is a logical place to start. Used for this purpose, behavioral rating scales can help to identify which behavioral domains are the most problematic, and also whether behaviors are consistent across teachers.

Using direct observation.   Data showing the amount of time the student remains on task with an age-appropriate level of independence, as well as the actual number of behaviors (e.g., out of seat, verbal outbursts) and the amount of time the teacher spends responding to the student, can be compelling. It is likely that several observations completed by personnel other than the classroom teacher, on different days and at different times, will be necessary to make the case that the student's presence has a detrimental effect on other students. Further, an observer can count the number of responses and total amount of time the teacher spends with the student. Using structured observation methods and protocols is likely to yield stronger evidence than will simple narrative observations.

Using teacher judgment.   Teacher judgment is part of any placement decision, as are the perspectives of the parents and the individual student. Teachers could be asked to estimate the amount of time and effort they spend with one individual as compared to other students in the class. Teachers might also be asked to compare the instructional needs of the target student with expectations for the curricular content or grade level they teach. Finally, teachers are in the position to observe the levels of social interaction and acceptance of individual students in relation to their classmates. Teacher judgment can be informative when the student's behavior differs considerably from normative expectations on valid rating scales, and direct classroom observations document that the behaviors are prominent, disruptive, and demanding of attention. A teacher's judgment that the student is inappropriately placed and might be better served in another setting is strengthened when supported by other assessment data.

Conclusion

Federal and state special education regulations favor but do not require that all educational programs be carried out in general education settings. These policies, however, do require that all students with disabilities receiving special education services be provided with FAPE in the LRE for each student. With the reauthorizations of IDEA in 1997 and 2004, FAPE changed from being whatever the schools and parents wanted it to be, to a program of instruction as close as possible to what is provided to every other student in the school. Regardless of what is taught, however, students vary in their need for structure, explicitness, and a variety of other factors that affect educational progress. For special education students, such needs must be determined and addressed through the IEP process before instructional placement can be logically addressed. Addressing placement in an *a priori* manner independent of data and thought (i.e., determining placement on the basis of disability category) is arbitrary and unjustified. We have discussed several forms of data that can be considered when evaluating placement decisions. We suggest that each assessment tool works in concert with the others to support decisions that are logical, respectful of the student's needs, and likely to lead to enhanced educational outcomes.

No single source of data, test, or procedure can be used in making educational decisions (IDEA, 2004). Consequently, no single source of data (e.g., state assessment, individual achievement test, teacher opinion, classroom grades) is sufficient to guide instructional placement decisions for students with disabilities. When various forms of data align to suggest similar conclusions, IEP teams can feel more assured of making appropriate placement decisions. The following case serves as an example.

Consider an individual student who is unable to pass the state proficiency test, attains low scores on an individual achievement test, is earning failing grades, and whose teachers express doubts about the adequacy of the current educational program. With these features in alignment, it is difficult to argue that the student was receiving FAPE. Something in the program (e.g., goal, kinds of services, amount of services) needs to be changed. Changing the program sometimes necessitates a change in placement, because not all actions can be carried out in the same place.

Conversely, data from various sources can align, but when few interventions have been tried and documentation of the efforts to support the student in the current environment is sparse or lacking, changes in placement are difficult to support even if the teachers and family agree on a more-restrictive alternative. To justify placement in a more-restrictive yet supportive environment, it is necessary to demonstrate in each case that FAPE cannot be or was not provided in the learning environment despite the use of supports, not simply that an individual with a disability is doing poorly in school.

When the sources of data conflict, legislation and case law suggest that state tests are likely to trump other assessments, with classroom grades (if they are in agreement with state test results) following close behind (S. Gordon, 2006). Regardless of the data source, however, an appropriate education that meets the unique needs of a student with disabilities requires more than minimal progress, and adequate assessment requires more than token efforts to recognize and respond to students' learning needs. By delivering a FAPE with as few changes as necessary to the experiences provided to other students, instruction is provided in the LRE. In contrast, delivering a general education that fails to provide the personalized benefits of FAPE for a student with disabilities does not constitute that student's LRE.

CHAPTER 23

Curriculum-Based Assessment

John Venn | *University of North Florida*

Assessment is the use of tests and other measures to make educational decisions. Decision making is the key element in the process (J. J. Venn, 2007). One level of decision making involves identifying students with disabilities and developing initial individual education programs (IEPs). Traditional assessment instruments, especially formal, standardized tests, are widely used at this level. Other purposes of assessment include instructional intervention and progress monitoring. Norm-referenced, formal assessments measure broad curriculum areas (e.g., reading, math, writing), and they are not necessarily linked to school curriculum. Without a link to curriculum, their usefulness for assessing classroom instruction and monitoring student progress is limited. To address these limitations, a variety of classroom-based procedures have been developed to evaluate the impact of instructional interventions on students and to monitor the progress of students in their curricula. Curriculum-based assessment (CBA) is one of the most widely used of these alternative procedures. CBA relies on measurement strategies and techniques that enable teachers to link their evaluations of student performance with the curriculum they use with their students.

This chapter provides an overview of CBA including a definition and description of the characteristics of CBA, an overview of several CBA strategies and procedures, and a discussion of some current issues regarding implementation of CBA. The chapter concludes with recommendations for teachers, decision makers, and researchers.

Defining Curriculum-Based Assessment

The term *curriculum-based assessment* refers to evaluation processes and procedures that use content taken directly from the material taught (Hall & Mengel, 2002). It is one form of criterion-referenced assessment that directly links evaluation with instructional programs in ways that inform teachers about the learning progress and the learning difficulties of their students. CBA relies on observation and recording of student performance in the classroom as the basis for making instructional decisions. The CBA process is a form of direct measurement, because when teachers use it, they assess what they teach (Witt, Elliott, Daly, Gresham, & Kramer, 1998). This differs significantly from indirect assessment with norm-referenced tests, which may not reflect the material taught in a particular school or classroom.

Although teachers may know in a general sense when their students are making adequate progress, teachers are imperfect judges of the performance levels of the students in their classrooms (see Hoge & Coladarci, 1989, for a review). CBA provides a structured way to measure precisely how well students perform in relation to specific class materials and lessons. For example, when teachers need to know the progress of their students in literacy, they can directly assess their students' performance in reading, spelling, and writing based on what they have taught. Frequent, ongoing use of brief CBA measures enables teachers to quickly determine when students are making adequate progress or failing to master particular skills or concepts (Witt et al., 1998). As a result, CBA helps teachers make a variety of instructional decisions, including determining present levels of educational performance in the curriculum, identifying strengths and weaknesses in specific skill areas, establishing priorities for intervention and remediation, monitoring progress in the curriculum, and assisting in IEP planning (L. S. Fuchs & Fuchs, 1986).

E. D. Jones, Southern, and Brigham (1998) refer to CBA as testing what is taught and teaching what is tested. This description highlights the strong connection between assessment and instruction, and this is a defining characteristic of CBA. Although CBA is often referred to as a type of informal assessment, E. D. Jones et al. point out that many CBA procedures are quite systematic, structured, and formal in their approach. When practitioners standardize their use of CBA, effectiveness is enhanced, and more consistent results are obtained. Regardless of the specific type of CBA used, several stages are common to most procedures, including analyzing the curriculum and identifying specific learning outcomes and criteria for success, selecting or designing appropriate assessment procedures, determining present levels of performance in the curriculum, collecting and displaying the assessment results, and making decisions based on the results (Payne, Marks, & Bogan, 2007).

This process is essentially a diagnostic and prescriptive procedure that involves assessing student performance and then teaching students the skills they have not acquired but need to learn next in the curriculum or in a particular subject or learning area. Once students have received targeted instruction in the identified knowledge or skill area, then CBA is useful in quickly and accurately re-assessing the students to determine their progress. If the student has mastered the skills, then the teacher may move to the next skills in the curriculum. If the student has not made progress, then the intervention approach may need to be modified. Thus, CBA is a continuous test–teach–test–teach cycle that combines informal assessment with instructional intervention programs. For these reasons, CBA is useful in the IEP process, especially in establishing IEP goals by providing efficient and effective measures of present levels of performance in specific skill areas. The same CBA strategies and procedures used to establish goals can be used repeatedly to evaluate student progress in reaching those goals.

Characteristics of Curriculum-Based Assessment

A variety of CBA approaches have been developed, and they share several common characteristics. First, CBA involves brief, direct, and ongoing measurement in that teachers use probes, or small and discrete assessments, that may take only a few minutes to administer and score. Second, CBA measures the specific skills being taught by the teacher. This makes it context and content specific. Third, CBAs are grounded in good teaching practice by enabling teachers to assess student progress as an integral part of the teaching and learning process. Finally, CBAs are learner centered in that they help teachers focus on the particular skills with which individual children need help rather than more general skills.

Direct measurement of the skills being taught in the curriculum is the key characteristic of CBA. This is accomplished by assessing a sample of items using content and materials from the instructional lessons and learning activities in the curriculum. In other words, the skills assessed are the skills taught. For example, performance in oral reading and spelling are directly measured by assessing words read and spelled correctly using the words taught in the curriculum. Conducting assessment in this manner makes CBA more precise than traditional assessment and connects CBA with the goals for individual students and for groups of students. Most CBA techniques and procedures are brief, taking from 1 to 5 minutes to complete. This means they are usually quick and easy to accurately administer and score. As a result, they can be given frequently to obtain an ongoing measure of student performance over time. Frequent measurement gives CBA a distinct advantage over traditional testing.

In contrast to the traditional testing, which is episodic at best and usually given only once, CBA evaluates ongoing performance over time. This produces a more accurate picture of how much and what students are learning, and it is sensitive to small changes in student performance. CBA also produces more than test score results. Data may be charted for visual analysis or used in various item and error pattern analysis procedures for identifying current performance, pinpointing emerging skills, and targeting skills in need of remediation. These characteristics mean that CBA is grounded in good instructional practice as an integral part of the teaching and learning process.

Reliability, Validity, and Fairness

Reliability, validity, and fairness are important characteristics of all assessments, including curriculum-based evaluations. The goal is to conduct assessment in ways that produce reliable and valid results that are fair for all students and free from possible sources of bias. According to experts (National Council of Accreditation for Teacher Education, n.d.; Stiggins, 2001), reliability, validity, and fairness have specific meanings as applied to CBA. Assessments are reliable when they produce consistent score results. In other words, the scores are dependable and similar over more than one administration of the same test or assessment. For example, if a teacher assesses math performance using a procedure such as error analysis on several occasions within a few days of each other, the results should be similar on each assessment.

Assessments are said to be valid to the extent that they measure what they are supposed to measure. Validity is really a question of accuracy and fairness. Teachers can enhance accuracy by reviewing their assessments to ensure they reflect the standards, knowledge, and skills their students are expected to demonstrate. Similarly, assessments are fair when they assess what was taught in the curriculum. Content mapping is an example of a strategy teachers can use to help to ensure fairness. Content maps, or curriculum maps, involve identifying what one plans to teach (e.g., in a project map), as well as what one actually teaches (e.g., in a diary map) (Hale, 2008). By systematically and accurately recording what has actually been taught in class, teachers can design assessments that match their curriculum, thereby ensuring that students have had opportunities to learn and practice what is being assessed.

The notion of fairness is perhaps the key measurement characteristic that teachers should consider in CBA. Another aspect of fairness and validity is freedom from bias. Teachers may reduce the possible sources of bias in CBAs by minimizing distractions during assessment such as noise, discomfort, and inappropriate seating or lighting. Teachers should also ensure that all assessments have adequate instructions, well-written test questions, and materials that are neatly arranged and clearly copied. Ways to reduce bias also include providing assessments with appropriate language (e.g., using vocabulary and language that is at the students' comprehension levels) and consistent scoring procedures. Assessments that are fair avoid discriminating against students, including students from culturally and linguistically diverse backgrounds and students with disabilities. Fairness also refers to how the assessment results are used. Therefore, CBAs should also produce consistent scores and results that teachers can use effectively as part of instruction (N. S. Cole & Zieky, 2001; Joint Committee on Testing Practices, 2005; D. Whittington, 1999).

Representative CBA Strategies and Procedures

CBA strategies are available for general and special education classroom use and for assessing student performance in a number of specific areas, especially literacy (Gansle, Gilbertson, & VanDerHeyden, 2006; Garcia, 2007; Marcotte & Hintze, 2009; Otaiba & Lake, 2007). In this chapter we highlight CBA strategies and procedures for assessing reading performance. The particular CBA procedures described in the following sections are miscue and error analysis, cloze, informal reading inventories, checklists and rating scales, and portfolios. We chose these because they are CBA strategies teachers are most likely to use in their classrooms on a daily basis. Furthermore, although this chapter focuses on the application of CBA to reading, these procedures represent the kinds of assessments available for other subjects as well. For each procedure, we provide a definition of the process, a description of the characteristics of the procedures, and a discussion of how it may be implemented.

Miscue and Error Analysis

Miscue and error analysis are among the most commonly used curriculum-based strategies for assessing reading. The error analysis process described by McLoughlin and Lewis (2008) includes several steps, beginning with selection of appropriate material for the student to read. The materials may be from a word list or passages from graded books used in the curriculum. Several levels of graded passages should be used, including passages at the independent, instructional, and frustration levels. Two copies of each passage are needed. The student reads one copy, and the teacher records errors on the other. Teachers may also create an audio recording of the student reading the passage so that they can go back and make sure that they have recorded and coded all reading errors accurately. Common reading errors include additions, substitutions, omissions, and reversals. A variety of approaches are available for identifying and coding errors in miscue analysis (Jarmulowicz & Hay, 2009; Larsen & Nippold, 2007; Layton & Koenig, 1998; McGuinness, 1997; C. Watson & Willows, 1995).

Miscue analysis is similar to error analysis but focuses more on the qualitative aspects of the reading process. In subjects such as math, error analysis involves examining students' responses to a curriculum-based work sample, such as a computation worksheet, to identify patterns in errors and underlying skill deficits. The teacher identifies the errors and underlying skill deficit(s) and then addresses them in subsequent instruction. For example, if a student makes multiple errors by adding numbers on subtraction problems, subsequent instruction might involve teaching the student to highlight the operation sign in order to remediate this error pattern. K. S. Goodman (1965, 1967) initially developed miscue analysis from linguistic studies of cues and miscues in reading, describing it as providing teachers with "windows on the reading process" (K. S. Goodman, 1965, p. 123). Goodman used the term *miscue* instead of *mistake* or *error* to describe student reading responses that do not match expected responses. A reading miscue occurs when students read a word that is not the word in print. Miscues are not considered errors; rather, they represent a student's best attempt to read the given passage and can provide important information on the strategies that the student does and does not use to read difficult material.

In addition to recording the type of miscues made, teachers analyze miscues to determine whether they change the meaning of the text. According to K. S. Goodman and Burke (1973), miscues that change the meaning may include graphic similarity (e.g., reading *house* instead of *horse*), sound similarity (e.g., reading *wrist* instead of *waist*), and grammatical function (e.g., reading *besides* instead of *both sides*). Kucer (2008) reported that reading accurately might not be as important as the type of miscue and the pattern of errors. For example, although it involves errors, when a student reads, "We both got into the car," it does not change the essential meaning of the phrase in text, "We both hopped in the car." However, reading, "We both hoped to get a car" does change the meaning of the phrase, signals a comprehension problem, and is therefore considered a more important miscue. Furthermore, errors that change the meaning of an entire passage may be more significant than other types of errors. For example, errors in clauses are less likely to disrupt comprehension than errors in passages that contain a significant story event.

Teachers may develop their own analysis from reading materials in their classroom, but a formal, standardized Reading Miscue Inventory (Y. Goodman, Watson, & Burke, 2005) is available. Extensive research (J. Brown, Goodman, & Marek, 1996; Ehri & McCormick, 2004; McKenna & Picard, 2006) has been conducted using miscue analysis to assess student reading performance, to inform reading instruction, and to investigate how students learn to read. The overall results of these studies support the reliability and validity of the process. Ehri and McCormick indicated that teachers should use error totals in their analysis of students' reading. According to McKenna and Picard (2006), error totals are particularly helpful in identifying instructional and independent reading levels of students. These totals help teachers select appropriate reading materials for their students. Further, miscue analysis can help measure how well students use decoding skills.

Unlike formal, standardized tests, which are clinical and episodic in nature, miscue and error analyses assess reading in an authentic, genuine manner using reading materials that are part of the student's curriculum. This produces both quantitative data and qualitative information for evaluating reading performance as it occurs during instruction. Most miscue and error analysis procedures focus on assessing how students use cues in oral reading rather than on directly assessing reading comprehension. Cues are what students rely on to read words they don't know. For example, multiple miscues that exhibit high sound similarity but that change the meaning of the text indicate that the student may be using phonetic cues (e.g., trying to sound out the word) but not attending to whether the word choice makes sense. Evaluating the pattern of errors provides useful diagnostic information about areas in need of remediation. Although some aspects of comprehension may be evaluated using miscue analysis, many teachers rely on cloze procedures for assessing the comprehension skills of their students.

Cloze

Cloze is a diagnostic tool for assessing reading comprehension. The procedure involves deleting every *n*th word, usually every fifth word, in an appropriate grade-level passage and having the student read the material while filling in the missing words (J. J. Venn, 2007). Depending on the particular cloze procedure, word choices may or may not be provided. To complete the task, students must rely on background knowledge, context clues, word meanings, language structures, grammar skills, and general understanding of the material. Cloze provides teachers with data and information to determine whether specific reading material is on their students' instructional level. The cloze scoring process involves determining the percentage of words the students successfully supply.

According to Chatel (2001), students who correctly provide between 44% and 57% of the missing words are reading material at their instructional level. The instructional level refers to reading material that is challenging for a student to understand but is manageable with instructional support. If students fail to correctly supply at least 44% of the words in a passage, the material is too difficult for them, and they are likely to become frustrated. At the frustration level, students have difficulty understanding the meaning of what they are reading because the material is too difficult for them. Students who supply greater than 57% of the words correctly are at the independent level and can easily read and comprehend the reading passage without instructional support.

Like many curriculum-based tools, cloze is useful for identifying reading comprehension difficulties and planning instruction. Chatel (2001) indicated all teachers have the knowledge and skills necessary to develop and use cloze procedures and that the same reading material that teachers use for diagnostic purposes may be used instructionally to help students develop their skills in using background knowledge and language skills. J. S. Shin, Deno, and Espin (2000) reported that a derivation of the cloze procedure (maze, as described in the following paragraph) provided a reliable and valid method of assessing the reading growth of 43 second graders who were evaluated monthly for the entire school year.

Many variations of cloze procedures are used in literacy, including using the process as a visual way to assess spelling of the words the student supplies (Mercer & Pullen, 2005), and maze, which is a form of cloze with choices provided to the student for each of the missing words in the passage. The maze procedure (J. S. Shin et al., 2000) involves deleting every seventh word and providing the student with three, multiple-choice alternatives. One alternative is the correct word and the other two are incorrect. A critical feature of the maze procedure is that the rate at which the student reads the passage is timed. Busch and Lembke (2005) provide an excellent guide for preparing, administering, and scoring maze measures. Research evidence supports the use of maze procedures for assessing the reading progress of students, including students with severe reading deficits (Faykus & McCurdy, 1998; R. Parker, Hasbrouck, & Tindal, 1992). As summarized by Busch and Lembke, research has shown that maze assessments demonstrate high alternate-forms reliability (i.e., student scores were consistent across different maze measures) and strong concurrent validity (i.e., students' scores on maze assessments correlated highly and positively with scores on other formal, standardized reading comprehension measures).

Informal Reading Inventories

Informal reading inventories (IRIs) are diagnostic tools for measuring reading performance. They consist of graded word lists for assessing word-decoding ability and graded reading passages for measuring oral reading, silent reading, and reading comprehension skills (S. G. Paris & Carpenter, 2003). The diagnostic procedure involves having students read passages that are below, at, and above their reading level to identify appropriate reading materials for students, to place students in reading groups, to determine strengths and areas in need of remediation, to evaluate progress over time, and to pinpoint gaps in the skills of struggling readers (Nilsson, 2008). In a review of informal reading inventories, Applegate, Quinn, and Applegate (2002) indicated that most IRIs are best at measuring reading recognition skills rather than reading comprehension abilities. Therefore, IRIs should be used together with other measures of reading to obtain a comprehensive picture of a student's reading strengths and weaknesses.

A variety of informal reading inventories are commercially available (e.g., Johns, 2005; Nilsson, 2008; Woods & Moe, 2006), but teachers may also construct their own IRIs from reading material in their curriculum (J. J. Venn, 2007). The process of constructing and using an IRI begins with the teacher's selecting appropriate passages from reading material in the curriculum. The passages should be about 50 to 100 words for elementary students and about 150 to 200 words for secondary students. Second, the teacher selects three to five passages; for example, two passages below the student's grade level, one passage on grade level, and two above the student's grade level. Next, the teacher makes two copies of each passage, and the student reads one copy aloud while the teacher records errors on the other copy. As an optional step, after the student finishes reading a passage, the teacher asks three to four comprehension questions a student should be able to answer. The questions include both factual (simple) and inferential (complex) questions. Finally, the teacher calculates the percentage of words read correctly.

Passages in which the student reads 95% or more of the words correctly can be considered to be at the student's independent level. *Independent* means the student can read the material easily. Teachers should make sure, for example, that students select material for pleasure reading that is at their independent reading level. Passages in which the student reads 90% to 95% of the words correctly can be considered to be at the student's instructional level, at which the student needs some support to read with fluency and for meaning. This means that reading material at this level is appropriate for use in instructional situations. Passages the student reads with an accuracy of below 90% are at the frustration level for the student. This means they are too difficult for the student to read independently and are generally not appropriate for instruction. In addition to calculating a percentage correct score, IRIs usually involve conducting a miscue analysis as part of the process of interpreting and analyzing the results for purposes of instruction and remediation. A summary of the steps in the process of conducting and scoring an IRI appears in Figure 23.1.

Figure 23.1 Steps in giving and scoring a teacher-made informal reading inventory.

1. Select two passages below, one passage at, and two above the student's grade level.
2. Make two copies of each passage.
3. Have the student read each passage, and record errors on a separate copy.
4. After the student is finished reading, ask three to four comprehension questions (optional).
5. Analyze the results.

Checklists and Rating Scales for Assessing Literacy

Teachers who want to systematically assess literacy behaviors in an efficient and effective manner often use diagnostic checklists and rating scales. A checklist is a list of skills or behaviors designed for recording student performance in a structured manner. Rating scales are like checklists except they include a scale or range of rating options for each item assessed (Oosterhof, 2009). Checklists and rating scales pinpoint behaviors quickly in an easily understood format. This makes them ideal tools for recording observations, documenting performance, and keeping progress data and notes. Diagnostic checklists are useful for assessing many literacy behaviors, including student reading strengths, areas for growth, and emerging skills. Checklists produce a permanent record and may be designed to measure improvement over time.

Checklists and rating scales are developed by taking broad skills and breaking them down into specific steps or subskills (McLoughlin & Lewis, 2008). For example, teachers often use informal diagnostic checklists to assess literacy skills such as oral reading. The diagnostic oral reading checklist appearing in Figure 23.1 (Hudson, Lane, & Pullen, 2005; J. J. Venn, 2007) provides a tool for assessing specific oral reading behaviors in a systematic, organized manner, and it provides a written record of student performance. Because checklists are quick and easy to create, administer, and score, teachers may use them to obtain data and information efficiently about student progress in ways that are connected with instruction. Teachers may use tools like this in a flexible manner, but they are perhaps most helpful when used systematically over time to measure progress (e.g., monthly or every other month).

The process of constructing a checklist begins with identifying the items that will make up the content. The content can be derived from the most important skills in a lesson or unit or the most important behaviors in a skill set, such as the oral reading behaviors in the sample in Figure 23.2. The items may also be obtained from the objectives, outcomes, or standards in the curriculum. The items should be written in a way that is measureable and reliable. Reliability is a key to developing checklists that produce consistent, dependable results. Reliability is improved by providing operational definitions, examples, and nonexamples for each target behavior. A suitable format for displaying and scoring the behaviors or skills in checklist form should also be developed. In addition, the best checklists produce a score or result that can be used to monitor progress. One way to score checklists is to simply count the number of skills mastered out of the total number of skills. For example, a student may have mastered 8 of the 10 skills, objectives, or standards (or 80%).

Although a paucity of research supports the efficacy of checklists, this informal tool has high content validity (i.e., the degree to which the intended content is assessed) when teachers construct checklists and rubrics that reflect key competencies, outcomes, and standards that students are expected to acquire in their particular curriculum. Checklists provide a valuable tool for identifying the skills and knowledge that students have mastered and those areas in need of remediation.

Portfolio Assessment

A portfolio is a systematic collection of student work that provides evidence of student learning. Portfolios emphasize student performance, and most focus on literacy skills although they are useful in all subjects in the curriculum. Portfolio assessment is a type of curriculum-based evaluation that relies on genuine samples of authentic student work to assess academic performance (J. J. Venn, 2007). Tone and Farr (1998) suggested that portfolios facilitate reflective teaching, learning, and assessment by emphasizing student participation in the instructional process. Student self-assessment is a key feature of portfolio evaluation.

The two major types of portfolios are process and product portfolios. Process portfolios are the major and more dynamic type that teachers most commonly use in their classrooms. Process portfolios include evidence of the process students work through as they develop mastery of skills, standards, and outcomes. For example, students may include their "sloppy copy," rough draft, and final paper to show their progress in developing a writing sample. Product portfolios, in contrast, focus on the final products of student work such as the best or final writing samples.

Electronic and digital portfolios are becoming more widely used as an alternative approach to assessing student progress. Whereas paper portfolios are static documents, electronic portfolios are more dynamic because they may include links to a variety of sources. Students

Figure 23.2   Checklist of oral reading behaviors.

Student: _____   Teacher: _____

Date: _____   School: _____

Description of passage, including grade level and length:

Reading Behavior	Yes	No	Notes
1. Reads with expression and intonation.			
2. Reads clearly with good articulation.			
3. Reads fluently at an appropriate rate.			
4. Not easily distracted.			
5. Not easily discouraged.			
6. Reads in a flowing manner.			
7. Quick word identification.			
8. Attempts new words.			
9. Uses decoding to read unfamiliar words.			
10. Follows punctuation.			
11. Makes use of context clues.			
12. Demonstrates good comprehension.			
13. Other noticeable behaviors (list).			

Observations: _____

_____

also have the opportunity to develop their technology skills when they use electronic portfolios. Fitzsimmons (2008) identified several advantages of electronic portfolios, including efficient display of benchmark learning examples and effective links to state and local learning outcomes. For example, in the state of Rhode Island, digital portfolios have replaced high-stakes standardized tests as the accountability measure for student demonstration of their proficiency (Archer, 2007). The future clearly points to even more widespread use of electronic portfolios in classrooms, schools districts, and entire states.

The portfolio assessment process includes several steps (J. J. Venn, 2007) and begins with selecting the portfolio contents. Other steps include constructing a management system, developing appropriate scoring protocols, and holding student conferences. The management system should include teacher responsibilities for managing the portfolios and student duties related to organizing and managing the materials that are part of the portfolio. Portfolio scoring is usually conducted by the teacher, but most student portfolios include student self-assessment materials such as writing and reading logs that include student reflections. Portfolios may be scored using holistic or analytic rubrics. Holistic scoring rubrics are usually brief forms that produce an overall score for the entire portfolio. In contrast, analytic rubrics are more detailed forms that score each portfolio entry individually, typically evaluating specific, prescribed aspects of each entry (e.g., grammar, spelling, cohesiveness, personal voice, completeness). Analytic scoring provides more specific data and information and is therefore more useful in instructional situations that require diagnosis and remediation of specific weaknesses.

Although portfolios are widely used in education, they tend to have low reliability, especially the informal portfolios developed by teachers (D. Miller, Linn, & Gronlund, 2009). For this reason, portfolios should be developed carefully, with attention to the scoring criteria and to using the most appropriate scoring rubric. The reliability of rubrics, especially holistic rubrics, has been examined (Jonsson & Svingby, 2007; Rezaei & Lovorn, 2010). In their review of research on scoring rubrics,

Jonsson and Svingby reported that although the reliability of rubrics was not always adequate, using rubrics generally improved the consistency of performance tests (e.g., portfolios). Moreover, their review indicated that factors such as using benchmarks (i.e., specific descriptions of what is required to earn each scoring point on a rubric), training in scoring rubrics, and using analytic and topic-specific rubrics are associated with more reliable scoring, More research is needed regarding how to make rubrics more useful as reliable and valid evaluation tools (N. Elliot, 2005; Hafner & Hafner, 2003).

Student self-assessment is a key element in all of these steps. For example, students should participate in the process of selecting the portfolio contents. Student conferences are a key part of portfolio teaching, learning, and assessment. In most portfolio systems, students have specific responsibilities to prepare for their conferences with the teacher, including identifying their learning goals and gauging their progress in meeting their goals. Students often write their goals on a portfolio conference record that can then become part of their portfolio contents after the conference is complete (J. J. Venn, 2007).

Issues in Curriculum-Based Assessment

Practitioners face a number of barriers in conducting CBA with high fidelity, or as designed. In addition to these barriers are concerns about how best to provide accommodations and modifications when using CBA. Each is considered in the following sections.

Barriers to High-Quality Curriculum-Based Assessment

The stumbling blocks that confront teachers in their efforts to conduct high-quality CBA are many, and these barriers are particularly evident with students who have special needs. In a review of these barriers, Stiggins (2001, 2007) identified negative feelings about assessment by teachers as a key obstacle. Problems may arise from the negative personal experiences many teachers have had with traditional assessment, which may have an impact on their view of the use of various assessment procedures in their classrooms. The teacher's negative experience may be coupled with similar negative assessment experiences of students with disabilities. Stiggins (2001, 2007) suggested that the general result is poor attitudes about assessment. More specifically, students with special needs often expect to fail tests based on their previous poor performance on many different assessments, including formal tests and informal curriculum-based evaluations.

Lack of institutional support for teachers who wish to conduct consistent and effective assessments is a second barrier cited by Stiggins (2007). Because students with special needs often present some of the most difficult assessment challenges, the need for support is especially evident in special education. Stiggins suggested that lack of support coupled with the many demands placed on teachers (e.g., pressure to focus on high-stakes testing) often result in incomplete classroom assessments simply because teachers do not have enough time to prepare, conduct, and analyze the results of CBAs of student performance. Best practices call for teachers to identify present levels of performance using appropriate assessments, develop individual learning goals and objectives for each student based on the assessment results, measure student progress in meeting the objectives, and revise the objectives based on student progress. It would appear that practitioners must receive meaningful support to successfully complete all of the complex and demanding assessment and intervention tasks expected of them.

Questions about Accommodations and Modifications

Accommodations provide students with disabilities the opportunity to demonstrate their skills and knowledge by removing the barriers preventing accurate measurement of a student's present levels of performance (Sireci, 2006). Similar to accommodations provided for high-stakes proficiency tests (see Chapter 24, this volume), accommodations in CBA may include changes in the setting, timing, scheduling, administration, or response method used (B. J. Case, 2005). Issues include how to identify appropriate accommodations, concerns about effectiveness, and how to create more flexible assessments that reduce the need for accommodations.

One ongoing issue is that teachers are often unsure about which accommodations to provide. Selecting the most appropriate accommodations is difficult because accommodations should be individualized to meet unique student needs, and there are many different accommodations (McKevitt & Elliott, 2003). Extended time and reduced distractions (e.g., using a separate room for the assessment) are two of the most common accommodations (Pitoniak & Royer, 2001). Sign language interpreters for deaf students, computers for word processing on essay tests, scribes who write for a student, and readers are other frequently used accommodations for classroom assessments. Further complicating the selection of accommodations is the absence of a sound research evidence base for many of the current policies guiding provision of accommodations (Sireci, Scarpati, & Li, 2005).

One possible solution to the problem of providing accommodations is the development of new, more flexible CBAs using Universal Design for Learning (UDL) techniques (Sireci, Li, & Scarpati, 2003). The term *UDL* refers to instruction that is accessible to all students including students with disabilities by presenting information in multiple and flexible formats and by providing multiple and flexible methods of expression and engagement for students (National Universal Design for Learning Task Force, 2007). It has been suggested that more widespread use of UDL would minimize the concerns about which accommodations should be available in different testing situations, though more research is clearly needed regarding the application of UDL principles and the use of CBA. UDL provides a way to develop CBAs and other assessments that are more flexible and can be adjusted to meet the unique and individual learning needs of many (although not all) students with disabilities without the need for accommodations. For example, the National Universal Design for Learning Task Force (2007) indicated that digital versions of student textbooks are becoming more readily available for students. Many digital textbooks are universally designed, and they provide text-to-speech decoding, research-based strategy supports, easily accessible glossary definitions for different levels of reading comprehension, and assessments that can be printed or taken on a computer.

Students with more severe disabilities may require modifications, which are more extensive changes in the assessment procedures than the changes typically afforded by accommodations. Modifications fundamentally change assessment procedures by altering the content, the level, or the administration procedure. Modifications, also referred to as *alternative assessments,* are provided to students with severe disabilities when it is determined typical assessments would not be appropriate, even with accommodations. Typical alternative assessments include portfolios, checklists, rating scales, or directly measuring skills using modified achievement standards (L. Cohen & Spenciner, 2007; Towles-Reeves, Kleinert, & Muhomba, 2009). Because guidelines, policies, and procedures for providing modifications are relatively new, clear and research-based guidelines for modifying CBAs for students with special needs do not yet exist.

Fortunately, teachers have considerable flexibility in how they provide accommodations and modifications in the classroom when using CBAs that are part of intervention programs. Teachers have much less flexibility when using formal, standardized, norm-referenced tests. Evidence (S. N. Elliott, McKevitt, & Kettler, 2002) supports the contention that most students with disabilities perform better on assessments when they receive accommodations. Therefore, teachers should implement appropriate accommodations when they use informal CBAs as well as when they give more formal, standardized tests.

Recommendations for Teachers, Decision Makers, and Researchers

Teachers, decision makers, and researchers face many challenges in further developing CBAs in ways that help students. The foremost challenge faced by teachers is building their knowledge and skills so that they can consistently and accurately use CBAs along with other assessments such as curriculum-based measurement (see Chapter 18, this volume) to plan and inform instruction, to develop remedial intervention programs, and to measure the progress of students with special needs. Given the current focus on inclusion of students with disabilities, teachers also need to become experts in providing accommodations and modifications for conducting CBAs in general education settings. For this to occur, decision makers must find new ways to support teachers as they build their competencies in using assessment as an integral part of the teaching and learning process.

The challenges faced by decision makers are many, including finding ways to provide additional support to practitioners as they strive to overcome the barriers to high-quality assessment in their classrooms. Some experts (Neil, 2008; Rothstein, Jacobsen, & Wilder, 2008) believe a major challenge is to develop policies that reduce the current overdependence on high-stakes test scores as the sole measure of school success. Rothstein et al. (2008) believe that state test-based, high-stakes accountability systems have failed to close the achievement gap, and they call for expansion of accountability measures to include local, curriculum-based evidence of student progress. According to Neil (2008), other nations with excellent educational systems rely either primarily on classroom assessments or on a combination of classroom evidence and results from high-stakes tests to account for student learning. For this to occur in the United States, decision makers, like teachers, need to develop their knowledge of CBA and measurement.

The challenges faced by researchers include conducting practical, applied investigations designed to assist teachers in strengthening the reliability and validity of CBA. This extends to the need for additional research on accommodations and modifications in the classroom. Although relatively new concepts to many educators, accommodations and modifications have much potential to assist students with special needs in the assessment process and during instruction. Researchers should also consider conducting more applied studies examining the efficacy of CBAs (e.g., does using CBAs result in improved student outcomes?). Findings from investigations such as these will clarify which CBAs are most effective in assessing student performance and improving student outcomes, which will in turn assist practitioners and decision makers in looking beyond high-stakes tests as the only useful measure of student progress.

Summary

This chapter has investigated a variety of topics associated with CBA for students with special needs. The chapter included discussions of representative procedures for assessing reading (i.e., miscue and error analysis, cloze, informal reading inventories, checklists and rating scales, and portfolios). Issues in CBA, including barriers to high-quality assessment and use of accommodations and modifications, were also addressed. The challenges that teachers, leaders, and researchers face in implementing CBA with fidelity were considered, with particular emphasis on the need to support teachers. Farr (1996), in a description of how to make assessment more student centered, expressed the hope that teachers, along with support from policy makers and researchers, will develop new ways to use CBA and related assessments as valuable tools in planning and delivering instruction, remediating weaknesses, and measuring student progress. Farr indicated the need to place confidence in the validity of teachers' decision-making abilities as part of the assessment process. The goal is to use CBA to support student learning with the emphasis on student accomplishments (Farr, 1991). It will be necessary for teachers, decision makers, and researchers to work together to create, refine, administer, and apply the results of CBAs that focus on this goal in order to ensure that all students achieve, grow, and progress to the maximum extent possible. Researchers need to provide more practical, applied CBA information that directly informs instruction. Decision makers must provide additional support for teachers to implement CBA. Teachers need to build their skills and knowledge in using CBA as an assessment tool that can help them measure student performance accurately, efficiently, and effectively.

CHAPTER 24

Accommodations for Assessment

Martha L. Thurlow, Sheryl S. Lazarus, and **Laurene L. Christensen** |
National Center on Educational Outcomes, University of Minnesota

*A*ccommodations have become an integral part of thinking about the participation of students with disabilities in assessment programs. Few books written today about state or district assessments fail to address in some way the need to provide accommodations to students with disabilities. In fact, several books have been written specifically about testing accommodations (Bolt & Roach, 2009; S. N. Elliott, Braden, & White, 2001; Laitusis & Cook, 2007).

Despite the increasing attention given to accommodations, confusion about terminology remains, complicated by the changing meaning of terms over time (Thurlow, 2007). As used today by most states and districts, *assessment accommodations* are defined as changes in test materials or procedures that *do not* alter the content being measured (Lazarus, Thurlow, Lail, & Christensen, 2009). *Assessment modifications,* in contrast, are defined as changes in test materials or procedures that *do* alter the content being measured. Federal law and regulations do not use the same terminology, instead referring almost exclusively to "accommodations," with clarification added as to whether the accommodation does or does not change the validity of assessment results. For consistency in this chapter, we use the term *accommodations* unless specifically citing a policy in which the term *modification* is used.

Accommodations generally are grouped into categories such as presentation, response, timing, scheduling, and setting. Sometimes categories are combined (e.g., timing and

scheduling), and sometimes categories are added (e.g., technology). Regardless of the specific categories used, accommodations include changes such as large-print editions of a test, allowing the student to mark in the test booklet rather than on a bubble sheet, giving the student extended time, and having the student take the test in an area away from other students, perhaps in a separate room.

In this chapter we provide a historical picture of accommodations, along with the theoretical, legal, and policy contexts in which accommodations have existed and changed in meaning over time. Then we describe the research base for three accommodations—extended time, reading aloud/oral presentation, and computer-based testing—including the extent to which the evidence addresses classroom, district, or state assessments. We conclude with an analysis of the strengths and weaknesses of the literature on accommodations for students with disabilities, along with recommendations for practice and future research.

Historical, Theoretical, Legal, and Policy Contexts for Accommodations

Historical Context

Accommodations have been a part of special education practice for a long time. Starting before the first federal special education law for public schools (Public

Law 94-142, Education for All Handicapped Children Act of 1975), policy makers recognized the importance of making adjustments in the workplace and higher educational institutions to provide for the challenges that a disability might create for doing an activity in exactly the same way as all other individuals. Specifically, Section 504 of the 1973 Rehabilitation Act extended civil rights to individuals with disabilities. It required that programs receiving federal funds provide reasonable accommodations to individuals with disabilities so that they can participate in employment, education, and other activities (Cortiella & Kaloi, 2009; T. E. C. Smith & Patton, 1998).

Although debate continues about what *reasonable accommodations* means in various settings, the Individuals with Disabilities Education Act (IDEA; 1990) used the terms *accommodations* and *modifications* to refer to changes made to instructional materials and procedures in schools. It was not until the 1997 reauthorization of IDEA that state and district assessments were referenced in the law. Requirements for the participation of students with disabilities in state- and district-wide assessments included a short statement that students must be provided accommodations as appropriate, if necessary. And, in the section addressing individualized education programs (IEPs), additional statements were provided to indicate that modifications to be used in state and district assessments must be identified in the IEP. The use of the term *modifications* in the 1997 reauthorization of IDEA was inconsistent with the use of this term by most states and districts, and in fact, was changed in the 2004 reauthorization of IDEA to refer simply to *accommodations.*

In 2001, the Elementary and Secondary Act (ESEA) was reauthorized as the No Child Left Behind Act (NCLB). This reauthorization raised the importance of attending to the participation and performance of students with disabilities on state assessments. Although the previous reauthorization of ESEA in 1994 (the Improving America's Schools Act) required that students with disabilities must participate in state assessments and their results must be reported and disaggregated from those of other students, it took the accountability provisions of NCLB for districts and schools to attend to these requirements. NCLB reflected the requirements of IDEA, although it never used the term *modifications,* instead referring generally to accommodations that produced valid results and accommodations that produced invalid results. Subsequent guidance and regulations indicated that students who participated in assessments using accommodations that produced invalid results would no longer be counted as participants in the assessment. Counting assessment participants was an important piece of NCLB accountability, because any school, district, or state that had fewer than 95% participation of students with disabilities (as well as other groups) would automatically be designated as not meeting the adequate yearly progress (AYP) accountability measure.

As the NCLB requirements for accommodations were emerging, states were carefully setting policies to distinguish between changes in materials or procedures that would produce valid results (accommodations) and those that would produce invalid results (modifications). Nearly all states used this terminology (or the somewhat parallel terms, *standard accommodation* versus *nonstandard accommodation*) to clarify the distinction between accommodations and modifications. This distinction in the area of assessment created considerable angst among many educators, who believed that whatever students received during instruction (whether an accommodation or a modification) should be allowed during assessment. This misperception arose, in part, from best practices recommendations that an accommodation should not be used for the first time during an assessment, but rather should be part of typical classroom practice (J. L. Elliott & Thurlow, 2006; Thurlow, Elliott, & Ysseldyke, 2003).

Theoretical Context

The provision of "reasonable" accommodations has been a topic of civil rights advocates for years. Attention to accommodations in testing has raised questions about the function of accommodations and the procedures needed to determine whether a change in materials or procedures actually results in a test that produces valid or invalid results. Linn suggested that the purpose of accommodations for students with disabilities on assessments is to remove "disadvantages due to disabilities that are irrelevant to the construct the test is intended to measure without giving unfair advantage to those being accommodated" (2002, p. 36). Defining and identifying what constitutes an "unfair advantage" has led to considerable debate about the best way to determine whether test results are more accurate (valid) when accommodations are used than when not used. It is generally easy to understand how eyeglasses (which could be considered an accommodation) result in more accurate test results than would requiring a student to take an assessment without them—as long as the test is not measuring how well the student sees, and as long as the student has a vision problem that is addressed by glasses. Although this example seems simple, decisions about whether other accommodations produce valid assessment results have not been so simple to understand. Policy makers have looked to research to determine whether an assessment accommodation produces valid results.

The theoretical basis for research designed to determine whether an accommodation alters the content measured by the test (and thus produces invalid results) has changed over time. S. E. Phillips (1994) was the first to argue that to be considered an accommodation, a change in testing procedures or materials would have to increase the performance of students with disabilities and not change the performance of students without disabilities. Often, this is referred to as the *interaction hypothesis.* Since then, other researchers have suggested the need to identify a differential boost—in other words, the performance of students without disabilities increases some as the result of an accommodation, but the performance of students with disabilities increases more, indicating that students with disabilities gain a larger increase in their scores than do students without disabilities (L. S. Fuchs & Fuchs, 1999; Sireci, Scarpati, & Li, 2005). According to Laitusis (2007), the differential boost approach to research is the best for determining whether an accommodation produces valid results and whether it removes variance irrelevant to the construct being assessed.

Access to instruction and to assessments is critical for students with disabilities. Making decisions about accommodations for these students is the responsibility of the IEP team, but IEP teams often are challenged by the need to differentiate between instructional accommodations that provide access and assessment accommodations that provide both access and valid results (Thurlow, Lazarus, & Christensen, 2008). Information from research about the effects of accommodations, along with decision-making training and tools for IEP teams (J. L. Elliott & Thurlow, 2006; Minnesota Department of Education, 2009), all contribute to sound policies and decision making about accommodations.

Legal and Policy Context

Legal concerns about the provision of instructional accommodations arise most often in relation to Section 504 of the 1973 Rehabilitation Act and the Americans with Disabilities Act. Concerns about accommodations for state and district assessment generally arise in relation to those assessments that are considered high stakes for students (Heubert & Hauser, 1999). Cases on testing

accommodations within the K–12 education system in Oregon (Disability Rights Advocates, 2001) and Alaska (*Noon v. Alaska State Board of Education & Early Development*, 2004; Volz, 2004) were settled out of court by the states addressing (usually expanding) the accommodations allowed during testing, as well as providing alternative routes for students to show their knowledge and skills. In California, the ruling in *Juleus Chapman et al. v. California Department of Education,* 2001 (Disability Rights Advocates, 2008) indicated that accommodations were not being allowed for use on the California High School Exit Exam even though students had used them during instruction. In resolving the issues related to accommodations, the court decided that students with disabilities could use accommodations that state policy did not allow for other students. If the student passed the test using these accommodations, however, the student would need to go through a waiver process to earn a regular diploma.

Accommodations allowed by states for use during state assessments are described in state policies and guidelines. Policies and guidelines have changed considerably over time, reflecting changes in the policy framework that surrounds accommodations (Lazarus et al., 2009). The National Center on Educational Outcomes (NCEO) has studied state assessment policies on accommodations since the early 1990s (see Thurlow, Ysseldyke, & Silverstein, 1993, 1995). Since 1999, NCEO has examined accommodations policies every 2 years. In 1992, 21 states had written policies. Since 2001, all states have written accommodations policies that summarize the various accommodations that are allowed or not allowed, or have specified other restrictions that may apply to assessment situations.

Table 24.1 shows some of the most frequently mentioned accommodations and modifications in state assessment policies. Even though the accommodations and modifications listed are the most frequently mentioned within each category, they reflect different numbers of states mentioning them. For example, large print and braille are mentioned in the policies of 49 states.

Table 24.1   Frequently Mentioned Accommodations in State Assessment Policies for 2006 to 2007

Presentation	Response	Timing/Scheduling	Setting
Braille edition	Proctor/scribe	With breaks	Individual
Large print	Computer/machine	Extended time	Small group
Read-aloud questions	Write in booklet	Beneficial time	Carrel
Sign interpret directions	Communication device	Multiple sessions	Separate room
Sign interpret questions	Brailler	Multiple days	Seat location

Source: Information from Christensen, L. L., Lazarus, S. S., Crone, M., & Thurlow, M. L. (2008). *2007 state policies on assessment participation and accommodations for students with disabilities* (Synthesis Report 69). Minneapolis, MN: University of Minnesota, National Center on Educational Outcomes.

In contrast, "with breaks" is mentioned by 45 states and extended time is mentioned by 40 states.

In addition to states' accommodations policies for state tests, testing companies write policies for local and district assessments. For example in 2009, Northwest Educational Assessments' (NWEA) Measures of Academic Progress (MAP) allowed the extended-time accommodation (Northwest Evaluation Association, 2009), while the Metropolitan 8 (MAT-8) allowed an accommodation of up to twice the usual time (B. J. Case, 2003) when assessing students with disabilities. In contrast, the Dynamic Indicators of Basic Early Literacy Skills (DIBELS) measures instructed schools not to enter assessments conducted under untimed or with extended time into the DIBELS data system—and further instructed that any scores obtained under extended or untimed situations should be used with caution (Good & Kaminski, 2002/2003).

A frequently mentioned accommodation is not necessarily an accommodation that is frequently used (Bolt & Thurlow, 2004; Thurlow, 2007). Accommodations designed for sensory disabilities (e.g., braille, large print, sign language interpretation) are nearly always mentioned and allowed for use during state assessments but are among the most infrequently used—presumably because of the low incidence of sensory disabilities (see Albus, Thurlow, & Bremer, 2009, for state data on accommodations used in states).

Research Base for Assessment Accommodations

The research base for accommodation policies has changed over time and continues to change. It relies on various kinds of evidence, including surveys, extant data analyses, quasi-experimental studies, and experimental studies. Studies that examined early data (e.g., 2001) found a positive relationship between the number of accommodations allowed in state policies and the participation rates for students with disabilities (Cox, Herner, Demczyk, & Nieberding, 2006) and found that differences in National Assessment of Educational Progress (NEAP) participation rates could be tied to differences in state accommodations policies (N. E. Anderson, Jenkins, & Miller, 1996). These studies found general effects but did not necessarily show effects of specific accommodations.

Although attention to the effects of accommodations has increased since 2000, literally hundreds of accommodations still could be studied. Researchers have focused on relatively few accommodations—sometimes because they are frequently allowed, sometimes because they are frequently used, sometimes because they are easy to apply and study, and sometimes because they are controversial and need evidence to support or refute their use. Further complicating the study of accommodations, students who use accommodations rarely use just one accommodation, but instead frequently use a combination of accommodations. This reflects the fact that the disability characteristics of students almost always require more than one accommodation. In fact, some accommodations in themselves create a need for a second accommodation (e.g., receiving a read aloud from a human reader precludes the student from being in the traditional testing setting and instead requires an individualized or perhaps small-group administration). All of these factors, as well as others (e.g., grade level, disability category), make it difficult to identify specific accommodations with strong overall evidence to support their use. Nevertheless, evidence does exist when research findings are considered in detail.

We have selected three accommodations to highlight in this chapter. They reflect a frequently used accommodation (extended time), a controversial accommodation (read aloud/oral presentation), and a new approach to accommodations (computer-based testing). Each of these accommodations is explored in the next section, with clarification of exactly what the accommodation entails and the ways in which it is treated in state policies, as well as the nature of the research base for each accommodation. In recent years, researchers have increasingly focused on validating accommodations; however, research seldom provides conclusive evidence about the effects of accommodations on validity. In fact, comprehensive reviews of the literature have concluded that, of all the assessment accommodations that have been studied, only extended time has convincing evidence of a differential boost for students with disabilities (Sireci et al., 2005). As noted earlier, these research results may be attributable to many factors, including differences in the students who were included in studies, differences in the need for the accommodation among the tested students, and differences in the assessment tasks that students completed (Thurlow, 2007).

To summarize the literature for the three accommodations included in this chapter, we initially used the following criteria to select studies:

1. The study was conducted or published during or after 2000.

2. The study reported the results of empirical research.

3. The study was published in a peer-reviewed journal that could be obtained through a secure university library system.

4. The study focused on the effects of accommodations for students with disabilities in kindergarten through 12th grade.

5. The study examined the effects of accommodations on achievement tests or college entrance exams.

We used the NCEO online Accommodations Bibliography (http://apps.cehd.umn.edu/nceo/accommodations/) to identify empirical research studies, and we included those involving extant data only if the number of studies for an accommodation was limited without them (this occurred only for the extended-time accommodation). We also searched the ERIC online catalog to look for any studies that may have been missed in the Accommodations Bibliography. We coded each study by type of methodology used (i.e., randomized experimental, quasi-experimental, or correlational). We also compiled data on the grade levels of the study participants, the particular disability categories (e.g., learning disabilities [LD]) represented, the content area studied, and the study's reported results.

Extended Time

Extended time as an accommodation allows a student to take longer than the time typically allowed to complete an assessment. As indicated in Figure 24.1, in 2007 the policies of 34 states allowed the use of the extended-time accommodation with no restrictions, and 4 additional states allowed its use in certain circumstances (Christensen, Lazarus, Crone, & Thurlow, 2008). Similar to many other accommodations, states have frequently changed how extended time was included in policy over the years: 26 states allowed the use of extended time with no restrictions in 2001; the number gradually increased to 39 states in 2005, and then dropped to 34 states in 2007. In more recent years, some states probably dropped mention of extended time as they moved toward untimed tests (Lazarus et al., 2009).

Appendix 24.1 (appears at the end of this chapter) shows the eight extended-time studies we identified that included K–12 students with disabilities that were published in 2000 or later. The reported studies

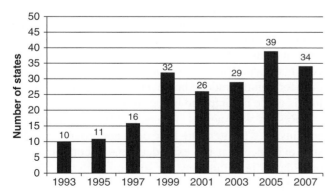

Figure 24.1 States that allow the use of extended time with no restrictions.

Source: Data from Christensen et al., 2008; Lazarus et al., 2009.

do not include studies of accommodations packages (i.e., extended time provided with other accommodations). The eight studies (A. S. Cohen, Gregg, & Deng, 2005; Crawford, Helwig, & Tindal, 2004; S. N. Elliott & Marquart, 2004; L. S. Fuchs, Fuchs, Eaton, Hamlett, Binkley, & Crouch, 2000; L. S. Fuchs, Fuchs, Eaton, Hamlett, & Karns, 2000; Lewandowski, Lovett, Parolin, Gordon, & Codding, 2007; Lewandowski, Lovett, & Rogers, 2008; Lindstrom & Gregg, 2007) all examined whether students with disabilities received a differential boost in scores (when compared to students without disabilities) when provided with the extended-time accommodation. The studies also examined whether both groups of students received a boost.

None of the studies conclusively found a differential boost for students with disabilities; though L. S. Fuchs, Fuchs, Eaton, Hamlett, and Karns (2000) found a differential boost on problem-solving classroom-based measures (CBMs) but not on the conventional test. Four of the eight studies (S. N. Elliott & Marquart, 2004; L. S. Fuchs, Fuchs, Eaton, Hamlett, Binkley, & Crouch, 2000; Lewandowski et al., 2007, 2008) concluded that a general (rather than differential) increase in the scores of both students with disabilities and students without disabilities occurred when extended time was used.

As shown in Appendix 24.1 (at the end of this chapter), the studies examined the effect of extended time on different content areas. Five studies examined the effect on math assessments (A. S. Cohen et al., 2005; S. N. Elliott & Marquart, 2004; L. S. Fuchs, Fuchs, Eaton, Hamlett, & Karns, 2000; Lewandowski et al., 2007; Lindstrom & Gregg, 2007); three studies examined the effect on a reading assessment (L. S. Fuchs, Fuchs, Eaton, Hamlett, Binkley, & Crouch, 2000; Lewandowski et al., 2008; Lindstrom & Gregg, 2007), and two studies examined the effect on a writing assessment (Crawford et al., 2004; Lindstrom & Gregg, 2007). The Lindstrom and Gregg study examined all three of these content areas.

Six of the studies included students with LD (A. S. Cohen et al., 2005; Crawford et al., 2004; L. S. Fuchs, Fuchs, Eaton, Hamlett, Binkley, & Crouch, 2000; L. S. Fuchs, Fuchs, Eaton, Hamlett & Karns, 2000; Lewandowski et al., 2008; Lindstrom & Gregg, 2007). Lindstrom and Gregg and Lewandowski et al. also included students with attention deficit hyperactivity disorder (ADHD). The S. N. Elliott and Marquart (2004) study included students with mild LD, emotional disabilities, behavior disabilities, mild physical disabilities, speech and language disabilities, and mild cognitive disabilities.

Two studies (A. S. Cohen et al., 2005; Lindstrom & Gregg, 2007) were correlational studies that used large extant data sets to compare the scores of accommodated students with the scores of nonaccommodated students. To explore whether students with extended time performed differently from other students, A. S. Cohen et al. analyzed data for ninth-grade students from the 2003 administration of the mathematics Florida Comprehensive Assessment Test (FCAT). Half were randomly selected from the group of students identified as having LD who used extended time (and no additional accommodations); the other half were randomly selected from the group of students without LD who used no accommodations. A. S. Cohen et al. found that "the results suggest that students' accommodation status is not a sufficiently useful explanatory variable for determining the cause of differential item functioning" (p. 231). Lindstrom and Gregg (2007) analyzed scores from the Scholastic Aptitude Reasoning Test for students with LD and/or ADHD who used extended time and for students without disabilities who did not use extended time. The analysis was conducted for the Critical Reading, Math, and Writing sections of the test. Although differences in mean scores were found across groups and there was greater variability in scores for students with disabilities, results of invariance analyses indicated that "the items measuring the constructs of critical thinking, reasoning, and writing appear to function in the same way for the two groups" (p. 92). Therefore, the authors suggested that extended time did not alter the constructs being assessed for students with LD and ADHD.

As is evident in Appendix 24.1 (at the end of this chapter), six studies had quasi-experimental designs (Crawford et al., 2004; S. N. Elliott & Marquart, 2004; L. S. Fuchs, Fuchs, Eaton, Hamlett, Binkley, & Crouch, 2000; L. S. Fuchs, Fuchs, Eaton, Hamlett, & Karns, 2000; Lewandowski et al., 2007, 2008). Lewandowski et al. (2007) compared how scores were affected for fifth- and seventh-grade students with ADHD and students without disabilities on a mathematics assessment when they had the extended-time accommodation. The extended-time accommodation was one and one half times the normal length of the test. The students with disabilities did not receive a differential boost, and the authors concluded that "although students with ADHD tended to work with less overall efficiency in terms of processing speed and task fluency, they do not benefit significantly more than nondisabled students when given extended time on a speed-based math task" (p. 17). Lewandowski et al. (2008) examined whether extended time affected the performance of high school students on a reading comprehension test. Half of the students had LD; half did not have an identified disability. Lewandowski et al. found that the scores of both groups of students were boosted, though the scores of students without disabilities were boosted more than the scores of the students with LD. The students with LD attempted the same number of questions as the other students when provided with the extended-time accommodation.

Two of the earliest studies examined the effect of extended time on fourth- and fifth-grade students' performance on CBMs. L. S. Fuchs, Fuchs, Eaton, Hamlett, Binkley, and Crouch (2000) analyzed how students with and without LD did on a reading assessment under standard and extended-time conditions. Both groups of students received a boost from the accommodation. L. S. Fuchs, Fuchs, Eaton, Hamlett, and Karns (2000) administered a short mathematics CBM to a group of fourth- and fifth-grade students, half without disabilities and half with LD. The measures covered three domains: computations, concepts and applications, and problem solving. The analysis found that students with LD tended to have a differential boost from extended time on problem-solving CBMs but not on the other CBMs.

S. N. Elliott and Marquart (2004) compared performance with and without extended time for three groups of eighth-grade students (students with disabilities, students without identified disabilities who were educationally at risk on the math test, and students without disabilities). The researchers found that the scores of all students were boosted when the extended-time accommodation was provided, though the scores were boosted the most for the struggling students who did not have identified disabilities. They also surveyed the participating students and found that most students preferred the extended-time administration; in general, however, students with disabilities less strongly supported the extended-time accommodation than the other two groups of students.

Crawford et al. (2004) was the only extended-time study of the eight that examined how a multiple-day administration affected performance. Crawford et al. compared how two groups of fifth- and eighth-grade students (students with LD, students without disabilities) performed on a 30-minute writing assessment with how they performed on an assessment completed over 3 days. The study included 213 fifth graders (including 42 students with LD) and 140 eighth graders (including 6 with LD). The findings were mixed. Crawford et al. reported a significant time by disability status interaction for fifth-grade participants, indicating that both groups of students performed better with extended time, but that students with LD received a greater benefit from the accommodation. The authors found no effect of extended time for eighth graders; however, few students with LD in this grade participated in the study.

Results vary across studies, and the results are inconclusive. The literature base does not provide conclusive evidence that the extended-time accommodation provides differential boost for students with disabilities. In fact, some evidence shows that extended time may often boost the scores of both students with and without disabilities. This suggests that it may be appropriate to allow extended time for all students.

Read-Aloud/Oral Presentation

Reading a test, or portion of a test, aloud to a student may occur in a variety of ways. One consideration is the portion of the test being read. It is often a good testing practice to read the directions aloud; still, in some states reading directions aloud is considered an accommodation. More controversial is the reading aloud of test questions and test passages. When these are read aloud, they may be read by a human reader, or they may be read by a computer. In some situations, these items may be provided orally via audio or video. In some cases, the read-aloud accommodation may be bundled with another accommodation, like extended time, small-group setting, or individual administration. Tindal and Fuchs (2000) also reported that having the test read aloud may be accompanied by cueing, rephrasing, and dictation (p. 55).

In their analysis of state accommodations policies, Christensen et al. (2008) noted that a majority of states ($n = 31$) allowed directions to be read aloud as an accommodation without any restrictions; of course, in some states reading the directions aloud is not considered an accommodation but rather is standard testing practice available for all students. Reading the questions aloud is allowed in nearly all states ($n = 49$); however, most states put some restriction on its use. For example, in 24 states, the accommodation is allowed only in certain circumstances, such as only in certain grades (e.g., high school) or in certain subject areas (e.g., science or mathematics). In 20 states, reading the questions aloud is allowed in limited circumstances; however, when students have questions read to them, their scores may be thrown out, or the students may be counted as nonparticipants. Only in three states is this accommodation allowed without any restrictions. Subtle changes have occurred over time in the number of states allowing the read-aloud accommodation without restrictions (see Figure 24.2).

The controversial nature of the read-aloud accommodation makes it an interesting subject of research.

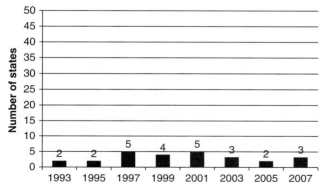

Figure 24.2 States that allow read-aloud/oral presentation with no restrictions.

Appendix 24.2 (at the end of this chapter) shows the eight studies of the read-aloud accommodation selected for review here. Studies that used a speech-to-text computer-based approach were excluded because they were confounded with the computer-based approach. In the studies reviewed here, the nature of the read-aloud accommodation itself varied. Two studies (Ketterlin-Geller, Yovanoff, & Tindal, 2007; McKevitt & Elliott, 2003) presented the read-aloud accommodation via audiotape. One study, conducted by Helwig, Rozek-Tedesco, and Tindal (2002), used a videotape to present the accommodation to students. Four studies (Elbaum, 2007; L. S. Fuchs, Fuchs, Eaton, Hamlett, & Karns, 2000; E. Johnson, 2000; Meloy, Deville, & Frisbie, 2002) described giving the accommodation to students by having someone read the questions aloud directly to the students. Of these four, only the Johnson and Meloy et al. studies mentioned using a process to train the readers to read a script verbatim. One additional study (Schulte, Elliott, & Kratochwill, 2001) did not describe the means by which the students received the read-aloud accommodation.

The study designs used to research the read-aloud accommodation were primarily experimental and quasi-experimental. Although the participants themselves were not chosen through a randomized control process, the determination of who received the accommodation was often made randomly. For example, Ketterlin-Geller, Yovanoff, et al. (2007) investigated two accommodations, the read-aloud questions accommodation and the simplified-language accommodation. The students in their study were assigned to one of the two accommodations randomly. Then, students took the assessment both with and without the accommodation. Ketterlin-Geller, Yovanoff, et al. found that students benefited from the read-aloud accommodation only when the level of language in the questions was challenging enough to interfere with the student's understanding of the content.

All eight studies considered here examined differential boost. Of these, five studies (L. S. Fuchs, Fuchs, Eaton, Hamlett, & Karns, 2000; Helwig et al., 2002; E. Johnson, 2000; Ketterlin-Geller, Yovanoff, et al., 2007; Schulte et al., 2001) found some support for using the accommodation in elementary school. For example, Schulte et al. (2001) found that elementary students with disabilities benefited more than their peers without disabilities when the math test was read aloud to them. In her meta-analysis of eight studies examining read-aloud accommodations for students with disabilities on math tests, Elbaum (2007) found that elementary students with LD received a differential boost from the read-aloud accommodation.

Studies examining the effect of the accommodation for middle school or high school (Elbaum, 2007;

Helwig et al., 2002; McKevitt & Elliott, 2003; Meloy et al., 2002) yielded more divided findings. Meloy et al. found that the read-aloud accommodation did provide a differential boost for students with LD in middle school. The other studies concluded that middle school students with disabilities received no differential boost with the use of this accommodation. For example, McKevitt and Elliott (2003) found no significant differential boost for students with disabilities who used the read-aloud accommodation, although all of the students (both those with and without disabilities) who used the accommodation did somewhat better than the students who used other teacher-recommended accommodations.

The content areas included in the read-aloud studies varied. Seven of the studies (Elbaum, 2007; L. S. Fuchs, Fuchs, Eaton, Hamlett, & Karns, 2000; Helwig et al., 2002; E. Johnson, 2000; Ketterlin-Geller, Yovanoff, et al., 2007; Meloy et al., 2002; Schulte et al., 2001) looked at the effect of the read-aloud accommodation for math. All of the studies found some benefit for students with disabilities when used in math, although the effects varied somewhat by grade, as noted earlier. Two of the studies also looked at effects for reading (McKevitt & Elliott, 2003; Meloy et al., 2002). Both of these studies found no differential boost for students with disabilities. Thus, the research suggests some benefit occurs for elementary students using the accommodation in math but not in reading.

Five of the studies included here (Elbaum, 2007; L. S. Fuchs, Fuchs, Eaton, Hamlett, & Karns, 2000; Helwig et al., 2002; Ketterlin-Geller, Yovanoff, et al., 2007; Meloy et al., 2002) identified students with LD as the target population. Helwig et al. found that elementary students with LD benefited from the accommodation. L. S. Fuchs et al. found that students with LD benefited on CBM when the CBM involved problem solving. Ketterlin-Geller, Yovanoff, et al., Meloy et al., and Elbaum found less conclusive results. Meloy et al. reported that both students with and without LD benefited from the accommodation. In the Ketterlin-Geller, Yovanoff, et al. study, students benefited from the accommodation only when the language level limited their interaction with the more challenging content. At the secondary level, Elbaum reported that students without disabilities benefited more from read-aloud accommodations than did students with LD. In conclusion, these five studies suggest that some benefit may exist in using the read-aloud accommodation with students who have LD. Still, many considerations, such as the conditions under which students will benefit, need further exploration before strong conclusions are drawn.

In both research and practice, the read-aloud accommodation has been, and remains, controversial. Since the beginning of the standards-based reform movement, states have frequently refined their policies on reading the test or parts of it to the student (see Lazarus et al., 2009). States look to research to show conclusive evidence that an accommodation is appropriate. Conclusive evidence has not yet emerged from research on read-aloud accommodations. Of those studies that have been conducted, a variety of approaches to implementing the accommodation have been used. Furthermore, most of the studies focused on mathematics as the content area, even though reading is the area of most interest to states setting policies. Just two of the studies reviewed here, McKevitt and Elliott (2003) and Meloy et al. (2002), looked at the read-aloud accommodation for reading.

Computer-Based Testing

Computer-based testing as an accommodation involves the provision of the assessment on a computer and may or may not include allowing the use of other accommodations (e.g., screen reader, highlighting key terms, spell-checker) via the computer. In an early summary of the empirical basis for defining accommodations, Tindal and Fuchs (2000) indicated that some of the changes that may be incorporated into computer-based testing might not typically be considered as accommodations but can nevertheless be "used to enhance access to tests for students with disabilities because changes are made in the manner in which items are displayed, sequenced, or presented (sequenced or paced)" (p. 30).

Figure 24.3 shows the number of states that allowed computer-based testing as an accommodation with no restrictions from 1993 to 2007. Figure 24.3 shows that the number of states that permitted this accommodation fluctuated. Just 11 states mentioned this accommodation in 1993, but by 1999, 28 states allowed the use of computer-based testing without restrictions. By 2003 the number was 37; after that the number dropped to 25 in 2005 and then increased again to 31 in 2007. These

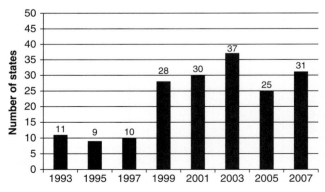

Figure 24.3   States that allow computer-based testing with no restrictions.

fluctuations are consistent with those observed for the extended-time and read-aloud accommodations.

Christensen et al. (2008) found that computer-based testing was identified as a response accommodation (i.e., used by students in documenting their response to test questions) for state-wide assessments by 43 states. Most states ($n = 31$) allowed this accommodation without restriction; the remaining states ($n = 12$) imposed some type of limitation on the accommodation (e.g., spell-checker must be disabled, cannot be used for writing assessment). States' accommodations policies generally did not identify computerized testing as a presentation accommodation but instead referred specifically to the use of screen readers or other approaches to reading the assessment to the student via computer.

Appendix 24.3 (at the end of this chapter) shows the computer-based accommodations studies that included students with disabilities of school age. The eight studies included in our analysis (M. B. Calhoon, Fuchs, & Hamlett, 2000; Dolan, Hall, Bannerjee, Chun, & Strangman, 2005; Hasselbring & Crossland, 1982; Hollenbeck, Rozek-Tedesco, Tindal, & Glasgow, 2000; Horton & Lovitt, 1994; Keen & Davey, 1987; Poggio, Glasnapp, Yang, & Poggio, 2005; Varnhagen & Gerber, 1984) examined whether a differential boost occurred for students with disabilities or a general increase in performance occurred for all students; the studies also examined the perceptions of the accommodation by students. All of these studies appeared in published journals, but at least half were published before 2000. We extended the dates we reviewed for this accommodation so that we could obtain a reasonable number of studies to examine. The limitation of including only those studies that were in journals available through the secure University of Minnesota library system eliminated several older studies that had been cited in summaries of accommodations research by Tindal and Fuchs (2000) and S. Thompson, Blount, and Thurlow (2002), including studies that specifically examined the effects of computer-based testing for students with disabilities (e.g., Barton & Sheinker, 2003; Burk, 1999).

Of the eight studies we examined, only four were designed in a way that allowed the researchers to determine whether a differential boost in performance existed for students with disabilities. Just one of these studies (Hollenbeck et al., 2000) found evidence of a differential boost in performance for students with disabilities. Hollenbeck et al. specifically looked at the performance of students who had diagnosed reading disabilities on a test of mathematics. These students were all in grade 7. Computer-based testing in which students determined their own pace in working through problems produced a differential boost

over a paper-and-pencil test for which a videotaped teacher presented information and paced test completion. Hollenbeck et al. actually found that not only was there a differential boost for students with reading disabilities, but that for those students without disabilities, there was a slight but nonsignificant negative effect on performance for the computer-based self-paced testing.

Five of the studies we examined (M. B. Calhoon et al., 2000; Dolan et al., 2005; Hasselbring & Crossland, 1982; Horton & Lovitt, 1994; Varnhagen & Gerber, 1984) showed a general (rather than differential) increase in performance. Three studies (Horton & Lovitt, 1994; Poggio et al., 2005; Varnhagen & Gerber, 1984) that could have detected a differential boost did not. Two studies (Dolan et al., 2005; Hasselbring & Crossland, 1982) included only students with disabilities.

As is evident in Appendix 24.3 (at the end of this chapter), the five studies that showed a general increase in performance varied widely in terms of content area (mathematics, one study; social studies, two studies, with one also looking at science; spelling, two studies), and student grade level (study grades: 9–12, 11 and 12, 3–8, 6–12, and 3). All students with disabilities in these studies had either LD or learning "handicaps." Two of the five studies provided additional information about the nature of the general increase in performance that they found. For example, Dolan et al. (2005) found that the difference between computer-based and paper-and-pencil tests emerged only when the item passages (in a social studies test) were "long" (meaning greater than 100 words in this study). In their study, students with LD were administered equivalent forms of the test in counterbalanced order for paper-and-pencil and computer-based tests. Students without disabilities were not included in this study. Also, the computer-based form had optional text-to-speech capability, meaning that students could use that feature or not, depending on their preferences. Students in this study reported that they would recommend the use of computer-based testing (with text to speech) for other students, and that they thought they performed better on the computer-based test.

Horton and Lovitt (1994) also found an increase in performance with computer-based testing, but results were mixed in their examination of social studies and science tests. Horton and Lovitt studied three groups of middle and high school students (students with LD, students in remedial programs, and normally achieving students). All students participated in each condition through an equivalent time-samples design in which students were "randomly assigned four times each to all experimental and control groups" (paragraph 30). The researchers found no differences between computer-based and paper-and-pencil tests when the items were interpretive questions; when the items were factual questions, computer-based testing produced increased performance over the paper-and-pencil format.

The finding of a general boost in performance for computer-based testing—higher performance for test takers regardless of whether they had a disability—is consistent with the concept of universally designed assessments (see S. J. Thompson, Thurlow, & Malouf, 2004). Universally designed assessments are designed to be accessible to the widest range of students, including those with and without disabilities, as long as what the test is intended to measure does not change.

Only two of the eight studies we examined (Keen & Davey, 1987; Poggio et al., 2005) indicated no statistical difference between computer-based and paper-and-pencil tests. The Keen and Davey study was published in the late 1980s, and the computer-based system may have not been as easy to use as more recent computer-based tests. Yet the study by Hasselbring and Crossland (1982) also was published in the 1980s and found an increase in performance with the computer-based test. Another unique aspect of the Keen and Davey study was that it focused on a test of reading—the only one of the eight studies that addressed this content area. It may be that something about a test of reading precludes a boost in performance from the computer-based platform.

The Poggio et al. (2005) study is a relatively recent study that was clearly designed to detect a differential boost if one existed. The researchers found, however, no statistical difference between the computer-based and the paper-and-pencil version on a math test. This study involved students taking equivalent forms of the test, with each student taking both the computer-based and the paper-and-pencil, with order counterbalanced across students. Poggio et al. also examined possible effects by type of question (i.e., knowledge, application) and found that performance was virtually identical for the two question types.

The variability in studies is typical of accommodations research; this variability was evident not only in the computer-based testing studies, but also in those focused on extended time and read aloud. In fact, similar variability exists in the research on many other accommodations that have been studied (see Johnstone, Altman, Thurlow, & Thompson, 2006; S. Thompson et al., 2002; Tindal & Fuchs, 2000; Zenisky & Sireci, 2007). Nevertheless, one can take away from this research that computer-based testing is a viable accommodation for students with disabilities. Beyond that, research suggests that computer-based testing may be an approach that provides greater accessibility for all students and something that should be pursued in the name of universally designed assessments.

This conclusion does not, on the other hand, detract from the suggestion that caution must be observed in implementing a computer-based test. Many accommodations and design features must first be explored (Dolan et al., 2009; S. J. Thompson, Quenemoen, & Thurlow, 2006).

Conclusion

Accommodations are an essential part of the instruction and assessment of students with disabilities. Yet, they are surrounded by controversy and confusion, especially when applied to assessments. Historically, assessment accommodations have taken a wandering pathway. First they were considered necessary just to provide access to assessments for students whose disabilities interfered with their ability to take the test (regardless of what happened to the construct being measured). They now are considered to be an essential part of the validity argument for assessments; to obtain valid results for students with disabilities, it is necessary to provide accommodations that help them show what they know and can do without interference from the barriers that their disabilities pose, as long as the accommodations do not change what the assessment is intended to measure.

The crux of the challenge for policy makers and educators is to determine which changes in testing materials or procedures actually alter what the test is intended to measure. The theory behind how this is shown has changed over time, from an interaction hypothesis to a differential-boost hypothesis. Nevertheless, research-based evidence has not produced clear results. In part, the lack of clarity about accommodations and their effects is due to all the confounding factors that surround the identification of students as having disabilities, the nature of specific disability categories, and the challenges of determining whether an individual student needs an accommodation. The research evidence presented in this chapter for three accommodations—extended time (which is frequently used), read aloud (which is controversial), and computer-based testing (which is relatively new)—dramatically reflects the variability in research findings. The variability spans not only the number and types of students included (although most participants with disabilities have LD), the content of the assessment, and the grade levels in which the studies were conducted, but also the nature of the research itself and whether packages of accommodations were included or just a single accommodation. All of these factors, and others, have an impact on the results obtained.

The accommodations research literature has shown many strengths in recent years. For example, there has been a general progression in methods toward more refined randomized experimental and quasi-experimental designs. Increasingly, studies include greater numbers of students and often attempt to reflect actual testing situations.

The weaknesses in the literature on the effects of accommodations are related in many ways to the challenges of conducting this research. For example, researchers study accommodations in numerous content areas, resulting in studies of an accommodation being conducted in content other than where the greatest practical questions actually exist (e.g., the read aloud, where many studies are in content areas other than reading). An additional weakness is that many studies involve relatively small numbers of students. This limitation reflects the difficulty of identifying students who may need an accommodation, and then securing their participation in a study.

Implications for Practice

Practitioners can take away from this review of accommodations both the conclusion that accommodations are important research-based practices for supporting the participation and performance of students with disabilities (Crawford, 2007) and the conclusion that the three accommodations that we included in this chapter are supported by some of the research. This is true despite the fact that research on most accommodations is still relatively limited, though the number of studies has increased over time, and that the research varies in terms of the students who are included, the nature of the test, and the methodology used to study the accommodation. It is the conditions of the research to which practitioners must attend as they consider how to use specific accommodations in their own environments. These conditions also suggest the importance of practitioners engaging in a process

of checking the effects of specific accommodations for individual students during classroom instruction and assessments (see J. L. Elliott & Thurlow, 2006; Thurlow et al., 2003).

It is important for practitioners also to realize that additional research, not reviewed here, suggests educators have difficulties making decisions about accommodations and implementing accommodations during instruction and assessment (Shriner & DeStefano, 2003). This research indicates that even with the improvements that have occurred in accommodations research, many contextual issues remain that contribute to the challenge of conducting research, as well as to the challenge of actually implementing accommodations effectively. Implementation research suggests a need for greater emphasis on training on appropriate accommodations and decision making about accommodations for instruction and assessment. Further, some research suggests the need for monitoring of the provision and effects of accommodations in actual testing situations (Christensen, Thurlow, & Wang, 2009; Thurlow et al., 2008).

Across the time that research on accommodations has been conducted, dating back to some of the early work at Educational Testing Services (Willingham et al., 1988), policy increasingly has pushed accommodation practices for testing. Some accommodations (e.g., extended time) have over time become considered good testing practice rather than accommodations (e.g., providing untimed tests). As good testing practices, they are available to all students. This trend supports the emphasis now being placed on universally designed assessments (S. J. Thompson et al., 2004), in which all students are considered from the beginning of test development, and tests are designed to meet the needs of the widest range of students, as long as the intent of the assessment is not compromised.

Appendix 24.1

Extended Time: Study Descriptions

Study	Type	Grades	Disabilities	Package	Content	Results
A. S. Cohen, Gregg, & Deng (2005)	C[1]	9	LD (*n* = 2,500; 1,250 per group)	No	M	Accommodated/ nonaccommodated status did little to explain differences in performance between students with LD and students without disabilities.
Crawford, Helwig, & Tindal (2004)	QE[2]	5, 8	LD (Grade 5: *n* = 213; 42 with LD; Grade 8: *n* = 140; 6 with LD)	No	W	Mixed results; grade-5 students (both students with LD and students without disabilities) benefited from extended time (over multiple days) on a writing performance assessment, and students with disabilities benefited the most; at grade 8, there was little effect of extended time.
S. N. Elliott & Marquart (2004)	QE[3]	8	Multiple[4] (*n* = 97; 23 with disabilities, 23 at risk in math, 51 without disabilities)	No	M	Scores of all three groups were boosted when the extended-time accommodation was provided—though the scores were boosted the most for the struggling students who did not have identified disabilities.
L. S. Fuchs, Fuchs, Eaton, Hamlett, Binkley, & Crouch (2000)[5]	QE[3]	4–5	LD (*n* = 365; approximately half with LD; 59 received extended time[5])	No	R	Scores of both groups (both students with LD and students without disabilities) boosted when extended time was provided.
L. S. Fuchs, Fuchs, Eaton, Hamlett, & Karns (2000)	QE[3]	4–5	LD (*n* = 400; approximately 200 per with LD; 145 received extended time[5])	No	M	Mixed results: Students with LD tended to have a differential boost on problem-solving CBMs, but not on conventional CBMs.
Lewandowski, Lovett, Parolin, Gordon, & Codding (2007)	QE[3]	5–7	ADHD (*n* = 65[6]; 27 in each group)	No	M	Scores of both groups (both students with ADHD and students without disabilities) boosted when extended time was provided.

Study	Type	Grades	Disabilities	Package	Content	Results
Lewandowski, Lovett, & Rogers (2008)	QE[3]	10–12	LD ($n = 64$; 32 per group)	No	R	Scores of both groups (both students with LD and students without disabilities) boosted when extended time was provided—but the scores of students without disabilities were boosted more. Students with LD were able to attempt as many items as students without disabilities.
Lindstrom & Gregg (2007)	C	HS[7]	LD, ADHD (1,517 with LD, 588 with ADHD, 371 with both)	No	R, M, W	Invariance analyses indicated that extended time did not alter the constructs of critical thinking, reasoning, and writing for students with LD and ADHD.

Note: Study Type: C = correlational; QE = quasi-experimental.

Grades: HS = high school.

Disabilities: ADHD = attention deficit/hyperactivity disorder; LD = learning disability.

Package: Yes = effect of more than one accommodation; No = effect of a single accommodation.

Content: M = math; R = reading; W = writing.

Results: CBM = curriculum-based measurement.

[1]Used extant data from the mathematics Florida Comprehensive Assessment Test (FCAT). Half of the cases were randomly selected from the group of students identified as having LD who used extended time (and no additional accommodations); the other half were randomly drawn from the group of students without LD who used no accommodations.

[2]All students participated in both conditions. Students completed the Oregon Statewide Assessment Test-Writing (OSAT-W) over a 3-day period; the 30-minute writing task was approximately 2 weeks before or after the OSAT-W.

[3]Study did not use random assignment to conditions, but instead had all students in all conditions, with counterbalancing of order.

[4]Included students with mild learning disabilities; emotional disabilities, behavior disabilities, mild physical disabilities, speech and language disabilities, and mild cognitive disabilities.

[5]Several accommodations were included in the study. Data-based rules and teacher judgment were used to determine which students would receive extended time.

[6]Several students were later excluded from study due to high scores on ADHD rating scales or high processing speed scores.

[7]Used extant data from the SAT Reasoning Test. Half of the cases were the group of students with LD, ADHD, or both who used extended time; the other half were randomly drawn from the group of students who used no accommodations.

Appendix 24.2

Read-Aloud/Oral Administration Study Descriptions

Study	Type	Grades	Disabilities[1]	Package	Content	Results
Elbaum (2007)	QE[2]	6–10	LD (n = 388)	No	M	Test administrator read each item aloud twice. Students without disabilities benefited more from accommodations than did students with LD, which was consistent with results of accompanying meta-analysis. Meta-analysis showed that elementary students with LD made greater gains with the accommodation than peers.
L. S. Fuchs, Fuchs, Eaton, Hamlett, & Karns (2000)[3]	QE	4–5	LD (n = 200)	Extended time, calculators	M	Teacher read the questions aloud. Students with LD benefited from accommodations on problem-solving CBMs but not on conventional CBMs.
Helwig, Rozek-Tedesco, & Tindal (2002)	QE[4]	4–8	LD (n = 200)	No	M	Read aloud was given through a video. Elementary students benefited from the accommodation; middle school students experienced no significant interaction.
E. Johnson (2000)	QE[4]	4	Students with IEPs (n = 38)	No	M	Trained proctors read the items verbatim. Study supports the use of the accommodation for math when students have a reading disability.
Ketterlin-Geller, Yovanoff, & Tindal (2007)	RE[5]	3	EBD (n = 1), CD (n = 10), LD (n = 11), UNS (n = 6)	Extended time	M	Students received the accommodation via audiotape. Students benefited from the accommodation only when the level of language limited interaction with challenging content.
McKevitt & Elliott (2003)	RE[6]	8	Students with IEPs (n = 40)	Small group	R	Students received the accommodation via audiotape. No differential benefit for students with disabilities using the accommodation was observed.

Study	Type	Grades	Disabilities[1]	Package	Content	Results
Meloy, Deville, & Frisbie (2002)	RE[7]	6–8	LD (*n* = 62)	No	R, M, S, U&E	Students were given the read-aloud accommodation as read via a script. Test scores were higher for both the LD group and the non-LD group in this study.
Schulte, Elliott, & Kratochwill (2001)	QE[4]	4	UNS (*n* = 43)	Yes	M	Test was read aloud to student. Students with disabilities benefited more from the accommodations than students without disabilities.

Note: Study Type: QE = quasi-experimental; RE = randomized experimental.
Disabilities: CD = communication disorder; EBD = emotional and behavioral disorder; IEP = individualized education program; LD = learning disability; UNS = unspecified.
Content: M = math; R = reading; S = science; U&E = usage and expression.
Results: CBM = curriculum-based measurement.
[1]Number is the number of students with disabilities; other groups (e.g., general education students, gifted students) are not reflected in this number.
[2]Classrooms were randomly assigned to one of four testing conditions.
[3]This study examined differential boost.
[4]Study did not use random assignment to conditions, but instead had all students in all conditions with counterbalancing of order.
[5]Study used a convenience sample of students, with random assignment to one of two accommodations under investigation. All students in each accommodation group took the assessment with and without accommodations.
[6]Students were selected to receive one of two treatment conditions using random assignment. In addition, two versions of the assessment were used, and selection of the assessment version was determined by a flip of a coin.
[7]Students who were LD and students who were not LD were randomly assigned to one of two treatment groups (with the read-aloud accommodation and without the accommodation).

Appendix 24.3

Computerized Testing Study Descriptions

Study	Type	Grades	Disabilities[1]	Package	Content	Results
M. B. Calhoon, Fuchs, & Hamlett (2000)	QE[2]	9–12	LD (*n* = 81)	Yes	M	Computer-based with computer reading or computer reading with video showed same increases in performance as teacher-read without computer; all produced higher scores than standard administration. No students without disabilities were included.
Dolan, Hall, Bannerjee, Chun, & Strangman (2005)	QE[2]	11, 12	LD (*n* = 10)	Yes	SS	No statistical difference overall for computer based versus paper-and-pencil, but a significant difference favoring the computer-based test when item passages were long (>100 words). No students without disabilities were included.
Hasselbring & Crossland (1982)	RE	3–8[3]	LD (*n* = 28; 14 per group)	No	SP	Computerized test boosted scores more than paper-and-pencil for students with LD. No students without disabilities were included.
Hollenbeck, Rozek-Tedesco, Tindal, & Glasgow (2000)	QE[2]	7	RD (*n* = 25)	No	M	Computer-based test with student pacing produced a differential boost over teacher-paced video presentation for students with disabilities compared to students without disabilities for whom a slight negative effect was found.
Horton & Lovitt (1994)	QE[4]	6–12[5]	LD (*n* = 13)	No	Sc, SS	Mixed results: computer-based favored for factual questions; no difference for interpretive questions for all students overall. No significant effects were observed for students with disabilities versus other groups.
Keen & Davey (1987)	RE	9–12	LD (*n* = 51; 25 computer, 26 paper/pencil)	No	R	No differences in performance between computer-based and paper-and-pencil. No students without disabilities were included.

Study	Type	Grades	Disabilities[1]	Package	Content	Results
Poggio, Glasnapp, Yang, & Poggio (2005)	QE[2]	7	LD (*n* = 31–32)	No	M	No statistical difference for computer-based versus paper-and-pencil for either students with disabilities or students without disabilities.
Varnhagen & Gerber (1984)	QE[1]	3	LH (*n* = 9)	No	SP	Paper-and-pencil boosted scores more than computerized test for both students with learning handicaps and students without disabilities.

Note: Study Type: QE = quasi-experimental; RE = randomized experimental.

Disabilities: LD = learning disability; LH = learning handicap; RD = reading disability.

Content: M = math; R = reading; Sc = science, SP = spelling, SS = social studies.

[1]Number is the number of students with disabilities; other groups (e.g., general education students, gifted students) are not reflected in this number.

[2]Study did not use random assignment to conditions, but instead had all students in all conditions, with counterbalancing of order.

[3]Study included ages 9 yr 9 mo to 14 yr 6 mo. Table shows estimated grades covered by those ages.

[4]Study design was an equivalent time samples design, with the computer-based and paper-and-pencil tests randomly assigned to all experimental and control groups.

[5]Student included middle school and high school students. Table shows estimated grades covered by those school levels.

Research-Based Strategies for Improving Outcomes for Targeted Groups of Learners

CHAPTER 25

Research-Based Practices in Early Childhood Special Education

Mary Jo Noonan and **Patricia Sheehey** | *University of Hawaii at Manoa*

*E*arly childhood special education (ECSE) addresses the needs of young children with disabilities, birth through age 8. The intent of ECSE is to optimize developmental outcomes for children with delays or disabilities by providing individualized, specialized services. ECSE has its roots in compensatory education: In 1972, Head Start began requiring that 10% of their enrollment be children who have disabilities (Economic Opportunity Act Amendments). Although the Education for All Handicapped Children Act (EHA) of 1975 mandated special education for school-age students, it *permitted* but did not *require* states to provide services to infants, toddlers, and preschoolers. Not until the EHA Amendments of 1986 were states mandated to provide preschool special education to 3- to 5-year-olds with disabilities. These amendments also provided grants and incentive monies to states to encourage them to develop early intervention services for infants and toddlers (birth through age 2) with disabilities.

Since the establishment of early intervention and preschool special education programs through the EHA Amendments of 1986, the numbers of infants and young children with disabilities served through EHA—now known as the Individuals with Disabilities Education Improvement Act (IDEA, 2004)—have grown steadily. The 2007 *Annual Report to Congress* (U.S. Department of Education, 2007b) indicated that slightly over

1 million young children, birth through age 5, received early intervention and preschool special education through IDEA (298,150 children received early intervention services, and 704,087 received preschool special education). The most frequently identified disabilities among the preschool children served through IDEA in 2005 were speech or language impairments (46.4%) and developmental delay (27.8%). Given that speech and language impairments and developmental delay are relatively mild disabilities, it is not surprising that approximately one third of these children received all of their special services in typical early childhood environments (U.S. Department of Education, 2007b).

Three major philosophical perspectives have influenced the development of research-based practices in ECSE: inclusion, natural environments, and developmentally appropriate practice. The philosophical perspective of *inclusion* has a long history dating back to the deinstitutionalization, normalization, and integration movements of the 1970s (cf., Schalock, Harber, & Genung, 1981; Scheerenberger, 1977; Wolfensberger, 1972). The basic tenet of these movements was that all individuals have a right to fully participate in society. For young children with disabilities, this means that most children should receive their specialized services in day-care and preschool programs that serve primarily children who do not have disabilities, rather than attend segregated preschools enrolling only children with disabilities (Division for Early Childhood [DEC] and the National Association for the Education of Young Children [NAEYC], 2009). As educational environments, quality early childhood programs provide children with disabilities a varied and rich curriculum of play, exploration, socialization, communication, and other developmental activities. And as social environments, inclusive early childhood programs afford children with disabilities and their families opportunities to develop friendships and social networks with children who do not have disabilities and their families.

Special education legislation also supports the philosophy of inclusion—especially the least restrictive environment (LRE) policy of the IDEA (2004). Furthermore, the effectiveness and feasibility of inclusive early childhood programs have been demonstrated since the early 1970s, when Head Start began requiring that 10% of its enrollment be children with disabilities (P.L. 92-424, Sec. 3[b]) and when the U.S. federal government funded the model, inclusive of ECSE preschool programs (cf., D. Bricker & Bricker, 1971; D. Bricker, Bricker, Iacino, & Dennison, 1976; W. Bricker & Bricker, 1976). Since these initial efforts, inclusive ECSE programs have shown their effectiveness throughout the United States, serving children with disabilities who have a wide range of special needs (cf., Guralnick, 2001).

The *natural environments* perspective was described in IDEA (1991) to clarify the meaning of least restrictive settings for young children who are not yet school age. According to IDEA, natural environments are "home and community settings in which children without disabilities participate" (Section 303.12), such as preschools, day-care settings, and other community groups serving same-age peers. The opportunity for young children to participate in these natural environments is further supported by the Americans with Disabilities Act (ADA, 1990), which prohibits private programs that serve the public from discriminating against individuals on the basis of disability. The perspective of natural environments exceeds the legal preference for these typical settings, however, and suggests that interventions be provided through *natural learning opportunities* within the settings. Natural learning opportunities are routines and activities that occur in the everyday lives of young children, especially routines and activities that appear to be of high interest to the child (Bruder, 2001; Dunst & Bruder, 2006). When children show high interest, they are focused and engaged in the routine or activity and their learning is enhanced (Dunst et al., 2001). Teaching through natural learning opportunities thereby uses the inherent motivational qualities of inclusive, natural environments (McWilliam & Casey, 2008).

And finally, the third perspective that has strongly influenced the development of research-based practices in ECSE is developmentally appropriate practice (DAP). DAP is a philosophy and a set of principles of the National Association for the Education of Young Children, the leading professional organization for early childhood education (Bredekamp, 1987; Bredekamp & Rosegrant, 1992; Copple & Bredekamp, 2009), which guides the development and assessment of high-quality early childhood programs. Programs that adhere to DAP *facilitate* learning by following children's interests and natural inquisitiveness. Children are encouraged to explore, and teachers respond by arranging related learning activities. Early academics are not the focus; instead, play, social, community, and daily living activities appropriate to the children's developmental levels make up the curriculum.

The earliest publications of DAP did not mention young children with disabilities, and subsequently, the professional community has addressed and debated the applicability and appropriateness of DAP for ECSE in the past (cf., Berkeley & Ludlow, 1989; Carta, Schwartz, Atwater, & McConnell, 1991; Cavallaro, Haney, & Cabello, 1993; J. E. Johnson & Johnson, 1992). Although it may not always provide sufficient structure, supports, and specialized instruction for young children with disabilities through its curricular approach, DAP has come to characterize most preschool settings that serve primarily children without disabilities and therefore represents the targeted inclusion model for most young children with disabilities. The challenge is to identify research-based intervention practices that can be implemented in programs that adhere to DAP (Hemmeter, 2000).

Review of Research-Based Practices

Together, the perspectives of inclusion, natural environments, and DAP have influenced the development of research-based practices for ECSE. Research-based practices are not just those shown to produce developmental gains for young children with disabilities; they are also practices that have been demonstrated to be successful and practical in inclusive and natural environments (Hemmeter, 2000). Two ECSE practices with empirical support for their effectiveness in natural contexts are (a) activity-based intervention (ABI) and (b) milieu teaching.

Activity-Based Intervention

As noted previously, a significant challenge of ECSE is to provide effective, specialized instruction to young children with disabilities in inclusive, natural environments. In a 1989 book chapter, D. Bricker and Cripe defined and proposed ABI as an approach for addressing this challenge. The chapter was soon followed by a detailed textbook on developing and implementing ABI (D. Bricker & Cripe, 1992). As suggested by the title of the approach, ABI provides interventions *during* activities, rather than *as* activities. More specifically, ABI is characterized by four major elements: (a) child-directed instructional interactions; (b) instruction embedded in child-directed, teacher directed, and routine activities; (c) logically occurring antecedents and consequences; and (d) functional and generative skill outcomes. It was developed as a framework for providing special education in conjunction with DAP (D. Bricker & Cripe, 1992).

In linking ABI and DAP, children with disabilities attend inclusive early childhood programs and participate in the same developmentally appropriate activities as their peers who do not have disabilities; specialized interventions are infused into the developmentally appropriate activities. This is in direct contrast to traditional, separate special education preschool programs where activities were defined by individualized education program (IEP) objectives and focused on developmental areas of need (e.g., "motor time," "language time"). A major difference in the two approaches is the *context* of instruction: In ABI, children's special needs are addressed *within* a developmentally appropriate activity; in separate special education preschool programs, children's intervention needs are addressed in isolation of contextually meaningful activities.

A second important difference between separate ECSE programs and inclusive programs that implement ABI is the manner in which specialized interventions are provided. Separate ECSE programs have primarily implemented highly structured, one-on-one, didactic behavioral interventions. Instead, ABI emphasizes a more general, incidental approach to intervention. Using ABI, the special education teacher is guided by broad goals and follows the child's interest to determine when and where to provide specialized instruction (D. Bricker & Cripe, 1992). This child-directed approach to intervention is exemplified in milieu teaching, the second research-based practice we discuss in this chapter.

Theoretical Underpinnings

As described by D. Bricker and Cripe (1992), the ABI model is based on several related conceptual and theoretical frameworks. These include theoretical assumptions of early intervention, a psychoeducational framework, and learning theories. Foundational assumptions of early intervention are two: (a) delays and/or disabilities can be positively affected by intervention, and (b) early

experiences are an important factor in early development. Related assumptions are that (a) young children with disabilities need more and/or different experiences than children who do not have disabilities; (b) personnel must be well-trained in providing formal, early intervention to address children's special needs; and (c) children with delays or disabilities experience improved developmental outcomes if they participate in early intervention. Taken together, these assumptions posit that young children with delays or disabilities will benefit from high-quality, specialized early intervention.

ABI curricula are contextualized by a psychoeducational framework that targets generative, functional, and adaptive skills (D. Bricker & Cripe, 1992). *Generative* means that a child can modify an existing response and formulate a novel and appropriate response to fit a new situation. This is sometimes referred to as response generalization (Carr, 1988). *Functional* skills are immediately useful responses. Pointing to a photo of a cup when a teacher says, "Show me the cup," may be considered nonfunctional; whereas handing a cup to the teacher when told, "Give me your cup if you want water," would be considered a functional skill. And finally, *adaptive* responses are those that are modified to fit a social or physical constraint or need. In other words, a child's repertoire should be flexible enough that if one response is ineffective, one or more additional responses can be used. ABI focuses on teaching generative, functional, and adaptive skills that help children meet the ever-changing demands of natural environments.

Interventions to teach generative, functional, and adaptive skills using ABI are influenced by the learning theories of Vygotsky, Piaget, and Dewey (D. Bricker, 1986; D. Bricker & Cripe, 1992). These three theories share the common thread that the child's interaction with the environment is fundamental to development and learning. Vygotsky's child development theory emphasized the role of social interaction in the learning process, and noted that interaction has a reciprocal effect: The environment affects the child, and the child, in turn, affects the environment (Vygotsky, 1978). While Piaget believed that child development was primarily a biological process, he stressed that it also required environmental interaction because of the feedback obtained through the interaction. Focusing on children's cognitive development, Piaget proposed that children construct their intelligence as they actively engage in the world (Piaget, 1954). Dewey (1916), an educational theorist, emphasized that learning is an experiential process. He suggested that children learn from *all* of their experiences; and educational goals are maximized when teachers orchestrate thoughtfully planned, sequenced, and well-organized activities that allow for children's full participation. D. Bricker and Cripe (1992) based ABI on three themes drawn from the theoretical frameworks of Vygotsky, Piaget, and Dewey: "1) the influence and interaction of both the immediate and larger social-cultural environment, 2) the need for active involvement by the learner, and 3) the enhancement of learning by engaging children in functional and meaningful activities" (p. 16).

Research Base

D. Bricker and Cripe (1992) summarized initial research on ABI in four manuscripts (Bailey & Bricker, 1985; D. Bricker, Bruder, & Bailey, 1982; D. Bricker & Gumerlock, 1988; D. Bricker & Sheehan, 1981). These studies were conducted as program evaluations of a model ABI demonstration project for infants and preschoolers with and without disabilities. All four studies were pretest/post-test comparisons, and included norm-referenced and criterion-referenced measures addressing developmental milestones and preacademic skills. Although none of these program evaluation studies included control/comparison groups, the data did indicate that children made significant progress over spans of 5 months to 2 years. In a more controlled single-subject alternating treatments study of object naming with six preschool children who were at risk or had developmental delays, results indicated that direct instruction was associated with more rapid skill acquisition than ABI; however, ABI was more effective in promoting generalization and maintenance of the newly acquired object names (Losardo & Bricker, 1994).

Concurrent with the development of ABI by Bricker and her colleagues, other researchers investigated what is probably the most distinctive feature of ABI, *embedded instruction*. Embedded instruction is also known as embedded learning opportunities (Dunst, Hamby, Trivette, Raab, & Bruder, 2000; Horn, Lieber, Li, Sandall, & Schwartz, 2000), routines-based instruction (Pretti-Frontczak, Barr, Macy, & Carter, 2003; Schepis, Reid, Ownbey, & Parsons, 2001), and participation-based practices (Campbell, 2004; Fleming, Sawyer, & Campbell, 2011). Consistent with the description in ABI, embedded instruction means that intervention to address the needs of children with disabilities is incorporated into ongoing, functional, age-appropriate activities. These activities can be in preschool, home, or community environments.

Researchers have shown that embedded instruction is an effective technique across a wide range of skill areas (Fox & Hanline, 1993; Grisham-Brown, Schuster, Hemmeter, & Collins, 2000; Horn et al., 2000; Kohler, Strain, Hoyson, & Jamieson, 1997; McBride & Schwartz, 2003), including communication (McBride & Schwartz, 2003; Peck, Killen, & Baumgart, 1989; Warren & Gazdag, 1990), social (Macy & Bricker, 2007; M. L. Venn & Wolery, 1992), play (Schepis et al., 2001),

self-help (McBride & Schwartz, 2003; Schepis et al., 2001; Sewell, Collins, Hemmeter, & Schuster, 1998), cognitive/preacademic (Daugherty, Grisham-Brown, & Hemmeter, 2001; McBride & Schwartz, 2003; M. L. Venn et al., 1993), and transition (Bakkaloglu, 2008). A number of teaching strategies have been used as the intervention method during embedded instruction, such as time delay (Daugherty et al., 2001; Grisham-Brown et al., 2000), incidental teaching (Bakkalogu, 2008; Horn et al., 2000; Macy & Bricker, 2007; Mudd & Wolery, 1987; Warren & Kaiser, 1986), discrete trial training/systematic instruction (Grisham-Brown et al., 2000; McBride & Schwartz, 2003; Sewell et al., 1998), and peer-based strategies (Kohler et al., 1997). And finally, research has demonstrated that embedded instruction can be implemented effectively in inclusive early childhood settings and home environments, even by relatively inexperienced student teachers, teaching assistants, and family members (Dunst et al., 2001; Fox & Hanline, 1993; Kaiser, Hancock, & Hester, 1998; Kohler et al., 1997; Macy & Bricker, 2007; Schepis et al., 2001).

Despite the large number of studies indicating that embedding is an effective strategy that does not require extensive training or support to implement, some studies have indicated that embedding is not used to the extent that it could be, even following training on its implementation (Horn et al., 2000; Pretti-Frontczak & Bricker, 2001). Pretti-Frontzcak and Bricker found that teachers were most likely to embed instruction during one-on-one activities and in situations that were more teacher directed than child directed. This finding was concerning for two reasons: first, one-on-one activities did not occur very often in the inclusive environments observed during the study, and thus, very little instruction was occurring for the targeted skills. Second, the procedure was designed to be implemented as teachers followed the children's lead. The multitude of demands on teachers' attention and responsibilities during the school day as well as their concerns about stigmatizing children with disabilities by implementing specialized interventions also seem to influence the extent to which the embedding strategy was implemented (Horn et al., 2000). Although Pretti-Frontzcak and Bricker emphasized that teachers must learn to identify opportunities for embedded instruction as they naturally occur, they also recommended that providing some planning—such as engineering opportunities for instruction (cf., Grisham-Brown et al., 2000) or establishing a minimum number of opportunities for instruction within an activity (cf., Macy & Bricker, 2007)—may help to increase teachers' use of embedding.

Unlike ABI, embedded instruction is not a comprehensive curricular approach; instead, it focuses solely on providing specially designed instruction to students with disabilities during meaningful, developmentally appropriate activities. Results of the related research on embedded instruction, however, lend support to ABI as a research-based practice in early childhood special education. ABI—and its most recognized component, embedded instruction—is now considered a recommended practice in ECSE (Sandall, Hemmeter, Smith, & McLean, 2005). Next we provide a description of the procedures for implementing embedded instruction as described in the ABI model.

Implementation of ABI/Embedded Instruction

In the following sections, we provide guidelines for planning and implementing ABI/embedded instruction.

Planning for ABI/embedded instruction. Planning the embedded instruction component of ABI involves three steps: First, the intervention itself must be developed; second, individual and group activity schedules are designed; and third, meaningful, age-appropriate activities are prepared (D. Bricker & Cripe, 1992). The intervention is a detailed instructional plan that is written in behavioral terms, specifying general antecedents (i.e., prompts or environmental arrangements provided *before* the child is expected to respond), responses (i.e., child behaviors that meet the objective), and consequences (i.e., teacher responses that correct, extend, or reinforce the child's behavior after its occurrence). The procedures delineated in the intervention are conducted in a similar manner each time it is embedded. For example, if an intervention to teach a child with physical disabilities to reach for a desired object is developed, it might be embedded one or more times during arrival at preschool, large-group morning circle, center activities, and snack time. When the intervention plan is implemented in each of these activities, the antecedents, response, and consequences will be nearly identical (some slight differences may be necessary to fit the activity). In this example, the antecedent could be that highly preferred items are placed within the child's reach, but at a distance requiring the child to extend her elbow and shoulder in order to obtain the items. The response could be stated as any arm movement that results in the child's touching the item. And the consequence might be that a teacher physically assists the child in grasping and obtaining the item as soon as the child touches the item. If the child doesn't reach the object within 6 seconds, the teacher assists the child in reaching and grasping the item.

When this intervention is embedded throughout the school day, the materials and activities will vary. During arrival at preschool, the child may reach for a book to look at while waiting for school to begin; in the

large-group morning circle, the child may reach for a magnifying glass to use in the science center for a new activity; and at snack time, the child may reach to indicate a preferred type of cracker. Because the intervention is implemented in a nearly identical manner each time it is embedded, the child is likely to learn that given a particular antecedent situation (e.g., when an item is out of reach), a specific response (e.g., reaching with extended shoulder and elbow) consistently results in a given consequence (e.g., obtaining a desired item). Thus, systematic instruction is provided across a variety of meaningful activities. The variety of activities, and the associated variations in materials, peers, adults, and other situational stimuli, have an added benefit of promoting generalization (Stokes & Baer, 1977).

The second step in planning embedded instruction in the ABI model is to design individual and group activity schedules. This step is critical because it ensures that children receive both one-on-one and group instruction. It also provides an accountability mechanism to ensure that children receive an adequate amount of instruction on priority objectives, while at the same time allowing teachers to schedule a manageable amount of embedded instruction. Individual and group activity schedules are created as matrices (Noonan & McCormick, 2006, pp. 94–95). The group activity schedule is created by listing the daily schedule of home, community, and/or classroom activities down the left side of a grid, and the children's names/objectives to be embedded throughout the day across the top of the grid. The schedule should include a balance of child-initiated (e.g., child-directed play during centers time), teacher-directed (e.g., group science lesson), and routine activities (e.g., cleanup in preparation for recess). Check marks are placed in the cells of the grid corresponding to objectives that will be taught during each activity (see Figure 25.1). A teacher can then review a group activity schedule before an activity and note which children's objectives are to be embedded during that activity.

The individual activity schedules are similar to the group activity schedules. Instead of placing check marks in the cells of the grid specifying when objectives are embedded, a brief description of how the objective will be addressed within the corresponding activity is noted in the cell. Continuing with the example discussed previously, "Reaches to indicate book choice" is written in the cell corresponding to morning arrival time in the schedule and the objective of "reaches for an item." The individual activity schedule is developed for each child and operationalizes the form that objectives take when embedded in activities.

Preparing activities is the third step in implementing embedded instruction in the ABI model. Selection or creation of activities is a critical step in ABI: activities

Figure 25.1 Group activity matrix.

Schedule	Students and Embedded Objectives					
	Jacob: makes two-word requests	**Sara:** names item	**Keoni:** takes two conversational turns	**Mia:** points to symbol on board	**Sam:** points to indicate choice	**Malia:** Looks at speaker and makes audible request
Arrival			✓	✓		✓
Group Exercise		✓			✓	
Snack	✓	✓	✓	✓	✓	✓
Hygiene		✓		✓		
Morning Circle	✓		✓	✓		✓
Centers	✓	✓				✓
Recess			✓		✓	
Lunch	✓				✓	✓

must be developmentally appropriate, that is, age appropriate, meaningful, and of high interest to the children (with and without disabilities). As indicated, the plans are written for child-directed activities, teacher-directed activities, and routines. The plan includes a detailed description/sequence of the activity, variations that might be included, and required materials. An example of a description/sequence of a "Trip to the Store" activity is provided by D. Bricker and Cripe (1992), and begins as follows:

> The activity area is set up as a pretend store. The interventionist is positioned at the cash register and the children are near the shelves or pushing shopping carts. The interventionist has materials such as bags and shopping lists behind the cash register at the beginning of the activity. (p. 117)

The description continues and explains that the children may decide how they get to the store, what they might talk about during the activity, and what they might do while in the store. The use of various materials (e.g., purses, play money, food items) is also described. The "variations" section of the activity plan suggests alternative approaches to the activity, such as stocking the store or shopping for a specific purpose, such as a birthday party. The intent of the activity plan is to provide a general guide (script) of the activity, keeping in mind the need for naturally or logically occurring opportunities to embed instruction on children's selected objectives. The activity plan also includes situations that facilitate learning opportunities (e.g., surprising students with items that are new to the classroom or are highly preferred items).

Implementing ABI/embedded instruction.   To implement ABI, activities are conducted as indicated on the activity schedules and activity plans. During an activity, the teacher carefully attends to the children with embedded objectives and watches for opportunities for instruction (transactions). The teacher is responsive to the children and may facilitate an instructional opportunity by following a child's lead and/or interacting in a reciprocal manner. If a preschool child is playing with toy cars and has an embedded objective to initiate interactions with peers, the teacher may begin by playing responsively with the child. For instance, the teacher may pick up a car and roll it behind the child's car. If the child directs the teacher to move the car along a particular path, the teacher complies and allows the child to lead the play. If the child changes the type of play with the car (perhaps moving the car toward the teacher's car), the teacher may reciprocate by moving the car in a novel fashion. By following the child's lead and interacting reciprocally, the teacher has entered the child's play. As the play continues, the teacher may use a number of strategies to embed learning opportunities to address the objective of initiating interaction with peers.

One example of an embedding strategy to teach social interactions is to bring a peer into proximity with a new and unique toy car. Novelty often attracts attention and may provide a naturalistic prompt for the target child to initiate interaction. When the target child shows attention in any way to the peer with the new toy car, the teacher responds to the child's interest by embedding and implementing the instructional plan (providing the prompts, corrections, and other consequences indicated in the plan) to teach the child to initiate interaction with a peer. Another strategy might be to introduce materials that have been shown to facilitate child interaction, such as building blocks. A peer can be guided to play next to the target child, building bridges and roads with blocks. When the child looks at or approaches the block roads or bridges, the teacher notices the learning opportunity and embeds the instructional plan.

Other strategies for embedding suggested by D. Bricker and Cripe (1992) include:

1. *Forgetfulness:* The teacher prompts a response from the child by *forgetting* to provide a necessary material or step for an activity. During tooth brushing, for example, toothbrushes and cups might be lined up on the counter, but the toothpaste is missing.

2. *Visible but unreachable:* Highly desirable items are placed in view, but at a distance beyond where a child can access them independently. This strategy prompts interaction to obtain the items.

3. *Violation of expectations:* A step or component of a familiar routine or activity is changed or omitted. Instead of saying, "And the pig says oink-oink," while reading a favorite story, the teacher might say, "And the pig says meow-meow." Similar to the forgetfulness strategy, the violation of expectations encourages or evokes a response from the child as the child is surprised and recognizes the error.

4. *Piece by piece:* When an activity involves several pieces or components, the teacher can provide one piece at a time, requiring the child to request each piece throughout the activity time (e.g., child must ask for each item of a tea set when setting a table).

5. *Assistance:* Materials that are highly desirable, but difficult to use independently (e.g., starting an electronic toy, putting on tie-shoes in preparation for recess), can encourage children to interact or attempt various problem-solving strategies, potentially including a target objective.

6. *Sabotage:* To promote problem solving and child interaction with materials, peers, or adults, the teacher can intentionally interrupt or interfere with the workings of an item. For example, a computer mouse can be hidden, or children can be told to get art materials only to find that the art cabinet is locked.

7. *Interruption or delay:* When used judiciously (as to not cause too much upset), stopping or pausing an activity or routine—especially a very familiar one—can be highly effective in prompting initiations

and requests from children. When singing the itsy-bitsy spider song with a toddler, for example, the teacher might pause the song's words and hand motions just after singing, "Down came the rain and . . ." prompting the child to look at the adult and either indicate what comes next (singing "washed the spider out," or taking the teacher's hands to make the washing-out motion) or requesting that the adult continue.

The techniques are designed to increase opportunities to embed instruction. The keys to embedded instruction are to ensure that instructional plans are implemented at times that are typical or logical for the targeted skills. Embedding instruction involves naturally occurring stimuli and consequences that will ultimately promote and support the maintenance and generalization of newly acquired skills. In summary, the components that must be present if an intervention is adhering to the guidelines of ABI (Losardo & Bricker, 1994) are listed in Table 25.1.

Table 25.1 Essential Activity-Based Intervention Components

Component	Characteristics
1. Nature of Transactions	• Teacher directs attention to child's interests, actions, and motivations.
	• Teacher follows child's lead.
	• Teacher responds reciprocally to child's initiations.
2. Goals and Objectives	• Teacher targets goals and objectives during naturally occurring opportunities.
	• Teacher ensures adequate instructional time by planning embedded goals and objectives.
	• Teacher plans beginning and end of transitions.
3. Antecedents and Consequences	• Teacher uses antecedents that are inherent or logical to the activity.
	• Teacher uses consequences that are inherent outcomes or are logical to the activity.
4. Generalization	• Teacher uses multiple antecedents to elicit a range of appropriate child responses.
	• Teacher assesses for generalization of newly acquired skills.

Source: Adapted, with permission, from p. 747 of Losardo, A. & Bricker, D. (1994). Activity-based intervention and direct instruction: A comparison study. *American Journal on Mental Retardation, 98,* 744–765.

Milieu Teaching

Perhaps the earliest demonstration of embedded instruction was Hart and Risley's (1968) language intervention study using incidental teaching, later subsumed under the naturalistic language teaching strategies known as milieu teaching (Hart & Rogers-Warren, 1978) and enhanced milieu teaching (EMT) (Kaiser, 1993). Incidental teaching was originally developed and demonstrated with preschoolers with language delays who were from economically disadvantaged backgrounds. The procedure was designed to address the challenges of generalizing newly acquired language skills to spontaneous use in new situations (Hart & Risley, 1980).

Incidental teaching is a child–adult teaching interaction that occurs during natural, unstructured times. A hallmark of incidental teaching is that teaching interactions follow the child's attentional lead. The teacher follows the child's attentional lead by approaching the child, moving to the child's level, and visually attending to what the child is attending to. Specifically, incidental teaching interactions occur in *child-selected* situations that are identified in advance as an *occasion for instruction,* such as, "when the child requests assistance, either verbally or nonverbally" (Hart & Risley, 1975, pp. 411–412). In addition to occurring under naturalistic conditions and following the child's lead, incidental teaching and its variations (milieu teaching and EMT) share the common features of using multiple examples to teach elaborated linguistic forms, explicitly prompting for child language, and providing natural consequences for children's use of targeted language (Kaiser, Yoder, & Keetz, 1992).

As described by Hart and Risley (1975), incidental teaching includes a series of decisions as the teacher responds to the child's request:

1. whether to use the occasion for incidental teaching; if yes, then

2. a decision concerning the language behavior to be obtained from the child, and

3. a decision concerning the cue to be used to initiate instruction, whether

    a. the cue of focused attention alone [following the child's attentional lead], or

    b. the cue of focused attention plus a verbal cue.

    And, if the child does not respond to the cue,

4. a decision concerning the degree of prompt to be used, whether

    a. fullest degree: a request for imitation

    b. medium degree: a request for partial imitation, or

    c. minimal degree: a request for the terminal language behavior. (p. 412)

This sequence of decision making is followed each time an incidental teaching interaction is implemented.

Theoretical Underpinnings

Developmental and behavioral perspectives have been described to explain the effectiveness of incidental and milieu teaching (Hart & Risley, 1980; Warren & Kaiser, 1986); Warren and Kaiser (1988) referred to these joint perspectives as an interactionist or hybrid framework. From a developmental perspective, incidental and milieu teaching mirror the natural social and communication interactions of parents who are responsive to their children (Bruner, 1975). For example, parents tend to reply to the meaning of their child's communication, rather than the grammatical correctness of the utterance. In other words, if a child says, "Want cookie," the parent might typically respond, "Oh, you'd like one of these chocolate chip cookies!" and gives the child the cookie. In contrast, it is unlikely for parents' replies to address the grammatical correctness of their children's requests (e.g., "No. Say, 'I want a cookie, please'"). In addition to responding to meaning rather than grammar, parents tend to reply with extensions and expansions, adding content and modeling more structure to the child's utterance. Researchers in child language development believe that this style of responsive parent interactions supports the development of more sophisticated language development (L. McCormick, 2003). Further, correcting grammar tends to interrupt communicative interactions and decrease subsequent language use.

Hart and Risley (1980) posited that, from a behavioral perspective, incidental teaching establishes language use as a generalized class of behavior. Children learn through incidental teaching that language use gains close, receptive adult attention and access to reinforcers. That is, the procedures of incidental teaching function to reinforce and thereby increase children's use of language. Moreover, language use transfers across settings and occasions because of reinforcement in a rich variety of stimulus conditions.

At a finer level of behavioral theoretical analysis, incidental teaching incorporates at least three stimulus conditions that promote generalization (Stokes & Baer, 1977). First, incidental teaching is conducted in natural environments that include a rich array of naturally maintaining reinforcers. As children acquire and demonstrate targeted language skills, the natural communities of reinforcers (e.g., adult attention, access to preferred items) function to maintain and increase future use of the new skills. Second, the varied array of stimulus conditions (e.g., requesting juice at snack time, requesting a favorite book during centers time, or requesting a peer-partner for a field trip) under which the child initiates language and responds with elaborations provides multiple exemplars, a procedure that promotes generalization. And third, the naturalistic conditions under which incidental teaching is implemented are inherently loosely structured, meaning that stimulus and response characteristics of environments change slightly from occasion to occasion because events rarely repeat in an identical manner. The fluid and changeable structure of the naturalistic environment functions as the *train-loosely* technique for facilitating generalization (Stokes & Baer, 1977). Together, the developmental and behavioral bases for incidental and milieu teaching provide a strong theoretical explanation for the effectiveness of the procedures.

Research Base

Beginning with the 1968 seminal study by Hart and Risley, incidental and milieu teaching have been shown to be effective strategies for increasing overall language use and rate (Halle, Baer, & Spradlin, 1981; Rogers-Warren & Warren, 1980); increasing vocabulary, linguistic complexity, and length (Hart & Risley, 1980; Warren, McQuarter, & Rogers-Warren, 1984); and teaching specific linguistic forms and functions in young children with delayed speech or mild developmental delays. The most important finding regarding incidental and milieu teaching strategies was their effectiveness in achieving generalization *concurrently* with the acquisition of new language skills (Alpert & Kaiser, 1992; Alpert & Rogers-Warren, 1984; Halle, Marshall, & Spradlin, 1979; Hart & Risley, 1974, 1975, 1980; Kaiser & Hester, 1994; Rogers-Warren & Warren, 1980; Warren et al., 1984). This was significant because it contradicted the widely held belief that generalization was an advanced stage of the learning process that could occur only after the stages of acquisition, maintenance, and fluency (R. H. Horner, Sprague, & Wilcox, 1982).

Linguistic forms and functions taught through incidental and milieu teaching include descriptive adjectives (Hart & Risley, 1968, 1974), prepositions (McGee, Krantz, & McClannahan, 1985), nouns and compound sentences (Hart & Risley, 1974), two- and three-word semantic relations (Hancock & Kaiser, 2002), receptive object labels (McGee, Krantz, Mason, & McClannahan, 1983), initiations (Halle et al., 1979), affirmations and negations (Neef, Walters, & Egel, 1984), requests (Cavallaro & Bambara, 1982; Halle et al., 1981), and responses to questions (Rogers-Warren & Warren, 1980; Warren et al., 1984). Milieu teaching has also been shown to be a research-based strategy for increasing nonverbal, prelinguistic requesting and commenting (Warren, Yoder, Gazdag, Kim, & Jones, 1993; Yoder, Warren, Kim, & Gazdag, 1994), as well as teaching the

use of augmentative/alternative communication systems such as sign language (Kaiser, Ostrosky, & Alpert, 1993; Oliver & Halle, 1982), communication boards (Kaiser et al., 1993), and voice output communication aids (Schepis, Reid, Behrmann, & Sutton, 1998).

Critical reviews have suggested that incidental and milieu teaching are most effective in teaching basic vocabulary and simple two- and three-word semantic relationships (e.g., agent–action–object) to children in the early stages of language development (Kaiser, 1993; Warren & Yoder, 1997, Yoder et al., 1995). Although initially developed and demonstrated with preschoolers from economically disadvantaged backgrounds (Hart & Risley, 1968, 1974, 1975) and with language delays (Alpert & Rogers-Warren, 1984; Rogers-Warren & Warren, 1980; Warren et al., 1984), their effectiveness has also been demonstrated with children who have disabilities such as developmental delay/intellectual disabilities (Halle et al., 1979; Halle et al., 1981; Kaiser et al., 1993; Oliver & Halle, 1982) and autism (Charlop-Christy & Carpenter, 2000; Hancock & Kaiser, 2002; McGee et al., 1985; Schepis et al., 1998).

One of the most appealing findings concerning incidental and milieu teaching strategies is that they can be implemented effectively in home and school environments, by parents (Alpert & Kaiser, 1992; Alpert & Rogers-Warren, 1984; Charlop-Christy & Carpenter, 2000; Kaiser & Hancock, 2003) and even siblings (Hancock & Kaiser, 1996). The effectiveness data on parents' implementing milieu teaching are compelling: In 2003, Kaiser and Hancock reported that 94% of the more than 200 parents trained to implement milieu teaching in their homes completed the training, and 97% of those completing the training reached the accuracy criterion. The training effectiveness and integrity resulted in secondary effects on their children (many of whom demonstrated significant language delays): nearly 90% of the children maintained and generalized language skills learned through the incidental teaching provided by their parents. Teachers have also been trained, with graphical feedback, to increase their use of milieu teaching (Casey & McWilliam, 2008).

The overwhelming majority of the research on incidental and milieu teaching has been conducted using single-subject research designs. This is both a weakness and a strength of the research base. It is a weakness because generalization of research findings is usually dependent on randomized assignment of participants and control groups. However, in the case of incidental and milieu teaching, with over 40 years of single-subject research studies (see reviews in Hancock & Kaiser, 2006; Kaiser et al., 1992; Warren & Kaiser, 1986), it can be considered a strength. The extensive number of replications across procedures and procedural variations, participant age groups (e.g., toddlers through adults), language needs/disabilities (e.g., speech delays, cognitive impairments, prelinguistic communicators, autism, disadvantaged backgrounds), targeted language responses, settings (e.g., home, school), and interventionists (e.g., researchers, graduate students, special education teachers, parents) builds a strong case for the generalizability of its effectiveness. Moreover, the single-subject research designs have allowed for cross-case intrasubject analyses that have suggested that the children who are likely to show the greatest improvements in language skills through incidental and milieu teaching are those who are verbally imitative, have at least 10 productive words, and have mean length of utterances between 1.0 and 3.5 words (Kaiser et al., 1992).

Implementation of Milieu Teaching

Incidental teaching is currently subsumed under the procedures of *milieu teaching* (Kaiser, 2000), a set of four language teaching procedures:

1. In the *model* procedure, the teacher notices the occasion for instruction, approaches the child, demonstrates the target communication response ("I need help"), and waits a few seconds. If the child imitates the model, the teacher provides what the child requested. If the child does not imitate within the specified time, the teacher judges the child's level of interest. If the teacher believes the child is still very interested, the teacher repeats the model and waits again. If the teacher believes the child is losing interest, the teacher repeats the model and gives the child the requested item.

2. The *mand-model* procedure builds on the *model* procedure by first offering a less-intrusive prompt than the model (a mand) when the teacher notices the child-determined occasion for instruction. Instead of modeling the target response, the teacher provides a mand (e.g., a directive, an indirect verbal prompt), such as, "Tell me what you need." If the child responds correctly, the teacher immediately provides what the child requested. If the child does not respond within the specified time period (usually 4 or 5 seconds) and the child's interest level is still high, the teacher repeats the mand; if the child's interest is waning, the teacher provides a model of the target response, for example, "I need help." From this point on, the *model* procedure is followed. In summary, one or two mands may be provided as prompts for the target response (depending on the child's level of interest); if the mand is an ineffective prompt, the teacher shifts to the model

procedure, and may provide one or two models (depending on the child's level of interest).

3. When a child has demonstrated acquisition of a target response but does not use that response frequently, consistently, or independently (as an initiation), the *delay* procedure is used. A less-intrusive procedure than the model or mand-model procedure, the delay procedure begins as all incidental teaching interactions begin, with the teacher noticing the child-determined occasion for instruction, approaching the child, and sharing the child's focus of attention. Unlike the model or mand-model procedure, the teacher says nothing. Instead, the teacher implements a delay by continuing to focus on the child and the child's activity and waiting expectantly for several seconds (usually 4 or 5 seconds) for the child to provide the target response. If the child responds correctly, the teacher immediately provides what the child requested. If the child does not respond and shows high interest, the teacher may continue to the delay for a few more seconds. If the child does not provide the target response, the teacher shifts to the mand-model procedure (if the child shows a moderate level of interest) or the model procedure (if the child shows a low level of interest).

4. And finally, the *incidental teaching* procedure includes the model, mand-model, and delay procedures with the teacher selecting one of the three procedures based on the difficulty level of the target response and the apparent level of child interest at the time. The model procedure is generally used with basic vocabulary, conversational, and imitation skills, or when the child's interest level appears to be relatively low. It is the most intrusive of the milieu teaching procedures, providing the child with a clear demonstration of the target response. The mand-model procedure is most appropriate for promoting generalization of new communication skills across situations and settings; the child should show at least a moderate level of interest. And the delay procedure is best-suited to highlighting environmental stimuli as the prompts to communication (e.g., the natural turn-taking pause in conversational turns or the attention of an adult); the child should show a high level of interest in having a need met.

Other variations of incidental/milieu teaching are EMT, which includes incidental teaching, plus two additional strategies—environmental arrangements and responsive interactions (Kaiser, Hemmeter, & Hester, 1997). Environmental arrangements and responsive interactions are general approaches to setting up the early childhood environment and responding to children in ways that encourage and promote communication. Increasing the overall quantity of communicative interactions, in turn, increases opportunities for incidental teaching.

Environmental arrangements in EMT are much like the environmental arrangements discussed earlier in the description of ABI:

1. Provide interesting materials and activities.

2. Place desired materials in sight but out of reach.

3. Offer small amounts of desired or required materials.

4. Offer choices frequently.

5. Provide activities in which the children will require assistance.

6. Create surprising, unexpected situations.

The common element in these strategies is that they create the need for children to communicate. Multiple environmental arrangement strategies can be used concurrently, and they can be used on a daily basis (although materials and activities should change in keeping with the preschool curriculum throughout the year).

The *responsive interaction* component of EMT requires that adults (e.g., teachers, parents) respond to children in ways that encourage communicative interactions and promote balanced communication exchanges (again, much like the *responsive* interactions described in ABI). When adults are responsive to children, they focus on and attend to the child and follow the child's lead. In EMT—with its specific goal of improving communication skills—adults then attempt to facilitate communication. The teacher might ask a question or comment on the child's play. If the child talks to the teacher, the teacher responds in a manner that encourages sustained conversation. For example, a child holds up a toy dinosaur and says, "blue." Rather than simply replying "Yes," and effectively ending the communication exchange, the teacher might say, "A blue dinosaur! What is your dinosaur doing?"

It is common to see the use of environmental arrangements and responsive interactions in high-quality preschool programs. Environmental arrangements ensure that the setting provides numerous prompts for communication, and responsive interactions ensure that children have adult communication partners who are focused and attentive to their interests. The third component of EMT is incidental teaching (as described previously). As noted, all incidental teaching interactions are embedded at child-determined occasions for instruction. This means that the occasion for instruction is planned ahead of time, and intervention occurs when the teacher observes the occasion (e.g., "When the child approaches a peer and watches the peer play," "When the child notices that a required item is missing and makes a one-word request").

Milieu teaching is a communication intervention approach in ECSE that has a well-established research base in promoting generalized communication skills. It is the most thoroughly researched embedded instruction procedure, beginning with the seminal incidental teaching study by Hart and Risley in 1968. Over the years it has evolved to a set of four milieu teaching procedures (developed primarily by Warren, Kaiser, and their colleagues; e.g., Kaiser et al., 1993; Warren & Gazdag, 1990) and more recently led to the conceptualization of EMT (by Kaiser and her colleagues; e.g., Kaiser & Hester, 1994). Although incidental teaching was originally developed for young children from economically disadvantaged backgrounds, a significant amount of research now demonstrates its effectiveness for young children with disabilities.

Summary

The philosophies of inclusion, natural environments, and DAP have influenced the development of research-based practices in ECSE. We have described two research-based practices, ABI and milieu teaching, that have been shown to be effective intervention approaches in inclusive, developmentally appropriate preschool programs. Diane Bricker and her colleagues (D. Bricker & Cripe, 1992) developed ABI, which provides special education through the use of embedded instruction in naturalistic environments. Incidental teaching, initially developed by Hart and Risley (1968, 1974, 1975, 1980), is an embedded intervention approach to facilitating language development. Incidental teaching is supported by an extensive research base and is now subsumed in a set of naturalistic language teaching procedures known as milieu teaching (Kaiser, 2000; Warren & Kaiser, 1986) and EMT (Kaiser et al., 1997). Both ABI and milieu teaching are well-established research-based procedures considered recommended practices in ECSE (Sandall et al., 2005).

CHAPTER 26

Teaching Students with High-Incidence Disabilities

Thomas E. Scruggs and **Margo A. Mastropieri** | *George Mason University*

Students with high-incidence disabilities—including the categories of learning disabilities, mild intellectual disabilities, and emotional disturbance—comprise nearly two thirds of the total population of school-age individuals with disabilities (Mastropieri & Scruggs, 2009; U.S. Department of Education, 2006a). Students in these high-incidence disability areas are generally thought to be able to master most, if not all, of the school's general education curriculum and very commonly receive instruction in general education settings. Students in high-incidence categories of exceptionality share a number of characteristics. Some (e.g., intellectual ability) are defining characteristics for particular disability areas (e.g., intellectual disability), whereas others are commonly found in conjunction with one or more categories. Two characteristics very commonly observed across high-incidence disability categories are difficulty with verbal learning and memory, skills and processes critically linked to successful school learning (see Mastropieri & Scruggs, 2009, Chapter 10).

Memory deficits have long been associated with intellectual disability (Kavale & Forness, 1992) and have accompanied many different early theoretical perspectives on this category. Intellectual disability has been associated with deficits in many aspects of memory functioning, including short-term (L. Henry, 2008) and long-term (Kavale & Forness, 1992) memory, as well as with procedural and declarative memory processes (Vakil, Shelef-Reshef, & Levy-Shiff, 1997).

Researchers in the 1970s began to identify verbal or semantic memory deficits as important characteristics of learning disabilities (Bauer, 1977; Torgesen, 1977; Torgesen & Goldman, 1977). Evidence of memory deficits accumulated in later years (e.g., Ceci, 1984; Cooney & Swanson, 1987), as researchers considered memory deficits in this population as automatic (e.g., spontaneous) or purposive (e.g., intentional strategic) processes (Brainerd, Kingma, & Howe, 1986; Wertlieb, 1992) and established the link between memory and literacy skills (Cornwall, 1992).

Verbal learning and memory have been studied in students with emotional disturbance less overall; however, sustained academic learning deficits (presumably one correlate of verbal learning) have been well documented for this population (Scruggs & Mastropieri, 1986; Reid, Gonzalez, Nordness, Trout, & Epstein, 2004), as have deficits in general information (Mastropieri, Jenkins, & Scruggs, 1985). Further, deficits in verbal learning and memory have commonly been associated with anxiety, depression, and aggressiveness (Günther, Holtkamp, Jolles, Herpertz-Dahlmann, & Konrad, 2004; Mueller, 1979; Seguin, Pihl, Harden, Tremblay, & Boulerice, 1995; Watts, 1995).

Deficits in verbal learning and memory are among the major contributors to another important characteristic of students with high-incidence disabilities: deficits in academic achievement. Given the close association between memory deficits and both academic learning and deficits in purposive (strategic) processing (Kavale & Forness, 1992; Mueller, 1979; Wertlieb, 1992), strategies intended to increase memory for school-related content would seem to be highly appropriate for students with high-incidence disabilities. In addition, because most of these students receive a large portion of their instruction in general education classrooms (Mastropieri & Scruggs, 2009), it also seems appropriate to develop methods for implementing learning strategies in general education classrooms in ways that minimize or eliminate the stigma of working with "specialized" materials. This would involve maximizing individual student engagement, providing appropriate instructional strategies (e.g., rehearsal, elaboration, active engagement), and finding ways to present instructional materials such that instruction can be individualized without appearing to single out individual students.

In this chapter, we describe some successful approaches to these complex problems. One relevant approach to memory and verbal learning deficits, which has received considerable research attention, is mnemonic instruction (Scruggs & Mastropieri, 1990). These strategies have been demonstrated to facilitate very substantial improvements in the amount of information students with high-incidence disabilities have been able to acquire and retain. Next, we describe some relevant approaches to the application of effective instructional strategies, including mnemonic elaboration, in inclusive general education classrooms. These approaches, described as differentiated curriculum enhancements (Scruggs, Mastropieri, Marshak, & Mills, 2009), have recently been employed to increase learning and memory of academic material for both general education and special education students. Finally, we discuss the strengths and weaknesses of these approaches to date and provide suggestions for future research.

Mnemonic Strategies

Whereas a mnemonic is any procedure or operation designed to improve memory, mnemonic strategies described in this chapter are those that involve "a specific reconstruction of target content intended to tie new information more closely to the learner's existing knowledge base and, therefore, facilitate retrieval" (Scruggs & Mastropieri, 1990, pp. 271–272). In this section, we review a number of mnemonic strategies (i.e., keyword method, pegword method, letter strategies,

and reconstructive elaborations) that share the same theoretical rationale of addressing learning needs by capitalizing on student strengths.

Rationale

Mnemonic strategies are intended to be useful because they build on familiarity or meaningfulness (Underwood & Shultz, 1960) and elaboration (Rohwer, Raines, Eoff, & Wagner, 1966; Scruggs & Cohn, 1983) to enhance learning (Mastropieri, Scruggs, & Levin, 1985). These types of mnemonics are expected to be of particular utility to individuals with high-incidence disabilities, because they minimize the effect of relative learning weaknesses (e.g., spontaneous strategy production, verbal fluency, memory for verbal information), while maximizing relative strengths (e.g., memory for pictures, memory for semantically or phonetically elaborated information; see Scruggs, Mastropieri, & Levin, 1987, for a discussion).

Types of Mnemonic Strategies
The Keyword Method

The keyword method has its roots as far back as ancient Greece (Yates, 1966), as do most mnemonic strategies, but its first appearance in modern experimental psychology was in an investigation by Atkinson (1975) on Russian vocabulary learning. The keyword method works by creating concrete, acoustically similar proxies for unfamiliar information and associating it with the to-be-remembered information. For example, to remember that *dorado* is a Spanish word for a type of fish, a keyword is first constructed for *dorado*. In this case, a good keyword would be "door," because it sounds like the first part of *dorado* and is easily pictured. Learners are then shown (or asked to imagine) a picture of the keyword and associated information interacting, for example, in a picture of a *fish* (meaning for *dorado*) knocking at a *door* (keyword for *dorado*). When asked for the meaning of *dorado,* then, learners are taught to first think of the keyword, *door,* think of the picture with the door in it, remember *what else* was in the picture (a fish), and retrieve the answer, fish (McLoone, Scruggs, Mastropieri, & Zucker, 1986). For another example, consider the scientific name, *ranidae,* which refers to the family of common frogs. A good keyword for ranidae would be *rain,* and a picture would be shown of a *frog* (or family of frogs) sitting in the *rain.* When asked the meaning of ranidae, then, learners first think of the keyword, *rain,* think of the picture with the rain in it, remember what else was in the picture (frog), and retrieve the answer, frogs (Mastropieri, Scruggs, Levin, Gaffney, & McLoone, 1985).

Table 26.1 Example Applications of Keyword Mnemonics

Subject Area	Target Word	Key Word	Meaning	Interactive Picture
English	Vituperation	Viper	Abusive speech	A *viper speaking abusively*
Foreign language	*Barca* (Italian)	Bark	Boat	A *barking dog* in a *boat*
Science	Erode	Road	To wear away, by wind or water	A *road, eroding* from wind and water runoff
Social studies	Lusitania	Lucy	Passenger ship sunk by German submarine	*Lucy* (from Peanuts) on the deck of a sinking passenger ship, shaking her fist at a submarine

Keywords have been shown to be very versatile, and have been applied in many domains, including foreign language vocabulary; English vocabulary; social studies content, including people, places, and concepts; and science concepts and classifications. Some examples of applications of keyword mnemonics in different subject areas are provided in Table 26.1. The keyword method, as with all mnemonic techniques, cannot be considered a panacea for all school learning. The keyword method is best when used to promote initial acquisition of unfamiliar names, facts, and concepts. Additional activities can easily be combined with the keyword method, including activities designed to promote fluency, comprehension, and applications.

The Pegword Method

Pegwords are rhyming proxies for numbers (e.g., *one* is *bun*, *two* is *shoe*, *three* is *tree*) and can be used when numbered or ordered information needs to be remembered. For example, to help students remember that a *rake* is an example of a third-class lever (fulcrum at one end, force applied in the middle), show them a picture of a *rake* leaning on a *tree* (pegword for *three*). To help students remember that insects have *six* legs, show a picture of *insects* on *sticks* (pegword for *six*). To help students remember that spiders have *eight* legs, show a picture of a *spider* weaving a web on a *gate* (pegword for *eight*).

Pegwords can also be combined with keywords when unfamiliar terms are associated with numbers. For example, to help students remember that Andrew Jackson was the *seventh* president, show a picture of angels playing *jacks* (keyword for Jackson) in *heaven* (pegword for seven) (Mastropieri, Scruggs, Bakken, & Whedon, 1997). Or, to help students remember that the mineral *wolframite* has a hardness level of approximately *four,* show a picture of a *wolf* (keyword for *wolframite*) at a *door* (pegword for *four*). When asked about wolframite, then, learners think of the keyword, *wolf,* think back to the picture of the wolf, remember

the wolf was at a door, remember that *door* is a pegword for *four,* and retrieve the answer, hardness level four (Mastropieri et al., 1986).

Additional information has also been successfully integrated into mnemonic pictures involving pegwords; for example, to teach that wolframite is hardness level four, is commonly *black* in color, and is used in the manufacture of tungsten for *lightbulb* filaments, show a picture of a *black* (color) *wolf* (keyword for *wolframite*) pulling a cord on a *lightbulb* (common use) in front of a *door* (pegword for *four*). Although this may seem a complicated strategy, it has been successfully employed with students with learning disabilities (e.g., Scruggs, Mastropieri, Levin, & Gaffney, 1985). Pegwords higher than 10 can include numbers for the teens (e.g., *lever* (11)) and combinations used for number decades (e.g., *twin* for 20, *twin doors* = 24).

Letter Strategies

Letter strategies are probably the most familiar of mnemonic strategies, as most individuals can remember learning that HOMES could represent the first letters of the Great Lakes (i.e., Huron, Ontario, Michigan, Erie, and Superior). Letter strategies include acronyms—in which each letter represents a word, as in the HOMES example; and acrostics—in which the first letters of words in a sentence are used to remember a list or sequence of information. For example, the sentence, "King Phillip's class ordered a family of gentle spaniels," could be used to prompt recall of the taxonomic order: kingdom, phylum, class, order, family, genius, species. The sentence, "My very educated mother just served us nine pizzas" has been used to prompt the recall of the planets in order: Mercury, Venus, Earth, Mars, Jupiter, Saturn, Uranus, Neptune, Pluto.

Letter strategies can also be combined with keywords. For example, in social studies, to remember that the members of the Central Powers during World War I were Turkey (Ottoman Empire), Austria-Hungary, and Germany, students can be shown a picture of children playing *TAG* (acronym for Turkey, Austria-Hungary, and Germany) in *Central Park* (keyword for *Central Powers*). When students are asked the names of the countries in the Central Powers, they remember the keyword, *Central Park,* think of the children playing *TAG* in Central Park, and remember the countries that begin with T, A, and G (Scruggs & Mastropieri, 1989b). Because letter strategies such as this provide only a first-letter prompt, teachers must be certain to practice the relevant names sufficiently so that students can remember them, given only the first letter.

Reconstructive Elaborations

School curriculum is complex and diverse, requiring a number of different mnemonic strategies to effectively encompass all important content. Scruggs and Mastropieri (1989b) suggested a model referred to as *reconstructive elaborations* to address this issue. They suggested considering the familiarity and concreteness of relevant content, and constructing mnemonic elaborations relative to these features (see also Mastropieri & Scruggs, 1989c). For example, *earthworm* is concrete and familiar to most learners and needs no reconstruction. To-be-associated information can simply be shown in a representative interactive picture (a *mimetic* reconstruction). For example, to remember that earthworms are *segmented,* have *many hearts,* and live *in the ground,* a picture can be developed of an earthworm with many segments, and showing a number of hearts, living in the ground. Similarly, to help students remember that many World War I soldiers became *ill* in the *trenches* (all familiar concepts), simply show a picture of *sick soldiers* in *trenches.*

Other content is familiar but not concrete. For example, the concept of *U.S. policy* may be familiar to students but not easy to represent. Therefore, teachers can use a *symbolic* reconstruction, in this case, the figure "Uncle Sam," to represent U.S. policy. For information that is unfamiliar, acoustic reconstructions in the form of the keyword method can be employed. These reconstructions also can be combined with letter strategies or pegwords, as needed, and have been effective in teaching content in U.S. history (Scruggs & Mastropieri, 1989a) and science (Scruggs & Mastropieri, 1992).

Description and Fidelity Checklist

Implementation of mnemonic instruction depends on development of appropriate mnemonic elaborations of target content. In most cases, this involves developing relevant illustrations. First, identify critical target content that students may have difficulty remembering. For example, a list of SAT vocabulary words may include the following:

Vocabulary Word	Meaning
Martinet	A strict disciplinarian
Turbulent	Violent, stormy
Truculent	Fierce, cruel, aggressive
Vociferous	Loud and noisy

Because vocabulary words lend themselves to the keyword method, construct a keyword for each target word. A good keyword is familiar to learners, sounds like an important part of the target word, and can be included in a picture. Good keywords for these words may include the following:

Vocabulary Word	Keyword	Meaning
Martinet	Martian	A strict disciplinarian
Turbulent	Turtle	Violent, stormy
Truculent	Truck	Fierce, cruel, aggressive
Vociferous	Voice	Loud and noisy

Now, create an illustration of the keyword and meaning interacting in some way that is memorable. This interaction is important so that the retrieval of the illustration prompts recall of the word meaning. For example, a good illustration for *martinet* would be a Martian being a strict disciplinarian, for example, in a school classroom. Possible mnemonic illustrations include the following:

Word	Keyword	Meaning	Picture
Martinet	Martian	A strict disciplinarian	A Martian being a strict disciplinarian
Turbulent	Turtle	Violent, stormy	A turtle swimming through a violent storm
Truculent	Truck	Fierce, cruel, aggressive	A truck with an aggressive driver
Vociferous	Voice	Loud and noisy	A baby with a loud and noisy voice

Once mnemonic elaborations have been constructed, it is best to develop mnemonic illustrations. Although imagery can also be used (by prompting students to imagine mnemonic pictures), it is generally less effective (Scruggs & Mastropieri, 1992). Good pictures should contain clear and direct representations of the necessary information, but not any additional information. For example, in our earlier research, we used no color, unless it was important for the mnemonic picture (as in the *wolframite* example, described previously). Fortunately, mnemonic illustrations, to be effective, do not need to be creative or particularly artistic, if they adequately portray the important information. Other alternatives are using stick figures and cutouts from magazines, selecting an artistic student to draw the appropriate illustrations, or using computer clip art to create relevant illustrations. Such clip art programs can be found installed with some computers, can be purchased at computer stores, or can be found online by searching (e.g., "turtle clip art") and selecting from the alternatives. For example, to represent a turtle in a violent storm, clip art for "turtle" and "storm" can be identified and combined into an effective mnemonic illustration, as shown in Figure 26.1. Such an illustration can be displayed on an overhead projector, on a PowerPoint slide, or on student handouts. The presentation should employ something like the following dialogue:

> *Turbulent* means *violent* or *stormy.* The keyword (or word clue) for *turbulent* is *turtle.* What is the keyword for *turbulent*? [students respond] Good, *turtle.* Remember this picture of a *turtle* in a *violent storm.* Remember this picture of what? [students respond] Good, a turtle in a violent storm. When I ask you for the meaning of *turbulent,* first think back to the keyword, which is . . .? [students respond] *Turtle,* good. Now think back to the picture of the turtle, and remember *what else* is in the picture. In this case, the turtle is . . .? [students respond] In a violent storm, good. So *turbulent* means . . .? [students respond] *Violent* or *stormy,* good. And what word means *violent* or *stormy?* [students respond] *Turbulent,* good.

In some cases, particularly in early stages of mnemonic instruction, students may reply that *turbulent* means *turtle.* In such cases, simply state that *turtle* is not the meaning, but it is the word clue that will help find the meaning, and then repeat the strategy.

Figure 26.1 Mnemonic illustration of *turbulent* = *violent* or *stormy.*

Turbulent (turtle)   **Violent, stormy**

It is also important to consider that mnemonic strategies are intended to facilitate recall of verbal information and are not in themselves strategies for facilitating comprehension. Although mnemonically trained students typically outperform traditionally taught students on comprehension tests (e.g., Mastropieri, Scruggs, & Fulk, 1990), this is because mnemonically instructed students recall more information, which they can bring to bear on comprehension tests. Nevertheless, it is important to determine that students taught mnemonically (or otherwise) understand what they are learning. For these purposes, comprehension strategies (e.g., content elaboration, discussion, examples, applications, hands-on activities, multimedia presentations) can be employed. Above all, memory and comprehension should not be looked at as mutually exclusive competitors, but as important components of all learning tasks. Although students might acquire new verbal information without comprehending it, it is also true that information must first be remembered before it can be employed in any meaningful way.

Table 26.2 provides other examples of how mnemonics might be applied, in this case in a U.S. history class. Examining the content for the World War I unit, a teacher may consider the target information shown in Table 26.2 (Scruggs & Mastropieri, 1989a). Using the method of reconstructive elaborations, effective mnemonic elaborations can be developed for the information, as represented in the table. The teacher then constructs the appropriate mnemonic pictures, using the methods described previously. In a U.S. history lesson, the teacher would select a number of mnemonic illustrations (usually, three to five in a lesson) to present along with the content, using dialogue such as the following:

> The *Zimmerman note* was an important cause of U.S. entry into World War I. Zimmerman was the German Foreign Secretary, who sent a coded note to Mexico asking them to join Germany against the United States, in case the United States entered the war on the side of the Allied Powers. In return, Germany promised former Mexican territory in Texas, Arizona, and New Mexico. This note was intercepted and decoded, caused public outrage in the United States, and contributed to the declaration of war against Germany and its allies.
>
> To help you remember about the Zimmerman note, remember the keyword for *Zimmerman, swimmer.* What is the keyword for *Zimmerman?* [students respond]. *Swimmer,* good. Now [shows picture] remember this picture of a *swimmer* swimming from Germany to Mexico with a *coded note* saying "Mexico: Join us." Remember this picture of what? [students respond]. Good, a *swimmer* with a *coded note.* So when I ask what the Zimmerman note is, what do you answer? [students respond]. Good, a coded note from Germany to Mexico.

Teachers should practice the content and the mnemonic strategy with students several times, until students

Table 26.2   Target Information from a Unit on World War I

Question	Response	Mnemonic Elaboration
What were the countries in the Central Powers?	Turkey (Ottoman Empire), Austria-Hungary, Germany	"TAG" (Turkey, Austria-Hungary, Germany) in *Central Park*
What were the countries in the Allied Powers?	France, Italy, Russia, England	"FIRE" (France, Italy, Russia, England) in an ALLIED van (keyword for *Allied Powers*)
Who was William Jennings Bryan?	Secretary of State, opposed war	A *lion* (keyword for *Bryan*) as secretary at a desk (Secretary of State), urging other animals to *stop fighting* (opposed war)
What was the first U.S. policy?	Not to get involved	*Uncle Sam* (symbol for U.S. policy) looking over at Europe and saying, "*It's not my fight*"
What was the *Lusitania*?	Passenger ship sunk by a German submarine	*Lucy* (keyword for *Lusitania*) on a sinking passenger ship sunk by a German submarine
What was the Zimmerman note?	Coded note from Germany to Mexico, urging Mexico to fight the United States	A *swimmer* (keyword for *Zimmerman*) carrying a coded note from Germany to Mexico
What were the conditions of trench warfare?	Unhealthy, many soldiers became sick	A mimetic (representational) picture of *sick soldiers* in *trenches*
Who was Eddie Rickenbacker?	U.S. flying ace, shot down many enemy airplanes	A *linebacker* (keyword for Rickenbacker) *flying* over a football field, *shooting down* enemy aircraft
Who was George M. Cohan?	Patriotic songwriter, wrote "Over There"	Someone asking a person with an ice cream *cone* (keyword for Cohan) "Where did you get that cone?" with person responding, "*Over There, Over There*"

can clearly retrieve the information. Although mnemonic strategies frequently improve memory, they must be presented clearly, practiced several times by students, and reviewed periodically to be maximally effective.

Fidelity Checklist

Mnemonic instruction is versatile and can be applied in different ways in many different subject areas. For example, Mastropieri et al. (1998) employed mnemonic instruction for important science vocabulary in the context of a hands-on unit on ecosystems. However, in all cases, the following steps should be taken:

- Critical target content identified
- Appropriate mnemonic elaborations constructed
- Clear, relevant mnemonic illustrations developed
- Appropriate delivery of strategy information, with questioning and feedback
- Sufficient guided and independent practice activities
- Periodic review of content and mnemonic strategies

Research Base
Applications

Mnemonic strategies are among the most thoroughly researched techniques in the field of special education and have been applied effectively in a wide variety of content areas, from English vocabulary instruction (Mastropieri, Scruggs, Levin, et al., 1985) to foreign language vocabulary (McLoone et al., 1986), state (Mastropieri & Scruggs, 1989b) and U.S. history (Mastropieri & Scruggs, 1988), and life and earth sciences (King-Sears, Mercer, & Sindelar, 1992; Scruggs & Mastropieri, 1992). These strategies have been successfully employed on elementary (Uberti, Scruggs, & Mastropieri, 2003) and secondary levels (Bulgren, Schumaker, & Deshler, 1994) as well as with students with learning disabilities (Mastropieri, Scruggs, & Levin, 1985), intellectual disability (Mastropieri, Scruggs, Whittaker, & Bakken, 1994), and emotional/behavioral disabilities (Mastropieri, Emerick, & Scruggs, 1988). In addition, students who are normally achieving (Scruggs et al., 1986) and those who are gifted (Scruggs & Mastropieri, 1988) have also benefitted from mnemonic strategies.

Settings

Most of the earlier investigations were conducted in laboratory-type settings, where participants were seen individually in a private area removed from the classroom (e.g., Mastropieri, Scruggs, Levin, et al., 1985). Once the potential efficacy of mnemonic strategies had been demonstrated in these laboratory studies, later investigations were conducted in special education classrooms over longer periods of time (e.g., Mastropieri & Scruggs, 1988). More recently, mnemonic strategy research has been conducted in inclusive classrooms (J. Fontana, Mastropieri, & Scruggs, 2007; Mastropieri, Sweda, & Scruggs, 2000; Uberti et al., 2003). J. Fontana et al. (2007) investigated the use of mnemonic strategies in high school history classes, and they reported that students who were English language learners (ELLs) benefited most from the strategies.

Diversity of Participants

Mnemonic strategy research studies have also included substantial diversity among participants. For example, African American students represented 49% of the sample in the Scruggs, Mastropieri, Brigham, and Sullivan (1992) investigation, 40% of the Scruggs and Mastropieri (1989a) investigation, and 56% of the Mastropieri and Scruggs (1988) investigation. Hispanic students represented 7% of the Scruggs and Mastropieri (1989b) investigation and 19% of the Scruggs, Mastropieri, McLoone, Levin, and Morrison (1987) investigation. In the second experiment of the Mastropieri et al. (1986) investigation, all of the participants were Native Americans. The Mastropieri, Scruggs, Levin, et al. (1985) investigation included 11% Hispanic and 6% Native American students. The J. Fontana et al. (2007) investigation, in inclusive high school history classes, included 17% African American, 19% Hispanic, and 7% Asian participants. As mentioned, in that investigation, the students who benefited most from the mnemonic strategies were ELLs.

Levels of Support and Fidelity of Implementation

In the earliest mnemonic laboratory investigations, researchers delivered the treatments, and all dialogue was read from prepared scripts at a prespecified pace (e.g., Mastropieri, Scruggs, & Levin, 1986; Mastropieri, Scruggs, Levin, et al., 1985). In some classroom applications (e.g., Mastropieri & Scruggs, 1988), teachers were given prepared scripts for the mnemonic portion of the classroom activities and a videotape model for implementing instruction, and observers attended class regularly and evaluated treatment fidelity (J. Fontana et al., 2007). In some inclusive classes (e.g., Mastropieri et al., 2000; Uberti et al., 2003), teachers had less support, developed their own materials, and were more independent with their implementation. Similarly positive outcomes were consistent across these investigations. In other inclusive implementations (J. Fontana et al., 2007; Marshak, Mastropieri, & Scruggs, 2009), fidelity was monitored through teacher logs and direct observation with checklists and was found to be high (e.g., 95% in the Marshak et al., 2009).

Meta-Analysis

Several quantitative research syntheses have been published on the effectiveness of mnemonic instruction in general (Levin, Anglin, & Carney, 1987) and for students with disabilities (Mastropieri & Scruggs, 1989b; Scruggs & Mastropieri, 2000). With respect to high-incidence disabilities, Mastropieri and Scruggs (1989a) summarized the outcomes of 24 experimental investigations of mnemonic instruction, involving 983 students, and reported a very large overall mean effect size of 1.62 ($SD = 0.79$) on criterion-referenced content and vocabulary tests. An effect size of this magnitude means that the average-performing student receiving mnemonic instruction would have scored at the 94.7th percentile of the comparison conditions, who generally received direct-instruction rehearsal, free study, or visual-spatial displays. Stated another way, the average proportion of items correct after instruction for all the comparison conditions, as reported in the original studies, was 43.8%, as compared with 75.0% correct for students instructed mnemonically, an overall difference of nearly 2-to-1.

An updated meta-analysis of mnemonic strategy instruction for students with high-incidence disabilities of 34 experiments was reported by Scruggs and Mastropieri (2000), who identified a virtually identical mean effect size of 1.62 ($SD = 0.84$). Effect sizes were found to be similar across a number of variables, including grade levels, content areas, type of disability of participants, laboratory or field-based setting, and whether Scruggs and Mastropieri were involved as authors. More recently, Wolgemuth, Cobb, and Alwell (2008) summarized all mnemonic research for students with high-incidence disabilities on the secondary level only and reported a mean overall effect size of 1.38. Taken together, these effect sizes are among the largest of any intervention in special education (Forness, 2001).

Adaptations and Modifications

Because mnemonic strategy instruction has itself been considered an adaptation for students who exhibit difficulty learning and remembering new content, adaptations or modifications have not been typically employed. In all cases, students received very direct, explicit instruction on the strategy and, specifically, how it was to be employed, with the assumption that students with high-incidence disabilities would need more support than other types of learners (Scruggs & Mastropieri, 1988). Researchers found that additional instructional sessions were necessary for students with intellectual disability to master mnemonic pegwords (Mastropieri et al., 1986), an issue probably associated with observed rhyming difficulties of students with this disability (M. S. Scott, Perou, Greenfield, & Swanson, 1993). In inclusive settings, it may be that all students do not require mnemonic strategies to learn content adequately. In such cases, adaptations have been created in the form of *differentiated curriculum enhancements,* which employ differential exposure to different instructional procedures (including mnemonics), in order to maximize learning for all students.

Differentiated Curriculum Enhancements

As students with high-incidence disabilities have moved from self-contained to more inclusive settings, concurrently addressing the needs of diverse learners has become a more important issue. One common approach to this problem is *differentiated instruction* (e.g., Tomlinson, 2001), in which students receive different materials or instructional strategies depending on their individual learning needs. One potential problem with such differentiation, however, is that students with high-incidence disabilities may be perceived to be receiving "dumbed-down" materials and instruction and may become stigmatized by this perception. To address this significant problem and to preserve the concept of appropriately differentiated instruction, a model referred to as *differentiated curriculum enhancements* was proposed (Mastropieri et al., 2006). Using this model, all students receive the same materials, and differentiation is built into the instructional program so that each student can differentially benefit, according to individual learning needs. In all cases, class-wide peer tutoring (Greenwood, 1997) or small-group learning is used to individualize instruction.

Rationale

Research has indicated that students with high-incidence disabilities, who generally exhibit relatively low levels of achievement, learn better when (a) time on task is maximized, (b) they are engaged with activities directly relevant to learning objectives, (c) they receive questioning directly relevant to learning objectives, and (d) to-be-learned information is elaborated and effectively linked to prior knowledge (Mastropieri & Scruggs, 2004, 2009). In addition, research has consistently supported the use of peer tutoring for increasing the outcomes of students with high-incidence disabilities (e.g., Greenwood, 1997; Osguthorpe & Scruggs, 1986; Sáenz, McMaster, Fuchs, & Fuchs, 2007). Differentiated curriculum enhancements represent an attempt to place these considerations within a context in which all students work with the same instructional materials. The differentiation occurs when students with special learning needs receive (a) more practice, (b) more time with lower-difficulty levels of the materials, or (c) elaborative learning strategies to be used when needed.

Description and Implementation Procedures

To date, three separate approaches have been applied to enhance learning in inclusive science and social studies classrooms. These approaches are (a) fact sheets, (b) differentiated activities, and (c) embedded mnemonic elaborations.

Fact Sheets

The simplest method of differentiated curriculum enhancements is the development of "fact sheets" to promote learning of critical content area information. Teachers develop a number of fact sheets and corresponding quizzes, which include questions and answers of relevance to unit tests or high-stakes (i.e., state proficiency) tests. For example, one question (of about five per sheet) might be "What kind of molecule is DNA?" with the answer, "Double helix molecule." These sheets are duplicated and placed in folders. Teachers then construct multiple-choice quizzes designed to match the content of fact sheets. Teachers select the frequency of quiz administration but typically administer them before and after a chapter of content. The multiple-choice format of the quizzes enables students to easily administer and score their partner's quizzes.

Students are placed in tutoring pairs using the following process. Students are (discreetly) listed from highest to lowest in terms of academic performance on the target content. Then, the list is divided in the middle. The highest-performing student on the first half of the list is paired with the highest-performing student in the second half of the list, the second highest on the first half with the second highest on the second half, and so on. In this way, student pairs differ in skill level, and the difference in skill level is similar in all peer-tutoring dyads. Students are then informed of their tutoring partners, and given the following directions, in sequence: get with your partner and pick up a tutoring folder; write date, time, and names on the record sheet; take out fact sheets, and begin asking and answering questions with your partner. Students are divided into groups (e.g., "Admirals" and "Generals"), where one group represents the higher-functioning partner.

The higher-functioning tutor begins asking questions of the other student. After a certain amount of time, the students switch roles. Students are provided with rules, including speaking with a quiet voice, cooperating with partners, and correcting responses appropriately. For instance, when a partner answers incorrectly, the tutor might say, "You missed that one, can you try again?" If partially correct, the tutor might say, "Almost—can you think of anything else?" If the partner does not answer within 3 seconds, the tutor might say, "The answer is ____," and then repeat the question. As students master the fact sheets, scores (based on number of correct responses) are recorded, and tutoring pairs move on to the next fact sheet (see also McMaster, Fuchs, & Fuchs, 2006, for a discussion of class-wide peer-tutoring procedures). At designated times partners administer and score quizzes that correspond with the fact sheets, and students record their own performance. Teams may or may not be established within a class to compete against one another.

Using fact sheets, all students receive the same materials, and tutoring sessions can be implemented two or three times a week, for 20 or 30 minutes. Differentiation occurs in the manner in which the fact sheets are implemented. That is, students work on individual fact sheets until they achieve mastery using a predetermined criteria such as 100% on two consecutive trials, pass the quiz, and record the score. Then students practice new fact sheets. Given the peer-tutoring framework, each student receives appropriate individualized practice with the materials as needed. Fact sheets are the simplest of the differentiated curriculum enhancements, with materials that are the easiest to develop and implement, and for this reason may be of particular value to teachers.

Essential components of implementing fact sheets that could be included on fidelity of implementation checklists include:

- Fact sheet materials are designed to cover critical content at appropriate level of difficulty.

- Teachers effectively start and monitor tutoring session.

- Students have appropriate tutoring materials.

- Students administer appropriate prequiz measures.

- Students tutor one another for designated amount of time.

- Students remain on task during tutoring.

- Students administer appropriate postquizzes.

- Students record performance and progress.

- Teachers and students make decisions based on data whether to proceed to the next level of fact sheets.

- Students replace tutoring materials.

- Teachers record anecdotal observation notes from the session.

Differentiated Activities

Some content does not lend itself as readily to question-and-answer tutoring formats. In such cases, students can work in small peer groups to complete comprehension/application tasks on relevant content, depending on student skill level. For example, students in a science unit on scientific methods may need to learn about independent and dependent variables, qualitative and quantitative research questions, and to include data into various graphs and charts. Activities can be provided at three graduated levels, progressing generally from identification (where students identify a correct response from an array) to production (where students produce the correct response) with prompting when needed, to production responses without prompts. As students complete activity areas, they progress toward more complicated applications of the same content.

For each level of difficulty, activity materials are created. For example, for the "Quantitative/Qualitative" activities, Level 1 materials can direct students to read statements on each of a series of cards, and identify whether it was a quantitative or qualitative statement. Level 2 materials may direct students to generate three quantitative and three qualitative observations from each of a series of illustrations, with prompting provided by partners when needed. The final level (Level 3) materials could direct students to generate quantitative and qualitative observations, without any prompting. For an activity on experimental design, students could be directed to match independent with dependent variables (Level 1), and then produce independent and dependent variables, and hypotheses, given one of a series of scenarios, with prompts when needed (Level 2) or without prompts (Level 3). Record-keeping sheets can also be developed, on which students record progress on each of the levels of each of the activities.

Differentiation occurs on several levels. First, some students may not require participation in all levels. For example, when students have demonstrated they have previously identified content, they may be told to skip the identification-level activities. Second, no specified time limit is associated with the activities. In this way students can repeat levels as necessary before proceeding to more advanced levels. Differentiated activities are appropriate when content includes comprehension and application objectives. These are more difficult to develop than fact sheets, and also require some creativity in coming up with relevant game-like activities for each unit. However, once developed (and preferably, laminated), materials can be used over and over again, over a period of years, with different classes. Essential components of implementing differentiated activities that could be included on fidelity of implementation checklists are highly similar to the one described for fact sheets. However, differentiated activities should be designed to directly reflect the learning objectives and be appropriate for the targeted difficulty levels.

Embedded Mnemonic Elaborations

Peer tutoring using fact sheets can also be combined with mnemonic or other elaborative strategies, to be used when needed. For example, tutors can be directed to ask tutoring partners the meaning of *mole* in a chemistry class (i.e., atomic weight in grams of a compound or element). Because *mole* is a complicated concept, additional questioning can be provided when students give the correct answer, such as, "Can you give me an example of a mole?" and, "What else is important about moles?" If tutoring partners have difficulty retrieving the meaning of *mole,* they can be shown a mnemonic elaboration, for example, a picture of a mole (the animal) sitting on a scale, getting its weight in grams. The tutor can read from a supplied script, for example, "To remember that a mole is the atomic weight in grams of a compound or element, remember this picture of a mole on a scale, getting its weight in grams. So, what is a mole?" Other mnemonic strategies could include, for example, for *groups* and *periods* in a periodic table, "*Groups* sounds like *grows,* and plants *grow* up and down, like the groups in the periodic table. *Periods* are at the end of sentences, and sentences are horizontal like the periods on the periodic table."

Embedded mnemonic elaborations are differentiated in that the mnemonic strategies are provided only if students are having difficulty remembering important words (they can be on a separate page or attached to the back of the tutoring sheet). Nevertheless, all students receive the same materials and can use as many, or as few, elaborations as needed. Essential components of implementing embedded mnemonic elaborations that could be included on fidelity of implementation checklists are highly similar to those described for fact sheets and for differentiated activities. However, embedded mnemonic elaborations should be designed to directly reflect the learning objectives and should be concrete, familiar, and meaningful for the targeted sample.

Research Base

Applications

To date, the applications of differentiated curriculum enhancements are far fewer than those of mnemonic strategy instruction, but the number of studies conducted is sufficient to draw some tentative conclusions (Scruggs, Mastropieri, Marshak, & Mills, 2009). These studies include investigations of the use of fact sheets (Mastropieri, Scruggs, & Marshak, 2008; McDuffie, Mastropieri, & Scruggs, 2009; Scruggs, Mastropieri, & Marshak, 2009), differentiated activities (Mastropieri et al., 2006; Simpkins, Mastropieri, & Scruggs, 2009),

and differentiated mnemonic elaborations (Marshak, 2008; Mastropieri, Scruggs, & Graetz, 2005). In each of these studies, students engaged in differentiated curriculum enhancements statistically outperformed students taught by traditional methods, including lecture, questioning, work sheet, and independent study activities.

Settings

Studies to date have been conducted mostly in junior high settings, with one study of Earth and physical science learning (Simpkins et al., 2009) conducted in fifth-grade classes, and one (Mastropieri et al., 2005) conducted in high school chemistry classes. In all cases, students were taught in inclusive science or social studies classrooms, both individually taught and co-taught.

Diversity

Considerable diversity was represented in this set of investigations. For example, the Simpkins et al. (2009) investigation included 23% Asian, 18% African American, 3% Hispanic, and 5% biracial participants. The Mastropieri et al. (2006) investigation included 27% African American, 17% Hispanic, 4% Asian, and 5% multiracial students; whereas the Marshak (2008) investigation included 12% African American, 16% Hispanic, 22% Asian, and 3% multiracial students. Students who were ELLs frequently participated in these studies, however, the sample sizes were often small, and in many cases students were also identified as having other primary disabilities. One qualitative study, however, specifically described ELLs' interaction with differentiated science curriculum enhancements (Norland, 2005). These students reported that the materials contributed to the learning success and that they enjoyed using them more than their traditional science instruction (Norland, 2005).

Levels of Support and Fidelity of Implementation

Although all studies in this area to date employed teachers as intervention agents, in every case teachers received considerable support from research staff, including materials development and training. In some investigations (e.g., Scruggs, Mastropieri, & Marshak, 2009), teachers played a role in content selection and material development. In all cases, teachers kept logs documenting their implementation practices, and classes were observed regularly with fidelity checklists to ensure materials and methods were implemented appropriately. Fidelity ranged from 95% to 100% in Scruggs, Mastropieri, and Marshak (2009) and was 95% in Marshak et al. (2009). In other investigations (e.g., J. Fontana et al., 2007;

McDuffie et al., 2009), implementation integrity was reported as number of minutes per teaching component across conditions.

Research Support

In all cases, students in classes employing differentiated curriculum enhancements outperformed students taught by more traditional methods. In the differentiated activities studies (Mastropieri et al., 2006; Simpkins et al., 2009), mean effect sizes were in the mid 0.30s. However, these included a significant effect for the standardized end-of-year high-stakes test in science in the Mastropieri et al. investigation. This outcome was somewhat surprising, because that study was conducted over a small proportion of the entire school year (12 weeks). It was hypothesized that the effect may have been greater because the content selected (scientific method) had applications to all other science units.

For the fact sheet investigations (Mastropieri et al., 2008; McDuffie et al., 2009; Scruggs, Mastropieri, & Marshak, 2009), effect sizes were somewhat higher, in the 0.50 to 0.60 range. These effect sizes are consistent with, or a little larger than, previous meta-analyses of peer tutoring (e.g., S. Cook, Scruggs, Mastropieri, & Casto, 1985–1986). The embedded mnemonic elaborations yielded much higher mean effect sizes, of 0.84 (general education) and 1.22 (special education), more consistent with effect sizes found in meta-analyses of mnemonic instruction in content area learning (Scruggs, Mastropieri, Berkeley, & Graetz, 2010). Overall, research outcomes to date have been in the moderate-to-high effect range and have been consistently positive. In addition, in all studies to date, students and teachers have commented positively on the procedures.

Overall, seven experimental studies on differentiated curriculum enhancements have been conducted in science and social studies, with implementation periods of 8 to 18 weeks ($M = 11.14$ weeks). All interventions produced a statistically significant advantage over traditional instruction. The studies included 940 students (702 general education students and 315 special education and ELL students). Across all models, the overall average effect size was 0.55 for typical learners and 0.76 for at-risk students, ELLs, and students with disabilities. The higher overall effect size for students with disabilities and other special learning needs may indicate that these students benefit differentially from enhanced practice, activities, and learning strategies. Nevertheless, the effect size of 0.55 for general education students is sufficiently substantial to merit the use of these strategies in inclusive classrooms.

Summary

Overall, existing research provides strong support for both mnemonic strategy instruction and differentiated curriculum enhancements. The research base for mnemonics is among the most substantial in special education; research supporting differentiated curriculum enhancements is more limited but includes a substantial number of students, classrooms, and content areas across seven replication studies. Perhaps one reason for the success of these approaches is that they interact favorably with the characteristics of students with high-incidence disabilities. It appears that students with problems with verbal learning and memory benefit from mnemonic strategies, and that generalized low achievement is ameliorated by increased academic engagement afforded by peer mediation and learning materials targeted to learning needs.

In spite of the observed positive outcomes, several limitations can be noted. Mnemonic instruction has been demonstrated to be very effective; however, these effects are generally limited to initial acquisition and retention of specified verbal content. Such objectives are of great importance but are not the only school learning objectives. Additional strategies are needed to address other objectives, such as fluency development, comprehension, and application. Future research could address how mnemonic instruction can effectively be combined into an integrated program of instruction, incorporating a variety of instructional objectives, over significant instructional periods.

Research in differentiated curriculum enhancements is recent and in need of further replication, particularly across grade levels and subject areas. In addition, evidence is needed about teacher receptivity to the approaches, particularly with respect to issues of materials development and classroom organization. Scruggs, Mastropieri, and McDuffie (2007) observed that general education teachers may be reluctant to depart significantly from traditional classroom routines, and strategies for encouraging teachers to implement more research-based practices in inclusive classrooms could be of particular importance.

Mnemonic strategies and differentiated curriculum enhancements represent only a small fraction of the range of instructional and behavioral strategies now available for students with high-incidence disabilities (see Parts 1 and 2 of this volume). Taken in conjunction with these other strategies, teachers have a wide variety of effective treatments available for substantially improving the school experiences of students with high-incidence disabilities.

CHAPTER 27

Teaching Individuals with Severe Intellectual Disability: *Effective Instructional Practices*

Susan R. Copeland and **Kay Osborn** | *University of New Mexico*

*B*efore beginning a discussion of effective interventions for persons identified as having severe intellectual disability, it is useful to first describe who these individuals are. The most widely used current definition of intellectual disability states that it is "characterized by significant limitations both in intellectual functioning and in adaptive behavior as expressed in conceptual, social, and practical adaptive skills. This disability originates before age 18" (Schalock et al., 2010, p. 5). To better provide services, researchers and others have further classified individuals within this broad disability based on a measure of the severity of their disability. Before 1992, IQ scores were the major method used to classify individuals with intellectual disability. Some organizations, such as the World Health Organization, continue to use this method of classification. According to this system, individuals scoring between 25 and 40 on a standardized assessment of intelligence were classified as having severe intellectual disability. Beginning in 1992, the American Association on Mental Retardation (now known as the American Association on Intellectual and Developmental Disability [AAIDD]) eliminated IQ-based categories and instead recommended categorization based on the level and intensity of individuals' needs for support (i.e., the activities, resources, or strategies that assist individuals to function more successfully in their environment) (Schalock et al., 2010). The underlying premise of a supports-based classification model is that provision of necessary supports will result in improved outcomes for the individual. In a supports-based classification system, individuals with severe intellectual disability would be those most likely to require support across the majority of areas of their life for sustained periods of time (Beirne-Smith, Patton, & Kim, 2006).

Research reviewed for this chapter spans several decades, so participants in reviewed studies were likely assigned classifications based on different systems, depending on the time period within which they were identified as having an intellectual disability. To ensure consistency in the manner in which we use the term *severe intellectual disability,* we will adhere to Beirne-Smith and colleagues' (2006) statement that "the 'severe' label encompasses the groups specifically designated as having moderate, severe, and profound levels of mental retardation" (p. 294).

General Learning Characteristics of Persons with Severe Intellectual Disability

Individuals with severe intellectual disability comprise a heterogeneous group (Beirne-Smith et al., 2006). Each individual has unique learning needs and also skill areas that are relative strengths. The effect of low expectations on the learning abilities of this group of individuals must be considered. Historically, educators and others have had few expectations for individuals with severe intellectual disability to acquire skills beyond basic functional tasks (Browder, Spooner, Wakeman, Trela, & Baker, 2006), which too often resulted in limited opportunities for these students to learn more complex skills. Given the pervasiveness of these limited opportunities, it is not always possible to make completely definitive conclusions about what these individuals can and cannot learn.

Nonetheless, a number of learning challenges widely observed with this group of individuals merit consideration when selecting content for instruction and instructional methods. Many individuals with severe intellectual disability, for example, experience difficulty in both understanding spoken language and producing it (Reichle, 1997). Because of the foundational nature of language, language and communication delays and impairments significantly affect all areas of learning. This includes social and behavioral skills and the ability to acquire related academic skills, such as literacy.

Difficulty attending to relevant cues in a given situation is another learning challenge for many persons with severe intellectual disability (K. W. Heller, Forney, Alberto, Best, & Schwartzman, 2009). Sensory and motor challenges may further affect the ability to focus or respond to instruction (K. W. Heller et al., 2009). A related problem is difficulty with memory, particularly short-term memory. These complexities, combined with language impairments, can affect the ability of individuals with severe intellectual disability to organize and synthesize several different skills needed to complete activities comprised of multiple components (L. Brown et al., 1983). For example, a student may have learned the component skills necessary to purchase lunch in the school cafeteria in a classroom setting (i.e., coin identification, basic sight-word vocabulary, social greeting responses). However, when faced with buying lunch in the actual cafeteria during the lunch period, the student may not be able to use the necessary skills to accomplish the task.

Another common learning challenge for persons with severe intellectual disability is transferring (generalizing) information learned in one context to a novel or different context or to novel materials or people (L. Brown et al., 1983). This problem requires instructors to teach in a manner that facilitates generalization, such as carefully selecting multiple teaching examples that represent the range of situations in which targeted skills may be needed (i.e., general case instruction), using authentic materials that are common to the environments that individuals will encounter, and teaching skills that are likely to be reinforced in natural settings (Fox, 1989).

Difficulty establishing social relationships is another widespread challenge for individuals with severe intellectual disability (K. W. Heller et al., 2009). Multiple factors contribute to this difficulty, such as having limited communication skills and trouble reading social cues, as well as a lack of access to peers because of receiving educational services exclusively with other individuals who also have significant limitations in social competence (Schwartz, Staub, Peck, & Gallucci, 2006). Effective means to address these issues seem to combine teaching social skills directly in inclusive settings where the skills will be used and where individuals with severe disability can observe competent peer models (Schwartz et al., 2006).

Researchers and others have developed and examined a number of highly effective instructional practices that assist persons with severe intellectual disability across the age range to acquire and use skills in many different environments. In the following sections, we describe three such research-based practices: prompting, task analysis, and self-management. Within each of these sections, we define the practice, describe the research base supporting it, describe how to implement it successfully with this population of students, and provide suggestions for continued research on the practice. We selected these three practices because of their foundational nature. These practices can be used in home, school (general and special education settings), community, and employment settings; and research supports their use with individuals ranging from young children to adults. All are derived from behavioral theory, specifically, from the field of applied behavior analysis.

Prompting

A prompt is a stimulus that sets the occasion for the targeted response when it is paired with the natural cue (i.e., the discriminative stimulus) (J. O. Cooper, Heron, & Heward, 2007). A prompt provides information that lets a student know how or when to perform a task. Educators use prompts to reduce errors when individuals are acquiring new skills but then fade the prompts as the new skill becomes more fluent. Prompts are considered to be an antecedent strategy (i.e., specific, planned actions before a student responds) and are derived from the field of applied behavior analysis (Browder, Ahlgrim-Delzell, Spooner, Mims, & Baker, 2009).

Response Prompts

Researchers categorize instructional prompts in several different ways. Response prompts are the actions a teacher takes before the student responds or after an incorrect response that help the student make a correct response (J. O. Cooper et al., 2007). These include verbal cues, gestures, modeling, or full or partial physical assistance. Prompts may be provided before a student responds, such as with simultaneous prompting, or provided in the form of feedback after a student responds (e.g., "That isn't correct. Do that problem again."). Research supports use of response prompts in teaching both discrete and chained (i.e., multistep) tasks (Wolery, Ault, Gast, Doyle, & Griffen, 1990).

Simultaneous prompting is a type of response prompt that is considered an errorless learning strategy. It may be effective for individuals with severe intellectual disability who become upset when they make a mistake or those who are easily confused by errors (Browder, 2001). When using this strategy, the teacher presents the natural cue for the targeted behavior and simultaneously provides the controlling prompt (Morse & Schuster, 2004). A controlling prompt is one that "consistently produces the target behavior" (Wolery et al., 1992, p. 240). For example, a teacher using this strategy to teach sight words shows the student a printed word (the natural cue) (e.g., milk) while simultaneously reading the word aloud (modeling the correct response), and then instructs the student to read the word using simultaneous prompting (e.g., "This word is *milk*. Read *milk*."). The teacher's model demonstrates to the student how to respond, increasing the likelihood of success.

After several trials using the simultaneous prompt, the teacher assesses the student's performance by presenting the natural cue without the prompt. These trials are called probes and occur before the instructional session so the teacher can assess whether stimulus control has shifted from the controlling prompt to the natural cue. Returning to our sight-word example, after one or more sessions using the model as a controlling prompt, the teacher would present the printed target word(s) and ask the student to read the word without providing the model. She would then record the student's performance and use this information to determine whether the student needed additional sessions with the simultaneous prompt or was ready to move to new words.

Morse and Schuster (2004) reviewed 17 studies examining simultaneous prompting on acquisition of both discrete and chained tasks in one-to-one and small-group instructional arrangements. Individuals with severe intellectual disability across the age range from preschool to adulthood made up a large segment of the participants in these studies (approximately 19 of 74 total participants). Findings indicated that simultaneous prompting was effective in helping participants with severe intellectual disability acquire a range of skills including communication, vocational, and self-care/domestic skills within school and vocational training settings. Participants acquired skills with generally low error rates and generalized and maintained the skills they learned.

Simultaneous prompting has also been used to teach academic skills. Rao and Kane (2009) used simultaneous prompting to teach two middle school students with intellectual disability (one who had severe intellectual disabilities) in a self-contained classroom to subtract decimals using regrouping. Both students acquired the skill, maintained it, and demonstrated generalization of the skill across settings, materials, and persons.

Morse and Schuster (2004) noted that simultaneous prompting is easy for teachers to learn and implement. It doesn't require students to have a wait time that teachers must monitor or for teachers to set up a predetermined hierarchy of prompts (e.g., starting with a verbal prompt, then using a model prompt if the student doesn't respond, and finally using a physical prompt if the student still does not respond). Use of a single controlling prompt rather than a hierarchy may also make it a more time-efficient procedure than other prompting methods.

Typically, teachers or other adults have been the instructors in studies examining response prompts. Nevertheless, some researchers have successfully trained parents to use response prompts to teach skills (e.g., Denny et al., 2000). Other researchers have examined use of response prompts to teach academic skills to small groups of students versus in one-to-one formats. Some of these groups have included individuals with severe intellectual disabilities as well as peers who are typically developing (e.g., Fickel, Schuster, & Collins, 1998; Schoen & Ogden, 1995). This group of studies demonstrated positive outcomes for all students in the instructional groups and support use of response prompts within general education settings, thereby adding evidence of their utility with students with diverse abilities.

Fading Response Prompts

To avoid prompt dependency, the teacher should transfer stimulus control from the prompt to the natural cue as soon as the student's performance warrants this. Researchers have developed several systems to promote stimulus transfer. These include the *most-to-least* prompting hierarchy (sometimes called *the system of most prompts*), the least-to-most prompting hierarchy (sometimes called *the system of least prompts*), graduated guidance, and time delay.

A *most-to-least prompting hierarchy* begins with the instructor providing the maximum level of prompt required for the individual to be successful and then fading to a less intrusive level of prompt as the individual begins to acquire the new skill (Demchak, 1990). Often this begins with a physical prompt, gradually moving to a verbal prompt, and then to no external prompt. This strategy has been used successfully to teach individuals with severe intellectual disability functional tasks such as self-care, dressing, and food preparation (Demchak, 1990).

When using the *least-to-most prompting hierarchy*, the teacher provides the natural cue and waits a predetermined amount of time for the student to respond (e.g., 3 seconds). If the student gives no response or an incorrect response, the teacher provides the least-intrusive level of prompt possible and again waits for the student to respond. If the student still gives no response, the teacher then provides the next most-intrusive prompt, and so on, until the student successfully responds. The system of least prompts has been used to teach both discrete and chained tasks and is one of the most widely used techniques for learners with severe intellectual disability (P. M. Doyle, Wolery, Ault, & Gast, 1988). Diverse tasks involving language, social, employment, self-care, and motor skills have been successfully taught to this group of learners using a system of least prompts.

Time delay is a stimulus-fading procedure with a strong evidence base (Browder et al., 2009). The two types of time delay are constant and progressive. A teacher using constant time delay secures the student's attention, presents the natural cue, asks the student to make the correct response, and then gives a several-second delay before providing an additional prompt. On the initial trials, the teacher uses a 0-second delay by modeling the correct response immediately after providing the natural cue (just like simultaneous prompting, described earlier). As soon as the student responds correctly, the teacher provides reinforcement for correct responding. Once the student has had several opportunities to succeed with a 0-second delay, the teacher increases the time-delay interval to a predetermined length (e.g., 4 seconds) and continues this delay interval until the student consistently responds without need of prompts. The increased delay gives the student an opportunity to make a correct response. If the student does not respond within the delay interval or makes a mistake, the teacher provides error correction and prompts the student to perform the task correctly (e.g., "No, write the number 6."). Constant time delay is an especially useful strategy for individuals who do best when they make

few errors in acquiring a new skill or who might become dependent on the teacher's prompts (U. C. Miller & Test, 1989). Numerous research studies have shown constant time delay effective in teaching discrete and chained tasks to individuals with severe intellectual disability in both one-to-one and small-group teaching formats using teachers and peer tutors to deliver instruction (e.g., B. C. Collins, Branson, & Hall, 1995; Schoen & Ogden, 1995).

With *progressive time delay*, the length of the delay after the 0-second delay trials is gradually and systematically extended across time (Demchak, 1990). The teacher may go from a zero delay to a 2-second delay for several sessions and then to a 4-second delay, then a 6-second delay, and so on. Although more complex to implement than constant time delay, it can be useful for persons who need a gradual withdrawal of prompts. For example, researchers have successfully used progressive time delay to teach purchasing skills (Frederick-Dugan, Test, & Varn, 1991), recreation skills (S. Chen, Zhang, Lange, Miko, & Joseph, 2001), and vocational skills (e.g., Walls, Dowler, Haught, & Zawlocki, 1984).

Graduated guidance, a variation of using physical prompts, is most often used with chained tasks (Snell & Brown, 2011). The teacher begins by using hand-over-hand guidance to assist the student to perform the targeted task. Next, the teacher moves his or her hand either slightly away from the student and shadows the required movement or changes the position of the physical prompt (J. O. Cooper et al., 2007). For example, to teach students to write their names, teachers first put their hand over their students' hands as students form the letter. Once students have acquired some fluency, teachers move their hand to students' wrists, then to students' elbows, and then fade the physical prompt completely. Graduated guidance has been used to successfully teach a range of functional and play skills to individuals with severe intellectual disability (e.g., Reese & Snell, 1991). Denny and colleagues (2000), for example, described parents using graduated guidance to teach their preschool child with severe intellectual and motor disabilities to feed himself and engage in a play activity. The mother used a four-level procedure to teach the child to spoon feed, and the mother and father used a three-level procedure to teach the child to roll a ball back and forth to another individual. The child maintained both skills across a 1-year period. Snell and Brown (2011) recommended using graduated guidance when other prompting systems have not succeeded and using it during early acquisition stages of learning a new task.

Comparison of Response Prompting Procedures

Research comparing use of each type of prompting system with individuals with severe intellectual disability in terms of efficiency (e.g., number of trials to criterion, number of errors) and effectiveness has found each of these systems more effective than simple error correction (P. M. Doyle et al., 1988). Constant and progressive time delays appear more efficient than a system of least prompts with both discrete and chained tasks (Demchak, 1990; Wolery et al., 1990, 1992). Comparisons between the most-to-least prompting and system of least prompts have yielded mixed results (P. M. Doyle et al., 1988). Demchak's review of the literature indicated that the most-to-least prompting might be more effective when teaching for acquisition, whereas the system of least prompts might be more effective in teaching for fluency (i.e., building accuracy and speed).

Stimulus Prompts

Many individuals with severe intellectual disability have difficulty attending to the relevant aspect of a stimulus, making it difficult to discriminate between two stimuli. Stimulus prompts (sometimes called *stimulus modification*) are changes to instructional materials that cue the student to make a correct discrimination (i.e., response) (J. O. Cooper et al., 2007). For example, color coding the start and stop buttons on a portable DVD player make it easier to choose correctly when operating the machine. Ault and colleagues (1989) reviewed research comparing stimulus prompts with other prompting systems and found stimulus prompts to produce fewer errors for individuals with severe intellectual disability than response prompting or simple error correction. Combining stimulus prompts with response-prompting methods was found to be especially effective.

Just as with response prompts, it is critical to transfer stimulus control from a stimulus prompt to the natural cue. The first method of stimulus transfer, stimulus fading, involves changing one or more dimensions of the stimulus prompt to make it more salient to the learner and fading this change over time. For example, in our previous DVD player example, we could make the color on the buttons more and more transparent across time until it is completely eliminated. Researchers have used this method successfully with learners with severe intellectual disability to teach skills such as word and shape recognition (e.g., McGee & McCoy, 1981; Schreibman, 1975; Sheehy, 2002; Strand & Morris, 1986).

Stimulus shaping, another stimulus transfer method that facilitates skill acquisition, is done by presenting incorrect items (i.e., distractor stimuli) with the natural stimulus that are initially very different from the natural stimulus on one or more dimensions (e.g., size and color). Over time, distractor stimuli are changed to be more like the natural stimulus, requiring the student to make increasingly fine discriminations between the two. For example,

to teach recognition of the letter *b,* the teacher would first pair it with letters that look very different (e.g., *w, z*) and gradually add pairings with letters of a similar shape (e.g., *p, d*). Using this method, individuals with severe intellectual disability have successfully learned skills such as self-care (Mosk & Bucher, 1984), number and word recognition (e.g., Repp, Karsh, & Lentz, 1990; B. F. Walsh & Lamberts, 1979), and discrimination between photographs (Graff & Green, 2004).

Utilizing Prompting with Fidelity

Selecting and implementing the most effective prompting strategy for a given individual requires paying careful attention to the individual's learning history and characteristics and to the type of task being taught. Figure 27.1 provides general considerations for implementation of the various response-prompting strategies based on reviews of the research. Many excellent resources describe in detail how to implement prompting strategies effectively (e.g., Dogoe & Banda, 2009; Morse & Schuster, 2004; Snell & Brown, 2011); the reader is encouraged to consult one of these for additional information on how to implement prompting as designed.

Summary

A broad research base that spans over 30 years and comprises over 100 studies supports the use of response and stimulus prompts to teach individuals with severe intellectual disability. Researchers examining prompting with this population have primarily used single-case research designs. Examination of the research in this area indicates that the majority of studies are methodologically sound. Researchers demonstrated reliable measurement of participants' behaviors, and many, but not all, assessed procedural fidelity.

Prompting often forms the underlying basis on which other instructional approaches are founded. For example, task analysis instruction, discussed in the next section, typically incorporates prompting to teach each task step. Given the strong empirical support for the use of prompting and the fact that it is more effective than simple error correction (P. M. Doyle et al., 1988), it is critical that educators and others understand how to use prompting effectively with individuals with severe intellectual disability.

One aspect of response prompting that appears to be under-researched is its use in general education and inclusive community settings. Researchers have expressed concern that use of highly specialized instructional practices, such as response prompting, within general education settings may stigmatize students with extensive

Figure 27.1 Checklist for use of response prompts.

Simultaneous Prompting

1. Select a task that is meaningful for the individual student.

2. Choose the least-intrusive controlling prompt that has been shown previously to be successful for that individual and that matches the features of the teaching task. Modeling has been used most often in research studies in this area (e.g., Rao & Kane, 2009).

3. Secure the student's attention before teaching on each trial during instruction.

4. Provide the target stimulus and the controlling prompt simultaneously (0-second delay). Consider providing a minimum of two instructional sessions at this level before conducting probe sessions.

5. Provide specific feedback after the student responds versus more general (e.g., "Good, you read *milk*" instead of "Great work").

6. Provide probe sessions immediately before each teaching session, and collect data on student's error rate. Use these data to determine when to introduce new items to instruction. Criterion most often used in research was 100% correct responding for 3 consecutive probe sessions (e.g., Fickel et al., 1998).

Most-to-Least Prompting Hierarchy

1. Choose which prompts fit the student's learning needs, and arrange in order from most to least intrusive; select a length of delay between the natural cue and the prompt (e.g., 3 second). Base this on knowledge of the student's prior learning.

2. Decide what will be the criterion to move from one prompt level to the next (e.g., 5 trials with 100% accuracy). Base this on the student's prior learning history.

3. Provide the natural cue (instruction for the task); wait using the delay time. If the student fails to respond or responds incorrectly, provide the first level of prompt. Reinforce any correct prompted or unprompted responses using specific feedback.

4. Collect data on student's error rates. Use these data to determine when to move up the prompt levels according to the predetermined criterion.

Least-to-Most Prompting Hierarchy

1. Choose which prompts fit the student's learning needs, and arrange in order from least to most intrusive; select the length of delay time between presentation of the natural cue and the prompt based on the student's prior learning history (e.g., 3 second). Note that the research literature generally used 4 or more prompt levels for individuals with severe intellectual disability.

2. Choose the criterion to move from one prompt level to the next (e.g., 5 trials with 100% accuracy). Base this on the student's prior learning history.

3. Provide the natural cue (instruction for the task); wait using the delay time (researchers have used 2- to 30-second delays, with most using 4- to 10-second delays; e.g., P. M. Doyle et al., 1988). If the student fails to respond or responds incorrectly, provide the first level of prompt. Reinforce any correct prompted or unprompted responses using specific feedback. If the student gives no response or an incorrect response, present the next most-intrusive prompt on the next trial.

4. Collect data on student's error rates. Use these data to determine when to move down the prompt levels according to the predetermined criterion.

Constant Time Delay

1. Choose the most effective prompt for the individual that is also the least intrusive; this should be based on the student's learning history.

2. Select the delay interval. Researchers have used 2- to 5-second delays; some experts recommend use of a 4-second delay (e.g., Snell & Brown, 2011). Consider the student's learning characteristics, the features of the task, and observations of peers who are typically developing performing the task.

3. Begin with one or more trials at 0-second delay (i.e., providing natural cue and controlling prompt simultaneously), and then move to trials using the predetermined delay interval. Criteria to increase the delay varied across studies; most researchers used 1, 2, or 3 consecutive correct 0-second delay sessions as the criterion to move to the longer interval (e.g., Dogoe & Banda, 2009).

Constant Time Delay *(continued)*

4. Interrupt errors with the predetermined prompt. Reinforce correct unprompted and prompted responses using specific feedback. Plan to thin the reinforcement schedule as the student becomes more proficient.

5. Collect data on student error rates, and use these to make instructional decisions. If errors do not decrease, return to several trials at 0-second delay.

Progressive Time Delay

1. Choose the most effective prompt for the individual that is also the least intrusive; this should be based on the student's learning history.

2. Select the delay intervals. Consider the student's learning characteristics, the features of the task, and observations of peers who are typically developing performing the task. Researchers have typically used 3- to 5-second delays (e.g., Collins et al., 1993).

3. Decide what will be criterion to move from one delay level (i.e., time interval) to another. Researchers have used varied criteria, ranging from 67% to 100% correct responding on a single trial to 100% correct on 2 to 5 consecutive trials (e.g., Collins et al., 1993).

4. Begin with one or more trials at 0-second delay (i.e., providing natural cue and controlling prompt simultaneously) and then move to trials using the first predetermined delay interval. After criterion is reached at this level, move to the next level, and so on.

5. Interrupt errors with the predetermined prompt. Reinforce correct unprompted and prompted responses using specific feedback. Plan to thin the reinforcement schedule as the student becomes more proficient.

6. Collect data on student error rates and use that information to make instructional decisions. If errors do not decrease, return to several trials at previous delay interval.

Graduated Guidance

1. Determine each level of physical guidance for the individual student (e.g., full physical prompt at hand, gradual lessening of pressure to light touch, shadowing). Selection should be based on student's individual learning characteristics. Arrange these in order from most intrusive to least intrusive.

2. Determine a delay interval to use before providing a level of physical guidance (researchers often used 5-second delay). Select a criterion for moving from one level to the next (e.g., 3 consecutive trials with 100% accuracy).

3. Provide the instruction to begin the task, use the predetermined wait time, and provide the first level of physical guidance if student does not respond or responds incorrectly. When student meets criterion, move to next level of physical guidance and so on until student is performing task independently.

4. Interrupt errors with the level of guidance used on a prior trial; reinforce correct prompted and unprompted responses using specific feedback.

5. Collect data on student error rates. Use these data to determine when to lessen physical guidance according to the predetermined criterion. Researchers' criteria varied, but many used 3 consecutive trials of correct response at one prompt level before moving to a less-intrusive prompt (Denny et al., 2000).

support needs or that their use might disrupt the typical routines in these settings (McDonnell, 1998). Some evidence suggests that prompting can be used within general education environments in nonstigmatizing ways with individuals with severe intellectual disability (e.g., see the work of McDonnell and colleagues on embedded instruction, e.g., Jameson, McDonnell, Johnson, Riesen, & Polychronis, 2007). A small group of studies has examined use of prompting strategies with students without disabilities. This is promising and is also an area in need of additional research. Finally, relatively few studies have investigated prompting to teach complex academic tasks (Dogoe & Banda, 2009). As educators provide more students with severe intellectual disability the opportunity to acquire academic skills, this is also an area for future research.

Task Analysis

Task analysis essentially involves breaking a complex skill or activity down into a series of smaller steps and teaching someone to perform the steps in sequence. Its origins, like many other successful practices for persons with severe disabilities, are within applied behavior analysis. The steps in a task analysis are called a *behavioral chain* (Alberto & Troutman, 2009). Each response in the behavior chain acts as a cue (i.e., a discriminative stimulus) for the next behavior in the chain. Individuals perform one step in the chain, which cues them to perform the next step, and so on until they reach the end of the chain and receive some type of reinforcement. Consider, for example, that many of us download driving directions from Mapquest to travel from where we live or work to a new destination. We carefully follow each step in the directions (task analysis), with each step prompting the next until we arrive at the desired location. Our reinforcement consists of the satisfaction of having arrived without getting lost.

Task analysis is one of the most commonly used instructional strategies with students with extensive support needs. Task analysis instruction may be especially helpful for individuals with severe intellectual disability because it supports difficulties with short-term memory by breaking a complex task down into single, discrete steps that can be mastered and chained together. A task analysis is also easily individualized for a student's particular needs. This feature can be particularly important for students with severe intellectual disability who may have additional conditions that affect their learning and require individualization. Reese and Snell (1991), for example, designed individualized task analyses for three young students with intellectual disability and accompanying sensory and motor difficulties that took into account each student's unique learning challenges (e.g., modifying steps for a child who had difficulty using one arm) so that all the students could succeed.

Task analyses are also useful instructional tools because they can perform several functions. These include serving as (a) an initial form of assessment to determine which component skills within a task or activity a student may have already mastered; (b) a plan for instruction (breaking down a task into teachable steps); and (c) a means of progress monitoring (collecting frequent information on student progress in acquiring a targeted skill) (F. Brown, Lehr, & Snell, 2011).

Types of Task Analyses

Behavior chains can be taught using three methods: forward chaining, backward chaining, and total task presentation. Forward chaining begins by teaching the first task step and then proceeding sequentially through the steps as each is mastered. Training does not proceed to the next step until a preset criterion is mastered on the first step. Researchers have used forward chaining to teach a variety of skills. For example, J. McDonnell and McFarland (1988) used forward chaining to teach four high school students with severe intellectual disability

to operate a commercial washing machine and laundry soap dispenser. They taught students these behavioral chains beginning with the first step. Once students could perform that step independently for three consecutive trials, instruction began on the next step in the chain and so on until the entire chain was performed independently.

Backward chaining, another method of teaching chained tasks, involves beginning instruction with the last step; and when that is mastered, teaching the last two steps, then the last three steps, and so on (Farlow & Snell, 2006). It has been widely used with individuals with severe intellectual disability (J. McDonnell & Laughlin, 1989). For example, Hagopian, Farrell, and Amari (1996) taught a 12-year-old boy with intellectual disability and autism to swallow liquids from a cup using a backward chaining procedure. They noted that if an individual does not display a target behavior at all or very infrequently, then backward chaining may be a useful instructional procedure. This may be because this method makes a more salient connection for the student between the final step (which can act as a natural reinforcer) and the preceding steps. In other words, it promotes understanding of how the steps are linked and creates more immediate access to reinforcement.

Total task presentation (sometimes called *whole task* or *total task approach*) requires teaching each step of the behavioral chain every time the skill is taught (J. O. Cooper et al., 2007). Many academic chains, such as addition with regrouping, are taught in this manner (Alberto & Troutman, 2009). An advantage of using this format is that the student can experience the functional outcome of the task (i.e., receive the natural reinforcer for the task) every time the skill is practiced (similar to backward chaining). This outcome may enhance students' understanding of why an activity is being taught and what is its purpose. However, with long and complex tasks, total task presentation may require large amounts of instructional time and may be so complicated that it interferes with student learning (Farlow & Snell, 2006). Despite this, numerous researchers have used total task presentation successfully in teaching a range of tasks: self-care and domestic skills (e.g., R. D. Horner & Keilitz, 1975; U. C. Miller & Test, 1989); purchasing skills (e.g., J. McDonnell & Laughlin, 1989; Morse & Schuster, 2004), cooking skills (e.g., Griffen, Wolery, & Schuster, 1992; Wright & Schuster, 1994), vocational skills (e.g., Chandler, Schuster, & Stevens, 1993; Walls et al., 1981), safety skills (e.g., B. C. Collins, Stinson, & Land, 1993), and academic skills (Rao & Kane, 2009).

Several researchers have compared the effectiveness of these three methods of teaching task analysis (e.g., J. McDonnell & McFarland, 1988; Walls et al., 1981). Results indicate that total task presentation is more efficient and effective in teaching complex, chained tasks to individuals with severe intellectual disability, although some results are mixed (J. McDonnell & Laughlin, 1989). Particular aspects of certain tasks or unique learning characteristics of some individuals likely make one method more effective than another in different circumstances. Therefore, teachers and other instructors should take into consideration their knowledge of the student and the task being taught when selecting the type of task analysis.

Task Analysis Instruction

A response prompt method typically is used to teach the steps of a task analysis, regardless of which task analysis format is being used. An examination of the literature indicates that all the response prompt procedures have been used to successfully teach chained tasks. Certain prompting systems seem more effective or efficient in certain situations, however. A comparison of using least-prompts hierarchies with constant time delay to teach chained tasks to individuals with severe intellectual disability found constant time delay most efficient (P. M. Doyle et al., 1988). Comparisons of the effectiveness of constant time delay versus a system of most prompts to teach chained tasks via task analysis have shown mixed results. U. C. Miller and Test (1989) compared these two prompting systems and found that although both methods assisted students with severe intellectual disability in acquiring task-analyzed laundry skills, constant time delay resulted in less instructional time and fewer student errors. However, J. McDonnell and Ferguson (1989) compared the two methods in teaching banking skills to high school students with severe disability and found time delay less efficient. These findings suggest that the instructor should take the learning characteristics of each student and the features of the task into consideration when selecting a prompting system to teach the task analysis.

Instruction using task analysis has been criticized by some experts as being too focused on teaching subskills and not focused on teaching for understanding (M. Carter & Kemp, 1996). Yet, careful construction of a task analysis can create opportunities for individuals to acquire more than merely the motor skills involved in a task (Browder, 2001). In fact, students can learn what F. Brown and colleagues (2011) called "extension skills" (p. 93) within the context of task analysis instruction. These critical skills include self-initiating the task, making choices, problem solving, using social or communication skills, or self-monitoring performance. K. J. Cooper and Browder (1998), for example, described a study in which three adults with severe intellectual disability increased independent performance on the steps of a purchasing task when choices were included within

the task analysis (e.g., selecting which door to enter the restaurant, selecting which food item to order). These individuals knew how to make choices but did not do so until choices were embedded within the task and they were taught to make selections. The authors suggested that adding choice-making instruction to the task analysis may have enhanced the participants' motivation to perform other task steps, or it may have increased the salience of the discriminative stimulus for each step, and thus helped participants recognize what behaviors were required.

Although most often teachers use task analysis instruction for one student at a time, research supports using small-group instruction (e.g., three to four students) to teach chained responses (Reese & Snell, 1991; Wall & Gast, 1999). Griffen and colleagues (1992), for example, described a study in which the classroom teacher taught three elementary students with moderate or severe intellectual disability to prepare snacks using a total task presentation format combined with constant time delay. The teacher taught each student one snack preparation task directly, while the other students merely observed and turned pages in a pictorial recipe book as the lesson progressed. The teacher praised the observers, gave them tokens, and prompted them to praise and give a token to the student being directly instructed. All the students acquired three snack preparation tasks, including those they had only observed. This research finding is promising because it indicates that students with severe disabilities can acquire skills through observational learning in small groups, thus increasing instructional efficiency.

Another promising line of research has investigated using peers who are typically developing to teach or model chained tasks with students with severe intellectual disability (Kohl & Stettner-Eaton, 1985). Werts and colleagues (1996), for example, taught 12 peers who were typically developing to model several school skill task chains (e.g., sharpening a pencil) while verbally describing each step as three students with disabilities, including one with severe intellectual disability, observed. Each of the students with disabilities acquired the targeted skills, and all generalized at least some of the new skills to different materials. These findings support the inclusion of students with severe intellectual disability within inclusive environments where they can acquire useful skills through observing competent peer models.

Some researchers have investigated the effect of requiring students to perform steps in a task chain in a specific, predetermined order, in comparison to letting the students perform the steps out of order as long as this did not keep them from completing the tasks successfully (called a *functional order*). Of course, some tasks should be completed in a specific order (e.g., crossing a street), but rearranging step order within other tasks will not necessarily affect the outcome. Wright and Schuster (1994), for example, taught four elementary students with moderate or severe disabilities to make two simple snacks, one using the specific task step format and one using the functional order format. Students acquired the preparation tasks using both formats and maintained them up to 3 weeks, but required fewer instructional sessions during the functional order task instruction. Three of the four students made fewer errors when taught with this format. Because reducing error rates is associated with increased instructional efficiency, this is a potentially useful strategy for teachers to consider as they design task analysis instruction.

Implementing Task Analysis Instruction with Fidelity

Research examining task analysis instruction for individuals with severe intellectual disability reveals a few key instructional considerations. A first critical decision in teaching with a task analysis is whether the student has all the prerequisite skills needed to perform the steps in the task analysis (Alberto & Troutman, 2009). If the student lacks one or more of these, then the first step is to teach these individual, necessary skills. Next, it is important to individualize the task analysis for the learner. Generally, learners with severe intellectual disability require smaller steps—more explicit individual skills—than do persons with no or milder disability. A next step is to determine which format to use in teaching the task. Although all three formats have been found to be effective, total task presentation seems in general to be more effective across most tasks for learners with severe intellectual disability. Finally, the instructor must select a prompting system with which to teach the task analysis. Results of studies comparing these methods are not completely clear. What seems most effective is to consider the student's past learning history and the specific features of the task to be taught. As with prompting, many excellent resources describe in detail how to use task analysis instruction (e.g., Browder, 2001); the reader is encouraged to consult one of these for additional information.

Summary

In summary, numerous research studies have examined task analysis instruction. Much of this research involved participants with severe intellectual disability ranging in age from preschool through adulthood. Tasks taught in these studies have included self-help, motor, community, leisure, vocational, and academic skills. However, we located only one study that examined a chained academic task taught to participants with severe intellectual

disability (Rao & Kane, 2009). This seems to be an area for future research, particularly, as students with severe disability should now be given access to the core academic content (IDEA, 2004).

The majority of studies examining the utility of task analysis as an instructional tool used single-case research designs. Research design and methodology in the studies were adequate. Not all studies assessed procedural fidelity, but the majority of the studies included many design components needed for quality single-case research.

Although some studies examining the utility of task analysis occurred in community settings or generalization was probed within inclusive school environments (e.g., the school cafeteria), the majority took place in settings where most of the individuals present had disabilities (e.g., self-contained classrooms). Only three of the studies located were conducted in general education settings (Arntzen, Halstadtro, & Halstadtro, 2003; Kohl & Stettner-Eaton, 1985; Werts et al., 1996). This finding substantiates Wolery and Schuster's (1997) observation that relatively little research that includes participants with severe disabilities has been conducted in inclusive settings. It is now required that these students have access to the general curriculum, and research indicates that providing this access to the curriculum within general education settings can be highly beneficial for students (Ryndak, Moore, Orlando, & Delano, 2008/2009). Researchers should, then, further examine some of the research-based strategies used in special education settings, such as task analysis, within general education settings. These strategies likely will be effective in general education settings, but more evidence is needed about implementation techniques that do not disrupt ongoing instruction or that inadvertently stigmatize students (J. McDonnell, 1998).

Self-Management

Self-management strategies are actions individuals take to manage or regulate their own behavior (Agran, King-Sears, Wehmeyer, & Copeland, 2003). These are sometimes called *student-directed learning strategies* because their use allows students to direct their learning rather than relying solely on teachers to do so (Agran et al., 2003). Self-management employs behavioral strategies that come from behavioral theory (J. O. Cooper et al., 2007). From this perspective, an individual who uses self-management engages in a behavior that affects or modifies the environment in some manner that makes it more likely that the target behavior will occur again (Agran et al., 2003). For example, checking off a picture representing a step on a task list helps individuals understand that this step is accomplished, and that they need to initiate the next step on the list.

Self-management strategies comprise some of the component skills of self-determination, which has been defined as the "skills, knowledge, and beliefs that enable [individuals] to engage in goal-directed, self-regulated, autonomous behavior" (Field, Martin, Miller, Ward & Wehmeyer, 1998, p. 2). Research has demonstrated that providing instruction on the component strategies of self-determination is highly effective in helping individuals improve a range of skills, including academic skills in core content areas (e.g., Fowler, Konrad, Walker, Test, & Wood, 2007). These instructional strategies also teach broader skills (e.g., problem solving) that individuals with severe intellectual disability can use across the lifespan in different life areas.

Additional advantages of self-management strategies are that they can be effective with behaviors that are not readily observable (e.g., problem solving). Consequently, an individual can use them even when an external change agent, such as a teacher, cannot easily observe the behavior. Self-management strategies can also help persons with severe intellectual disability to gain increased control of their lives. These individuals may look frequently to others to guide their behavior rather than manage it themselves. Acquiring self-management skills can decrease reliance on external assistance and help them provide their own supports. Individuals may be motivated to use self-management strategies because they, not someone else, direct their own actions. This may result in higher performance rates of target behaviors than in teacher-directed interventions (Fantuzzo, Polite, Cook, & Quinn, 1988).

Self-management strategies also facilitate maintenance and generalization of newly acquired behaviors because individuals can provide their own prompts and consequences across settings. Indeed, L. K. Koegel and colleagues (1999) considered self-management to be a pivotal behavior because acquiring a self-management strategy allows an individual to apply it to a wide range of behaviors across settings and people without need for an external change agent to be present. Because many individuals with severe intellectual disability struggle with generalizing skills, this is an important benefit for this population of learners. Some experts have suggested that self-management strategies can increase instructional efficiency because teachers will spend less time managing students' behaviors if the students are taught to manage their own behaviors (Ganz, 2008). Ganz also suggested that learning to implement self-management instruction is relatively simple and does not require obtaining materials or resources beyond those found in most classrooms. This characteristic makes it appealing to classroom teachers and others who often work with large numbers of students and have limited time and resources to develop instructional materials.

Individuals with diverse abilities have used self-management to acquire new skills, build fluency of previously acquired skills, and facilitate generalization of skills across settings, materials, time, and persons. Self-management strategies have assisted individuals with severe intellectual disability improve performance of a variety of skills including social (e.g., C. Hughes et al., 2000), employment (e.g., S. C. Moore, Agran, & Fodor-Davis, 1989), classroom (Agran et al., 2005), recreational (e.g., C. Hughes et al., 2004), and academic skills (e.g., Copeland, Hughes, Agran, Wehmeyer, & Fowler, 2002).

Numerous self-management strategies are available. In the following sections, we describe two of the most widely used strategies: antecedent prompts and self-monitoring. We describe the research base supporting both strategies and offer research-based suggestions about successful implementation with individuals with severe intellectual disability. We also refer readers to additional sources that provide extensive information on implementation of both strategies (e.g., Agran et al., 2003; Ganz, 2008).

Antecedent Prompts

Antecedent prompts are cues added to the environment that help individuals guide their behavior. They differ from consequences, which are stimuli that occur after a behavior and affect its future occurrence, because antecedent prompts are used before a behavior to signal a response. Many people use antecedent prompts in their daily lives. Writing the date for an important meeting on a calendar is a form of antecedent prompting. Seeing the written date prompts you to gather your materials and attend the meeting. Similarly, individuals with disabilities may use visual, tactile, or auditory prompts to assist them in learning the steps for a new behavior or remembering to initiate a behavior. Some individuals require these prompts only temporarily, but others may continue to need them each time they perform a targeted skill (Agran et al., 2003).

Antecedent prompts have many benefits for persons with severe intellectual disability, such as increasing independence. Some individuals may master a skill but may not always be certain when to use the skill. Rather than relying on others for cues to begin a task, use of antecedent prompts allows individuals to initiate and complete tasks on their own. These prompts can also act as a memory aid for individuals who have difficulty with short-term memory that hampers their ability to complete complicated routines or activities. Antecedent prompts can provide the support needed to successfully complete complex tasks. Because these prompts typically are easily moved from one setting to another (i.e., they are portable), an individual can easily use them across different settings and with different tasks, thus facilitating generalization of learned skills.

Types of Antecedent Prompts

Picture prompts are a common form of antecedent prompts that can include graphic images, line drawings, or photographs. Research supports their successful use with individuals with severe intellectual disability across the age span to increase independent performance of many different types of skills such as social (e.g., C. Hughes et al., 2000), vocational (e.g., Lancioni & O'Reillly, 2001), leisure (Bambara & Ager, 1992), and functional tasks (e.g., Irvine, Erickson, Singer, & Stahlberg, 1992), among others. These prompts have been used with both multicomponent tasks (e.g., assembly tasks) and to help individuals perform a series of activities (e.g., follow an activity schedule).

Auditory prompts are another form of antecedent prompting that research has found is successful in teaching new skills to individuals with severe intellectual disability. Skills taught have included vocational (e.g., Grossi, 1998) and functional skills (e.g., Lancioni, Klaase, & Goossens, 1995). Most often, researchers have used a portable audio cassette player to provide either single- or multiple-word prompts to participants. Post and Storey (2002) noted that auditory prompting has been used to (a) help individuals remember to perform steps in complex multistep tasks, (b) stay focused on a task long enough to complete it, and (c) reduce errors in completing tasks. In a review of the auditory-prompting literature, Mechling (2007) stated that auditory-prompting systems may be easier for individuals with physical disabilities to use than systems that require manipulation of the picture prompts. Post and Storey (2002) also pointed out in their review of this literature that some participants in research studies were able to fade their use of auditory prompts once they had acquired the targeted skills.

Recently, researchers have begun to examine the use of computer-based systems to provide antecedent prompts, teaching skills ranging from daily living, employment, and school routines (Mechling, 2007). Mechling listed several advantages of computerized systems. First, computer use is a highly valued skill in our society, so prompting systems making use of this technology may be less stigmatizing than systems based on use of picture cards. It is also possible to easily individualize a computerized prompting system for an individual's needs. Use of touch screens, for example, can be helpful for individuals with physical challenges who may have difficulty manipulating a picture card system. Computerized systems also combine auditory and picture cues, for example, in video clips. Computers can also be used to provide varied types of cues, which can help individuals with severe intellectual disability attend more consistently to the task. Handheld computers are also small and easily portable, which is another advantage for their use across settings.

Several studies have compared computerized systems with picture prompts and have found computerized systems to be more effective in teaching persons with severe intellectual disability to complete daily living and vocational tasks (e.g., Davies, Stock, & Wehmeyer, 2003). Researchers speculated that these systems helped participants focus on the relevant cues within the task so that they made more correct decisions in completing the task steps. Generalization may also be enhanced with this type of antecedent prompting (e.g., Cihak, Kessler, & Alberto, 2006).

Implementing Antecedent Prompt Interventions with Fidelity

Implementing picture prompt interventions requires matching of the type of graphic to the individual's unique learning needs. Some persons with severe intellectual disability will do best with actual photographs, and others may be able to use line drawings or other graphic images. Organization of the graphic cues is another area for consideration. Short tasks can be represented with a few pictures arranged sequentially. More complex tasks will require a different arrangement. A common solution for complex tasks is to place photographs of each step of the task within a booklet. Individuals refer to each picture as they complete each step of the task. Copeland and Hughes (2000), for example, taught two high school students with severe intellectual disabilities to successfully and independently complete multistep work tasks using a picture prompt strategy that included self-monitoring. Students learned to refer to a picture of a task step, perform the step, and then turn the page to the next step, complete it, and so on, until the entire task was finished.

When teaching individuals to use auditory prompts, some researchers have interspersed verbal task step instructions with music (e.g., C. A. Davis, Brady, Williams, & Burta, 1992), and others have used a tone (beep) to cue participants to pause the audio and perform the verbalized step. Other researchers (e.g., Mechling & Gast, 1997) have taught students with intellectual disability to perform tasks by combining both auditory prompts and visual prompts. These researchers pointed out that using two sensory systems may be a way to provide additional information about task completion to students with extensive support needs.

Teaching individuals with severe intellectual disability to use computer prompting systems requires similar considerations to picture and auditory prompting.

Selection of graphics, complexity of auditory prompts, size (complexity) of prompted steps, and physical access of the device (e.g., using a touch screen, pushing keys) must be based on the individual's unique learning characteristics. Additional considerations include device cost and availability of someone to provide technical support.

Self-Monitoring

Self-monitoring, the most widely used and researched self-management strategy, is often used in conjunction with other self-management strategies (J. O. Cooper et al., 2007). Self-monitoring requires individuals to observe one of their behaviors and indicate its occurrence in some way, such as by making a checkmark on a form. Self-monitoring assists students in becoming more aware of their own behavior. D. J. Smith and Nelson (1997) noted that becoming more aware of one's own behavior, called *reactivity,* may act as a discriminative stimulus for that behavior.

Self-monitoring can be used to increase or decrease a behavior and typically is used with behaviors a student already knows how to perform (Agran et al., 2003). In other words, it can be useful in increasing the fluency of a behavior or in maintaining it across time, but not for learning a new behavior. Individuals can be taught to self-monitor specific behaviors (e.g., check off each step that is required to access a favorite Web site as it is completed) or can learn to self-monitor broader categories of behavior such as on-task behavior (Agran et al., 2003). This makes it a very flexible strategy that can be applied to widely varying situations.

Individuals with severe intellectual disability have used self-monitoring with a range of skills including academic (e.g., L. K. Koegel et al., 1999), social (e.g., C. Hughes et al., 2002), exercise (e.g., D. N. Ellis, Cress, & Spellman, 1992), and vocational (e.g., Ganz & Sigafoos, 2005) behaviors. Individuals have used self-monitoring strategies to increase independence of previously acquired skills and decrease problem behaviors (e.g., L. K. Koegel et al., 1999). Interventions have been used successfully in both general and special education settings across age ranges from kindergarten to adulthood (see Ferretti, Cavalier, Murphy, & Murphy, 1993; Ganz, 2008). In addition to adults, peers who are typically developing have successfully taught individuals with severe intellectual disability to self-monitor (e.g., Gilberts, Agran, Hughes, & Wehmeyer, 2001).

Implementing Self-Monitoring Interventions with Fidelity

When teaching an individual with severe intellectual disability to self-monitor, it is important to explicitly teach the individual to recognize the target behavior when it occurs and to select a form of marking its occurrence based on the individual's age, ability level, and learning characteristics (e.g., checking a small box on a form each time an elementary student raises his hand). Researchers have frequently used modeling and role-play to explicitly teach the self-monitoring system selected. Often researchers set criteria for accurate self-monitoring that must be met before the individual begins independent self-monitoring (e.g., self- and teacher-recording of the occurrence of behavior must match on 80% of opportunities). However, research indicates that even if the individual's self-recorded data are not completely accurate, positive behavioral changes often result (e.g., Gilberts et al., 2001). If the individual fails to maintain self-monitoring after initial training, some researchers have provided brief booster sessions to retrain participants in the system, which has proved successful with a variety of participants across settings and tasks (e.g., Ganz & Sigafoos, 2005).

Summary

As with the other reviewed practices, a solid empirical basis supports teaching individuals with severe intellectual disability to use antecedent prompts and self-monitoring to self-manage their behaviors. Most studies in this area employed single-case research designs and were methodologically sound. Most, however, used an intervention package, meaning that more than one strategy was used within an intervention (e.g., antecedent prompts and self-monitoring), making it difficult to isolate the individual effects of a particular strategy. Studies included participants across the age range from kindergarten to adulthood and examined self-management with diverse skill areas and across environments. Because self-management has been documented to decrease reliance on others and to promote generalization of skills, it is especially promising for use within inclusive school and community settings.

Despite the documented effectiveness of self-management strategies with individuals with severe intellectual disability, research has shown that these individuals may not be given opportunities to acquire these valuable skills. Wehmeyer and colleagues (2000) surveyed 1,200 high school teachers of students with disabilities regarding self-management instruction. Although the majority of the responding teachers recognized the importance and potential benefit of teaching self-management strategies to their students, 41% of them did not think that their students had the resources or skills to do this successfully. Teachers of students with severe intellectual disability were less likely than teachers of students with other disabilities to provide self-management instruction and less likely to recognize potential benefits of providing this instruction. This finding is troubling, because self-management strategies increase independence and autonomy, promote generalization of adaptive skills, and may be an effective way to increase access to the general curriculum for individuals with severe intellectual disability. Future research should investigate how to increase acceptance of this important strategy among instructors of individuals with severe intellectual disability.

Conclusion

Individuals with severe intellectual disability have significant learning challenges that affect all aspects of their lives. The instructional practices reviewed within this chapter address the particular learning characteristics of this group in ways that help them successfully acquire new knowledge and skills. Studies examining these practices provide a strong research-based foundation for their effectiveness.

Because of low expectations frequently held about the learning potential of individuals with severe intellectual disability, these individuals have not always been provided opportunities to acquire complex skills. Thankfully, expectations are changing, and increasingly these individuals receive challenging and meaningful instruction in content areas valued by society within settings that include individuals with and without disabilities. Researchers and practitioners now have the challenge of taking the instructional strategies found to be effective with learners with severe intellectual disabilities such as those reviewed in this chapter, and extend their use within inclusive school, community, and employment settings.

CHAPTER 28

Effective Reading Interventions for English Language Learners Who Are Struggling Readers or Identified with Learning Disabilities

Kathleen A. King Thorius | *Indiana University—Indianapolis*

Alfredo J. Artiles and **Amanda L. Sullivan** | *Arizona State University*

Setting the Context

As the U.S. population grows and becomes more diverse, so does the enrollment of public schools, which comprises 43% racial minority students and students who are learning English (Planty et al., 2008). In the West, Latino/a students constitute nearly 45% of the 7.9 million students in the region, and 22% of students are considered English Language Learners (ELLs). This increasing diversity, paired with anti-immigrant and anti-bilingual discourses (Chávez, 2008), further complicates the educational opportunities and outcomes for the 10.8 million students classified as Limited English Proficient (LEP),[1] the majority of whom speak Spanish as their primary language (Planty et al., 2008).

Educators are increasingly challenged to meet the educational needs of students who are ELLs, yet barriers to effective supports exist. For example, in states with large ELL populations, teachers reported having received little professional development to prepare them to teach these students (Gándara, Maxwell-Jolly, & Driscoll, 2005). Further, many educators view students' linguistic diversity as a problem rather than a resource that enriches teaching and learning (G. Law & Lane, 1987; Obiakor, 1999). Such attitudes manifest themselves in low expectations expressed in watered down, fragmented curriculum for students of diverse abilities, languages, and cultures (Steinberg & Kincheloe, 2004). Consequently, these students have a greater chance of receiving low grades, dropping out, and not going on to postsecondary schools (Durán, 2008).

Authors' note: The second author acknowledges the support of the Equity Alliance at ASU under grant #S004D080027 awarded by the U.S. Department of Education. Funding agencies' endorsement of the ideas expressed in this manuscript should not be inferred.

[1]The phrases *Limited English Proficient* and *English Language Learner,* and their respective acronyms, *LEP* and *ELL,* are similar in meaning. The primary difference is that LEP students are identified through testing, while ELL is a more general term referring to any student who is learning English as a second or additional language. Therefore, while Planty et al. (2008) reported on LEP students, this term also refers to ELLs.

Latino/a students, who are disproportionately represented in the ELL population, continue to have the highest dropout rate in the United States as compared to all other ethnic groups (U.S. Department of Education, 2010a), and the Education Trust (2009) reports that 4 of every 10 Latino/a children who enroll in U.S. schools fail to graduate.

Moreover, students who are ELLs may have a higher probability of being placed in special education in some school contexts, and researchers have expressed concern that such educational decisions are made without ensuring access to high-quality opportunities to learn, providing instruction in the students' primary language, or ensuring the application of culturally and linguistically appropriate pre-referral interventions (Bernhard et al., 2006). Many ELLs, who often have immigrant backgrounds, do not receive curriculum in a language they understand and are taught by educators who only speak English and may not know or use techniques for working effectively with them (Suárez-Orozco, Roos, & Suárez-Orozco, 2000). Scholars point out that increasing special education referrals are also affected by (a) providing instructional services to foster English proficiency and academic content mastery simultaneously and (b) premature exiting from language support programs (Ochoa, Robles-Piña, Garcia, & Breunig, 1999).

Unfortunately, the connection between language and disability is not fully understood. For many educators, distinguishing between limited English proficiency and reading disability is exceedingly difficult (Keller-Allen, 2006); educators often confuse language acquisition with learning problems (Artiles & Klingner, 2006). In addition, no instruments are available to reliably assess limited English proficiency versus potential learning disability (LD) (Keller-Allen, 2006). These challenges have contributed to questions as to whether ELLs are misidentified for special education because educators do not adequately understand language acquisition processes and the influence of language acquisition on the academic content mastery (R. E. Case & Taylor, 2005) or, conversely, because educators fail to identify students with LD for special education because they are ELLs (Zehler et al., 2003). Indeed, emerging evidence indicates that ELLs in the Southwestern United States are overrepresented in special education (Artiles, Klingner, Sullivan, & Fierros, 2010; Artiles, Rueda, Salazar, & Higerada, 2005; De Valenzuela, Copeland, Qi, & Park, 2006). Further, the rate of ELLs identified as LD is growing significantly, quite often related to reading difficulties (Artiles, Trent, & Palmer, 2004; Donovan & Cross, 2002; Losen & Orfield, 2002).

Not surprisingly, emerging research has demonstrated teacher ratings of literacy skills and reading proficiency are significant predictors of eventual special education placement (Samson & Lesaux, 2009). However, considering the high proportion of ELLs who struggle academically, a significant challenge for researchers, policy makers, and practitioners is to elucidate whether disabilities or other factors shape ELLs' poor educational performance. Scholars have discussed that ELLs' disproportionate special education placement is likely shaped by complex interactions between factors such as ELLs' limited access to effective instruction and interventions, structural barriers (e.g., low funding, low teacher quality), and systematic disadvantages (e.g., poverty rates) (Artiles & Klingner, 2006). Thus, the necessity for supporting educators' development of culturally responsive research-based practices for intervening with struggling ELLs' literacy cannot be understated.

Exploring ELLs' Literacy Needs

The literacy outcomes of ELLs differ from those who are language-majority learners (i.e., students for whom English is their primary language). ELLs tend to perform less well on reading and writing assessments than their English-speaking peers; the gap is smaller on math, science, and social studies tests (Abedi, 2006). Nationwide, less than 20% of ELLs met state standards in reading (Genesee, Lindholm-Leary, Saunders, & Christian, 2005) and large-scale reading assessments show that at all grade levels, ELLs perform nearly 2 standard deviations below peers (Durán, 2008). Factors that contribute to these disparities vary across multiple levels (e.g., student, teacher, family, community/culture) and include demographics (e.g., economic status) (Snow, Burns, & Griffin 1998), sociocultural influences (Goldenberg, Rueda, & August, 2006), instructional quality (Téllez & Waxman, 2006), and those related to the developmental processes associated with literacy in second-language learners (Francis, Rivera, Lesaux, Kieffer, & Rivera, 2006). Despite considerable educational and language research around supporting ELLs' literacy development, a large research–practice gap remains.

This chapter offers a description of research-based practices that are effective in improving literacy outcomes for ELLs who are either identified as struggling readers or as having LD. The implications for this chapter are twofold. First, we hope educators may apply this review and description of effective research-based practices to a better understanding of how the research on literacy for ELLs is grounded. The goal of such awareness is to provide educators and leaders at different levels of the educational system with insights about how a general literacy curriculum is conceptualized; what underlying assumptions exist about the nature and purpose of literacy for ELLs who are struggling learners, and in turn, how are literacy interventions designed and implemented to support ELLs' literacy development?

Second, we hope educators find this chapter a useful support to increase their capacity to design, select, and implement literacy interventions with ELLs who are struggling to read or who have been identified with LD, while being mindful of histories of marginalization and unfavorable outcomes many students in such groups have faced in U.S. schools (e.g., Gitlin, Buendía, Crosland, & Doumbia, 2003; Valdés, 2001). Implications for this enhanced understanding of appropriate literacy interventions are improved instruction and support for ELLs, including better services for ELLs identified as having LD, as well as the prevention of unwarranted referrals for special education eligibility evaluations and the reduction of disproportionate representation of ELLs in special education for literacy difficulties.

Definition of Terms

First, we define what we mean by *intervention* and describe multiple positions held by those who design, implement, and study interventions with regard to what *reading* or *literacy* entails. Although *reading* and *literacy* are sometimes used interchangeably, specific definitions of each term appear to inform particular types of supports, which we discuss in detail in subsequent sections. *Intervention* is a word commonly used in education policy, practice, and research, yet its meaning is rarely addressed in sources on the subject. Even in the federal No Child Left Behind Act, despite the call for educational practitioners to apply "scientifically based research" to guide their decisions about which interventions to implement to have an impact on student achievement, the criteria for defining an intervention are not provided. For the purposes of this chapter, we use the following definition of *intervention:* "The direct manipulation by the researchers of psychological, medical, or educational variables for the purpose of assessing learning efficiency, learning accuracy, learning understanding or the combination of all three" (L. Swanson, 2000, pp. 4–5). In this chapter we focus on interventions to improve reading/literacy performance for ELLs. This is one of the most critical issues in the national education policy and practice discourse, because federal and state policies require success on standardized measures of reading for all student subgroups and schools experience difficulties understanding and implementing curriculum and instruction that ensure this outcome.

Two competing conceptualizations of literacy account for opposite ends in a continuum that defines conceptions of literacy (Snow, 2006) and guides the research and practice of designing and implementing literacy interventions with ELLs who are struggling to read, who have been identified with LD, or both. One side of the continuum defines literacy as a set of discrete skills to be taught explicitly; skills that, when applied by readers, allow them to obtain meaning from print for a functional purpose (Lyon, 1998; Reyna, 2004). Reviews of research demonstrate that these skills, commonly referred to as the five core areas of reading instruction (i.e., phonemic awareness, phonics, fluency, vocabulary, and comprehension), apply similarly to

reading instruction for ELLs (August & Shanahan, 2006; Shanahan & Beck, 2006). On the other side of this continuum are conceptions of literacy as an integrated, collaborative, empowering social activity that can be understood and facilitated by attending to the process by which readers make sense of texts (Gee, 1996; Street, 1995).

Proponents of either end of this continuum have engaged in long-standing debate, in which skill-based approaches to teaching reading were pitted against process-oriented approaches. Buried deep within the debate, which raged during the 1980s and 1990s, are assumptions about literacy's nature and purpose. These assumptions become more complex as related to a particular group of students with histories of exclusion and marginalization in U.S. schools (Willis & Harris, 2000). Testing these assumptions requires that we ask: (a) What are the goals of literacy development for ELLs in schools? (b) How has literacy been used as a political tool that has both afforded and constrained social access and power for ELLs? (c) What are individuals' and groups' reasons for becoming literate (Ladson-Billings, 1992)? These questions underlie competing views of literacy that shaped our approach to this review of literacy interventions for ELLs who are struggling readers and those identified with LD.

We review research on two categories of literacy interventions for these groups of ELLs. The first of these are interventions grounded in the notion that literacy is a set of cognitive reading and writing skills that collectively allow one to advance socially, economically, and engage in individual decision making. This first group of interventions bases effective interventions for ELLs on the teaching of specific subskills delivered as *explicit* or *direct* instruction. The second category of literacy interventions we review are those grounded in the notion that literacy is a sociocultural process between the learner and the text, which therefore emphasizes the provision of opportunities for individuals to engage in *reciprocal, interaction-oriented* strategies of reading and more broadly defined literacy practices as part of a larger process of inquiry. Finally, we provide a model of literacy and accompanying interventions for ELLs grounded in the research base of both literacy models, with approaches that use the resources of the multiple literacies ELLs bring to their classrooms to develop basic literacy skills.

Review Methods

To locate research studies as a basis for our description of effective literacy interventions for ELLs struggling with reading or identified with LD, we conducted a title, abstract, and full-text search of the ERIC and EBSCO host databases for research-based journal articles published between 2003 and 2008. This is the 5-year period immediately following the unprecedented emphasis placed on the academic achievement of students classified as Limited

English Proficient by the 2002 reauthorization of the Elementary and Secondary Education Act (i.e., No Child Left Behind Act) and its Title III, the English Language Acquisition, Language Enhancement, and Academic Achievement Act. To find articles concerned with the particular groups of children on whom this chapter is focused, we used the keywords *English* AND *Learner* AND *disability* OR *struggling* AND *reading* OR *literacy*. Our search excluded articles about research with ELLs who were not having learning difficulties at school.

Participants in Identified Studies

Articles were coded on the basis of the target group identified for the interventions and the type of intervention used. We found 16 studies that appeared in a total of 11 educational research journals. Of the 16 articles, 14 were focused on ELLs identified as struggling readers (i.e., at risk for reading failure or for identification as having LD). The remaining articles were concerned with ELLs who struggled with reading within *both* special and general education; no articles researched interventions *solely* for ELLs who were eligible for and received special education.

Types of Interventions in Research

We found a pattern in the types of interventions that corresponded with the two ends of the literacy continuum in the relevant literature: (a) interventions concerned with the direct instruction of a specific set of reading subskills and (b) interventions focused on social, reciprocal (i.e., transactional) interactions around text, primarily concerned with students' literacy as making meaning from texts. Descriptive features (i.e., intervention, setting, participants, measures, duration, level of support, fidelity, and outcomes) of the studies reviewed are provided in Appendix 28.1, at the end of this chapter.

In the subsequent sections, we describe briefly these two broad categories of interventions located in the recent literature by highlighting the features of each and, given the relatively few studies located, providing an overview of each.

Research-Based Literacy Interventions for ELLs

Interventions for Specific Reading Subskills

Just under 88% (i.e., 14 of 16) of the studies included in this review of the literature were grounded in the premise that effective instruction and intervention for ELLs who are struggling, ELLs identified with LD, or both is based

on the teaching of specific reading subskills. Some studies focused more explicitly on intervention in one specific subskill (e.g., phonological awareness, or the ability to recognize the many ways sounds function in words). Others used a combination of several skills, either as a prepackaged literacy intervention program such as *Reading Recovery* (e.g., Scull & Bianco, 2008) or as an intervention for which the researchers combined a number of interventions to account for various dimensions of decoding, fluency, and comprehension (e.g., Linan-Thompson, Vaughn, Hickman-Davis, & Kouzekanani, 2003).

Interventions Targeting Phonological Awareness Skills

Of the articles that reported results of interventions implemented around one specific reading subskill, several demonstrated the effectiveness of intensive phonological awareness instruction for ELLs. For instance, a study with ELL kindergarteners by Leafstedt, Richards, and Gerber (2004) found that when intensive phonological awareness instruction was provided as an intervention within one self-contained kindergarten class, students demonstrated significantly greater growth in word reading as compared to students in another class who did not receive this intervention. Vaughn and colleagues (S. Vaughn, Linan-Thompson, et al., 2006; S. Vaughn, Mathes, et al., 2006) demonstrated the efficacy of intervention consisting of explicit instruction in oral language and reading skills based on lesson plans of integrated literacy content strands. The experimental group intervention was delivered in small-group settings for 50 minutes every day and led to improved ELL performance on letter naming, phonological awareness, word attack, and comprehension compared to peers receiving standard English reading interventions. It is important to note that although both of these studies demonstrated the intervention's efficacy, the intervention for the S. Vaughn, Linan-Thompson, et al. (2006) study involved students who were considered at risk for reading problems in Spanish; the intervention was conducted only in Spanish, and effects were observed in Spanish, but not English. In contrast, the S. Vaughn, Mathes, et al. (2006) study involved students who were assessed to be at risk for reading problems in both Spanish and English. The intervention was delivered in English. Effects were strongest on English measures but were evident on some Spanish measures.

M. M. Gerber et al. (2004) demonstrated the positive relationship between strong foundational primary language skills and reading skill acquisition in English as a second language. This study looked at an intensive phonological skills training intervention for Spanish-speaking kindergarteners considered to be at risk. The intervention model focused on direct instruction strategies, in addition to the support for the development of phonological skills.

Interventions Based on Prepackaged Literacy Programs

Five research studies on prepackaged literacy intervention programs investigated the efficacy of the following published materials with ELLs who were struggling readers, some of whom were identified with LD: *Reading Recovery, Fast ForWord Language, Reading Mastery,* and *Read Well.* Two studies assessed the efficacy of *Reading Recovery* (Kelly, Gomez-Bellenge, Chen, & Schulz, 2008; Scull & Bianco, 2008). Kelly et al. (2008) analyzed data collected as part of the national program evaluation for *Reading Recovery.* Participants were among the lowest 20% in reading performance at their school in the fall of their first grade year. Among children who completed the full *Reading Recovery* intervention, 69% of ELL students and 76% of Native English Speaking (NES) children achieved grade-level performance in reading at the end of the school year. The authors concluded that, although the ELLs' achievement on levels of text reading and phonological awareness was significantly lower than their NES peers, the effect ($d = 0.18$) was not large enough to exclude ELLs from *Reading Recovery* as an effective intervention and considered it part of the spectrum of best practice for ELLs who are struggling readers.

Scull and Bianco (2008) approached the study of *Reading Recovery* from a more critical stance, in response to earlier findings that a percentage of ELLs continued to struggle with literacy, even after receiving the *Reading Recovery* intervention. The researchers used ethnographic observation strategies and analysis of the nature of specific examples of teaching and learning in *Reading Recovery* with 10 young (6.5 to 8 years) ELLs identified as progressing below expected levels, and their 10 literacy teachers, compared to a group of students who were making "accelerated" progress. The authors found that student progress was related to teachers' capacity to understand the varying skill levels of students and to match supports to their level of need. Teacher–learner interactions were the key mechanism by which ELLs became more independent learners. One type of interaction the authors found particularly supportive in this acceleration was teachers' "verbal accompaniment to reading" (p. 145). Furthermore, the authors concluded that oral language is of central importance as a contributor to early literacy development.

Fast ForWord Language is a program that provides students with instruction in receptive English language skills through the use of interactive exercises that provide ELLs practice discriminating nonverbal and verbal sounds, recognizing vocabulary, and comprehending language. These exercises lengthen and, at times, amplify portions of recorded sounds students listen to, with the aim of speeding up the learning of English by ELLs. The method employed by Troia (2004) is based on findings of August and Hakuta (1997) that demonstrated some ELLs' difficulty with the perception of phonemes that were not part of their native language. Researchers assigned first- through sixth-grade ELLs ($n = 191$) to a treatment and control group, and used a pre- and post-test design with a no-contact control group. The author reported limited statistically significant differences between the treatment and control group; of the five domains (English language proficiency, oral language competence, phonological processing, basic reading, and classroom behavior), the treatment group showed significantly greater gains in the basic reading domain only. Based on this finding, Troia questioned media claims of *Fast ForWord's* efficacy, its popularity with educators and researchers, and called for additional research on the effectiveness of this program and caution when applying it systematically as an intervention for ELLs who are struggling readers.

The last program studied within the period included in this review was the *Reading Mastery* program, in combination with a parent training component entitled *Incredible Years* (Webster-Stratton, 1992). The *Reading Mastery* intervention was delivered as a 2-year supplemental reading program for 299 students "at risk for reading failure" (p. 66), in kindergarten through third grade, who were randomly assigned to a treatment and control group (Gunn, Biglan, Smolkowski, & Ary, 2005). *Reading Mastery* focuses specifically on the development of fluency and decoding, and students' capacity in these areas was assessed before intervention, once a year in the spring during the intervention years, and then annually for 2 more years. Students who were Latino and non-Latino, and who were both ELLs and non-ELLs, benefited from the intervention as much as or significantly more than non-Latino students (all of whom spoke only English) with matched baseline achievement levels. Evidence of smaller intervention effects on the non-Latino students was demonstrated, but effects for ELLs and non-ELLs as separate groups were not provided. Instead, on the basis of 84% of the Latino students' parents reporting that the primary language of the home was Spanish, the authors concluded that supplemental instruction focused on the development of word-recognition skills that is part of the *Reading Mastery* program is an effective intervention for both ELL and non-ELL students at risk for reading failure.

Multiple-Strategy Interventions Targeting Reading Skills

The remaining intervention studies with the target group of children used methods that combined strategies for teaching a number of specific reading subskills. For example, Lovett et al. (2008) investigated how struggling readers from varied linguistic backgrounds responded to phonologically based reading interventions by randomly assigning 166 struggling elementary students to one of three reading intervention programs (the *Phonological and Strategy Training (PHAST) Decoding Program;* the *Phonological Analysis and Blending/Direct Instruction Decoding Program,* with spelling and writing components added; or the *PHAST Decoding Program* with additional spelling and writing components) or to a special education curricular control group. The authors found that all of the interventions were significantly more effective than the special education curriculum exposure and that, regardless of students' first language, growth rate and outcomes for the three interventions were not statistically different.

A similar study by Denton, Wexler, Vaughn, and Bryan (2008) also divided students between an intervention group and a control group that provided their school's remedial or special education classes. The intervention included 40 minutes of daily small-group instruction with a modified version of the Wilson Reading System (Wilson, 1996) for 38 students, of whom a majority were Spanish-speaking ELLs identified with what the authors termed "significant reading disabilities" (p. 79). The authors found that in general, the intervention was no more effective than the control instruction, and they recommended further design and study of effective interventions for ELLs with identified disabilities.

K. Y. Tam, Heward, and Heng (2006), in a multiple-baseline across-subjects design, provided three components of reading instruction—vocabulary instruction, error correction, and fluency building on oral reading rate and comprehension—with five ELL struggling elementary school readers. There were two intervention conditions: The first provided students with a new passage during each intervention session; the second condition used the same passage each session until a predetermined criterion was achieved. Each student received between 73 and 79 intervention sessions. Despite these differences in conditions, the students improved fluency and comprehension under both; and in the second condition, four of the five reached the predetermined fluency criterion.

Kamps and colleagues (2007) found that second-tier direct instruction of a reading subskills intervention delivered in a three-tiered model of intervention (i.e., Response to Intervention; RtI) was effective with ELLs across urban and suburban schools, compared to instruction provided in nontreatment schools. The participants consisted of 170 ELLs and 148 English-only speakers. The ELLs in the experimental schools received an intervention that combined elements of three direct-instruction curricula: *Reading Mastery* (Engelmann & Bruner, 1995), *Early Interventions in Reading* (Mathes & Torgesen, 2005a),

and *Read Well* (Sprick, Howard, & Fidanque, 1998). For second-grade students only, the *Read Naturally* (Ihnot, 1991) program was also implemented, and materials from the *Open Court* program (Adams, Bereiter, McKeough, Case, Roit, Hirschberg, et al., 2002) were used as reading texts. Nonexperimental schools provided students with an "ESL/balanced literacy intervention," which focused on word study, writing activities, and group and individual story reading in addition to primary reading instruction. Overall, ELLs in the experimental schools had a statistically higher performance level on all outcome measures (i.e., $p < 0.001$) as compared to control schools, especially for students who received the intervention in small groups.

Linan-Thompson et al. (2003) studied the impact of an intervention that combined research-based instructional strategies for ELLs and effective skill-based reading interventions based on research with monolingual English speakers. The intervention, which consisted of 58 sessions provided 30 minutes daily for 13 weeks in small groups of two to three students, focused on specific activities that addressed students' oral reading fluency, phonological awareness, instructional level reading, word study (word analysis strategies), and writing. Practices grounded in research on effective instruction for ELLs included the provision of opportunities for students to learn skills in isolation and then practice them in context, redundancy in the daily lesson format, frequent guided and independent skill practice opportunities, and discussion between students about what they were learning. The researchers found a statistically significant time effect (e.g., significant increases from pretest to post-test measures) on all reading subskills incorporated in the intervention (Linan-Thompson et al., 2003).

Finally, Sáenz, Fuchs, and Fuchs (2005) studied the impact of Peer-Assisted Learning Strategies (PALS) for 132 third- through sixth-grade ELLs identified with LD and their classroom peers of all achievement levels, implemented three times a week for 15 weeks. Six classes were randomly assigned to the PALS condition, and six classes to a control condition. The PALS intervention is a reciprocal whole-class peer-tutoring strategy that includes a different literacy focus at different grade levels (Sáenz et al., 2005). The PALS Grades 2 to 6, the intervention studied, is focused on increasing strategic reading, reading fluency, and comprehension. ELLs were paired with students who were low, medium, and high achieving, and pairings were switched every 3 to 4 weeks. Within the pairs, both students were tutors and tutees. The students who participated in PALS significantly outperformed those who did not on reading comprehension questions answered correctly across student groups, after a 15-week intervention. The largest effect size (1.03) was associated with ELL students with LD. Large and moderate effect sizes that were not statistically significant were achieved, respectively, for ELL students with LD for words read correctly and correct words selected on a maze measure. Notably, although a classroom teacher facilitated this intervention strategy, this was the only intervention study in the identified research pool in which students worked collaboratively to support each other's literacy development, rather than a teacher or instructional staff member holding responsibility for direct intervention delivery.

For the most part, the research reviewed appeared to measure literacy in relation to the interventions designed and implemented to improve a set of cognitive skills measurable by standardized tests (e.g., S. Vaughn, Linan-Thompson, et al., 2006, S. Vaughn, Mathes, et al., 2006) or locally normed curriculum-based assessments (e.g., Scull & Bianco, 2008). The emphasis on the development of basic literacy skills by ELLs, particularly those who are struggling, those with disabilities, or both, is important in order for them to access the general education curriculum and experience favorable participation and outcomes. However, the autonomous model of literacy (Street, 1984), as these intervention studies appear to reflect, has been criticized in relation to an assumption that teaching and learning of literacy skills can occur independently of the cultural context in which they are applied (Street, 1995). This criticism has highlighted the emphasis in the autonomous model on one standard form of literacy (i.e., English language practices used among U.S. middle class speakers) and that a major goal of becoming literate is to demonstrate mastery of this standard set of cognitive skills (Delpit, 1986). This pattern of reading instruction has been documented as prevalent by research on instruction provided for the lowest reading groups and remedial reading classes, as well as in reading lessons with ELLs (Au & Raphael, 2000).

Interventions for Reading as a Reciprocal, Interaction-Oriented Process

We located only two research articles on literacy interventions for ELLs who were struggling readers or identified with disabilities, despite over a decade having past since Gee (2000) promoted "a broader view of both what constitutes empirical research and what sorts of empirical evidence are relevant to complex issues that integrally involve culture, social interaction, institutions, and cognition" (p. 126). These two studies differed markedly in terms of sample size, methods, and implications.

The first study focused on the relationship between a struggling high school ELL and tutor in a summer university tutoring course (J. Cohen, 2007). The tutoring focused on intensive strategy instruction between 13 graduate students and 13 ELL readers and writers.

The 4-week program included a variety of interactions around texts, writing, and discussing literacy content. Interactions included think alouds, K-W-L charts (described later), reading aloud quietly, and mental imagery of what was read (Gambrell & Jawitz, 1993) as a way to monitor comprehension. These were taught and practiced in pairs with tutors and in whole-group sessions. Students selected a person about whom they wanted to research and present about at the course end. One student participant, Mario, selected Julio Cesar Chavez, a famous boxer from his Mexican hometown. The discussion between the researcher/tutor and Mario emphasized how Mario would have reacted to the situations Chavez encountered throughout his life and career. Lower-level texts about Chavez were provided in both English and Spanish. Throughout the intervention, Mario learned to make K-W-L charts (Ogle, 1986) about what he already Knew (K), what he Wanted to know (W), and what he had Learned after interacting with the text (L), with his tutor, and during sustained silent reading periods.

Findings indicated that Mario reported liking reading, and he visited the library and checked out books on his own, which was new for him. He got a B in his high school English class, and he reported getting along better with teachers and feeling more confident about reading. Additionally, the research design used the Qualitative Reading Inventory—3 (Leslie & Caldwell, 2001) as a pre- and post-assessment. The preassessment was applied to the design of Mario's literacy instructional plan. On the preassessment, although Mario was able to decode most words, he had limited reading comprehension, while at the end of the course, he answered all reading comprehension questions without difficulty.

The final study presented results of a 1-year language intervention program called the Early Authors Program (EAP) (Bernhard et al., 2006), which is grounded in principles of transformative education (Freire, 1970) as well as other sources including Bransford, Brown, and Cocking's *How People Learn* model (2000), and Cummins's Academic Expertise framework (2000). The intervention randomly selected 367 children enrolled at early childhood centers in Miami Dade County and placed them in experimental ($n = 280$) and control ($n = 87$) groups.

The primary component of the EAP involved preschool ELLs writing and illustrating autobiographical bilingual books, which were shared with peers, parents, and teachers. The program also included on-site coaching from literacy specialists who supported educators to implement the EAP in technology-enriched classrooms. Other EAP elements included (a) monthly parent meetings to facilitate families' roles in reading and communicating with their children about their self-created texts and (b) training for assessors of children's performance on pre- and post-test measures that measured expressive language, auditory comprehension, cognition, and fine motor skills and were administered in Spanish or English, depending on students' dominant language. Students demonstrated improved language and early literacy scores, expressed pride in themselves as readers, and developed "affective bonds to literacy" (Bernhard et al., 2006, p. 2399).

The literacy interventions employed in these two research studies focused on providing students with opportunities to engage in inquiry, connect with self-selected and self-generated texts, and learn strategies for making meaning of texts, in order to enhance multiple forms of literacy, including oral language development. These interventions characterize what has been called an *ideological model of literacy* (e.g., Street, 1995), which emphasizes the purposes of and uses for literacy within a social system and does not focus on the teaching of discrete and separate reading subskills. Criticisms of these types of approaches, and of this conceptualization of literacy, argue that such practices rely on context and authentic texts as a proxy for decoding skills (G. R. Lyon, 1998).

Good, Research-Based Practices for Supporting Literacy Development of ELLs Who Are Struggling Readers or Identified with LD

To provide concrete illustrations of how research-based interventions can be applied with struggling ELL readers, we present in this section a detailed description of two strategies, one explicit and one reciprocal, supported by the reviewed research. Further, we expand these strategies by providing teachers with a set of considerations to guide their use of these interventions within the unique local contexts of their own classrooms.

Before we present these examples, we discuss briefly what is regarded as "best practice" and offer guidelines to consider when identifying "good practices." We address this point as a means to transcend simplistic analyses of the intervention research literature that tend to focus on narrow aspects of the interventions at the expense of considering equally substantive aspects in the design and implementation of interventions. Although a universally accepted notion of what constitutes a best practice does not seem to exist, we find the definition of best practice presented by the United Nations Educational, Scientific, and Cultural Organization (UNESCO) useful for the purposes of this chapter. Best practices, according to UNESCO (n.d.), are innovative (i.e., they are new and creative) solutions to common problems, demonstrate positive and tangible impact, have sustainable effect, and serve as a model for policy and practice elsewhere. We ask, therefore, what should be considered when identifying good practices?

What Are Good Practices?

To call any one practice or group of practices *best* is to suggest that there is one superior way to teach, which neglects careful consideration of context within which the practice is to be applied. Alexander's (1996) model of good practice is a potentially useful heuristic in this discussion; it consists of five considerations that interact and balance each other and that view good practice as an aspiration as much as an accomplishment. The first two shape teaching in general and inform the latter three, which together contribute to a model of *good practice:*

1. *Political considerations:* Practices are shaped by institutional and historical norms, as well as the expectations of professionals, parents, communities, and other political players.

2. *Pragmatic considerations:* Practices are implemented within an awareness of the opportunities and constraints of a particular educational context (e.g., district, school, classroom).

3. *Conceptual considerations:* The practice is shaped by the essential elements of teaching, learning, and the curriculum, and the relationship between them.

4. *Value considerations:* The practice is shaped by views about students' needs, societal needs, and necessary knowledge, all of which inform what is taught.

5. *Empirical considerations:* Evidence supports the effectiveness of the practice to result in learning.

Good, research-based practices in ELL literacy interventions provide students with direct instruction in a set of reading subskills relevant to the development of access to and understanding of written language. Simultaneously, however, such practices incorporate the multiple literacies that students who are ELLs bring to their classrooms and connect them to literacy practices with purposes of developing oral language through engaging students in social interaction with texts and those around them. Further, "good, research-based practice" in literacy intervention for ELLs includes teachers' analysis of and attention to the contexts of their classrooms within which they are creating the opportunities for struggling ELLs to improve their literacy skills, as much as any specific set of replicable recommendations that teachers are to deliver to students.

We expect, therefore, that this discussion will help us transcend simplistic policy, research, or practice questions about interventions that privilege exclusively empirical considerations. Although it is critical to maintain empirical considerations at the center of discussions about good practice, it is also necessary to take into account the comprehensive perspective we outline in this section. Next, we describe in more detail two reading interventions used for ELLs who struggle with reading. We encourage readers to bring to bear the considerations about good practice that we outline in this section as they review these exemplars.

Supplemental Direct Instruction of Phonological Awareness

A report published by the National Center for Education Evaluation and Regional Assistance (Gersten et al., 2007) recommended focused, intensive small-group interventions for elementary-grade ELLs who are struggling readers. This recommendation parallels those included in the reviewed literacy interventions that we described as skills-based approaches. The research provides evidence of the effectiveness of direct small-group instruction in a combined set of skills: phonological awareness, phonics, reading fluency, vocabulary, and comprehension. Based on our review of the recent research literature for this type of instruction for ELLs who are struggling readers or who are identified as having LD (Gunn et al., 2005; S. Vaughn, Linan-Thompson, et al., 2006; S. Vaughn, Mathes, et al., 2006), we decided to focus on a particular subset of these areas for direct instruction—phonological awareness—because it was the only reading subskill included across all 14 skills-based intervention studies.

Phonemic awareness, the basis for learning phonics, is the understanding that the sounds of spoken language are combined together to form words. *Phonological awareness* refers to the ability to key in on and manipulate phonemes, the smallest units of sound connected with independent meaning, into spoken words (Adams, Foorman, Lundberg, & Beeler, 1998). A core assumption of this type of intervention is that ELLs, particularly those who are struggling readers, need early, direct, and intensive instruction in phonological awareness in order to develop the building blocks for decoding skills. Research shows that as early as kindergarten it is possible to identify ELLs who are at risk for becoming struggling readers in relationship to their weaknesses with phonological awareness (Gunn et al., 2005; Leafstedt et al., 2004). Additional research shows that many schools delay in addressing the needs of ELLs who are experiencing reading difficulty, and instead take the approach that these students are simply learning English and developing literacy skills in typical ways due to their limited oral proficiency in English (Limbos & Geva, 2001). It is very important, it is argued, not to delay intervention until English proficiency is gained.

As summarized briefly in the preceding section entitled "Multiple-Strategy Interventions Targeting Reading Skills," Linan-Thompson et al. (2003) provided supplementary phonological awareness instruction as part of a focused literacy intervention for ELLs with Spanish as their primary language who were struggling readers. Of all the 14 skills-based intervention studies we reviewed (which were grounded in previous research on effective literacy interventions for monolingual English speakers who were

also struggling readers), this was the only skill-based intervention study that also incorporated strategies vetted in previous research on effective instructional strategies for ELLs. To provide sufficient detail so that readers can apply findings from this study to their own practice, we next detail Linan-Thompson and colleagues' approach to phonological awareness in combination with the instructional strategies for ELLs. Phonological awareness intervention was provided 5 minutes per day, following a period of 5 minutes of intervention in fluent reading, and followed by 10 minutes of instructional level reading and 5 minutes of word-study activities within a 30-minutes' total intervention block. Specifically, the phonological awareness portion of the intervention block consisted of students engaging in activities in which they had to "blend, segment, delete, substitute, and manipulate phonemes in words" (Linan-Thompson et al., 2003, p. 228). Teachers used activities from existing programs (e.g., *Ladders to Literacy,* Notari-Syverson, O'Conner, & Vadasy, 1998; *Phonemic Awareness in Young Children: A Classroom Curriculum,* Adams et al., 1998) and also created their own, grounded in research on effective instruction for ELLs, to assist students with auditory recognition of words, one strategy involved the teacher's showing picture cards while pronouncing the words illustrated by the cards. Another strategy informed by ELL instruction research was teacher identification of real and nonsense words; many real words encountered in the phonological awareness activities were not already part of the students' vocabulary, so teachers provided quick definitions of real words and identified nonsense words as students practiced blending, segmenting, and other phonemic manipulations of presented words. Further, if students could already manipulate phonemes efficiently in Spanish, the phonological awareness intervention focused instead on teachers' direct instruction of sounds that are similar in both Spanish and English, and then on those that are often more difficult for students who speak Spanish to distinguish, "such as minimal contrast pairs (e.g., /d/ and /th/)" (Linan-Thompson et al., 2003, p. 229). The 13-week intervention was conducted in small groups of two to three students per teacher for 30 minutes per day. For further reference, blending and segmenting are listed in a table of subskills most commonly addressed in phonological awareness interventions (see Table 28.1), because they have been found to have the greatest impact on overall phonological awareness (Yopp, 1988).

Considerations for Phonological Awareness Interventions with ELLs

When implementing phonological awareness interventions, a number of considerations are necessary to make them appropriate for ELLs. First, a primary focus in learning another language is on making meaning of sounds one hears in order to comprehend what is being said. However, many phonological awareness interventions instead

Table 28.1   Examples of Subskills Addressed in Phonological Awareness Interventions

Specific Skill	Example
Blending	Teacher: What word do you get when you put together these four sounds? /m/ /e/ /s/ /a/? Students: Mesa
Segmenting	Teacher: How many sounds are in *map*? Students: /m/ /a/ /p/ three (students tap out sounds on table as they say them).
Deleting	Teacher: What is *hand* without the /h/? Students: *Hand* without the /h/ is *and.*
Substituting	Teacher: The word is *grade*. Change /d/ to /p/. What's the new word? Students: *Grape.*
Discriminating between real and nonsense words	Teacher: Which word is real? *Table* or *Pable?* Students: *Table.*

ask ELLs to manipulate individual meaningless units of speech. Phonological awareness for ELLs therefore should be paired with strong support for language learning in comprehensible contexts (Cummins, 2000). Further, although English and some languages, such as Spanish, share similar sounds and have many polysyllabic words, some languages, such as Mandarin and Thai, have many monosyllabic words with very few final consonant sounds that may have many different meanings, depending on the speaker's tone. These variations across languages may mean some students, especially those experiencing reading difficulties, will struggle to discriminate sounds in words because of differences in their primary language structure. Thus, phonological awareness interventions may better support students when incorporating knowledge about the structure of the ELLs' primary language.

Intervention Concerned with Sociocultural Process of Literacy

The EAP (Bernhard et al., 2006, 2008), as mentioned earlier, is a literacy program that provides ELL struggling readers with opportunities to be writers and readers of their own books, supported by adults who facilitate this process. The EAP is one of several literacy interventions concerned with multiple forms of literacy described by Ada and Campoy (2003). The EAP intervention (Bernhard et al., 2006) included several components as students self-authored their own identity texts (i.e., autobiographies), facilitated by a teacher or other instructional personnel over a 12-month period. Educators required professional development to facilitate their effective teaching; they attended three community events in which the principles of

the program were presented, in addition to 2 days of on-site training led by bilingual literacy specialists.

Students authored, read, and used their books with each other, teachers, and their families and caregivers over the intervention period. Parents were involved in the authorship process by guiding students along the way. Four 2-hour meetings with parents/family members were held over the course of the intervention. During the meetings, family members participated in writing activities based on prompts about their life histories, which formed the basis for discussions about key themes in family writing. Additionally, teachers taught students to recite poems and rhymes in their home language. The EAP intervention provided teachers with books and other texts that included "children's oral folklore, including traditional art, literature, and sayings" (Bernhard et al., 2006, p. 2390). Teachers received training in how to relate letters of the alphabet with letters in children's names and with those of their family members and friends. Students who participated in the EAP demonstrated significant improvement in language skills compared to children in the control group, as measured by pre- and post-assessment with the Learning Accomplishment Profile–Diagnostic Edition (LAP-D; Nehring, Nehring, Bruni, & Randolph, 1992) and the Preschool Language Scale–Revised Fourth Edition (PLS-R; Zimmerman, Steiner, & Evatt Pond, 2002).

Bernhard et al. (2006) caution that the EAP is not a program that should or could be replicated exactly, because it is so highly driven by the context within which it is enacted and is informed by the settings, students, and families who participate in it. Instead, they recommend that similar interventions should adhere to the principles that inform the approaches presented in the study and should account for the unique resources and needs of the students in the processes of authorship and sharing of texts detailed within the program design. For further reference, these principles are listed and described in Table 28.2.

Conclusion and the Road Ahead: Toward Culturally Responsive Literacy Interventions for ELLs Who Are Struggling Readers or Identified with LD

Despite the unprecedented growth of the ELL population in schools around the United States and their long-standing negative educational outcomes, relatively few intervention studies have been conducted regarding literacy for this population in recent years. The theoretical underpinnings of the existing research continue to index the opposing views that have historically pervaded in the debates about reading and literacy. On one hand,

Table 28.2   Principles of Process-Oriented Literacy Intervention

Principle	Description
Student authorship of bilingual autobiographical texts	Students author books in which they are featured as protagonists of their life story.
Teacher facilitation of authorship process	Teachers engage in professional learning in the principles of the intervention and in their classrooms by bilingual literacy specialists to support students in the authorship process. Teachers have access to material resources that allow students' books to be published in high-quality format (e.g., laid out on computer, printed in black and white and color, bound, laminated).
Family facilitation of authorship process	Families receive training over time in community settings from bilingual literacy specialists about how to (a) support their children in developing ideas about self to include in auto-biographical texts, (b) assist their children with taking pictures or finding print objects to be included in their texts, and (c) involve family members in related writing activities of their own.
Teacher-led instruction on phonological awareness grounded in students' cultural and linguistic contexts	Teachers instruct students to recite poems and rhymes in their home language through the use of texts that included "children's oral folklore, including traditional art, literature, and sayings" (Bernhard et al., p. 2390). Teachers receive training by bilingual literacy specialists about how to relate letters of the alphabet with letters in children's names and in the names of their family members and friends.
Students' texts used as school curriculum and family resources	Students' texts are frequently used as the basis for school and home storytelling and literature-based discussion with teachers, other students, and family members.

Source: Information from Bernhard, J. K., Cummins, J., Campoy, F. I., Ada, A. F., Winsler, A., & Bleiker, C. (2006). Identity texts and literacy development among preschool English language learners: Enhancing learning opportunities for children at risk for learning disabilities. *Teachers College Record, 108,* 2380–2405.

the bulk of the work is founded on a skill-based perspective, partly because federal and state funding have prioritized this model (M. L. Smith, 2004). Moreover, more skill-oriented research has been produced because this perspective has received greater attention over time in the special education research community, where most of this research is conducted (L. Swanson, 2000; L. Swanson, Trainin, Necoechea, & Hammill, 2003). On the other hand, the bulk of process-oriented literacy research has historically relied on qualitative methodologies, which have a different approach to the transportability of findings across populations and contexts (Flood, Heath, & Lapp, 2008; C. Lee & Smagorinsky, 1999).

With the goal of transcending unproductive dichotomies in intervention work and as a means to pose a challenge to this field for future research, we conclude with discussion of a third model: culturally responsive literacy interventions for ELLs who are struggling with reading, identified with LD, or both. We frame this model as a set of the most promising practices from both types of interventions (i.e., skills based and socioculturally based) described earlier.

Culturally Responsive Literacy Interventions

Culturally responsive literacy interventions bridge a gap between the models discussed previously, while addressing histories of marginalization that many ELL groups have experienced in U.S. schools. Specifically, these interventions provide explicit, small-group instruction in discrete reading skills that are informed by knowledge of students' primary language structures. Further, these interventions engage students in the use of authentic texts and purposes for using texts in ways that draw on and build on the multiple ways of being literate that ELLs bring into classrooms. ELLs use their cultures and languages as a basis for understanding themselves and others, as a foundation for structuring social interactions around literacy practices, and to provide frameworks for conceptualizing new learning and knowledge (Ladson-Billings, 1992) as they receive direct instruction in reading subskills. Culturally responsive literacy interventions are:

1. *Relevant:* They use the cultural knowledge, prior experiences, and performance styles of diverse students to make learning more appropriate and effective; teaching to and through the strengths of ELLs (Gay, 2000).

2. *Multifaceted:* Their goals are to develop a variety of forms of literacy in ELLs, to provide opportunities to participate in critical inquiry about their world, and to work for social change. Multiple literacies include language-based, mathematical, scientific, historical, cultural, and political aspects (Ladson-Billings, 1992).

3. *Explicit:* ELLs receive direct instruction in basic literacy skills required in order to fully participate in the dominant culture (Delpit, 1988).

Table 28.3   Practitioner Considerations in Designing Culturally Responsive Literacy Interventions

Element	Questions
Goal of Instruction	How do I establish students' ownership of literacy as the overarching goal of the curriculum, while maintaining a systematic instruction in the cognitive processes of reading and writing?
	How do I make literacy personally meaningful and viewed as useful for the student's own purposes?
Role of Home Language	How do I allow students' primary language to exist in the classroom and build upon this language to achieve English literacy proficiency?
Instructional Materials	In what ways can I use materials that present diverse cultures in an authentic manner? Does the literature accurately depict the experiences of diverse groups?
	How do I increase students' motivation to read, their appreciation and understanding of their own language and cultural heritage, and their valuing of their own life experiences as a topic for writing?
Classroom Management and Interaction with Students	How do I create and adjust the classroom environment (organization and management system) to allow for genuine literacy activities through which students can feel ownership and learn through collaboration and engage in conversations with rules more like those for everyday talk rather than for classroom recitation?
Relationship to the Community	How do I make stronger links to the community, restructure the power relationships between the school and community, and involve parents and other community members in the school?
	How do I make specific connections to communities to which students belong?
Instructional Methods	In what ways can I provide students with authentic literacy activities, while providing instruction in specific literacy skills needed for full participation in the culture of power?
	How do I teach basic literacy skills within authentic literacy activities?
Assessment	What strategies could I use to prepare and analyze my assessments prior to implementation that would help reduce or eliminate sources of bias and more accurately reflect students' literacy achievement?

Source: Reprinted with permission from National Center for Culturally Responsive Educational Systems (2008). *Culturally responsive literacy. Professional Learning Series.* Tempe, AZ: Author.

We also wish to engage teachers in consideration of their unique classroom and community contexts as they implement the types of interventions described here. Thus, we provide a list of considerations for practitioners as they design culturally responsive literacy interventions (see Table 28.3). The questions in the table first appeared in our work with the National Center for Culturally Responsive Educational Systems, as part of a larger professional learning module on Culturally Responsive Literacy (National Center for Culturally Responsive Educational Systems, 2008). They are grouped by elements for improving school literacy learning of students of diverse backgrounds (Au, 1998) and reflect key areas of research on school literacy learning.

To conclude, we identified specific strategies with demonstrated effectiveness in promoting acquisition of reading subskills and other literacy practices. However, much work remains related to the advancement of a model that integrates insights derived from alternative models of reading and literacy. Furthermore, educators face substantial challenges in the institutionalization and scaling up of the research knowledge produced in this domain of study. It is encouraging that the bulk of intervention studies focused on prevention, that is, on ELLs who struggle with learning to read before diagnosis with LD. This is a needed perspective that can save significant resources to school districts (e.g., assessment costs) while enhancing the power of general education to address the needs of all students. Simultaneously, our review clearly suggests an urgent need to invest in research that addresses the needs of ELLs with LD, particularly because students in this disability category constitute the largest population served under IDEA funding. The increasing investment in preventive approaches as well as the growing concern with the seamless integration of general and special education are undoubtedly welcome developments that we expect will benefit significantly the growing population of ELLs in U.S. schools. We hope to see the consolidation of such trends in years to come.

Appendix 28.1

Summary Information on Interventions Reviewed

Study	Intervention	Setting	Participants	Measures	Duration	Level of Support	Fidelity Measures	Outcome
Bernhard et al., 2006	Early Authors Program	32 child-care centers in Miami-Dade County	1,179 randomly selected children ages 2–4	Learning Accomplishment Profile—Diagnostic Edition; Preschool Language Scale—Revised Fourth Edition; teacher survey of literacy skills; Early Steps to Reading Success survey	1 year	Support provided to classroom teachers by 13 trained literacy specialists	Not reported	Significant gains in language development compared to pretest measures and control children; prevented increasing lag compared to national age norm groups
J. Cohen, 2007	Summer literacy program of individualized instruction, Sustained Silent Reading, dialogue journals, and whole-group activities	Collaborative program between university and school district	One 17-year-old ELL	Qualitative Reading Inventory—3	4-week, full-day program	Individualized tutoring and group instruction by trained graduate students	Not reported	Increased enjoyment of reading, transactions with text, completion of oral reading activities, improved responses to reading comprehension items
Denton, Wexler, Vaughn, & Bryan, 2008	Modified phonics-based remedial program incorporating ESL practice, vocabulary instruction, fluency, and comprehension strategies	Southwest, urban middle school serving predominantly Hispanic, economically disadvantaged population	38 sixth- to eighth-grade students with DIBELS words correct per minute <80; randomly assigned to treatment or typical practice group	Peabody Picture Vocabulary Test in English and Spanish (receptive vocabulary); WJ-III Passage Comprehension, Letter-Word Identification, and Word Attack subtests; DIBELS reading fluency; Test of Word Reading Efficiency; Social Skills Rating System	47–55 daily 40-min sessions over 13 weeks	Instructional groupings of 2–4 students taught by 2 teachers with ≥10 hr training and ongoing coaching	Observations 3 times using treatment integrity checklist; rating between 91% and 98% for both teachers	Improved Sight Word Efficiency on the TOWRE

Study	Intervention	Setting	Participants	Measures	Duration	Level of Support	Fidelity Measures	Outcome
M. M. Gerber et al., 2004	Core Intervention Model: supplemental direct instruction in phonological skills	3 California school districts of predominantly Latino students identified as ELLs	37 Spanish-speaking kindergartners	Phonological awareness tasks (rime, onset detection, and phoneme segmentation); WJ-III English Word Attack and Letter-Word Identification	10 half-hr sessions	Small-group, direct instruction provided by trained bilingual undergraduates	Monitoring and feedback by senior researchers	Significant gains from beginning of kindergarten to end of 1st grade; caught up with high-performing peers
Gunn et al., 2005	Supplemental Reading Program emphasizing instruction in phonemic awareness and phonics; Incredible Years parent training program; Contingencies for Learning Academic and Social Skills	13 schools across 4 communities in Oregon	148 K–3 students identified with poor reading skills (n = 80) or aggressive social behavior (n = 80) (17 in special education; 27 receiving Title I services)	WJ-III English Word Attack, Letter-Word Identification, Vocabulary, Comprehension; Oral Reading Fluency words/minute	30 min daily for 3 days/week for 6–7 mo in 1st year, 9 mo in 2nd year	30 min/day supplemental reading instruction, parent training, social skills intervention, provided by 9 instructional assistants with 10 hr of training	Weekly observations during first month, monthly observations thereafter, 90% to 100% fidelity reported across observations	Significant improvement in letter-word identification, oral reading fluency, and reading comprehension relative to control group; continued improvement in reading fluency following intervention
Kamps et al., 2007	Small-group direct instruction in phonemic awareness, letter-sound recognition, decoding, fluency, and comprehension skills	16 Kansas schools over a 5-year period	170 ELL and 148 English-only 1st- and 2nd-grade students	DIBELS, Woodcock Reading Mastery Test	Not stated	Groups of 3–6 students using *Reading Mastery, Early Interventions in Reading, Read Well,* or *Reading Naturally* by general education teachers or reading specialists	Fidelity checklists of procedures, instructional features, instruction in key skills, and management features; mean scores of 82% to 98% across schools	Significant gains in Nonsense Word Fluency and Oral Reading Fluency; direct instruction intervention more effective than ESL literacy services

Study	Intervention	Setting	Participants	Measures	Duration	Delivery	Fidelity	Outcomes
Kelly et al., 2008	*Reading Recovery* intensive tutorial intervention	U.S. schools participating in *Reading Recovery*	8,581 ELLs from schools throughout U.S.	An Observation Survey of Early Literacy Achievement	Average of 15–16 weeks	Daily, individual 30-min lessons from 12–20 weeks from a trained teacher	Not reported	69% achieved grade-level performance
Leafstedt, Richards, & Gerber, 2004	Intensive phonological awareness direct instruction based on Core Intervention Model	Semi-rural California community of predominantly Spanish-speaking families	1 kindergarten class of ELLs ($n = 18$)	WJ-III Word Identification, Word Attack	300 min over 10 weeks (15 min twice per week)	Intensive instruction provided by researcher to groups of 3–5 students using Early Reading Project Curriculum	Not reported	Significant growth in word reading compared to ELLs receiving general kindergarten instruction ($n = 46$)
Linan-Thompson et al., 2003	Supplemental reading instruction in English	11 schools participating in a multistate longitudinal project	26 ELLs identified as at risk for reading difficulty	Texas Primary Reading Inventory; Woodcock Reading Mastery Test—Revised; Test of Reading Fluency; DIBELS—Segmentation Fluency; Woodcock-Muñoz Language Survey	30 min daily for 13 weeks (58 sessions)	Small groups	Not reported	Significant gains from pre- to post-test measures on all outcome measures
Lovett et al., 2008	Remedial reading instruction emphasizing word attack and word identification, randomly assigned to 1 of 3 groups focusing on (a) decoding only, (b) decoding plus writing and spelling, (c) phonological analysis plus writing and spelling	16 schools from a diverse, urban school district in Toronto, Canada	166 students identified with reading disabilities (76 ELL, 90 non-ELL)	Comprehensive Tests of Phonological Processing, Woodcock Reading Mastery Tests—Revised	1 hr daily for 4–5 weeks, totaling 105 hr	Intervention classes taught by certified special education teachers, grouped by reading level	Fidelity checked once for every 35 hr of instruction	No differences in outcomes between ELL and non-ELL groups; significant gains in overall scores and growth rates over students receiving equivalent amount of special education reading instruction

Study	Intervention	Setting	Participants	Measures	Duration	Level of Support	Fidelity Measures	Outcome
Sáenz, Fuchs, & Fuchs, 2005	PALS: reciprocal, class-wide peer-tutoring strategy	12 transitional, bilingual education classrooms in a South Texas school district	132 native Spanish-speaking ELLs, 3rd to 6th grades, 10 with learning disabilities	Comprehensive Reading Assessment Battery	35 min, 3 times per week for 15 weeks	Classes taught by teachers who completed full-day PALS workshop	Observation checklist assessed during weeks 6 and 12 by 2 observers, 100% at Time 1, mean accuracy between 93% and 95%	More growth in reading comprehension for ELLs with and without LD relative to comparison group receiving normal instruction
Scull & Bianco, 2008	*Reading Recovery* intensive tutorial intervention	10 schools in Victoria, Australia	10 students 6 to 8 years old, 4 ELLs	Observations, survey of early literacy achievement, record of reading difficulty level	30 min daily instruction for 12–20 weeks	Individualized instruction by teachers with at least 2 years' experience teaching RR	Not stated	Improved independent reading confidence and skill
K. Y. Tam, Heward, & Heng, 2006	Intervention program of vocabulary instruction, error correction, and fluency building	Public elementary school of 500 students	5 ELLs, 3 with disabilities	Reading rate, correct answers to comprehension questions	65 daily sessions	Individualized instruction by researcher	Not stated	4 of 5 reached fluency criterion of 100 words correct per minute
Troia, 2004	*Fast ForWord Language* computer-assisted instructional program, training in auditory perception and spoken language comprehension skills	7 rural public schools in Central Washington	99 first- to sixth-grade ELLs, 92 in control group	Lindamood Auditory Conceptualization Test; WJ-III Sound Blending, Word Identification, Word Attack; experimental rhyming and segmentation tasks	Five 20-min computer exercises per day for 4 weeks	Individualized computer-based exercises	Not stated	Greater gains compared to control group in basic reading, with greater gains among students with lower English proficiency in word recognition

Study	Intervention	Setting	Participants	Measures	Duration	Instruction format	Fidelity	Outcomes
S. Vaughn, Linan-Thompson, et al., 2006	Direct instruction in oral language and reading in Spanish following predetermined lesson plans of integrated literacy content strands	20 classrooms in 7 schools from 3 school districts	69 first-grade, Spanish-speaking ELLs	Woodcock Language Proficiency Battery—Revised	50 min/day for 8 mo	Small-group (3–5 students) instruction by 6 trained bilingual intervention teachers	Intervention validity checklist, field notes, teacher checklists of daily preparedness	Higher performance in Spanish on measures of basic reading and reading comprehension relative to student receiving standard interventions
S. Vaughn, Mathes, et al., 2006	Direct instruction in oral language and reading in English following predetermined lesson plans of integrated literacy content strands	14 classrooms in 4 schools in 2 districts in Texas	48 first-grade, Spanish-speaking ELLs	Letter naming, letter-sound identification, Comprehensive Tests of Phonological Processing; Test of Phonological Processes—Spanish; Woodcock Language Proficiency Battery—R: English and Spanish Forms; DIBELS	50 min/day for 7 mo	Small-group (3–5 students) instruction by 4 trained bilingual reading interventionists	Intervention validity checklist, field notes, teacher checklists of daily preparedness	Higher performance in letter naming, phonological awareness, word attack, and comprehension compared to students receiving standard instruction. Largest effects on these performance measures were in English; smaller effects on outcomes were in Spanish

Note: DIBELS = Dynamic Indicators of Basic Early Literacy Skills; ELL = English Language Learner; ESL = English as a Second Language; LD = Learning Disability; PALS = Peer-Assisted Learning Strategies; RR = Reading Recovery; WJ-III = Woodcock-Johnson III Tests of Achievement.

CHAPTER 29

Teaching Students with Language Disorders

Laura M. Justice | *The Ohio State University*

Sandra Gillam | *Utah State University*

Anita McGinty | *University of Virginia*

T he term *language* refers to the socially shared code of symbols that people use to represent the world to others using speech (spoken language), sign (sign language), or writing (written language). Language, which draws on a set of basic and higher-order processes based largely within the left hemisphere of the human brain, is often confused with such closely related terms as *speech* and *communication*. Speech is the neuromuscular process through which humans express language, whereas communication is the process through which information is shared between humans using speech, language, and other means, such as gestures and facial expressions (Justice, 2010).

Language processes are often differentiated into two modalities—comprehension (i.e., the reception of language) and expression (i.e., the production of language)—and four domains. These domains consist of (a) grammar, referring to the set of rules that govern word and sentence structure (e.g., using the conjunction *and* to join two independent clauses); (b) semantics, referring to the set of rules that govern word meanings and word relationships (e.g., recognizing that *couch* and *chair* are categorically related); (c) phonology, referring to the set of rules that govern speech sounds (e.g., knowing that the sound /g/ never follows the sound /n/ at the start of spoken English words); and (d) pragmatics, referring to the set of rules

that govern the social use of language (e.g., entering conversations using specific strategies, such as commenting on the topic currently being discussed).

Language involves a highly complex set of processes specific to the human species that facilitates participation in life from home to the community. Language abilities are intricately tied to children's ability to form attachment relationships with their earliest caregivers, to succeed academically, and to form positive peer relationships. Beyond the years of schooling, language ability is necessary to perform most if not all activities required to participate fully in society, including basic and advanced work functions (e.g., responding to e-mail, leading meetings) and civic functions (e.g., voting by ballot). Given the relevance of language skill to human development from birth forward, it is not surprising that educators are greatly concerned when children are not meeting their full potential in language acquisition, as may be the case when children have a language disorder.

Language disorders are a specific type of disability that can affect individuals across the lifespan, from infants to the elderly. A language disorder occurs when one's language skills or processes in any one of the four domains are not consistent with expectations based on normative references (i.e., the language abilities expected based on a person's age and social background, including educational history). A long history of developmental research has informed our understanding of when specific language skills and processes typically emerge during the course of human development (as well as how variability in developmental experiences can have an impact on emergence of language), and these normative references are useful for identifying when language acquisition is not proceeding at a typical rate. For instance, we generally expect infants to begin to babble by about 6 months of age and to produce their first word by about 12 months. By 18 months, it is common to see children begin to combine two words to make very short sentences (e.g., *mommy up*). Such developmental data make it possible to recognize when language development is not following its expected courses (e.g., Ganger & Brent, 2004). For instance, in infancy, characteristics of a language disorder typically include (a) delayed use of babbling and restricted range of babbled sounds, (b) delayed gesturing and other nonverbal means of communicating, and (c) delayed production of the first word. In addition, infants with language disorder will accrue their first 50 vocabulary words relatively slowly and will begin to combine words to make two-word sentences later than other children (Rescorla, Roberts, & Dahlsgaard, 1997; Scarborough, 1990).

Language disorders, when present from infancy forward, are referred to as *developmental language disorders* to distinguish them from language disorders that occur later in life, often because of some sort of acquired brain damage (most commonly stroke or a traumatic brain injury). Language disorders that result from damage to the brain are typically described as acquired language disorders, or aphasia. In this chapter, we focus exclusively on developmental language disorders. Some cases of developmental language disorder occur for no known reason; in such instances, a significant disability in the area of language is the child's only impairment, as the language disorder occurs in the absence of any intellectual (e.g., cognitive disability), neurological (e.g., autism), motor (e.g., cerebral palsy), or sensory (e.g., hearing loss) disturbances. When a language disorder occurs in isolation, it is referred to as *primary language disorder* or, more commonly, *specific language impairment (SLI)*. SLI affects an estimated 7% to 10% of school-age children, thereby making it one of the most common reasons for which children receive special education services (Tomblin et al., 1997). Language disorders can also occur concomitantly with other disabilities; for instance, children who experience cognitive disability (e.g., Down syndrome), autism, and hearing loss often experience a language disorder as a result of their primary disability.

Whether a language disorder is a child's primary disability or occurs secondary to another type of impairment, difficulties with language ability can cause children to have significant challenges in two pivotal areas of development: (a) social competence, including engagement and interactions with parents, teachers, and peers; and (b) academic achievement, including the development of skills specific to reading development and the use of these skills to gain access to the entire curriculum. Because of its far-reaching impact on children's social and academic development, treatment of language disorders is a significant component of special education services for children within public schooling. In fact, the costs of such services are estimated at $36 billion annually (J. Chambers, Parrish, & Harr, 2004).

Intervention for language disorders is often introduced early in a child's life, perhaps as early as infancy for children who exhibit specific recognizable conditions that heighten risks for language disorders. This includes early-identified cognitive disability (e.g., as associated with fetal alcohol syndrome and Down syndrome) and significant hearing loss, as well as prematurity/low birth weight. Intervention for children who are not yet talking (e.g., babies with Down syndrome) will focus on helping them to develop *prelinguistic* skills, such as engaging in periods of sustained attention with their caregivers and babbling (Warren, Yoder, Gazdag, Kim, & Jones, 1993). In the years following infancy, including toddlerhood and the preschool years, most language disorders are recognized among children who do not exhibit other identifiable disabilities, because this is when children must draw on their linguistic resources to interact with the world around them (e.g., by producing sentences to make requests and to ask questions). Warning signs that can signal presence of a language disorder include (a) having a very small vocabulary and having difficulty learning new words; (b) using very short sentences and omitting grammatical markers (e.g., plurals, articles) when other children are using them; and (c) being unable to use language instrumentally with peers and others, such as asking questions to gain information and making requests. These and other indicators of language disorders characterizing children in the preschool and primary grades appear in Table 29.1.

Educators, parents, and allied professionals (e.g., speech-language pathologists) use a number of practices to address the core language difficulties of children with language disorders. These practices can vary substantially with respect to *how* they go about changing a child's language abilities; for instance, one practice may feature the child's participation in highly decontextualized repeated drill-and-practice routines with a professional, whereas another practice may feature the child's participation in classroom-based curricular activities with a peer. Often, decisions about the specific techniques one uses (the *how* of intervention) are based on one's theoretical paradigm and personal experience. As a general rule, a variety of practices are potentially

Table 29.1 Common Indicators of Language Disorder

Age	Language Difficulties
Infancy and toddlerhood	Delayed production of babbling
	Late appearance of first word
	Delayed use of simple grammatical markers (present progressive -*ing*, plural -*s*, possessive -*'s*)
	Late emergence of two- and three-word combinations
	Less variety of verbs
	Slow development of pronouns
Preschool	Omission of *to be* verbs (e.g., "he going," "dolly coming")
	Omission of articles
	Pronoun errors
	Shorter sentence length
	Lack of coherence in stories
	Problems comprehending complex directions
	Overreliance on nonspecific nouns
	Difficulty initiating conversations with peers
	Difficulty sustaining conversations over multiple turns
	Limited diversity in vocabulary
Early and later elementary	Word-finding problems
	Slow naming speed and naming errors (e.g., *shoes* for *pants*)
	Use of earlier-developing pronoun forms
	Difficulty maintaining conversational topics over multiple turns
	Difficulty/reluctance initiating conversation with peers
	Difficulty understanding abstract vocabulary terms
	Shorter sentence length
	Lack of coherence in connected discourse (e.g., story retelling)
	Problems with reading development (including reading comprehension)
	Problems comprehending figurative language (e.g., riddles, idioms)

Sources: Conti-Ramsden & Jones (1997); Leonard (2000); McGregor & Leonard (1995); Ratner & Harris (1994); Watkins, Rice, & Molz (1993).

effective for bringing about change in a child's language abilities. What seems to be particularly important is that a selected language-intervention practice is offered with reasonable intensity/frequency and explicitly targets the

domains of language developing slowly (Fey, Cleave, & Long, 1997; S. Gillam, Gillam, Petersen, & Bingham, 2008; J. Law, Garrett, & Nye, 2004).

In the remainder of this chapter, we'll discuss two specific language-intervention practices adhering to these parameters that also have a reasonable amount of quality research supporting their effectiveness with children with language disorders: *focused stimulation* and *story structure intervention*. We have selected these two practices not only because they are scientifically supported but also because they represent how approaches may vary when used with younger versus older children. Specifically, focused stimulation is primarily used with toddlers and preschoolers, whereas story structure intervention is primarily used with school-age children.

Review of Effective Practices

Focused Stimulation

Definition and Overview

Focused stimulation is a language-intervention practice commonly used with toddlers and preschoolers exhibiting significantly delayed language development. To implement this practice, a parent, teacher, or therapist provides *highly concentrated presentations* of specific linguistic targets, which include words, sounds, or grammatical structures, within such naturalistic routines as play or storybook reading (Girolametto, Pearce, & Weitzman, 1996, p. 1275; see also Fey, 1986). These "presentations" often take the form of repeated *models, contrasts,* and *recasts.* Contrasts and models tend to follow and thus build on the child's communicative contributions. These three examples target the child's use of "is" as a main (copula) verb:

Example 1: *Teacher (models):* This boy *is* sad. The boy *is* so sad.

Child: He sad.

Teacher (recasts): He *is* sad.

Example 2: *Child:* He sad.

Teacher (recasts): Is he sad?

Example 3: *Child:* Him sad.

Teacher (contrasts and recasts): He is sad.

In the first example, the teacher initially models the targeted form. The child responds and omits the targeted form, to which the teacher then recasts the child's utterance to model again the targeted form. Note that the teacher's recast retains the child's statement verbatim with the exception of providing the copula form. In the third example, the teacher uses a contrast for the pronoun form (*him/he*) along with the recast for the copula form: the teacher uses the correct form of the subjective pronoun (*he*) as contrasted against the child's form (*him*): Models, contrasts, and recasts can be used to target a variety of specific linguistic structures, including such semantic targets as individual words and word combinations (Girolametto et al., 1996):

Example 1: *Child:* That. (individual word)

> *Teacher (models, recasts):* That's a *baby.*

Example 2: *Child:* Baby sleeping. (word combination)

> *Teacher (models, recasts):* The *little baby's* sleeping. He's a *little baby.*

Phonological targets might include eliminating cluster reduction (i.e., when the child reduces consonant clusters to single sounds) and eliminating final consonant deletion (Tyler & Sandoval, 1994).

Example 1: *Child:* It's a "tain." (cluster reduction)

> *Teacher (recasts, contrasts):* It's a *train.* Is it a tain or a *train?*

Example 2: *Child:* My "boa." (final consonant deletion)

> *Teacher (recasts, models):* That's your *boat.* It's a *boat.*

Grammatical targets might include use of articles and use of word inflections (e.g., *-ing* for present progressive) (Cleave & Fey, 1997).

Example 1: *Child:* I need book. (use of articles)

> *Teacher (recasts, models):* You want *the* book.

Example 2: *Child:* He walk. (use of word inflections)

> *Teacher (recasts):* He is *walking.*

In addition to using models, recasts, and contrasts to provide children with high-density exposure to targeted linguistic forms, focused stimulation procedures also commonly feature several additional strategies designed to elicit the child's productions of targeted forms explicitly. These descriptions and definitions are adapted from Cleave and Fey's (1997) description of each strategy. The first strategy involves using *false assertions and feigned misunderstandings* designed to evoke responses from the child that include targeted forms, as in this false assertion which evokes the child's use of the targeted present-progressive verb form:

Example 1: *Adult (pointing to a sleeping baby):* The baby is *eating.*

> *Child:* No, baby sleeping.

Forced-choice questions are another strategy for eliciting the child's production of targeted forms, as in this example designed to elicit the child's use of subjective pronouns:

Example 1: *Adult (holding two baby dolls):* Do you want *him* or *her?*

The third strategy is *requests for elaboration,* which are used specifically to elicit the child's use of more complex sentence structures and to include omitted information:

Example 1: *Child:* Want that one.

> *Adult:* Which one do you want?
>
> *Child:* That one.
>
> *Adult:* Why do you want that one?
>
> *Child:* That one strawberry.
>
> *Adult:* Oh, you like strawberry. That's your favorite flavor.

An important aspect of focused stimulation is that it is to be implemented within naturalistic contexts. This approach to intervention is designed to leverage children's desire to communicate with others in functional circumstances that approximate typical communicative experiences. Within these naturalistic contexts, such as interactive play, the adult might use specific strategies to manipulate the environment so as to encourage the child's use of targeted words, sounds, or grammatical structures (Cleave & Fey, 1997). For instance, again drawing on our goal for a child to use *is* as a main verb, a teacher might engage a child in an activity that involves taking turns, such as building a tower out of blocks in which opportunities to add to the tower are rotated across teacher and child. During the activity, the teacher might withhold blocks from the child (e.g., place them behind her back) so that the child must communicate to participate in the activity; this is sometimes referred to as *sabotage.* This presents the opportunity for the teacher to model the targeted grammatical form frequently, as in "It *is* my turn" and "It *is* your turn." Should the child comment "It my turn," this also provides the opportunity for the teacher to recast the child's contribution by responding, "It *is* your turn."

A particularly important feature of focused stimulation concerns the selection of linguistic targets (also called *goals*), which requires careful examination of the child's current vocabulary, phonological, or grammatical abilities. In other words, goal selection is highly individualized. Goals are typically selected based on (a) communicative need (the goal will in some way help a child communicate more effectively) and (b) readiness (the child shows some cognitive readiness for the goal) (Cleave & Fey, 1997). For instance, vocabulary goals for a given child might be a small set of words that are highly functional to a child (e.g., *eat, want, my, bottle*) and are comprehended but are not used in any context. That the words are comprehended suggests that the child may be "ready" to use the words productively. Grammatical goals for a child might represent grammatical forms used infrequently and inconsistently; a typical benchmark for selection of a grammatical form as an appropriate target for intervention is use of the form less than 50% of the time in obligatory contexts (Cleave & Fey, 1997). Selection of goals for a specific child typically requires one to have a strong understanding of typical language development (so as to select developmentally appropriate targets) as well as sophisticated knowledge of that child's language abilities across grammar, semantics, phonology, and pragmatics. This knowledge is typically attained not only by standardized assessments but also through language-sampling procedures, in which children's language production is studied and analyzed across a variety of different contexts, including everyday routines.

Theoretical Underpinnings

Focused stimulation is highly influenced by social-interactionist theories of language acquisition. Interactionist perspectives view language acquisition as a psychobiological process in which "frequent, relatively well-tuned affectively positive verbal interactions" are critical for supporting language growth in early childhood (Chapman, 2000, p. 43). This perspective emphasizes the importance of children's socially embedded, mediated interactions with more knowledgeable conversational partners as a critical developmental mechanism (Bruner, 1983; Justice & Ezell, 1999). Within such interactions, the more knowledgeable partner (e.g., teacher) fine-tunes her verbal input to scaffold the child's communicative engagement and gradual movement from dependent to more independent levels of linguistic skill in semantics, phonology, grammar, and pragmatics. This partner is seen as a critical resource for fostering the language skills of children with language disorders, in that she can provide "enhanced or optimized levels" of linguistic input that provide increased opportunities for children to learn specific dimensions of language (Girolametto et al., 1996, p. 1274). Drawing on the perspective that interactions with others is a critical context in which children acquire language skills, focused stimulation embeds intervention within naturalistic conversational routines; within these routines, the adult provides the child with highly concentrated exposures to specific language-acquisition targets, based on the theory that children with language-learning difficulties may require a higher concentration of exposures to specific words, sounds, or grammatical forms to acquire them.

Developmental research provides considerable empirical support for social-interactionist perspectives regarding the influence of linguistic input on children's rate of language acquisition (e.g., Baumwell, Tamis-LeMonda, & Bornstein, 1997; Hart & Risley, 1995; Pellegrini, Galda, Jones, & Perlmutter, 1995; Tamis-LeMonda, Bornstein, & Baumwell, 2001). Although much of this research has focused on parents and their children, some studies have looked outside the home to study associations between the linguistic input children hear in other environments and their rate of language growth. For instance, Girolametto and Weitzman (2002) described the rate of child-care providers' use of specific language-modeling strategies (e.g., imitations, labeling, expansions) to explain variation in preschoolers' semantic and syntactic skills. Additionally, a number of studies (several of which we describe shortly) have directly tested the effects of focused stimulation for accelerating the language growth of children with language disorders, supporting the efficacy of this approach (e.g., Cleave & Fey, 1997; Girolametto et al., 1996).

Implementation Guide

Implementation of focused stimulation typically involves three primary considerations: (a) establishing and manipulating the intervention context, (b) selecting intervention targets, and (c) implementing focused stimulation procedures. Figure 29.1 provides an overview of each of these three components of focused stimulation based on published reports in the literature (Cleave & Fey, 1997; Fey, Long, & Finestack, 2003; Girolametto et al., 1996). It is also worth noting that a comprehensive manual for implementing a variation of focused stimulation is available from the nonprofit Hanen Centre, located in Canada; this guide (*It Takes Two to Talk;* Pepper & Weitzman, 2004) was developed specifically for parents as a means to support their use of focused stimulation procedures within the home environment with their toddlers with language disabilities. This manual presents complex concepts regarding language facilitation in parent-friendly terms and offers numerous examples of specific facilitation techniques. Also available is a teacher-oriented manual, *Learning Language and Loving It* (LLLI; Weitzman & Greenberg, 2002), which was designed to teach early childhood educators how to use focused stimulation procedures with young children in their classrooms. The Hanen Centre has implementation checklists available for LLLI that can be used to promote teachers' learning of these techniques (Girolametto & Weitzman, 2002, includes a copy in the appendix).

Research Base

Among the variety of language-intervention approaches available in the research literature, focused stimulation is likely the most strongly supported. This support is

Figure 29.1 Implementation guide for focused stimulation.

A. Intervention Context

— Intervention implemented in naturalistic contexts/activities

— Intervention features natural adult–child conversations

— Context manipulated to entice child to engage in communicative participation (e.g., withholding objects, use of interesting toys)

B. Intervention Targets

— Targets selected based on analysis of conversational language sample

— Targets represent obstacles to child's communication success

— Targets are linguistic forms that the child uses infrequently and/or inconsistently

C. Intervention Procedures

1. Adult provides a high density of linguistic targets by using:

— **simple models** of linguistic targets in a range of possible contexts

— **recasts** that follow the child's use of linguistic targets

— **contrasts** between target forms and more advanced forms

2. Adult elicits child's attempts at linguistic targets by:

— **false assertions** and **feigned misunderstandings**

— **forced-choice questions**

— **requests for elaborations**

Sources: Cleave & Fey (1997); Fey (1986); Fey, Long, & Finestack (2003); Girolametto, Pearce, & Weitzman (1996).

derived in part from descriptive or correlational studies that support a positive and significant relationship between child exposure to specific stimulation procedures (e.g., recasts) and their language gains (Girolametto & Weitzman, 2002; M. W. Smith & Dickinson, 1994). Girolametto and Weitzman, for instance, reported correlations of 0.51, 0.41, and 0.48 between day-care providers' use of three stimulation strategies combined (i.e., models, expansions, recasts) and preschool-age children's verbal productivity, syntactic complexity, and lexical diversity. Perhaps more convincingly, experimental studies training parents, teachers, and therapists to use specific stimulation techniques have consistently shown these strategies to foster early language achievements in young children (e.g., K. Cole, Dale, & Mills, 1991; Fey, Cleave, & Long, 1997; Fey, Krulik, Loeb, &

Proctor-Williams, 1999; Fey & Loeb, 2002). We describe two such studies here to illustrate the type of evidence available in support of this approach to language intervention with young children.

Focused stimulation with toddlers with vocabulary delays. Girolametto and colleagues (1996) conducted a randomized controlled trial of focused stimulation as implemented by parents of toddlers with expressive vocabulary delays. A total of 25 mother–child dyads participated, with 12 dyads assigned to an experimental treatment group, and the remainder ($n = 13$) assigned to a control group. Demographically, the sample comprised primarily middle- to upper-socioeconomic status (SES) families, all of whom were native English speakers. Children ranged in age from 23 to 33 months of age, and all had significant delays in vocabulary development (i.e., all were in the lower fifth percentile on a standardized measure of language expression, based on parent report).

Parents assigned to the treatment group participated in an 11-week program involving eight 2.5-hour evening training sessions (completed as a group) and three home visits; training sessions and home visits were conducted by certified speech-language pathologists (SLPs). The parent training used the Hanen Centre's variation of focused stimulation and taught parents how to use specific stimulation techniques, particularly modeling and recasting, to target 10 vocabulary words across a variety of naturalistic contexts within the home environment. Treatment fidelity was assessed for all parents, to include attendance data showing that parents completed training sessions and observation data showing that parents used the stimulation techniques they were taught.

To assess the efficacy of focused stimulation for these toddlers with expressive-vocabulary delays, researchers assessed children's vocabulary growth pre- and post-intervention, using several measures, including parent report of child vocabulary size based on a standardized parent questionnaire and analysis of children's vocabulary expression during structured observations. Compared to children in the control group, at post-intervention the children whose parents used focused stimulation had significantly larger vocabularies and used a significantly greater variety of words when interacting with their parents. Study findings suggest that parent implementation of focused stimulation within the home environment is an efficacious means for promoting the vocabulary development of toddlers with vocabulary delays.

Focused stimulation with preschoolers with SLI. A hallmark characteristic of SLI is its negative impacts on children's development of grammar (e.g., Rice & Wexler, 1996; Rice, Wexler, & Hershberger, 1998). Children with SLI, during the preschool years, commonly exhibit late onset of specific grammatical forms (e.g., objective pronouns: *she, he, they*) as well as protracted use of more immature forms (e.g., substituting subjective pronouns for objective pronouns: *Her did it*). A number of experimental studies have sought specifically to determine whether focused stimulation procedures are efficacious for resolving the grammatical deficits of preschoolers with SLI (see Cleave & Fey, 1997; Fey et al., 1997; Fey, Cleave, Long, & Hughes, 1993).

Likely the most extensive study addressing this question to date was that of Fey and colleagues, described in a 1993 publication. This study involved 30 children with SLI who ranged in age from 42 to 70 months. All had grammar-specific deficits in conjunction with additional difficulties with language (e.g., vocabulary and phonological weaknesses). The children were randomly assigned to one of three groups, two of which involved focused stimulation, and one of which involved a delayed-treatment (control, *n* = 9) group. The two focused stimulation groups, comprising a total of 21 children, featured a planned comparison of parent- and clinician-implemented language interventions (*n* = 10 and *n* = 11, respectively). As this design indicates, in addition to assessing the efficacy of focused stimulation for influencing the language skills of children with SLI, this study also sought to compare the efficacy of parent- and clinician-implemented treatment variations.

Children in both treatment conditions received focused stimulation for 4.5 months. Children in the clinician-implemented condition received treatment in three sessions per week by a licensed SLP, consisting of one 1-hour individual session and two 1-hour group sessions involving four to six children. Children in the parent-implemented condition received treatment at home by their parents, who completed weekly 2-hour group sessions (in which only parents participated) for 12 weeks and then monthly for two additional months. For children in both treatment groups, four specific grammatical goals were selected for each child, and one goal was targeted each week; goals were cycled through the course of the 4.5 month treatment. Focused stimulation procedures used by clinicians and parents largely adhered to those listed in Figure 29.1.

The effects of the focused stimulation treatment programs on children's language development were determined using a single measure of grammatical complexity collected from children pre- and post-intervention. Children in the control group exhibited no gains on the grammatical complexity measure from pre- to post-test, whereas children in both treatment programs exhibited gains on the magnitude of about 1 standard deviation unit. This is generally considered to be a large treatment effect. Interestingly, the difference between the two treatment conditions (parent- or clinician-implemented) was not statistically significant, indicating that whether children received focused stimulation from an SLP or a parent was not an important consideration when considering intervention efficacy. In this regard, findings of this study converge with those discussed previously concerning parental implementation of focused stimulation with their toddlers experiencing vocabulary delays.

Story Structure Intervention

Definition and Overview

Story structure intervention is a practice commonly used with school-age children who have a language disorder. It is designed to increase children's comprehension and production of relatively "large" units of language (e.g., stories, also called *narratives*). Story structure instruction typically involves teaching the components of a story, modeling the use of the components in stories, identifying story elements, answering questions about stories, retelling stories, or generating new stories containing the elements that were taught. Many of the instructional strategies include graphic visual representations of specific elements, ideas, and causal connections contained in stories, which we refer to as *story maps*. Originally, the goal of story structure instruction was to improve children's reading comprehension (Z. T. Davis, 1994; Gardill & Jitendra, 1999; Reutzel, 1985a, 1985b; Short & Ryan, 1984). However, later studies of story structure instruction have focused on improving children's story-telling skills. A number of story elements have been taught in story structure intervention, often called story grammar (D. Hughes, McGillivray, & Schmidek, 1997; Labov, 1972; N. L. Stein & Glenn, 1979); elements of story grammar often taught in the intervention are summarized in Figure 29.2.

Some story grammar elements are associated with more sophisticated conceptual and linguistic knowledge than others. For example, for a child to understand or employ the use of *planning* in a story, he must have knowledge of mental state verbs such as *thought* or *decided* and attribute them to characters. Plans are usually expressed with a complex syntactic structure called a *clausal complement* (e.g., "Superman thought he should save Lois Lane."), in which the object of the mental state verb is an entire clause. Similarly, *internal responses* require an understanding of the ways characters feel about events in the story and how they may motivate their actions. Attributing mental states and feelings to characters can be particularly difficult for children with language problems (J. Ford & Milosky, 2003; Spackman, Fujiki, & Brinton, 2006) or with

Figure 29.2 Elements of story structure often targeted in story structure instruction.

Character	Agents who perform actions in stories
Setting	References to time or place in stories
Initiating events	Central problems in the story requiring some action be taken for resolution
Internal responses	Statements indicating how characters feel about an initiating event
Plan	Character's thoughts about potential solutions to a problem
Attempts	Actions taken by a character to resolve a central problem
Complications	Obstacles impeding the resolution of central problems
Consequences	Statements about whether actions taken by characters in response to central problems were successful or unsuccessful
Reactions	Statements indicating how characters feel about the consequences
Closing	Statements that bring the story to a close or explain the general meaning of the story

autism spectrum disorders (Bartsch & Wellman, 1995; Silliman et al., 2003; Wellman, 1990) and may require more explicit, intensive instruction. Thus, decisions regarding the kinds of story grammar elements to include in story structure instruction will involve careful consideration of a child's level of conceptual development as well as linguistic proficiency.

Educators can use story maps to specifically teach children the causal connections between story elements, as in the following example:

$$\text{Character} \rightarrow \text{Problem} \rightarrow \text{Action}$$
$$\rightarrow \text{Consequence} \rightarrow \text{Reaction}$$

In this story map, the character encounters a problem and takes a corresponding action, which is then followed by a consequence and a subsequent reaction. These story grammar elements occur in temporal order, as indicated by the direction of the arrows, and these elements together form the basis for understanding the story. The story also involves a causal order of events; for instance, the problem "causes" the character to act, which in turn results in a consequence.

The use of "why" questioning techniques has been recommended as a useful way to highlight causal networks in stories (Trabasso & Magliano, 1996). For example, using the example from the preceding causal map, a teacher or clinician might ask, "Why did [character] do [action]?" The correct answer would require the child to make a causal connection between the *problem* in the story and the *action* taken by the character to solve that problem, as in "Eleanor *ran away* (action) *because* (causal connection) *the bear was chasing her* (initiating event/problem)."

Theoretical Underpinnings

Teaching procedures commonly associated with story structure intervention, particularly the use of story maps and graphic organizers, align well with the theoretical literature on text structure (see Hoggan & Strong, 1994). Mapping allows a visual depiction of the overall structure and theme of the story as well as the sequence of events. The theory of text structure (Kintsch & van Dijk, 1978) is relevant to the story structure approach because it includes descriptions of text microstructure (e.g., vocabulary, sentences), macrostructure (e.g., overall structure or theme of the text, specific to different genres), and cohesion (i.e., devices used to relate microstructures to each other and to the macrostructure). Kintsch and van Dijk proposed that comprehension is accomplished by integrating these sources of information to construct a coherent situational representation of the text through the use of semantic relationships and causal connections contained therein.

Schema theory (Rumelhart, 1975; N. L. Stein & Glenn, 1979) is another theoretical basis for the use of story structure instruction that focuses on story episodes in comprehension instruction. Helping children gain explicit knowledge of text structures may improve the conceptual knowledge that supports their understanding and use of oral and written discourse structures. *Text structure* refers to the ways in which texts are organized: in narrative stories, a common text structure is problem–solution, whereas in expository text, a common text structure is compare–contrast. Text structures are associated with specific vocabulary as well as specific grammatical forms. Comprehension processes can be facilitated through knowledge of underlying text structure (Graesser, Singer, & Trabasso, 1994; Trabasso, Secco, & van den Broek, 1984). One of the most salient features of narrative texts is its predictable and stable causal structure (Trabasso, van den Broek, & Suh, 1989). Adults and children are better able to recall relevant information and answer comprehension questions about texts when they attend to the underlying text structures that are contained therein (Goldman & Varnhagen, 1986; Trabasso & Magliano, 1996; Trabasso & van den Broek, 1985; Trabasso, Suh, Payton, & Jain, 1995). Providing children with a highly specific scaffold or story map for narrative discourse should improve a child's understanding of the "structure" of oral and written texts. This knowledge may

Figure 29.3   Implementation guide for story structure intervention.

A. Intervention Context

— Intervention implemented in literature-based contexts/activities

— Intervention features identification of story grammar elements and causal connections using visual graphic organizers or symbols

— Complexity of stories manipulated to highlight different linguistic targets (e.g., subordinated adverbial clauses, relative clauses, causal compliments, later developing infinitives)

B. Intervention Targets

— Intervention targets story grammar elements (character, setting, initiating event, internal response, attempts, complication, consequence, ending)

— Intervention targets causal connection words (e.g., *because, so, since, therefore, thus*)

— Intervention targets linguistic forms that the child uses infrequently, inconsistently, or both in narrative production (e.g., subordinated adverbial clauses, relative clauses, causal compliments, later-developing infinitives) to improve story complexity and use of literate language

C. Intervention Procedures

1. Adult models, scaffolds, and supports independence in:

— **identification** of story grammar elements and causal connections in a variety of contexts (e.g., listening and reading, question-answer)

— **production** or use of story grammar elements and causal connections in supported and self-generated stories (e.g., retelling sequenced pictures, wordless picture books and single scenes, drawing/pictography)

— **contrasts** between complete (e.g., initiating event, attempt, consequence), incomplete (e.g., initiating event, attempt), and complex (initiating event, attempt, complication, consequence) episodes

2. Adult highlights linguistic forms, causal connections, or both through the use of contingent facilitation strategies:

— **modeling/demonstration** (Adult: She ran BECAUSE she was afraid of the bear.)

— **prompts/questions** (Child: She ran away. Adult: Why do you think she ran away?)

— **vertical structuring** (e.g., Child: The girl is running. Adult: Why is she running? Child: She sees a bear. Adult: The girl is running BECAUSE she sees a bear.)

— **growth-relevant recasts** (e.g., Child: That girl is running. Adult: Yes, she is running SO THAT the bear can't catch her.)

Source: Information from Gillam, S., Gillam, R., Petersen, D., & Bingham, C. (2008). *Narrative language intervention program: Promoting oral language development.* Technical session presented at The Annual Convention of the American Speech Language and Hearing Association, Chicago, IL.

be applied regularly to future encounters with similar texts (Pearson & Duke, 2002) to aid in comprehension and generation of summaries.

Implementation Guide

Figure 29.3 provides a general implementation guide for story structure interventions. In general, story maps may be developed for an entire story or for certain subcomponents of a story (e.g., mapping a cause-and-effect sequence of events); as a result, these may be very specific or more general in nature. As may be seen in Figure 29.4, a story map may be used to elaborate on any one aspect of story grammar with which children may be having particular problems or to assist them in deeper processing of information for use in elaboration. The story map shown in Figure 29.5 was designed to assist children in thinking

Figure 29.4   Story map for character elaboration.

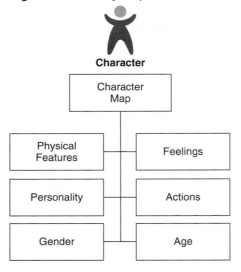

Figure 29.5   Child-generated story map based on a clinician-led, progressive, group story-generation activity.

Source: Information from Gillam, S., Gillam, R., Petersen, D., & Bingham, C. (2008). *Narrative language intervention program: Promoting oral language development*. Technical session presented at The Annual Convention of the American Speech Language and Hearing Association, Chicago, IL.

about the attributes of the characters who took part in the story for use in answering more elaborative questions after reading. As a rule, there is considerable flexibility in using story maps to promote language and reading skills.

Research Base

The practice of teaching story structure through the use of story maps and graphic organizers has been widely applied in regular and special education contexts. School-age children who are developing typically as well as those with a wide range of disabilities—including learning disabilities, reading disabilities, and language disorders—have been shown to benefit from various approaches to story structure instruction (Boulinea, Fore, Hagan-Burke, & Burke, 2004; J. Fitzgerald & Spiegel, 1983; C. J. Gordon & Pearson, 1983; Hayward & Schnieder, 2000; Idol, 1987; Montgomery & Kahn, 2003; Nathanson, Crank, Saywitz, & Ruegg, 2007; Nolte & Singer, 1985; H. Singer & Donlan, 1982; L. A. Swanson, Fey, Mills, & Hood, 2005; Westerveld & Gillon, 2008). Most of the early studies on story structure focused on improving reading comprehension rather than language expression. However, more recent research has begun to explore the effectiveness of story structure intervention for improving aspects of spoken language ability, including the ability to summarize, retell, and generate narrative stories.

Several well-conducted studies have provided empirical support for the use of story structure intervention for children with language disorders and, more generally, learning disabilities (see Hayward & Schnieder, 2000; Nathanson et al., 2007; Westerveld & Gillon, 2008). As an example, Nathanson and colleagues (2007) investigated the effects of story structure instruction for improving children's recall of a history lesson. Study participants were 39 children with learning disabilities, 7 to 12 years old, who were randomly assigned to either a story structure instruction group, referred to as *narrative elaboration treatment (NET)*, or a control group. Children in the NET group were given verbal descriptions and simple cue cards depicting information in four overarching categories: (a) character details, (b) setting details, (c) actions/behaviors, and (d) feelings of characters. After explaining the meaning of the cue cards, teachers used a think-aloud process to demonstrate their use. Children practiced describing pictures and used the cue cards to recount video vignettes. During training, children received corrective feedback with respect to the completeness and accuracy of their recounts and their accuracy in using the pictorial cues. Children in the control condition performed similar storytelling activities but did not receive instruction in using cue cards. Instead, these children were told to "do their best" and "remember as much information as you can" when describing pictures and recounting the video vignettes.

All the children in the study had participated in a history lesson 2 weeks before the intervention sessions. Each child received individual instruction in recalling the video vignettes in two 30-minute sessions held 2 days apart. At the end of the second session, children participated in free- and prompted-recall tasks regarding the previous history lesson. Children were asked to recount what they remembered about the history lesson they had received 2 weeks earlier. Children in the NET group recalled 25% more information from history lessons during free recall (Cohen's $d = 0.37$) than children in the control group, although this difference did not reach statistical significance. However, for cued-recall children, the NET group recalled significantly more information (Cohen's $d = 2.87$) than children in the motivating instructions group. The results of this study are very encouraging because they suggest that the use of story maps or visual graphic organizers may be useful in improving the content and quality of information children report even after a significant delay between exposure to information and oral reporting of the information.

Researchers have begun to investigate whether instruction in story structure is associated with gains in narrative production and general language skills such as syntax or morphology (e.g., L. A. Swanson et al., 2005). As an example, S. Gillam et al. (2008) sought to determine whether a story structure instruction program improved the comprehension and production of narratives and general language abilities for 16 children with language disorders between the ages of 6 and 9 years. Children were randomly assigned to a socialization-first or concurrent-socialization group. Children in the socialization-first group engaged in free play together for 4 weeks (i.e., the control block). After the free-play block, these children received narrative intervention from SLPs for 4 weeks (i.e., the intervention block). The concurrent socialization group stayed at home and did not receive any services for 4 weeks (i.e., the control block), then received narrative intervention followed by free play each day for 4 weeks (i.e., the cross-over intervention block). The focus of the 4-week intervention was on story structure, emphasizing both story retelling and story generation in the context of simple and complex episodes. As in earlier studies of story structure instruction (e.g., L. A. Swanson et al., 2005; Westerveld & Gillon, 2008) graphic organizers or story maps were used to teach the elements of story grammar and to assist children in retelling and generating their own stories. Children were seen in groups of three or four for 90 minutes, 4 days per week by certified SLPs in a university setting.

The basic session format included instruction on meaning of the story element icons. Then, clinicians and children created stories using the icons. The visual icons representing story structures were also used during story comprehension activities to cue children to answer questions about specific information related to particular story elements. Children participated in group retelling activities, progressive story generation tasks, and independent story generation tasks with and without the visual icons to assist them. In group retelling, children listened to stories that they had heard repeatedly and then received all of the relevant icons in a random fashion. For example, Child A might be given icons representing *character, plan,* and *resolution;* Child B might be given *setting, complication,* and *consequence;* and Child C might be given *initiating event, internal response,* and *attempts.* As the group retold the story, each child was responsible for filling in the story grammar elements represented on their cue cards in the appropriate order in the story. Progressive story generation involved a similar process, except children drew stick figures of elements in their "group-created" stories on story maps containing the icons and later without the icons. An example of a child's map of a story generated through progression is shown in Figure 29.5. In this map, a spider and a fly are the characters; the basic premise of the story is as follows:

> The spider wants to live in his web and catch flies, but he has a medical issue regarding his spinner mechanism, which has made him sad. He decides to get some medication for his spinner. After obtaining the medication, he applies it to his spinner. The medicine heals his spinner, and he builds a web for future fly catching and yummy meals and is very happy about it.

Independent story generation was similar to progressive story generation, except children designed and told their own stories using the story structure instruction process with and without icons. Children took turns telling their peer's independently generated stories while peers tracked story grammar elements on Bingo cards containing the iconic representations. Children were tested immediately after random assignment (pretest), after the control blocks (midtest), and after intervention (post-test) with the Test of Narrative Language (TNL; R. B. Gillam & Pearson, 2004) and the Clinical Evaluation of Language Fundamentals, Fourth Edition (CELF-4; Semel, Wiig, & Secord, 2003). Children did not make improvements in narration (TNL) or in general language proficiency (CELF-4) after the control blocks. After the intervention blocks, children in both groups made significant improvements on the TNL production composite score but not on the TNL comprehension composite score or on the CELF-4 standard score. The results suggest that for some children with language disorders, a narrative intervention program that focused on story structure using story structure procedures was associated with significant gains in oral narrative production but not in narrative comprehension (TNL) or in general language proficiency.

This finding is similar to that of L. A. Swanson et al. (2005), in which researchers reported that story structure intervention resulted in improved oral narrative skills but not in general language abilities. In the S. Gillam et al. (2008) study, the findings may reflect the intensive focus on storytelling rather than story comprehension or specific grammatical or syntactic targets. That is, children spent the majority of their time developing and producing stories, and less time answering questions about them. Instruction in more authentic contexts and texts may be required to activate the mechanisms involved in bringing about change in specific linguistic domains (morphology, syntax). In terms of the comprehension findings, children with language disorders may require the same type of intensive, explicit instruction and practice in story comprehension that they received in story production. That is, children with language disorders do not appear to be adept at transferring skill from one situation (e.g., story production activities) to another (e.g., story comprehension activities) or in generalizing information or knowledge that they have in one context to another.

To summarize, the use of story structure instruction to improve the comprehension and production of oral stories is generally well-supported in the literature for increasing the language skills of children developing typically as well as those with language disorders and more general learning disabilities. The research that has been summarized in this chapter supports the use of story mapping procedures within story structure instructional programs. Specifically, good results have been obtained when children are explicitly taught the components of a story using visual (graphic) representations of specific story elements or story content. Researchers typically model the use of the target story components in stories and ask children to identify story elements in model stories, answer questions about stories, retell stories using the graphic representations as guides, or generate new stories containing the elements that were taught.

One limitation in the research base related to story structure intervention using story mapping procedures is the lack of high-quality, randomized, clinical trials with large numbers of children with language disorders. To date, we are aware of no meta-analyses, systematic reviews, or large-scale randomized controlled trials examining this approach for improving story comprehension or production. Positive outcomes for story structure interventions have been demonstrated in a range of contexts with a variety of interventionists. Children have been shown to benefit from instruction provided in intensive individual intervention contexts delivered by SLPs as well as in less-intensive group settings delivered by regular and special educators, SLPs, and teachers of English Language Learners. Practitioners can feel relatively comfortable that children will respond favorably to story structure interventions that involve (a) explicit instruction with the use of visual, graphic organizers in the context of stories, (b) repetitive practice in identification and use of story elements and

causal connections, (c) frequent opportunities for children to generate their own stories, and (d) directed practice in answering questions about story grammar elements and causal connections contained in texts.

In addition, we also want to point out several shortcomings associated with current approaches to story structure instruction. Most approaches have focused on teaching children to produce simple single-episode narratives. These narrative language targets are qualitatively and quantitatively different from the longer and more complex age- and content-appropriate narratives that students routinely encounter in daily academic instruction (J. Lynch et al., 2008). In addition, existing narrative interventions often focus on story retelling to the exclusion of story generation or do not place enough emphasis on language features such as vocabulary, sentence structure, and causal connections. We were surprised to note that there were no studies of the generalization from oral story comprehension and production to reading comprehension and writing in children with language disorders. Story structure instruction may need to include explicit print-based experiences within the context of authentic literature in order to support generalizations to broader language skills and to written language. Finally, additional research is necessary to tease apart the underlying mechanisms that contribute to positive outcomes in other language abilities such as grammatical morphology and syntax and the associated procedures that will facilitate their emergence.

Conclusion

A variety of intervention approaches are available to address the language difficulties of children with language disorders, many of which can be used in classroom settings; however, not all approaches have a sufficient research base showing their efficacy or effectiveness. Two approaches to language intervention described in this chapter, focused stimulation and story structure intervention, have reasonable research support demonstrating the positive effects that might be expected with their use. Focused stimulation involves highly concentrated delivery of targeted language forms and functions in naturalistic contexts and is typically used with toddlers and preschoolers. Story structure intervention involves explicit teaching of story grammar and other aspects of narratives using story maps and graphic organizers. Both interventions require professionals to have a well-developed understanding of a child's linguistic strengths and needs to select appropriate targets for intervention. Nonetheless, the extant literature also suggests that both interventions can be used by a range of potential interventionists, including parents, teachers, and allied professionals, such as SLPs.

CHAPTER 30

Teaching Students with Autism Spectrum Disorders

Rose Iovannone | *University of South Florida*

The education of students with autism spectrum disorders (ASD) presents ongoing and increased programming challenges to education professionals (National Research Council, 2001b). Although substantial research related to autism, including etiology, characteristics, and interventions has been conducted, it remains a complex and not fully understood developmental disorder that begins at a very young age and continues throughout the lifespan of an individual. Contributing to the ongoing challenges are the widely disparate display of atypical characteristics and patterns of behavior, uneven developmental rates, diversity in responding to interventions, and reported increase in prevalence (e.g., in 2010 the Centers for Disease Control and Prevention [CDC] reported that the prevalence of ASD had risen to 1 in 110 children).

To date, the characteristics of ASD have been distributed into a triad of domain impairments consisting of social interaction, communication, and repetitive behaviors and fixated interests (American Psychiatric Association, *Diagnostic and Statistical Manual of Mental Disorders,* 4th ed. [DSM-IV], 1994). Examples of social interaction impairments include difficulties using and understanding nonverbal behavior, lack of spontaneous sharing and social-emotional reciprocity, and failure to develop peer relationships. Features of communication impairment are manifested by a delay

or lack of development of spoken language, difficulty initiating and maintaining conversation, repetitive and idiosyncratic use of language, and lack of pretend play. Repetitive behaviors and fixated interests include preoccupations with restricted areas of focus, inflexible adherence to routines, recurring movements, and preoccupation with parts of objects. Although the DSM-IV provides thresholds of the number of symptoms to be displayed within each domain, the specific features and intensity of symptoms exhibited by individuals within the spectrum are heterogeneous; thus, the needs of individuals with ASD are diverse, which further contributes to the challenge of effective education. In addition to the core features used for diagnostic purposes, students with ASD manifest unique learning characteristics such as stimulus overselectivity, reduced motivation, behavioral excesses, and generalization difficulties that require specialized attention and intervention before planning instruction (Simpson & Myles, 1998).

Developing defensible instructional programs is daunting, primarily due to the paucity of agreement on appropriate practices for students with ASD (Detrich, 2008). Although the literature related to interventions for students with ASD is plentiful, it is remarkably varied, lacks a unifying theory, and can create more confusion than clarification. In addition, new, unproven treatments continue to inundate the media and Internet—treatments that require professionals and parents to differentiate between practices that have strong empirical evidence and those that have no or inadequate efficacy (Detrich, 2008).

Since the 1990s, researchers have attempted to respond to the lack of program guidance by offering reports identifying and describing the core factors shared by effective interventions for young children with ASD. Reports have originated from states and provinces (e.g., New York Department of Health, 1999; Perry & Condillac, 2003), specialized task forces and councils (e.g., Hurth, Shaw, Izeman, Whaley, & Rogers, 1999; National Research Council, 2001), and various individual authors (e.g., Dawson & Osterling, 1997; Dunlap & Robbins, 1991; M. D. Powers, 1992; Simpson, 2005). Although the outcomes of the reports are varied, researchers generally agree on the core features present in most effective programs for young children with ASD, including structured learning environments, specialized curriculum, early initiation of intervention, instructional foundation built on behavioral principles, and active family involvement. These reports have contributed valuable programming guidance to educational professionals, yet they are primarily focused on features present in early intervention programs.

More recently, the National Autism Center (2009) prepared a comprehensive report called the National Standards Project that evaluated the strength of research evidence for educational and behavioral strategies currently used for individuals with ASD, aged birth through 21 years. The report used a threshold method to establish the category of evidence for each practice. After identifying and evaluating 775 intervention articles to be included in the review, 38 treatments were identified. Four hierarchical categories provided the evidential basis, with interventions identified as (a) established, (b) emerging, (c) unestablished, or (d) ineffective/harmful. Of the 38 treatments, 11 were identified as established or having multiple studies showing effectiveness for students with ASD, 22 were classified as emerging or having few studies showing effectiveness, and 5 were assigned as unestablished or having limited or low-quality research. No treatments were identified as ineffective or harmful.

Even with the provision of the reports of recommended practices, educators continue to need specific and clear teaching guidelines to support students with ASD. An early attempt to provide such guidelines was made by Iovannone, Dunlap, Huber, and Kincaid (2003) by reviewing the literature on young children with ASD and identifying six core components of effective educational practices: (a) systematic instruction, (b) individualized supports and services, (c) comprehensible and structured learning environments, (d) specialized

curriculum focus, (e) functional approach to problem behavior, and (f) family involvement. The same components were further described by Dunlap and Iovannone (2008), with additional guidelines addressing pertinent issues and the infrastructure needed when developing programs for students with ASD. This chapter provides details on two of the six components and their application in typical school contexts. Specifically, we discuss information regarding programs with specialized curricular focus (specifically, peer social-mediation techniques) and a functional approach to problem behavior (specifically, individualized positive behavior support).

Peer-Mediated Interventions to Enhance Social Skills

Social interaction difficulties of individuals with ASD have major, widespread impact on their ability to access inclusive educational and community environments and can lead to social isolation and a reduced quality of life. In comparison to their peers who are typically developing, students with ASD present with qualitatively different social behaviors that are evident at a very young age and include impairments in joint social attention, symbolic play, and nonverbal behaviors such as smiling and eye contact (Clifford & Dissanayake, 2008). As they grow older, the social difficulties students with ASD display effect play skills and social interaction overtures necessary for developing and maintaining friendships.

Given the importance of social relationships, considerable research has been devoted to exploring interventions designed to address the lack of reciprocal social behaviors. Some of the most effective practices for increasing and improving the social behaviors of learners with ASD are those in which peers are the primary interventionists and are taught to interact with specific students with ASD. A wide variety of peer-assisted or peer-mediated interventions exist and have been implemented with learners with ASD, including peer management (nonacademic), peer tutoring (academic), peer modeling, and peer participation in group contingencies (Kohler & Strain, 1990).

All of the variations of peer-mediated interventions are similar in conceptualization: They begin with identifying a student (for our purposes in this chapter, one with ASD) who has social difficulties and one (or more) typically developing peer(s) with intact social behaviors who have opportunities to frequently interact with the learner with ASD. Specific procedural training on how to interact with and support the learner with ASD is provided to the peer. After implementing the intervention with the learner with ASD, the peer is provided ongoing, systematic support and reinforcement to ensure continuation of interactions and strategies. The results of the numerous studies using peer-mediated techniques have shown that the practice is very effective in increasing social skills of students with ASD (e.g., Harper, Symon, & Frea, 2008; Owen-DeSchryver, Carr, Cale, & Blakeley-Smith, 2008; Strain, Kerr, & Ragland, 1979) as well as generalizing and sustaining social skills (e.g., C. D. Jones & Schwartz, 2004; Kamps et al., 1992; Strain & Hoyson, 2000). For the purposes of this chapter, a detailed description of Peer-Mediated Instruction and Intervention (PMI), based on a nonacademic peer-management framework, illustrates the implementation of peer-mediated interventions.

Steps of Peer-Mediated Instruction

Step 1: Get Buy-in from Faculty

Before starting PMI, it is important to have administrative, faculty, and parental support for implementing the practice. Although activities are intended to occur during social times throughout the school day, typical peers will be asked to leave their classrooms for small periods of time to receive training from adults and to serve as the social skills peer mediator for the student with ASD.

Step 2: Select Peers

Peers who are typically developing and who are close to the chronological age of the student with ASD will be recruited to participate in the intervention. Literature has identified that peers with the following characteristics are the most appropriate for participation and have the greatest promise of successful performance (Neitzel, Boyd, Odom, & Edmondson-Pretzel, 2008; Snell & Janney, 2000; Strain & Odom, 1986): competent social skills, well-respected and liked by others, present in classes with focus student or has a similar schedule (if young), ability to attend to tasks or activities at an age-appropriate duration (e.g., 5 to 10 minutes), good school attendance, history of positive interactions with the focus student, generally persistent and positive about individual differences, and willing to participate.

After acquiring parental permission for participation, cohorts of three to six peers for each focus student should be formed, with the intent of having one or two peers paired with the student with ASD for each scheduled social interaction. The cohort allows for rotation of peer pairs, which increases the focus student's acquisition and generalization of specific skills due to exposure to multiple peers over an extended period of time (i.e., minimum of 3 to 4 months). After 4 months, additional peers should be selected and added to the cohort to further enhance skill generalization (E. W. Carter & Kennedy, 2006; Utley, Mortweet, & Greenwood, 1997).

Step 3: Provide Training to Selected Peers

Once appropriate peers have been selected, a block of time is scheduled for direct training. The specific content and number of training sessions depend on the amount of time allotted, the age of the peers, and the quantity and complexity of the interventions. In general, four to five training sessions may be needed for peers to feel competent implementing the strategies with the student with ASD (Strain & Odom, 1986). Training occurs in two distinct sections: the first provides awareness of disabilities, and the second focuses on specific intervention strategies that will be implemented with the student with ASD.

Training content generally begins with appreciation of individual differences. Peers discuss similarities and differences of their friends, classmates, family members, and acquaintances. During this part of the training, a brief description of ASD is provided, specifically, behaviors related to social interaction. The training content is adjusted for the chronological age of the typical peers; for younger students, it is concrete and factual, focusing on observable behaviors, while older students may receive more information about the characteristics in addition to concrete examples. For elementary-age and older peers, relevant information about the student with ASD is also discussed, including social activity preferences that will be used in determining when peer support will be provided.

The next section of training concentrates on teaching peers the specific strategies designed to increase the social skills of the learner with ASD. It is best to present only one strategy at each session so that the peers have ample time to learn it, see it modeled by the trainer, practice it by role-playing with the trainer, and receive feedback on their performance. Examples of typical PMI strategies for young children include organizing play (e.g., "Let's play. Do you want to play with the ball or the puzzles?"), sharing (e.g., "Here is a puzzle piece. Put it in."), providing assistance (e.g., "Do you need help with that puzzle piece?"), and delivering affection and praise (e.g., "Way to go!") (Strain & Odom, 1986). At elementary and middle school grade levels, social behaviors emphasized include initiating and responding to interactions; starting, maintaining, and ending conversations; giving and accepting compliments; taking turns and sharing; asking for help and assisting others; and entering into ongoing social activities and inviting others to participate (Kamps et al., 1992; Thiemann & Goldstein, 2004). More recent literature suggests placing increased emphasis on teaching peers of all ages to make comments about activities, objects, and actions (e.g., "I like to swing." "Swinging is fun.") for the purpose of providing the student with ASD a model of conversational phrases commonly used in an age-appropriate manner (R. L. Koegel & Koegel, 2006).

Figure 30.1   Sample script for peer-mediated instruction—elementary.

Target Skill: Asking a Friend to Play

Introductory Lesson

Teacher: Today, we are going to talk about how to get Noah to play with you during recess. One way is to ask Noah to do something he likes. What is one thing Noah likes to do? (If students do not respond, prompt as necessary.)

Trained Peers: Play with trains.

Teacher: Yes, Noah likes trains. When you ask Noah to play with you, first get his attention by looking at him or touching him on the shoulder and say, *"Hey, Noah. Let's play. Here,"* and put the train in his hand. How are you going to get Noah to play with you?

Trained Peers: Get his attention, say, *"Hey, Noah, let's play. Here,"* and put the train in his hand.

Once targeted skills are selected and the activity preferences of the learner with ASD are considered, peers are asked for examples of age-appropriate words and phrases that can be used that will elicit the desired social behaviors during the preferred activities. Having peers, rather than teachers, generate the phrases ensures that the language used will be age appropriate and will be more natural and comfortable for use by the trained peers. Scripts or other visual cues can be created that include actions to perform and suggestions for responses (Sasso, Mundschenk, Melloy, & Casey, 1998). The script can also be provided as a visual prompt for engaging in the peer-mediated activities. Figure 30.1 gives an example of a script appropriate for an elementary student.

The peers use modeling and role-playing techniques to practice the strategies in relevant activities. Initially, the teacher models by role-playing the use of scripts with a peer acting the part of the student with ASD. Next, peers role-play with each other to increase competency in using the skills. The teacher provides prompts to cue peers of accurate use of the strategies and delivers feedback and reinforcement following each role-play practice.

Step 4: Introduce and Practice Strategy Implementation with Student with ASD in a Structured Social Setting

After peers are sufficiently trained, a time is scheduled to practice the strategies with the student with ASD. A brief social period (e.g., 5 to 10 minutes) is scheduled in which the teacher, similar to Step 3, presents the activity, gives cues to the peers to implement the trained strategies with the student with ASD, and provides them with reinforcement and feedback. The cueing and prompting of the trained peers has been shown to be a vital ingredient in enhancing the strategy's impact on increasing the targeted social behaviors of students with ASD (Storey, Smith, & Strain, 1993). After peers demonstrate competent use of the strategies with the student with ASD,

they can implement them in daily, natural activities with a planned fading of adult prompts and feedback.

Step 5: Implement Strategies in Naturalistic Settings

It is important to determine all of the naturally occurring social activities and routines throughout the day that present opportunities in which the trained peers will use PMI to interact with the learner with ASD. A lesson-planning matrix that identifies key events in which interactions can occur can be a valuable tool for this purpose. After determining appropriate daily opportunities for social interaction activities, the teacher chooses those that can be scheduled consistently (e.g., daily) for 10 to 15 minutes and considers preferred activities for both the focus student and peers to enhance motivation for participating. Then, the teacher selects one or two social skills to be targeted during the social session. For example, responding to play initiations and participating for a brief time (e.g., 2 minutes) can be targeted skills for an elementary student during recess time. This information is provided to the peers, along with a menu of strategies to be implemented that are appropriate for eliciting the selected behaviors. A rotating schedule, identifying which of the trained peers within the cohort will support the student with ASD during the scheduled time, is a useful tool to identify the activity, target skills, interventions, and peer schedule (see Figure 30.2 for an example).

Over time, it is important for the adult to turn more responsibility for initiating the social interactions over to the trained peers. Initially, the adult is in close proximity to the peers and provides verbal prompts, feedback, and reinforcement as necessary. As peers become more proficient in using the strategies, one way to fade support is the adults' carefully eliminating prompts and distancing themselves from physical proximity. Also, the adults can replace verbal prompts and feedback with visual cues and gradually fade the visual tools until peers are

Figure 30.2   Peer-planning form schedule.

Student: <u>Noah</u>	Peer Cohort: <u>Joey, Elijah, Gustavo, Jeff</u>			Week of: <u>10/1/13</u>	
Activity	*Peer Schedule*				
	Monday	Tuesday	Wednesday	Thursday	Friday
	Joey, Elijah	Joey, Gustavo	Elijah, Jeff	Gustavo, Jeff	Joey, Elijah
	Target Skills				
Free Time 10:00–10:15	Respond to request to play	Respond to request to play	Respond to request to play	Respond to request to play Take turns	Respond to request to play Take turns
Recess 12:00–12:30	Respond to request to play	Respond to request to play	Respond to request to play	Respond to request to play Take turns	Respond to request to play Take turns
Lunch 12:30–1:00	Respond a minimum of one time to a comment Use peers' names	Respond a minimum of one time to a comment Use peers' names	Respond a minimum of one time to a comment Use peers' names	Respond a minimum of one time to a comment Use peers' names	Respond a minimum of two times to a comment Use peers' names

performing independently (Odom, Chandler, Ostrosky, McConnell, & Reaney, 1992).

Step 6: Evaluate, Monitor, and Provide Follow-Up Support

Data should be collected to evaluate the effectiveness of the peer-mediated intervention and the fidelity of implementation. Initially, teachers may take the primary role of collecting data, but as the adults fade out their support, the trained peers can measure the focus student's interactions as well as self-monitor their use of peer-mediated strategies. In addition, measurements of teacher fidelity in presenting the PMI procedures to peers should be reviewed. Figure 30.3 shows an example of a fidelity measure that can be used to evaluate the degree to which the teacher implemented the program.

Regularly scheduled debriefing meetings are held to provide follow-up support to the trained peers on a consistent basis. During debriefing sessions, data are reviewed to ensure that the intervention is associated with desirable outcomes for the student with ASD and that the trained peers are implementing the strategies as intended. Group problem solving and identification of any needed adaptations, as well as development of next steps, also occur within the recurring meetings. Trained peers can give their perspective on additional social interaction goals that are relevant for the targeted student with ASD and suggest intervention strategies. Achievements are celebrated during this meeting, and trained peers are provided reinforcement. Although most peer mediators are

intrinsically reinforced, it is recommended that various forms of recognition be provided to peers for the time and efforts they exert. Some examples of appropriate reinforcement include verbal praise for specific activities, certificates of recognition, or social events with food that can take place at the end of problem-solving meetings.

Research Support

The extant literature includes numerous research studies examining the effectiveness of PMI to increase, sustain, and generalize social interaction skills of students with ASD. The majority of the studies have focused on young children (i.e., preschool), although recent years have shown an emerging research base examining the use of PMI with older students (i.e., 6 to 13 years of age). Studies focused on young children have shown that PMI is effective in increasing the number and the duration of reciprocal social interactions between children with ASD and trained peers as well as the number of social initiations for play (e.g., Kohler, Greteman, Raschke, & Highnam, 2007; C. Nelson, McDonnell, Hohnston, Crompton, & Nelson, 2007). Studies targeting elementary-aged students have used PMI strategies to increase social engagement while concurrently decreasing stereotypic behaviors (S. Lee, Odom, & Loftin, 2007), to increase social communication skills of students with high-functioning ASD (K. M. Chung et al., 2007), and to enhance social overtures between students with ASD and peers in inclusive settings (Owen-DeSchryver et al., 2008). Studies have explored using a combination of

Figure 30.3   Sample fidelity measure for peer-mediated instruction.

Teacher: Smith Student: Noah Date: 10/5/13 Type of Measure (circle): Observation Self-Assessment		
Procedures	*Was the step implemented?*	*Fidelity Score* *Y = 1* *N = 0* *NA = NA*
1. Obtained faculty buy-in	Y/N/NA	
2. Recruited multiple peers (3–5 per target student) to participate	Y/N/NA	
3. Obtained parental consent	Y/N/NA	
4. Scheduled training sessions for peers	Y/N/NA	
5. Determined daily activities/routines in which peers and Noah will implement PMI	Y/N/NA	
6. Prepared and gathered all necessary materials for training peers	Y/N/NA	
7. Presented training on appreciation of individual differences to peers	Y/N/NA	
8. Discussed reasons for PMI, expectations, and responsibilities with peers	Y/N/NA	
9. Introduced target skills and presented strategies/script	Y/N/NA	
10. Engaged peers to practice by Q&A and demonstration	Y/N/NA	
11. Engaged peers in role-playing exercises with teacher	Y/N/NA	
12. Engaged peers in role-playing exercises with each other	Y/N/NA	
13. Provided prompts/cues to peers as necessary	Y/N/NA	
14. Delivered appropriate reinforcement to peers and feedback	Y/N/NA	
15. Conducted debriefing session at end of lesson, and provided specific reinforcement and feedback	Y/N/NA	
16. Scheduled a time for peers to practice with Noah before beginning PMI in scheduled routines	Y/N/NA	
17. Provided prompts/cues to peers as necessary	Y/N/NA	
18. Delivered appropriate reinforcement to peers and feedback	Y/N/NA	
19. Conducted debriefing session at end of lesson and provided specific reinforcement and feedback	Y/N/NA	
20. Upon implementation, provided ongoing support to peers by giving them scripts, cues, and other tools to be used	Y/N/NA	
21. Provided prompts/cues to peers as necessary	Y/N/NA	
22. Delivered appropriate reinforcement to peers and feedback	Y/N/NA	
23. Conducted debriefing session at end of lesson, and provided specific reinforcement and feedback	Y/N/NA	
24. Held problem-solving meetings (weekly/biweekly) with peers to celebrate, discuss status, and decide on next steps	Y/N/NA	
25. Systematically faded level of support as peer competence increased	Y/N/NA	
26. Used rotating schedule of peer trainers and identified targeted skills within activities	Y/N/NA	
Implementation Score **(Total Y's/Total Y's + N's in column)**		

Note: Y = 1; N = 0; NA = not applicable.

PMI and pivotal response training during recess to increase social skills (Blauvelt-Harper, Symon, & Frea, 2008) and to explore the effectiveness of using multiple peer trainers to generalize intervention effects (Pierce & Schreibman, 1997). Thiemann and Goldstein (2004) extended the PMI research by combining it with written text cues to increase the number and quality of social interactions as well as to improve specific social behaviors.

In comparison to studies conducted with young children, relatively fewer studies have explored the effectiveness of PMI with older students (e.g., middle school, high school). However, L. Morrison, Kamps, Garcia, and Parker (2001) conducted a study that included four students with ASD whose ages were from 10 to 13 years. A group of peers were trained in PMI and self-monitoring strategies. Results indicated that the combination of PMI and self-monitoring increased the quantity of social initiations and length of social interactions along with specific social skill behaviors of the students with ASD.

Finally, Strain and Hoyson (2000) reported on the longitudinal outcomes of a comprehensive intervention approach, Learning Experiences: An Alternative Program for Preschoolers and Parents (LEAP), for children with ASD. The LEAP model, described in detail in Hoyson, Jamieson, and Strain (1984), includes daily peer-mediated interventions embedded in multiple social opportunities throughout the day. Data collected over a period of several years from six children with ASD who were the first recipients of the LEAP procedures showed an increase of intervals engaged in positive social interactions from entry into the program (2%) to exit (23%) and sustainability at age 10 (24%), lending further support for the use of peer trainers to improve and generalize appropriate social behaviors.

In summary, PMI strategies have been effective in increasing the social competence skills of students with ASD. The technique has been successfully used for young students (e.g., preschool) and for older students (e.g., elementary school, middle school). The technology is well developed, is feasible for use by typical school personnel, and is suitable for application in an expansive range of environments.

Functional Approach to Problem Behaviors

Students with ASD frequently display problem behaviors that can be a formidable challenge to address through typical behavior interventions used by teachers. Limited communication skills as well as deficits in social behaviors contribute to the unique types and quality of behavior problems experienced by students with ASD (Heal, Borthwick-Duffy, & Saunders, 1996; R. L. Koegel, Koegel, & Surratt, 1992). Typographies of problem behavior are varied and can include self-injury, pica, tantrums, physical aggression, disruptions, noncompliance, and stereotypy (R. H. Horner, Diemer, & Brazeau, 1992; Reichle, 1990). Problem behaviors are often cited as the primary reason for excluding students with ASD from inclusive educational and community settings and serve as a barrier in delivering effective and meaningful educational instruction (Sprague & Rian, 1993).

An impressive body of research has been conducted on the effectiveness of using function-based supports to decrease problem behaviors and increase prosocial, appropriate behaviors for students with ASD (National Research Council, 2001b). In recent decades, the field has shifted focus from contingency-based interventions to delivering more comprehensive behavior approaches that emphasize contextual adjustments to prevent problem behaviors; teach new, appropriate replacement skills; and change the way others respond to behaviors so that the new skills will be reinforced and repeated and problem behaviors will be extinguished (E. G. Carr et al., 2002).

The emerging approach, referred to as *positive behavior support (PBS),* is based on the wealth of applied research taken from the core concepts of operant learning theory (e.g., J. O. Cooper, Heron, & Heward, 2007; B. F. Skinner, 1953) and principles of ecological and contextual systems theories that have contributed to the current work in school-based positive behavior support (E. G. Carr et al., 2002). The theory is framed within a three-pronged contingency model in which antecedent (i.e., environmental) events set the stage for problem behavior occurrence that is immediately followed by consequences (e.g., positive reinforcer, punishment) that either strengthen or weaken the behavior (Harrower, Fox, Dunlap, & Kincaid, 2000).

As a first step to intervention in a PBS approach, a functional behavior assessment (FBA) is conducted to identify the contextual conditions eliciting problem behavior and resulting consequences that serve to reinforce and maintain problem behavior. This information leads to development of a hypothesis from which a function-based support plan is built that includes the identification and manipulation of three key components: (a) antecedents associated with identified patterns of responding to prevent problem behavior; (b) strategies for teaching new skills to replace problem behaviors; and (c) consequences, particularly contingent positive reinforcement. The aim is to promote conditions that allow new, appropriate behaviors to occur more frequently and to change responses to problem behavior in order to render them no longer effective or efficient for obtaining the desired outcome (i.e., escape, obtain). Individualized PBS expands on traditional behavioral interventions by collaborating with stakeholders (i.e., teachers), ensuring that interventions have social and ecological validity and contextual fit, and broadening the targeted goals of intervention that impact quality of life (E. G. Carr et al., 2002).

Recently, a randomized controlled trial exploring the efficacy of implementing a standardized model of function-based behavior intervention based on the components of PBS was conducted, and outcomes indicated that students receiving the intervention, Prevent-Teach-Reinforce (PTR), had significantly improved outcomes in comparison to the students who received "services as usual" (Iovannone et al., 2009). The intervention is manualized (Dunlap, Iovannone, Kincaid, et al., 2010), with the steps feasible for use by typical school personnel in school settings and detailed in such a way they can be implemented with fidelity across settings. The PTR model, a functional approach to problem behavior, consists of five basic steps that are common to most FBA approaches: (a) forming a team, (b) identifying goals of intervention, (c) conducting an FBA and developing a hypothesis, (d) building a comprehensive function-based support plan, and (e) evaluating and monitoring the impact of the behavior support plan. The following section provides details for each step.

Steps of a Function-Based Approach to Problem Behavior

Step 1: Forming a Team

A team is formed that includes people who have a vested interest in improving the life of the focus student and who will be committed to actively participating in the process. The team includes individuals who have direct knowledge of the student's behavior, such as the primary classroom teacher, paraeducators, primary caregivers, and others with whom the student interacts consistently (e.g., teachers of art, music, PE; speech pathologists; related service providers). In addition, the team includes at least one person who has knowledge of behavioral principles and experience in facilitating FBAs (e.g., school psychologist, special educator, behavior analyst/specialist, guidance counselor, social worker), as well as an individual who has knowledge of the context in which the interventions will be implemented and has the ability to access resources (e.g., administrator).

To enhance team cohesiveness, the roles and responsibilities of each team member should be established before participating in any activities. Deciding the manner in which each team member will provide input and determining how consensus will be reached will increase the likelihood that meetings will be run efficiently and effectively in an environment that is collaborative and nonthreatening. One team member who has competence in collaborative consultation techniques and has a sound knowledge of behavioral principles should be designated as the facilitator.

Step 2: Identifying Goals of Intervention

The primary purpose of Step 2 is to identify and define the behaviors of greatest concern as the targets of intervention. During this step, the team will develop a method of collecting data that is simple to use yet provides enough information to make decisions about the impact of the intervention on student behavior change. Team members identify both the problem behaviors they wish to see decreased, as well as appropriate behaviors to be increased. Once they identify those behaviors, the team clearly describes them in operational terms that are observable and measurable. The definition includes the physical and auditory behaviors that the student performs when engaged in the problem behavior. For example, if the team identifies tantrums as a problem behavior of concern, team members list the behaviors they have observed the student doing when he is engaged in tantrums and develop an operational definition. For one team, tantrum behaviors may include screaming at a high pitch and volume, dropping body to the floor on back, and kicking feet against persons who approach. Another student's tantrum behavior may be defined differently, depending on the actual behaviors exhibited during the episodes.

After the team identifies and defines behaviors, they prioritize the behaviors that are of greatest concern. Although FBA processes can be conducted for more than one problem behavior, it can be quite time-consuming and possibly overwhelming to do so; therefore, the team may wish to start with the one or two behaviors that are considered the most disruptive or severe and are reducing the student's access to inclusive environments and educational instruction.

Next, the team agrees on methods of collecting data on the targeted behaviors and establishes a data plan that includes who will collect the data and how often. Data should be collected frequently (i.e., minimum two times a week, with daily collection preferred) and in a way that is both practical for the teacher and sensitive to behavior variations. Although many observational data methods exist (i.e., interval, partial interval, time sampling), not all teachers are adequately trained to use these techniques, and they can be time-consuming. An emerging method for assessing social behavior, called Direct Behavior Rating (DBR), has been the subject of several recent studies. DBR is a hybrid data technology combining features of systematic direct observation with the efficiency of rating scales (Chafouleas, Riley-Tillman, & Christ, 2009). With DBR, an individual observes the student's behavior and evaluates it by rating its occurrence using a Likert-type scale with anchors representing a standardized coding system (Pelham, Fabiano, & Massetti, 2005). For example, a 5-point scale can be created in which anchor 5 represents the most undesirable presence of the behavior (i.e., excessive frequency, duration, or intensity), a 3 can represent an average presence for that particular student, and a

Figure 30.4 Sample behavior rating scale.

Student: Noah		Teacher: Smith		Routine/time for measurement: Transition from preferred to nonpreferred activities																	
Behavior	Date																					
Screaming	Ear penetrating	5	5	5	5	5	5	5	5	5	5	5	5	5	5	5	5	5	5	5
	Outside voice	4	4	4	4	4	4	4	4	4	4	4	4	4	4	4	4	4	4	4
	Loud inside voice	3	3	3	3	3	3	3	3	3	3	3	3	3	3	3	3	3	3	3
	Inside voice	2	2	2	2	2	2	2	2	2	2	2	2	2	2	2	2	2	2	2
	Soft squeal	1	1	1	1	1	1	1	1	1	1	1	1	1	1	1	1	1	1	1
Hitting	≥5 times	5	5	5	5	5	5	5	5	5	5	5	5	5	5	5	5	5	5	5
	4 times	4	4	4	4	4	4	4	4	4	4	4	4	4	4	4	4	4	4	4
	3 times	3	3	3	3	3	3	3	3	3	3	3	3	3	3	3	3	3	3	3
	2 times	2	2	2	2	2	2	2	2	2	2	2	2	2	2	2	2	2	2	2
	0–1 time	1	1	1	1	1	1	1	1	1	1	1	1	1	1	1	1	1	1	1
Asking for a Break	≥5 times	5	5	5	5	5	5	5	5	5	5	5	5	5	5	5	5	5	5	5
	4 times	4	4	4	4	4	4	4	4	4	4	4	4	4	4	4	4	4	4	4
	3 times	3	3	3	3	3	3	3	3	3	3	3	3	3	3	3	3	3	3	3
	2 times	2	2	2	2	2	2	2	2	2	2	2	2	2	2	2	2	2	2	2
	0–1 time	1	1	1	1	1	1	1	1	1	1	1	1	1	1	1	1	1	1	1

Note: Definitions of Behaviors: Screaming—high pitched, loud piercing cry; Hitting—open-handed slap, pinching delivered to peers and adults; Asking for a break—using voice-output device to ask for a break when transitioning from preferred to nonpreferred activities.

1 can represent the goal of intervention. An example of a DBR is shown in Figure 30.4. The scale is individualized and reflects the team's prioritized problem and appropriate behaviors, operational definitions, and estimates of behavioral occurrence. The scale can be used to measure behavior presence during a specific routine or time (e.g., centers, math class, writing activities, independent work time), a partial day (e.g., morning, afternoon), or the entire day. At the end of the specified time period, the teacher simply circles the rating that best represents her estimate of behavior performance. Recent studies have shown that DBR has the potential of being both efficient and a reliable and valid method of teacher data collection (Riley-Tillman, Chafouleas, Sassu, Chanese, & Glazer, 2008).

Step 3: Conducting a Functional Behavior Assessment and Developing a Hypothesis

The primary purposes of an FBA are to identify the environmental events consistently associated with the presence of problem and appropriate behaviors, to identify the function(s) of the problem behavior in the specific events, and to lay the framework for building an effective behavior support plan (O'Neill et al., 1997). Since the late 1990s the field of special education has seen an increased focus on developing FBA procedures and accompanying tools that are "school-friendly" while adhering to the foundational behavioral theory. The techniques include development of forms to record direct observations (e.g., O'Neill et al., 1997) and creation of indirect procedures such as checklists and interviews (e.g., Dunlap, Iovannone, Kincaid, et al., 2010; T. M. Scott & Nelson, 1999). In determining the resources to commit to conducting the FBA, the team should attempt to match the intensity of the method with the intensity of the problem behavior (i.e., more severe and complicated problem behavior warrants more intense FBA resources). Regardless of the intensity of the FBA method selected, the assessment should include a way of identifying the events and contexts in which the target problem behavior occurs and does not occur and the consequences or responses that follow the problem behavior.

After the FBA data are collected, the team organizes the information, identifies patterns, and develops a hypothesis statement that summarizes the patterns and surmises the function of the problem behavior. The subsequent hypothesis statement will include, at a minimum, three distinct components: (a) the antecedents to the problem behaviors, (b) the specific behavior that is the focus of the FBA, and (c) the purpose or function of the behavior. An example of a hypothesis statement is:

> *When presented with an academic demand to start a nonpreferred activity or when transitioning from a preferred to a nonpreferred activity, Noah will scream at a high pitch and loud volume for an extended amount of time. As a result, he delays the nonpreferred activity or transition and gets adult attention.*

Once the team reaches consensus on the hypothesis, they are ready to begin to build a function-based support plan.

Step 4: Building a Comprehensive Function-Based Support Plan

After completion of the hypothesis statement, the team develops an individualized behavior support plan. The plan includes strategies linked to the hypothesis components (a) to prevent the problem behavior from occurring, (b) to teach new and appropriate skills that replace the problem behavior, and (c) to arrange responding consequences that reinforce the performance of the new skill so that it is repeated and reinforcement of the problem behavior discontinues.

Prevention strategies aim to alter the circumstances related to behavioral occurrence (i.e., antecedents) in a way that makes the event less aversive, thereby eliminating a need for the student to perform the target behavior. Taking our hypothesis example in the preceding section, one antecedent situation identified is transition from preferred to nonpreferred activities. In this case, the team will design support strategies that modify the transition so that it no longer is a predicting event occasioning the problem behavior. Examples of transitional support interventions are providing visual or auditory transition warnings, developing a visual support (e.g., visual schedule) that prepares the student for transitions, presenting visual checklists or auditory supports that describe appropriate transition behaviors, or giving the student some choices about how the transition will occur.

When the team selects the new skill to be taught that replaces the problem behavior, they carefully consider the function of the behavior and discuss appropriate, alternate ways of getting the same outcomes (e.g., escape; delay or avoidance of an activity, a person, an object, or sensory stimuli; obtaining access to an activity, attention from others, an object, or a sensory event). For example, if a student is screaming to protest and delay a nonpreferred activity, the team would decide which behavior they would prefer the student to perform that would result

in the same outcome (delay the nonpreferred activity) but in an acceptable method. In this case, the team may want to teach the student to request a brief delay of the transition or ask for a time to calm down before transitioning. In selecting the replacement behavior, the team ensures that it is a skill that is already present in the student's repertoire and can be performed as effortlessly as the problem behavior.

Finally, the team develops a strategy to reinforce the use of the replacement skill. Again, they use the function listed on the hypothesis as a guide in identifying an effective approach. That is, if the student's hypothesized function of the problem behavior is to escape, and the new skill they will teach the student is to ask for a break, the reinforcement strategy is to grant the student's request and permit a short delay. In addition to identifying the reinforcement that follows student use of the replacement behavior, the team also considers how to change the current method of responding when the problem behavior occurs so that it defeats the behavior's function. For example, if the student was removed to a cool down after displaying problem behavior resulting in a delay of a nonpreferred activity, the new response strategy may be for the teacher to calmly and efficiently redirect or prompt the student to use the new request for break behavior. When developing the reinforcement strategy, the team carefully ensures that the new behavior results in the student's getting the outcome just as quickly and efficiently as did the problem behavior.

Effective behavior support plans describe each of the intervention strategies with enough detail so that the teacher and any other staff or interventionist understands its implementation. This may be effectively achieved by task analyzing each intervention and including when to do the intervention, what to say to the student, and the specific physical actions that comprise the strategy. To enhance the likelihood of teacher willingness to implement the strategies, careful attention should be given to the classroom context so that the intervention developed is one that is feasible for teachers to do within the classroom dynamics and matched to their skill levels. Moreover, methods for training the teacher how to use the strategy should be prescribed as a part of the plan. Figure 30.5 shows a sample function-based intervention plan developed for the hypothesis described in Step 3.

The next consideration for Step 4 is to plan how the team will provide the teacher with follow-up support and ensure that the interventions are being implemented with fidelity. As discussed in the PMI section, before making any changes to the intervention plan or probing reasons for lack of impact of the plan on student behavior, it is important to first decide if the interventions are being

Figure 30.5   Sample function-based support plan.

Hypothesis: *When presented with an academic demand to start a nonpreferred activity or when transitioning from a preferred to a nonpreferred activity, Noah will scream at a high pitch and loud volume for an extended amount of time. As a result, he delays the nonpreferred activity or transition and he gets adult attention.*

Prevent Interventions	*Teach Interventions*	*Reinforce Interventions*
Providing Choices Noah will be given choices before transitioning from preferred to nonpreferred activities. Choices will be from the following: (a) within—Noah can choose the materials he will use to do the activities; (b) when—Noah can choose the sequence of activities. Steps: 1. Immediately before transitioning, tell Noah, *"Noah, for* (nonpreferred activity), *do you want to use the marker or the pencil to do* (activity)? OR *"Noah, we have 3 things to do in the math center* (show the mini-task schedule icons). *Which do you want to do first?* (Have Noah put icon selected in the first spot on the mini-task schedule.) *Which do you want to do second?* Repeat sequence. 2. Have Noah put each completed activity in the finished pocket.	**Replacement Behavior: Ask for a break** Noah will be taught to ask for a break using his voice-output device (VOD) and will select what he needs to calm down. Steps: 1. Immediately before a transition to a nonpreferred activity, prompt Noah to use his VOD to ask for a break by saying, *"Noah, do you need a break?"* 2. Initially, physically prompt Noah to push the icon for break by using hand-over-hand. 3. When Noah presses the break icon, say *"Noah, you asked for a break. What do you need to calm down?"* Present him with the choices. 4. Initially use hand-over-hand prompting to assist Noah in selecting his calming activity. 5. After he selects the activity say, *"Noah, calm down with a break for 1 minute."*	**Reinforce Replacement Behavior: Ask for a break** Each time Noah asks for a break, honor his request and choices. Steps: 1. When Noah requests a break, say *"Thank you for asking for a break."* 2. When Noah selects his calming activity say, *"Thank you for telling us what you need to calm down."* 3. Use flat affect, flat verbal tone when Noah requests break and choices. Do not provide attention while he is engaged in his calming activity. 4. Use a warm tone of voice with all other peers while Noah is engaged in calming activity. 5. When Noah transitions from the calming activity to the nonpreferred activity, warmly say, *"Thank you, Noah, for joining us!"* **Discontinue Reinforcing Problem Behavior** If Noah engages in screaming or hitting, redirect him to use his VOD to request a break. Steps: 1. Using flat affect and no eye contact, physically prompt Noah to use his VOD to request a break. Say, *"What do you need?"* 2. Repeat sequence for replacement behavior.

implemented accurately. Figure 30.6 provides a fidelity measure sample that can be used as an observational measure as well as a self-assessment. Once it is confirmed that the plan is doable and is implemented with fidelity by the teacher, the team is ready to evaluate the effectiveness of the plan.

Step 5: Evaluating and Monitoring the Impact of the Behavior Support Plan

The evaluation and monitoring step establishes a plan for evaluating the effectiveness of the supports on the student behavior and for making data-based decisions about whether and how to change the behavior support plan. Student outcome data, used consistently throughout Steps 2 through 5, are reviewed to determine whether behavior change is headed in the desired direction. If behavior is changing as desired, several options are

available for the next steps. Teams may decide to expand the interventions for use in other times or routines, systematically fade components of the intervention, or identify another behavior target and add to the plan. The latter option is particularly appealing in cases of multiple behaviors occurring under different situations for different functions. By building on the plan gradually, it is less likely the teacher and/or student will be overwhelmed.

If the student's behavior data indicate a trend that is undesirable, showing no change or worsening of the situation, the team should first examine the fidelity data and, if necessary, address implementation issues. If the fidelity data indicate the teacher has consistently implemented the plan as intended, but the student data show no improvement, the team should revisit the FBA data and hypothesis to determine if the function is correct. For example, suppose the hypothesized function of a student's screaming behavior was to get

Figure 30.6 Sample fidelity measure for function-based support plan.

Intervention Strategies	Was the step implemented?	Fidelity Score Y = 1 N = 0 NA = NA
Prevent Intervention—Providing Choices with Mini-Task Schedule		
1. Presented a valid choice (within or when)	Y/N/NA	
2. Presented the choice prior to transition from preferred to nonpreferred activity	Y/N/NA	
3. Honored the choices	Y/N/NA	
Teach Intervention—Replacement Behavior—Ask for a Break		
1. Prior to transitioning from preferred to nonpreferred activity, prompted Noah to request a break using his Voice Output Device	Y/N/NA	
2. After requesting a break, prompted Noah to select the activity/object for his break time	Y/N/NA	
Reinforce Intervention—Reinforced Replacement Behavior		
1. Immediately after requesting a break, presented the choice activities for calming down	Y/N/NA	
2. Immediately after Noah makes his choice, released him to the activity	Y/N/NA	
3. Used a flat affect and minimal attention while engaged in choice	Y/N/NA	
4. Used a warm tone with peers while Noah engaged in choice	Y/N/NA	
5. Welcomed Noah with a warm tone upon ending break and transitioning to the activity	Y/N/NA	
Discontinue Reinforcing Problem Behavior		
1. If Noah engaged in screaming or hitting behaviors, used flat affect, no eye contact, and minimal verbage to redirect him to use his VOD to request a break.	Y/N/NA	
Implementation Score **(Total Y's/Total Y's + N's in column)**		

Note: Y = 1; N = 0; NA = not applicable.

attention and the plan included a replacement behavior designed to allow the student attention. However, if the primary function of screaming was actually to escape, the plan then does not match the purpose of the behavior. By changing the replacement behavior to one that allows the student escape and examining the student data after the new intervention is implemented, the team can then determine the accuracy of the new hypothesis. A new FBA may need to be conducted, particularly if the behavior is significantly intense and/or occurs in multiple contexts with multiple functions. The team would then develop a revised or new behavior support plan based on the new FBA data and resulting hypothesis.

It is important for the team to continue to review both student performance and fidelity data throughout the process. The information allows the team to make data-based decisions for continuing, discontinuing, or changing the support plan. Using data allows the team to document areas of weakness within the plan, evaluate student progress toward desired goals, identify interventions that require supplemental teacher training, and determine next steps.

Research Support

Addressing problem behaviors through the functional behavior process has been repeatedly documented as effective by extant literature. Functional approaches have been effectively used with students with ASD for a wide range of problem behaviors such as physical aggression and self-injurious behaviors (Christensen et al., 2009; O'Reilly, Sigafoos, Lancioni, Edrisinha, & Andrews, 2005), elopement (Perrin, Perrin, Hill, & DiNovi, 2008), and compliance (Stager, Singer, & Horner, 1987). Research using individualized function-based supports for students with ASD has examined the effectiveness of use by people holding diverse roles including speech-language pathologists (Bopp, Brown, & Mirenda, 2004), families (Lucyshyn et al., 2007; Najdowski et al., 2008; Smith-Bird & Turnbull, 2005), as well as preschool program staff (Duda, Dunlap, Fox, Lentini, & Clarke, 2004).

FBA-derived strategies have been shown to be effective for a wide age range including young children (Dunlap & Fox, 1999), elementary-aged students (Lang et al., 2008), and adolescents (Butler & Luiselli, 2007).

More recently, Iovannone et al. (2009) and Dunlap, Iovannone, Wilson, et al. (2010) reported on a randomized controlled trial that examined the effectiveness of a model of function-based supports, PTR, as compared to services as usual for students in grades K–8. Although the study's sample of 245 did not focus solely on students with ASD, they were represented with 24 students (10% of the participants). Results of the study showed that students receiving the PTR intervention increased their social skills and academic engagement, and decreased their problem behaviors at a significant degree, when compared with their control counterparts.

Summary

The literature related to students with ASD is diverse and often consists of unfounded recommendations. The recent attempts to describe and define practices that are supported by research are helpful for the field in selecting interventions. This chapter describes two strategies that have been shown to be efficacious through a multitude of studies. Although the method in which the strategies will be included in educational programs must be flexible to meet the diversity of characteristics displayed by students with ASD, the steps described for each provide a firm foundation for delivery of effective instruction for these students.

It is imperative that educators become proficient in applying social and behavior interventions. Outside of families, education is the main source of treatment for students with ASD (National Research Council, 2001b). Educational environments provide wide-ranging natural opportunities for meaningful social exchanges and appropriate behavior skills that will build mastery. In addition, the deficits in social skills and behaviors experienced by individuals with ASD impact all areas of human life (National Research Council, 2001b). Without receiving instruction in these core areas, students with ASD will have marked difficulties making and sustaining friendships, engaging in activities with others, gaining access to inclusive environments, engaging in academic instruction, securing or keeping competitive employment, and attaining a high quality of life. Both of the interventions described in this chapter—peer-mediated interventions to enhance social skills and a functional approach to problem behavior—have shown to fit contextually within typical school settings, are easy for teachers to learn, and can be generalized to multiple environments. Both are individualized to meet unique student needs and circumstances and include tools to monitor progress and treatment fidelity. Certainly, more research will be conducted in the future to further substantiate these approaches as research-based strategies; however, both interventions currently enjoy a well-established infrastructure of research support and technology as well as guidelines for implementation that should prove helpful for educational professionals and lead to important life-altering outcomes for students with ASD.

CHAPTER 31

Effective Practices for Promoting Literacy with Individuals Who Have Physical Disabilities

Mari Beth Coleman | *University of Tennessee*

Kathryn Wolff Heller | *Georgia State University*

Reading and writing skills are critical for participation in school, employment, and life activities. Literacy opens doors to academic success; concept development; career possibilities; personal fulfillment; and, in this age of ever-expanding technology, access to real-time information, multimodal text experiences, and social networking (Barone & Wright, 2008; Browning, 2002; Hansford & Adlington, 2009). For individuals who have physical disabilities that impact their ability to perform manual tasks, the ability to read and write is even more essential with regard to an individual's being included in less-restrictive educational settings, finding employment, having access to resources and information, and participating in leisure activities (K. W. Heller, Coleman-Martin, & Swinehart-Jones, 2006; Peterson-Karlan, Hourcade, & Parette, 2008). When speech limitations accompany a physical disability, literacy becomes crucial for an individual to be able to communicate (K. W. Heller, 2010). This chapter discusses the barriers to literacy experienced by individuals with physical disabilities and two literacy interventions that have a small, but important, research base with this population: the Nonverbal Reading Approach and the use of assistive technology to promote writing.

Characteristics of Individuals with Physical Disabilities That Impede Literacy Acquisition

The causes and impacts of physical disabilities are, quite possibly, more varied than in any other disability category. Even two individuals who have the same diagnosis (e.g., spastic quadriplegic cerebral palsy) may be on extreme ends between mild and profound in terms of their physical limitations and cognitive abilities (K. W. Heller, 2009b). The term referring to physical disabilities in federal legislation is *orthopedic impairments*. The Individuals with Disabilities Education Improvement Act of 2004 provides this definition:

> Orthopedic impairment means a severe orthopedic impairment that adversely affects a child's educational performance. The term includes impairments caused

by congenital anomaly (e.g., clubfoot, absence of some member, etc.), impairments caused by disease (e.g., poliomyelitis, bone tuberculosis, etc.), and impairments from other causes (e.g., cerebral palsy, amputations, and fractures or burns that cause contractures). [20 U.S.C. § 1401 (3); 1401(30)]

Orthopedic impairment is a disability category in which services across different states and even different school systems vary tremendously. Less than one third of states continue to have separate licensure for teachers of students with orthopedic impairments. Often, the cross-categorical certification of special educators creates a situation where students with physical disabilities are served in less-restrictive environments by teachers who are not prepared to deal with their physical, health, and disability-related educational needs, or they are placed in classrooms where their physical and health needs can be met but the instruction does not sufficiently challenge them cognitively and academically (K. W. Heller & Swinehart-Jones, 2003). K. W. Heller, Fredrick, Dykes, Best, and Cohen (1999) found that one third of cross-categorically licensed teachers who were directly responsible for teaching students with physical disabilities reported feeling unprepared in 60% of the knowledge and skills identified as critical for working with this population. Because students with physical disabilities often require specialized instruction and adaptations to succeed in reading and writing, it is critical to identify interventions that overcome barriers to learning faced by these students and to disseminate knowledge of these strategies to teachers responsible for providing their literacy instruction.

A number of barriers impede successful literacy acquisition for people who have physical disabilities, and these must be addressed in the context of literacy instruction. Barriers to literacy vary depending on the type of disability (e.g., neuromotor impairment, degenerative condition), functional impact of the disability (e.g., sensory loss, health and endurance factors, background experiences), psychosocial impact on the individual (e.g., self-concept, behavioral and emotional functioning), and environmental factors (e.g., physical, learning, and attitudinal barriers) (K. W. Heller, 2009a).

The type of disability may have an impact on an individual's acquisition of literacy skills. Neuromotor impairments resulting from damage to the brain (e.g., cerebral palsy, traumatic brain injury) or requiring intracranial medical intervention (e.g., shunting for hydrocephaly in individuals with spina bifida) might result in learning difficulties more significant than a musculoskeletal disability (e.g., scoliosis, arthritis) (Iddon, Morgan, Loveday, Sahakian, & Pickard, 2004; Vermeer & Dekker, 1993). Whereas the physical impact of a neuromotor impairment initially may be more significant than that of a degenerative condition (e.g., muscular

dystrophy, spinal muscular atrophy), issues surrounding the loss of abilities and death and dying may have an impact on a child's progress in learning literacy (K. W. Heller, Mezei, & Schwartzman, 2009). The type of disability also plays a role in learning because of the specific functional effects of different disabilities.

Many physical disabilities result in the loss of functional abilities due to atypical motor patterns or restricted motor abilities (K. W. Heller, 2009a). The inability to engage with reading and writing materials and to explore the surrounding environment poses important obstacles in early development of literacy skills and basic concepts. The early print experiences of young children without disabilities are very different from those of children with severe physical disabilities. Often, young children will select books from the bookshelf, crawl up into an adult's lap, and engage in a shared reading experience. Children with physical disabilities often do not have the ability to select materials or turn pages in a book, and their parents may have difficulty holding them in their laps while reading. These factors make early literacy learning different for children with physical disabilities. When another barrier, impaired speech, is present, early literacy learning becomes increasingly adult directed. Young children often request the same book repeatedly; however, children who have both physical and verbal limitations cannot do so and thus miss out on the repeated exposure to text that is so important for development of early literacy skills (K. W. Heller & Coleman-Martin, 2007). Different early literacy experiences paired with different experiences of the surrounding world (e.g., not playing in the dirt or going to the mall because of mobility difficulties) can play a major factor in the development of concepts necessary for reading comprehension and written productivity.

Many physical disabilities, such as cerebral palsy and spina bifida, are accompanied by concomitant impairments such as decreased visual acuity or visual perception and problems related to memory, attention, or cognitive processing (Junkala & Talbot, 1982; Rowley-Kelly & Reigel, 1993). Finally, functional effects that may impact literacy development of individuals with physical disabilities include physical and health factors such as fatigue, lack of endurance, pain, and medication effects (K. W. Heller, 2009a). These functional barriers often contribute to or interact with psychosocial and environmental factors to impair development of reading and writing abilities.

Psychosocial factors such as behavioral, emotional, and social functioning; motivation; and self-efficacy can play a part in reading and writing for individuals with physical disabilities. Behavioral challenges can arise from ineffective discipline and decreased expectations related to the presence of a disability. Some individuals with physical disabilities have lower self-concept or self-esteem that can impact performance in academics or life activities (K. W. Heller, 2009a). They may fail to develop appropriate social skills because of isolation or decreased social opportunities (G. A. King, Schultz, Steel, Gilpin, & Cathers, 1993; Magill-Evans & Restall, 1991). Lower self-efficacy and higher levels of learned helplessness have been noted in individuals with physical disabilities, which may impact motivation to read and write (K. W. Heller, 2009a; S. F. Tam, 2000). Because learning happens through social engagement with adults and peers, all of these psychosocial factors may have a direct impact on the development of literacy skills.

Finally, environmental barriers such as decreased access to materials, limited participation, ineffective learning environments, and decreased expectations can impede an individual with a physical disability from achieving his full potential in reading and writing (K. W. Heller, 2009a). When upper limb function is impaired or problems with positioning are present, access to books and other printed materials as well as writing utensils or keyboards may be limited. Hemmingson and Borell (2002) found that barriers of time, pace, and space had a detrimental effect on the participation in general education classrooms by children with physical disabilities. Because the general education classroom must accommodate large numbers of students, the pace of instruction and amount of time devoted to mastery learning and the amount of space devoted to accessibility may not meet the needs of students with significant physical disabilities. Mike (1995) found that as little as 30 minutes per day was allocated for literacy instruction in a classroom for students with severe physical disabilities because of the increased focus on meeting the physical and health needs of the students.

As previously mentioned, most states do not have certification in orthopedic impairments. Thus, teacher-preparation programs in those states may not provide specific training in teaching literacy to students with physical disabilities. Even in states that continue to have separate teacher licensure in this area, some school systems do not have teachers who are trained to provide literacy instruction that meets the specific needs of students with physical disabilities. One other environmental factor is the incorrect assumption by many people that physical disability is always accompanied by limited learning capacity, which may lead to decreased expectations and inappropriate literacy instruction for students who have physical disabilities.

To reiterate, numerous potential barriers to learning reading and writing exist for individuals who have physical disabilities. Depending on the type of disability, an individual may experience one or more functional or psychosocial effects that may impact learning. Additionally, environmental barriers may exist that result in inappropriate literacy instruction for students with physical disabilities. Despite the barriers that impede literacy and the increased need for strong literacy skills for individuals who have physical disabilities, the literature examining effective interventions for promoting literacy with this population is sparse (Browning, 2002; Ferreira, Rönnberg, Gustafson, & Wengelin, 2007; Koppenhaver, Hendrix, & Williams, 2007). Two interventions demonstrated to be effective in promoting literacy for individuals with physical disabilities are the Nonverbal Reading Approach and assistive technology for writing.

The Nonverbal Reading Approach

Definition and Theoretical Underpinnings of the Nonverbal Reading Approach

One effective practice that was originally developed for students with physical disabilities is the Nonverbal Reading Approach (NRA; K. W. Heller, Fredrick, & Diggs, 1999). The NRA is a systematic instructional strategy for teaching decoding skills to students who have severe speech impairments in addition to their physical disabilities, such as those with severe spastic quadriplegia cerebral palsy who have dysarthric speech (i.e., poor articulation) or anarthric speech (i.e., no intelligible speech). It has also been used with students who have disabilities such as autism, stroke, and intellectual disabilities with speech and physical disabilities. The approach is designed to be used in conjunction with phonics-based reading programs (K. W. Heller & Alberto, 2010). It uses the strategies of guided practice, inner speech, self-instruction, diagnostic distractor arrays, and error analysis.

The NRA has been used to teach students specific words in a phonics-based reading program, as well as to teach students a strategy to use when encountering unknown words. It has been used to effectively improve word-recognition and reading levels in conjunction with the Direct Instruction curriculum (K. W. Heller, Fredrick, & Diggs, 1999), to promote generalization or faster acquisition of decoding unknown words with similar phoneme sequences (K. W. Heller, Fredrick, Tumlin, & Brineman, 2002), to promote decoding when paired with computer-based instruction (Coleman-Martin, Heller, Cihak, & Irvine, 2005), and as a self-instruction strategy to promote decoding unknown words (K. W. Heller & Alberto, 2010; Swinehart-Jones & Heller, 2009).

The theoretical basis of the NRA originates with Lev Vygotsky, who theorized about the development of inner speech and its relationship to thought through the influences of the sociocultural experience (Vygotsky, 1934/1986).

According to Vygotsky, children develop from using language to communicate to using language to guide and monitor their activity. Language, in the form of inner speech, therefore can be used in a self-regulatory capacity, and students can be taught to use inner speech in self-instruction strategies (Diaz, Neal, & Amaya-Williams, 1990). Using the NRA, students are taught to use inner speech as a self-instruction strategy to decode words and monitor progress. This can be an advantage for children who lack the ability to speak or to speak understandably.

Speech production has been found to be important for decoding words, and students with limited speech production are at risk of developing limited reading skills (Peeters, Verhoeven, de Moor, & van Balkom, 2009). However, studies have shown that speech production (i.e., articulatory coding) is not an essential part of the process used for subvocal rehearsal or phonological coding (Baddeley & Wilson, 1985; Bishop & Robson, 1989; Foley & Pollatsek, 1999; Peeters, Verhoeven, & de Moor, 2009; Vallar & Cappa, 1987). For example, in one study by Foley and Pollatsek (1999), children with no intelligible speech and those with severe speech production impairments were able to accurately use phonological coding for reading and short-term memory tasks in the absence of speech. These findings support the use of inner speech to teach word decoding and self-instruction.

Description of the Nonverbal Reading Approach: Guided Practice

The NRA consists of: (a) a guided practice procedure for teaching the target words and decoding process, (b) an evaluation procedure, and (c) expansion strategies. The purpose of the guided practice portion of the NRA is to teach students their targeted words as well as teach them a procedure for decoding unknown words. In this procedure, students are taught to use inner speech to decode words, in a manner similar to that of a more advanced reader (instead of decoding aloud as a beginning reader would do). This allows students who have difficulty speaking to put their efforts into correctly decoding the words subvocally and concentrating on the correct sounds, rather than struggling to pronounce sounds that will sound inaccurate because of their speech impairment. The main part of the guided practice portion of the NRA is a three-step decoding sequence using inner speech and self-instruction of the sequence.

Three-Step Decoding with Inner Speech

The three-step decoding process of the NRA focuses on using inner speech. The teacher needs to consistently use the same phrase when directing students to use inner speech, such as, "Think the sound," "Quietly say the sound to yourself," "Silently say the sound," or "Say in your head the sound." Teachers should not use the cue "Say the sound in your head," because students may start to vocalize the moment they hear, "Say the sound" before the teacher has a chance to say the rest of the cue. Students may need to be taught directly the concept of using inner speech. This can be done by presenting the student with known items and saying, "Think what this is. Don't say it aloud. Are you doing it? Are you saying it in your head?" Games and songs like BINGO that substitute saying a letter or item with a clap or other action may also assist with teaching the use of inner speech.

Students are taught to decode words using a three-step decoding process with inner speech (see Figure 31.1). In Step 1, the student sounds out each letter (or groups of letters) using inner speech while the teacher models the sounds aloud. For example, for the word *man,* the student is shown the first letter, *m,* and is told to "Say in your head this sound" (or a similar phrase) while the teacher models "/mmm/" aloud. This continues for all of the sounds of the word. Step 2 consists of slowly blending together the letters (or groups of letters). For the word *man,* the teacher directs the student to use inner speech to say all of the sounds together without stopping between the sounds while the teacher says "/mmmaaannn/." In Step 3, the word is blended quickly and the student is told to "Say it in your head fast," as the teacher says the word (e.g., /man/) (K. W. Heller & Alberto, 2010).

Motoric Indicators with the Three-Step Decoding Process

Because using inner speech is a covert process, it is not possible to know with absolute certainty that the student is using inner speech or is using it correctly. However, the teacher can look for indications that the student is using inner speech, such as seeing the student visually track across the written word, attend to the written word, correctly decode the word during the evaluation process, or engage in a motoric indicator.

A motoric indicator is any type of observable movement that the student engages in simultaneously with each step of the decoding process. Not only do motoric indicators provide an observable behavior for the teacher to see, they may also assist the student in remembering the decoding steps. Some examples of movements used by students include moving a finger left to right near the word for each of the three steps, moving an arm up and down, leaning the body forward, and eye blinking. The movement should involve minimal effort for the student to make, and it is important that it does not interfere with the concentration needed to decode the words with inner speech. The use of the motoric indicator is optional.

Figure 31.1   Steps of the Nonverbal Reading Approach.

Guided Practice Component of the Nonverbal Reading Approach

1. *Introduction.* The teacher shows the word to the student and says, "Look at this word. I'll say the sounds, and you think the sound in your head."

2. *Step 1 of saying each sound/unit.* The teacher shows only the first letter of the word (or first word unit) by covering other letters with a piece of paper and says, "Think in your head this sound (unit)," and the teacher models the sound aloud. The teacher uncovers the next letter (or unit), repeats this process, and continues until all of the sounds (word unit) have been modeled.

3. *Step 2 of blending the sounds/units.* The teacher shows the student the word and says, "In your head, think the sounds all together without stopping between the sounds," as the teacher provides a model by slowly saying the word aloud while pointing to the letters across the word.

4. *Step 3 of saying the sounds fast to make a word.* The teacher says, "Think it in your head fast." The teacher then says the word aloud as it would be pronounced when reading text and pointing quickly across the word.

Evaluation Component of the Nonverbal Reading Approach

1. *Introduction.* The teacher says, "I am going to test you on some words. Sound them out first in your head using the three steps, and then I will give you choices." The teacher shows the student the target word and says, "Sound out this word" (or provides guidance by telling the student the steps to decode the word as in the guided practice component, but without providing the sounds).

2. *Provides diagnostic distractor array.* The teacher says, "I'll give you four choices. Listen to your choices. Your choices are: [choice 1], [choice 2], [choice 3], [choice 4]." "Is it [choice 1]?" (waits 3 to 5 seconds for student response). "Is it [choice 2]?" and so on. The teacher gives choices without any cueing.

3. *Records student response.* The teacher watches the student to indicate her choice (e.g., head nod, vocalization, eye blink) and accurately records the one the student selected.

4. *Responding to student's selection.* If the student gave a correct answer, the teacher confirms the correct selection (and gives praise or reinforcement). If the student gives an incorrect answer, the teacher goes through the guided practice procedure while providing sounds.

5. *Error analysis.* The teacher analyzes the data after the session for error patterns to determine additional instructional needs and possible changes in distractor arrays.

In some cases, students may engage in a motoric indicator spontaneously. If that does not occur, a motoric indicator can be selected for use if the teacher elects to have one in place. However, for some students, introducing a motoric indicator after they have learned the three-step decoding process may be better, so their attention is not divided between learning the steps and learning a corresponding movement.

Teaching Self-Instruction of the Nonverbal Reading Approach

One of the goals of the NRA is not only to have students learn the words being targeted for instruction but to be able to decode unknown words. Teachers consistently need to teach students to learn the three-step decoding process and to apply it to unknown words. Some strategies that may be used to teach students to learn the three-step decoding process are systematic instruction of the three steps, modeling the three steps and gradually fading teacher support, using prompt cards with the steps, programming the steps on the students' augmentative and alternative communication (AAC) devices, and using mnemonics. Once the three-step decoding process is learned, teachers need to instruct students when to use it on their own. This can be facilitated by intentionally introducing unknown words and prompting students, "What do you do if you don't know the word?" and prompting them (e.g., on their AAC device, motioning to their prompt card) to use the three-step decoding process. Students then use the strategy, and teachers assess if they did it correctly.

Some students like the use of mnemonics to help remember the steps. One mnemonic is SAM, which can stand for, "Say the sounds, All together, Make it fast"—corresponding to each of the three decoding steps.

Another mnemonic is SAMS, which may be more appropriate if the student is reading sentences. It stands for Say the sounds, All together, Make it fast, and check if it makes Sense. The last step serves as a self-reflection step to help the students determine if the word they decoded fits the sentence they are reading.

Optional Components

Teachers may add some optional components to the guided practice portion of the NRA. For example, some students can make noises or approximations of letter sounds and want to say the word aloud. Teachers have the option of first modeling the word before sounding it out and having students say the word aloud as well as they can before guiding students through the three-step decoding strategy using inner speech.

Supplementary instruction is often provided along with teaching the decoding process using the NRA. For example, the teacher may compare the word to a previously learned word, examine prefixes or suffixes, provide definitions, and have the student spell and write the word. Often these activities are part of the phonics curriculum that is being used in conjunction with the NRA.

Description of the Nonverbal Reading Approach: Evaluation Component

After using guided practice to teach students to decode words, the teacher will need to evaluate if the students decoded properly. The evaluation component of the NRA consists of several steps: (a) the student decodes the word, (b) the teacher provides a diagnostic distractor array, (c) the student receives confirmation and praise for a correct response or goes through a correction procedure, and (d) the teacher performs an error analysis.

The evaluation component begins by the teacher presenting the word and directing the student to sound out the word using the three-step decoding process and inner speech. For students who have not learned the three steps independently, the teacher guides the students through the steps using the same procedure in the guided practice component, but the teacher does not provide the sounds. This process helps the students learn the decoding steps and decode the targeted word. Next, the teacher encourages the students to remember the word that was just decoded and then listen closely to the verbally presented choices and select the one that matches what the students just decoded. It is important that the teacher uses a diagnostic distractor array when selecting the choices for the student to choose from.

Diagnostic Distractor Arrays

A diagnostic distractor array provides choices to the student designed to evaluate the student's acquisition of the targeted material, which in this case is whether the student correctly decoded the word. Most diagnostic distractor arrays consist of the correct answer and two or three additional choices that have been carefully selected to determine if the student correctly decoded the word. Choices are typically presented orally to the student as the student looks at the written word she decoded. Teachers must be cautious not to inadvertently cue the student to the correct word through intonation or emphasis when saying the words in the diagnostic distractor array.

There is a difference between simply providing an array of words and a diagositc distractor array. For example, if the student was shown the word *dog,* asked to sound it out, and then was given the verbal choices of *cat, rabbit, dog,* and *car,* a correct answer would indicate only that the student knows the first letter sound or some other sound in the word *dog.* In a diagnostic distractor array, the carefully chosen array assists the teacher in pinpointing the student's errors and helps ensure that the student knows the word. Initially, a diagnostic distractor array may begin by including a word with a different beginning sound, a word with a different ending, and a word with a different vowel sound. In our *dog* example, a diagnostic distractor array could consist of *hog, dug, dog, dot.* If the student selected *dot,* she may not be sounding out the word until the end or may be confusing the *g* and *t* sound. If the student selected *dug,* she appears to have vowel-sound confusion. If the student selected *hog,* she appears not to be sounding out the beginning sound.

Student Response and Consequence

Students should be told when they answer correctly and should be given praise or other reinforcement as appropriate. If the student makes an incorrect response, the teacher should go through a correction procedure that consists of using the guided practice component of the NRA, as well as any additional instruction (e.g., providing more repetition on the word or the sounds that are being confused). In addition, the teacher should record the distractor array that was used and the choice the student made for each word for later error analysis.

Error Analysis

An error analysis is a careful examination of the type of errors the student is making within the trial as well as any error patterns across the different targeted words.

In our *dog* example, let's say the student selects *dot*. And for another choice, the teacher sees that for the word *rat* the student selected *rag*. This may indicate that the student is confusing *g* and *t*. The student needs additional instruction for the *g* and *t*-sounds. Also, other diagnostic distractor arrays will need to be examined. For example, after teaching *g* and *t,* the student is answering correctly for the word *dog* and *rat*; however, for a third word, *fit,* which the student has always answered correctly, the teacher sees that the distractors never included a choice with a *g* sound. In this case, the teacher would provide the word *fig* as one of the choices the next time she assesses the word *fit* to be sure the student is no longer confusing *g* and *t* and that the student really knows that word. Careful analysis is important to correctly identify and address any decoding errors that may be occurring.

Description of the Nonverbal Reading Approach: Expansion Strategies

The NRA involves students in a process of (a) sounding out words nonverbally with guided practice, (b) sounding out words using the NRA independently (i.e., self-directed instruction) with words in isolation and words in sentences, and (c) achieving automaticity on targeted words (i.e., recognizing words without decoding them). As the student gains automaticity on targeted words, the teacher should present the word and ask, "Do you know what this word is?" If no, the teacher may say, "What do you do if you don't know the word?" and wait for the student to respond (e.g., on his AAC device). If the student does not respond or responds incorrectly, the teacher can prompt: "Sound it out in your head" or "SAM." If the student indicates that he knows the word, the teacher may skip having the student sound out the word and assess his mastery of the word by using a diagnostic distractor array (Heller & Alberto, 2010).

The NRA should be integrated into other reading activities, such as reading connected text (e.g., sentences, stories), checking for comprehension, promoting fluency, as well as spelling and writing. Often, students will need assistive technology to gain access to writing and will need augmentative communication and other adaptations to promote reading and writing skills.

Research Supporting the Nonverbal Reading Approach

The NRA is based on best practices in phonics instruction and is adapted to include inner speech and self-instruction. Owing to the paucity of researchers who investigate reading strategies with students with severe physical disabilities, the research supporting the NRA is still in its infancy, with further investigations still under way. Currently, four research articles and additional review articles and book chapters have focused on the NRA (Coleman-Martin et al., 2005; Heller & Alberto, 2010; K. W. Heller & Coleman-Martin, 2007; K. W. Heller, Fredrick, & Diggs, 1999; K. W. Heller, Fredrick, Tumlin, & Brineman, 2002; Swinehart-Jones & Heller, 2009).

K. W. Heller, Fredrick, and Diggs (1999) examined the use of the NRA in conjunction with Direct Instruction reading programs (Reading Mastery and Corrective Reading) over the course of a school year (9 months), with three students who had severe physical disabilities and anarthric or severe dysarthric speech. This pilot study used a case study format to investigate word-reading acquisition and reading gains. By the end of the study, participants showed gains in the number of words learned, with improvements ranging from 85 words to 261 words over the study (mastering 58% to 88% of the words taught). All three participants made gains in word identification on standardized achievement tests (7-month gain, 1-year gain, and a 2.5-month gain for a student who was ill 44% of the academic year). This study was considered successful due to the percentage of words learned by each student, as well as the amount of gain they had made before the study compared with the gain made after the intervention. For example, a 15-year-old participant had made only kindergarten-level gains in word recognition for all the years she was in school before the study, but she was able to make a 7-month gain in word recognition in the one academic year of this intervention. She also went from reading single words to reading paragraphs with automaticity.

Heller, Fredrick, and Diggs (1999) reported a second study that examined the importance of using diagnostic distractor arrays. This study used a reversal design (ABAB) to compare percent of correct responses for words with which students were unfamiliar using grossly dissimilar arrays (i.e., arrays in which word choices were dissimilar along multiple dimensions) (A) and diagnostic distractor arrays (B). When assessed with grossly dissimilar arrays, students had high percentages of correct responses (80% to 100%). However, when the same unknown words were presented using diagnostic distractor arrays, students were unable to guess the correct words (0% to 20% accuracy). This demonstrated that the diagnostic distractor arrays were far more accurate than grossly dissimilar arrays for assessing word identification for nonverbal individuals. It appears that students could guess the correct response on grossly dissimilar arrays by only partially decoding the word (e.g., beginning sound). This introductory study showed positive effects of using the NRA with Direct Instruction curricula and emphasized the importance of using diagnostic distractor arrays.

K. W. Heller et al. (2002) taught students words using the NRA and then examined whether the students could generalize their decoding skills to unknown words with similar phoneme sequences. A multiple-baseline probe design was used across three students with severe physical and speech disabilities. Graphic analysis and error examination indicated that the NRA was effective in teaching decoding skills with students ranging from 0% to 30% accuracy during baseline and reaching 80% to 100% accuracy for multiple sessions during intervention. These skills generalized to unknown words with little or no additional instruction (reaching 80% accuracy or higher).

The guided practice procedure of the NRA has been delivered through computer-assisted instruction (CAI) to teach word decoding to students with cerebral palsy, autism, and stroke (Coleman-Martin et al., 2005). In this study, a multiple-conditions design with drop-down baselines was used to investigate using the NRA with three students across three conditions of: (a) teacher-only instruction, (b) teacher and CAI, and (c) CAI alone. The study was not meant to determine which condition was better, but to examine if students would be able to correctly identify word sets instructed by CAI alone, after successful completion of the first two conditions (which is thought to be a typical natural progression from teacher-directed to computer-directed instruction). Baselines ranged from 0% to 20%, and all participants reached criteria in each of the three conditions (80% accuracy or above for two consecutive sessions). The results indicated that the guided practice component of the NRA can be effectively delivered through computer-assisted instruction, which has the potential to allow students time to practice decoding independently.

The most recent research article examined the effect of NRA on learning targeted words as well as the three-step decoding process as a self-instruction strategy (Swinehart-Jones & Heller, 2009). A changing-criterion design demonstrated that four students with cerebral palsy learned their targeted words as they used the decoding strategy along with motoric indicators with 0 words correct at baseline to all 10 words correct by the end of the intervention. After learning to use the three-step decoding process of the NRA with their 10 targeted words, classroom teachers used the NRA with the reading curriculum. Students were observed and evaluated for independent use of the decoding strategy, and all four students were found to use the three-step decoding process independently 6 months after initially being taught to use the strategy.

Assistive Technology to Promote Writing

Definition and Theoretical Underpinnings of Assistive Technology for Writing

Another practice that assists individuals with physical disabilities in overcoming barriers to literacy is assistive technology (AT). The Individuals with Disabilities Education Improvement Act of 2004 states, "*Assistive technology device* means any item, piece of equipment, or product system, whether acquired commercially off the shelf, modified, or customized, that is used to increase, maintain, or improve the functional capabilities of a child with a disability." Additionally, the law stipulates that the term "assistive technology" includes services that assist a child with a disability with selection, acquisition, or use of an AT device [20 U.S.C. § 1401 (1); 1401(2)]. Assistive technology opens doors to participation in a wide array of activities and settings not otherwise afforded to people with physical disabilities. Stumbo, Martin, and Hedrick (2009) found that, "appropriately chosen and implemented assistive technology" (p. 108) is imperative for adults with physical disabilities to participate on levels approaching that of peers without disabilities in education, employment, and independent living. Because AT encompasses such a wide array of devices and services, this chapter will focus on how AT devices for writing can increase access to writing and written productivity for individuals with physical disabilities.

As previously described, individuals with physical disabilities face many barriers that restrict their level of achievement in writing. Assistive technology often provides a means for individuals with disabilities to overcome such barriers. Although AT may prove beneficial for many individuals with disabilities, the presence of a physical disability often results in increased reliance on AT solutions for writing as compared to other disabilities. Parette and Peterson-Karlan (2007) defined AT as "a tool that allows a person to do a task they could not do without the tool *at the expected performance level*" (pp. 388–389). The use of AT devices and software for writing may bridge the gap between the individual's performance level and *"expected performance level"* by compensating for the functional effects of decreased motor abilities and concomitant sensory impairments as well as environmental barriers such as decreased access to writing materials and lower expectations from school personnel. Furthermore, AT can help to compensate for decreased achievement in written productivity due to differences in memory, attention, and cognition, as well as psychosocial factors such as lack of motivation and feelings of self-efficacy. The compensatory nature of AT to overcome these barriers can be associated with a theory originally developed to conceptualize human–machine interactions, Baker's Basic Ergonomic Equation (Edyburn, 2001).

Baker's Basic Ergonomic Equation was reconceptualized by T. W. King (1999) as a way to examine how human factors impact the use of AT. This theory suggests the use of AT will succeed only if the user's motivation to perform a task using the AT device is greater than the sum of the cognitive effort, physical effort, linguistic effort, and time load needed to perform the task with the device (T. W. King, 1999). When an individual has a physical disability that results in decreased ability to use writing implements or type on a standard keyboard, the physical process of writing may demand so much attention that little attention is allocated to the process of composing text. Assistive technologies such as (a) low-tech (i.e., nonelectronic, inexpensive) devices that facilitate hand-writing (e.g., pencil grips, adapted paper, slant boards) or access to keyboarding (e.g., hand braces, key guards, mouth sticks) or (b) high-tech software (e.g., standard or adaptive word processors, speech recognition software) can provide an individual with a means of access less taxing physically and requiring less cognitive attention to be placed on the physical aspect of writing (Coleman & Heller, 2009). The reduced levels of attention, memory, and cognition of some individuals with physical disabilities may be aided by software that provides structure and support for written productivity such as talking word processors that support struggling writers through auditory feedback or software that provides graphic organizers to help with the organization and structure of written works. These supports may reduce the cognitive and linguistic effort required for writing, thus requiring lower levels of motivation for task completion than writing without the use of technology. However, some AT for writing requires advanced cognitive and linguistic processes for writers with physical disabilities.

Individuals with extremely limited motor abilities may need to gain access to a computer with a single switch. For writing, this involves the use of an onscreen keyboard with scanning. Scanning is the process where the computer highlights letters in sequence and the user activates his switch when the desired letter is highlighted. Usually, to make scanning faster, the sequence involves scanning each row of the keyboard until the user activates the switch indicating the desired letter is in that row and then highlighting across the row until the desired letter is reached (i.e., row–column scanning). Because this process for word processing requires multiple steps to "type" each letter, scanning poses a higher cognitive load on the user than is generally required for keyboarding. In light of Baker's Basic Ergonomic Equation, writing via scanning requires heavy cognitive

and physical effort; the AT user must have a high level of motivation to complete the writing task for this technology to be effective.

In the areas of access and written productivity, word-prediction software, which provides a list of possible words based on the first letters typed, may assist with reducing the number of keystrokes required to type a word and may improve spelling; however, it demands a shift of attention from the writing content to the word list being provided, thus increasing the cognitive load (Peterson-Karlan et al., 2008). This principle also applies to hand-held spelling checkers, or spelling checkers or dictionary features built in to word processors. If those supports are necessary for single-word production, attention is shifted and the writing process is slowed. The increased physical, cognitive, and linguistic demands placed on the task of writing by the presence of a physical disability generally slow the process. As suggested by Baker's Basic Ergonomic Equation, for an AT device to succeed in promoting writing for an individual, she must have a level of motivation that supersedes these demands.

When examined in light of Baker's Basic Ergonomic Equation, the potential impact of AT on writing for individuals with physical disabilities is evident; when motivation exceeds the additional effort required, AT can successfully enhance the communication of individuals with physical disabilities. However, the number of intervention studies addressing AT interventions for writing with this population is limited. In the following sections, the small body of research on AT for writing for students with physical disabilities is addressed along with implications for future research and practice.

Research on Assistive Technology for Writing with Students Who Have Physical Disabilities

Although ATs specifically designed for individuals with physical disabilities are available (e.g., switches, enlarged keyboards, computer input devices), technology designed for others often is equally beneficial for someone with a physical disability. For example, a word processor may be helpful to someone who physically can write with a pen or pencil (e.g., making writing faster and more legible), whereas it is assistive (i.e., necessary) for another person whose motor limitations impede hand-writing. Furthermore, individuals with physical disabilities who have learning and cognitive impairments may be benefited equally by software designed to compensate for learning or intellectual disabilities. See Figure 31.2 for examples of AT for writing.

Assistive technology for writing can be categorized as providing access to writing or to promote written productivity. In some cases, the technology serves in both

Figure 31.2   Examples of assistive technology for writing for individuals with physical disabilities.

Assistive Technology for Access to Writing

Low-Tech Assistive Technology for Handwriting

    Writing Implements

        Felt-tip pens (require less pressure, easier to see)

        Pencil grip

        Larger-surface pens or pencils (commercially available or built-up with foam)

        Weighted pencil or pen to decrease extraneous movements or tremors

        Hand brace to provide grip and stability

        Mouthstick or headstick with pencil/pen holder

    Paper Adaptations or Stabilization

        Paper with darker or larger lines

        Paper with raised lines or use of writing guides

        Stabilization of paper with tape, clipboards, or nonslip material (e.g., Dycem)

        Use of a slanted surface (e.g., notebook or slant board)

Electronic Solutions for Access to Writing

    Portable word processors

    Word processing software

    Accessibility features for typing (e.g., sticky keys, filter keys)

    Hand, head, or mouth pointers used for typing

    Different keyboard layouts (e.g., ABC, Dvorak)

    Adaptive keyboards (e.g., smaller, larger, onscreen)

    Adaptive input devices (e.g., trackball, joystick, head-controlled mouse emulators)

    Switches to control scanning on onscreen keyboards

Assistive Technology to Increase Written Productivity or Written Expression

    Word walls or picture dictionaries (low-tech or computerized)

    Handheld spell checkers

    Features in standard word processors (e.g., spell check, grammar check, dictionary, thesaurus)

    Adaptive word processors (e.g., talking word processors, symbol processors)

    Graphic organizer software to increase writing organization and structure

    Speech recognition software

    Word prediction software

    Augmentative communication devices used for writing

---

capacities. Small bodies of literature examine the use of AT for access to writing and AT for increased written productivity for individuals with physical disabilities.

Assistive Technology for Access to Writing

One issue that limits research on AT for access to writing for people with physical disabilities is that there are almost as many solutions as there are individuals who need the technology. Often an individual needs a combination of technologies such as a pencil grip and slant board for documents requiring short answers and a computer with a keyguard and word processing software for more extensive writing (Coleman & Heller, 2009). In a study that examined the use of constant time delay to teach spelling to students with physical disabilities (Coleman-Martin & Heller, 2004), each of the three participants required different ATs for writing. One student used specially lined paper and a slant board to write her responses, one typed on a standard laptop keyboard, and one used a trackball to type her answers on an onscreen keyboard. These adaptations made accessing the task of spelling possible for the three students, and all three achieved criterion (i.e., 100% accuracy for three sessions) for spelling three sets of words.

Studies have explored the impact of other AT devices on writing. Lancioni et al. (2008) noted that head-controlled devices for computer access might be laborious and tiring when used for a long time. They compared the impact of a voice-detecting sensor to a pressure switch to activate an onscreen scanning keyboard for two boys with extensive physical disabilities. Both participants indicated a preference for the voice-detecting sensor, but mean writing time per letter was better with the pressure sensor for one and with the voice-detecting sensor for the other. Similar studies in the education and rehabilitation engineering literature have explored the use of various input devices for writing (e.g., tongue-activated light sensor, eye-tracking devices, acoustically controlled mouse pointer, morse code keyboard emulators, tilt sensors), often with results that show variable performance based on individual needs and abilities of the participants (e.g., Felton, Lewis, Wills, Radwin, & Williams, 2007; LoPresti, Brienza, Angelo, & Gilbertson, 2003; Yang, Chuang, Yang, & Luo, 2003). Although no single AT solution meets the needs of all individuals with physical disabilities, a couple of important points can be drawn from this research literature.

First, teachers and therapists of students with physical disabilities need to be aware of the wide array of AT available to provide access to writing for these students. The second issue is that devices should be adjustable to make them more efficient for individual students' needs. Simpson, Koester, and LoPresti (2006) proposed that,

"Because each person's disability is unique, tuning these devices to each user's strengths and limitations is critical for success in many cases" (p. 127). Advancements in AT already allow individuals with significant physical disabilities to write using movements as small as an eye blink. Researchers are working on technologies that will provide computer access through neural signals for people with severely limited physical movements (e.g., advanced amyotrophic lateral sclerosis) (Felton et al., 2007). As AT that provides access to writing for individuals with physical disabilities advances, barriers to successful literacy are torn down and doors to communication and participation open for even those with the most severe physical limitations.

Assistive Technology to Promote Written Productivity

Several types of technology can be used to increase written productivity for individuals with physical disabilities. For children who are at the emergent stages of writing, software is available that combines symbols and pictures (e.g., *Boardmaker Plus, Writing With Symbols*) to promote early sentence building and other early writing skills. Talking word processors (e.g., *Write:OutLoud, IntelliTalk*) or symbol word processors (e.g., *Writing With Symbols* 2000) provide immediate auditory feedback, visual feedback, or both, to writers who struggle with spelling and grammar. Software that provides graphic or advanced organizers (e.g., *Inspiration, Draft: Builder*) can assist students with organizing thoughts and correctly structuring their writing (Sitko, Laine, & Sitko, 2005). One type of software, word prediction, was designed to increase writing fluency for individuals with physical disabilities by decreasing keystrokes, but much of the research has shown it to be more effective in promoting spelling and only increasing writing fluency in some cases of students with severe physical disabilities who type at extremely slow rates (Mirenda, Turoldo, & McAvoy, 2006; Tumlin & Heller, 2004). One type of software that has implications for students with physical disabilities, as well as the general population, is speech recognition. Speech recognition has the ability to increase production of written material, which can be beneficial for students with physical disabilities.

Speech recognition software for individuals with physical disabilities. Speech recognition software allows users to dictate into a microphone and have their speech converted to text or to computer functions. Speech recognition software is generally marketed as a productivity tool for people without disabilities because most people speak at rates that are considerably faster than they are able to type. The average speaking rate of adults

without disabilities is approximately 125 to 160 words per minute as compared to written speed of approximately 15 to 25 words per minute (De La Paz & Graham, 1997; Feng, Karat, & Sears, 2005). Speech recognition software can be used to dictate into word processing documents, e-mail, web browsers, and other programs, and to operate basic computer functions. The use of speech recognition software requires the user to dictate the desired text, punctuation (e.g., "comma," "question mark," "end quote"), and commands (e.g., "new paragraph," "tab," "caps on," "page up") within a word processing document. If the program does not recognize words or phrases, the user can select the incorrect text through voice commands (e.g., "select *commonly misunderstood great*") and restate the correct phrase to correct the text (e.g., *"commonly misunderstood phrase"*). Additionally, some speech recognition programs offer the ability to control functions on the screen such as the mouse cursor, and opening and closing files through spoken commands (e.g., "move mouse left," "double click").

Over the years, speech recognition software has progressed from requiring the person to speak one word at a time (discrete speech recognition) to allowing the user to speak at a normal rate (continuous speech recognition). Most speech recognition programs come with templates so that, right out of the box, they can recognize some speech, but they require training by the user to increase accurate recognition of the individual's speech. Typically, this involves the user reading passages while the software creates voice files based on the user's speech. The user's voice files are integrated with the preprogrammed templates to increase the software's accuracy in recognizing the user's speech. Generally, options are available for performing additional training of the software, which will result in higher percentages of recognition accuracy. In addition to training the software to recognize the user's voice, the user needs explicit instruction for controlling the software.

Inadequate training time or inefficient training is one of the causes for AT abandonment for individuals with physical disabilities (Coleman, 2011). Training the use of speech recognition software is especially important, given that the use of speech recognition software requires users to speak differently during the dictation process than during normal speech (e.g., dictate punctuation, enunciate more clearly) and learn numerous commands. When first introducing the software to a user, it is important to discuss dictation style. Continuous speech recognition software does not require users to speak one word at a time; however, accuracy will be decreased if users speak too rapidly, run words together, drop sounds, or insert extraneous sounds (e.g., "um") as many people do in normal conversational speech. Thus, one of the first steps is to have the user practice using a dictation vocal pattern. One mother of a high school speech recognition user called it his "radio announcer's voice."

Another early step in training someone to use speech recognition software is teaching basic commands such as turning the microphone on and off (e.g., "stop listening") and the use of punctuation and capitalization (e.g., "cap that"). Having a written list of commands available for reference is useful for most new users of speech recognition software. One of the most crucial parts of training is error correction. If a user can access a keyboard and mouse, a combination of voice and physical input may be used to make corrections. Otherwise, the user will need to learn numerous commands to correct recognition errors or make changes to text. Most speech recognition software learns a user's voice as recognition errors are corrected. Excessive use of certain correction commands that are intended for replacement of recognition errors (e.g., "scratch that") instead of commands to replace text that was recognized correctly that the user wishes to change (e.g., "select . . .") may decrease the software's recognition accuracy (Koester, 2006). One final area of training is using navigation features and commands to control the program. For some users, it is faster to use the keyboard, mouse, or other input device to perform tasks such as moving the cursor and saving files; in this case, training on voice commands for those features will not be necessary. Individuals without such access methods will need to learn numerous additional commands.

Speech recognition increases the potential for independent production of written text for writers who have physical or written expression limitations. Because speech recognition does not require physical manipulation of a keyboard (physical or onscreen), it may provide a solution to writing for individuals with extremely limited motor abilities (Rosen & Yampolsky, 2000). Speaking, for most individuals, is faster, less laborious, and less fatiguing than manual text entry (Koester, 2004). For individuals with physical disabilities, the reduction of physical effort may mean successful writing experiences that cannot be achieved by handwriting or physically entering text into the computer. Additionally, the fact that speech recognition does not require the user to spell or produce words letter-by-letter makes speech recognition a viable method of writing for individuals who struggle with written expression. This has the potential to decrease cognitive and linguistic load and possibly decrease the loss of ideas that can be lost in the process of transcribing text (De La Paz, 1999).

Although speech recognition may be effectively used to promote writing, there are some considerations regarding its appropriateness for certain students. First, the software does not assist the user in learning the writing process. Writing instruction can be used in conjunction with speech recognition software so that the user learns how to spell and construct text in written rather than spoken form, if the goal is for the student to learn to read, print, and spell. Also, the differences in spoken language and more formal writing would need to be taught. A second consideration is the noise level of the classroom affecting the software program by typing extraneous noises as words. Newer versions of the software are more efficient at filtering intentional speech from extraneous noise, but background noise is a consideration when deciding the environments in which to use speech recognition software. The user's privacy and the potential of disturbing others in the environment must also be considered.

Another potential issue is that the speech recognition user must have adequate reading skills to be able to recognize whether the software is correctly transcribing his speech. Most speech recognition programs have a feature that will read the printed text to the user; however, if reading and spelling skills are not adequate, the individual may still have difficulty making corrections to his writing. Another consideration is that the process for correcting errors can be tedious and frustrating, especially for individuals who have no physical ability to gain access to the keyboard (MacArthur & Cavalier, 2004). Some speech recognition users may not see increased productivity as compared to typing due to the increased length of time required to correct errors with speech recognition compared to keyboard entry (Karat, Horn, Halverson, & Karat, 2000; A. L. Kotler & Tam, 2002). Finally, the commands and special words that the user must memorize to use speech recognition may cause an increased burden on memory (Koester, 2004).

A small but growing research base supports the use of speech recognition for increasing writing access and quality of written products for individuals with physical disabilities. A. L. Kotler and Tam (2002) investigated the impact of discrete-utterance (i.e., dictating one word at a time) speech recognition software on the speed and recognition accuracy of six adults with physical disabilities as well as disadvantages of the use of speech recognition software. While continuous speech recognition software is more commonly used, discrete-utterance speech recognition may provide more accurate recognition, and thus more efficient text generation, for individuals who have significant speech difficulties or poor breath support (e.g., individuals who use ventilators). Participants in this study were unable to effectively use a keyboard due to functional physical limitations resulting from neuromotor and degenerative conditions (e.g., cerebral palsy, muscular dystrophy, scleroderma).

Interviews indicated that speech recognition resulted in faster speeds of text generation for participants than previously used computer access methods. However, some participants reported that the recognition accuracy of the software was not acceptable. With regard to accuracy of the speech recognition software for recognition of single words, results ranged from 62.4% to 94.4%. In dictation of formatting and correction commands, the average recognition accuracy of the software ranged from 91.5% to 99.6%. It was noted that background noise, fatigue, and illnesses that affected voice quality may have played a part in decreased accuracy of speech recognition. Other disadvantages noted were voice-related problems, fatigue, and the limited confidentiality when dictating text into speech recognition software. While the results of this study generally suggest a positive impact of the use of discrete-utterance speech recognition software on writing for most of the users, A. L. Kotler and Tam (2002) cautioned that users who have the ability to type may not see the benefit of increased speed of text generation and may experience vocal or general fatigue with use of discrete-utterance software.

Through surveying 24 adults with physical disabilities who were experienced users of speech recognition technology, Koester (2004) found that most users were generally satisfied with the performance of their speech recognition systems and reported that dictation to the computer was less painful and fatiguing than using a keyboard for input. The participants in this study who typed at slow rates (<15 wpm) showed increased production of text when using speech recognition. In 2006, Koester examined 20 different factors (e.g., specific equipment, training and experience, usage techniques, user characteristics) that influence writing performance by 23 experienced speech recognition users with physical disabilities through survey and video analysis of software usage. Bivariate and multivariate analyses were used to evaluate the effect of variables on recognition accuracy and text entry rate. Of the 20 independent variables examined, results indicate that using appropriate correction strategies, the amount of time spent on the computer, manual typing speed, and the speed with which the speech recognition system recognized user's speech were the only significant indicators of better writing performance with speech recognition software. The most influential factor was participants' use of the "scratch that" feature for correction of recognition errors. As mentioned, "scratch that" is a correction strategy intended for correction of speech recognition errors, and incorrect use of this command, to have the software disregard correctly recognized speech when the user wanted to change what was written, resulted in less-accurate recognition overall because the software is designed to learn from its mistakes. Interestingly, the amount of training time was not a significant factor in better writing performance; however,

it could be argued that more appropriate training might result in more efficient use of speech recognition software if users are trained in the appropriate corrections techniques (e.g., correct use of "scratch that").

Garrett et al. (2011) compared the use of speech recognition software to word processing for creating first drafts of writing products for five high school students with physical disabilities (i.e., spina bifida, muscular dystrophy, cerebral palsy, and spinal muscular atrophy) and concomitant disabilities (e.g., Asperger's syndrome, visual impairments). They examined the areas of writing fluency, writing accuracy, type of word errors, recall of intended meaning, and length through a single-subject alternating treatments design. For all of their participants, the use of speech recognition software resulted in increased writing fluency and length of written products. However, the participants experienced varying levels of accuracy with the speech recognition software, which resulted in frustration.

For individuals with physical disabilities who also have dysarthric (i.e., motor impaired) speech, speech recognition software may not be viable. A few studies have focused on ways to increase the capability of the speech recognition software to recognize dysarthric speech. A. L. Kotler and Thomas-Stonell (1997) found that speech training for the user can increase the accuracy of speech recognition. Hux, Rankin-Erickson, Manasse, and Lauritzen (2000) found that the quality of the speech recognition software program had an impact on the accuracy of recognition for a user with dysarthric speech but did not have a substantial impact for a user without a speech impairment. M. Parker, Cunningham, Enderby, Hawley, and Green (2006) investigated the use of a speaker-dependent speech recognition system (i.e., every word must be trained by the user) for providing access to electronic devices such as a television, lamp, compact disc player, and radio by individuals with severely dysarthric speech. Unlike speaker-independent speech recognition that comes with user templates and does not require training of every word, this type of technology has the potential for increased accuracy because of its lack of reliance on "normal" articulation patterns. M. Parker et al. found positive effects for four of seven participants and mixed results for the other participants. Although this study did not address speech recognition for writing directly, accurate speech recognition is a prerequisite for individuals with physical disabilities and dysarthric speech to be able to use this software effectively to enhance writing. As this type of speech recognition system improves, individuals with physical disabilities and dysarthric speech may someday be able to use speech recognition software fluently.

As speech recognition technology continues to improve, it will continue to open doors to writing for individuals with physical disabilities. Future research should explore options for making speech recognition more effective for these users, including instruction in the use of speech recognition, writing, and features of the software that make it easier and more accurate for individual users (e.g., individuals who have motor speech impairments). Additionally, there is a crucial need for exploring writing interventions for individuals who use AAC devices. In 2004, D. C. Millar, Light, and McNaughton stated, "In fact, at present, there are no evidence-based writing instructional programs available to guide teachers in the development of instructional activities that have been appropriately modified for individuals who use AAC" (p. 165). Years later, their study, which examined the use of direct instruction and writer's workshop methods in conjunction with AAC devices for children with physical disabilities, is the only one we located that focused solely on providing an intervention for writing with the use of AAC. Because individuals who use AAC devices need to write to communicate messages that are not stored in their devices, we recommend that researchers examine how AAC users can increase their achievement in writing.

Summary

Individuals with physical disabilities face many barriers to acquisition of literacy skills including those based on the type of disability, functional impact of the disability, psychosocial impact of the disability, and environmental factors. Although the research base demonstrating effective practices for promoting literacy for individuals with physical disabilities is limited, some practices have evidentiary support for use with this population. In the area of reading, the NRA is an effective method for overcoming the barrier of limited or absent speech by teaching students to decode through inner speech and giving teachers a way to evaluate student learning. AT can overcome numerous barriers by promoting access to writing and increased written production for individuals with physical disabilities. One particularly promising AT solution is speech recognition software. This software may overcome barriers that prevent access to writing due to functional physical limitations for individuals with physical disabilities.

There is a critical need for research investigating interventions that are effective for promoting literacy for individuals with physical disabilities. Although research from other disability areas (e.g., learning disabilities) can provide some insight to teaching literacy to individuals with physical disabilities, the diversity in physical, cognitive, and academic abilities of this population makes it difficult to generalize research findings. Overall, there is a need to examine strategies that are effective in promoting reading, decoding, fluency, and comprehension for students with physical disabilities. Studies that examine the expansion strategies of the NRA are needed to investigate application of this method to reading fluency and comprehension. As in reading, there is a comprehensive need for research in the area of writing for individuals with physical disabilities. More research is needed to examine how specific features and improvements in writing software can increase writing speed and decrease fatigue during writing for individuals with limited fine motor abilities. Additionally, the impact of AT for writing (e.g., talking word processors, graphic organizer software) on the quality of writing for individuals with physical disabilities should be explored.

In summary, two practices, the NRA for reading and AT for writing, have been demonstrated to be effective for increasing literacy skills for individuals with physical disabilities. Teachers of students with physical disabilities should be instructed in the use of both of these interventions. It is especially important that teachers are educated in the individual needs of their students, which must be considered when implementing reading and writing interventions. For example, when implementing the NRA, teachers must tailor instruction to support the student's reading level and must adjust assessment procedures to incorporate the student's best means of responding. With regard to AT, teachers should consider low-tech to high-tech devices or combinations of devices and strategies that result in maximum outcomes in writing for a student with a physical disability. Future research should focus on finding additional strategies that are effective in helping students with physical disabilities overcome barriers to literacy and acquire the reading and writing abilities necessary to have more fulfilled and productive lives.

CHAPTER 32

Teaching Students Who Have Sensory Disabilities

Deborah Chen and **Rachel Friedman Narr** | *California State University, Northridge*

Diane P. Wormsley | *North Carolina Central University*

S tudents who have sensory disabilities belong to one of three low-incidence and heterogeneous groups: those who are deaf or hard of hearing (DHH); those who are blind, have a visual impairment (VI), or deaf-blind (DB); and those with additional intellectual, motor, or other disabilities. Lack of or limited access to comprehensible auditory or visual information influences the development of communication, language, and literacy skills; therefore, instructional practices have focused on these learning needs. In this chapter, we identify three selected practices: (a) teaching visual phonics to students who are DHH, (b) early identification of braille as the primary literacy medium for students who are blind or have a VI, and (c) the use of tangible symbols with learners who are DB. It should be noted that "person-first" language is not universally acknowledged in the fields of sensory disabilities and has been rejected by some adults with these disabilities. For example, "deaf teachers" (referring to teachers who are deaf), "deaf and hard-of-hearing students," or "blind adults" are the terms preferred by many individuals.

Visual Phonics with Deaf and Hard-of-Hearing Students

Description of Students

The Individuals with Disabilities Education Act (IDEA, 2004) differentially defines *deafness* as "a hearing impairment that is so severe that the child is impaired in processing linguistic information through hearing, with or without amplification, that adversely affects a child's educational performance," and *hearing impairment* as "an impairment in hearing, whether permanent or fluctuating, that adversely affects a child's educational performance but that is not included under the definition of deafness in this section." When DHH learners acquire a complete first language (whether spoken or signed), they can develop linguistic and academic skills commensurate with age-expected levels (Mayberry, 2010). Underachievement in reading may be related to pervasive delays in receptive and expressive language development (spoken or signed), lack of access to important elements of spoken English (phonological information), as well as the sheer difficulty of learning a second language (presumably English) through reading and writing alone. Research indicates that DHH learners struggle with all facets of the reading process including word identification, vocabulary, syntax, figurative language use in written language, and comprehension skills (Paul, 2009). However, when DHH children attain a comprehensible language, the reading process becomes more natural and more easily navigated (Chamberlain & Mayberry, 2008). DHH students may be considered English Language Learners (ELLs) or Limited English Proficient (LEP), whether they enter school with impoverished language abilities due to lack of exposure to and interaction with comprehensible input (either spoken English or in signed language) or because they have learned a signed language as their first language.

Theoretical Underpinnings

Acquisition of a natural signed language (e.g., American Sign Language [ASL]) provides the strong language base necessary for DHH students (Chamberlain & Mayberry, 2008; C. Mayer & Akamatsu, 2003). Because of the innate visual abilities of DHH students, even those with advanced technology such as cochlear implants or digital hearing aids, visually based instruction builds on their strengths. Understanding that text is made up of individual phonemes represented through letter combinations in print (i.e., the alphabetic principle) is at the core of learning to read text. This principle is clearly challenging for DHH students, who frequently do not internalize all the elements of spoken English. Recognizing the need to help DHH learners "crack the code," teachers have used a variety of multimodal strategies (e.g., providing speech-reading cues, making up signs or gestures to accompany phonemes, sitting close to the student to maximize auditory cues, asking the student to attempt production of phonemes or words) that provide limited amounts of information about the phonological code of spoken English. The internal representations formed are likely incomplete (Leybaert & Alegria, 2003), so these strategies remain generally problematic (Luckner, Sebald, Cooney, Young, & Muir, 2005/2006; Trezek, Wang, & Paul, 2010).

Description and Implementation of Practice

See the Sound/Visual Phonics (commonly referred to as Visual Phonics) provides a means of making phonemes of spoken English visually accessible to DHH learners. Visual Phonics is a system of hand and grapheme cues that represent the 44 to 46 phonemes in spoken English. Visual Phonics is not a communication system. Teachers use it instructionally to convey phonemic information in single words. Visual Phonics is a supplement to any reading curriculum; its hand and grapheme cues can be used to represent sound-based (typically auditory) information.

The hand cues used in Visual Phonics are manual productions of phonemic information. These hand cues were designed to imitate the speech-articulatory features of each phoneme. For example, the /t/ sound is represented by a hand cue produced by using the index finger and thumb, with the rest of the hand closed, and the index finger flicking up off the thumb. Each hand cue is distinct, making each phoneme fully perceptible by the hand cue alone. The cues are ideal for providing visually accessible phonemic information for isolated phonemes, syllables, or words. They are not appropriate for use in communicative contexts, and although speech production of the phonemes can accompany the hand cues, it is not necessary to distinguish each phoneme. For this reason, deaf teachers can also effectively use Visual Phonics because spoken production is not necessary. Some teachers and other professionals may also use Visual Phonics to enhance students' articulation skills.

A written symbol system representing each phoneme accompanies the Visual Phonics hand cues. The written symbols roughly portray the hand cues. For example, the symbol [ɟ] is used to represent the /t/ sound described above. Teachers report having mixed interest in using the written symbols, depending on the grades they are teaching and the purposes of the lessons (Narr & Cawthon, 2010). Written symbols can be helpful for making spelling patterns more transparent or for making phonic associations.

Because Visual Phonics is a supplemental system that can be used with any reading program or curriculum, its application to instruction is flexible. A teacher incorporates Visual Phonics into reading and spelling lessons where phonemic awareness and phonic concepts of English are presented. The connection between word recognition (decoding) and vocabulary (semantics) must be discretely taught to many DHH learners.

Because learning decoding skills through audition alone (sound out the word) is frequently impractical, students are taught to use other cues for decoding through Visual Phonics, such as lip movements from reading speech on other people's mouths (speech reading), sight word recognition, and structural and morphemic analysis of words (identifying affixes and word parts). The goal for DHH readers is to internalize the visual properties of written words and associate those properties with the word meaning. These supplemental word analysis cues help with word recognition and vocabulary retention and recall. Many reading curricula are structured around themes so that these skills and strategies are contextualized for the learners. DHH learners often require additional instruction in background knowledge and vocabulary due to their impoverished language development. When this instruction is infused into reading lessons, discrete instruction related to word recognition skills with the use of Visual Phonics can occur simultaneously.

Three general components are associated with the implementation of Visual Phonics:

1. *Teacher training:* To learn Visual Phonics, teachers and other professionals should attend a 10- to 14-hour training provided by a licensed International Communication Learning Institute (ICLI) trainer. Mastery is gained through practice and continued use of the system.

2. *Identify specific parts of the reading and spelling lesson with which to apply Visual Phonics:* If a specific reading curriculum or program is used, the teacher should review the content and identify how phonemic awareness, phonics, spelling, or vocabulary are to be taught.

3. *Visual Phonics instruction:* Table 32.1 demonstrates how Visual Phonics is incorporated to supplement the phonics part of a reading lesson. It also shows additional instructional strategies for DHH learners. The written symbols can be used at the discretion of the teacher to teach and reinforce spelling patterns.

Table 32.1 A Common Phonics Kindergarten Lesson with Visual Phonics Supplement

Phonics Lesson-Building Words: Segmenting and Blending Short u Words	*Teacher Says/Signs and Does*	*Supplement with Visual Phonics*	*Additional Instructional Strategies for DHH Learners*
Display Letter Cards *a, b, d, g, h, i, j, m, n, p, r, t, u,* and *w.* Using the Letter Cards, model how to build *hug.*	"First I'll stretch out the sounds: /h/ / u/ /g/. How many sounds do you hear? The first sound is /h/. I'll put up an *h* to spell that. The next sound is /u/. What letter spells that? The last sound is /g/. What letter should I choose for that?"	1. Say/Sign the word *hug* first. When giving the Visual Phonics cues, lean to the left to provide the "sounds" /h/ /u/ /g/ to differentiate the phoneme hand cue from a sign (Trezek, Wang, & Paul, 2010). 2. Ask "How many sounds do you hear/see?" 3. Put the *h* Letter Card on the board, and give the /h/ hand cue again. 4. Say/Sign, "The next sound is /u/." Give the hand cue. "What letter spells that?" 5. Say/Sign, "The next sound is /g/." Provide the hand cue. "What letter should I choose for that?"	Students need to know the concepts associated with each word. Preteach the vocabulary in the lesson: such as *hug, bug, rug, dug, mug.* Fingerspell 3-letter words instead of using a sign. This helps spelling and word-recognition skills.
Next remove the *h.* "Which letter should I add to build *hug*?"	Model how to read *hug* by blending /h/ with /u/ and /g/.	1. Use the hand cues for /h/ /u/ /g/, presenting each cue slowly to form the word *hug.* 2. Alternate fingerspelling the word *hug,* describing the meaning, and presenting the hand cues for the word, which helps to create a strong association between the word structure and the word meaning (Padden & Ramsey, 2000).	
Continue making and blending short *u* words by substituting *d, r, m,* and *t.*	Model several more words using these strategies.	Repeat the procedure explained above, substituting the appropriate letters and hand cues.	Encourage students to build their own words using letter blocks or letter cards. Keep the focus on word meaning.

Research Base

Research on Visual Phonics is growing. Trezek and her colleagues (Trezek & Malmgren, 2005; Trezek & Wang, 2006; Trezek, Wang, Woods, Gampp, & Paul, 2007) have published most widely in this area, documenting the effectiveness of using Visual Phonics with a variety of structured reading instructional curricula with DHH students. Narr (2008) also examined the use of Visual Phonics in reading instruction, looking specifically at decoding and rhyme judgment skills with DHH students. Narr and Cawthon (2010) conducted a national survey of 200 teachers using Visual Phonics and found that teachers overwhelmingly indicated it was easy to use, engaging to students, and beneficial for improving phonemic awareness and decoding skills. Results show that Visual Phonics is a promising tool for providing accessible information to DHH learners as they learn how to decode text.

Trezek and Malmgren (2005) demonstrated that Visual Phonics could be used effectively with 23 DHH middle school students in an urban school district in the Midwest. The 8-week intervention consisted of a daily treatment package for 45 minutes that included Direct Instruction lessons that were supplemented with Visual Phonics, Baldi (a computerized avatar that demonstrates production of phonemes; see Massaro & Light, 2004), and a pictorial glossary accompanying Baldi to facilitate vocabulary instruction within the lessons. Instruction was conducted using Total Communication (typically a combination of speech, audition, and sign language). The intervention group ($n = 12$) and comparison group ($n = 13$) were matched for hearing levels that ranged from slight to profound, grade equivalence in reading, and chronological age. Teachers for the intervention and comparison groups both held K–12 certification for DHH students, and both had more than 25 years of teaching experience. Neither teacher had prior experience with Direct Instruction, Visual Phonics, or the computer program Baldi. The teacher for the intervention group was trained by one of the researchers for a full day on the contents of the Direct Instruction lessons, Visual Phonics cues applicable within the lessons, and how to use Baldi, all as part of the treatment package for the study. A procedural reliability form and a reading instruction log sheet were used to monitor and document the fidelity of the treatment package implementation.

Teachers in the comparison group continued to use one of three district-approved reading programs in their instruction (Trezek & Malmgren, 2005). Pretest and post-test scores on a researcher-designed measure of phonemic awareness and pseudoword decoding were used to determine the effects of the treatment package. At pretest, students with better hearing in both the intervention and comparison groups scored higher than students with lower hearing levels. At post-test, students in the intervention group scored higher than students in the comparison group, regardless of hearing levels; that is, students' hearing levels did not correlate with scores on the phonemic awareness and pseudo-word decoding measure. For the comparison group, a correlation was found between hearing level and performance on the post-assessment. Although the findings do not attribute the higher assessment scores to any one part of the treatment package (Direct Instruction, Visual Phonics, or Baldi), they demonstrate that students can learn and apply phonic knowledge to reading tasks, despite being DHH.

Another study conducted by Trezek and Wang (2006) examined whether 13 kindergarten and first-grade DHH students demonstrated improvements in early reading skills after participating in a phonics-based reading curriculum with Visual Phonics as a supplement to instruction. Students had hearing levels within the severe-to-profound range, and two had cochlear implants. They were divided into three cohorts, based on their classroom placement, receiving instruction in Total Communication using Direct Instruction Reading Mastery I curriculum (Engelmann & Bruner, 1995, as cited in Trezek & Wang, 2006) for an average of 48 lessons over 8 months. Visual Phonics was used to teach the phonemic aspects of the curriculum. Three teachers of DHH students with three semesters of prior experience using Direct Instruction and Visual Phonics provided the instruction.

Subtests of the Wechsler Individual Achievement Test—II (Psychological Corporation, 2002) were used to measure reading achievement. The Word Reading subtest was administered to the four kindergarten students, and the Word Reading, Pseudoword Decoding, and Reading Comprehension subtests were administered to the nine first graders. All students demonstrated statistically significant gains as indicated by comparison of pretest and post-test performance on both the Word Reading and Pseudoword Decoding subtests. Reading Comprehension subtests scores were also characterized by large gains, although they were not statistically significant. Student achievement was not related to hearing levels, again demonstrating that both deaf and hard-of-hearing students can benefit from phonics instruction.

In a more recent investigation, Trezek and her colleagues (2007) assessed performance on early reading measures of 20 DHH students in four kindergarten and first-grade classes using a district-developed phonics-based literacy program supplemented by Visual Phonics. Students had mild-to-profound hearing losses, and half had cochlear implants. Three of the classrooms used Total

Communication, and one used an oral/aural approach. Four teachers certified to work with DHH students were trained to use Visual Phonics over a 1-month period before the study. The first author provided monitoring and consultation on the reading curriculum implementation and use of Visual Phonics. Reading instruction occurred daily for 90 minutes.

Scores on several subtests of the Dominie Reading and Writing Assessment Portfolio (DeFord, 2001) were used to measure student performance at the beginning and end of the academic year. The Sentence Writing Phoneme, Sentence Writing Spelling, and Phonemic Awareness Segmentation subtests were given to the nine kindergarten students. The same three subtests, in addition to the Phonemic Awareness Deletion, Phonics Onsets, and Phonics Rimes subtests, were given to the 11 first-grade students. Pretest scores on the reading and writing measures for all DHH students were within average ranges at the beginning of the school year, which the authors suggested may have been due to the students' participation in at least 2 years of preschool. Post-test performance showed the students significantly improved on the early reading measures, although those scores were lower than expected on several subtests when compared to the hearing normative sample for the assessments. Because all students took part in the same curriculum with the supplement of Visual Phonics, it is unclear whether participation in the phonics-based reading curriculum or the use of Visual Phonics, or a combination of the two, affected the students' performance. Taken together, Trezek's studies demonstrate the value of Visual Phonics with phonics-based reading curricula with DHH students.

Narr (2008) examined the relationships between phonological awareness, decoding using Visual Phonics symbols, reading performance, and length of time in literacy instruction with Visual Phonics for 10 DHH students in one class, grades kindergarten through third grade. Participants' hearing levels ranged from severe to profound. One teacher with over 8 years' experience using Visual Phonics delivered academic instruction through sign-supported English and American Sign Language. Reading performance was teacher reported through several curriculum-based measures and ranged between late-kindergarten and mid-second grade levels. Six of the ten students were reading at or above their grade levels. Phonological awareness skills were determined through a rhyme judgment task, and decoding abilities were determined through a picture and Visual Phonics symbols (word) matching task. Students were required to "decipher" the written word and match it with the accurate picture, demonstrating they could decode words and associate them with meaning. The students were able to make rhyme judgments and decode with greater than chance accuracy. Although no relationship was found between reading performance and rhyme judgment, or reading performance and length of time instructed with Visual Phonics, a positive relationship was found between reading ability and decoding ability. Although this study did not include a comparison group, these findings, however limited, show DHH children can use Visual Phonics to learn these skills and apply them to an accurate internal construct for vocabulary.

Summary

Research evidence related to Visual Phonics is just starting to catch up with over 20 years of use in isolated classrooms. Anecdotal evidence and word-of-mouth have propagated its dissemination and implementation. The few quasi-experimental studies that exist and are reviewed here support the efficacy of using Visual Phonics as a tool to teach early reading skills with DHH learners.

Strengths of the Research Base

Trezek's studies examined the use of Visual Phonics as a supplement to reading instruction using direct instruction. Each study demonstrated that Visual Phonics is a viable and effective tool for teaching the phonemic elements of reading to DHH learners. Two reviews of research previously acknowledged that this kind of instruction is typically omitted when teaching reading to DHH learners (Luckner et al., 2005/2006; Schirmer & McGough, 2005), primarily because of a lack of reliable and comprehensible access to phonemic information. Each of the studies reviewed previously in this discussion were conducted in self-contained classrooms where manual communication was used and the participants were functionally deaf or hard of hearing. Although this may be considered a potential limitation, it strengthens the ability to generalize across students with varying hearing levels. Each of Trezek's studies also demonstrated a high degree of social validity. The teachers who participated had not been using Visual Phonics for a long time, and although they had consultative support from the researcher, it showed that the Visual Phonics as a supplemental tool could be learned and implemented with fidelity in a reasonably short amount of time.

Limitations of the Research Base

The Trezek and Malmgren (2005) study was the only one that included a comparison group, so it is difficult to identify a causal effect on student performance within the other studies. Studies were characterized by small sample sizes, typical of research with low-incidence populations.

Possibilities of bias also existed within each study. The researchers, teachers, or both participated as examiners, allowing for the possibility of assessor bias. Both Trezek and colleagues (2005, 2006, 2007) and Narr (Narr, 2008; Narr & Cawthon, 2010) also reported they are Visual Phonics trainers, and in each of Trezek's studies, she provided the teacher training before interventions. Finally, improved overall reading achievement is the ultimate goal of these investigations; however, only Trezek and Wang (2006) included a measure of reading comprehension. The other studies measured discrete skills related to phonemic awareness and phonics/decoding. Consistent and clear gains in overall reading achievement are inconclusive from this research.

Recommendations for Future Research

A paucity of research addresses teaching phonemic awareness and phonic skills to DHH learners. With the use of Visual Phonics providing comprehensible access to phonemic information to such students, the effect of learning these skills on overall reading achievement requires further investigation. Researchers should expand investigations to include a variety of curricula and reading programs examining not only discrete skills but also how learning discrete skills (using Visual Phonics) contributes to improvements in overall reading comprehension. Longitudinal studies could demonstrate the progression of skill development, documenting when the use of Visual Phonics can be faded out. Larger sample sizes will allow further differentiation of instruction, giving insight into the characteristics of students who benefit most from acquiring these discrete skills. Finally, the use of Visual Phonics provides learners with multiple means of representation as required by the principles of Universal Design for Learning (Center for Applied Special Technology [CAST], 2008), an approach to instruction that is gaining popularity in the research literature on teaching students with special needs. Future research could examine how, using vision as an unimpaired sensory pathway, deaf *and* hard-of-hearing learners can gain access to information traditionally considered "auditory."

Professional development and implementation fidelity require further exploration. There is no research on training procedures for professionals learning Visual Phonics that subsequently investigates how training effects implementation. Furthermore, understanding how teachers integrate and implement instruction using Visual Phonics has not been examined.

Summative Recommendations for Practice

Strong language skills are a requisite for learning to read; therefore, developing those skills should be the primary focus of professionals working with young DHH children and their families. When DHH students are ready to develop the complex skills required for learning to read, Visual Phonics can be used as a tool for teaching phonemic awareness and phonic skills.

Early Identification of Braille as the Primary Reading Medium for Students with Visual Impairments

Description of Students

Approximately 1 in 1,000 school-age children has a visual impairment (VI). About 10% of this population is blind, with the remainder having various degrees of vision loss (Council for Exceptional Children [CEC], 2007). The American Printing House (APH) 2008 Federal Quota Census data (APH, 2009) includes only 58,388 legally blind students nationally. This population is very heterogeneous, varying in degree of vision, functional use of vision, and the media used for reading. Moreover, about 60% of these children have multiple disabilities (Ferrell, Shaw, & Deitz, 1998).

Learners who are blind or have severe VI need to develop fluency in reading and writing. Because fluency in reading develops over time (Pikulski, 2006), disruptions in the student's developmental process of learning to read can disrupt the eventual attainment of fluency in reading. Early identification of potential braille readers is critical to promote essential early experiences with braille that will allow these children to learn to read and write using braille as their literacy medium from kindergarten.

Description and Implementation of Practice

The IDEA requires that the individualized education program (IEP) team consider braille for a child who has a VI unless a reason is identified for not considering this literacy medium (IDEA, 2004). It is important to make the determination as early as possible if a child who has VI is likely to be a braille reader. To determine whether a child should learn to read using braille or print, or both, the teacher certified in visual impairments (TVI) should collaborate with the IEP team to conduct a learning media assessment (LMA) that includes information on the eye condition, including whether it is degenerative and likely to result in progressive vision loss; a functional vision evaluation; information on sensory functioning (i.e., visual, tactile, and auditory); and information on additional disabilities. Results of the assessment are used to determine whether the primary literacy medium would be print or braille. The TVI may need to educate the team, including the parents, as to the consequences of delaying instruction in braille. Once braille has been identified as either the primary or secondary literacy medium, it must be purposefully and systematically inserted into the child's literacy environment.

Parents and classroom teachers need assistance from the TVI to provide a braille-rich literacy environment that will facilitate learning to read braille. Exposure to braille in books, braille writing equipment, braille labels and letters, and role models of braille readers and writers should be included along with the typical language-rich activities necessary for learning to read. Beginning in kindergarten, students should have daily formal instruction in braille reading and writing. Whether the initial reading curriculum is a braille adaptation of the school's reading curriculum, or whether the TVI introduces a specialized braille curriculum for teaching reading in braille, instruction should be provided on a daily basis similar to what is provided for sighted print readers.

Theoretical Underpinnings

According to Steinman, LeJeune, and Kimbrough (2006), the development of braille reading skills follows the same developmental progression as print reading (Chall, 1983), with the exception that fluency building may extend over a longer period for braille readers until all braille contractions are introduced. Braille reading involves learning more symbols than are involved in print reading, and the number of symbols introduced each year varies according to the learner (Wall Emerson, Holbrook, & D'Andrea, 2009). Steinman and colleagues anticipate that students who are learning braille will be continually moving between Chall's Stage 1 level of reading (learning grapheme–phoneme correspondence) and subsequent stages, at least until they have learned the entire character set for braille reading. Depending on how contractions are introduced to students, this can take them up through third grade (Rex, Koenig, Wormsley, & Baker, 1994), although many students learn all contractions by the end of first or second grade (Wall Emerson, Holbrook, et al., 2009).

When all the symbols are learned, students can begin to concentrate in earnest on fluency building. Even those students with VI who begin braille reading in kindergarten are not necessarily on a par with their sighted peers in terms of their reading rates or achievement (Wall Emerson, Sitar, Erin, Wormsley, & Herlich, 2009). However, when braille instruction is not begun early, students who are braille readers fall even further behind their sighted peers in reading comprehension and fluency. In other words, the later braille is identified as the students' primary literacy medium, the later reading and writing instruction in braille will begin, and the more likely it is that the student will be hopelessly behind her peers in learning to read and write. Early identification of braille occurs most often when a highly qualified TVI is available in the school district who has experience in assessing students with VI, when TVIs have adequate instruction and experience in using the LMA to determine the literacy medium, and when TVIs are confident in their ability to teach braille and understand the importance of early, daily instruction in braille reading and writing (Spungin, 1990).

Research Base

Koenig and Holbrook (1995) developed the most commonly used LMA to be performed by a TVI with other members of the individualized family services plan (IFSP)/IEP team, including parents. Since its development, LMA has become an accepted practice in the field of blindness and VI, although tests of validity and reliability of this procedure are yet to be conducted. Other assessments of learning and literacy media have followed the Koenig and Holbrook model, with some combining functional vision assessment and LMA (Sanford & Burnett, 2008).

Sharpe, McNear, and Bosma (1995) created an inventory of items rated by a national sample of 225 TVIs, administrators, and university professors to include in their own LMA, which had many similarities to the original LMA (Koenig & Holbrook, 1995). A developmentally appropriate LMA modeled on the Koenig and Holbrook LMA has been adapted for early intervention (Anthony, 2003). Although still somewhat subjective, the LMA provides information to guide the decision about the literacy medium for a child who has VI.

Hatton and Erickson (2005) surveyed 184 adults who were blind or had VI, ages 22 to 75, who had at least a 4-year college degree and who had VI before age 6 years. When asked what would have made it easier for them to read and write, the group that used braille as their primary literacy medium ($n = 85$) listed their three most frequent responses as having more accessible resources (47.1%), having caregivers learn braille (34.1%), and having braille taught earlier (27.1%). Of those who did not use braille, the most frequent response again was having more accessible resources (39.7%) and the second was having braille taught earlier (25%). Approximately a quarter of the group surveyed, therefore, felt that having braille taught earlier would have made it easier for them to learn to read and write.

Koenig and Holbrook (2000) conducted a Delphi study with 40 professionals (university faculty, program administrators, and experienced TVIs) in the field of VI to gain consensus on the length of instruction time, the number of days per week, and the length of time overall for particular developmental phases in reading. Respondents agreed that development of early formal literacy skills ("prebraille") requires 30 to 60 minutes a day and that development of beginning braille literacy skills (first through third grade) needs 1 to 2 hours of daily instruction.

S. Millar (1974) examined tactile short-term memory in four related experiments with blind and sighted subjects. One of the conditions, delay after stimulus presentation, was shown to have detrimental effects on memory. As S. Millar stated, "the longer-term memory evolves, or is accessed, only with continual trials" (p. 262). Rex and colleagues (1994) suggested that the rapid decay of tactile memory contributes to difficulty learning and retaining braille characters. In reviewing the research on neuroscience and the impact of brain plasticity on braille reading, Hannan (2006) found neurological evidence for the brain's reorganizing itself to accommodate a tactile reading skill. "Lack of practice or reinforcement of skills causes atrophy" (p. 410). These findings support the recommendation for consistent delivery of daily braille instruction and continuous use of braille to enhance learning.

Early introduction of braille contributes to building fluency in reading. S. D. Trent and Truan (1997) interviewed 30 adolescent braille readers at the Tennessee School for the Blind, tested their reading rates, and separated them into three groups according to their rates of reading. The fastest readers were those who had learned braille from the beginning of their schooling. These researchers conclude that it is difficult, if not impossible, for students introduced to braille in the third grade or later to catch up with those who learned braille when they began school. Using a case study approach, Truan and Trent (1997) examined three adolescent males who had learned braille in late adolescence due to deteriorating eye conditions. In each case the reading rates were low, between 21 and 28 words per minute (wpm).

Wormsley (1996) reported on the reading rates of 22 elementary school braille readers (ages 6 to 12) obtained during an entire school year. The four fastest readers (highest rates 91 to 145 wpm) all began braille at ages 5 or 6 and had received 4 to 5 years of braille instruction up to the time of the study. However, these learners also were among the students with the highest IQ scores. The four slowest readers (highest rates 17 to 30 wpm) began their braille instruction at ages 6 to 9, had 1 to 2 years of braille instruction, and had lower IQ scores.

Knowlton and Wetzel (1996) reported on the reading rates of 23 braille reading adults, ages 23 to 68 years, who had learned to read from the beginning of their reading instruction at 5 to 7 years of age. These adults read 65 to 185 wpm for oral reading tasks, with a mean of 135 wpm. In contrast, Bruteig (1987) studied the reading rates of 35 adventitiously blinded adults ages 20 to 70 who learned braille after already learning to read print; Bruteig found rates of reading between 15 and 70 wpm, with a mean of 38.7 wpm.

The studies reviewed (as summarized in Appendix 32.1, at the end of this chapter) emphasize the need for early identification of potential braille readers and timely introduction of braille. When braille is ultimately to be a student's literacy medium, delaying its introduction means inhibiting the student's ability to build fluency that will enable him to gain access to the general education curriculum.

General Strengths

Although sparse, the research on reading rates of braille readers provides evidence that early identification of braille as the primary literacy medium and early introduction of braille reading and writing instruction can have beneficial effects on the development of fluent reading speeds. The combination of a Delphi study approach (Koenig & Holbrook, 2000) with the research provided by S. Millar (1974), Rex and colleagues (1994), and Hannan (2006) on tactual memory demonstrate that daily reading instruction is essential for these readers, just as it is for print readers.

General Limitations

Studies conducted have limited numbers of participants partly due to the low-incidence population. Studies with braille readers have varied in the age of subjects, degree of VI, and focus of the investigation. The limited number of researchers focusing on literacy and the lack of a concerted and unified effort to coordinate research with this population have resulted in scattered and fragmented information.

Although results of the studies reported here are fairly consistent in terms of the reading rates reported, the rates are still slow and do not approach the norms for print readers. For example, Wall Emerson, Holbrook, et al. (2009) reported on the results of the ABC Braille study, a longitudinal study of 40 young braille readers from kindergarten through fourth grade. The results showed that their overall oral reading rates did not keep pace compared with the oral reading rate norms for their sighted peers. Edmonds and Pring (2006) matched 17 children who have VI with 17 sighted children on decoding age. The groups were comparable to each other in their ability to infer, but when chronological age was compared, the children who have VI were on average a year older. These research studies suggest that even those students who were identified as braille readers and who had braille instruction from kindergarten fell behind their sighted print-reading age peers in fluency and other reading skills. These studies also seem to suggest that simply identifying braille as the literacy medium and beginning braille reading and writing instruction in kindergarten are perhaps not early enough.

Although there is a rich research base on the emergent and early literacy experiences of sighted children leading to their success in learning to read and write, there is a dearth of research on early intervention with children who are blind and potential braille readers (Erickson & Hatton, 2007; Erickson, Hatton, Roy, Fox, & Renne, 2007; Murphy, Hatton, & Erickson, 2008). No intervention studies have been conducted on the effectiveness of strategies commonly used to promote the emergent and early literacy skills of young children with visual impairments.

Recommendations for Future Research

Because children with VI are so heterogeneous, the use of well-designed, qualitative, small-group, and single-subject studies would contribute to the development of a research base. For example, a series of longitudinal case studies following students as they progress to formal learning of reading and writing through braille, print, or both as their literacy medium and through their elementary schooling would be a rich source of evidence. Research should examine the efficacy of LMA for determining the literacy media, the influence of an enriched emergent literacy environment, and the early introduction of a literacy medium to young children with VI along with daily instruction in braille reading and writing using various approaches on children's literacy skills and outcomes. Moreover, just as research has identified the significance of early literacy experiences for sighted children in their development of literacy skills, it follows that early intervention with children who are potential braille readers would also be important. To facilitate the early introduction of braille reading and writing in kindergarten, research is needed to examine the determination of literacy media in the preschool years.

Summative Recommendations for Practice

Although the research based specifically on instructional practices with young children who are potential braille readers is sparse, research-based practices support early identification of potential braille readers and early introduction to daily instruction in braille reading and writing in order for them to develop fluent reading. A concerted effort is needed to promote these practices that will support the successful literacy outcomes for students who are blind or VI.

Tangible Symbols with Students Who Are Deaf-Blind

Description of Students

The most recent report from the National Deaf-Blind Child Count (National Consortium on Deaf-Blindness [NCDB], 2009) identifies 9,200 infants, children, and young adults (between birth and 21 years) as "deaf-blind." These learners vary greatly in degree of visual impairment and hearing loss and in the nature of their additional disabilities, with the majority having some usable vision or hearing. At one extreme, some children have mild hearing loss and functional vision; and at the other, some children are totally blind and have profound hearing loss. Furthermore, more than 90% of children who are deaf-blind (DB) have additional disabilities, such as cognitive impairments (66%), orthopedic or other physical impairments (57%), complex health care needs (38%), behavior challenges (9%), and other problems (30%) (Killoran, 2007).

The combination of hearing loss with visual impairment has a severe influence on communication skills (D. Chen, 2005). As demonstrated in the memorable example of Helen Keller's first understanding of a word, "water," children who are totally DB need specific supports and experiences to develop an understanding of symbols. Although the majority of learners who are DB have some functional vision, hearing, or both, the lack of access to clear information through the visual and/or auditory senses and the additional disabilities further complicate the development of symbolic language.

Definition and Implementation of Practice

Objects, textures, and other concrete representations that facilitate memory, cognitive, and communication skills have been used with learners who are DB. These so-called "tangible symbols" are defined as three-dimensional (e.g., objects) and two-dimensional (e.g., photographs) symbols that are permanent and can be manipulated by the learner as a means of expressive communication (Rowland & Schweigert, 1989). Other terms, such as objects of reference (Aiken, Buultjens, Clark, Eyre, & Pease, 2000), object cues (D. Chen & Downing, 2006), object symbols (Bloom, 1990), and tangible cues (Trief, 2007), are also found in the literature. All these terms refer to concrete items (e.g., object, picture, textured form) that are initially used to (a) promote the learner's understanding of the daily routine, activity sequences or options, people, places, events, or things (i.e., receptive communication); and (b) provide a means by which the learner can make requests, refusals, or choices (i.e., expressive communication). Tangible symbols provide a means of communicative exchange for a child who does not understand abstract symbols and should be used to supplement spoken and signed communication (D. Chen & Downing, 2006).

Effective intervention with learners who are DB requires a systematic approach to (a) select an appropriate mode of communication and instructional procedures that will overcome the limitations of combined visual impairments and hearing loss and (b) promote use of the selected mode (Sigafoos, Didden, Schlosser, Green, O'Reilly, & Lancioni, 2008). A literature review suggests the following sequence of planning and implementation of tangible symbols (D. Chen & Downing, 2006; Murray-Branch, Udvari-Solner, & Bailey, 1991; Rowland & Schweigert, 1989, 2000; Turnell & Carter, 1994):

1. Conduct an authentic interdisciplinary assessment of the learner's communication skills, preferences, and interests. Provide an interdisciplinary team to address considerations related to the child's vision, hearing, cognitive, and motor skills in developing an individualized tangible symbol communication system. Use ecological and preference inventories to identify opportunities that are likely to motivate the learner's communication interactions.

2. Draw on assessment results to develop an individualized intervention plan and materials to support the learner's communication skills. Results should reveal (a) high-frequency vocabulary that the learner will be motivated to use, (b) types of materials that the learner is likely to touch and manipulate, and (c) the starting point for the appropriate level of representation based on perceptual features from the learner's perspective. For example, if a child enjoys the playground swing and holds on to the chain attached on each side of the swing, then an appropriate tangible symbol to represent "swing" would be a 3-inch piece of chain.

3. Begin with a limited number of selected tangible symbols to represent frequently occurring and motivating activities, and teach the learner to indicate choices, express desires, or initiate conversations. Selected items should be tactilely salient and distinctive from each other. Increase the array of tangible symbols to represent different referents as the learner demonstrates recognition and understanding of selected symbols.

4. Gradually increase the use of abstract symbolic representations. At first, objects selected as tangible symbols must be those that are used in the actual activity in order for the child to understand what they represent. For example, a lunch ticket that is required to purchase lunch may be used as a referent for the upcoming activity. Once the learner associates the selected object (tangible symbol) with its referent, fade the use of concrete objects, and introduce more abstract tangible symbols to increase the distance between the "tangible symbol" and its referent.

5. Select tangible symbols that are easy for the child to discriminate and small enough to be portable. Avoid the use of miniatures whose similarities to their referents are purely visual (e.g., plastic dog to refer to a pet).

6. Organize the learner's tangible symbols to be accessible to the student and to be used consistently across activities, people, and environments (e.g., a partitioned box for an activity schedule, a binder separated by categories, a communication board). Write the intended message on the tangible symbol or on the material that holds the tangible symbol.

7. Implement use of the tangible-symbol communication system consistently in daily activities through systematic and direct instruction using behavioral strategies (e.g., reinforcement, prompting, fading). Once the learner understands its meaning, include the tangible symbol with others to offer a choice. Present the tangible symbol for the preferred referent with a foil (i.e., symbol without a referent) or a tangible symbol that represents a disliked referent.

8. Collect trial-by-trial data on the learner's expressive use of tangible symbols, and analyze these data at least weekly to identify any need for changing instruction.

9. Implement opportunities for generalization of tangible symbols across settings and people. Learners should have consistent access to their communication systems wherever they are. Further, communication partners need to be trained to engage the learner in communication using her preferred system.

Theoretical Underpinnings

The use of tangible symbols in the field of deaf-blindness is derived from theories of early symbolic communication. According to Werner and Kaplan (1963), children develop symbols first by associating objects or topics with concrete representations and gradually making abstract or distant (i.e., not intrinsic) associations (i.e., words) through "distancing" processes termed *denaturalization* and *decontextualization*. Denaturalization is the decreasing need for similarity between the communicative act and that which it represents. The continuum ranges from expressions in which the communicative act and its meaning are the same (e.g., the student puts the teacher's hand on the cookie jar to request a cookie), to the most denaturalized or abstract communicative act, using speech or sign to make a request. Decontextualization is the process through which the meaning of the communicative act becomes constant regardless of where it appears and who uses it. For example, an identical object (e.g., cup) used in and to represent the activity (e.g., snack) is a concrete and proximal representation that is understood within a specific context; whereas an arbitrary symbol (e.g., the printed or spoken word *snack*) is an abstract and distal representation whose meaning is understood no matter where it is used.

Decades ago, van Dijk (1967) introduced the systematic use of objects to facilitate communication with children who are DB. He drew on the work of Werner and Kaplan's (1963) concept of distancing to help children learn ways to characterize and recognize people, objects, animals, and events. These characteristics are used to help the child develop concepts of time, for example, by using objects to depict a tangible sequence of daily activities, as well as events and activities (e.g., going to the beach), by using a "memory" book or box that contains artifacts related to the experience.

Pierce (1932, as cited in E. Bates, Benigni, Bretherton, Camaioni, & Volterra, 1979) identified three types of signs or symbolic means (e.g., words or pictures): index, icon, and symbol. An index is a sign that is part of or participates in the object or event that it represents (e.g., a lunch ticket to indicate "lunch time"). An icon is a sign that is related to its referent through some physical, visual, or tactile resemblance; but unlike an index, an icon is not a component of the activity (e.g., a toy cup to indicate "lunch time"). A symbol is a sign related to its referent only through conventions agreed upon by its users (e.g., a textured shape to indicate lunch time that is a match to the one attached to the door of the cafeteria, the label "lunch time" in braille or print). Tangible symbols are thought to be effective with learners who are DB because they are concrete indices or icons whose representations are easy to understand and perceive. Further, they provide a scaffold to the development of symbols because "distancing" can be encouraged through use of progressively more varied and abstract objects and symbols (Bruce, 2005).

Research Base

Although tangible symbols (objects and other concrete representations) have been used for decades both nationally and internationally with learners who are DB (Aiken et al., 2000; Bloom, 1990; Rowland & Schweigert, 1989; van Dijk, 1967), research on this practice is limited. Appendix 32.2, at the end of this chapter, identifies studies, sample size, age range, characteristics, research design, and key findings of available studies. The majority of participants had sensory impairments, intellectual disabilities, physical disabilities, and medical problems.

Murray-Branch and colleagues (1991) evaluated the use of textured symbols with two high-school-aged girls who were DB and had additional disabilities. Although one learner understood 28 receptive tactile signs, she used only four signs, infrequently and often incorrectly; the other learner communicated through facial expressions and vocalizations. Textured symbols were selected as a communication means because they motivated manual searching, were portable, and were easy to discriminate. After 3 months of systematic direct individual instruction (three to four times a day) in daily, naturally occurring activities (at least 10 opportunities in each activity), both learners demonstrated use of multiple textured symbols to make requests and indicate choices for preferred items and activities. One girl learned to use 3 and the other used 20 symbols. The intervention included generalization of textured symbols use across environments and people. No reliability data were reported.

Rowland and Schweigert (1989) examined the use of tangible symbols with nine school-age participants with severe intellectual impairments, visual impairments, and hearing loss. Case studies are reported for two children (a 6-year-old girl and a 4.5-year-old boy) with severe-to-profound hearing loss, VI or blindness, and severe intellectual disabilities. Training involved offering a high-preference item to the learner and prompting the learner to select its tangible symbol representation (from an array of one to three symbols) and give it to the teacher. Correct selection was reinforced by the preferred activity or item. Findings revealed that all nine learners acquired 16 to 98 symbols (mean of 43) in 10 to 19 months of training (mean of 14.5 months). On average, participants required 13.4 training sessions to acquire the first three symbols, which decreased to an average of 6.5 training sessions for the last three symbols across home and school settings. Some learners also acquired two-dimensional symbols (line drawings) and manual signs. Learners demonstrated increased communication development as measured by the Wisconsin Behavior Rating Scale (Song et al., 1980) and the Callier Azusa Scale-H (Stillman & Battle, 1986). The majority used tangible symbols in typical classroom activities as measured by observational data during three 1-hour observations per month. Communicative behavior (presymbolic and symbolic) was scored for each 30-second interval, and reliability was calculated on 20% of the observations. This study used a pre and post-test design and lacked a control group.

Rowland and Schweigert (2000) implemented the use of tangible symbols (i.e., objects, textures, and pictures) with 41 learners (3 to 18 years, mean of 6 years; 24 males and 17 females) who had severe and multiple disabilities. Most did not understand speech, signs, or printed words.

Some communicated through gestures, and seven had a few spoken words and used a few (one to eight) tangible symbols. Seven had both visual impairment and hearing loss. The Communication Matrix (Rowland, 1996) and Levels of Representation Pretest (Rowland & Schweigert, 1990) were administered to determine the learner's expressive communication level and what level of symbolic representation, if any, would be meaningful to that individual. Learners without intentional communicative behaviors were first taught to use presymbolic communication behaviors (e.g., hand movements, vocalizations) for intentional communication (e.g., make requests, gain attention, establish joint attention). Once these were accomplished, then tangible symbols were introduced.

Intervention began with one-symbol arrays and increased quickly to two- and three-symbol arrays, with some learners making selections from a book of symbols. The initial communication function was requesting, with some learners moving to comments and labels. Learners were required to point to or touch a symbol while looking at the communication partner or give it to the communication partner before obtaining the motivating referent. Intervention involved direct individual instruction by project staff for approximately 15 minutes during each school day for an average of 6.5 months. Results indicate that 35 of the 41 children acquired the use of tangible symbols (average of 12 to 22 symbols) for expressive communication, and some progressed to using abstract symbols including speech. Two of the seven learners who were DB failed to acquire any tangible symbols. Learners were considered to have acquired a new symbol when they independently made the correct selection from an array of at least three symbols for at least 80% of the trials over two consecutive sessions. A reliability probe conducted by the project coordinator during observation of 40% of all direct intervention sessions during 5 consecutive days resulted in a mean of 92% agreement. Data from monthly videotapes were compared to data collected during the intervention session. Mean interobserver agreement on direct observation sessions was 90%. Reliability checks obtained on 20% of the monthly videotapes of intervention sessions resulted in a mean kappa coefficient of 0.89. This study used a pre–post-test design but did not include baseline data, control group, or sufficient detail to enable replication.

Trief (2007) implemented the use of tangible symbols with 25 learners (4 to 16 years) who were blind or VI with additional disabilities. Ten were totally blind, and 15 had low vision. A total of 28 tangible symbols that consisted of whole or parts of objects embedded in a cardboard card represented daily activities and places in the school. Learners were asked to select the corresponding symbol from an array of two cues and hand it to the communication partner for the activity to begin.

They were introduced to different symbols depending on their daily activities. Data were collected and compared from the beginning (September) to the end of the school year (June). Five learners learned the referents of all 28 symbols, 10 learners identified 1 to 20 symbols, and 10 students (who had the most severe cognitive, physical, and visual disabilities) failed to learn any symbols. This study is an intervention study that does not provide baseline information or sufficient detail for replication. Although this sample did not include learners who are DB, they had similar additional disabilities and communication difficulties. This study was also included as the most recent of those investigating the use of tangible symbols and focused on the daily school schedule rather than targeting high-preference objects or activities.

Turnell and Carter (1994) found that an 8-year-old boy who had a VI, hearing loss, and other severe and multiple disabilities learned to use three tangible symbols to make requests. These tangible symbols represented high-preference activities and items: a bike, a spinning toy, and a walking frame. Instruction involved three sessions a day each, with five trials, for a total of 15 trials a day over 9 school weeks. This study used a multiple-probe design across symbols.

Summary

The few available studies on the use of tangible symbols with learners who are DB or VI with significant multiple disabilities highlight the diversity of these students in terms of sensory status, abilities, and learning needs. These characteristics contribute to the challenges of building an evidence base on effective practices.

General Strengths

All studies included an interdisciplinary team (e.g., special education teacher, speech and language pathologist, occupational or physical therapist) approach in the development of selected symbols and used ecological inventories to identify frequently occurring activities. With the exception of Trief (2007), studies focused on high-preference activities and used systematic and direct instruction. The majority of learners acquired the use of tangible symbols for making requests and choices. Tangible symbols appeared to serve as a scaffold to symbolic communication (manual signs or speech) for a few learners.

General Limitations

The extremely heterogeneous and low-incidence nature of school-age children labeled as "deaf-blind" is reflected in the various descriptions used by researchers and presents a challenge to rigorous research designs (e.g., matched intervention and control groups). Thus, evidence on the use of tangible symbols causing improved communication outcomes is inconclusive. Moreover, available studies of tangible symbols with learners who are DB were conducted more than 9 to 20 years ago, with a majority of learners in segregated classrooms. Another limitation is the general lack of emphasis on family involvement in the development and implementation of the communication intervention. Further, available research findings do not provide evidence by which to determine selection of a specific type of tangible symbol (index, icon, or symbol) that is likely to be easily understood and acquired by a particular learner.

Recommendations for Future Research

The evidence base for use of tangible symbols with learners who are DB should be expanded through a series of carefully designed single-subject studies that target learners with specific characteristics. This way, participants could be selected according to age, educational experience, degree of visual impairment and hearing loss, other disabilities, and communication level; and these studies could be replicated. Investigations could examine whether different types of tangible symbols (index, icon, or symbol) differ in their ease and rate of acquisition to guide the decision-making process for individual learners. Further, instruction and generalization could be implemented across environments and people. Participants should also include learners who are fully included in general education settings to identify ways to support communication with peers. Another source of evidence should be to examine communication intervention studies with learners who have a VI, hearing loss, and significant additional disabilities to identify potential interventions that may be appropriate for learners who are DB.

Summative Recommendations for Practice

To address the diverse abilities and needs of learners who are DB, an interdisciplinary team approach and family–professional collaboration are essential. Ecological and preference inventories are required to identify the initial vocabulary that should be translated into tangible symbols. Moreover, carefully planned and sequenced direct and individualized instruction with behavioral strategies and data collection are required to support the learner's acquisition of these symbols.

Conclusion

Clearly, research on instructional practices with students who have sensory disabilities is urgently needed. The promise of using Visual Phonics with DHH students should continue to be evaluated as the research base grows through extending the instructional settings and further defining the characteristics of DHH students for whom this practice is most beneficial. Similarly, the effects of early identification of students with VI who require braille as their primary reading medium will continue to be examined. Further research on tangible symbols is needed to reveal how they may scaffold the development of symbolic communication (i.e., expressive speech or sign production).

Access to participants with low-incidence disabilities and research could be increased through the development of national collaborative efforts among researchers with similar interests. Further, practitioners should be encouraged to contribute to the evidence base through systematic implementation of instruction and careful documentation, which could lead to publication of their instructional practices with learners who are DHH or DB, have a VI, or are blind.

Appendix 32.1

Available Studies on Braille Reading

Study	Sample Size	Age (Years)	Characteristics	Research Design	Findings
S. D. Trent & Truan (1997)	30	Adolescents	Scored at sixth-grade level of Gilmore Oral Reading Test. Grouped according to reading speed as well as age at which they lost vision.	Interview plus collection of data on Gilmore Oral Reading	Fastest readers were all in congenital/preschool group for onset; late-blinded group included students from middle and lowest reading groups.
Truan & Trent (1997)	3	17, 14, 18	Progressive vision loss resulting in severe visual impairment and learning braille in late adolescence.	Case study	Reading rates of 26, 28, and 21 wpm, respectively.
Wormsley (1996)	22	6–12	Braille as primary reading medium.	Time Series Design/ Case studies	Four fastest readers all began braille at age 5 or 6; had received 4–5 years of instruction; had high IQ scores. Four slowest readers began braille at ages 6–9; had 1–2 years of instruction; had lower IQ scores.
Knowlton & Wetzel (1996)	23	23–68	Braille reading as primary mode from ages 5–7.	4 x 3 factorial design: reading task with four levels, and presentation task with three levels.	Oral reading speeds ranged from 65–185 wpm (Mean = 135 wpm).
Bruteig (1987)	35	20–71	Late-blinded adults	Reading rate data on narrative texts in both contracted and uncontracted to compare speeds.	Silent reading rates of 15–70 wpm (Mean = 38.7 wpm).

Appendix 32.2

Available Studies on Tangible Symbols

Study	Sample Size	Age (Years)	Characteristics	Research Design	Findings
Murray-Branch et al. (1991)	2	15–19	Blind, HL, cerebral palsy, severe–profound intellectual disability, microcephaly medical problems	Case study Intervention study	3–20 symbols used for requests and choices
Rowland & Schweigert (1989)	9	"school age"	VI, severe–profound HL intellectual disability	Pre–post (Case study for 2)	16–98 symbols used for requests and choices
Rowland & Schweigert (2000)	41 (7 DB)	3–18	VI, HL, physical disabilities, seizure disorders, autism, intellectual disability	Pre–post	35 acquired 3–35 symbols for requests and choices
Trief (2007)	25	4–16	VI, moderate–severe intellectual disabilities, physical disabilities, seizure disorders	Intervention study	15 acquired 1–28 symbols to label activity
Turnell & Carter (1994)	1	8	Moderate HL, VI, athetoid quadriplegia, intellectual disability seizures	Multiple probe across symbols	3 symbols used for requests

Note: DB = deaf-blind; HL = hearing loss; VI = visual impairment including blindness.

CHAPTER 33

Teaching for Transition to Adulthood

David W. Test, Kelly R. Kelley, and **Dawn A. Rowe** | *University of North Carolina at Charlotte*

Throughout all stages of life, individuals experience many transitions. Graduating from high school and pursuing a productive adulthood is one of the more significant transitions that adolescents face with long-term outcomes. Many changes take place for individuals with and without disabilities as they complete high school and move into adulthood, specifically in the areas of employment, education, and independent living. Halpern (1992) defined this transition as "a period of floundering that occurs for at least the first several years after leaving school as adolescents attempt to assume a variety of adult roles in their communities" (p. 203). For individuals with disabilities, this transition period is critical because the choices and actions made can affect them for a lifetime.

Numerous postschool outcome data continue to illustrate that individuals with disabilities have poor postschool outcomes compared to individuals without disabilities in education, employment, and independent living. Although reports of postschool outcomes for students with disabilities have shown some improvement since the first National Longitudinal Transition Study (NLTS), conducted from 1985 to 1993, they continue to remain dismal when compared to their peers without disabilities (Blackorby & Wagner, 1996; M. Wagner, Newman, Cameto, Garza, & Levine, 2005). Young adults with disabilities are performing much lower than their peers in postschool life skill areas essential to becoming productive members of society (i.e., education,

employment, independent living, and community living). In evaluating data across disability categories such as specific learning disabilities, emotional disturbances, and mental retardation based on the most recent National Longitudinal Transition Study (NLTS2) results, outcomes across disability categories also show variation (Newman, Wagner, Cameto, & Knokey, 2009).

For example, comparisons of postsecondary program enrollment results vary widely. In terms of education, Newman et al. (2009) reported 45% of youth with disabilities had pursued postsecondary education within 4 years of leaving high school compared to 53% of youth in the general population. In terms of education, students with disabilities who completed high school were three times more likely to be enrolled in postsecondary education than were students who did not complete high school (Newman et al., 2009). Postsecondary attendance up to 4 years after leaving high school ranged from 27% to 78% across all students with disabilities. In comparing disability categories, 47% of students with learning disabilities, 34% of students with emotional disturbances, and 27% of individuals with mental retardation reported participation in postsecondary programs (i.e., vocational, technical, community, and university). Despite the reported 89% of youth with disabilities intending to finish their degree or certificate programs, only 29% of the students reported completion of the programs, with the remaining 71% of participants with disabilities not graduating or completing their postsecondary programs.

In terms of employment, 57% of youth with disabilities leaving high school were employed outside of the home compared to 67% of the general population (Newman et al., 2009). Employment status fluctuated greatly in comparison to the NLTS2 (Wagner, Newman, Cameto, Levine, & Garza, 2006) data. Again, employment rates varied across disability categories. For example, 64% of students with learning disabilities, 42% of students with emotional disturbances, and 31% of individuals with mental retardation were currently working at the time of the interviews (Newman et al., 2009).

Twenty-five percent of youth with disabilities as compared to 28% of the general population reported living independently (Newman et al., 2009). Across disability categories, 29% of individuals with learning disabilities, 22% with emotional disturbances, and 14% with mental retardation reported living independently. Although at least 56% of youth with disabilities reported having savings accounts and 28% reported having credit cards in their name, few could live independently or provide for additional family members because 89% had annual incomes of $25,000 or less, and more than half of these youth earned less than $5,000 per year. Although these results have changed for the better over time, there continues to be room for improvement.

One way to help improve postschool outcomes is to use research-based practices and predictors to guide educational practices in secondary education settings. Test, Fowler, et al. (2009) conducted a literature review to identify research-based practices (i.e., practices supported by high-quality studies that use experimental research designs) in secondary transition. Overall, 32 secondary-transition research-based practices were identified. The majority of practices (*n* = 25; 78.1%) involved teaching students specific transition skills, such as self-determination skills and daily living skills. In addition, community-based instruction (CBI) was identified as a research-based practice.

Although these research-based practices were designed to teach students specific transition-related skills, to date, experimental studies have not measured the impact of these skills on postschool outcomes. As a result, Test, Mazzotti, et al. (2009) conducted a second literature review that included rigorous correlational research in secondary transition to identify the research-based predictors that correlated with improved postschool outcomes in education, employment, or independent living. Based on results of this review, 16 research-based, in-school predictors of postschool outcomes were identified. The three research-based practices most closely associated with positive postschool outcomes were: (a) self-advocacy/self-determination skills were

related to higher postschool education and employment outcomes; (b) self-care/independent living skills were related to higher postschool education, employment, and independent living outcomes; and (c) community experiences and paid employment/work experience were related to higher postschool outcomes in education, employment, and independent living.

In conclusion, based on high-quality experimental and correlational research, both self-determination skills and CBI have been identified as research-based instructional practices and predictors of postschool success. As a result, the remainder of this chapter provides more detail on each of these practices by first defining each one, providing a brief overview of the research base for each practice, and then describing examples of how to implement each practice.

Self-Determination
What Is Self-Determination?

One area that is currently receiving much attention in the research literature is self-determination. Self-determination is a construct based primarily on social psychology theories (Wehmeyer, 1992). For example, Deci and Ryan (1985) theorized that self-determination represents an innate human need to control one's life. Next, behavioral theory describes self-determination in terms of self-control, as individuals directing their own behavior. Finally, social learning theorists view self-determination as closely related to self-efficacy, individuals' belief that they can perform a certain behavior. As a result, Wehmeyer (1992) suggested

> Self-determination refers to the attitudes and abilities required to act as the primary causal agent in one's life and to make choices regarding one's actions free from undue external influence or interference. It involves autonomy (acting according to one's own priorities or principals [sic]), self-actualization (the full development of one's unique talents and potentials) and self-regulation (cognitive or self-controlled medication of one's behavior). (p. 304)

For teachers to promote self-determination in their classrooms more easily, the concept of self-determination has been divided into a number of teachable components (e.g., Field & Hoffman, 1994; Ward, 1988; Wehmeyer, 1996b) including choice/decision making, goal setting/attainment, problem solving, self-evaluation/management, self-advocacy, person-centered individualized education program (IEP) planning, relationships with others, and self-awareness. Two specific strategies, the Self-Advocacy Strategy and the Self-Directed IEP, are examined in following sections in this chapter.

What Does Research Say About Self-Determination Skills?

Cobb, Lehmann, Newman-Gonchar, and Alwell (2009) identified seven narrative and systematic reviews published since 2000 on self-determination that concluded that self-determination interventions were effective. Furthermore, self-determination skills have been identified as a research-based predictor of postschool success (Test, Mazzotti, et al., 2009). For example, Benitez, Lattimore, and Wehmeyer (2005) found that teaching self-determination skills in high school was positively correlated with improved postschool outcomes for students with disabilities. Wehmeyer and Palmer (2003) found that self-determination skills in high school were significant predictors of postschool education and independent living success. When used in combination with Direct Instruction strategies, self-determination strategies have resulted in improved academic performance by both students with learning disabilities (Konrad, Fowler, Walker, Test, & Wood, 2007) and developmental disabilities (Fowler, Konrad, Walker, Test, & Wood, 2007).

Finally, Test, Fowler, et al. (2009) identified teaching self-determination skills as a research-based instructional practice based on their literature review of high-quality experimental research (using both group and single-subject designs). Similarly, Test and colleagues' (2004) review of the literature on interventions designed to increase students' involvement in their IEP process found that using the IEP process is an excellent way to increase student self-determination skills. Test et al. (2004) found that students with widely varying disabilities can be actively involved in the IEP process and that both published curricula designed to teach students skills to enhance their participation before IEP meetings and person-centered planning strategies were effective in increasing students' involvement in their IEP meetings. Two research-based practices that teach self-determination strategies via the IEP process are the Self-Advocacy Strategy (Van Reusen & Bos, 1994; Test & Neale, 2004) and the Self-Directed IEP (Allen, Smith, Test, Flowers, & Wood, 2001; Arndt, Konrad, & Test, 2006; J. E. Martin, Van Dycke, Christensen, et al., 2006).

The Self-Advocacy Strategy

The Self-Advocacy Strategy is a motivation strategy designed to prepare students to participate in any education or transition-planning meeting. Prerequisites include a willingness to learn the strategy and the ability to communicate (i.e., through gestures or words). The Self-Advocacy Strategy consists of five steps that can be taught over a series of seven lessons. The five steps are presented using the acronym "I PLAN" to help students remember the steps in the strategy:

1. *I*nventory your strengths, areas to improve or to learn, goals, and choices for learning or accommodations. In this first step, students complete an inventory sheet that they can use at their meetings. This inventory identifies strengths, areas to improve or to learn, goals, and choices for learning or accommodations.

2. *P*rovide your inventory information. In the second step, students use their inventory sheet during discussion in the IEP meeting.

3. *L*isten and respond. The third step involves students' learning the proper times to listen (e.g., when someone is making a statement, when someone is asking a question) and respond (e.g., when someone asks a question, when you have information to add).

4. *A*sk questions. The fourth step involves teaching students how to ask questions when they don't understand what people are saying.

5. *N*ame your goals. The last step teaches students to name the goals they would like included in their IEP.

Based on criteria used by Test, Fowler, et al. (2009), the Self-Advocacy Strategy was identified as having a moderate level of evidence based on one high-quality group experimental study (Van Reusen & Bos, 1994) and four acceptable-quality single-subject studies (Hammer, 2004; Lancaster, Schumaker, & Deshler, 2002; Test & Neale, 2004; Van Reusen, Deshler, & Schumaker, 1989). Research studies documenting the positive effects of the Self-Advocacy Strategy have involved both males and females, aged 12 to 17, identified as having mild-to-moderate disabilities to participate in their IEP meeting. In addition, students who served as participants in these studies were identified as Caucasian, Hispanic, African American, Native American, or Asian Pacific Islander. The Self-Advocacy Strategy has been taught using both teacher-led instruction and technology-guided instruction using hypermedia and CD-ROM. For example, Test and Neale (2004) taught the Self-Advocacy Strategy in ten 20- to 45-minute tutoring sessions over 2 weeks to four students with mild disabilities. Figure 33.1 is the research-to-practice lesson plan for using the Self-Advocacy Strategy. Research-to-practice lessons provide teachers with basic information needed to develop a lesson plan including an objective, setting and materials, content to be taught, teaching procedures, and an evaluation strategy. All material in a research-to-practice lesson plan starter is taken directly from one of the published articles used by Test, Fowler, et al. (2009) to establish the research base for the practice.

Figure 33.1 Research-to-practice lesson plan starter for using the Self-Advocacy Strategy.

Objective: To teach students to enhance the quality of their verbal contributions and self-determination skills using the Self-Advocacy Strategy

Setting and Materials:

Setting: Classroom

Materials:

1. The Self-Advocacy Strategy for Education and Transition Planning Manual
2. Tape recorder or video camera (optional for recording student responses)

Content Taught:

The Self-Advocacy Strategy is a motivation and self-determination strategy designed to prepare students to participate in education or transition-planning conferences. The strategy consists of five steps using the acronym "I PLAN" to help cue students to remember the steps for using this strategy.

Step 1: I = "Inventory." Students list their strengths, areas to improve or to learn, education and transition goals, accommodations needed, and choices for learning on an inventory sheet.

Step 2: P = "Provide Your Inventory Information." Focuses on teaching students how to provide input during the meeting.

Step 3: L = "Listen and Respond." Relates to listening to others' statements or questions and responding appropriately.

Step 4: A = "Ask Questions." Involves asking appropriate questions to gather needed information.

Step 5: N = "Name your Goals." Communicates personal goals and ideas on actions to be taken.

Ten lessons are taught to the students one-on-one, with lessons ranging from 20 to 45 minutes each. The entire curriculum can be taught in approximately 2 weeks.

Teaching Procedures:

1. Give the pretest by asking the students the 10 questions listed below before beginning instruction, and record or score their responses based on a 4-point scale (see evaluation).
2. Teach the lessons and specific instructional phases as outlined in the teacher's handbook of the Self-Advocacy Strategy.
3. Ask students the 10 questions again, and record their responses after phase three (model and prepare), four (verbal practice), five (practice and feedback), and six (practice and feedback), which also mark specific mastery points of the Self-Advocacy Strategy.
4. When possible, ask the students the 10 questions during their actual IEP meeting to see if the skills are generalized to other settings and conditions.

Evaluation:

a. (Student's Name), what do you think are your strongest study or learning skills?

b. Can you tell me what you think are your weakest study or learning skills?

c. What skills do you want to improve or learn over this next year that will help you to do better in school or get along better with other people?

d. Can you tell me about any activities or materials that teachers have shared with you in the past that have helped you learn your school subjects?

e. Are there any after-school activities, such as sports, jobs, or clubs, in which you want to become involved?

f. Many students at your age have begun to think about careers or jobs they might like after they finish high school. Upon graduating from school, what kind of job or career would you like to pursue?

g. What types of study or learning activities work best for you?

h. What size learning or study group works best for you?

i. I'm sure you've taken a lot of tests during your years in school. Can you name or describe the type of test items on which you do best when taking tests over material you have learned?

j. Is there anything we've overlooked or something you'd like to say about school, or any other area you are concerned about?

Score the student responses to pretest/post-test questions using a 4-point scale:

0 = student does not respond or does not know the answer

1 = student response is not related to the specific question asked

2 = student response is related to the question, but is not specific enough

3 = student responds to the question appropriately and with specific details

Note: Lesson plan based on: Test, D. W., & Neale, M. (2004). Using the *Self-Advocacy Strategy* to increase middle graders' IEP participation. *Journal of Behavioral Education, 13,* 135–145.

Source: Based on National Secondary Transition Technical Assistance Center (NSTTAC) Lesson Plan Starters. National Secondary Transition Technical Assistance Center. (2008). *IEP meeting participation using the Self-Advocacy Strategy (2).* Charlotte, NC: NSTTAC. Retrieved from http://nsttac.appstate.edu/sites/default/files/assets/pdf/5.pdf.

The Self-Directed IEP

The Self-Directed IEP (J. E. Martin, Marshall, Maxson, & Jerman, 1997) consists of 11 steps students can follow to lead their own IEP meeting. Steps are organized across 11 lessons taught in six to ten 45-minute sessions. The Self-Directed IEP package also includes assessments, videotape, and student workbook. The 11 steps are:

1. *Begin meeting by stating the purpose:* Students learn how to explicitly state the purpose of the meeting (e.g., review goals).

2. *Introduce everyone:* Students learn who is required to be at an IEP meeting and who else they would like to invite, as well as practice introducing these individuals.

3. *Review past goals and performance:* Students state their goals and learn which actions can be taken to help meet their goals.

4. *Ask for others' feedback:* Students learn what feedback is and the different ways they can receive feedback on their goals.

5. *State your school and transition goals:* Students identify their interests, skills, and needs, and the goals they would like to achieve in school.

6. *Ask questions if you don't understand:* Students learn how to ask questions for clarification.

7. *Deal with differences in opinion:* Students learn the LUCK strategy (Listening to other person's opinion, Using a respectful tone of voice, Compromising or Changing your opinion if necessary, and Knowing and stating the reasons for your opinion).

8. *State the support you will need to reach your goal:* Students learn about the supports that will help them in achieving their goals.

9. *Summarize your current goals:* Students restate their goals and the actions they will take to meet those goals as well as state how they would receive feedback in meeting those goals.

10. *Close meeting by thanking everyone:* Students learn how to bring closure to the meeting by using closing statements and thanking everyone for attending.

11. *Work on IEP goals all year:* Students are reminded to work on their goals all year by taking actions, receiving feedback, and gaining support to accomplish these goals.

The Self-Directed IEP can be easily implemented by following the guidelines in the teacher's workbook. Each lesson follows the format listed in the research-to-practice lesson plan starter in Figure 33.2, under "Teaching Procedures."

Based on criteria used by Test, Fowler, et al. (2009), the Self-Directed IEP has a moderate level of evidence based on one high-quality group experimental study (J. E. Martin, Van Dycke, Christensen, et al., 2006) and has been used to teach both males and females, aged 12 to 21, identified as having mild-to-moderate disabilities to participate in their IEP meeting. In addition, students who served as participants in this study were identified as Caucasian, Hispanic, African American, and Native American.

Community-Based Instruction

What Is Community-Based Instruction?

CBI (sometimes referred to as *in vivo training*) is defined as instruction of functional skills that takes place in the community where target skills would naturally occur (L. Brown et al., 1983). It is a reality-based training program in which a student works and trains at selected community businesses, services, and other places, with desired outcomes being competitive employment and independent performance of living skills (Wehman & Kregel, 2003). The primary theory underlying CBI is that more naturalistic instructional arrangements allow students opportunities to respond to actual stimuli rather than simulations, thereby alleviating problems with generalizing skills taught (P. E. Bates, Cuvo, Miner, & Korabek, 2001; L. Brown et al., 1983). CBI provides opportunities for students to generalize newly learned skills to community settings in addition to opportunities for students with disabilities to be included in society with individuals without disabilities (Wolfe, 1994). This section describes CBI as a practice for teaching functional skills, including two examples of such skills.

What Does Research Say About CBI?

Research has shown that using CBI results in increased acquisition and generalization of employment and life skills for students with disabilities (P. E. Bates et al., 2001; Branham, Collins, Schuster, & Kleinert, 1999; Cihak, Alberto, Kessler, & Taber, 2004; Westling & Fox, 2009). Many skills that have been taught using CBI include laundry skills (P. E. Bates et al., 2001; P. Taylor, Collins, Schuster, & Kleinert, 2002), grocery shopping (Alcantara, 1994; P. E. Bates et al., 2001; Morse & Schuster, 2000), vocational skills, initiating requests, job training (P. E. Bates et al., 2001), leisure skills (Schloss et al., 1995), and safety skills (Taber, Alberto, Hughes, & Seltzer, 2002). When used in combination with appropriate

Figure 33.2 Research-to-practice lesson plan starter for using the Self-Directed IEP.

Objective: To teach students to participate in IEP meetings through the use of the Self-Directed IEP multimedia package modified for nonreaders.

Setting/Materials:

Setting: High school classroom

Materials: Self-Directed IEP Multimedia Package (includes teacher's manual, student workbook, two videos)

Content Taught: (Note: Not all steps were included in this study)

Instructional Unit 1: Leading Meeting

Step 1: Begin Meeting by Stating a Purpose

Step 2: Introduce Everyone

Step 3: Review Past Goals and Performance

Step 10: Close Meeting by Thanking Everyone

Instructional Unit 2: Reporting Interests

Step 5: State Your School and Transition Goals

Instructional Unit 3: Reporting Skills

Step 5: State Your School and Transition Goals

Instructional Unit 4: Reporting Options

Step 9: Summarize Your Goals

Teaching Procedures:

Within each step a similar format is followed:

    a. Review of prior steps, as needed.

    b. Preview lesson content and instruction on new vocabulary used.

    c. Videotape material provides model and sample situations used for guided practice.

    d. Workbook activities (e.g., teacher reads aloud, writes on overhead, and leads class discussion in place of workbook activities when needed) used to practice each step.

    e. Teacher demonstrates and students practice for real IEP meetings.

    f. Brief student skill evaluation.

    g. Ask students to relate skills to other situations, wrap up.

    h. Picture prompts are used for students with limited reading, writing, and cognitive skills.

Evaluation:

1. **Five Mock IEP Meetings.** After each instructional unit is completed, a mock IEP meeting is held using the following format:

    a. **State the Purpose of the Meeting:** (Name of Student), why are we having this meeting today?

    b. **Introduce Everyone:** (Name of Student), who is attending this meeting? (May point to self and other members of the meeting and say, "Who is that?/Who am I?")

    c. **Review Past Performance and Goals:** (Name of Student), do you think you have worked hard in school so far? What have you been working on?

    d. **Student Interests:** Great, (Name of Student). Before we look at new goals, let's talk about your interests. This discussion will help determine your new goals.

        – What do you want to learn about in school?

        – We have visited several job sites. What do you think you want to do after you graduate from high school?

        – What are some of your personal interests? What sports do you like to play or activities do you like to participate in? (Probe if necessary by providing examples of sports, activities, etc.)

(continued)

Figure 33.2 Research-to-practice lesson plan starter for using the Self-Directed IEP. (*continued*)

 - If you were going to live on your own or with a roommate, what daily living skills would you be interested in learning about?
 - After you graduate from high school, where do you want to live?
 - What community activities would you like to participate in?

e. **Skills and Limits:** For each area, which skills are you strong in and what skills do you need?

f. **Options and Goals:** OK, now we are going to write down several options for education (replace *education* with each of the areas). From these options, we are going to write goals for each of the transition areas.

 - You have mentioned several school subjects that you are interested in. What other school subjects would you like to learn about? Repeat this format for all areas (use pictorial representations of the student's options if needed).
 - Now, from your options, we are going to determine goals for you to work on. Talk to student about reasonable goals.

g. **Closing the Meeting:** Now that we have finished determining your goals, it's time to end the meeting. Let's review.

 - (Name of Student), what are your new goals? Great job!
 - (Name of Student), would you please bring our meeting to a close? (Cue for student to shake hands and say thank you.)

2. **Student Performance in Mock and Real IEP Meetings Is Measured Using Choicemaker Curriculum Checklist:**

Students are assessed on expressing both skills and limits in the areas of education, employment, personal, daily skills, housing, and community participation.

3. **Real IEP Meetings:**

The first real IEP meeting is held before any instruction begins. The second IEP meeting is held after all instruction and mock IEP meetings are completed.

a. (Name of Student), do you know why we are here today? Please tell us.

b. (Name of Student), please introduce the people attending your meeting.

c. Let's look at past goals and your progress toward them. (Cue for student to tell how well student did meeting past goals.)

d. OK, before we get started, let's talk about your interests, (Name of Student). Is there anything you would like to learn about in school?

e. What do you want to do after you graduate?

f. What are some skills that you would need to have to learn, live, or work on your own?

g. What are some skills limits?

h. I see you have some options for each transition area (referring to list of options created prior to the meeting). Please tell us a few.

i. Great. Now, let's decide on a goal for you to work toward. (Cue for student to state goal in each transition area.)

j. Nice job. Let's finish signing all of the paperwork, and then we will end this meeting.

k. What are some goals you are going to work toward? Thank you. (Cue for student to say thanks and shake hands.)

Note: Lesson plan based on: Allen, S., Smith, A., Test, D., Flowers, C., & Wood, W. (2001). The effects of *Self-Directed IEP* on student participation in IEP meetings. *Career Development for Exceptional Individuals, 24,* 107–120.

Source: Based on National Secondary Transition Technical Assistance Center (NSTTAC) Lesson Plan Starters. National Secondary Transition Technical Assistance Center. (2008). *IEP meeting participation: Using Choicemaker Self-Directed IEP.* Charlotte, NC: NSTTAC. Retrived from http://nsttac.appstate.edu/sites/default/files/assets/pdf/1_and_8.pdf.

nonintrusive instructional techniques—such as least-to-most prompts, nonexclusionary time-out, and data collection using a notepad or stopwatch—CBI has been found to be a socially valid teaching method (Wolfe, 1994). In a recent literature review on CBI, Walker, Uphold, Richter, and Test (2010) identified 23 studies that taught functional skills using CBI in one of four domains: vocational, daily living, community, and recreation. The two most common skills taught using CBI in these studies were grocery shopping ($n = 6$; 26.1%) and employment skills ($n = 4$; 17.4%). Overall, studies reviewed showed increases in target skill acquisition for participants.

Because CBI is an essential component of transition programming and has been identified as a research-based practice leading to improved postschool outcomes (Test, Fowler, et al., 2009), it is important to include CBI in the educational programming of students with disabilities at all grade levels and across functional content areas such as grocery shopping and employment skills.

Teaching Grocery Shopping

Teaching grocery shopping skills includes instruction on making a shopping list, locating items in a grocery store, locating and then purchasing items from a shopping list, and choosing items that are more economical or the better buy. The instructional practices associated with teaching grocery shopping include various levels and orders of prompting (e.g., least-to-most, most-to-least), picture or written task analysis, computer assisted, simulated, and CBI. Based on criteria used by Test, Fowler, et al. (2009),

using CBI to teach grocery shopping has been identified as having a moderate level of evidence based on one high-quality quasi-experimental group study (P. E. Bates et al., 2001) and on two acceptable single-subject studies (B. Ferguson & McDonnell, 1991; Gaule, Nietupski, & Certo, 1985). Research studies using CBI to teach grocery shopping involved both male and female participants, ages 17 to 20, identified as having mild-to-severe intellectual disabilities. None of the studies provided information on ethnicity.

Grocery shopping skills have been taught using CBI in a variety of ways. For example, Gaule et al. (1985) taught students how to prepare a shopping list using a picture recipe in the classroom and then taught locating and purchasing items using an adapted picture shopping list in a grocery store (see Figure 33.3 for the

Figure 33.3   Research-to-practice lesson plan starter for grocery shopping.

Objective: To teach students to prepare a shopping list, locate and obtain items from the supermarket, and purchase obtained items.

Setting/Materials:

Settings: Community grocery store and high school classroom

Materials:

1. Pictorial Meal Preparation Manual:

    a. The manual contains picture recipes and is used to generate shopping lists for supermarket items.

    b. The first page contains pictures of necessary food items, as well as utensils needed in preparing the meal.

    c. To simplify the development of the shopping list, as appropriate, the teacher may circle all of the food items on the page so students do not have to discriminate between food and nonfood items.

2. Adaptive shopping list:

    a. An adaptive shopping aid is placed in a three-ring binder that can be opened and put in the seat section of a shopping cart.

    b. The shopping aid contains pictures of all of the items for each student's recipe.

    c. Adjacent to each picture is a square that denotes the approximate cost. Each square represents a 50-cent interval. Thus, a quart of milk that costs $1.49 has three squares.

    d. Another feature of the shopping aid is the money line on which students mark off the number of squares to determine approximate cost. Students count number of dollars available for shopping and use a marking pen to indicate available funds for shopping.

Content Taught:

1. Shopping list preparation (taught in classroom)

    a. Obtain the adaptive shopping list from its storage area.

    b. Check off each food item depicted in the recipe on the shopping list.

    c. Erase checks from pictures of grocery items on hand.

    d. Count the number of $1.00 bills available for shopping.

    e. Mark a line designating the number of dollars available on the money line found on the shopping aid.

2. Locating and obtaining items from the supermarket (taught in community)

    a. Enter the store.

    b. Obtain a cart.

(continued)

Figure 33.3 Research-to-practice lesson plan starter for grocery shopping. (*continued*)

---

    c. Place the open shopping aid in the seat of the cart.

    d. Obtain the needed supermarket items within 30 minutes.

    e. Cross out each item depicted on the shopping aid as it is obtained.

    f. Check off the appropriate number of squares for each item on the money line when the item is obtained.

3. Purchasing obtained items (taught in community)

    a. Enter the checkout lane with the cart.

    b. Give the appropriate number of dollars to the clerk.

    c. Receive and put away any change.

    d. Pick up the sack of items.

    e. Exit store.

Teaching Procedures:

1. Shopping list preparation

    a. At the beginning of each instructional session, the teacher demonstrates the steps in the task sequence.

    b. Three to five individual instructional trials are given to the student with the number of trials given dependent on the available time.

    c. Each trial consists of presentation cues and materials indicated on task analysis.

    d. The student is allowed to perform the task steps until the sequence is completed correctly or until an error is made.

    e. Verbal praise is used to reinforce correct performance.

    f. Incorrect responses are followed by: (a) verbal prompt, (b) teacher modeling correct response and required imitation by student, and (c) verbal cues to perform task step and physical guidance.

    g. Following error correction, student is allowed to proceed to next step.

    h. After percentage of correctly performed task steps on initial instructional trial reaches 50% on 3 consecutive days, teacher demonstration at the beginning of the session is discontinued.

2. Locating and obtaining items from the supermarket

    a. The reinforcement and correction procedures are identical to shopping list preparation, with the exception that no teacher model is provided on arrival at the supermarket.

3. Purchasing obtained items

    a. The reinforcement and correction procedures are identical to locating and obtaining items from the supermarket.

Evaluation:

Evaluate the student's performance by collecting data on the percentage of steps correct on the task analyses.

Note: Lesson plan based on: Gaule, K., Nietupski, J., & Certo, N. (1985). Teaching supermarket shopping skills using an adaptive shopping list. *Education and Training of the Mentally Retarded, 20,* 53–59.

Source: From National Secondary Transition Technical Assistance Center (NSTTAC) Lesson Plan Starters. National Secondary Transition Technical Assistance Center. (2008). *Grocery shopping.* Charlotte, NC: NSTTAC. Retrieved from http://nsttac.appstate.edu/sites/default/files/assets/pdf/49.pdf.

research-to-practice lesson plan starter). Locating and purchasing items at the grocery store have been taught using prompting systems, written and picture task analyses, and combinations of prompting and task analyses (Alcantara, 1994; P. E. Bates et al., 2001; B. Ferguson & McDonnell, 1991; J. McDonnell, Horner, & Williams, 1984; Mechling, 2004; Morse & Schuster, 2000). Purchasing has also been taught in the community using the dollar-more strategy and an adapted number line (J. McDonnell et al., 1984; Sandknop, Schuster, Wolery, & Cross, 1992). Finally, Nietupski, Welch, and Wacker

(1983) taught students to acquire, maintain, and transfer purchasing skills at community grocery stores using a calculator.

Teaching Employment Skills

Teaching employment skills includes a range of instructional topics including time management and self-monitoring for completing vocational tasks, cleaning public restrooms, and performing clerical tasks such as operating a copying machine. The instructional practices associated with employment skills include various levels and orders of prompting (e.g., least-to-most, most-to-least), picture or written task analysis, constant time delay, CBI, and simulated instruction paired with CBI. Based on criteria used by Test, Fowler, et al. (2009), using CBI to teach employment skills has been identified as having a moderate level of evidence based on one acceptable-quality group-design experimental study (P. E. Bates et al., 2001), one high-quality single-subject study (DiPipi-Hoy, Jitendra, & Kern, 2009), and one acceptable-quality single-subject study (Cihak et al., 2004). Research that successfully used CBI to teach employment skills has involved both male ($n = 36$) and female participants ($n = 13$), ages 16 to 20, identified as having mild-to-moderate intellectual disabilities. None of the studies provided information on ethnicity.

Employment skills have been taught using CBI in a variety of ways. More specifically, P. E. Bates et al. (2001) taught students how to clean a public restroom using a 43-step task analysis. Next, Cihak et al. (2004) taught students how to operate a copying machine using 3-second time delay and least-to-most prompting (see Figure 33.4 for the research-to-practice lesson plan starter). Finally, DiPipi-Hoy et al. (2009) taught students to use digital

Figure 33.4   Research-to-practice lesson plan starter for employment skills.

Objective: To teach students to make collated photocopies using simulated and community-based instruction on the same day

Setting/Materials:

Setting: Local print shop and classroom

Materials:

1. Copy machine with top feeder tray and key pad
2. Camera to take photographs of photocopy machine
3. Photo album
   a. For each of 12 steps in the task analysis, create 4 photographs that correspond to the step
      (i.e., a total of 128 photographs) including:
      i. photograph depicting correct action being performed in the relevant setting.
      ii. photograph depicting correct materials, but wrong manipulation.
      iii. photograph depicting an out-of-sequence action.
      iv. photograph depicting an action associated with the task, but not included in the training sequence.

Content Taught:

Task Analysis:

1. Place the original newsletter on the feeder tray.
2. Enter a four-digit PIN code.
3. Press the ID button.
4. Press the number 5 for the number of copies.
5. Press the collate button.
6. Press the OK button.
7. Press the start button.
8. Remove the original from the upper tray.
9. Remove the copies from the bottom tray.

Teaching Procedures:

1. On the same day, provide training in the classroom before community-based instruction. For example, provide instruction using the simulated procedures on Monday morning, and provide community-based instruction on Monday afternoon.
2. During classroom instruction, use the photo album to provide instruction.
   a. Tell students to pretend they are going to make copies using a photocopy machine.
   b. Present the photo album to the student.

(continued)

Figure 33.4 Research-to-practice lesson plan starter for employment skills. (*continued*)

---

   c. Tell students to visually scan the photos on the album cover and point to the picture indicating the task they would complete.

   d. Present task materials to the student.

   e. Open the album and ask, "What is the first thing you do?"

   f. Tell students to put a finger on the photo that depicts what is next on each photo page.

   g. Use a system of least prompts with a 3-second interval between each prompt level. To assist a student in successfully identifying the photos depicting steps to complete the task, prompts should be provided in the following order:

      i. Verbal prompt (e.g., "Do you see where the writing is"?)

      ii. Gesture (e.g., pointing to discriminative stimulus on page opposite the 4 photos)

      iii. Gesture plus verbal explanation (e.g., pointing to the discriminative stimulus on page opposite the 4 photos and providing a verbal explanation)

      iv. Modeling plus verbal explanation (e.g., pointing to correct picture and plus providing verbal explanation)

      v. Physical assistance plus verbal explanation (e.g., holding the student's wrist, guiding the correct response, and providing an explanation)

3. Provide training at a photocopy machine in a community print shop.

   a. Tell students that they are going to make copies using a photocopy machine.

   b. Use a system of least prompts with a 3-second interval between each prompt level.

   c. To assist a student in successfully completing the task, prompts should be provided in the following order:

      i. Verbal prompt (e.g., "Do you see where the writing is"?)

      ii. Gesture (e.g., pointing to discriminative stimulus on the machine)

      iii. Gesture plus verbal explanation (e.g., pointing to the discriminative stimulus and providing a verbal explanation)

      iv. Modeling plus verbal explanation (e.g., demonstrating appropriate actions plus verbal explanation)

      v. Physical assistance plus verbal explanation (e.g., holding the student's wrist, guiding the correct response, and providing an explanation)

Evaluation:

Collect student performance data on the number of steps completed independently and correctly.

Note: Lesson plan based on: Cihak, D. F., Alberto, P. A., Kessler, K., & Taber, T. A. (2004). An investigation of instructional scheduling arrangements for community based instruction. *Research in Developmental Disabilities, 25,* 67–88.

Source: From National Secondary Transition Technical Assistance Center (NSTTAC) Lesson Plan Starters. National Secondary Transition Technical Assistance Center. (2008). *Grocery shopping.* Charlotte, NC: NSTTAC. Retrieved from http://nsttac.appstate.edu/sites/default/files/assets/pdf/49.pdf.

watches in the classroom and community employment settings to manage their time and monitor work tasks. A majority of the research base with employment paired simulated instruction with CBI. However, when instruction took place immediately after simulation within community settings, employment skills were taught within settings such as a florist, print shop, public restroom, recreational camp, and veterinarian's office (P. E. Bates et al., 2001; Cihak et al., 2004; DiPipi-Hoy et al., 2009).

Instructional Approaches

The instructional approaches often used in teaching self-determination skills and when using CBI to teach grocery shopping and employment skills are based on a behavioral framework. Based on the principles of applied behavior analysis (see J. O. Cooper, Heron, & Heward, 2007), Heward and Orlansky (1984) identified seven characteristics common to using a behavioral approach to instruction: (a) specifying the skill or behavior to be learned (often using task analysis); (b) using direct and continuous measurement; (c) using techniques that can be replicated by others; (d) requiring learners to repeatedly perform the target skill during each instructional session; (e) providing immediate feedback (usually in the form of positive reinforcement or specific corrective feedback); (f) systematically using and withdrawing cues and prompts (e.g., modeling, physical guidance, time-delay, least-to-most prompting); and (g) designing instruction to help learners generalize newly acquired skills to new, untrained settings. The lesson plan starters included in this chapter incorporate many of these seven characteristics of a behavior approach to teaching, because all have specific objectives and specify content to be taught (often in the form of a task analysis), have specific instructional strategies that include both prompting and feedback strategies, and incorporate a method that can be used to directly and continuously evaluate the effects of instruction.

Analysis of the Research Base

The practices described in this chapter were taken from the literature review conducted by the National Secondary Transition Technical Assistance Center and reported by Test, Fowler, et al. (2009). As part of their systematic review, published research studies were reviewed using the quality indicators for group and quasi-experimental research proposed by Gersten et al. (2005) or the quality indicators for single-subject research proposed by R. H. Horner et al. (2005). As a result, the research base used in this chapter consisted of studies that were of acceptable or high quality as defined by Gersten et al. or Horner et al. However, the review of the literature was not comprehensive; that is, once the number of studies needed to establish a practice had reached a "strong" level of evidence, further articles on that practice were not reviewed. Given this background, the remainder of this section summarizes the general strengths and limitations of the research base reviewed for self-determination (specifically, for the Self-Advocacy Strategy and the Self-Directed IEP) and CBI, and it provides recommendations for future research and practice in relation to these practices.

Strengths of the Research Base

In general, the research reviewed (in previous sections) for self-determination, including the Self-Advocacy Strategy and the Self-Directed IEP, and CBI, including grocery shopping and employment skills, had many strengths. Specific to their methodology, the researchers described (a) participants, the process for selecting participants, and setting; (b) dependent variables with operational precision and measured them over time with a quantifiable index; and (c) independent variables with operational precision and measures of treatment fidelity. By supplying this level of detail, these studies provide practitioners with the specificity needed to use their professional judgment to decide not only if the practice might be successful with their students in their settings, but also how to teach each skill.

The single-subject studies reviewed included a baseline phase and repeated measures of the dependent variable over time; provided at least three demonstrations of experimental effect at different points in time to control for common threats to internal validity; and

replicated experimental effects across participants, settings, or materials to establish external validity. In addition, they included measures of interrater reliability. The use of high-quality experimental designs (i.e., valid, single-subject research designs such as multiple baseline and reversal designs, and group experimental and quasi-experimental designs) ensures practitioners that a functional relationship existed between the intervention used in the studies and changes in student behavior; that is, self-determination and CBI resulted in improved student outcomes. Given these strengths of the literature base on self-determination and CBI, practitioners can be confident that these interventions should result in similar changes in their students' behavior if implemented with integrity.

Weaknesses of Research Base

In general, the research for self-determination (as reviewed in previous sections), including the Self-Advocacy Strategy, the Self-Directed IEP, and using CBI to teach grocery shopping and employment skills, also had several weaknesses. Most studies lacked formal measures of social validity. In secondary transition, social validity data are typically gathered by collecting consumer satisfaction on the goals, procedures, or outcomes of an intervention from students, teachers, or parents. Although it is important to know that an intervention works, if consumers do not value the goals, if they believe the procedures are too difficult to implement, or if they are not satisfied with the outcomes, the specific interventions will probably not be used in a classroom. In these cases, potentially effective practices may go unused by many teachers. Therefore, it is important to have interventions that are effective but also socially valid. Group studies also lacked descriptions of fidelity of implementation and evidence of adequate reliability for outcome measures. Without evidence that the intervention was implemented as designed and data collected were reliable, research consumers should be cautious about placing their full confidence in study findings. As a result, practitioners should be cautious about using practices that do not have such evidence and even more diligent than usual in planning for and evaluating the generalization of these skills.

Although the research-based practices identified by this review do provide practitioners with strategies for teaching specific skills, the experimental literature reviewed did not correlate student skill development with improved postschool outcomes. The limitations in the experimental research base point to the ongoing need for research but also highlight the fact that as special educators use research to guide practice, they need to remain steadfast in connecting individual student outcomes with practices used. Especially until experimental studies begin to measure the longitudinal impact of interventions, practitioners should collect their own data to link their instructional practices to development of student skills that predict postschool success (Test, Fowler, et al., 2009).

Suggestions for Future Research

The limitations of the current research base provide direction for next steps in examining the effectiveness of self-determination, including the Self-Advocacy Strategy, the Self-Directed IEP, and using CBI to teach grocery shopping and employment skills. First, it is important that future research examine maintenance and generalization of all skills taught. Maintenance (i.e., the student's ability to demonstrate the skill over time) and generalization (i.e., the students' ability to demonstrate the skill in settings beyond those in which the skills were taught) are critical elements for using skills that have been learned and are, therefore, important outcomes to intervention research. For practitioners to have the best information to use when selecting possible practices for use in their classrooms, researchers need to expand their examinations of the maintenance and generalization of self-determination and CBI.

Future research also needs to measure the social validity of the goals, procedures, and outcomes of transition skills instruction from the viewpoints of parents, teachers, and students to determine if skills taught are relevant for everyday living. Moreover, given that self-determination focuses on helping individuals gain greater control over their lives, it would seem that, at a minimum, social validity data would always be collected from students. In addition to adding measures of social validity, future research should also investigate the use of new and innovative technologies. The use of technology can also help build in strategies to ensure generalization and maintenance of newly learned skills. For example, using a handheld media device to list the steps in a task analysis will allow students to have the directions on how to perform the task wherever they go.

Over and above improving specific aspects of research design (e.g., social validity, implementation fidelity) and examining critical aspects of the practices (e.g., generalization, use of technology), it is important that researchers systematically study the effects of self-determination and CBI through more research and replication of findings. Many of the secondary-transition related skills that could be taught using CBI (e.g., managing finances, physical fitness, travel, healthy living, engaging in civic activities, maintaining employment) do not appear to have a substantial research base. Future research studies in these areas must be designed to meet the quality indicators for group or single-subject designs, conducted with measured and reported integrity, and have their results linked with postschool outcomes such as employment, education/training, and quality of life.

Recommendations for Practice

Although much remains to do in relation to bolstering the research base, the practices highlighted in this chapter for self-determination and CBI are research-based approaches that focus on modifiable predictors of critical postschool outcomes (e.g., Test, Fowler, et al., 2009). To maximize effectiveness of the practices, practitioners should consider a few implications for implementing them. The primary argument for using CBI as a teaching strategy is to maximize the potential for skill generalization (P. E. Bates et al., 2001). To maximize instructional time while in the community, it may be necessary to develop simulated training opportunities in addition to CBI. For example, simulated classroom training might be used to provide students with repeated opportunities to practice the skill of paying for groceries if they are having trouble mastering the skill at the grocery store. In this case, a teacher could provide students with multiple opportunities to practice paying for items in the classroom, whereas at the grocery store only one opportunity to respond would occur per day. Not surprisingly, researchers recommend that any simulated instructional opportunities should share as many characteristics as possible with the natural environment where the new behavior is expected to be performed, to ensure generalization to the community (P. E. Bates et al., 2001; Nietupski, Hamre-Nietupski, Clancy, & Veerhusen, 1986).

In relation to self-determination skills, consider having students with limited verbal skills develop PowerPoint slides to use to guide their IEP meetings (Parent & Wehman, 2011). Both of the research-based practices for enhancing self-determination skills described in this chapter, the Self-Advocacy Strategy and the Self-Directed IEP, provide a framework for developing the content to be used. In addition, student voices can be added to PowerPoint presentations for individuals who may be too shy to speak in front of the IEP team.

Conclusion

In conclusion, this chapter provides practitioners with a starting point for implementing several research-based practices in the area of secondary transition. Are they guaranteed to work? Not always and not for every individual. But practitioners can be confident that the practices described in this chapter will produce the positive effects described in the review of research with most of their students when implemented as designed. Teachers should, then, use these strategies first when teaching self-determination skills to involve students in the IEP process and should use CBI to teach functional skills such as grocery shopping or employment skills.

References

Abedi, J. (2006). Psychometric issues in the ELL assessment and special education eligibility. *Teachers College Record, 108,* 2282–2303.

Abrams, L., Flood, J., & Phelps, L. (2006). Psychopharmacology in the schools. *Psychology in the Schools, 43,* 493–501.

Achenbach, T. (1991a). *Manual for the Child Behavior Checklist/4-18 and 1991 Profile.* Burlington, VT: University of Vermont Department of Psychiatry.

Achenbach, T. M. (1991b). *Integrative guide for the 1991 CBCL/4-18, YRS, & TRF profiles.* Burlington: University of Vermont, Department of Psychiatry.

Ada, A. F., & Campoy, I. (2003). *Authors in the classroom: A transformative education process.* Boston: Allyn & Bacon.

Adams, M. J. (1990). *Beginning to read: Thinking and learning about print.* Cambridge, MA: The MIT Press.

Adams, M. J., Bereiter, C., McKeough, A., Case, R., Roit, M., Hirschberg, J., et al. (2002). *Open Court Reading.* Columbus, OH: McGraw-Hill.

Adams, M. J., Foorman, B. R., Lundberg, I., & Beeler, T. (1998). *Phonemic awareness in young children: A classroom curriculum.* Baltimore: Brookes.

Adelman, H. S., & Taylor, L. (2003). On sustainability of project innovation as systemic change. *Journal of Educational and Psychological Consultation, 14*(1), 1–25.

Ager, C., & Cole, C. (1991). A review of cognitive-behavioral interventions for children and adolescents with behavioral disorders. *Behavioral Disorders, 16,* 276–287.

Agran, M., Alper, S., Cavin, M., Sinclair, T., Wehmeyer, M., & Hughes, C. (2005). Using self-monitoring to increase following-direction skills of students with moderate to severe diabilities in general education. *Education & Training in Developmental Disabilities, 40,* 3–13.

Agran, M., King-Sears, M. E., Wehmeyer, M. L., & Copeland, S. R. (2003). *Teachers' guides to inclusive practices: Student-directed learning strategies.* Baltimore: Brookes.

Ahearn, E. M. (2009). State eligibility requirements for specific learning disabilities. *Communication Disorders Quarterly, 30*(2), 120–128.

Aiken, S., Buultjens, M., Clark, C., Eyre, J. T., & Pease, L. (2000). *Teaching children who are deafblind: Contact, communication and learning.* London: David Fulton.

Al Otaiba, S., & Fuchs, D. (2002). Characteristics of children who are unresponsive to early literacy intervention: A review of the literature. *Remedial and Special Education, 23,* 300–316.

Al Otaiba, S., & Fuchs, D. (2006). Who are the young children for whom best practices in reading are ineffective? An experimental and longitudinal study. *Journal of Learning Disabilities, 39,* 414–418.

Al Otaiba, S., Schatschneider, C., & Silverman, E. (2005). Tutor assisted intensive learning strategies in kindergarten: How much is enough? *Exceptionality, 13,* 195–208.

Al Otaiba, S., & Torgesen, J. K. (2007). Effects from intensive standardized kindergarten and first grade interventions for the prevention of reading difficulties. In S. R. Jimerson, M. K. Burns, & A. M. VanDerHeyden (Eds.), *Handbook of response to intervention: The science and practice of assessment and intervention* (pp. 212–222). New York: Springer.

Alberto, P. A., & Troutman, A. C. (2009). *Applied behavior analysis for teachers* (8th ed.). Upper Saddle River, NJ: Pearson.

Albus, D., Thurlow, M., & Bremer, C. (2009). *Achieving transparency in the public reporting of 2006–2007 assessment results* (Technical Report 53). Minneapolis, MN: University of Minnesota, National Center on Educational Outcomes.

Alcantara, P. R. (1994). Effects of videotape instructional package on purchasing skills of children with autism. *Exceptional Children, 61,* 40–55.

Alexander, R. (1996). In search of good primary practice. In P. Woods (Ed.), *Contemporary issues in teaching and learning* (pp. 57–72). New York: Routledge.

Algozzine, B. (1977). The emotionally disturbed child: Disturbed or disturbing. *Journal of Abnormal Child Psychology, 5,* 205–211.

Allen, S. K., Smith, A. C., Test, D. W., Flowers, C., & Wood, W. M. (2001). The effects of self-directed IEP on student participation in IEP meetings. *Career Development for Exceptional Individuals, 24*(2), 107–120.

Allen-Meares, P. (2008). Assessing the adaptive behavior of youths: Multicultural responsivity. *Social Work, 53*(4), 307–316.

Allor, J. H., Mathes, P. G., Champlin, T., & Cheatham, J. P. (2009). Research-based techniques for teaching early reading skills to students with intellectual disabilities. *Education and Training in Developmental Disabilities, 44,* 356–366.

Allor, J. H., Mathes, P. G., Jones, F. G., Champlin, T., & Cheatham, J. P. (2010). Individualized research-based reading instruction for students with intellectual disabilities. *Teaching Exceptional Children, 42,* 6–12.

Allor, J. H., Mathes, P. G., Roberts, J. K., Cheatham, J., & Champlin, T. (2010). Comprehensive reading instruction for students with intellectual disabilities: Findings from the first three years of a longitudinal study. *Psychology in the Schools, 47,* 445–466.

Allor, J. H., Mathes, P. G., Roberts, K. R., Jones, F. G., & Champlin, T. (2010). Teaching students with moderate intellectual disabilities to read: An experimental examination of a comprehensive reading intervention. *Education and Training in Autism and Developmental Disabilities, 45,* 3–22.

Alpert, C. L., & Kaiser, A. (1992). Training parents as milieu language teachers. *Journal of Early Intervention, 16,* 31–52.

Alpert, C. L., & Rogers-Warren, A. K. (1984). *Mothers as incidental language trainers of their language-disordered children.* Unpublished manuscript, University of Kansas, Lawrence.

Alves, A. J., & Gottlieb, J. (1986). Teacher interactions with mainstreamed handicapped students and their nonhandicapped peers. *Learning Disability Quarterly, 9,* 77–83.

Alvin Independent School Dist. v. A.D. ex rel. Patricia F, 30. 503 M33d7 8 (5th Cir. 2007).

Amanda J. v. Clark County School District, 260 F.3d 1106 (9th Cir. 2001).

American Printing House for the Blind (APH). (2009). Distribution of eligible students based on the federal quota census of January 2, 2009 (Fiscal Year 2008). Retrieved from http://www.aph .org/about/ar2008.pdf

American Psychiatric Association. (1994). *Diagnostic and statistical manual of mental disorders* (4th ed.). Washington, DC: American Psychiatric Publishing.

American Psychological Association [APA] Board of Educational Affairs Task Force on Classroom Violence Directed Against Teachers. (2011). *Understanding and preventing violence directed against teachers.* Washington, DC: American Psychological Association. Retrieved from http://www.apa.org/ed/schools/cpse/activities/classroom-violence.aspx

Americans with Disabilities Act of 1990, 42 U.S.C. § 12101.

Analysis of comments and changes to 2006 IDEA Part B Regulations, 71 Federal Register, 46565 and 46664, August 14, 2006.

Anderson, N. E., Jenkins, F. F., & Miller, K. E. (1996). *NAEP inclusion criteria and testing accommodations: Findings from the NAEP 1995 field test in mathematics.* Washington, DC: National Center for Education Statistics.

Anderson, R. C., Hiebert, E. F., Scott, J. A., & Wilkinson, L. A. (1985). *Becoming a nation of readers: The report of the Commission on Reading.* Washington, DC: The National Institute of Education.

Ang, R., & Hughes, J. (2001). Differential benefits of skills training with antisocial youth based on group composition: A meta-analytic investigation. *School Psychology Review, 31,* 164–185.

Anthony, T. L. (2003). *Individual Sensory Learning Profile Interview (ISLPI).* Chapel Hill, NC: Early Intervention Training Center for Infants and Toddlers with Visual Impairments, FPG Child Development Institute, UNC-CH. Retrieved from http://www.fpg.unc.edu/~edin/Resources/modules/VCM/4/session_files/handouts/VCM4_HandoutK_ISLP.pdf

Applegate, M. D., Quinn, K. B., & Applegate, A. J. (2002). Levels of thinking required by comprehension questions in informal reading inventories. *The Reading Teacher, 56,* 174–180.

Archer, J. (2007). Digital portfolios: An alternative approach to assessing progress. *Education Week, 26*(30), 38.

Ardoin, S. P., Martens, B. K., & Wolfe, L. A. (1999). Using high-probability instruction sequences with fading to increase student compliance during transitions. *Journal of Applied Behavior Analysis, 32,* 339–351.

Arndt, S. A., Konrad, M., & Test, D. W. (2006). Effects of *Self-Directed IEP* on student participation in planning meetings. *Remedial and Special Education, 27,* 194–207.

Arntzen, E., Halstadtro, A., & Halstadtro, M. (2003). Training play behavior in a 5-year-old boy with developmental disabilities. *Journal of Applied Behavior Analysis, 36,* 367–370.

Arreaga-Mayer, C., Terry, B. J., & Greenwood, C. R. (1998). Classwide peer tutoring. In K. Topping & S. Ehly (Eds.), *Peer-assisted learning* (pp. 105–119). Mahwah, NJ: Erlbaum.

Artiles, A. J. (2003). Special education's changing identity: Paradoxes and dilemmas in views of culture and space. *Harvard Educational Review, 73*(2), 164–202.

Artiles, A. J., & Klingner, J. K. (2006). Forging a knowledge base on English language learners with special needs: Theoretical, population, and technical issues. *Teachers College Record, 108,* 2187–2194.

Artiles, A. J., Klingner, J., Sullivan, A., & Fierros, E. (2010). Shifting landscapes of professional practices: English learner special education placement in English-only states. In P. Gándara & M. Hopkins (Eds.), *Forbidden language: English learners and restrictive language policies* (pp. 102–117). New York: Teachers College Press.

Artiles, A. J., Rueda, R., Salazar, J. J., & Higareda, I. (2005). Within-group diversity in minority disproportionate representation: English language learners in urban school districts. *Exceptional Children, 71,* 283–300.

Artiles, A. J., Trent, S. C., & Palmer, J. (2004). Culturally diverse students in special education. In J. A. Banks & C. M. Banks (Eds.), *Handbook of research on multicultural education* (2nd ed., pp. 716–735). San Francisco: Jossey-Bass.

Arunachalam, V. (2001). The science behind tradition. *Current Science, 80,* 1272–1275.

Association for Supervision and Curriculum Development (ASCD). (2002). *Teaching students with learning disabilities: Using learning strategies* [DVD]. Alexandria, VA: Author.

Atkinson, R. (1975). Mnemotechnics in second language learning. *American Psychologist, 30,* 821–828.

Au, K. H. (1998). Social constructivism and the school literacy learning of students of diverse backgrounds. *The Journal of Literacy Research, 30,* 297–319.

Au, K., & Raphael, T. (2000). Equity and literacy in the next millennium. *Reading Research Quarterly, 35,* 170–188.

August, D., & Hakuta, K. (Eds.). (1997). *Improving schooling for language minority children: A research agenda.* Washington, DC: National Academy Press.

August, D. L., & Shanahan, T. (2006). Synthesis: Instruction and professional development. In D. L. August & T. Shanahan (Eds.), *Developing literacy in a second language: Report of the National Literacy Panel.* Mahwah, NJ: Erlbaum.

Ault, M. J., Wolery, M., Doyle, P. M., & Gast, D. L. (1989). Review of comparative studies in the instruction of students with moderate and severe handicaps. *Exceptional Children, 55,* 346–356.

Austin, J. L., & Agar, G. (2005). Helping young children follow their teachers' directions: The utility of high-probability command sequences in pre-K and kindergarten classrooms. *Education and Treatment of Children, 28*(3), 222–236.

Baddeley, A., & Wilson, B. (1985). Phonological coding and short term memory in patients without speech. *Journal of Memory and Language, 24,* 490–502.

Baer, D., Wolfe, M., & Risley, T. (1968). Some current dimensions of applied behavior analysis. *Journal of Applied Behavior Analysis, 1,* 91–97.

Bailey, E., & Bricker, D. (1985). Evaluation of a three-year early intervention demonstration project. *Topics in Early Childhood Special Education, 5*(2), 52–65.

Baker, J. A., Clark, T. P., Maier, K. S., & Viger, S. (2008). The differential influence of instructional context on the academic engagement of students with behavior problems. *Teaching and Teacher Education, 24,* 1876–1883.

Baker, J., & Zigmond, N. (1995). The meaning and practice of inclusion for students with learning disabilities. *Journal of Special Education, 29,* 163–180.

Baker, L., & Brown, A. C. (1984). Metacognitive skills and reading. In P. D. Pearson, M. Kamil, R. Barr, & P. Mosenthal (Eds.), *Handbook of reading research* (Vol. 1, pp. 353–394). White Plains, NY: Longman.

Baker, S., Gersten, R., & Lee, D. (2002). A synthesis of empirical research on teaching mathematics to low-achieving students. *The Elementary School Journal, 103,* 51–73.

Baker, S., & Smith, S. (1999). Starting off on the right foot: The influence of four principles of professional development in improving literacy instruction in two kindergarten programs. *Learning Disabilities Research and Practice, 14,* 239–253.

Baker, S., & Smith, S. (2001). Linking school assessments to research-based practices in beginning reading: Improving programs and outcomes for students with and without disabilities. *Teacher Education and Special Education, 24,* 315–322.

Baker, S. K., Chard, D. J., Ketterlin-Geller, L. R., Apichatabutra, C., & Doabler, C. (2009). Teaching writing to at-risk students: The quality of evidence for self-regulated strategy development. *Exceptional Children, 75,* 303–318.

Baker, S. K., Simmons, D. C., & Kameenui, E. J. (1995). *Vocabulary acquisition: Synthesis of the research.* (Technical Report No. 13.) Eugene: University of Oregon, National Center to Improve the Tools of Educators.

Bakkaloglu, H. (2008). The effectiveness of activity-based intervention program on the transition skills of children with developmental disabilities aged between 3 and 6 years. *Educational Sciences: Theory and Practice, 8,* 393–406.

Ball, D., & Bass, H. (2003). Making mathematics reasonable in school: What research says about the NCTM Standards. In J. Kilpatrick, G. Martin, & D. Schifter (Eds.), *A research companion to principles and standards for school mathematics* (pp. 27–44). Reston, VA: National Council of Teachers of Mathematics.

Bambara, L. M., & Ager, C. (1992). Using self-scheduling to prompt self-directed leisure activity in home and community settings. *Journal of the Association for Persons with Severe Handicaps, 17,* 67–76.

Bambara, L. M., Koger, F., Katzer, T., & Davenport, T. A. (1995). Embedding choice in the context of daily routines: An experimental case study. *Journal of the Association for Persons with Severe Handicaps, 20,* 185–195.

Banda, D. R., & Kubina, R. M., Jr. (2006). The effects of a high-probability request sequencing technique in enhancing transition behaviors. *Education and Treatment of Children, 29*(3), 507–516.

Bandura, A. (1976). Self-reinforcement: Theoretical and methodological considerations. *Behaviorism, 4*(2), 135–155.

Bandura, A. (1979). Self-efficacy: Toward a unifying theory of behavioral change. *Psychological Review, 84,* 191–215.

Bandura, A. (1993). Perceived self-efficacy in cognitive development and functioning. *Educational Psychologist, 28,* 117–148.

Barker, L. (2003). Computer-assisted vocabulary acquisition: The CSLU vocabulary tutor in oral-deaf education. *Journal of Deaf Studies and Deaf Education, 8,* 187–198.

Barnard-Brak, L., & Lechtenberger, D. (2009). Student IEP participation and academic achievement across time. *Remedial and Special Education, 30,* 1–7.

Barnett, D., Elliot, N., Graden, J., Ihlo, T., Macmann, G., Natntais, M., & Prasse, D. (2006). Technical adequacy for response to intervention practices. *Assessment for Effective Intervention, 32,* 20–31.

Barney, T., Klovin, I., & Bhate, S. R. (1981). School phobia: A therapeutic trial with clomipramine and short-term outcome. *British Journal of Psychiatry, 138,* 110–122.

Barone, D., & Wright, T. E. (2008). Literacy instruction with digital and media technologies. *Reading Teacher, 62,* 292–302.

Barrish, H., Saunders, M., & Wolf, M. M. (1969). Good Behavior Game: Effects of individual contingencies for group consequences on disruptive behavior in a classroom. *Journal of Applied Behavior Analysis, 2,* 119–124.

Barton, K. E., & Sheinker, A. (2003). *Comparability and accessibility: On line versus on paper writing prompt administration and scoring across students with various abilities.* Monterey, CA: CTB-McGraw-Hill.

Bartsch, K., & Wellman, H. M. (1995). *Children talk about the mind.* New York: Oxford University Press.

Bateman, B. D. (2007a). *From gobbledygook to clearly written IEP goals*. Verona, WI: IEP Resources/Attainment.

Bateman, B. D. (2007b). Law and the conceptual foundations of special education practice. In J. B. Crockett, M. M. Gerber, & T. J. Landrum (Eds.), *Achieving the radical reform of special education: Essays in honor of James M. Kauffman* (pp. 95–114). Mahwah, NJ: Erlbaum.

Bateman, B. D. (2011). Individual education programs for students with disabilities. In J. M. Kauffman & D. P. Hallahan (Eds.), *Handbook of special education* (pp. 91–106). New York: Routledge.

Bateman, B. D., & Linden, M. A. (2006). *Better IEPs: How to develop legally correct and educationally useful programs* (4th ed.). Verona, WI: IEP Resources/Attainment.

Bates, E., Benigni, L., Bretherton, I., Camaioni, L., & Volterra, V. (1979). *The emergence of symbols. Cognition and communication in infancy.* New York: Academic Press.

Bates, P. E., Cuvo, T., Miner, C. A., & Korabek, C. A. (2001). Simulated and community-based instruction involving persons with mild and moderate mental retardation. *Research in Developmental Disabilities, 22,* 95–115.

Bauer, R. (1977). Short-term memory in learning disabled and nondisabled children. *Bulletin of the Psychonomic Society, 10,* 128–130.

Baumann, J. F., Edwards, E. C., Boland, E. M., Olejnik, S., & Kame'enui, E. J. (2003). Vocabulary tricks: Effects of instruction in morphology and context on fifth-grade students' ability to derive and infer word meanings. *American Educational Research Journal, 40,* 447–494.

Baumann, J. F., Edwards, E. C., Font, G., Tereshinski, C. A., Kame'enui, E. J., & Olejnik, S. F. (2002). Teaching morphemic and contextual analysis to fifth-grade students. *Reading Research Quarterly, 37,* 150–176.

Baumwell, L., Tamis-LeMonda, C. S., & Bornstein, M. H. (1997). Maternal verbal sensitivity and child language comprehension. *Infant Behavior and Development, 20,* 247–258.

Bauwens, J., & Hourcade, J. J. (1995). *Cooperative teaching: Rebuilding the schoolhouse for all students.* Austin, TX: Pro-Ed.

Bauwens, J., Hourcade, J., & Friend, M. (1989). Cooperative teaching: A model for general and special education integration. *Remedial and Special Education, 10,* 17–22.

Beals, V. L. (1983). *The effects of large group instruction on the acquisition of specific learning strategies by learning disabled adolescents.* Unpublished doctoral dissertation, University of Kansas, Lawrence, KS.

Beck, A. T., Rush, A. J., Shaw, B. F., & Emery, G. (1979). *Cognitive therapy of depression.* New York: Guilford Press.

Beck, I., & McKeown, M. (1981). Developing questions that promote comprehension: The story map. *Language Arts, 58,* 913–918.

Beck, I. L., & McKeown, M. G. (1991). Conditions of vocabulary acquisition. In R. Barr, M. Kamil, P. Mosenthal, & P. D. Pearson (Eds.), *Handbook of reading research* (Vol. 2, pp. 789–814). New York: Longman.

Beck, I. L., & McKeown, M. G. (2007). Increasing young low-income children's oral vocabulary repertoires through rich and focused instruction. *The Elementary School Journal, 107,* 251–271.

Beck, I. L., McKeown, M. G., & Kucan, L. (2002). *Bringing words to life: Robust vocabulary instruction.* New York: Guilford Press.

Beelmann, A., Pfingsten, U., & Losel, F. (1994). Effects of training social competence in children: A meta-analysis of recent evaluation studies. *Journal of Clinical Child Psychology, 23,* 260–271.

Behar, L., & Stringfield, S. (1974). *Preschool Behavior Questionnaire, Scale and Manual.* Durham, NC: Learning Institute of North Carolina.

Beirne-Smith, M. (1991). Peer tutoring in arithmetic for children with learning disabilities. *Exceptional Children, 57,* 330–337.

Beirne-Smith, M., Patton, J. R., & Kim, S. H. (2006). *Mental retardation* (7th ed.). Upper Saddle River, NJ: Merrill/Pearson.

Belfiore, P. J., Basile, S. P., & Lee, D. L. (2008). Using a high-probability sequence to increase classroom compliance: The role of behavioral momentum. *Journal of Behavioral Education, 17,* 160–171.

Belfiore, P. J., Lee, D. L., Scheeler, M. C., & Klein, D. (2002). Implications of behavioral momentum and academic achievement for students with behavior disorders: Theory, application, and practice. *Psychology in the Schools, 39*(2), 171–179.

Belfiore, P. J., Lee, D. L., Vargas, A. U., & Skinner, C. H. (1997). Effects of high-preference single-digit mathematics problem completion on multiple-digit mathematics problem performance. *Journal of Applied Behavior Analysis, 30,* 327–330.

Benitez, D. T., Lattimore, J., & Wehmeyer, M. L. (2005). Promoting the involvement of students with emotional and behavioral disorders in career and vocational planning and decision making: The self-determined career development model. *Behavioral Disorders, 30,* 431–447.

Bennett, R. E. (1982). Cautions for the use of informal measures in the educational assessment of exceptional children. *Journal of Learning Disabilities, 15,* 337–339.

Bergeron, R., Floyd, R. G., & Shands, E. I. (2008). States' eligibility guidelines for mental retardation: An update and consideration of part scores and unreliability of IQs. *Education and Training in Developmental Disabilities, 43*(1), 123–131.

Berkeley, T. R., & Ludlow, B. L. (1989). Toward a reconceptualization of the developmental model. *Topics in Early Childhood Special Education, 9,* 51–66.

Bernhard, J. K., Cummins, J., Campoy, F. I., Ada, A. F., Winsler, A., & Bleiker, C. (2006). Identity texts and literacy development among preschool English language learners: Enhancing learning opportunities for children at risk for learning disabilities. *Teachers College Record, 108,* 2380–2405.

Bernhard, J. K., Winsler, A., Bleiker, C., Ginieniewicz, J., & Madigan, A. (2008). Read my story: Promoting early literacy among diverse, urban, preschool children in poverty with the Early Authors Program. *Journal of Education for Students Placed at Risk, 13*(1), 76–105.

Bernhardt, A., & Forehand, R. (1975). The effects of labeled and unlabeled praise upon lower and middle class children. *Journal of Experimental Child Psychology, 19,* 536–543.

Berninger, V., Mizokawa, D., & Bragg, R. (1991). Theory-based diagnosis and remediation of writing disabilities. *Journal of School Psychology, 29,* 57–79.

Berninger, V. W., Winn, W. D., Stock, P., Abbott, R. D., Eschen, K., Lin, S., et al. (2008). Tier 3 specialized writing instruction for students with dyslexia. *Reading and Writing, 21,* 95–129.

Bernstein, G. A., Borchardt, C. M., Perwin, A. R., Crosby, R. D., Kushner, M. G., Thuras, P. D., et al. (2000). Imipramine plus cognitive behavioral therapy in treatment of school refusal. *Journal of the American Academy of Child and Adolescent Psychiatry, 39,* 276–283.

Bernstein, G. A., Garfinkel, B. D., & Borchardt, C. M. (1990). Comparative studies of pharmachotherapy for school refusal. *Journal of the American Academy of Child and Adolescent Psychiatry, 29,* 773–781.

Biederman, J. (1987). Clonazepam in the treatment of prepubertal children with panic-like symptoms. *Journal of Clinical Psychiatry, 1,* 38–41.

Biglan, A., & Dow, M. G. (1981). Toward a second-generation model: A problem-specific approach. In L. P. Rehm (Ed.), *Behavior therapy for depression: Present status and future directions* (pp. 97–131). New York: Academic Press.

Bird, H. R., Canino, G. J., Davies, M., Ramirez, R., Chavez, L., Duarte, C., & Shen, S. (2005). The Brief Impairment Scale (BIS): A multidimensional scale of functional impairment for children and adolescents. *Journal of the American Academy of Child and Adolescent Psychiatry, 44,* 699–707.

Birmaher, B., Axelson, D. A., Monk, K., Kalas, C., Clark, D. B., Ehmann, M., et al. (2003). Fluoxetine for the treatment of childhood anxiety disorders. *Journal of the American Academy of Child and Adolescent Psychiatry, 42,* 415–423.

Bishop, D., & Robson, J. (1989). Unimpaired short-term memory and rhyme judgment in congenitally speechless individuals: Implications for the notion of "articulatory coding." *Quarterly Journal of Experimental Psychology, 41,* 123–140.

Blachman, B. A., Tangel, D. M., Bail, E. W., Black. R., & McGraw, C. K. (1999). Developing phonological awareness and word recognition skills: A two-year intervention with low-income, inner-city children. *Reading and Writing: An Interdisciplinary Journal, 11,* 239–273.

Blackorby, J., & Wagner, M. (1996). Longitudinal postschool outcomes of youth with disabilities: Findings from the National Longitudinal Transition Study. *Exceptional Children, 62,* 399–413.

Blauvelt-Harper, C., Symon, J. B. G., & Frea, W. D. (2008). Recess is time-in: Using peers to improve social skills of children with autism. *Journal of Autism and Developmental Disabilities, 28,* 815–826. doi: 10.1007s10803-007-0449-2

Blick, D. W., & Test, D. W. (1987). Effects of self-recording on high-school students' on-task behavior. *Learning Disability Quarterly, 10,* 203–213.

Bloom, Y. (1990). *Object symbols: A communication option.* Sydney, Australia: North Rocks Press.

Blue-Banning, M., Summers, J. A., Frankland, H. C., Nelson, L. L., & Beegle, G. (2004). Dimensions of family and professional partnerships: Constructive guidelines for collaboration. *Exceptional Children, 70,* 167–184.

Board of Education of the Hendrick Hudson School District v. Rowley, 458 U.S. 176 (1982).

Boardman, A. G., Arguelles, M. E., Vaughn, S., Hughes, M. T., & Klingner, J. (2005). Special education teachers' views of research-based practices. *Journal of Special Education, 39,* 168–180.

Bolt, S., & Roach, A. T. (2009). *Inclusive assessment and accountability: A guide to accommodations for students with diverse needs.* New York: Guilford Press.

Bolt, S. E., & Thurlow, M. L. (2004). Five of the most frequently allowed testing accommodations in state policy: Synthesis of research. *Remedial and Special Education, 25,* 141–152.

Bolt, S. E., & Ysseldyke, J. E. (2006). Comparing DIF across math and reading/language arts tests for students receiving a read-aloud accommodation. *Applied Measurement in Education, 19,* 329–355.

Boone, R. (1992). Involving culturally diverse parents in transition planning. *Career Development for Exceptional Individuals, 15,* 205–221.

Boone, R., & Higgins, K. (1993). Hypermedia basal readers: Three years of school-based research. *Journal of Special Education Technology, 12,* 86–106.

Bopp, K. D., Brown, K. E., & Mirenda, P. (2004). Speech-language pathologists' roles in the delivery of positive behavior support for individual with developmental disabilities. *American Journal of Speech-Language Pathology, 13,* 5–10.

Bos, C. S., & Vaughn, S. (2006). *Strategies for teaching students with learning and behavior problems* (6th ed.). Upper Saddle River, NJ: Pearson/Allyn & Bacon.

Bosseler, A., & Massaro, D. (2003). Development and evaluation of a computer-animated tutor for vocabulary and language learning in children with autism. *Journal of Autism and Developmental Disorders, 33,* 653–672.

Botvin, G. (2004). Advancing prevention science and practice: Challenges, critical issues, and future directions. *Prevention Science, 5,* 69–72.

Boudah, D., Schumaker, J., & Deshler, D. (1997). Collaborative instruction: Is it an effective option for inclusion in secondary classrooms? *Learning Disability Quarterly, 20,* 293–316.

Boulinea, T., Fore, C., Hagan-Burke, S., & Burke, M. (2004). Use of story-mapping to increase the story-grammar text comprehension of elementary students with learning disabilities. *Learning Disability Quarterly, 27,* 105–121.

Bowers, F., Cook, C. R., Jensen, M. E., Snyder, T., & McEachern, A. (2008). Generalization and maintenance of positive peer reporting intervention for peer-rejected youth. *International Journal of Cognitive Behavior Therapy, 4,* 230–246.

Bowers, F. E., McGinnis, J. C., Friman, P. C., & Ervin, R. A. (1999). Merging research and practice: The example of positive peer reporting applied to social rejection. *Education and Treatment of Children, 22,* 218–226.

Bowers, F. E., Woods, D. W., Carolyn, W. D., & Friman, P. C. (2000). Using positive peer reporting to improve the social interactions and acceptance of socially isolated adolescents in residential care: a systematic replication. *Journal of Applied Behavioral Analysis, 33,* 239–242.

Braconnier, A., Le Coent, R., & Cohen, D. (2003). Paroxine versus clomipramine in adolescents with severe major depression: A double-blind, randomized, multicenter trial. *Journal of the American Academy of Child and Adolescent Psychiatry, 42,* 22–29.

Brainerd, C., Kingma, J., & Howe, M. (1986). Long-term memory development and learning disability: Storage and retrieval loci of disabled/nondisabled differences. In S. Ceci (Ed.), *Handbook of cognitive, social, and neuropsychological aspects of learning disabilities* (Vol. 1, pp. 161–184). Hillsdale, NJ: Erlbaum.

Branham, R. S., Collins, B. C., Schuster, J. W., & Kleinert, H. (1999). Teaching community skills to students with moderate disabilities: Comparing combined techniques of classroom simulation, videotape modeling, and community-based instruction. *Education and Training in Mental Retardation and Developmental Disabilities, 2,* 170–181.

Bransford, J., Brown, A., & Cocking, R. (Eds.) (2000). *How people learn.* Washington, DC: National Academies Press.

Bredekamp, S. (Ed.). (1987). *Developmentally appropriate practice in early childhood programs serving children from birth through age 8.* Washington, DC: National Association for Education of Young Children.

Bredekamp, S., & Rosegrant, T. (1992). *Reaching potentials: Appropriate curriculum and assessment for young children* (Vol. 1). Washington, DC: National Association for Education of Young Children.

Brent, D. A., Holder, D., Kolko D. J., Birmaher, B., Baugher, M., Roth, C., et al. (1997). A clinical psychotherapy trial for adolescent depression comparing cognitive, family, and supportive therapy. *Archives of General Psychiatry, 54,* 877–885.

Breznitz, Z. (2006). *Fluency in reading: Synchronization of processes.* Mahwah, NJ: Erlbaum.

Bricker, D. (1986). *Early education of at-risk and handicapped infants, toddlers, and preschool children.* Glenview, IL: Scott, Foresman.

Bricker, D., & Bricker, W. (1971). *Toddler research and intervention project report: Year 1 (IMRID Behavioral Sciences Monograph No. 20).* Nashville, TN: George Peabody College, Institute of Mental Retardation & Intellectual Development.

Bricker, D., Bricker, W., Iacino, R., & Dennison, L. (1976). *Intervention strategies for the severely and profoundly handicapped child.* (Vol. 1). New York: Grune & Stratton.

Bricker, D., Bruder, M., & Bailey, E. (1982). Developmental integration of preschool children. *Analysis and Intervention in Developmental Disabilities, 2,* 207–222.

Bricker, D., & Cripe, J. J. (1989). Activity-based intervention. In D. Bricker (Ed.), *Early education of at risk handicapped infants, toddlers, and preschoolers* (pp. 251–274). Palo Alto, CA: VORT Corp.

Bricker, D., & Cripe, J. (1992). *An activity-based approach to early intervention.* Baltimore: Brookes.

Bricker, D., & Gumerlock, S. (1988). Application of a three-level evaluation plan for monitoring child progress and program effects. *Journal of Special Education, 22,* 66–81.

Bricker, D., & Sheehan, R. (1981). Effectiveness of an early intervention program as indexed by child change. *Journal of the Division for Early Childhood, 4,* 11–27.

Bricker, W. A., & Bricker, D. (1974). An early language training strategy. In R. L. Schiefelbush & L. L. Lloyd (Eds.), *Language perspective: Acquisition, retardation, and intervention.* Baltimore: University Park Press.

Bricker, W., & Bricker, D. (1976). The infant, toddler, and preschool research and intervention project. In T. Tjossem (Ed.), *Intervention strategies for high risk infants and young children* (pp. 545–572). Baltimore: University Park Press.

Brigham, F. J., & Brigham, M. S. P. (2010). Preventive instruction: Response to intervention can catch students before their problems become insurmountable. *The American School Board Journal, 197*(6), 32–33.

Brigham, F. J., Scruggs, T. E., & Mastropieri, M. A. (1992). The effect of teacher enthusiasm on the learning

and behavior of learning disabled students. *Learning Disabilities Research & Practice, 7,* 68–73.

Brigham, M. M., Brigham, F. J., & Lloyd, J. W. (2002). *Balancing interventions and accommodations: Educating, equalizing, or equivocating?* Paper presented at the annual conference of Teacher Educators of Children with Behavior Disorders, Tempe, AZ.

Bronfenbrenner, U. (1979). *The ecology of human development.* Cambridge, MA Harvard University Press.

Brophy, J., & Good, T. L. (1986). Teacher behavior and student achievement. In M. C. Wittrock (Ed.), *Handbook of research on teaching* (3rd ed., pp. 328–375). New York: Macmillan.

Brouwers, A., & Tomic, W. (2000). A longitudinal study of teacher burnout and perceived self-efficacy in classroom management. *Teaching and Teacher Education, 16,* 239–253.

Browder, D. (2001). *Curriculum and assessment for students with moderate and severe disabilities.* New York: Guilford Press.

Browder, D. M., Ahlgrim-Delzell, L., Spooner, F., Mims, P. J., & Baker, J. N. (2009). Using time delay to teach literacy to students with severe disabilities. *Exceptional Children, 75,* 343–364.

Browder, D. M., Spooner, F., Wakeman, S., Trela, K., & Baker, J. N. (2006). Aligning instruction with academic content standards: Finding the link. *Research & Practice for Persons with Severe Disabilities, 31,* 309–321.

Brown, A. L., & Palincsar, A. S. (1987). Reciprocal teaching of comprehension strategies. In J. D. Day & J. G. Borkowski (Eds.), *Intelligence and exceptionality: New directions for theory, assessment, and instructional practice* (pp. 81–132). Norwood, NJ: Ablex.

Brown, F., Lehr, D., & Snell, M. (2011). Conducting and using student assessment. In M. E. Snell & F. Brown (Eds.), *Instruction of students with severe disabilities* (7th ed.). Upper Saddle River, NJ: Pearson.

Brown, F., & Snell, M. E. (2006). Meaningful assessment. In M. E. Snell & F. Brown (Eds.), *Instruction of students with severe disabilities* (6th ed., pp. 67–110). Upper Saddle River, NJ: Merrill/Pearson.

Brown, J., Goodman, K. S., & Marek, A. M. (Eds.). (1996). *Studies in miscue analysis: An annotated bibliography.* Newark, DE: International Reading Association.

Brown, L., Nisbet, J., Ford, A., Sweet, M., Shiraga, B., York, J., & Loomis, R. (1983). The critical need for nonschool instruction in educational programs for severely handicapped students. *Journal of the Association for the Severely Handicapped, 8,* 71–77.

Brown-Chidsey, R., & Steege, M. W. (2005). *Response to intervention: Principles and strategies for effective practice.* New York: Guilford Press.

Browning, N. (2002). Literacy of children with physical disabilities: A literature review. *Canadian Journal of Occupational Therapy, 69,* 176–182.

Bruce, S. M. (2005). The application of Werner and Kaplan's concept of "distancing" to children who are deaf-blind. *Journal of Visual Impairment & Blindness, 99,* 464–477.

Bruder, M. B. (2000). Family-centered early intervention: Clarifying our values for the new millennium. *Topics in Early Childhood Special Education, 20,* 105–115.

Bruder, M. B. (2001). Infants and toddlers: Outcomes and ecology. In M. J. Guralnick (Ed.), *Early childhood inclusion: Focus on change* (pp. 203–228). Baltimore: Brookes.

Bruininks, R. H., Woodcock, R. W., Weatherman, R. F., & Hill, B. K. (1996). *Scales of Independent Behavior—Revised.* Itasca, IL: Riverside Publishing.

Bruner, J. S. (1975). The ontogenesis of speech acts. *Journal of Child Language, 2,* 1–19.

Bruner, J. (1983). *Child's talk.* New York: Norton.

Bruteig, J. M. (1987). The reading rates for contracted and uncontracted braille of blind Norwegian adults. *Journal of Visual Impairment and Blindness, 81,* 19–23.

Bryant, D. P., Bryant, B. R., Gersten, R., Scammacca, N., & Chavez, M. (2008). Mathematics intervention for first- and second-grade students with mathematics difficulties: The effects of tier 2 intervention delivered as booster lessons. *Remedial and Special Education, 29*(1), 20–32.

Bryant, D. P., Bryant, B. R., Gersten, R., Scammacca, N., Funk, C., & Winter, A. (2008). The effects of tier 2 intervention on first-grade mathematics performance. *Learning Disability Quarterly, 31*(2), 47–63.

Bryant, D., Goodwin, M., Bryant, B., & Higgins, K. (2003). Vocabulary instruction for students with learning disabilities: A review of the research. *Learning Disability Quarterly, 26,* 117–128.

Bryant, D. P., Vaughn, S., Linan-Thompson, S., Ugel, N., Hamff, A., & Hougen, M. (2000). Reading outcomes for students with and without reading disabilities in general education middle-school content area classes. *Learning Disability Quarterly, 23,* 238–252.

Buikema, J. L., & Graves, M. F. (1993). Teaching students to use context cues to infer word meanings. *Journal of Reading, 36,* 450–457.

Bulgren, J., Deshler, D. D., & Lenz, B. K. (2007). Engaging adolescents with LD in higher order thinking about history concepts using integrated content enhancement routines. *Journal of Learning Disabilities, 40,* 121–133.

Bulgren, J. A., Deshler, D. D., & Schumaker, J. B. (1997). Use of a recall enhancement routine and strategies in inclusive secondary classes. *Learning Disabilities Research and Practice, 12,* 198–208.

Bulgren, J. A., Deshler, D. D., & Schumaker, J. B. (1998). *Reasoning strategies and teaching routines for use in mainstream content classrooms.* Final research report submitted to the U.S. Department of Education, Special Education Services.

Bulgren, J. A., Deshler, D. D., Schumaker, J. B., & Lenz, B. K. (2000). The use and effectiveness of analogical instruction in diverse secondary content classrooms. *Journal of Educational Psychology, 92,* 426–441. doi:10.1037/0022-0663.92.3.426

Bulgren, J. A., Lenz, B. K., Deshler, D. D., & Schumaker, J. B. (2001). *The question exploration routine.* Lawrence, KS: Edge Publications.

Bulgren, J. A., Lenz, B. K., Schumaker, J. B., Deshler, D. D., & Marquis, J. G. (2002). The use and effectiveness of a comparison routine in diverse secondary content classrooms. *Journal of*

Educational Psychology, 94, 356–371. doi:10.1037/0022-0663.94.2.356

Bulgren, J. A., Marquis, J. G., Lenz, B. K., Deshler, D. D., & Schumaker, J. B. (2009). Effectiveness of question exploration to enhance students' written expression of content knowledge and comprehension. *Reading and Writing Quarterly, 25,* 271–289.

Bulgren, J. A., Marquis, J. G., Lenz, B. K., Deshler, D. D., & Schumaker, J. B. (2011). The effectiveness of a question-exploration routine for enhancing the content learning of secondary students. *Journal of Educational Psychology, 103,* 578–593.

Bulgren, J. A., & Schumaker, J. B. (2006). Teaching practices that optimize curriculum access. In D. D. Deshler & J. B. Schumaker (Eds.), *Teaching adolescents with disabilities: Accessing the general education curriculum* (pp. 79–120). Thousand Oaks, CA: Corwin Press.

Bulgren, J. A., Schumaker, J. B., & Deshler, D. D. (1988). Effectiveness of a concept teaching routine in enhancing the performance of LD students in secondary-level mainstream classes. *Learning Disabilities Quarterly, 11*(1), 3–17.

Bulgren, J. A., Schumaker, J. B., & Deshler, D. D. (1994). The effects of a recall enhancement routine on the test performance of secondary students with and without learning disabilities. *Learning Disabilities Research & Practice, 9*(1), 2–11.

Bullock, C., & Normand, M. P. (2006). The effects of a high-probability instruction sequence and response-independent reinforcer delivery on child compliance. *Journal of Applied Behavior Analysis, 39*(4), 495–499.

Burk, M. (1999). *Computerized test accommodations.* Washington, DC: A.U. Software.

Burke, M. D., & Hagan-Burke, S. (2007). Concurrent criterion-related validity of early literacy for middle of first grade. *Assessment for Effective Intervention, 32,* 66–77.

Burke, M., Hagan-Burke, S., & Sugai, G. (2003). The efficacy of function-based interventions for students with learning disabilities who exhibit escape-motivated behaviors: Preliminary results from a single-case experiment.

Learning Disability Quarterly, 26, 15–25.

Burns, B. J., Costello, E. J., Angold, A., Tweed, D., Stangle, D., Farmer, E. M. Z., et al. (1995). Children's mental health service use across service sectors. *Health Affairs, 14,* 148–159.

Burns, M. K., Appleton, J. A., & Stehouwer, J. D. (2005). Meta-analytic review of responsiveness-to-intervention research: Examining field-based and research-implemented models. *Journal of Psychoeducational Assessment, 23,* 381–394.

Burns, M. K., & Coolong-Chaffin, M. (2006). Response-to-intervention: Role for and effect on school psychology. *School Psychology Forum, 1*(1), 3–15.

Burns, M. K., Dean, V. J., & Klar, S. (2004). Using curriculum-based assessment in the responsiveness to intervention diagnostic model for learning disabilities. *Assessment for Effective Intervention, 29*(3), 47–56.

Burns, M. K., Deno, S. L., & Jimerson, S. R. (2007). Toward a unified response-to-intervention model. In S. R. Jimerson, M. K., Burns, & A. M. VanDerHeyden (Eds.), *Handbook of response to intervention* (pp. 428–440). New York: Springer.

Burns, M. K., & Gibbons, K. (2008). *Response to intervention implementation in elementary and secondary schools: Procedures to assure scientific-based practices.* New York: Routledge.

Burns, M. K., Jacob, S., & Wagner, A. R. (2008). Ethical and legal issues associated with using response-to-intervention to assess learning disabilities. *Journal of School Psychology, 46*(3), 263–279.

Burns, M. K., Peters, R., & Noell, G. H. (2008). Using performance feedback to enhance the implementation integrity of the problem-solving team process. *Journal of School Psychology, 46,* 537–550.

Burns, M. K., Scholin, S. E., Kosciolek, S., & Livingston, S. (2010). Reliability of decision-making frameworks for response to intervention for reading. *Journal of Psychoeducational Assessment, 28,* 102–114.

Burns, M. K., & Senesac, B. K. (2005). Comparison of dual discrepancy criteria for diagnosis of unresponsiveness

to intervention. *Journal of School Psychology, 43,* 393–406.

Burns, M. K., & Symington, T. (2002). A meta-analysis of prereferral intervention teams: Systemic and student outcomes. *Journal of School Psychology, 40,* 437–447.

Burns, M. K., Tucker, J. A., Frame, J., Foley, S., & Hauser, A. (2000). Interscorer, alternate-form, internal consistency, and test–retest reliability of Gickling's model of curriculum-based assessment for reading. *Journal of Psychoeducational Assessment, 18,* 353–360.

Burns, M. K., & VanDerHeyden, A. M. (2006). Using response to intervention to assess learning disabilities: Introduction to the special series. *Assessment for Effective Intervention, 32,* 3–5.

Burns, M. K., VanDerHeyden, A. M., & Boice, C. H. (2008). Best practices in delivery of intensive academic interventions. In A. Thomas & J. Grimes (Eds.), *Best practices in school psychology* (5th ed.). Bethesda, MD: National Association of School Psychologists.

Burns, M. K., VanDerHeyden, A. M., & Jiban, C. (2006). Assessing the instructional level for mathematics: A comparison of methods. *School Psychology Review, 35,* 401–418.

Burns, M. K., & Wagner, D. (2008). Determining an effective intervention within a brief experimental analysis for reading: A meta-analytic review. *School Psychology Review, 37,* 126–136.

Burns, M. K., Wiley, H. I., & Viglietta, E. (2008). Best practices in facilitating problem-solving teams. In A. Thomas & J. Grimes (Eds.), *Best practices in school psychology* (5th ed.). Bethesda, MD: National Association of School Psychologists.

Burns, M. K., & Ysseldyke, J. E. (2009). Reported prevalence of evidence-based instructional practices in special education. *Journal of Special Education, 43,* 3–11.

Bus, A. G., van Ijzendoorn, M. H., & Pellegrini, A. D. (1995). Joint book reading makes for success in learning to read. A meta-analysis on intergenerational transmission of literacy. *Review of Educational Research, 65,* 1–21.

Busch, T. W., & Lembke, E. S. (2005). *Teaching tutorial 5: Progress monitoring in reading using the CBM maze*

procedure. Web-based tutorial published on the Division for Learning Disabilities Web site. Available from http://www.dldcec.org

Butler, L. R., & Luiselli, J. K. (2007). Escape-maintained problem behavior in a child with autism: Antecedent functional analysis and intervention evaluation of noncontingent escape and instructional fading. *Journal of Positive Behavior Interventions, 9,* 195–202.

Cable, A. (2007). *An oral narrative intervention for second graders with poor oral narrative ability.* Unpublished doctoral dissertation. University of Texas–Austin.

Cain, K., Oakhill, J., & Elbro, C. (2003). The ability to learn new word meanings from context by school-age children with and without language comprehension difficulties. *Journal of Child Language, 30,* 681–694.

Caldarella, P., & Merrell, K. (1997). Common dimensions of social skills in children and adolescents: Taxonomy of positive social behaviors. *School Psychology Review, 26,* 265–279.

Caldarella, P., Young, E. L., Richardson, M. J., Young, B. J., & Young, K. R. (2008). Validation of the Systematic Screening for Behavior Disorders in middle and junior high school. *Journal of Emotional and Behavioral Disorders, 16*(2), 105–117.

Calhoon, B., Al Otaiba, S., Greenberg, D., King, A., & Avalos, A. (2006). Boosting the intensity of reading instruction for culturally diverse first grade students: The promise of peer-assisted learning strategies. *Learning Disabilities: Research & Practice, 21,* 261–272.

Calhoon, M. B., Fuchs, L. S., & Hamlett, C. L. (2000). Effects of computer-based test accommodations on mathematics performance assessments for secondary students with learning disabilities. *Learning Disability Quarterly, 23,* 271–282.

Callahan, K., & Radenmacher, J. A. (1999). Using self-management strategies to increase the on-task behavior of a student with autism. *Journal of Positive Behavior Interventions, 1,* 117–122.

Callicott, K. J. (2003). Culturally sensitive collaboration within person-centered planning. *Focus on Autism and Other*

Developmental Disabilities, 18(1), 60–68.

Campbell, P. H. (2004). Participation-based services: Promoting children's participation in natural settings. *Young Exceptional Children, 8,* 20–29.

Caprara, G., Barbaranelli, C., Pastorelli, C., Bandura, A., & Zimbardo, P. (2000). Prosocial foundations of children's academic achievement. *Psychological Science, 11,* 302–305.

Cardemil, E. V., Reivich, K. J., & Seligman, E. P. (2002). The prevention of depressive symptoms in low-income minority middle school students. *Prevention and Treatment, 5,* 8–38.

Carlisle, J. F., Fleming, J., & Gudbrandsen, B. (2000). Incidental word learning in science classes. *Contemporary Educational Psychology, 25,* 184–211.

Carlo, M. S., August, D., Snow, C. E., Lively, T. J., & White, C. E. (2004). Closing the gap: Addressing the vocabulary needs of English-language learners in bilingual and mainstream classrooms. *Reading Research Quarterly, 39,* 188–215.

Carlson, J. I., Luiselli, J. K., Slyman, A., & Markowski, A. (2008). Choice-making as intervention for public disrobing children with developmental disabilities. *Journal of Positive Behavior Intervention, 10,* 86–90.

Carnine, D. W. (1976). Effects of two teacher-presentation rates on off-task behavior, answering correctly, and participation. *Journal of Applied Behavior Analysis, 9,* 199–206.

Carnine, D. (1997). Bridging the research-to-practice gap. *Exceptional Children, 63,* 513–521.

Carnine, D. (2000). *Why education experts resist effective practices: And what it would take to make education more like medicine.* Washington, DC: Thomas B. Fordham Foundation.

Carnine, D., & Stein, M. (1981). Organisational strategies and practice procedures for teaching basic facts. *Journal of Research in Mathematics Education, 12*(1), 65–69.

Caron, E. A., & McLaughlin, M. J. (2002). Indicators of beacons of excellence: What do they tell us about collaborative practices? *Journal of Educational and Psychological Consultation, 13,* 285–314.

Carr, E. G. (1988). Functional equivalence as a mechanism of response generalization. In R. H. Horner, G. Dunlap, & K. L. Koegel (Eds.), *Generalization and maintenance: Life-style changes in applied settings* (pp. 221–241). Baltimore: Brookes.

Carr, E. G., & Carlson, J. I. (1993). Reduction of severe behavior problems in the community using multicomponent treatment approach. *Journal of Applied Behavior Analysis, 26,* 157–172.

Carr, E. G., Dunlap, G., Horner, R. H., Koegel, R. L., Turnbull, A. P., Sailor, W., et al. (2002). Positive behavior support: Evolution of an applied science. *Journal of Positive Behavior Interventions, 4,* 4–16, 20.

Carr, J. E., Nicolson, A. C., & Higbee, T. S. (2000). Evaluation of a brief multiple-stimulus preference assessment in a naturalistic context. *Journal of Applied Behavior Analysis, 33,* 353–357.

Carr-George, C., Vannest, K. J., Willson, V., & Davis, J. L. (2009). The participation and performance of students with emotional and behavioral disorders in a state accountability assessment in reading. *Behavioral Disorders, 35,* 66–78.

Carson, P. M., & Eckert, T. L. (2003). An experimental analysis of mathematics instructional components: Examining the effects of student-selected versus empirically-selected interventions. *Journal of Behavioral Education, 12,* 35–54.

Carta, J. J., Schwartz, I. S., Atwater, J. B., & McConnell, S. R. (1991). Developmentally appropriate practice: Appraising its usefulness for young children with disabilities. *Topics in Early Childhood Special Education, 11,* 1–20.

Carter, D. R., & Horner, R. H. (2007). Adding functional behavioral assessment to First Step to Success. *Journal of Positive Behavior Interventions, 9,* 229–238.

Carter, E. W., & Kennedy, C. H. (2006). Promoting access to the general curriculum using peer support strategies. *Research and Practice for Persons with Severe Disabilities, 32,* 284–292.

Carter, E. W., Sisco, L. G., Brown, L., Brickham, D., & Al-Khabbaz, Z. A. (2008). Peer interactions and academic engagement of youth with developmental disabilities in inclusive middle and high school classrooms. *American Journal on Mental Retardation, 113,* 479–494.

Carter, M., & Kemp, C. R. (1996). Strategies for task analysis in special education. *Educational Psychology, 16,* 155–176.

Case, B. J. (2003). *Accommodations for the Metropolitan8: Meeting the needs of all students.* Upper Saddle River, NJ: Pearson Education. Retrieved from http://pearsonassess.com/NR/rdonlyres/1E23DAFB-0131046C2-938F-E077F4900777/0/AccommodationfortheMAT8_Rev1_Final.pdf

Case, B. J. (2005). *Accommodations to improve instruction and assessment of students who are deaf or hard of hearing.* Retrieved from http://pearsonassess.com/NR/rdonlyres/318B76DB-853A-449F-A02E-CC53C8CFD1DB/0/Deaf.pdf

Case, L. P., Harris, K. R., & Graham, S. (1992). Improving the mathematical problem-solving skills of students with learning disabilities: Self-regulated strategy development. *Journal of Special Education, 26,* 1–19.

Case, R. E., & Taylor, S. S. (2005). Language difference or learning disability? Answers from a linguistic perspective. *The Clearinghouse, 78*(3), 127–130.

Casey, A. M., & McWilliam, R. A. (2008). Graphical feedback to increase teachers' use of incidental teaching. *Journal of Early Intervention, 30,* 251–268.

Cassel, J., & Reid, R. (1996). Use of a self-regulated strategy intervention to improve word problem-solving skills of students with mild disabilities. *Journal of Behavioral Education, 6,* 153–172.

Catone, W. V., & Brady, S. A. (2005). The inadequacy of individual educational program (IEP) goals for high school students with word-level reading difficulties. *Annals of Dyslexia, 55*(1), 53–78.

Cavallaro, C. C., & Bambara, L. (1982). Two strategies for teaching language during free play. *Journal of the Association for the Severely Handicapped, 7,* 80–93.

Cavallaro, C. C., Haney, M., & Cabello, B. (1993). Developmentally appropriate strategies for promoting full participation in early childhood settings. *Topics in Early Childhood Special Education, 13,* 293–307.

Ceci, S. (1984). A developmental study of learning disabilities and memory. *Journal of Experimental Child Psychology, 38,* 352–371.

Center for Applied Special Technology (CAST). (2008). *Universal design for learning (UDL) guidelines-Version 1.0.* Retrieved from http://www.cast .org/publications/UDLguidelines/ .html

Centers for Disease Control and Prevention. (2010). *CDC study: An average of 1 in 110 children have an ASD.* Retrieved from http://www.cdc.gov/ Features/CountingAutism

Chabris, C., & Simons, D. (2010). *The invisible gorilla: And other ways our intuitions deceive us.* New York: Crown.

Chafouleas, S. M., Riley-Tillman, T. C., & Christ, T. J. (2009). Direct behavior rating (DBR): An emerging method for assessing social behavior within a tiered intervention system. *Assessment for Effective Intervention, 34,* 195–200.

Chall, J. (1967, 1983). *Learning to read: The great debate.* New York: McGraw-Hill. (Updated Edition, 1983).

Chall, J. (1983). *Stages of reading development.* New York: McGraw Hill.

Chamberlain, C., & Mayberry, R. (2008). American sign language syntactic and narrative comprehension in skilled and less skilled readers: Bilingual and bimodal evidence for the linguistic basis for reading. *Applied Psycholinguistics, 29,* 367–388.

Chambers, C. R., & Childre, A. L. (2005). Fostering family-professional collaboration through person-centered IEP meetings: The "true directions" model. *Young Exceptional Children, 8*(3), 20–28.

Chambers, J., Parrish, T., & Harr, J. (2004). *What are we spending on special education services in the United States, 1999–2000?* Palo Alto, CA: American Institutes for Research, Center for Special Education Finance.

Chambless, D. L., & Hollon, S. D. (1998). Defining empirically supported therapies. *Journal of Consulting and Clinical Psychology, 66,* 7–18.

Chan, L. K. S., & Cole, P. G. (1986). The effects of comprehension monitoring training on learning disabled and regular class students. *Remedial and Special Education, 7*(4), 43–40.

Chandler, M. A. (2009, November 19). Alternative test may inflate score gains. *The Washington Post.* Retrieved from http://www.washingtonpost.com/ wp-dyn/content/article/2009/11/18/ AR2009111801796.html

Chandler, W., Schuster, J. W., & Stevens, K. B. (1993). Teaching employment skills to adolescents with mild to moderate disabilities using a constant time delay procedure. *Education and Training in Mental Retardation and Developmental Disabilities, 28,* 155–168.

Chapman, R. (2000). Children's language learning: An interactionist perspective. *Journal of Child Psychology and Psychiatry, 41,* 33–54.

Chard, D. J., & Kame'enui, E. J. (2000). Struggling first-grade readers: The frequency and progress of their reading. *The Journal of Special Education, 34,* 28–38.

Chard, D., Ketterlin-Geller, L. R., Baker, S. K., Doabler, C., & Apichatabutra, C. (2009). Repeated reading interventions for students with learning disabilities: Status of the evidence. *Exceptional Children, 75,* 263–281.

Chard, D. J., Pikulski, J. J., & McDonagh, S. (2006). Fluency: The link between decoding and comprehension for struggling readers. In T. Rasinski, C. Blachowicz, & K. Lems (Eds.), *Teaching reading fluency* (pp. 39–61). New York: Guilford.

Charlebois, P., & Leblanc, M. (1994). Methodological issues in multiple-gating screening procedures for antisocial behaviors in elementary students. *Remedial and Special Education, 15*(1), 44–54.

Charlier, B. L., & Leybaert, J. (2000). The rhyming skills of deaf children educated with phonetically augmented speechreading. *Quarterly Journal of Experimental Psychology, 53A,* 349–375.

Charlop-Christy, M. H., & Carpenter, M. H. (2000). Modified incidental teaching sessions: A procedure for parents to increase spontaneous speech in their children with autism. *Journal of Positive Behavior Interventions, 2,* 98–112.

Chatel, R. G. (2001). Diagnostic and instructional uses of the Cloze procedure. *New England Reading Association Journal, 37,* 3–7.

Chávez, L. (2008). *The Latino threat: Constructing immigrants, citizens and the nation.* Stanford, CA: Stanford University Press.

Chen, D. (2005). Young children who are deaf-blind: Implications for professionals in deaf and hard of hearing services. *Volta Review, 104,* 273–287.

Chen, D., & Downing, J. E. (2006). *Tactile strategies for children with visual impairments and multiple disabilities: Promoting communication and learning skills.* New York: AFB Press.

Chen, S., Zhang, J., Lange, E., Miko, P., & Joseph, D. (2001). Progressive time delay procedure for teaching motor skills to adults with severe mental retardation. *Adapted Physical Activity Quarterly, 18,* 35–48.

Cheney, D., Blum, C., & Walker, B. (2004). An analysis of leadership teams' perceptions of positive behavior support and the outcomes of typically developing and at-risk students in their schools. *Assessment for Effective Intervention, 30,* 7–24.

Cheney, D., Flower, A., & Templeton, T. (2008). Applying response to intervention metrics in the social domain for students at risk for developing emotional and behavioral disorders. *Journal of Special Education, 42,* 108–126.

Chiang, B., Rylance, B. J., Bongers, J., & Russ, S. (1998). *School psychologist ratio and caseload: A statewide survey.* (Wisconsin Educators' Caseload Efficacy Project Research Report No. 3). Oshkosh, WI: University of Wisconsin Oshkosh.

Childre, A., & Chambers, C. R. (2005). Family perceptions of student centered planning and IEP meetings. *Education and Training in Developmental Disabilities, 40,* 217–233.

Christ, T. J. (2006). Short term estimates of growth using curriculum-based measurement of oral reading fluency: Estimates of standard error of the slope to construct confidence intervals. *School Psychology Review, 35,* 128–133.

Christ, T., & Davie, J. (2009). Empirical evaluation of Read Naturally effects. A randomized control trial. Retreived from http://www.readnaturally.com/ pdf/UofMnReadNaturallyStudy.pdf

Christensen, L., Young, K., & Marchant, M. (2004). The effects of a peer-mediated positive behavior support program on socially appropriate classroom behavior. *Education and Treatment of Children, 27,* 199–234.

Christensen, L. L., Lazarus, S. S., Crone, M., & Thurlow, M. L. (2008). *2007 state policies on assessment participation and accommodations for students with disabilities* (Synthesis Report 69). Minneapolis, MN: University of Minnesota, National Center on Educational Outcomes.

Christensen, L. L., Thurlow, M. L., & Wang, T. (2009). *Improving accommodations outcomes: Monitoring assessment accommodations for students with disabilities*. Minneapolis, MN: National Center on Educational Outcomes with Council of Chief State School Officers.

Christiansen, T. J., Ringdahl, J. E., Bosch, J. J., Falcomata, T. S., Luke, J. R., & Andelman, M. S. (2009). Constipation associated with self-injurious and aggressive behavior exhibited by a child diagnosed with autism. *Education and Treatment of Children, 32*, 89–103.

Christle, C. A., & Yell, M. L. (2010). Individualized educational programs: Legal requirements and research findings. *Exceptionality, 18*(3), 109–123.

Christoff, K. A., Scott, W. O. N., Kelley, M. L., Schlundt, D., Baer, G., & Kelly, J. A. (1985). Social skills and social problem-solving for shy young adolescents. *Behavior Therapy, 16*, 468–477.

Christou, C., & Philippou, G. (1999). Role of schemas in one-step word problems. *Educational Research and Evaluation, 5*, 269–289.

Chung, K. H., & Tam, Y. H. (2005). Effects of cognitive-based instruction on mathematical problem solving by learners with mild intellectual disabilities. *Journal of Intellectual and Developmental Disability, 30*, 207–216.

Chung, K. M., Reavis, S., Mosconi, M., Drewry, J., Matthews, T., & Tasse, M. J. (2007). Peer-mediated social skills training program for young children with high-functioning autism. *Research in Developmental Disabilities, 28*, 423–436.

Cihak, D. F., Alberto, P. A., Kessler, K., & Taber, T. A. (2004). An investigation of instructional scheduling arrangements for community-based instruction. *Research in Developmental Disabilities, 25*, 67–88.

Cihak, D. F., Kessler, K. B., & Alberto, P. A. (2006). Generalized use of a handheld prompting system. *Research in Developmental Disabilities, 28*, 397–408.

Claes, C., Van Hove, G., Vandevelde, S., van Loon, J., & Schalock, R. L. (2010) Person-centered planning: Analysis of research and effectiveness. *Intellectual and Developmental Disabilities, 48*, 432–453.

Clark, E. (1995). Review of the Developing Skills Checklist. In J. C. Conoley & J. C. Impara (Eds.), *The twelfth mental measurements yearbook* (pp. 278–281). Lincoln, NE: Buros Institute of Mental Measurements.

Clarke-Edmands, S. (2004). *S.P.I.R.E.®*. Cambridge, MA: Educators Publishing Service.

Cleave, P. L., & Fey, M. E. (1997). Two approaches to the facilitation of grammar in children with language impairments: Rationale and description. *American Journal of Speech-Language Pathology, 6*, 22–32.

Clifford, S. M., & Dissanayake, C. (2008). The early development of joint attention in infants with autistic disorder using home video observations and parental interview. *Journal of Autism and Developmental Disorders, 38*, 791–805.

Clonan, S., McDougal, J., Clark, K., & Davison, S. (2007). Use of office discipline referrals in school-wide decision making: A practical example. *Psychology in the Schools, 44*(1), 19–27.

Cobb, B., Lehmann, J., Newman-Gonchar, R., & Alwell, M. (2009). Self-determination for students with disabilities: A narrative metasynthesis. *Career Development for Exceptional Individuals, 32*, 108–114.

Cohen, A. S., Gregg, N., & Deng, M. (2005). The role of extended time and item content on a high-stakes mathematics test. *Learning Disabilities Research and Practice, 20*, 225–233.

Cohen, J. (1977). *Statistical power analysis for the behavioral sciences* (rev. ed.). New York: Academic Press.

Cohen, J. (1988). *Statistical power analysis for the behavioral sciences* (2nd ed.). Hillsdale, NJ: Erlbaum.

Cohen, J. (2007). A case study of a high school English-language learner and his reading. *Journal of Adolescent & Adult Literacy, 51*, 164–176.

Cohen, L., & Spenciner, L. (2007). *Assessment of children and youth with special needs* (3rd ed.). Upper Saddle River, NJ: Merrill/Pearson Education.

Coie, J. D., & Dodge, K. A. (1983). Continuities and changes in children's social status: A five-year longitudinal study. *Merrill-Palmer Quarterly, 29*, 261–282.

Coie, J., Dodge, K., & Coppotelli, H. (1982). Dimensions and types of social status: A cross-age perspective. *Developmental Psychology, 18*, 557–570.

Coie, J. D., Watt, M. F., West, S. G., Hawkins, J. D., Asarnow, J. R., Markman, H. J., . . . Long, B. (1993). The science of prevention: A conceptual framework and some directions for a national research program. *American Psychologist, 48*, 1013–1022.

Cole, C. L., & Levinson, T. R. (2002). Effects of within-activity choices on the challenging behavior of children with severe developmental disabilities. *Journal of Positive Behavior Interventions, 4*, 29–37.

Cole, K., Dale, P., & Mills, P. (1991). Individual differences in language delayed children's responses to direct and interactive preschool instruction. *Topics in Early Childhood Special Education, 11*, 99–124.

Cole, N. S., & Zieky, M. J. (2001). The new faces of fairness. *Journal of Educational Measurement, 38*, 369–382.

Coleman, M. B. (2011). Successful implementation of assistive technology to promote access to curriculum and instruction for students with physical disabilities. *Physical Disabilities: Education and Related Services, 30*(2), 2–22.

Coleman, M. B., & Heller, K. W. (2009). Assistive technology considerations. In K. W. Heller, P. E. Forney, P. A. Alberto, S. J. Best, & M. N. Swartzman (Eds.), *Understanding physical, health, and multiple disabilities* (2nd ed., pp. 139–153). Upper Saddle River, NJ: Pearson Education.

Coleman, M., Wheeler, L., & Webber, J. (1993). Research on interpersonal problem-solving training: A review. *Remedial and Special Education, 14*, 25–36.

Coleman-Martin, M. B., & Heller, K. W. (2004). Using a modified constant prompt-delay procedure to teach spelling to students with physical disabilities. *Journal of Applied Behavior Analysis, 37*, 469–480.

Coleman-Martin, M. B., Heller, K. W., Cihak, D. F., & Irvine, K. L. (2005).

Using computer-assisted instruction and the nonverbal reading approach to teach work identification. *Focus on Autism and Other Developmental Disabilities, 20,* 80–90.

Collins, B. C., Branson, T., A., & Hall, M. (1995). Teaching generalized reading of cooking product labels to adolescents with mental disabilities through the use of key words taught by peer tutors. *Education and Training in Mental Retardation and Developmental Disabilities, 30,* 64–75.

Collins, B. C., Stinson, D. M., & Land, L. (1993). A comparison of in vivo and simulation prior to in vivo instruction in teaching generalized safety skills. *Education and Training in Mental Retardation, 28,* 128–142.

Collins, K. A., Westra, H. A., Dozois, D. J., & Burns, D. D. (2004). Gaps in accessing treatment for anxiety and depression: Challenges for the delivery of care. *Clinical Psychology Review, 24,* 583–616.

Colvin, G. (2004). *Managing the cycle of acting-out behavior in the classroom.* Eugene, OR: Behavior Associates.

Colvin, G., Sugai, G., Good, R. H., III, & Lee, Y. Y. (1997). Using active supervision and precorrection to improve transition behaviors in an elementary school. *School Psychology Quarterly, 12,* 344–363.

Colvin, G., Sugai, G., & Patching, B. (1993). Pre-correction: An instructional approach for managing predictable problem behaviors. *Intervention in School and Clinic, 28,* 143–150.

Committee for Children. (2007). *Second steps violence prevention.* Seattle, WA: Author.

Compton, D. L., Fuchs, D., Fuchs, L. S., & Bryant, J. D. (2006). Selecting at-risk readers in first grade for early intervention: A two-year longitudinal study of decision rules and procedures. *Journal of Educational Psychology, 98,* 394–409.

Cone, J. D., Delawyer, D. D., & Wolfe, V.V. (1985). Assessing parent participation: The parent/family involvement index. *Exceptional Children, 51,* 417–424.

Conley, D. T. (2008). *Rethinking college readiness. New Directions for Higher Education,* 3–13. doi:10.1002/he.321

Conley, M. W. (2008). Cognitive strategy instruction for adolescents: What we know

about the promise, what we don't know about the potential. *Harvard Educational Review, 78,* 84–106.

Connell, M. C., & Carta, J. J. (1993). Building independence during in-class transitions: Teaching in-class transition skills to preschoolers with developmental delays through choral-response-based self-assessment and contingent praise. *Education and Treatment of Children, 16*(2), 160–174.

Conroy, M. A., Sutherland, K. S., Snyder, A., Al-Hendaawi, M., & Vo, A. (2009). Creating a positive classroom atmosphere: Teachers use of effective praise and feedback. *Beyond Behavior, 18,* 18–26.

Conroy, M. A., Sutherland, K. S., Snyder, A. L., & Marsh, S. (2008). Classwide interventions: Effective instruction makes a difference. *Teaching Exceptional Children, 40*(6), 24–30.

Conti-Ramsden, G., & Jones, M. (1997). Verb use in specific language impairment. *Journal of Speech, Language, and Hearing Research, 40,* 1298–1313.

Conway, T. (2001). Intensive remedial instruction for children with severe reading disabilities: Immediate and long-term outcomes for two instructional approaches. *Journal of Learning Disabilities, 34,* 33–58.

Cook, B. G., Landrum, T. J., Tankersley, M., & Kauffman, J. M. (2003). Bringing research to bear on practice: Effecting evidence-based instruction for students with emotional or behavioral disorders. *Education and Treatment of Children, 26,* 325–361.

Cook, B. G., & Schirmer, B. R. (2006). An overview and analysis of the role of evidence-based practices in special education. In B. G. Cook & B. R. Schirmer (Eds.), *What is special about special education: The role of evidence-based practices* (pp. 175–185). Austin, TX: Pro-Ed.

Cook, B. G., & Smith, G. J. (2012). Leadership and instruction: Evidence-based practices in special education. In J. B. Crockett, B. S. Billingsley, & M. L. Boscardin (Eds.), *Handbook of leadership and administration for special education.* London: Routledge.

Cook, B. G., Tankersley, M., Cook, L., & Landrum, T. J. (2008). Evidence-based practices in special education: Some practical considerations. *Intervention in School & Clinic, 44*(2), 69–75.

Cook, B. G., Tankersley, M., & Harjusola-Webb, S. (2008). Evidence-based special education and professional wisdom: Putting it all together. *Intervention in School and Clinic, 44,* 105–111.

Cook, B. G., Tankersley, M., & Landrum, T. J. (2009). Determining evidence-based practices in special education. *Exceptional Children, 75,* 365–383.

Cook, C. R., Gresham, F. M., Kern, L., Barreras, R.B., Thornton, S., & Crews, S. D. (2008). Social skills training with secondary EBD students: A review and analysis of the meta-analytic literature. *Journal of Emotional and Behavioral Disorders, 16,* 131–144.

Cook, L., Cook, B. G., Landrum, T. J., & Tankersley, M. (2008). Examining the role of group experimental research in establishing evidenced-based practices. *Intervention in School & Clinic, 44*(2), 76–82.

Cook, L., & Friend, M. (1996). Co-teaching: Guidelines for creating effective practices. In E. L. Meyer, G. A. Vergason, & R. J. Whelan (Eds.), *Strategies for teaching exceptional children in inclusive settings* (pp. 309–330). Denver, CO: Love.

Cook, S., Scruggs, T. E., Mastropieri, M. A., & Casto, G. C. (1985–1986). Handicapped students as tutors. *Journal of Special Education, 19,* 483–492.

Cook, T. D., Habib, F. N., Phillips, M., Settersten, R. A., Shagle, S. C., & Degimencioglu, S. M. (1999). Comer's school development program in Prince George's County, Maryland: A theory-based evaluation. *American Educational Research Journal, 36,* 543–597.

Cooney, J., & Swanson, H. (1987). Memory and learning disabilities: An overview. In H. L. Swanson (Ed.), *Advances in learning and behavioral disabilities: Memory and learning disabilities* (Suppl. 2, pp. 1–40). Greenwich, CT: JAI Press.

Cooper, J. D., & Pikulski, J. J. (2003). *A world of animals.* California Teacher's Edition. Kindergarten. Boston, MA: Houghton Mifflin.

Cooper, J. O., Heron, T. E., & Heward, W. L. (2007). *Applied behavior analysis* (2nd ed.). Upper Saddle River, NJ: Merrill/Pearson.

Cooper, K. J., & Browder, D. M. (1998). Enhancing choice and participation for adults with severe disabilities in community-based instruction.

Journal of the Association for Persons with Severe Handicaps, 23, 252–260.

Copeland, S. R., & Hughes, C. (2000). Acquisition of a picture prompt strategy to increase independent performance. *Education & Training in Mental Retardation & Developmental Disabilities, 35,* 294–305.

Copeland, S. R., Hughes, C., Agran, M., Wehmeyer, M., & Fowler, S. E. (2002). An intervention package to support high school students with mental retardation in general education classrooms. *American Journal on Mental Retardation, 107,* 32–45.

Copple, C., & Bredekamp, S. (Eds.). (2009). *Developmentally appropriate practice in early childhood programs serving children from birth through age 8* (3rd ed.). Washington, DC: National Association for Education of Young Children.

Cornwall, A. (1992). The relationship of phonological awareness, rapid naming, and verbal memory to severe reading and spelling disability. *Journal of Learning Disabilities, 25,* 532–538.

Cortiella, C. (2006). *NCLB and IDEA: What parents of students with disabilities need to know and do.* Minneapolis, MN: University of Minnesota: National Center on Educational Outcomes.

Cortiella, C., & Kaloi, L. (2009). *Understanding the Americans with Disabilities Act Amendments Act and Section 504 of the Rehabilitation Act* (Panel Advocacy Brief). New York: National Center for Learning Disabilities.

Costello, E. J., Erkanli, A., & Angold, A. (2006). Is there an epidemic of child or adolescent depression? *Journal of Child Psychology and Psychiatry, 47,* 1263–1271.

Coughlin, J., & Montague, M. (2011). The effects of cognitive strategy instruction on the mathematical problem solving of students with spina bifida. *Journal of Special Education, 45,* 171–183.

Council for Exceptional Children. (2007). *Blindness and visual impairment.* Retrieved from http://www.cec.sped.org/AM/Template.cfm?Section=Home&CONTENTID=7568&TEMPLATE=/CM/ContentDisplay.cfm

Council for Exceptional Children. (2009). *What every special educator must know: Ethics, standards, and guidelines* (6th ed.). Arlington, VA: Council for Exceptional Children.

Cox, M. L., Herner, J. G., Demczyk, M. J., & Nieberding, J. L. (2006). Provision of testing accommodations for students with disabilities on statewide tests: Statistical links with participation and discipline rates. *Remedial and Special Education, 27*(6), 346–354.

Coyle, C., & Cole, P. (2004). A videotaped self-modeling and self-monitoring treatment program to decrease off-task behavior in children with autism. *Journal of Intellectual & Developmental Disability, 29,* 3–15.

Coyne, M. D., Kame'enui, E. J., & Simmons, D. C. (2001). Prevention and intervention in beginning reading: Two complex systems. *Learning Disabilities: Research & Practice, 16,* 62–73.

Coyne, M. D., McCoach, B., & Kapp, S. (2007). Vocabulary intervention for kindergarten students: Comparing extended instruction to embedded instruction and incidental exposure. *Learning Disability Quarterly, 30,* 74–89.

Coyne, M. D., McCoach, D. B., Loftus, S., Zipoli, R., & Kapp, S. (2009). Direct vocabulary instruction in kindergarten: Teaching for breadth versus depth. *The Elementary School Journal, 110,* 1–18.

Coyne, M. D., Simmons, D., Kame'enui, E., & Stoolmiller, M. (2004). Teaching vocabulary during shared storybook readings: An examination of differential effects. *Exceptionality, 12,* 145–162.

Coyne, M. D., Simmons, D., Kame'enui, E., Stoolmiller, M., Santoro-Edwards, L., Smith, S. B., & Kaufman, N. (2007). Attributes of effective and efficient kindergarten reading intervention: An examination of instructional time and design specificity. *Journal of Learning Disabilities, 40,* 331–347.

Crain-Thoreson, C., & Dale, P. (1999). Enhancing linguistic performance: Parents and teachers as book reading partners for children with language delays. *Topics in Early Childhood Special Education, 19,* 28–39.

Cramer, K. A., Post, T. R., & del Mas, R. C. (2002). Initial fraction learning by fourth- and fifth-grade students: A comparison of the effects of using commercial curricula with the effects of using the rational number project curriculum. *Journal for Research in Mathematics Education, 33,* 111–144.

Crawford, L. (2007). *State testing accommodations: A look at their value and validity.* New York: National Center for Learning Disabilities.

Crawford, L., Helwig, R., & Tindal, G. (2004). Writing performance assessments: How important is extended time? *Journal of Learning Disabilities, 37,* 132–142.

Crews, S. D., Bender, H., Gresham, F. M., Kern, L., Vanderwood, M., & Cook, C. R. (2007). Risk and protective factors of emotional and/or behavioral disorders in children and adolescents: A "mega"-analytic synthesis. *Behavioral Disorders, 32,* 64–77.

Crockett, J. B. (2008). IEPs, the least restrictive environment, and placement. In K. E. Lane, M. A. Gooden, J. F. Mead, P. Pauken, & S. Eckes (Eds.), *The principal's legal handbook* (4th ed., pp. 243–268). Dayton, OH: Education Law Association.

Crone, D. A., Horner, R. H., & Hawken, L. S. (2004). *Responding to problem behavior in schools: The behavior education program.* New York: Guilford.

Crowe, L., Norris, J., & Hoffman, P. (2000). Facilitating storybook interactions between mothers and their preschoolers with language impairment. *Communications Disorders Quarterly, 21,* 131–146.

Cullinan, D., & Sabornie, E. J. (2004). Characteristics of emotional disturbance in middle and high school students. *Journal of Emotional and Behavioral Disorders, 12,* 157–167.

Cumming, J., & Elkins, J. (1999). Lack of automaticity in the basic addition facts as a characteristic of arithmetic learning problems and instructional needs. *Mathematical Cognition, 5,* 149–180.

Cummins, J. (2000). *Language, power and pedagogy: Bilingual children in the crossfire.* Clevedon, England: Multilingual Matters Ltd.

Cunningham, A. E., & Stanovich, K. E. (1997). Early reading acquisition and its relationship to reading experience and ability 10 years later. *Developmental Psychology, 33,* 934–945.

Curry, J. F. (2001). Specific psychotherapies for childhood and adolescent depression. *Biological Psychiatry, 49,* 1091–1100.

Curtis, M. E. (1987). Vocabulary testing and vocabulary instruction. In M. G. McKeown & M. E. Curtis (Eds.), *The nature of vocabulary acquisition.* Hillsdale, NJ: Erlbaum.

Cutler, L., & Graham, S. (2008). Primary grade writing instruction: A national survey. *Journal of Educational Psychology, 100,* 907–919.

Cutler, W. W. (2000). *Parents and schools: The 150-year struggle for control in American education.* Chicago: University of Chicago Press.

Dabkowski, D. M. (2004). Encouraging active parent participation in IEP team meetings. *Teaching Exceptional Children, 36*(3), 34–39.

Dacy, B. J. S., Nihalani, P. K., Cestone, C. M., & Robinson, D. H. (2011). (Lack of) support for prescriptive statements in teacher education textbooks. *The Journal of Educational Research, 104,* 1–6.

Dalton, B., & Proctor, C. P. (2008). The changing landscape of text and comprehension in the age of new literacies. In J. Coiro, M. Knobel, C. Lankshear, & D. Leu (Eds.), *Handbook of research on new literacies* (pp. 297–324). Mahwah, NJ: Erlbaum.

Daly, E. J., III, Witt, J. C., Martens, B. K., & Dool, E. J. (1997). A model for conducting a functional analysis of academic performance problems. *School Psychology Review, 26,* 554–574.

Dammann, J. E., & Vaughn, S. (2001). Science and sanity in special education. *Behavioral Disorders, 27,* 21–29.

Daniel, G. E. (2003). *Effects of cognitive strategy instruction on the mathematical problem solving of middle school students with learning disabilities.* Unpublished doctoral dissertation, Ohio State University.

Daniel, P. T. K. (2008). "Some benefit" or "Maximum benefit": Does the No Child Left Behind Act render greater educational entitlement to students with disabilities. *Journal of Law & Education, 37,* 347–365.

Darch, C., & Gersten, R. (1985). The effects of teacher presentation rate and praise on LD students' oral reading performance. *British Journal of Educational Psychology, 55,* 295–303.

Darch, C. B., & Thorpe, H. W. (1977). The principal game: A group consequence procedure to increase classroom on-task behavior. *Psychology in the Schools, 14,* 341–347.

Darveaux, D. X. (1984). The good behavior game plus merit: Controlling disruptive behavior and improving student motivation. *School Psychology Review, 13,* 510–514.

Dattilo, J., & Rusch, F. R. (1985). Effects of choice on leisure participation for persons with severe handicaps. *The Association for Persons with Severe Handicaps, 10,* 194–199.

Daugherty, S., Grisham-Brown, J., & Hemmeter, M. L. (2001). The effects of embedded skill instruction on the acquisition of target and nontarget skills in preschoolers with developmental delays. *Topics in Early Childhood Special Education, 21,* 213–221.

Davies, D. K., Stock, S. E., & Wehmeyer, M. L. (2003). A palmtop computer-based intelligent aid for individuals with intellectual disabilities to increase independent decision making. *Research & Practice for Persons with Severe Disabilities, 28,* 182–193.

Davies, G., McMahon, R., Flessati, E., & Tiedemann, G. (1984). Verbal rationales and modeling as adjuncts to a parenting technique for child compliance. *Child Development, 55,* 1290–1298.

Davis, C. A., Brady, M. P., Hamilton, R., McEvoy, M. A., & Williams, R. E. (1994). Effects of high-probability requests on the social interactions of young children with severe disabilities. *Journal of Applied Behavior Analysis, 27*(4), 619–637.

Davis, C. A., Brady, M. P., Williams, R. E., & Burta, M. (1992). The effects of self-operated auditory prompting tapes on the performance fluency of persons with severe mental retardation. *Education and Training in Mental Retardation, 27,* 39–50.

Davis, C. A., Brady, M. P., Williams, R. E., & Hamilton, R. (1992). Effects of high-probability requests on the acquisition and generalization of responses to requests in young children with behavior disorders. *Journal of Applied Behavior Analysis, 25*(4), 905–916.

Davis, C. A., & Reichle, J. E. (1996). Variant and invariant high-probability requests: Increasing appropriate behaviors in children with emotional-behavioral disorders. *Journal of Applied Behavior Analysis, 29*(4), 471–482.

Davis, C. A., Reichle, J. E., & Southard, K. L. (2001). High-probability requests and preferred item as a distracter: Increasing successful transitions in children with problem behavior. *Education and Treatment of Children, 23*(4), 423–440.

Davis, Z. T. (1994). Effects of prereading story-mapping on elementary readers' comprehension. *Journal of Educational Research, 7,* 353–360.

Dawson, G., & Osterling, J. (1997). Early intervention in autism. In M. Guralnick (Ed.), *The effectiveness of early intervention* (pp. 307–326). Baltimore: Brookes.

De Groot, E. V. (2002). Learning through interviewing: Students and teachers talk about learning and schooling. *Educational Psychologist, 37,* 41–52.

De La Paz, S. (1999). Composing via dictation and speech recognition systems: Compensatory technology for students with learning disabilities. *Learning Disabilities Quarterly, 22,* 173–182.

De La Paz, S. (2001). Teaching writing to students with attention deficit disorder and specific language impairment. *The Journal of Educational Research, 95,* 37–47.

De La Paz, S., & Graham, S. (1997). Effects of dictation and advanced planning instruction on the composing of students with writing and learning problems. *Journal of Educational Psychology, 89,* 203–222.

De La Paz, S., & MacArthur, S. (2003). Knowing the how and why of history: Expectations for secondary students with and without learning disabilities. *Learning Disability Quarterly, 26,* 142–154.

De Valenzuela, J., Copeland, S., Qi, C., & Park, M. (2006). Examining educational equity: Revisiting the disproportionate representation of minority students in special education. *Exceptional Children, 72,* 425–441.

DeBaryshe, B. (1993). Joint picture-book reading correlates of early oral language skills. *Journal of Child Language, 20,* 455–461.

DeBaryshe, D., Patterson, G., & Capaldi, D. (1993). A performance model for academic achievement in early adolescent boys. *Developmental Psychology, 29,* 795–804.

Deci, E. L., & Ryan, R. H. (1985). *Intrinsic motivation and self-determination in human behavior.* New York: Plenum.

DeFord, D. (2001). *Dominie reading and writing assessment portfolio* (3rd ed.). Carlsbad, CA: Dominie Press.

Della Toffalo, D. A., & Milke, R. M. (2008). Test reviews: Dynamic assessment of test accommodations. *Journal of Psychoeducational Assessment, 26,* 83–91.

Delpit, L. (1986). Skills and other dilemmas of a progressive Black educator. *Harvard Educational Review, 56,* 379–385.

Delpit, L. (1988). The silenced dialogue: Power and pedagogy in educating other people's children. *Harvard Educational Review, 58,* 280–298.

Delquadri, J., Greenwood, C. R., Whorton, D., Carta, J. J., & Hall, R. V. (1986). Classwide peer tutoring. *Exceptional Children, 52,* 535–542.

Demchak, M. (1990). Response prompting and fading methods: A review. *American Journal on Mental Retardation, 94,* 603–615.

Dennis, R., & Giangreco, M. F. (1996). Creating conversation: Reflections on cultural sensitivity in family interviewing. *Exceptional Children, 63,* 103–116.

Dennis, R. E., Williams, W., Giangreco, M. F., & Cloninger, C. J. (1993). Quality of life as a context for planning and evaluation of services for people with disabilities. *Exceptional Children, 59,* 499–512.

Denny, M., Martella-Marchand, N., Martella, R. C., Reilly, J. R., Reilly, J. F., & Cleanthous, C. C. (2000). Using parent-delivered graduated guidance to teach functional living skills to a child with Cri du Chat syndrome. *Education and Treatment of Children, 23,* 441–454.

Deno, S. L. (1985). Curriculum-based measurement: The emerging alternative. *Exceptional Children, 52,* 219–232.

Deno, S. L. (2003). Developments in curriculum-based measurement. *Journal of Special Education, 37,* 184–192.

Deno, S. L. (2006). Developments in curriculum-based measurement. In B. G. Cook & B. R. Schirmer (Eds.), *What is special about special education: The role of evidence-based practices* (pp. 100–112). Austin, TX: Pro-Ed.

Deno, S. L., Fuchs, L. S., Marston, D., & Shin, J. (2001). Using curriculum-based measurement to establish growth standards for students with learning disabilities. *School Psychology Review, 30,* 507–526.

Deno, S. L., Marston, D., & Mirkin, P. K. (1982). Valid measurement procedures for continuous evaluation of written expression. *Exceptional Children, 48,* 368–371.

Deno, S. L., & Mirkin, P. K. (1977). *Data-based program modification: A manual.* Reston, VA: Council for Exceptional Children.

Deno, S. L., Mirkin, P. K., & Chiang, B. (1982). Identifying valid measures of reading. *Exceptional Children, 49,* 36–45.

Deno, S. L., Mirkin, P. K., Lowry, L., & Kuehnle, K. (1980). *Relationships among simple measures of spelling and performance on standardized achievement tests* (Research Report No. 21). Minneapolis: Institute for Research on Learning Disabilities, University of Minnesota.

Denton, C. A., Wexler, J., Vaughn, S., & Bryan, D. (2008). Intervention provided to linguistically diverse middle school students with severe reading difficulties. *Learning Disabilities Research & Practice, 23,* 79–89.

Depry, R. L., & Sugai, G. (2002). The effect of active supervision and pre-correction on minor behavioral incidents in a sixth-grade general education classroom. *Journal of Behavioral Education, 11,* 255–267.

Deshler, D. D., & Schumaker, J. B. (2006). *Teaching adolescents with disabilities: Accessing the general education curriculum.* Thousand Oaks, CA: Corwin Press.

Deshler, D. D., Schumaker, J. B., & Lenz, B. K. (1984). Cognitive and academic interventions for learning disabled adolescents: Part I. *Journal of Learning Disabilities, 17,* 108–116.

Deshler, D. D., Schumaker, J. B., Lenz, B. K., Bulgren, J. A., Hock, M. F., Knight, J., & Ehren, B. J. (2001). Ensuring content-area learning by secondary students with learning disabilities. *Learning Disabilities Research and Practice, 16*(2), 96–108.

Detrich, R. (2008). Evidence-based, empirically supported, or best practice? A guide for the scientist-practitioner. In J. K. Luiselli, D. C. Russo, W. P. Christian, & S. M. Wilczynski (Eds.), *Effective practices for children with autism: Educational and behavioral support interventions that work* (pp. 3–26). New York: Oxford.

Dewey, J. (1916). *Democracy and education: An introduction to the philosophy of education.* New York: Macmillan.

Dewitz, P., Jones, J., & Leahy, S. (2009). Comprehension strategy instruction in core reading programs. *Reading Research Quarterly, 44,* 102–126.

Diaz, R. M., Neal, C. J., & Amaya-Williams, M. (1990). The social origin of self-regulation. In L. C. Moll (Ed.), *Vygotsky and education: Instructional implications and applications of sociohistorical psychology* (pp. 127–154). New York: Cambridge University Press.

Dickson, D. (2003). Let's not get too romantic about traditional knowledge. *Science Development Network.* Retrieved from http://www.scidev .net/en/editorials/lets-not-get-too-romantic-about-traditional-knowl .html

Dieker, L. A. (2001). What are the characteristics of "effective" middle and high school co-taught teams for students with disabilities? *Preventing School Failure, 46*(1), 14–23.

DiGangi, S. A., Maag, J. W., & Rutherford, R. B. (1991). Self-graphing of on-task behavior: Enhancing the reactive effects of self-monitoring on on-task behavior and academic performance. *Learning Disability Quarterly, 14,* 221–230.

Diken, I. H., & Rutherford, R. B. (2005). First Step to Success Early Intervention Program: A study of effectiveness with Native-American children. *Education and Treatment of Children, 28,* 444–465.

Dinkes, R., Kemp, J., & Baum, K. (2009). *Indicators of School Crime and Safety: 2008* (NCES 2009–022/NCJ 226343). National Center for Education Statistics, Institute of Education Sciences, U.S. Department of Education, and Bureau of Justice Statistics, Office of Justice Programs, U.S. Department of Justice. Washington, DC.

Dinkes, R., Kemp, J., Baum, K., & Snyder, T. (2008). *Indicators of school crime and safety: 2008.* Washington, DC: National Center for Education Statistics, Institute of Education Sciences, U.S. Department of Education, and Bureau of Justice Statistics, Office of Justice Programs, U.S. Department of Justice.

DiPerma, J., & Elliott, S. N. (2000). *Academic competence evaluation scales.* San Antonio, TX: Psychological Corporation.

DiPerma, J., & Elliott, S. N. (2002). Promoting academic enablers to improve student achievement: An introduction to the mini-series. *School Psychology Review, 31,* 293–297.

DiPerma, J. C., Volpe, R. J., & Elliott, S. N. (2002). A model of academic enablers and elementary reading/language arts achievement. *School Psychology Review, 31,* 298–312.

DiPipi-Hoy, C., Jitendra, A. K., & Kern, L. (2009). Effects of time management instruction on adolescents' ability to self-manage time in a vocational setting. *Journal of Special Education, 43,* 145–159.

Disability Rights Advocates. (2001). *Do no harm—High stakes testing and students with learning disabilities.* Oakland, CA: Author.

Disability Rights Advocates. (2008). *Chapman v. California Department of Education.* Retrieved from http://www.dralegal.org/cases/education_testing/chapman_v_ca.php

Dishion, T. J., & Patterson, G. R. (2006). The development and ecology of antisocial behavior in children and adolescents. In D. Cicchetti & D. J. Cohen (Eds.), *Developmental psychopathology* (2nd ed., pp. 503–541). Hoboken, NJ: Wiley.

Division for Early Childhood and the National Association for the Education of Young Children. (2009). *Early childhood inclusion: A joint position statement of the Division for Early Childhood (DEC) and the National Association for the Education of Young Children (NAEYC).* Chapel Hill, NC: The University of North Carolina, FPG Child Development Institute.

Dodge, K. (1986). A social information processing model of social competence in children. In M. Perlmutter (Ed.), *Minnesota symposium on child psychology* (Vol. 18, pp. 77–125). Hillsdale, NJ: Erlbaum.

Dogoe, M., & Banda, D. R. (2009). Review of recent research using constant time delay to teach chained tasks to persons with developmental disabilities. *Education and Training in Developmental Disabilities, 44,* 177–186.

Dolan, R. P., Burling, K. S., Harms, M., Beck, R., Hanna, E., Jude, J., Murray, E. A., Rose, D. H., & Way, W. (2009). *Universal design for computer-based testing guidelines.* Iowa City, IA: Pearson.

Dolan, R. P., Hall, T. E., Bannerjee, M., Chun, E., & Strangman, N. (2005). Applying principles of universal design to test design: The effect of computer-based read-aloud on test performance of high school students with learning disabilities. *The Journal of Technology, Learning, and Assessment, 3*(7). Retrieved from http://www.jtla.org

Dole, J. A., Duffy, G. G., Roehler, L. R., & Pearson, P. D. (1991). Moving from the old to the new: Research on reading comprehension instruction. *Review of Educational Research, 61,* 239–264.

Donovan, M. S., & Cross, C. T. (Eds.). (2002). *Minority students in special and gifted education.* Washington, DC: National Academies Press.

Dowell, H. A., Storey, K., & Gleason, M. (1994). A comparison of programs designed to improve the descriptive writing of students labeled learning disabled. *Developmental Disabilities Bulletin, 22,* 73–91.

Downing, J. A. (2002). Individualized behavior contracts. *Intervention in School and Clinic, 37,* 168–172.

Doyle, P. M., Wolery, M., Ault, M. J., & Gast, D. L. (1988). System of least prompts: A literature review of procedural parameters. *Journal of the Association for Persons with Severe Handicaps, 13,* 28–40.

Doyle, W. (1986). Classroom organization and management. In M. C. Wittrock (Ed.), *Handbook of research on teaching* (3rd ed., pp. 392–431). New York: Macmillan.

Drasgow, E., & Yell, M. L. (2001). Functional behavioral assessments: Legal requirements and challenges. *The School Psychology Review, 30,* 239–251.

Drasgow, E., Yell, M. L., & Robinson, T. R. (2001). Developing legally and educationally appropriate IEPs: Federal law and lessons learned from the Lovaas hearings and cases. *Remedial and Special Education, 22,* 359–373.

Drummond, T. (1994). *The Student Risk Screening Scale (SRSS).* Grants Pass, OR: Josephine County Mental Health Program.

Dryfoos, J. (1990). *Adolescents at risk: Prevalence and prevention.* New York: Oxford University Press.

Ducharme, J. M., Atkinson, L., & Poulton, L. (2001). Errorless compliance training with physically abusive mothers: A single-case approach. *Child Abuse and Neglect, 6,* 855–868.

Ducharme, J. M., & DiAdamo, C. (2005). An errorless approach to management of child noncompliance in a special education setting. *School Psychology Review, 34,* 107–115.

Ducharme, J. M., DiPadova, T., & Ashworth, M. (2010). Errorless compliance training to reduce extreme conduct problems and intrusive control strategies in home and school settings. *Clinical Case Studies, 9,* 16.

Ducharme, J. M., & Drain, T. (2004). Errorless academic compliance training: Improving generalized cooperation with parental requests in children with autism. *Journal of the American Academy of Child and Adolescent Psychiatry, 43,* 469–487.

Ducharme, J. M., & Harris, K. (2005). Errorless embedding for children with on-task and conduct difficulties: Rapport-based, success-focused intervention in the classroom. *Behavior Therapy, 36,* 213–222.

Ducharme, J., Harris, K., Milligan, K., & Pontes, E. (2003). Sequential evaluation of reinforced compliance and graduated request delivery for the treatment of noncompliance in children with developmental disabilities. *Journal of Autism and Developmental Disabilities, 33,* 519–526.

Ducharme, J., & Popynick, M. (1993). Errorless compliance to parental requests: Treatment effects and generalization. *Behavior Therapy, 24,* 209–226.

Ducharme, J., Popynick, M., Pontes, E., & Steele, S. (1996). Errorless compliance to parental requests: Group parent training with parent observation data and long-term follow-up. *Behavior Therapy, 27,* 353–372.

Ducharme, J., Sanjuan, E., & Drain, T. (2007). Errorless compliance training: Success-focused behaviors treatment of children with Asperger syndrome. *Behavior Modification, 31,* 329–346.

Ducharme, J. M., & Worling, D. E. (1994). Behavioral momentum and stimulus fading in the acquisition and maintenance of child compliance in the home. *Journal of Applied Behavior Analysis, 27*(4), 639–647.

Duda, M. A., Dunlap, G., Fox, L., Lentini, R., & Clarke, S. (2004). An experimental evaluation of positive behavior support in a community preschool program. *Topics in Early Childhood Special Education, 24,* 143–155.

Dunlap, G., DePerczel, M., Clarke, S., Wilson, D., Wright, S., et al. (1994). Choice making to promote adaptive behavior for students with emotional and behavioral challenges. *Journal of Applied Behavior Analysis, 27,* 505–518.

Dunlap, G., & Fox, L. (1999). A demonstration of behavioral support for young children with autism. *Journal of Positive Behavior Interventions, 1,* 77–87.

Dunlap, G., & Iovannone, R. (2008). Essential components for effective autism educational programs. In J. K. Luiselli, D. C. Russo, W. P. Christian, & S. M. Wilczynski (Eds.), *Effective practices for children with autism: Educational and behavioral support interventions that work* (pp. 111–136). New York: Oxford.

Dunlap, G., Iovannone, R., Kincaid, D., Wilson, K., Christiansen, K., Strain, P., & English, C. (2010). *Prevent-Teach-Reinforce: A school-based model of individualized positive behavior support.* Baltimore: Brookes.

Dunlap, G., Iovannone, R., Wilson, K., Strain, P., & Kincaid, D. (2010). Prevent-Teach-Reinforce: A standardized model of school-based behavioral intervention. *Journal of Positive Behavior Interventions, 12,* 9–22.

Dunlap, G., & Robbins, F. R. (1991). Current perspectives in service delivery for young children with autism. *Comprehensive Mental Health Care, 1,* 177–194.

Dunlap, G., White, R., Vera, A., Wilson, D., & Panacek, L. (1996). The effects of multi-component, assessment-based curricular modifications on the classroom behavior of children with emotional and behavioral disorders.

Journal of Behavioral Education, 6, 481–500.

Dunst, C. J. (2000). Revisiting "Rethinking early intervention." *Topics in Early Childhood Special Education, 20,* 95–104.

Dunst, C. J., & Bruder, M. B. (2006). Early intervention service coordination models and service coordinator practices. *Journal of Early Intervention, 28,* 155–165.

Dunst, C. J., Bruder, M. B., Trivette, C. M., Hamby, D., Raab, M., & McLean, M. (2001). Characteristics and consequences of everyday natural learning opportunities. *Topics in Early Childhood Special Education, 21,* 68–92.

Dunst, C. J., Hamby, D., Trivette, C. M., Raab, M., & Bruder, M. B. (2000). Everyday family and community life and children's naturally occurring learning opportunities. *Journal of Early Intervention, 23,* 151–164.

DuPaul, G. J., & Eckert, T. L. (1994). The effects of social skills curricula: Now you see them, now you don't. *School Psychology Quarterly, 9,* 113–132.

Durán, R. P. (2008). Assessing English-language learners' achievement. *Review of Research in Education, 32,* 292–327.

Durkin, D. (1978–1979). What classroom observations reveal about reading comprehension instruction. *Reading Research Quarterly, 14,* 481–533.

Durlak, J. A., Fuhrman, T., & Lampman, C. (1991). Effectiveness of cognitive-behavior therapy for maladapting children: A meta-analysis. *Psychological Bulletin, 110,* 204–214.

Dweck, C. S. (2007). The perils and promises of praise. *Educational Leadership, 65*(2), 34–39.

Dwyer, K. P., Osher, D., & Warger, W. (1998). *Early warning, timely response: A guide to safe schools.* Washington, DC: U.S. Department of Education.

Dyer, K. (1987). The competition of autistic stereotyped behavior with usual and specially assessed reinforcers. *Research in Developmental Disabilities, 8,* 607–626.

Dyer, K., Dunlap, G., & Winterling, V. (1990). Effects of choice making on the serious problem behaviors of students with severe handicaps. *Journal of Applied Behavior Analysis, 23,* 515–524.

Dyson, A. H. (1986). What are we teaching? Applying error analysis to school activities. *Reading Research and Instruction, 25,* 71–79.

Eads, J. R. (1991). *Classroom teacher mediated generalization of a sentence writing strategy to the regular classroom by nine middle school students with learning disabilities.* Unpublished educational specialist thesis, Northeast Missouri State University, Kirksville, MO.

Ebbers, S. M., & Denton, C. A. (2008). A root awakening: vocabulary instruction for older students with reading difficulties. *Learning Disabilities Research and Practice, 23,* 90–102.

Economic Opportunity Amendments of 1972, Pub. L. No. 92-424.

Eddy, J. M., Reid, J. B., & Curry, V. (2002). The etiology of youth antisocial behavior, delinquency and violence and a public health approach to prevention. In M. Shinn, H. Walker, & G. Stoner (Eds.), *Interventions for academic and behavior problems: II. Preventive and remedial approaches.* Bethesda, MD: National Association for School Psychologists.

Edelman, S., Knutson, J., Osborn, D., & Giangreco, M. F. (1995). Heidi's inclusion in junior high: Transition and educational planning for a student with deaf-blindness. *Deaf-Blind Perspectives 2*(3), 1–6.

Edens, K., & Potter, E. (2006). How students "unpack" the structure of a word problem: Graphic representations and problem solving. *School Science and Mathematics, 108,* 184–196.

Edmonds, C. J., & Pring, L. (2006). Generating inferences from written and spoken language: A comparison of children with visual impairment and children with sight. *British Journal of Developmental Psychology, 24,* 337–351.

Edmonds, M. S., Vaughn, S., Wexler, J., Reutebuch, C., Cable, A., Tackett, K. K., & Schnakenberg, J. W. (2009). Synthesis of reading interventions and effects on reading outcomes for older struggling readers. *Review of Educational Research, 79,* 262–300.

Education for All Handicapped Children Act of 1975 § 1401 *et seq.*

Education for All Handicapped Children Act of 1979, Pub. L. No. 94-142, 20 U.S.C. 1400 *et seq.*

Education for All Handicapped Children Act Amendments of 1986, Pub. L. No. 99-457, 20 U.S.C. 1400 *et seq.*

Education Trust. (2009). *Education Watch National Report.* Washington, DC: Author.

Edyburn, D. L. (2001). Models, theories, and frameworks: Contributions to understanding special education technology. *Special Education Technology Practice, 4*(2), 16–24.

Ehri, L. C. (1997). Sight word learning in normal readers and dyslexics. In B. Blachman (Ed.), *Foundations of reading acquisition and dyslexia* (pp. 163–189). Mahwah, NJ: Erlbaum.

Ehri, L. C. (2002). Phases of acquisition in learning to read words and implications for teaching. *British Journal of Educational Psychology: Monograph Series, 1,* 7–28.

Ehri, L. C., & McCormick, S. (2004). Phases of word learning: Implications for Instruction with delayed and disabled readers. In R. B. Ruddell, M. R. Ruddell, & H. Singer (Eds.), *Theoretical models and processes of reading* (5th ed., pp. 365–389). Newark, DE: International Reading Association.

Elbaum, B. (2007). Effects of an oral testing accommodation on the mathematics performance of secondary students with and without learning disabilities. *The Journal of Special Education, 40,* 218–229.

Elbaum, B., Vaughn, S., Hughes, M. T., Moody, S. W., & Schumm, J. S. (2000). How reading outcomes of students with disabilities are related to instructional grouping formats: A meta-analytic review. In R. M. Gersten, E. P. Schiller, & S. Vaughn (Eds.), *Contemporary special education research: Syntheses of the knowledge base on critical instructional issues* (pp. 105–135). Mahwah, NJ: Erlbaum.

Elbro, C., & Arnbak, E. (1996). The role of morpheme recognition and morphological awareness in dyslexia. *Annals of Dyslexia, 46,* 209–240.

Elkind, J., Cohen, K., & Murray, C. (1993). Using computer-based readers to improve reading comprehension in students with dyslexia. *Annals of Dyslexia, 43,* 238–259.

Elksnin, L., & Elksnin, N. (2006). *Teaching social-emotional skills at school and home.* Denver: Love.

Elley, W. (1989). Vocabulary acquisition from listening to stories. *Reading Research Quarterly, 24,* 174–187.

Elliot, N. (2005). *On a scale: A social history of writing assessment in America.* New York: Peter Lang.

Elliott, J., Lee, S. W., & Tollefson, N. (2001). A reliability and validity study of the Dynamic Indicators of Basic Early Literacy Skills—Modified. *School Psychology Review, 30,* 33–49.

Elliott, J., & Morrison, D. (2008). *Response to intervention blueprints for implementation: District level.* Alexandria, VA: National Association of State Directors of Special Education.

Elliott, J. L., & Thurlow, M. L. (2006). *Improving test performance of students with disabilities on district and state assessments* (2nd ed.). Thousand Oaks, CA: Corwin.

Elliott, S. N., Braden, J. P., & White, J. (2001). *Assessing one and all: Educational accountability and students with disabilities.* Alexandria, VA: Council for Exceptional Children.

Elliott, S. N., & Busse, R. T. (2004). Assessment and evaluation of students' behavior and intervention outcomes: The utility of rating scale methods. In R. B. Rutherford, M. M. Quinn, & S. R. Mathur (Eds.), *Handbook of research in emotional and behavioral disorders* (pp. 123–142). New York: Guilford Press.

Elliott, S. N., & Gresham, F. M. (1991). *Social skills intervention guide.* Bloomington, MN: Pearson Assessments.

Elliott, S. N., & Gresham, F. M. (2007). *Social skills improvement system: Classwide intervention program.* Bloomington, MN: Pearson Assessments.

Elliott, S. N., & Marquart, A. M. (2004). Extended time as a testing accommodation: Its effects and perceived consequences. *Exceptional Children, 70,* 349–367.

Elliott, S. N., McKevitt, B. C., & Kettler, R. J. (2002). Testing accommodations research and decision-making: The case of "good" scores being highly valued but difficult to achieve for all students. *Measurement and Evaluation in Counseling and Development, 35,* 153–166.

Ellis, A. K. (2005). *Research on educational innovations* (4th ed.). Larchmont, NY: Eye on Education.

Ellis, D. N., Cress, P. J., & Spellman, C. R. (1992). Using timers and lap counters to promote self-management of independent exercise in adolescents with mental retardation. *Education and Training in Mental Retardation, 27,* 51–59.

Ellis, J. D., & Bulgren, J. (2009). *Improving teaching of scientific argumentation skills.* Paper presented at the annual meeting of the Association for Science Teacher Educators, Hartford, CT.

Embry, D. D. (2002). The Good Behavior Game: A best practice candidate as a universal behavioral vaccine. *Clinical Child and Family Psychology Review, 5,* 273–297.

Emslie, G., Heiligenstein, J. H., Wagner, K. D., Hoog, S. L., Ernest, D. E., Brown, E., et al. (2002). Fluoxetine for acute treatment of depression in children and adolescents: A placebo-controlled randomized clinical trial. *Journal of the American Academy of Child and Adolescent Psychiatry, 41,* 1205–1215.

Engelmann, S. (1997). Theory of mastery and acceleration. In J. W. Lloyd, E. J. Kameenui, & D. J. Chard (Eds.), *Issues in educating students with disabilities* (pp. 177–195). Mahwah, NJ: Erlbaum.

Engelmann, S., & Bruner, E. C. (1995). *SRA reading mastery rainbow edition.* Chicago, IL: SRA/McGraw-Hill.

Engelmann, S., & Carnine, D. W. (1982). *Theory of instruction: Principles and applications.* New York: Irvington.

Engelmann, S., & Colvin, G. (1983). *Generalized compliance training: A direct-instruction program for managing severe behavior problems.* Austin: Pro-Ed.

Englert, C. S., & Thomas, C. C. (1987). Sensitivity to text structure in reading and writing: A comparison between learning disabled and non-learning disabled students. *Learning Disability Quarterly, 10,* 93–105.

Epstein, J. S. (2009). *School, family and community partnerships.* Thousand Oaks, CA: Corwin Press.

Epstein, M., Patton, J. R., Polloway, E. A., & Foley, R. (1992). Educational services for students with behavior disorders: A review of Individualized Education Programs. *Teacher Education and Special Education, 15*(1), 41–48.

Epstein, M. H., & Sharma, H. M. (1998). *Behavioral and Emotional Rating Scale (BERS)*. Austin, TX: Pro-Ed.

Epstein, M. H., & Walker, H. M. (2002). Special education: Best practices and First Step to Success. In B. J. Burns & K. Hoagwood (Eds.), *Community treatment for youth: Evidence-based interventions for severe emotional and behavioral disorders* (pp. 179–197). New York: Oxford University Press.

Erickson, K. A., & Hatton, D. (2007). Expanding understanding of emergent literacy: Empirical support for a new framework. *Journal of Visual Impairment and Blindness, 101*, 261–277.

Erickson, K. A., Hatton, D., Roy, V., Fox, D., & Renne, D. (2007). Literacy in early intervention for children with visual impairments: Insights from individual cases. *Journal of Visual Impairment and Blindness, 101*, 80–95.

Ervin, R. A., Johnston, E. S., & Friman, P. C. (1998). Positive peer reporting to improve the social interactions of a socially rejected girl. *Proven Practice: Prevention and Remediation Solutions for Schools, 1*, 17–21.

Ervin, R. A., Miller, P. M., & Friman, P. C. (1996). Feed the hungry bee: using positive peer reports to improve the social interactions and acceptance of a socially rejected girl in residential care. *Journal of Applied Behavior Analysis, 29*, 251–253.

Ervin, R. A., Schaughency, E., Goodman, S. D., McGlinchey, M. T., & Matthews, A. (2006). Merging research and practice agendas to address reading and behavior school-wide. *School Psychology Review, 35*, 198–223.

Espin, C. A., Busch, T. W., Shin, J., & Kruschwitz, R. (2001). Curriculum-based measurement in the content areas: Validity of vocabulary-matching as an indicator of performance in social studies. *Learning Disabilities Research and Practice, 16*(3), 142–151.

Espin, C. A., De La Paz, S., Scierka, B. J., & Roelofs, L. (2005). Relation between curriculum-based measures in written expression and quality and completeness of expository writing for middle-school students. *Journal of Special Education, 38*, 208–217.

Espin, C., Shin, J., & Busch, T. W. (2000). *Formative evaluation* (Current Practice Alerts No. 2). Reston, VA: Division for Learning Disabilities & Division for Research of the Council for Exceptional Children.

Espin, C. A., Shin, J., & Busch, T. W. (2005). Curriculum-based measurement in the content areas: Vocabulary-matching as an indicator of social studies learning. *Journal of Learning Disabilities, 38*, 353–363.

Espin, C. L., & Wallace, T. (2004). *Descriptive analysis of curriculum-based measurement literature*. Working Document. University of Minnesota Institute for Research on Progress Monitoring.

Espin, C., Wallace, T., Lembke, R., Campbell, H., & Long, J. D. (2010). Creating a progress-monitoring system in reading for middle-school students: Tracking progress toward meeting high-stakes standards. *Learning Disabilities Research & Practice, 25*, 60–75.

Espin, C., Wallace, T., Campbell, H., Lembke, E. S., Long, J. D., & Ticha, R. (2008). Curriculum-based measurement in writing: Predicting the success of high-school students on state standards tests. *Exceptional Children, 74*, 174–193.

Espin, C., Wallace, T., Lembke, E. S., Campbell, H., & Long, J. D. (2010). Examining the effects of oral reading and maze tasks as curriculum-based measures for secondary students. *Learning Disabilities Research and Practice, 25*(2), 60–75.

Etscheidt, S., & Curran, C. M. (2010). Peer-reviewed research and individualized education programs: An examination of intent and impact. *Exceptionality, 18*, 138–150.

Evans, I. M., & Meyer, L. (1990). Toward a science in support of meaningful outcomes: A response to Horner et al. *Journal of the Association for Persons with Severe Handicaps, 15*, 133–135.

Evans, M. D., Hollon, S. D., DeRubeis, R. J. Piasecki, J. M., Grove, W. M., Garvey, M. J., et al. (1992). Differential relapse following cognitive therapy and pharmacotherapy for depression. *Archives of General Psychiatry, 49*, 802–808.

Fairbanks, S., Sugai, G., Guardino, D., & Lathrop, M. (2007). Response to intervention: examining classroom behavior support in second grade. *Exceptional Children, 73*, 288–310.

Fantuzzo, J. W., Polite, K., Cook, D. M., & Quinn, G. (1988). An evaluation of the effectiveness of teacher-vs.-student-management classroom interventions. *Psychology in the Schools, 25*, 154–163.

Farlow, L. J., & Snell, M. E. (2006). Teaching self-care skills. In M. E. Snell & F. Brown (Eds.), *Instruction of students with severe disabilities* (6th ed., pp. 328–374). Upper Saddle River, NJ: Pearson.

Farr, R. (1991). The assessment puzzle. *Educational Leadership, 49*, 95.

Farr, R. (1996). I have a dream about assessment. *The Reading Teacher, 49*, 424.

Faykus, S. P., & McCurdy B. L. (1998). Evaluating the sensitivity of the maze as an index of reading proficiency for students who are severely deficient in reading. *Education and Treatment of Children, 21*, 1–21.

Feil, E. G., & Severson, H. H. (1995). Identification of critical factors in the assessment of preschool behavior problems. *Education and Treatment of Children, 18*(3), 261–272.

Feil, E. G., Walker, H., Severson, H., & Ball, A. (2000). Proactive screening for emotional/behavioral concerns in Head Start preschools: Promising practices and challenges in applied research. *Behavioral Disorders, 26*(1), 13–25.

Felton, E. A., Lewis, N. L., Wills, S. A., Radwin, R. G., & Williams, J. C. (2007). *Neural signal based control of the Dasher Writing System*. Paper presented at the 3rd International IEEE EMBS Conference on Neural Engineering, Kohala Coast, Hawaii.

Feng, J., Karat, C. M., & Sears, A. (2005). How productivity improves in hands-free continuous dictation tasks: Lessons learned from a longitudinal study. *Interacting with Computers, 17*, 265–289.

Ferguson, B., & McDonnell, J. (1991). A comparison of serial and concurrent sequencing strategies in teaching generalized grocery item location to students with moderate handicaps. *Education and Training in Mental Retardation, 26*, 292–304.

Ferguson, C. (2008). *The school-family connection: Looking at the larger picture*. Austin, TX: Southwest Educational Development Laboratories.

Ferreira, J., Rönnberg, J., Gustafson, S., & Wengelin, Å. (2007). Reading, why not?: Literacy skills in children with motor and speech impairments. *Communication Disorders Quarterly, 28,* 236–251.

Ferrell, K. A., Shaw, A. R., & Deitz, S. J. (1998). *Project PRISM: A longitudinal study of developmental patterns of children who are visually impaired. (Final Report, CFDA 84-023C, Grant H023C10188).* Greeley: University of Northern Colorado, Division of Special Education.

Ferretti, R. P., Cavalier, A. R., Murphy, M. J., & Murphy, R. (1993). The self-management of skills by persons with mental retardation. *Research in Developmental Disabilities, 14,* 189–205.

Fey, M. E. (1986). *Language intervention with young children.* Newton, MA: Allyn & Bacon.

Fey, M. E., Cleave, P. L., & Long, S. H. (1997). Two models of grammar facilitation in children with language impairments. *Journal of Speech, Language, and Hearing Research, 40,* 5–19.

Fey, M. E., Cleave, P. L., Long, S. H., & Hughes, D. L. (1993). Two approaches to the facilitation of grammar in children with language impairment: An experimental evaluation. *Journal of Speech and Hearing Research, 36,* 141–157.

Fey, M. E., Krulik, T. E., Loeb, D. F., & Proctor-Williams, K. (1999). Sentence recast use by parents of children with typical language and children with specific language impairment. *American Journal of Speech-Language Pathology, 8,* 273–286.

Fey, M. E., & Loeb, D. F. (2002). An evaluation of the facilitative effects of inverted yes-no questions on the acquisition of auxiliary verbs. *Journal of Speech, Language, and Hearing Research, 45,* 160–174.

Fey, M. E., Long, S. H., & Finestack, L. H. (2003). Ten principles of grammar facilitation for children with specific language impairments. *American Journal of Speech-Language Pathology, 12,* 3–15.

Fickel, K. M., Schuster, J., & Collins, B. C. (1998). Teaching different tasks using different stimuli in a heterogeneous small group. *Journal of Behavioral Education, 8,* 219–244.

Field, S., & Hoffman, A. (1994). Development of a model for self-determination. *Career Development for Exceptional Individuals, 17,* 159–169.

Field, S., Martin, J., Miller, R., Ward, M., & Wehmeyer, M. (1998). *A practical guide to teaching self-determination.* Reston, VA: Council for Exceptional Children.

Filter, K. J., & Horner, R. H. (2009). Function-based academic interventions for problem behavior. *Education and Treatment of Children, 32,* 1–19.

Finn, J. E., & Kohler, P. D. (2009). A compliance evaluation of the Transition Outcomes Project. *Career Development for Exceptional Individuals, 32*(1), 17–29.

First, C. G. (1994). *The effects of sentence combining on the written expression skills of students with serious emotional disturbances.* Unpublished doctoral dissertation, University of the Pacific, Stockton, CA.

Fishbein, J. E., & Wasik, B. H. (1981). Effect of the Good Behavior Game on disruptive library behavior. *Journal of Applied Behavior Analysis, 14,* 89–93.

Fisher, W. W., Adelinis, J. D., Thompson, R. H., Worsdell, A. S., & Zarcone, J. R. (1998). Functional analysis and treatment of destructive behavior maintained by termination of "don't" (and symmetrical "do") requests. *Journal of Applied Behavior Analysis, 31*(3), 339–356.

Fitzgerald, G., Koury, K., & Mitchem, K. (2008). Research on computer-mediated instruction for students with high incidence disabilities. *Journal of Educational Computing Research, 38*(2), 201–233.

Fitzgerald, J., & Spiegel, D. L. (1983). Enhancing children's reading comprehension through instruction in narrative structure. *Journal of Reading Behavior, 15,* 1–17.

Fitzpatrick, M., & Knowlton, E. (2009). Bringing evidence-based self-directed intervention practices to the trenches for students with emotional and behavioral disorders. *Preventing School Failure, 53,* 253–266.

Fitzsimmons, D. (2008). Digital portfolios in visual arts classrooms. *Art Education, 61*(5), 47–55.

Flannery, K. B., Newton, S., Horner, R. H., Slovic, R., Blumberg, R., & Ard, W. R. (2000). The impact of person centered planning on the content and organization of individual supports. *Career Development of Exceptional Individuals, 23,* 123–137.

Flavell, J. H. (1979). Metacognition and cognitive monitoring: A new area of cognitive developmental inquiry. *American Psychologist, 34,* 906–911.

Fleming, J. L., Sawyer, L. B., & Campbell, P. H. (2011). Early intervention providers' perspectives about implementing participation-based practices. *Topics in Early Childhood Special Education, 30,* 233–244.

Fletcher, J. M., Coulter, W. A., Reschly, D. J., & Vaughn, S. (2004). Alternative approach to the definition and identification of learning disabilities: Some questions and answers. *Annals of Dyslexia, 54,* 304–331.

Flood, J., Heath, S. B., & Lapp, D. (Eds.). (2008). *Handbook of research on teaching literacy through the communicative and visual arts.* New York: Routledge.

Foegen, A. (2008). Algebra progress monitoring and interventions for students with learning disabilities. *Learning Disability Quarterly, 31,* 65–78.

Foegen, A., & Deno, S. L. (2001). Identifying growth indicators for low-achieving students in middle-school mathematics. *Journal of Special Education, 35,* 4–16.

Foegen, A., Jiban, C., & Deno, S. (2007). Progress monitoring in mathematics: A review of the literature. *Journal of Special Education, 41,* 121–139.

Foegen, A., Olson, J. R., & Impecoven-Lind, L. (2008). Developing progress monitoring measures for secondary mathematics: An illustration in algebra. *Assessment for Effective Intervention, 33,* 240–249.

Foley, B. E., & Pollatsek, A. (1999). Phonological processing and reading abilities in adolescents and adults with severe congenital speech impairments. *Augmentative and Alternative Communication, 15,* 156–173.

Fontana, J., Scruggs, T. E., & Mastropieri, M. A. (2007). Mnemonic strategy instruction in inclusive secondary social studies classes. *Remedial and Special Education, 28,* 345–355.

Fontana, K. C. (2005). The effects of co-teaching on the achievement of eighth grade students with learning disabilities. *The Journal of At-Risk Issues, 11,* 17–23.

Foorman, B. R., Francis, D. J., Fletcher, J. M., Schatschneider, C., & Mehta, P. (1998). The role of instruction in learning to read: Preventing reading failure in at-risk children. *Journal of Educational Psychology, 90,* 37–55.

Ford, A., Olmi, J., Edwards, R., & Tingstrom, D. (2001). The sequential introduction of compliance training components with elementary-aged children in general education classroom settings. *School Psychology Quarterly, 16,* 142–157.

Ford, J., & Milosky, L. (2003). Inferring emotional reactions in social situations: Differences in children with language impairment. *Journal of Speech, Language, and Hearing Research, 46,* 21–30.

Fore, C., III, Hagan-Burke, S., Burke, M., Boon, R., & Smith, S. (2008). Academic achievement and class placement: Do students with specific learning disabilities achieve more in one class placement than another? *Education and Treatment of Children, 31,* 1–18.

Forehand, R., & McMahon, R. (1981). *Helping the non-compliant child.* New York: Guilford Press.

Forehand, R., & Scarboro, M. (1975). An analysis of children's oppositional behavior. *Journal of Abnormal Child Psychology, 3,* 27–31.

Forehand, R., Wells, K., & Sturgis, E. (1978). Predictors of child noncompliant behaviors in the home. *Journal of Consulting and Clinical Psychology, 46,* 179.

Forest, M., & Lusthaus, E. (1987). The kaleidoscope: Challenge to the cascade. In M. Forest (Ed.), *More education/ integration* (pp. 1–16). Downsview, Ontario: G. Allan Roeher Institute.

Forness, S. R. (2001). Special education and related services: What have we learned from meta-analysis? *Exceptionality, 9,* 185–197.

Forness, S. R., Freeman, S. F., & Paparella, T. (2006). Recent randomized clinical trials comparing behavioral interventions and psychopharmacologic treatments for students with EBD. *Behavioral Disorders, 31,* 284–296.

Foster, M., Berger, M., & McLean, M. (1981). Re-thinking a good idea: A reassessment of parent involvement. *Topics in Early Childhood Special Education, 1,* 55–65.

Fowler, C. H., Konrad, M., Walker, A. R., Test, D. W., & Wood, W. M. (2007). Self-determination interventions' effects on the academic performance of students with developmental disabilities. *Education and Training in Developmental Disabilities, 42,* 270–285.

Fox, L. (1989). Stimulus generalization of skills and persons with profound mental handicaps. *Education and Training in Mental Retardation, 24,* 219–229.

Fox, L., & Hanline, M. F. (1993). A preliminary evaluation of learning within developmentally appropriate early childhood settings. *Topics in Early Childhood Special Education, 13,* 308–327.

Francis, D., Rivera, M., Lesaux, N., Kieffer, M., & Rivera, H. (2006). *Practical guidelines for the education of English language learners: Research-based recommendations for instruction and academic interventions.* Portsmouth, NH: RMC Research Corporation, Center on Instruction.

Francis, D. J., Shaywitz, S. E., Stuebing, K. K., Shaywitz, B. A., & Fletcher, J. M. (1996). Developmental lag versus deficit models of reading disability: A longitudinal, individual growth curve analysis. *Journal of Educational Psychology, 88,* 3–17.

Frederick-Dugan, A., Test, D. W., & Varn, L. (1991). Acquisition and generalization of purchasing skills using a calculator by students who are mentally retarded. *Education and Training in Mental Retardation, 26,* 381–387.

Freedman, D. H. (2010). *Wrong: Why experts keep failing us—and how to know when not to trust them.* New York: Little, Brown.

Freire, P. (1970). *Pedagogy of the oppressed.* New York: Herder and Herder.

Frey, K. S., Hirschstein, M. K., & Guzzo, B. A. (2000). Second step: Preventing aggression by promoting social competence. *Journal of Emotional and Behavioral Disorders, 8,* 102–112.

Friend, M., & Cook, L. (1992). *Interactions: Collaboration skills for school professionals.* New York: Longman.

Friend, M., & Cook, L. (2003). *Interactions: Collaboration skills for school professionals* (4th ed.). Upper Saddle River, NJ: Allyn & Bacon/ Pearson.

Friend, M., Hurley-Chamberlain, D., & Cook, L. (2006, April). *NCLB and IDEA: Disaster or golden opportunity for co-teaching?* Paper presented at the convention of the Council for Exceptional Children, Salt Lake City, UT.

Fuchs, D., & Deshler, D. D. (2007). What we need to know about responsiveness to intervention and shouldn't be afraid to ask. *Learning Disabilities Research & Practice, 22*(2), 129–136.

Fuchs, D., & Fuchs, L. S. (1998). Researchers and teachers working together to adapt instruction for diverse learners. *Learning Disabilities Research and Practice, 13,* 126–137.

Fuchs, D., & Fuchs L. S. (2005). Peer-assisted learning strategies: Promoting word recognition, fluency, and reading comprehension in young children. *Journal of Special Education, 39,* 34–44.

Fuchs, D., & Fuchs, L. S. (2006). New directions in research, introduction to response to intervention: What, why, and how valid is it? *Reading Research Quarterly, 41,* 93–99.

Fuchs, D., Fuchs, L. S., & Burish, P. (2000). Peer-assisted learning strategies: An evidence-based practice to promote reading achievement. *Learning Disabilities Research and Practice, 15,* 85–91.

Fuchs, D., Fuchs, L. S., Mathes, P. G., & Simmons, D. C. (1997). Peer-assisted learning strategies: Making classrooms more responsive to academic diversity. *American Educational Research Journal, 34,* 174–206.

Fuchs, D., Fuchs, L. S., Svenson, E., Thompson, A., Yen, L., McMaster, K. N., Al Otaiba, S., & Yang, N. J. (2000). *Peabody peer assisted learning strategies: First grade reading.* Unpublished training manual, Vanderbilt University, Nashville, TN.

Fuchs, D., Fuchs, L. S., Thompson, A., Al Otaiba, S., Yen, L., & Braun, M. (2000). *Peer-assisted learning strategies: Kindergarten: A teacher's manual.* Unpublished training manual, Vanderbilt University, Nashville, TN.

Fuchs, D., Fuchs, L. S., Thompson, A., Svenson, E., Al Otaiba, S., Yang, N., . . . Saenz, L. (2001). Peer-assisted learning strategies in reading: Extensions to kindergarten/first grade and high school. *Remedial and Special Education, 22,* 15–21.

Fuchs, D., Mock, D., Morgan, P. L., & Young, C. L. (2003). Responsiveness-to-intervention: Definitions, evidence, and implications for the learning disabilities construct. *Learning Disabilities Research & Practice, 18,* 157–171.

Fuchs, L. S. (2003). Assessing intervention responsiveness: Conceptual and technical issues. *Learning Disabilities: Research & Practice, 18,* 172–186.

Fuchs, L. S. (2004). The past, present, and future of curriculum-based measurement research. *School Psychology Review, 33,* 188–192.

Fuchs, L. S., & Deno, S. L. (1991). Effects of curriculum within curriculum-based measurement. *Exceptional Children, 58,* 232–244.

Fuchs, L. S., & Deno, S. L. (1994). Must instructionally useful performance assessment be based in the curriculum? *Exceptional Children, 61,* 15–24.

Fuchs, L. S., Deno, S. L., & Mirkin, P. K. (1984). Effects of frequent curriculum-based measurement and evaluation on pedagogy, student achievement, and student awareness of learning. *American Educational Research Journal, 21,* 449–460.

Fuchs, L. S., & Fuchs, D. (1986). Effects of systematic formative evaluation on student achievement: A meta-analysis. *Exceptional Children, 53,* 199–208.

Fuchs, L. S., & Fuchs, D. (1992). Identifying a measure for monitoring student progress. *School Psychology Review, 21,* 45–58.

Fuchs, L. S., & Fuchs, D. (1999). Fair and unfair testing accommodations. *School Administrator, 56,* 24–29.

Fuchs, L. S., & Fuchs, D. (2001). Helping teachers formulate sound test accommodation decisions for students with learning disabilities. *Learning Disabilities Research & Practice, 16,* 174–181.

Fuchs, L. S., & .Fuchs, D. (2002). *What is scientifically-based research on progress monitoring?* (Technical report). Nashville, TN: Vanderbilt University.

Fuchs, L. S., & Fuchs, D. (2003). Enhancing the mathematical problem solving of students with mathematics disabilities. In H. L. Swanson, K. R. Harris, & S. E. Graham (Eds.), *Handbook on learning disabilities* (pp. 306–322). New York: Guilford.

Fuchs, L. S., Fuchs, D., Compton, D. L., Bryant, J. D., Hamlett, C. L., & Seethaler, P. M. (2007). Mathematics screening and progress monitoring at first grade: Implications for response to intervention. *Exceptional Children, 73,* 311–330.

Fuchs, L. S., Fuchs, D., Craddock, C., Hollenbeck, K. N., Hamlett, C. L., & Schatschneider, C. (2008). Effects of small-group tutoring with and without validated classroom instruction on at-risk students' math problem solving: Are two tiers of prevention better than one? *Journal of Educational Psychology, 100,* 491–509.

Fuchs, L. S., Fuchs, D., Eaton, S., & Hamlett, C. (2003). *Dynamic assessment of test accommodations.* San Antonio, TX: PsychCorp.

Fuchs, L. S., Fuchs, D., Eaton, S. B., Hamlett, C., Binkley, E., & Crouch, R. (2000). Using objective data sources to enhance teacher judgments about test accommodations. *Exceptional Children, 67,* 67–81.

Fuchs, L. S., Fuchs, D., Eaton, S. B., Hamlett, C. L., & Karns, K. M. (2000). Supplementing teacher judgments of mathematics test accommodations with objective data sources. *School Psychology Review, 29*(1), 66–85.

Fuchs, L. S., Fuchs, D., Finelli, R., Courey, S. J., & Hamlett, C. L. (2004). Expanding schema-based transfer instruction to help third graders solve real-life mathematical problems. *American Educational Research Journal, 41,* 419–445.

Fuchs, L. S., Fuchs, D., & Hamlett, C. L. (1989). Effects of instrumental use of curriculum-based measurement to enhance instructional programs. *Remedial and Special Education, 10,* 42–52.

Fuchs, L. S., Fuchs, D., & Hamlett, C. L. (1993). Technological advances linking the assessment of students' academic proficiency to instructional planning. *Journal of Special Education Technology, 12,* 49–62.

Fuchs, L. S., Fuchs, D., Hamlett, C. L., & Appleton, A. C. (2002). Explicitly teaching for transfer: Effects on the mathematical problem-solving performance of students with mathematics disabilities. *Learning Disabilities Research & Practice, 17,* 90–106.

Fuchs, L. S., Fuchs, D., Hamlett, C. L., Phillips, N. B., & Bentz, J. (1994). Classwide curriculum-based measurement: Helping general educators meet the challenge of student diversity. *Exceptional Children, 60,* 518–537.

Fuchs, L. S., Fuchs, D., Hamlett, C. L., & Stecker, P. M. (1990). The role of skills analysis in curriculum-based measurement in math. *School Psychology Review, 19,* 6–22.

Fuchs, L. S., Fuchs, D., Hosp, M. K., & Hamlett, C. L. (2003). The potential for diagnostic analysis within curriculum-based measurement. *Assessment for Effective Intervention, 28*(3–4), 13–22.

Fuchs, L. S., Fuchs, D., & Kazdan, S. (1999). Effects of peer-assisted learning strategies on high-school students with serious reading problems. *Remedial and Special Education, 20,* 309–318.

Fuchs, L. S., Fuchs, D., & Maxwell, S. (1988). The validity of informal reading comprehension measures. *Remedial and Special Education, 9*(2), 20–28.

Fuchs, L. S., Powell, S. R., Seethaler, P. M., Cirino, P. T., Fletcher, J. M., Fuchs, D., Hamlett, C. L., & Zumeta, R. O. (2009). Remediating number combination and word problem deficits among students with mathematics difficulties: A randomized control trial. *Journal of Educational Psychology, 101,* 561–576.

Fuchs, L. S., Seethaler, P. M., Powell, S. R., Fuchs, D., Hamlett, C. L., & Fletcher, J. M. (2008). Effects of preventative tutoring on the mathematical problem solving of third-grade students with math and reading difficulties. *Exceptional Children, 74,* 155–173.

Fuchs, L. S., Tindal, G., & Deno, S. L. (1984). Methodological issues in curriculum-based reading assessment. *Diagnostique, 9,* 191–207.

Fukkink, R. G., & deGlopper, K. (1998). Effects of instruction in deriving word meaning from context: A meta-analysis. *Review of Educational Research, 68,* 450–469.

Fulk, B. M., Brigham, F. J., & Lohman, D. (1998). Motivation and self-regulation: A comparison of students with learning and behavior problems. *Remedial & Special Education, 19,* 300–309.

Furney, K. S., & Salembier, G. (2000). Rhetoric and reality: A review of the literature on parent and student participation in the IEP and transition planning process. In D. R. Johnson & E. J. Emanuel (Eds.), *Issues influencing the future of transition programs* and services in the United States (pp. 111–126). Minneapolis: National Transition Network, Institute on Community Integration.

Fuson, K. C., & Willis, G. B. (1989). Second graders' use of schematic drawings in solving addition and subtraction word problems. *Journal of Educational Psychology, 81,* 514–520.

Gable, R. A., Hester, P. H., Rock, M. L., & Hughes, K. G. (2009). Back to basics: Rules, praise, ignoring, and reprimands revisited. *Intervention in School and Clinic, 44,* 195–205.

Gajria, M., Jitendra, A. K., Sood, S., & Sacks, S. (2007). Comprehension of expository text in students with LD: A research synthesis. *Journal of Learning Disabilities, 40,* 210–225.

Galagan, J. E. (1985). Psychoeducational testing: Turn out the lights, the party's over. *Exceptional Children, 52,* 288–299.

Gallagher, J., & Desimone, L. (1995). Lessons learned from implementation of the IEP: Applications to the IFSP. *Topics in Early Childhood Education, 15*(3), 353–378.

Gallagher, W. (1993). *The power of place: How our surroundings shape our thoughts, emotions, and actions.* New York: Poseidon Press.

Gallimore, R., & Tharp, R. (1990). Teaching mind in society. In L.C. Moll (Ed.), *Vygotsky and education* (pp. 175–205). New York: Cambridge Press.

Gambrell, L.B., & Jawitz, P. B. (1993). Mental imagery, text illustrations, and children's story comprehension and recall. *Reading Research Quarterly, 28,* 264–276.

Gándara, P., Maxwell-Jolly, J., & Driscoll, A. (2005). *Listening to teachers of English language learners: A survey of California's teachers' challenges, experiences, and professional development needs.* Santa Barbara, CA: UC Linguistic Minority Research Institute.

Ganger, J., & Brent, M. R. (2004). Reexamining the vocabulary spurt. *Developmental Psychology, 40,* 621–632.

Gansle, K. A., Gilbertson, D. N., & VanDerHeyden, A. M. (2006). Elementary school teachers' perceptions of curriculum-based measures of written expression. *Practical Assessment, Research & Evaluation, 11,* 1–17.

Gansle, K. A., & Noell, G. H. (2007). The fundamental role of intervention implementation in assessing resistance to intervention. In S. Jimerson, M. K. Burns, & A. M. VanDerHeyden (Eds.), *Handbook of response to intervention: The science and practice of assessment and intervention* (pp. 244–254). New York: Springer.

Gansle, K. A., Noell, G. H., VanDer Heyden, A. M., Naquin, G. M., & Slider, N. J. (2002). Moving beyond total words written: The reliability, criterion validity, and time cost of alternative measure for curriculum-based measurement in writing. *School Psychology Review, 31*(4), 477–497.

Ganz, J. B. (2008). Self-monitoring across age and ability levels: Teaching students to implement their own positive behavioral interventions. *Preventing School Failure, 53,* 39–48.

Ganz, J. B., & Sigafoos, J. (2005). Self-monitoring: Are young adults with MR and autism able to utilize cognitive strategies independently? *Education and Training in Developmental Disabilities, 40,* 24–33.

Garcia, T. (2007). Facilitating the reading process. *Teaching Exceptional Children, 39,* 12–17.

Gardill, M. C., & Jitendra, A. K. (1999). Advanced story-map instruction: Effects on the reading comprehension of students with learning disabilities. *The Journal of Special Education, 33,* 2–17.

Garrett, J., Heller, K., Fowler, L., Alberto, P., Fredrick, L., & O'Rourke, C. (2011). Using speech recognition software to increase writing fluency for individuals with physical disabilities. *Journal of Special Education Technology, 26*(1), 25–41.

Gast, D. L. (2010). *Single subject research in behavioral sciences.* New York: Routledge.

Gately, S., & Gately, F., Jr. (2001). Understanding co-teaching components. *Teaching Exceptional Children, 33,* 40–47.

Gaule, K., Nietupski, J., & Certo, N. (1985). Teaching supermarket shopping skills using an adaptive shopping list. *Education and Training of the Mentally Retarded, 20,* 53–59.

Gay, G. (2000). *Culturally responsive teaching: Theory, research, and practice.* New York: Teachers College Press.

Geary, D. C. (1990). A componential analysis of an early learning deficit in mathematics. *Journal of Exceptional Child Psychology, 33,* 386–404.

Geary, D. (1994). *Children's mathematical development.* Washington, DC: American Psychological Association.

Gee, J. P. (1996). *Social linguistics and literacies: Ideology in discourses.* London/Bristol, PA: Taylor & Francis.

Gee, J. P. (2000). The limits of reframing: A response to Professor Snow. *Journal of Reading Behavior, 32,* 121–128.

Geenan, S., Powers, L. E., & Lopez-Vasquez, A. (2001). Multicultural aspects of parent involvement in transition planning. *Exceptional Children, 67,* 265–282.

Geffre et al., v. Leola School District 44-2 CIV 06-1047 (U.S. Dist. LEXIS 88278 2009).

Geller, B., Reising, D., Leonard, H. L., Riddle, M. A., & Walsh, B. T. (1999). Critical review of tricyclic antidepressant use in children and adolescents. *Journal of the American Academy of Child and Adolescent Psychiatry, 38,* 513–516.

Genesee, F., Lindholm-Leary, K., Saunders, W., & Christian, D. (2005). English language learners in U.S. schools: An overview of research findings. *Journal of Education for Students Placed at Risk, 10,* 363–385.

Gerber, M. M. (2005). Teachers are still the test. Limitations of response to instruction strategies for identifying children with learning disabilities. *Journal of Learning Disabilities, 38,* 516–524.

Gerber, M. M., Jimenez, T., Leafstedt, J., Villaruz, J., Richards, C., & English, J. (2004). English reading effects of small-group intensive intervention in Spanish for K-1 English learners. *Learning Disabilities Research & Practice, 19,* 239–251.

Gerber, M. M., & Semmel, M. I. (1984). Teacher as imperfect test: Reconceptualizing the referral process. *Educational Psychologist, 19,* 137–148.

Gerber, P. L., Banbury, M. M., & Miller, J. H. (1986). Special educators' perceptions of parental participation in the Individual Education Plan process. *Psychology in the Schools, 23,* 158–163.

Gersten, R., Baker, S. K., Shanahan, T., Linan-Thompson, S., Collins, P., & Scarcella, R. (2007). *Effective literacy and English language instruction for English learners in the elementary grades: A practical guide*. Washington, DC: National Center for Education Evaluation and Regional Assistance, Institute of Education Sciences, U.S. Department of Education.

Gersten, R., Beckmann, S., Clarke, B., Foegen, A., Marsh, L., Star, J. R., & Witzel, B. (2009a). *Assisting students struggling with mathematics: Response to intervention (RtI) for elementary and middle schools*. IES Practice Guide. National Center for Education Evaluation and Regional Assistance. Washington, DC: U.S. Department of Education.

Gersten, R., Beckmann, S., Clarke, B., Foegen, A., Marsh, L., Star, J. R., & Witzel, B. (2009b). *Assisting students struggling with mathematics: Response to Intervention (RtI) for elementary and middle schools* (NCEE 2009-4060). Washington, DC: National Center for Education Evaluation and Regional Assistance, Institute of Education Sciences, U.S. Department of Education. Retrieved from http://ies.ed.gov/ncee/wwc/publications/practiceguides/

Gersten, R., Chard, D., & Baker, S. (2000). Factors enhancing sustained use of research-based instructional practices. *Journal of Learning Disabilities, 33*, 445–457.

Gersten, R., Chard, D., Jayanthi, M., Baker, S., Morphy, P., & Flojo, J. (2009). Mathematics instruction for students with learning disabilities: A meta-analysis of instructional components. *Review of Educational Research, 79*, 1202–1242.

Gersten, R., Compton, D., Connor, C. M., Dimino, J., Santoro, L., Linan-Thompson, S., & Tilly, W. D. (2008). *Assisting students struggling with reading: Response to Intervention and multi-tier intervention for reading in the primary grades. A practice guide*. (NCEE 2009-4045). Washington, DC: National Center for Education Evaluation and Regional Assistance, Institute of Education Sciences, U.S. Department of Education. Retrieved from http://ies.ed.gov/ncee/wwc/publications/practiceguides/

Gersten, R., Fuchs, L. S., Compton, D. L., Coyne, M. D., Greenwood, C. R., & Innocenti, K. S. (2005). Quality indicators for group experimental and quasi-experimental research in special education. *Exceptional Children, 71*, 149–164.

Gersten, R., Fuchs, L. S., Williams, J. P., & Baker, S. (2001). Teaching reading comprehension strategies to students with learning disabilities: A review of research. *Review of Educational Research, 71*, 279–320.

Gersten, R., Vaughn, S., & Brengelman, S. U. (1996). Grading and academic feedback for special education students and students with learning difficulties. In T. R. Guskey (Ed.), *Communicating student learning: ASCD yearbook, 1996* (pp. 47–57). Alexandria, VA: Association for Supervision and Curriculum Development.

Giangreco, M. F., Cloninger, C. J., Dennis, R. E., & Edelman, S. W. (1993). National expert validation of COACH: Congruence with exemplary practice and suggestions for improvement. *Journal of the Association for Persons with Severe Handicaps, 18*, 109–120.

Giangreco, M. F., Cloninger, C. J., & Iverson, V. S. (2011). *Choosing outcomes and accommodations for children (COACH): A guide to educational planning for students with disabilities* (3rd ed.). Baltimore: Brookes.

Giangreco, M. F., Cloninger, C., Mueller, P., Yuan, S., & Ashworth, S. (1991). Perspectives of parents whose children have dual sensory impairments. *Journal of the Association for Persons with Severe Handicaps, 16*, 14–24.

Giangreco, M. F., Dennis, R., Edelman, S., & Cloninger, C. (1994). Dressing your IEPs for the general education climate: Analysis of IEP goals and objectives for students with multiple disabilities. *Remedial and Special Education, 15*, 288–296.

Giangreco, M. F., Edelman, S., Dennis, R., & Cloninger, C. J. (1995). Use and impact of COACH with students who are deaf-blind. *Journal of the Association for Persons with Severe Handicaps, 20*, 121–135.

Giangreco, M. F., Edelman, S.W, Nelson, C., Young, M. R., & Kiefer-O'Donnell, R. (1999). Improving support service decision-making: Consumer feedback regarding updates to VISTA. *International Journal of Disability, Development and Education, 46*, 463–473.

Giangreco, M. F., Whiteford, T., Whiteford, L., & Doyle, M. B. (1998). Planning for Andrew: A case study of COACH and VISTA use in an inclusive early childhood program. *International Journal of Disability, Development and Education, 45*, 375–396.

Gilberts, G. H., Agran, M., Hughes, C., & Wehmeyer, M. (2001). The effects of peer delivered self-monitoring strategies on the participation of students with severe disabilities in general education classrooms. *Journal of the Association for Persons with Severe Handicaps, 26*, 25–36.

Gillam, R. B., & Pearson, N. A. (2004). *Test of narrative language*. Austin, TX: Pro-Ed.

Gillam, S., Gillam, R., Petersen, D., & Bingham, C. (2008). *Narrative language intervention program: Promoting oral language development*. Technical session presented at The Annual Convention of the American Speech Language and Hearing Association, Chicago, IL.

Gillham, J. E., Shatte, A. J., & Freres, D. R. (2000). Preventing depression: A review of cognitive-behavioral and family interventions. *Applied & Preventive Psychology, 9*, 63–88.

Gilliam, W. S., & Shahar, G. (2006). Prekindergarten expulsion and suspension: Rates and predictors in one state. *Infants and Young Children, 19*, 228–245.

Girolametto, L., Pearce, P.S., & Weitzman, E. (1996). Interactive focused stimulation for toddlers with expressive vocabulary delays. *Journal of Speech and Hearing Research, 39*, 1275.

Girolametto, L., & Weitzman, E. (2002). Responsiveness of child care providers in interactions with toddlers and preschoolers. *Language, Speech, and Hearing Services in Schools, 33*, 268–281.

Gitlin, A., Buendía, E., Crosland, K., & Doumbia, F. (2003). The production of margin and center: Welcoming–unwelcoming of immigrant students. *American Educational Research Journal, 40*, 91–122.

Gittelman-Klein, R., & Klein, D. F. (1971). Controlled impramine treatment of school phobia. *Archives of General Psychiatry, 25*, 204–207.

Giumento, A. (1990). *The effectiveness of two intervention procedures on the acquisition and generalization of object labels by young children who are at-risk or have developmental delays.* Unpublished doctoral dissertation, University of Oregon, Eugene.

Glover, T. A., & Albers, C. A. (2007). Considerations for evaluating universal screening assessments. *Journal of School Psychology, 45,* 117–135.

Goerss, B. L., Beck, I. L., & McKeown, M. G. (1999). Increasing remedial students' ability to derive word meaning from context. *Reading Psychology, 20,* 151–175.

Goldenberg, C., Rueda, R., & August, D. (2006). Synthesis: Sociocultural contexts and literacy development. In D. August & T. Shanahan (Eds.), *Report of the national literacy panel on language minority youth and children* (pp. 249–267). Mahwah, NJ: Erlbaum.

Goldman, R. W. (1994). A free appropriate education in the least restrictive environment: Promises made, promises broken by the Individuals with Disabilities Education Act. *Dayton Law Review, 20,* 243–291.

Goldman, S., & Varnhagen, C. K. (1986). Memory for embedded and sequential story structures. *Journal of Memory and Language, 25,* 401–418.

Goldstein, H., & Ferrell, D. R. (1987). Augmenting communicative interaction between handicapped and nonhandicapped preschool children. *Journal of Speech and Hearing Disorders, 52,* 200–211.

Goldstein, S., Strickland, B., Tumbull, A. P., & Curry, L. (1980). An observational analysis of the IEP conference. *Exceptional Children, 46,* 278–286.

Golly, A., Sprague, J., Walker, H. M., Beard, K., & Gorham, G. (2000). The First Step to Success program: An analysis of outcomes with identical twins across multiple baselines. *Behavioral Disorders, 25,* 170–182.

Golly, A. M., Stiller, B., & Walker, H. M. (1998). First Step to Success: Replication and social validation of an early intervention program. *Journal of Emotional and Behavioral Disorders, 6,* 243–250.

Good, R. H., Bank, N., & Watson, J. M. (Eds.). (2003). *Indicadores dinamicos del exito en la lectura* [Dynamic indicators of basic early literacy skills].

Eugene, OR: Institute for the Development of Educational Achievement.

Good, R. H., Gruba, J., & Kaminski. R. A. (2001). Best practices in using Dynamic Indicators of Basic Early Literacy Skills (DIBELS) in an outcomes-driven model. In A. Thomas & J. Grimes (Eds.), *Best practices in school psychology* (Vol. 4, pp. 679–700). Washington, DC: National Association of School Psychologists.

Good, R. H., & Kaminski, R. A. (2002, revised July 2, 2003). *Dynamic Indicators of Basic Literacy Skills^{TM} 6th Edition DIBELS^{TM}.* Eugene, OR: Institute for the Development of Educational Achievement. Retrieved from http://dibels.uoregon.edu/Dibels

Good, R. H., & Kaminski, R. A. (Eds.). (2007). *Dynamic indicators of basic early literacy skills* (6th ed.). Eugene, OR: Institute for the Development of Educational Achievement.

Good, R. H., III, Simmons, D. C., & Kame'enui, E. J. (2001). The importance and decision-making utility of a continuum of fluency-based indicators of foundational reading skills for third-grade high-stakes outcomes. *Scientific Studies of Reading, 5,* 257–289.

Goodman, K. S. (1965). A linguistic study of cues and miscues in reading. *Elementary English, 42,* 639–643.

Goodman, K. S. (1967). Reading: A psycholinguistic guessing game. *Journal of the Reading Specialist, 6,* 126–135.

Goodman, K. S. (1969). Analysis of oral reading miscues: Applied psycholinguistics. *Reading Research Quarterly, 5,* 9–30.

Goodman, K. S., & Burke, C. L. (1973). *Theoretically based studies of patterns of miscues in oral reading performance.* Washington, DC: U.S. Department of Health, Education and Welfare. (ERIC Document Reproduction Service No. ED 079 708)

Goodman, R. (1997). The Strengths and Difficulties Questionnaire: A research note. *Journal of Child Psychology and Psychiatry, 38,* 581–586.

Goodman, R. (2001). Psychometric properties of the Strengths and Difficulties Questionnaire (SDQ). *Journal of the American Academy of Child and Adolescent Psychiatry, 40,* 1337–1345.

Goodman, R., Meltzer, H., & Bailey, V. (1998). The Strengths and Difficulties Questionnaire: A pilot study on

the validity of the self-report version. *European Child and Adolescent Psychiatry, 7,* 125–130.

Goodman, Y., Watson, D., & Burke, C. (2005). *Reading miscue inventory.* Katonah, NY: Owen.

Gordon, C. J., & Pearson, P. D. (1983). *The effects of instruction in metacomprehension and inferencing on children's comprehension abilities* (Tech. Rep. No. 277). Urbana, IL: University of Illinois, Center for the Study of Reading.

Gordon, S. (2006). Making sense of the inclusion debate under IDEA. *Brigham Young University Education and Law Journal, 189*(1), 176–213.

Gottfredson, D. C., Gottfredson, G. D., & Hybl, L. G. (1993). Managing adolescent behavior: A multiyear, multischool study. *American Educational Research Journal, 30,* 179–215.

Gough, P. B. (1996). How children learn to read and why they fail. *Annals of Dyslexia, 46,* 3–20.

Graae, F., Milner, J., Rizzotto, L., & Klein, R. G. (1994). Clonazepam in childhood anxiety disorders. *Journal of the American Academy of Child and Adolescent Psychiatry, 33,* 372–376.

Graden, J. L., Stollar, S. A., & Poth, R. L. (2007). The Ohio integrated systems model: Overview and lessons learned. In S. Jimerson, M. K. Burns, & A. M. VanDerHeyden (Eds.), *Handbook of response to intervention: The science and practice of assessment and intervention* (pp. 288–299). New York: Springer.

Graesser, A. C., Baggett, W., & Williams, K. (1996). Question-driven explanatory reasoning. *Applied Cognitive Psychology, 10*(7), 17–31. doi:10.1002/(SICI)1099-0720 (199611)10:7<17::AID-ACP435> 3.0.CO;2-7

Graesser, A. C., McNamara, D. S., & VanLehn, K. (2005). Scaffolding deep comprehension strategies through point&query, autotutor, and iSTART. *Educational Psychologist, 40,* 225–234. doi:10.1207/s15326985ep4004_4

Graesser, A. C., Person, N. K., & Hu, X. (2002). Improving comprehension through discourse processing. In D. F. Halpern & M. D. Hakel (Eds.), *Applying the science of learning to university teaching and beyond: New directions for teaching and learning* (pp. 33–44). San Francisco, CA: Wiley Periodicals.

Graesser, A. C., Singer, M., & Trabasso, T. (1994). Constructing inferences during narrative text comprehension. *Psychological Review, 101,* 371–395.

Graff, R. B., & Green, G. (2004). Two methods for teaching simple visual discriminations to learners with severe disabilities. *Research in Developmental Disabilities, 25,* 295–307.

Graham, S. (1990). The role of production factors in learning disabled students' compositions. *Journal of Educational Psychology, 82,* 781–791.

Graham, S. (1999). Handwriting and spelling instruction for students with learning disabilities: A review. *Learning Disabilities Quarterly, 22,* 78–98.

Graham, S. (2006). Strategy instruction and the teaching of writing: A meta-analysis. In C. MacArthur, S. Graham, & J. Fitzgerald (Eds.), *Handbook of writing research* (pp. 187–207). New York: Guilford.

Graham, S., & Harris, K. R. (2003). Students with learning disabilities and the process of writing: A meta-analysis of SRSD studies. In H. L. Swanson, K. R. Harris, & S. Graham (Eds.), *Handbook of learning disabilities* (pp. 323–344). New York: Guilford Press.

Graham, S., & Harris, K. R. (2006). Preventing writing difficulties: Providing additional handwriting and spelling instruction to at-risk children in first grade. *Teaching Exceptional Children, 39,* 64–66.

Graham, S., & Harris, K. R. (2009). Almost 30 years of writing research: Making sense of it all with the *Wrath of Khan*. *Learning Disabilities Research & Practice, 24,* 58–68.

Graham, S., Harris, K. R., & Fink, B. (2000). Is handwriting causally related to learning to write? Treatment of handwriting problems in beginning writers. *Journal of Educational Psychology, 92,* 620–633.

Graham, S., Harris, K. R., & Fink-Chorzempa, B. (2002). Contributions of spelling instruction to the spelling, writing, and reading of poor spellers. *Journal of Educational Psychology, 94,* 669–686.

Graham, S., Harris, K. R., & Loynachan, C. (1996). The directed spelling thinking activity: Applications with high frequency words. *Learning Disabilities Research and Practice, 11,* 34–40.

Graham, S., Harris, K. R., & Mason, L. (2005). Improving the writing performance, knowledge, and motivation of struggling young writers: The effects of self-regulated strategy development. *Contemporary Educational Psychology, 30,* 207–241.

Graham, S., Harris, K. R., Mason, L. H., Fink-Chorzempa, B., Moran, S., & Saddler, B. How do primary grade teachers teach handwriting? (2008). *Reading and Writing: An Interdisciplinary Journal, 21,* 49–69.

Graham, S., Loynachan, C., & Harris, K. R. (1993). The basic spelling vocabulary list. *Journal of Educational Research, 86,* 363–368.

Graham, S., & MacArthur, C. (1988). Improving learning disabled students' skills at revising essays produced on a word processor: Self-instructional strategy training. *The Journal of Special Education, 22,* 133–152.

Graham, S., Morphy, P., Harris, K., Fink-Chorzempa, B., Saddler, B., Moran, S., & Mason, L. (2008). Teaching spelling in the primary grades: A national survey of instructional practices and adaptations. *American Educational Research Journal, 45,* 796–825.

Graham, S., & Perin, D. (2007). A meta-analysis of writing instruction for adolescent students. *Journal of Educational Psychology, 99,* 445–476.

Grandy, S. E., & Peck, S. M. (1997). The use of functional assessment and self-management with a first grader. *Family Behavior Therapy, 19,* 29–43.

Graves, A. W., Gersten, R., & Haager, D. (2004). Literacy instruction in multiple language first-grade classrooms: Linking student outcomes to observed instructional practice. *Learning Disabilities: Research & Practice, 19,* 262–272.

Graves, M. F. (2006). *The vocabulary book: Learning and instruction.* New York: Teachers College Press.

Gravois, T. A., & Gickling, E. (2008). Best practices in instructional assessment. In A. Thomas & J. Grimes (Eds.), *Best practices in school psychology* (Vol. 4, pp. 503–518). Bethesda, MD: National Association of School Psychologists.

Gravois, T. A., & Rosenfield, S. A. (2006). Impact of instructional consultation teams on the disproportionate referral and placement of minority students in special education. *Remedial and Special Education, 27,* 45–52.

Greene, G. (1996). Empowering culturally and linguistically diverse families in the transition planning process. *Journal for Vocational Special Needs Education, 19*(1), 26–30.

Greenspan, S. (2006). Functional concepts in mental retardation: Finding the natural essence of an artificial category. *Exceptionality, 14*(4), 205–224.

Greenwood, C. (1997). Classwide peer tutoring. *Behavior and Social Issues, 7,* 53–57.

Greenwood, C. R., & Abbott, M. (2001). The research-to-practice gap in special education. *Teacher Education and Special Education, 24,* 276–289.

Greenwood, C. R., Carta, J. J., & Hall, R. V. (1988). The use of peer-tutoring strategies in classroom management and educational instruction. *School Psychology Review, 17,* 258–275.

Greenwood, C. R., Hart, B., Walker, D., & Risley, T. (1994). The opportunity to respond and academic performance revisited: A behavioral theory of developmental retardation and its prevention. In R. Gardner, D. M. Sainato, J. O. Cooper, T. E. Heron, W. L. Heward, J. W. Eshleman, & T. A. Grossi (Eds.), *Behavior analysis in education: Focus on measurably superior instruction* (pp. 213–223). Pacific Grove, CA: Brooks/Cole.

Greenwood, C. R., Horton, B. T., & Utley, C. A. (2002). Academic engagement: Current perspectives on research and practice. *School Psychology Review, 31,* 328–349.

Gresham, F. M. (1981a). Assessment of children's social skills. *Journal of School Psychology, 19,* 120–134.

Gresham, F. M. (1981b). Social skills training with handicapped children: A review. *Review of Educational Research, 51,* 139–176.

Gresham, F. M. (1983). Social validity in the assessment of children's social skills: Establishing standards for social competency. *Journal of Psychoeducational Assessment, 1,* 297–307.

Gresham, F. M. (1985). Utility of cognitive-behavioral procedures for social skills training with children: A critical review. *Journal of Abnormal Child Psychology, 13,* 411–423.

Gresham, F. M. (1986). Conceptual issues in the assessment of social competence in children. In P. Strain, M. Guralnick, & H. Walker (Eds.), *Children's social behavior: Development, assessment, and modification* (pp. 143–180). New York: Academic Press.

Gresham, F. M. (1989). Assessment of treatment integrity in school consultation and prereferral intervention. *School Psychology Review, 18,* 37–50.

Gresham, F. M. (1995). Student Self-Concept Scale: Description and relevance to students with emotional and behavioral disorders. *Journal of Emotional & Behavioral Disorders, 3,* 19–26.

Gresham, F. M. (1997). Social competence and students with behavior disorders: Where we've been, where we are, and where we should go. *Education and Treatment of Children, 20,* 233–250.

Gresham, F. M. (1998). Social skills training: Should we raze, remodel, or rebuild? *Behavioral Disorders, 24,* 19–25.

Gresham, F. M. (2002a). Best practices in social skills training. In A. Thomas & J. Grimes (Eds.), *Best practices in school psychology* (4th ed., pp. 1029–1040). Bethesda, MD: National Association of School Psychologists.

Gresham, F. M. (2002b). Responsiveness to intervention: An alternative approach to the identification of learning disabilities. In R. Bradley & L. Danielson (Eds.), *Identification of learning disabilities: Research to practice. The LEA series on special education and disability* (pp. 467–519). Mahwah, NJ: Erlbaum.

Gresham, F. M. (2002c). Teaching social skills to high-risk children and youth: Preventive and remedial strategies. In M. Shinn, H. Walker, & G. Stoner (Eds.), *Interventions for academic and behavior problems: Preventive and remedial approaches* (2nd ed., pp. 403–432). Bethesda, MD: National Association of School Psychologists.

Gresham, F. M. (2005). Response to intervention: An alternative means of identifying students as emotionally disturbed. *Education and Treatment of Children, 28*(4), 328–344.

Gresham, F. M. (2007). Evolution of the response-to-intervention concept: Empirical foundations and recent developments. In S. R. Jimerson, M. K., Burns, & A. M. VanDerHeyden (Eds.), *Handbook of response to intervention* (pp. 10–24). New York: Springer.

Gresham, F. M., Cook, C. R., Crews, S. D., & Kern, L. (2004). Social skills training for children and youth with emotional and behavioral disorders: Validity considerations and future directions. *Behavioral Disorders, 30,* 32–46.

Gresham, F. M., & Elliot, S. N. (1984). Assessment and classification of children's social skills: A review of methods and issues. *School Psychology Review, 13,* 292–301.

Gresham, F. M., & Elliott, S. N. (1990). *Social Skills Rating System.* Bloomington, MN: Pearson Assessments.

Gresham, F. M., & Elliott, S. N. (2008). *Social skills improvement system-rating scales.* Bloomington, MN: Pearson Assessments.

Gresham, F. M., Elliott, S. N., & Evans-Fernandez, S. (1992). *Student Self-Concept Scale.* Circle Pine, MN: American Guidance Service.

Gresham, F. M., & Gansle, K. A. (1992). Misguided assumptions of DSM-III-R: Implications for school psychological practice. *School Psychology Quarterly, 7,* 79–95.

Gresham, F. M., Gansle, K. A., & Noell, G. H. (1993). Treatment integrity in applied behavior analysis with children. *Journal of Applied Behavior Analysis, 26,* 257–263.

Gresham, F. M., & Kern, L. (2004). Internalizing behavior problems in children and adolescents. In R. Rutherford, M. M. Quinn, & S. R. Mather (Eds.), *Handbook of research in emotional and behavioral disorders* (pp. 262–281). New York: Guilford Press.

Gresham, F. M., & Lopez, M. F. (1996). Social validation: A unifying concept for school-based consultation research and practice. *School Psychology Quarterly, 11,* 204–227.

Gresham, F. M., Sugai, G., & Horner, R. (2001). Interpreting outcomes of social skills training for students with high-risk disabilities. *Exceptional Children, 67,* 331–344.

Gresham, F. M., Sugai, G., Horner, R., Quinn, M., & McInerney, M. (1998). *Classroom and schoolwide practices that support students' social competence: A synthesis of research.* Washington, DC: Office of Special Education Programs.

Gresham, F. M., Van, M. B., & Cook, C. R. (2006). Social skills training for teaching replacement behaviors: Remediation of acquisition deficits for at-risk children. *Behavioral Disorders, 30,* 32–46.

Grieger, T., Kauffman, J. M., & Grieger, R. M. (1976). Effects of peer reporting on cooperative play and aggression of kindergarten children. *Journal of School Psychology, 14,* 307–313.

Griffen, A. K., Wolery, M., & Schuster, J. W. (1992). Triadic instruction of chained food preparation responses: Acquisition and observational learning. *Journal of Applied Behavior Analysis, 25,* 193–204.

Grimes, J., Kurns, S., Tilly, III, W. D. (2006). Sustainability: an enduring commitment to success. *School Psychology Review, 35,* 224–243.

Grisham-Brown, J., Pretti-Frontczak, K., Hemmeter, M. L., & Ridgley, R. (2002). Teaching IEP goals and objectives in the context of classroom routines and activities. *Young Exceptional Children, 6*(1), 18–27.

Grisham-Brown, J. L., Schuster, J. W., Hemmeter, M. L., & Collins, B. C. (2000). Using embedded strategies to teach preschoolers with significant disabilities. *Journal of Behavior Education, 10,* 139–162.

Grossi, T. A. (1998). Using a self-operated auditory prompting system to improve the work performance of two employees with severe disabilities. *Journal of the Association for the Severely Handicapped, 23,* 149–154.

Gulchak, D. (2008). Using a mobile handheld computer to teach a student with an emotional and behavioral disorder to self-monitor attention. *Education and Treatment of Children, 31,* 567–581.

Gunn, B., Biglan, A., Smolkowski, K., & Ary, D. (2005). The efficacy of supplemental instruction in decoding skills for Hispanic and non-Hispanic students in early elementary school. *Journal of Special Education, 34,* 90–113.

Gunter, P. L., Hummel, J. H., & Venn, M. L. (1998). Are effective academic instructional practices used to teach students with behavior disorders? *Beyond Behavior, 9,* 5–11.

Gunter, P. L., & Sutherland, K. S. (2005). Active student responding. In G. Sugai & R. Horner (Eds.), *Encyclopedia of behavior modification and cognitive behavior therapy: Vol. 3. Educational applications* (pp. 1131–1132). Thousand Oaks, CA: Sage.

Günther, T., Holtkamp, K., Jolles, J., Herpertz-Dahlmann, B., & Konrad, K. (2004). Verbal memory and aspects of attentional control in children and adolescents with anxiety disorders or depressive disorders. *Journal of Affective Disorders, 82,* 265–269.

Guralnick, M. J. (2001). *Early childhood inclusion: Focus on change.* Baltimore: Brookes.

Guthrie, J. T., & Davis, M. H. (2003). Motivating struggling readers in middle school through an engagement model of classroom practice. *Reading & Writing Quarterly, 19*(1), 59–86.

Guthrie, J. T., & Wigfield, A. (2000). Engagement and motivation in reading. In M. Kamil, R. Barr, P. Mosenthal, & P. D. Pearson (Eds.), *Handbook of reading research* (Vol. 3, pp. 403–422). New York: Longman.

Haager, D., & Klinger, J. (2005). *Differentiating instruction in inclusive classrooms: The special educator's guide.* Upper Saddle River, NJ: Pearson Education.

Hafner, J. C., & Hafner, P. M. (2003). Quantitative analysis of the rubric as an assessment tool: An empirical study of student peer-group rating. *International Journal of Science Education, 25*(12), 1509–1528.

Hage, S. M., Romano, J. L., Conye, R. K., Kenny, M., Matthews, C., Schwartz, J. P., & Waldo, M. (2007). Best practice guidelines on prevention, practice, research, training, and social advocacy for psychologists. *Journal of Counseling Psychologists, 35,* 493–566.

Hagopian, L. P., Farrell, D. A., & Amari, A. (1996). Treating total liquid refusal with backward chaining and fading. *Journal of Applied Behavior Analysis, 29,* 573–575.

Hains, A. A. (1992). Comparison of cognitive-behavioral stress management techniques with adolescent boys. *Journal of Counseling and Development, 70,* 600–605.

Hains, A. A., & Szyjakowski, M. (1990). A cognitive stress-reduction intervention program for adolescents. *Journal of Counseling Psychology, 37,* 79–84.

Hale, J. A. (2008). *Curriculum mapping: Planning, implementing, and sustaining the process.* Thousand Oaks, CA: Corwin Press.

Hale, J. B., Naglieri, J. A., Kaufman, A. S., & Kavale, K. A. (2004). Specific learning disability classification in the new Individuals with Disabilities Education Act: The danger of good ideas. *The School Psychologist, 58*(1), 6–13.

Hall, T. E., Hughes, C. A., & Filbert, M. (2000). Computer assisted instruction in reading for students with learning disabilities: A research synthesis. *Education and Treatment of Children, 23,* 173–193.

Hall, T., & Mengel, M. (2002). *Curriculum-based evaluations.* Wakefield, MA: National Center on Accessing the General Curriculum. Retrieved from http://www.cast.org/publications/ncac/ncac_curriculumbe.html

Hallahan, D. P., & Sapona, R. (1983). Self-monitoring of attention within learning disabled children: Past research and current issues. *Journal of Learning Disabilities, 16,* 616–620.

Halle, J. W., Baer, D. M., & Spradlin, J. E. (1981). Teachers' generalized use of delay as a stimulus control procedure to increase language use in handicapped children. *Journal of Applied Behavior Analysis, 14,* 387–400.

Halle, J. W., Marshall, A. M., & Spradlin, J. E. (1979). Time delay: A technique to increase language use and facilitate generalization in retarded children. *Journal of Applied Behavior Analysis, 12,* 431–440.

Hallenbeck, B. A., & Kauffman, J. M. (1995). How does observational learning affect the behavior of students with emotional or behavioral disorders? A review of research. *Journal of Special Education, 29,* 45–71.

Halpern, A. S. (1992). Transition: Old wine in new bottles. *Exceptional Children, 58,* 202–211.

Halpern, A. S., Herr, C. M., Wolf, N. K., Doren, B., Johnson, M. D., & Lawson, J. D. (1997). *Next S.T.E.P.: Student transition and educational planning.* Austin, TX: Pro-Ed.

Hammen, C., & Rudolph, R. D. (1996). Childhood depression. In E. J. Mash & R. A. Barkley (Eds.), *Child psychopathology* (pp. 153–195). New York: Guilford Press.

Hammer, M. R. (2004). Using the self-advocacy strategy to increase student participation in IEP conferences. *Intervention in School and Clinic, 39,* 295–300.

Hancock, T. B., & Kaiser, A. P. (1996). Siblings' use of milieu teaching at home. *Topics in Early Childhood Special Education, 16,* 168–190.

Hancock, T. B., & Kaiser, A. P. (2002). The effects of trainer-implemented enhanced milieu teaching on the social communication of children with autism. *Topics in Early Childhood Special Education, 22,* 39–54.

Hancock, T. B., & Kaiser, A. P. (2006). Enhanced milieu teaching. In R. J. McCauley & M. C. Fey (Eds.), *Treatment of language disorders in children.* Baltimore, MD: Paul H. Brookes.

Hannan, C. K. (2006). Review of research: Neuroscience and the impact of brain plasticity on braille reading. *Journal of Visual Impairment and Blindness, 100,* 397–413.

Hansford, D., & Adlington, R. (2009). Digital spaces and young people's online authoring: Challenges for teachers. *Australian Journal of Language & Literacy, 32*(1), 55–68.

Harchik, A. E., & Putzier, V. S. (1990). The use of high-probability requests to increase compliance with instructions to take medication. *Journal of the Association for Persons with Severe Handicaps (JASH), 15*(1), 40-43.

Hargrave, A., & Senechal, M. (2000). A book reading intervention with preschool children who have limited vocabularies: The benefits of regular reading and dialogic reading. *Early Childhood Research Quarterly, 15,* 75–90.

Harper, C. B., Symon, J. B. G., & Frea, W. D. (2008). Recess is time-in: Using peers to improve social skills of children with autism. *Journal of Autism and Developmental Disorders, 38,* 815–826.

Harrington, R., Whittaker, J., & Shoebridge, P. (1998). Psychological treatment of depression in children and adolescents: A review of treatment research. *British Journal of Psychiatry, 173,* 291–298.

Harris, A., & Jacobson, M. (1980). A comparison of the Fry, Spache, and Harris-Jacobson Readability formulas for primary grades. *The Reading Teacher, 33*(8), 920–924.

Harris, C. A., Miller, S. P., & Mercer, C. D. (1995). Teaching initial multiplication skills to students with disabilities in general education classrooms. *Learning Disabilities Research & Practice, 10,* 180–195.

Harris, K. R. (1982). Cognitive-behavior modification: Applications with exceptional students. *Focus on Exceptional Children, 15,* 1–16.

Harris, K. R., & Graham, S. (1999). Programmatic intervention research: Illustrations from the evolution of self-regulated strategy development. *Learning Disability Quarterly, 22,* 251–262.

Harris, K. R., & Graham, S. (2007). Marconi invented the television so people who couldn't afford radio could hear the news: The research on teaching powerful composition strategies we have, and the research we need. In M. Pressley (Ed.), *Shaping literacy achievement: Research we have, research we need* (pp. 175–198). New York: Guilford.

Harris, K. R., & Graham, S. (2009). Self-regulated strategy development in writing: Premises, evolution, and the future. *British Journal of Educational Psychology Monograph Series II, Number 6—Teaching and Learning Writing, 1*(1), 113–135.

Harris, K. R., Graham, S., Brindle, M., & Sandmel, K. (2009). Metacognition and children's writing. In D. Hacker, J. Dunlosky, & A. Graesser (Eds.), *Handbook of metacognition in education* (pp. 131–153). Mahwah, NJ: Erlbaum.

Harris, K. R., Graham. S., & Mason, L. (2003). Self-regulated strategy development in the classroom: Part of a balanced approach to writing instruction for students with disabilities. *Focus on Exceptional Children, 35,* 1–16.

Harris, K. R., Graham, S., & Mason, L. (2006). Improving the writing, knowledge, and motivation of struggling young writers: Effects of Self-Regulated Strategy Development with and without peer support. *American Educational Research Journal, 43,* 295–340.

Harris, K. R., Graham, S., Mason, L. H., & Friedlander, B. (2008). *Powerful writing strategies for all students.* Baltimore: Brookes.

Harris, L. (1991). *The Metropolitan Life Survey of the American Teacher, 1991, The first year: New teachers' expectations and ideals.* New York: Metropolitan Life Insurance Company.

Harris, T., & Hodges, R. (1985). *The literacy dictionary.* Newark, DE: International Reading Association.

Harris-Murri, N., King, K., & Rostenberg, D. (2006). Reducing disproportionate minority representation in special education programs for students with emotional disturbances: Toward a culturally responsive response to intervention model. *Education and Treatment of Children, 29*(4), 779–799.

Harrison, P., & Oakland, T. (2003). *Adaptive Behavior Assessment System,* 2nd edition. San Antonio, TX: The Psychological Corporation.

Harrower, J. D., Fox, L., Dunlap, G., & Kincaid, D. (2000). Functional assessment and comprehensive early intervention. *Exceptionality, 8,* 189–204.

Harry, B. (1992a). An ethnographic study of cross-cultural communication with Puerto Rican-American families in the special education system. *American Educational Research Journal, 29,* 471–494.

Harry, B. (1992b). Making sense of disability: Low-income, Puerto Rican parents' theory of the problem. *Exceptional Children, 59,* 27–40.

Harry, B. (2008). Collaboration with culturally and linguistically diverse families: Ideal vs. reality. *Exceptional Children, 74,* 372–388.

Harry, B., Allen, N., & McLaughlin, M. (1995). Communication versus compliance: African-American parents' involvement in special education. *Exceptional Children, 61,* 364–377.

Harry, B., Klingner, J. K., Sturges, K. M., & Moore, R. F. (2002). Of rocks and soft places: Using qualitative methods to investigate disproportionality. In D. J. Losen & G. Orfield (Eds.), *Racial inequity in special education* (pp. 71–92). Cambridge, MA: Civil Rights Project at Harvard University, Harvard Education Press.

Hart, B., & Risley, T. R. (1968). Establishing use of descriptive adjectives in the spontaneous speech of disadvantaged preschool children. *Journal of Applied Behavior Analysis, 1,* 109–120.

Hart, B., & Risley, T. R. (1974). Using preschool materials to modify the language of disadvantaged children. *Journal of Applied Behavior Analysis, 7,* 243–256.

Hart, B., & Risley, T. R. (1975). Incidental teaching of language in the preschool. *Journal of Applied Behavior Analysis, 8,* 411–420.

Hart, B., & Risley, T. R. (1980). In vivo language interventions: Unanticipated general effects. *Journal of Applied Behavior Analysis, 13,* 407–432.

Hart, B., & Risley, T. R. (1995). *Meaningful differences in the everyday experience of young American children.* Baltimore: Brookes.

Hart, B., & Rogers-Warren, A. K. (1978). A milieu approach to teaching language. In R. L. Schiefelbusch (Ed.), *Language intervention strategies* (pp. 193–235). Baltimore: University Park Press.

Hasazi, S., Furney, K. S., & DeStefano, L. (1999). Implementing the IDEA transition mandates. *Exceptional Children, 65,* 555–566.

Hasbrouck, J. E., Ihnot, C., & Rogers, G. (1999). Read Naturally: A strategy to increase oral reading fluency. *Reading Research and Instruction, 39*(1), 27–37.

Hasbrouck, J., & Tindal, G. (2005). *Oral reading fluency: 90 years of measurement* (Tech. Rep.No. 33). Eugene, OR: University of Oregon, College of Education, Behavioral Research and Teaching.

Hasselbring, T. S., & Crossland, C. L. (1982). Application of microcomputer technology to spelling assessment of learning disabled students. *Learning Disability Quarterly, 5,* 80–82.

Hatton, D. D., & Erickson, K. (2005, November). *Highly literate individuals with visual impairments: Practical applications from research.* Paper presented at the Seventh Biennial Getting in Touch with Literacy Conference, Denver, CO.

Hawken, L. S., MacLeod, S. K., & Rawlings, L. (2007). Effects of the behavior education program (BEP) on office discipline referrals of elementary school students. *Journal of Positive Behavior Interventions, 9,* 94–102.

Hawkins, R. (1991). Is social validity what we are interested in? Argument for a functional approach. *Journal of Applied Behavior Analysis, 24,* 205–213.

Haydon, T., Mancil, G. R., & Van Loan, C. (2009). Using opportunities to respond in a general education classroom: A case study. *Education and Treatment of Children, 32,* 267–278.

Haydon, T., & Scott, T. M. (2008). Using common sense in common settings: Active supervision and pre-correction in the morning gym. *Intervention in School and Clinic, 43,* 283–290.

Haynes, R. S., Derby, K. M., McLaughlin, T. F., & Weber, K. P. (2002). A comparison of forced-choice preferences assessment procedures using a parent and novel therapist. *Journal of Positive Behavior Interventions, 4,* 176–181.

Hayward, D., & Schnieder, P. (2000). Effectiveness of teaching story grammar knowledge to pre-school children with language impairment. An exploratory study. *Child Language Teaching and Therapy, 30,* 255–284.

Heal, L. W., Borthwick-Duffy, S. A., & Saunders, R. R. (1996). Assessment of quality of life. In Mulick & Anton (Eds.). *Manual of diagnosis and professional practice in mental retardation* (pp. 199–209). Washington, DC: American Psychological Association.

Heflinger, C. R., Cook, V. J., & Thackrey, M. (1987). Identification of mental retardation by the System of Multicultural Pluralistic Assessement: Nondiscriminatory or nonexistent? *Journal of School Psychology, 25,* 177–183.

Hegarty, M., & Kozhevnikov, M. (1999). Types of visual-spatial representations and mathematical problem solving. *Journal of Educational Psychology, 91,* 684–689.

Hegarty, M., Mayer, R. E., & Monk, C. A. (1995). Comprehension of arithmetic word problems: A comparison of successful and unsuccessful problem solvers. *Journal of Educational Psychology, 87,* 18–32.

Heller, K. A., Holtzman, W. H., & Messick, S. (1982). *Placing children in special education: Theories and recommendations.* Washington, DC: National Academy Press.

Heller, K. W. (2009a). Learning and behavioral characteristics of students with physical, health, or multiple disabilities. In K. W. Heller, P. E. Forney, P. A. Alberto, S. J. Best, & M. N. Swartzman (Eds.), *Understanding physical, health, and multiple disabilities* (2nd ed., pp. 18–34). Upper Saddle River, NJ: Pearson Education.

Heller, K. W. (2009b). Understanding disabilities and effective teaming. In K. W. Heller, P. E. Forney, P. Alberto, S. J. Best, & M. N. Schwartzman (Eds.), *Understanding physical, health, and multiple disabilities* (2nd ed., pp. 3–17). Upper Saddle River, NJ: Pearson Education.

Heller, K. W. (2010). Writing instruction and adaptations. In S. Best, K. W. Heller, & J. Bigge (Eds.), *Teaching individuals with physical, health, or multiple disabilities* (6th ed., pp. 407–431). Upper Saddle River, NJ: Merrill/Pearson Education.

Heller, K. W., & Alberto, P. A. (2010). Reading instruction and adaptations. In S. Best, K.W. Heller, & J. Bigge (Eds.), *Teaching individuals with physical, health, or multiple disabilities* (6th ed.) (pp. 375–406). Upper Saddle River, NJ: Pearson.

Heller, K. W., & Coleman-Martin, M. B. (2007). Strategies for promoting literacy for students who have physical disabilities. *Communication Disorders Quarterly, 28,* 69–72.

Heller, K. W., Coleman-Martin, M. B., & Swinehart-Jones, D. (2006). *Strategies for promoting literacy with students who have physical disabilities* (3rd ed.). Atlanta, GA: Georgia Bureau for Students with Physical and Health Impairments.

Heller, K. W., Forney, P. E., Alberto, P. A., Best, S. J., & Schwartzman, M. N. (2009). *Understanding physical, health, and multiple disabilities* (2nd ed.). Upper Saddle River, NJ: Pearson.

Heller, K. W., Fredrick, L. D., & Diggs, C. A. (1999). Teaching reading to students with severe speech and physical impairments using the nonverbal reading approach. *Physical Disabilities: Education and Related Services, 18,* 3–34.

Heller, K. W., Fredrick, L. D., Dykes, M. K., Best, S. J., & Cohen, E. T. (1999). A national perspective of competencies for teachers of individuals with physical and health disabilities. *Exceptional Children, 65,* 219–234.

Heller, K. W., Fredrick, L. D., Tumlin, J., & Brineman, D. G. (2002). Teaching decoding for generalization using the Nonverbal Reading Approach. *Journal of Developmental and Physcial Disabilities, 14,* 19–35.

Heller, K. W., Mezei, P., & Schwartzman, M. N. (2009). Muscular dystrophies. In K. W. Heller, P. E. Forney, P. Alberto, S. J. Best, & M. N. Schwartzman (Eds.), *Understanding physical, health, and multiple disabilities* (2nd ed., pp. 232–247). Upper Saddle River, NJ: Pearson.

Heller, K. W., & Swinehart-Jones, D. (2003). Supporting the educational needs of students with orthopedic impairments. *Physical Disabilities: Education and Related Services, 22,* 3–24.

Heller, R., & Greenleaf, C. (2007). *Literacy instruction in the content areas: Getting to the core of middle and high school improvement.* Washington, DC: Alliance for Excellent Education.

Helwig, R., Rozek-Tedesco, M., & Tindal, G. (2002). An oral versus a standard administration of a large-scale mathematics test. *The Journal of Special Education, 36,* 39–47.

Hemmeter, M. L. (2000). Classroom-based interventions: Evaluating the past and looking toward the future. *Topics in Early Childhood Special Education, 20,* 56–61.

Hemmingson, H., & Borell, L. (2002). Environmental barriers in mainstream schools. *Child: Care, Health & Development, 28*(1), 57–63.

Henderlong, J., & Lepper, M. R. (2002). The effects of praise on children's intrinsic motivation: A review and synthesis. *Psychological Bulletin, 128,* 774–795.

Henderson, A. T., & Mapp, K. L. (2002). *A new wave of evidence: The impact of school, family, and community connection on student achievement.* Austin, TX: Southwest Education Development Laboratory.

Henggeler, S.W., Mihalic, S. F., Rone, L., Thomas, C., & Timmons-Mitchell, J. (1998). *Multisystemic therapy: Blueprints for violence prevention, Book Six* (D. S. Elliott, Series Editor). Boulder, CO: Center for the Study and Prevention of Violence, Institute of Behavioral Science, University of Colorado.

Henry, L. (2008). Short-term memory coding in children with intellectual disabilities. *American Journal on Mental Retardation, 113,* 187–200.

Henry, M. (1993). Morphological structure: Latinate and Greek roots and affixes as upper grade code strategies. *Reading and Writing: An Interdisciplinary Journal, 5,* 227–241.

Henry, M. (1996). *Parent–school collaboration: Feminist organizational structures and school leadership.* Albany, NY: State University of New York Press.

Herrnstein, R. J. (1961). Relative and absolute strength of response as a function of frequency of reinforcement. *Journal of the Experimental Analysis of Behavior, 4,* 267–272.

Herrnstein, R. J. (1970). On the law of effect. *Journal of the Experimental Analysis of Behavior, 13,* 243–266.

Hersh, R., & Walker, H. M. (1983). Great expectations: Making schools effective for all students. *Policy Studies Review, 2,* 147–188.

Heshusius, L. (2004). Special education knowledges: The inevitable struggle with the "self." In D. J. Gallagher, L. Heshusius, R. P. Lano, & T. M. Skrtic (Eds.), *Challenging orthodoxy in special education: Dissenting voices.* (pp. 283–309) Denver, CO: Love.

Hess, F. M., & Brigham, F. J. (2007). How federal special education policy affects schooling in Virginia. In M. Burns (Ed.), *Taking sides: Clashing views in special education* (3rd ed., pp. 139–149). New York: McGraw-Hill.

Hess, F., & Petrilli, M. (2006). *No Child Left Behind primer.* New York: Peter Lang.

Heubert, J. P., & Hauser, R. M. (1999). *High stakes: Testing for tracking, promotion, and graduation.* Washington, DC: National Academy Press.

Heward, W. L. (1994). Three "low tech" strategies for increasing the frequency of active student response during group instruction. In R. Gardner, III, D. M. Sainato, J. O. Cooper, T. E. Heron, W. L. Heward, J. Eshleman, & T. A. Grossi (Eds.), *Behavior analysis in education: Focus on measurably superior instruction* (pp. 283–320). Pacific Grove, CA: Brooks/Cole.

Heward, W. L., & Orlansky, M. D. (1984). *Exceptional children* (2nd ed.). Columbus, OH: Merrill.

Hiebert, B., & Murdock, J. (1994). Comparing three computer-aided instruction output modes to teach vocabulary words to students with learning disabilities. *Learning Disabilities Research & Practice, 9,* 136–141.

Hiebert, E. H. (2009). *Reading more, reading better.* New York: Guilford Press.

Hiebert, J. (2003). What research says about the NCTM Standards. In J. Kilpatrick, G. Martin, & D. Schifter (Eds.), *A research companion to principles and standards for school mathematics* (pp. 5–26). Reston, VA: National Council of Teachers of Mathematics.

Higgins, E. L., & Raskind, M. H. (2005). The compensatory effectiveness of the Quicktionary Reading Pen II on the reading comprehension of students with learning disabilities. *Journal of Special Education Technology, 20,* 31–39.

Hill, C. C. (2006). *The Individualized Education Program: An Analysis of IEP litigation from 2000 to present* (Doctoral dissertation). (UMI No.32-52012.)

Hilt-Panahon, A., Kern, L., Divatia, A., & Gresham, F. (2007). School-based interventions for students with or at-risk for depression: A review of the literature. *Advances in School Mental Health Promotion, 1,* 32–41.

Hintze, J. M., Christ, T. J., & Keller, L. A. (2002). The generalizability of CBM survey-level mathematics assessment: Just how many samples do we need? *School Psychology Review, 31,* 514–528.

Hobbs, S., Forehand, R., & Murray, R. (1978). Effects of various durations of timeout on the noncompliant behavior of children. *Behavior Therapy, 9,* 652–656.

Hock, M. F., Pulvers, K. A., Deshler, D. D., & Schumaker, J. B. (2001). The effects of an after-school tutoring program on the academic performance of at-risk students and students with LD. *Remedial and Special Education, 22,* 172–186.

Hoff, K. E., & DuPaul, G. J. (1998). Reducing disruptive behavior in general education classrooms: The use of self-management strategies. *School Psychology Review, 27,* 290–303.

Hoff, K. E., & Ronk, M. J. (2006). Increasing pro-social interactions using peers: Extension of positive peer-reporting methods. *Journal of Evidenced-Based Practices for Schools, 7,* 27–42.

Hoffman, P. R., Norris, J. A., & Monjure, J. (1990). Comparison of process targeting and whole language treatments for phonologically delayed preschool children. *Language, Speech, and Hearing Services in Schools, 21,* 102–109.

Hoge, R. D., & Coladarci, T. (1989). Teacher-based judgments of academic achievement: A review of literature. *Review of Educational Research, 59,* 297–313.

Hoggan, K., & Strong, C. (1994). The magic of "Once upon a time": Narrative teaching strategies. *Language, Speech, and Hearing Services in Schools, 25,* 76–89.

Hogue, A., Henderson, C. E., Dauber, S., Barajas, P. C., Fried, A., & Liddle, H. A. (2008). Treatment adherence, competence, and outcome in individual and family therapy for adolescent behavior problems. *Journal of Consulting and Clinical Psychology, 76,* 544–555.

Holdnack, J. A., & Weiss, L. G. (2006). IDEA 2004: Anticipating implications for clinical practice—Integrating assessment and intervention. *Psychology in the Schools, 43,* 871–882.

Hollenbeck, K., Rozek-Tedesco, M. A., Tindal, G., & Glasgow, A. (2000). An exploratory study of student-paced versus teacher-paced accommodations for large-scale math tests. *Journal of Special Education Technology, 15,* 27–36.

Hollinger, J. (1987). Social skills for behaviorally disordered children as preparation for mainstreaming: Theory, practice, and new directions. *Remedial and Special Education, 8,* 17–27.

Hoover-Dempsey, K. V., Walker, J. M. T., Jones, K. P., & Reed, R. P. (2002). Teachers involving parents (TIP): Results of an in-service teacher education program for enhancing parental involvement. *Teaching and Teacher Education, 18,* 843–867.

Hops, H., & Walker, H.M. (1988). CLASS: Contingencies for learning academic and social skills. Seattle, WA: Educational Achievement Systems.

Horn, E., Lieber, J., Li, S., Sandall, S., & Schwartz, I. (2000). Supporting young children's IEP goals in inclusive settings through embedded learning opportunities. *Topics in Early Childhood Education, 20,* 208–223.

Horner, R. D., & Keilitz, I. (1975). Training mentally retarded adolescents to brush their teeth. *Journal of Applied Behavior Analysis, 8,* 301–309.

Horner, R. H. (2000). Positive behavior supports. In M. L. Wehmeyer & J. R. Patton (Eds.), *Mental retardation in the 21st century* (pp. 181–196). Austin, TX: Pro-Ed.

Horner, R. H, & Billingsley, F. F. (1988). The effects of competing behavior on the generalization and maintenance of adaptive behavior in applied settings. In R. Horner, G. Dunlap, & R. Koegel (Eds.), *Generalization and maintenance: Lifestyle changes in applied settings* (pp. 197–220). Baltimore: Brookes.

Horner, R. H., Carr, E. G., Halle, J., McGee, G., Odom, S., & Wolery, M. (2005). The use of single-subject research to identify evidence-based practice in special education. *Exceptional Children, 71,* 165–179.

Horner, R. H., Day, H. M., Sprague, J. R., O'Brien, M., & Heathfield, L. T. (1991). Interspersed requests: A nonaversive procedure for reducing aggression and self-injury during instruction. *Journal of Applied Behavior Analysis, 24*(2), 265–278.

Horner, R. H., Diemer, S. M., & Brazeau, K. C. (1992). Educational support for students with severe problem behaviors in Oregon: A descriptive analysis from the 1987–88 school year. *Journal of the Association for Persons with Severe Handicaps, 17,* 154–169.

Horner, R. H., Sprague, J., & Wilcox, B. (1982). General case programming for community activities. In B. Wilcox & G. T. Bellamy (Eds.), *Design of high school programs for severely handicapped students* (pp. 61–98). Baltimore: Brookes.

Horner, R. H., & Sugai, G. (2000). School-wide behavior support: An emerging initiative. *Journal of Positive Behavior Interventions, 2,* 231–232.

Horner, R. H., Sugai, G., Smolkowski, K., Eber, L., Nakasato, J., Todd, A., et al.

(2009). A randomized, wait-list controlled effectiveness trial assessing school-wide positive behavior support in elementary schools. *Journal of Positive Behavior Interventions, 11*(3), 133–144.

Horner, R. H., Todd, A. W., Lewis-Palmer, T., Irvin, L. K., Sugai, G., & Boland, J. B. (2004). The school-wide evaluation tool (SET): A research instrument for assessing school-wide positive behavior support. *Journal of Positive Behavior Interventions, 6,* 3–12.

Horton, S. V., & Lovitt, T. C. (1994). A comparison of two methods of administering group reading inventories to diverse learners. *Remedial and Special Education, 15,* 378–390.

Hosp, J. L. (2008). Best practice in aligning academic assessment with instruction. In A. Thomas & J. Grimes (Eds.), *Best practices in school psychology* (Vol. 5, pp. 363–376). Bethesda, MD: National Association of School Psychologists.

Hosp, J. L., & Hosp, M. K. (2001). Behavior differences between African-American and Caucasian students: Issues for assessment and intervention. *Education & Treatment of Children, 24*(3), 336–350.

Hosp, M. K., & Fuchs, L. S. (2005). Using CBM as an indicator of decoding, word reading, and comprehension: Do the relations change with grade? *School Psychology Review, 34,* 9–26.

Houlihan, D., & Brandon, P. K. (1996). Compliant in a moment: A commentary on Nevin. *Journal of Applied Behavior Analysis, 29*(4), 549–555.

Houlihan, D., Jacobson, L., & Brandon, P. K. (1994). Replication of a high-probability request sequence with varied interprompt times in a preschool setting. *Journal of Applied Behavior Analysis, 27*(4), 737–738.

Houlihan, D., & Jones, R. N. (1990). Exploring the reinforcement of compliance with do and don't requests and their side effects: A partial replication and extension. *Psychological Reports, 67,* 439–448.

Howell, K. W., & Nolet, V. (2000). *Curriculum-based evaluation: Teaching and decision making.* Atlanta, GA: Wadsworth.

Hoyson, M., Jamieson, B., & Strain, P. S. (1984). Individualized group

instruction of normally developing and autistic-like children: The LEAP curriculum model. *Journal of Educational Psychology, 55,* 95–41.

Hudson, R. F., Lane, H. B., & Pullen, P. C. (2005). Reading fluency assessment and instruction: What, why, and how? *The Reading Teacher, 58,* 702–715.

Hudson, R. F., Mercer, C. D., & Lane, H. (2000). *Exploring reading fluency: A paradigmatic overview.* Unpublished manuscript, University of Florida, Gainesville.

Huebner, E. S., & Gould, K. (1991). Multidisciplinary teams revisited: Current perceptions of school psychologists regarding team functioning. *School Psychology Review, 20*(3), 428–434.

Huefner, D. S. (2000). The risks and opportunities of the IEP requirements of IDEA '97. *Journal of Special Education, 33,* 195–204.

Huefner, D. S. (2008). Updating the FAPE standard under IDEA. *Journal of Law & Education, 37,* 367–379.

Hughes, C., Copeland, S. R., Agran, M., Wehmeyer, M. L., Rodi, M. S., & Presley, J. A. (2002). Using self-monitoring to improve performance in general education high school classes. *Education and Training in Mental Retardation and Developmental Disabilities, 37,* 262–272.

Hughes, C., Fowler, S. E., Copeland, S. R., Agran, M., Wehmeyer, M. L., & Church-Pupke, P. (2004). Supporting high school students to engage in recreational activities with peers. *Behavior Modification, 28,* 3–27.

Hughes, C., Rung, L. L., Wehmeyer, M. L., Agran, M., Copeland, S. R., & Bogseon, H. (2000). Self-prompted communication book use to increase social interaction among high school students. *Journal of the Association for Persons with Severe Handicaps, 25,* 153–166.

Hughes, C. A., & Ruhl, K. L. (1987). The nature and extent of special educator contacts with students' parents. *Teacher Education and Special Education, 10*(4), 180–184.

Hughes, D., McGillivray, L., & Schmidek, M. (1997). *Guide to narrative language: Procedures for assessment.* Eau Claire, WI: Thinking Publications.

Hunt, P., & Goetz, L. (1997). Research on inclusive educational programs, practices, and outcomes for students with severe disabilities. *Journal of Special Education, 31*(1), 3–29.

Hunt, P., Goetz, L., & Anderson, J. (1986). The quality of IEP objectives associated with placement on integrated versus segregated school sites. *The Journal of the Association for Persons with Severe Handicaps, 11*, 125–130.

Hurth, J., Shaw, E., Izeman, S. G., Whaley, K., & Rogers, S. J. (1999). Areas of agreement about effective practices among programs serving young children with autism spectrum disorder. *Infants and Young Children, 12*, 17–26.

Hutchinson, N. L. (1993). Effects of cognitive strategy instruction on algebra problem solving of adolescents with learning disabilities. *Learning Disability Quarterly, 16*, 34–63.

Hux, K., Rankin-Erickson, J., Manasse, N., & Lauritzen, E. (2000). Accuracy of three speech recognition systems: Case study of dysarthric speech. *Augmentative and Alternative Communication, 16*, 186–196.

Huynh, H., & Barton, K. (2006). Performance of students with disabilities under regular and oral administration of a high stakes reading examination. *Applied Measurement in Education, 19*, 21–39.

Huynh, H., Meyer, J. P., & Gallant, D. J. (2004). Comparability of student performance between regular and oral administrations for a high-stakes mathematics test. *Applied Measurement in Education, 17*, 39–57.

Hyatt, K. J., Iddings, A. C. D., & Ober, S. (2005). Inclusion: A catalyst for school reform. *Teaching Exceptional Children Plus, 1*(3), Retrieved from http:// escholarship.bc.edu/cgi/viewcontent .cgi?article=1078&context= education/tecplus

Iddon, J. L., Morgan, D. J. R., Loveday, C., Sahakian, B. J., & Pickard, J. D. (2004). Neuropsychological profile of young adults with spina bifida with or without hydrocephalus. *Journal of Neurology Neurosurgery and Psychiatry, 75*, 1112–1118.

Idol, L. (1987). Group story mapping: A comprehension strategy for both skilled and unskilled readers. *Journal of Learning Disabilities, 20*(4), 196–205.

Ihnot, C. (1991). *Read naturally.* St. Paul, MN: Read Naturally.

Ikeda, M. J., & Gustafson, J. K. (2002). *Heartland AEA 11's problem solving process: Impact on issues related to special education* (Research Report. No. 2002-01). Johnston, IA: Heartland Area Education Agency.

Ikeda, M. J., Rahn-Blakeslee, A., Niebling, B. C., Gustafson, J. K., Allison, R., & Stumme, J. (2007). The Heartland Area Educational Agency 11 problem-solving approach: An overview and lesson learned. In S. R. Jimerson, M. K., Burns, & A. M. VanDerHeyden (Eds.), *Handbook of response to intervention* (pp. 255–268). New York: Springer.

Improving America's Schools Act of 1994, The Safe and Drug-Free Schools and Communities Act (1994).

Inclusive Solutions. (n.d.). *Person centered planning.* Retrieved from http:// www.inclusive-solutions.com/pcplanning.asp

Individuals with Disabilities Education Act of 1990, Pub. L. No. 101-476, 104 Stat. 1142.

Individuals with Disabilities Education Act of 1991, Pub. L. No. 102-119, 105 Stat. 587.

Individuals with Disabilities Education Act of 1997, Pub. L. No. 105-17, 105 Stat. 37.

Individuals with Disabilities Education Improvement Act of 2004, Pub. L. No. 108-446, 118 Stat. 2647.

Interactive Collaborative Autism Network. (n.d.). *Person centered planning.* Retrieved from http://www .autismnetwork.org/modules/social/ pcp/index.html

Iovannone, R., Dunlap, G., Huber, H., & Kincaid, D. (2003). Effective educational practices for students with autism spectrum disorders. *Focus on Autism and Other Developmental Disabilities, 18*, 150–165.

Iovannone, R., Greenbaum, P., Wei, W., Kincaid, D., Dunlap, G., & Strain, P. (2009). Randomized controlled trial of a tertiary behavior intervention for students with problem behaviors: Preliminary outcomes. *Journal of Emotional and Behavioral Disorders, 17*, 213–225.

Irvine, A. B., Erickson, A. M., Singer, G. H. S., & Stahlberg, D. (1992). A coordinated program to transfer self-management skills from school

to home. *Education and Training in Mental Retardation, 27*, 241–254.

Isaacs, A., & Carroll, W. (1999). Strategies for basic fact instruction. *Teaching Children Mathematics, 5*, 508–515.

Iwata, B. A., Dorsey, M. F., Slifer, K. J., Bauman, K. E., & Richman, G. S. (1982). Toward a functional analysis of self-injury. *Analysis and Intervention in Developmental Disabilities, 2*, 3–20.

Jackson, L., Ryndak, D. L., & Billingsly, F. (2000). Useful practices in inclusive education: A preliminary view of what experts in moderate to severe disabilities are saying. *Journal of the Association for Persons with Severe Handicaps, 25*, 129–141.

Jacob, S., & Hartshorne, T. S. (2007). *Ethics and law for school psychologists* (5th ed.). Hoboken, NJ: John Wiley & Sons.

Jacobsen, E. (1938). *Progressive relaxation.* Chicago: University of Chicago Press.

Jameson, J. M., McDonnell, J., Johnson, J. W., Riesen, T., & Polychronis, S. (2007). A comparison of one-to-one embedded instruction in the general education classroom and one-to-one massed practice instruction in the special education classroom. *Education and Treatment of Children, 30*, 23–44.

Janvier, C. (1987). *Problems of representation in the teaching and learning of mathematics.* Hillsdale, NJ: Erlbaum.

Jarmulowicz, L., & Hay, S. E. (2009). Derivational morphophonology: Exploring morphophonology: Exploring errors in third graders' production [part of a forum on morphology and literacy]. *Language, Speech, and Hearing Services in Schools, 40*, 299–311.

Jaspers, M. W. M., & Van Lieshout, E. C. D. M. (1994). The evaluation of two computerized instruction programs for arithmetic word-problem solving by educable mentally retarded children. *Learning and Instruction, 4*, 193–215.

Jaycox, L. H., Reivich, K. J., Gillham, J., & Seligman, M. E. P. (1994). Prevention of depressive symptoms in school children. *Behaviour Research and Therapy, 32*, 801–816.

Jegatheesan, B., Miller, P., & Fowler, S. (2010). Autism from a religious perspective: A study of parental beliefs in South Asian Muslim immigrant families. *Focus on Autism and Other*

Developmental Disabilities, 25(2), 98–109.

Jenkins, J. R., Graff, J. J., & Miglioretti, D. L. (2009). Estimating reading growth using intermittent CBM progress monitoring. *Exceptional Children, 75*(2), 151–163.

Jenkins, J. R., & Jewell, M. (1993). Examining the validity of two measures for formative teaching: Reading aloud and maze. *Exceptional Children, 59,* 421–432.

Jenkins, J. R., Matlock, B., & Slocum, T. A. (1989). Approaches to vocabulary instruction: The teaching of individual word meanings and practice deriving word meaning from context. *Reading Research Quarterly, 24,* 215–235.

Jenkins, J. R., Vadasy, P. F., Firebaugh, M., & Profilet, C. (2000). Tutoring first-grade struggling readers in phonological reading skills. *Learning Disabilities: Research & Practice, 15,* 75–84.

Jennings, J. L., & Beveridge, A. A. (2009). How does test exemption affect schools' and students' academic performance? *Educational Evaluation and Policy Analysis, 31,* 153–175.

Jensen, T., Orquiz, P., & Gillam, S. (April, 2009). Narrative language intervention for English language learners. *National Conference on Undergraduate Research.* LaCrosse, WI (poster session).

Jeynes, W. H. (2005). A meta-analysis of the relation of parental involvement to urban elementary school student academic achievement. *Urban Education, 40,* 237–239.

Jimenez, R. T., Garcia, G. E., & Pearson, P. D. (1995). Three children, two languages, and strategic reading: Case studies in bilingual/monolingual reading. *American Educational Research Journal, 32,* 67–97.

Jitendra, A. K. (2007). *Solving math word problems: Teaching students with learning disabilities using schema-based instruction.* Austin, TX: Pro-Ed.

Jitendra, A. K. (2008). Using schema-based instruction to make appropriate sense of word problems. *Perspectives on Language and Literacy, 34*(2), 20–24.

Jitendra, A. K., DiPipi, C. M., & Perron-Jones, N. (2002). An exploratory study of word problem-solving instruction for middle school students with learning disabilities: An emphasis on conceptual and procedural understanding. *Journal of Special Education, 36,* 23–38.

Jitendra, A. K., Edwards, L. L., Sacks, G., & Jacobson, L. A. (2004). What research says about vocabulary instruction for students with learning disabilities. *Exceptional Children, 70,* 299–322.

Jitendra, A. K., Griffin, C., Haria, P., Leh, J., Adams, A., & Kaduvetoor, A. (2007). A comparison of single and multiple strategy instruction on third grade students' mathematical problem solving. *Journal of Educational Psychology, 99,* 115–127.

Jitendra, A. K., Griffin, C., McGoey, K., Gardill, C., Bhat, P., & Riley, T. (1998). Effects of mathematical word problem solving by students at risk or with mild disabilities. *Journal of Educational Research, 91,* 345–356.

Jitendra, A. K., & Hoff, K. (1996). The effects of schema-based instruction on mathematical word problem solving performance of students with learning disabilities. *Journal of Learning Disabilities, 29,* 422–431.

Jitendra, A. K., Hoff, K., & Beck, M. (1999). Teaching middle school students with learning disabilities to solve multistep word problems using a schema-based approach. *Remedial and Special Education, 20,* 50–64.

Jitendra, A. K., Sczeniak, E., & Deatline-Buchman, A. (2005). An exploratory validation of curriculum-based mathematical word problem-solving tasks as indicators of mathematics proficiency for third graders. *School Psychology Review, 34,* 358–371.

Jitendra, A. K., Star, J., Starosta, K., Leh, J., Sood, S., Caskie, G., . . . & Mack, T. (2009). Improving students' learning of ratio and proportion problem solving: The role of schema-based instruction. *Contemporary Educational Psychology, 34,* 250–264.

Jitendra, A., & Xin, A. (1997). Mathematical word problem solving instruction for students with mild disabilities and students at risk for failure: A research synthesis. *Journal of Special Education, 30,* 412–438.

Johns, J. L. (2005). *Basic reading inventory* (9th ed.). Dubuque, IA: Kendall/Hunt.

Johnson, C. S. (2005). *Teaching sentence writing preskills to middle school students with mild to moderate disabilities.* Unpublished master's thesis, California State University, Fullerton, CA.

Johnson, D. W., & Johnson, R. (1989). *Cooperation and competition: Theory and research.* Edina, MN: Interaction Book Company.

Johnson, D. W., & Johnson, R. (2009). An educational psychology success story: Social interdependence theory and cooperative learning. *Educational Researcher, 38,* 365–380.

Johnson, D. W., Johnson, R., & Holubec, E. (2008). *Cooperation in the classroom* (8th ed.). Edina, MN: Interaction Book Company.

Johnson, E. (2000). The effects of accommodations on performance assessments. *Remedial and Special Education, 21,* 261–267.

Johnson, J. E., & Johnson, K. M. (1992). Clarifying the developmental perspective in response to Carta, Schwartz, Atwater, & McConnell. *Topics in Early Childhood Special Education, 12,* 439–457.

Johnson, S. M., Wahl, G., Martin, S., & Johansson, S. (1973). How deviant is the normal child: A behavioral analysis of the preschool child and his family. In R. D. Rubin, J. P. Brady, & J. D. Henderson (Eds.), *Advances in behavioral therapy* (Vol. 4). New York: Academic Press.

Johnson-Gros, K. N., & Shriver, M. D. (2006). Compliance training and positive peer reporting with a 4-year old in a preschool classroom. *Journal of Evidence-Based Practices for Schools, 7,* 167–185.

Johnstone, C. J., Altman, J., Thurlow, M. L., & Thompson, S. J. (2006). *A summary of research on the effects of test accommodations: 2002 through 2004* (Technical Report 45). Minneapolis, MN: University of Minnesota, National Center on Educational Outcomes.

Joint Committee on Testing Practices. (2005). Code of fair testing practices in education (rev.). *Educational Measurement, 24,* 2–9.

Jolivette, K., McCormick, K., McLaren, E., & Steed, E. A. (2009). Opportunities for young children to make choices in a model interdisciplinary and inclusive preschool program. *Infants and Young Children, 22,* 279–289.

Jolivette, K., Ridgely, R., & White, A. (2002). Choice-making strategies: Information for families. *Center for*

Effective Collaboration and Practice. Retrieved from http://cecp.air.org/familybriefs/docs/choice_at_home/pdf

Jolivette, K., Stichter, J. P., & McCormick, K. M. (2002). Making choices—improving behavior—engaging in learning. *Teaching Exceptional Children, 34,* 24–29.

Jolivette, K., Stichter, J. P., Sibilisky, S., Scott, T. M., & Ridgely, R. (2002). Naturally occurring opportunities for preschool children with or without disabilities to make choices. *Education and Treatment of Children, 25,* 396–414.

Jolivette, K., Wehby, J. H., Canale, J., & Massey, N. G. (2001). Effects of choice-making opportunities on the behavior of students with emotional and behavioral disorders. *Behavioral Disorders, 26,* 131–145.

Jones, C. D., & Schwartz, I. S. (2004). Siblings, peers, and adults: Differential affects of models for children with autism. *Topics in Early Childhood Special Education, 24,* 187–198.

Jones, E. D., Southern, W. S., & Brigham, F. J. (1998). Curriculum-based assessment: Testing what is taught and teaching what is tested. *Intervention in School and Clinic, 33,* 239–249.

Jones, K. M., Young, M. M., & Friman, P. C. (2000). Increasing peer praise of socially rejected delinquent youth: Effects on cooperation and acceptance. *School Psychology Quarterly, 15,* 30–39.

Jones, M. L. (2009). A study of novice special educators' views of evidence-based practices. *Teacher Education and Special Education, 32*(2), 101–120.

Jonsson, A. & Svingby, G. (2007). The use of scoring rubrics: Reliability, validity and educational consequences. *Educational Research Review, 2,* 130–144.

Jordan, N. C., & Hanich, L. (2000). Mathematical thinking in second-grade children with different forms of LD. *Journal of Learning Disabilities, 33,* 567–578.

Juel, C. (1988). Learning to read and write: A longitudinal study of 54 children from first through fourth grades. *Journal of Educational Psychology, 80,* 443–447.

Juleus Chapman et al. v. California Department of Education et al., 2001, No. C01-1780.

Junkala, J., & Talbot, M. L. (1982). Cognitive styles of students with cerebral palsy. *Perceptual and Motor Skills, 55,* 403–410.

Justice, L. M. (2010). *Communication sciences and disorders: A contemporary perspective* (2nd ed.). Upper Saddle River, NJ: Merrill/Pearson.

Justice, L. M., & Ezell, H. K. (1999). Vygotskian theory and its application to assessment: An overview for speech-language pathologists. *Contemporary Issues in Communication Science and Disorders, 26,* 111–118.

Kaestle, C. F. (2001). The common school. In S. Mondale & S. B. Patton (Eds.), *School: The story of American public education* (pp. 11–17). Boston: Beacon Press.

Kaestle, C., Campbell, A., Finn, J., Johnson, S., & Mikulecky, L. (2001). *Adult literacy and education in America.* Washington, DC: National Center for Education Statistics.

Kahn, J. S., Kehle, T. J., Jenson, W. R., & Clark, E. (1990). Comparison of cognitive-behavioral, relaxation, and self-modeling interventions for depression among middle school students. *School Psychology Review, 19,* 196–211.

Kaiser, A. P. (1993). Parent-implemented language intervention: An environmental systems perspective. In A. P. Kaiser & D. B. Gray (Eds.), *Enhancing children's communication: Research foundations for intervention* (Vol. 2, pp. 63–84). Baltimore: Brookes.

Kaiser, A. P. (2000). Teaching functional communication skills. In M. E. Snell & F. Brown (Eds.), *Instruction of students with severe disabilities* (4th ed., pp. 347–370). Upper Saddle River, NJ: Merrill/Pearson.

Kaiser, A. P., & Hancock, T. B. (2003). Teaching parents new skills to support their young children's development. *Infants and Young Children, 16*(1), 9–21.

Kaiser, A. P., Hancock, T. B., & Hester, P. P. (1998). Parents as cointerventionists: Research on applications of naturalistic language teaching procedures. *Infants and Young Children, 10*(4), 46–55.

Kaiser, A. P., Hemmeter, M. L., & Hester, P. P. (1997). The facilitative effects

of input on children's language development: Contributions from studies on enhanced milieu teaching. In L. B. Adamson & M. A. Romski (Eds.), *Communication and language acquisition: Discoveries from atypical development* (pp. 267–294). Baltimore: Brookes.

Kaiser, A. P., & Hester, P. P. (1994). Generalized effects of enhanced milieu teaching. *Journal of Speech & Hearing Research, 37,* 1320–1341.

Kaiser, A. P., Ostrosky, M. M., & Alpert, C. L. (1993). Training teachers to use environmental arrangement and milieu teaching with nonvocal preschool children. *Journal of the Association for Persons with Severe Handicaps, 18,* 188–199.

Kaiser, A., Yoder, P., & Keetz, A. (1992). Evaluating milieu teaching. In S. F. Warren & J. Reichle (Eds.), *Causes and effects in communication and language intervention* (pp. 9–47). Baltimore: Brookes.

Kalberg, J. R., Lane, K. L., & Lambert, W. (2012). The utility of conflict resolution and social skills interventions with middle school students at risk for antisocial behavior: A methodological illustration. *Remedial and Special Education, 33,* 23–38.

Kalberg, J. R., Lane, K. L., & Menzies, H. M. (2010). Using systematic screening procedures to identify students who are nonresponsive to primary prevention efforts: Integrating academic and behavioral measures. *Education and Treatment of Children, 33,* 561–584.

Kalyanpur, M., & Harry, B. (1999). *Culture in special education: Building reciprocal family-professional relationships.* Baltimore: Brookes.

Kalyuga, S. (2006). Rapid cognitive assessment of learners' knowledge structures. *Learning and Instruction, 16,* 1–11.

Kamins, M. L., & Dweck, C. S. (1999). Person versus process praise and criticism: Implications for contingent self-worth and coping. *Developmental Psychology, 35,* 835–847.

Kamphaus, R. W., & Reynolds, C. R. (2007). *BASC-2 behavior and emotional screening system (BASC-2 BESS).* San Antonio, TX: Pearson.

Kamps, D., Abbott, M., Greenwood, C., Arreaga-Mayer, C., Wills, H., Longstaff, J., . . . Walton, C. (2007). Use of evidence-based, small group reading instruction for English language learners in elementary grades: Second tier intervention. *Learning Disabilities Quarterly, 30,* 153–168.

Kamps, D. M., Leonard, B. R., Vernon, S., Dugan, E. P., Delquadri, J. C., Gershon, B., Wade, L., & Folk, L. (1992). Teaching social skills to students with autism to increase peer interactions in an integrated first-grade classroom. *Journal of Applied Behavior Analysis, 25,* 281–288.

Kamps, D., Wendland, M., & Culpepper, M. (2006). Active teacher participation in functional behavior assessment for students with emotional and behavior disorders in general education classrooms. *Behavioral Disorders, 31,* 128–146.

Karat, J., Horn, D. B., Halverson, C. A., & Karat, C. M. (2000, April). *Overcoming unusabilty: Developing efficient strategies in speech recognition systems.* Paper presented at the CHI 2000, AMC Conference on Human Factors in Computer Systems, The Hague, Netherlands.

Kartub, D. T., Taylor-Greene, S., March, R. E., & Horner, R. H. (2000). Reducing hallway noise: A systems approach. *Journal of Positive Behavior Intervention, 2,* 179–182.

Katz, J., & Mirenda, P. (2002) Including students with developmental disabilities in general education classrooms: Educational benefits. *International Journal of Special Education, 17*(2), 14–24.

Katz, L. A., & Carlisle, J. F. (2009). Teaching students with reading difficulties to be close readers: A feasibility study. *Language, Speech and Hearing Services in Schools, 40,* 325–340.

Kauffman, J. M. (1996). Research to practice issues. *Behavioral Disorders, 22,* 55–60.

Kauffman, J. M. (2001). *Characteristics of emotional and behavioral disorders of children and youth* (7th ed.). Upper Saddle River, NJ: Merrill/Pearson.

Kauffman, J. M. (2010). *The tragicomedy of public education: Laughing and crying, thinking and fixing.* Verona, WI: Full Court Press.

Kauffman, J. M., & Brigham, F. J., (2009). *Working with troubled children.* Verona, WI: Full Court Press.

Kauffman, J. M., & Hallahan, D. P. (2005). *Special education: What it is and why we need it.* Boston: Allyn & Bacon.

Kauffman, J. M., & Konold, T. R. (2007). Making sense in education: Pretense (including No Child Left Behind) and realities in rhetoric and policy about schools and schooling. *Exceptionality, 15,* 75–96.

Kauffman, J. M., & Landrum, T. (2009). *Characteristics of emotional and behavioral disorders of children and youth* (8th ed.). Upper Saddle River, NJ: Merrill/Pearson.

Kauffman, J. M., & Lloyd, J. W. (1995). A sense of place: The importance of placement issues in contemporary special education. In J. M. Kauffman, J. W. Lloyd, D. P. Hallahan & T. A. Astuto (Eds.), *Issues in educational placement: Students with emotional and behavioral disorders* (pp. 3–19). Hillsdale, NJ: L. Erlbaum.

Kaufman, A. S., & Kaufman, N. L. (2004). *Kaufman Test of Educational Achievement, Second Edition (KTEA-II).* Circle Pines, MN: American Guidance Service.

Kavale, K. A. (2002). Mainstreaming to full inclusion: From orthogenesis to pathogenesis of an idea. *International Journal of Disability, Development and Education, 49,* 201–214.

Kavale, K. A., & Forness, S. R. (1985). *The science of learning disabilities.* San Diego, CA: College-Hill Press.

Kavale, K. A., & Forness, S. R. (1992). Learning difficulties and memory problems in mental retardation: A meta-analysis of theoretical perspectives. In T. E. Scruggs & M. A. Mastropieri (Eds.), *Advances in learning and behavioral disabilities* (Vol. 7, pp. 177–222). Greenwich, CT: JAI Press.

Kavale, K. A., & Forness, S. R. (2000). Policy decision in special education: The role of meta-analysis. In R. M. Gersten, E. P. Schiller, & S. Vaughn (Eds.), *Contemporary special education research: Syntheses of the knowledge base on critical instructional issues* (pp. 281–326). Mahwah, NJ: L. Erlbaum.

Kavale, K. A., Kauffman, J. M., Bachmeier, R. J., & LeFever, G. B. (2008). Response-to-intervention: Separating the rhetoric of self-congratulation from the reality of specific learning disability identification. *Learning Disability Quarterly, 31*(3), 135–150.

Kavale, K. A., & Reese, J. H. (1992). The character of learning disabilities. *Learning Disability Quarterly, 15,* 74–94.

Kazdin, A. (1977). Assessing the clinical or applied significance of behavior change through social validation. *Behavior Modification, 1,* 427–452.

Kazdin, A. E. (1987). Treatment of anti-social behavior in children: Current status and future directions. *American Psychological Association, 102,* 187–203.

Kazdin, A. E. (2010). *Single case research designs: Methods for clinical and applied settings* (2nd ed.). New York: Oxford University Press.

Kazdin, A. E., & Marciano, P. L. (1998). Childhood and adolescent depression. In E. J. Mash & R. A. Barkley (Eds.), *Treatment of childhood disorders* (2nd ed, pp. 211–248). New York: Guilford Press.

Keen, S., & Davey, B. (1987). Effects of computer-presented text on LD adolescents reading behaviors. *Learning Disabilities Quarterly, 19,* 283–290.

Kellam, S., Ling, X., Merisca, R., Brown, C., & Ialongo, N. (1998). The effect of the level of aggression in the first grade classroom on the course and malleability of aggressive behavior into middle school. *Development and Psychopathology, 10,* 165–185.

Keller, M. B., Neal, R. D., Strober, M., Klein, R. G., Kutcher, S. P., Birmaher, B., et al. (2001). Efficacy of paroxetine in the treatment of adolescent major depression: A randomized, controlled trial. *Journal of the American Academy of Child and Adolescent Psychiatry, 40,* 762–772.

Keller-Allen, C. (2006). *English language learners with disabilities: Identification and other state policies and issues.* Alexandria, VA: Project Forum.

Kelly, P. R., Gomez-Bellenge, F. X., Chen, J., & Schulz, M. M. (2008). Learner outcomes for English language learner low readers in an early intervention. *TESOL Quarterly, 42,* 235–260.

Kemp, C., & Carter, M. (2006). Active and passive task related behavior, direction following and the inclusion of children with disabilities. *Education and Training in Developmental Disabilities, 41,* 14–27.

Kendall, P. C., Stark, K. D., & Adam, T. (1990). Cognitive deficit or cognitive distortion of childhood depression. *Journal of Abnormal Childhood Psychology, 18*(3), 255–270.

Kennedy, C. H., Itkonen, T., & Lindquist, K. (1995). Comparing interspersed requests and social comments as antecedents for increasing student compliance. *Journal of Applied Behavior Analysis, 28,* 97–98.

Kennedy, C. H., Long, T., Jolivette, K., Cox, J., Tang, J., & Thompson, T. (2001). Facilitating general education participation for students with behavior problems by linking positive behavior supports and person-centered planning. *Journal of Emotional and Behavioral Disorders, 9,* 161–171.

Kennedy, M., & Deshler, D. (2010). Literacy instruction, technology, and students with learning disabilities: Research we have, research we need. *The Free Library.* Retrieved from http://www.thefreelibrary.com/Literacy instruction, technology, and students with learning...-a0242754548

Kern, L., Bambara, L., & Fogt, J. (2002). Classwide curricular modification to improve the behavior of students with emotional and behavioral disorders. *Behavioral Disorders, 27,* 317–326.

Kern, L., Childs, K. E., Dunlap, G., Clarke, S., & Falk, G. D. (1994). Using assessment-based curricular intervention to improve the classroom behavior of a student with emotional and behavioral challenges. *Journal of Applied Behavior Analysis, 27,* 7–19.

Kern, L., & Clemens, N. H. (2007). Antecedent strategies to promote appropriate classroom behavior. *Psychology in the Schools, 44,* 65–75.

Kern, L., Delaney, B., Clarke, S., Dunlap, G., & Childs, K. (2001). Improving classroom behavior of students with emotional and behavioral disorders using individualized curricular modifications. *Journal of Emotional and Behavioral Disorders, 9,* 239–247.

Kern, L., DuPaul, G. J., Volpe, R., Sokol, N., Lutz, J. G., Arbolino, L., et al. (2007). Multi-setting assessment-based intervention for young children at-risk for ADHD: Initial effects on academic and behavioral functioning. *School Psychology Review, 36*(2), 237–255.

Kern, L., Hilt, A., & Gresham, F. (2004). An evaluation of the functional behavioral assessment process used with students with or at risk for emotional and behavioral disorders. *Education and Treatment of Children, 27,* 440–452.

Kern, L., Mantegna, M. E., Vorndran, C. M., Bailin, D., & Hilt, A. (2001). Choice of task sequence to reduce problem behaviors. *Journal of Positive Behavior Interventions, 3,* 3–10.

Kern, L., & Manz, P. (2004). A look at current validity issues of school-wide behavior support. *Behavioral Disorders, 30,* 47–59.

Kern, L., & State, T. M. (2009). Incorporating choice and preferred activities into classwide instruction. *Beyond Behavior, 18,* 3–11.

Ketterlin-Geller, L. R., Alonzo, J., Braun-Monegan, J., & Tindal, G. (2007). Recommendations for accommodations: Implications of (in)consistency. *Remedial and Special Education, 28,* 194–206.

Ketterlin-Geller, L., Yovanoff, P., & Tindal, G. (2007). Developing a new paradigm for conducting research on accommodations in mathematics testing. *Exceptional Children, 73*(3), 331–347.

Keyes, M. W., & Owens-Johnson, L. (2003). Developing person-centered IEPs. *Intervention in School & Clinic, 38,* 145–152.

Killoran, J. (2007). *The national deaf-blind child count 1998–2005 in review.* The National Technical Assistance Consortium for Children and Young Adults Who Are Deaf-Blind. Retrieved from http://nationaldb.org/documents/products/Childcountreview0607Final.pdf

Killu, K., Sainato, D. M., Davis, C. A., Ospelt, H., & Paul, J. N. (1998). Effects of high-probability request sequences on preschoolers' compliance and disruptive behavior. *Journal of Behavioral Education, 8*(3), 347–368.

Kilpatrick, J., Swafford, J., & Finell, B. (Eds.). (2001). *Adding it up: Helping children learn mathematics.* Washington, DC: National Academy Press.

Kim, A., Vaughn, S., Klingner, J. K., Woodruf, A. L., Reutebuch, C. K., & Kouzekanani, K. (2006). Improving the reading comprehension of middle school students with disabilities through computer-assisted collaborative strategic reading. *Remedial and Special Education, 27,* 235–249.

Kim, A., Vaughn, S., Wanzek, J., & Wei, S. (2004). Graphic organizers and their effects on the reading comprehension of students with LD. *Journal of Learning Disabilities, 37,* 105–118.

Kindler, A. (2002). *Survey of the states' limited English proficient students and available educational programs and services, 2000–2001 summary report.* Washington, DC: National Clearinghouse for English Language Acquisition and Language Instruction Educational Programs.

King, A. (1994). Guiding knowledge construction in the classroom: Effects of teaching children how to question and how to explain. *American Educational Research Journal, 31,* 358-368. doi:10.3102/00028312031002338

King, F. J., Goodson, L., & Rohani, F. (1998). *Higher order thinking skills.* Center for Advancement and Learning. Retrieved from http://www.cala.fsu.edu/portfolio?chosen_service=Assessment+and+Test+Development

King, G. A., Schultz, I. Z., Steel, K., Gilpin, M., & Cathers, T. (1993). Self-evaluation and self-concept of adolescents with physical disabilities. *The American Journal of Occupational Therapy, 47,* 132–140.

King, T. W. (1999). *Assistive technology: Essential human factors.* Boston, MA: Allyn & Bacon.

King-Sears, M. E., Mercer, C. D., & Sindelar, P. (1992). Toward independence with keyword mnemonics: A strategy for science vocabulary instruction. *Remedial and Special Education, 13,* 22–33.

Kintsch, W., & van Dijk, T. A. (1978). Toward a model of text comprehension and production. *Psychological Review, 85,* 363–394.

Kirby v. Cabell Board of Education, 46 IDELR 156 (D. W.VA. 2006).

Kiuhara, S., Graham, S., & Hawken, L. (2009). Teaching writing to high school students: A national survey. *Journal of Educational Psychology, 101,* 136–160.

Klecan-Aker, J., Flahive, L. K., & Fleming, S. (1997). Teaching storytelling to a group of children with learning disabilities: A look at treatment outcomes. *Contemporary Issues in Communication Science and Disorders, 24,* 23–32.

Klein, R. G., Koplewicz, H. S., & Kanner, A. (1992). Imipramine treatment of children with separation anxiety disorder. *Journal of the American Academy of Child and Adolescent Psychiatry, 31,* 21–28.

Kleinert, H. L., Haig, J., Kearns, J. F., & Kennedy, S. (2000). Alternate assessments: Lessons learned and roads to be taken. *Exceptional Children, 67,* 51–66.

Kleinert, H. L., & Kearns, J. F. (2001). *Measuring outcomes and supports for students with disabilities.* Baltimore: Brookes.

Klem, A. M., & Connell, J. P. (2004). Relationships matter: Linking teacher support to student engagement and achievement. *The Journal of School Health, 74,* 262–273.

Klingner, J. K. (2004). Assessing reading comprehension. *Assessment for Effective Intervention, 29,* 59–70.

Klingner, J. K., Arguelles, M. E., Hughes, M. T., & Vaughn, S. (2001). Examining the school-wide "spread" of research-based practices. *Learning Disability Quarterly, 24,* 221–234.

Klingner, J. K., & Edwards, P. A. (2006). Cultural considerations with response to intervention models. *Reading Research Quarterly, 41*(1), 108–117.

Klingner, J. K., Urbach, J., Golos, D., Brownell, M., & Menon, S. (2008, April). *How do special education teachers promote reading comprehension?* Paper presented at the annual meeting of the American Educational Research Association, New York.

Klingner, J. K., & Vaughn, S. (1996). Reciprocal teaching of reading comprehension strategies for students with learning disabilities who use English as a second language. *Elementary School Journal, 96,* 275–293.

Klingner, J. K., & Vaughn, S. (1999). Promoting reading comprehension, content learning, and English acquisition through collaborative strategic reading (CSR). *The Reading Teacher, 52,* 738–747.

Klingner, J. K., & Vaughn, S. (2000). The helping behaviors of fifth graders while using collaborative strategic reading during ESL content classes. *TESOL Quarterly, 34,* 69–98.

Klingner, J. K., Vaughn, S., Arguelles, M. E., Hughes, M. T., & Leftwich, S. A. (2004). Collaborative strategic reading: Real world lessons from classroom teachers. *Remedial and Special Education, 25,* 291–302.

Klingner, J. K., Vaughn, S., & Boardman, A. (2007). *Teaching reading comprehension to students with learning difficulties.* New York: Guilford Press.

Klingner, J. K., Vaughn, S., Boardman, A. G., & Swanson, E. (2012). *Now we get it!: Boosting comprehension with Collaborative Strategic Reading.* San Francisco, CA: Jossey-Bass.

Klingner, J. K., Vaughn, S., Dimino, J., Schumm, J. S., & Bryant, D. (2001). *Collaborative strategic reading: Strategies for improving comprehension.* Longmont, CO: Sopris West.

Klingner, J. K., Vaughn. S., Hughes, M. T., & Arguelles, M. E. (1999). Sustaining research-based practices in reading: A 3-year follow-up. *Remedial and Special Education, 20,* 263–274.

Klingner, J. K., Vaughn, S., Hughes, S. T., Schumm, J. S., & Elbaum, B. (1998). Outcomes for students with and without learning disabilities in inclusive classrooms. *Learning Disabilities Research and Practice, 13,* 153–161.

Klingner, J. K., Vaughn, S., & Schumm, J. S. (1998). Collaborative strategic reading during social studies in heterogeneous fourth-grade classrooms. *The Elementary School Journal, 99,* 3–22.

Klingner, J. K., Vaughn, S., Schumm, J. S., Cohen, P., & Forgan, J. W. (1998). Inclusion or pull-out: Which do students prefer? *Journal of Learning Disabilities, 31,* 148–158.

Kloo, A., & Zigmond, N. (2008). Coteaching revisited: Redrawing the blueprint. *Preventing School Failure, 52*(2), 12–20.

Knapczyk, D. R. (1988). Reducing aggressive behaviors in special and regular class settings by training alternative social responses. *Behavioral Disorders, 14,* 27–39.

Knapczyk, D. R. (1992). Effects of developing alternative responses on the aggressive behavior of adolescents. *Behavioral Disorders, 17,* 247–263.

Knowlton, M., & Wetzel, R. (1996). Braille reading rates as a function of reading tasks. *Journal of Visual Impairment and Blindness, 90,* 227–236.

Koegel, L. K., Koegel, R. L., Harrower, J. K., & Carter, C. M. (1999). Pivotal response intervention I: Overview of approach. *Journal of the Association for Persons with Severe Handicaps, 24,* 174–185.

Koegel, R. L., & Koegel, L. K. (2006). *Pivotal response treatments for autism: Communication, social, & academic development.* Baltimore: Brookes.

Koegel, R. L., Koegel, L. K., & Surratt, A. (1992). Language intervention and disruptive behavior in pre-school children with autism. *Journal of Autism and Developmental Disabilities, 22,* 141–153.

Koenig, A. J., & Holbrook, M. C. (1995). *Learning media assessment of students with visual impairments: A resource guide for teachers* (2nd ed.). Austin, TX: Texas School for the Blind and Visually Impaired.

Koenig, A. J., & Holbrook, M. C. (2000). Ensuring high-quality instruction for students in braille literacy programs. *Journal of Visual Impairment & Blindness, 94,* 677–694.

Koester, H. H. (2004). Usage, performance, and satisfaction outcomes for experienced users of automatic speech recognition. *Journal of Rehabilitation Research & Development, 41,* 739–754.

Koester, H. H. (2006). Factors that influence the performance of experienced speech recognition users. *Assistive Technology, 18,* 56–76.

Kohl, F. L., & Stettner-Eaton, B. A. (1985). Fourth graders as trainers of cafeteria skills to severely handicapped students. *Education and Training of the Mentally Retarded, 20,* 60–68.

Kohler, F. W., & Greenwood, C. R. (1986). Toward a technology of generalization: The identification of natural contingencies of reinforcement. *The Behavior Analyst, 9,* 19–26.

Kohler, F. W., Greteman, C., Raschke, D., & Highnam, C. (2007). Using a buddy skills package to increase the social interactions between a preschooler with autism and her peers. *Topics in Early Childhood Special Education, 27,* 155–163. doi: 10.1177/02711214070270030601

Kohler, F. W., & Strain, P. S. (1990). Peer-assisted interventions: Early promises, notable achievements, and future aspirations. *Child Psychology Review, 10,* 441–452.

Kohler, F. W., Strain, P. S., Hoyson, M., & Jamieson, B. (1997). Merging naturalistic teaching and peer-based strategies to address the IEP objectives of preschoolers with autism: An examination of structural and child behavior outcomes. *Focus on Autism and Other Developmental Disabilities, 12,* 196–206.

Kolich, E. M. (1991). Effects of computer assisted vocabulary training on word knowledge. *Journal of Educational Research, 84,* 177–182.

Konrad, M., Fowler, C. H., Walker, A. R., Test, D. W., & Wood, W. M. (2007). Effects of self-determination interventions on the academic skills of students with learning disabilities. *Learning Disabilities Quarterly, 30,* 89–113.

Koppenhaver, D. A., Hendrix, M. P., & Williams, A. R. (2007). Toward evidence-based literacy interventions for children with severe and multiple disabilities. *Seminars in Speech & Language, 28*(1), 79–89.

Kortteinen, H., Närhi, V., & Ahonen, T. (2009). Does IQ matter in adolescents' reading disability? *Learning and Individual Differences, 19,* 257–261. doi:10.1016/j.lindif.2009.01.003

Kotler, A. L., & Tam, C. (2002). Effectiveness of using discreet utterance speech recognition software. *Augmentative and Alternative Communication, 18,* 137–146.

Kotler, A. L., & Thomas-Stonell, N. (1997). Effects of speech training on the accuracy of speech recognition for an individual with a speech impairment. *Augmentative and Alternative Communication, 13,* 71–80.

Kotler, J., & McMahon, R. (2003). Compliance and noncompliance in anxious, aggressive, and socially competent children: The impact of the Child's Game. *Behavior Therapy, 35,* 495–512.

Kozlow, M., & Bellamy, P. (2004). *Experimental study on the impact of the 6+1 Trait Writing Model on student achievement.* Portland, OR: Northwest Regional Educational Laboratory.

Kratochwill, T. R., Clements, M. A., & Kalymon, K. M. (2007). Response to intervention: Conceptual and methodological issues in implementation. In S. R. Jimerson, M. K. Burns, &

A. M. VanDerHeyden (Eds.), *Handbook of response to intervention* (pp. 25–52). New York: Springer.

Krom, D. M., & Prater, M. A. (1993). IEP goals for intermediate-aged students with mild mental retardation. *Career Development for Exceptional Individuals, 16,* 87–95.

Kucer, S. B. (2008). Speed, accuracy, and comprehension in the reading of elementary students. *Journal of Reading Education, 34,* 33–38.

Kuhn, M. R., & Stahl, S. A. (1998). Teaching children to learn word meanings from context: A synthesis and some questions. *Journal of Literacy Research, 30,* 119–138.

Kupersmidt, J., Coie, J., & Dodge, K. (1990). The role of peer relationships in the development of disorder. In S. Asher & J. Coie (Eds.), *Peer rejection in childhood* (pp. 274–308). New York: Cambridge University Press.

Kurns, S., & Tilly, W. D. (2008). *Response to intervention blueprints for implementation: School building level.* Alexandria, VA: National Association of State Directors of Special Education.

Kutcher, S., & Mackenzie. S. (1988). Successful clonazepam treatment of adolescents with panic disorder. *Journal of Clinical Psychopharmacology, 8,* 299–301.

LaBerge, D., & Samuels, S. A. (1974). Toward a theory of automatic information processing. *Cognitive Psychology, 6,* 293–323.

Labov, W. (1972). *Language in the inner city.* Philadelphia: University of Pennsylvania Press.

Ladd, G. W., Kochenderfer, B. J., & Coleman, C. C. (1997). Classroom peer acceptance, friendship, and victimization: Distinct relational systems that contribute uniquely to children's school adjustment. *Child Development, 68*(6), 1181–1197.

Ladson-Billings, G. (1992). Reading between the lines and beyond the pages: A culturally relevant approach to literacy teaching. *Theory into Practice, 31,* 312–320.

Laitusis, C. C. (2007). Research designs and analysis for studying accommodations on assessments. In C. C. Laitusis & L. L. Cook (Eds.), *Large-scale assessment and accommodations: What works?* (pp. 67–79). Arlington, VA: Council for Exceptional Children.

Laitusis, C. C., & Cook, L. L. (2007). *Large-scale assessment and accommodations: What works?* Arlington, VA: Council for Exceptional Children.

Lake, S. E. (2010). *Slippery slope! The IEP missteps every team must know—and how to avoid them.* Horsham, PA: LRP Publications.

Lambert, N., Nihira, K., & Leland, H. (1993). *AAMR Adaptive Behavior Scale-School: 2nd Edition.* Austin, TX: American Association on Mental Retardation.

Lamory, S. (2002). The effects of culture on special education services: Evil eyes, prayer meetings, and IEPs. *Teaching Exceptional Children, 34*(5), 67–71.

Lancaster, P., & Lancaster, S. (2003). *The self-advocacy strategy* [CD-ROM]. Lawrence, KS: Edge Enterprises.

Lancaster, P. E., Schumaker, J. B., & Deshler, D. D. (2002). The development and validation of an interactive hypermedia program for teaching a self-advocacy strategy to students with disabilities. *Learning Disability Quarterly, 25,* 277–302.

Lancioni, G. E., Klaase, M., & Goossens, A. (1995). Brief report: Pictorial vs. auditory prompt systems for promoting independent task performance in adolescents with multiple handicaps. *Behavioral Interventions, 10,* 237–244.

Lancioni, G. E., & O'Reilly, M. F. (2001). Self-management of instruction cues for occupation: Review of studies with people with severe and profound developmental disabilities. *Research in Developmental Disabilities, 22,* 41–65.

Lancioni, G. E., O'Reilly, M. F., & Emerson, E. (1996). A review of choice research with people with severe and profound developmental disabilities. *Research in Developmental Disabilities, 17,* 391–411.

Lancioni, G. E., Singh, N. N., O'Reilly, M. F., Sigafoos, J., Green, V., Chiapparino, C., & Oliva, D. (2008). A voice-detecting sensor and a scanning keyboard emulator to support word writing by two boys with extensive motor disabilities. *Research in Developmental Disabilities, 30,* 203–209.

Landrum, T. J. (2000). Assessment for eligibility: Issues in identifying students with emotional or behavioral disorders. *Assessment for Effective Intervention 26*(1), 41–49.

Landrum, T. J., Cook, B. G., Tankersley, M. T., & Fitzgerald, S. (2002). Teachers' perceptions of the trustworthiness, useability, and accessibility of information from different sources. *Remedial and Special Education, 23*(1), 42–48.

Landrum, T. J., Cook, B. G., Tankersley, M., & Fitzgerald, S. (2007). Teacher perceptions of the usability of intervention information from personal versus data-based sources. *Education and Treatment of Children, 30*, 27–42.

Landrum, T., & Lloyd, J. (1992). Generalization in social behavior research with children and youth who have emotional or behavioral disorders. *Behavior Modification, 16*, 593–616.

Landrum, T. J., & McDuffie, K. A. (2010). Learning styles in the age of differentiated instruction. *Exceptionality, 18*, 6–17.

Landrum, T. J., & Tankersley, M. (2004). Science at the schoolhouse: An uninvited guest. *Journal of Learning Disabilities, 37*, 207–212.

Landrum, T. J., Tankersley, M., & Kauffman, J. M. (2003). What is special about special education for students with emotional and behavioral disorders? *Journal of Special Education, 37*, 148–156.

Lane, K. L. (2007). Identifying and supporting students at risk for emotional and behavioral disorders within multi-level models: Data driven approaches to conducting secondary interventions with an academic emphasis. *Education and Treatment of Children, 30*, 135–164.

Lane, K. L., Barton-Arwood, S. M., Spencer, J. L., & Kalberg, J. R. (2007). Teaching elementary school educators to design, implement, and evaluate functional assessment-based interventions: Successes and challenges. *Preventing School Failure, 51*, 35–46.

Lane, K. L., & Beebe-Frankenberger, M. (2004). *School-based interventions: The tools you need to succeed.* Upper Saddle River, NJ: Pearson Education.

Lane, K. L., Bruhn, A. L., Crnobori, M. L., & Sewell, A. L. (2009). Designing functional assessment-based interventions using a systematic approach: A promising practice for supporting challenging behavior (pp. 341–370). In T. E. Scruggs &

M. A. Mastropieri (Eds.), *Policy and practice: Advances in learning and behavioral disabilities* (Vol. 22). Bingley, UK: Emerald.

Lane, K. L., Bruhn, A. L., Eisner, S. L., & Kalberg, J. R. (in press). Score reliability and validity of the Student Risk Screening Scale: A psychometrically-sound, feasible tool for use in urban middle schools. *Journal of Emotional and Behavioral Disorders.*

Lane, K. L., & Eisner, S. (2007). *Behavior screening at the elementary level.* Paper presented at Metropolitan Nashville Public Schools, Nashville, TN.

Lane, K. L., Harris, K., Graham, S., Driscoll, S. A., Sandmel, K., Morphy, P., Hebert, M., House, E., & Schatschneider, C. (2011). Self-regulated strategy development at tier-2 for second-grade students with writing and behavioral difficulties: A randomized control trial. *Journal of Research on Educational Effectiveness, 4*, 322–353.

Lane, K. L., Harris, K. R., Graham, S., Weisenbach, J., Brindle, M., & Morphy, P. (2008). The effects of self-regulated strategy development on the writing performance of second grade students with behavioral and writing difficulties. *Journal of Special Education, 41*, 234–253.

Lane, K. L., Kalberg, J. E., Bruhn, A. L., Driscoll, S. A., Wehby, J. H., & Elliott, S. N. (2009). Assessing social validity of school-wide positive behavior support plans: Evidence for the reliability and structure of the Primary Intervention Rating Scale. *School Psychology Review, 38*, 135–144.

Lane, K. L., Kalberg, J. R., Bruhn, A. L., Mahoney, M. E., & Driscoll, S. A. (2008). Primary prevention programs at the elementary level: Issues of treatment integrity, systematic screening, and reinforcement. *Education and Treatment of Children, 31*, 465–494.

Lane, K. L., Kalberg, J. R., & Edwards, C. (2008). An examination of school-wide interventions with primary level efforts conducted in elementary schools: Implications for school psychologists. In D. H. Molina (Ed.) *School psychology: 21st century issues and challenges* (pp. 253–278). New York: Nova Science.

Lane, K. L., Kalberg, J. R., & Menzies, H. M. (2009). *Developing schoolwide programs to prevent and manage problem

behaviors: A step-by-step approach.* New York: Guilford Press.

Lane, K. L., Kalberg, J. R., Menzies, H. M., Bruhn, A., Eisner, S., & Crnobori, M. (2011). Using systematic screening data to assess risk and identify students for targeted supports: Illustrations across the K–12 continuum. *Remedial and Special Education, 32*, 39–54.

Lane, K. L., Kalberg, J. R., Parks, R. J., & Carter, E. W. (2008). Student Risks Screening Scale: Initial evidence for score reliability and validity at the high school level. *Journal of Emotional and Behavioral Disorders, 16*, 178–190.

Lane, K. L., Kalberg, J. R., & Shepcaro, J. C. (2009). An examination of quality indicators of function-based interventions for students with emotional or behavioral disorders attending middle and high schools. *Exceptional Children, 75*, 321–340.

Lane, K. L., & Menzies, H. M. (2002). The effects of a school-based primary intervention program: Preliminary outcomes. *Preventing School Failure, 47*, 26–32.

Lane, K. L., & Menzies, H. M. (2003). A school-wide intervention with primary and secondary levels of support for elementary students: Outcomes and considerations. *Education and Treatment of Children, 26*, 431–451.

Lane, K. L., & Menzies, H. M. (2005). Teacher-identified students with and without academic and behavioral concerns: characteristics and responsiveness. *Behavioral Disorders, 31*, 65–83.

Lane, K. L., Menzies, H., Bruhn, A., & Crnobori, M. (2011). *Managing challenging behaviors in schools: Research-based strategies that work.* New York: Guilford.

Lane, K. L., Menzies, H. M, Oakes, W. P., & Kalberg, J. R. (2012). *Systematic screenings of behavior to support instruction: From preschool to high school.* New York: Guilford.

Lane, K. L., Robertson, E. J., & Graham-Bailey, M. A. L. (2006). An examination of school-wide interventions with primary level efforts conducted in secondary schools: Methodological considerations. In T. E. Scruggs & M. A. Mastropieri (Eds.), *Applications of research methodology: Advances in learning and behavioral disabilities*

(Vol. 19; pp. 157–199). Oxford, UK: Elsevier.

Lane, K. L., Robertson, E. J., & Wehby, J. H. (2002). *Primary Intervention Rating Scale.* Unpublished rating scale.

Lane, K. L., Smither, R., Huseman, R., Guffey, J., & Fox, J. (2007). A function-based intervention to decrease disruptive behavior and increase academic engagement. *Journal of Early and Intensive Behavioral Intervention, 3.4–4.1,* 348–364.

Lane, K. L., Umbreit, J., & Beebe-Frankenberger, M. (1999). A review of functional assessment research with students with or at-risk for emotional and behavioral disorders. *Journal of Positive Behavioral Interventions, 1,* 101–111.

Lane, K. L., & Wehby, J. (2002). Addressing antisocial behavior in the schools: A call for action. *Academic Exchange Quarterly, 6,* 4–9.

Lane, K. L., Wehby, J., Menzies, H. M., Doukas, G. L., Munton, S. M., & Gregg, R. M. (2003). Social skills instruction for students at risk for antisocial behavior: The effects of small-group instruction. *Behavioral Disorders, 28,* 229–248.

Lane, K. L., Wehby, J. H., Menzies, H. M., Gregg, R. M., Doukas, G. L., & Munton, S. M. (2002). Early literacy instruction for first-grade students at-risk for antisocial behavior. *Education and Treatment of Children, 25,* 438–458.

Lane, K. L., Wehby, J., Robertson, E. J., & Rogers, L. (2007). How do different types of high school students respond to positive behavior support programs? Characteristics and responsiveness of teacher-identified students. *Journal of Emotional and Behavioral Disorders, 15,* 3–20.

Lane, K. L., Weisenbach, J. L., Phillips, A., & Wehby, J. H. (2007). Designing, implementing, and evaluating function-based interventions using a systematic, feasible approach. *Behavioral Disorders, 32,* 122–139.

Lane, K. L., Wolery, M., Reichow, B., & Rogers, L. (2006). Describing baseline conditions: Suggestions for study reports. *Journal of Behavioral Education, 16,* 224–234.

Lang, R., O'Reilly, M., Machalicek, W., Lancioni, G., Rispoli, M., & Chan, J. M. (2008). A preliminary comparison of functional analysis results when conducted in contrived versus natural settings. *Journal of Applied Behavior Analysis, 41,* 441–445.

Langer, J., & Applebee, A. N. (1987). *How writing shapes thinking.* Urbana, IL: National Council of Teachers of English.

Lannie, A. L., & McCurdy, B. L. (2007). Preventing disruptive behavior in the urban classroom: Effects of the Good Behavior Game on student and teacher behavior. *Education and Treatment of Children, 30,* 85–98.

Larsen, J. A., & Nippold, M. A. (2007). Morphological analysis in school-age children: Dynamic assessment of a word learning strategy. *Language, Speech, and Hearing Services in Schools, 38,* 201–212.

Lau, M. Y., Sieler, J. D., Muyskens, P., Canter, A., Vankeuren, B., & Marston, D. (2006). Perspectives on the use of the problem-solving model from the viewpoint of a school psychologist, administrator, and teacher from a large Midwest urban school district. *Psychology in the Schools, 43,* 117–127.

Law, J., Garrett, Z. & Nye, C. (2004). The efficacy of treatment for children with developmental speech and language delay/disorder. *Journal of Speech, Language, and Hearing Research, 47,* 924–943.

Law, S. G., & Lane, D. S. (1987). Multicultural acceptance by teacher education students. *Journal of Instructional Psychology, 14,* 3–9.

Layton, C. A., & Koenig, A. J. (1998). Increasing reading fluency in elementary students with low vision through repeated readings. *Journal of Visual Impairment & Blindness, 92,* 276–292.

Lazarus, S. S., Thurlow, M. L., Lail, K. E., & Christensen, L. (2009). A longitudinal analysis of state accommodations policies: Twelve years of change 1993–2005. *Journal of Special Education, 43,* 67–80.

Leafstedt, J. M., Richards, C. R., & Gerber, M. M. (2004). Effectiveness of explicit phonological-awareness instruction for at-risk English learners. *Learning Disabilities Research & Practice, 19,* 252–261.

Leafstedt, J. M., Richards, C., LaMonte, M., & Cassidy, D. (2007). Perspectives on co-teaching: Views from high school students with learning disabilities. *Learning Disabilities: A Multidisciplinary Journal, 14*(3), 177–184.

Lee, C., & Smagorinsky, P. (Eds.). (1999). *Vygotskian perspectives on literacy research: Constructing meaning through collaborative inquiry.* New York: Cambridge University Press.

Lee, D. L., Belfiore, P. J., & Ferko, D. (2006). Using pre and post low-p latency to assess behavioral momentum: A preliminary investigation. *Journal of Behavioral Education, 15*(4), 203–214.

Lee, D. L., & Laspe, A. K. (2003). Using high-probability request sequences to increase journal writing. *Journal of Behavioral Education, 12*(4), 261–273.

Lee, S., Odom, S. I., & Loftin, R. (2007). Social engagement with peers and stereotypic behavior of children with autism. *Journal of Positive Behavior Interventions, 9,* 67–79. doi:10.1177/10983007070090020401

Lee, Y., Sugai, G., & Horner, R. H. (1999). Using an instructional intervention to reduce problem and off-task behaviors, *Journal of Positive Behavior Interventions, 1,* 195–204.

Leedy, A., Bates, P., & Safran, S. P. (2004). Bridging the research-to-practice gap: Improving hallway behavior using positive behavior supports. *Behavioral Disorders, 29,* 130–139.

Leff, S. S., Costigan, T., & Power, T. J. (2003). Using participatory research to develop a playground-based prevention program. *Journal of School Psychology, 42,* 3–21.

Lembke, E. S., & Foegen, A. (2009). Identifying early numeracy indicators for kindergarten and first-grade students. *Learning Disabilities Research & Practice, 24,* 12–20.

Lembke, E. S., Foegen, A., Whittaker, T. A., & Hampton, D. (2008). Establishing technically adequate measures of progress in early numeracy. *Assessment for Effective Intervention, 33,* 206–214.

Lenz, B. K., & Bulgren, J. A. (1995). Promoting learning in the content areas. In P. A. Cegelka & W. H. Berdine (Eds.), *Effective instruction for students with learning problems* (pp. 385–417). Needham Heights, MA: Allyn & Bacon.

Lenz, B. K., Schumaker, J. B., & Deshler, D. D. (1991, March). *Planning in the face of academic diversity: Whose questions should we be answering?* Paper presented at the American Educational Research Association Conference, Chicago.

Lenz, B. K., Schumaker, J. B., Deshler, D. D., & Beals, V. L. (1984). *The word identification strategy* (Learning Strategies Curriculum). Lawrence: University of Kansas.

Leonard, L. B. (2000). *Children with specific language impairment.* Cambridge, MA: MIT Press.

Lerner, J. W. (2002). *Learning disabilities: Theories, diagnosis, and teaching strategies* (8th ed.). Boston: Houghton-Mifflin.

Leslie, L., & Caldwell, J. (2001). *Qualitative Reading Inventory-3.* Boston, MA: Allyn & Bacon.

Leu, D. J., Jr., Kinzer, C. K., Coiro, J., & Cammack, D. (2004). Toward a theory of new literacies emerging from the Internet and other information and communication technologies. In R. B. Ruddell & N. Unrau (Eds.), *Theoretical models and processes of reading* (5th ed., pp. 1568–1611). Newark: International Reading Association.

Levin, J., Anglin, G., & Carney, R. (1987). On empirically validating functions of pictures in prose. In D. Willows & H. Houghton (Eds.), *The psychology of illustration, volume 1: Instructional issues* (pp. 51–85). New York: Springer-Verlag.

Levine, D. U., & Lezotte, L. W. (1990). *Unusually effective schools: A review and analysis of research and practice.* Madison, WI: National Center for Effective Schools Research and Development.

Lewandowski, L. J., Lovett, B. J., Parolin, R., Gordon, M., & Codding, R. S. (2007). Extended time accommodations and the mathematics performance of students with and without ADHD. *Journal of Psychoeducational Assessment, 25,* 17–28.

Lewandowski, L. J., Lovett, B. J., & Rogers, C. L. (2008). Extended time as a testing accommodation for students with reading disabilities: Does a rising tide lift all ships? *Journal of Psychoeducational Assessment, 26,* 315–324.

Lewinsohn, P. M. (1974). A behavioral approach to depression. In R. J. Friedman & M. M. Katz (Eds.), *The psychology of depression: Contemporary theory and research* (pp. 157–184). New York: Wiley.

Lewinsohn, P. M., Munoz, R., Youngren, M. A., & Zeiss, A. (1978). *Control your depression.* Upper Saddle River, NJ: Prentice-Hall.

Lewis, T. J., Colvin, G., & Sugai, G. (2000). The effects of pre-correction and active supervision on the recess behavior of elementary students. *Education and Treatment of Children, 23,* 109–121.

Lewis, T. J., Powers, L. J., Kelk, M. J., & Newcomer, L. L. (2002). Reducing problem behaviors on the playground: An investigation of the application of schoolwide positive behaviors supports. *Psychology in the Schools, 39,* 181–190.

Lewis, T. J., & Sugai, G. (1999). Effective behavior support: A systems approach to proactive schoolwide management. *Focus on Exceptional Children, 31,* 1–24.

Lewis, T. J., Sugai, G., & Colvin, G. (1998). Reducing problem behavior through a school-wide system of effective behavioral support: Investigation of a school-wide social skills training program and contextual intervention. *School Psychology Review, 27,* 446–459.

Leybaert, J., & Alegria, J. (2003). The role of cued speech in language development of deaf children. In M. Marschark & P. E. Spencer (Eds.), *Oxford handbook of deaf studies, language, and education.* New York: Oxford University Press.

Liaupsin, C. J., Umbreit, J., Ferro, J. B., Urso, A., & Upreti, G. (2006). Improving academic engagement through systematic, function-based intervention. *Education and Treatment of Children, 29,* 573–591.

Libster, L. R. (2008). *The efficacy of positive peer reporting procedures for use with neglected-status students in general education classrooms.* Unpublished master's thesis, Louisiana State University.

Lien-Thorne, S., & Kamps, D. (2005). Replication study of the First Step to Success early intervention program. *Behavioral Disorders, 31,* 18–32.

Limbos, M. M., & Geva, E. (2001). Accuracy of teacher assessments of second-language students at risk for reading disability. *Journal of Learning Disabilities, 34,* 136–151.

Linan-Thompson, S., Vaughn, S., Hickman-Davis, P., & Kouzekanani, K. (2003). Effectiveness of supplemental reading instruction for second-grade English language learners with reading difficulties. *Elementary School Journal, 103,* 221–238.

Lindstrom, J. H., & Gregg, N. (2007). The role of extended time on the SAT for students with learning disabilities and/or attention-deficit/hyperactivity disorder. *Learning Disabilities Research and Practice, 22,* 85–95.

Linn, R. L. (2002). Validation of the uses and interpretations of results of state assessment and accountability systems. In G. Tindal & M. Haladyna (Eds.), *Large-scale assessment programs for all students.* Mahwah, NJ: Erlbaum.

Lithner, J. (2008). A research framework for creative and imitative reasoning. *Educational Studies in Mathematics, 67,* 255–276.

Lloyd, J. W. (2002). There's more to identifying learning disability than discrepancy. In R. Bradley, L. Danielson, & D. P. Hallahan (Eds.), *Identification of learning disabilities: Research to practice* (pp. 427–435). Mahwah, NJ: Erlbaum.

Lloyd, J. W., Pullen, P. C., Tankersley, M., & Lloyd, P. A. (2006). Critical dimensions of experimental studies and research syntheses that help define effective practice. In B. G. Cook & B. R. Schirmer (Eds.), *What is special about special education? Examining the role of evidence-based practices* (pp. 136–153). Austin, TX: Pro-Ed.

Lloyd, J., Saltzman, N. J., & Kauffman, J. M. (1981). Predictable generalization in academic learning as a result of preskills and strategy training. *Learning Disability Quarterly, 4,* 203–216.

Lo, Ya-yu., & Cartledge, G. (2006). FBA and BIP: Increasing the behavior adjustment of African American Boys in Schools. *Council for Children with Behavioral Disorders, 31,* 147–161.

Locke, W. R., & Fuchs, L. S. (1995). Effects of peer-mediated reading instruction on the on-task behavior and social interactions of children with behavior disorders. *Journal of Emotional and Behavioral Disorders, 3,* 92–99.

Loeber, R., Dishion, T. J., & Patterson, G. R. (1984). Multiple gating: A multistage assessment procedure for identifying youths at risk for delinquency. *Journal of Research on Crime and Delinquency, 21,* 7–32.

Logan, G. D. (1988). Toward an instance theory of automatization. *Psychological Review, 95,* 492–527.

Lohrmann-O'Rourke, S., Knoster, T., Sabatine, K., Smith, D., Horvath, B., & Llewellyn, G. (2000). School-wide application of PBS in the Bangor area school district. *Journal of Positive Behavior Interventions, 2,* 238–240.

LoPresti, E. F., Brienza, D. M., & Angelo, J. (2002). Head-operated computer controls: Effect of control method on performance for subjects with and without disability. *Interacting with Computers, 14,* 359–377.

LoPresti, E. F., Brienza, D. M., Angelo, J., & Gilbertson, L. (2003). Neck range of motion and use of computer head controls. *Journal of Rehabilitation Research & Development, 40,* 199–212.

Losardo, A., & Bricker, D. (1994). Activity-based intervention and direct instruction: A comparison study. *American Journal on Mental Retardation, 98,* 744–765.

Losel, F., & Beelmann, A. (2003). Effects of child skills training in preventing antisocial behavior: A systematic review of randomized evaluations. *Annals AAPSS, 857,* 84–109.

Losen, D. J., & Orfield, G. (2002). *Racial inequity in special education.* Cambridge, MA: Harvard Education Press.

Lovett, M. W., De Palma, M., Steinbach, K., Temple, M., Benson, N., & Lacerenza, L. (2008). Interventions for reading difficulties: A comparison of response to intervention by ELL and EFL struggling readers. *Journal of Learning Disabilities, 41,* 333–352.

Lovett, M. W., Lacerenza, L., & Borden, S. L. (2000). Putting struggling readers on the PHAST track: A program to integrate phonological and strategy-based remedial reading instruction and maximize outcomes. *Journal of Learning Disabilities, 33,* 458–476.

Lovett, M. W., Steinbach, K. A., & Frijters, J. C. (2000). Remediating the core deficits of developmental reading disability: A Double-Deficit perspective. *Journal of Learning Disabilities, 33,* 334–358.

Luckner, J. L., Sebald, A. M., Cooney, J., Young, J., & Muir, S. G. (2005/2006). An examination of the evidence-based literacy research in deaf education. *American Annals of the Deaf, 150,* 443–456.

Lucyshyn, J. M., Albin, R. W., Horner, R. H., Mann, J. C., Mann, J. A., & Wadsworth, G. (2007). Family implementation of positive behavior support for a child with autism: Longitudinal, single-case, experimental, and descriptive replication and extension. *Journal of Positive Behavior Interventions, 5,* 131–150.

Luiselli, J. K., Putnam, R. F., & Sunderland, M. (2002). Longitudinal evaluation of behavior support intervention in a public middle school. *Journal of Positive Behavior Intervention, 4,* 182–188.

Lundeen, C., & Lundeen, D. (1993, November). *Effectiveness of mainstreaming with collaborative teaching.* Paper presented at the annual convention of the American Speech–Language-Hearing Association, Anaheim, CA. (ERIC Document Reproduction Service No. ED 368 127)

Lusthaus, C. S., Lusthaus, E. W., & Gibbs, H. (1981). Parents' role in the decision process. *Exceptional Children, 48,* 256–257.

Lynch, E. C., & Beare, P. L. (1990). The quality of IEP objectives and their relevance to instruction for students with mental retardation and behavioral disorders. *Remedial and Special Education, 11*(2), 48–55.

Lynch, E. W., & Stein, R. (1983). Perspectives on parent participation in special education. *Exceptional Education Quarterly, 3,* 56–63.

Lynch, J., van den Broek, P., Kremer, K., Kendeou, P., White, M., & Lorch, E. (2008). The development of narrative comprehension and its relation to other early reading skills. *Reading Psychology, 29,* 327–333.

Lyon, G. R. (1998). Why reading is not a natural process. *Educational Leadership, 55*(6), 14–18.

Lyon, G. R., Fletcher, J. M., Shaywitz, S. E., Shaywitz, B. A., Torgesen, J. K., Wood, F. B., . . . Olson, R.K. (2001). Rethinking learning disabilities. In C. E. Finn, Jr., R. A. J. Rotherham, & C. R. Hokanson, Jr. (Eds.), *Rethinking special education for a new century* (pp. 259–287). Washington, DC: Thomas B. Fordham Foundation and Progressive Policy Institute.

Lytle, R. K., & Bordin, J. (2001). Enhancing the IEP team: Strategies for teachers and professionals. *Teaching Exceptional Children, 33*(5), 40–44.

Maag, J. W. (2004). *From theoretical implications to practical applications* (2nd ed.). Belmont, CA: Thompson Wadsworth.

Maag, J. W. (2005). Social skills training for youth with emotional and behavioral disorders and learning disabilities: Problems, conclusions, and suggestions. *Exceptionality, 13,* 155–172.

Maag, J. W. (2006). Social skills training for students with emotional and behavioral disorders; A review of reviews. *Behavioral Disorders, 32,* 5–17.

Maag, J. W., & Larson, P. J. (2004). Training a general education teacher to apply functional assessment. *Education and Treatment of Children, 27,* 26–36.

Maag, J. W., Reid, R., & DiGangi, S. A. (1993). Differential effects of self-monitoring, attention, accuracy, and productivity. *Journal of Applied Behavior Analysis, 26,* 329–344.

MacArthur, C. A., & Cavalier, A. R. (2004). Dictation and speech recognition technology as test accommodations. *Exceptional Children, 71,* 43–58.

MacArthur, C., Schwartz, S., & Graham, S. (1991). Effects of a reciprocal peer revision strategy in special education classrooms. *Learning Disability Research and Practice, 6,* 201–210.

Maccini, P., Gagnon, J. C., & Hughes, C. A. (2002). Technology-based interventions for secondary students with learning disabilities. *Learning Disability Quarterly, 25,* 247–262.

Mace, F. C. (1996). In pursuit of general behavioral relations. *Journal of Applied Behavior Analysis, 29,* 557–563.

Mace, F. C., Hock, M. L., Lalli, J. S., West, B. J., Belfiore, P. J., Pinter, E., & Brown, D. K. (1988). Behavioral momentum in the treatment of noncompliance. *Journal of Applied Behavior Analysis, 21*(2), 123–141.

Mace, F. C., Mauro, B. C., Boyajian, A. E., & Eckert, T. L. (1997). Effects of reinforcer quality on behavioral momentum: Coordinated applied and basic research. *Journal of Applied Behavior Analysis, 30,* 1–20.

MacMillan, D. L., & Forness, S. R. (1998). The role of IQ in special education placement decisions: Primary and determinative or peripheral and inconsequential? *Remedial and Special Education, 19*(4), 239.

MacMillan, D. L., Gresham, F., & Forness, S. (1996). Full inclusion: An empirical perspective. *Behavioral Disorders, 21,* 145–159.

MacMillan, D. L., & Siperstein, G. N. (2002). Learning disabilities as operationally defined by schools. In R. Bradley, L. Danielson, & D. P. Hallahan (Eds.), *Identification of learning disabilities: Research to practice* (pp. 287–333). Mahwah, NJ: Erlbaum.

MacMillan, D. L., & Turnbull, A. P. (1983). Parent involvement in special education: Respecting individual preferences. *Education and Training of the Mentally Retarded, 18,* 4–9.

Macy, M. G., & Bricker, D. D. (2007). Embedding individualized social goals into routine activities in inclusive early childhood classrooms. *Early Childhood Development and Care, 177,* 107–120.

Madelaine, A., & Wheldall, K. (2005). Identifying low-progress readers: Comparing teacher judgment with a curriculum-based measurement procedure. *International Journal of Disability, Development and Education, 52,* 33–42.

Madison Wisconsin Metropolitan School District. (n.d.). *Student intervention monitoring system.* Retrieved from http://dpi.wi.gov/rti/sims2.html

Madsen, C., Becker, W., & Thomas, D. (1968). Rules, praise, and ignoring: Elements of classroom elementary control. *Journal of Applied Behavior Analysis, 1,* 139–150.

Mager, R. (1962). *Preparing instructional objectives.* Palo Alto, CA: Fearon Press.

Magiera, K. A., & Simmons, R. J. (2005). *The Magiera-Simmons quality indicator model of co-teaching.* Fredonia, NY: Excelsior Educational Service.

Magiera, K., Simmons, R., & Hance, S. (2008). Secondary co-teaching: A quality process. *Impact on Instructional Improvement, 34*(1), 18–25.

Magiera, K., Simmons, R., Marotta, A., & Battaglia, B. (2005). A co-teaching model: A response to students with disabilities and their performance on NYS assessments. *School Administrators Association of New York Journal, 34*(2), 9–12.

Magiera, K., Smith, C., Zigmond, N., & Gebauer, K. (2005). Benefits of co-teaching in secondary mathematics classes. *Teaching Exceptional Children, 37*(3), 20–24.

Magiera, K., & Zigmond, N. (2005). Co-teaching in middle school classrooms under routine conditions: Does the instructional experience differ for SWDs in co-taught and solo-taught classes? *Learning Disabilities Research and Practice, 20,* 79–85.

Magill-Evans, J. E., & Restall, G. (1991). Self-esteem of persons with cerebral palsy: from adolescence to adulthood. *The American Journal of Occupational Therapy, 45,* 819–825.

Malecki, C. K. (1998). *The influence of elementary students' social behaviors on academic achievement.* Unpublished doctoral dissertation, University of Wisconsin-Madison.

Malecki, C. K., & Demaray, M. K. (2007). Social behavior assessment and response to intervention. In S. R. Jimerson, M. K. Burns, & A. M. VanDerHeyden (Eds.), *Handbook of response to intervention* (pp. 161–171). New York: Springer.

Malecki, C. K., & Elliott, S. N. (2002). Children's social behaviors as predictors of academic achievement: A longitudinal analysis. *School Psychology Quarterly, 17,* 1–23.

Malouf, D. B., & Schiller, E. P. (1995). Practice and research in special education. *Exceptional Children, 61,* 414–424.

March, J. S., Biederman, J., Wolkow, R., Safferman, A., Mardekian, J., Cook, E. H., et al. (1998). Sertraline in children and adolescents with obsessive-compulsive disorder: A multicenter randomized controlled trial. *Journal of the American Medical Association, 280,* 1252–1293.

March, R. E., & Horner, R. H. (2002). Feasibility and contributions of functional behavioral assessment in schools. *Journal of Emotional and Behavioral Disorders, 10,* 158–170.

March, R., Lewis-Palmer, T., Brown, D., Crone, D., Todd, A.W., & Carr, E. (2000). *Functional assessment checklist for teachers and staff (FACTS).* Educational and Community Supports. University of Oregon, Eugene.

Marcotte, A. M., & Hintze, J. M. (2009). Incremental and predictive utility of formative assessment methods of reading comprehension. *Journal of School Psychology, 47,* 315–335.

Mardell, C., & Goldenberg, D. S. (1998). *DIAL-3: Developmental Indicators for the Assessment of Learning, 3rd Edition.* Bloomington, MN: Pearson Assessment.

Margolis, H., & McCabe, P. (2004). Resolving struggling readers' homework difficulties: A social cognitive perspective. *Reading Psychology, 25,* 225–260.

Mariage, T., & Patriarca, L. (2007). Meeting the spirit of AYP through school reform: Systems of individuation and differentiation are needed to meet all stakeholders' needs. *Focus on Results, 9*(4), GATA 07-01.

Marr, M. B., Aduette, B., White, R., Ellis, E., & Algozzine, B. (2002). School-wide discipline and classroom ecology. *Special Services in the Schools, 18,* 55–72.

Marshak, L. (2008). *Curriculum enhancements in inclusive social studies classrooms: Effects on students with and without disabilities.* Unpublished doctoral dissertation, Fairfax, VA: George Mason University, College of Education and Human Development.

Marshak, L., Mastropieri, M. A., & Scruggs, T. E. (April, 2009). *Peer tutoring with strategic mnemonic instruction in inclusive history classes: Effects for middle school students with and without disabilities.* Paper presented at the annual meeting of the American Educational Research Association, San Diego.

Marshall, S. P. (1995). *Schemas in problem solving.* New York: Cambridge University Press.

Marston, D. (1982). *The technical adequacy of direct, repeated measurement of academic skills in low-achieving elementary students.* Unpublished doctoral dissertation, Minneapolis: University of Minnesota.

Marston, D. B. (1989). A curriculum-based measurement approach to assessing academic performance: What it is and why do it. In M. R. Shinn (Ed.), *Curriculum-based measurement: Assessing special children.* New York: Guilford.

Marston, D., Muyskens, P., Lau, M., & Canter, A. (2003). Problem-solving model for decision making with high-incidence disabilities: The Minneapolis experience. *Learning Disabilities: Research & Practice, 18*(3), 187–200.

Martens, B. K. (1992). Contingency and choice: The implications of matching theory for classroom instruction. *Journal of Behavioral Education, 2,* 121–137.

Martens, B. K., & Houk, J. L. (1989). The application of Herrnstein's Law of Effect to disruptive and on-task behavior of a retarded adolescent girl. *Journal of the Experimental Analysis of Behavior, 51,* 17–27.

Martens, B. K., Lochner, D. G., & Kelly, S. Q. (1992). The effects of variable-interval reinforcement on academic engagement: A demonstration of matching theory. *Journal of Applied Behavior Analysis, 25,* 143–151.

Martin, A. J., Linfoot, K., & Stephenson, J. (1999). How teachers respond to concerns about misbehavior in their classroom. *Psychology in the Schools, 36,* 347–358.

Martin, J. E., Marshall, L. H., Maxson, L. M., & Jerman, R. L. (1997). *The self-directed IEP.* Longmont, CO: Sopris West.

Martin, J. E., Marshall, L. H., & Sale, P. (2004). A 3-year study of middle, junior high and high school IEP meetings. *Exceptional Children, 70,* 285–297.

Martin, J. E., Van Dycke, J. L., Christensen, W. R., Greene, B. A., Gardner, J. E., & Lovett, D. L. (2006). Increasing student participation in their transition IEP meetings: Establishing the self-directed IEP as an evidenced-based practice. *Exceptional Children, 72,* 299–316.

Martin, J. E., Van Dycke, J. L., Greene, B. A., Gardner, J. E., Christensen, W. R., Woods, L. L., & Lovett, D. L. (2006). Direct observation of teacher-directed IEP meetings: Establishing the need for student IEP meeting instruction. *Exceptional Children, 72,* 187–200.

Martin, K. F., Lloyd, J. W., Kauffman, J. M., & Coyne, M. (1995). Teachers' perceptions of educational placement decisions for pupils with emotional or behavioral disorders. *Behavioral Disorders, 20,* 106–117.

Marvin, C., & Mirenda, P. (1993). Home literacy experiences of preschoolers enrolled in head start and special education programs. *Journal of Early Intervention, 17,* 351–367.

Mason, L. (2008). Teaching spelling in the primary grades: A national survey of instructional practices and adaptations. *American Educational Research Journal, 45,* 796–825.

Mason, L. H. (2010). Literacy instruction for students with special needs. In E. Baker, B. McGaw, & P. Peterson (Eds.), *International encyclopedia of education* (3rd ed., pp. 759–766). Oxford, UK: Elsevier.

Mason, L. H., & Graham, S. (2008). Writing instruction for adolescents with learning disabilities: Programs of intervention research. *Learning Disabilities Research and Practice, 23,* 103–112.

Mason, L. H., & Shriner, J. G. (2008). Self-regulated strategy development for writing an opinion essay: Effects for six students with emotional/behavioral disorders. *Reading and Writing: An Interdisciplinary Journal, 21,* 71–93.

Massaro, D. W., & Light, J. (2004). Using visible speech to train perception and production of speech for individuals with hearing loss. *Journal of Speech, Language, and Hearing Research, 47,* 304–320.

Mastropieri, M. A., Emerick, K., & Scruggs, T. E. (1988). Mnemonic instruction of science concepts. *Behavioral Disorders, 14,* 48–56.

Mastropieri, M. A., Jenkins, V., & Scruggs, T. E. (1985). Academic and intellectual characteristics of behaviorally disordered children and youth. *Severe Behavior Disorders Monographs, 8,* 86–104.

Mastropieri, M. A., & Scruggs, T. E. (1988). Increasing the content area learning of learning disabled students: Research implementation. *Learning Disabilities Research, 4,* 17–25.

Mastropieri, M. A., & Scruggs, T. E. (1989a). Constructing more meaningful relationships: Mnemonic instruction for special populations. *Educational Psychology Review, 1,* 83–111.

Mastropieri, M. A., & Scruggs, T. E. (1989b). Mnemonic social studies instruction: Classroom applications. *Remedial and Special Education, 10*(3), 40–46.

Mastropieri, M. A., & Scruggs, T. E. (1989c). Reconstructive elaborations: Strategies that facilitate content learning. *Learning Disabilities Focus, 4,* 73–77.

Mastropieri, M. A., & Scruggs, T. E. (1992). Science for students with disabilities. *Review of Educational Research, 62,* 377–411. doi: 10.3102/00346543062004377

Mastropieri, M. A., & Scruggs, T. E. (2004). Effective classroom instruction. In C. Spielberger (Ed.), *Encyclopedia of applied psychology* (pp. 687–691). Oxford, UK: Elsevier.

Mastropieri, M. A., & Scruggs, T. E. (2009). *The inclusive classroom: Strategies for effective differentiated instruction* (4th ed.). Upper Saddle River, NJ: Merrill/Pearson Education.

Mastropieri, M. A., Scruggs, T. E., Bakken, J. P., & Whedon, C. (1996). Reading comprehension: A synthesis of research in learning disabilities. In T. E. Scruggs & M. A. Mastropieri (Eds.), *Advances in learning and behavioral disabilities* (pp. 277–303). Greenwhich, CT: JAI Press.

Mastropieri, M. A., Scruggs, T. E., Bakken, J. P., & Whedon, C. (1997). Using mnemonic strategies to teach information about U.S. presidents: A classroom-based investigation. *Learning Disability Quarterly, 20,* 13–21.

Mastropieri, M. A., Scruggs, T. E., & Fulk, B. M. (1990). Teaching abstract vocabulary with the keyword method: Effects on recall and comprehension. *Journal of Learning Disabilities, 23*(2), 92–96, 107.

Mastropieri, M. A., Scruggs, T. E., & Graetz, J. E. (2003). Reading comprehension instruction for secondary students: Challenges for struggling students and teachers. *Learning Disability Quarterly, 26,* 103–116.

Mastropieri, M. A., Scruggs, T. E., & Graetz, J. (2005). Cognition and learning in inclusive high school chemistry classes. In T. E. Scruggs & M. A. Mastropieri (Eds.), *Cognition and learning in diverse settings: Advances in learning and behavioral disabilities* (Vol. 18, pp. 107–118). Oxford, UK: Elsevier.

Mastropieri, M. A., Scruggs, T. E., & Levin, J. R. (1985). Maximizing what exceptional students can learn: A review of research on the keyword method and related mnemonic techniques. *Remedial and Special Education, 6*(2), 39–45.

Mastropieri, M. A., Scruggs, T. E., & Levin, J. R. (1986). Direct vs. mnemonic instruction: Relative benefits for exceptional learners. *Journal of Special Education, 20,* 299–308.

Mastropieri, M. A., Scruggs, T. E., Levin, J. R., Gaffney, J., & McLoone, B. (1985). Mnemonic vocabulary instruction for learning disabled students. *Learning Disability Quarterly, 8,* 57–63.

Mastropieri, M. A., Scruggs, T. E., Mantzicopoulos, P. Y., Sturgeon, A., Goodwin, L., & Chung, S. (1998). "A place where living things affect and depend on each other": Qualitative and quantitative outcomes associated with inclusive science teaching. *Science Education, 82,* 163–179.

Mastropieri, M. A., Scruggs, T. E., & Marshak, L. (2008). Training teachers, parents, and peers to implement effective teaching strategies for content area learning. In T. E. Scruggs & M. A. Mastropieri (Eds.), *Personnel preparation: Advances in learning and behavioral disabilities* (Vol. 21, pp. 311–329). Bingley, UK: Emerald.

Mastropieri, M. A., Scruggs, T. E., Norland, J., Berkeley, S., McDuffie, K., Tornquist, E. H., & Conners, N. (2006). Differentiated curriculum enhancement in inclusive middle school science: Effects on classroom and high-stakes tests. *Journal of Special Education, 40,* 130–137.

Mastropieri, M. A., Scruggs, T. E., Whittaker, M. E. S., & Bakken, J. P. (1994). Applications of mnemonic strategies with students with mental disabilities. *Remedial and Special Education, 15*(1), 34–43.

Mastropieri, M. A., Sweda, J., & Scruggs, T. E. (2000). Putting mnemonic strategies to work in an inclusive classroom. *Learning Disabilities Research & Practice, 15,* 69–74.

Mather, N., & Kaufman, N. (2006). Introduction to the special issue, part one: It's about the *what,* the *how well,* and the *why. Psychology in the Schools, 43*(7), 747–752.

Mathes, P. G., & Babyak, A. O. (2001). The effects of Peer-Assisted Literacy Strategies for first-grade readers with and without additional mini-skills lessons. *Learning Disabilities: Research & Practice, 16,* 28–44.

Mathes, P. G., Denton, C. A., Fletcher, J. M., Anthony, J. L., Francis, D. J., & Schatschneider, C. (2005). The effects of theoretically different instruction and student characteristics on the skills of struggling readers. *Reading Research Quarterly, 40*(2), 148–182.

Mathes, P. G., Howard, J. K., Allen, S. H., & Fuchs, D. (1998). Peer-assisted learning strategies for first grade readers: Responding to the needs of diverse learners. *Reading Research Quarterly, 33,* 62–94.

Mathes, P. G., Kethley, C., Nimon, K., Denton, C. A., & Ware, P. (2009). *A test of proven early intervention in high poverty schools: Do results generalize to more challenging contexts?* Unpublished manuscript.

Mathes, P., & Torgesen, J. (2005a). *Early interventions in reading.* New York: McGraw Hill/SRA.

Mathes, P. G., & Torgesen, J. K. (2005b) *Early interventions in reading, Level 1.* Columbus, OH: SRA/McGraw-Hill.

Mathes, P. G., Torgesen, J. K., Allen, S. H., & Allor, J. H. (2001). *First-grade PALS: Peer-Assisted Literacy Strategies.* Longmont, CO: Sopris West.

Mathes, P. G., Torgesen, J. K., & Allor, J. H. (2001). The effects of Peer-Assisted Learning Strategies for first grade readers with and without additional computer assisted instruction in phonological awareness. *American Educational Research Journal, 38,* 371–410.

Mathes, P. G., Torgesen, J. K., & Clancy-Menchetti, J. (2001). *K-PALS: Kindergarten Peer-Assisted Literacy Strategies.* Longmont, CO: Sopris West.

Mathur, S., & Rutherford, R. (1991). Peer-mediated interventions promoting social skills for children and youth with behavioral disorders. *Education and Treatment of Children, 14,* 227–242.

Mattingly, D. J., Prislin, R., McKenzie, T. L., Rodriguez, J. L., & Kayzar, B. (2002). Evaluating evaluations: The case of parent involvement programs. *Review of Educational Research, 72,* 549–576.

Mattingly, J. C., & Bott, D. A. (1990). Teaching multiplication facts to students with learning problems. *Exceptional Children, 56,* 438–450.

May, K. (2009). By reason thereof: Causation and eligibility under the Individuals with Disabilities Education Act. *BYU Education and Law Journal,* (1), 173–195.

May, S., Ard, W., III, Todd, A. W., Horner, R. H., Glasgow, A., Sugai, G., & Sprague, J. (2000). *School-wide Information System (SWIS ©).* Eugene: University of Oregon, Educational and Community Supports.

Mayberry, R. (2010). Early language acquisition and adult language ability: What sign language reveals about the critical period for language. In M. Marschark & P. Spencer (Eds.), *The Oxford handbook of deaf studies, language, and education, Volume 2.* New York: Oxford University Press.

Mayer, C., & Akamatsu, C. (2003). Bilingualism and literacy. In M. Marschark & P. Spencer (Eds.), *The Oxford handbook of deaf studies, language, and education.* New York: Oxford University Press.

Mayer, G. R. (1995). Preventing antisocial behavior in the schools. *Journal of Applied Behavior Analysis, 28,* 467–478.

Mayer, G. R., Butterworth, T., Nafpaktitis, M., & Sulzer-Azaroff, B. (1983). Preventing school vandalism and improving discipline: A three-year study. *Journal of Applied Behavior Analysis, 16,* 355–369.

Mayer, R. E. (1985). Mathematical ability. In R. J. Sternberg (Ed.), *Human abilities: Information processing approach* (pp. 127–150). San Francisco, CA: Freeman.

Mayer, R. E. (1999). *The promise of educational psychology Vol. I: Learning in the content areas.* Upper Saddle River, NJ: Merrill/Pearson.

Mayer, R. E., & Hegarty, M. (1996). The process of understanding mathematics problems. In R. J. Sternberg & T. Ben-Zeev (Eds.), *The nature of mathematical thinking* (pp. 29–53). Hillsdale, NJ: Erlbaum.

McBride, B. J., & Schwartz, I. S. (2003). Effects of teaching early interventionists to use discrete trials during ongoing classroom activities. *Topics in Early Childhood Special Education, 23,* 5–18.

McCauley, E., Burke, P., Mitchell, J. R., & Moss, S. (1988). Cognitive attributes of depression in children and adolescents. *Journal of Consulting and Clinical Psychology, 56*(6), 903–908.

McComas, J. J., Wacker, D. P., & Cooper, L. J. (1998). Increasing compliance with medical procedures: Application of the high-probability request procedure to a toddler. *Journal of Applied Behavior Analysis, 31*(2), 287–290.

McComas, J. J., Wacker, D. P., Cooper, L. J., Asmus, J. M., Richman, D., & Stoner, B. (1996). Brief experimental analysis of stimulus prompts for accurate responding on academic tasks in an outpatient clinic. *Journal of Applied Behavior Analysis, 29,* 397–401.

McComas, J. J., Wacker, D. P., Cooper, L. J., Peck, S., Golonka, Z., Millard, T., & Richman, D. (2000). Effects of the high-probability request procedure: Patterns of responding to low-probability requests. *Journal of Developmental and Physical Disabilities, 12*(2), 157–171.

McConaughy, S. H., Kay, P. L., & Fitzgerald, M. (1999). The achieving, behaving, caring project for preventing ED: Two-year outcomes. *Journal of Emotional and Behavioral Disorders, 7,* 224–239.

McCormick, K. M., Jolivette, K., & Ridgely, R. (2003). Choice making as an intervention strategy for young children. *Young Exceptional Children, 6,* 3–10.

McCormick, L. (2003). Introduction to language acquisition. In L. McCormick, D. F. Loeb, & R. L. Schiefelbusch (Eds.), *Supporting children with communication difficulties in inclusive settings: School-based language intervention* (2nd ed., pp. 1–42). Boston: Allyn & Bacon.

McCurdy, B. L., Manella, M. C., & Eldridge, N. (2003). Positive behavior support in urban schools: Can we prevent the escalation of antisocial behavior? *Journal of Positive Behavior Interventions, 5,* 158–170.

McDonnell, A. (1993). Ethical considerations in teaching compliance to individuals with mental retardation. *Education and Training in Mental Retardation, 28,* 3–12.

McDonnell, J. (1998). Instruction for students with severe disabilities in general education settings. *Education and Training in Mental Retardation and Developmental Disabilities, 33,* 199–215.

McDonnell, J., & Ferguson, B. (1989). A comparison of time delay and decreasing prompt hierarchy strategies in teaching baking skills to students with moderate handicaps. *Journal of Applied Behavior Analysis, 22,* 85–91.

McDonnell, J., Horner, R. H., & Williams, J. A. (1984). Comparison of three strategies for teaching generalized grocery purchasing to high school students with severe handicaps. *The Journal of the Association for Persons with Severe Handicaps, 9,* 123–133.

McDonnell, J., & Laughlin, B. (1989). A comparison of backward ad concurrent chaining strategies in teaching community skills. *Education and Training in Mental Retardation, 24,* 230–238.

McDonnell, J., & McFarland, S. (1988). A comparison of forward and concurrent chaining strategies in teaching Laundromat skills to students with severe handicaps. *Research in Developmental Disabilities, 9,* 177–194.

McDougall, D. (1998). Research on self-management techniques used by students with disabilities in general education settings. *Remedial and Special Education, 19,* 310–320.

McDuffie, K. A., Landrum, T. J., & Gelman, J. (2008). Co-teaching and students with emotional and behavioral disorders. *Beyond Behavior, 17*(2), 11–16.

McDuffie, K. A., Mastropieri, M. A., & Scruggs, T. E. (2009). Differential effects of peer tutoring in co-taught and non co-taught classes: Results for content learning and student-teacher interactions. *Exceptional Children, 75,* 493–510.

McGahee-Kovac, M. (1995). *Student-led IEPs.* Washington, DC: National Information Center for Children and Youth with Disabilities.

McGee, G. G., Krantz, P. J., Mason, D., & McClannahan, L. E. (1983). A modified incidental-teaching procedure for autistic youth: Acquisition and generalization of receptive object labels. *Journal of Applied Behavior Analysis, 16,* 329–338.

McGee, G. G., Krantz, P. J., & McClannahan, L. E. (1985). The

facilitative effects of incidental teaching on preposition use by autistic children. *Journal of Applied Behavior Analysis, 18,* 17–31.

McGee, G. G., & McCoy, J. F. (1981). Training procedures for acquisition and retention of reading in retarded youth. *Applied Research in Mental Retardation, 2*(3), 263–276.

McGregor, K., & Leonard, L. B. (1995). Intervention for word-finding deficits in children. In M. Fey, J. Windsor, & S. Warren (Eds.), *Language intervention: Preschool through the elementary years* (pp. 85–105). Baltimore: Brookes.

McGuinness, D. (1997). Decoding strategies as predictors of reading skill: A follow-on study [study of first- and third-grade children]. *Annals of Dyslexia, 47,* 117–150.

McIntosh, K., Campbell, A., Carter, D., & Zumbo, B. (2009). Concurrent validity of office discipline referrals and cut points used in schoolwide positive behavior support. *Behavioral Disorders, 34*(2), 100–113.

McIntosh, R., Vaughn, S., Schumm, J. S., Haager, D., & Lee, O. (1993). Observations of students with learning disabilities in general education classrooms. *Exceptional Children, 60,* 249–262.

McIntosh, R., Vaughn, S., & Zaragoza, N. (1991). A review of social interventions for students with learning disabilities. *Journal of Learning Disabilities, 24,* 451–458.

McIntyre, S. B., Test, D. W., Cooke, N. L., & Beattie, J. (1991). Using count-bys to increase multiplication facts fluency. *Learning Disability Quarterly, 14,* 82–88.

McKenna, M. C., & Picard, M. (2006). Revisiting the role of miscue analysis in effective teaching. *The Reading Teacher, 60,* 378–380.

McKeown, M. G. (1986). The acquisition of word meaning from context by children of high and low ability. *Reading Research Quarterly, 20,* 482–496.

McKevitt, B., & Elliott, S. (2003). Effects and perceived consequences of using read-aloud and teacher-recommended test accommodations on a reading achievement test. *School Psychology Review, 32,* 583–600.

McLaughlin, C. A., & Davis, C.A. (2010). *Using high-probability requests in the classroom to decrease challenging behaviors.* Paper presented at the International Conference on Autism, Intellectual Disabilities, and Other Developmental Disabilities, Maui, HI.

McLaughlin, M. J. (2002). Examining special and general education collaborative practices in exemplary schools. *Journal of Educational and Psychological Consultation, 13,* 279–284.

McLaughlin, M. J., & Warren, S. H. (1995). *Individual education programs: Issues and options for change* (Final Report for the Office of Special Education Programs). Alexandria, VA: National Association of State Directors of Special Education.

McLeod, B. D., Southam-Gerow, M. A., & Weisz, J. R. (2009). Conceptual and methodological issues in treatment integrity measurement. *School Psychology Review, 38,* 541–546.

McLoone, B. B., Scruggs, T. E., Mastropieri, M. A., & Zucker, S. F. (1986). Memory strategy instruction and training with LD adolescents. *Learning Disabilities Research, 2,* 45–53.

McLoughlin, J. A., & Lewis, R. B. (2008). *Assessing students with special needs* (7th ed.). Upper Saddle River, NJ: Merrill/Pearson.

McMahon, R., & Forehand, R. (2003) *Helping the noncompliant child: Family-based treatment for oppositional behavior* (2nd ed.). New York: Guilford Press.

McMahon, S. D., & Washburn, J. J. (2003). Violence prevention: An evaluation of program effects with urban African-American students. *Journal of Primary Prevention, 24,* 43–62.

McMaster, K. L., Fuchs, D., & Fuchs, L. S. (2006). Research on peer-assisted learning strategies: The promise and limitations of peer-mediated instruction. *Reading and Writing Quarterly: Overcoming Learning Difficulties, 22,* 5–25.

McMaster, K. L., Fuchs, D., & Fuchs, L. S. (2007). Promises and limitations of peer-assisted learning strategies in reading. *Learning Disabilities: A Contemporary Journal, 5,* 97–112.

McMaster, K. L., Fuchs, D., Fuchs, L. S., & Compton, D. L. (2005). Responding to nonresponders: An experimental field trial of identification and intervention methods. *Exceptional Children, 71,* 445–464.

McMaster, K. L., Fuchs, D., Saenz, L., Lemons, C., Kearns, D., Yen, L., . . . Fuchs, L. S. (2010). Scaling up PALS: The importance of implementing evidence-based practice with fidelity and flexibility. *New Times for DLD, 28*(1), 1–3. Retrieved from http://www.teachingld.org/pdf/NewTimes_ScalingUpPals2010.pdf

McMaster, K. L., & Wagner, D. (2007). Monitoring response to general education instruction. In S. R. Jimerson, M. K. Burns, & A. M. VanDerHeyden (Eds.), *Handbook of response to intervention: The science and practice of assessment and intervention* (pp. 223–233). New York: Springer.

McNair, J., & Rusch, F. R. (1991). Parent involvement in transition programs. *Mental Retardation, 29,* 93–101.

McNamara, K., & Hollinger, C. (2003). Intervention-based assessment: Evaluation rates and eligibility findings. *Exceptional Children, 69,* 181–194.

McWilliam, R. A., & Casey, A. M. (2008). *Engagement of every child in the preschool classroom.* Baltimore: Brookes.

McWilliam, R. A., Tocci, L., & Harbin, G. L. (1998). Family-centered services: Service providers' discourse and behavior. *Topics in Early Childhood Special Education, 18,* 206–221.

Mead, J. F., & Paige, M. A. (2008). *Board of Education of Hendrick Hudson v. Rowley:* An examination of its precedential impact. *Journal of Law & Education, 37,* 329–345.

Mechling, L. C. (2004). Effects of multimedia, computer-based instruction on grocery shopping fluency. *Journal of Special Education Technology, 19,* 23–34.

Mechling, L. C. (2007). Assistive technology as a self-management tool for prompting students with intellectual disabilities to initiate and complete daily tasks: A literature review. *Education and Training in Developmental Disabilities, 42,* 252–269.

Mechling, L. C., & Gast, D. L. (1997). Combination audio-visual self-prompting system for teaching chained tasks to students with intellectual disabilities. *Education and Training in Mental Retardation and Developmental Disabilities, 32,* 138–153.

Mellard, D. F., & Johnson, E. (2008). *RTI: A practitioner's guide to implementing response to intervention.* Thousand Oaks, CA: Corwin Press.

Meloy, L., Deville, C., & Frisbie, D. (2002). The effect of a read aloud accommodation on test scores of students with and without a learning disability in reading. *Remedial and Special Education, 23,* 248–255.

Menlove, R. R., Hudson, P. J., & Suter, D. (2001). A field of IEP dreams: Increasing general education teacher participation in the IEP development process. *Teaching Exceptional Children, 33*(5), 28–33.

Mercer, C. D., & Pullen, P. C. (2005). *Students with learning disabilities* (7th ed.). Upper Saddle River, NJ: Merrill/Pearson Education.

Merrell, K. W. (2001). *Helping students overcome depression and anxiety: A practical guide.* New York: Guilford Press.

Merrell, K. W., & Gimpel, G. A. (1998). *Social skills of children and adolescents: Conceptualization, assessment, treatment.* Mahwah, NJ: Erlbaum.

Merulla, E., & McKinnon, A. (1982). 'Stuck' on Deno's cascade. *Journal of Learning Disabilities, 15,* 94–96.

Messick, S. (1988). The once and future issues of validity: Assessing the meaning and consequences of measurement. In H. Wainer & H. I. Braun (Eds.), *Test validity* (pp. 22–45). Hillsdale, NJ: Erlbaum.

Messick, S. (1995). Validity of psychological assessment: Validation of inferences from persons' responses and performances as scientific inquiry into score meaning. *American Psychologist, 50,* 741–179.

Metzler, C. W., Biglan, A., Rusby, J. C., & Sprague, J. R. (2001). Evaluation of a comprehensive behavior management program to improve school-wide positive behavior support. *Education and Treatment of Children, 24,* 448–479.

Meyer, A., & Rose, D. H. (1998). *Learning to read in the computer age.* Cambridge, MA: Brookline.

Meyer, L., & Evans, I. (1989). *Nonaversive intervention for behavior problems: A manual for home and community.* Brookes: Baltimore, MD.

Michnowicz, L. L., McConnell, S. R., Peterson, C. A., & Odom, S. L.

(1995). Social goals and objectives of preschool IEPs: A content analysis. *Journal of Early Intervention, 19,* 273–282.

Mike, D. G. (1995). Literacy and cerebral palsy: Factors influencing literacy learning in a self-contained setting. *Journal of Reading Behavior, 27,* 627–642.

Millar, D. C., Light, J. C., & McNaughton, D. B. (2004). The effect of direct instruction and writer's workshop on the early writing skills of children who use augmentative and alternative communication. *Augmentative and Alternative Communication, 20,* 164–178.

Millar, S. (1974). Tactile short-term memory by blind and sighted children. *British Journal of Psychology, 65,* 253–263.

Miller, D., Linn, R., & Gronlund, N. (2009). *Measurement and assessment in teaching* (10th ed.). Upper Saddle River, NJ: Allyn & Bacon/Pearson.

Miller, M. J., Lane, K. L., & Wehby, J. (2005). Social skills instruction for students with high incidence disabilities: An effective, efficient approach for addressing acquisition deficits. *Preventing School Failure, 49,* 27–40.

Miller, S. P., & Mercer, C. D. (1993). Using data to learn about concrete-semiconcrete-abstract instruction for students with math disabilities. *Learning Disabilities Research & Practice, 8,* 89–96.

Miller, U. C., & Test, D. W. (1989). A comparison of constant time delay and most-to-least prompting in teaching laundry skills to students with moderate mental retardation. *Education and Training in Mental Retardation, 24,* 363–370.

Miner, C. A., & Bates, P. E. (1997). The effect of person centered planning on the IEP/Transition Planning process. *Education and Training in Mental Retardation and Developmental Disabilities, 32,* 105–112.

Minnesota Department of Education. (2009). *Minnesota manual of accommodations: A guide to selecting, administering, and evaluating the use of test administration accommodations for students with disabilities.* Roseville, MN: Author.

Mirenda, P., Turoldo, K., & McAvoy, C. (2006). The impact of word prediction software on the written output of students with physical disabilities. *Journal of Special Education Technology, 21*(3), 5–12.

Moffitt, T. E. (1993). Adolescence-limited and life-course-persistent antisocial behavior: A developmental taxonomy. *Psychological Review, 100,* 674–701.

Montague, M. (1992). The effects of cognitive and metacognitive strategy instruction on mathematical problem solving of middle school students with learning disabilities. *Journal of Learning Disabilities, 25,* 230–248.

Montague, M. (2003). *Solve It: A mathematical problem-solving instructional program.* Reston, VA: Exceptional Innovations.

Montague, M., & Applegate, B. (1993). Mathematical problem-solving characteristics of middle school students with learning disabilities. *Journal of Special Education, 27,* 175–201.

Montague, M., Applegate, B., & Marquard, K. (1993). Cognitive strategy instruction and mathematical problem-solving performance of students with learning disabilities. *Learning Disabilities Research and Practice, 29,* 251–261.

Montague, M., & Bos, C. (1986). The effect of cognitive strategy training on verbal math problem solving performance of learning disabled adolescents. *Journal of Learning Disabilities, 19,* 26–33.

Montague, M., & Dietz, S. (2009). Evaluating the evidence base for cognitive strategy instruction and mathematical problem solving. *Exceptional Children, 75,* 285–382.

Montague, M., Enders, C., & Dietz, S. (2009). The effects of Solve It! on middle school students' math problem solving and math self-efficacy. Unpublished raw data.

Montague, M., Enders, C., & Dietz, S. (2010, February). *The effects of Solve It! on middle school students' math problem solving.* Paper presented at the Pacific Coast Research Conference, Coronado, CA.

Montali, J., & Lewandowski, L. (1996). Bimodal reading: Benefits of a talking computer for average and less skilled readers. *Journal of Learning Disabilities, 29,* 271–279.

Montgomery, J., & Kahn, N. (2003). You are going to be an author: Adolescent narratives as intervention. *Communication Disorders Quarterly, 24,* 143–152.

Mooney, P., Ryan, J., Uhing, B., Reid, R., & Epstein, M. (2005). A review of self-management interventions targeting academic outcomes for students with emotional and behavioral disorders. *Journal of Behavioral Education, 14,* 203–221.

Moore, M., & Calvert, S. (2000). Brief report: Vocabulary acquisition for children with autism: Teacher or computer instruction. *Journal of Autism and Developmental Disorders, 30,* 359–362.

Moore, S. C., Agran, M., & Fodor-Davis, J. (1989). Using self-management strategies to increase the production rates of workers with severe handicaps. *Education and Training in Mental Retardation, 24,* 324–332.

Moran, M. R., Schumaker, J. B., & Vetter, A. F. (1981). *Teaching a paragraph organization strategy to learning disabled adolescents* (Research Rep. No. 54). Lawrence, KS: Institute for Research in Learning Disabilities.

Moreau, M., & Fidrych-Puzzo, H. (1994). *The story grammar marker.* Easthampton, MA: Discourse Skills Productions.

Morgan, P. (2006). Increasing task engagement using preference or choice-making: Some behavioral and methodological factors affecting their efficacy as classroom interventions. *Remedial and Special Education, 27,* 176–187.

Moroz, K. B., & Jones, K. M. (2002). The effects of positive peer reporting on children's social involvement. *School Psychology Review, 31,* 235–245.

Morris, R. D., Lovett, M., Wolf, M., Sevcik, R., Steinbeach, K., Frijters, J. C., & Shapiro, M. B. (2010). Multiple-component remediation for developmental reading disabilities: IQ, socioeconomic status, and race as factors in remedial outcome. *Journal of Learning Disabilities,* doi:10.1177/0022219409355472

Morrison, J. Q., & Jones, K. M. (2007). The effects of positive peer reporting as a class-wide positive behavioral support. *Journal of Behavioral Education, 16,* 111–124.

Morrison, L., Kamps, D., Garcia, J., & Parker, D. (2001). Peer mediation and monitoring strategies to improve initiations and social skills for students with autism. *Journal of Positive Behavior Interventions, 3,* 237–250. doi:10.1177/109830070100300405

Morse, T. E., & Schuster, J. W. (2000). Teaching elementary students with moderate intellectual disabilities how to shop for groceries. *Exceptional Children, 66,* 273–288.

Morse, T. E., & Schuster, J. W. (2004). Simultaneous prompting: A review of the literature. *Education and Training in Developmental Disabilities, 39,* 153–168.

Mosk, M. D., & Bucher, B. (1984). Prompting and stimulus shaping procedures for teaching visual-motor skills to retarded children. *Journal of Applied Behavior Analysis, 17,* 23–34.

Mostert, M. P. (Ed.). (2010). Empirically unsupported interventions in special education [special issue]. *Exceptionality, 18*(1).

Mostert, M. P., & Crockett, J. B. (2000). Reclaiming the history of special education for more effective practice. *Exceptionality, 8,* 133–143.

Mount, B., & Zwernik, K. (1988). *It's never too early, it's never too late: A booklet about personal futures planning.* St. Paul, MN: Minnesota Governor's Planning Council on Developmental Disabilities.

Mudd, J. M., & Wolery, M. (1987). Training Head Start teachers to use incidental teaching. *Journal of the Division for Early Childhood, 11*(2), 124–133.

Mueller, J. H. (1979). Anxiety and encoding processes in memory. *Personality and Social Psychology Bulletin, 5,* 288–294.

Muller, E., Friend, M., & Hurley-Chamberlain, D. (2009). State-level approaches to co-teaching. *In Forum Brief Policy Analysis,* 1–7.

Murawski, W. W. (2006). Student outcomes in co-taught secondary English classes: How can we improve? *Reading and Writing Quarterly, 22,* 227–247.

Murawski, W. W., & Swanson, H. L. (2001). A meta-analysis of co-teaching research: Where are the data? *Remedial and Special Education, 22,* 258–267.

Murphy, J. L., Hatton, D., & Erickson, K. (2008). Exploring the early literacy practices of teachers of infants, toddlers, and preschoolers with visual impairments. *Journal of Visual Impairment and Blindness, 102,* 133–146.

Murray-Branch, J., Udvari-Solner, A., & Bailey, B. (1991). Textured communication systems for individuals with severe intellectual and dual sensory impairments. *Language, Speech, and Hearing Services in Schools, 22,* 260–268.

Musson, J. E., Thomas, M. K., Towles-Reeves, E., & Kearns, J. F. (2010). An analysis of state alternate assessment participation guidelines. *The Journal of Special Education, 44,* 67–78.

Naglieri, J. A. (1997). *Naglieri Nonverbal Ability Test.* San Antonio, TX: The Psychological Corporation.

Nagy, W. E. (2007). Metalinguistic awareness and the vocabulary-comprehension connection. In R. K. Wagner, A. E. Muse, & K. R. Tannenbaum (Eds.), *Vocabulary acquisition: Implications for reading comprehension* (pp. 52–77). New York: Guilford.

Nagy, W. E., & Anderson, R. C. (1984). The number of words in printed school English. *Reading Research Quarterly, 19,* 304–330.

Nagy, W. E., & Scott, J. A. (2000). Vocabulary processes. In M. L. Kamil, P. B. Mosenthal, P. D. Pearson, & R. Barr (Eds.), *Handbook of reading research* (Vol. 3, pp. 269–284). Mahwah, NJ: Erlbaum.

Najdowski, A. C., Wallace, M. D., Penrod, B., Tarbox, J., Reagon, K., & Higbee, T. S. (2008). Caregiver-conducted experimental functional analyses of inappropriate mealtime behavior. *Journal of Applied Behavior Analysis, 41,* 459–465.

Narr, R. F. (2008). Phonological awareness and decoding in deaf/hard of hearing students who use Visual Phonics. *Journal of Deaf Studies and Deaf Education, 13,* 405–416.

Narr, R. F., & Cawthon, S. (2010). The "Wh" questions of visual phonics: What, who, where, when, and why. *Journal of Deaf Studies and Deaf Education,* Advance online publication. doi:10.1093/deafed/enq038

Nash, H., & Snowling, M. (2006). Teaching new words to children with poor existing vocabulary knowledge: A controlled evaluation of the definition and context methods. *International Journal of Language and Communication Disorders, 41,* 335–354.

Nathan, M. J., & Kim, S. (2009). Regulation of teacher elicitations in the mathematics classroom. *Cognition and Instruction, 27,* 91–120.

Nathan, R. G., & Stanovich, K. E. (1991). The causes and consequences in differences in reading fluency. *Theory in Practice, 30*(3), 176–184.

Nathanson, R., Crank, J., Saywitz, K., & Ruegg, E. (2007). Enhancing the oral narratives of children with learning disabilities. *Reading & Writing Quarterly, 23,* 315–331.

National Assessment of Educational Progress. (2009). *The nation's report card.* Washington, DC: Author.

National Assessment of Educational Progress, National Center for Education Statistics. (2007). *The nation's report card: Reading 2007.* Washington, DC: National Center for Education Statistics.

National Autism Center. (2009). *National standards report: National standards project—Addressing the need for evidence-based practice guidelines for autism spectrum disorders.* Randolph, MA: National Autism Center.

National Center for Culturally Responsive Educational Systems. (2008). *Culturally responsive literacy.* Professional Learning Series. Tempe, AZ: Author.

National Center on Educational Restructuring and Inclusion. (1995). *National study of inclusive education* (2nd ed.). New York: Author.

National Commission on Writing. (2007). *2007 survey: Learning to write.* Retrieved from www.collegeboard.com

National Consortium on Deaf-Blindness (NCDB). (2009). *2009 national deaf-blind child count maps.* Retrieved from http://www.nationaldb.org/censusMaps.php

National Council of Teachers of Mathematics. (2000). *Principles and standards for school mathematics.* Reston, VA: Author.

National Council of Teachers of Mathematics. (2006). *Curriculum focal points.* Reston, VA: Author.

National Council of Teachers of Mathematics. (2009). *Focus in Grade 1.* Reston, VA: Author.

National Council on Accreditation for Teacher Education. (n.d.). *Assessing the assessments: Fairness, accuracy, consistency, and the avoidance of bias in NCATE standard 2.* Washington, DC: Author.

National Early Literacy Panel. (2008). *Executive summary. Developing early literacy: Report of the National Early Literacy Panel (NELP).* Louisville, KY: National Institute for Literacy.

National Institute of Child Health and Human Development. (2000). *Report of the National Reading Panel: Teaching children to read: An evidence-based assessment of the scientific research literature on reading and its implications for reading instruction: Reports of the sub-groups.* Washington, DC: U.S. Department of Health and Human Services, National Institute on Health.

National Mathematics Advisory Panel. (2008). *Foundations for success: The final report of the National Mathematics Advisory Panel.* Washington, DC: U.S. Department of Education.

National Reading Panel. (2000a). National Institute of Child Health and Human Development. *Report of the National Reading Panel. Teaching children to read: An evidence-based assessment of the scientific research literature on reading and its implications for reading instruction* (NIH Publication No. 00-4769). Washington, DC: U.S. Government Printing Office.

National Reading Panel. (2000b). National Institute of Child Health and Human Development. *Report of the National Reading Panel. Teaching children to read: an evidence-based assessment of the scientific research literature on reading and its implications for reading instruction: Reports of the subgroups* (NIH Publication No. 00-4754). Washington, DC: U.S. Government Printing Office.

National Research Council. (2001a). Adding it up: Helping children learn mathematics. In J. Kilpatrick, J. Swafford, & B. Findell (Eds.), *Mathematics Learning Study Committee, Center for Education, Division of Behavioral and Social Sciences and Education.* Washington, DC: National Academy Press.

National Research Council. (2001b). *Educating children with autism.* Committee on Educational Interventions for Children with Autism, Division of Behavioral and Social Sciences and Autism. Washington, DC: National Academy Press.

National Research Council. (2009). *Mathematic learning in early childhood: Paths toward excellence and equity.* Washington, DC: Author.

National Secondary Transition Technical Assistance Center Research to Practice Lesson Plan Starter Library. Retrieved from http://www.nsttac.org/LessonPlanLibrary/Main.aspx

National Secondary Transition Technical Assistance Center. (n.d.). Research to practice lesson plan starter: IEP meeting involvement using person-centered planning. Retrieved from http://www.nsttac.org/LessonPlanLibrary/2_27_35.pdf

National Universal Design for Learning Task Force. (2007). Universal design for learning classroom scenarios. Retrieved from http://www.advocacyinstitute.org/UDL/classroom_scenarios.shtml

Neef, N. A., Shafer, M. S., Egel, A. L., Cataldo, M. F., & Parrish, J. M. (1983). The class specific effects of compliance training with *do* and *don't* requests: Analogue analysis and classroom application. *Journal of Applied Behavior Analysis, 16,* 81–99.

Neef, N. A., Walters, J., & Egel, A. L. (1984). Establishing generative yes/no responses in developmentally disabled children. *Journal of Applied Behavior Analysis, 17,* 453–460.

Nehring, A. D., Nehring, E. E., Bruni, J. R., & Randolph, P. L. (1992). *Learning accomplishment profile-diagnostic standardized assessment.* Lewisville, NC: Kaplan Press.

Neil, M. (2008). *Improving accountability: A review of grading education.* Boston: National Center for Fair and Open Testing. Retrieved from http://www.fairtest.org/improving-accountability-review-grading-education

Neiman, S., & DeVoe, J. F. (2009). *Crime, violence, discipline, and safety in U.S. public schools: Findings from the school survey on crime and safety: 2007–08* (NCES 2009-326). Washington, DC: National

Center for Education Statistics, Institute of Education Sciences, U.S. Department of Education.

Neitzel, J., Boyd, B., Odom, S. L., & Edmondson-Pretzel, R. (2008). *Peer-mediated instruction and intervention for children and youth with autism spectrum disorders: Online training module.* Chapel Hill, NC: National Professional Development Center on Autism Spectrum Disorders, FPG Child Development Institute, UNC-Chapel Hill.

Nelson, C., McDonnell, A. P., Hohnston, S. S., Crompton, A., & Nelson, A. R. (2007). Keys to Play: A strategy to increase the social interactions of young children with autism and their typically developing peers. *Education and Training in Developmental Disabilities, 42,* 165–181.

Nelson, J. R. (1996). Designing schools to meet the needs of students who exhibit disruptive behaviors. *Journal of Emotional and Behavioral Disorders, 4,* 147–161.

Nelson, J. R., Benner, G. J., & Gonzalez, J. (2003). Learner characteristics that influence the treatment effectiveness of early literacy interventions: A meta-analytic review. *Learning Disabilities: Research & Practice, 18,* 255–267.

Nelson, J. R., Benner, G. J., Lane, K. L., & Smith, B. W. (2004). Academic achievement of K–12 students with emotional and behavioral disorders. *Exceptional Children, 71,* 59–73.

Nelson, J. R., Benner, G. J., Reid, R. C., Epstein, M. H., & Currin, D. (2002). The convergent validity of office discipline referrals with the CBCL-TRF. *Journal of Emotional and Behavioral Disorders, 10,* 181–188.

Nelson, J. R., Martella, R., & Galand, B. (1998). The effects of teaching school expectations and establishing a consistent consequence on formal office disciplinary actions. *Journal of Emotional and Behavioral Disorders, 6,* 153–161.

Nelson, J. R., Martella, R. M., & Marchand-Martella, N. (2002). Maximizing student learning: The effects of a comprehensive school-based program for preventing problem behaviors. *Journal of Emotional and Behavioral Disorders, 10,* 136–148.

Netzel, D. M., & Eber, L. (2003). Shifting from reactive to proactive discipline in an urban school district: A change in focus through PBIS implementation. *Journal of Positive Behavior Interventions, 5,* 71–79.

Nevin, A. I. (2006). Can co-teaching provide quality education? Let the data tell us. [Review of the book *The Magiera-Simmons quality indicator model of co-teaching*]. *Remedial and Special Education, 27,* 250–251.

Nevin, J. A. (1996). The momentum of compliance. *Journal of Applied Behavior Analysis, 29,* 535–547.

Nevin, J. A., Mandell, C., & Atak, J. R. (1983). The analysis of behavioral momentum. *Journal of Applied Behavior Analysis, 39,* 49–59.

New York Department of Health. (1999). *Clinical practice guideline: Report of the recommendations. Autism/ pervasive developmental disorders: Assessment and intervention for young children (age 0–3 years).* Albany, NY: New York Department of Health.

Newborg, J. (2005). *Battelle Developmental Inventory, 2nd Edition: Examiner's manual.* Itasca, IL: Riverside.

Newcomb, A., Bukowski, W., & Pattee, L. (1993). Children's peer relations: A meta-analytic review of popular, rejected, neglected, controversial, and average sociometric status. *Psychological Bulletin, 113,* 99–128.

Newcomer, L. L., & Lewis, T. J. (2004). Functional behavioral assessment: An investigation of assessment reliability and effectiveness of function-based interventions. *Journal of Emotional and Behavioral Disorders, 12,* 168–181.

Newman, L., Wagner, M., Cameto, R., & Knokey, A. M. (2009). *The post-high school outcomes of youth with disabilities up to 4 years after high school. A report from the National Longitudinal Transition Study–2 (NLTS2)* (NCSER 2009-3017). Menlo Park, CA: SRI International.

Nickles, J. L., Cronis, T. G., Justen, J. E. I., & Smith, G. J. (1992). Individualized education programs: A comparison of students with BD, LD, and MMR. *Intervention in School and Clinic, 28*(1), 41–44.

Niesyn, M. (2009). Strategies for success: Evidence-based instructional practices for students with emotional and behavioral disorders. *Preventing School Failure, 53,* 227–233.

Nietupski, J., Hamre-Nietupski, S., Clancy, P., & Veerhusen, K. (1986). Guidelines for making simulation an effective adjunct to in vivo community instruction. *Journal of the Association for Persons with Severe Handicaps, 11,* 12–18.

Nietupski, J., Welch, J., & Wacker, D. (1983). Acquisition, maintenance, and transfer of grocery item purchasing skills by moderately and severely handicapped students. *Education and Training in Mental Retardation, 18,* 279–286.

Nilsson, N. L. (2008). A critical analysis of eight Informal Reading Inventories. *The Reading Teacher, 61,* 526–536.

Nishioka, V. (2001). *Similarities and differences in the personal and ecological characteristics of middle school boys with emotional disturbance, learning disabilities, and social maladjustment.* Eugene: Institute on Violence and Destructive Behavior, University of Oregon.

No Child Left Behind Act of 2001, Pub. L. No. 107-110, 115 Stat. 1425 *et seq.* (2001).

No Child Left Behind Act of 2001, Pub. L. No. 107-110, 115 Stat. 1425 (2002).

No Child Left Behind Act, 2001, 20 U.S.C. 70 § 6301 *et seq.* (2002).

Noell, G. H., Duhon, G. J., Gatti, S. L., & Connell, J. E. (2002). Consultation, follow-up, and implementation of behavior management interventions in general education. *School Psychology Review, 31,* 217–234.

Noell, G. H., & Gansle, K. A. (2006). Assuring the form has substance: Treatment plan implementation as the foundation of assessing response to intervention. *Assessment for Effective Intervention, 32*(1), 32–39.

Noell, G. H., Gresham, F. M., & Gansle, K. A. (2002). Does treatment integrity matter? A preliminary investigation of instructional implementation and mathematics performance. *Journal of Behavioral Education, 11,* 51–67.

Noell, G. H., Witt, J. C., Slider, N. J., Connell, J. E., Gatti, S. L., Williams, K. L., & Duhon, G. J. (2005). Treatment implementation following behavioral consultation in schools: A comparison of three follow-up strategies. *School Psychology Review, 34,* 87–106.

Nolet, V. (2005). *Accessing the general curriculum: Including students with disabilities in standards-based reform* (2nd ed.). Thousand Oaks, CA: Corwin Press.

Nolet, V., & McLaughlin, M. J. (2000). *Accessing the general curriculum: Including students with disabilities in standards-based reform.* Thousand Oaks, CA: Corwin Press

Nolte, R., & Singer, H. (1985). Active comprehension: Teaching a process of reading comprehension and its effects on achievement. *The Reading Teacher, 39,* 24–31.

Noon v. Alaska State Board of Education & Early Development, Case No. A04-0057 CV (JKS) (Settle Agreement). 2004.

Noonan, M. J., & McCormick, L. (2006). *Young children with disabilities in natural environments: Methods and procedures.* Baltimore: Brookes.

Noonan, M. J., McCormick, L., & Heck, R. (2003). The co-teacher relationship scale: Applications for professional development. *Education and Training in Developmental Disabilities, 38,* 113–120.

Norland, J. J. (2005). *English Language Learners interactions with various science curriculum features.* (Doctoral dissertation.) Available from Proquest Dissertation and Theses database. (UMI No. 885692991)

Northwest Evaluation Association. (2003). *Technical manual for the NWEA measures of academic progress and achievement level tests.* Lake Oswego, OR: Author.

Northwest Evaluation Association. (2009). *Testing season checklist: A complete guide to your MAP testing season.* Retrieved from http://www.nwea.org/support/checklist.aspx?key=TestImplementation

Notari, A. R. (1988). The utility of a criterion-referenced instrument in the development of individual education plan goals for infants and young children. *Dissertation Abstracts International, 49*(7), 1767A. (UMI No. AAT88-14193)

Notari-Syverson, A., O'Conner, R. E., & Vadasy, P. F. (1998). *Ladders to literacy.* Baltimore: Brookes.

Nunes, T., & Bryant, P. (Eds.). (2006). *Improving literacy by teaching morphemes.* London: Routledge.

O'Brien, C. L., & O'Brien, J. (2000). *The origins of person-centered planning: A community of practice perspective.* Atlanta, GA: Responsive Systems Associates. Retrieved from http://thechp.syr.edu/PCP_History.pdf

O'Brien, J., & Lyle, C. (1987). *Framework for accomplishment.* Decatur, GA: Responsive Systems Associates.

O'Connor, R. E. Notari-Syverson, A., & Vadasy, P. F. (1998). *Ladders to Literacy: A kindergarten activity book.* Baltimore: Brookes.

O'Leary, E., L. M., & Doty, D. (2001). *Transition requirements checklist.* Washington, DC: U.S. Department of Education Office of Special Education.

O'Neill, R., Horner, R., Albin, R., Sprague, J., Storey, K., & Newton, J. (1997). *Functional assessment and program development for problem behavior: A practical handbook.* Pacific Grove, CA: Brooks/Cole.

O'Reilly, M., Sigafoos, J., Lancioni, G., Edrisinha, C., & Andrews, A. (2005). An examination of the effects of a classroom activity schedule on levels of self-injury and engagement for a child with severe autism. *Journal of Autism and Developmental Disorders, 35,* 305–311.

O'Shaughnessy, T. E., & Swanson, H. L. (2000). A comparison of two reading interventions for children with reading disabilities. *Journal of Learning Disabilities, 33,* 257–277.

Obiakor, F. E. (1999). Teacher expectations of minority exceptional learners: Impact on accuracy of self-concepts. *Exceptional Children, 65,* 39–53.

Ochoa, S. H., Robles-Piña, E., Garcia, S. B., & Breunig, N. (1999). School psychologists' perspectives on referrals of language minority students. *Multiple Voices for Exceptional Learners, 3,* 1–14.

Odom, S. L., Chandler, L. K., Ostrosky, M., McConnell, S. R., & Reaney, S. (1992). Fading teacher prompts from peer-initiation interventions for young children with disabilities. *Journal of Applied Behavior Analysis, 25,* 307–317.

Odom, S. L., McConnell, S. R., Ostrosky, M., Peterson, C., Skellenger, A., Spicuzza, R., . . . Favazza, P. C. (1993). *Play time/social time: Organizing your classroom to build interaction skills.* Tucson, AZ: Communication Skill Builders.

Office of Special Education Programs. (2009). *28th Annual report to Congress on the implementation of the Individuals with Disabilities Education Act, 2006.* Washington, DC: U.S. Department of Education, Office of Special Education and Rehabilitative Services, Office of Special Education Programs.

Ogle, D. M. (1986). K-W-L: A teaching model that develops active reading of expository text. *The Reading Teacher, 39,* 564–570.

Oliver, C. B., & Halle, J. W. (1982). Language training in the everyday environment: Teaching functional sign use to a retarded child. *Journal of the Association for the Severely Handicapped, 8,* 50–62.

Olmeda, R., & Kauffman, J. (2003). Sociocultural considerations in social skills research with African American students with emotional and behavioral disorders. *Journal of Developmental and Physical Disabilities, 15,* 101–121.

Olson, R. K., & Wise, B. W. (1992). Reading on the computer with orthographic and speech feedback: An overview of the Colorado Remedial Reading Project. *Reading and Writing: An Interdisciplinary Journal, 4,* 107–144.

Omanson, R. (1982). An analysis of narratives: Identifying central, supportive, and distracting content. *Discourse Processes, 5,* 195–224.

Oosterhof, A. (2009). *Developing and using classroom assessments* (4th ed.). Upper Saddle River, NJ: Pearson.

Osguthorpe, R. T., & Scruggs, T. E. (1986). Special education students as tutors: A review and analysis. *Remedial and Special Education, 7*(4), 15–26.

Otaiba, S., & Lake, V. E. (2007). Preparing special educators to teach reading and use curriculum-bases assessments. *Reading and Writing, 20,* 591–617.

Overton, S., McKenzie, L., King, K., & Osborne, J. (2002). Replication of the First Step to Success model: A multiple-case study of implementation effectiveness. *Behavioral Disorders, 28*(1), 40–56.

Overton, T. (2009). *Assessing learners with special needs: An applied approach* (6th ed.). Upper Saddle River, NJ: Merrill/Pearson.

Owen, R. L., & Fuchs, L.S. (2002). Mathematical problem-solving strategy instruction for third-grade students with learning disabilities. *Remedial and Special Education, 23,* 268–278.

Owen-DeSchryver, J. S., Carr, E. G., Cale, S. I., & Blakely-Smith, A. (2008). Prompting social interactions between students with autism spectrum disorders and their peers in inclusive school settings. *Focus on Autism and Other Developmental Disabilities, 23,* 15–28.

Padden, C., & Ramsey, C. (2000). American Sign Language and reading ability in deaf children. In C. Chamberlain, J. P. Morford, & R. I. Mayberry (Eds.), *Language acquisition by eye* (pp. 165–189). Mahwah, NJ: Erlbaum.

Paine, S. C., Radicchi, J. Rosellini, L. C., Deutchman, L., & Darch, C. B. (1983). *Structuring your classroom for academic success.* Champaign, IL: Research Press.

Palincsar, A. S. (1986). The role of dialogue in providing scaffolded instruction. *Educational Psychologist, 21,* 73–98.

Palincsar, A. S., & Brown, A. L. (1984). The reciprocal teaching of comprehension-fostering and comprehension-monitoring activities. *Cognition and Instruction, 1,* 117–175.

Palincsar, A. S., & Brown, D. S. (1987). Enhancing instructional time through attention to metacognition. *Journal of Learning Disabilities, 20*(2), 66–75.

Parent, W., & Wehman, P. (2011). Writing the transition individualized education program. In P. Wehman (Ed.). *Essentials of transition planning* (pp. 95–109). Baltimore: Brookes.

Parette, H. P., & Peterson-Karlan, G. R. (2007). Facilitating student achievement with assistive technology. *Education and Training in Developmental Disabilities, 42,* 387–397.

Paris, A. H., Lipson, M. Y., & Wixson, K. K. (1983). Becoming a strategic reader. *Contemporary Educational Psychology, 8,* 293–316.

Paris, A. H., Wasik, B. A., & Turner, J. C. (1991). The development of strategic readers. In R. Barr, M. L. Kamil,

B. P. Mosenthal, & P. D. Pearson (Eds.), *Handbook of reading research* (Vol. 2, pp. 609–640). New York: Longman.

Paris, S. G., & Carpenter, R. D. (2003). FAQs about IRIs. *Reading Teacher, 56,* 578–581.

Parker, J., & Asher, S. (1987). Peer relations and later personal adjustment: Are low-accepted children at-risk? *Psychological Bulletin, 102,* 357–389.

Parker, M., Cunningham, S., Enderby, P., Hawley, M., & Green, P. (2006). Automatic speech recognition and training for severely dysarthric users of assistive technology: The STARDUST project. *Clinical Linguistics and Phonetics, 20*(2/3), 149–156.

Parker, R., Hasbrouck, J. E., & Tindal, G. (1992). The maze as a classroom-based reading measure: Construction methods, reliability, and validity. *The Journal of Special Education, 26,* 195–218.

Parnes, S. J. (1988). *Visionizing: State-of-the-art processes for encouraging innovative excellence.* East Aurora, NY: D.O.K. Publishing.

Parnes, S. J. (1992). *Source book for creative problem-solving: A fifty year digest of proven innovation processes.* Buffalo, NY: Creative Education Foundation Press.

Parrish, J., Cataldo, M., Kolko, D., Neef N., & Egel, A. (1986). Experimental analysis of response covariation among compliant and inappropriate behaviors. *Journal of Applied Behavior Analysis, 19,* 241–254.

Pashler, H., Bain, P. M., Bottge, B. A., Graesser, A., Koedinger, K., McDaniel, M., & Metcalfe, J. (2007). *Organizing instruction and study to improve student learning.* IES Practice Guide (NCER 2007-2004). Jessup, MD: National Center for Education Research.

Passolunghi, M. C., & Siegel, L. S. (2001). Short-term memory, working memory, and inhibitory control in children with specific arithmetic learning disabilities. *Journal of Experimental Child Psychology, 80,* 44–57.

Patberg, J. P., Graves, M. F., & Stibbe, M. A. (1984). Effects of active teaching and practice in facilitating students' use of context clues. In J. A. Niles & L. A. Harris (Eds.), *Changing perspectives on research in reading/language processing and instruction: Thirty-third Yearbook of the National Reading Conference* (pp. 146–151). Rochester, NY: National Reading Conference.

Patterson, G. R. (1982). *Coercive family process.* Eugene, OR: Castalia.

Patterson, G. R., DeBaryshe, B. D., & Ramsey, E. (1989). A developmental perspective on antisocial behavior. *American Psychologist, 44,* 329–335.

Patterson, G. R., & Reid, J. B. (1973). Intervention for families of aggressive boys: A replication study. *Behavior Research and Therapy, 11,* 383–394.

Patterson, G. R., Reid, J. B., & Dishion, T. J. (1992). *Antisocial boys.* Eugene, OR: Castalia.

Patton, B., Jolivette., K., & Ramsey, M. (2006). Students with emotional and behavioral disorders can manage their own behavior: Implications for practice. *Teaching Exceptional Children, 39,* 14–21.

Paul, P. V. (2009). *Language and deafness* (4th ed.). Sudbury, MA: Jones and Bartlett.

Paykel, E. S., Scott, J., Teasdale, J. D., Johnson, A. L., Garland, A., Moore, R., et al. (1999). Prevention of relapse in residual depression by cognitive therapy: A controlled trial. *Archives of General Psychiatry, 56,* 829–835.

Payne, L. D., Marks, L. J., & Bogan, B. L. (2007). Using curriculum-based assessment to address the academic and behavioral deficits of students with emotional and behavioral disorders. *Beyond Behavior, 16*(3), 3–6.

Pearpoint, J., O'Brien, J., & Forest, M. (1993). *PATH: A workbook for planning positive possible futures.* Toronto, Canada: Inclusion Press.

Pearson Education. (2008). *AIMSweb.* Upper Saddle River, NJ: Author.

Pearson Scott Foresman. (Ed.). (2008). *Scott Foresman, reading street.* Glenview, IL: Pearson Education.

Pearson, P. D., & Duke, N. K. (2002). Comprehension instruction in the primary grades. In C. Collins-Block & M. Pressley (Eds.), *Comprehension instruction: Research based best practices* (pp. 247–258). New York: Guilford Press.

Peck, C. A., Killen, C. C., & Baumgart, D. (1989). Increasing implementation of special education instruction in mainstream preschools: Direct and generalized effects of nondirective consultation. *Journal of Applied Behavior Analysis, 22,* 197–210.

Peck, S. M., Wacker, D. P., Berg, W. K., Cooper, L. J., Brown, K. A., et al. (1996). Choice-making treatment of young children's severe behavior problems. *Journal of Applied Behavior Analysis, 29,* 263–290.

Pediatric OCD Treatment Study Team. (2004). Cognitive-behavior therapy, sertraline, and their combination for children and adolescents with obsessive-compulsive disorder: The pediatric OCD treatment study (POTS) randomized controlled trial. *Journal of the American Medical Association, 292*(16), 1969–1976.

Peeters, M., Verhoeven, L., & de Moor, J. (2009). Predictors of verbal working memory in children with cerebral palsy. *Research in Developmental Disabilities, 30,* 1502–1511.

Peeters, M., Verhoeven, L., de Moor, J., & van Balkom, H. (2009). Importance of speech production for phonological awareness and word decoding: The case of children with cerebral palsy. *Research in Developmental Disabilities, 30,* 712–726.

Pelham, W. F., Fabiano, G. A., & Massetti, G. M. (2005). Evidence-based assessment of attention deficit hyperactivity disorder in children and adolescents. *Journal of Clinical Child and Adolescent Psychology, 34,* 449–476.

Pellegrini, A. D., Galda, L., Jones, I., & Perlmutter, J. (1995). Joint reading between mothers and their Head Start children: Vocabulary development in two text formats. *Discourse Processes, 19,* 441–463.

Penno, D. A., Frank, A. R., & Wacker, D. P. (2000). Instructional accommodations for adolescent students with severe emotional or behavioral disorders. *Behavioral Disorders, 25,* 325–343.

Pepper, J., & Weitzman, E. (2004). *It takes two to talk: A practical guide for parents of children with language delays* (2nd ed.). Toronto: The Hanen Centre.

Perfetti, C. A. (1977). Language comprehension and fast decoding: Some psycholinguistic prerequisites for skilled reading comprehension. In J. T. Guthrie (Ed.), *Cognition, curriculum and comprehension* (pp. 20–41). Newark, DE: International Reading Association.

Perfetti, C. (1985). *Reading ability.* New York: Oxford University Press.

Perfetti, C. A., Landi, N., & Oakhill, J. (2005). The acquisition of reading comprehension skill. In M. J. Snowling & C. Hulme (Eds.), *The science of reading: A handbook* (pp. 227–247). Oxford: Blackwell.

Perkins, D., & Salomon, G. (1992). *Transfer of learning: Contribution to the international encyclopedia of education* (2nd ed.). Oxford, England: Pergamon Press.

Perrin, C. J., Perrin, S. H., Hill, E. A., & DiNovi, K. (2008). Brief functional analysis and treatment of elopement in preschoolers with autism. *Behavioral Interventions, 23,* 87–95.

Perry, A., & Condillac, R. A. (2003). *Evidence-based practices for children and adolescents with autism spectrum disorder: Review of the literature and practice guide.* Toronto: Children's Mental Health, Ontario.

Peterson-Karlan, G., Hourcade, J. J., & Parette, P. (2008). A review of assistive technology and writing skills for students with physical and educational disabilities. *Physical Disabilities: Education and Related Services, 26*(2), 13–32.

Phillips, L. M., Norris, S. P., Osmond, W. C., & Maynard, A. M. (2002). Relative reading achievement: A longitudinal study of 187 children from first through sixth grades. *Journal of Educational Psychology, 94,* 3–13.

Phillips, S. E. (1994). High stakes testing accommodations: Validity versus disabled rights. *Applied Measurement in Education, 7,* 93–120.

Piaget, J. (1954). *The construction of reality in the child.* New York: Basic Books.

Piazza, C., Fisher, W., Hagopian, L., Bowman, L., & Toole. L. (1996). Using a choice assessment to predict reinforce effectiveness. *Journal of Applied Behavior Analysis, 29,* 1–9.

Pierce, K., & Schreibman, L. (1997). Multiple peer use of pivotal response training to increase social behaviors of classmates with autism: Results from trained and untrained peers. *Journal of Applied Behavior Analysis, 30,* 156–160.

Pikulski, J. J. (2006). Fluency: A developmental and language perspective. In S. J. Samuels & A. E. Farstrup (Eds.), *What research has to say about fluency instruction.* Newark, DE: International Reading Association.

Pikulski, J. J., & Chard, D. J. (2005). Fluency: Bridge between decoding and reading comprehension. *Reading Teacher, 58,* 510–519.

Pinnell, G. S., Pikulski, J. J., Wizson, K. K., Campbell, J. R., Gough, P. B., & Beatty, A. S. (1995). *Listening to children read aloud.* Washington, DC: Office of Educational Research and Improvement, U.S. Department of Education.

Pitoniak, M. J., & Royer, J. M. (2001). Testing accommodations for examinees with disabilities: A review of psychometric, legal, and social policy issues. *Review of Educational Research, 71*(1), 53–104.

Planty, M., Hussar, W., Snyder, T., Provasnik, S., Kena, G., Dinkes, R., . . . Kemp, J. (2008). *The condition of education 2008* (NCES 2008-031). Washington, DC: National Center for Education Statistics, Institute of Education Sciences, U.S. Department of Education.

Poduska, J. M., Kellam, S. G., Wang, W., Brown, C. H., Ialongo, N. S., & Toyinbo, P. (2008). Impact of the Good Behavior Game, a universal classroom-based behavior intervention, on young adult service use for problems with emotions, behavior, or drugs or alcohol. *Drug and Alcohol Dependence, 95,* 529–545.

Poggio, J., Glasnapp D. R., Yang, X., & Poggio, A. J. (2005). A comparative evaluation of score results from computerized and paper & pencil mathematics testing in a large scale state assessment program. *The Journal of Technology, Learning, and Assessment, 3*(6). Retrieved from http://www.jtla.org

Pomplun, M., Frey, S., & Becker, D. (2002). The score equivalence of paper-and-pencil and computerized versions of a speeded test of reading comprehension. *Educational and Psychological Measurement, 62*(2), 337–354. Retrieved from http://epm.sagepub.com

Poponi, D. M. (2009). *The relationship between student outcomes and parental involvement in multidisciplinary IEP team meetings.* Retrieved from http://digitalcommons.pcom.edu/psychology_dissertations/116

Porter, A., McMaken, J., Hwang, J., & Yang, R. (2011). Common core standards: The new U.S. intended curriculum. *Educational Researcher, 40*(3), 103–116.

Post, M., & Storey, K. (2002). A review of using auditory prompting systems with persons who have moderate to severe disabilities. *Education and Training in Mental Retardation and Developmental Disabilities, 37,* 317–327.

Powers, K. M., Gil-Kashiwabara, E., Geenen, S. J., Powers, L. E., Balandran, J., & Palmer, C. (2005). Mandates and effective transition planning practices reflected in IEPs. *Career Development for Exceptional Individuals, 28*(1), 47–59.

Powers, M. D. (1992). Early intervention for children with autism. In D. E. Berkell (Ed.), *Autism: Identification, education, and treatment* (pp. 225–252). Hillsdale, NJ: Erlbaum.

Prater, M. A., Hogan, S., & Miller, S. R. (1992). Using self-monitoring to improve on-task behavior and academic skills of an adolescent with mild handicaps across special and regular education settings. *Education & Treatment of Children, 15,* 43–55.

Preciado, J. A., Horner, R. H., & Baker, S. K. (2009). Using a function-based approach to decrease problem behaviors and increase academic engagement for Latino English language learners. *Journal of Special Education, 42,* 227–240.

President's Commission on Excellence in Special Education. (2001). *A new era: Revitalizing special education for children and their families.* Washington, DC: Education Publications Center, U.S. Department of Education.

Pressley, M. (2002). Conclusion: Improving comprehension strategy instruction: A path for the future. In C. C. Block, L. B. Gambrel, & M. Pressley (Eds.), *Improving comprehension instruction* (pp. 385–399). San Francisco: Jossey-Bass.

Pressley, M. (2006). *Reading instruction that works: The case for balanced teaching* (3rd ed.). New York: Guilford Press.

Pressley, M., & Afferbach, P. (1995). *Verbal protocols of reading: The nature of constructively responsive reading.* Hillsdale, NJ: Erlbaum.

Pressley, M., Borkowski, J. G., & Schneider, W. (1987). Cognitive strategies: Good strategy users coordinate metacognition and knowledge. In R. Vasta & G. Whitehurst (Eds.), *Annals of child development* (Vol. 5, pp. 89–98). New York: JAI Press.

Pressley, M., El-Dinary, P. B., Gaskins, I., Schuder, T., Bergman, J., Almasi, J., & Brown, R. (1992). Beyond direct explanation: Transactional instruction of reading comprehension strategies. *The Elementary School Journal, 92,* 513–555.

Pressley, M., Wood, E., Woloshyn, V. E., Martin, V., King, A., & Menke, D. (1992). Encouraging mindful use of prior knowledge: Attempting to construct explanatory answers facilitates learning. *Educational Psychologist, 27*(1), 91–109. doi:10.1207/s15326985ep2701_7

Pretti-Frontczak, K. L., Barr, D. M., Macy, M., & Carter, A. (2003). Research and resources related to activity-based intervention, embedded learning opportunities, and routines-based instruction. *Topics in Early Childhood Special Education, 23,* 29–39.

Pretti-Frontczak, K., & Bricker, D. (2000). Enhancing the quality of individual education plan (IEP) goals and objectives. *Journal of Early Intervention, 23*(2), 92–105.

Pretti-Frontczak, K. L., & Bricker, D. D. (2001). Use of the embedding strategy by early childhood education and early childhood special education teachers. *Infant and Toddler Intervention: The Transdisciplinary Journal, 11,* 111–128.

Pretti-Frontczak, K., & Bricker, D. (2004). *An activity-based approach to early intervention* (3rd ed.). Baltimore: Brookes.

Prewitt, P. N. (1992). The relationship between the Kaufman Brief Intelligence Test (K-BIT) and the WISC-R with referred students. *Psychology in the Schools, 29,* 25–27.

Proctor, C. P., Dalton, B., & Grisham, D. (2007). Scaffolding English language learners and struggling readers in a multimedia hypertext environment with embedded strategy instruction and vocabulary support. *Journal of Literacy Research, 39,* 71–93.

Proctor, C. P., Uccelli, P., Dalton, B., & Snow, C. E. (2009). Understanding depth of vocabulary online with bilingual and monolingual children. *Reading and Writing Quarterly, 25,* 311–333.

Psychological Corporation. (2002). *Wechsler Individual Achievement Test* (2nd ed.). San Antonio, TX: Harcourt Assessment.

Pugach, M. C., & Johnson., L. J. (1989). The challenge of implementing collaboration between general and special education. *Exceptional Children, 56,* 232–236.

Purkey, S. C., & Smith, M. S. (1985). School reform: The district policy implications of the effective schools literature. *Elementary School Journal, 85,* 353–389.

Quinn, M. M., Gable, R. A., Fox, J., Rutherford, R. B., Van Acker, R., & Conroy, M. (2001). Putting quality functional assessment into practice in schools: A research agenda on behalf of E/BD students. *Education and Treatment of Children, 24,* 261–275.

Quinn, M., Kavale, K., Mathur, S., Rutherford, R., & Forness, S. (1999). A meta-analysis of social skill interventions for students with emotional and behavioral disorders. *Journal of Emotional and Behavioral Disorders, 7,* 54–64.

Ramsey, M. L., Jolivette, K., Patterson, D. P., & Kennedy, C. (2010). Using choice to increase time on task, task completion, and accuracy for students with emotional/ behavior disorders in a residential facility. *Education and Treatment of Children, 33*(1), 1–21.

RAND Reading Study Group. (2002). *Reading for understanding: Towards an R & D program in reading comprehension.* Santa Monica, CA: RAND. Retrieved from http://www.rand.org/pubs/monograph_reports/2005/MR1465.pdf

Rao, S. S. (2000). Perspectives of an African-American mother on parent-professional relationships in special education. *Mental Retardation, 38,* 475–488.

Rao, S., & Kane, M. T. (2009). Teaching students with cognitive impairment chained mathematical task of decimal subtraction using simultaneous prompting. *Education and Training in Developmental Disabilities, 44,* 244–256.

Rasheed, S. A., Fore, C., & Miller, S. (2006). Person-centered planning: Practices, promises, and provisos. *The Journal for Vocational Special Needs Education, 28*(3), 47–59.

Rasinski, T. V., Ruetzel, D. R., Chard, D., & Linan-Thompson, S. (2010). Reading fluency. In M. L. Kamil, P. D. Pearson, E. Birr Moje, & P. P. Afflerbach (Eds.), *Handbook of reading research* (Vol. 4, pp. 286–319). New York: Routledge.

Ratner, V. L., & Harris, L. R. (1994). *Understanding language disorders: The impact on learning.* Eau Claire, WI: Thinking Publications.

Ray, K. P., Skinner, C. H., & Watson, T. S. (1999). Transferring stimulus control via momentum to increase compliance in a student with autism: A demonstration of collaborative consultation. *The School Psychology Review, 28*(4), 622–628.

Rea, P. J., McLaughlin, V. L., & Walther-Thomas, C. (2002). Outcomes for students with learning disabilities in inclusive and pullout programs. *Exceptional Children, 68,* 203–222.

Reese, G. M., & Snell, M. E. (1991). Putting on and removing coats and jackets: The acquisition and maintenance of skills by children with severe multiple disabilities. *Education and Training in Mental Retardation, 26,* 398–410.

Reeve, P., & Hallahan, D. (1994). Practical questions about collaboration between general and special educators. *Focus on Exceptional Children, 26,* 1–12.

Reichle, J. (1990). *National Working Conference on Positive Approaches to the Management of Excess Behavior: Final report and recommendations.* Minneapolis, MN: Institute on Community Integration, University of Minnesota.

Reichle, J. (1997). Communication intervention with persons who have severe disabilities. *Journal of Special Education, 31,* 110–134.

Reid, J. B. (1993). Prevention of conduct disorder before and after school

entry: Relating interventions to developmental findings. *Development and Psychopathology, 5,* 243–262.

Reid, R., Gonzalez, J. E., Nordness, P. D., Trout, A., & Epstein, M. H. (2004). A meta-analysis of the academic status of students with emotional/behavioral disturbance. *The Journal of Special Education, 38,* 130–143.

Reinking, D., & Pickle, J. M. (1993). Using a formative experiment to study how computers affect reading and writing in classrooms. In D. J. Leu & C. K. Kinzer (Eds.), *Examining central issues in literacy research, theory, and practice* (pp. 263–270). Chicago: National Reading Conference.

Reiter, S., Kutcher, S., & Gardner, D. (1992). Anxiety disorders in children and adolescents: Clinical and related issues in pharmacological treatment. *Canadian Journal of Psychiatry, 37,* 432–438.

Renaissance Learning. (1998). *STAR math.* Wisconsin Rapids, WI: Author.

Renaissance Learning. (2003). *STAR early literacy.* Wisconsin Rapids, WI: Author.

Repp, A. C., Karsh, K. G., & Lenz, M. W. (1990). Discrimination training for persons with developmental disabilities: A comparison of the task demonstration model and the standard prompting hierarchy. *Journal of Applied Behavior Analysis, 23,* 43–52.

Reschly, D. J. (1996). Functional assessments and special education decision making. In W. Stainback & S. Stainback (Eds.), *Controversial issues confronting special education: Divergent perspectives* (2nd ed., pp. 115–128). Boston: Allyn & Bacon.

Reschly, D. J. (2005). Learning disabilities identification: Primary intervention, secondary intervention, and then what? *Journal of Learning Disabilities, 38*(6), 510–515.

Reschly, D. J., & Grimes, J. P. (2002). Best practices in intellectual assessment. In A. Thomas & J. Grimes (Eds.), *Best practices in school psychology* (Vol. 4, pp. 1337–1350). Bethesda, MD: National Association of School Psychologists.

Reschly, D. J., & Hosp, J. L. (2004). State LD identification policies and practices. *Learning Disability Quarterly, 27*(4), 197–213.

Reschly, D. J., & Wilson, M. S. (1995). School psychology faculty and practitioners: 1986 to 1991 trends in demographic characteristics, roles, satisfaction, and system reform. *School Psychology Review, 24,* 62–80.

Rescorla, L., Roberts, J., & Dahlsgaard, K. (1997). Late talkers at 2: Outcome at age 3. *Journal of Speech, Language, and Hearing Research, 40,* 556–566.

Research Unit on Pediatric Psychopharmacology Anxiety Study Group. (2001). Fluvoxamine for the treatment of anxiety disorders in children and adolescents. *New England Journal of Medicine, 344,* 1279–1285.

Research Unit on Pediatric Psychopharmacology Anxiety Study Group. (2002). Treatment of pediatric anxiety disorders: An open-label extension of the research units on pediatric psychopharmacology anxiety study. *Journal of Child and Adolescent Psychopharmacology, 12,* 175–188.

Reutzel, R. (1985a). Reconciling schema theory with the basal reading lesson. *The Reading Teacher, 39,* 194–197.

Reutzel, R. (1985b). Story maps improve comprehension. *Reading Teacher, 38,* 400–404.

Rex, E. J., Koenig, A. J., Wormsley, D. P., & Baker, R. L. (1994). *Foundations of braille literacy.* New York: AFB Press.

Reyna, V. (2004). Why scientific research: The importance of evidence in changing educational practice. In P. McCardle & V. Chhabra (Eds.), *The voice of evidence in reading research.* Baltimore: Brookes.

Reynolds, C. R., & Kamphaus, R. W. (1992). *Behavior Assessment System for Children, 2nd Edition: Manual.* Circle Pines, MN: American Guidance.

Reynolds, W. M., & Coats, K. I. (1986). A comparison of cognitive-behavioral therapy and relaxation training for the treatment of depression in adolescents. *Journal of Consulting and Clinical Psychology, 54,* 653–660.

Reynolds, W. M., & Stark, K. D. (1987). School-based intervention strategies for the treatment of depression in children and adolescents. In S. G. Forman (Ed.), *School-based affective and social intervention* (pp. 67–88). New York: Haworth Press.

Rezaei, A., & Lovorn, M. (2010). Reliability and validity of rubrics for assessment through writing. *Assessing Writing, 15,* 18–39.

Rhode, G., Jenson, W. R., & Reavis, H. K. (1992). *The tough kid book: Practical classroom applications.* Longmont, CO: Sopris West.

Rhode, G., Morgan, D. P., & Young, K. R. (1983). Generalization and maintenance of treatment gains of behaviorally disordered handicapped students from resource rooms to regular classroom using self-evaluation procedures. *Journal of Applied Behavior Analysis, 16,* 171–188.

Rice, M. L., & Wexler, K. (1996). Toward tense as a clinical marker of specific language impairment in English-speaking children. *Journal of Speech and Hearing Research, 39,* 1239–1257.

Rice, M. L., Wexler, K., & Hershberger, S. (1998). The longitudinal course of tense acquisition in children with specific language impairment. *Journal of Speech, Language, and Hearing Research, 41,* 1412–1431.

Riddle, M. A., Geller, B., & Ryan, N. (1993). Case study: Another sudden death in a child treated with desipramine. *Journal of American Academy of Child and Adolescent Psychiatry, 32,* 792–797.

Riley-Tillman, T. C., Chafouleas, S. M., Sassu, K. A., Chanese, J. A. M., & Glazer, A. D. (2008). Examining the agreement of direct behavior ratings and systematic direct observation data for on-task and disruptive behavior. *Journal of Positive Behavior Intervention, 10,* 136–143.

Robbins, C., & Ehri, L. C. (1994). Reading storybooks to kindergartners helps them learn new vocabulary words. *Journal of Educational Psychology, 86,* 54–64.

Roberts, G., Torgesen, J. K., Boardman, A., & Scammacca, N. (2008). Evidence-based strategies for reading instruction in older students with learning disabilities. *Learning Disabilities Research and Practice, 23,* 63–69.

Roberts, L. M., Marshall, J., Nelson, R., & Albers, C. A. (2001). Curriculum-based assessment procedures embedded within functional behavioral assessments: Identifying escape-motivated behaviors in a general education classroom. *School Psychology Review, 30,* 264–272.

Roberts, M., McMahon, R., Forehand, R., & Humphreys, L. (1978). The effect of parental instruction-giving on child compliance. *Behavior Therapy, 9,* 793–798.

Robertson, E. J., & Lane, K. L. (2007). Supporting middle school students with academic and behavioral concerns within the context of a three-tiered model of support: Findings of a secondary prevention program. *Behavioral Disorders, 33,* 5–22.

Robinson, C., Menchetti, B., & Torgesen, J. (2002). Toward a two-factor theory of one type of mathematics disabilities. *Learning Disabilities Research & Practice, 17,* 81–89.

Rock, M. L. (2005). Use of strategic self-monitoring to enhance academic engagement, productivity, and accuracy of students with and without exceptionalities. *Journal of Positive Behavior Interventions, 7,* 3–17.

Rodger, S. (1995). Individual education plans revisited: A review of the literature. *International Journal of Disability, Development, and Education, 42,* 221–239.

Rogers, L., & Graham, S. (2008). A meta-analysis of single subject design writing intervention research. *Journal of Educational Psychology, 100,* 879–906.

Rogers-Warren, A., & Warren, S. F. (1980). Mands for verbalization: Facilitating the display of newly-taught language. *Behavior Modification, 4,* 361–382.

Rohwer, W. D., Jr., Raines, J. M., Eoff, J., & Wagner, M. (1966). The development of elaborative propensity in adolescence. *Journal of Experimental Child Psychology, 23,* 472–492.

Romaniuk, C., Miltenberger, R., Conyers, C., Jenner, N., Jurgens, M., & Ringenberg, C. (2002). The influence of activity choices on problem behaviors maintained by escape versus attention. *Journal of Applied Behavior Analysis, 35,* 349–362.

Romano, J. P., & Roll, D. (2000). Expanding the utility of behavior momentum for youth with developmental disabilities. *Behavioral Interventions, 15,* 99–111.

Root, P. (1996). *Mrs. Potter's pig.* Cambridge, MA: Candelwick Publishing.

Rortverdt, A. K., & Miltenberger, R. G. (1994). Analysis of a high-probability instructional sequence and time-out in the treatment of child noncompliance. *Journal of Applied Behavior Analysis, 27*(2), 327–330.

Rose, D., & Meyer, A. (2002). *Teaching every student the digital age.* Alexandria, VA: ASCD.

Rose, D. H., & Meyer, A. (2006). *A practical reader in universal design for learning.* Cambridge, MA: Harvard Education Press.

Rosen, K., & Yampolsky, S. (2000). Automatic speech recognition and a review of its functioning with dysarthric speech. *Augmentative and Alternative Communication, 16,* 48–60.

Rosenbaum, M. S., & Drabman, R. S. (1979). Self-control training in the classroom: A review and critique. *Journal of Applied Behavior Analysis, 12,* 467–485.

Rosenberg, M., Bott, D., Majsterek, D., Chiang, B., Gartland, D., Wesson, C., . . . Wilson, R. (1992). Minimum standards for the description of participants in learning disabilities research. *Learning Disability Quarterly, 15,* 65–70.

Rosenshine, B., Meister, C., & Chapman, S. (1996). Teaching students to generate questions: A review of the intervention studies. *Review of Educational Research, 66*(2), 181–221. doi:10.2307/1170607

Rosenshine, B., & Stevens, R. (1986). Teaching functions. In M. C. Wittrock (Ed.), *Handbook of research on teaching* (3rd ed.). New York: Macmillan.

Rosenthal, R., Rosnow, R. L., & Rubin, D. B. (2000). *Contrasts and effect sizes in behavioral research: A correlational approach.* New York: Cambridge University Press.

Rosman, N. J. S. (1994). *Effects of varying the special educator's role within an algebra class on math attitude and achievement.* Master's thesis, University of South Dakota, Vermillion (ERIC Document Reproduction Service No. ED381 993).

Rothstein, R., Jacobsen, R., & Wilder, T. (2008). *Grading education: Getting accountability right.* Williston, VT: Teachers College Press.

Rouet, J. F., Vidal-Abarca, E., Erboul, A. B., & Millogo, V. (2001). Effects of information search tasks on the comprehension of instructional text. *Discourse Processes, 31*(2), 163–186. doi:10.1207/S15326950DP3102_03

Rowland, C. (1996). *Communication matrix.* Portland, OR: Oregon Health Sciences University.

Rowland, C., & Schweigert, P. (1989). Tangible symbols: Symbolic communication for individuals with sensory impairments. *Augmentative and Alternative Communication, 5,* 226–234.

Rowland, C., & Schweigert, P. (1990). *Tangible symbol systems.* Tucson, AZ: Communication Skill Builders.

Rowland, C., & Schweigert, P. (2000). Tangible symbols, tangible outcomes. *Augmentative and Alternative Communication, 16,* 61–78.

Rowley-Kelly, F. L., & Reigel, D. H. (1993). *Teaching the student with spina bifida.* Baltimore: Brookes.

Rozalski, M., Stewart, A., & Miller, J. (2010). How to determine the Least Restrictive Environment for students with disabilities. *Exceptionality, 18,* 151–163.

Rudell, R. B., & Unrau, N. J. (Eds.) (2004). *Theoretical models and processes of reading* (5th ed.). Newark, DE: International Reading Association.

Rumelhart, D. E. (1975). Notes on a schema for stories. In D. G. Brown & A. Collins (Eds.), *Representation and understanding: Studies in cognitive science* (pp. 211–236). New York: Academic Press.

Rushton, J. L., Clark, S. J., & Freed, G. L. (2000). Primary care role in the management of childhood depression: A comparison of pediatricians and family care physicians. *Pediatrics, 205,* 957–962.

Russo, D. C., Cataldo, M. F., & Cushing, P. J. (1981). Compliance training and behavioral covariation in the treatment of multiple behavior problems. *Journal of Applied Behavior Analysis, 14*(3), 209–222.

Rust, J., & Golombok, S. (2009). *Modern psychometrics: The science of psychological assessment* (3rd ed.). New York: Routledge.

Rutter, R. (1979). Protective factors in children's responses to stress and disadvantage. In M. W. Kent & J. E. Rolf (Eds.), *Primary prevention of psychopathology: Vol. 3. Social competence in children* (pp. 49–74). Hanover, NH: University Press of New England.

Ryndak, D. L., Moore, M. A., Orlando, A. M., & Delano, M. (2008/2009). Access to the general curriculum: The mandate and the role of context in research-based practice for students with extensive support needs. *Research and Practice for Persons with Severe Disabilities, 33/34,* 199–213.

Rynn, M. A., Siqueland, L., & Rickels, K. (2001). Placebo-controlled trial of sertraline in the treatment of children with generalized anxiety disorder. *American Journal of Psychiatry, 158,* 2008–2014.

Sáenz, L. M, Fuchs, L. S., & Fuchs D. (2005). Peer-assisted learning strategies for English language learners with learning disabilities. *Exceptional Children, 71,* 231–247.

Sáenz, L. M., McMaster, K. L., Fuchs, D., & Fuchs, L. S. (2007). Peer-assisted learning strategies in reading for students with different learning needs. *Cognitive Education and Psychology, 6,* 395–410.

Safe and Drug-Free Schools and Communities Act of 1994, Pub. L. No. 103-382, 4001-4133, 108 Stat. 3518 (codified as amended at 20 U.S.C. 7101-7143 [2000]).

Sagan, C. (1996). *The demon-haunted world: Science as a candle in the dark.* New York: Ballantine Books.

Salahu-Din, D., Persky, H., & Miller, J. (2008). *The Nation's Report Card: Writing 2007* (NCES 2008-468). National Center for Education Statistics, Institute of Education Sciences, U.S. Department of Education, Washington, DC.

Salembier, G., & Furney, K. S. (1994). Promoting self-advocacy and family participation in transition planning. *Journal for Vocational Special Needs Education, 17*(1), 12–17.

Salembier, G., & Furney, K. S. (1997). Facilitating participation: Parents' perceptions of their involvement in the IEP/transition planning process. *Career Development for Exceptional Individuals, 20*(1), 29–42.

Salend, S. J., Gordon, J., & Lopez-Vona, K. (2002). Evaluating cooperative teaching teams. *Intervention in School and Clinic, 37,* 195–200.

Salend, S. J., Reynolds, C. J., & Coyle, E. M. (1989). Individualizing the Good Behavior Game across type and frequency of behavior with emotionally disturbed adolescents. *Behavior Modification, 13,* 108–126.

Sallee, F., Hilal, R., Dougherty, D., Beach, K., & Nesbitt, L. (1998). Platlet serotonin transporter in depressed children and adolescants: 3H-paroxetine platelet binding before and after sertraline. *Journal of the American Academy of Child and Adolescent Psychiatry, 37,* 777–784.

Sallee, F., Vrindavanam, N., Deas-Nesmith, D., Carson, S., & Sethuraman, G. (1997). Pulse intravenous clomipramine for depressed adolescents: Double-blind controlled trial. *American Journal of Psychiatry, 154,* 668–673.

Sameroff, A. J. (1983). Developmental systems: Contexts and evolution. In P. H. Mussen (Gen. Ed.) & W. Kessen (Vol. Ed.), *Handbook of child psychology: Vol. 1. History, theory, and methods* (4th ed., pp. 237–294). New York: Wiley.

Sameroff, A. J., Seifer, R., Barocas, R., Zax, M., & Greenspan, R. (1987). Intelligence quotient scores of 4-year-old children: Social environmental risk factors. *Pediatrics, 79,* 343–350.

Samson, J. F., & Lesaux, N. K. (2009). Language-minority learners in special education: Rates and predictors of identification for services. *Journal of Learning Disabilities, 42,* 148–162.

Sanchez-Fort, M. R., Brady, M. P., & Davis, C. A. (1995). Using high-probability requests to increase low-probability communication behavior in young children with severe disabilities. *Education and Training in Mental Retardation and Developmental Disabilities, 30*(2), 151–165.

Sandall, S., Hemmeter, M. L., Smith, B. J., & McLean, M. E. (Eds.). (2005). *DEC recommended practices: A comprehensive guide for practical application in early intervention/ early childhood special education.* Longmont, CO: Sopris West.

Sandknop, P. A., Schuster, J. W., Wolery, M., & Cross, D. P. (1992). The use of an adaptive device to teach students with moderate mental retardation to select lower priced grocery items. *Education and Training in Mental Retardation, 27,* 219–229.

Sandler, C., & Sugai, G. (2009). Effective behavior and instructional support: A district model for early identification of reading and behavior problems. *Journal of Positive Interventions and Supports, 11,* 35–46.

Sandmel, K., Brindle, M., Harris, K. R., Lane, K., Graham, S., Little, A., Nackel, J., & Mathias, R. (2009). Making it work: Differentiating tier two writing instruction with self-regulated strategies development in tandem with schoolwide positive behavioral support for second graders. *Teaching Exceptional Children, 42*(2), 22–33.

Sandomierski, T., Kincaid, D., & Algozzine, B. (2007). Response to intervention and Positive Behavior Support: Brothers from different mothers or sisters with different misters? *Positive Behavior Interventions and Supports Newsletter, 4*(2). Retrieved from http://pbis.org/news/ New/Newsletters/Newsletter4-2.aspx

Sanford, L., & Burnett, R. (2008). *Functional vision and learning media assessment. A practitioner's guide.* Louisville, KY: American Printing House for the Blind.

Santamaría, L. J., & Thousand, J. S. (2004). Collaboration, co-teaching, and differentiated instruction: A process-oriented approach to whole schooling. *International Journal of Whole Schooling, 1*(1), 13–27.

Santos, R. M., & Lignugaris-Kraft, B. (1999). The effects of direct questions on preschool children's responses to indirect requests. *Journal of Behavioral Education, 9,* 193–210.

Sasso, G. M., Conroy, M., A., Stichter, J. P., & Fox, J. J. (2001). Slowing down the bandwagon: The misapplication of functional assessment for students with emotional or behavioral disorders. *Behavioral Disorders, 26,* 282–296.

Sasso, G. M., Mundschenk, N. A., Melloy, K. J., & Casey, S. D. (1998). A comparison of the effects of organismic and setting variables on the social interaction behavior of children with developmental disabilities and autism. *Focus on Autism and Other Developmental Disabilities, 13,* 2–16.

Satcher, D. (2001). *Youth violence: A report of the Surgeon General.* Washington, DC: Office of the Surgeon General, U.S. Department of Health & Human Services.

Sattler, J. M., & Hoge, R. D. (2006). *Assessment of children: Behavioral, social, and clinical foundations* (5th ed.). La Mesa, CA: Sattler.

Saxon, K. (March 22, 2005). Co-teaching and school reform: A case study. *Academic Exchange Quarterly.* Retrieved from http://goliath.ecnext .com/coms2/gi_0199-4327562/ Co-teaching-and-school-reform.html

Scarboro, M., & Forehand, R. (1975). Effects of response contingent isolation and ignoring on compliance and oppositional behavior of children. *Journal of Experimental Child Psychology, 19,* 252–264.

Scarborough, H. (1990). Very early language deficits in dyslexic children. *Child Development, 61,* 1728–1743.

Scarborough, H. S., & Dobrich, W. (1994). On the efficacy of reading to preschoolers. *Developmental Review, 14,* 245–302.

Schalock, R. L., Borthwick-Duffy, S. A., Bradley, V. J., Buntinx, W. H. E., Coulter, D. L., Craig, E. M., . . . Yeager, M. H. (2010). *Intellectual disability: Definition, classification, and systems of supports* (11th ed.). Washington, DC: American Association on Intellectual and Developmental Disabilities.

Schalock, R. L., Harber, R. S., & Genung, T. (1981). Community integration of mentally retarded adults: Community placement and program success. *American Journal of Mental Deficiency, 85,* 478–488.

Scheerenberger, R. C. (1977). Deinstitutionalization in perspective. In J. Paul, D. Stedman, & G. Neufeld (Eds.), *Deinstitutionalization program and policy development* (pp. 3–14). Syracuse: Syracuse University Press.

Schepis, M. M., Reid, D. H., Behrmann, M. M., & Sutton, K. A. (1998). Increasing communicative interactions of young children with autism using a voice output communication aid and naturalistic teaching. *Journal of Applied Behavior Analysis, 31,* 561–578.

Schepis, M. M., Reid, D. H., Ownbey, J., & Parsons, M. B. (2001). Training support staff to embed teaching within natural routines of young children with disabilities in an inclusive preschool. *Journal of Applied Behavior Analysis, 34,* 313–327.

Schirmer, B. R., & McGough, S. M. (2005). Teaching reading to children who are deaf: Do the conclusions of the National Reading Panel apply? *Review of Educational Research, 75,* 83–117.

Schloss, P. J., Alper, S., Young, H., Arnold-Reid, G., Aylward, M., & Dudenhoeffer, S. (1995). Acquisition of functional sight words in community-based recreation settings. *The Journal of Special Education, 29,* 84–96.

Schloss, P., Schloss, C., Wood, C., & Kiehl, W. (1986). A critical review of social skills research with behaviorally disordered students. *Behavioral Disorders, 12,* 1–14.

Schmidt, J. L., Deshler, D. D., Schumaker, J. B., & Alley, G. R. (1988). Effects of generalization instruction on the written language performance of adolescents with learning disabilities in the mainstream classroom. *Reading, Writing, and Learning Disabilities, 4,* 291–309.

Schneider, B. (1992). Didactic methods for enhancing children's peer relationships. *Clinical Psychology Review, 12,* 363–382.

Schneider, B., & Byrne, B. (1985). Children's social skills training: A meta-analysis. In B. Schneider, K. Rubin, & J. Ledingham (Eds.), *Children's peer relations: Issues in assessment and intervention* (pp. 175–190). New York: Springer-Verlag.

Schoen, S. F. (1983). The status of compliance technology: Implications for programming. *The Journal of Special Education, 17,* 438–496.

Schoen, S. F., & Ogden, S. (1995). Impact of time delay, observational learning, and attentional cuing upon word recognition during integrated small-group instruction. *Journal of Autism & Developmental Disorders, 25,* 503–519.

Schreibman, L. (1975). Effects of within-stimulus and extra-stimulus prompting on discrimination learning in autistic children. *Journal of Applied Behavior Analysis, 8,* 91–112.

Schulte, A., Elliott, S., & Kratochwill, T. (2001). Effects of testing accommodations on standardized mathematics test scores: An experimental analysis of the performances of students with and without disabilities. *School Psychology Review, 30,* 527–547.

Schumaker, J., Bulgren, J., Deshler, D., & Lenz, B. K. (1998). *The recall enhancement routine.* Lawrence, KS: The University of Kansas Center for Research on Learning.

Schumaker, J. B., & Deshler, D. D. (1992). Validation of learning strategy interventions for students with LD: Results of a programmatic research effort. In Y. L. Wong (Ed.), *Contemporary intervention research in learning disabilities: An international perspective.* New York: Springer-Verlag.

Schumaker, J. B., & Deshler, D. D. (2003). Can students with LD become competent writers? *Learning Disabilities Quarterly, 26,* 129–141.

Schumaker, J. B., & Deshler, D. D. (2009). Adolescents with learning disabilities as writers: Are we selling them short? *Learning Disabilities Research and Practice, 24,* 81–92.

Schumaker, J. B., & Deshler, D. D. (2010). Using a tiered intervention model in secondary schools to improve academic outcomes in subject-area courses. In M. Shinn & H. Walker (Ed.), *Interventions for achievement and behavior problems in a three-tier model including RTI* (pp. 609–632). Bethesda, MD: National Association of School Psychologists.

Schumaker, J. B., Deshler, D. D., Lenz, B. K., Bulgren, J. B., & Davis, B. (2006). *Strategies for helping adolescents with disabilities access the general education curriculum.* Lawrence, KS: University of Kansas Center for Research on Learning.

Schumaker, J. B., Deshler, D. D., & McKnight, P. (2002). Ensuring success in the secondary general education curriculum through the use of teaching routines. In M. A. Shinn, H. M. Walker, & G. Stoner (Eds.), *Interventions for academic and behavior problems II: Preventive and remedial approaches* (pp. 791–823). Bethesda, MD: NASP Publications.

Schumaker, J. B., & Lyerla, K. D. (1991). *The paragraph writing strategy: Instructor's manual.* Lawrence, KS: The University of Kansas Center for Research on Learning.

Schumaker, J. B., & Sheldon, J. (1985). *Proficiency in the sentence writing strategy: Instructor's manual.* Lawrence, KS: The University of Kansas Center for Research on Learning.

Schumm, J. S., & Vaughn, S. (1995). General education teacher planning: What can students with learning disabilities expect? *Exceptional Children, 61,* 335–353.

Schumm, J. S., Vaughn, S., & Harris, J. (1997). Pyramid power for cooperative planning. *Teaching Exceptional Children, 29,* 62–66.

Schunk, D. H. (2004). *Learning theories: An educational perspective.* Upper Saddle River, NJ: Merrill/Pearson.

Schwartz, I. S., Staub, D., Peck, C. A., & Gallucci, C. (2006). Peer relationships. In M. E. Snell & F. Brown (Eds.), *Instruction of students with severe disabilities* (6th ed.). Upper Saddle River, NJ: Merrill/Pearson.

Scott, M. S., Perou, R., Greenfield, D. B., & Swanson, L. (1993). Rhyming skills: Differentiating among mildly mentally retarded, learning disabled, and normally achieving students. *Learning Disabilities Research & Practice, 8,* 215–222.

Scott, T. M. (2001). A schoolwide example of positive behavioral support. *Journal of Positive Behavior Interventions, 3,* 88–94.

Scott, T. M., & Barrett, S. B. (2004). Using staff and student time engaged in disciplinary procedures to evaluate the impact of school-side PBS. *Journal of Positive Behavior Interventions, 6,* 21–27.

Scott, T. M., & Nelson, C. M. (1999). Using functional assessment to develop effective intervention plans: A practical classroom application. *Journal of Positive Behavioral Support, 1,* 242–251.

Scruggs, T. E., & Cohn, S. J. (1983). Learning characteristics of verbally gifted students. *Gifted Child Quarterly, 27,* 169–172.

Scruggs, T. E., & Mastropieri, M. A. (1986). Academic characteristics of behaviorally disordered and learning disabled children. *Behavioral Disorders, 11,* 184–190.

Scruggs, T. E., & Mastropieri, M. A. (1988). Acquisition and transfer of learning strategies by gifted and nongifted students. *Journal of Special Education, 22,* 153–166.

Scruggs, T. E., & Mastropieri, M. A. (1989a). Mnemonic instruction of learning disabled students: A field-based evaluation. *Learning Disability Quarterly, 12,* 119–125.

Scruggs, T. E., & Mastropieri, M. A. (1989b). Reconstructive elaborations: A model for content area learning. *American Educational Research Journal, 26,* 311–327.

Scruggs, T. E., & Mastropieri, M. A. (1990). Mnemonic instruction for learning disabled students: What it is and what it does. *Learning Disability Quarterly, 13,* 271–281.

Scruggs, T. E., & Mastropieri, M. A. (1992). Classroom applications of mnemonic instruction: Acquisition, maintenance, and generalization. *Exceptional Children, 58,* 219–229.

Scruggs, T. E., & Mastropieri, M. A. (2000). The effectiveness of mnemonic instruction for students with learning and behavior problems: An update and research synthesis. *Journal of Behavioral Education, 10,* 163–173.

Scruggs, T.E., & Mastropieri, M. A. (2013). Teaching students with high-incidence disabilities. In B.G. Cook & M. Tankersley (Eds.), *Research-based practices in special education.* Columbus, OH: Pearson.

Scruggs, T.E., Mastropieri, M.A., Berkeley, S., & Graetz, J. (2010). Do special education interventions improve learning of secondary content? A meta-analysis. *Remedial and Special Education, 31,* 437–449.

Scruggs, T. E., Mastropieri, M. A., Brigham, F. J., & Sullivan, G. S. (1992). Effects of mnemonic reconstructions on the spatial learning of adolescents with learning disabilities. *Learning Disability Quarterly, 15,* 154–162.

Scruggs, T. E., Mastropieri, M. A., Casto, G. (1987). The quantitative synthesis of single-subject research: Methodology and validation. *Remedial and Special Education, 8,* 24–33.

Scruggs, T. E., Mastropieri, M. A., & Levin, J. R. (1986). Can children effectively re-use the same mnemonic pegwords? *Educational Communication and Technology Journal, 34,* 83–88.

Scruggs, T. E., Mastropieri, M. A., & Levin, J. R. (1987). Implications of mnemonic strategy research for theories of learning disabilities. In H. L. Swanson (Ed.), *Memory and learning disabilities: Advances in learning and behavior disabilities*

(pp. 225–244). Greenwich, CT: JAI Press.

Scruggs, T. E., Mastropieri, M. A., Levin, J. R., & Gaffney, J. S. (1985). Facilitating the acquisition of science facts in learning disabled students. *American Educational Research Journal, 22,* 575–586.

Scruggs, T. E., Mastropieri, M. A., & Marshak, L. (2009). *Peer-mediated instruction in inclusive secondary social studies classrooms: A randomized field trial.* Fairfax, VA: George Mason University, College of Education and Human Development.

Scruggs, T. E., Mastropieri, M. A., Marshak, L., & Mills, S. (2009, April). *How to differentiate instruction without differentiating it: Results of recent research.* Paper presented at the annual meeting of the Council for Exceptional Children, San Diego.

Scruggs, T. E., Mastropieri, M. A., & McDuffie, K. A. (2007). Co-teaching in inclusive classrooms: A meta-synthesis of qualitative research. *Exceptional Children, 73,* 392–416.

Scruggs, T. E., Mastropieri, M. A., McLoone, B. B., Levin, J.R., & Morrison, C. (1987). Mnemonic facilitation of learning disabled students' memory for expository prose. *Journal of Educational Psychology, 79,* 27–34.

Scull, J. A., & Bianco, J. L. (2008). Successful engagement in early literacy intervention. *Journal of Early Childhood Literacy, 8,* 123–150.

Scullin, M. H. (2006). Large state-level fluctuations in mental retardation classifications related to introduction of renormed intelligence test. *American Journal of Mental Retardation, 111*(5), 322–335.

Seeley, J. R., Small, J. W., Walker, H. M., Feil, E. G., Severson, H. H., Golly, A. M., & Forness, S. R. (2009). Efficacy of the *First Step to Success* intervention for students with ADHD. *School Mental Health, 1,* 37–48.

Seguin, J. R., Pihl, R. O., Harden, P. W., Tremblay, R. E., & Boulerice, B. (1995). Cognitive and neuropsychological characteristics of physically aggressive boys. *Journal of Abnormal Psychology, 104,* 614–624.

Self, H., Benning, A., Marston, D., & Magnusson, D. (1991) Cooperative teaching project: A model for students at risk. *Exceptional Children, 58,* 26–33.

Semel, E., Wiig, E. H., & Secord, W. A. (2003). *Clinical Evaluation of Language Fundamentals, Fourth Edition (CELF-4).* Toronto, Canada: Psychological Corporation/Harcourt Assessment.

Senechal, M. (1997). The differential effect of storybook reading on preschoolers' acquisition of expressive and receptive vocabulary. *Journal of Child Language, 24,* 123–138.

Severson, H. H., Walker, H. M., Hope-Doolittle, J., Kratochwill, T. R., & Gresham, F. M. (2007). Proactive, early screening to detect behaviorally at-risk students: Issues, approaches, emerging innovations, and professional practices. *Journal of School Psychology, 45,* 193–223.

Sewell, T. J., Collins, B. C., Hemmeter, M. L., & Schuster, J. W. (1998). Using simultaneous prompting within an activity-based format to teach dressing skills to preschoolers with developmental delays. *Journal of Early Intervention, 21,* 132–145.

Seybert, A., Dunlap, G., & Ferro, J. (1996). The effects of choice-making on the problem behaviors of high school students with intellectual disabilities. *Journal of Behavioral Education, 6,* 49–65.

Shanahan, T., & Beck, I. L. (2006). Effective literacy teaching for English-language learners. In D. L. August & T. Shanahan (Eds.), *Developing literacy in a second language: Report of the National Literacy Panel.* Mahwah, NJ: Erlbaum.

Shapiro, E. S., Edwards, L., & Zigmond, N. (2005). Progress monitoring of mathematics among students with learning disabilities. *Assessment for Effective Intervention, 30*(2), 15–32.

Shapiro, J. P., Burgoon, J. D., Welker, C. J., & Clough, J. B. (2002). Evaluation of the peacemakers program: School-based violence prevention for students in grades four through eight. *Psychology in the Schools, 39,* 87–100.

Share, D. L., Jorm, A. F., MacLean, R., & Matthews, R. (1984). Sources of individual differences in reading acquisition. *Journal of Educational Psychology, 76,* 1309–1324.

Sharpe, M., McNear, D., & Bosma, J. (1995). The development of a scale to facilitate reading mode decisions. *Journal of Visual Impairment & Blindness, 89,* 83–89.

Shearin, A., Roessler, R., & Schriner, K. (1999). Evaluating the transition component in IEPs of secondary students with disabilities. *Rural Special Education Quarterly, 18*(2), 22–35.

Sheehy, K. (2002). The effective use of symbols in teaching word recognition to children with severe learning difficulties: A comparison of word alone, integrated picture cueing and the handle technique. *International Journal of Disability, Development, and Education, 49,* 47–59.

Shermer, M. (2002). *Why people believe weird things.* New York: Henry Holt.

Shevin, M., & Klein, N. K. (1984). The importance of choice-making skills for students with severe disabilities. *Journal of the Association for Persons with Severe Handicaps, 9,* 159–166.

Shin, J. S., Deno, S. L., & Espin, C. (2000). Technical adequacy of the maze task for curriculum-based measurement of reading growth. *Journal of Special Education, 34,* 164–172.

Shinn, M. R. (1989). *Curriculum-based measurement: Assessing special children.* New York: Guilford Press.

Shinn, M. R. (1998). *Advanced applications of curriculum-based measurement.* New York: Guilford Press.

Shinn, M. R., Good, R. H., Knutson, N., Tilly, W. D., & Collins, V. L. (1992). Curriculum-based measurement reading fluency: A confirmatory analysis of its relation to reading. *School Psychology Review, 21,* 459–479.

Shinn, M. R., Habedank, L., & Good, R. H. (1993). The effects of classroom reading performance data on general education teachers' and parents' attitudes about reintegration. *Exceptionality, 4,* 205–228.

Shinn, M. R., & Marston, D. (1985). Differentiating mildly handicapped, low-achieving and regular education students: A curriculum-based measurement approach. *Remedial and Special Education, 6,* 31–45.

Shinn, M. R., & McConnell, S. M. (1994). Improving general education instruction: Relevance to school psychologists. *School Psychology Review 23*(3), 351–371.

Shinn, M. R., Ysseldyke, J. E., Deno, S. L., & Tindal, G. (1986). A comparison of differences between students labeled learning disabled and low achieving on measures of classroom performance. *Journal of Learning Disabilities, 19,* 545–552.

Shogren, K. A., Faggella-Luby, M. N., Bae, A. J., & Wehmeyer, M. L. (2004). The effect of choice-making as an intervention for problem behavior: A meta-analysis. *Journal of Positive Behavior Interventions, 6,* 228–237.

Shores, R. E., & Wehby, J. H. (1999). Analyzing social behavior of children with emotional and behavioral disorders in classrooms. *Journal of Emotional and Behavioral Disorders, 7,* 194–199.

Short, E. J., & Ryan, E. B. (1984). Metacognitive differences between skilled and less skilled readers: Remediating deficits through story grammar and attribution training. *Journal of Educational Psychology, 76,* 225–235.

Shriner, J. G., Carty, S.J., Trach, J., Weber, R., & Yell, M. (April, 2008). *Research on standards-based IEPs: Development of a web-based decision model.* Paper presented at the annual meeting of the Council of Exceptional Children, Boston.

Shriner, J. G., & Destefano, L. (2003). Participation and accommodation in state assessment: The role of Individualized Education Programs. *Exceptional Children, 69,* 147–161.

Shulman, L. (1985). On teaching problem-solving and the solving of the problems of teaching. In E. A. Silver (Ed.), *Teaching and learning mathematical problem solving: Multiple research perspectives* (pp. 439–450). New Jersey: Erlbaum.

Siegler, R. S. (2007). Cognitive variability. *Developmental Science, 10,* 104–109.

Sigafoos, F., & Dempsey, R. (1992). Assessing choice making among children with multiple disabilities. *Journal of Applied Behavior Analysis, 25,* 747–755.

Sigafoos, J., Didden, R., Schlosser, R., Green, V. A., O'Reilly, M. F., & Lancioni, G. E. (2008). A review of intervention studies on teaching AAC to individuals who are deaf and blind. *Journal of Developmental and Physical Disabilities, 20,* 71–99.

Sigafoos, J., Roberts, D., Couzens, D., & Kerr, M. (1993). Providing opportunities for choice-making and turn-taking to adults with multiple disabilities. *Journal of Developmental and Physical Disabilities, 5,* 297–310.

Sileo, T. W., Sileo, A. P., & Prater, M. A. (1996). Parent and professional partnerships in special education: Multicultural considerations. *Intervention in School and Clinic, 31,* 145–153.

Silliman, E., Diehl, S., Huntley-Bahr, R., Hnath-Chisolm, T., Zenko, C., & Friedman, S. (2003). A new look at theory of mind tasks by adolescents with ASD. *Language Speech and Hearing Services in Schools, 34,* 236–252.

Silver, E. A. (1985). Research on teaching mathematical problem solving: Some underrepresented themes and needed directions. In E.A. Silver (Ed.), *Teaching and learning mathematical problem solving: Multiple research perspectives* (pp. 247–266). Hillsdale, NJ: Erlbaum.

Simeon, J., & Ferguson, B. (1987). Alprazolam effects in children with anxiety disorders. *Canadian Journal Psychiatry, 32,* 570–574.

Simmons, D., Fuchs, L., & Fuchs, D. (1995). Effects of explicit teaching and peer-mediated instruction on the reading achievement of learning disabled and low-performing students. *Elementary School Journal, 95,* 387-407.

Simmons, D., Fuchs, D., Fuchs, L. S., Pate, J., & Mathes, P. (1994). Importance of instructional complexity and role reciprocity to classwide peer tutoring. *Learning Disabilities Research and Practice, 9,* 203–212.

Simmons, D. C., Fuchs, L. S., Fuchs, D., Mathes, P. G., & Hodge, J. (1995). Effects of explicit teaching and peer-mediated instruction on the reading achievement of learning disabled and low performing students. *Elementary School Journal, 95,* 387–408.

Simmons, R. J., & Magiera, K. (2007). Evaluation of co-teaching in three high schools within one school district: How do you know when you are TRULY co-teaching? *Teaching Exceptional Children Plus,* 3(3) Article 4. Retrieved from http://escholarship.bc.edu/education/tecplus/vol3/iss3/art4

Simmons, R., Magiera, K., Cummings, B., & Arena, M. (2008). Co-teaching in secondary mathematics: How the special education teacher fits into the equation. *New York State Mathematics Teachers' Journal,* 58(1), 12–25.

Simon, J. B. (2006). Perceptions of the IEP requirement. *Teacher Education and Special Education, 29,* 225–235.

Simpkins, P. M., Mastropieri, M. A., & Scruggs, T. E. (2009). Differentiated curriculum enhancements in inclusive 5th grade science classes. *Remedial and Special Education, 30,* 300–308.

Simpson, R. (2005). Evidence-based practices and students with autism spectrum disorder. *Focus on Autism and Other Developmental Disabilities, 20,* 140–149.

Simpson, R., Koester, H., & LoPresti, E. (2006). Evaluation of an adaptive row/column scanning system. *Technology and Disability, 18,* 127–138.

Simpson, R., & Myles, B. (1998). Understanding and responding to the needs of students with autism. In R. Simpson & B. Myles (Eds.), *Educating children and youth with autism: Strategies for effective practice* (pp. 1–24). Austin, TX: Pro-Ed.

Singer, G. H., Singer, J., & Horner, R. H. (1987). Using pretask requests to increase the probability of compliance for students with severe disabilities. *Journal of the Association for Persons with Severe Handicaps, 12,* 287–291.

Singer, H., & Donlan, D. (1982). Active comprehension: Problem-solving schema with question generation for comprehension of complex short stories. *Reading Research Quarterly, 17,* 166–186.

Sireci, S. G. (2006). *Test accommodations and test validity: Issues, research findings, and unanswered questions.* Amherst, MA: University of Massachusetts [PowerPoint Slides]. Retrieved from cehd.umn.edu/NCEO/Teleconferences/tele12/

Sireci, S. G., Li, S., & Scarpati, S. (2003). *The effects of test accommodations on test performance: A review of the literature.* Retrieved from www.education.umn.edu/NCEO/OnlinePubs/TestAccommLitReview.pdf

Sireci, S. G., Scarpati, S., & Li, S. (2005). Test accommodations for students with disabilities: An analysis of the interaction hypothesis. *Review of Educational Research, 75,* 457–490.

Sitko, M. C., Laine, C. J., & Sitko, C. J. (2005). Writing tools: Technology and strategies for struggling writers. In D. L. Edyburn, K. Higgins, & R. Boone (Eds.), *Handbook of special education technology research and practice* (pp. 571–598). Whitefish Bay, WI: Knowledge by Design.

Skiba, R. J., Poloni-Staudinger, L., Gallini, S., Simmons, A. B., & Feggins-Azziz, R. (2006). Disparate access: The disproportionality of African American students with disabilities across educational environments. *Exceptional Children, 72*(4), 411–424.

Skinner, B. F. (1953). *Science and human behavior.* New York: Macmillan.

Skinner, C. H., Belfiore, P. J., Mace, H. W., Williams-Wilson, S., & Johns, G. A. (1997). Altering response typography to increase response efficiency and learning rates. *School Psychology Quarterly, 12,* 54–64.

Skinner, C. H., Fletcher, P. A., & Henington, C. (1996). Increasing learning rates by increasing student responses rates: A summary of research. *School Psychology Quarterly, 11,* 313–325.

Skinner, C. H., Ford, J. M., & Yunker, B. D. (1991). A comparison of instructional response requirements on the multiplication performance of behaviorally disordered students. *Behavioral Disorders, 17,* 56–65.

Skinner, C. H., Neddenriep, C. E., Robinson, S. L., Ervin, R., & Jones, K. (2002). Altering educational environments through positive peer reporting: Prevention and remediation of social problems associated with behavioral disorders. *Psychology in the Schools, 39,* 191–202.

Skinner, C. H., & Shapiro, E. S. (1989). A comparison of taped-words and drill interventions on reading fluency in adolescents with behavior disorders. *Education and Treatment of Children, 12,* 123–133.

Skinner, C. H., Smith, E. S., & McLean, J. E. (1994). The effects of intertribal interval duration on sight-word learning rates in children with behavioral disorders. *Behavioral Disorders, 19,* 98–107.

Skinner, D. G., Correa, V., Skinner, M., & Bailey, D. (2001). Role of religion in the lives of Latino families of young children with developmental delays. *American Journal on Mental Retardation, 106,* 297–313.

Slate, J. R., & Saudargas, R. A. (1986). Differences in the classroom behaviors of behaviorally disordered and regular class children. *Behavioral Disorders, 12,* 45–53.

Smith, A. (2003). Scientifically based research and evidence-based education: A federal policy context. *Research and Practice for Persons with Severe Disabilities, 28,* 126–132.

Smith, B. W., & Sugai, G. (2000). A self-management functional assessment-based behavior support plan for a middle school student with EBD. *Journal of Positive Behavior Interventions, 2,* 208–217.

Smith, D. J., & Nelson, R. (1997). Goal setting, self-monitoring, and self-evaluation for students with disabilities. In M. Agran (Ed.), *Student-directed learning: Teaching self-determination skills* (pp. 80–110). Pacific Grove, CA: Brookes/Cole.

Smith, M. L. (2004). *Political spectacle and the fate of American schools.* New York: Routledge-Falmer.

Smith, M. W., & Dickinson, D. K. (1994). Describing oral language opportunities and environments in head start and other preschool classrooms. *Early Childhood Research Quarterly, 9,* 345–366.

Smith, R. G., & Iwata, B. A. (1997). Antecedent influences on behavioral disorders. *Journal of Applied Behavior Analysis, 30,* 343–375.

Smith, S. W. (1987). *Program evaluation for procedural and substantive efficacy* (PEPSE). Unpublished manuscript. University of Kansas, Special Education Department, Lawrence, KS.

Smith, S. W. (1990a). Comparison of individualized education programs (IEPs) of students with behavioral disorders and learning disabilities. *The Journal of Special Education, 24,* 85–100.

Smith, S. W. (1990b). Individualized education programs (IEPs) in special education: From intent to acquiescence. *Exceptional Children, 57,* 6–14.

Smith, S. W., Daunic, A. P., & Taylor, G. G. (2007). Treatment validity in applied educational research: Expanding the adoption and application of measures to ensure evidence-based practices (Report). *Education and Treatment of Children, November 1.*

Smith, T. E. C., & Patton, J. R. (1998). *Section 504 and public schools: A practical guide for determining eligibility, developing accommodation plans, and documenting compliance.* Austin, TX: Pro-Ed.

Smith-Bird, E., & Turnbull, A. P. (2005). Linking positive behavior support to family quality-of-life outcomes. *Journal of Positive Behavior Interventions, 7,* 174–180.

Smith-Bird, E., Turnbull, A. P., & Koegel, R. L. (2005). Linking positive behavior support to family quality-of-life outcomes. *Journal of Positive Behavior Interventions, 7,* 174–180.

Smull, M. W., & Sanderson, H. (2005). *Essential lifestyle planning for everyone.* London: Sanderson.

Snell, M. E., & Brown, F. (2011). Selecting teaching strategies and arranging educational environments. In M. E. Snell & F. Brown (Eds.), *Instruction of students with severe disabilities* (7th ed.). Upper Saddle River, NJ: Pearson.

Snell, M. E., & Janney, R. (2000). *Social relationships and peer support.* Baltimore: Brookes.

Snow, C. (2006). What counts as literacy in early childhood? In K. McCartney & D. Phillips (Eds.), *Handbook of early child development* (pp. 274–294). Oxford: Blackwell.

Snow, C. E., Burns, M. S., & Griffin, P. (1998). *Preventing reading difficulties in young children.* Washington, DC: National Academies Press.

Snyder, E. P., & Shapiro, E. S. (1997). Teaching students with emotional/behavioral disorders the skills to participate in the development of their own IEPs. *Behavioral Disorders, 22,* 246–259.

Snyder, J., & Stoolmiller, M. (2002). Reinforcement and coercion mechanisms in the development of antisocial behavior: The family. In J. Reid, G. Patterson, & J. Snyder (Eds.), *Antisocial behavior in children and adolescents: A developmental analysis and model for intervention* (pp. 65–100). Washington, DC: American Psychological Association.

Song, A., Jones, S., Lippert, J., Metzger, K., Miller, J., & Borreca, C. (1980). *Wisconsin behavior rating scale.* Madison, WI: Wisconsin Central Center for the Developmentally Disabled.

Sonntag, C. M., & McLaughlin, T. F. (1984). The effects of training students in paragraph writing. *Education and Treatment of Children, 7,* 49–59.

Sontag, J. C., & Schacht, R. (1994). An ethnic comparison of parent participation and information needs in early intervention. *Exceptional Children, 60,* 422–433.

Sopko, K. M. (2003). *The IEP: A synthesis of current literature since 1997* (Information Analyses). Alexandria, VA: National Association of State Directors of Special Education.

Spackman, M. P., Fujiki, M., & Brinton, B. (2006). Understanding emotions in context: The effects of language impairment on children's ability to infer emotional reactions. *International Journal of Language & Communication Disorders, 41,* 173–188.

Spann, S. J., Kohler, F. W, & Soenksen, D. (2003). Examining parents' involvement in and perceptions of special education services: An interview with families in a parent support group. *FOCUS on Autism and Other Developmental Disabilities, 18,* 228–237.

Sparrow, S. S., Cicchetti, D. V., & Balla, D. A. (2005). *Vineland Adaptive Behavior Scales, 2nd Edition.* Minneapolis, MN: Pearson Assessment.

Special Education Elementary Longitudinal Study. (2005). *SEELS data documentation and dictionary: Introduction.* Washington, DC: U.S. Office of Special Education Programs.

Spectrum K12 School Solutions. (2009). Response to intervention adoption survey 2009. *Towson, MD: Author.*

Speece, D. L. (2002). Classification of learning disabilities: Convergence, expansion, and caution. In R. Bradley, L. Danielson, & D. Hallahan (Eds.), *Learning disabilities: Research to practice* (pp. 279–285). Mahwah, NJ: Erlbaum.

Speece, D. L., & Case, L. P. (2001). Classification in context: An alternative approach to identifying early reading disability. *Journal of Educational Psychology, 93,* 735–749.

Spicuzza, R., Ysseldyke, J., Lemkuil, A., Kosciolek, S., Boys, C., & Teeluchsingh, E. (2001). Effects of curriculum-based monitoring on classroom instruction and math achievement. *Journal of School Psychology, 39,* 521–542.

Sprague, J. R., & Rian, V. (1993). *Support systems for students with severe problems in Indiana: A descriptive analysis of school structure and student demographics.* Unpublished manuscript. Bloomington, IN: Indiana University Institute for the Study of Developmental Disabilities.

Sprague, J., Walker, H., Golly, A., White, K., Myers, D. R., & Shannon, T. (2001). Translating research into effective practice: The effects of a universal staff and student intervention on indicators of discipline and school safety. *Education and Treatment of Children, 24,* 495–511.

Sprick, M., Howard, L., & Fidanque, A. (1998). *Read well.* Longmont, CO: Sopris West.

Spungin, S. (1990). *Braille literacy: Issues for blind persons, families, professionals and producers of braille.* New York: AFB Press.

Stading, M., Williams, R. L., & McLaughlin, T. F. (1996). Effects of a copy, cover, and compare procedure on multiplication facts mastery with a third grade girl with learning disabilities in a home setting. *Education & Treatment of Children, 19*(4), 425–434.

Stager, G. H., Singer, J., & Horner, R. H. (1987). Using pretask requests to increase the probability of compliance for students with severe disabilities. *Journal of the Association for Persons with Severe Handicaps, 12,* 287–291.

Stahr, B., Cushing, D., Lane, K., & Fox, J. (2006). Efficacy of a function-based intervention in decreasing off-task behavior exhibited by a student with ADHD. *Journal of Positive Behavior Interventions, 8,* 201–211.

Stanovich, K. E. (1986). Matthew effects in reading: Some consequences in individual differences in the acquisition of literacy. *Reading Research Quarterly, 21,* 360–407.

Starr, M. S., Kambe, G., Miller, B., & Keith, R. (2002) Basic functions of language, reading and reading disability. In E. Witruk, A. D. Friederici, & T. Lachmann (Eds.), *Neuropsychology and cognition* (Vol. 20, pp. 121–136). Dordrecht, Netherlands: Kluwer Academic Publishers.

Stecker, P. M., & Fuchs, L. S. (2000). Effecting superior achievement using curriculum-based measurement: The importance of individual progress monitoring. *Learning Disability Research and Practice, 15,* 128–134.

Stecker, P. M., Fuchs, L. S., & Fuchs, D. (2005). Using curriculum-based measurement to improve student achievement: A review of research. *Pyschology in the Schools, 42,* 795–818.

Stecker, S. K., Roser, N. L., & Martinez, M. G. (1998). Understanding oral reading fluency. In T. Shanahan & F. V. Rodrigues-Brown (Eds.), *47th Yearbook of the National Reading Conference* (pp. 295–310). Chicago: National Reading Conference.

Stein, M., Kinder, D., Silbert, J., & Carnine, D. W. (2006). *Designing effective mathematics instruction: A direct instruction approach* (4th ed.). Upper Saddle River, NJ: Prentice Hall.

Stein, N. L., & Glenn, C. (1979). An analysis of story comprehension in elementary school children. In R. O. Freedle (Ed.), *New directions in discourse processing* (vol. 2, pp. 53–120). Norwood, NJ: Ablex.

Steinberg, S., & Kincheloe, J. (2004). *19 urban questions: Teaching in the city.* New York: Peter Lang.

Steinman, B. A., LeJeune, B. J., & Kimbrough, B. T. (2006). Developmental stages of reading processes in children who are blind and sighted. *Journal of Visual Impairment & Blindness, 100,* 36–46.

Sternberg, R. (1985). *Beyond IQ.* Cambridge, MA: Cambridge University.

Stevens, V., De Bourdeaudhuij, I., & Van Oost, P. (2000). Bullying in Flemish schools: An evaluation of anti-bullying intervention in primary and secondary schools. *British Journal of Educational Psychology, 70,* 195–210.

Stiggins, R. J. (2001). *Student-involved classroom assessment* (3rd ed.). Upper Saddle River, NJ: Merrill/ Pearson.

Stiggins, R. J. (2005). From formative assessment to assessment FOR learning: A path to success in standards-based schools. *Phi Delta Kappan, 87,* 324–328.

Stiggins, R. J. (2007). Five assessment myths and their consequences. *Education Week, 27*(8), 28–29. Retrieved from www.childrensprogress.com/ documents/2007_10_07_Education-Week.pdf

Stillman, R., & Battle, C. W. (1986). *Callier-Azusa Scale H: Cognition and communication.* Dallas, TX: University of Texas at Dallas.

Stith, S., Pruitt, I., Dees, J., Fronce, M., Green, N., Som, A., & Linkh, D. (2006). Implementing community-based prevention programming: A review of the literature. *Journal of Primary Prevention, 27,* 599–617.

Stoddard, B., & MacArthur, C. A. (1993). A peer editor strategy: Guiding learning-disabled students in response and revision. *Research in the Teaching of English, 27,* 76–103.

Stokes, T. F., & Baer, D. M. (1977). An implicit technology of generalization. *Journal of Applied Behavior Analysis, 10,* 349–367.

Stokes, T. F., & Osnes, P. G. (1989). An operant pursuit of generalization. *Behavior Therapy, 20,* 337–355.

Storey, K., Smith, D., & Strain, P. (1993). Use of classroom assistants and peer-mediated intervention to increase integration in preschool settings. *Exceptionality, 4*(1), 1–16.

Stormont, M. A., Smith, S. C., & Lewis, T. J. (2007). Teacher implementation of precorrection and praise statements in Head Start classrooms as a component of a program-wide system of positive behavior support. *Journal of Behavior Education, 16,* 280–290.

Stouthamer-Loeber, M., & Loeber, R. (2002). Lost opportunities for intervention: Undetected markers for the development of serious juvenile delinquency. *Criminal Behaviour and Mental Health, 12,* 69–82.

Straetmans, G., & Eggen, T. (1998). Comparison of test administration procedures for placement decisions in a mathematics course. *Educational Research and Evaluation, 4,* 259–275.

Strain, P. S., & Hoyson, M. (2000). The need for longitudinal, intensive social skill intervention: LEAP follow-up outcomes for children with autism. *Topics in Early Childhood Special Education, 20,* 116–122. doi:10.1177/027112140002000207

Strain, P. S., Kerr, M. M., & Ragland, E. U. (1979). Effects of peer-mediated social initiations and prompting/reinforcement procedures on the social behavior of autistic children. *Journal of Autism and Developmental Disorders, 9,* 41–54.

Strain, P. S., & Odom, S. L. (1986). Effective intervention for social skill development of exceptional children. *Exceptional Children, 52,* 543–551.

Strand, S. C., & Morris, R. C. (1986). Programmed training of visual discriminations: A comparison of techniques. *Applied Research in Mental Retardation, 7,* 165–181.

Strangman, N., & Dalton, B. (2005). Technology for struggling readers: A review of the research. In D. Edyburn, K. Higgins, & R. Boone (Eds.), *Handbook of special education technology research and practice* (pp. 549–569). Whitefish Bay, WI: Knowledge by Design.

Street, B. V. (1984). *Literacy in theory and practice.* Cambridge: Cambridge University Press.

Street, B. V. (1995). *Social literacies: Critical approaches to literacy in development, ethnography, and education.* London/New York: Longman.

Stuebing, K. K., Fletcher, J. M., LeDoux, J. M., Lyon, G. R., Shaywitz, S. E., & Shaywitz, B. A. (2002). Validity of IQ-discrepancy classifications of reading disabilities: A meta-analysis. *American Educational Research Journal, 39*(2), 469–518.

Stumbo, N. J., Martin, J. K., & Hedrick, B. N. (2009). Assistive technology: Impact on education, employment, and independence of individuals with physical disabilities. *Journal of Vocational Rehabilitation, 30,* 99–110.

Suárez-Orozco, M., Roos, P. M., & Suárez-Orozco, C. (2000). Culture, education, and legal perspective on immigration: Implications for school reform. In J. P. Heubert (Ed.), *Law and school reform: Six strategies for promoting educational equity* (pp. 160–204). New Haven, CT: Yale University Press.

Sugai, G., & Horner, R. H. (2002). The evolution of discipline practices: School-wide positive behavior supports. *Child & Family Behavior Therapy, 24,* 25–50.

Sugai, G., & Horner, R. H. (2006). A promising approach for expanding and sustaining school-wide positive behavior support. *School Psychology Review, 35,* 245–260.

Sugai, G., Horner, R., & Gresham, F. M. (2002). Behaviorally effective school environments. In M. Shinn, H. Walker, & G. Stoner (Eds.), *Interventions for academic and behavior problems* (2nd ed., pp. 315–350). Bethesda, MD: National Association of School Psychologists.

Sugai, G., Horner, R., & Todd, A. W. (2000). *Effective Behavior Support (EBS) Survey: Assessing and planning behavior support in schools.* Eugene: University of Oregon.

Sugai, G., Lewis-Palmer, T., Todd, A., & Horner, R. H. (2001). *School-wide evaluation tool.* Eugene: University of Oregon.

Sulzby, E. (1985). Children's emergent reading of favorite storybooks: A developmental study. *Reading Research Quarterly, 20,* 458–481.

Sutherland, K. S., Alder, N., & Gunter, P. L. (2003). The effect of increased rates of opportunities to respond on the classroom behavior of students with emotional/behavioral disorders. *Journal of Emotional and Behavioral Disorders, 11,* 239–248.

Sutherland, K. S., & Oswald, D. (2005). The relationship between teacher and student behavior in classrooms for students with emotional and behavioral disorders: Transactional processes. *Journal of Child and Family Studies, 14,* 1–14.

Sutherland, K. S., & Singh, N. N. (2004). Learned helplessness and students with EBD: Deprivation in the classroom. *Behavioral Disorders, 29,* 169–181.

Sutherland, K. S., & Wehby, J. H. (2001). Exploring the relationship between increased opportunities to respond to academic requests and the academic and behavioral outcomes of students with emotional and behavioral disorders: A review. *Remedial and Special Education, 22,* 113–121.

Sutherland, K. S., Wehby, J. H., & Copeland, S. R. (2000). Effect of varying rates of behavior-specific praise on the on-task behavior of students with EBD. *Journal of Emotional & Behavioral Disorders, 8*(1), 2–8.

Sutherland, K. S., Wehby, J. H., & Yoder, P. J. (2002). Examination of the relationship between teacher praise and opportunities for students with EBD to respond to academic requests. *Journal of Emotional and Behavior Disorders, 10*(1), 5–13.

Swanson, E. A., Wexler, J., & Vaughn, S. (2009). Text reading and students with learning difficulties. In E. H. Hiebert (Ed.), *Reading more, reading better* (pp. 210–230). New York: Guilford Press.

Swanson, H. L. (1990). Instruction derived from the strategy deficit model: Overview of principles and procedures. In T. E. Scruggs & B. Y. L. Wong (Eds.), *Intervention research in learning disabilities* (pp. 34–65). New York: Springer-Verlag.

Swanson, H. L. (1993). Principles and procedures in strategy use. In L. Meltzer (Ed.), *Strategy assessment and instruction for students with learning disabilities* (pp. 61–92). Austin, TX: Pro-Ed.

Swanson, H. L. (1999). *Interventions for students with learning disabilities: A meta-analysis of treatment outcomes.* New York: Guilford Press.

Swanson, H. L., & Beebe-Frankenberger, M. (2004). The relationship between working memory and mathematical problem solving in children at risk and not at risk for math disabilities. *Journal of Education Psychology, 96,* 471–491.

Swanson, H. L., & Deshler, D. D. (2003). Instructing adolescents with learning disabilities: Converting a meta-analysis to practice. *Journal of Learning Disabilities, 36*(2), 124–135. doi:10.1177/002221940303600205

Swanson, H. L., & Hoskyn, M. (2001a). Instructing adolescents with learning disabilities: A component and composite analysis. *Learning Disabilities Research & Practice, 16,* 109–119.

Swanson, H. L., & Hoskyn, M. (2001b). A meta-analysis of intervention research for adolescent students with learning disabilities. *Learning Disabilities Research & Practice, 16,* 109–119.

Swanson, H. L., Hoskyn, M., & Lee, C. (1999). *Interventions for students with learning disabilities: A meta-analysis of treatment outcomes.* New York: Guilford Press.

Swanson, H. L., & Sachs-Lee, C. (2000). A meta-analysis of single-subject-design intervention research for students with LD. *Journal of Learning Disabilities, 33,* 114–136.

Swanson, L. (2000). What instruction works for students with learning disabilities: Summarizing the results from a meta-analysis of intervention studies. In R. M. Gersten, E. P. Schiller, & S. Vaughn (Eds.), *Contemporary special education research* (pp. 1–30). Mahwah, NJ: Erlbaum.

Swanson, L. A., Fey, M. E., Mills, C. E., & Hood, L. S. (2005). Use of narrative-based language intervention with children who have specific language impairment. *American Journal of Speech-Language Pathology, 14,* 131–143.

Swanson, L., Trainin, G., Necoechea, D. M., & Hammill, D. (2003). Rapid naming, phonological awareness, and reading: A meta-analysis of the correlation evidence. *Review of Educational Research, 73,* 407–440.

Sweet, A. P., & Snow, C. (2002). Reconceptualizing reading comprehension. In C. C. Block, L. B. Gambrell, & M. Pressley (Eds.), *Improving reading comprehension instruction: Rethinking research, theory, and classroom practice* (pp. 17–53). San Francisco, CA: Jossey-Bass.

Sweller, J. (2005). Implications of cognitive load theory for multimedia learning. In R. Mayer (Ed.), *Cambridge handbook of multimedia learning* (pp. 19–30). New York: Cambridge University Press.

Sweller, J., Chandler, P., Tierney, P., & Cooper, M. (1990). Cognitive load as a factor in the structuring of technical material. *Journal of Experimental Psychology: General, 119,* 176–192.

Swinehart-Jones, D., & Heller, K. W. (2009). Teaching students with severe speech and physical impairments strategy using internal speech and motoric indicators. *The Journal of Special Education, 43,* 131–144.

Taber, T. A., Alberto, P. A., Hughes, M., & Seltzer, A. (2002). A strategy for students with moderate disabilities when lost in the community. *Research and Practice for Persons with Severe Disabilities, 27,* 141–152.

Taft, R., & Mason, L. H. (2011). Examining effect of writing interventions: Spotlighting results for students with primary disabilities other than learning disabilities. *Remedial and Special Education, 32,* 359–370.

Talbott, E., Lloyd, J. W., & Tankersley, M. (1995). Effects of reading comprehension interventions with students with learning disabilities. *Learning Disability Quarterly, 17,* 223–232.

Tam, K. Y., Heward, W. L., & Heng, M. A. (2006). A reading instruction intervention program for English-Language Learners who are struggling readers. *Journal of Special Education, 40,* 79–93.

Tam, S. F. (2000). The effects of a computer skill training programme adopting social comparison and self-efficacy enhancement strategies on self-concept and skill outcome in trainees with physical disabilities. *Disability and Rehabilitation, 22,* 655–664.

Tamis-LeMonda, C. S., Bornstein, M. H., & Baumwell, L. (2001). Maternal responsiveness and children's achievement of language milestones. *Child Development, 72,* 748–767.

Tankersley, M., Harjusola-Webb, S., & Landrum, T. J. (2008). Using single-subject research to establish the evidence base of special education. *Intervention in School and Clinic, 44,* 83–90.

Tawney, J. W., & Gast, D. L. (1984). *Single subject research in special education.* Columbus, OH: Merrill.

Taylor, P., Collins, B. C., Schuster, J. W., & Kleinert, H. (2002). Teaching laundry skills to high school students with disabilities: Generalization of targeted skills and nontargeted information. *Education and Training in Mental Retardation and Developmental Disabilities, 37,* 172–183.

Taylor, S. J. (1988). Caught in the continuum: A critical analysis of the principle of the least restrictive environment. *Journal of the Association for Persons with Severe Handicaps, 13*(1), 41–53.

Taylor-Greene, S., Brown, D., Nelson, L. Longton, J., Gassman, T., Cohen, J., Swartz, J., Horner, R. H., Sugai, G., & Hall, S. (1997). School-wide behavioral support: Starting the year off right. *Journal of Behavioral Education, 7,* 99–112.

Taylor-Greene, S. J., & Kartub, D. T. (2000). Durable implementation of school-wide behavior support. *Journal of Positive Behavior Support, 2,* 233–235.

Téllez, K., & Waxman, H. (2006). *Preparing quality educators for English language learners: Research, policies, and practices.* Mahwah, NJ: Erlbaum.

Templeton, J. (1990). Social skills training for behavior-problem adolescents: A review. *Journal of Partial Hospitalization, 6,* 49–60.

Test, D. W., Fowler, C. H., Richter, S. M., Mazzotti, V., White, J., Walker, A. R., . . . Kortering, L. (2009). Evidence-based practices in secondary transition. *Career Development for Exceptional Individuals, 32,* 115–128.

Test, D. W., Mason, C., Hughes, C., Konrad, M., Neale, M., & Wood, W. M. (2004). Student involvement in individualized education program meetings: A review of the literature. *Exceptional Children, 70*(4), 391–412.

Test, D. W., Mazzotti, V. L., Mustian, A. L., Fowler, C. H., Kortering, L., & Kohler, P. (2009). Evidence-based secondary transition predictors for improving post-school outcomes for students with disabilities. *Career Development for Exceptional Individuals, 32,* 160–181.

Test, D. W., & Neale, M. (2004). Using the *Self-Advocacy Strategy* to increase middle graders' IEP participation. *Journal of Behavioral Education, 13,* 135–145.

Therrien, W. J. (2004). Fluency and comprehension gains as a result of repeated reading: A meta-analysis. *Remedial and Special Education, 25,* 252–261.

Thevenot, C., Devidal, M., Barrouillet, P., & Fayol, M. (2007). Why does placing the question before an arithmetic word problem improve performance?

A situation model account. *The Quarterly Journal of Experimental Psychology, 60,* 43–56.

Thiemann, K. S., & Goldstein, H. (2004). Effects of peer training and written text cueing on social communication of school-age children with pervasive developmental disorder. *Journal of Speech, Language, and Hearing Research, 47,* 126–144. doi:1092-4388/04/4701-0126

Thomas, J. D., Presland, I. E., Grant, M. D., & Glynn, T. (1978). Natural rates of teacher approval and disapproval in grade-7 classrooms. *Journal of Applied Behavior Analysis, 11,* 91–94.

Thompson, R. H., White, K. R., & Morgan, D. P. (1982). Teacher-student interactions patterns in classrooms with mainstreamed mildly handicapped students. *American Educational Research Journal, 19,* 220–236.

Thompson, S., Blount, A., & Thurlow, M. (2002). *A summary of research on the effects of test accommodations: 1999 through 2001* (Technical Report 34). Minneapolis, MN: University of Minnesota, National Center on Educational Outcomes.

Thompson, S. J., Quenemoen, R. F., & Thurlow, M. L. (2006). Factors to consider in the design of inclusive online assessments. In M. Hricko (Ed.), *Online assessment and measurement: foundations and challenges* (pp. 102–117). Hershey, PA: Information Science Publishing.

Thompson, S. J., Thurlow, M. L., & Malouf, D. (2004, May). Creating better tests for everyone through universally designed assessments. *Journal of Applied Testing Technology, 10*(2). Retrieved on *date* from http://www.testpublishers.org/atp .journal.htm

Thompson, T., Symons, F. J., & Felce, D. (2000). Principles of behavioral observation: Assumptions and strategies. In T. Thompson, D. Felce, & F. J. Symons (Eds.), *Behavioral observation: Technology and applications in developmental disabilities* (pp. 3–16). Baltimore: Brookes.

Thousand, J. S., & Villa, R. A. (1989). Enhancing success in heterogeneous schools. In S. Stainback, W. Stainback, & M. Forest (Eds.), *Educating all students in the mainstream of regular education* (pp. 89–103). Baltimore: Brookes.

Thurlow, M. L. (2000). Standards-based reform and students with disabilities: Reflections on a decade of change. *Focus on Exceptional Children, 33*(3), 1–16.

Thurlow, M. L. (2007). State policies and accommodations: Issues and implications. In C. C. Laitusis & L. L. Cook (Eds.), *Large-scale assessment and accommodations: What works?* (pp. 13–22). Arlington, VA: Council for Exceptional Children.

Thurlow, M., Altman, J., & Vang, M. (2009). *Annual performance report: 2006–2007 State assessment data.* Minneapolis, MN: University of Minnesota National Center on Educational Outcomes (NCEO). Retrieved from http://www.cehd .umn.edu/nceo/OnlinePubs/APR-report2006-2007.pdf

Thurlow, M. L., Elliott, J. E., & Ysseldyke, J. E. (2003). *Testing students with disabilities: Practical strategies for complying with district and state requirements* (2nd ed.). Thousand Oaks, CA: Corwin.

Thurlow, M. L., Lazarus, S. S., & Christensen, L. L. (2008). Role of assessment accommodations in accountability. *Perspectives on Language and Learning, 34*(4), 17–20.

Thurlow, M. L., & Thompson, S. J. (2004). Inclusion of students with disabilities in state and district assessments. In J. E. Wall & G. R. Walz (Eds.), *Measuring up: Assessment issues for teachers, counselors, and administrators* (pp. 161–176). Austin, TX: Pro-Ed.

Thurlow, M. L., Ysseldyke, J. E., & Silverstein, B. (1993). *Testing accommodations for students with disabilities: A review of the literature* (Synthesis Report 4). Minneapolis, MN: University of Minnesota, National Center on Learning Disabilities.

Thurlow, M. L., Ysseldyke, J. E., & Silverstein, B. (1995). Testing accommodations for students with disabilities. *Remedial and Special Education, 16,* 260–270.

Tiger, J. H., Hanley, G. P., & Hernandez, E. (2006). An evaluation of the value of choice with preschool children. *Journal of Applied Behavior Analysis, 39,* 1–16.

Tilly, W. D. (2003, December). *How many tiers are needed for successful prevention and early intervention? Heartland Area Education Agency's evolution from four to three tiers.* Paper presented at the National Research Center on Learning Disabilities Responsiveness-to-Intervention Symposium, Kansas City, MO.

Tilly, W. D., Reschly, D. J., & Grimes, J. (1999). Eligibility determination in problem solving systems: Conceptual foundations and critical components. In D. J. Reschly, W. D. Tilly, III, & J. P. Grimes (Eds.), *Special education in transition* (pp. 221–251). Longmont, CO: Sopris West.

Timmons, J. R., & Whitney-Thomas, J. (1998). The most important member: Facilitating the focus person's participation in person centered planning. *Research in Practice, 4*(1), 3–6.

Tincani, M., & Crozier, S. (2008). Comparing brief and extended wait-time during small group instruction for children with challenging behavior. *Journal of Behavioral Education, 17,* 79–92.

Tindal, G. A. (1992). Evaluating instructional programs using curriculum-based measurement: *Preventing School Failure, 36,* 39–44.

Tindal, G., & Fuchs, L. (2000). *A summary of research on test changes: An empirical basis for defining accommodations.* Lexington, KY: Mid-South Regional Resource Center. (ERIC Document Reproduction Service No. ED 442 245)

Tindal, G., Fuchs, L., Fuchs, D. Shinn, M., Deno, S., & Germann, G. (1983). *The technical adequacy of a basal reading series mastery test: The Scott-Foresman reading program* (Research Report No. 128). Minneapolis: Institute for Research on Learning Disabilities.

Tindal, G., Germann, G., & Deno, S. L. (1983). *Descriptive research on the Pine County norms: A compilation of findings* (Research Report No. 132). Minneapolis: University of Minnesota Institute for Research on Learning Disabilities.

Tindal, G., & Nolet, V. (1995). Curriculum-based measurement in middle and high schools: Critical thinking skills in content areas. *Focus on Exceptional Children, 27,* 1–22.

Tindal, G. A., & Parker, R. (1991). Identifying measures for evaluating written expression. *Learning Disabilities Research and Practice, 6,* 211–218.

Tingstrom, D. H., Sterling-Turner, H. E., & Wilczynski, S. M. (2002). The Good Behavior Gamer: 1969–2002. *Behavior Modification, 30,* 225–253.

Todd, A., Haugen, L., Anderson, K., & Spriggs, M. (2002). Teaching recess: Low-cost efforts producing effective results. *Journal of Positive Behavior Interventions, 4,* 46–52.

Todd, A. W., Horner, R. H., & Sugai, G. (1999). Self-monitoring and self-recruited praise: Effects on problem behavior, academic engagement, and work completion in a typical classroom. *Journal of Positive Behavior Interventions, 1,* 66–76.

Tomblin, J. B., Records, N., Buckwalter, P., Zhang, X., Smith, E., & O'Brien, M. (1997). Prevalence of specific language impairment in kindergarten children. *Journal of Speech, Language, and Hearing Research, 40,* 1245–1260.

Tomesen, M., & Aarnoutse, C. (1998). Effects of an instructional programme for deriving word meanings. *Educational Studies, 24,* 107–128.

Tomlinson, C. (1999). *The differentiated classroom: Responding to the needs of all learners.* Alexandria, VA: ASCD.

Tomlinson, C. A. (2001). *How to differentiate instruction in mixed-ability classrooms* (2nd ed.). Alexandria, VA: Association for Supervision and Curriculum Development.

Tomlinson, C. A. (2003). *Fulfilling the promise of the differentiated classroom: Strategies and tools for responsive teaching.* Alexandria, VA: Association for Supervision and Curriculum Development.

Tone, B., & Farr, R. C. (1998). *Portfolio and performance assessment: Helping students evaluate their progress as readers and writers.* Fort Worth, TX: Harcourt Brace.

Torgesen, J. K. (1977). Memorization process in reading-disabled children. *Journal of Educational Psychology, 69,* 571–578.

Torgesen, J. K. (1998). Catch them before they fall: Identification and assessment to prevent reading failure in young children. *American Educator, 22,* 32–39.

Torgesen, J. K., Alexander, A. W., Wagner, R. K., Rashotte, C. A., Voeller, K. K. S., & Conway, T. (2001). Intensive remedial instruction for children with severe reading disabilities: Immediate and long-term outcomes from two instructional approaches. *Journal of Learning Disabilities, 34,* 33–58, 78.

Torgesen, J. K., & Bryant, B. R. (1994). *Test of phonological awareness.* Burlingame, CA: Psychological and Educational Publications.

Torgesen, J. K., & Goldman, T. (1977). Verbal rehearsal and short-term memory in reading disabled children. *Child Development, 48,* 56–60.

Torgesen, J. K., & Licht, B. (1983). The learning disabled child as an inactive learner: Restrospect and prospects. In J. D. McKineey & L. Feagans (Eds.), *Current topics in learning disabilities* (Vol. 1, pp. 3–32). Norwood, NJ: Ablex.

Torgesen, J. K., Rashotte, C. A., & Alexander, A. W. (2001). Principles of fluency instruction in reading: Relationships with established empirical outcomes. In M. Wolf (Ed.), *Dyslexia, fluency, and the brain* (pp. 307–331). Timonium, MD: York Press.

Tournaki, N. (2003). The differential effects of teaching addition through strategy instruction versus drill and practice to students with and without learning disabilities. *Journal of Learning Disabilities, 36,* 449–558.

Towles-Reeves, E., Kleinert, H., & Muhomba, M. (2009). Alternate assessment: Have we learned anything new? *Exceptional Children, 75,* 233–252.

Trabasso, T. (2005). The role of causal reasoning in understanding narratives. In T. Trabasso, J. Sabatini, D. Massaro, & R. Calfee (Eds.), *From orthography to pedagogy: Essays in honor of Richard L. Venezky* (pp. 81–106). Mahwah, NJ: Erlbaum.

Trabasso, T., & Magliano, J. P. (1996). How do children understand what they read and what can we do to help them? In M. F. Graves, P. van den Broek, & B. M. Taylor (Eds.), *The first R: Every child's right to read* (pp. 160–187). New York: Teachers College Press.

Trabasso, T., Secco, T., & van den Broek, P. W. (1984). Casual cohesion and story coherence. In H. Mandl, N. L. Stein, & T. Trabasso (Eds.), *Learning and comprehension of text* (pp. 83–111). Hillsdale, NJ: Erlbaum.

Trabasso, T., Suh, S., Payton, P., & Jain, R. (1995). Explanatory inferences and other strategies during comprehension and their effect on recall. In R. F. Lorch & E. J. O'Brien (Eds.), *Sources of coherence in reading* (pp. 219–239). Hillsdale, NJ: Erlbaum.

Trabasso, T., & van den Broek, P. (1985). Casual thinking and the representation of narrative events. *Journal of Memory and Language, 24,* 612–630.

Trabasso, T., van den Broek, P., & Suh, S. (1989). Logical necessity and transitivity of causal relations in stories. *Discourse Processes, 12,* 1–25.

Trainor, A. A. (2007). Person-centered planning in two culturally distinct communities: Responding to divergent needs and preferences. *Career Development for Exceptional Individuals, 30,* 92–103.

Treatment for Adolescents with Depression Study (TADS) Team. (2004). Fluoxetine, cognitive-behavioral therapy, and their combination for adolescents with depression. *Journal of American Medical Association, 292,* 807–820.

Trent, S. C. (1998). False starts and other dilemmas of a secondary general education collaborative teacher. *Journal of Learning Disabilities, 31,* 503–514.

Trent, S. D., & Truan, M. B. (1997). Speed, accuracy, and comprehension of adolescent braille readers in a specialized school. *Journal of Visual Impairment & Blindness, 91,* 494–500.

Trezek, B. J., & Malmgren, K. W. (2005). The efficacy of utilizing a phonics treatment package with middle school deaf and hard of hearing students. *Journal of Deaf Studies and Deaf Education, 10,* 256–271.

Trezek, B. J., & Wang, Y. (2006). Implications of utilizing a phonics-based reading curriculum with children who are deaf or hard of hearing.

Journal of Deaf Studies and Deaf Education, 11, 202–213.

Trezek, B. J., Wang, Y., & Paul, P. V. (2010). *Reading and deafness: Theory, research, and practice.* Clifton Park, NY: Delmar, Cengage Learning.

Trezek, B. J., Wang, Y., Woods, D. G., Gampp, T. L., & Paul, P. V. (2007). Using visual phonics to supplement beginning reading instruction for students who are deaf/hard of hearing. *Journal of Deaf Studies and Deaf Education, 12,* 373–384.

Trief, E. (2007). The use of tangible cues for children with multiple disabilities and visual impairment. *Journal of Visual Impairment & Blindness, 101,* 613–619.

Troia, G. A. (2004). Migrant students with limited English proficiency: Can Fast ForWord Language make a difference in their language skills and academic achievement? *Remedial and Special Education, 25,* 353–366.

Truan, M. B., & Trent, S. D. (1997). Impact of adolescents' adjustment to progressive vision loss on braille reading skills: Case studies. *Journal of Visual Impairment and Blindness, 91,* 301–308.

Trussell, R. P., Lewis, T. J., & Stichter, J. P. (2008). The impact of targeted classroom interventions and function-based behavior interventions on problem behaviors of students with emotional/behavioral disorders. *Behavioral Disorders, 33,* 153–166.

Tumlin, J., & Heller, K. W. (2004). Using word prediction software to increase typing fluency with students with physical disabilities. *Journal of Special Education Technology, 19,* 5–14.

Turnbull, A., Edmonson, H., Griggs, P., Wickham, D., Sailor, W., Freeman, R., Guess, D., Lassen, S., McCart, A., Park, J., Riffel, L., Turnbull, R., & Warren, J. (2002). A blueprint for school-wide positive behavior support: Implementation of three components. *Exceptional Children, 58,* 377–402.

Turnbull, A. P., & Turnbull, H. R. (1990). *Families, professionals, and exceptionality: A special partnership.* Upper Saddle River, NJ: Merrill/ Pearson.

Turnbull, A., Turnbull, R., Erwin, E. J., Soodak, L. C., & Shogren, K. A. (2011). *Families, professionals, and exceptionality: Positive outcomes through partnerships and trust* (6th ed.). Upper Saddle River, NJ: Pearson.

Turnbull, A. P., Zuna, N., Hong, J. Y., Hu, X., Kyzar, K., Obremski, S., . . . Stowe, M. (2010). Knowledge-to-action guides: Preparing families to be partners in making educational decisions. *Teaching Exceptional Children, 42*(3), 42–53.

Turnbull, H. R., III. (2005). Individuals with Disabilities Education Act Reauthorization: Accountability and personal responsibility. *Remedial and Special Education, 26,* 320–326.

Turnbull, H. R., Turnbull, A., & Wheat, M. (1982). Assumptions about parent participation: A legislative history. *Exceptional Education Quarterly, 3*(2), 1–8.

Turnell, R., & Carter, M. (1994). Establishing a repertoire of requesting for a student with severe and multiple disabilities using tangible symbols and naturalistic time delay. *Australia and New Zealand Journal of Developmental Disabilities, 19,* 193–207.

Turton, A. M., Umbreit, J., Liaupsin, C. J., & Bartley, J. (2007). Function-based intervention for an adolescent with emotional and behavioral disorders in Bermuda. *Behavioral Disorders, 33,* 23–32.

Tylenda, B., Beckett, J., & Barrett, R. P. (2007). Assessing mental retardation using standardized intelligence tests. In J. L. Matson (Ed.), *Handbook of assessment in persons with intellectual disability* (Vol. 34, pp. 27–97). Boston: Elsevier.

Tyler, A. A., & Sandoval, K. T. (1994). Preschoolers with phonological and language disorders: Treating different linguistic domains. *Language, speech, and hearing services in schools, 25,* 215–234.

Uberti, H. Z., Scruggs, T. E., & Mastropieri, M. A. (2003). Keywords make the difference! Mnemonic instruction in inclusive classrooms. *Teaching Exceptional Children, 35*(3), 56–61.

Ukrainetz, T. A. (1998a). Stickwriting stories: A quick and easy narrative representation strategy. *Language,* *Speech, and Hearing Services in Schools, 29,* 197–206.

Ukrainetz-McFadden, T. (1998b). The immediate effects of pictographic representation on children's narratives. *Child Language Teaching and Therapy, 14,* 51–67.

Umbreit, J. (1995). Functional assessment and intervention in a regular classroom setting for the disruptive behavior of a student with attention deficit hyperactivity disorder. *Behavioral Disorders, 20,* 267–278.

Umbreit, J., & Blair, K. W. (1996). The effects of preference, choice, and attention on problem behavior at school. *Education and Training in Mental Retardation and Developmental Disabilities,* June, 151–161.

Umbreit, J., Ferro, J., Liaupsin, C., & Lane, K. (2007). *Functional behavioral assessment and function-based intervention: An effective, practical approach.* Upper Saddle River, NJ: Pearson.

Umbreit, J., Lane, K. L., & Dejud, C. (2004). Improving classroom behavior by modifying task difficulty: effects of increasing the difficult of too-easy tasks. *Journal of Positive Behavior Interventions, 6,* 13–20.

Underwood, B. J., & Shultz, R. W. (1960). *Meaningfulness and verbal learning.* Chicago: Lippincott.

United Nations Educational, Scientific and Cultural Organization. (n.d.) *Best practices.* Retrieved from http://www .unesco.org/new/en/social-and-human-sciences/themes/social-transformations/ international-migration/best-practices/

Urdan, T., & Schoenfelder, E. (2006). Classroom effects on student motivation: Goal structures, social relationships, and competence beliefs. *Journal of School Psychology, 44,* 331–349.

U.S. Department of Education. (2001). *The No Child Left Behind Act of 2001.* Retrieved from: http://www .ed.gov/legislation/ESEA02/

U.S. Department of Education. (2004). *The Individuals with Disabilities Education Improvement Act of 2004.* Retrieved from http://idea.ed.gov

U.S. Department of Education. (2006a). *Twenty-eighth annual report to congress on the implementation of the Individuals with Disabilities Education Act, Parts B and C.* Retrieved from http://www2.ed.gov/about/

reports/annual/osep/2006/parts-b-c/index.html

U.S. Department of Education. (2006b). *26th Annual (2004) Report to Congress on the Implementation of the Individuals with Disabilities Education Act, Vol. 1.* Washington, DC: Author. Retrieved from http://www.ed.gov/about/reports/annual/osep/2004/26th-vol-1-front.pdf

U.S. Department of Education. (2007a). *Modified academic achievement standards: Non-regulatory guidance.* Washington, DC: Author. Retrieved from http://www.ed.gov/policy/speced/guid/nclb/twopercent.doc.

U.S. Department of Education. (2007b). *The 29th annual report to Congress on the implementation of the Individuals with Disabilities Education Act.* Washington, DC: Author.

U.S. Department of Education, National Center for Education Statistics. (2010a). *The condition of education 2010.* Washington, DC: Author.

U.S. Department of Education. (2010b). *Memo: A Response to Intervention (RTI) process cannot be used to delay–deny an evaluation of eligibility under the Individuals with Disabilities Education Act (IDEA).* Retrieved from http://www5.esc13.net/thescoop/special/files/2011/01/RTI-Memo-1-21-111.pdf.

U.S. Department of Education, Office of Special Education and Rehabilitative Services, Office of Special Education Programs. (2009). *28th Annual report to Congress on the implementation of the Individuals with Disabilities Education Act, Vol. 1.* Washington, DC: Author. Retrieved from http://www.ed.gpv/about/reports/annual/osep/2004/26th-vol-1-front.pdf.

Utley, C. A., Mortweet, S. L., & Greenwood, C. R. (1997). Peer-mediated instruction and interventions. *Focus on Exceptional Children, 27,* 167–181.

Vacc, N. A., Vallecorsa, A. L., Parker, A., Bonner, S., Lester, C., Richardson, S., & Yates, C. (1985). Parents' and educators' participation in IEP conferences. *Education and Treatment of Children, 8*(2), 153–162.

Vadasy, P. F., Jenkins, J. R., Antil, L. R., Wayne, S. K., & O'Connor, R. E. (1997). Community-based early reading intervention for at-risk first graders. *Learning Disabilities: Research & Practice, 12,* 29–39.

Vadasy, P. F., Jenkins, J. R., & Pool, K. (2000). Effects of tutoring in phonological and early reading skills on students at risk for reading disabilities. *Journal of Learning Disabilities, 33,* 579–590.

Vadasy, P. F., Sanders, E. A., & Abbott, R. D. (2008). Effects of supplemental early reading intervention at 2-year follow up: Reading skill growth patterns and predictors. *Scientific Studies of Reading, 12*(1), 51–89.

Vadasy, P. F., Sanders, E. A., & Peyton, J. A. (2006). Code-oriented instruction for kindergarten students at risk for reading difficulties: A randomized field trial with paraeducator implementers. *Journal of Educational Psychology, 98,* 508–528.

Vadasy, P. F., Wayne, S. K., O'Connor, R. E., Jenkins, J. R., Pool, K., Firebaugh, M., . . . Peyton, J. (2004). *Sound Partners: A supplementary, one-to-one tutoring program in phonics based early reading skills.* Longmont, CO: Sopris West.

Vakil, E., Shelef-Reshef, E., & Levy-Shiff, R. (1997). Procedural and declarative memory processes: Individuals with and without mental retardation. *American Journal on Mental Retardation, 102,* 147–160.

Valdés, G. (2001). *Learning and not learning English.* New York: Teachers College Press.

Vallar, G., & Cappa, S. F. (1987). Articulation and verbal short-term memory. Evidence from anarthria. *Cognitive Neuropsychology, 4,* 55–78.

Van Acker, R., Grant, S. H., & Henry, D. (1996). Teacher and student behavior as a function of risk for aggression. *Education and Treatment of Children, 19,* 316–334.

van Dijk, J. (1967). The first steps of deaf-blind children towards language. *The International Journal for the Education of the Blind, 15*(4), 112–114.

van Dijk, T., & Kintsch, W. (1983). *Strategies of discourse comprehension.* New York: Academic Press.

van Garderen, D., & Montague, M. (2003). Visual-spatial representation, mathematical problem solving, and students of varying abilities. *Learning Disabilities Research & Practice, 18,* 246–254.

Van Reusen, A. K., & Bos, C. S. (1990). IPLAN: Helping students communicate in planning conferences. *Teaching Exceptional Children, 22*(4), 30–32.

Van Reusen, A. K., & Bos, C. S. (1994). Facilitating student participation in the individualized education programs through motivation strategy instruction. *Exceptional Children, 60,* 466–475.

Van Reusen, A. K., Deshler, D. D., & Schumaker, J. B. (1989). Effects of a student participation strategy in facilitating the involvement of adolescents with learning disabilities in the individualized educational program planning process. *Learning Disabilities, 1,* 23–34.

Vandercook, T., York, J., & Forest, M. (1989). The McGill Action Planning System (MAPS): A strategy for building the vision. *Journal of the Association for Persons with Severe Handicaps, 14,* 205–215.

VanDerHeyden, A. M., & Burns, M. K. (2005). Using curriculum-based assessment and curriculum-based measurement to guide elementary mathematics instruction: Effect on individual and group accountability scores. *Assessment for Effective Intervention, 30*(3), 15–29.

VanDerHeyden, A. M., & Burns, M. K. (2010). *Essentials of Response to Intervention.* New York: Wiley.

VanDerHeyden, A. M., Witt, J. C., & Gilbertson, D. A. (2007). Multi-year evaluation of the effects of a Response to Intervention (RtI) model on identification of children for special education. *Journal of School Psychology, 45,* 225–256.

VanDerHeyden, A. M., Witt, J. C., & Naquin, G. (2003). Development and validation of a process for screening referrals to special education. *School Psychology Review, 32,* 204–227.

Vansickle, T. (2004). Types and uses of tests. In J. E. Wall & G. R. Walz (Eds.), *Measuring up: Assessment issues for teachers, counselors, and administrators* (pp. 21–31). Austin, TX: Pro-Ed.

Varley, C., & McClellan, J. (1997). Case study: Additional sudden deaths with tricyclic antidepressants. *Journal of the American Academy of Child and Adolescent Psychiatry, 36,* 390–394.

Varnhagen, S., & Gerber, M. M. (1984). Use of microcomputers for spelling assessment: Reasons to be cautious. *Learning Disability Quarterly, 7,* 266–270.

Vaughn, B., & Horner, R. H. (1995). Effects of concrete versus verbal choice systems on problem behavior. *Augmentative and Alternative Communication, 11,* 89–92.

Vaughn, B., & Horner, R. H. (1997). Identifying instructional tasks that occasion problem behaviors and assessing the effects of student versus teacher choice among these tasks. *Journal of Applied Behavior Analysis, 30,* 299–312.

Vaughn, S., Bos, C. S., Harrell, J. E., & Lasky, B. A. (1988). Parent participation in the initial placement/IEP conference: Ten years after mandated involvement. *Journal of Learning Disabilities, 21,* 82–89.

Vaughn, S., Bos, C., & Schumm, J. (2006). *Teaching exceptional, diverse, and at-risk students in the general education classroom* (3rd ed.). Upper Saddle River, NJ: Allyn & Bacon/Pearson.

Vaughn, S., Chard, D. J., Bryant, D. P., Coleman, M., Tyler, B., Linan-Thompson, S., & Kouzekanani, K. (2000). Fluency and comprehension interventions for third-grade students. *Remedial and Special Education, 21,* 325–335.

Vaughn, S., Cirino, P. T., Linan-Thompson, S., Mathes, P. G., Carlson, C. D., Cardenas-Hagan, . . . Francis, D. (2006). Effectiveness of a Spanish intervention and an English intervention for English-Language Learners at risk for reading problems. *American Educational Research Journal, 43,* 449–479.

Vaughn, S., Elbaum, B. E., Schumm, J. S., & Hughes, M. T. (1998). Social outcomes for students with and without learning disabilities in inclusive classrooms. *Journal of Learning Disabilities, 31,* 428–436.

Vaughn, S., Gersten, R., & Chard, D. J. (2000). The underlying message in learning disabilities intervention research: Findings from research syntheses. *Exceptional Children, 67,* 99–114.

Vaughn, S., Hughes, M. T., Moody, S., & Elbaum, B. (2001). Instructional grouping for reading for students with LD: Implications for practice. *Intervention in School and Clinic, 36*(3), 131–137.

Vaughn, S., Hughes, M. T., Schumm, J. S., & Klingner, J. K. (1998). A collaborative effort to enhance reading and writing instruction in inclusion classrooms. *Learning Disability Quarterly, 21,* 57–74.

Vaughn, S., & Klingner, J. K. (1998). Students' perceptions of inclusion and resource room settings. *The Journal of Special Education, 32,* 79–88.

Vaughn, S., Linan-Thompson, S., Mathes, P. G., Cirino, P. T., Carlson, C. D., Hagan, E. C., . . . Francis, D. J. (2006). Effectiveness of Spanish intervention and an English Intervention for first-grade English Language Learners at risk for reading difficulties. *Journal of Learning Disabilities, 39,* 56–73.

Vaughn, S., Mathes, P., Linan-Thompson, S., Cirino, P., Carlson, C., Pollard-Durodola, S., . . . Francis, D. J. (2006). Effectiveness of an English intervention for first-grade English language learners at risk for reading problems. *The Elementary School Journal, 107,* 154–180.

Vaughn, S., Schumm, J. S., & Arguelles, M. E. (1997). The ABCDE's of co-teaching. *Teaching Exceptional Children, 30*(2), 4–10.

Vellutino, F. R., Scanlon, D. M., Sipay, E. R., Small, S. G., Pratt, A., Chen, R., & Denckla, M. B. (1996). Cognitive profiles of difficult-to-remediate and readily remediated poor readers: Early intervention as a vehicle for distinguishing between cognitive and experiential deficits as basic causes of specific reading disability. *Journal of Educational Psychology, 88*(4), 601–638.

Velosa, J. F., & Riddle, M. A. (2000). Pharmacologic treatment of anxiety disorders in children and adolescents. *Pharmacology, 9,* 119–133.

Venn, J. J. (2007). *Assessing students with special needs* (4th ed.). Upper Saddle River, NJ: Merrill/Pearson Education.

Venn, M. L., & Wolery, M. (1992). Increasing daycare staff members' interactions during caregiving routines. *Journal of Early Intervention, 16,* 304–319.

Venn, M. L., Wolery, M., Wertz, M. G., Morris, A., DeCesare, L. D., & Cuffs, M. S. (1993). Embedding instruction in art activities to teach preschoolers with disabilities to imitate their peers. *Early Childhood Research Quarterly, 8,* 277–294.

Vermeer, A., & Dekker, L. F. D. (1993). Assessment of learning potential in children with cerebral palsy. *Issues in Special Education & Rehabilitation, 8,* 83–90.

Villa, R., Thousand, J., & Nevin, A. (2008). *A guide to co-teaching: Practical tips for facilitating student learning* (2nd ed.). Thousand Oaks, California: Corwin Press.

Voltz, D. L., Elliot, R. N., Jr., & Cobb, H. B. (1994). Collaborative teacher roles: Special and general educators. *Journal of Learning Disabilities, 27,* 527–535.

Volz, M. (2004, August 3). *Disabled students in Alaska to get special accommodations during high school exit exams in settlement.* Retrieved from www.SignOnSanDiego.com.

von Mizener, B. H., & Williams, R. L. (2009). The effects of student choices on academic performance. *Journal of Positive Behavior Intervention, 11,* 110–128.

Vygotsky, L. S. (1978). *Mind in society: The development of higher psychological processes.* (M. Cole, V. John-Steiner, S. Scribner, & E. Souberman, Eds.). Cambridge, MA: Harvard University Press.

Vygotsky, L. (1934/1986). *Thought and language.* Cambridge, MA: MIT Press.

Wagner, M., Kutash, K., Duchnowski, A. J., Epstein, M. H., & Sumi, W. C. (2005). The children and youth we serve: A national picture of the characteristics of students with emotional disturbances receiving special education. *Journal of Emotional and Behavioral Disorders, 13*(2), 79–96.

Wagner, M., Newman, L., Cameto, R., Garza, N., & Levine, P. (2005). *After high school: A first look at the postschool experiences of youth with disabilities. A report from the National Longitudinal Transition Study-2 (NLTS2).* Menlo Park, CA: SRI International.

Wagner, M., Newman, L., Cameto, R., Levine, P., & Garza, N. (2006). An overview of findings from Wave 2 of the National Longitudinal Transition Study-2 (NLTS2). *National Center for Special Education Research.* (ERIC Document Reproduction Service No. ED495660). Menlo Park, CA: SRI International. Available at www.nlts2.org/reports/2006_08/ nlts2_report_2006_08_complete.pdf.

Wagner, R. K., Muse, A. E., & Tannenbaum, K. R. (2007). Promising avenues for better understanding: Implications of vocabulary development for reading comprehension. In R. K. Wagner, A. E. Muse, & K. R. Tannenbaum (Eds.), *Vocabulary acquisition: Implications for reading comprehension* (pp. 276–291). New York: Guilford.

Walker, A. R., Uphold, N. M., Richter, S., & Test, D. W. (2010). A review of literature on community based instruction across grade levels. *Education and Training in Developmental Disabilities, 45,* 242–267.

Walker, B., Cheney, D., Stage, S., & Blum, C. (2005). Schoolwide screening and positive behavior supports: Identifying and supporting students at risk for school failure. *Journal of Positive Behavior Interventions, 7,* 194–204.

Walker, G. R. (1993). Noncompliant behavior of people with mental retardation. *Research in Developmental Disabilities, 14,* 87–105.

Walker, H. M. (2003, February 20). *Comments on accepting the Outstanding Leadership Award from the Midwest Symposium for Leadership in Behavior Disorders.* Kansas City, KS: Author.

Walker, H. M., Forness, S., Kauffman, J., Epstein, M., Gresham, F. M., Nelson, C. M., & Strain, P. (1998). Macro-social validation: Referencing outcomes in behavioral disorders to societal issues and problems. *Behavioral Disorders, 24,* 130–140.

Walker, H. M., Horner, R. H., Sugai, G., Bullis, M., Sprague, J. R., Bricker, D., & Kauffman, M. J. (1996). Integrated approaches to preventing antisocial behavior patterns among school-age children and youth. *Journal of Emotional and Behavioral Disorders, 4,* 193–256.

Walker, H. M., Irvin, L., Noell, J., & Singer, G. (1992). A construct score approach to the assessment of social competence: Rationale, technological considerations, and anticipated outcomes. *Behavior Modification, 16,* 448–474.

Walker, H. M., Kavanagh, K., Stiller, B., Golly, A., Severson, H. H., & Feil, E. G. (1998). First Step to Success: An early intervention approach for preventing school antisocial behavior. *Journal of Emotional and Behavioral Disorders, 6*(2), 66–80.

Walker H. M., & McConnell, S. (1995). *Walker-McConnell Scale of Social Competence and School Adjustment.* Florence, KY: Thomson Learning.

Walker, H. M., Nishioka, V. M., Zeller, R., Severson, H. H., & Feil, E. G. (2000). Causal factors and potential solutions for the persistent underidentification of students having emotional or behavioral disorders in the context of schooling. *Assessment for Effective Intervention, 26*(1), 29–39.

Walker, H. M., Ramsey, E., & Gresham, F. M. (2004). *Antisocial behavior at school: Evidence-based practices.* Belmont, CA: Wadsworth/Thomson Learning.

Walker, H. M., Seeley, J. R., Small, J., Severson, H. H., Graham, B., Feil, E. G., Serna, L., Golly, A. M., & Forness, S. R. (2009). A randomized controlled trial of the *First Step to Success* early intervention: Demonstration of program efficacy outcomes within a diverse, urban school district. *Journal of Emotional and Behavioral Disorders, 17,* 197–212.

Walker, H. M., & Severson, H. (1992a). *Systematic screening for behavior disorders: Technical manual.* Longmont, CO: Sopris West.

Walker, H. M., & Severson, H. H. (1992b). *Systematic screening for behavior disorders (SSBD): User's guide and technical manual.* Longmont, CO: Sopris West.

Walker, H. M., & Severson, H. H. (2002). Developmental prevention of at-risk outcomes for vulnerable antisocial children and youth. In K. L. Lane, F. M. Gresham, & T. E. O'Shaughnessy (Eds.), *Interventions for children with or at risk for emotional and behavioral disorders* (pp. 177–194). Boston, MA: Allyn & Bacon.

Walker, H. M., Severson, H. H., & Feil, E. G. (1994). *Early Screening Project (E.S.P.): A proven child find process.* Longmont, CO: Sopris West.

Walker, H. M., Severson, H. H., & Feil, E. G. (1995). *User manual. Early Screening Project: A proven child find process.* Longmont, CO: Sopris West.

Walker, H. M., Severson, H. H., Feil, E. G., Stiller, B., & Golly, A. (1998). First step to success: Intervening at the point of school entry to prevent antisocial behavior. *Psychology in the Schools, 35*(3), 259–269.

Walker, H. M., Severson, H., & Haring, N. (1985). *Standardized screening and identification of behavior disordered pupils in the elementary age range: Rationale, procedure, and guidelines.* Eugene: Oregon Research Institute.

Walker, H. M., Severson, H., Nicholson, F., Kehel, T., Jenson, W. R., & Clark, E. (1994). Replication of the Systematic Screening for Behavior Disorders (SSBD) procedure for the identification of at-risk children. *Journal of Emotional and Behavioral Disorders, 2*(2), 66–77.

Walker, H. M., Severson, H., Stiller, B., Wiliams, G., Haring, N., Shinn, M., & Todis, B. (1988). Systematic screening of pupils in the elementary age range at risk for behavior disorders: Development and trial testing of a Multiple Gating model. *Remedial and Special Education, 9*(3), 8–14.

Walker, H. M., Severson, H., Todis, B. J., Block-Pedego, A. E., Williams, G. J., Haring, N. G., & Barckley, M. (1990). Systematic Screening for Behavior Disorders (SSBD): Further validation, replication, and normative data. *Remedial and Special Education, 11,* 32–46.

Walker, H. M., Sprague, J. R., Perkins-Rowe, K. A., Beard-Jordan, K. Y., Seibert, B. M., Golly, A. M., Severson, H. H., & Feil, E. G. (2005). The First Step to Success program: Achieving secondary prevention outcomes for behaviorally at-risk children through early intervention. In M. H. Epstein, K. Kutash, & A. J. Duchnowski (Eds.), *Outcomes for children and youth with emotional and behavioral disorders and their families: Programs and evaluation best practices* (2nd ed., pp. 501–523). Austin, TX: Pro-Ed.

Walker, H. M., Stiller, B., Golly, A., Kavanagh, K., Severson, H., & Feil, E. (1997). *First Step to Success: Helping young children overcome antisocial behavior (an early intervention program for grades K–3)*. Longmont, CO: Sopris West.

Walker, H. M., Stiller, B., Severson, H., Feil, E., & Golly, A. (1998). First Step to Success: Intervening at the point of school entry to prevent antisocial behavior patterns. *Psychology in the Schools, 35,* 259–269.

Wall, M. E., & Gast, D. L. (1999). Acquisition of incidental information during instruction for a response-chain skill. *Research in Developmental Disabilities, 20,* 31–50.

Wall Emerson, R., Holbrook, C., & D'Andrea, F. M. (2009). Acquisition of literacy skills in young blind children: Results from the ABC Braille Study. *Journal of Visual Impairment and Blindness, 103,* 610–624.

Wall Emerson, R., Sitar, D., Erin, J. N., Wormsley, D. P., & Herlich, S. L. (2009). The effect of consistent structured reading instruction on high and low literacy achievement in young children who are blind. *Journal of Visual Impairment and Blindness, 103,* 595–609.

Wallace, G. W., & Bott, D. A. (1989). Statement-pie: A strategy to improve the paragraph writing skills of adolescents with learning disabilities. *Journal of Learning Disabilities, 22,* 541–553.

Wallace, T., Espin, C. A., McMaster, K., Deno, S. L., & Foegen, A. (2007). CBM progress monitoring within a standards-based system. *The Journal of Special Education, 41,* 66–67.

Walls, R. T., Dowler, D. L., Haught, P. A., & Zawlocki, R. J. (1984). Progressive delay and unlimited delay of prompt in forward chaining and whole task training strategies. *Education and Training of the Mentally Retarded, 19,* 276–284.

Walls, R. T., Zane, T., & Ellis, W. B. (1981). Forward and backward chaining, and who task methods. *Behavior Modification, 5,* 61–74.

Walsh, B. F., & Lamberts, F. (1979). Errorless discrimination and picture fading as techniques for teaching sight words to TMR students.

American Journal of Mental Deficiency, 84, 473–479.

Walsh, J. M., & Snyder, D. (1993, April). *Cooperative teaching: An effective model for all students.* Paper presented at the annual convention of the Council for Exceptional Children, San Antonio, TX. (ERIC Document Reproduction Service No. ED361930)

Walther-Thomas, C. S. (1997). Co-teaching experiences: The benefits and problems that teachers and principals report over time. *Journal of Learning Disabilities, 30,* 395–408.

Walther-Thomas, C., Korinek, L., McLaughlin, V., & Williams, B. (2000). *Collaboration for inclusive education: Developing successful programs.* Needham Heights, MA: Allyn & Bacon.

Ward, M. J. (1988). The many facets of self-determination. *NICHCY transition summary: National Information Center for Children and Youth with Disabilities, 5,* 2–3.

Warren, S. F., Fey, M. E., & Yoder, P. J. (2007). Differential treatment intensity research: A missing link to creating optimally effective communication interventions. *Mental Retardation and Developmental Disabilities, 13,* 70–77.

Warren, S. F., & Gazdag, G. (1990). Facilitating early language development with milieu teaching procedures. *Journal of Early Intervention, 14,* 62–86.

Warren, S. F., & Kaiser, A. P. (1986). Incidental language teaching: A critical review. *Journal of Speech and Hearing Disorders, 51,* 291–299.

Warren, S. F., & Kaiser, A. P. (1988). Research in early language intervention. In S. L. Odom & M. B. Karnes (Eds.), *Early intervention for infants and children with handicaps: An empirical base* (pp. 89–108). Baltimore: Brookes.

Warren, S. F., McQuarter, R. J., & Rogers-Warren, A. K. (1984). The effects of mands and models on the speech of unresponsive socially isolate children. *Journal of Speech and Hearing Disorders, 47,* 42–52.

Warren, S. F., & Yoder, P. J. (1997). Emerging model of communication and language intervention. *Mental*

Retardation and Developmental Disabilities, 3, 358–362.

Warren, S. F., Yoder, P. J., Gazdag, G.E., Kim, K., & Jones, H.A. (1993). Facilitating prelinguistic communication skills in young children with developmental delay. *Journal of Speech and Hearing Research, 36,* 83–97.

Wasik, B., Bond, M. A., & Hindman, A. (2006). The effects of a language and literacy intervention on head start children and teachers. *Journal of Educational Psychology, 98,* 63–74.

Watkins, R., Rice, M., & Molz, C. (1993). Verb use by language-impaired and normally developing children. *First Language, 37,* 133–143.

Watson, C., & Willows, D. M. (1995), Information-processing patterns in specific reading disability. *Journal of Learning Disabilities, 28,* 216–231.

Watson, S. T., & Robinson, S. L. (1998). A behavior analytic approach to treating depression. In T. S. Watson & F. M. Gresham (Eds.), *Handbook of child behavior therapy: Issues in clinical child psychology* (pp. 393–411). New York: Plenum Press.

Watts, F. N. (1995). Depression and anxiety. In A. D. Baddeley, B. A. Wilson, & F. N. Watts (Eds.), *Handbook of memory disorders* (pp. 293–317). Oxford, UK: John Wiley & Sons.

Wayman, M. M., Wallace, T., Wiley, H. I., Ticha, R., & Espin, C. A. (2007). Literature synthesis on curriculum-based measurement in reading. *Journal of Special Education, 41,* 85–120.

Weber, M. C. (2009). The IDEA eligibility mess. *Buffalo Law Review, 57,* 83–160.

Webster-Stratton, C. (1998). Parent training with low-income clients: Promoting parental engagement through a collaborative approach. In J. R. Lutzker (Ed.), *Child abuse: A handbook of theory, research and treatment* (pp. 183–210). New York: Plenum Press.

Webster-Stratton, C. (2006). *The incredible years: A trouble-shooting guide for parents of children aged 3–8.* Seattle, WA: Incredible Years Press.

Wechsler, D. (2004). *The Wechsler Intelligence Scale for Children—4th Edition.* London: Pearson Assessment.

Wehby, J. H., & Hollahan, M. S. (2000). Effects of high-probability requests on the latency to initiate academic tasks. *Journal of Applied Behavior Analysis, 33*(2), 259–262.

Wehby, J. H., Lane, K. L., & Falk, K. B. (2005). An inclusive approach to improving early literacy skills of students with emotional and behavioral disorders. *Behavior Disorders, 30,* 155–169.

Wehby, J. H., Symons, F. J., Canale, J. A., & Go, F. J. (1998). Teaching practices in classrooms for students with emotional and behavioral disorders: Discrepancies between recommendations and observations. *Behavioral Disorders, 24,* 51–56.

Wehman, P., & Kregel, J. (2003). *Functional curriculum for elementary, middle, and secondary age students with special needs.* Austin, TX: Pro-Ed.

Wehmeyer, M. L. (1992). Self-determination and the education of students with mental retardation. *Education and Training in Mental Retardation, 27,* 302–314.

Wehmeyer, M. L. (1996a). Self-determination as an educational outcome: Why is it important to children, youth and adults with disabilities? In D. J. Sands & M. L. Wehmeyer (Eds.), *Self-determination across the lifespan: Independence and choice for people with disabilities* (pp. 15–34). Baltimore: Brookes.

Wehmeyer, M. L. (1996b). Self-determination in youth with severe cognitive disabilities: From theory to practice. In L. E. Powers, G. H. S. Singer, & J. Sowers (Eds.), *On the road to autonomy: Promoting self-competence for children and youth with disabilities* (pp. 17–36). Baltimore: Brookes.

Wehmeyer, M. (2005). Self-determination and individuals with severe disabilities: Re-examining meanings and misinterpretations. *Research and Practice in Severe Disabilities, 30,* 113–120.

Wehmeyer, M. L., Agran, M., & Hughes, C. (2000). A national survey of teachers' promotion of self-determination and student-directed learning. *Journal of Special Education, 34,* 58–68.

Wehmeyer, M. L., & Field, S. (2007). *Instructional and assessment strategies to promote the self-determination of students with disabilities.* Thousand Oaks, CA: Corwin Press.

Wehmeyer, M. L., & Palmer, S. B. (2003). Adult outcomes for students with cognitive disabilities three-years after high school: The impact of self-determination. *Education and Training in Developmental Disabilities, 38,* 131–144.

Weiss, M. P. (2004). Co-teaching as science in the schoolhouse: More questions than answers. *Journal of Learning Disabilities, 37,* 218–223.

Weiss, M. P., & Brigham, F. J. (2000). Co-teaching and the model of shared responsibility: What does the research support. In T. E. Scruggs & M. A. Mastropieri (Eds.), *Advances in learning and behavioral disabilities: Educational interventions* (pp. 217–246). Stamford, CT: JAI Press.

Weiss, M. P., & Lloyd, J. W. (2001). Structure and effective teaching. In D. P. Hallahan & B. K. Keogh (Eds.), *Research and global perspectives in learning disabilities: Essays in honor of William M. Cruickshank* (pp. 131–145). Mahwah, NJ: Erlbaum.

Weiss, M., & Lloyd, J. (2002). Congruence between roles and actions of secondary special educators in co-taught and special education settings. *The Journal of Special Education, 36*(2), 58–68.

Weissberg, R. P., Kumpfer, K. L., & Seligman, M. E. P. (2003). Prevention that works for children and youth. *American Psychologist, 58,* 425–432.

Weisz, J. R., Thurber, C. A., Sweeney, L., Proffitt, V. D., & LeGagnoux, G. L. (1997). Brief treatment of mild-moderate child depression using primary and secondary control enhancement training. *Journal of Counseling and Clinical Psychology, 65,* 703–707.

Weitzman, E., & Greenberg, J. (2002). *Learning language and loving it: A guide to promoting children's social, language, and literacy development in early childhood settings* (2nd ed.). Toronto, Canada: The Hanen Centre.

Welch, M. (2000). Descriptive analysis of team teaching in two elementary classrooms: A formative experimental approach. *Remedial and Special Education, 21,* 366–376.

Wellman, H. M. (1990). *The child's theory of mind.* Cambridge, MA: MIT Press.

Wentzel, K. R. (1993). Does being good make the grade? Social behavior and academic competence in middle school. *Journal of Educational Psychology, 85,* 357–364.

Werner, H., & Kaplan, B. (1963). *Symbol formation: An organismic-developmental approach to language and expression of thought.* New York: John Wiley.

Wertlieb, E. C. (1992). Automatic and purposive semantic processing in learning disabled individuals. *Journal of Special Education, 23,* 450–462.

Werts, M. G., Caldwell, N. K., & Wolery, M. (1996). Peer modeling of response chains: Observational learning by students with disabilities. *Journal of Applied Behavior Analysis, 29,* 53–66.

West, R. P., & Sloane, H. N. (1986). Teacher presentation rate and point delivery rate: Effect on classroom disruption, performance accuracy, and response rate. *Behavior Modification, 10,* 267–286.

Westby, C. E. (1984). Development of Narrative Language Abilities. In G. P. Wallach & K. G. Butler (Eds.), *Language learning disabilities in school-age children* (pp. 103–127). Baltimore: Williams & Wilkins.

Westerveld, M. F., & Gillon, G. T. (2008). Oral narrative intervention for children with mixed reading disability. *Child Language Teaching and Therapy, 24,* 31–54.

Westling, D. L., & Fox, L. (2009). *Teaching students with severe disabilities* (4th ed.). Upper Saddle River, NJ: Merrill/Pearson.

What Works Clearinghouse. (2006, September). *WWC intervention report: Enhanced proactive reading. A practice guide.* Washington, DC: National Center for Education Evaluation and Regional Assistance, Institute of Education Sciences, U.S. Department of Education. Retrieved from http://ies.ed.gov/ncee/wwc/.

Whitbread, K. M., Bruder, M. B., Fleming, G., & Park, H. J. (2007). Collaboration in special education: Parent-professional training. *Teaching Exceptional Children, 39*(4), 6–14.

Whitby, P. (2009). *The effects of a modified learning strategy on the multiple step mathematical word problem solving ability of middle school students with high-functioning autism or Aspergers' disorder.* Unpublished doctoral dissertation, University of Central Florida.

White, K. R., Taylor, M. J., & Moss, V. D. (1992). Does research support claims about the benefits of involving parents in early intervention programs? *Review of Educational Research, 62,* 91–125.

White, M. A. (1975). Natural rates of teacher approval and disapproval in the classroom. *Journal of Applied Behavior Analysis, 8,* 367–372.

Whitehurst, G. J., Arnold, D., Epstein, J., Angell, A., Smith, M., & Fischel, J. (1994). A picture book reading intervention in day care and home for children from low-income families. *Developmental Psychology, 30,* 679–689.

Whitehurst, G. J., Falco, F., Lonigan, C. J., Fischal, J. E., DeBaryshe, B. D., Valdez-Manchaca, M. C., & Caulfield, M. (1988). Accelerating language development through picturebook reading. *Development Psychology, 24,* 552–559.

Whittington, C. J., Kendall, T., Fonagy, P., Cottrell, D., Cotgrove, A., & Boddington, E. (2004). Selective serotonin reuptake inhibitors in childhood depression: Systematic review of published versus unpublished data. *The Lancet, 363,* 1341–1345.

Whittington, D. (1999). Making room for values and fairness: Teaching reliability and validity in the classroom context. *Educational Measurement, 18,* 14–21.

Wigfield, A., & Karpathian, M. (1991). Who am I and what can I do? Children's self-concepts and motivation in achievement situations. *Educational Psychologist, 26,* 233–261.

Wiley, A. L., Siperstein, G. N., Bountress, K. E., Forness, S. R., & Brigham, F. J. (2009). School context and the academic achievement of students with emotional disturbance. *Behavioral Disorders, 33,* 198–210.

Wiley, A. L., Siperstein, G. N., Forness, S. R., & Brigham, F. J. (2010). School context and the problem behavior and social skills of students with emotional disturbance. *Journal of Child and Family Studies, 19,* 451–461.

Wilkinson, G. S. (1993). *Wide Range Achievement Test* (3rd ed.). Wilmington, DE: Wide Range.

Wilkinson, L. A. (2008). Self-management for children with high-functioning autism spectrum disorders. *Intervention in School and Clinic, 43,* 150–157.

Williams, D. M., & Collins, B. C. (1994). Teaching multiplication facts to students with learning disabilities: Teacher-selected versus student-selected material prompts within the delay procedure. *Journal of Learning Disabilities, 27,* 589–597.

Williams, J. P. (1998). Improving comprehension of disabled readers. *Annals of Dyslexia, 48,* 213–238.

Williams, J. P. (2000). *Strategic processing of text: Improving reading comprehension for students with learning disabilities* (Report No. EDO-EC-00-8). Reston, VA: Council for Exceptional Children. (ERIC Document Reproduction Service No. ED449596)

Willingham, W. W., Ragosta, M., Bennett, R. E., Braun, H., Rock, D. A., & Powers, D. E. (1988). *Testing handicapped people.* Needham Heights, MA: Allyn & Bacon.

Willis, A., & Harris, V. (2000). Political acts: Literacy learning and teaching. *Reading Research Quarterly, 35,* 72–88.

Wilson, B. (1996). *Wilson reading system.* Millbury, MA: Wilson Language Training.

Wilson, B. A. (2000). *Wilson reading system.* Oxford, MA: Wilson Language Training.

Wise, B., Olson, R., Anstett, M., Andrews, L., Terjak, M., Schneider, V., & Kostuch, J. (1989). Implementing a long-term computerized remedial program with synthetic speech feedback: Hardware, software, and real-world issues. *Behavior Research Methods, Instruments, and Computers, 21,* 173–189.

Wise, B., Ring, J., & Olson, R. K. (2000). Individual differences in gains from computer assisted-remedial reading with more emphasis on phonological analysis or accurate reading in context. *Journal of Experimental Child Psychology, 77,* 197–235.

Witt, J. C., & Elliott, S. N. (1985). Acceptability of classroom intervention strategies. In T. R. Kratochwill (Ed.), *Advances in school psychology* (Vol. 4., pp. 251–288). Mahwah, NJ: Erlbaum.

Witt, J. C., Elliott, S. N., Daly, III, E. J., Gresham, F. M., & Kramer, J. J. (1998). *Assessment of at-risk and special needs children* (2nd ed.). Boston, MA: McGraw-Hill.

Witt, J. C., & VanDerHeyden, A. M. (2007). The System to Enhance Educational Performance (STEEP): Using science to improve achievement. In S. R. Jimerson, M. K., Burns, & A. M. VanDerHeyden (Eds.), *Handbook of Response to Intervention* (pp. 148–171). New York: Springer.

Wolery, M., Ault, M. J., Gast, D. L., Doyle, P. M., & Griffen, A. K. (1990). Comparison of constant time delay and the system of least prompts in teaching chained tasks. *Education and Training in Mental Retardation, 25,* 243–257.

Wolery, M., & Gast, D. L. (1984). Effective and efficient procedures for the transfer of stimulus control. *Topics in Early Childhood Special Education, 4,* 55–77.

Wolery, M., Holombe, A., Cybriwsky, C., Doyle, P. M., Schuster, J. W., Ault, M. J., & Gast, D. L. (1992). Constant time delay with discrete responses. A review of effectiveness and demographic, procedural, and methodological parameters. *Research in Developmental Disabilities, 13,* 239–266.

Wolery, M., & Schuster, J. W. (1997). Instructional methods with students who have significant disabilities. *Journal of Special Education, 31,* 61–79.

Wolf, M. M. (1978). Social validity: The case for subjective measurement or how applied behavior analysis is finding its heart. *Journal of Applied Behavior Analysis, 11,* 203–214.

Wolf, M., & Bowers, P. (1999). The "Double-Deficit Hypothesis" for the developmental dyslexias. *Journal of Educational Psychology, 91*(3), 1–24.

Wolf, M., Barzillai, M., Gottwald, S., Miller, L., Spencer, K., Norton, E., Lovett, M., & Morris, R. (2009). The RAVE-O intervention: Connecting neuroscience to the classroom. *Mind Brain and Education, 3*(2), 84–93.

Wolf, M., & Bowers, P. (2000). The question of naming-speed deficits in developmental reading disability: An introduction to the Double-Deficit hypothesis. *Journal of Learning Disabilities, 33,* 322–324.

Wolf, M., Bowers, P. G., & Biddle, K. (2000). Naming speed processes, timing, and reading: A conceptual review. *Journal of Learning Disabilities, 33,* 387–407.

Wolf, M., Gottwald, S., & Orkin, M. (2009). Serious word play: How multiple linguistic emphases in RAVE-O instruction improve multiple reading skills. *Perspectives on Language Literacy,* 21–24.

Wolf, M., & Katzir-Cohen, T. (2001). Reading fluency and its intervention. *Scientific Studies of Reading, 5,* 211–238.

Wolf, M., Miller, L., & Donnelly, K. (2000). RAVE-O: A comprehensive fluency-based reading intervention program. *Journal of Learning Disabilities, 33,* 375–386.

Wolfe, P. S. (1994). Judgment of the social validity of instructional strategies used in community-based instructional sites. *Journal of the Association of Persons with Severe Handicaps, 19,* 43–51.

Wolfensberger, W. (1972). *The principle of normalization in human services.* Downsview, Ontario: National Institute on Mental Retardation.

Wolgemuth, J. R., Cobb, B. R., & Alwell, M. (2008). The effects of mnemonic interventions on academic outcomes for youth with disabilities: A systematic review. *Learning Disabilities Research & Practice, 23,* 1–10.

Wolraich, M. L. (2003). The use of psychotropic medications in children: An American view. *Journal of Child Psychology and Psychiatry, 44,* 159–168.

Wong, B. Y. L., Harris, K. R., Graham, S., & Butler, D. L. (2003). Cognitive strategies instruction research in learning disabilities. In H. L. Swanson, K. R. Harris, & S. Graham (Eds.). *Handbook of learning disabilities* (pp. 383–402). New York: Guilford Press.

Wood, B. K., Umbreit, J., Liaupsin, C. J., & Gresham, F. M. (2007). A treatment integrity analysis of function-based interventions. *Education and Treatment of Children, 30,* 105–120.

Wood, D., Frank, A., & Wacker, D. (1998). Teaching multiplication facts to students with learning disabilities. *Journal of Applied Behavior Analysis, 31,* 323–338.

Wood, L., & Hood, E. (2004). Shared storybook readings with children who have little or no functional speech: A language intervention tool for students who use augmentative and alternative communication. *Perspectives in Education, 22,* 101–114.

Woodcock, R. W. (1987). *Woodcock Reading Mastery Tests–Revised.* Circles Pines, MN: American Guidance Service.

Woodcock, R. W., & Johnson, M. B. (1990). *Woodcock-Johnson Psycho-Educational Battery—Revised.* Allen, TX: DLM Teaching Resources.

Woodcock, R. W., McGrew, K. S., & Mather, N. (2001). *Woodcock-Johnson III Tests of Achievement.* Itasca, IL: Riverside.

Woods, M. L., & Moe, A. J. (2006). *Analytical reading inventory* (8th ed.). Upper Saddle River, NJ: Merrill/Pearson Education.

Woodward, J. (2006). Developing automaticity in multiplication facts: Integrating strategy instruction with timed practice drills. *Learning Disability Quarterly, 29,* 269–289.

Woodward, J., & Rieth, H. (1997). An historical review of technology research in special education. *Review of Educational Research, 67,* 503–536.

Wormsley, D. P. (1996). Reading rates of young braille-reading children. *Journal of Visual Impairment and Blindness, 90,* 278–282.

Wright, C. W., & Schuster, J. W. (1994). Accepting specific versus functional student responses within training chained tasks. *Education and Training in Mental Retardation and Developmental Disabilities, 29,* 43–56.

Wright-Gallo, G. L., Higbee, T. S., Reagon, K. A., & Davey, B. J. (2006). Classroom-based functional analysis and intervention for students with emotional/behavioral disorders. *Education and Treatment of Children, 29,* 421–436.

Xin, J., & Rieth, H. (2001). Video-assisted vocabulary instruction for elementary school students with learning disabilities. *Information Technology in Childhood Education Annual, 13,* 87–143.

Xin, Y. P. (2008). The effects of schema-based instruction in solving mathematics word problems: An emphasis on prealgebraic conceptualization of multiplicative relations. *Journal for Research in Mathematics Education, 39,* 526–551.

Xin, Y. P., Jitendra, A. K., & Deatline-Buchman, A. (2005). Effects of mathematical word problem solving instruction on students with learning problems. *Journal of Special Education, 39,* 181–192.

Xin, Y. P., Wiles, B., & Lin, Y. Y. (2008). Teaching conceptual model based word problem story grammar to enhance mathematics problem solving. *Journal of Special Education, 42,* 163–178.

Xin, Y. P., & Zhang, D. (2009). Exploring a conceptual model-based approach to teaching situated word problems. *Journal of Educational Research, 102,* 427–441.

Yang, C. H., Chuang, L. Y., Yang, C. H., & Luo, C. H. (2003). Morse code application for wireless environmental control systems for severely disabled individuals. *IEEE Transactions on Neural Systems and Rehabilitation Engineering, 2*(4), 463–469.

Yates, R. A. (1966). *The art of memory.* Chicago: University of Chicago Press.

Yeager, C., & McLaughlin, T. (1995). The use of a time-out ribbon and precision requests to improve child compliance in the classroom: A case study. *Child and Family Behavior Therapy, 17*(4), 1–9.

Yeaton, W., & Sechrest, L. (1981). Critical dimensions in the choice and maintenance of successful treatments: Strength, integrity, and effectiveness. *Journal of Counsulting and Clinical Psychology, 49,* 156–167.

Yell, M. L. (2006). *The law and special education* (2nd ed.). Upper Saddle River, NJ: Merrill/Pearson Education.

Yell, M. L. (2009). Developing educationally meaningful and legally correct Individualized Education Programs. In M. L. Yell, N. B. Meadows, E. Dragsow, & J. G. Shriner, *Evidence based practices for educating students with emotional and behavioral disorders* (pp. 190–214). Upper

Saddle River, NJ: Merrill/Pearson Education.

Yell, M. L., & Crockett, J. B. (2011). Free Appropriate Public Education. In J. M. Kauffman & D. P. Hallahan (Eds.), *Handbook of special education* (pp. 77–90). New York: Routledge.

Yell, M. L., & Drasgow, E. (2000). Litigating a free appropriate public education: The Lovaas hearings and cases. *Journal of Special Education, 33,* 206–215.

Yell, M. L., Drasgow, E., & Oh, I. (April, 2008). *Development of an evaluation instrument to assess the procedural and substantive quality of IEPs: The IEP Quality Indicator Scale (IQUIS).* Paper presented at the annual meeting of the Council of Exceptional Children, Boston, MA.

Yell, M. L., Meadows, N. B., Drasgow, E., & Shriner, J. G. (2009). *Evidence-based practices of educating students with emotional and behavioral disorders.* Upper Saddle River, NJ: Pearson.

Yell, M. L., Rogers, D., & Rogers, E. L. (1998). The legal history of special education: What a long, strange trip it's been! *Remedial and Special Education, 19,* 219–238.

Yell, M. L., & Stecker, P. M. (2003). Developing legally correct and educationally meaningful IEPs using curriculum-based measurement. *Assessment for Effective Intervention, 28*(3/4), 73–88.

Yoder, P. J., Kaiser, A. P., Goldstein, H., Alpert, C., Mousetis, L. Kaczmarek, L., & Fischer, R. (1995). An exploratory comparison of milieu teaching and responsive interaction in classroom applications. *Journal of Early Intervention, 19,* 218–242.

Yoder, P., Warren, S., Kim, K., & Gazdag, G. (1994). Facilitating prelinguistic communication skills in young children with developmental delay II: Systematic replication and extension. *Journal of Speech and Hearing Research, 37,* 841–851.

Yopp, H. K. (1988). The validity and reliability of phonemic awareness tests. *Reading Research Quarterly, 23,* 159–177.

Yoshida, R. K., Fenton, K. S., Kaufman, M. J., & Maxwell, J. (1978). Parental involvement in the special education pupil planning process: The school's perspective. *Exceptional Children, 44,* 531–534.

Ysseldyke, J. E. (2005). Assessment and decision making for students with learning disabilities: What if this is as good as it gets? *Learning Disability Quarterly, 28,* 125–128.

Ysseldyke, J. E., & McLeod, S. (2007). Using technology tools to monitor Response to Intervention. In S. Jimerson, M. K. Burns, & A. M. VanDerHeyden (Eds.), *Handbook of Response to Intervention: The science and practice of assessment and intervention* (pp. 396–407). New York: Springer.

Ysseldyke, J., Thurlow, M., Bielinski, J., House, A., Moody, M., & Haigh, J. (2001). The relationship between instructional and assessment accommodations in an inclusive state accountability system. *Journal of Learning Disabilities, 34,* 212–220.

Zaragoza, N., Vaughn, S., & McIntosh, R. (1991). Social skills interventions and children with behavior problems: A review. *Behavioral Disorders, 16,* 260–275.

Zarcone, J. R., Iwata, B. A., Hughes, C. E., & Vollmer, T. R. (1993). Momentum versus extinction effects in the treatment of self-injurious escape behavior. *Journal of Applied Behavior Analysis, 26,* 135–136.

Zarcone, J. R., Iwata, B. A., Mazaleski, J. L., & Smith, R. G. (1994). Momentum and extinction effects on self-injurious escape behavior and noncompliance. *Journal of Applied Behavior Analysis, 27*(4), 649–658.

Zawaiza, T. B. W., & Gerber, M. M. (1993). Effects of explicit instruction on community college students with learning disabilities. *Learning Disabilities Quarterly, 16,* 64–79.

Zehler, A. M., Fleischman, H. L., Hopstock, P. J., Stephenson, T. G., Pendzick, M. L., & Sapru, S. (2003). *Descriptive study of services to LEP students and LEP students with disabilities: Policy report—Summary of findings related to LEP and SPED-LEP student.* Washington, DC: Development Associates, Inc.

Zenisky, A. L., & Sireci, S. G. (2007). *A summary of the research on the effects of test accommodations: 2005–2006* (Technical Report 47). Minneapolis, MN: University of Minnesota, National Center on Educational Outcomes.

Zettel, J. J., & Ballard, J. (1982). The Education for All Handicapped Children Act of 1975 (P.L. 94-142): Its history, origins, and concepts. In J. Ballard, B. Ramirez, & F. Weintraub (Eds.), *Special education in America: Its legal and governmental foundations* (pp. 11–22). Reston, VA: Council for Exceptional Children.

Zigmond, N. (1996). Organization and management of general education classrooms. In D. Speece & B. Keogh (Eds.), *Research on classroom ecologies: Implications for inclusion of children with learning disabilities* (pp. 163–190). Hillsdale, NJ: Erlbaum.

Zigmond, N. (2003). Where should SWDs receive special education services? Is one place better than another? *Journal of Special Education, 37,* 193–199.

Zigmond, N. (2006). Reading and writing in co-taught secondary school social studies classrooms: A reality check. *Reading and Writing Quarterly, 22,* 249–268.

Zigmond, N., Kloo, A., & Volonino, V. (2009). What, where, and how? Special education in the climate of full inclusion. *Exceptionality, 17,* 189–204.

Zigmond, N., & Magiera, K. (2001). *Co-teaching* (Current Practice Alerts No. 6, pp. 1–4). Reston, VA: Division for Learning Disabilities & Division for Research of the Council for Exceptional Children.

Zigmond, N., & Matta, D. (2004). Value added of the special education teacher on secondary school co-taught classes. In T. E. Scruggs & M. A. Mastropieri (Eds.), *Research in secondary schools: Advances in learning and behavioral disabilities* (Vol. 17, pp. 55–76). Oxford, UK: Elsevier Science/JAI.

Zimmerman, I. L., Steiner, V. G., & Evatt Pond, R. (2002). *Preschool Language Scale-Revised* (PLS-R) (4th ed.). San Antonio, TX: Psychological Corporation.

Zinth, J. D. (2007). *Standard graduation requirements.* Denver, CO: Education Commission of the States. Retrieved from http://mb2.ecs.org/reports/Report.aspx?id=735.

Name Index

Subject Index

AAC (augmentative and alternative communication) devices, 339, 413, 415, 422
AAMR Adaptive Behavior Scale, 255
ABC (Antecedent-Behavior-Consequence) worksheets, 143
ABI. *See* Activity-based intervention (ABI)
Academic achievement
    academic engagement and, 153, 155
    curriculum-based measurement and, 235–248
    high-incidence disabilities and, 343, 349, 352
    placement decisions and, 289
    reading proficiency and, 239
    social skills and, 215
Academic enablers, 215
Academic engagement
    classroom contexts and, 154
    defined, 153–154
    externalizing behaviors and, 192
    First Step to Success and, 197
    Good Behavior Game, 158–160
    opportunities to respond, 154–158, 163–164
    practice recommendations, 164
    recommendations for future research, 163–164
    research strengths and limitations, 153, 154, 161–163
    students with disabilities and, 153
    teacher praise, 157, 160–162, 163, 164
Academic skills outcomes
    arithmetic combinations and, 61–72
    content areas and, 98–115
    co-teaching and, 116–124
    curriculum-based assessment and, 302
    early literacy instruction and, 11–23
    functional assessment-based intervention and, 203
    mathematics reasoning and, 73–85
    positive behavior support and, 129, 135
    prompts and, 355, 359
    reading comprehension and, 33–46
    reading fluency and, 24–32
    research-based practices in, 7
    research-to-practice gap and, 6
    vocabulary and, 47–60
    written expression and, 86–97
Access to writing. *See also* Written expression
    physical disabilities, 418–419, 422
Accommodations. *See also* Assessment accommodations
    curriculum-based assessment, 308–309
    false negatives and, 292

    individualized education programs and, 278, 279–280, 282, 284, 312
    placement decisions and, 291
Accommodations Bibliography, 315
Accountability, No Child Left Behind Act of 2001, 235
Accuracy, speech recognition, 421
Achievement tests. *See specific tests*
Acquisition deficits, 216, 222
Activity-based intervention (ABI)
    developmentally appropriate practices and, 332–333
    group activity matrix, 336
    implementation, 333, 335–337, 341
    research on, 334–335
    theoretical underpinnings, 333–334
ADA (Americans with Disabilities Act), 332
Adaptations
    mnemonic strategies and, 348–349
    physical disabilities and, 415
    special-needs students and, 23
Adaptive behavior, 255
Adaptive Behavior Assessment System-Second Edition (ABAS-II), 255
Adaptive skills, 333
ADD (attention deficit disorder), 152
Adequate yearly progress (AYP), 312
ADHD. *See* Attention deficit hyperactivity disorder (ADHD)
Adjustment disorder, 180
Adult-assisted learning structures, 102–103
Adverse impact on classmates, placement decisions, 298–299
Aggressive, coercive behavior. *See also* Antisocial behavior
    autism spectrum disorders and, 407
    early intervention and, 193–194
    as externalizing behavior, 192–193, 214
    First Step to Success and, 193, 194–198, 203–204, 205–206
    functional assessment-based interventions and, 198–203, 204, 207–212
    function-based approach to problem behaviors, 407
    verbal learning deficits and, 342
Alphabetic principle
    early literacy instruction and, 11, 12, 15, 21
    reading comprehension and, 33–34
    reading fluency and, 25
    Response to Intervention and, 230
Alphabet Practice activities, 88
Alprazolam, 190
Alternative assessments. *See* Modifications

Alternative explanations, determining effective practices, 4
Alvin Independent School Dist. v. A.D. ex rel. Patricia F (2007), 291, 298
Amanda J. v. Clark County School District (2001), 274
American Association on Intellectual and Developmental Disability (AAIDD), 353
American Association on Mental Retardation, 353
American Sign Language (ASL), 424, 427
Americans with Disabilities Act (ADA), 332
AM/RT. *See* Anxiety management/relaxation training (AM/RT)
Amyotropic lateral sclerosis, 419
Analytic rubrics, 307–308
Anarthric speech, 411, 415
Anorexia nervosa, 180
Antecedent-Behavior-Consequence (ABC) worksheets, 143
Antecedent procedures, 154–155, 158, 162
Antecedent prompts
    description of, 354–359, 363–365
    implementation of, 364–365
    types of, 364
Antisocial behavior. *See also* Aggressive, coercive behavior
    academic failure and, 193
    as externalizing behavior, 192
    First Step to Success and, 194–198
    functional assessment-based intervention and, 198–203
    increase in, 127
Anxiety
    as internalizing problem, 179, 214
    pharmacologic interventions and, 186–191
    verbal learning deficits and, 342
Anxiety management/relaxation training (AM/RT)
    definition and theory for effectiveness, 184
    implementation, 184–185
    internalizing behaviors and, 179, 184–186
    research on, 185–186, 190–191
    as tertiary support, 139
Appropriate services, placement decisions, 288
Are We Really Co-Teachers Scale, 121
Arithmetic combinations
    instructional practices for, 63–72
    instruction-related difficulties with, 62–63
    mathematical achievement and, 61–62
    rationale and theoretical framework for teaching, 63–64